I0788148

POETRY AND POLITICS

OLD WESTERN CULTURE READER

VOLUME 14

POETRY AND POLITICS

OLD WESTERN CULTURE READER

VOLUME 14

Companion to Early Moderns: Poetry and Politics,
a great books curriculum by Roman Roads Press

ROMAN ROADS PRESS

MOSCOW, IDAHO

Poetry and Politics: Old Western Culture Reader, Volume 14

Copyright © 2019 Roman Roads Media, LLC

Published by Roman Roads Press
Moscow, Idaho
romanroadspress.com

Series Editor: Daniel Foucachon
Cover Design: Valerie Anne Bost, Daniel Foucachon, and Rachel Rosales
Interior Layout: Valerie Anne Bost and Carissa Hale
Edmund Burke Editor and Latin Translations: Josiah Roberts

Printed in the United States of America

Poetry and Politics: Old Western Culture Reader, Volume 14
Roman Roads Media, LLC
ISBN: 978-1-944482-90-9 (Hardback), 978-1-944482-48-0 (paperback)

Version 1.1.0   October 2021

This is a companion reader for the Old Western Culture curriculum by Roman Roads Press. To find out more about this course, visit www.romanroadspress.com.

OLD WESTERN CULTURE

Great Books Reader Series

THE GREEKS

VOLUME 1	*The Epics*
VOLUME 2	*Drama & Lyric*
VOLUME 3	*The Histories*
VOLUME 4	*The Philosophies*

THE ROMANS

VOLUME 5	*The Aeneid*
VOLUME 6	*The Historians*
VOLUME 7	*Early Christianity*
VOLUME 8	*Nicene Christianity*

CHRISTENDOM

VOLUME 9	*Early Medievals*
VOLUME 10	*Defense of the Faith*
VOLUME 11	*The Medieval Mind*
VOLUME 12	*The Reformation*

EARLY MODERNS

VOLUME 13	*Rise of England*
VOLUME 14	*Politics and Poetry*
VOLUME 15	*The Enlightenment*
VOLUME 16	*The Novels*

CONTENTS

Essay on Criticism

Alexander Pope

Part I

'Tis hard to say, if greater want of skill
Appear in writing or in judging ill;
But, of the two, less dang'rous is th' offence
To tire our patience, than mislead our sense.
Some few in that, but numbers err in this,
Ten censure wrong for one who writes amiss;
A fool might once himself alone expose,
Now one in verse makes many more in prose.

'Tis with our judgments as our watches, none
Go just alike, yet each believes his own.   10
In poets as true genius is but rare,
True taste as seldom is the critic's share;
Both must alike from Heav'n derive their light,
These born to judge, as well as those to write.
Let such teach others who themselves excel,
And censure freely who have written well.
Authors are partial to their wit, 'tis true,
But are not critics to their judgment too?

Yet if we look more closely we shall find
20 Most have the seeds of judgment in their mind;

Nature affords at least a glimm'ring light;
The lines, tho' touch'd but faintly, are drawn right.
But as the slightest sketch, if justly trac'd,
Is by ill colouring but the more disgrac'd,
So by false learning is good sense defac'd;
Some are bewilder'd in the maze of schools,
And some made coxcombs Nature meant but fools.
In search of wit these lose their common sense,
And then turn critics in their own defence:
30   Each burns alike, who can, or cannot write,
Or with a rival's, or an eunuch's spite.
All fools have still an itching to deride,
And fain would be upon the laughing side.
If Mævius scribble in Apollo's spite,
There are, who judge still worse than he can write.

Some have at first for wits, then poets pass'd,
Turn'd critics next, and prov'd plain fools at last;
Some neither can for wits nor critics pass,
As heavy mules are neither horse nor ass.
40   Those half-learn'd witlings, num'rous in our isle
As half-form'd insects on the banks of Nile;
Unfinish'd things, one knows not what to call,
Their generation's so equivocal:
To tell 'em, would a hundred tongues require,
Or one vain wit's, that might a hundred tire.

But you who seek to give and merit fame,
And justly bear a critic's noble name,
Be sure your self and your own reach to know,
How far your genius, taste, and learning go;
50   Launch not beyond your depth, but be discreet,
And mark that point where sense and dulness meet.

Nature to all things fix'd the limits fit,
And wisely curb'd proud man's pretending wit:

As on the land while here the ocean gains,
In other parts it leaves wide sandy plains;
Thus in the soul while memory prevails,
The solid pow'r of understanding fails;
Where beams of warm imagination play,
The memory's soft figures melt away.
One science only will one genius fit; 60
So vast is art, so narrow human wit:
Not only bounded to peculiar arts,
But oft in those, confin'd to single parts.
Like kings we lose the conquests gain'd before,
By vain ambition still to make them more;
Each might his sev'ral province well command,
Would all but stoop to what they understand.

   First follow NATURE, and your judgment frame
By her just standard, which is still the same:
Unerring Nature, still divinely bright, 70
One clear, unchang'd, and universal light,
Life, force, and beauty, must to all impart,
At once the source, and end, and test of art.
Art from that fund each just supply provides,
Works without show, and without pomp presides:
In some fair body thus th' informing soul
With spirits feeds, with vigour fills the whole,
Each motion guides, and ev'ry nerve sustains;
Itself unseen, but in th' effects, remains.
Some, to whom Heav'n in wit has been profuse, 80
Want as much more, to turn it to its use;
For wit and judgment often are at strife,
Though meant each other's aid, like man and wife.
'Tis more to guide, than spur the Muse's steed;
Restrain his fury, than provoke his speed;
The winged courser, like a gen'rous horse,
Shows most true mettle when you check his course.

Those RULES of old discover'd, not devis'd,
Are Nature still, but Nature methodis'd;
90   Nature, like liberty, is but restrain'd
By the same laws which first herself ordain'd.

Hear how learn'd Greece her useful rules indites,
When to repress, and when indulge our flights:
High on Parnassus' top her sons she show'd,
And pointed out those arduous paths they trod;
Held from afar, aloft, th' immortal prize,
And urg'd the rest by equal steps to rise.
Just precepts thus from great examples giv'n,
She drew from them what they deriv'd from Heav'n.
100   The gen'rous critic fann'd the poet's fire,
And taught the world with reason to admire.
Then criticism the Muse's handmaid prov'd,
To dress her charms, and make her more belov'd;
But following wits from that intention stray'd;
Who could not win the mistress, woo'd the maid;
Against the poets their own arms they turn'd,
Sure to hate most the men from whom they learn'd.
So modern 'pothecaries, taught the art
By doctor's bills to play the doctor's part,
110   Bold in the practice of mistaken rules,
Prescribe, apply, and call their masters fools.
Some on the leaves of ancient authors prey,
Nor time nor moths e'er spoil'd so much as they:
Some drily plain, without invention's aid,
Write dull receipts how poems may be made:
These leave the sense, their learning to display,
And those explain the meaning quite away.

You then whose judgment the right course would steer,
Know well each ANCIENT'S proper character;
120   His fable, subject, scope in ev'ry page;
Religion, country, genius of his age:

Without all these at once before your eyes,
Cavil you may, but never criticise.
Be Homer's works your study and delight,
Read them by day, and meditate by night;
Thence form your judgment, thence your maxims bring,
And trace the Muses upward to their spring;
Still with itself compar'd, his text peruse;
And let your comment be the Mantuan Muse.

    When first young Maro in his boundless mind   130
A work t' outlast immortal Rome design'd,
Perhaps he seem'd above the critic's law,
And but from Nature's fountains scorn'd to draw:
But when t' examine ev'ry part he came,
Nature and Homer were, he found, the same.
Convinc'd, amaz'd, he checks the bold design,
And rules as strict his labour'd work confine,
As if the Stagirite o'erlook'd each line.
Learn hence for ancient rules a just esteem;
To copy nature is to copy them.   140

    Some beauties yet, no precepts can declare,
For there's a happiness as well as care.
Music resembles poetry, in each
Are nameless graces which no methods teach,
And which a master-hand alone can reach.
If, where the rules not far enough extend,
(Since rules were made but to promote their end)
Some lucky LICENCE answers to the full
Th' intent propos'd, that licence is a rule.
Thus Pegasus, a nearer way to take,   150
May boldly deviate from the common track.
Great wits sometimes may gloriously offend,
And rise to faults true critics dare not mend;
From vulgar bounds with brave disorder part,
And snatch a grace beyond the reach of art,

Which, without passing through the judgment, gains
The heart, and all its end at once attains.
In prospects, thus, some objects please our eyes,
Which out of nature's common order rise,
160   The shapeless rock, or hanging precipice.
But tho' the ancients thus their rules invade,
(As kings dispense with laws themselves have made)
Moderns, beware! or if you must offend
Against the precept, ne'er transgress its end;
Let it be seldom, and compell'd by need,
And have, at least, their precedent to plead.
The critic else proceeds without remorse,
Seizes your fame, and puts his laws in force.

I know there are, to whose presumptuous thoughts
170   Those freer beauties, ev'n in them, seem faults.
Some figures monstrous and misshap'd appear,
Consider'd singly, or beheld too near,
Which, but proportion'd to their light, or place,
Due distance reconciles to form and grace.
A prudent chief not always must display
His pow'rs in equal ranks, and fair array,
But with th' occasion and the place comply,
Conceal his force, nay seem sometimes to fly.
Those oft are stratagems which errors seem,
180   Nor is it Homer nods, but we that dream.

Still green with bays each ancient altar stands,
Above the reach of sacrilegious hands,
Secure from flames, from envy's fiercer rage,
Destructive war, and all-involving age.
See, from each clime the learn'd their incense bring!
Hear, in all tongues consenting pæans ring!
In praise so just let ev'ry voice be join'd,
And fill the gen'ral chorus of mankind!
Hail, bards triumphant! born in happier days;

Immortal heirs of universal praise!   190
Whose honours with increase of ages grow,
As streams roll down, enlarging as they flow!
Nations unborn your mighty names shall sound,
And worlds applaud that must not yet be found!
Oh may some spark of your celestial fire
The last, the meanest of your sons inspire,
(That on weak wings, from far, pursues your flights;
Glows while he reads, but trembles as he writes)
To teach vain wits a science little known,
T' admire superior sense, and doubt their own!   200

PART II

Of all the causes which conspire to blind
Man's erring judgment, and misguide the mind,
What the weak head with strongest bias rules,
Is pride, the never-failing vice of fools.
Whatever Nature has in worth denied,
She gives in large recruits of needful pride;
For as in bodies, thus in souls, we find
What wants in blood and spirits, swell'd with wind;
Pride, where wit fails, steps in to our defence,
And fills up all the mighty void of sense!   210
If once right reason drives that cloud away,
Truth breaks upon us with resistless day;
Trust not yourself; but your defects to know,
Make use of ev'ry friend—and ev'ry foe.

A little learning is a dang'rous thing;
Drink deep, or taste not the Pierian spring:
There shallow draughts intoxicate the brain,
And drinking largely sobers us again.
Fir'd at first sight with what the Muse imparts,
In fearless youth we tempt the heights of arts,   220

While from the bounded level of our mind,
Short views we take, nor see the lengths behind,
But more advanc'd, behold with strange surprise
New, distant scenes of endless science rise!
So pleas'd at first, the tow'ring Alps we try,
Mount o'er the vales, and seem to tread the sky;
Th' eternal snows appear already past,
And the first clouds and mountains seem the last;
But those attain'd, we tremble to survey
230   The growing labours of the lengthen'd way,
Th' increasing prospect tires our wand'ring eyes,
Hills peep o'er hills, and Alps on Alps arise!

    A perfect judge will read each work of wit
With the same spirit that its author writ,
Survey the whole, nor seek slight faults to find,
Where nature moves, and rapture warms the mind;
Nor lose, for that malignant dull delight,
The gen'rous pleasure to be charm'd with wit.
But in such lays as neither ebb, nor flow,
240   Correctly cold, and regularly low,
That shunning faults, one quiet tenour keep;
We cannot blame indeed—but we may sleep.
In wit, as nature, what affects our hearts
Is not th' exactness of peculiar parts;
'Tis not a lip, or eye, we beauty call,
But the joint force and full result of all.
Thus when we view some well-proportion'd dome,
(The world's just wonder, and ev'n thine, O Rome!'
No single parts unequally surprise;
250   All comes united to th' admiring eyes;
No monstrous height, or breadth, or length appear;
The whole at once is bold, and regular.

    Whoever thinks a faultless piece to see,
Thinks what ne'er was, nor is, nor e'er shall be.

In ev'ry work regard the writer's end,
Since none can compass more than they intend;
And if the means be just, the conduct true,
Applause, in spite of trivial faults, is due.
As men of breeding, sometimes men of wit,
T' avoid great errors, must the less commit: 260
Neglect the rules each verbal critic lays,
For not to know such trifles, is a praise.
Most critics, fond of some subservient art,
Still make the whole depend upon a part:
They talk of principles, but notions prize,
And all to one lov'd folly sacrifice.

Once on a time, La Mancha's knight, they say,
A certain bard encount'ring on the way,
Discours'd in terms as just, with looks as sage,
As e'er could Dennis of the Grecian stage;   270
Concluding all were desp'rate sots and fools,
Who durst depart from Aristotle's rules.
Our author, happy in a judge so nice,
Produc'd his play, and begg'd the knight's advice,
Made him observe the subject and the plot,
The manners, passions, unities, what not?
All which, exact to rule, were brought about,
Were but a combat in the lists left out.
"What! leave the combat out?" exclaims the knight;
"Yes, or we must renounce the Stagirite."   280
"Not so by Heav'n" (he answers in a rage)
"Knights, squires, and steeds, must enter on the stage."
So vast a throng the stage can ne'er contain.
"Then build a new, or act it in a plain."

Thus critics, of less judgment than caprice,
Curious not knowing, not exact but nice,
Form short ideas; and offend in arts
(As most in manners) by a love to parts.

Some to conceit alone their taste confine,
290 And glitt'ring thoughts struck out at ev'ry line;
Pleas'd with a work where nothing's just or fit;
One glaring chaos and wild heap of wit.
Poets, like painters, thus, unskill'd to trace
The naked nature and the living grace,
With gold and jewels cover ev'ry part,
And hide with ornaments their want of art.
True wit is nature to advantage dress'd,
What oft was thought, but ne'er so well express'd,
Something, whose truth convinc'd at sight we find,
300 That gives us back the image of our mind.
As shades more sweetly recommend the light,
So modest plainness sets off sprightly wit.
For works may have more wit than does 'em good,
As bodies perish through excess of blood.

Others for language all their care express,
And value books, as women men, for dress:
Their praise is still—"the style is excellent":
The sense, they humbly take upon content.
Words are like leaves; and where they most abound,
310 Much fruit of sense beneath is rarely found.
False eloquence, like the prismatic glass,
Its gaudy colours spreads on ev'ry place;
The face of Nature we no more survey,
All glares alike, without distinction gay:
But true expression, like th' unchanging sun,
Clears, and improves whate'er it shines upon,
It gilds all objects, but it alters none.
Expression is the dress of thought, and still
Appears more decent, as more suitable;
320 A vile conceit in pompous words express'd,
Is like a clown in regal purple dress'd:
For diff'rent styles with diff'rent subjects sort,
As several garbs with country, town, and court.

Some by old words to fame have made pretence,
Ancients in phrase, mere moderns in their sense;
Such labour'd nothings, in so strange a style,
Amaze th' unlearn'd, and make the learned smile.
Unlucky, as Fungoso in the play,
These sparks with awkward vanity display
What the fine gentleman wore yesterday!   330
And but so mimic ancient wits at best,
As apes our grandsires, in their doublets dress'd.
In words, as fashions, the same rule will hold;
Alike fantastic, if too new, or old;
Be not the first by whom the new are tried,
Not yet the last to lay the old aside.

    But most by numbers judge a poet's song;
And smooth or rough, with them is right or wrong:
In the bright Muse though thousand charms conspire,
Her voice is all these tuneful fools admire,   340
Who haunt Parnassus but to please their ear,
Not mend their minds; as some to church repair,
Not for the doctrine, but the music there.
These equal syllables alone require,
Tho' oft the ear the open vowels tire,
While expletives their feeble aid do join,
And ten low words oft creep in one dull line,
While they ring round the same unvaried chimes,
With sure returns of still expected rhymes.
Where'er you find "the cooling western breeze",   350
In the next line, it "whispers through the trees":
If "crystal streams with pleasing murmurs creep",
The reader's threaten'd (not in vain) with "sleep".
Then, at the last and only couplet fraught
With some unmeaning thing they call a thought,
A needless Alexandrine ends the song,
That, like a wounded snake, drags its slow length along.
Leave such to tune their own dull rhymes, and know

What's roundly smooth, or languishingly slow;
360   And praise the easy vigour of a line,
Where Denham's strength, and Waller's sweetness join.
True ease in writing comes from art, not chance,
As those move easiest who have learn'd to dance.
'Tis not enough no harshness gives offence,
The sound must seem an echo to the sense.
Soft is the strain when Zephyr gently blows,
And the smooth stream in smoother numbers flows;
But when loud surges lash the sounding shore,
The hoarse, rough verse should like the torrent roar.
370   When Ajax strives some rock's vast weight to throw,
The line too labours, and the words move slow;
Not so, when swift Camilla scours the plain,
Flies o'er th' unbending corn, and skims along the main.
Hear how Timotheus' varied lays surprise,
And bid alternate passions fall and rise!
While, at each change, the son of Libyan Jove
Now burns with glory, and then melts with love;
Now his fierce eyes with sparkling fury glow,
Now sighs steal out, and tears begin to flow:
380   Persians and Greeks like turns of nature found,
And the world's victor stood subdu'd by sound!
The pow'r of music all our hearts allow,
And what Timotheus was, is Dryden now.

Avoid extremes; and shun the fault of such,
Who still are pleas'd too little or too much.
At ev'ry trifle scorn to take offence,
That always shows great pride, or little sense;
Those heads, as stomachs, are not sure the best,
Which nauseate all, and nothing can digest.
390   Yet let not each gay turn thy rapture move,
For fools admire, but men of sense approve;
As things seem large which we through mists descry,
Dulness is ever apt to magnify.

   Some foreign writers, some our own despise;
The ancients only, or the moderns prize.
Thus wit, like faith, by each man is applied
To one small sect, and all are damn'd beside.
Meanly they seek the blessing to confine,
And force that sun but on a part to shine;
Which not alone the southern wit sublimes,   400
But ripens spirits in cold northern climes;
Which from the first has shone on ages past,
Enlights the present, and shall warm the last;
(Though each may feel increases and decays,
And see now clearer and now darker days.)
Regard not then if wit be old or new,
But blame the false, and value still the true.
Some ne'er advance a judgment of their own,
But catch the spreading notion of the town;
They reason and conclude by precedent,   410
And own stale nonsense which they ne'er invent.
Some judge of authors' names, not works, and then
Nor praise nor blame the writings, but the men.
Of all this servile herd, the worst is he
That in proud dulness joins with quality,
A constant critic at the great man's board,
To fetch and carry nonsense for my Lord.
What woeful stuff this madrigal would be,
In some starv'd hackney sonneteer, or me?
But let a Lord once own the happy lines,   420
How the wit brightens! how the style refines!
Before his sacred name flies every fault,
And each exalted stanza teems with thought!

   The vulgar thus through imitation err;
As oft the learn'd by being singular;
So much they scorn the crowd, that if the throng
By chance go right, they purposely go wrong:
So Schismatics the plain believers quit,

And are but damn'd for having too much wit.

430   Some praise at morning what they blame at night;
But always think the last opinion right.
A Muse by these is like a mistress us'd,
This hour she's idoliz'd, the next abus'd;
While their weak heads, like towns unfortified,
Twixt sense and nonsense daily change their side.
Ask them the cause; they're wiser still, they say;
And still tomorrow's wiser than today.
We think our fathers fools, so wise we grow;
Our wiser sons, no doubt, will think us so.
440   Once school divines this zealous isle o'erspread;
Who knew most Sentences, was deepest read;
Faith, Gospel, all, seem'd made to be disputed,
And none had sense enough to be confuted:
Scotists and Thomists, now, in peace remain,
Amidst their kindred cobwebs in Duck Lane.
If Faith itself has different dresses worn,
What wonder modes in wit should take their turn?
Oft, leaving what is natural and fit,
The current folly proves the ready wit;
450   And authors think their reputation safe
Which lives as long as fools are pleased to laugh.

      Some valuing those of their own side or mind,
Still make themselves the measure of mankind;
Fondly we think we honour merit then,
When we but praise ourselves in other men.
Parties in wit attend on those of state,
And public faction doubles private hate.
Pride, Malice, Folly, against Dryden rose,
In various shapes of Parsons, Critics, Beaus;
460   But sense surviv'd, when merry jests were past;
For rising merit will buoy up at last.
Might he return, and bless once more our eyes,

New Blackmores and new Milbourns must arise;
Nay should great Homer lift his awful head,
Zoilus again would start up from the dead.
Envy will merit, as its shade, pursue,
But like a shadow, proves the substance true;
For envied wit, like Sol eclips'd, makes known
Th' opposing body's grossness, not its own.
When first that sun too powerful beams displays,   470
It draws up vapours which obscure its rays;
But ev'n those clouds at last adorn its way,
Reflect new glories, and augment the day.

Be thou the first true merit to befriend;
His praise is lost, who stays till all commend.
Short is the date, alas, of modern rhymes,
And 'tis but just to let 'em live betimes.
No longer now that golden age appears,
When patriarch wits surviv'd a thousand years:
Now length of Fame (our second life) is lost,   480
And bare threescore is all ev'n that can boast;
Our sons their fathers' failing language see,
And such as Chaucer is, shall Dryden be.
So when the faithful pencil has design'd
Some bright idea of the master's mind,
Where a new world leaps out at his command,
And ready Nature waits upon his hand;
When the ripe colours soften and unite,
And sweetly melt into just shade and light;
When mellowing years their full perfection give,   490
And each bold figure just begins to live,
The treacherous colours the fair art betray,
And all the bright creation fades away!

Unhappy wit, like most mistaken things,
Atones not for that envy which it brings.
In youth alone its empty praise we boast,

But soon the short-liv'd vanity is lost:
Like some fair flow'r the early spring supplies,
That gaily blooms, but ev'n in blooming dies.
500   What is this wit, which must our cares employ?
The owner's wife, that other men enjoy;
Then most our trouble still when most admir'd,
And still the more we give, the more requir'd;
Whose fame with pains we guard, but lose with ease,
Sure some to vex, but never all to please;
'Tis what the vicious fear, the virtuous shun;
By fools 'tis hated, and by knaves undone!

If wit so much from ign'rance undergo,
Ah let not learning too commence its foe!
510   Of old, those met rewards who could excel,
And such were prais'd who but endeavour'd well:
Though triumphs were to gen'rals only due,
Crowns were reserv'd to grace the soldiers too.
Now, they who reach Parnassus' lofty crown,
Employ their pains to spurn some others down;

And while self-love each jealous writer rules,
Contending wits become the sport of fools:
But still the worst with most regret commend,
For each ill author is as bad a friend.
520   To what base ends, and by what abject ways,
Are mortals urg'd through sacred lust of praise!
Ah ne'er so dire a thirst of glory boast,
Nor in the critic let the man be lost!
Good nature and good sense must ever join;
To err is human; to forgive, divine.

But if in noble minds some dregs remain,
Not yet purg'd off, of spleen and sour disdain,
Discharge that rage on more provoking crimes,
Nor fear a dearth in these flagitious times.

No pardon vile obscenity should find,   530
Though wit and art conspire to move your mind;
But dulness with obscenity must prove
As shameful sure as impotence in love.
In the fat age of pleasure, wealth, and ease,
Sprung the rank weed, and thriv'd with large increase:
When love was all an easy monarch's care;
Seldom at council, never in a war:
Jilts ruled the state, and statesmen farces writ;
Nay wits had pensions, and young Lords had wit:
The fair sat panting at a courtier's play,   540
And not a mask went unimprov'd away:
The modest fan was lifted up no more,
And virgins smil'd at what they blush'd before.
The following licence of a foreign reign
Did all the dregs of bold Socinus drain;
Then unbelieving priests reform'd the nation,
And taught more pleasant methods of salvation;
Where Heav'n's free subjects might their rights dispute,
Lest God himself should seem too absolute:
Pulpits their sacred satire learned to spare,   550
And Vice admired to find a flatt'rer there!
Encourag'd thus, wit's Titans brav'd the skies,
And the press groan'd with licenc'd blasphemies.
These monsters, critics! with your darts engage,
Here point your thunder, and exhaust your rage!
Yet shun their fault, who, scandalously nice,
Will needs mistake an author into vice;
All seems infected that th' infected spy,
As all looks yellow to the jaundic'd eye.

Part III

   Learn then what morals critics ought to show,   560
For 'tis but half a judge's task, to know.

'Tis not enough, taste, judgment, learning, join;
In all you speak, let truth and candour shine:
That not alone what to your sense is due,
All may allow; but seek your friendship too.

    Be silent always when you doubt your sense;
And speak, though sure, with seeming diffidence:
Some positive, persisting fops we know,
Who, if once wrong, will needs be always so;
570   But you, with pleasure own your errors past,
And make each day a critic on the last.

    'Tis not enough, your counsel still be true;
Blunt truths more mischief than nice falsehoods do;
Men must be taught as if you taught them not;
And things unknown proposed as things forgot.
Without good breeding, truth is disapprov'd;
That only makes superior sense belov'd.

    Be niggards of advice on no pretence;
For the worst avarice is that of sense.
580   With mean complacence ne'er betray your trust,
Nor be so civil as to prove unjust.
Fear not the anger of the wise to raise;
Those best can bear reproof, who merit praise.

    'Twere well might critics still this freedom take,
But Appius reddens at each word you speak,
And stares, *Tremendous*! with a threatening eye,
Like some fierce tyrant in old tapestry!
Fear most to tax an honourable fool,
Whose right it is, uncensur'd, to be dull;
590   Such, without wit, are poets when they please,
As without learning they can take degrees.
Leave dangerous truths to unsuccessful satires,
And flattery to fulsome dedicators,

Whom, when they praise, the world believes no more,
Than when they promise to give scribbling o'er.
'Tis best sometimes your censure to restrain,
And charitably let the dull be vain:
Your silence there is better than your spite,
For who can rail so long as they can write?
Still humming on, their drowsy course they keep,   600
And lash'd so long, like tops, are lash'd asleep.
False steps but help them to renew the race,
As after stumbling, jades will mend their pace.
What crowds of these, impenitently bold,
In sounds and jingling syllables grown old,
Still run on poets, in a raging vein,
Even to the dregs and squeezings of the brain,
Strain out the last, dull droppings of their sense,
And rhyme with all the rage of impotence!

Such shameless bards we have; and yet 'tis true,   610
There are as mad, abandon'd critics too.
The bookful blockhead, ignorantly read,
With loads of learned lumber in his head,
With his own tongue still edifies his ears,
And always list'ning to himself appears.
All books he reads, and all he reads assails,
From Dryden's Fables down to Durfey's Tales.
With him, most authors steal their works, or buy;
Garth did not write his own *Dispensary*.
Name a new play, and he's the poet's friend,   620
Nay show'd his faults—but when would poets mend?
No place so sacred from such fops is barr'd,
Nor is Paul's church more safe than Paul's churchyard:
Nay, fly to altars; there they'll talk you dead:
For fools rush in where angels fear to tread.
Distrustful sense with modest caution speaks;
It still looks home, and short excursions makes;
But rattling nonsense in full volleys breaks;

And never shock'd, and never turn'd aside,
630 Bursts out, resistless, with a thund'ring tide.

But where's the man, who counsel can bestow,
Still pleas'd to teach, and yet not proud to know?
Unbias'd, or by favour or by spite;
Not dully prepossess'd, nor blindly right;
Though learn'd, well-bred; and though well-bred, sincere;
Modestly bold, and humanly severe?
Who to a friend his faults can freely show,
And gladly praise the merit of a foe?
Blest with a taste exact, yet unconfin'd;
640 A knowledge both of books and human kind;
Gen'rous converse; a soul exempt from pride;
And love to praise, with reason on his side?

Such once were critics; such the happy few,
Athens and Rome in better ages knew.
The mighty Stagirite first left the shore,
Spread all his sails, and durst the deeps explore:
He steer'd securely, and discover'd far,
Led by the light of the Mæonian Star.
Poets, a race long unconfin'd and free,
650 Still fond and proud of savage liberty,
Receiv'd his laws; and stood convinc'd 'twas fit,
Who conquer'd nature, should preside o'er wit.

Horace still charms with graceful negligence,
And without methods talks us into sense,
Will, like a friend, familiarly convey
The truest notions in the easiest way.
He, who supreme in judgment, as in wit,
Might boldly censure, as he boldly writ,
Yet judg'd with coolness, though he sung with fire;
660 His precepts teach but what his works inspire.
Our critics take a contrary extreme,

They judge with fury, but they write with fle'me:
Nor suffers Horace more in wrong translations
By wits, than critics in as wrong quotations.

See Dionysius Homer's thoughts refine,
And call new beauties forth from ev'ry line!
Fancy and art in gay Petronius please,
The scholar's learning, with the courtier's ease.

In grave Quintilian's copious work we find
The justest rules, and clearest method join'd;   670
Thus useful arms in magazines we place,
All rang'd in order, and dispos'd with grace,
But less to please the eye, than arm the hand,
Still fit for use, and ready at command.

Thee, bold Longinus! all the Nine inspire,
And bless their critic with a poet's fire.
An ardent judge, who zealous in his trust,
With warmth gives sentence, yet is always just;
Whose own example strengthens all his laws;
And is himself that great sublime he draws.   680

Thus long succeeding critics justly reign'd,
Licence repress'd, and useful laws ordain'd;
Learning and Rome alike in empire grew,
And arts still follow'd where her eagles flew;
From the same foes, at last, both felt their doom,
And the same age saw learning fall, and Rome.
With tyranny, then superstition join'd,
As that the body, this enslav'd the mind;
Much was believ'd, but little understood,
And to be dull was constru'd to be good;   690
A second deluge learning thus o'er-run,
And the monks finish'd what the Goths begun.

At length Erasmus, that great, injur'd name,

(The glory of the priesthood, and the shame!)
Stemm'd the wild torrent of a barb'rous age,
And drove those holy Vandals off the stage.

    But see! each Muse, in Leo's golden days,
Starts from her trance, and trims her wither'd bays!
Rome's ancient genius, o'er its ruins spread,
Shakes off the dust, and rears his rev'rend head!
Then sculpture and her sister-arts revive;
Stones leap'd to form, and rocks began to live;
With sweeter notes each rising temple rung;
A Raphael painted, and a Vida sung.
Immortal Vida! on whose honour'd brow
The poet's bays and critic's ivy grow:
Cremona now shall ever boast thy name,
As next in place to Mantua, next in fame!

    But soon by impious arms from Latium chas'd,
Their ancient bounds the banished Muses pass'd;
Thence arts o'er all the northern world advance;
But critic-learning flourish'd most in France.
The rules a nation born to serve, obeys,
And Boileau still in right of Horace sways.
But we, brave Britons, foreign laws despis'd,
And kept unconquer'd, and uncivilis'd,
Fierce for the liberties of wit, and bold,
We still defied the Romans, as of old.
Yet some there were, among the sounder few
Of those who less presum'd, and better knew,
Who durst assert the juster ancient cause,
And here restor'd wit's fundamental laws.
Such was the Muse, whose rules and practice tell
"Nature's chief master-piece is writing well."
Such was Roscommon—not more learn'd than good,
With manners gen'rous as his noble blood;
To him the wit of Greece and Rome was known,

And ev'ry author's merit, but his own.
Such late was Walsh—the Muse's judge and friend,
Who justly knew to blame or to commend; 730
To failings mild, but zealous for desert;
The clearest head, and the sincerest heart.
This humble praise, lamented shade! receive,
This praise at least a grateful Muse may give:
The Muse, whose early voice you taught to sing,
Prescrib'd her heights, and prun'd her tender wing,
(Her guide now lost) no more attempts to rise,
But in low numbers short excursions tries:
Content, if hence th' unlearn'd their wants may view,
The learn'd reflect on what before they knew: 740
Careless of censure, nor too fond of fame,
Still pleas'd to praise, yet not afraid to blame,
Averse alike to flatter, or offend,
Not free from faults, nor yet too vain to mend.

The Iliad of Homer

Alexander Pope

Translator

The Contention of Achilles and Agamemnon

In the war of Troy, the Greeks having sacked some of the neighbouring towns, and taken from thence two beautiful captives, Chryseis and Briseis, allotted the first to Agamemnon, and the last to Achilles. Chryses, the father of Chryseis, and priest of Apollo, comes to the Grecian camp to ransom her; with which the action of the poem opens, in the tenth year of the siege. The priest being refused, and insolently dismissed by Agamemnon, entreats for vengeance from his god; who inflicts a pestilence on the Greeks. Achilles calls a council, and encourages Chalcas to declare the cause of it; who attributes it to the refusal of Chryseis. The king, being obliged to send back his captive, enters into a furious contest with Achilles, which Nestor pacifies; however, as he had the absolute command of the army, he seizes on Briseis in revenge. Achilles in discontent withdraws himself and his forces from the rest of the Greeks; and complaining to Thetis, she supplicates Jupiter to render them sensible of the wrong done to her son, by giving victory

to the Trojans. Jupiter, granting her suit, incenses Juno: between
whom the debate runs high, till they are reconciled by the address
of Vulcan.

The time of two-and-twenty days is taken up in this book: nine
during the plague, one in the council and quarrel of the princes,
and twelve for Jupiter's stay with the Æthiopians, at whose return
Thetis prefers her petition. The scene lies in the Grecian camp,
then changes to Chrysa, and lastly to Olympus.

BOOK I

Achilles' wrath, to Greece the direful spring
Of woes unnumber'd, heavenly goddess, sing!
That wrath which hurl'd to Pluto's gloomy reign
The souls of mighty chiefs untimely slain;
Whose limbs unburied on the naked shore,
Devouring dogs and hungry vultures tore.
Since great Achilles and Atrides strove,
Such was the sovereign doom, and such the will of Jove!
Declare, O Muse! in what ill-fated hour
10   Sprung the fierce strife, from what offended power
Latona's son a dire contagion spread,
And heap'd the camp with mountains of the dead;
The king of men his reverent priest defied,
And for the king's offence the people died.
For Chryses sought with costly gifts to gain
His captive daughter from the victor's chain.
Suppliant the venerable father stands;
Apollo's awful ensigns grace his hands
By these he begs; and lowly bending down,
20   Extends the sceptre and the laurel crown
He sued to all, but chief implored for grace
The brother-kings, of Atreus' royal race
'Ye kings and warriors! may your vows be crown'd,

And Troy's proud walls lie level with the ground.
May Jove restore you when your toils are o'er
Safe to the pleasures of your native shore.
But, oh! relieve a wretched parent's pain,
And give Chryseis to these arms again;
If mercy fail, yet let my presents move,
And dread avenging Phoebus, son of Jove.'   30
The Greeks in shouts their joint assent declare,
The priest to reverence, and release the fair.
Not so Atrides; he, with kingly pride,
Repulsed the sacred sire, and thus replied:
'Hence on thy life, and fly these hostile plains,
Nor ask, presumptuous, what the king detains
Hence, with thy laurel crown, and golden rod,
Nor trust too far those ensigns of thy god.
Mine is thy daughter, priest, and shall remain;
And prayers, and tears, and bribes, shall plead in vain;   40
Till time shall rifle every youthful grace,
And age dismiss her from my cold embrace,
In daily labours of the loom employ'd,
Or doom'd to deck the bed she once enjoy'd
Hence then; to Argos shall the maid retire,
Far from her native soil and weeping sire.'

An Essay on Man

Alexander Pope

Epistle I

To Henry St. John, Lord Bolingbroke

Awake, my St. John! leave all meaner things
To low ambition, and the pride of kings.
Let us (since life can little more supply
Than just to look about us and to die)
Expatiate free o'er all this scene of man;
A mighty maze! but not without a plan;
A wild, where weeds and flow'rs promiscuous shoot;
Or garden, tempting with forbidden fruit.
Together let us beat this ample field,
Try what the open, what the covert yield; 10
The latent tracts, the giddy heights explore
Of all who blindly creep, or sightless soar;
Eye Nature's walks, shoot folly as it flies,
And catch the manners living as they rise;
Laugh where we must, be candid where we can;
But vindicate the ways of God to man.

1

Say first, of God above, or man below,
What can we reason, but from what we know?
Of man what see we, but his station here,
From which to reason, or to which refer?
Through worlds unnumber'd though the God be known,
'Tis ours to trace him only in our own.
He, who through vast immensity can pierce,
See worlds on worlds compose one universe,
Observe how system into system runs,
What other planets circle other suns,
What varied being peoples ev'ry star,
May tell why Heav'n has made us as we are.
But of this frame the bearings, and the ties,
The strong connections, nice dependencies,
Gradations just, has thy pervading soul
Look'd through? or can a part contain the whole?

Is the great chain, that draws all to agree,
And drawn supports, upheld by God, or thee?

2

Presumptuous man! the reason wouldst thou find,
Why form'd so weak, so little, and so blind?
First, if thou canst, the harder reason guess,
Why form'd no weaker, blinder, and no less!
Ask of thy mother earth, why oaks are made
Taller or stronger than the weeds they shade?
Or ask of yonder argent fields above,
Why Jove's satellites are less than Jove?

Of systems possible, if 'tis confest
That Wisdom infinite must form the best,

Where all must full or not coherent be,
And all that rises, rise in due degree;
Then, in the scale of reas'ning life, 'tis plain
There must be somewhere, such a rank as man:
And all the question (wrangle e'er so long)
Is only this, if God has plac'd him wrong?   50

Respecting man, whatever wrong we call,
May, must be right, as relative to all.
In human works, though labour'd on with pain,
A thousand movements scarce one purpose gain;
In God's, one single can its end produce;
Yet serves to second too some other use.
So man, who here seems principal alone,
Perhaps acts second to some sphere unknown,
Touches some wheel, or verges to some goal;
'Tis but a part we see, and not a whole.   60

When the proud steed shall know why man restrains
His fiery course, or drives him o'er the plains:
When the dull ox, why now he breaks the clod,
Is now a victim, and now Egypt's God:
Then shall man's pride and dulness comprehend
His actions', passions', being's, use and end;
Why doing, suff'ring, check'd, impell'd; and why
This hour a slave, the next a deity.

Then say not man's imperfect, Heav'n in fault;
Say rather, man's as perfect as he ought: 70
His knowledge measur'd to his state and place,
His time a moment, and a point his space.
If to be perfect in a certain sphere,
What matter, soon or late, or here or there?
The blest today is as completely so,
As who began a thousand years ago.

3

Heav'n from all creatures hides the book of fate,
All but the page prescrib'd, their present state:
From brutes what men, from men what spirits know:
80   Or who could suffer being here below?
The lamb thy riot dooms to bleed today,
Had he thy reason, would he skip and play?
Pleas'd to the last, he crops the flow'ry food,
And licks the hand just rais'd to shed his blood.
Oh blindness to the future! kindly giv'n,
That each may fill the circle mark'd by Heav'n:
Who sees with equal eye, as God of all,
A hero perish, or a sparrow fall,
Atoms or systems into ruin hurl'd,
90   And now a bubble burst, and now a world.

Hope humbly then; with trembling pinions soar;
Wait the great teacher Death; and God adore!
What future bliss, he gives not thee to know,
But gives that hope to be thy blessing now.
Hope springs eternal in the human breast:
Man never is, but always to be blest:
The soul, uneasy and confin'd from home,
Rests and expatiates in a life to come.

Lo! the poor Indian, whose untutor'd mind
100   Sees God in clouds, or hears him in the wind;
His soul, proud science never taught to stray
Far as the solar walk, or milky way;
Yet simple nature to his hope has giv'n,
Behind the cloud-topt hill, an humbler heav'n;
Some safer world in depth of woods embrac'd,
Some happier island in the wat'ry waste,
Where slaves once more their native land behold,
No fiends torment, no Christians thirst for gold.

To be, contents his natural desire,
He asks no angel's wing, no seraph's fire;   110
But thinks, admitted to that equal sky,
His faithful dog shall bear him company.

4

Go, wiser thou! and, in thy scale of sense
Weigh thy opinion against Providence;
Call imperfection what thou fanciest such,
Say, here he gives too little, there too much:
Destroy all creatures for thy sport or gust,
Yet cry, if man's unhappy, God's unjust;
If man alone engross not Heav'n's high care,
Alone made perfect here, immortal there: 120
Snatch from his hand the balance and the rod,
Rejudge his justice, be the God of God.
In pride, in reas'ning pride, our error lies;
All quit their sphere, and rush into the skies.
Pride still is aiming at the blest abodes,
Men would be angels, angels would be gods.
Aspiring to be gods, if angels fell,
Aspiring to be angels, men rebel:
And who but wishes to invert the laws
Of order, sins against th' Eternal Cause.   130

5

Ask for what end the heav'nly bodies shine,
Earth for whose use? Pride answers, "'Tis for mine:
For me kind Nature wakes her genial pow'r,
Suckles each herb, and spreads out ev'ry flow'r;
Annual for me, the grape, the rose renew,
The juice nectareous, and the balmy dew;
For me, the mine a thousand treasures brings;

For me, health gushes from a thousand springs;
Seas roll to waft me, suns to light me rise;
140   My foot-stool earth, my canopy the skies."

But errs not Nature from this gracious end,
From burning suns when livid deaths descend,
When earthquakes swallow, or when tempests sweep
Towns to one grave, whole nations to the deep?
"No, ('tis replied) the first Almighty Cause
Acts not by partial, but by gen'ral laws;
Th' exceptions few; some change since all began:
And what created perfect?"—Why then man?
If the great end be human happiness,
150   Then Nature deviates; and can man do less?
As much that end a constant course requires
Of show'rs and sunshine, as of man's desires;
As much eternal springs and cloudless skies,
As men for ever temp'rate, calm, and wise.
If plagues or earthquakes break not Heav'n's design,
Why then a Borgia, or a Catiline?
Who knows but he, whose hand the lightning forms,
Who heaves old ocean, and who wings the storms,
Pours fierce ambition in a Cæsar's mind,
160   Or turns young Ammon loose to scourge mankind?
From pride, from pride, our very reas'ning springs;
Account for moral, as for nat'ral things:
Why charge we Heav'n in those, in these acquit?
In both, to reason right is to submit.

Better for us, perhaps, it might appear,
Were there all harmony, all virtue here;
That never air or ocean felt the wind;
That never passion discompos'd the mind.
But ALL subsists by elemental strife;
170   And passions are the elements of life.

The gen'ral order, since the whole began,
Is kept in nature, and is kept in man.

6

What would this man? Now upward will he soar,
And little less than angel, would be more;
Now looking downwards, just as griev'd appears
To want the strength of bulls, the fur of bears.
Made for his use all creatures if he call,
Say what their use, had he the pow'rs of all?
Nature to these, without profusion, kind,
The proper organs, proper pow'rs assign'd;   180
Each seeming want compensated of course,
Here with degrees of swiftness, there of force;
All in exact proportion to the state;
Nothing to add, and nothing to abate.
Each beast, each insect, happy in its own:
Is Heav'n unkind to man, and man alone?
Shall he alone, whom rational we call,
Be pleas'd with nothing, if not bless'd with all?

The bliss of man (could pride that blessing find)
Is not to act or think beyond mankind;   190
No pow'rs of body or of soul to share,
But what his nature and his state can bear.
Why has not man a microscopic eye?
For this plain reason, man is not a fly.
Say what the use, were finer optics giv'n,
T' inspect a mite, not comprehend the heav'n?
Or touch, if tremblingly alive all o'er,
To smart and agonize at ev'ry pore?
Or quick effluvia darting through the brain,
Die of a rose in aromatic pain?   200
If nature thunder'd in his op'ning ears,

And stunn'd him with the music of the spheres,
How would he wish that Heav'n had left him still
The whisp'ring zephyr, and the purling rill?
Who finds not Providence all good and wise,
Alike in what it gives, and what denies?

7

Far as Creation's ample range extends,
The scale of sensual, mental pow'rs ascends:
Mark how it mounts, to man's imperial race,
210   From the green myriads in the peopled grass:
What modes of sight betwixt each wide extreme,
The mole's dim curtain, and the lynx's beam:
Of smell, the headlong lioness between,
And hound sagacious on the tainted green:
Of hearing, from the life that fills the flood,
To that which warbles through the vernal wood:
The spider's touch, how exquisitely fine!
Feels at each thread, and lives along the line:
In the nice bee, what sense so subtly true
220   From pois'nous herbs extracts the healing dew:
How instinct varies in the grov'lling swine,
Compar'd, half-reas'ning elephant, with thine:
'Twixt that, and reason, what a nice barrier;
For ever sep'rate, yet for ever near!
Remembrance and reflection how allied;
What thin partitions sense from thought divide:
And middle natures, how they long to join,
Yet never pass th' insuperable line!
Without this just gradation, could they be
230   Subjected, these to those, or all to thee?
The pow'rs of all subdu'd by thee alone,
Is not thy reason all these pow'rs in one?

8

See, through this air, this ocean, and this earth,
All matter quick, and bursting into birth.
Above, how high, progressive life may go!
Around, how wide! how deep extend below!
Vast chain of being, which from God began,
Natures ethereal, human, angel, man,
Beast, bird, fish, insect! what no eye can see,
No glass can reach! from infinite to thee,   240
From thee to nothing!—On superior pow'rs
Were we to press, inferior might on ours:
Or in the full creation leave a void,
Where, one step broken, the great scale's destroy'd:
From nature's chain whatever link you strike,
Tenth or ten thousandth, breaks the chain alike.

And, if each system in gradation roll
Alike essential to th' amazing whole,
The least confusion but in one, not all
That system only, but the whole must fall.   250
Let earth unbalanc'd from her orbit fly,
Planets and suns run lawless through the sky;
Let ruling angels from their spheres be hurl'd,
Being on being wreck'd, and world on world;
Heav'n's whole foundations to their centre nod,
And nature tremble to the throne of God.
All this dread order break—for whom? for thee?
Vile worm!—Oh madness, pride, impiety!

9

What if the foot ordain'd the dust to tread,
Or hand to toil, aspir'd to be the head?   260
What if the head, the eye, or ear repin'd

To serve mere engines to the ruling mind?
Just as absurd for any part to claim
To be another, in this gen'ral frame:
Just as absurd, to mourn the tasks or pains,
The great directing Mind of All ordains.

All are but parts of one stupendous whole,
Whose body Nature is, and God the soul;
That, chang'd through all, and yet in all the same,
270   Great in the earth, as in th' ethereal frame,
Warms in the sun, refreshes in the breeze,
Glows in the stars, and blossoms in the trees,
Lives through all life, extends through all extent,
Spreads undivided, operates unspent,
Breathes in our soul, informs our mortal part,
As full, as perfect, in a hair as heart;
As full, as perfect, in vile man that mourns,
As the rapt seraph that adores and burns;
To him no high, no low, no great, no small;
280   He fills, he bounds, connects, and equals all.

10

Cease then, nor order imperfection name:
Our proper bliss depends on what we blame.
Know thy own point: This kind, this due degree
Of blindness, weakness, Heav'n bestows on thee.
Submit.—In this, or any other sphere,
Secure to be as blest as thou canst bear:
Safe in the hand of one disposing pow'r,
Or in the natal, or the mortal hour.
All nature is but art, unknown to thee;
290   All chance, direction, which thou canst not see;
All discord, harmony, not understood;
All partial evil, universal good:

And, spite of pride, in erring reason's spite,
One truth is clear, Whatever is, is right.

Epistle II

1

Know, then, thyself, presume not God to scan;
The proper study of mankind is man.
Placed on this isthmus of a middle state,
A being darkly wise, and rudely great:
With too much knowledge for the sceptic side,
With too much weakness for the stoic's pride,
He hangs between; in doubt to act, or rest;
In doubt to deem himself a god, or beast;
In doubt his mind or body to prefer;
Born but to die, and reasoning but to err;   10
Alike in ignorance, his reason such,
Whether he thinks too little, or too much:
Chaos of thought and passion, all confused;
Still by himself abused, or disabused;
Created half to rise, and half to fall;
Great lord of all things, yet a prey to all;
Sole judge of truth, in endless error hurled:
The glory, jest, and riddle of the world!

Go, wondrous creature! mount where science guides,
Go, measure earth, weigh air, and state the tides;   20
Instruct the planets in what orbs to run,
Correct old time, and regulate the sun;
Go, soar with Plato to th' empyreal sphere,
To the first good, first perfect, and first fair;
Or tread the mazy round his followers trod,

And quitting sense call imitating God;
As Eastern priests in giddy circles run,
And turn their heads to imitate the sun.
Go, teach Eternal Wisdom how to rule—
30   Then drop into thyself, and be a fool!

Superior beings, when of late they saw
A mortal man unfold all Nature's law,
Admired such wisdom in an earthly shape
And showed a Newton as we show an ape.

Could he, whose rules the rapid comet bind,
Describe or fix one movement of his mind?
Who saw its fires here rise, and there descend,
Explain his own beginning, or his end?
Alas, what wonder! man's superior part
40   Unchecked may rise, and climb from art to art;
But when his own great work is but begun,
What reason weaves, by passion is undone.
Trace Science, then, with Modesty thy guide;
First strip off all her equipage of pride;
Deduct what is but vanity or dress,
Or learning's luxury, or idleness;
Or tricks to show the stretch of human brain,
Mere curious pleasure, or ingenious pain;
Expunge the whole, or lop th' excrescent parts
50   Of all our vices have created arts;
Then see how little the remaining sum,
Which served the past, and must the times to come!

2

Two principles in human nature reign;
Self-love to urge, and reason, to restrain;
Nor this a good, nor that a bad we call,
Each works its end, to move or govern all

And to their proper operation still,
Ascribe all good; to their improper, ill.
Self-love, the spring of motion, acts the soul;
Reason's comparing balance rules the whole. 60
Man, but for that, no action could attend,
And but for this, were active to no end:
Fixed like a plant on his peculiar spot,
To draw nutrition, propagate, and rot;
Or, meteor-like, flame lawless through the void,
Destroying others, by himself destroyed.
Most strength the moving principle requires;
Active its task, it prompts, impels, inspires.
Sedate and quiet the comparing lies,
Formed but to check, deliberate, and advise. 70
Self-love still stronger, as its objects nigh;
Reason's at distance, and in prospect lie:
That sees immediate good by present sense;
Reason, the future and the consequence.
Thicker than arguments, temptations throng.
At best more watchful this, but that more strong.
The action of the stronger to suspend,
Reason still use, to reason still attend.
Attention, habit and experience gains;
Each strengthens reason, and self-love restrains. 80
Let subtle schoolmen teach these friends to fight,
More studious to divide than to unite;
And grace and virtue, sense and reason split,
With all the rash dexterity of wit.
Wits, just like fools, at war about a name,
Have full as oft no meaning, or the same.
Self-love and reason to one end aspire,
Pain their aversion, pleasure their desire;
But greedy that, its object would devour,
This taste the honey, and not wound the flower: 90
Pleasure, or wrong or rightly understood,
Our greatest evil, or our greatest good.

3

Modes of self-love the passions we may call;
'Tis real good, or seeming, moves them all:
But since not every good we can divide,
And reason bids us for our own provide;
Passions, though selfish, if their means be fair,
List under Reason, and deserve her care;
Those, that imparted, court a nobler aim,
100   Exalt their kind, and take some virtue's name.

In lazy apathy let stoics boast
Their virtue fixed; 'tis fixed as in a frost;
Contracted all, retiring to the breast;
But strength of mind is exercise, not rest:
The rising tempest puts in act the soul,
Parts it may ravage, but preserves the whole.
On life's vast ocean diversely we sail,
Reason the card, but passion is the gale;
Nor God alone in the still calm we find,
110   He mounts the storm, and walks upon the wind.

Passions, like elements, though born to fight,
Yet, mixed and softened, in his work unite:
These, 'tis enough to temper and employ;
But what composes man, can man destroy?
Suffice that Reason keep to Nature's road,
Subject, compound them, follow her and God.
Love, hope, and joy, fair pleasure's smiling train,
Hate, fear, and grief, the family of pain,
These mixed with art, and to due bounds confined,
120   Make and maintain the balance of the mind;
The lights and shades, whose well-accorded strife
Gives all the strength and colour of our life.
Pleasures are ever in our hands or eyes;
And when in act they cease, in prospect rise:

Present to grasp, and future still to find,
The whole employ of body and of mind.
All spread their charms, but charm not all alike;
On different senses different objects strike;
Hence different passions more or less inflame,
As strong or weak, the organs of the frame;   130
And hence once master passion in the breast,
Like Aaron's serpent, swallows up the rest.

As man, perhaps, the moment of his breath
Receives the lurking principle of death;
The young disease that must subdue at length,
Grows with his growth, and strengthens with his strength:
So, cast and mingled with his very frame,
The mind's disease, its ruling passion came;
Each vital humour which should feed the whole,
Soon flows to this, in body and in soul: 140
Whatever warms the heart, or fills the head,
As the mind opens, and its functions spread,
Imagination plies her dangerous art,
And pours it all upon the peccant part.

Nature its mother, habit is its nurse;
Wit, spirit, faculties, but make it worse;
Reason itself but gives it edge and power;
As Heaven's blest beam turns vinegar more sour.

We, wretched subjects, though to lawful sway,
In this weak queen some favourite still obey: 150
Ah! if she lend not arms, as well as rules,
What can she more than tell us we are fools?
Teach us to mourn our nature, not to mend,
A sharp accuser, but a helpless friend!
Or from a judge turn pleader, to persuade
The choice we make, or justify it made;
Proud of an easy conquest all along,

She but removes weak passions for the strong;
So, when small humours gather to a gout,
160 The doctor fancies he has driven them out.

Yes, Nature's road must ever be preferred;
Reason is here no guide, but still a guard:
'Tis hers to rectify, not overthrow,
And treat this passion more as friend than foe:
A mightier power the strong direction sends,
And several men impels to several ends:
Like varying winds, by other passions tossed,
This drives them constant to a certain coast.
Let power or knowledge, gold or glory, please,
170 Or (oft more strong than all) the love of ease;
Through life 'tis followed, even at life's expense;
The merchant's toil, the sage's indolence,
The monk's humility, the hero's pride,
All, all alike, find reason on their side.

The eternal art, educing good from ill,
Grafts on this passion our best principle:
'Tis thus the mercury of man is fixed,
Strong grows the virtue with his nature mixed;
The dross cements what else were too refined,
180 And in one interest body acts with mind.

As fruits, ungrateful to the planter's care,
On savage stocks inserted, learn to bear;
The surest virtues thus from passions shoot,
Wild nature's vigour working at the root.
What crops of wit and honesty appear
From spleen, from obstinacy, hate, or fear!
See anger, zeal and fortitude supply;
Even avarice, prudence; sloth, philosophy;
Lust, through some certain strainers well refined,
190 Is gentle love, and charms all womankind;

Envy, to which th' ignoble mind's a slave,
Is emulation in the learned or brave;
Nor virtue, male or female, can we name,
But what will grow on pride, or grow on shame.

Thus Nature gives us (let it check our pride)
The virtue nearest to our vice allied:
Reason the bias turns to good from ill
And Nero reigns a Titus, if he will.
The fiery soul abhorred in Catiline,
In Decius charms, in Curtius is divine: 200
The same ambition can destroy or save,
And makes a patriot as it makes a knave.

4

This light and darkness in our chaos joined,
What shall divide? The God within the mind.

Extremes in nature equal ends produce,
In man they join to some mysterious use;
Though each by turns the other's bound invade,
As, in some well-wrought picture, light and shade,
And oft so mix, the difference is too nice
Where ends the virtue or begins the vice.   210

Fools! who from hence into the notion fall,
That vice or virtue there is none at all.
If white and black blend, soften, and unite
A thousand ways, is there no black or white?
Ask your own heart, and nothing is so plain;
'Tis to mistake them, costs the time and pain.

5

Vice is a monster of so frightful mien,

As, to be hated, needs but to be seen;
Yet seen too oft, familiar with her face,
220   We first endure, then pity, then embrace.
But where th' extreme of vice, was ne'er agreed:
Ask where's the north? at York, 'tis on the Tweed;
In Scotland, at the Orcades; and there,
At Greenland, Zembla, or the Lord knows where.
No creature owns it in the first degree,
But thinks his neighbour farther gone than he;
Even those who dwell beneath its very zone,
Or never feel the rage, or never own;
What happier nations shrink at with affright,
230   The hard inhabitant contends is right.

6

Virtuous and vicious every man must be,
Few in th' extreme, but all in the degree,
The rogue and fool by fits is fair and wise;
And even the best, by fits, what they despise.
'Tis but by parts we follow good or ill;
For, vice or virtue, self directs it still;
Each individual seeks a several goal;
But Heaven's great view is one, and that the whole.
That counter-works each folly and caprice;
240   That disappoints th' effect of every vice;
That, happy frailties to all ranks applied,
Shame to the virgin, to the matron pride,
Fear to the statesman, rashness to the chief,
To kings presumption, and to crowds belief:
That, virtue's ends from vanity can raise,
Which seeks no interest, no reward but praise;
And build on wants, and on defects of mind,
The joy, the peace, the glory of mankind.

Heaven forming each on other to depend,

A master, or a servant, or a friend,   250
Bids each on other for assistance call,
Till one man's weakness grows the strength of all.
Wants, frailties, passions, closer still ally
The common interest, or endear the tie.
To these we owe true friendship, love sincere,
Each home-felt joy that life inherits here;
Yet from the same we learn, in its decline,
Those joys, those loves, those interests to resign;
Taught half by reason, half by mere decay,
To welcome death, and calmly pass away.   260

Whate'er the passion, knowledge, fame, or pelf,
Not one will change his neighbour with himself.
The learned is happy nature to explore,
The fool is happy that he knows no more;
The rich is happy in the plenty given,
The poor contents him with the care of Heaven.
See the blind beggar dance, the cripple sing,
The sot a hero, lunatic a king;
The starving chemist in his golden views
Supremely blest, the poet in his muse.   270

See some strange comfort every state attend,
And pride bestowed on all, a common friend;
See some fit passion every age supply,
Hope travels through, nor quits us when we die.

Behold the child, by Nature's kindly law,
Pleased with a rattle, tickled with a straw:
Some livelier plaything gives his youth delight,
A little louder, but as empty quite:
Scarves, garters, gold, amuse his riper stage,
And beads and prayer-books are the toys of age: 280
Pleased with this bauble still, as that before;
Till tired he sleeps, and life's poor play is o'er.

Meanwhile opinion gilds with varying rays
Those painted clouds that beautify our days;
Each want of happiness by hope supplied,
And each vacuity of sense by pride:
These build as fast as knowledge can destroy;
In folly's cup still laughs the bubble, joy;
One prospect lost, another still we gain;
290 And not a vanity is given in vain;
Even mean self-love becomes, by force divine,
The scale to measure others' wants by thine.
See! and confess, one comfort still must rise,
'Tis this: Though man's a fool, yet God is wise.

EPISTLE III

1

Here, then, we rest: "The Universal Cause
Acts to one end, but acts by various laws."
In all the madness of superfluous health,
The trim of pride, the impudence of wealth,
Let this great truth be present night and day;
But most be present, if we preach or pray.

Look round our world; behold the chain of love
Combining all below and all above.
See plastic Nature working to this end,
10 The single atoms each to other tend,
Attract, attracted to, the next in place
Formed and impelled its neighbour to embrace.
See matter next, with various life endued,
Press to one centre still, the general good.
See dying vegetables life sustain,

See life dissolving vegetate again:
All forms that perish other forms supply
(By turns we catch the vital breath, and die),
Like bubbles on the sea of matter borne,
They rise, they break, and to that sea return.   20
Nothing is foreign: parts relate to whole;
One all-extending, all-preserving soul
Connects each being, greatest with the least;
Made beast in aid of man, and man of beast;
All served, all serving: nothing stands alone;
The chain holds on, and where it ends, unknown.

Has God, thou fool! worked solely for thy good,
Thy joy, thy pastime, thy attire, thy food?
Who for thy table feeds the wanton fawn,
For him as kindly spread the flowery lawn: 30
Is it for thee the lark ascends and sings?
Joy tunes his voice, joy elevates his wings.
Is it for thee the linnet pours his throat?
Loves of his own and raptures swell the note.
The bounding steed you pompously bestride,
Shares with his lord the pleasure and the pride.
Is thine alone the seed that strews the plain?
The birds of heaven shall vindicate their grain.
Thine the full harvest of the golden year?
Part pays, and justly, the deserving steer: 40
The hog, that ploughs not nor obeys thy call,
Lives on the labours of this lord of all.

Know, Nature's children all divide her care;
The fur that warms a monarch, warmed a bear.
While man exclaims, "See all things for my use!"
"See man for mine!" replies a pampered goose:
And just as short of reason he must fall,
Who thinks all made for one, not one for all.

Grant that the powerful still the weak control;

50   Be man the wit and tyrant of the whole:
Nature that tyrant checks; he only knows,
And helps, another creature's wants and woes.
Say, will the falcon, stooping from above,
Smit with her varying plumage, spare the dove?
Admires the jay the insect's gilded wings?
Or hears the hawk when Philomela sings?
Man cares for all: to birds he gives his woods,
To beasts his pastures, and to fish his floods;
For some his interest prompts him to provide,
60   For more his pleasure, yet for more his pride:
All feed on one vain patron, and enjoy
The extensive blessing of his luxury.
That very life his learned hunger craves,
He saves from famine, from the savage saves;
Nay, feasts the animal he dooms his feast,
And, till he ends the being, makes it blest;
Which sees no more the stroke, or feels the pain,
Than favoured man by touch ethereal slain.
The creature had his feast of life before;
70   Thou too must perish when thy feast is o'er!

To each unthinking being, Heaven, a friend,
Gives not the useless knowledge of its end:
To man imparts it; but with such a view
As, while he dreads it, makes him hope it too;
The hour concealed, and so remote the fear,
Death still draws nearer, never seeming near.
Great standing miracle! that Heaven assigned
Its only thinking thing this turn of mind.

2

Whether with reason, or with instinct blest,
80   Know, all enjoy that power which suits them best;
To bliss alike by that direction tend,

And find the means proportioned to their end.
Say, where full instinct is the unerring guide,
What pope or council can they need beside?
Reason, however able, cool at best,
Cares not for service, or but serves when pressed,
Stays till we call, and then not often near;
But honest instinct comes a volunteer,
Sure never to o'er-shoot, but just to hit;
While still too wide or short is human wit;   90
Sure by quick nature happiness to gain,
Which heavier reason labours at in vain,
This too serves always, reason never long;
One must go right, the other may go wrong.
See then the acting and comparing powers
One in their nature, which are two in ours;
And reason raise o'er instinct as you can,
In this 'tis God directs, in that 'tis man.

Who taught the nations of the field and wood
To shun their poison, and to choose their food?   100
Prescient, the tides or tempests to withstand,
Build on the wave, or arch beneath the sand?
Who made the spider parallels design,
Sure as Demoivre, without rule or line?
Who did the stork, Columbus-like, explore
Heavens not his own, and worlds unknown before?
Who calls the council, states the certain day,
Who forms the phalanx, and who points the way?

3

God in the nature of each being founds
Its proper bliss, and sets its proper bounds: 110
But as He framed a whole, the whole to bless,
On mutual wants built mutual happiness:
So from the first, eternal order ran,

And creature linked to creature, man to man.
Whate'er of life all-quickening ether keeps,
Or breathes through air, or shoots beneath the deeps,
Or pours profuse on earth, one nature feeds
The vital flame, and swells the genial seeds.
Not man alone, but all that roam the wood,
120 Or wing the sky, or roll along the flood,
Each loves itself, but not itself alone,
Each sex desires alike, till two are one.
Nor ends the pleasure with the fierce embrace;
They love themselves, a third time, in their race.
Thus beast and bird their common charge attend,
The mothers nurse it, and the sires defend;
The young dismissed to wander earth or air,
There stops the instinct, and there ends the care;
The link dissolves, each seeks a fresh embrace,
130 Another love succeeds, another race.
A longer care man's helpless kind demands;
That longer care contracts more lasting bands:
Reflection, reason, still the ties improve,
At once extend the interest and the love;
With choice we fix, with sympathy we burn;
Each virtue in each passion takes its turn;
And still new needs, new helps, new habits rise.
That graft benevolence on charities.
Still as one brood, and as another rose,
140 These natural love maintained, habitual those.
The last, scarce ripened into perfect man,
Saw helpless him from whom their life began:
Memory and forecast just returns engage,
That pointed back to youth, this on to age;
While pleasure, gratitude, and hope combined,
Still spread the interest, and preserved the kind.

4

Nor think, in Nature's state they blindly trod;
The state of nature was the reign of God:
Self-love and social at her birth began,
Union the bond of all things, and of man.   150
Pride then was not; nor arts, that pride to aid;
Man walked with beast, joint tenant of the shade;
The same his table, and the same his bed;
No murder clothed him, and no murder fed.
In the same temple, the resounding wood,
All vocal beings hymned their equal God:
The shrine with gore unstained, with gold undressed,
Unbribed, unbloody, stood the blameless priest:
Heaven's attribute was universal care,
And man's prerogative to rule, but spare.   160
Ah! how unlike the man of times to come!
Of half that live the butcher and the tomb;
Who, foe to nature, hears the general groan,
Murders their species, and betrays his own.
But just disease to luxury succeeds,
And every death its own avenger breeds;
The fury-passions from that blood began,
And turned on man a fiercer savage, man.

See him from Nature rising slow to art!
To copy instinct then was reason's part;   170
Thus then to man the voice of Nature spake—
"Go, from the creatures thy instructions take:
Learn from the birds what food the thickets yield;
Learn from the beasts the physic of the field;
Thy arts of building from the bee receive;
Learn of the mole to plough, the worm to weave;
Learn of the little nautilus to sail,
Spread the thin oar, and catch the driving gale.
Here too all forms of social union find,

180   And hence let reason, late, instruct mankind:
      Here subterranean works and cities see;
      There towns aërial on the waving tree.
      Learn each small people's genius, policies,
      The ant's republic, and the realm of bees;
      How those in common all their wealth bestow,
      And anarchy without confusion know;
      And these for ever, though a monarch reign,
      Their separate cells and properties maintain.
      Mark what unvaried laws preserve each state,
190   Laws wise as nature, and as fixed as fate.
      In vain thy reason finer webs shall draw,
      Entangle justice in her net of law,
      And right, too rigid, harden into wrong;
      Still for the strong too weak, the weak too strong.
      Yet go! and thus o'er all the creatures sway,
      Thus let the wiser make the rest obey;
      And, for those arts mere instinct could afford,
      Be crowned as monarchs, or as gods adored."

5

      Great Nature spoke; observant men obeyed;
200   Cities were built, societies were made:
      Here rose one little state: another near
      Grew by like means, and joined, through love or fear.
      Did here the trees with ruddier burdens bend,
      And there the streams in purer rills descend?
      What war could ravish, commerce could bestow,
      And he returned a friend, who came a foe.
      Converse and love mankind might strongly draw,
      When love was liberty, and Nature law.
      Thus States were formed; the name of king unknown,
210   'Till common interest placed the sway in one.
      'Twas virtue only (or in arts or arms,
      Diffusing blessings, or averting harms)

The same which in a sire the sons obeyed,
A prince the father of a people made.

6

'Till then, by Nature crowned, each patriarch sate,
King, priest, and parent of his growing state;
On him, their second providence, they hung,
Their law his eye, their oracle his tongue.
He from the wondering furrow called the food,
Taught to command the fire, control the flood,   220
Draw forth the monsters of the abyss profound,
Or fetch the aërial eagle to the ground.
'Till drooping, sickening, dying they began
Whom they revered as God to mourn as man:
Then, looking up, from sire to sire, explored
One great first Father, and that first adored.
Or plain tradition that this all begun,
Conveyed unbroken faith from sire to son;
The worker from the work distinct was known,
And simple reason never sought but one: 230
Ere wit oblique had broke that steady light,
Man, like his Maker, saw that all was right;
To virtue, in the paths of pleasure, trod,
And owned a Father when he owned a God.
Love all the faith, and all the allegiance then;
For Nature knew no right divine in men,
No ill could fear in God; and understood
A sovereign being but a sovereign good.
True faith, true policy, united ran,
This was but love of God, and this of man.   240

Who first taught souls enslaved, and realms undone,
The enormous faith of many made for one;
That proud exception to all Nature's laws,
To invert the world, and counter-work its cause?

Force first made conquest, and that conquest, law;
'Till superstition taught the tyrant awe,
Then shared the tyranny, then lent it aid,
And gods of conquerors, slaves of subjects made:
She, 'midst the lightning's blaze, and thunder's sound,
250 When rocked the mountains, and when groaned the ground,
She taught the weak to bend, the proud to pray,
To power unseen, and mightier far than they:
She, from the rending earth and bursting skies,
Saw gods descend, and fiends infernal rise:
Here fixed the dreadful, there the blest abodes;
Fear made her devils, and weak hope her gods;
Gods partial, changeful, passionate, unjust,
Whose attributes were rage, revenge, or lust;
Such as the souls of cowards might conceive,
260 And, formed like tyrants, tyrants would believe.
Zeal then, not charity, became the guide;
And hell was built on spite, and heaven on pride,
Then sacred seemed the ethereal vault no more;
Altars grew marble then, and reeked with gore;
Then first the flamen tasted living food;
Next his grim idol smeared with human blood;
With heaven's own thunders shook the world below,
And played the god an engine on his foe.

So drives self-love, through just and through unjust,
270 To one man's power, ambition, lucre, lust:
The same self-love, in all, becomes the cause
Of what restrains him, government and laws.
For, what one likes if others like as well,
What serves one will when many wills rebel?
How shall he keep, what, sleeping or awake,
A weaker may surprise, a stronger take?
His safety must his liberty restrain:
All join to guard what each desires to gain.
Forced into virtue thus by self-defence,

Even kings learned justice and benevolence: 280
Self-love forsook the path it first pursued,
And found the private in the public good.

'Twas then, the studious head or generous mind,
Follower of God, or friend of human-kind,
Poet or patriot, rose but to restore
The faith and moral Nature gave before;
Re-lumed her ancient light, not kindled new;
If not God's image, yet His shadow drew:
Taught power's due use to people and to kings,
Taught nor to slack, nor strain its tender strings,   290
The less, or greater, set so justly true,
That touching one must strike the other too;
Till jarring interests, of themselves create
The according music of a well-mixed state.
Such is the world's great harmony, that springs
From order, union, full consent of things:
Where small and great, where weak and mighty, made
To serve, not suffer, strengthen, not invade;
More powerful each as needful to the rest,
And, in proportion as it blesses, blest;   300
Draw to one point, and to one centre bring
Beast, man, or angel, servant, lord, or king.

For forms of government let fools contest;
Whate'er is best administered is best:
For modes of faith let graceless zealots fight;
His can't be wrong whose life is in the right:
In faith and hope the world will disagree,
But all mankind's concern is charity:
All must be false that thwart this one great end;
And all of God, that bless mankind or mend.   310

Man, like the generous vine, supported lives;
The strength he gains is from the embrace he gives.

On their own axis as the planets run,
Yet make at once their circle round the sun;
So two consistent motions act the soul;
And one regards itself, and one the whole.

Thus God and Nature linked the general frame,
And bade self-love and social be the same.

Epistle IV

Oh Happiness! our being's end and aim!
Good, pleasure, ease, content! whate'er thy name:
That something still which prompts th' eternal sigh,
For which we bear to live, or dare to die,
Which still so near us, yet beyond us lies,
O'er-look'd, seen double, by the fool, and wise.
Plant of celestial seed! if dropt below,
Say, in what mortal soil thou deign'st to grow?
Fair op'ning to some court's propitious shine,
Or deep with di'monds in the flaming mine?
Twin'd with the wreaths Parnassian laurels yield,
Or reap'd in iron harvests of the field?
Where grows?—where grows it not? If vain our toil,
We ought to blame the culture, not the soil:
Fix'd to no spot is happiness sincere,
'Tis nowhere to be found, or ev'rywhere:
'Tis never to be bought, but always free,
And fled from monarchs, St. John! dwells with thee.

Ask of the learn'd the way? The learn'd are blind;
This bids to serve, and that to shun mankind;
Some place the bliss in action, some in ease,
Those call it pleasure, and contentment these;
Some sunk to beasts, find pleasure end in pain;

Some swell'd to gods, confess e'en virtue vain;
Or indolent, to each extreme they fall,
To trust in ev'ry thing, or doubt of all.

Who thus define it, say they more or less
Than this, that happiness is happiness?

Take nature's path, and mad opinion's leave;
All states can reach it, and all heads conceive;   30
Obvious her goods, in no extreme they dwell;
There needs but thinking right, and meaning well;
And mourn our various portions as we please,
Equal is common sense, and common ease.

Remember, man, "the Universal Cause
Acts not by partial, but by gen'ral laws";
And makes what happiness we justly call
Subsist not in the good of one, but all.
There's not a blessing individuals find,
But some way leans and hearkens to the kind: 40
No bandit fierce, no tyrant mad with pride,
No cavern'd hermit, rests self-satisfy'd:
Who most to shun or hate mankind pretend,
Seek an admirer, or who would fix a friend:
Abstract what others feel, what others think,
All pleasures sicken, and all glories sink:
Each has his share; and who would more obtain,
Shall find the pleasure pays not half the pain.

Order is heav'n's first law; and this confest,
Some are, and must be, greater than the rest,   50
More rich, more wise; but who infers from hence
That such are happier, shocks all common sense.
Heav'n to mankind impartial we confess,
If all are equal in their happiness:
But mutual wants this happiness increase;

All nature's diff'rence keeps all nature's peace.
Condition, circumstance is not the thing;
Bliss is the same in subject or in king,
In who obtain defence, or who defend,
In him who is, or him who finds a friend:
Heav'n breathes thro' ev'ry member of the whole
One common blessing, as one common soul.
But fortune's gifts if each alike possest,
And each were equal, must not all contest?
If then to all men happiness was meant,
God in externals could not place content.

Fortune her gifts may variously dispose,
And these be happy call'd, unhappy those;
But heav'n's just balance equal will appear,
While those are plac'd in hope, and these in fear:
Not present good or ill, the joy or curse,
But future views of better, or of worse.
Oh sons of earth! attempt ye still to rise,
By mountains pil'd on mountains, to the skies?
Heav'n still with laughter the vain toil surveys,
And buries madmen in the heaps they raise.

Know, all the good that individuals find,
Or God and nature meant to mere mankind,
Reason's whole pleasure, all the joys of sense,
Lie in three words, health, peace, and competence
But health consists with temperance alone;
And peace, oh virtue! peace is all thy own.
The good or bad the gifts of fortune gain;
But these less taste them, as they worse obtain.
Say, in pursuit of profit or delight,
Who risk the most, that take wrong means, or right?
Of vice or virtue, whether blest or curst,
Which meets contempt, or which compassion first?
Count all th' advantage prosp'rous vice attains,

'Tis but what virtue flies from and disdains: 90
And grant the bad what happiness they would,
One they must want, which is, to pass for good.

Oh blind to truth, and God's whole scheme below,
Who fancy bliss to vice, to virtue woe!
Who sees and follows that great scheme the best,
Best knows the blessing, and will most be blest.
But fools the good alone unhappy call,
For ills or accidents that chance to all.
See Falkland dies, the virtuous and the just!
See god-like Turenne prostrate on the dust! 100
See Sidney bleeds amid the martial strife!
Was this their virtue, or contempt of life?
Say, was it virtue, more tho' heav'n ne'er gave,
Lamented Digby! sunk thee to the grave?
Tell me, if virtue made the son expire,
Why, full of days and honour, lives the sire?
Why drew Marseilles' good bishop purer breath,
When nature sicken'd and each gale was death!
Or why so long (in life if long can be)
Lent heav'n a parent to the poor and me? 110

What makes all physical or moral ill?
There deviates nature, and here wanders will.
God sends not ill; if rightly understood,
Or partial ill is universal good,
Or change admits, or nature lets it fall,
Short, and but rare, till man improv'd it all.
We just as wisely might of heav'n complain
That righteous Abel was destroy'd by Cain,
As that the virtuous son is ill at ease,
When his lewd father gave the dire disease. 120
Think we, like some weak prince, th' eternal cause
Prone for his fav'rites to reverse his laws?

Shall burning Ætna, if a sage requires,
Forget to thunder, and recall her fires?
On air or sea new motions be imprest,
Oh blameless Bethel! to relieve thy breast?
When the loose mountain trembles from on high
Shall gravitation cease, if you go by?
Or some old temple, nodding to its fall,
130   For Chartres' head reserve the hanging wall?

But still this world (so fitted for the knave)
Contents us not. A better shall we have?
A kingdom of the just then let it be:
But first consider how those just agree.
The good must merit God's peculiar care;
But who, but God, can tell us who they are?
One thinks on Calvin heav'n's own spirit fell;
Another deems him instrument of hell;
If Calvin feel heav'n's blessing, or its rod,
140   This cries there is, and that, there is no God.
What shocks one part will edify the rest,
Nor with one system can they all be blest.
The very best will variously incline,
And what rewards your virtue, punish mine.
Whatever is, is right.—This world, 'tis true,
Was made for Cæsar—but for Titus too;
And which more blest, who chain'd his country, say,
Or he whose virtue sigh'd to lose a day?

"But sometimes virtue starves, while vice is fed."
150   What then? is the reward of virtue bread?
That vice may merit, 'tis the price of toil;
The knave deserves it, when he tills the soil,
The knave deserves it, when he tempts the main,
Where folly fights for kings, or dives for gain.
The good man may be weak, be indolent;
Nor is his claim to plenty, but content.

But grant him riches, your demand is o'er?
"No, shall the good want health, the good want pow'r?"
Add health and pow'r, and ev'ry earthly thing,
"Why bounded pow'r? why private? why no king?   160
Nay, why external for internal giv'n?
Why is not man a God, and earth a heav'n?"
Who ask and reason thus, will scarce conceive
God gives enough, while he has more to give:
Immense the pow'r, immense were the demand;
Say, at what part of nature will they stand?

What nothing earthly gives, or can destroy,
The soul's calm sunshine, and the heart-felt joy,
Is virtue's prize: a better would you fix?
Then give humility a coach and six,   170
Justice a conq'ror's sword, or truth a gown,
Or public spirit its great cure, a crown.
Weak, foolish man! will heav'n reward us there
With the same trash mad mortals wish for here?
The boy and man an individual makes,
Yet sigh'st thou now for apples and for cakes?
Go, like the Indian, in another life
Expect thy dog, thy bottle, and thy wife,
As well as dream such trifles are assign'd,
As toys and empires, for a god-like mind.   180
Rewards, that either would to virtue bring
No joy, or be destructive of the thing:
How oft by these at sixty are undone
The virtues of a saint at twenty-one!

To whom can riches give repute, or trust,
Content, or pleasure, but the good and just?
Judges and senates have been bought for gold,
Esteem and love were never to be sold.
Oh fool! to think God hates the worthy mind,
The lover and the love of human-kind,   190

Whose life is healthful, and whose conscience clear,
Because he wants a thousand pounds a year.

Honour and shame from no condition rise;
Act well your part, there all the honour lies.
Fortune in men has some small diff'rence made
One flaunts in rags, one flutters in brocade;
The cobler apron'd, and the parson gown'd,
The frier hooded, and the monarch crown'd.
"What differ more (you cry) than crown and cowl?"
200   I'll tell you, friend! a wise man and a fool.
You'll find, if once the monarch acts the monk,
Or, cobler-like, the parson will be drunk,
Worth makes the man, and want of it, the fellow;
The rest is all but leather or prunella.

Stuck o'er with titles and hung round with strings,
That thou may'st be by kings, or whores of kings.
Boast the pure blood of an illustrious race,
In quiet flow from Lucrece to Lucrece:
But by your fathers' worth if your's you rate,
210   Count me those only who were good and great.
Go! if your ancient, but ignoble blood
Has crept thro' scoundrels ever since the flood,
Go! and pretend your family is young;
Nor own your fathers have been fools so long.
What can ennoble sots, or slaves, or cowards?
Alas! not all the blood of all the Howards.

Look next on greatness; say where greatness lies.
"Where, but among the heroes and the wise?"
Heroes are much the same, the point's agreed,
220   From Macedonia's madman to the Swede;
The whole strange purpose of their lives, to find
Or make, an enemy of all mankind!
Not one looks backward, onward still he goes,

Yet ne'er looks forward farther than his nose.
No less alike the politic and wise;
All sly slow things, with circumspective eyes:
Men in their loose unguarded hours they take,
Not that themselves are wise, but others weak.
But grant that those can conquer, these can cheat;
'Tis phrase absurd to call a villain great: 230
Who wickedly is wise, or madly brave,
Is but the more a fool, the more a knave.
Who noble ends by noble means obtains,
Or failing, smiles in exile or in chains,
Like good Aurelius let him reign, or bleed
Like Socrates, that man is great indeed.

What's fame? a fancy'd life in others' breath,
A thing beyond us, ev'n before our death.
Just what you hear, you have, and what's unknown
The same (my Lord) if Tully's, or your own.   240
All that we feel of it begins and ends
In the small circle of our foes or friends;
To all beside as much an empty shade
An Eugene living, as a Cæsar dead;
Alike or when, or where they shone, or shine,
Or on the Rubicon, or on the Rhine.
A wit's a feather, and a chief a rod;
An honest man's the noblest work of God.
Fame but from death a villain's name can save,
As justice tears his body from the grave;   250
When what t' oblivion better were resign'd,
Is hung on high, to poison half mankind.
All fame is foreign, but of true desert;
Plays round the head, but comes not to the heart:
One self approving hour whole years out-weighs
Of stupid starers, and of loud huzzas;
And more true joy Marcellus exil'd feels,
Than Cæsar with a senate at his heels.

In parts superior what advantage lies?
260 Tell (for you can) what is it to be wise?
'Tis but to know how little can be known;
To see all others' faults, and feel your own:
Condemn'd in bus'ness or in arts to drudge,
Without a second, or without a judge:
Truths would you teach, or save a sinking land?
All fear, none aid you, and few understand.
Painful pre-eminence! yourself to view
Above life's weakness, and its comforts too.

Bring then these blessings to a strict account;
270 Make fair deductions; see to what they 'mount:
How much of other each is sure to cost;
How each for other oft is wholly lost;
How inconsistent greater goods with these;
How sometimes life is risqu'd, and always ease:
Think, and if still the things thy envy call,
Say, would'st thou be the man to whom they fall?
To sigh for ribbands if thou art so silly,
Mark how they grace Lord Umbra, or Sir Billy.
Is yellow dirt the passion of thy life;
280 Look but on Gripus, or on Gripus' wife.
If parts allure thee, think how Bacon shin'd,
The wisest, brightest, meanest of mankind:
Or ravish'd with the whistling of a name,
See Cromwell, damn'd to everlasting fame!
If all, united, thy ambition call,
From ancient story learn to scorn them all.
There, in the rich, the honour'd, fam'd and great,
See the false scale of happiness complete!
In hearts of kings, or arms of queens who lay,
290 How happy those to ruin, these betray.
Mark by what wretched steps their glory grows,
From dirt and sea-weed as proud Venice rose;
In each how guilt and greatness equal ran,

And all that rais'd the hero, sunk the man:
Now Europe's laurels on their brows behold,
But stain'd with blood, or ill-exchang'd for gold:
Then see them broke with toils, or sunk in ease,
Or infamous for plunder'd provinces.
Oh, wealth ill-fated! which no act of fame
E'er taught to shine, or sanctify'd from shame!   300
What greater bliss attends their close of life?
Some greedy minion, or imperious wife,
The trophy'd arches, story'd halls invade,
And haunt their slumbers in the pompous shade.
Alas! not dazzled with their noon-tide ray,
Compute the morn and ev'ning to the day;
The whole amount of that enormous fame,
A tale, that blends their glory with their shame!

Know then this truth, enough for man to know,
"Virtue alone is happiness below."   310
The only point where human bliss stands still,
And tastes the good without the fall to ill;
Where only merit constant pay receives,
Is blest in what it takes, and what it gives;
The joy unequal'd, if its end it gain,
And if it lose, attended with no pain:
Without satiety, tho' e'er so bless'd,
And but more relish'd as the more distress'd:
The broadest mirth unfeeling folly wears,
Less pleasing far than virtue's very tears;   320
Good, from each object, from each place acquir'd,
For ever exercis'd, yet never tir'd;
Never elated, while one man's oppress'd;
Never dejected, while another's bless'd;
And where no wants, no wishes can remain,
Since but to wish more virtue, is to gain.

See the sole bliss Heav'n could on all bestow!

Which who but feels can taste, but thinks can know:
Yet poor with fortune, and with learning blind,
330   The bad must miss, the good, untaught, will find;
Slave to no sect, who takes no private road,
But looks through nature up to nature's God:
Pursues that chain which links th' immense design,
Joins heav'n and earth, and mortal and divine;
Sees, that no being any bliss can know,
But touches some above, and some below;
Learns, from this union of the rising whole,
The first, last purpose of the human soul;
And knows where faith, law, morals, all began,
340   All end, in love of God, and love of man.

For him alone, hope leads from goal to goal,
And opens still, and opens on his soul;
Till lengthen'd on to faith, and unconfin'd,
It pours the bliss that fills up all the mind.
He sees, why nature plants in man alone
Hope of known bliss, and faith in bliss unknown:
(Nature, whose dictates to no other kind
Are giv'n in vain, but what they seek they find)
Wise is her present; she connects in this
350   His greatest virtue with his greatest bliss;
At once his own bright prospect to be blest,
And strongest motive to assist the rest.
Self-love thus push'd to social, to divine,
Gives thee to make thy neighbour's blessing thine.
Is this too little for the boundless heart?
Extend it, let thy enemies have part:
Grasp the whole worlds of reason, life, and sense,
In one close system of benevolence:
Happier as kinder, in whate'er degree,
360   And height of bliss but height of charity.

God loves from whole to parts: but human soul

Must rise from individual to the whole.
Self-love but serves the virtuous mind to wake
As the small pebble stirs the peaceful lake;
The centre mov'd, a circle strait succeeds,
Another still, and still another spreads;
Friend, parent, neighbour, first it will embrace;
His country next; and next all human race;
Wide and more wide, th' o'erflowings of the mind
Take ev'ry creature in, of ev'ry kind;   370
Earth smiles around, with boundless bounty blest,
And heav'n beholds its image in his breast.

Come then, my friend, my genius, come along;
Oh master of the poet, and the song!
And while the muse now stoops, or now ascends,
To man's low passions, or their glorious ends,
Teach me, like thee, in various nature wise,
To fall with dignity, with temper rise;
Form'd by thy converse, happily to steer
From grave to gay, from lively to severe;   380
Correct with spirit, eloquent with ease,
Intent to reason, or polite to please.
Oh! while along the stream of time thy name
Expanded flies, and gathers all its fame;
Say, shall my little bark attendant sail,
Pursue the triumph, and partake the gale?
When statesmen, heroes, kings, in dust repose,
Whose sons shall blush their fathers were thy foes,
Shall then this verse to future age pretend
Thou wert my guide, philosopher, and friend?   390
That, urg'd by thee, I turn'd the tuneful art
From sounds to things, from fancy to the heart;
For wit's false mirror held up nature's light;
Shew'd erring pride, whatever is, is right;
That reason, passion, answer one great aim;
That true self-love and social are the same;

That virtue only makes our bliss below;
And all our knowledge is, ourselves to know.

Ode on Solitude

Alexander Pope

Happy the man, whose wish and care
   A few paternal acres bound,
Content to breathe his native air,
     In his own ground.

Whose herds with milk, whose fields with bread,
   Whose flocks supply him with attire,
Whose trees in summer yield him shade,
     In winter fire.

Blest, who can unconcernedly find
   Hours, days, and years slide soft away,
In health of body, peace of mind,
     Quiet by day,

Sound sleep by night; study and ease,
   Together mixed; sweet recreation;
And innocence, which most does please,
     With meditation.

Thus let me live, unseen, unknown;
   Thus unlamented let me die;
Steal from the world, and not a stone
     Tell where I lie.

DE DESCRIPTIONE TEMPORUM

C.S. Lewis

Inaugural Lecture from The Chair of Medieval and Renaissance Literature at Cambridge University, 1954

Speaking from a newly founded Chair, I find myself freed from one embarrassment only to fall into another. I have no great predecessors to overshadow me; on the other hand, I must try (as the theatrical people say) 'to create the part.' The responsibility is heavy. If I miscarry, the University might come to regret not only my election—an error which, at worst, can be left to the great healer—but even, which matters very much more, the foundation of the Chair itself. That is why I have thought it best to take the bull by the horns and devote this lecture to explaining as clearly as I can the way in which I approach my work; my interpretation of the commission you have given me.

What most attracted me in that commission was the combination 'Medieval and Renaissance.' I thought that by this formula the University was giving official sanction to a change which has been coming over historical opinion within my own lifetime. It is temperately summed up by Professor Seznec in the words: 'As the Middle Ages and the Renaissance come to be better known, the traditional antithesis between them grows less marked.' Some scholars might go further than Professor Seznec, but very few, I believe, would now oppose him. If we are sometimes unconscious of the change, that is not because we have not shared it but because it has been gradual and imperceptible. We recognize it most clearly if we are suddenly brought face to face with the old view in its full vigour. A good experiment is to re-read the first chapter of J. M. Berdan's *Early Tudor Poetry*. It is still in many ways a useful book; but it is now difficult to read that chapter without a smile. We begin with twenty-nine pages (and they contain several misstatements) of unrelieved gloom about grossness, superstition, and cruelty to children, and on the twenty-ninth comes the sentence, 'The first rift in this darkness is the Copernican doctrine'; as if a new hypothesis in astronomy would naturally make a man stop hitting his daughter about the head. No scholar could now write quite like that. But the old picture, done in far cruder colours, has survived among the weaker brethren, if not (let us hope) at Cambridge, yet certainly in that Western darkness from which you have so lately bidden me emerge. Only last summer a young gentleman whom I had the honour of examining described Thomas Wyatt as 'the first man who scrambled ashore out of the great, dark surging sea of the Middle Ages.' This was interesting because it showed how a stereotyped image can obliterate a man's own experience. Nearly all the medieval texts which the syllabus had required him to study had in reality led him into formal gardens where every passion was subdued to a ceremonial and every problem of conduct was dovetailed into a complex and rigid moral theology.

From the formula 'Medieval and Renaissance,' then, I inferred that the University was encouraging my own belief that the barrier between those two ages has been greatly exaggerated, if indeed it was not largely a figment of Humanist propaganda. At the very least, I was ready to welcome any increased flexibility in our conception of history. All lines of demarcation between what we call 'periods' should be subject to constant revision. Would that we could dispense with them altogether! As a great Cambridge historian has said: 'Unlike dates, periods are not facts. They are retrospective conceptions that we form about past events, useful to focus discussion, but very often leading historical thought astray.' The actual temporal process, as we meet it in our lives (and we meet it, in a strict sense, nowhere else) has no divisions, except perhaps those 'blessed barriers between day and day,' our sleeps. Change is never complete, and change never ceases. Nothing is ever quite finished with; it may always begin over again. (This is one of the sides of life that Richardson hits off with wearying accuracy.) And nothing is quite new; it was always somehow anticipated or prepared for. A seamless, formless continuity-in-mutability is the mode of our fife. But unhappily we cannot as historians dispense with periods. We cannot use for literary history the technique of Mrs. Woolf's *The Waves*. We cannot hold together huge masses of particulars without putting into them some kind of structure. Still less can we arrange a term's work or draw up a lecture list. Thus we are driven back upon periods. All divisions will falsify our material to some extent; the best one can hope is to choose those which will falsify it least. But because we must divide, to reduce the emphasis on any one traditional division must, in the long run, mean an increase of emphasis on some other division. And that is the subject I want to discuss. If we do not put the Great Divide between the Middle Ages and the Renaissance, where should we put it? I ask this question with the full consciousness that, in the reality studied, there is no Great Divide. There is nothing in history that quite corresponds to a coastline or a watershed in geography. If, in spite of this, I still think my question worth asking, that is certainly not because I claim for my answer more than a methodological value, or even much of that. Least of all would I wish it to be any less subject than others to continual attack and speedy revision. But I believe that the discussion is as good a way as any other of explaining how I look at the work you have given me. When I have finished it, I shall at least have laid the cards on the table and you will know the worst.

The meaning of my title will now have become plain. It is a chapter-heading borrowed from Isidore. In that chapter Isidore is engaged in dividing history, as he knew it, into its periods; or, as he calls them, *aetates*. I shall be doing the same. Assuming that we do not put our great frontier between the Middle Ages and the Renaissance, I shall consider the rival claims of certain other divisions which have been, or might be, made. But, first, a word of warning. I am not, even on the most Lilliputian scale, emulating Professor Toynbee or Spengler. About everything that could be called 'the philosophy of history' I am a desperate sceptic. I know nothing of the future, not even whether there will be any future. I don't know whether past history has been necessary or contingent. I don't know whether the human tragi-comedy is now in Act I or Act V; whether our present disorders are those of infancy or of old age. I am merely considering how we should arrange or schematize those facts—ludicrously few in comparison with the totality which survive to us (often by accident) from the past. I am less like a botanist in a forest than a woman arranging a few cut flowers for the drawing room. So, in some degree, are the greatest historians. We can't get into the real forest of the past; that is part of what the word past means.

The first division that naturally occurs to us is that between Antiquity and the Dark Ages—the fall of the Empire, the barbarian invasions, the christening of Europe. And of course no possible revolution in historical thought will ever make this anything less than a massive and multiple change. Do not imagine that I mean to belittle it. Yet I must observe that three things have happened since, say, Gibbon's time, which make it a shade less catastrophic for us than it was for him.

1. The partial loss of ancient learning and its recovery at the Renaissance were for him both unique events. History furnished no rivals to such a death and such a re-birth. But we have lived to see the second death of ancient learning. In our time something which was once the possession of all educated men has shrunk to being the technical accomplishment of a few specialists. If we say that this is not total death, it may be replied that there was no total death in the Dark Ages either. It could even be argued that Latin, surviving

as the language of Dark Age culture, and preserving the disciplines of Law and Rhetoric, gave to some parts of the classical heritage a far more living and integral status in the life of those ages than the academic studies of the specialists can claim in our own. As for the area and the tempo of the two deaths, if one were looking for a man who could not read Virgil though his father could, he might be found more easily in the twentieth century than in the fifth.

2. To Gibbon the literary change from Virgil to *Beowulf* or the *Hildebrand*, if he had read them, would have seemed greater than it can to us. We can now see quite clearly that these barbarian poems were not really a novelty comparable to, say, *The Waste Land* or Mr. Jones's *Anathemata*. They were rather an unconscious return to the spirit of the earliest classical poetry. The audience of Homer, and the audience of the *Hildebrand*, once they had learned one another's language and metre, would have found one another's poetry perfectly intelligible. Nothing new had come into the world.

3. The christening of Europe seemed to all our ancestors, whether they welcomed it themselves as Christians, or, like Gibbon, deplored it as humanistic unbelievers, a unique, irreversible event. But we have seen the opposite process. Of course the un-christening of Europe in our time is not quite complete; neither was her christening in the Dark Ages. But roughly speaking we may say that whereas all history was for our ancestors divided into two periods, the pre-Christian and the Christian, and two only, for us it falls into three—the pre-Christian, the Christian, and what may reasonably be called the post-Christian. This surely must make a momentous difference. I am not here considering either the christening or the un-christening from a theological point of view. I am considering them simply as cultural changes. When I do that, it appears to me that the second change is even more radical than the first. Christians and Pagans had much more in common with each other than either has with a post-Christian. The gap between those who worship different gods is not so wide as that between those who worship and those who do not. The Pagan and Christian ages alike are

ages of what Pausanias would call the δρώμενον, the externalised and enacted idea; the sacrifice, the games, the triumph, the ritual drama, the Mass, the tournament, the masque, the pageant, the epithalamium, and with them ritual and symbolic costumes, *trabea* and laticlave, crown of wild olive, royal crown, coronet, judge's robes, knight's spurs, herald's tabard, coat-armour, priestly vestment, religious habit—for every rank, trade, or occasion its visible sign. But even if we look away from that into the temper of men's minds, I seem to see the same. Surely the gap between Professor Ryle and Thomas Browne is far wider than that between Gregory the Great and Virgil. Surely Seneca and Dr. Johnson are closer together than Burton and Freud?

You see already the lines along which my thought is working; and indeed it is no part of my aim to save a surprise for the end of the lecture. If I have ventured, a little, to modify our view of the transition from 'the Antique' to 'the Dark,' it is only because I believe we have since witnessed a change even more profound.

The next frontier which has been drawn, though not till recently, is that between the Dark and the Middle Ages. We draw it somewhere about the early twelfth century. This frontier clearly cannot compete with its predecessor in the religious field; nor can it boast such drastic redistribution of populations. But it nearly makes up for these deficiencies in other ways. The change from Ancient to Dark had, after all, consisted mainly in losses. Not entirely. The Dark Ages were not so unfruitful in progress as we sometimes think. They saw the triumph of the *codex* or hinged book over the roll or *volumen*—a technical improvement almost as important for the history of learning as the invention of printing. All exact scholarship depends on it. And if—here I speak under correction—they also invented the stirrup, they did something almost as important for the art of war as the inventor of Tanks. But in the main, they were a period of retrogression: worse houses, worse drains, fewer baths, worse roads, less security. (We notice in *Beowulf* that an old sword is expected to be better than a new one.) With the Middle Ages we reach a period of widespread and brilliant improvement.

The text of Aristotle is recovered. Its rapid assimilation by Albertus Magnus and Thomas Aquinas opens up a new world of thought. In architecture new solutions of technical problems lead the way to new aesthetic effects. In literature the old alliterative and assonantal metres give place to that rhymed and syllabic verse which was to carry the main burden of European poetry for centuries. At the same time the poets explore a whole new range of sentiment. I am so far from underrating this particular revolution that I have before now been accused of exaggerating it. But 'great' and 'small' are terms of comparison. I would think this change in literature the greatest if I did not know of a greater. It does not seem to me that the work of the Troubadours and Chrestien and the rest was really as great a novelty as the poetry of the twentieth century. A man bred on the *Chanson de Roland* might have been puzzled by the *Lancelot*. He would have wondered why the author spent so much time on the sentiments and so (comparatively) little on the actions. But he would have known that this was what the author had done. He would, in one important sense, have known what the poem was 'about.' If he had misunderstood the intention, he would at least have understood the words. That is why I do not think the change from 'Dark' to 'Middle' can, on the literary side, be judged equal to the change which has taken place in my own lifetime. And of course in religion it does not even begin to compete.

A third possible frontier remains to be considered. We might draw our line somewhere towards the end of the seventeenth century, with the general acceptance of Copernicanism, the dominance of Descartes, and (in England) the foundation of the Royal Society. Indeed, if we were considering the history of thought (in the narrower sense of the word) I believe this is where I would draw my line. But if we are considering the history of our culture in general, it is a different matter. Certainly the sciences then began to advance with a firmer and more rapid tread. To that advance nearly all the later, and (in my mind) vaster, changes can be traced. But the effects were delayed. The sciences long remained like a lion-cub whose gambols delighted its master in private; it had not yet tasted man's blood. All through the eighteenth century the tone of the common mind remained ethical, rhetorical, juristic, rather than scientific, so that Johnson could truly say, 'the knowledge of external nature, and the sciences which that knowledge requires or includes, are not the great or the frequent business of the human mind.' It is easy to see why. Science was not the business of Man because Man had not yet become the business of science. It dealt chiefly with the inanimate; and it threw off few technological by-products. When Watt makes his engine, when Darwin starts monkeying with the ancestry of Man, and Freud with his soul, and the economists with all that is his, then indeed the lion will have got out of its cage. Its liberated presence in our midst will become one of the most important factors in everyone's daily life. But not yet; not in the seventeenth century.

It is by these steps that I have come to regard as the greatest of all divisions in the history of the West that which divides the present from, say, the age of Jane Austen and Scott. The dating of such things must of course be rather hazy and indefinite. No one could point to a year or a decade in which the change indisputably began, and it has probably not yet reached its peak. But somewhere between us and the Waverley Novels, somewhere between us and *Persuasion*, the chasm runs. Of course, I had no sooner reached this result than I asked myself whether it might not be an illusion of perspective. The distance between the telegraph post I am touching and the next telegraph post looks longer than the sum of the distances between all the other posts. Could this be an illusion of the same sort? We cannot pace the periods as we could pace the posts. I can only set out the grounds on which, after frequent reconsideration, I have found myself forced to reaffirm my conclusion.

1. I begin with what I regard as the weakest; the change, between Scott's age and ours, in political order. On this count my proposed frontier would have serious rivals. The change is perhaps less than that between Antiquity and the Dark Ages. Yet it is very great; and I think it extends to all nations, those we call democracies as well

as dictatorships. If I wished to satirise the present political order I should borrow for it the name which *Punch* invented during the first German War: *Govertisetnent*. This is a portmanteau word and means 'government by advertisement.' But my intention is not satiric; I am trying to be objective. The change is this. In all previous ages that I can think of the principal aim of rulers, except at rare and short intervals, was to keep their subjects quiet, to forestall or extinguish widespread excitement and persuade people to attend quietly to their several occupations. And on the whole their subjects agreed with them. They even prayed (in words that sound curiously old-fashioned) to be able to live 'a peaceable life in all godliness and honesty' and 'pass their time in rest and quietness.' But now the organisation of mass excitement seems to be almost the normal organ of political power. We live in an age of 'appeal if drives,' and 'campaigns.' Our rulers have become like schoolmasters and are always demanding 'keenness.' And you notice that I am guilty of a slight archaism in calling them 'rulers.' 'Leaders' is the modern word. I have suggested elsewhere that this is a deeply significant change of vocabulary. Our demand upon them has changed no less than theirs on us. For of a ruler one asks justice, incorruption, diligence, perhaps clemency; of a leader, dash, initiative, and (I suppose) what people call 'magnetism' or 'personality.'

On the political side, then, this proposed frontier has respectable, but hardly compulsive, qualifications.

2. In the arts I think it towers above every possible rival. I do not think that any previous age produced work which was, in its own time, as shatteringly and bewilderingly new as that of the Cubists, the Dadaists, the Surrealists, and Picasso has been in ours. And I am quite sure that this is true of the art I love best, that is, of poetry. This question has often been debated with some heat, but the heat was, I think, occasioned by the suspicion (not always ill-grounded) that those who asserted the unprecedented novelty of modern poetry intended thereby to discredit it. But nothing is farther from my purpose than to make any judgement of value, whether favourable

or the reverse. And if once we can eliminate that critical issue and concentrate on the historical fact, then I do not see how anyone can doubt that modern poetry is not only a greater novelty than any other 'new poetry' but new in a new way, almost in a new dimension. To say that all new poetry was once as difficult as ours is false; to say that any was is an equivocation. Some earlier poetry was difficult, but not in the same way. Alexandrian poetry was difficult because it presupposed a learned reader; as you became learned you found the answers to the puzzles. Skaldic poetry was unintelligible if you did not know the *kenningar*, but intelligible if you did. And— this is the real point—all Alexandrian men of letters and all skalds would have agreed about the answers. I believe the same to be true of the dark conceits in Donne; there was one correct interpretation of each and Donne could have told it to you. Of course you might misunderstand what Wordsworth was 'up to' in *Lyrical Ballads*; but everyone understood what he said. I do not see in any of these the slightest parallel to the state of affairs disclosed by a recent symposium on Mr. Eliot's *Cooking Egg*. Here we find seven adults (two of them Cambridge men) whose fives have been specially devoted to the study of poetry discussing a very short poem which has been before the world for thirty-odd years; and there is not the slightest agreement among them as to what, in any sense of the word, it means. I am not in the least concerned to decide whether this state of affairs is a good thing, or a bad thing. I merely assert that it is a new thing. In the whole history of the West, from Homer—I might almost say from the *Epic of Gilgamesh*—there has been no bend or break in the development of poetry comparable to this. On this score my proposed division has no rival to fear.

3. Thirdly, there is the great religious change which I have had to mention before: the un-christening. Of course there were lots of sceptics in Jane Austen's time and long before, as there are lots of Christians now. But the presumption has changed. In her days some kind and degree of religious belief and practice were the norm: now, though I would gladly believe that both kind and degree have improved, they are the exception. I have already argued that this

change surpasses that which Europe underwent at its conversion. It is hard to have patience with those Jererniahs, in Press or pulpit, who warn us that we are 'relapsing into Paganism.' It might be rather fun if we were. It would be pleasant to see some future Prime Minister trying to kill a large and lively milk-white bull in Westminster Hall. But we shan't. What lurks behind such idle prophecies, if they are anything but careless language, is the false idea that the historical process allows mere reversal; that Europe can come out of Christianity 'by the same door as in she went' and find herself back where she was. It is not what happens. A post-Christian man is not a Pagan; you might as well think that a married woman recovers her virginity by divorce. The post-Christian is cut off from the Christian past and therefore doubly from the Pagan past.

4. Lastly, I play my trump card. Between Jane Austen and us, but not between her and Shakespeare, Chaucer, Alfred, Virgil, Homer, or the Pharaohs, comes the birth of the machines. This lifts us at once into a region of change far above all that we have hitherto considered. For this is parallel to the great changes by which we divide epochs of pre-history. This is on a level with the change from stone to bronze, or from a pastoral to an agricultural economy. It alters Man's place in nature. The theme has been celebrated till we are all sick of it, so I will here say nothing about its economic and social consequences, immeasurable though they are. What concerns us more is its psychological effect. How has it come about that we use the highly emotive word 'stagnation,' with all its malodorous and malarial overtones, for what other ages would have called 'permanence'? Why does the word 'primitive' at once suggest to us clumsiness, inefficiency, barbarity? When our ancestors talked of the primitive church or the primitive purity of our constitution they meant nothing of that sort. (The only pejorative sense which Johnson gives to Primitive in his Dictionary is, significantly, 'Formal; affectedly solemn; Imitating the supposed gravity of old times.') Why does 'latest' in advertisements mean 'best'? Well, let us admit that these semantic developments owe something to the nineteenth-century belief in spontaneous progress which itself

owes something either to Darwin's theorem of biological evolution or to that myth of universal evolutionism which is really so different from it, and earlier. For the two great imaginative expressions of the myth, as distinct from the theorem—Keats's *Hyperion* and Wagner's *Ring*—are pre-Darwinian. Let us give these their due. But I submit that what has imposed this climate of opinion so firmly on the human mind is a new archetypal image. It is the image of old machines being superseded by new and better ones. For in the world of machines the new most often really is better and the primitive really is the clumsy. And this image, potent in all our minds, reigns almost without rival in the minds of the uneducated. For to them, after their marriage and the births of their children, the very milestones of life are technical advances. From the old push-bike to the motor-bike and thence to the little car; from gramophone to radio and from radio to television; from the range to the stove; these are the very stages of their pilgrimage. But whether from this cause or from some other, assuredly that approach to life which has left these footprints on our language is the thing that separates us most sharply from our ancestors and whose absence would strike us as most alien if we could return to their world. Conversely, our assumption that everything is provisional and soon to be superseded, that the attainment of goods we have never yet had, rather than the defence and conservation of those we have already, is the cardinal business of life, would most shock and bewilder them if they could visit ours.

I thus claim for my chosen division of periods that on the first count it comes well up to scratch; on the second and third it arguably surpasses all; and on the fourth it quite clearly surpasses them without any dispute. I conclude that it really is the greatest change in the history of Western Man.

At any rate, this conviction determines my whole approach to my work from this Chair. I am not preparing an excuse in advance lest I should hereafter catch myself lecturing either on the *Epic of Gilgamesh* or on the Waverley Novels. The field 'Medieval and Renaissance' is already far too wide for my powers. But you see how to me the appointed area must primarily appear as a specimen of something far larger, something which had already begun when the *Iliad* was composed and was still almost unimpaired when Waterloo was fought. Of course within that immense period there are all sorts of differences. There are lots of convenient differences between the area I am to deal with and other areas; there are important differences within the chosen area. And yet despite all this, that whole thing, from its Greek or pre-Greek beginnings down to the day before yesterday, seen from the vast distance at which we stand today, reveals a homogeneity that is certainly important and perhaps more important than its interior diversities. That is why I shall be unable to talk to you about my particular region without constantly treating things which neither began with the Middle Ages nor ended with the end of the Renaissance. In that way I shall be forced to present to you a great deal of what can only be described as Old European, or Old Western, Culture. If one were giving a lecture on Warwickshire to an audience of Martians (no offence: Martians may be delightful creatures) one might loyally choose all one's *data* from that county: but much of what you told them would not really be Warwickshire lore but 'common tellurian.'

The prospect of my becoming, in such halting fashion as I can, the spokesman of Old Western Culture, alarms me. It may alarm you. I will close with one reassurance and one claim.

First, for the reassurance. I do not think you need fear that the study of a dead period, however prolonged and however sympathetic, need prove an indulgence in nostalgia or an enslavement to the past. In the individual fife, as the psychologists have taught us, it is not the remembered but the forgotten past that enslaves us. I think the same is true of society. To study the past does indeed liberate us from the present, from the idols of our own market-place. But I think it liberates us from the past too. I think no class of men are less enslaved to the past than historians. The unhistorical are usually, without knowing it, enslaved to a fairly recent past. Dante read Virgil. Certain other medieval authors evolved the legend of Virgil as a great magician. It was the more recent past, the whole quality of mind evolved during a few preceding centuries, which impelled them to do so. Dante was freer; he also knew more of the past. And you will be no freer by coming to misinterpret Old Western Culture as quickly and deeply as those medievals misinterpreted Classical Antiquity; or even as the Romantics misinterpreted the Middle Ages. Such misinterpretation has already begun. To arrest its growth while arrest is still possible is surely a proper task for a university.

And now for the claim: which sounds arrogant but, I hope, is not really so. I have said that the vast change which separates you from Old Western has been gradual and is not even now complete. Wide as the chasm is, those who are native to different sides of it can still meet; are meeting in this room. This is quite normal at times of great change. The correspondence of Henry More and Descartes is an amusing example; one would think the two men were writing in different centuries. And here comes the rub. I myself belong far more to that Old Western order than to yours. I am going to claim that this, which in one way is a disqualification for my task, is yet in another a qualification. The disqualification is obvious. You don't want to be lectured on Neanderthal Man by a Neanderthaler, still less on dinosaurs by a dinosaur. And yet, is that the whole story? If a live dinosaur dragged its slow length into the laboratory, would we not all look back as we fled? What a chance to know at last how it really moved and looked and smelled and what noises it made! And if the Neanderthaler could talk, then, though his lecturing technique might leave much to be desired, should we not almost certainly learn from him some things about him which the best modern anthropologist could never have told us? He would tell us without knowing he was telling. One thing I know: I would give a great deal to hear any ancient Athenian, even a stupid one, talking about Greek tragedy. He would know in his bones so much that we seek in vain. At any moment some chance phrase might, unknown to him, show us where modem scholarship had been on the wrong track for years. Ladies and gentlemen, I stand before you somewhat as that Athenian might stand. I read as a native texts that you must read as foreigners. You see why I said that the claim was not really arrogant; who can be proud of speaking fluently his mother tongue or knowing his way about his father's house? It is my settled conviction that in order to read Old Western literature aright you must suspend most of the responses and unlearn most of the habits you have acquired in reading modern literature. And because this is the judgement of a native, I claim that, even if the defence of my conviction is weak, the fact of my conviction is a historical *datum* to which you should give full weight. That way, where I fail as a critic, I may yet be useful as a specimen. I would even dare to go further. Speaking not only for myself but for all other Old Western men whom you may meet, I would say, use your specimens while you can. There are not going to be many more dinosaurs.

LETTERS AND SPEECHES

Edmund Burke

LETTER TO RICHARD CHAMPION, ESQ.

March, 1776

MY DEAR CHAMPION,

I do not know which was best in the intention, the zeal of our worthy friend for a good public cause, or yours for a friend whom you love for the natural reason of having obliged him. I ought not, perhaps, to put a public and private cause upon a par; but there is so much belonging to goodness in the latter, that it compensates for the superior dignity in the former; and whatever besides is wanting to make the scale even, is thrown in by a man's partiality to himself. Be that as it may, pray, my dear Champion, do not let these little disputes go beyond the heat of the moment, or leave any sort of soreness behind them. If we do, we play the game of that unhappy set of men whose business is, and ever has been, to divide the men whose cause they pretended to be engaged in. It is to this point all their speeches, writings, and intrigues of all sorts, tend. They have been hitherto, in some sort, disappointed; disappoint them completely. This I beg may be the case, I should be unhappy and mortified beyond measure, if a difference of opinion on a point, after all, of mere speculation, should produce the least coolness between those who for every public and every private reason, should live in the warmest friendship, and who are mutually deserving it from each other, and from everybody else. What is all this matter? Those who wished to quiet America by concession, thought it best to make that concession at the least possible diminution of the reputation and authority of this country. This was the principle of those who acted in a responsible situation for that measure, in 1766. In this possibly they were wrong. Others thought they ought rather to have convicted their country of robbery, and to have given up the object, not as a liberal donation, but as a restitution of stolen goods. They thought that there were speculative bounds, with regard to legislative power, on which they could maintain one part whilst they abandoned others. They thought it dangerous to trust themselves with indefinite powers. They had reason; because they made such use of them, in a twelvemonth after they had denied their legal existence, as to bring on the present unhappy consequences. Now, if any friend of ours thinks, from the theory and practice of these gentlemen, that their hands ought to have been tied from doing mischief, I am sure I am more inclined to praise his zeal, than to blame his error, if he be in a mistake. We are on the right side; it becomes us to be reasonable. Let Dr. Price rail at the Declaratory Act of 1766. His friends have so abused it, that it is but too natural. Let him rail at this declaration, as those rail at free-will, who have sinned in consequence of it. Once for all, my dear friend, be again without a shadow, a relish, a smutch, a tinge, anything, the slightest that can be imagined, of anger, at the honest opinion of one of the worthiest men in the world. All comes from the best cause in the world. Adieu, my dear friend; salute your worthy family in the name of all here.

Your ever affectionate friend, and humble servant,
EDM. BURKE.

LETTER TO SAMUEL SPAN, ESQ., MASTER OF THE SOCIETY OF MERCHANT ADVENTURERS OF BRISTOL

Beaconsfield, 23d April, 1778

SIR,

I am honored with your letter of the 13th, in answer to mine, which accompanied the resolutions of the House relative to the trade of Ireland.

You will be so good as to present my best respects to the Society, and to assure them that it was altogether unnecessary to remind me of the interest of the constituents. I have never regarded anything else, since I had a seat in parliament. Having frequently and maturely considered that interest, and stated it to myself in almost every point of view, I am persuaded that, under the present circumstances, I cannot more effectually pursue it, than by giving all the support in my power to the propositions which I lately transmitted to the Hall.

The fault I find in the scheme is, that it falls extremely short of that liberality in the commercial system, which, I trust, will one day be adopted. If I had not considered the present resolutions, merely as preparatory to better things, and as a means of shewing experimentally, that justice to others is not always folly to ourselves, I should have contented myself with receiving them in a cold and silent acquiescence. Separately considered, they are matters of no very great importance. But they aim, however imperfectly, at a right principle. I submit to the restraint to appease prejudice: I accept the enlargement, so far as it goes, as the result of reason and of sound policy.

We cannot be insensible of the calamities which have been brought upon this nation by an obstinate adherence to narrow and restrictive plans of government. I confess, I cannot prevail on myself to take them up, precisely at a time when the most decisive experience has taught the rest of the world to lay them down.

The propositions in question did not originate from me, or from my particular friends. But when things are so right in themselves, I hold it my duty not to enquire from what hands they come. I opposed the American measures upon the very same principle on which I support those that relate to Ireland. I was convinced that the evils which have arisen from the adoption of the former, would be infinitely aggravated by the rejection of the latter.

Perhaps Gentlemen are not yet fully aware of the situation of their country, and what its exigencies absolutely require. I find that we are still disposed to talk at our ease, and as if all things were to be regulated by our good pleasure. I should consider it as a fatal symptom, if, in our present distressed and adverse circumstances, we should persist in the errors which are natural only to prosperity. One cannot indeed sufficiently lament the continuance of that spirit of delusion, by which, for a long time past, we have thought fit to measure our necessities by our inclinations. Moderation, prudence, and equity are far more suitable to our condition than loftiness, and confidence, and rigor. We are threatened by enemies of no small magnitude, whom, if we think fit, we may despise, as we have despised others; but they are enemies who can only cease to be truly formidable by our entertaining a due respect for their power. Our danger will not be lessened by our shutting our eyes to it; nor will our force abroad be increased by rendering ourselves feeble, and divided at home.

There is a dreadful schism in the British nation. Since we are not able to reunite the empire, it is our business to give all possible vigor and soundness to those parts of it which are still content to be governed by our councils. Sir, it is proper to inform you, that our measures must be healing. Such a degree of strength must be communicated to all the members of the state, as may enable them to defend themselves, and to co-operate in the defense of the whole. Their temper too must be managed, and their good affections cultivated. They may then be disposed to bear the load with cheerfulness, as a contribution towards what may be called with truth and propriety, and not by an empty form of words, a common cause. Too little dependence cannot be had, at this time of day, on names and prejudices. The eyes of mankind are opened; and communities must be held together by an evident and solid interest. God forbid, that our conduct should demonstrate to the world, that Great Britain can, in no instance whatsoever, be brought to a sense of rational and equitable policy, but by coercion and force of arms!

I wish you to recollect, with what powers of concession, relatively to commerce, as well as to legislation, his Majesty's Commissioners to the United Colonies have sailed from England within this week. Whether these powers are sufficient for their purposes, it is not now my business to examine. But we all know that our resolutions in favor of Ireland are trifling and insignificant, when compared with the concessions to the Americans. At such a juncture, I would implore every man, who retains the least spark of regard to the yet remaining honor and security of this country, not to compel others to an imitation of their conduct; or by passion and violence, to force them to seek in the territories of the separation, that freedom, and those advantages, which they are not to look for whilst they remain under the wings of their ancient government.

After all, what are the matters we dispute with so much warmth? Do we in these resolutions bestow anything upon Ireland? Not a shilling. We only consent to leave to them, in two or three instances, the use of the natural faculties which God has given to them, and to all mankind. Is Ireland united to the crown of Great Britain for no other purpose, than that we should counteract the bounty of Providence in her favor? And in proportion as that bounty has been liberal, that we are to regard it as an evil, which is to be met with in every sort of corrective? To say that Ireland interferes with us, and therefore must be checked, is, in my opinion, a very mistaken, and a very dangerous principle. I must beg leave to repeat what I took the liberty of suggesting to you in my last letter, that Ireland is a country, in the same climate, and of the same natural qualities and productions, with this; and has consequently no other means of growing wealthy in herself, or, in other words, of being useful to us, but by doing the very same things which we do, for the same purposes. I hope that in Great Britain we shall always pursue, without exception, every means of prosperity; and of course, that

Ireland will interfere with us in something or other; for either, in order to limit her, we must restrain ourselves, or we must fall into that shocking conclusion, that we are to keep our yet remaining dependency, under a general and indiscriminate restraint, for the mere purpose of oppression. Indeed, Sir, England and Ireland may flourish together. The world is large enough for us both. Let it be our care, not to make ourselves too little for it.

I know it is said, that the people of Ireland do not pay the same taxes, and therefore ought not in equity to enjoy the same benefits with this. I had hopes that the unhappy phantom of a compulsory equal taxation had haunted us long enough. I do assure you, that until it is entirely banished from our imaginations, (where alone it has, or can have any existence) we shall never cease to do ourselves the most substantial injuries. To that argument of equal taxation, I can only say, that Ireland pays as many taxes as those who are the best judges of her powers[1] are of opinion she can bear. To bear more she must have more ability; and in the order of nature, the advantage must precede the charge. This disposition of things, being the law of God, neither you nor I can alter it. So that if you will have more help from Ireland, you must previously supply her with more means. I believe it will be found, that if men are suffered freely to cultivate their natural advantages, a virtual equality of contribution will come in its own time, and will flow by an easy descent, through its own proper and natural channels. An attempt to disturb that course, and to force nature, will only bring on universal discontent, distress and confusion.

You tell me, Sir, that you prefer an union with Ireland to the little regulations which are proposed in Parliament. This union is a great question of state, to which, when it comes properly before me in my parliamentary capacity, I shall give an honest and unprejudiced consideration. However, it is a settled rule with me to make the most of my actual situation; and not to refuse to do a proper thing, because there is something else more proper, which I am not able to do. This union is a business of difficulty; and on the principles

---

1 The Irish Parliament.

of your letter, a business impracticable. Until it can be matured into a feasible and desirable scheme, I wish to have as close an union of interest and affection with Ireland, as I can have; and that, I am sure, is a far better thing than any nominal union of government.

France, and indeed most extensive empires, which by various designs and fortunes have grown into one great mass, contain many Provinces that are very different from each other in privileges and modes of government; and they raise their supplies in different ways; in different proportions; and under different authorities; yet none of them are for this reason curtailed of their natural rights; but they carry on trade and manufactures with perfect equality. In some way or other the true balance is found; and all of them are properly poised and harmonized. How much have you lost by the participation of Scotland in all your commerce? The external trade of England has more than doubled since that period; and I believe your internal (which is the most advantageous) has been augmented at least fourfold. Such virtue there is in liberality of sentiment, that you have grown richer even by the partnership of poverty.

If you think that this participation was a loss, commercially considered, but that it has been compensated by the share which Scotland has taken in defraying the public charge—I believe you have not very carefully looked at the public accounts. Ireland, Sir, pays a great deal more than Scotland; and is perhaps as much, and as effectually united to England as Scotland is. But if Scotland, instead of paying little, had paid nothing at all, we should be gainers, not losers by acquiring the hearty co-operation of an active intelligent people, towards the increase of the common stock; instead of our being employed in watching and counteracting them, and their being employed in watching and counteracting us, with the peevish and churlish jealousy of rivals and enemies on both sides.

I am sure, Sir, that the commercial experience of the merchants of Bristol, will soon disabuse them of the prejudice, that they can trade no longer, if countries more lightly taxed, are permitted to deal in the same commodities at the same markets. You know, that in fact, you trade very largely where you are met by the goods of all nations. You even pay high duties, on the import of your goods, and afterwards undersell nations less taxed, at their own markets; and where goods of the same kind are not charged at all. If it were otherwise, you could trade very little. You know that the price of all sorts of manufacture is not a great deal enhanced, (except to the domestic consumer) by any taxes paid in this country. This I might very easily prove.

The same consideration will relieve you from the apprehension you express, with relation to sugars, and the difference of the duties paid here and in Ireland. Those duties affect the interior consumer only; and for obvious reasons, relative to the interest of revenue itself, they must be proportioned to his ability of payment; but in all cases in which sugar can be an object of commerce, and therefore (in this view) of rivalship, you are sensible that you are at least on a par with Ireland. As to your apprehensions concerning the more advantageous situation of Ireland, for some branches of commerce (for it is so but for some), I trust you will not find them more serious. Millford Haven, which is at your door, may serve to shew you, that the mere advantage of ports is not the thing which shifts the seat of commerce from one part of the world to the other. If I thought you inclined to take up this matter on local considerations, I should state to you that I do not know any part of the kingdom so well situated for an advantageous commerce with Ireland as Bristol; and that none would be so likely to profit of its prosperity as our city. But your profit and theirs must concur. Beggary and bankruptcy are not the circumstances which invite to an intercourse with that or with any country; and I believe it will be found invariably true, that the superfluities of a rich nation furnish a better object of trade than the necessities of a poor one. It is the interest of the commercial world that wealth should be found everywhere.

The true ground of fear, in my opinion is this; that Ireland, from the vicious system of its internal polity, will be a long time before it can derive any benefit from the liberty now granted, or from anything else. But as I do not vote advantages in hopes that they may not be enjoyed, I will not lay any stress upon this consideration. I rather wish that the Parliament of Ireland may, in its own wisdom, remove these impediments, and put their country in a condition to avail itself of its natural advantages. If they do not, the fault is with them, and not with us.

I have written this long letter, in order to give all possible satisfaction to my constituents with regard to the part I have taken in this affair. It gave me inexpressible concern to find that my conduct had been a cause of uneasiness to any of them. Next to my honor and conscience, I have nothing so near and dear to me as their approbation. However, I had much rather run the risk of displeasing than of injuring them; if I am driven to make such an option. You obligingly lament that you are not to have me for your advocate; but if I had been capable of acting as an advocate in opposition to a plan so perfectly consonant to my known principles, and to the opinions I had publicly declared on an hundred occasions, I should only disgrace myself, without supporting with the smallest degree of credit or effect, the cause you wished me to undertake. I should have lost the only thing which can make such abilities as mine of any use to the world now or hereafter; I mean that authority which is derived from an opinion, that a member speaks the language of truth and sincerity; and that he is not ready to take up or lay down a great political system for the convenience of the hour; that he is in parliament to support his opinion of the public good, and does not form his opinion in order to get into parliament, or to continue in it. It is in a great measure for your sake that I wish to preserve this character. Without it, I am sure, I should be ill able to discharge, by any service, the smallest part of that debt of gratitude and affection which I owe you for the great and honorable trust you have reposed in me. I am, with the highest regard and esteem.

Sir,

Your most obedient and humble servant,

E. B.

Speech on Moving His Resolutions for a Conciliation With The Colonies.

March 22, 1775

I hope, sir, that, notwithstanding the austerity of the Chair, your good nature will incline you to some degree of indulgence towards human frailty. You will not think it unnatural, that those who have an object depending, which strongly engages their hopes and fears, should be somewhat inclined to superstition. As I came into the House full of anxiety about the event of my motion, I found to my infinite surprise that the grand penal bill, by which we had passed sentence on the trade and sustenance of America, is to be returned to us from the other House.[2] I do confess, I could not help looking on this event as a fortunate omen. I look upon it as a sort of providential favor; by which we are put once more in possession of our deliberative capacity, upon a business so very questionable in its nature, so very uncertain in its issue. By the return of this bill, which seemed to have taken its flight forever, we are at this very instant nearly as free to choose a plan for our American Government, as we were on the first day of the session. If, sir, we incline to the side of conciliation, we are not at all embarrassed (unless we please to make ourselves so) by any incongruous mixture of coercion and restraint. We are therefore called upon, as it were by a superior warning voice, again to attend to America; to attend to the whole of it together; and to review the subject with an unusual degree of care and calmness.

Surely it is an awful subject; or there is none so on this side of the grave. When I first had the honor of a seat in this House, the

---

2 "The act to restrain the trade and commerce of the provinces of Massachusetts Bay and New Hampshire, and colonies of Connecticut and Rhode Island, and Providence Plantation, in North America, to Great Britain, Ireland, and the British Islands in the West Indies; and to prohibit such provinces and colonies from carrying on any fishery on the banks of Newfoundland, and other places therein mentioned, under certain conditions and limitations."

affairs of that continent pressed themselves upon us, as the most important and most delicate object of Parliamentary attention. My little share in this great deliberation oppressed me. I found myself a partaker in a very high trust; and having no sort of reason to rely on the strength of my natural abilities for the proper execution of that trust, I was obliged to take more than common pains to instruct myself in everything which relates to our Colonies. I was not less under the necessity of forming some fixed ideas, concerning the general policy of the British Empire. Something of this sort seemed to be indispensable; in order, amidst so vast a fluctuation of passions and opinions, to concenter my thoughts; to ballast my conduct; to preserve me from being blown about by every wind of fashionable doctrine. I really did not think it safe, or manly, to have fresh principles to seek upon every fresh mail which should arrive from America.

At that period, I had the fortune to find myself in perfect concurrence with a large majority in this House. Bowing under that high authority, and penetrated with the sharpness and strength of that early impression, I have continued ever since, without the least deviation, in my original sentiments. Whether this be owing to an obstinate perseverance in error, or to a religious adherence to what appears to me truth and reason, it is in your equity to judge.

Sir, Parliament, having an enlarged view of objects, made, during this interval, more frequent changes in their sentiments and their conduct than could be justified in a particular person upon the contracted scale of private information. But though I do not hazard anything approaching to a censure on the motives of former Parliaments to all those alterations, one fact is undoubted; that under them the state of America has been kept in continual agitation. Everything administered as remedy to the public complaint, if it did not produce, was at least followed by, an heightening of the distemper; until, by a variety of experiments, that important country has been brought into her present situation—a situation, which I will not miscall, which I dare not name; which I scarcely know how to comprehend in the terms of any description.

In this posture, sir, things stood at the beginning of the session. About that time, a worthy member[3] of great Parliamentary experience who, in the year 1766, filled the chair of the American committee with much ability, took me aside; and, lamenting the present aspect of our politics, told me things were come to such a pass that our former methods of proceeding in the House would be no longer tolerated. That the public tribunal (never too indulgent to a long and unsuccessful opposition) would now scrutinize our conduct with unusual severity. That the very vicissitudes and shiftings of ministerial measures, instead of convicting their authors of inconstancy and want of system, would be taken as an occasion of charging us with a predetermined discontent, which nothing could satisfy; whilst we accused every measure of vigor as cruel, and every proposal of lenity as weak and irresolute. The public, he said, would not have patience to see us play the game out with our adversaries: we must produce our hand. It would be expected that those, who for many years had been active in such affairs, should show that they had formed some clear and decided idea of the principles of Colony government; and were capable of drawing out something like a platform of the ground, which might be laid for future and permanent tranquility.

I felt the truth of what my honorable friend represented: but I felt my situation too. His application might have been made with far greater propriety to many other gentlemen. No man was indeed ever better disposed, or worse qualified, for such an undertaking than myself. Though I gave so far into his opinion that I immediately threw my thoughts into a sort of Parliamentary form, I was by no means equally ready to produce them. It generally argues some degree of natural impotence of mind, or some want of knowledge of the world, to hazard plans of government, except from a seat of authority. Propositions are made, not only ineffectually, but somewhat disreputably, when the minds of men are not properly disposed for their reception; and for my part, I am not ambitious of ridicule; not absolutely a candidate for disgrace.

---

3 Mr. Rose Fuller.

Besides, sir, to speak the plain truth, I have in general no very exalted opinion of the virtue of paper government; nor of any politics in which the plan is to be wholly separated from the execution. But when I saw that anger and violence prevailed every day more and more; and that things were hastening towards an incurable alienation of our Colonies; I confess, my caution gave way. I felt this as one of those few moments in which decorum yields to an higher duty. Public calamity is a mighty leveler; and there are occasions when any, even the slightest, chance of doing good must be laid hold on, even by the most inconsiderable person.

To restore order and repose to an empire so great and so distracted as ours, is, merely in the attempt, an undertaking that would ennoble the flights of the highest genius, and obtain pardon for the efforts of the meanest understanding. Struggling a good while with these thoughts, by degrees I felt myself more firm. I derived, at length, some confidence from what in other circumstances usually produces timidity. I grew less anxious, even from the idea of my own insignificance. For, judging of what you are, by what you ought to be, I persuaded myself, that you would not reject a reasonable proposition, because it had nothing but its reason to recommend it. On the other hand, being totally destitute of all shadow of influence, natural or adventitious, I was very sure that, if my proposition were futile or dangerous; if it were weakly conceived, or improperly timed, there was nothing exterior to it of power to awe, dazzle, or delude you. You will see it just as it is; and you will treat it just as it deserves.

The proposition is peace. Not peace through the medium of war; not peace to be hunted through the labyrinth of intricate and endless negotiations; not peace to arise out of universal discord, fomented, from principle, in all parts of the Empire; not peace to depend on the juridical determination of perplexing questions; or the precise marking the shadowy boundaries of a complex government. It is simple peace; sought in its natural course, and its ordinary haunts. It is peace sought in the spirit of peace; and laid in principles purely pacific. I propose, by removing the ground of the difference, and by restoring the former unsuspecting confidence of the Colonies in the Mother Country, to give permanent satisfaction to your people; and (far from a scheme of ruling by discord) to reconcile them to each other in the same act, and by the bond of the very same interest, which reconciles them to British government.

My idea is nothing more. Refined policy ever has been the parent of confusion; and ever will be so, as long as the world endures. Plain good intention, which is as easily discovered at the first view, as fraud is surely detected at last, is, let me say, of no mean force in the government of mankind. Genuine simplicity of heart is an healing and cementing principle. My plan, therefore, being formed upon the most simple grounds imaginable, may disappoint some people, when they hear it. It has nothing to recommend it to the prurience of curious ears. There is nothing at all new and captivating in it. It has nothing of the splendor of the project, which has been lately laid upon your table by the noble lord in the blue ribband.[4] It does not propose to fill your lobby with squabbling Colony agents who will require the interposition of your mace, at every instant, to keep the peace amongst them. It does not institute a magnificent auction of finance, where captivated provinces come to general ransom by bidding against each other, until you knock down the hammer, and determine a proportion of payments, beyond all the powers of algebra to equalize and settle.

---

4 "That when the governor, council, or assembly, or general court, of any of his majesty's provinces or colonies in America, shall propose to make provision, according to the condition, circumstances, and situation, of such province or colony, for contributing their proportion to the common defense (such proportion to be raised under the authority of the general court, or general assembly, of such province or colony, and disposable by parliament) and shall engage to make provision also for the support of the civil government, and the administration of justice, in such province or colony, it will be proper, if such proposal shall be approved by his majesty, and the two houses of parliament, and for so long as such provision shall be made accordingly, to forbear, in respect of such province or colony, to levy any duty, tax, or assessment, or to impose any farther duty, tax, or assessment, except such duties as it may be expedient to continue to levy or impose, for the regulation of commerce; the net produce of the duties last mentioned to be carried to the account of such province or colony respectively." Resolution moved by Lord North in the committee; and agreed to by the house, 27 Feb. 1775.

The plan, which I shall presume to suggest, derives, however, one great advantage from the proposition and registry of that noble lord's project. The idea of conciliation is admissible. First, the house, in accepting the resolution moved by the noble lord, has admitted, notwithstanding the menacing front of our address, notwithstanding our heavy bill of pains and penalties—that we do not think ourselves precluded from all ideas of free grace and bounty.

The house has gone farther; it has declared conciliation admissible, previous to any submission on the part of America. It has even shot a good deal beyond that mark, and has admitted, that the complaints of our former mode of exerting the right of taxation were not wholly unfounded. That right thus exerted is allowed to have had something reprehensible in it; something unwise, or something grievous: since, in the midst of our heat and resentment, we, of ourselves, have proposed a capital alteration; and, in order to get rid of what seemed so very exceptionable, have instituted a mode that is altogether new; one that is, indeed, wholly alien from all the ancient methods and forms of Parliament.

The principle of this proceeding is large enough for my purpose. The means proposed by the noble lord for carrying his ideas into execution, I think indeed, are very indifferently suited to the end; and this I shall endeavor to show you before I sit down. But, for the present, I take my ground on the admitted principle. I mean to give peace. Peace implies reconciliation; and where there has been a material dispute, reconciliation does in a manner always imply concession on the one part or on the other. In this state of things, I make no difficulty in affirming that the proposal ought to originate from us. Great and acknowledged force is not impaired, either in effect or in opinion, by an unwillingness to exert itself. The superior power may offer peace with honor and with safety. Such an offer from such a power will be attributed to magnanimity. But the concessions of the weak are the concessions of fear. When such a one is disarmed, he is wholly at the mercy of his superior; and he loses forever that time and those chances, which, as they happen to all men, are the strength and resources of all inferior power.

The capital leading questions on which you must this day decide, are these two. First, whether you ought to concede; and secondly, what your concession ought to be. On the first of these questions we have gained (as I have just taken the liberty of observing to you) some ground. But I am sensible that a good deal more is still to be done. Indeed, sir, to enable us to determine both on the one and the other of these great questions with a firm and precise judgment, I think it may be necessary to consider distinctly the true nature and the peculiar circumstances of the object which we have before us. Because after all our struggle, whether we will or not, we must govern America, according to that nature, and to those circumstances; and not according to our own imaginations; not according to abstract ideas of right; by no means according to mere general theories of government, the resort to which appears to me, in our present situation, no better than arrant trifling. I shall therefore endeavor, with your leave, to lay before you some of the most material of these circumstances in as full and as clear a manner as I am able to state them.

The first thing that we have to consider with regard to the nature of the object is—the number of people in the Colonies. I have taken for some years a good deal of pains on that point. I can by no calculation justify myself in placing the number below two millions of inhabitants of our own European blood and color; besides at least 500.000 others, who form no inconsiderable part of the strength and opulence of the whole. This, sir, is, I believe, about the true number. There is no occasion to exaggerate, where plain truth is of so much weight and importance. But whether I put the present numbers too high or too low, is a matter of little moment. Such is the strength with which population shoots in that part of the world, that state the numbers as high as we will, whilst the dispute continues, the exaggeration ends. Whilst we are discussing any given magnitude, they are grown to it. Whilst we spend our time in deliberating on the mode of governing two millions, we shall find we have millions more to manage. Your children do not grow faster from infancy to manhood, than they spread from families to communities, and from villages to nations.

I put this consideration of the present and the growing numbers in the front of our deliberation; because, sir, this consideration will make it evident to a blunter discernment than yours, that no partial, narrow, contracted, pinched, occasional system will be at all suitable to such an object. It will show you, that it is not to be considered as one of those minima which are out of the eye and consideration of the law; not a paltry excrescence of the state; not a mean dependent, who may be neglected with little damage, and provoked with little danger. It will prove that some degree of care and caution is required in the handling such an object; it will show that you ought not, in reason, to trifle with so large a mass of the interests and feelings of the human race. You could at no time do so without guilt; and be assured you will not be able to do it long with impunity.

But the population of this country, the great and growing population, though a very important consideration, will lose much of its weight if not combined with other circumstances. The commerce of your Colonies is out of all proportion beyond the numbers of the people. This ground of their commerce indeed has been trod some days ago, and with great ability, by a distinguished person[5] at your bar. This gentleman, after thirty-five years—it is so long since he first appeared at the same place to plead for the commerce of Great Britain—has come again before you to plead the same cause, without any other effect of time than that, to the fire of imagination and extent of erudition, which even then marked him as one of the first literary characters of his age, he has added a consummate knowledge in the commercial interest of his country, formed by a long course of enlightened and discriminating experience.

Sir, I should be inexcusable in coming after such a person with any detail; if a great part of the members who now fill the House

____

5 Mr. Glover.

had not the misfortune to be absent when he appeared at your bar. Besides, sir, I propose to take the matter at periods of time somewhat different from his. There is, if I mistake not, a point of view from whence, if you will look at this subject, it is impossible that it should not make an impression upon you.

I have in my hand two accounts; one a comparative state of the export trade of England to its Colonies, as it stood in the year 1704, and as it stood in the year 1772. The other a state of the export trade of this country to its Colonies alone, as it stood in 1772, compared with the whole trade of England to all parts of the world (the Colonies included) in the year 1704. They are from good vouchers; the latter period from the accounts on your table, the earlier from an original manuscript of Davenant, who first established the Inspector-General's office, which has been ever since his time so abundant a source of Parliamentary information.

The export trade to the Colonies consists of three great branches. The African, which, terminating almost wholly in the Colonies, must be put to the account of their commerce; the West Indian; and the North American. All these are so interwoven, that the attempt to separate them would tear to pieces the contexture of the whole; and, if not entirely destroy, would very much depreciate the value of all the parts. I therefore consider these three denominations to be what in effect they are, one trade.

The trade to the Colonies, taken on the export side, at the beginning of this century, that is, in the year 1704, stood thus:

Exports to North America, and the West Indies	£483,265
To Africa	86,665
	£569.930

In the year 1772, which I take as a middle year between the highest and lowest of those lately laid on your table, the account was as follows:

To North America, and the West Indies   £4.791.734
To Africa   866.398

To which if you add the export trade from Scotland,
which had in 1704 no existence   364.000
                                     £6.024.171

From five hundred and odd thousand, it has grown to six millions. It has increased no less than twelve-fold. This is the state
of the Colony trade, as compared with itself at these two periods,
within this century;—and this is matter for meditation. But this is
not all. Examine my second account. See how the export trade to
the Colonies alone in 1772 stood in the other point of view, that is,
as compared to the whole trade of England in 1704.

The whole export trade of England, including
that to the Colonies, in 1704   £6.509.000
Export to the Colonies alone, in 1772   6.024.000
Difference   £485.000

The trade with America alone is now within less than £500,000
of being equal to what this great commercial nation, England,
carried on at the beginning of this century with the whole world! If
I had taken the largest year of those on your table, it would rather
have exceeded. But, it will be said, is not this American trade an
unnatural protuberance that has drawn the juices from the rest of
the body? The reverse. It is the very food that has nourished every
other part into its present magnitude. Our general trade has been
greatly augmented; and augmented more or less in almost every
part to which it ever extended; but with this material difference;
that of the six millions which in the beginning of the century
constituted the whole mass of our export commerce, the Colony
trade was but one twelfth part; it is now (as a part of sixteen
millions) considerably more than a third of the whole. This is the
relative proportion of the importance of the Colonies at these two
periods: and all reasoning concerning our mode of treating them

must have this proportion as its basis; or it is a reasoning weak, rotten, and sophistical.

Mr. Speaker, I cannot prevail on myself to hurry over this great consideration. It is good for us to be here. We stand where we have an immense view of what is, and what is past. Clouds indeed, and darkness, rest upon the future. Let us however, before we descend from this noble eminence, reflect that this growth of our national prosperity has happened within the short period of the life of man. It has happened within sixty-eight years. There are those alive whose memory might touch the two extremities. For instance, my Lord Bathurst might remember all the stages of the progress. He was in 1704 of an age at least to be made to comprehend such things. He was then old enough *acta parentum jam legere, et quae sit po-terit cognoscere virtus*[6]—Suppose, sir, that the angel of this auspicious youth, foreseeing the many virtues which made him one of the most amiable, as he is one of the most fortunate men of his age, had opened to him in vision that when, in the fourth generation, the third Prince of the House of Brunswick had sat twelve years on the throne of that nation, which (by the happy issue of moderate and healing councils) was to be made Great Britain, he should see his son, Lord Chancellor of England, turn back the current of hereditary dignity to its fountain, and raise him to an higher rank of peerage, whilst he enriched the family with a new one—If amidst these bright and happy scenes of domestic honor and prosperity, that angel should have drawn up the curtain, and unfolded the rising glories of his country, and whilst he was gazing with admiration on the then commercial grandeur of England, the genius should point out to him a little speck, scarce visible in the mass of the national interest, a small seminal principle, rather than a formed body, and should tell him: "Young man, there is America—which at this day serves for little more than to amuse you with stories of savage men, and uncouth manners; yet shall, before you taste of death, show itself equal to the whole of that commerce which now

---

6 To read the deeds of forefathers, and learn what virtue is.

attracts the envy of the world. Whatever England has been growing to by a progressive increase of improvement, brought in by varieties of people, by succession of civilizing conquests and civilizing settlements in a series of seventeen hundred years, you shall see as much added to her by America in the course of a single life!"

If this state of his country had been foretold to him, would it not require all the sanguine credulity of youth, and all the fervid glow of enthusiasm, to make him believe it? Fortunate man, he has lived to see it! Fortunate indeed, if he lives to see nothing that shall vary the prospect, and cloud the setting of his day!

Excuse me, sir, if turning from such thoughts I resume this comparative view once more. You have seen it on a large scale; look at it on a small one. I will point out to your attention a particular instance of it in the single province of Pennsylvania. In the year 1704 that province called for £11,459 in value of your commodities, native and foreign. This was the whole. What did it demand in 1772? Why nearly fifty times as much; for in that year the export to Pennsylvania was £507,909 nearly equal to the export to all the Colonies together in the first period.

I choose, sir, to enter into these minute and particular details; because generalities, which in all other cases are apt to heighten and raise the subject, have here a tendency to sink it. When we speak of the commerce with our colonies, fiction lags after truth; invention is unfruitful, and imagination cold and barren.

So far, sir, as to the importance of the object in the view of its commerce, as concerned in the exports from England. If I were to detail the imports, I could show how many enjoyments they procure, which deceive the burden of life; how many materials which invigorate the springs of national industry, and extend and animate every part of our foreign and domestic commerce. This would be a curious subject indeed—but I must prescribe bounds to myself in a matter so vast and various.

I pass therefore to the Colonies in another point of view, their agriculture. This they have prosecuted with such a spirit, that, be-sides feeding plentifully their own growing multitude, their annual export of grain, comprehending rice, has some years ago exceeded a million in value. Of their last harvest, I am persuaded, they will export much more. At the beginning of the century, some of these Colonies imported corn from the Mother Country. For some time past, the Old World has been fed from the New. The scarcity which you have felt would have been a desolating famine; if this child of your old age, with a true filial piety, with a Roman charity, had not put the full breast of its youthful exuberance to the mouth of its exhausted parent.

As to the wealth which the Colonies have drawn from the sea by their fisheries, you had all that matter fully opened at your bar. You surely thought those acquisitions of value; for they seemed even to excite your envy; and yet the spirit by which that enterpris-ing employment has been exercised, ought rather, in my opinion, to have raised your esteem and admiration. And pray, sir, what in the world is equal to it? Pass by the other parts, and look at the manner in which the people of New England have of late carried on the whale fishery. Whilst we follow them among the jumbling mountains of ice, and behold them penetrating into the deepest frozen recesses of Hudson's Bay, and Davis's Straights, whilst we are looking for them beneath the Arctic Circle, we hear that they have pierced into the opposite region of polar cold, that they are at the Antipodes, and engaged under the frozen serpent of the south. Falkland Island, which seemed too remote and romantic an object for the grasp of national ambition, is but a stage and resting-place in the progress of their victorious industry. Nor is the equinoctial heat more discouraging to them, than the accumulated winter of both the poles. We know that whilst some of them draw the line and strike the harpoon on the coast of Africa, others run the lon-gitude, and pursue their gigantic game along the coast of Brazil. No sea but what is vexed by their fisheries. No climate that is not witness to their toils. Neither the perseverance of Holland, nor the activity of France, nor the dexterous and firm sagacity of English enterprise, ever carried this most perilous mode of hardy industry to the extent to which it has been pushed by this recent people; a people who are still, as it were, but in the gristle, and not yet hardened into the bone of manhood. When I contemplate these things; when I know that the Colonies in general owe little or nothing to any care of ours, and that they are not squeezed into this happy form by the constraints of watchful and suspicious government, but that through a wise and salutary neglect, a generous nature has been suffered to take her own way to perfection: when I reflect upon these effects, when I see how profitable they have been to us, I feel all the pride of power sink, and all presumption in the wisdom of human contrivances melt, and die away within me. My rigor relents. I pardon something to the spirit of liberty.

I am sensible, sir, that all which I have asserted in my detail, is admitted in the gross; but that quite a different conclusion is drawn from it. America, gentlemen say, is a noble object. It is an object well worth fighting for. Certainly it is, if fighting a people be the best way of gaining them. Gentlemen in this respect will be led to their choice of means by their complexions and their habits. Those who understand the military art, will of course have some predilection for it. Those who wield the thunder of the state, may have more confidence in the efficacy of arms. But I confess, possibly for want of this knowledge, my opinion is much more in favor of prudent management, than of force; considering force not as an odious, but a feeble instrument, for preserving a people so numerous, so active, so growing, so spirited as this, in a profitable and subordinate connection with us.

First, sir, permit me to observe, that the use of force alone is but temporary. It may subdue for a moment; but it does not remove the necessity of subduing again: and a nation is not governed, which is perpetually to be conquered.

My next objection is its uncertainty. Terror is not always the effect of force; and an armament is not a victory. If you do not succeed, you are without resource; for, conciliation failing, force remains; but, force failing, no further hope of reconciliation is left. Power and authority are sometimes bought by kindness; but they can never be begged as alms, by an impoverished and defeated violence.

A further objection to force is, that you impair the object by your very endeavors to preserve it. The thing you fought for is not the thing which you recover; but depreciated, sunk, wasted, and consumed in the contest. Nothing less will content me than whole America. I do not choose to consume its strength along with our own; because in all parts it is the British strength that I consume. I do not choose to be caught by a foreign enemy at the end of this exhausting conflict; and still less in the midst of it. I may escape; but I can make no insurance against such an event. Let me add, that I do not choose wholly to break the American spirit, because it is the spirit that has made the country.

Lastly, we have no sort of experience in favor of force as an instrument in the rule of our Colonies. Their growth and their utility has been owing to methods altogether different. Our ancient indulgence has been said to be pursued to a fault. It may be so. But we know, if feeling is evidence, that our fault was more tolerable than our attempt to mend it; and our sin far more salutary than our penitence.

These, sir, are my reasons for not entertaining that high opinion of untried force by which many gentlemen, for whose sentiments in other particulars I have great respect, seem to be so greatly captivated. But there is still behind a third consideration concerning this object which serves to determine my opinion on the sort of policy which ought to be pursued in the management of America, even more than its population and its commerce—I mean its temper and character.

In this character of the Americans, a love of freedom is the predominating feature, which marks and distinguishes the whole: and as an ardent is always a jealous affection, your Colonies become suspicious, restive, and intractable whenever they see the least attempt to wrest from them by force, or shuffle from them by chicane, what they think the only advantage worth living for. This fierce spirit of liberty is stronger in the English Colonies probably than in any other people of the earth; and this from a great variety of powerful causes; which, to understand the true temper of their minds, and the direction which this spirit takes, it will not be amiss to lay open somewhat more largely.

First, the people of the Colonies are descendants of Englishmen. England, sir, is a nation which still, I hope, respects and formerly adored her freedom. The Colonists emigrated from you,when this part of your character was most predominant; and they took this bias and direction the moment they parted from your hands. They are therefore not only devoted to liberty, but to liberty according to English ideas, and on English principles. Abstract liberty, like other mere abstractions, is not to be found. Liberty inheres in some sensible object; and every nation has formed to itself some favorite point, which by way of eminence becomes the criterion of their happiness. It happened, you know, sir, that the great contests for freedom in this country were from the earliest times chiefly upon the question of taxing. Most of the contests in the ancient commonwealths turned primarily on the right of election of magistrates; or on the balance among the several orders of the state. The question of money was not with them so immediate. But in England it was otherwise. On this point of taxes the ablest pens and most eloquent tongues have been exercised; the greatest spirits have acted and suffered. In order to give the fullest satisfaction concerning the importance of this point, it was not only necessary for those who in argument defended the excellence of the English constitution, to insist on this privilege of granting money as a dry point of fact, and to prove that the right had been acknowledged in ancient parchments, and blind usages, to reside in a certain body called an house of commons. They went much further; they attempted to prove, and they succeeded, that in theory it ought to be so, from the particular nature of a house of commons, as an immediate representative of the people; whether the old records had delivered this oracle or not. They took infinite pains to inculcate, as a fundamental principle, that, in all monarchies, the people must in effect themselves mediately or immediately possess the power of granting their own money, or no shadow of liberty could subsist. The Colonies draw from you, as with their life-blood, these ideas and principles. Their love of liberty, as with you, fixed and attached on this specific point of taxing. Liberty might be safe, or might be endangered in twenty other particulars, without their being much pleased or alarmed. Here they felt its pulse; and as they found that beat, they thought themselves sick or sound. I do not say whether they were right or wrong in applying your general arguments to their own case. It is not easy indeed to make a monopoly of theorems and corollaries. The fact is that they did thus apply those general arguments; and your mode of governing them, whether through lenity or indolence, through wisdom or mistake, confirmed them in the imagination that they, as well as you, had an interest in these common principles.

They were further confirmed in this pleasing error by the form of their provincial legislative assemblies. Their governments are popular in an high degree; some are merely popular; in all, the popular representative is the most weighty; and this share of the people in their ordinary government never fails to inspire them with lofty sentiments, and with a strong aversion from whatever tends to deprive them of their chief importance.

If anything were wanting to this necessary operation of the form of government, religion would have given it a complete effect. Religion, always a principle of energy, in this new people is no way worn out or impaired; and their mode of professing it is also one main cause of this free spirit. The people are Protestants; and of that kind which is the most adverse to all implicit submission of mind and opinion. This is a persuasion not only favorable to liberty, but built upon it. I do not think, sir, that the reason of this averseness in the dissenting churches from all that looks like absolute government is so much to be sought in their religious tenets, as in their history. Everyone knows that the Roman Catholic religion is at least co-eval with most of the governments where it prevails; that it has generally gone hand in hand with them; and received great favor and every kind of support from authority. The Church of England too was formed from her cradle under the nursing care of regular government. But the dissenting interests have sprung up in direct opposition to all the ordinary powers of the world; and could justify that opposition only on a strong claim to natural liberty. Their very existence depended on the powerful and unremitted assertion of that claim. All Protestantism, even the most cold and passive, is a sort of dissent. But the religion most prevalent in our Northern Colonies is a refinement on the principle of resistance; it is the dissidence of dissent; and the protestantism of the Protestant religion. This religion, under a variety of denominations, agreeing in nothing but in the communion of the spirit of liberty, is predominant in most of the northern provinces; where the Church of England, notwithstanding its legal rights, is in reality no more than a sort of private sect, not composing most probably the tenth of the people. The Colonists left England when this spirit was high; and in the emigrants was the highest of all: and even that stream of foreigners, which has been constantly flowing into these Colonies, has, for the greatest part, been composed of dissenters from the establishments of their several countries, and have brought with them a temper and character far from alien to that of the people with whom they mixed.

Sir, I can perceive by their manner, that some gentlemen object to the latitude of this description; because in the Southern Colonies the Church of England forms a large body, and has a regular establishment. It is certainly true. There is, however, a circumstance attending these colonies which in my opinion fully counterbalances this difference, and makes the spirit of liberty still more high and haughty than in those to the northward. It is that in Virginia and the Carolinas they have a vast multitude of slaves. Where this is the case in any part of the world, those who are free are by far the most proud and jealous of their freedom. Freedom is to them not only an enjoyment, but a kind of rank and privilege. Not seeing there that freedom, as in countries where it is a common blessing, and as broad and general as the air, may be united with much abject toil, with great misery, with all the exterior of servitude, liberty looks amongst them, like something that is more noble and liberal. I do not mean, sir, to commend the superior morality of this sentiment, which has at least as much pride as virtue in it; but I cannot alter the nature of man. The fact is so; and these people of the Southern Colonies are much more strongly, and with an higher and more stubborn spirit, attached to liberty than those to the northward. Such were all the ancient commonwealths; such were our Gothic ancestors; such in our days were the Poles; and such will be all masters of slaves, who are not slaves themselves. In such a people the haughtiness of domination combines with the spirit of freedom, fortifies it, and renders it invincible.

Permit me, sir, to add another circumstance in our Colonies, which contributes no mean part towards the growth and effect of this intractable spirit. I mean their education. In no country perhaps in the world is the law so general a study. The profession itself is numerous and powerful; and in most provinces it takes the lead. The greater number of the deputies sent to the Congress were lawyers. But all who read, and most do read, endeavor to obtain some smattering in that science. I have been told by an eminent bookseller that in no branch of his business, after tracts of popular devotion, were so many books as those on the law exported to the plantations. The Colonists have now fallen into the way of printing them for their own use. I hear that they have sold nearly as many of Blackstone's Commentaries in America as in England. General Gage marks out this disposition very particularly in a letter on your table. He states that all the people in his government are lawyers, or smatterers in law; and that in Boston they have been enabled, by successful chicane, wholly to evade many parts of one of your capital penal constitutions. The smartness of debate will say that this knowledge ought to teach them more clearly the rights of legislature, their obligations to obedience, and the penalties of rebellion.

All this is mighty well. But my honorable and learned friend on the floor,[7] who condescends to mark what I say for animadversion[8], will disdain that ground. He has heard as well as I that when great honors and great emoluments do not win over this knowledge to the service of the state, it is a formidable adversary to government. If the spirit be not tamed and broken by these happy methods, it is stubborn and litigious. *Abeunt studia in mores.*[9] This study renders men acute, inquisitive, dexterous, prompt in attack, ready in defense, full of resources. In other countries, the people, more simple and of a less mercurial cast, judge of an ill principle in government only by an actual grievance; here they anticipate the evil, and judge of the pressure of the grievance by the badness of the principle. They augur misgovernment at a distance; and snuff the approach of tyranny in every tainted breeze.

The last cause of this disobedient spirit in the Colonies is hardly less powerful than the rest, as it is not merely moral, but laid deep in the natural constitution of things. Three thousand miles of ocean lie between you and them. No contrivance can prevent the effect of this distance in weakening government. Seas roll, and months pass, between the order and the execution; and the want of a speedy explanation of a single point is enough to defeat a whole system. You have, indeed, winged ministers of vengeance, who carry your bolts in their pounces to the remotest verge of the sea. But there a power steps in that limits the arrogance of raging passions and furious elements, and says, "So far shalt thou go, and no farther." Who are you, that should fret and rage, and bite the chains of nature?—Nothing worse happens to you than does to all nations who have extensive empire; and it happens in all the forms into which empire can be thrown. In large bodies, the circulation of power must be less vigorous at the extremities. Nature has said it. The Turk cannot govern Egypt, and Arabia, and Kurdistan, as he governs Thrace; nor has he the same dominion in Crimea and Algiers,

---

7   The Attorney General.

8   Criticism or censure

9   "Studies turn into habits."

which he has at Brusa and Smyrna. Despotism itself is obliged to truck and huckster. The sultan gets such obedience as he can. He governs with a loose rein, that he may govern at all; and the whole of the force and vigor of his authority in his center is derived from a prudent relaxation in all his borders. Spain, in her provinces, is, perhaps, not so well obeyed, as you are in yours. She complies too; she submits; she watches times. This is the immutable condition, the eternal law of extensive and detached empire.

Then, sir, from these six capital sources—of descent, of form, of government, of religion in the Northern Provinces, of manners in the Southern, of education, of the remoteness of situation from the first mover of government—from all these causes a fierce spirit of liberty has grown up. It has grown with the growth of the people in your Colonies, and increased with the increase of their wealth; a spirit that, unhappily meeting with an exercise of power in England, which, however lawful, is not reconcilable to any ideas of liberty much less with theirs, has kindled this flame, that is ready to consume us.

I do not mean to commend either the spirit in this excess, or the moral causes which produce it. Perhaps a more smooth and accommodating spirit of freedom in them would be more acceptable to us. Perhaps ideas of liberty might be desired more reconcilable with an arbitrary and boundless authority. Perhaps we might wish the Colonists to be persuaded that their liberty is more secure when held in trust for them by us (as their guardians during a perpetual minority) than with any part of it in their own hands. But the question is not whether their spirit deserves praise or blame—what, in the name of God, shall we do with it? You have before you the object; such as it is, with all its glories, with all its imperfections on its head. You see the magnitude; the importance; the temper; the habits; the disorders. By all these considerations, we are strongly urged to determine something concerning it. We are called upon to fix some rule and line for our future conduct which may give a little stability to our politics, and prevent the return of such unhappy deliberations as the present. Every such return will bring the matter before us in a still more intractable form. For what astonishing and incredible things have we not seen already? What monsters have not been generated from this unnatural contention? Whilst every principle of authority and resistance has been pushed, upon both sides, as far as it would go, there is nothing so solid and certain, either in reasoning or in practice, that has been not shaken. Until very lately, all authority in America seemed to be nothing but an emanation from yours. Even the popular part of the Colony Constitution derived all its activity, and its first vital movement, from the pleasure of the Crown. We thought, sir, that the utmost which the discontented Colonists could do was to disturb authority; we never dreamt they could of themselves supply it; knowing in general what an operose[10] business it is, to establish a government absolutely new. But having, for our purposes in this contention, resolved that none but an obedient assembly should sit, the humors of the people there, finding all passage through the legal channel stopped, with great violence broke out another way. Some provinces have tried their experiment, as we have tried ours; and theirs has succeeded. They have formed a government sufficient for its purposes without the bustle of a revolution, or the troublesome formality of an election. Evident necessity, and tacit consent, have done the business in an instant. So well they have done it that lord Dunmore (the account is among the fragments on your table) tells you that the new institution is infinitely better obeyed than the ancient government ever was in its most fortunate period. Obedience is what makes government, and not the names by which it is called; not the name of governor, as formerly, or committee, as at present. This new government has originated directly from the people; and was not transmitted through any of the ordinary artificial media of a positive constitution. It was not a manufacture ready formed, and transmitted to them in that condition from England. The evil arising from hence is this; that the Colonists having once found the possibility of enjoying the advantages of order, in the midst of a struggle for liberty, such struggles will not henceforward seem so

---

10   Involving or displaying much industry or effort.

terrible to the settled and sober part of mankind, as they had appeared before the trial.

Pursuing the same plan of punishing by the denial of the exercise of government to still greater lengths, we wholly abrogated the ancient government of Massachusetts. We were confident that the first feeling, if not the very prospect of anarchy, would instantly enforce a complete submission. The experiment was tried. A new, strange, unexpected face of things appeared. Anarchy is found tolerable. A vast province has now subsisted, and subsisted in a considerable degree of health and vigor, for near a twelvemonth, without governor, without public council, without judges, without executive magistrates. How long it will continue in this state, or what may arise out of this unheard-of situation, how can the wisest of us conjecture? Our late experience has taught us that many of those fundamental principles, formerly believed infallible, are either not of the importance they were imagined to be; or that we have not at all adverted to some other far more important, and far more powerful principles, which entirely over-rule those we had considered as omnipotent. I am much against any further experiments, which tend to put to the proof any more of these allowed opinions, which contribute so much to the public tranquility. In effect, we suffer as much at home by this loosening of all ties and this concussion of all established opinions, as we do abroad. For in order to prove that the Americans have no right to their liberties, we are every day endeavoring to subvert the maxims, which preserve the whole spirit of our own. To prove that the Americans ought not to be free, we are obliged to depreciate the value of freedom itself; and we never seem to gain a paltry advantage over them in debate, without attacking some of those principles, or deriding some of those feelings, for which our ancestors have shed their blood.

But, sir, in wishing to put an end to pernicious experiments, I do not mean to preclude the fullest enquiry. Far from it. Far from deciding on a sudden or partial view, I would patiently go round and round the subject, and survey it minutely in every possible aspect. Sir, if I were capable of engaging you to an equal attention, I would state, that, as far as I am capable of discerning, there are but three ways of proceeding relative to this stubborn spirit, which prevails in your Colonies, and disturbs your government. These are— to change that spirit, as inconvenient, by removing the causes; to prosecute it as criminal; or to comply with it as necessary. I would not be guilty of an imperfect enumeration; I can think of but these three. Another has indeed been started—that of giving up the Colonies; but it met so slight a reception, that I do not think myself obliged to dwell a great while upon it. It is nothing but a little sally of anger; like the forwardness of peevish children; who, when they cannot get all they would have, are resolved to take nothing.

The first of these plans—to change the spirit as inconvenient, by removing the causes—I think is the most like a systematic proceeding. It is radical in its principle; but it is attended with great difficulties, some of them little short, as I conceive, of impossibilities. This will appear by examining into the plans which have been proposed.

As the growing population in the Colonies is evidently one cause of their resistance, it was last session mentioned in both houses by men of weight, and received not without applause, that in order to check this evil, it would be proper for the Crown to make no further grants of land. But to this scheme there are two objections. The first, that there is already so much unsettled land in private hands as to afford room for an immense future population, although the Crown not only withheld its grants, but annihilated its soil. If this be the case, then the only effect of this avarice of desolation, this hoarding of a royal wilderness, would be to raise the value of the possessions in the hands of the great private monopolists, without any adequate check to the growing and alarming mischief of population.

But, if you stopped your grants, what would be the consequence? The people would occupy without grants. They have already so occupied in many places. You cannot station garrisons in every part of these deserts. If you drive the people from one place, they will carry on their annual tillage, and remove with their flocks and herds to another. Many of the people in the back settlements are already little attached to particular situations. Already they have topped the Appalachian Mountains. From thence they behold before them an immense plain, one vast, rich, level meadow; a square of five hundred miles. Over this they would wander, without a possibility of restraint; they would change their manners with the habits of their life; would soon forget a government, by which they were disowned; would become Hordes of English Tartars; and, pouring down upon your unfortified frontiers a fierce and irresistible cavalry, become masters of your governors and your counsellors, your collectors and comptrollers, and of all the slaves that adhered to them. Such would and, in no long time, must be the effect of attempting to forbid as a crime, and to suppress as an evil, the command and blessing of Providence, "increase and multiply."

Such would be the happy result of an endeavor to keep as a lair of wild beasts that earth which God, by an express charter, has given to the children of men. Far different, and surely much wiser, has been our policy hitherto. Hitherto we have invited our people by every kind of bounty to fixed establishments. We have invited the husbandman to look to authority for his title. We have taught him piously to believe in the mysterious virtue of wax and parchment. We have thrown each tract of land, as it was peopled, into districts; that the ruling power should never be wholly out of sight. We have settled all we could; and we have carefully attended every settlement with government.

Adhering, sir, as I do, to this policy, as well as for the reasons I have just given, I think this new project of hedging-in population to be neither prudent nor practicable.

To impoverish the Colonies in general, and in particular to arrest the noble course of their marine enterprises, would be a more easy task. I freely confess it. We have shown a disposition to a system of this kind; a disposition even to continue the restraint after the offence; looking on ourselves as rivals to our Colonies, and persuaded that of course we must gain all that they shall lose. Much mischief we may certainly do. The power inadequate to all other things is often more than sufficient for this. I do not look on the direct and immediate power of the Colonies to resist our violence as very formidable. In this, however, I may be mistaken. But when I consider that we have Colonies for no purpose but to be serviceable to us, it seems to my poor understanding a little preposterous, to make them unserviceable, in order to keep them obedient. It is, in truth, nothing more than the old, and, as I thought, exploded problem of tyranny which proposes to beggar its subjects into submission. But, remember, when you have completed your system of impoverishment, that nature still proceeds in her ordinary course; that discontent will increase with misery; and that there are critical moments in the fortune of all states, when they, who are too weak to contribute to your prosperity, may be strong enough to complete your ruin. *Spoliatis arma supersunt.*[11]

The temper and character which prevail in our Colonies, are, I am afraid, unalterable by any human art. We cannot, I fear, falsify the pedigree of this fierce people, and persuade them that they are not sprung from a nation in whose veins the blood of freedom circulates. The language in which they would hear you tell them this tale would detect the imposition; your speech would betray you. An Englishman is the unfittest person on earth to argue another Englishman into slavery.

I think it is nearly as little in our power to change their republican religion, as their free descent; or to substitute the Roman Catholic, as a penalty; or the Church of England, as an improvement. The mode of inquisition and dragooning is going out of fashion in the old world; and I should not confide much to their efficacy in the new. The education of the Americans is also on the same unalterable bottom with their religion. You cannot persuade them to burn their books of curious science; to banish their lawyers from their courts of law; or to quench the lights of their assemblies

---

11 The despoiled still have their weapons.

by refusing to choose those persons who are best read in their privileges. It would be no less impracticable to think of wholly annihilating the popular assemblies in which these lawyers sit. The army, by which we must govern in their place, would be far more chargeable to us; not quite so effectual; and perhaps, in the end, full as difficult to be kept in obedience.

With regard to the high aristocratic spirit of Virginia and the Southern Colonies, it has been proposed, I know, to reduce it by declaring a general enfranchisement of their slaves. This project has had its advocates and panegyrists; yet I never could argue myself into any opinion of it. Slaves are often much attached to their masters. A general wild offer of liberty would not always be accepted. History furnishes few instances of it. It is sometimes as hard to persuade slaves to be free, as it is to compel freemen to be slaves; and in this auspicious scheme we should have both these pleasing tasks on our hands at once. But when we talk of enfranchisement, do we not perceive that the American master may enfranchise too; and arm servile hands in defense of freedom? A measure to which other people have had recourse more than once, and not without success, in a desperate situation of their affairs.

Slaves as these unfortunate black people are, and dull as all men are from slavery, must they not a little suspect the offer of freedom from that very nation which has sold them to their present masters? From that nation, one of whose causes of quarrel with those masters, is their refusal to deal any more in that inhuman traffic? An offer of freedom from England would come rather oddly, shipped to them in an African vessel, which is refused an entry into the ports of Virginia or Carolina, with a cargo of three hundred Angola negroes. It would be curious to see the Guinea captain attempting at the same instant to publish his proclamation of liberty, and to advertise his sale of slaves.

But let us suppose all these moral difficulties got over. The ocean remains. You cannot pump this dry; and as long as it continues in its present bed, so long all the causes which weaken authority by distance will continue.

"Ye gods, annihilate but space and time, and make two lovers happy!"—was a pious and passionate prayer;—but just as reasonable, as many of the serious wishes of very grave and solemn politicians.

If then, sir, it seems almost desperate to think of any alterative course for changing the moral causes (and not quite easy to remove the natural) which produce prejudices irreconcilable to the late exercise of our authority—but that the spirit infallibly will continue, and, continuing, will produce such effects, as now embarrass us—the second mode under consideration is to prosecute that spirit in its overt acts as criminal.

At this proposition, I must pause a moment. The thing seems a great deal too big for my ideas of jurisprudence. It should seem, to my way of conceiving such matters, that there is a very wide difference in reason and policy between the mode of proceeding on the irregular conduct of scattered individuals, or even of bands of men who disturb order within the state, and the civil dissensions which may, from time to time, on great questions, agitate the several communities which compose a great empire. It looks to me to be narrow and pedantic, to apply the ordinary ideas of criminal justice to this great public contest. I do not know the method of drawing up an indictment against an whole people. I cannot insult and ridicule the feelings of millions of my fellow-creatures, as sir Edward Coke insulted one excellent individual (Sir Walter Raleigh) at the bar. I am not ripe to pass sentence on the gravest public bodies entrusted with magistracies of great authority and dignity, and charged with the safety of their fellow-citizens, upon the very same title that I am. I really think, that for wise men, this is not judicious; for sober men, not decent; for minds tinctured with humanity, not mild and merciful.

Perhaps, sir, I am mistaken in my idea of an empire, as distinguished from a single state or kingdom. But my idea of it is this;

that an empire is the aggregate of many states, under one common head; whether this head be a monarch, or a presiding republic. It does, in such constitutions, frequently happen (and nothing but the dismal, cold, dead uniformity of servitude can prevent its happening) that the subordinate parts have many local privileges and immunities. Between these privileges, and the supreme common authority, the line may be extremely nice. Of course disputes, often too, very bitter disputes, and much ill blood, will arise. But though every privilege is an exemption (in the case) from the ordinary exercise of the supreme authority, it is no denial of it. The claim of a privilege seems rather, *ex vi termini*[12], to imply a superior power. For to talk of the privileges of a state or of a person, who has no superior, is hardly any better than speaking nonsense. Now, in such unfortunate quarrels, among the component parts of a great political union of communities, I can scarcely conceive anything more completely imprudent, than for the head of the empire to insist that, if any privilege is pleaded against his will, or his acts, that his whole authority is denied; instantly to proclaim rebellion, to beat to arms, and to put the offending provinces under the ban. Will not this, sir, very soon teach the provinces to make no distinctions on their part? Will it not teach them that the government, against which a claim of liberty is tantamount to high-treason, is a government to which submission is equivalent to slavery? It may not always be quite convenient to impress dependent communities with such an idea.

We are, indeed, in all disputes with the Colonies, by the necessity of things, the judge. It is true, sir. But, I confess, that the character of judge in my own cause is a thing that frightens me. Instead of filling me with pride, I am exceedingly humbled by it. I cannot proceed with a stern, assured, judicial confidence, until I find myself in something more like a judicial character. I must have these hesitations as long as I am compelled to recollect that, in my little reading upon such contests as these, the sense of mankind has, at least, as

---

12　From the force of the word.

often decided against the superior as the subordinate power. Sir, let me add too, that the opinion of my having some abstract right in my favor, would not put me much at my ease in passing sentence; unless I could be sure that there were no rights which, in their exercise under certain circumstances, were not the most odious of all wrongs, and the most vexatious of all injustice. Sir, these considerations have great weight with me when I find things so circumstanced that I see the same party, at once a civil litigant against me in a point of right; and a culprit before me, while I sit as a criminal judge, on acts of his, whose moral quality is to be decided upon the merits of that very litigation. Men are every now and then put, by the complexity of human affairs, into strange situations; but justice is the same, let the judge be in what situation he will.

There is, sir, also a circumstance which convinces me that this mode of criminal proceeding is not (at least in the present stage of our contest) altogether expedient; which is nothing less than the conduct of those very persons who have seemed to adopt that mode, by lately declaring a rebellion in Massachusetts Bay, as they had formerly addressed to have traitors brought hither under an Act of Henry the Eighth, for trial. For though rebellion is declared, it is not proceeded against as such; nor have any steps been taken towards the apprehension or conviction of any individual offender, either on our late or our former address; but modes of public coercion have been adopted, and such as have much more resemblance to a sort of qualified hostility towards an independent power than the punishment of rebellious subjects. All this seems rather inconsistent; but it shows how difficult it is to apply these juridical ideas to our present case.

In this situation, let us seriously and coolly ponder. What is it we have got by all our menaces, which have been many and ferocious? What advantage have we derived from the penal laws we have passed, and which, for the time, have been severe and numerous? What advances have we made towards our object by the sending of a force, which, by land and sea, is no contemptible strength? Has the disorder abated? Nothing less. When I see things in this situation, after such confident hopes, bold promises, and active exertions, I cannot, for my life, avoid a suspicion, that the plan itself is not correctly right.

If then the removal of the causes of this spirit of American liberty be, for the greater part, or rather entirely, impracticable; if the ideas of criminal process be inapplicable, or, if applicable, are in the highest degree inexpedient, what way yet remains? No way is open, but the third and last—to comply with the American spirit as necessary; or, if you please, to submit to it, as a necessary evil.

If we adopt this mode—if we mean to conciliate and concede— let us see of what nature the concession ought to be. To ascertain the nature of our concession, we must look at their complaint. The Colonies complain that they have not the characteristic mark and seal of British freedom. They complain that they are taxed in a Parliament in which they are not represented. If you mean to satisfy them at all, you must satisfy them with regard to this complaint. If you mean to please any people, you must give them the boon which they ask; not what you may think better for them, but of a kind totally different. Such an act may be a wise regulation, but it is no concession: whereas our present theme is the mode of giving satisfaction.

Sir, I think you must perceive, that I am resolved this day to have nothing at all to do with the question of the right of taxation. Some gentlemen startle—but it is true: I put it totally out of the question. It is less than nothing in my consideration. I do not indeed wonder, nor will you, sir, that gentlemen of profound learning are fond of displaying it on this profound subject. But my consideration is narrow, confined, and wholly limited to the policy of the question. I do not examine whether the giving away a man's money be a power excepted and reserved out of the general trust of government; and how far all mankind, in all forms of polity, are entitled to an exercise of that right by the charter of nature. Or whether, on the contrary, a right of taxation is necessarily involved in the general principle of legislation, and inseparable from the ordinary supreme power. These are deep questions, where great names militate against each other; where reason is perplexed; and an appeal to authorities only thickens the confusion. For high and reverend authorities lift up their heads on both sides; and there is no sure footing in the middle. This point is the great Serbonian bog, betwixt Damiata and Mount Casius old, where armies whole have sunk.[13] I do not intend to be overwhelmed in that bog, though in such respectable company. The question with me is not whether you have a right to render your people miserable; but whether it is not your interest to make them happy. It is not what a lawyer tells me I may do; but what humanity, reason, and justice, tell me, I ought to do. Is a politic act the worse for being a generous one? Is no concession proper, but that which is made from your want of right to keep what you grant? Or does it lessen the grace or dignity of relaxing in the exercise of an odious claim, because you have your evidence-room full of titles, and your magazines stuffed with arms to enforce them? What signify all those titles, and all those arms? Of what avail are they when the reason of the thing tells me that the assertion of my title is the loss of my suit; and that I could do nothing but wound myself by the use of my own weapons?

Such is steadfastly my opinion of the absolute necessity of keeping up the concord of this Empire by a unity of spirit, though in a diversity of operations, that, if I were sure the Colonists had, at their leaving this country, sealed a regular compact of servitude; that they had solemnly abjured all the rights of citizens; that they had made a vow to renounce all ideas of liberty for them and their posterity, to all generations; yet I should hold myself obliged to conform to the temper I found universally prevalent in my own day, and to govern two million of me, impatient of servitude, on the principles of freedom. I am not determining a point of law; I am restoring tranquility; and the general character and situation of a people must determine what sort of government is fitted for them. That point nothing else can or ought to determine.

---

13   *Paradise Lost*, II., 392-394

My idea, therefore, without considering whether we yield as matter of right, or grant as matter of favor, is to admit the people of our Colonies into an interest in the Constitution; and, by recording that admission in the journals of Parliament, to give them as strong an assurance as the nature of the thing will admit that we mean for ever to adhere to that solemn declaration of systematic indulgence.

Some years ago, the repeal of a revenue act, upon its understood principle, might have served to show that we intended an unconditional abatement of the exercise of a taxing power. Such a measure was then sufficient to remove all suspicion; and to give perfect content. But unfortunate events, since that time, may make something further necessary; and not more necessary for the satisfaction of the Colonies, than for the dignity and consistency of our own future proceedings.

I have taken a very incorrect measure of the disposition of the house, if this proposal in itself would be received with dislike. I think, sir, we have few American financiers. But our misfortune is we are too acute; we are too exquisite in our conjectures of the future, for men oppressed with such great and present evils. The more moderate among the opposers of Parliamentary concession freely confess that they hope no good from taxation; but they apprehend the Colonists have further views; and if this point were conceded, they would instantly attack the trade laws. These gentlemen are convinced that this was the intention from the beginning; and the quarrel of the Americans with taxation was no more than a cloak and cover to this design. Such has been the language even of a gentleman of real moderation, and of a natural temper well-adjusted to fair and equal government.[14] I am, however, sir, not a little surprised at this kind of discourse whenever I hear it; and I am the more surprised, on account of the arguments which I constantly find in company with it, and which are often urged from the same mouths, and on the same day.

---

14 Mr. Rice.

For instance, when we allege that it is against reason to tax a people under so many restraints in trade as the Americans, the noble lord in the blue ribband shall tell you[15] that the restraints on trade are futile and useless; of no advantage to us, and of no burden to those on whom they are imposed; that the trade to America is not secured by the Acts of Navigation, but by the natural and irresistible advantage of a commercial preference.

Such is the merit of the trade laws in this posture of the debate. But when strong internal circumstances are urged against the taxes; when the scheme is dissected; when experience and the nature of things are brought to prove, and do prove, the utter impossibility of obtaining an effective revenue from the Colonies; when these things are pressed, or rather press themselves, so as to drive the advocates of Colony taxes to a clear admission of the futility of the scheme; then, sir, the sleeping trade laws revive from their trance; and this useless taxation is to be kept sacred, not for its own sake, but as a counterguard and security of the laws of trade.

Then, sir, you keep up revenue laws which are mischievous, in order to preserve trade laws that are useless. Such is the wisdom of our plan in both its members. They are separately given up as of no value; and yet one is always to be defended for the sake of the other. But I cannot agree with the noble lord, nor with the pamphlet from whence he seems to have borrowed these ideas, concerning the inutility of the trade laws. For without idolizing them, I am sure they are still, in many ways, of great use to us; and in former times, they have been of the greatest. They do confine, and they do greatly narrow, the market for the Americans. But my perfect conviction of this does not help me in the least to discern how the revenue laws form any security whatsoever to the commercial regulations; or that these commercial regulations are the true ground of the quarrel; or that the giving way in any one instance of authority, is to lose all that may remain unconceded.

---

15 Lord North.

One fact is clear and indisputable. The public and avowed origin of this quarrel was on taxation. This quarrel has indeed brought on new disputes on new questions; but certainly the least bitter, and the fewest of all, on the trade laws. To judge which of the two be the real radical cause of quarrel, we have to see whether the commercial dispute did, in order of time, precede the dispute on taxation? There is not a shadow of evidence for it. Next, to enable us to judge whether at this moment a dislike to the trade laws be the real cause of quarrel, it is absolutely necessary to put the taxes out of the question by a repeal. See how the Americans act in this position, and then you will be able to discern correctly what is the true object of the controversy, or whether any controversy at all will remain. Unless you consent to remove this cause of difference, it is impossible, with decency, to assert that the dispute is not upon what it is avowed to be. And I would, sir, recommend to your serious consideration, whether it be prudent to form a rule for punishing people, not on their own acts, but on your conjectures? Surely it is preposterous at the very best. It is not justifying your anger, by their misconduct; but it is converting your ill-will into their delinquency.

But the Colonies will go further—alas! alas! When will this speculating against fact and reason end? What will quiet these panic fears which we entertain of the hostile effect of a conciliatory conduct? Is it true that no case can exist in which it is proper for the sovereign to accede to the desires of his discontented subjects? Is there anything peculiar in this case, to make a rule for itself? Is all authority of course lost, when it is not pushed to the extreme? Is it a certain maxim, that, the fewer causes of dissatisfaction are left by government, the more the subject will be inclined to resist and rebel?

All these objections being in fact no more than suspicions, conjectures, divinations; formed in defiance of fact and experience; they did not, sir, discourage me from entertaining the idea of a conciliatory concession, founded on the principles which I have just stated.

In forming a plan for this purpose, I endeavored to put myself in that frame of mind which was the most natural, and the most reasonable; and which was certainly the most probable means of securing me from all error. I set out with a perfect distrust of my own abilities; a total renunciation of every speculation of my own; and with a profound reverence for the wisdom of our ancestors, who have left us the inheritance of so happy a constitution, and so flourishing an empire, and what is a thousand times more valuable, the treasury of the maxims and principles which formed the one, and obtained the other.

During the reigns of the kings of Spain of the Austrian family, whenever they were at a loss in the Spanish councils, it was common for their statesmen to say, that they ought to consult the genius of Philip the Second. The genius of Philip the Second might mislead them; and the issue of their affairs showed that they had not chosen the most perfect standard. But, sir, I am sure that I shall not be misled when, in a case of constitutional difficulty, I consult the genius of the English Constitution. Consulting at that oracle (it was with all due humility and piety) I found four capital examples in a similar case before me: those of Ireland, Wales, Chester, and Durham.

Ireland, before the English conquest, though never governed by a despotic power, had no Parliament. How far the English Parliament itself was at that time modelled according to the present form, is disputed among antiquarians. But we have all the reason in the world to be assured that a form of Parliament, such as England then enjoyed, she instantly communicated to Ireland; and we are equally sure that almost every successive improvement in constitutional liberty, as fast as it was made here, was transmitted thither. The feudal baronage, and the feudal knighthood, the roots of our primitive Constitution, were early transplanted into that soil; and grew and flourished there. Magna Charta, if it did not give us originally the House of Commons, gave us at least an House of Commons of weight and consequence. But your ancestors did not churlishly sit down alone to the feast of Magna Charta. Ireland was made immediately a partaker. This benefit of English laws and liberties, I confess, was not at first extended to all Ireland. Mark the consequence. English authority and English liberties had exactly the same boundaries. Your standard could never be advanced an inch before your privileges. Sir John Davis shows beyond a doubt that the refusal of a general communication of these rights was the true cause why Ireland was five hundred years in subduing; and after the vain projects of a military government, attempted in the reign of Queen Elizabeth, it was soon discovered that nothing could make that country English, in civility and allegiance, but your laws and your forms of legislature. It was not English arms, but the English Constitution, that conquered Ireland. From that time, Ireland has ever had a general Parliament, as she had before a partial Parliament. You changed the people; you altered the religion; but you never touched the form or the vital substance of free government in that kingdom. You deposed kings; you restored them; you altered the succession to theirs, as well as to your own Crown; but you never altered their Constitution; the principle of which was respected by usurpation; restored with the restoration of monarchy, and established, I trust, forever, by the glorious Revolution. This has made Ireland the great and flourishing kingdom that it is; and from a disgrace and a burden intolerable to this nation, has rendered her a principal part of our strength and ornament. This country cannot be said to have ever formally taxed her. The irregular things done in the confusion of mighty troubles, and on the hinge of great revolutions, even if all were done that is said to have been done, form no example. If they have any effect in argument, they make an exception to prove the rule. None of your own liberties could stand a moment if the casual deviations from them, at such times, were suffered to be used as proofs of their nullity. By the lucrative amount of such casual breaches in the Constitution, judge what the stated and fixed rule of supply has been in that kingdom. Your Irish pensioners would starve if they had no other fund to live on than taxes granted by English authority. Turn your eyes to those popular grants from whence all your great supplies are come; and learn to respect that only source of public wealth in the British Empire.

My next example is Wales. This country was said to be reduced by Henry the Third. It was said more truly to be so by Edward the First. But though then conquered, it was not looked upon as any part of the realm of England. Its old Constitution, whatever that might have been, was destroyed; and no good one was substituted in its place. The care of that tract was put into the hands of Lords Marchers[16]—a form of government of a very singular kind; a strange heterogeneous monster, something between hostility and government; perhaps it has a sort of resemblance, according to the modes of those times, to that of Commander in Chief at present, to whom all civil power is granted as secondary. The manners of the Welsh nation followed the genius of the government: The people were ferocious, restive, savage, and uncultivated; sometimes composed, never pacified. Wales, within itself, was in perpetual disorder; and it kept the frontier of England in perpetual alarm. Benefits from it to the state, there were none. Wales was only known to England by incursion and invasion.

Sir, during that state of things Parliament was not idle. They attempted to subdue the fierce spirit of the Welsh by all sorts of rigorous laws. They prohibited by statute the sending all sorts of arms into Wales, as you prohibit by proclamation (with something more of doubt on the legality) the sending arms to America. They disarmed the Welsh by statute, as you attempted (but still with more question on the legality) to disarm New England by an instruction. They made an act to drag offenders from Wales into England for trial, as you have done (but with more hardship) with regard to America. By another act, where one of the parties was an Englishman, they ordained that his trial should be always by English. They made acts to restrain trade, as you do; and they prevented the Welsh

---

16 These lords were given permission by the English kings to take from the Welsh as much land as they could. They built their castles on the boundary line between the two countries, and when they were not quarrelling among themselves waged a guerilla warfare against the Welsh. The Lords Marchers, because of special privileges and the peculiar circumstances of their life, were virtually kings—petty kings, of course.

from the use of fairs and markets, as you do the Americans from fisheries and foreign ports. In short, when the statute-book was not quite so much swelled as it is now, you find no less than fifteen acts of penal regulation on the subject of Wales.

Here we rub our hands—a fine body of precedents for the authority of Parliament and the use of it!—I admit it fully; and pray add likewise to these precedents that all the while Wales rid this kingdom like an incubus, that it was an unprofitable and oppressive burden, and that an Englishman travelling in that country could not go six yards from the high road without being murdered.

The march of the human mind is slow. Sir, it was not until after two hundred years discovered that, by an eternal law, Providence had decreed vexation to violence; and poverty to rapine. Your ancestors did however at length open their eyes to the ill husbandry of injustice. They found that the tyranny of a free people could of all tyrannies the least be endured; and that laws made against a whole nation were not the most effectual methods for securing its obedience. Accordingly, in the twenty-seventh year of Henry the Eighth the course was entirely altered. With a preamble stating the entire and perfect rights of the Crown of England, it gave to the Welsh all the rights and privileges of English subjects. A political order was established; the military power gave way to the civil; the Marches were turned into Counties. But that a nation should have a right to English liberties, and yet no share at all in the fundamental security of these liberties—the grant of their own property—seemed a thing so incongruous that eight years after, that is, in the thirty-fifth of that reign, a complete and not ill proportioned representation by counties and boroughs was bestowed upon Wales, by Act of Parliament. From that moment, as by a charm, the tumults subsided; obedience was restored; peace, order, and civilization followed in the train of liberty. When the day-star of the English Constitution had arisen in their hearts, all was harmony within and without—

Simul alba nautis
Stella refulsit,

Defluit saxis agitatus humor:
Concidunt venti, fugiuntque nubes:
Et minax (quod sic voluere) ponto
Unda recumbit.[17]

The very same year the County Palatine of Chester received the same relief from its oppressions, and the same remedy to its disorders. Before this time Chester was little less distempered than Wales. The inhabitants, without rights themselves, were the fittest to destroy the rights of others; and from thence Richard the Second drew the standing army of archers, with which for a time he oppressed England. The people of Chester applied to Parliament in a petition penned as I shall read to you:

To the King our Sovereign Lord, in most humble wise shown unto your excellent Majesty, the inhabitants of your Grace's County Palatine of Chester, that where the said County Palatine of Chester is and hath been always hitherto exempt, excluded and separated out and from your High Court of Parliament, to have any Knights and Burgesses within the said Court; by reason whereof the said inhabitants have hitherto sustained manifold disherisons, losses and damages, as well in their lands, goods, and bodies, as in the good, civil, and politic governance and maintenance of the commonwealth of their said country: (2.) And for as much as the said inhabitants have always hitherto been bound by the Acts and Statutes made and ordained by your said Highness, and your most noble progenitors, by authority of the said Court, as far forth as other counties, cities, and boroughs have been, that have had their Knights and Burgesses within your said Court of Parliament, and yet have had neither Knight ne Burgess there for the said County Palatine; the said inhabitants, for lack thereof, have been oftentimes touched and grieved with acts and statutes made within the said Court, as well derogatory unto the most ancient jurisdictions, liberties, and privileges of your said County Palatine, as prejudicial unto the common wealth, quietness, rest, and peace of your Grace's most bounden subjects inhabiting within the same.

---

17   As the bright star shines on the sailors, the turbulent water flows off the rocks. The winds fall, and the clouds flee, and (as they willed it [Castor and Pollux]) the threatening wave sinks into the sea.

What did Parliament with this audacious address? Reject it as a libel? Treat it as an affront to government? Spurn it as a derogation from the rights of legislature? Did they toss it over the table? Did they burn it by the hands of the common hangman? They took the petition of grievance, all rugged as it was, without softening or temperament, unpurged of the original bitterness and indignation of complaint; they made it the very preamble to their Act of redress; and consecrated its principle to all ages in the sanctuary of legislation.

Here is my third example. It was attended with the success of the two former. Chester, civilized as well as Wales, has demonstrated that freedom and not servitude is the cure of anarchy; as religion, and not atheism, is the true remedy for superstition. Sir, this pattern of Chester was followed in the reign of Charles the Second with regard to the County Palatine of Durham, which is my fourth example. This county had long lain out of the pale of free legislation. So scrupulously was the example of Chester followed, that the style of the preamble is nearly the same with that of the Chester Act; and without affecting the abstract extent of the authority of Parliament, it recognizes the equity of not suffering any considerable district in which the British subjects may act as a body, to be taxed without their own voice in the grant.

Now if the doctrines of policy contained in these preambles, and the force of these examples in the Acts of Parliament, avail anything, what can be said against applying them with regard to America? Are not the people of America as much Englishmen as the Welsh? The preamble of the act of Henry the Eighth says the Welsh speak a language no way resembling that of his Majesty's English subjects. Are the Americans not as numerous? If we may trust the learned and accurate judge Barrington's account of North Wales, and take that as a standard to measure the rest, there is no comparison. The people cannot amount to above 200,000; not a tenth part of the number in the Colonies. Is America in rebellion? Wales was hardly ever free from it. Have you attempted to govern America by penal statutes? You made fifteen for Wales. But your legislative authority is perfect with regard to America; was it less perfect in Wales, Chester, and Durham? But America is virtually represented. What! Does the electric force of virtual representation more easily pass over the Atlantic than pervade Wales, which lies in your neighborhood; or than Chester and Durham, surrounded by abundance of representation that is actual and palpable? But, sir, your ancestors thought this sort of virtual representation, however ample, to be totally insufficient for the freedom of the inhabitants of territories that are so near, and comparatively so inconsiderable. How then can I think it sufficient for those which are infinitely greater, and infinitely more remote?

You will now, sir, perhaps imagine that I am on the point of proposing to you a scheme for a representation of the Colonies in Parliament. Perhaps I might be inclined to entertain some such thought; but a great flood stops me in my course. *Opposuit natura*[18]—I cannot remove the eternal barriers of the creation. The thing in that mode, I do not know to be possible. As I meddle with no theory, I do not absolutely assert the impracticability of such a representation. But I do not see my way to it; and those who have been more confident, have not been more successful. However, the arm of public benevolence is not shortened; and there are often several means to the same end. What nature has disjoined in one way, wisdom may unite in another. When we cannot give the benefit as we would wish, let us not refuse it altogether. If we cannot give the principal, let us find a substitute. But how? Where? What substitute?

Fortunately I am not obliged for the ways and means of this substitute to tax my own unproductive invention. I am not even obliged to go to the rich treasury of the fertile framers of imaginary commonwealths; not to the republic of Plato, not to the Utopia of More; not to the Oceana of Harrington. It is before me—it is at my feet,

---

18 Nature opposes.

And the rude swain treads daily on it with his clouted shoon.[19]

I only wish you to recognize, for the theory, the ancient constitutional policy of this kingdom with regard to representation, as that policy has been declared in Acts of Parliament; and, as to the practice, to return to that mode which an uniform experience has marked out to you, as best; and in which you walked with security, advantage, and honor, until the year 1763.

My resolutions therefore mean to establish the equity and justice of a taxation of America, by grant, and not by imposition. To mark the legal competency of the Colony Assemblies for the support of their government in peace, and for public aids in time of war. To acknowledge that this legal competency has had a dutiful and beneficial exercise; and that experience has shown the benefit of their grants, and the futility of parliamentary taxation as a method of supply.

These solid truths compose six fundamental propositions. There are three more resolutions corollary to these. If you admit the first set, you can hardly reject the others. But if you admit the first, I shall be far from solicitous whether you accept or refuse the last. I think these six massive pillars will be of strength sufficient to support the temple of British concord. I have no more doubt than I entertain of my existence that, if you admitted these, you would command an immediate peace; and with but tolerable future management, a lasting obedience in America. I am not arrogant in this confident assurance. The propositions are all mere matters of fact; and if they are such facts as draw irresistible conclusions even in the stating, this is the power of truth, and not any management of mine.

Sir, I shall open the whole plan to you together with such observations on the motions as may tend to illustrate them where they may want explanation. The first is a resolution:

---

19   Milton, *Comus*, 6, 34, 35

> *That the Colonies and Plantations of Great Britain in North Amer-*
> *ica, consisting of fourteen separate Governments, and containing two*
> *millions and upwards of free inhabitants, have not had the liberty and*
> *privilege of electing and sending any Knights and Burgesses, or others*
> *to represent them in the High Court of Parliament.*

This is a plain matter of fact, necessary to be laid down, and (excepting the description) it is laid down in the language of the Constitution; it is taken nearly verbatim from Acts of Parliament.

The second is like unto the first:

> *That the said Colonies and Plantations have been liable to, and bound-*
> *en by, several subsidies, payments, rates, and taxes, given and granted*
> *by Parliament, though the said Colonies and Plantations have not*
> *their Knights and Burgesses, in the said High Court of Parliament, of*
> *their own election, to represent the condition of their country; by lack*
> *whereof they have been oftentimes touched and grieved by subsidies*
> *given, granted, and assented to, in the said Court, in a manner preju-*
> *dicial to the common wealth, quietness, rest, and peace of the subjects*
> *inhabiting within the same.*

Is this description too hot or too cold, too strong or too weak? Does it arrogate too much to the supreme legislature? Does it lean too much to the claims of the people? If it runs into any of these errors, the fault is not mine. It is the language of your own ancient Acts of Parliament. *Non meus hic sermo, sed quae praecepit Ofellus, rusti-cus, abnormis sapiens.*[20] It is the genuine produce of the ancient rustic, manly, home-bred sense of this country—I did not dare to rub off a particle of the venerable rust that rather adorns and preserves, than destroys the metal. It would be a profanation to touch with a tool the stones which construct the sacred altar of peace. I would not violate with modern polish the ingenuous and noble roughness of these truly Constitutional materials. Above all things, I was re-solved not to be guilty of tampering, the odious vice of restless and unstable minds. I put my foot in the tracks of our forefathers;

---

20 This word is not mine, it is what Ofellus taught—plain, but extraordinarily wise.

where I can neither wander nor stumble. Determining to fix articles
of peace, I was resolved not to be wise beyond what was written; I
was resolved to use nothing else than the form of sound words; to
let others abound in their own sense; and carefully to abstain from
all expressions of my own. What the law has said, I say. In all things
else I am silent. I have no organ but for her words. This, if it be not
ingenious, I am sure is safe.

There are indeed words expressive of grievance in this second
resolution which those who are resolved always to be in the right
will deny to contain matter of fact, as applied to the present case;
although Parliament thought them true with regard to the counties
of Chester and Durham. They will deny that the Americans were
ever "touched and grieved" with the taxes. If they consider nothing in taxes but their weight as pecuniary impositions, there might
be some pretense for this denial. But men may be sorely touched
and deeply grieved in their privileges, as well as in their purses.
Men may lose little in property by the act which takes away all their
freedom. When a man is robbed of a trifle on the highway, it is
not the two-pence lost that constitutes the capital outrage. This is
not confined to privileges. Even ancient indulgencies withdrawn,
without offence on the part of those who enjoyed such favors, operate as grievances. But were the Americans then not touched and
grieved by the taxes, in some measure, merely as taxes? If so, why
were they almost all either wholly repealed or exceedingly reduced?
Were they not touched and grieved, even by the regulating duties
of the sixth of George the Second? Else why were the duties first
reduced to one third in 1764, and afterwards to a third of that third
in the year 1766? Were they not touched and grieved by the Stamp
Act? I shall say they were, until that tax is revived. Were they not
touched and grieved by the duties of 1767, which were likewise
repealed, and which, Lord Hillsborough tells you (for the ministry)
were laid contrary to the true principle of commerce? Is not the
assurance given by that noble person to the Colonies of a resolution to lay no more taxes on them, an admission that taxes would
touch and grieve them? Is not the resolution of the noble lord in

the blue ribband, now standing on your journals, the strongest of all proofs that Parliamentary subsidies really touched and grieved them? Else, why all these changes, modifications, repeals, assurances, and resolutions?

The next proposition is:

That, from the distance of the said Colonies, and from other circumstances, no method hath hitherto been devised for procuring a representation in Parliament for the said Colonies.

This is an assertion of a fact. I go no further on the paper; though in my private judgment, an useful representation is impossible; I am sure it is not desired by them; nor ought it perhaps by us; but I abstain from opinions.

The fourth Resolution is:

That each of the said Colonies hath within itself a body, chosen in part, or in the whole, by the freemen, freeholders, or other free inhabitants thereof, commonly called the General Assembly, or General Court, with powers legally to raise, levy, and assess, according to the several usage of such Colonies, duties and taxes towards defraying all sorts of public services.

This competence in the Colony Assemblies is certain. It is proved by the whole tenor of their Acts of Supply in all the Assemblies, in which the constant style of granting is "an aid to his Majesty," and Acts granting to the Crown have regularly for near a century passed the public offices without dispute. Those who have been pleased paradoxically to deny this right, holding that none but the British Parliament can grant to the Crown, are wished to look to what is done, not only in the Colonies, but in Ireland, in one uniform unbroken tenor every session. Sir, I am surprised, that this doctrine should come from some of the law servants of the Crown. I say, that if the Crown could be responsible, his Majesty—but certainly the Ministers, and even these law officers themselves, through whose hands the Acts pass, biennially in Ireland, or annually in the Colonies—are in an habitual course of committing impeachable offences. What habitual offenders have been all Presidents of the Council, all Secretaries of State, all First Lords of Trade, all Attorneys and all Solicitors General! However, they are safe; as no one impeaches them; and there is no ground of charge against them, except in their own unfounded theories.

The fifth Resolution is also a resolution of fact:

> *That the said General Assemblies, General Courts, or other bodies legally qualified as aforesaid, have at sundry times freely granted several large subsidies and public aids for his Majesty's service, according to their abilities, when required thereto by letter from one of his Majesty's principal Secretaries of State; and that their right to grant the same, and their cheerfulness and sufficiency in the said grants, have been at sundry times acknowledged by Parliament.*

To say nothing of their great expenses in the Indian wars; and not to take their exertion in foreign ones, so high as the supplies in the year 1695; not to go back to their public contributions in the year 1710; I shall begin to travel only where the journals give me light; resolving to deal in nothing but fact, authenticated by Parliamentary record; and to build myself wholly on that solid basis.

On the 4th of April 1748,[21] a Committee of this House came to the following resolution:

> *Resolved:*
>
> *That it is the opinion of this Committee, that it is just and reasonable that the several Provinces and Colonies of Massachusetts Bay, New Hampshire, Connecticut, and Rhode Island, be reimbursed the expenses they have been at in taking and securing to the Crown of Great Britain, the Island of Cape Breton, and its dependencies.*

These expenses were immense for such Colonies. They were above £200,000 sterling; money first raised and advanced on their public credit.

---

21 Journals of the house, Vol. XXV.

On the 28th of January 1756,[22] a message from the King came to us, to this effect:

> *His Majesty, being sensible of the zeal and vigor with which his faithful subjects of certain Colonies in North America have exerted themselves in defense of his Majesty's just rights and possessions, recommends it to this House to take the same into their consideration, and to enable his Majesty to give them such assistance as may be a proper reward and encouragement.*

On the 3rd of February 1756,[23] the House came to a suitable Resolution, expressed in words nearly the same as those of the message: but with the further addition, that the money then voted was as an encouragement to the Colonies to exert themselves with vigor. It will not be necessary to go through all the testimonies which your own records have given to the truth of my Resolutions. I will only refer you to the places in the Journals:

> *Vol. XXVII—16th and 19th May, 1757.*
> *Vol. XXVIII—June 1st, 1758—April 26th and 30th, 1759—March 26th and 31st, and April 28th, 1760—Jan. 9th and 20th, 1761.*
> *Vol. XXIX—Jan. 22d and 26th, 1762—March 14th and 17th, 1763.*

Sir, here is the repeated acknowledgment of Parliament, that the Colonies not only gave, but gave to satiety. This nation has formally acknowledged two things: first, that the Colonies had gone beyond their abilities, Parliament having thought it necessary to reimburse them; secondly, that they had acted legally and laudably in their grants of money, and their maintenance of troops, since the compensation is expressly given as reward and encouragement. Reward is not bestowed for acts that are unlawful; and encouragement is not held out to things that deserve reprehension. My Resolution therefore does nothing more than collect into one proposition,

---

22 Journals of the House, Vol. XXVII.

23 Ibid.

what is scattered through your Journals. I give you nothing but your own; and you cannot refuse in the gross, what you have so often acknowledged in detail. The admission of this, which will be so honorable to them and to you, will, indeed, be mortal to all the miserable stories, by which the passions of the misguided people have been engaged in an unhappy system. The people heard, indeed, from the beginning of these disputes, one thing continually dinned in their ears, that reason and justice demanded that the Americans, who paid no taxes, should be compelled to contribute. How did that fact of their paying nothing stand when the taxing system began? When Mr. Grenville began to form his system of American revenue, he stated in this House that the Colonies were then in debt two millions six hundred thousand pounds sterling money; and was of opinion they would discharge that debt in four years. On this state, those untaxed people were actually subject to the payment of taxes to the amount of six hundred and fifty thousand a year. In fact, however, Mr. Grenville was mistaken. The funds given for sinking the debt did not prove quite so ample as both the Colonies and he expected. The calculation was too sanguine: the reduction was not completed till some years after, and at different times in different Colonies. However, the taxes after the war continued too great to bear any addition with prudence or propriety; and when the burdens imposed in consequence of former requisitions were discharged, our tone became too high to resort again to requisition. No Colony, since that time, ever has had any requisition whatsoever made to it.

We see the sense of the Crown, and the sense of Parliament, on the productive nature of a revenue by grant. Now, search the same Journals for the produce of the revenue by imposition. Where is it? Let us know the volume and the page? What is the gross, what is the net produce? To what service is it applied? How have you appropriated its surplus? What, can none of the many skillful index-makers, that we are now employing, find any trace of it? Well, let them and that rest together. But are the Journals, which say nothing of the revenue, as silent on the discontent? Oh no! A child may find it. It is the melancholy burden and blot of every page.

I think then I am, from those Journals, justified in the sixth and last Resolution, which is:

> *That it hath been found by experience, that the manner of granting the said supplies and aids, by the said General Assemblies, hath been more agreeable to the said Colonies, and more beneficial, and conducive to the public service, than the mode of giving and granting aids in Parliament, to be raised and paid in the said Colonies.*

This makes the whole of the fundamental part of the plan. The conclusion is irresistible. You cannot say that you were driven by any necessity to an exercise of the utmost rights of legislature. You cannot assert that you took on yourselves the task of imposing Colony taxes from the want of another legal body that is competent to the purpose of supplying the exigencies of the state without wounding the prejudices of the people. Neither is it true that the body so qualified, and having that competence, had neglected the duty.

The question now, on all this accumulated matter, is: whether you will choose to abide by a profitable experience or a mischievous theory; whether you choose to build on imagination or fact; whether you prefer enjoyment or hope; satisfaction in your subjects or discontent?

If these propositions are accepted, everything which has been made to enforce a contrary system, must, I take it for granted, fall along with it. On that ground, I have drawn the following Resolution, which, when it comes to be moved, will naturally be divided in a proper manner:

> *That it may be proper to repeal an Act, made in the seventh year of the reign of his present Majesty, entitled An Act for granting certain duties in the British Colonies and Plantations in America; for allowing a drawback of the duties of customs upon the exportation from this Kingdom, of coffee and cocoa-nuts of the produce of the said Colonies or Plantations; for discontinuing the drawbacks payable on China earthen-ware exported to America; and for more effectually preventing the clandestine running of goods in the said Colonies and Plantations.—And that it*

> *may be proper to repeal an Act, made in the fourteenth year of the reign of his present Majesty, entitled An Act to discontinue in such manner, and for such time, as are therein mentioned, the landing and discharging, lading or shipping, of goods, wares, and merchandize, at the town and within the harbor of Boston, in the Province of Massachusetts Bay, in North America.—And that it may be proper to repeal an Act, made in the fourteenth year of the reign of his present Majesty, entitled An Act for the impartial administration of justice, in the cases of persons questioned for any acts done by them, in the execution of the law, or for the suppression of riots and tumults, in the Province of Massachusetts Bay in New England.—And that it may be proper to repeal an Act, made in the fourteenth year of the reign of his present Majesty, entitled An Act for the better regulating the government of the Province of the Massachusetts Bay in New England.—And also that it may be proper to explain and amend an Act, made in the thirty-fifth year of the reign of King Henry the Eighth, entitled An Act for the trial of treasons committed out of the King's dominions.*

I wish, sir, to repeal the Boston Port Bill, because (independently of the dangerous precedent of suspending the rights of the subject during the King's pleasure) it was passed, as I apprehend, with less regularity, and on more partial principles, than it ought. The corporation of Boston was not heard before it was condemned. Other towns, full as guilty as she was, have not had their ports blocked up. Even the Restraining Bill of the present session does not go to the length of the Boston Port Act. The same ideas of prudence which induced you not to extend equal punishment to equal guilt even when you were punishing, induce me, who mean not to chastise, but to reconcile, to be satisfied with the punishment already partially inflicted.

Ideas of prudence, and accommodation to circumstances, prevent you from taking away the charters of Connecticut and Rhode Island, as you have taken away that of Massachusetts Bay, though the Crown has far less power in the two former Provinces than it enjoyed in the latter; and though the abuses have been full as great, and as flagrant, in the exempted as in the punished. The same reasons of prudence and accommodation have weight with me in restoring the charter of Massachusetts Bay. Besides, sir, the Act which changes the charter of Massachusetts is in many particulars so exceptionable that, if I did not wish absolutely to repeal, I would by all means desire to alter it; as several of its provisions tend to the subversion of all public and private justice. Such, among others, is the power in the Governor to change the sheriff at his pleasure; and to make a new returning officer for every special cause. It is shameful to behold such a regulation standing among English laws.

The Act for bringing persons accused of committing murder under the orders of Government to England for trial is but temporary. That Act has calculated the probable duration of our quarrel with the Colonies; and is accommodated to that supposed duration. I would hasten the happy moment of reconciliation; and therefore must, on my principle, get rid of that most justly obnoxious Sct.

The Act of Henry the Eighth, for the Trial of Treasons, I do not mean to take away, but to confine it to its proper bounds and original intention; to make it expressly for trial of treasons (and the greatest treasons may be committed) in places where the jurisdiction of the Crown does not extend.

Having guarded the privileges of local legislature, I would next secure to the Colonies a fair and unbiassed judicature; for which purpose, sir, I propose the following Resolution:

> *That, from the time when the General Assembly or General Court of any Colony or Plantation in North America, shall have appointed by Act of Assembly, duly confirmed, a settled salary to the offices of the Chief Justice and other Judges of the Superior Court, it may be proper, that the said Chief Justice and other Judges of the Superior Courts of such Colony, shall hold his and their office and offices during their good behavior; and shall not be removed therefrom, but when the said removal shall be adjudged by his Majesty in Council, upon a hearing on complaint from the General Assembly, or on a complaint from the Governor or Council or the House of Representatives severally, of the Colony in which the said Chief Justice and other Judges have exercised the said offices.*

The next Resolution relates to the Courts of Admiralty. It is this:

That it may be proper to regulate the Courts of Admiralty or Vice Admiralty, authorized by the 15th chap. of the 4th of George the Third, in such a manner as to make the same more commodious to those who sue, or are sued, in the said Courts, and to provide for the more decent maintenance of the Judges in the same.

These courts I do not wish to take away; they are in themselves proper establishments. This court is one of the capital securities of the Act of Navigation. The extent of its jurisdiction, indeed, has been increased; but this is altogether as proper, and is, indeed, on many accounts, more eligible, where new powers were wanted, than a court absolutely new. But courts incommodiously situated, in effect, deny justice;[24] and a court, partaking in the fruits of its own condemnation, is a robber. The Congress complain, and complain justly, of this grievance.

These are the three consequential propositions. I have thought of two or three more, but they come rather too near detail, and to the province of executive government, which I wish Parliament always to superintend, never to assume. If the first six are granted, congruity will carry the latter three. If not, the things that remain unrepealed will be, I hope, rather unseemly incumbrances on the building than very materially detrimental to its strength and stability.

Here, sir, I should close; but that I plainly perceive some objections remain, which I ought, if possible, to remove. The first will be, that, in resorting to the doctrine of our ancestors, as contained in the preamble to the Chester Act, I prove too much; that the grievance from a want of representation, stated in that preamble, goes to the whole of legislation as well as to taxation. And that the Colonies grounding themselves upon that doctrine, will apply it to all parts of legislative authority.

---

24   The solicitor-general informed Mr. B. when the resolutions were separately moved, that the grievance of the judges partaking of the profits of the seizure had been redressed by office; accordingly the resolution was amended.

To this objection, with all possible deference and humility, and wishing as little as any man living to impair the smallest particle of our supreme authority, I answer that the words are the words of Parliament, and not mine; and that all false and inconclusive inferences drawn from them are not mine; for I heartily disclaim any such inference. I have chosen the words of an Act of Parliament, which Mr. Grenville, surely a tolerably zealous and very judicious advocate for the sovereignty of Parliament, formerly moved to have read at your table in confirmation of his tenets. It is true that Lord Chatham considered these preambles as declaring strongly in favor of his opinions. He was a no less powerful advocate for the privileges of the Americans. Ought I not from hence to presume that these preambles are as favorable as possible to both, when properly understood; favorable both to the rights of Parliament, and to the privilege of the dependencies of this Crown? But, sir, the object of grievance in my resolution I have not taken from the Chester, but from the Durham Act, which confines the hardship of want of representation to the case of subsidies; and which therefore falls in exactly with the case of the Colonies. But whether the unrepresented Counties were de jure or de facto[25] bound, the preambles do not accurately distinguish; nor indeed was it necessary; for, whether de jure or de facto, the legislature thought the exercise of the power of taxing, as of right or as of fact without right, equally a grievance and equally oppressive.

I do not know that the Colonies have, in any general way or in any cool hour, gone much beyond the demand of immunity in relation to taxes. It is not fair to judge of the temper or dispositions of any man or any set of men when they are composed and at rest, from their conduct or their expressions in a state of disturbance and irritation. It is besides a very great mistake to imagine that mankind follow up practically any speculative principle, either of government or of freedom, as far as it will go in argument and logical illation. We Englishmen, stop very short of the principles upon

---

25   De jure: according to law. De facto: according to fact.

which we support any given part of our Constitution; or even the whole of it together. I could easily, if I had not already tired you, give you very striking and convincing instances of it. This is nothing but what is natural and proper. All government, indeed every human benefit and enjoyment, every virtue, and every prudent act, is founded on compromise and barter. We balance inconveniencies; we give and take; we remit some rights, that we may enjoy others; and we choose rather to be happy citizens, than subtle disputants. As we must give away some natural liberty to enjoy civil advantages, so we must sacrifice some civil liberties for the advantages to be derived from the communion and fellowship of a great empire. But in all fair dealings the thing bought must bear some proportion to the purchase paid. None will barter away the immediate jewel of his soul. Though a great house is apt to make slaves haughty, yet it is purchasing a part of the artificial importance of a great empire too dear, to pay for it all essential rights, and all the intrinsic dignity of human nature. None of us who would not risk his life, rather than fall under a government purely arbitrary. But, although there are some amongst us who think our Constitution wants many improvements to make it a complete system of liberty, perhaps none who are of that opinion would think it right to aim at such improvement by disturbing his country, and risking everything that is dear to him. In every arduous enterprise, we consider what we are to lose, as well as what we are to gain; and the more and better stake of liberty every people possess, the less they will hazard in a vain attempt to make it more. These are the cords of man. Man acts from adequate motives relative to his interest; and not on metaphysical speculations. Aristotle, the great master of reasoning, cautions us, and with great weight and propriety, against this species of delusive geometrical accuracy in moral arguments, as the most fallacious of all sophistry.

The Americans will have no interest contrary to the grandeur and glory of England, when they are not oppressed by the weight of it; and they will rather be inclined to respect the acts of a superintending legislature when they see them the acts of that power,

which is itself the security, not the rival, of their secondary importance. In this assurance, my mind most perfectly acquiesces; and I
confess, I feel not the least alarm from the discontents which are
to arise, from putting people at their ease; nor do I apprehend the
destruction of this empire from giving, by an act of free grace and
indulgence, to two millions of my fellow citizens, some share of
those rights upon which I have always been taught to value myself.

It is said indeed that this power of granting vested in American Assemblies, would dissolve the unity of the Empire which
was preserved, entire, although Wales, and Chester, and Durham
were added to it. Truly, Mr. Speaker, I do not know what this unity
means; nor has it ever been heard of, that I know, in the constitutional policy of this country. The very idea of subordination of
parts, excludes this notion of simple and undivided unity. England
is the head; but she is not the head and the members too. Ireland
has ever had from the beginning a separate, but not an independent, legislature; which, far from distracting, promoted the union
of the whole. Everything was sweetly and harmoniously disposed
through both islands for the conservation of English dominion,
and the communication of English liberties. I do not see that the
same principles might not be carried into twenty islands, and with
the same good effect. This is my model with regard to America,
as far as the internal circumstances of the two countries are the
same. I know no other unity of this Empire than I can draw from
its example during these periods, when it seemed to my poor understanding more united than it is now, or than it is likely to be by
the present methods.

But since I speak of these methods, I recollect, Mr. Speaker,
almost too late, that I promised, before I finished, to say something of the proposition of the[26] noble lord on the floor, which
has been so lately received, and stands on your Journals. I must
be deeply concerned whenever it is my misfortune to continue a
difference with the majority of this House. But as the reasons for

---

26 Lord North.

that difference are my apology for thus troubling you, suffer me to state them in a very few words. I shall compress them into as small a body as I possibly can, having already debated that matter at large, when the question was before the committee.

First, then, I cannot admit that proposition of a ransom by auction—because it is a mere project. It is a thing new; unheard of; supported by no experience; justified by no analogy; without example of our ancestors, or root in the Constitution. It is neither regular Parliamentary taxation, nor Colony grant. *Experimentum in corpore vili*[27] is a good rule which will ever make me adverse to any trial of experiments on what is certainly the most valuable of all subjects: the peace of this Empire.

Secondly, it is an experiment which must be fatal in the end to our Constitution. For what is it but a scheme for taxing the Colonies in the anti-chamber of the noble lord and his successors? To settle the quotas and proportions in this House is clearly impossible. You, sir, may flatter yourself, you shall sit a state auctioneer with your hammer in your hand, and knock down to each Colony as it bids. But to settle (on the plan laid down by the noble lord) the true proportional payment for four or five and twenty governments, according to the absolute and the relative wealth of each, and according to the British proportion of wealth and burden, is a wild and chimerical notion. This new taxation must therefore come in by the back-door of the Constitution. Each quota must be brought to this House ready formed; you can neither add nor alter. You must register it. You can do nothing further. For on what grounds can you deliberate either before or after the proposition? You cannot hear the counsel for all these provinces, quarrelling each on its own quantity of payment, and its proportion to others. If you should attempt it, the Committee of Provincial Ways and Means, or by whatever other name it will delight to be called, must swallow up all the time of Parliament.

---

27 Experiment on a worthless body.

Thirdly, it does not give satisfaction to the complaint of the Colonies. They complain that they are taxed without their consent; you answer that you will fix the sum at which they shall be taxed. That is, you give them the very grievance for the remedy. You tell them indeed, that you will leave the mode to themselves. I really beg pardon: it gives me pain to mention it; but you must be sensible that you will not perform this part of the compact. For, suppose the Colonies were to lay the duties which furnished their contingent upon the importation of your manufactures; you know you would never suffer such a tax to be laid. You know, too, that you would not suffer many other modes of taxation. So that when you come to explain yourself, it will be found that you will neither leave to themselves the quantum nor the mode; nor indeed anything. The whole is delusion from one end to the other.

Fourthly, this method of ransom by auction, unless it be universally accepted, will plunge you into great and inextricable difficulties. In what year of our Lord are the proportions of payments to be settled? To say nothing of the impossibility that Colony agents should have general powers of taxing the Colonies at their discretion; consider, I implore you, that the communication by special messages, and orders between these agents and their constituents on each variation of the case, when the parties come to contend together, and to dispute on their relative proportions, will be a matter of delay, perplexity, and confusion, that never can have an end.

If all the Colonies do not appear at the outcry, what is the condition of those Assemblies who offer, by themselves or their agents, to tax themselves up to your ideas of their proportion? The refractory Colonies who refuse all composition will remain taxed only to your old impositions; which, however grievous in principle, are trifling as to production. The obedient Colonies in this scheme are heavily taxed; the refractory remain unburdened. What will you do? Will you lay new and heavier taxes by Parliament on the disobedient? Pray consider in what way you can do it. You are perfectly convinced that in the way of taxing, you can do nothing but at the ports. Now suppose it is Virginia that refuses to appear at your auction, while Maryland and North Carolina bid handsomely for their ransom, and are taxed to your quota? How will you put these Colonies on a par? Will you tax the tobacco of Virginia? If you do, you give its death-wound to your English revenue at home, and to one of the very greatest articles of your own foreign trade. If you tax the import of that rebellious Colony, what do you tax but your own manufactures, or the goods of some other obedient, and already well-taxed Colony? Who has said one word on this labyrinth of detail, which bewilders you more and more as you enter into it? Who has presented, who can present you, with a clue, to lead you out of it? I think, sir, it is impossible, that you should not recollect that the Colony bounds are so implicated in one another (you know it by your other experiments in the bill for prohibiting the New-England fishery) that you can lay no possible restraints on almost any of them which may no be presently eluded, if you do not confound the innocent with the guilty, and burden those whom upon every principle you ought to exonerate. He must be grossly ignorant of America who thinks that, without falling into this confusion of all rules of equity and policy, you can restrain any single Colony, especially Virginia and Maryland, the central, and most important of them all.

Let it also be considered that, either in the present confusion you settle a permanent contingent, which will and must be trifling; and then you have no effectual revenue: or you change the quota at every exigency; and then on every new repartition you will have a new quarrel.

Reflect besides that when you have fixed a quota for every Colony, you have not provided for prompt and punctual payment. Suppose one, two, five, ten years arrears. You cannot issue a Treasury Extent against the failing Colony. You must make new Boston Port Bills, new restraining laws, new acts for dragging men to England for trial. You must send out new fleets, new armies. All is to begin again. From this day forward the Empire is never to know an hour's tranquility. An intestine fire will be kept alive in the bowels of the

Colonies, which one time or other must consume this whole Empire. I allow indeed that the empire of Germany raises her revenue and her troops by quotas and contingents; but the revenue of the empire, and the army of the empire, is the worst revenue, and the worst army, in the world.

Instead of a standing revenue, you will therefore have a perpetual quarrel. Indeed, the noble lord who proposed this project of a ransom by auction seemed himself to be of that opinion. His project was rather designed for breaking the union of the Colonies, than for establishing a revenue. He confessed, he apprehended that his proposal would not be to their taste. I say, this scheme of disunion seems to be at the bottom of the project; for I will not suspect that the noble lord meant nothing but merely to delude the nation by an airy phantom which he never intended to realize. But, whatever his views may be; as I propose the peace and union of the Colonies as the very foundation of my plan, it cannot accord with one whose foundation is perpetual discord.

Compare the two. This I offer to give you is plain and simple. The other, full of perplexed and intricate mazes. This is mild; that harsh. This is found by experience effectual for its purposes; the other is a new project. This is universal; the other calculated for certain Colonies only. This is immediate in its conciliatory operation; the other remote, contingent, full of hazard. Mine is what becomes the dignity of a ruling people: gratuitous, unconditional, and not held out as matter of bargain and sale. I have done my duty in proposing it to you. I have indeed tired you by a long discourse; but this is the misfortune of those to whose influence nothing will be conceded, and who must win every inch of their ground by argument. You have heard me with goodness. May you decide with wisdom! For my part, I feel my mind greatly disburdened by what I have done today. I have been the less fearful of trying your patience, because on this subject I mean to spare it altogether in future. I have this comfort, that in every stage of the American affairs, I have steadily opposed the measures that have produced the confusion, and may bring on the destruction, of this Empire. I now go so far as to risk a proposal of my own. If I cannot give peace to my country, I give it to my conscience.

But what (says the financier) is peace to us without money? Your plan gives us no revenue. No! But it does—for it secures to the subject the power of refusal; the first of all revenues. Experience is a cheat, and fact a liar, if this power in the subject of proportioning his grant, or of not granting at all, has not been found the richest mine of revenue ever discovered by the skill or by the fortune of man. It does not indeed vote you £152,750:11:2¾ths, nor any other paltry limited sum. But it gives the strong box itself, the fund, the bank, from whence only revenues can arise amongst a people sensible of freedom: *Posita luditur arca.*[28] Cannot you in England; cannot you at this time of day; cannot you, an House of Commons, trust to the principle which has raised so mighty a revenue, and accumulated a debt of near 140 millions in this country? Is this principle to be true in England, and false everywhere else? Is it not true in Ireland? Has it not hitherto been true in the Colonies? Why should you presume that, in any country, a body duly constituted for any function, will neglect to perform its duty, and abdicate its trust? Such a presumption would go against all government in all modes. But, in truth, this dread of penury of supply, from a free assembly, has no foundation in nature. For first observe that, besides the desire which all men have naturally of supporting the honor of their own government; that sense of dignity, and that security to property, which ever attends freedom, has a tendency to increase the stock of the free community. Most may be taken where most is accumulated. And what is the soil or climate where experience has not uniformly proved, that the voluntary flow of heaped-up plenty, bursting from the weight of its own rich luxuriance, has ever run with a more copious stream of revenue, than could be squeezed from the dry husks of oppressed indigence, by the straining of all the politic machinery in the world.

Next we know that parties must ever exist in a free country. We

---

28 Once the bets are placed, they play.

know too that the emulations of such parties, their contradictions, their reciprocal necessities, their hopes, and their fears, must send them all in their turns to him that holds the balance of the state. The parties are the gamesters; but government keeps the table, and is sure to be the winner in the end. When this game is played, I really think it is more to be feared that the people will be exhausted, than that government will not be supplied. Whereas, whatever is got by acts of absolute power ill obeyed, because odious, or by contracts ill kept, because constrained; will be narrow, feeble, uncertain, and precarious.

Ease would retract vows made in pain, as violent and void.

I, for one, protest against compounding our demands: I declare against compounding, for a poor limited sum, the immense, ever-growing, eternal debt, which is due to generous government from protected freedom. And so may I speed in the great object I propose to you, as I think it would not only be an act of injustice, but would be the worst economy in the world, to compel the Colonies to a sum certain, either in the way of ransom, or in the way of compulsory compact.

But to clear up my ideas on this subject: a revenue from America transmitted hither—do not delude yourselves—you never can receive it. No, not a shilling. We have experience that from remote countries it is not to be expected. If, when you attempted to extract revenue from Bengal, you were obliged to return in loan what you had taken in imposition; what can you expect from North America? For certainly, if ever there was a country qualified to produce wealth, it is India; or an institution fit for the transmission, it is the East-India company. America has none of these aptitudes. If America gives you taxable objects on which you lay your duties here, and gives you, at the same time, a surplus by a foreign sale of her commodities to pay the duties on these objects which you tax at home, she has performed her part to the British revenue. But with regard to her own internal establishments, she may, I doubt not she will, contribute in moderation. I say in moderation; for she ought not to be permitted to exhaust herself. She ought to be reserved to a war; the weight of which, with the enemies that we are most likely to have, must be considerable in her quarter of the globe. There she may serve you, and serve you essentially.

For that service, for all service, whether of revenue, trade, or empire, my trust is in her interest in the British Constitution. My hold of the Colonies is in the close affection which grows from common names, from kindred blood, from similar privileges, and equal protection. These are ties which, though light as air, are as strong as links of iron. Let the Colonies always keep the idea of their civil rights associated with your government—they will cling and grapple to you; and no force under heaven will be of power to tear them from their allegiance. But let it be once understood that your government may be one thing, and their privileges another; that these two things may exist without any mutual relation; the cement is gone; the cohesion is loosened; and everything hastens to decay and dissolution. As long as you have the wisdom to keep the sovereign authority of this country as the sanctuary of liberty, the sacred temple consecrated to our common faith, wherever the chosen race and sons of England worship freedom, they will turn their faces towards you. The more they multiply, the more friends you will have; the more ardently they love liberty, the more perfect will be their obedience. Slavery they can have anywhere. It is a weed that grows in every soil. They may have it from Spain, they may have it from Prussia. But until you become lost to all feeling of your true interest and your natural dignity, freedom they can have from none but you. This is the commodity of price of which you have the monopoly. This is the true Act of Navigation which binds to you the commerce of the Colonies, and through them secures to you the wealth of the world. Deny them this participation of freedom, and you break that sole bond, which originally made, and must still preserve, the unity of the Empire. Do not entertain so weak an imagination, as that your registers and your bonds, your affidavits and your sufferances, your cockets and your clearances, are what form the great securities of your commerce. Do not dream that your letters of office, and your instructions, and your suspending clauses, are the things that hold together the great contexture of this mysterious whole. These things do not make your government. Dead instruments, passive tools as they are, it is the spirit of English communion that gives all their life and efficacy to them. It is the spirit of the English Constitution which, infused through the mighty mass, pervades, feeds, unites, invigorates, vivifies, every part of the Empire, even down to the minutest member.

Is it not the same virtue which does everything for us here in England? Do you imagine then, that it is the Land Tax Act which raises your revenue? that it is the annual vote in the Committee of Supply which gives you your army? or that it is the Mutiny Bill which inspires it with bravery and discipline? No! Surely no! It is the love of the people; it is their attachment to their government from the sense of the deep stake they have in such a glorious institution, which gives you your army and your navy, and infuses into both that liberal obedience, without which your army would be a base rabble, and your navy nothing but rotten timber.

All this, I know well enough, will sound wild and chimerical to the profane herd of those vulgar and mechanical politicians who have no place among us; a sort of people who think that nothing exists but what is gross and material; and who therefore, far from being qualified to be directors of the great movement of empire, are not fit to turn a wheel in the machine. But to men truly initiated and rightly taught, these ruling and master principles, which, in the opinion of such men as I have mentioned, have no substantial existence, are in truth everything, and all in all. Magnanimity in politics is not seldom the truest wisdom; and a great empire and little minds go ill together. If we are conscious of our situation, and glow with zeal to fill our place as becomes our station and ourselves, we ought to auspicate all our public proceedings on America, with the old warning of the church, *Sursum corda!*[29] We ought to elevate our minds to the greatness of that trust to which the order of Providence has called us. By adverting to the dignity

---

29 Lift up your hearts!

of this high calling, our ancestors have turned a savage wilderness into a glorious empire; and have made the most extensive, and the only honorable conquests; not by destroying, but by promoting the wealth, the number, the happiness, of the human race. Let us get an American revenue as we have got an American empire. English privileges have made it all that it is; English privileges alone will make it all it can be.

In full confidence of this unalterable truth, I now (*quod felix faustumque sit*[30])—lay the first stone of the Temple of Peace; and I move you,

> *That the Colonies and Plantations of Great Britain in North America, consisting of fourteen separate governments, and containing two millions and upwards of free inhabitants, have not had the liberty and privilege of electing and sending any Knights and Burgesses, or others, to represent them in the High Court of Parliament.*

Upon this resolution, the previous question was put, and carried—for the previous question 270—against it 78.

As the propositions were opened separately in the body of the speech, the reader perhaps may wish to see the whole of them together, in the form in which they were moved for.

Moved:

> *That the Colonies and Plantations of Great Britain in North America, consisting of fourteen separate governments, and containing two millions and upwards of free inhabitants, have not had the liberty and privilege of electing and sending any Knights and Burgesses, or others, to represent them in the High Court of Parliament."*
>
> *That the said Colonies and Plantations have been made liable to, and bounden by, several subsidies, payments, rates, and taxes, given and granted by Parliament; though the said Colonies and Plantations have not their Knights and Burgesses, in the said High Court of*

---

30 May it be happy and fortunate.

Parliament, of their own election, to represent the condition of their country; by lack whereof, they have been oftentimes touched and grieved by subsidies given, granted, and assented to, in the said Court, in a manner prejudicial to the commonwealth, quietness, rest, and peace, of the subjects inhabiting within the same.

That, from the distance of the said Colonies, and from other circumstances, no method hath hitherto been devised for procuring a representation in Parliament for the said Colonies.

That each of the said Colonies hath within itself a body, chosen, in part or in the whole, by the freemen, freeholders, or other free inhabitants thereof, commonly called the General Assembly, or General Court; with powers legally to raise, levy, and assess, according to the several usage of such Colonies, duties and taxes towards defraying all sorts of public services.[31]

That the said General Assemblies, General Vourts, or other bodies, legally qualified as aforesaid, have at sundry times freely granted several large subsidies and public aids for his Majesty's service, according to their abilities, when required thereto by letter from one of his Majesty's principal Secretaries of State; and that their right to grant the same, and their cheerfulness and sufficiency in the said grants, have been at sundry times acknowledged by Parliament.

That it hath been found by experience, that the manner of granting the said supplies and aids, by the said General Assemblies, hath been more agreeable to the inhabitants of the said Colonies, and more beneficial and conducive to the public service, than the mode of giving and granting aids and subsidies in Parliament to be raised and paid in the said Colonies.

That it may be proper to repeal an Act, made in the 7th year of the reign of his present Majesty, entitled An Act for granting certain duties in the British Colonies and Plantations in America; for allowing a draw-back of the duties of customs, upon the exportation from this Kingdom, of coffee and cocoa-nuts, of the produce of the said Colonies or Plantations; for discontinuing the draw-backs payable on China earthen-ware exported to America; and for more effectually preventing the clandestine running of goods in the said Colonies and Plantations.

31　The first four motions and the last had the previous question put on them. The others were negatived. The words in Italics were, by an amendment that was carried, left out of the motion; which will appear in the journals, though it is not the practice to insert such amendments in the votes.

That it may be proper to repeal an Act, made in the 14th year of the reign of his present Majesty, entitled An Act to discontinue, in such manner, and for such time, as are therein mentioned, the landing and discharging, lading or shipping of goods, wares, and merchandize, at the town, and within the harbor, of Boston, in the Province of Massachusetts Bay, in North America.

That it may be proper to repeal an Act made in the 14th year of the reign of his present Majesty, entitled An Act for the impartial administration of justice, in cases of persons questioned for any acts done by them in the execution of the law, or for the suppression of riots and tumults, in the Province of Massachusetts Bay, in New England.

That it is proper to repeal an Act, made in the 14th year of the reign of his present Majesty, entitled An Act for the better regulating the government of the Province of the Massachusetts Bay in New England.

That it is proper to explain and amend an Act made in the 35th year of the reign of King Henry the Eighth entitled An Act for the trial of treasons committed out of the King's dominions."

That, from the time when the General Assembly or General Court, of any Colony or Plantation, in North America, shall have appointed, by act of assembly duly confirmed, a settled salary to the offices of the Chief Justice and Judges of the Superior Courts, it may be proper that the said Chief Justice and other Judges of the Superior Courts of such Colony shall hold his and their office and offices during their good behavior; and shall not be removed therefrom, but when the said removal shall be adjudged by his Majesty in Council, upon a hearing on complaint from the General Assembly, or on a complaint from the governor, or council, or the House of Representatives, severally, of the Colony in which the said Chief Justice and other Judges have exercised the said office.

That it may be proper to regulate the Courts of Admiralty or Vice Admiralty, authorized by the 15th chapter of the 4th of George the Third, in such a manner as to make the same more commodious to those who sue, or are sued, in the said Courts; and to provide for the more decent maintenance of the Judges of the same.

Reflections on the Revolution in France

Edmund Burke

On the Form of This Work

It may not be unnecessary to inform the reader that the following *Reflections* had their origin in a correspondence between the Author and a very young gentleman at Paris, who did him the honor of desiring his opinion upon the important transactions which then, and ever since, have so much occupied the attention of all men. An answer was written sometime in the month of October 1789, but it was kept back upon prudential considerations. That letter is alluded to in the beginning of the following sheets. It has been since forwarded to the person to whom it was addressed. The reasons for the delay in sending it were assigned in a short letter to the same gentleman. This produced on his part a new and pressing application for the Author's sentiments.

The Author began a second and more full discussion on the subject. This he had some thoughts of publishing early in the last spring; but, the matter gaining upon him, he found that what he had undertaken not only far exceeded the measure of a letter, but that its importance required rather a more detailed consideration than at that time he had any leisure to bestow upon it. However, having thrown down his first thoughts in the form of a letter, and, indeed, when he sat down to write, having intended it for a private letter, he found it difficult to change the form of address when his sentiments had grown into a greater extent and had received another direction. A different plan, he is sensible, might be more favorable to a commodious division and distribution of his matter.

I
REVOLUTION and ITS SUPPORTERS

Greeting and Introduction

Dear Sir,

You are pleased to call again, and with some earnestness, for my thoughts on the late proceedings in France. I will not give you reason to imagine that I think my sentiments of such value as to wish myself to be solicited about them. They are of too little consequence to be very anxiously either communicated or withheld. It was from attention to you, and to you only, that I hesitated at the time when you first desired to receive them. In the first letter I had the honor to write to you, and which at length I send, I wrote neither for, nor from, any description of men, nor shall I in this. My errors, if any, are my own. My reputation alone is to answer for them.

You see, sir, by the long letter I have transmitted to you, that though I do most heartily wish that France may be animated by a spirit of rational liberty, and that I think you bound, in all honest policy, to provide a permanent body in which that spirit may reside, and an effectual organ by which it may act, it is my misfortune to entertain great doubts concerning several material points in your late transactions.

Constitutional Society and Revolution Society:
The Author Disassociates from Them

You imagined, when you wrote last, that I might possibly be reckoned among the approvers of certain proceedings in France, from the solemn public seal of sanction they have received from two clubs of gentlemen in London, called the Constitutional Society and the Revolution Society.

I certainly have the honor to belong to more clubs than one, in which the constitution of this kingdom and the principles of the glorious Revolution are held in high reverence, and I reckon myself among the most forward in my zeal for maintaining that constitution and those principles in their utmost purity and vigor. It is because I do so, that I think it necessary for me that there should be no mistake. Those who cultivate the memory of our Revolution and those who are attached to the constitution of this kingdom will take good care how they are involved with persons who, under the pretext of zeal toward the Revolution and constitution, too frequently wander from their true principles and are ready on every occasion to depart from the firm but cautious and deliberate spirit which produced the one, and which presides in the other. Before I proceed to answer the more material particulars in your letter, I shall beg leave to give you such information as I have been able to obtain of the two clubs which have thought proper, as bodies, to interfere in the concerns of France, first assuring you that I am not, and that I have never been, a member of either of those societies.

The first, calling itself the Constitutional Society, or Society for Constitutional Information, or by some such title, is, I believe, of seven or eight years standing. The institution of this society appears to be of a charitable and so far of a laudable nature; it was intended for the circulation, at the expense of the members, of many books which few others would be at the expense of buying, and which might lie on the hands of the booksellers, to the great loss of a useful body of men. Whether the books, so charitably circulated, were ever as charitably read is more than I know. Possibly several of them have been exported to France and, like goods not in request here, may with you have found a market. I have heard much talk of the lights to be drawn from books that are sent from hence. What improvements they have had in their passage (as it is said some liquors are meliorated by crossing the sea) I cannot tell; but I never heard a man of common judgment or the least degree of information speak a word in praise of the greater part of the publications circulated by that society, nor have their proceedings been accounted, except by some of themselves, as of any serious consequence.

Your National Assembly seems to entertain much the same opinion that I do of this poor charitable club. As a nation, you reserved the whole stock of your eloquent acknowledgments for the Revolution Society when their fellows in the Constitutional were, in equity, entitled to some share. Since you have selected the Revolution Society as the great object of your national thanks and praises, you will think me excusable in making its late conduct the subject of my observations. The National Assembly of France has given importance to these gentlemen by adopting them; and they return the favor by acting as a committee in England for extending the principles of the National Assembly. Henceforward we must consider them as a kind of privileged persons, as no inconsiderable members in the diplomatic body. This is one among the revolutions which have given splendor to obscurity, and distinction to undiscerned merit. Until very lately I do not recollect to have heard of this club. I am quite sure that it never occupied a moment of my thoughts, nor, I believe, those of any person out of their own set. I find, upon inquiry, that on the anniversary of the Revolution in 1688, a club of dissenters, but of what denomination I know not, have long had the custom of hearing a sermon in one of their churches; and that afterwards they spent the day cheerfully, as other clubs do, at the tavern. But I never heard that any public measure or political system, much less that the merits of the constitution of any foreign nation, had been the subject of a formal proceeding at their festivals, until, to my inexpressible surprise, I found them in a sort of public capacity, by a congratulatory address, giving an authoritative sanction to the proceedings of the National Assembly in France.

In the ancient principles and conduct of the club, so far at least as they were declared, I see nothing to which I could take exception. I think it very probable that for some purpose new members may have entered among them, and that some truly Christian politicians, who love to dispense benefits but are careful to conceal the hand which distributes the dole, may have made them the instruments of their pious designs. Whatever I may have reason to suspect concerning private management, I shall speak of nothing as of a certainty but what is public.

For one, I should be sorry to be thought, directly or indirectly, concerned in their proceedings. I certainly take my full share, along with the rest of the world, in my individual and private capacity, in speculating on what has been done or is doing on the public stage in any place ancient or modern; in the republic of Rome or the republic of Paris; but having no general apostolical mission, being a citizen of a particular state and being bound up, in a considerable degree, by its public will, I should think it at least improper and irregular for me to open a formal public correspondence with the actual government of a foreign nation, without the express authority of the government under which I live.

I should be still more unwilling to enter into that correspondence under anything like an equivocal description, which to many, unacquainted with our usages, might make the address, in which I joined, appear as the act of persons in some sort of corporate capacity acknowledged by the laws of this kingdom and authorized to speak the sense of some part of it. On account of the ambiguity and uncertainty of unauthorized general descriptions, and of the deceit which may be practiced under them, and not from mere formality, the House of Commons would reject the most sneaking petition for the most trifling object, under that mode of signature to which you have thrown open the folding doors of your presence chamber, and have ushered into your National Assembly with as much ceremony and parade, and with as great a bustle of applause, as if you have been visited by the whole representative majesty of the whole English nation. If what this society has thought proper to send forth had been a piece of argument, it would have signified little whose argument it was. It would be neither the more nor the less convincing on account of the party it came from. But this is only a vote and resolution. It stands solely on authority; and in this case it is the mere authority of individuals, few of whom appear. Their signatures ought, in my opinion, to have been annexed to their instrument. The world would then have the means of knowing how many they are; who they are; and of what value their opinions may be, from their personal abilities, from their knowledge, their experience, or their lead and authority in this state. To me, who am but a plain man, the proceeding looks a little too refined and too ingenious; it has too much the air of a political stratagem adopted for the sake of giving, under a high-sounding name, an importance to the public declarations of this club which, when the matter came to be closely inspected, they did not altogether so well deserve. It is a policy that has very much the complexion of a fraud.

Considering Circumstances Before Supporting Political Movements

I flatter myself that I love a manly, moral, regulated liberty as well as any gentleman of that society, be he who he will; and perhaps I have given as good proofs of my attachment to that cause in the whole course of my public conduct. I think I envy liberty as little as they do to any other nation. But I cannot stand forward and give praise or blame to anything which relates to human actions, and human concerns, on a simple view of the object, as it stands stripped of every relation, in all the nakedness and solitude of metaphysical abstraction. Circumstances (which with some gentlemen pass for nothing) give in reality to every political principle its distinguishing color and discriminating effect. The circumstances are what render every civil and political scheme beneficial or noxious to mankind. Abstractedly speaking, government, as well as liberty, is good; yet could I, in common sense, ten years ago, have felicitated France on her enjoyment of a government (for she then had a government) without inquiry what the nature of that government was, or how it was administered? Can I now congratulate the same nation upon its freedom? Is it because liberty in the abstract may be classed amongst the blessings of mankind, that I am seriously to felicitate a madman, who has escaped from the protecting restraint and wholesome darkness of his cell, on his restoration to the enjoyment of light and liberty? Am I to congratulate a highwayman and murderer who has broken from prison upon the recovery of his natural rights? This would be to act over again the scene of the criminals condemned to the galleys, and their heroic deliverer, the metaphysical Knight of the Sorrowful Countenance.[1]

When I see the spirit of liberty in action, I see a strong principle at work; and this, for a while, is all I can possibly know of it. The wild gas, the fixed air, is plainly broke loose; but we ought to suspend our judgment until the first effervescence is a little subsided, till the liquor is cleared, and until we see something deeper than the agitation of a troubled and frothy surface. I must be tolerably sure, before I venture publicly to congratulate men upon a blessing, that they have really received one. Flattery corrupts both the receiver and the giver, and adulation is not of more service to the people than to kings. I should, therefore, suspend my congratulations on the new liberty of France until I was informed how it had been combined with government, with public force, with the discipline and obedience of armies, with the collection of an effective and well-distributed revenue, with morality and religion, with the solidity of property, with peace and order, with civil and social manners. All these (in their way) are good things, too, and without them

---

1 Don Quixote releases a group of galley-bound slaves who in turn pummel and rob him and his companion Sancho.

liberty is not a benefit whilst it lasts, and is not likely to continue long. The effect of liberty to individuals is that they may do what they please; we ought to see what it will please them to do, before we risk congratulations which may be soon turned into complaints. Prudence would dictate this in the case of separate, insulated, private men, but liberty, when men act in bodies, is power. Considerate people, before they declare themselves, will observe the use which is made of power and particularly of so trying a thing as new power in new persons of whose principles, tempers, and dispositions they have little or no experience, and in situations where those who appear the most stirring in the scene may possibly not be the real movers.

The Revolution Party's Approach

All these considerations, however, were below the transcendental dignity of the Revolution Society. Whilst I continued in the country, from whence I had the honor of writing to you, I had but an imperfect idea of their transactions. On my coming to town, I sent for an account of their proceedings, which had been published by their authority, containing a sermon of Dr. Price, with the Duke de Rochefoucault's and the Archbishop of Aix's letter, and several other documents annexed. The whole of that publication, with the manifest design of connecting the affairs of France with those of England by drawing us into an imitation of the conduct of the National Assembly, gave me a considerable degree of uneasiness. The effect of that conduct upon the power, credit, prosperity, and tranquility of France became every day more evident. The form of constitution to be settled for its future polity became more clear. We are now in a condition to discern, with tolerable exactness, the true nature of the object held up to our imitation. If the prudence of reserve and decorum dictates silence in some circumstances, in others prudence of a higher order may justify us in speaking our thoughts. The beginnings of confusion with us in England are at present feeble enough, but, with you, we have seen an infancy still more feeble growing by moments into a strength to heap mountains upon mountains and to wage war with heaven itself. Whenever our neighbor's house is on fire, it cannot be amiss for the engines to play a little on our own. Better to be despised for too anxious apprehensions than ruined by too confident a security.

Solicitous chiefly for the peace of my own country, but by no means unconcerned for yours, I wish to communicate more largely what was at first intended only for your private satisfaction. I shall still keep your affairs in my eye and continue to address myself to you. Indulging myself in the freedom of epistolary communication, I beg leave to throw out my thoughts and express my feelings just as they arise in my mind, with very little attention to formal method. I set out with the proceedings of the Revolution Society, but I shall not confine myself to them. Is it possible I should? It appears to me as if I were in a great crisis, not of the affairs of France alone, but of all Europe, perhaps of more than Europe. All circumstances taken together, the French revolution is the most astonishing that has hitherto happened in the world. The most wonderful things are brought about, in many instances by means the most absurd and ridiculous, in the most ridiculous modes, and apparently by the most contemptible instruments. Everything seems out of nature in this strange chaos of levity and ferocity, and of all sorts of crimes jumbled together with all sorts of follies. In viewing this monstrous tragicomic scene, the most opposite passions necessarily succeed and sometimes mix with each other in the mind: alternate contempt and indignation, alternate laughter and tears, alternate scorn and horror.

Introducing the Sermon of Dr. Price

It cannot, however, be denied that to some this strange scene appeared in quite another point of view. Into them it inspired no other sentiments than those of exultation and rapture. They saw nothing in what has been done in France but a firm and temperate exertion of freedom, so consistent, on the whole, with morals and with piety as to make it deserving not only of the secular applause of dashing Machiavellian politicians, but to render it a fit theme for all the devout effusions of sacred eloquence.

On the forenoon of the fourth of November last, Doctor Richard Price, a non-conforming minister of eminence, preached, at the dissenting meeting house of the Old Jewry,[2] to his club or society, a very extraordinary miscellaneous sermon, in which there are some good moral and religious sentiments, and not ill expressed, mixed up in a sort of porridge of various political opinions and reflections; but the Revolution in France is the grand ingredient in the cauldron. I consider the address transmitted by the Revolution Society to the National Assembly, through Earl Stanhope, as originating in the principles of the sermon and as a corollary from them. It was moved by the preacher of that discourse. It was passed by those who came reeking from the effect of the sermon without any censure or qualification, expressed or implied. If, however, any of the gentlemen concerned shall wish to separate the sermon from the resolution, they know how to acknowledge the one and to disavow the other. They may do it: I cannot.

For my part, I looked on that sermon as the public declaration of a man much connected with literary caballers and intriguing philosophers, with political theologians and theological politicians both at home and abroad. I know they set him up as a sort of oracle, because, with the best intentions in the world, he naturally philippizes and chants his prophetic song in exact unison with their designs.

That sermon is in a strain which I believe has not been heard in this kingdom, in any of the pulpits which are tolerated or encouraged in it, since the year 1648, when a predecessor of Dr. Price, the Rev. Hugh Peters, made the vault of the king's own chapel at St. James's ring with the honor and privilege of the saints, who, with the "high praises of God in their mouths, and a two-edged sword in their hands, were to execute judgment on the heathen,

---

2 A street in central London known for its dissenting chapel.

and punishments upon the people; to bind their kings with chains, and their nobles with fetters of iron." Few harangues from the pulpit, except in the days of your league in France or in the days of our Solemn League and Covenant in England, have ever breathed less of the spirit of moderation than this lecture in the Old Jewry. Supposing, however, that something like moderation were visible in this political sermon, yet politics and the pulpit are terms that have little agreement. No sound ought to be heard in the church but the healing voice of Christian charity. The cause of civil liberty and civil government gains as little as that of religion by this confusion of duties. Those who quit their proper character to assume what does not belong to them are, for the greater part, ignorant both of the character they leave and of the character they assume. Wholly unacquainted with the world in which they are so fond of meddling, and inexperienced in all its affairs on which they pronounce with so much confidence, they have nothing of politics but the passions they excite. Surely the church is a place where one day's truce ought to be allowed to the dissensions and animosities of mankind.

This pulpit style, revived after so long a discontinuance, had to me the air of novelty, and of a novelty not wholly without danger. I do not charge this danger equally to every part of the discourse. The hint given to a noble and reverend lay divine, who is supposed high in office in one of our universities, and other lay divines "of rank and literature" may be proper and seasonable, though somewhat new. If the noble Seekers should find nothing to satisfy their pious fancies in the old staple of the national church, or in all the rich variety to be found in the well-assorted warehouses of the dissenting congregations, Dr. Price advises them to improve upon non-conformity and to set up, each of them, a separate meeting house upon his own particular principles. It is somewhat remarkable that this reverend divine should be so earnest for setting up new churches and so perfectly indifferent concerning the doctrine which may be taught in them. His zeal is of a curious character. It is not for the propagation of his own opinions, but of any opinions. It is not for the diffusion of truth, but for the spreading of contradiction.

Let the noble teachers but dissent, it is no matter from whom or from what. This great point once secured, it is taken for granted their religion will be rational and manly. I doubt whether religion would reap all the benefits which the calculating divine computes from this "great company of great preachers." It would certainly be a valuable addition of nondescripts to the ample collection of known classes, genera and species, which at present beautify the *hortus siccus* of dissent.[3] A sermon from a noble duke, or a noble marquis, or a noble earl, or baron bold would certainly increase and diversify the amusements of this town, which begins to grow satiated with the uniform round of its vapid dissipations. I should only stipulate that these new Mess-Johns in robes and coronets should keep some sort of bounds in the democratic and leveling principles which are expected from their titled pulpits. The new evangelists will, I dare say, disappoint the hopes that are conceived of them. They will not become, literally as well as figuratively, polemic divines, nor be disposed so to drill their congregations that they may, as in former blessed times, preach their doctrines to regiments of dragoons and corps of infantry and artillery. Such arrangements, however favorable to the cause of compulsory freedom, civil and religious, may not be equally conducive to the national tranquility. These few restrictions I hope are no great stretches of intolerance, no very violent exertions of despotism.

But I may say of our preacher *"utinam nugis tota illa dedisset tempora saevitiae."*[4]—All things in this his fulminating bull are not of so innoxious a tendency. His doctrines affect our constitution in its vital parts. He tells the Revolution Society in this political sermon that his Majesty "is almost the only lawful king in the world because [he is] the only one who owes his crown to the choice of his people." As to the kings of the world, all of whom (except one) this arch-pontiff of the rights of men, with all the plenitude and with more than the boldness of the papal deposing power in

---

3 The "dry garden" of dissent.

4 "If only he had spent on trifles all that time he devoted to cruelty!"

its meridian fervor of the twelfth century, puts into one sweeping clause of ban and anathema and proclaims usurpers by circles of longitude and latitude, over the whole globe, it behooves them to consider how they admit into their territories these apostolic missionaries who are to tell their subjects they are not lawful kings. That is their concern. It is ours, as a domestic interest of some moment, seriously to consider the solidity of the only principle upon which these gentlemen acknowledge a king of Great Britain to be entitled to their allegiance.

This doctrine, as applied to the prince now on the British throne, either is nonsense and therefore neither true nor false, or it affirms a most unfounded, dangerous, illegal, and unconstitutional position. According to this spiritual doctor of politics, if his Majesty does not owe his crown to the choice of his people, he is no lawful king. Now nothing can be more untrue than that the crown of this kingdom is so held by his Majesty. Therefore, if you follow their rule, the king of Great Britain, who most certainly does not owe his high office to any form of popular election, is in no respect better than the rest of the gang of usurpers who reign, or rather rob, all over the face of this our miserable world without any sort of right or title to the allegiance of their people. The policy of this general doctrine, so qualified, is evident enough. The propagators of this political gospel are in hopes that their abstract principle (their principle that a popular choice is necessary to the legal existence of the sovereign magistracy) would be overlooked, whilst the king of Great Britain was not affected by it. In the meantime the ears of their congregations would be gradually habituated to it, as if it were a first principle admitted without dispute. For the present it would only operate as a theory, pickled in the preserving juices of pulpit eloquence, and laid by for future use. *Condo et compono quae mox depromere possim.*[5] By this policy, whilst our government is soothed with a reservation in its favor, to which it has no claim, the security which it has in common with all governments, so far as opinion is security, is taken away.

---

5 I store and arrange that I may later retrieve (Horace).

Thus these politicians proceed while little notice is taken of their doctrines; but when they are examined by the plain meaning of their words and the direct tendency of their doctrines, then equivocations and slippery constructions come into play. When they say the king owes his crown to the choice of his people and is therefore the only lawful sovereign in the world, they will perhaps tell us they mean to say no more than that some of the king's predecessors have been called to the throne by some sort of choice, and therefore he owes his crown to the choice of his people. Thus, by a miserable subterfuge, they hope to render their proposition safe by rendering it nugatory. They are welcome to the asylum they seek for their offence, since they take refuge in their folly. For if you admit this interpretation, how does their idea of election differ from our idea of inheritance?

And how does the settlement of the crown in the Brunswick line derived from James the First come to legalize our monarchy rather than that of any of the neighboring countries? At some time or other, to be sure, all the beginners of dynasties were chosen by those who called them to govern. There is ground enough for the opinion that all the kingdoms of Europe were, at a remote period, elective, with more or fewer limitations in the objects of choice. But whatever kings might have been here or elsewhere a thousand years ago, or in whatever manner the ruling dynasties of England or France may have begun, the king of Great Britain is, at this day, king by a fixed rule of succession according to the laws of his country; and whilst the legal conditions of the compact of sovereignty are performed by him (as they are performed), he holds his crown in contempt of the choice of the Revolution Society, who have not a single vote for a king amongst them, either individually or collectively, though I make no doubt they would soon erect themselves into an electoral college if things were ripe to give effect to their claim. His Majesty's heirs and successors, each in his time and order, will come to the crown with the same contempt of their choice with which his Majesty has succeeded to that he wears.

Whatever may be the success of evasion in explaining away the gross error of fact, which supposes that his Majesty (though he holds it in concurrence with the wishes) owes his crown to the choice of his people, yet nothing can evade their full explicit declaration concerning the principle of a right in the people to choose; which right is directly maintained and tenaciously adhered to. All the oblique insinuations concerning election have their foundation in this proposition and are referable to it. Lest the foundation of the king's exclusive legal title should pass for a mere rant of adulatory freedom, the political divine proceeds dogmatically to assert that, by the principles of the Revolution, the people of England have acquired three fundamental rights, all which, with him, compose one system and lie together in one short sentence, namely, that we have acquired a right:

(1) to choose our own governors.
(2) to cashier them for misconduct.
(3) to frame a government for ourselves.

This new and hitherto unheard-of bill of rights, though made in the name of the whole people, belongs to those gentlemen and their faction only. The body of the people of England have no share in it. They utterly disclaim it. They will resist the practical assertion of it with their lives and fortunes. They are bound to do so by the laws of their country made at the time of that very Revolution which is appealed to in favor of the fictitious rights claimed by the Society which abuses its name.

II
DR. PRICE'S THREE
FUNDAMENTAL RIGHTS

These gentlemen of the old Jewry, in all their reasonings on the Revolution of 1688, have a revolution which happened in England about forty years before and the late French revolution, so much before their eyes and in their hearts that they are constantly confounding all the three together. It is necessary that we should separate what they confound. We must recall their erring fancies to the acts of the Revolution which we revere, for the discovery of its true principles. If the principles of the Revolution of 1688 are anywhere to be found, it is in the statute called the Declaration of Right. In that most wise, sober, and considerate declaration, drawn up by great lawyers and great statesmen, and not by warm and inexperienced enthusiasts, not one word is said, nor one suggestion made, of a general right "to choose our own governors, to cashier them for misconduct, and to form a government for ourselves."

To Choose Our Own Governors

This Declaration of Right (the act of the 1st of William and Mary, sess. 2, ch. 2) is the cornerstone of our constitution as reinforced, explained, improved, and in its fundamental principles forever settled. It is called, "An Act for declaring the rights and liberties of the subject, and for settling the succession of the crown." You will observe that these rights and this succession are declared in one body and bound indissolubly together.

A few years after this period, a second opportunity offered for asserting a right of election to the crown. On the prospect of a total failure of issue from King William, and from the Princess, afterwards Queen Anne, the consideration of the settlement of the crown and of a further security for the liberties of the people again came before the legislature. Did they this second time make any provision for legalizing the crown on the spurious revolution principles of the Old Jewry? No. They followed the principles which prevailed in the Declaration of Right, indicating with more precision the persons who were to inherit in the Protestant line. This act also incorporated, by the same policy, our liberties and an hereditary succession in the same act. Instead of a right to choose our own governors, they declared that the succession in that line (the Protestant line drawn from James the First), was absolutely necessary "for the peace, quiet, and security of the realm," and that it was equally urgent on them "to maintain a certainty in the succession thereof, to which the subjects may safely have recourse for their protection." Both these acts, in which are heard the unerring, unambiguous oracles of revolution policy, instead of countenancing the delusive, gypsy predictions of a "right to choose our governors," prove to a demonstration how totally adverse the wisdom of the nation was from turning a case of necessity into a rule of law.

Unquestionably, there was at the Revolution, in the person of King William, a small and a temporary deviation from the strict order of a regular hereditary succession; but it is against all genuine principles of jurisprudence to draw a principle from a law made in a special case and regarding an individual person. *Privilegium non transit in exemplum.*[6] If ever there was a time favorable for establishing the principle that a king of popular choice was the only legal king, without all doubt it was at the Revolution. Its not being done at that time is a proof that the nation believed it ought not to be done at any time. There is no person so completely ignorant of our history as not to know that the majority in parliament of both parties were so little disposed to anything resembling that principle that at first they were determined to place the vacant crown, not on the head of the Prince of Orange, but on that of his wife Mary, daughter of King James, the eldest born of the issue of that king, which they acknowledged as undoubtedly his. It would be to repeat a very trite story, to recall to your memory all those circumstances which demonstrated that their accepting King William was not properly a choice; but to all those who did not wish, in effect, to recall King James or to deluge their country in blood and again to bring their religion, laws, and liberties into the peril they had just escaped, it was an act of necessity, in the strictest moral sense in which necessity can be taken.

---

6 A special case does not become the exemplar.

In the very act in which for a time, and in a single case, parliament departed from the strict order of inheritance in favor of a prince who, though not next, was, however, very near in the line of succession, it is curious to observe how Lord Somers, who drew the bill called the Declaration of Right, has comported himself on that delicate occasion. It is curious to observe with what address this temporary solution of continuity is kept from the eye, whilst all that could be found in this act of necessity to countenance the idea of an hereditary succession is brought forward, and fostered, and made the most of, by this great man and by the legislature who followed him. Quitting the dry, imperative style of an act of parliament, he makes the Lords and Commons fall to a pious, legislative exclamation and declare that they consider it "as a marvelous providence and merciful goodness of God to this nation to preserve their said Majesties' royal persons most happily to reign over us on the throne of their ancestors, for which, from the bottom of their hearts, they return their humblest thanks and praises."—The legislature plainly had in view the act of recognition of the first of Queen Elizabeth, chap. 3rd, and of that of James the First, chap. 1st, both acts strongly declaratory of the inheritable nature of the crown; and in many parts they follow, with a nearly literal precision, the words and even the form of thanksgiving which is found in these old declaratory statutes.

The two Houses, in the act of King William, did not thank God that they had found a fair opportunity to assert a right to choose their own governors, much less to make an election the only lawful title to the crown. Their having been in a condition to avoid the very appearance of it, as much as possible, was by them considered as a providential escape. They threw a political, well-wrought veil over every circumstance tending to weaken the rights which in the meliorated order of succession they meant to perpetuate, or which might furnish a precedent for any future departure from what they had then settled forever. Accordingly, that they might not relax the nerves of their monarchy, and that they might preserve a close conformity to the practice of their ancestors, as it appeared in the declaratory statutes of Queen Mary and Queen Elizabeth, in the next clause they vest, by recognition, in their Majesties all the legal prerogatives of the crown, declaring "that in them they are most fully, rightfully, and entirely invested, incorporated, united, and annexed." In the clause which follows, for preventing questions by reason of any pretended titles to the crown, they declare (observing also in this the traditional language, along with the traditional policy of the nation, and repeating as from a rubric the language of the preceding acts of Elizabeth and James) that on the preserving "a certainty in the *succession* thereof, the unity, peace, and tranquility of this nation doth, under God, wholly depend."

They knew that a doubtful title of succession would but too much resemble an election, and that an election would be utterly destructive of the "unity, peace, and tranquility of this nation," which they thought to be considerations of some moment. To provide for these objects and, therefore, to exclude forever the Old Jewry doctrine of "a right to choose our own governors," they follow with a clause containing a most solemn pledge, taken from the preceding act of Queen Elizabeth, as solemn a pledge as ever was or can be given in favor of an hereditary succession, and as solemn a renunciation as could be made of the principles by this Society imputed to them: The Lords spiritual and temporal, and Commons, do, in the name of all the people aforesaid, most humbly and faithfully submit themselves, their heirs and posterities forever; and do faithfully promise that they will stand to maintain, and defend their said Majesties, and also the limitation of the crown, herein specified and contained, to the utmost of their powers, etc. etc.

So far is it from being true that we acquired a right by the Revolution to elect our kings that, if we had possessed it before, the English nation did at that time most solemnly renounce and abdicate it, for themselves and for all their posterity forever. These gentlemen may value themselves as much as they please on their Whig principles, but I never desire to be thought a better Whig than Lord Somers, or to understand the principles of the Revolution better than those, by whom it was brought about, or to read in the

Declaration of Right any mysteries unknown to those whose penetrating style has engraved in our ordinances, and in our hearts, the words and spirit of that immortal law.

It is true that, aided with the powers derived from force and opportunity, the nation was at that time, in some sense, free to take what course it pleased for filling the throne, but only free to do so upon the same grounds on which they might have wholly abolished their monarchy and every other part of their constitution. However, they did not think of such bold changes within their commission. It is indeed difficult, perhaps impossible, to give limits to the mere abstract competence of the supreme power, such as was exercised by parliament at that time, but the limits of a moral competence subjecting, even in powers more indisputably sovereign, occasional will to permanent reason and to the steady maxims of faith, justice, and fixed fundamental policy, are perfectly intelligible and perfectly binding upon those who exercise any authority, under any name or under any title, in the state. The House of Lords, for instance, is not morally competent to dissolve the House of Commons, no, nor even to dissolve itself, nor to abdicate, if it would, its portion in the legislature of the kingdom. Though a king may abdicate for his own person, he cannot abdicate for the monarchy. By as strong, or by a stronger reason, the House of Commons cannot renounce its share of authority. The engagement and pact of society, which generally goes by the name of the constitution, forbids such invasion and such surrender. The constituent parts of a state are obliged to hold their public faith with each other and with all those who derive any serious interest under their engagements, as much as the whole state is bound to keep its faith with separate communities. Otherwise competence and power would soon be confounded and no law be left but the will of a prevailing force. On this principle the succession of the crown has always been what it now is, an hereditary succession by law; in the old line it was a succession by the common law; in the new, by the statute law operating on the principles of the common law, not changing the substance, but regulating the mode and describing the persons. Both these descriptions of law are of the same force and are derived from an equal authority emanating from the common agreement and original compact of the state, *communi sponsione reipublicae*,[7] and as such are equally binding on king and people, too, as long as the terms are observed and they continue the same body politic.

It is far from impossible to reconcile, if we do not suffer ourselves to be entangled in the mazes of metaphysical sophistry, the use both of a fixed rule and an occasional deviation: the sacredness of an hereditary principle of succession in our government with a power of change in its application in cases of extreme emergency. Even in that extremity (if we take the measure of our rights by our exercise of them at the Revolution), the change is to be confined to the guilty part only, to the part which produced the necessary deviation; and even then it is to be effected without a decomposition of the whole civil and political mass for the purpose of originating a new civil order out of the first elements of society.

A state without the means of some change is without the means of its conservation. Without such means it might even risk the loss of that part of the constitution which it wished the most religiously to preserve. The two principles of conservation and correction operated strongly at the two critical periods of the Restoration and Revolution, when England found itself without a king. At both those periods the nation had lost the bond of union in their ancient edifice; they did not, however, dissolve the whole fabric. On the contrary, in both cases they regenerated the deficient part of the old constitution through the parts which were not impaired. They kept these old parts exactly as they were, that the part recovered might be suited to them. They acted by the ancient organized states in the shape of their old organization, and not by the organic *moleculae*[8] of a disbanded people. At no time, perhaps, did the sovereign legislature manifest a more tender regard to that fundamental principle of British constitutional policy than at the time of the

---

7 Consent of the whole commonwealth.

8 Small groups or factions.

Revolution, when it deviated from the direct line of hereditary succession. The crown was carried somewhat out of the line in which it had before moved, but the new line was derived from the same stock. It was still a line of hereditary descent, still an hereditary descent in the same blood, though an hereditary descent qualified with Protestantism. When the legislature altered the direction, but kept the principle, they showed that they held it inviolable.

On this principle, the law of inheritance had admitted some amendment in the old time, and long before the era of the Revolution. Some time after the Conquest, great questions arose upon the legal principles of hereditary descent. It became a matter of doubt whether the heir per capita or the heir *per stirpes* was to succeed; but whether the heir per capita gave way when the heirdom *per stirpes* took place, or the Catholic heir when the Protestant was preferred, the inheritable principle survived with a sort of immortality through all transmigrations—*multosque per annos stat fortuna domus, et avi numerantur avorum.*[9] This is the spirit of our constitution, not only in its settled course, but in all its revolutions. Whoever came in, or however he came in, whether he obtained the crown by law or by force, the hereditary succession was either continued or adopted.

The gentlemen of the Society for Revolution see nothing in that of 1688 but the deviation from the constitution; and they take the deviation from the principle for the principle. They have little regard to the obvious consequences of their doctrine, though they must see that it leaves positive authority in very few of the positive institutions of this country. When such an unwarrantable maxim is once established, that no throne is lawful but the elective, no one act of the princes who preceded this era of fictitious election can be valid. Do these theorists mean to imitate some of their predecessors who dragged the bodies of our ancient sovereigns out of the quiet of their tombs? Do they mean to attaint and disable backward all the kings that have reigned before the Revolution, and

---

9 The fortune of the household withstands throughout the years, and fathers and their fathers are added to their line.

consequently to stain the throne of England with the blot of a continual usurpation? Do they mean to invalidate, annul, or to call into question, together with the titles of the whole line of our kings, that great body of our statute law which passed under those whom they treat as usurpers, to annul laws of inestimable value to our liberties—of as great value at least as any which have passed at or since the period of the Revolution? If kings who did not owe their crown to the choice of their people had no title to make laws, what will become of the statute *de tallagio non concedendo*, of the petition of right, and of the act of habeas corpus? Do these new doctors of the rights of men presume to assert that King James the Second, who came to the crown as next of blood, according to the rules of a then unqualified succession, was not to all intents and purposes a lawful king of England before he had done any of those acts which were justly construed into an abdication of his crown? If he was not, much trouble in parliament might have been saved at the period these gentlemen commemorate. But King James was a bad king with a good title, and not a usurper. The princes who succeeded, according to the act of parliament which settled the crown on the Electress Sophia and on her descendants, being Protestants, came in as much by a title of inheritance as King James did. He came in according to the law as it stood at his accession to the crown; and the princes of the House of Brunswick came to the inheritance of the crown, not by election, but by the law as it stood at their several accessions of Protestant descent and inheritance, as I hope I have shown sufficiently.

The law by which this royal family is specifically destined to the succession is the act of the 12th and 13th of King William. The terms of this act bind "us and our heirs, and our posterity, to them, their heirs, and their posterity," being Protestants, to the end of time, in the same words as the Declaration of Right had bound us to the heirs of King William and Queen Mary. It therefore secures both an hereditary crown and an hereditary allegiance. On what ground, except the constitutional policy of forming an establishment to secure that kind of succession which is to preclude a choice of the people forever, could the legislature have fastidiously rejected the fair and abundant choice which our country presented to them and searched in strange lands for a foreign princess from whose womb the line of our future rulers were to derive their title to govern millions of men through a series of ages?

The Princess Sophia was named in the act of settlement of the 12th and 13th of King William for a stock and root of inheritance to our kings, and not for her merits as a temporary administratrix of a power which she might not, and in fact did not, herself ever exercise. She was adopted for one reason, and for one only, because, says the act, "the most excellent Princess Sophia, Electress and Duchess Dowager of Hanover, is daughter of the most excellent Princess Elizabeth, late Queen of Bohemia, daughter of our late sovereign lord King James the First, of happy memory, and is hereby declared to be the next in succession in the Protestant line etc., etc., and the crown shall continue to the heirs of her body, being Protestants." This limitation was made by parliament, that through the Princess Sophia an inheritable line not only was to be continued in future, but (what they thought very material) that through her it was to be connected with the old stock of inheritance in King James the First, in order that the monarchy might preserve an unbroken unity through all ages and might be preserved (with safety to our religion) in the old approved mode by descent, in which, if our liberties had been once endangered, they had often, through all storms and struggles of prerogative and privilege, been preserved. They did well. No experience has taught us that in any other course or method than that of an hereditary crown our liberties can be regularly perpetuated and preserved sacred as our hereditary right. An irregular, convulsive movement may be necessary to throw off an irregular, convulsive disease. But the course of succession is the healthy habit of the British constitution. Was it that the legislature wanted, at the act for the limitation of the crown in the Hanoverian line, drawn through the female descendants of James the First, a due sense of the inconveniences of having two or three, or possibly more, foreigners in succession to the British throne?

No! They had a due sense of the evils which might happen from such foreign rule, and more than a due sense of them. But a more decisive proof cannot be given of the full conviction of the British nation that the principles of the Revolution did not authorize them to elect kings at their pleasure, and without any attention to the ancient fundamental principles of our government, than their continuing to adopt a plan of hereditary Protestant succession in the old line, with all the dangers and all the inconveniences of its being a foreign line full before their eyes and operating with the utmost force upon their minds.

A few years ago I should be ashamed to overload a matter so capable of supporting itself by the then unnecessary support of any argument; but this seditious, unconstitutional doctrine is now publicly taught, avowed, and printed. The dislike I feel to revolutions, the signals for which have so often been given from pulpits; the spirit of change that is gone abroad; the total contempt which prevails with you, and may come to prevail with us, of all ancient institutions when set in opposition to a present sense of convenience or to the bent of a present inclination: all these considerations make it not unadvisable, in my opinion, to call back our attention to the true principles of our own domestic laws; that you, my French friend, should begin to know, and that we should continue to cherish them. We ought not, on either side of the water, to suffer ourselves to be imposed upon by the counterfeit wares which some persons, by a double fraud, export to you in illicit vessels as raw commodities of British growth, though wholly alien to our soil, in order afterwards to smuggle them back again into this country, manufactured after the newest Paris fashion of an improved liberty.

The people of England will not ape the fashions they have never tried, nor go back to those which they have found mischievous on trial. They look upon the legal hereditary succession of their crown as among their rights, not as among their wrongs; as a benefit, not as a grievance; as a security for their liberty, not as a badge of servitude. They look on the frame of their commonwealth, such as it stands, to be of inestimable value, and they conceive the undisturbed succession of the crown to be a pledge of the stability and perpetuity of all the other members of our constitution.

I shall beg leave, before I go any further, to take notice of some paltry artifices which the abettors of election, as the only lawful title to the crown, are ready to employ in order to render the support of the just principles of our constitution a task somewhat invidious. These sophisters substitute a fictitious cause and feigned personages, in whose favor they suppose you engaged whenever you defend the inheritable nature of the crown. It is common with them to dispute as if they were in a conflict with some of those exploded fanatics of slavery, who formerly maintained what I believe no creature now maintains, "that the crown is held by divine hereditary and indefeasible right."—These old fanatics of single arbitrary power dogmatized as if hereditary royalty was the only lawful government in the world, just as our new fanatics of popular arbitrary power maintain that a popular election is the sole lawful source of authority. The old prerogative enthusiasts, it is true, did speculate foolishly, and perhaps impiously too, as if monarchy had more of a divine sanction than any other mode of government; and as if a right to govern by inheritance were in strictness indefeasible in every person who should be found in the succession to a throne, and under every circumstance, which no civil or political right can be. But an absurd opinion concerning the king's hereditary right to the crown does not prejudice one that is rational and bottomed upon solid principles of law and policy. If all the absurd theories of lawyers and divines were to vitiate the objects in which they are conversant, we should have no law and no religion left in the world. But an absurd theory on one side of a question forms no justification for alleging a false fact or promulgating mischievous maxims on the other.

To Cashier Them for Misconduct

The second claim of the Revolution Society is "a right of cashiering their governors for misconduct." Perhaps the apprehensions our ancestors entertained of forming such a precedent as that "of cashiering for misconduct" was the cause that the declaration of the act, which implied the abdication of King James, was, if it had any fault, rather too guarded and too circumstantial. But all this guard and all this accumulation of circumstances serves to show the spirit of caution which predominated in the national councils in a situation in which men irritated by oppression, and elevated by a triumph over it, are apt to abandon themselves to violent and extreme courses; it shows the anxiety of the great men who influenced the conduct of affairs at that great event to make the Revolution a parent of settlement, and not a nursery of future revolutions.

No government could stand a moment if it could be blown down with anything so loose and indefinite as an opinion of "misconduct." They who led at the Revolution grounded the virtual abdication of King James upon no such light and uncertain principle. They charged him with nothing less than a design, confirmed by a multitude of illegal overt acts, to subvert the Protestant church and state, and their fundamental, unquestionable laws and liberties; they charged him with having broken the original contract between king and people. This was more than misconduct. A grave and overruling necessity obliged them to take the step they took, and took with infinite reluctance, as under that most rigorous of all laws. Their trust for the future preservation of the constitution was not in future revolutions. The grand policy of all their regulations was to render it almost impracticable for any future sovereign to compel the states of the kingdom to have again recourse to those violent remedies. They left the crown what, in the eye and estimation of law, it had ever been—perfectly irresponsible. In order to lighten the crown still further, they aggravated responsibility on ministers of state. By the statute of the 1st of King William, sess. 2nd, called "the act for declaring the rights and liberties of the subject, and for settling the succession of the crown," they enacted that the ministers should serve the crown on the terms of that declaration. They secured soon after the frequent meetings of parliament, by which the whole government would be under the constant inspection and active control of the popular representative and of the magnates of the kingdom. In the next great constitutional act, that of the 12th and 13th of King William, for the further limitation of the crown and better securing the rights and liberties of the subject, they provided "that no pardon under the great seal of England should be pleadable to an impeachment by the Commons in parliament." The rule laid down for government in the Declaration of Right, the constant inspection of parliament, the practical claim of impeachment, they thought infinitely a better security, not only for their constitutional liberty, but against the vices of administration, than the reservation of a right so difficult in the practice, so uncertain in the issue, and often so mischievous in the consequences, as that of "cashiering their governors."

Dr. Price, in this sermon, condemns very properly the practice of gross, adulatory addresses to kings. Instead of this fulsome style, he proposes that his Majesty should be told, on occasions of congratulation, that "he is to consider himself as more properly the servant than the sovereign of his people." For a compliment, this new form of address does not seem to be very soothing. Those who are servants in name, as well as in effect, do not like to be told of their situation, their duty, and their obligations. The slave, in the old play, tells his master, *"Haec commemoratio est quasi exprobatio."*[10] It is not pleasant as compliment; it is not wholesome as instruction. After all, if the king were to bring himself to echo this new kind of address, to adopt it in terms, and even to take the appellation of Servant of the People as his royal style, how either he or we should be much mended by it I cannot imagine. I have seen very assuming letters, signed "Your most obedient, humble servant." The proudest denomination that ever was endured on earth took a title of still greater humility than that which is now proposed for sovereigns

---

10 That reminder is almost a reproof.

by the Apostle of Liberty. Kings and nations were trampled upon by the foot of one calling himself "the Servant of Servants;" and mandates for deposing sovereigns were sealed with the signet of "the Fisherman."

I should have considered all this as no more than a sort of flippant, vain discourse, in which, as in an unsavory fume, several persons suffer the spirit of liberty to evaporate, if it were not plainly in support of the idea and a part of the scheme of "cashiering kings for misconduct." In that light it is worth some observation.

Kings, in one sense, are undoubtedly the servants of the people because their power has no other rational end than that of the general advantage; but it is not true that they are, in the ordinary sense (by our constitution, at least), anything like servants; the essence of whose situation is to obey the commands of some other and to be removable at pleasure. But the king of Great Britain obeys no other person; all other persons are individually, and collectively too, under him and owe to him a legal obedience. The law, which knows neither to flatter nor to insult, calls this high magistrate not our servant, as this humble divine calls him, but "our sovereign Lord the king;" and we, on our parts, have learned to speak only the primitive language of the law, and not the confused jargon of their Babylonian pulpits.

As he is not to obey us, but as we are to obey the law in him, our constitution has made no sort of provision toward rendering him, as a servant, in any degree responsible. Our constitution knows nothing of a magistrate like the Justicia of Aragon, nor of any court legally appointed, nor of any process legally settled, for submitting the king to the responsibility belonging to all servants. In this he is not distinguished from the Commons and the Lords, who, in their several public capacities, can never be called to an account for their conduct, although the Revolution Society chooses to assert, in direct opposition to one of the wisest and most beautiful parts of our constitution, that "a king is no more than the first servant of the public, created by it, and responsible to it"

Ill would our ancestors at the Revolution have deserved their fame for wisdom if they had found no security for their freedom but in rendering their government feeble in its operations, and precarious in its tenure; if they had been able to contrive no better remedy against arbitrary power than civil confusion. Let these gentlemen state who that representative public is to whom they will affirm the king, as a servant, to be responsible. It will then be time enough for me to produce to them the positive statute law which affirms that he is not.

The ceremony of cashiering kings, of which these gentlemen talk so much at their ease, can rarely, if ever, be performed without force. It then becomes a case of war, and not of constitution. Laws are commanded to hold their tongues amongst arms, and tribunals fall to the ground with the peace they are no longer able to uphold. The Revolution of 1688 was obtained by a just war, in the only case in which any war, and much more a civil war, can be just. *Justa bella quibus necessaria.*[11] The question of dethroning or, if these gentlemen like the phrase better, "cashiering kings" will always be, as it has always been, an extraordinary question of state, and wholly out of the law—a question (like all other questions of state) of dispositions and of means and of probable consequences rather than of positive rights. As it was not made for common abuses, so it is not to be agitated by common minds. The speculative line of demarcation where obedience ought to end and resistance must begin is faint, obscure, and not easily definable. It is not a single act, or a single event, which determines it. Governments must be abused and deranged, indeed, before it can be thought of; and the prospect of the future must be as bad as the experience of the past. When things are in that lamentable condition, the nature of the disease is to indicate the remedy to those whom nature has qualified to administer in extremities this critical, ambiguous, bitter potion to a distempered state. Times and occasions and provocations will teach their own lessons. The wise will determine from the gravity of the

---

11 Wars are just when they are necessary.

case; the irritable, from sensibility to oppression; the high-minded, from disdain and indignation at abusive power in unworthy hands; the brave and bold, from the love of honorable danger in a generous cause; but, with or without right, a revolution will be the very last resource of the thinking and the good.

To Frame a Government for Ourselves

The third head of right, asserted by the pulpit of the Old Jewry, namely, the "right to form a government for ourselves," has, at least, as little countenance from anything done at the Revolution, either in precedent or principle, as the two first of their claims. The Revolution was made to preserve our ancient, indisputable laws and liberties and that ancient constitution of government which is our only security for law and liberty. If you are desirous of knowing the spirit of our constitution and the policy which predominated in that great period which has secured it to this hour, pray look for both in our histories, in our records, in our acts of parliament, and journals of parliament, and not in the sermons of the Old Jewry and the after-dinner toasts of the Revolution Society. In the former you will find other ideas and another language. Such a claim is as ill-suited to our temper and wishes as it is unsupported by any appearance of authority. The very idea of the fabrication of a new government is enough to fill us with disgust and horror. We wished at the period of the Revolution, and do now wish, to derive all we possess as an inheritance from our forefathers. Upon that body and stock of inheritance we have taken care not to inoculate any shoot alien to the nature of the original plant. All the reformations we have hitherto made have proceeded upon the principle of reverence to antiquity; and I hope, nay, I am persuaded, that all those which possibly may be made hereafter will be carefully formed upon analogical precedent, authority, and example.

Our oldest reformation is that of Magna Charta. You will see that Sir Edward Coke, that great oracle of our law, and indeed all the great men who follow him, to Blackstone, are industrious to prove the pedigree of our liberties. They endeavor to prove that the ancient charter, the Magna Charta of King John, was connected with another positive charter from Henry I, and that both the one and the other were nothing more than a reaffirmance of the still more ancient standing law of the kingdom. In the matter of fact, for the greater part these authors appear to be in the right; perhaps not always; but if the lawyers mistake in some particulars, it proves my position still the more strongly, because it demonstrates the powerful prepossession toward antiquity, with which the minds of all our lawyers and legislators, and of all the people whom they wish to influence, have been always filled, and the stationary policy of this kingdom in considering their most sacred rights and franchises as an inheritance.

In the famous law of the 3rd of Charles I, called the Petition of Right, the parliament says to the king, "Your subjects have inherited this freedom," claiming their franchises not on abstract principles "as the rights of men," but as the rights of Englishmen, and as a patrimony derived from their forefathers. Selden and the other profoundly learned men who drew this Petition of Right were as well acquainted, at least, with all the general theories concerning the "rights of men" as any of the discoursers in our pulpits or on your tribune; full as well as Dr. Price or as the Abbe Sieyes. But, for reasons worthy of that practical wisdom which superseded their theoretic science, they preferred this positive, recorded, hereditary title to all which can be dear to the man and the citizen, to that vague speculative right which exposed their sure inheritance to be scrambled for and torn to pieces by every wild, litigious spirit.

The same policy pervades all the laws which have since been made for the preservation of our liberties. In the 1st of William and Mary, in the famous statute called the Declaration of Right, the two Houses utter not a syllable of "a right to frame a government for themselves." You will see that their whole care was to secure the religion, laws, and liberties that had been long possessed, and had been lately endangered. "Taking into their most serious consideration the best means for making such an establishment, that their religion, laws, and liberties might not be in danger of being again subverted," they auspicate all their proceedings by stating as some of those best means, "in the first place" to do "as their ancestors in like cases have usually done for vindicating their ancient rights and liberties, to declare"—and then they pray the king and queen "that it may be declared and enacted that all and singular the rights and liberties asserted and declared are the true ancient and indubitable rights and liberties of the people of this kingdom."

You will observe that from Magna Charta to the Declaration of Right it has been the uniform policy of our constitution to claim and assert our liberties as an entailed inheritance derived to us from our forefathers, and to be transmitted to our posterity—as an estate specially belonging to the people of this kingdom, without any reference whatever to any other more general or prior right. By this means our constitution preserves a unity in so great a diversity of its parts. We have an inheritable crown, an inheritable peerage, and a House of Commons and a people inheriting privileges, franchises, and liberties from a long line of ancestors.

English Law in Harmony with Nature

This policy appears to me to be the result of profound reflection, or rather the happy effect of following nature, which is wisdom without reflection, and above it. A spirit of innovation is generally the result of a selfish temper and confined views. People will not look forward to posterity, who never look backward to their ancestors. Besides, the people of England well know that the idea of inheritance furnishes a sure principle of conservation and a sure principle of transmission, without at all excluding a principle of improvement. It leaves acquisition free, but it secures what it acquires. Whatever advantages are obtained by a state proceeding on these maxims are locked fast as in a sort of family settlement,

grasped as in a kind of mortmain forever. By a constitutional policy, working after the pattern of nature, we receive, we hold, we
transmit our government and our privileges in the same manner in
which we enjoy and transmit our property and our lives. The institutions of policy, the goods of fortune, the gifts of providence are
handed down to us, and from us, in the same course and order. Our
political system is placed in a just correspondence and symmetry
with the order of the world and with the mode of existence decreed to a permanent body composed of transitory parts, wherein,
by the disposition of a stupendous wisdom, molding together the
great mysterious incorporation of the human race, the whole, at
one time, is never old or middle-aged or young, but, in a condition
of unchangeable constancy, moves on through the varied tenor of
perpetual decay, fall, renovation, and progression. Thus, by preserving the method of nature in the conduct of the state, in what
we improve we are never wholly new; in what we retain we are never wholly obsolete. By adhering in this manner and on those principles to our forefathers, we are guided not by the superstition of
antiquarians, but by the spirit of philosophic analogy. In this choice
of inheritance we have given to our frame of polity the image of a
relation in blood, binding up the constitution of our country with
our dearest domestic ties, adopting our fundamental laws into the
bosom of our family affections, keeping inseparable and cherishing
with the warmth of all their combined and mutually reflected charities our state, our hearths, our sepulchers, and our altars.

Through the same plan of a conformity to nature in our artificial
institutions, and by calling in the aid of her unerring and powerful instincts to fortify the fallible and feeble contrivances of our
reason, we have derived several other, and those no small, benefits
from considering our liberties in the light of an inheritance. Always
acting as if in the presence of canonized forefathers, the spirit of
freedom, leading in itself to misrule and excess, is tempered with
an awful gravity. This idea of a liberal descent inspires us with a
sense of habitual native dignity which prevents that upstart insolence almost inevitably adhering to and disgracing those who are

the first acquirers of any distinction. By this means our liberty becomes a noble freedom. It carries an imposing and majestic aspect. It has a pedigree and illustrating ancestors. It has its bearings and its ensigns armorial. It has its gallery of portraits, its monumental inscriptions, its records, evidences, and titles. We procure reverence to our civil institutions on the principle upon which nature teaches us to revere individual men: on account of their age and on account of those from whom they are descended. All your sophisters cannot produce anything better adapted to preserve a rational and manly freedom than the course that we have pursued, who have chosen our nature rather than our speculations, our breasts rather than our inventions, for the great conservatories and magazines of our rights and privilege.

III
FRENCH REVOLT vs. ENGLISH REFORM

You might, if you pleased, have profited of our example and have given to your recovered freedom a correspondent dignity. Your privileges, though discontinued, were not lost to memory. Your constitution, it is true, whilst you were out of possession, suffered waste and dilapidation; but you possessed in some parts the walls and in all the foundations of a noble and venerable castle. You might have repaired those walls; you might have built on those old foundations. Your constitution was suspended before it was perfected, but you had the elements of a constitution very nearly as good as could be wished. In your old states you possessed that variety of parts corresponding with the various descriptions of which your community was happily composed; you had all that combination and all that opposition of interests; you had that action and counteraction which, in the natural and in the political world, from the reciprocal struggle of discordant powers, draws out the harmony of the universe. These opposed and conflicting interests which you considered as so great a blemish in your old and in our present constitution interpose a salutary check to all precipitate resolutions. They render deliberation a matter, not of choice, but of necessity; they make all change a subject of compromise, which naturally begets moderation; they produce temperaments preventing the sore evil of harsh, crude, unqualified reformations, and rendering all the headlong exertions of arbitrary power, in the few or in the many, forever impracticable. Through that diversity of members and interests, general liberty had as many securities as there were separate views in the several orders, whilst, by pressing down the whole by the weight of a real monarchy, the separate parts would have been prevented from warping and starting from their allotted places.

You had all these advantages in your ancient states, but you chose to act as if you had never been molded into civil society and had everything to begin anew. You began ill, because you began by despising everything that belonged to you. You set up your trade without a capital. If the last generations of your country appeared without much luster in your eyes, you might have passed them by and derived your claims from a more early race of ancestors. Under a pious predilection for those ancestors, your imaginations would have realized in them a standard of virtue and wisdom beyond the vulgar practice of the hour; and you would have risen with the example to whose imitation you aspired. Respecting your forefathers, you would have been taught to respect yourselves. You would not have chosen to consider the French as a people of yesterday, as a nation of lowborn servile wretches until the emancipating year of 1789. In order to furnish, at the expense of your honor, an excuse to your apologists here for several enormities of yours, you would not have been content to be represented as a gang of Maroon slaves suddenly broke loose from the house of bondage, and therefore to be pardoned for your abuse of the liberty to which you were not accustomed and ill fitted. Would it not, my worthy friend, have been wiser to have others consider you what I, for one, always thought you, a generous and gallant nation, long misled to your disadvantage by your high and romantic sentiments of fidelity, honor, and loyalty; that events had been unfavorable to you, but that you were not enslaved through any illiberal or servile disposition; that in your most devoted submission you were actuated by a principle of public spirit, and that it was your country you worshiped in the person of your king? Had you made it to be understood that in the delusion of this amiable error you had gone further than your wise ancestors, that you were resolved to resume your ancient privileges, whilst you preserved the spirit of your ancient and your recent loyalty and honor; or if, diffident of yourselves and not clearly discerning the almost obliterated constitution of your ancestors, you had looked to your neighbors in this land who had kept alive the ancient principles and models of the old common law of Europe meliorated and adapted to its present state—by following wise examples you would have given new examples of wisdom to the world. You would have rendered the cause of liberty venerable in the eyes of every worthy mind in every nation. You would have shamed despotism from the earth by showing that freedom was not only reconcilable, but auxiliary to law, as it is when well-disciplined. You would have had an unoppressive but a productive revenue. You would have had a flourishing commerce to feed it. You would have had a free constitution, a potent monarchy, a disciplined army, a reformed and venerated clergy, a mitigated but spirited nobility to lead your virtue, not to overlay it; you would have had a liberal order of commons to emulate and to recruit that nobility; you would have had a protected, satisfied, laborious, and obedient people, taught to seek and to recognize the happiness that is to be found by virtue in all conditions; in which consists the true moral equality of mankind, and not in that monstrous fiction which, by inspiring false ideas and vain expectations into men destined to travel in the obscure walk of laborious life, serves only to aggravate and embitter that real inequality which it never can remove, and which the order of civil life establishes as much for the benefit of those whom it must leave in a humble state as those whom it is able to exalt to a condition more splendid, but not more happy. You had a smooth and easy career of felicity and glory laid open to you, beyond anything recorded in the history of the world, but you have shown that difficulty is good for man.

Adverse Results of the Unnatural Revolt

Compute your gains: see what is got by those extravagant and presumptuous speculations which have taught your leaders to despise all their predecessors, and all their contemporaries, and even to despise themselves until the moment in which they become truly despicable. By following those false lights, France has bought undisguised calamities at a higher price than any nation has purchased the most unequivocal blessings! France has bought poverty by crime! France has not sacrificed her virtue to her interest, but she has abandoned her interest, that she might prostitute her virtue. All other nations have begun the fabric of a new government, or the reformation of an old, by establishing originally or by enforcing with greater exactness some rites or other of religion. All other people have laid the foundations of civil freedom in severer manners and a system of a more austere and masculine morality. France, when she let loose the reins of regal authority, doubled the license of a ferocious dissoluteness in manners and of an insolent irreligion in opinions and practice, and has extended through all ranks of life, as if she were communicating some privilege or laying open some secluded benefit, all the unhappy corruptions that usually were the disease of wealth and power. This is one of the new principles of equality in France.

France, by the perfidy of her leaders, has utterly disgraced the tone of lenient council in the cabinets of princes, and disarmed it of its most potent topics. She has sanctified the dark, suspicious maxims of tyrannous distrust, and taught kings to tremble at (what will hereafter be called) the delusive plausibilities of moral politicians. Sovereigns will consider those who advise them to place an unlimited confidence in their people as subverters of their thrones, as traitors who aim at their destruction by leading their easy good-nature, under specious pretenses, to admit combinations of bold and faithless men into a participation of their power. This alone (if there were nothing else) is an irreparable calamity to you and to mankind. Remember that your parliament of Paris told your king that, in calling the states together, he had nothing to fear but the prodigal excess of their zeal in providing for the support of the throne. It is right that these men should hide their heads. It is right that they should bear their part in the ruin which their counsel has brought on their sovereign and their country. Such sanguine declarations tend to lull authority asleep; to encourage it rashly to engage in perilous adventures of untried policy; to neglect those provisions, preparations, and precautions which distinguish benevolence from imbecility, and without which no man can answer for the salutary effect of any abstract plan of government or of freedom. For want of these, they have seen the medicine of the state corrupted into its poison. They have seen the French rebel against a mild and lawful monarch with more fury, outrage, and insult than ever any people has been known to rise against the most illegal usurper or the most sanguinary tyrant. Their resistance was made to concession, their revolt was from protection, their blow was aimed at a hand holding out graces, favors, and immunities.

This was unnatural. The rest is in order. They have found their punishment in their success: laws overturned; tribunals subverted; industry without vigor; commerce expiring; the revenue unpaid, yet the people impoverished; a church pillaged, and a state not relieved; civil and military anarchy made the constitution of the kingdom; everything human and divine sacrificed to the idol of public credit, and national bankruptcy the consequence; and, to crown all, the paper securities of new, precarious, tottering power, the discredited paper securities of impoverished fraud and beggared rapine, held out as a currency for the support of an empire in lieu of the two great recognized species that represent the lasting, conventional credit of mankind, which disappeared and hid themselves in the earth from whence they came, when the principle of property, whose creatures and representatives they are, was systematically subverted.

Were all these dreadful things necessary? Were they the inevitable results of the desperate struggle of determined patriots, compelled to wade through blood and tumult to the quiet shore of a tranquil and prosperous liberty? No! nothing like it. The fresh ruins of France, which shock our feelings wherever we can turn our eyes, are not the devastation of civil war; they are the sad but instructive monuments of rash and ignorant counsel in time of profound peace. They are the display of inconsiderate and presumptuous, because unresisted and irresistible, authority. The persons who have thus squandered away the precious treasure of their crimes, the persons who have made this prodigal and wild waste of public evils (the last stake reserved for the ultimate ransom of the state) have met in their progress with little or rather with no opposition at all. Their whole march was more like a triumphal procession than the progress of a war. Their pioneers have gone before them and demolished and laid everything level at their feet. Not one drop of their blood have they shed in the cause of the country they have ruined. They have made no sacrifices to their projects of greater consequence than their shoe buckles, whilst they were imprisoning their king, murdering their fellow citizens, and bathing in tears and plunging in poverty and distress thousands of worthy men and worthy families. Their cruelty has not even been the base result of fear. It has been the effect of their sense of perfect safety, in authorizing treasons, robberies, rapes, assassinations, slaughters, and burnings throughout their harassed land. But the cause of all was plain from the beginning.

The Composition of the National Assembly

This unforced choice, this fond election of evil, would appear perfectly unaccountable if we did not consider the composition of the National Assembly. I do not mean its formal constitution, which, as it now stands, is exceptionable enough, but the materials of which, in a great measure, it is composed, which is of ten thousand times greater consequence than all the formalities in the world. If we were to know nothing of this assembly but by its title and function, no colors could paint to the imagination anything more venerable. In that light the mind of an inquirer, subdued by such an awful image as that of the virtue and wisdom of a whole people collected into a focus, would pause and hesitate in condemning things even of the very worst aspect. Instead of blamable, they would appear only mysterious. But no name, no power, no function, no artificial institution whatsoever can make the men of whom any system of authority is composed any other than God, and nature, and education, and their habits of life have made them. Capacities beyond these the people have not to give. Virtue and wisdom may be the objects of their choice, but their choice confers neither the one nor the other on those upon whom they lay their ordaining hands. They have not the engagement of nature, they have not the promise of revelation, for any such powers.

After I had read over the list of the persons and descriptions elected into the *Tiers Etat*,[12] nothing which they afterwards did could appear astonishing. Among them, indeed, I saw some of known rank, some of shining talents; but of any practical experience in the state, not one man was to be found. The best were only men of theory. But whatever the distinguished few may have been, it is the substance and mass of the body which constitutes its character and must finally determine its direction. In all bodies, those who will lead must also, in a considerable degree, follow. They must conform their propositions to the taste, talent, and disposition of those whom they wish to conduct; therefore, if an assembly is viciously or feebly composed in a very great part of it, nothing but such a supreme degree of virtue as very rarely appears in the world, and for that reason cannot enter into calculation, will prevent the men of talent disseminated through it from becoming only the expert instruments of absurd projects! If, what is the more likely event, instead of that unusual degree of virtue, they should be actuated by sinister ambition and a lust of meretricious glory, then the feeble part of the assembly, to whom at first they conform, becomes in

---

12 The "Third Estate" (composed of the common people) was renamed the National Assembly shortly before the French Revolution and replaced by the Legislative Assembly in 1791.

its turn the dupe and instrument of their designs. In this political traffic, the leaders will be obliged to bow to the ignorance of their followers, and the followers to become subservient to the worst designs of their leaders.

To secure any degree of sobriety in the propositions made by the leaders in any public assembly, they ought to respect, in some degree perhaps to fear, those whom they conduct. To be led any otherwise than blindly, the followers must be qualified, if not for actors, at least for judges; they must also be judges of natural weight and authority. Nothing can secure a steady and moderate conduct in such assemblies but that the body of them should be respectably composed, in point of condition in life or permanent property, of education, and of such habits as enlarge and liberalize the understanding.

In the calling of the States-General of France, the first thing that struck me was a great departure from the ancient course. I found the representation for the Third Estate composed of six hundred persons. They were equal in number to the representatives of both the other orders. If the orders were to act separately, the number would not, beyond the consideration of the expense, be of much moment. But when it became apparent that the three orders were to be melted down into one, the policy and necessary effect of this numerous representation became obvious. A very small desertion from either of the other two orders must throw the power of both into the hands of the third. In fact, the whole power of the state was soon resolved into that body. Its due composition became therefore of infinitely the greater importance.

Judge, Sir, of my surprise when I found that a very great proportion of the assembly (a majority, I believe, of the members who attended) was composed of practitioners in the law. It was composed, not of distinguished magistrates, who had given pledges to their country of their science, prudence, and integrity; not of leading advocates, the glory of the bar; not of renowned professors in universities—but for the far greater part, as it must in such a number, of the inferior, unlearned, mechanical, merely instrumental members of the profession. There were distinguished exceptions, but the general composition was of obscure provincial advocates, of stewards of petty local jurisdictions, country attorneys, notaries, and the whole train of the ministers of municipal litigation, the fomenters and conductors of the petty war of village vexation. From the moment I read the list, I saw distinctly, and very nearly as it has happened, all that was to follow.

The degree of estimation in which any profession is held becomes the standard of the estimation in which the professors hold themselves. Whatever the personal merits of many individual lawyers might have been, and in many it was undoubtedly very considerable, in that military kingdom no part of the profession had been much regarded except the highest of all, who often united to their professional offices great family splendor, and were invested with great power and authority. These certainly were highly respected, and even with no small degree of awe. The next rank was not much esteemed; the mechanical part was in a very low degree of repute.

Whenever the supreme authority is vested in a body so composed, it must evidently produce the consequences of supreme authority placed in the hands of men not taught habitually to respect themselves, who had no previous fortune in character at stake, who could not be expected to bear with moderation, or to conduct with discretion, a power which they themselves, more than any others, must be surprised to find in their hands. Who could flatter himself that these men, suddenly and, as it were, by enchantment snatched from the humblest rank of subordination, would not be intoxicated with their unprepared greatness? Who could conceive that men who are habitually meddling, daring, subtle, active, of litigious dispositions and unquiet minds would easily fall back into their old condition of obscure contention and laborious, low, unprofitable chicane? Who could doubt but that, at any expense to the state, of which they understood nothing, they must pursue their private interests, which they understand but too well? It was not an event depending on chance or contingency. It was inevitable; it was necessary; it was planted in the nature of things. They must join (if their capacity did not permit them to lead) in any project which could procure to them a litigious constitution; which could lay open to them those innumerable lucrative jobs which follow in the train of all great convulsions and revolutions in the state, and particularly in all great and violent permutations of property. Was it to be expected that they would attend to the stability of property, whose existence had always depended upon whatever rendered property questionable, ambiguous, and insecure? Their objects would be enlarged with their elevation, but their disposition and habits, and mode of accomplishing their designs, must remain the same.

Well! but these men were to be tempered and restrained by other descriptions, of more sober and more enlarged understandings. Were they then to be awed by the supereminent authority and awful dignity of a handful of country clowns who have seats in that assembly, some of whom are said not to be able to read and write, and by not a greater number of traders who, though somewhat more instructed and more conspicuous in the order of society, had never known anything beyond their counting house? No! Both these descriptions were more formed to be overborne and swayed by the intrigues and artifices of lawyers than to become their counterpoise. With such a dangerous disproportion, the whole must necessarily be governed by them. To the faculty of law was joined a pretty considerable proportion of the faculty of medicine. This faculty had not, any more than that of the law, possessed in France its just estimation. Its professors, therefore, must have the qualities of men not habituated to sentiments of dignity. But supposing they had ranked as they ought to do, and as with us they do actually, the sides of sickbeds are not the academies for forming statesmen and legislators. Then came the dealers in stocks and funds, who must be eager, at any expense, to change their ideal paper wealth for the more solid substance of land. To these were joined men of other descriptions, from whom as little knowledge of, or attention to, the interests of a great state was to be expected, and as little regard to the stability of any institution; men formed to be instruments, not controls. Such in general was the composition of the *Tiers Etat* in the National Assembly, in which was scarcely to be perceived the slightest traces of what we call the natural landed interest of the country.

We know that the British House of Commons, without shutting its doors to any merit in any class, is, by the sure operation of adequate causes, filled with everything illustrious in rank, in descent, in hereditary and in acquired opulence, in cultivated talents, in military, civil, naval, and politic distinction that the country can afford. But supposing, what hardly can be supposed as a case, that the House of Commons should be composed in the same manner as the *Tiers Etat* in France, would this dominion of chicane be borne with patience or even conceived without horror? God forbid I should insinuate anything derogatory to that profession which is another priesthood, administering the rights of sacred justice. But whilst I revere men in the functions which belong to them, and would do as much as one man can do to prevent their exclusion from any, I cannot, to flatter them, give the lie to nature. They are good and useful in the composition; they must be mischievous if they preponderate so as virtually to become the whole. Their very excellence in their peculiar functions may be far from a qualification for others. It cannot escape observation that when men are too much confined to professional and faculty habits and, as it were, inveterate in the recurrent employment of that narrow circle, they are rather disabled than qualified for whatever depends on the knowledge of mankind, on experience in mixed affairs, on a comprehensive, connected view of the various, complicated, external and internal interests which go to the formation of that multifarious thing called a state.

After all, if the House of Commons were to have a wholly professional and faculty composition, what is the power of the House of Commons, circumscribed and shut in by the immovable barriers of laws, usages, positive rules of doctrine and practice, counterpoised by the House of Lords, and every moment of its existence at the discretion of the crown to continue, prorogue, or dissolve us? The power of the House of Commons, direct or indirect, is indeed great; and long may it be able to preserve its greatness and the spirit belonging to true greatness at the full; and it will do so as long as it can keep the breakers of law in India from becoming the makers of law for England. The power, however, of the House of Commons, when least diminished, is as a drop of water in the ocean, compared to that residing in a settled majority of your National Assembly. That assembly, since the destruction of the orders, has no fundamental law, no strict convention, no respected usage to restrain it. Instead of finding themselves obliged to conform to a fixed constitution, they have a power to make a constitution which shall conform to their designs. Nothing in heaven or upon earth can serve as a control on them. What ought to be the heads, the hearts, the dispositions that are qualified or that dare, not only to make laws under a fixed constitution, but at one heat to strike out a totally new constitution for a great kingdom, and in every part of it, from the monarch on the throne to the vestry of a parish? But "fools rush in where angels fear to tread." In such a state of unbounded power for undefined and undefinable purposes, the evil of a moral and almost physical inaptitude of the man to the function must be the greatest we can conceive to happen in the management of human affairs.

Having considered the composition of the Third Estate as it stood in its original frame, I took a view of the representatives of the clergy. There, too, it appeared that full as little regard was had to the general security of property or to the aptitude of the deputies for the public purposes, in the principles of their election. That election was so contrived as to send a very large proportion of mere country curates to the great and arduous work of remodeling a state: men who never had seen the state so much as in a picture—men who knew nothing of the world beyond the bounds of an obscure village; who, immersed in hopeless poverty, could regard all property, whether secular or ecclesiastical, with no other eye than that of envy; among whom must be many who, for the smallest hope of the meanest dividend in plunder, would readily join in any attempts upon a body of wealth in which they could hardly look to have any share except in a general scramble. Instead of balancing the power of the active chicaners in the other assembly, these curates must necessarily become the active coadjutors, or at best the passive instruments, of those by whom they had been habitually guided in their petty village concerns. They, too, could hardly be the most conscientious of their kind who, presuming upon their incompetent understanding, could intrigue for a trust which led them from their natural relation to their flocks and their natural spheres of action to undertake the regeneration of kingdoms. This preponderating weight, being added to the force of the body of chicane in the *Tiers Etat*, completed that momentum of ignorance, rashness, presumption, and lust of plunder, which nothing has been able to resist.

To observing men it must have appeared from the beginning that the majority of the Third Estate, in conjunction with such a deputation from the clergy as I have described, whilst it pursued the destruction of the nobility, would inevitably become subservient to the worst designs of individuals in that class. In the spoil and humiliation of their own order these individuals would possess a sure fund for the pay of their new followers. To squander away the objects which made the happiness of their fellows would be to them no sacrifice at all. Turbulent, discontented men of quality, in proportion as they are puffed up with personal pride and arrogance, generally despise their own order. One of the first symptoms they discover of a selfish and mischievous ambition is a profligate disregard of a dignity which they partake with others. To be attached to the subdivision, to love the little platoon we belong to in society, is the first principle (the germ as it were) of public affections. It is the first link in the series by which we proceed toward a love to our country and to mankind. The interest of that portion of social arrangement is a trust in the hands of all those who compose it; and as none but bad men would justify it in abuse, none but traitors would barter it away for their own personal advantage.

There were in the time of our civil troubles in England (I do not know whether you have any such in your assembly in France) several persons, like the then Earl of Holland, who by themselves or their families had brought an odium on the throne by the prodigal dispensation of its bounties toward them, who afterwards joined in the rebellions arising from the discontents of which they were themselves the cause; men who helped to subvert that throne to which they owed, some of them, their existence, others all that power which they employed to ruin their benefactor. If any bounds are set to the rapacious demands of that sort of people, or that others are permitted to partake in the objects they would engross, revenge and envy soon fill up the craving void that is left in their avarice. Confounded by the complication of distempered passions, their reason is disturbed; their views become vast and perplexed; to others inexplicable, to themselves uncertain. They find, on all sides, bounds to their unprincipled ambition in any fixed order of things. Both in the fog and haze of confusion all is enlarged and appears without any limit.

When men of rank sacrifice all ideas of dignity to an ambition without a distinct object and work with low instruments and for low ends, the whole composition becomes low and base. Does not something like this now appear in France? Does it not produce something ignoble and inglorious—a kind of meanness in all the prevalent policy, a tendency in all that is done to lower along with individuals all the dignity and importance of the state? Other revolutions have been conducted by persons who, whilst they attempted or affected changes in the commonwealth, sanctified their ambition by advancing the dignity of the people whose peace they troubled. They had long views. They aimed at the rule, not at the destruction, of their country. They were men of great civil and great military talents, and if the terror, the ornament of their age. They were not like Jew brokers, contending with each other who could best remedy with fraudulent circulation and depreciated paper the wretchedness and ruin brought on their country by their degenerate councils. The compliment made to one of the great bad men of the old stamp (Cromwell) by his kinsman, a favorite poet of that time, shows what it was he proposed, and what indeed to a great degree he accomplished, in the success of his ambition:

Still as you rise, the state exalted too,
Finds no distemper whilst 'tis changed by you;
Changed like the world's great scene, when without noise
The rising sun night's vulgar lights destroys.

These disturbers were not so much like men usurping power as asserting their natural place in society. Their rising was to illuminate and beautify the world. Their conquest over their competitors was by outshining them. The hand that, like a destroying angel, smote the country communicated to it the force and energy under which it suffered. I do not say (God forbid), I do not say that the virtues of such men were to be taken as a balance to their crimes; but they were some corrective to their effects. Such was, as I said, our Cromwell. Such were your whole race of Guises, Condes, and Colignis. Such the Richelieus, who in more quiet times acted in the spirit of a civil war. Such, as better men, and in a less dubious cause, were your Henry the Fourth and your Sully, though nursed in civil confusions and not wholly without some of their taint. It is a thing to be wondered at, to see how very soon France, when she had a moment to respire, recovered and emerged from the longest and most dreadful civil war that ever was known in any nation. Why? Because among all their massacres they had not slain the mind in their country. A conscious dignity, a noble pride, a generous sense of glory and emulation was not extinguished. On the contrary, it was kindled and inflamed. The organs also of the state, however shattered, existed. All the prizes of honor and virtue, all the rewards, all the distinctions remained. But your present confusion, like a palsy, has attacked the fountain of life itself. Every person in your country, in a situation to be actuated by a principle of honor, is disgraced and degraded, and can entertain no sensation of life except in a mortified and humiliated indignation. But this generation will quickly pass away. The next generation of the nobility will resemble the artificers and clowns, and money-jobbers usurers, and Jews, who will be always their fellows, sometimes their masters.

IV
INEQUALITY IN THE NATURAL ORDER

Believe me, sir, those who attempt to level, never equalize. In all societies, consisting of various descriptions of citizens, some description must be uppermost. The levelers, therefore, only change and pervert the natural order of things; they load the edifice of society by setting up in the air what the solidity of the structure requires to be on the ground. The association of tailors and carpenters, of which the republic (of Paris, for instance) is composed, cannot be equal to the situation into which by the worst of usurpations—a usurpation on the prerogatives of nature—you attempt to force them.

Inequality in Honor

The Chancellor of France, at the opening of the states, said, in a tone of oratorical flourish, that all occupations were honorable. If he meant only that no honest employment was disgraceful, he would not have gone beyond the truth. But in asserting that anything is honorable, we imply some distinction in its favor. The occupation of a hairdresser or of a working tallow-chandler cannot be a matter of honor to any person—to say nothing of a number of other more servile employments. Such descriptions of men ought not to suffer oppression from the state; but the state suffers oppression if such as they, either individually or collectively, are permitted to rule. In this you think you are combating prejudice, but you are at war with nature.

I do not determine whether this book be canonical, as the Gallican church (till lately) has considered it, or apocryphal, as here it is taken. I am sure it contains a great deal of sense and truth.[13]

I do not, my dear Sir, conceive you to be of that sophistical, captious spirit, or of that uncandid dullness, as to require, for every general observation or sentiment, an explicit detail of the correctives and exceptions which reason will presume to be included in all the general propositions which come from reasonable men. You do not imagine that I wish to confine power, authority, and distinction to blood and names and titles. No, Sir. There is no qualification for government but virtue and wisdom, actual or presumptive. Wherever they are actually found, they have, in whatever state, condition, profession, or trade, the passport of Heaven to human place and honor. Woe to the country which would madly and impiously reject the service of the talents and virtues, civil, military, or religious, that are given to grace and to serve it, and would condemn to obscurity everything formed to diffuse luster and glory around a state. Woe to that country, too, that, passing into the opposite extreme, considers a low education, a mean contracted view of things, a sordid, mercenary occupation as a preferable title to command. Everything ought to be open, but not indifferently, to every man. No rotation; no appointment by lot; no mode of election operating in the spirit of sortition or rotation can be generally good in a government conversant in extensive objects. Because they have no tendency, direct or indirect, to select the man with a view to the duty or to accommodate the one to the other. I do not hesitate to say that the road to eminence and power, from obscure condition, ought not to be made too easy, nor a thing too much of course. If rare merit be the rarest of all rare things, it ought to pass through some sort of probation. The temple of honor ought to be seated on an eminence. If it be opened through virtue, let it be remembered, too, that virtue is never tried but by some difficulty and some struggle.

---

13 Referring to the book of Ecclesiasticus, by Yeshua ben Sira. Not regarded as canonical by Protestants, but seen as useful for some instruction.

Inequality in Property

Nothing is a due and adequate representation of a state that does not represent its ability as well as its property. But as ability is a vigorous and active principle, and as property is sluggish, inert, and timid, it never can be safe from the invasion of ability unless it be, out of all proportion, predominant in the representation. It must be represented, too, in great masses of accumulation, or it is not rightly protected. The characteristic essence of property, formed out of the combined principles of its acquisition and conservation, is to be unequal. The great masses, therefore, which excite envy and tempt rapacity must be put out of the possibility of danger. Then they form a natural rampart about the lesser properties in all their gradations. The same quantity of property, which is by the natural course of things divided among many, has not the same operation. Its defensive power is weakened as it is diffused. In this diffusion each man's portion is less than what, in the eagerness of his desires, he may flatter himself to obtain by dissipating the accumulations of others. The plunder of the few would indeed give but a share inconceivably small in the distribution to the many. But the many are not capable of making this calculation; and those who lead them to rapine never intend this distribution.

The power of perpetuating our property in our families is one of the most valuable and interesting circumstances belonging to it, and that which tends the most to the perpetuation of society itself. It makes our weakness subservient to our virtue, it grafts benevolence even upon avarice. The possessors of family wealth, and of the distinction which attends hereditary possession (as most concerned in it), are the natural securities for this transmission. With us the House of Peers is formed upon this principle. It is wholly composed of hereditary property and hereditary distinction, and made, therefore, the third of the legislature and, in the last event, the sole judge of all property in all its subdivisions. The House of Commons, too, though not necessarily, yet in fact, is always so composed, in the far greater part. Let those large proprietors be what they will—and they have their chance of being amongst the best—they are, at the very worst, the ballast in the vessel of the commonwealth. For though hereditary wealth and the rank which goes with it are too much idolized by creeping sycophants and the blind, abject admirers of power, they are too rashly slighted in shallow speculations of the petulant, assuming, short-sighted coxcombs of philosophy. Some decent, regulated preeminence, some preference (not exclusive appropriation) given to birth is neither unnatural, nor unjust, nor impolitic.

It is said that twenty-four millions ought to prevail over two hundred thousand. True; if the constitution of a kingdom be a problem of arithmetic. This sort of discourse does well enough with the lamp-post for its second; to men who may reason calmly, it is ridiculous. The will of the many and their interest must very often differ, and great will be the difference when they make an evil choice. A government of five hundred country attorneys and obscure curates is not good for twenty-four millions of men, though it were chosen by eight and forty millions, nor is it the better for being guided by a dozen of persons of quality who have betrayed their trust in order to obtain that power. At present, you seem in everything to have strayed out of the high road of nature. The property of France does not govern it. Of course, property is destroyed and rational liberty has no existence. All you have got for the present is a paper circulation and a stock-jobbing constitution; and as to the future, do you seriously think that the territory of France, upon the republican system of eighty-three independent municipalities (to say nothing of the parts that compose them), can ever be governed as one body or can ever be set in motion by the impulse of one mind? When the National Assembly has completed its work, it will have accomplished its ruin. These commonwealths will not long bear a state of subjection to the republic of Paris. They will not bear that this body should monopolize the captivity of the king and the dominion over the assembly calling itself national. Each will keep its own portion of the spoil of the church to itself, and it will not suffer either that spoil, or the more just fruits of their industry, or the natural produce of their soil to be sent to swell the insolence or pamper the luxury of the mechanics of Paris. In this they will see none of the equality, under the pretense of which they have been tempted to throw off their allegiance to their sovereign as well as the ancient constitution of their country. There can be no capital city in such a constitution as they have lately made. They have forgot that, when they framed democratic governments, they had virtually dismembered their country. The person whom they persevere in calling king has not power left to him by the hundredth part sufficient to hold together this collection of republics. The republic of Paris will endeavor, indeed, to complete the debauchery of the army, and illegally to perpetuate the assembly, without resort to its constituents, as the means of continuing its despotism. It will make efforts, by becoming the heart of a boundless paper circulation, to draw everything to itself; but in vain. All this policy in the end will appear as feeble as it is now violent.

V

PRINCIPLES of the REVOLUTION

If this be your actual situation, compared to the situation to which you were called, as it were, by the voice of God and man, I cannot find it in my heart to congratulate you on the choice you have made or the success which has attended your endeavors. I can as little recommend to any other nation a conduct grounded on such principles, and productive of such effects. That I must leave to those who can see farther into your affairs than I am able to do, and who best know how far your actions are favorable to their designs. The gentlemen of the Revolution Society, who were so early in their congratulations, appear to be strongly of opinion that there is some scheme of politics relative to this country in which your proceedings may, in some way, be useful. For your Dr. Price, who seems to have speculated himself into no small degree of fervor upon this subject, addresses his audience in the following very remarkable words: "I cannot conclude without recalling particularly to your recollection a consideration which I have more than once alluded to, and which probably your thoughts have been all along anticipating; a consideration with which my mind is impressed more than I can express. I mean the consideration of the favorableness of the present times to all exertions in the cause of liberty."

It is plain that the mind of this political preacher was at the time big with some extraordinary design; and it is very probable that the thoughts of his audience, who understood him better than I do, did all along run before him in his reflection and in the whole train of consequences to which it led.

Before I read that sermon, I really thought I had lived in a free country; and it was an error I cherished, because it gave me a greater liking to the country I lived in. I was, indeed, aware that a jealous, ever-waking vigilance to guard the treasure of our liberty, not only from invasion, but from decay and corruption, was our best wisdom and our first duty. However, I considered that treasure rather as a possession to be secured than as a prize to be contended for. I did not discern how the present time came to be so very favorable to all exertions in the cause of freedom. The present time differs from any other only by the circumstance of what is doing in France. If the example of that nation is to have an influence on this, I can easily conceive why some of their proceedings which have an unpleasant aspect and are not quite reconcilable to humanity, generosity, good faith, and justice are palliated with so much milky, good nature toward the actors, and borne with so much heroic fortitude toward the sufferers. It is certainly not prudent to discredit the authority of an example we mean to follow. But allowing this, we are led to a very natural question: What is that cause of liberty, and what are those exertions in its favor to which the example of France is so singularly auspicious? Is our monarchy to be annihilated, with all the laws, all the tribunals, and all the ancient corporations of the kingdom? Is every landmark of the country to be done away in favor of a geometrical and arithmetical constitution? Is the House of Lords to be voted useless? Is episcopacy to be abolished? Are the church lands to be sold to Jews and jobbers or given to bribe new-invented municipal republics into a participation in sacrilege? Are all the taxes to be voted grievances, and the revenue reduced to a patriotic contribution or patriotic presents? Are silver shoebuckles to be substituted in the place of the land tax and the malt tax for the support of the naval strength of this kingdom? Are all orders, ranks, and distinctions to be confounded, that out of universal anarchy, joined to national bankruptcy, three or four thousand democracies should be formed into eighty-three, and that they may all, by some sort of unknown attractive power, be organized into one? For this great end, is the army to be seduced from its discipline and its fidelity, first, by every kind of debauchery and, then, by the terrible precedent of a donative in the increase of pay? Are the curates to be seduced from their bishops by holding out to them the delusive hope of a dole out of the spoils of their own order? Are the citizens of London to be drawn from their allegiance by feeding them at the expense of their fellow subjects? Is a compulsory paper currency to be substituted in the place of the legal coin of this kingdom? Is what remains of the plundered stock of public revenue to be employed in the wild project of maintaining two armies to watch over and to fight with each other? If these are the ends and means of the Revolution Society, I admit that they are well assorted; and France may furnish them for both with precedents in point.

At Odds with English Government

I see that your example is held out to shame us. I know that we are supposed a dull, sluggish race, rendered passive by finding our situation tolerable, and prevented by a mediocrity of freedom from ever attaining to its full perfection. Your leaders in France began by affecting to admire, almost to adore, the British constitution; but as they advanced, they came to look upon it with a sovereign contempt. The friends of your National Assembly amongst us have full as mean an opinion of what was formerly thought the glory of their country. The Revolution Society has discovered that the English nation is not free. They are convinced that the inequality in our representation is a "defect in our constitution so gross and palpable as to make it excellent chiefly in form and theory." That a representation in the legislature of a kingdom is not only the basis of all constitutional liberty in it, but of "all legitimate government; that without it a government is nothing but a usurpation;"—that "when the representation is partial, the kingdom possesses liberty only partially; and if extremely partial, it gives only a semblance; and if not only extremely partial, but corruptly chosen, it becomes a nuisance." Dr. Price considers this inadequacy of representation as our fundamental grievance; and though, as to the corruption of this semblance of representation, he hopes it is not yet arrived to its full perfection of depravity, he fears that "nothing will be done towards gaining for us this essential blessing, until some great abuse of power again provokes our resentment, or some great calamity again alarms our fears, or perhaps till the acquisition of a pure and equal representation by other countries, whilst we are mocked with the shadow, kindles our shame." To this he subjoins a note in these words. "A representation chosen chiefly by the treasury, and a few thousands of the dregs of the people, who are generally paid for their votes."

You will smile here at the consistency of those democratists who, when they are not on their guard, treat the humbler part of the community with the greatest contempt, whilst, at the same time, they pretend to make them the depositories of all power. It would require a long discourse to point out to you the many fallacies that lurk in the generality and equivocal nature of the terms "inadequate representation." I shall only say here, in justice to that old-fashioned constitution under which we have long prospered, that our representation has been found perfectly adequate to all the purposes for which a representation of the people can be desired or devised. I defy the enemies of our constitution to show the contrary. To detail the particulars in which it is found so well to promote its ends would demand a treatise on our practical constitution. I state here the doctrine of the Revolutionists only that you and others may see what an opinion these gentlemen entertain of the constitution of their country, and why they seem to think that some great abuse of power or some great calamity, as giving a chance for the blessing of a constitution according to their ideas, would be much palliated to their feelings; you see why they are so much enamored of your fair and equal representation, which being once obtained, the same effects might follow. You see they consider our House of Commons as only "a semblance," "a form," "a theory," "a shadow," "a mockery," perhaps "a nuisance."

These gentlemen value themselves on being systematic, and not without reason. They must therefore look on this gross and palpable defect of representation, this fundamental grievance (so they call it) as a thing not only vicious in itself, but as rendering our whole government absolutely illegitimate, and not at all better than a downright usurpation. Another revolution, to get rid of this illegitimate and usurped government, would of course be perfectly justifiable, if not absolutely necessary. Indeed, their principle, if you observe it with any attention, goes much further than to an alteration in the election of the House of Commons; for, if popular representation, or choice, is necessary to the legitimacy of all government, the House of Lords is, at one stroke, bastardized and corrupted in blood. That House is no representative of the people at all, even in "semblance or in form." The case of the crown is altogether as bad. In vain the crown may endeavor to screen itself against these gentlemen by the authority of the establishment made on the Revolution. The Revolution which is resorted to for a title, on their system, wants a title itself. The Revolution is built, according to their theory, upon a basis not more solid than our present formalities, as it was made by a House of Lords, not representing anyone but themselves, and by a House of Commons exactly such as the present, that is, as they term it, by a mere "shadow and mockery" of representation.

Something they must destroy, or they seem to themselves to exist for no purpose. One set is for destroying the civil power through the ecclesiastical; another, for demolishing the ecclesiastic through the civil. They are aware that the worst consequences might happen to the public in accomplishing this double ruin of church and state, but they are so heated with their theories that they give more than hints that this ruin, with all the mischiefs that must lead to it and attend it, and which to themselves appear quite certain, would not be unacceptable to them or very remote from their wishes. A man amongst them of great authority and certainly of great talents, speaking of a supposed alliance between church and state, says, "perhaps we must wait for the fall of the civil powers before this most unnatural alliance be broken. Calamitous no doubt will that time be. But what convulsion in the political world ought to be a subject of lamentation if it be attended with so desirable an effect?" You see with what a steady eye these gentlemen are prepared to view the greatest calamities which can befall their country.

At Odds with Any Government

It is no wonder, therefore, that with these ideas of everything in their constitution and government at home, either in church or state, as illegitimate and usurped, or at best as a vain mockery, they look abroad with an eager and passionate enthusiasm. Whilst they are possessed by these notions, it is vain to talk to them of the practice of their ancestors, the fundamental laws of their country, the fixed form of a constitution whose merits are confirmed by the solid test of long experience and an increasing public strength and national prosperity. They despise experience as the wisdom of unlettered men; and as for the rest, they have wrought underground a mine that will blow up, at one grand explosion, all examples of antiquity, all precedents, charters, and acts of parliament. They have "the rights of men." Against these there can be no prescription, against these no agreement is binding; these admit no temperament and no compromise; anything withheld from their full demand is so much of fraud and injustice. Against these their rights of men let no government look for security in the length of its continuance, or in the justice and lenity of its administration. The objections of these speculators, if its forms do not square with their theories, are as valid against such an old and beneficent government as against the most violent tyranny or the greenest usurpation. They are always at issue with governments, not on a question of abuse, but a question of competency and a question of title. I have nothing to say to the clumsy subtlety of their political metaphysics. Let them be their amusement in the schools—*"Illa se jactet in aula Aeolus, et clauso ventorum carcere regnet"*[14]—but let them not break prison to burst like a Levanter to sweep the earth with their hurricane and to break up the fountains of the great deep to overwhelm us.

VI

THE TRUE RIGHTS OF MAN AND THE PURPOSE OF GOVERNMENT

Far am I from denying in theory, full as far is my heart from withholding in practice (if I were of power to give or to withhold) the real rights of men. In denying their false claims of right, I do not mean to injure those which are real, and are such as their pretended rights would totally destroy. If civil society be made for the advantage of man, all the advantages for which it is made become his right. It is an institution of beneficence; and law itself is only beneficence acting by a rule. Men have a right to live by that rule; they have a right to do justice, as between their fellows, whether their fellows are in public function or in ordinary occupation. They have a right to the fruits of their industry and to the means of making their industry fruitful. They have a right to the acquisitions of their parents, to the nourishment and improvement of their offspring, to instruction in life, and to consolation in death. Whatever each man can separately do, without trespassing upon others, he has a right to do for himself; and he has a right to a fair portion of all which

---

14 Let Aeolus toss about in that hall, and reign—sealed off, in the prison of the winds.

society, with all its combinations of skill and force, can do in his favor. In this partnership all men have equal rights, but not to equal things. He that has but five shillings in the partnership has as good a right to it as he that has five hundred pounds has to his larger proportion. But he has not a right to an equal dividend in the product of the joint stock; and as to the share of power, authority, and direction which each individual ought to have in the management of the state, that I must deny to be amongst the direct original rights of man in civil society; for I have in my contemplation the civil social man, and no other. It is a thing to be settled by convention.

If civil society be the offspring of convention, that convention must be its law. That convention must limit and modify all the descriptions of constitution which are formed under it. Every sort of legislative, judicial, or executive power are its creatures. They can have no being in any other state of things; and how can any man claim under the conventions of civil society rights which do not so much as suppose its existence—rights which are absolutely repugnant to it? One of the first motives to civil society, and which becomes one of its fundamental rules, is that no man should be judge in his own cause. By this each person has at once divested himself of the first fundamental right of uncovenanted man, that is, to judge for himself and to assert his own cause. He abdicates all right to be his own governor. He inclusively, in a great measure, abandons the right of self-defense, the first law of nature. Men cannot enjoy the rights of an uncivil and of a civil state together. That he may obtain justice, he gives up his right of determining what it is in points the most essential to him. That he may secure some liberty, he makes a surrender in trust of the whole of it.

Abstract Perfection and Practical Defect

Government is not made in virtue of natural rights, which may and do exist in total independence of it, and exist in much greater clearness and in a much greater degree of abstract perfection; but their abstract perfection is their practical defect. By having a right to everything they want everything. Government is a contrivance of human wisdom to provide for human wants. Men have a right that these wants should be provided for by this wisdom. Among these wants is to be reckoned the want, out of civil society, of a sufficient restraint upon their passions. Society requires not only that the passions of individuals should be subjected, but that even in the mass and body, as well as in the individuals, the inclinations of men should frequently be thwarted, their will controlled, and their passions brought into subjection. This can only be done by a power out of themselves, and not, in the exercise of its function, subject to that will and to those passions which it is its office to bridle and subdue. In this sense the restraints on men, as well as their liberties, are to be reckoned among their rights. But as the liberties and the restrictions vary with times and circumstances and admit to infinite modifications, they cannot be settled upon any abstract rule; and nothing is so foolish as to discuss them upon that principle.

The moment you abate anything from the full rights of men, each to govern himself, and suffer any artificial, positive limitation upon those rights, from that moment the whole organization of government becomes a consideration of convenience. This it is which makes the constitution of a state and the due distribution of its powers a matter of the most delicate and complicated skill. It requires a deep knowledge of human nature and human necessities, and of the things which facilitate or obstruct the various ends which are to be pursued by the mechanism of civil institutions. The state is to have recruits to its strength, and remedies to its distempers. What is the use of discussing a man's abstract right to food or medicine? The question is upon the method of procuring and administering them. In that deliberation I shall always advise to call in the aid of the farmer and the physician rather than the professor of metaphysics.

The science of constructing a commonwealth, or renovating it, or reforming it, is, like every other experimental science, not to be taught a priori. Nor is it a short experience that can instruct us in that practical science, because the real effects of moral causes are not always immediate; but that which in the first instance is prejudicial may be excellent in its remoter operation, and its excellence may arise even from the ill effects it produces in the beginning. The reverse also happens: and very plausible schemes, with very pleasing commencements, have often shameful and lamentable conclusions. In states there are often some obscure and almost latent causes, things which appear at first view of little moment, on which a very great part of its prosperity or adversity may most essentially depend. The science of government being therefore so practical in itself and intended for such practical purposes—a matter which requires experience, and even more experience than any person can gain in his whole life, however sagacious and observing he may be—it is with infinite caution that any man ought to venture upon pulling down an edifice which has answered in any tolerable degree for ages the common purposes of society, or on building it up again without having models and patterns of approved utility before his eyes.

These metaphysical rights entering into common life, like rays of light which pierce into a dense medium, are by the laws of nature refracted from their straight line. Indeed, in the gross and complicated mass of human passions and concerns the primitive rights of men undergo such a variety of refractions and reflections that it becomes absurd to talk of them as if they continued in the simplicity of their original direction. The nature of man is intricate; the objects of society are of the greatest possible complexity; and, therefore, no simple disposition or direction of power can be suitable either to man's nature or to the quality of his affairs. When I hear the simplicity of contrivance aimed at and boasted of in any new political constitutions, I am at no loss to decide that the artificers are grossly ignorant of their trade or totally negligent of their duty. The simple governments are fundamentally defective, to say no worse of them. If you were to contemplate society in but one point of view, all these simple modes of polity are infinitely captivating. In effect each would answer its single end much more perfectly than the more complex is able to attain all its complex purposes. But it is better that the whole should be imperfectly and anomalously answered than that, while some parts are provided for with great exactness, others might be totally neglected or perhaps materially injured by the over-care of a favorite member.

The pretended rights of these theorists are all extremes; and in proportion as they are metaphysically true, they are morally and politically false. The rights of men are in a sort of middle, incapable of definition, but not impossible to be discerned. The rights of men in governments are their advantages; and these are often in balances between differences of good, in compromises sometimes between good and evil, and sometimes between evil and evil. Political reason is a computing principle: adding, subtracting, multiplying, and dividing, morally and not metaphysically or mathematically, true moral denominations.

By these theorists the right of the people is almost always sophistically confounded with their power. The body of the community, whenever it can come to act, can meet with no effectual resistance; but till power and right are the same, the whole body of them has no right inconsistent with virtue, and the first of all virtues, prudence. Men have no right to what is not reasonable and to what is not for their benefit; for though a pleasant writer said, *liceat perire poetis*,[15] when one of them, in cold blood, is said to have leaped into the flames of a volcanic revolution, *ardentem frigidus Aetnam insiluit*,[16] I consider such a frolic rather as an unjustifiable poetic license than as one of the franchises of Parnassus; and whether he was a poet, or divine, or politician that chose to exercise this kind of right, I think that more wise, because more charitable, thoughts would urge me rather to save the man than to preserve his brazen slippers as the monuments of his folly.

The kind of anniversary sermons to which a great part of what

---

15   Let it be allowed for poets to die.

16   Coldly, he leaps into Mt. Etna.

I write refers, if men are not shamed out of their present course in commemorating the fact, will cheat many out of the principles, and deprive them of the benefits, of the revolution they commemorate. I confess to you, Sir, I never liked this continual talk of resistance and revolution, or the practice of making the extreme medicine of the constitution its daily bread. It renders the habit of society dangerously frail; it is taking periodical doses of mercury sublimate and swallowing down repeated provocatives of cantharides to our love of liberty.

This distemper of remedy, grown habitual, relaxes and wears out, by a vulgar and prostituted use, the spring of that spirit which is to be exerted on great occasions. It was in the most patient period of Roman servitude that themes of tyrannicide made the ordinary exercise of boys at school—*cum perimit saevos classis numerosa tyrannos.*[17] In the ordinary state of things, it produces in a country like ours the worst effects, even on the cause of that liberty which it abuses with the dissoluteness of an extravagant speculation. Almost all the high-bred republicans of my time have, after a short space, become the most decided, thorough-paced courtiers; they soon left the business of a tedious, moderate, but practical resistance to those of us whom, in the pride and intoxication of their theories, they have slighted as not much better than Tories. Hypocrisy, of course, delights in the most sublime speculations, for, never intending to go beyond speculation, it costs nothing to have it magnificent. But even in cases where rather levity than fraud was to be suspected in these ranting speculations, the issue has been much the same. These professors, finding their extreme principles not applicable to cases which call only for a qualified or, as I may say, civil and legal resistance, in such cases employ no resistance at all. It is with them a war or a revolution, or it is nothing. Finding their schemes of politics not adapted to the state of the world in which they live, they often come to think lightly of all public principle, and are ready, on their part, to abandon for a very trivial interest what they

---

17　When a large class kills the raging tyrants.

find of very trivial value. Some, indeed, are of more steady and persevering natures, but these are eager politicians out of parliament who have little to tempt them to abandon their favorite projects. They have some change in the church or state, or both, constantly in their view. When that is the case, they are always bad citizens and perfectly unsure connections. For, considering their speculative designs as of infinite value, and the actual arrangement of the state as of no estimation, they are at best indifferent about it. They see no merit in the good, and no fault in the vicious, management of public affairs; they rather rejoice in the latter, as more propitious to revolution. They see no merit or demerit in any man, or any action, or any political principle any further than as they may forward or retard their design of change; they therefore take up, one day, the most violent and stretched prerogative, and another time the wildest democratic ideas of freedom, and pass from one to the other without any sort of regard to cause, to person, or to party.

VII
ASSESSMENT OF REV. PRICE

In France, you are now in the crisis of a revolution and in the transit from one form of government to another—you cannot see that character of men exactly in the same situation in which we see it in this country. With us it is militant; with you it is triumphant; and you know how it can act when its power is commensurate to its will. I would not be supposed to confine those observations to any description of men or to comprehend all men of any description within them—No! far from it. I am as incapable of that injustice as I am of keeping terms with those who profess principles of extremities and who, under the name of religion, teach little else than wild and dangerous politics. The worst of these politics of revolution is this: they temper and harden the breast in order to prepare it for the desperate strokes which are sometimes used in extreme occasions. But as these occasions may never arrive, the mind receives a gratuitous taint; and the moral sentiments suffer not a little when no political purpose is served by the depravation. This sort of people are so taken up with their theories about the rights of man that they have totally forgotten his nature. Without opening one new avenue to the understanding, they have succeeded in stopping up those that lead to the heart. They have perverted in themselves, and in those that attend to them, all the well-placed sympathies of the human breast.

This famous sermon of the Old Jewry breathes nothing but this spirit through all the political part. Plots, massacres, assassinations seem to some people a trivial price for obtaining a revolution. Cheap, bloodless reformation, a guiltless liberty appear flat and vapid to their taste. There must be a great change of scene; there must be a magnificent stage effect; there must be a grand spectacle to rouse the imagination grown torpid with the lazy enjoyment of sixty years' security and the still unanimating repose of public prosperity. The preacher found them all in the French Revolution. This inspires a juvenile warmth through his whole frame. His enthusiasm kindles as he advances; and when he arrives at his peroration it is in a full blaze. Then viewing, from the Pisgah of his pulpit, the free, moral, happy, flourishing and glorious state of France as in a bird's-eye landscape of a promised land, he breaks out into the following rapture: What an eventful period is this! I am thankful that I have lived to it; I could almost say, Lord, now lettest thou thy servant depart in peace, for mine eyes have seen thy salvation. I have lived to see a diffusion of knowledge, which has undermined superstition and error. I have lived to see the rights of men better understood than ever; and nations panting for liberty which seemed to have lost the idea of it. I have lived to see thirty millions of people, indignant and resolute, spurning at slavery, and demanding liberty with an irresistible voice. Their king led in triumph and an arbitrary monarch surrendering himself to his subjects.

Before I proceed further, I have to remark that Dr. Price seems rather to overvalue the great acquisitions of light which he has obtained and diffused in this age. The last century appears to me to have been quite as much enlightened. It had, though in a different place, a triumph as memorable as that of Dr. Price; and some of the great preachers of that period partook of it as eagerly as he has done in the triumph of France. On the trial of the Rev. Hugh Peters for high treason, it was deposed that, when King Charles was brought to London for his trial, the Apostle of Liberty in that day conducted the triumph. "I saw," says the witness, "his Majesty in the coach with six horses, and Peters riding before the king, triumphing." Dr. Price, when he talks as if he had made a discovery, only follows a precedent, for after the commencement of the king's trial this precursor, the same Dr. Peters, concluding a long prayer at the Royal Chapel at Whitehall (he had very triumphantly chosen his place), said, "I have prayed and preached these twenty years; and now I may say with old Simeon, Lord, now lettest thou thy servant depart in peace, for mine eyes have seen thy salvation." Peters had not the fruits of his prayer, for he neither departed so soon as he wished, nor in peace. He became (what I heartily hope none of his followers may be in this country) himself a sacrifice to the triumph which he led as pontiff.

They dealt at the Restoration, perhaps, too hardly with this poor good man. But we owe it to his memory and his sufferings that he had as much illumination and as much zeal, and had as effectually undermined all the superstition and error which might impede the great business he was engaged in, as any who follow and repeat after him in this age, which would assume to itself an exclusive title to the knowledge of the rights of men and all the glorious consequences of that knowledge.

After this sally of the preacher of the Old Jewry, which differs only in place and time, but agrees perfectly with the spirit and letter of the rapture of 1648, the Revolution Society, the fabricators of governments, the heroic band of cashierers of monarchs, electors of sovereigns, and leaders of kings in triumph, strutting with a proud consciousness of the diffusion of knowledge of which every member had obtained so large a share in the donative, were in haste to make a generous diffusion of the knowledge they had thus gratuitously received. To make this bountiful communication, they adjourned from the church in the Old Jewry to the London Tavern, where the same Dr. Price, in whom the fumes of his oracular tripod were not entirely evaporated, moved and carried the resolution or address of congratulation transmitted by Lord Stanhope to the National Assembly of France.

I find a preacher of the gospel profaning the beautiful and prophetic utterance, commonly called *nunc dimittis*, made on the first presentation of our Saviour in the Temple, and applying it with an inhuman and unnatural rapture to the most horrid, atrocious, and afflicting spectacle that perhaps ever was exhibited to the pity and indignation of mankind. This "leading in triumph," a thing in its best form unmanly and irreligious, which fills our preacher with such unhallowed transports, must shock, I believe, the moral taste of every well-born mind. Several English were the stupefied and indignant spectators of that triumph. It was (unless we have been strangely deceived) a spectacle more resembling a procession of American savages, entering into Onondaga after some of their murders called victories and leading into hovels hung round with scalps their captives, overpowered with the scoffs and buffets of women as ferocious as themselves, much more than it resembled the triumphal pomp of a civilized martial nation—if a civilized nation, or any men who had a sense of generosity, were capable of a personal triumph over the fallen and afflicted.

VIII
ACTIONS of the REVOLUTION OPPOSED to ENGLISH MANNERS

Mockery of Justice

This, my dear Sir, was not the triumph of France. I must believe that, as a nation, it overwhelmed you with shame and horror. I must believe that the National Assembly find themselves in a state of the greatest humiliation in not being able to punish the authors of this triumph or the actors in it, and that they are in a situation in which any inquiry they may make upon the subject must be destitute even of the appearance of liberty or impartiality. The apology of that assembly is found in their situation; but when we approve what they must bear, it is in us the degenerate choice of a vitiated mind.

With a compelled appearance of deliberation, they vote under the dominion of a stern necessity. They sit in the heart, as it were, of a foreign republic: they have their residence in a city whose constitution has emanated neither from the charter of their king nor from their legislative power. There they are surrounded by an army not raised either by the authority of their crown or by their command, and which, if they should order to dissolve itself, would instantly dissolve them. There they sit, after a gang of assassins had driven away some hundreds of the members, whilst those who held the same moderate principles, with more patience or better hope, continued every day exposed to outrageous insults and murderous threats. There a majority, sometimes real, sometimes pretended, captive itself, compels a captive king to issue as royal edicts, at third hand, the polluted nonsense of their most licentious and giddy coffeehouses. It is notorious that all their measures are decided before they are debated. It is beyond doubt that, under the terror of the bayonet and the lamp-post and the torch to their houses, they are obliged to adopt all the crude and desperate measures suggested by clubs composed of a monstrous medley of all conditions, tongues, and nations. Among these are found persons, in comparison of whom Catiline would be thought scrupulous and Cethegus a man of sobriety and moderation. Nor is it in these clubs alone that the public measures are deformed into monsters. They undergo a previous distortion in academies, intended as so many seminaries for these clubs, which are set up in all the places of public resort. In these meetings of all sorts every counsel, in proportion as it is daring and violent and perfidious, is taken for the mark of superior genius. Humanity and compassion are ridiculed as the fruits of superstition and ignorance. Tenderness to individuals is considered as treason to the public. Liberty is always to be estimated perfect, as property is rendered insecure. Amidst assassination, massacre, and confiscation, perpetrated or meditated, they are forming plans for the good order of future society. Embracing in their arms the carcasses of base criminals and promoting their relations on the title of their offences, they drive hundreds of virtuous persons to the same end, by forcing them to subsist by beggary or by crime.

The Assembly, their organ, acts before them the farce of deliberation with as little decency as liberty. They act like the comedians of a fair before a riotous audience; they act amidst the tumultuous cries of a mixed mob of ferocious men, and of women lost to shame, who, according to their insolent fancies, direct, control, applaud, explode them, and sometimes mix and take their seats amongst them, domineering over them with a strange mixture of servile petulance and proud, presumptuous authority. As they have inverted order in all things, the gallery is in the place of the house. This assembly, which overthrows kings and kingdoms, has not even the physiognomy and aspect of a grave legislative body—*nec color imperii, nec frons ulla senatus.*[18] They have a power given to them, like that of the evil principle, to subvert and destroy, but none to construct, except such machines as may be fitted for further subversion and further destruction.

Who is it that admires, and from the heart is attached to, national

---

18 Neither the appearance of an empire nor the pretense of a senate.

representative assemblies, but must turn with horror and disgust from such a profane burlesque, and abominable perversion of that sacred institute? Lovers of monarchy, lovers of republics must alike abhor it. The members of your assembly must themselves groan under the tyranny of which they have all the shame, none of the direction, and little of the profit. I am sure many of the members who compose even the majority of that body must feel as I do, notwithstanding the applauses of the Revolution Society. Miserable king! Miserable assembly! How must that assembly be silently scandalized with those of their members who could call a day which seemed to blot the sun out of heaven *"un beau jour!"*[19] How must they be inwardly indignant at hearing others who thought fit to declare to them "that the vessel of the state would fly forward in her course toward regeneration with more speed than ever," from the stiff gale of treason and murder which preceded our preacher's triumph! What must they have felt whilst, with outward patience and inward indignation, they heard, of the slaughter of innocent gentlemen in their houses, that "the blood spilled was not the most pure!" What must they have felt, when they were besieged by complaints of disorders which shook their country to its foundations, at being compelled coolly to tell the complainants that they were under the protection of the law, and that they would address the king (the captive king) to cause the laws to be enforced for their protection; when the enslaved ministers of that captive king had formally notified to them that there were neither law nor authority nor power left to protect? What must they have felt at being obliged, as a felicitation on the present new year, to request their captive king to forget the stormy period of the last, on account of the great good which he was likely to produce to his people; to the complete attainment of which good they adjourned the practical demonstrations of their loyalty, assuring him of their obedience when he should no longer possess any authority to command?

This address was made with much good nature and affection,

---

19 A happy day!

to be sure. But among the revolutions in France must be reckoned a considerable revolution in their ideas of politeness. In England we are said to learn manners at second-hand from your side of the water, and that we dress our behavior in the frippery of France. If so, we are still in the old cut and have not so far conformed to the new Parisian mode of good breeding as to think it quite in the most refined strain of delicate compliment (whether in condolence or congratulation) to say, to the most humiliated creature that crawls upon the earth, that great public benefits are derived from the murder of his servants, the attempted assassination of himself and of his wife, and the mortification, disgrace, and degradation that he has personally suffered. It is a topic of consolation which our ordinary of Newgate would be too humane to use to a criminal at the foot of the gallows. I should have thought that the hangman of Paris, now that he is liberalized by the vote of the National Assembly and is allowed his rank and arms in the herald's college of the rights of men, would be too generous, too gallant a man, too full of the sense of his new dignity to employ that cutting consolation to any of the persons whom the *leze nation* might bring under the administration of his executory power.

A man is fallen indeed when he is thus flattered. The anodyne draught of oblivion, thus drugged, is well calculated to preserve a galling wakefulness and to feed the living ulcer of a corroding memory. Thus to administer the opiate potion of amnesty, powdered with all the ingredients of scorn and contempt, is to hold to his lips, instead of "the balm of hurt minds," the cup of human misery full to the brim and to force him to drink it to the dregs.

Shameful Treatment of the Royal Family

Yielding to reasons at least as forcible as those which were so delicately urged in the compliment on the new year, the king of France will probably endeavor to forget these events and that compliment. But history, who keeps a durable record of all our acts and exercises her awful censure over the proceedings of all sorts of sovereigns, will not forget either those events or the era of this liberal refinement in the intercourse of mankind. History will record that on the morning of the 6th of October, 1789, the king and queen of France, after a day of confusion, alarm, dismay, and slaughter, lay down, under the pledged security of public faith, to indulge nature in a few hours of respite and troubled, melancholy repose. From this sleep the queen was first startled by the sentinel at her door, who cried out to her to save herself by flight—that this was the last proof of fidelity he could give—that they were upon him, and he was dead. Instantly he was cut down. A band of cruel ruffians and assassins, reeking with his blood, rushed into the chamber of the queen and pierced with a hundred strokes of bayonets and poniards the bed, from whence this persecuted woman had but just time to fly almost naked, and, through ways unknown to the murderers, had escaped to seek refuge at the feet of a king and husband not secure of his own life for a moment.

This king, to say no more of him, and this queen, and their infant children (who once would have been the pride and hope of a great and generous people) were then forced to abandon the sanctuary of the most splendid palace in the world, which they left swimming in blood, polluted by massacre and strewed with scattered limbs and mutilated carcasses. Thence they were conducted into the capital of their kingdom.

Two had been selected from the unprovoked, unresisted, promiscuous slaughter, which was made of the gentlemen of birth and family who composed the king's body guard. These two gentlemen, with all the parade of an execution of justice, were cruelly and publicly dragged to the block and beheaded in the great court of the palace. Their heads were stuck upon spears and led the procession, whilst the royal captives who followed in the train were slowly moved along, amidst the horrid yells, and shrilling screams, and frantic dances, and infamous contumelies, and all the unutterable abominations of the furies of hell in the abused shape of the vilest of women. After they had been made to taste, drop by drop, more than the bitterness of death in the slow torture of a journey of twelve miles, protracted to six hours, they were, under a guard composed of those very soldiers who had thus conducted them through this famous triumph, lodged in one of the old palaces of Paris, now converted into a bastille for kings.

Is this a triumph to be consecrated at altars? To be commemorated with grateful thanksgiving? To be offered to the divine humanity with fervent prayer and enthusiastic ejaculation? These Theban and Thracian orgies, acted in France and applauded only in the Old Jewry, I assure you, kindle prophetic enthusiasm in the minds but of very few people in this kingdom, although a saint and apostle, who may have revelations of his own and who has so completely vanquished all the mean superstitions of the heart, may incline to think it pious and decorous to compare it with the entrance into the world of the Prince of Peace, proclaimed in a holy temple by a venerable sage, and not long before not worse announced by the voice of angels to the quiet innocence of shepherds.

At first I was at a loss to account for this fit of unguarded transport. I knew, indeed, that the sufferings of monarchs make a delicious repast to some sort of palates. There were reflections which might serve to keep this appetite within some bounds of temperance. But when I took one circumstance into my consideration, I was obliged to confess that much allowance ought to be made for the Society, and that the temptation was too strong for common discretion—I mean, the circumstance of the Io Paean of the triumph, the animating cry which called "for all the *bishops* to be hanged on the lampposts," might well have brought forth a burst of enthusiasm on the foreseen consequences of this happy day. I allow to so much enthusiasm some little deviation from prudence. I allow this prophet to break forth into hymns of joy and thanksgiving on an event which appears like the precursor of the Millennium and the projected fifth monarchy in the destruction of all church establishments.

There was, however, (as in all human affairs there is) in the midst of this joy something to exercise the patience of these worthy gentlemen and to try the longsuffering of their faith. The actual murder of the king and queen, and their child, was wanting to the other auspicious circumstances of this "beautiful day." The actual murder of the bishops, though called for by so many holy utterances, was also wanting. A group of regicide and sacrilegious slaughter was indeed boldly sketched, but it was only sketched. It unhappily was left unfinished in this great history-piece of the massacre of innocents. What hardy pencil of a great master from the school of the rights of man will finish it is to be seen hereafter. The age has not yet the complete benefit of that diffusion of knowledge that has undermined superstition and error; and the king of France wants another object or two to consign to oblivion, in consideration of all the good which is to arise from his own sufferings and the patriotic crimes of an enlightened age.

IX
EXTRACT of M. DE LALLY TOLLENDAL'S SECOND LETTER to a FRIEND

Let us speak of the position I have taken; my conscience is well able to justify it:—Neither this guilty city, nor this still more guilty assembly are worthy of my self-justification; but I set great store by you, and the people who think like you, not condemning me. My health, I swear, is making my duties impossible; but even putting them aside it was beyond my strength to bear any longer the horror I felt at this blood,—these heads, a queen almost slaughtered,—this king,—led as a slave,—entering Paris, surrounded by his murderers, and preceded by the heads of his unfortunate officers—these perfidious janissaries, these murderers, these cannibalistic women, THIS SHOUT OF "ALL BISHOPS TO THE GALLOWS" as the king enters his capital with two bishops from his council in his carriage—a gunshot, which I witnessed shot at one of the queen's carriages. M. Bailly calling it a beautiful day,—the assembly having declared coldly that morning that it was beneath their dignity

> *to all go and fawn around the king—M. Mirabeau saying with impunity in this assembly that the ship of state, far from being stopped in its journey, would launch itself ever more swiftly towards its regeneration—M. Barnave, laughing with him, when rivers of blood were flowing all around us, the virtuous Mounier, escaping by a miracle from twenty murderers who had wanted to make his head yet another trophy: This—is what made me swear never to set foot again in this Cave of Cannibals [the National Assembly] where I no longer had the strength to raise my voice, where for six weeks I had raised it in vain.*
>
> *I, Mounier, and all the honest people, thought that the final effort we could make in doing the right thing was to leave. I had not the slightest idea of fear. I would strenuously defend myself against that. On the road I still received from the people, less guilty than those who intoxicated them with fury, cheers, and applause, which might have flattered some, but which made me tremble. It was the indignation, the horror, the physical convulsions, that the mere sight of blood invoked in me that I gave in to. We can brave death once; we can brave it several times, if it be useful. But no power under Heaven, no public or private opinion has the right to condemn me to suffer a thousand futile torments every minute, and to perish from despair, from rage, in the middle of their triumphs, from the crime that I could not put a stop to. Let them outlaw me, let them confiscate my property. I will till the land, and I will never see them again.—That is my justification. You can read it, show it to people, let it be copied; too bad for those who don't understand it; I will not have been wrong in giving it to them.[20]*

This military man had not so good nerves as the peaceable gentleman of the Old Jewry—see Mons. Mounier's narrative of these transactions; a man also of honor and virtue, and talents, and therefore a fugitive.

Although this work of our new light and knowledge did not go to the length that in all probability it was intended it should be carried, yet I must think that such treatment of any human creatures must be shocking to any but those who are made for accomplishing

---

20   Translated from the original French by Margaret Morrison.

revolutions. But I cannot stop here. Influenced by the inborn feelings of my nature, and not being illuminated by a single ray of this new-sprung modern light, I confess to you, Sir, that the exalted rank of the persons suffering, and particularly the sex, the beauty, and the amiable qualities of the descendant of so many kings and emperors, with the tender age of royal infants, insensible only through infancy and innocence of the cruel outrages to which their parents were exposed, instead of being a subject of exultation, adds not a little to any sensibility on that most melancholy occasion.

I hear that the august person who was the principal object of our preacher's triumph, though he supported himself, felt much on that shameful occasion. As a man, it became him to feel for his wife and his children, and the faithful guards of his person that were massacred in cold blood about him; as a prince, it became him to feel for the strange and frightful transformation of his civilized subjects, and to be more grieved for them than solicitous for himself. It derogates little from his fortitude, while it adds infinitely to the honor of his humanity. I am very sorry to say it, very sorry indeed, that such personages are in a situation in which it is not unbecoming in us to praise the virtues of the great.

I hear, and I rejoice to hear, that the great lady, the other object of the triumph, has borne that day (one is interested that beings made for suffering should suffer well), and that she bears all the succeeding days, that she bears the imprisonment of her husband, and her own captivity, and the exile of her friends, and the insulting adulation of addresses, and the whole weight of her accumulated wrongs, with a serene patience, in a manner suited to her rank and race, and becoming the offspring of a sovereign distinguished for her piety and her courage; that, like her, she has lofty sentiments; that she feels with the dignity of a Roman matron; that in the last extremity she will save herself from the last disgrace; and that, if she must fall, she will fall by no ignoble hand.

It is now sixteen or seventeen years since I saw the queen of France, then the dauphiness, at Versailles, and surely never lighted on this orb, which she hardly seemed to touch, a more delightful vision. I saw her just above the horizon, decorating and cheering the elevated sphere she just began to move in—glittering like the morning star, full of life and splendor and joy. Oh! What a revolution! And what a heart must I have to contemplate without emotion that elevation and that fall! Little did I dream when she added titles of veneration to those of enthusiastic, distant, respectful love, that she should ever be obliged to carry the sharp antidote against disgrace concealed in that bosom; little did I dream that I should have lived to see such disasters fallen upon her in a nation of gallant men, in a nation of men of honor and of cavaliers. I thought ten thousand swords must have leaped from their scabbards to avenge even a look that threatened her with insult. But the age of chivalry is gone. That of sophisters, economists; and calculators has succeeded; and the glory of Europe is extinguished forever. Never, never more shall we behold that generous loyalty to rank and sex, that proud submission, that dignified obedience, that subordination of the heart which kept alive, even in servitude itself, the spirit of an exalted freedom. The unbought grace of life, the cheap defense of nations, the nurse of manly sentiment and heroic enterprise, is gone! It is gone, that sensibility of principle, that chastity of honor which felt a stain like a wound, which inspired courage whilst it mitigated ferocity, which ennobled whatever it touched, and under which vice itself lost half its evil by losing all its grossness.

X

DANGER IN OVERTHROWING CUSTOMS

This mixed system of opinion and sentiment had its origin in the ancient chivalry; and the principle, though varied in its appearance by the varying state of human affairs, subsisted and influenced through a long succession of generations even to the time we live in. If it should ever be totally extinguished, the loss I fear will be great. It is this which has given its character to modern Europe. It is this which has distinguished it under all its forms of government, and distinguished it to its advantage, from the states of Asia and possibly from those states which flourished in the most brilliant periods of the antique world. It was this which, without confounding ranks, had produced a noble equality and handed it down through all the gradations of social life. It was this opinion which mitigated kings into companions and raised private men to be fellows with kings. Without force or opposition, it subdued the fierceness of pride and power, it obliged sovereigns to submit to the soft collar of social esteem, compelled stern authority to submit to elegance, and gave a domination, vanquisher of laws, to be subdued by manners.

But now all is to be changed. All the pleasing illusions which made power gentle and obedience liberal, which harmonized the different shades of life, and which, by a bland assimilation, incorporated into politics the sentiments which beautify and soften private society, are to be dissolved by this new conquering empire of light and reason. All the decent drapery of life is to be rudely torn off. All the superadded ideas, furnished from the wardrobe of a moral imagination, which the heart owns and the understanding ratifies as necessary to cover the defects of our naked, shivering nature, and to raise it to dignity in our own estimation, are to be exploded as a ridiculous, absurd, and antiquated fashion.

On this scheme of things, a king is but a man, a queen is but a woman; a woman is but an animal, and an animal not of the highest order. All homage paid to the sex in general as such, and without distinct views, is to be regarded as romance and folly. Regicide, and parricide, and sacrilege are but fictions of superstition, corrupting jurisprudence by destroying its simplicity. The murder of a king, or a queen, or a bishop, or a father are only common homicide; and if the people are by any chance or in any way gainers by it, a sort of homicide much the most pardonable, and into which we ought not to make too severe a scrutiny.

On the scheme of this barbarous philosophy, which is the offspring of cold hearts and muddy understandings, and which is as void of solid wisdom as it is destitute of all taste and elegance, laws are to be supported only by their own terrors and by the concern which each individual may find in them from his own private speculations or can spare to them from his own private interests. In the groves of their academy, at the end of every vista, you see nothing but the gallows. Nothing is left which engages the affections on the part of the commonwealth. On the principles of this mechanic philosophy, our institutions can never be embodied, if I may use the expression, in persons, so as to create in us love, veneration, admiration, or attachment. But that sort of reason which banishes the affections is incapable of filling their place. These public affections, combined with manners, are required sometimes as supplements, sometimes as correctives, always as aids to law. The precept given by a wise man, as well as a great critic, for the construction of poems is equally true as to states: *Non satis est pulchra esse poemata, dulcia sunto.*[21] There ought to be a system of manners in every nation which a well-informed mind would be disposed to relish. To make us love our country, our country ought to be lovely.

But power, of some kind or other, will survive the shock in which manners and opinions perish; and it will find other and worse means for its support. The usurpation which, in order to subvert ancient institutions, has destroyed ancient principles will hold power by arts similar to those by which it has acquired it. When the old feudal and chivalrous spirit of fealty, which, by freeing kings from fear, freed both kings and subjects from the precautions of tyranny, shall be extinct in the minds of men, plots and assassinations will be anticipated by preventive murder and preventive confiscation, and that long roll of grim and bloody maxims which form the political code of all power not standing on its own honor and the honor of those who are to obey it. Kings will be tyrants from policy when subjects are rebels from principle.

When ancient opinions and rules of life are taken away, the loss cannot possibly be estimated. From that moment we have no

---

21 It is not enough for poems to be beautiful, they must be pleasant.

compass to govern us; nor can we know distinctly to what port we steer. Europe, undoubtedly, taken in a mass, was in a flourishing condition the day on which your revolution was completed. How much of that prosperous state was owing to the spirit of our old manners and opinions is not easy to say; but as such causes cannot be indifferent in their operation, we must presume that on the whole their operation was beneficial.

We are but too apt to consider things in the state in which we find them, without sufficiently adverting to the causes by which they have been produced and possibly may be upheld. Nothing is more certain than that our manners, our civilization, and all the good things which are connected with manners and with civilization have, in this European world of ours, depended for ages upon two principles and were, indeed, the result of both combined: I mean the spirit of a gentleman and the spirit of religion. The nobility and the clergy, the one by profession, the other by patronage, kept learning in existence, even in the midst of arms and confusions, and whilst governments were rather in their causes than formed. Learning paid back what it received to nobility and to priesthood, and paid it with usury, by enlarging their ideas and by furnishing their minds. Happy if they had all continued to know their indissoluble union and their proper place! Happy if learning, not debauched by ambition, had been satisfied to continue the instructor, and not aspired to be the master! Along with its natural protectors and guardians, learning will be cast into the mire and trodden down under the hoofs of a swinish multitude.

If, as I suspect, modern letters owe more than they are always willing to own to ancient manners, so do other interests which we value full as much as they are worth. Even commerce and trade and manufacture, the gods of our economical politicians, are themselves perhaps but creatures, are themselves but effects which, as first causes, we choose to worship. They certainly grew under the same shade in which learning flourished. They, too, may decay with their natural protecting principles. With you, for the present at least, they all threaten to disappear together. Where trade and manufactures are wanting to a people, and the spirit of nobility and religion remains, sentiment supplies, and not always ill supplies, their place; but if commerce and the arts should be lost in an experiment to try how well a state may stand without these old fundamental principles, what sort of a thing must be a nation of gross, stupid, ferocious, and, at the same time, poor and sordid barbarians, destitute of religion, honor, or manly pride, possessing nothing at present, and hoping for nothing hereafter?

I wish you may not be going fast, and by the shortest cut, to that horrible and disgustful situation. Already there appears a poverty of conception, a coarseness, and a vulgarity in all the proceedings of the Assembly and of all their instructors. Their liberty is not liberal. Their science is presumptuous ignorance. Their humanity is savage and brutal.

It is not clear whether in England we learned those grand and decorous principles and manners, of which considerable traces yet remain, from you or whether you took them from us. But to you, I think, we trace them best. You seem to me to be *gentis incunabula nostrae*.[22] France has always more or less influenced manners in England; and when your fountain is choked up and polluted, the stream will not run long, or not run clear, with us or perhaps with any nation. This gives all Europe, in my opinion, but too close and connected a concern in what is done in France. Excuse me, therefore, if I have dwelt too long on the atrocious spectacle of the 6th of October, 1789, or have given too much scope to the reflections which have arisen in my mind on occasion of the most important of all revolutions, which may be dated from that day—I mean a revolution in sentiments, manners, and moral opinions. As things now stand, with everything respectable destroyed without us, and an attempt to destroy within us every principle of respect, one is almost forced to apologize for harboring the common feelings of men.

---

22 The cradle of our people.

Losing Natural Sense of Wrong and Right

Why do I feel so differently from the Reverend Dr. Price and those of his lay flock who will choose to adopt the sentiments of his discourse?—For this plain reason: because it is natural I should; because we are so made as to be affected at such spectacles with melancholy sentiments upon the unstable condition of mortal prosperity and the tremendous uncertainty of human greatness; because in those natural feelings we learn great lessons; because in events like these our passions instruct our reason; because when kings are hurled from their thrones by the Supreme Director of this great drama and become the objects of insult to the base and of pity to the good, we behold such disasters in the moral as we should behold a miracle in the physical order of things. We are alarmed into reflection; our minds (as it has long since been observed) are purified by terror and pity, our weak, unthinking pride is humbled under the dispensations of a mysterious wisdom. Some tears might be drawn from me if such a spectacle were exhibited on the stage. I should be truly ashamed of finding in myself that superficial, theatric sense of painted distress whilst I could exult over it in real life. With such a perverted mind I could never venture to show my face at a tragedy. People would think the tears that Garrick formerly, or that Siddons not long since, have extorted from me were the tears of hypocrisy; I should know them to be the tears of folly.

Indeed, the theatre is a better school of moral sentiments than churches, where the feelings of humanity are thus outraged. Poets who have to deal with an audience not yet graduated in the school of the rights of men and who must apply themselves to the moral constitution of the heart would not dare to produce such a triumph as a matter of exultation. There, where men follow their natural impulses, they would not bear the odious maxims of a Machiavellian policy, whether applied to the attainments of monarchical or democratic tyranny. They would reject them on the modern as they once did on the ancient stage, where they could not bear even the hypothetical proposition of such wickedness in the mouth of a personated tyrant, though suitable to the character he sustained. No theatric audience in Athens would bear what has been borne in the midst of the real tragedy of this triumphal day: a principal actor weighing, as it were, in scales hung in a shop of horrors, so much actual crime against so much contingent advantage; and after putting in and out weights, declaring that the balance was on the side of the advantages. They would not bear to see the crimes of new democracy posted as in a ledger against the crimes of old despotism, and the bookkeepers of politics finding democracy still in debt, but by no means unable or unwilling to pay the balance. In the theater, the first intuitive glance, without any elaborate process of reasoning, will show that this method of political computation would justify every extent of crime. They would see that on these principles, even where the very worst acts were not perpetrated, it was owing rather to the fortune of the conspirators than to their parsimony in the expenditure of treachery and blood. They would soon see that criminal means once tolerated are soon preferred. They present a shorter cut to the object than through the highway of the moral virtues. Justifying perfidy and murder for public benefit, public benefit would soon become the pretext, and perfidy and murder the end, until rapacity, malice, revenge, and fear more dreadful than revenge could satiate their insatiable appetites. Such must be the consequences of losing, in the splendor of these triumphs of the rights of men, all natural sense of wrong and right.

Louis XVI Was No Tyrant

But the reverend pastor exults in this "leading in triumph," because truly Louis the Sixteenth was "an arbitrary monarch;" that is, in other words, neither more nor less than because he was Louis the Sixteenth, and because he had the misfortune to be born king of France, with the prerogatives of which a long line of ancestors and a long acquiescence of the people, without any act of his, had put him in possession. A misfortune it has indeed turned out to him that he was born king of France. But misfortune is not crime, nor is indiscretion always the greatest guilt. I shall never think that a prince the acts of whose whole reign was a series of concessions to his subjects, who was willing to relax his authority, to remit his prerogatives, to call his people to a share of freedom not known, perhaps not desired, by their ancestors—such a prince, though he should be subjected to the common frailties attached to men and to princes, though he should have once thought it necessary to provide force against the desperate designs manifestly carrying on against his person and the remnants of his authority—though all this should be taken into consideration, I shall be led with great difficulty to think he deserves the cruel and insulting triumph of Paris and of Dr. Price. I tremble for the cause of liberty from such an example to kings. I tremble for the cause of humanity in the unpunished outrages of the most wicked of mankind. But there are some people of that low and degenerate fashion of mind, that they look up with a sort of complacent awe and admiration to kings who know to keep firm in their seat, to hold a strict hand over their subjects, to assert their prerogative, and, by the awakened vigilance of a severe despotism, to guard against the very first approaches to freedom. Against such as these they never elevate their voice. Deserters from principle, listed with fortune, they never see any good in suffering virtue, nor any crime in prosperous usurpation.

If it could have been made clear to me that the king and queen of France (those I mean who were such before the triumph) were inexorable and cruel tyrants, that they had formed a deliberate scheme for massacring the National Assembly (I think I have seen something like the latter insinuated in certain publications), I should think their captivity just. If this be true, much more ought to have been done, but done, in my opinion, in another manner. The punishment of real tyrants is a noble and awful act of justice; and it has with truth been said to be consolatory to the human mind. But if I were to punish a wicked king, I should regard the dignity in avenging the crime. Justice is grave and decorous, and in its punishments rather seems to submit to a necessity than to make a choice. Had Nero, or Agrippina, or Louis the Eleventh, or

Charles the Ninth been the subject; if Charles the Twelfth of Sweden, after the murder of Patkul, or his predecessor Christina, after the murder of Monaldeschi, had fallen into your hands, Sir, or into mine, I am sure our conduct would have been different.

If the French king, or king of the French (or by whatever name he is known in the new vocabulary of your constitution), has in his own person and that of his queen really deserved these unavowed, but unavenged, murderous attempts and those frequent indignities more cruel than murder, such a person would ill deserve even that subordinate executive trust which I understand is to be placed in him, nor is he fit to be called chief in a nation which he has outraged and oppressed. A worse choice for such an office in a new commonwealth than that of a deposed tyrant could not possibly be made. But to degrade and insult a man as the worst of criminals and afterwards to trust him in your highest concerns as a faithful, honest, and zealous servant is not consistent to reasoning, nor prudent in policy, nor safe in practice. Those who could make such an appointment must be guilty of a more flagrant breach of trust than any they have yet committed against the people. As this is the only crime in which your leading politicians could have acted inconsistently, I conclude that there is no sort of ground for these horrid insinuations. I think no better of all the other calumnies.

English Honor Requires Condemnation of the Revolution

In England, we give no credit to them. We are generous enemies; we are faithful allies. We spurn from us with disgust and indignation the slanders of those who bring us their anecdotes with the attestation of the flower-de-luce on their shoulder. We have Lord George Gordon fast in Newgate; and neither his being a public proselyte to Judaism, nor his having, in his zeal against Catholic priests and all sorts of ecclesiastics, raised a mob (excuse the term, it is still in use here) which pulled down all our prisons, have preserved to him a liberty of which he did not render himself worthy by a virtuous use of it. We have rebuilt Newgate and tenanted the mansion. We have prisons almost as strong as the Bastille for those who dare to libel the queens of France. In this spiritual retreat, let the noble libeler remain. Let him there meditate on his Talmud until he learns a conduct more becoming his birth and parts, and not so disgraceful to the ancient religion to which he has become a proselyte; or until some persons from your side of the water, to please your new Hebrew brethren, shall ransom him. He may then be enabled to purchase with the old boards of the synagogue and a very small poundage on the long compound interest of the thirty pieces of silver (Dr. Price has shown us what miracles compound interest will perform in 1790 years), the lands which are lately discovered to have been usurped by the Gallican church. Send us your Popish archbishop of Paris, and we will send you our Protestant Rabbi. We shall treat the person you send us in exchange like a gentleman and an honest man, as he is; but pray let him bring with him the fund of his hospitality, bounty, and charity, and, depend upon it, we shall never confiscate a shilling of that honorable and pious fund, nor think of enriching the treasury with the spoils of the poor-box.

To tell you the truth, my dear Sir, I think the honor of our nation to be somewhat concerned in the disclaimer of the proceedings of this society of the Old Jewry and the London Tavern. I have no man's proxy. I speak only for myself when I disclaim, as I do with all possible earnestness, all communion with the actors in that triumph or with the admirers of it. When I assert anything else as concerning the people of England, I speak from observation, not from authority, but I speak from the experience I have had in a pretty extensive and mixed communication with the inhabitants of this kingdom, of all descriptions and ranks, and after a course of attentive observations begun early in life and continued for nearly forty years. I have often been astonished, considering that we are divided from you but by a slender dyke of about twenty-four miles, and that the mutual association between the two countries has lately been very great, to find how little you seem to know of us. I suspect that this is owing to your forming a judgment of this nation from certain publications which do very erroneously, if they do at all, represent the opinions and dispositions generally prevalent in England. The vanity, restlessness, petulance, and spirit of intrigue, of several petty cabals, who attempt to hide their total want of consequence in bustle and noise, and puffing, and mutual quotation of each other, makes you imagine that our contemptuous neglect of their abilities is a mark of general acquiescence in their opinions. No such thing, I assure you. Because half a dozen grasshoppers under a fern make the field ring with their importunate chirp, whilst thousands of great cattle, reposed beneath the shadow of the British oak, chew the cud and are silent, pray do not imagine that those who make the noise are the only inhabitants of the field; that, of course, they are many in number, or that, after all, they are other than the little, shriveled, meager, hopping, though loud and troublesome, insects of the hour.

I almost venture to affirm that not one in a hundred amongst us participates in the "triumph" of the Revolution Society. If the king and queen of France, and their children, were to fall into our hands by the chance of war, in the most acrimonious of all hostilities (I deprecate such an event, I deprecate such hostility), they would be treated with another sort of triumphal entry into London. We formerly have had a king of France in that situation; you have read how he was treated by the victor in the field, and in what manner he was afterwards received in England. Four hundred years have gone over us, but I believe we are not materially changed since that period. Thanks to our sullen resistance to innovation, thanks to the cold sluggishness of our national character, we still bear the stamp of our forefathers. We have not (as I conceive) lost the generosity and dignity of thinking of the fourteenth century, nor as yet have we subtilized ourselves into savages. We are not the converts of Rousseau; we are not the disciples of Voltaire; Helvetius has made no progress amongst us. Atheists are not our preachers; madmen are not our lawgivers. We know that we have made no discoveries, and we think that no discoveries are to be made in morality, nor many in the great principles of government, nor in the ideas of liberty, which were understood long before we were born, altogether as well as they will be after the grace has heaped its mold upon our presumption and the silent tomb shall have imposed its law on our pert loquacity. In England we have not yet been completely embowelled of our natural entrails; we still feel within us, and we cherish and cultivate, those inbred sentiments which are the faithful guardians, the active monitors of our duty, the true supporters of all liberal and manly morals. We have not been drawn and trussed, in order that we may be filled, like stuffed birds in a museum, with chaff and rags and paltry blurred shreds of paper about the rights of men. We preserve the whole of our feelings still native and entire, unsophisticated by pedantry and infidelity. We have real hearts of flesh and blood beating in our bosoms. We fear God; we look up with awe to kings, with affection to parliaments, with duty to magistrates, with reverence to priests, and with respect to nobility. Why? Because when such ideas are brought before our minds, it is natural to be so affected; because all other feelings are false and spurious and tend to corrupt our minds, to vitiate our primary morals, to render us unfit for rational liberty, and, by teaching us a servile, licentious, and abandoned insolence, to be our low sport for a few holidays, to make us perfectly fit for, and justly deserving of, slavery through the whole course of our lives.

Value in Prejudice and Wisdom from the Past

You see, Sir, that in this enlightened age I am bold enough to confess that we are generally men of untaught feelings, that, instead of casting away all our old prejudices, we cherish them to a very considerable degree, and, to take more shame to ourselves, we cherish them because they are prejudices; and the longer they have lasted and the more generally they have prevailed, the more we cherish them. We are afraid to put men to live and trade each on his own private stock of reason, because we suspect that this stock in each man is small, and that the individuals would do better to avail themselves of the general bank and capital of nations and of ages. Many of our men of speculation, instead of exploding general prejudices, employ their sagacity to discover the latent wisdom which prevails in them. If they find what they seek, and they seldom fail, they think it more wise to continue the prejudice, with the reason involved, than to cast away the coat of prejudice and to leave nothing but the naked reason; because prejudice, with its reason, has a motive to give action to that reason, and an affection which will give it permanence. Prejudice is of ready application in the emergency; it previously engages the mind in a steady course of wisdom and virtue and does not leave the man hesitating in the moment of decision skeptical, puzzled, and unresolved. Prejudice renders a man's virtue his habit, and not a series of unconnected acts. Through just prejudice, his duty becomes a part of his nature.

Your literary men and your politicians, and so do the whole clan of the enlightened among us, essentially differ in these points. They have no respect for the wisdom of others, but they pay it off by a very full measure of confidence in their own. With them it is a sufficient motive to destroy an old scheme of things because it is an old one. As to the new, they are in no sort of fear with regard to the duration of a building run up in haste, because duration is no object to those who think little or nothing has been done before their time, and who place all their hopes in discovery. They conceive, very systematically, that all things which give perpetuity are mischievous, and therefore they are at inexpiable war with all establishments. They think that government may vary like modes of dress, and with as little ill effect; that there needs no principle of attachment, except a sense of present convenience, to any constitution of the state. They always speak as if they were of opinion that there is a singular species of compact between them and their magistrates which binds the magistrate, but which has nothing reciprocal in it, but that the majesty of the people has a right to dissolve it without any reason but its will. Their attachment to their country itself is only so far as it agrees with some of their fleeting projects; it begins and ends with that scheme of polity which falls in with their momentary opinion.

These doctrines, or rather sentiments, seem prevalent with your new statesmen. But they are wholly different from those on which we have always acted in this country.

I hear it is sometimes given out in France that what is doing among you is after the example of England. I beg leave to affirm that scarcely anything done with you has originated from the practice or the prevalent opinions of this people, either in the act or in the spirit of the proceeding. Let me add that we are as unwilling to learn these lessons from France as we are sure that we never taught them to that nation. The cabals here who take a sort of share of your transactions as yet consist of but a handful of people. If, unfortunately, by their intrigues, their sermons, their publications, and by a confidence derived from an expected union with the counsels and forces of the French nation, they should draw considerable numbers into their faction, and in consequence should seriously attempt anything here in imitation of what has been done with you, the event, I dare venture to prophesy, will be that, with some trouble to their country, they will soon accomplish their own destruction. This people refused to change their law in remote ages from respect to the infallibility of popes, and they will not now alter it from a pious implicit faith in the dogmatism of philosophers, though the former was armed with the anathema and crusade, and though the latter should act with the libel and the lamp-iron.

Formerly, your affairs were your own concern only. We felt for them as men, but we kept aloof from them because we were not citizens of France. But when we see the model held up to ourselves, we must feel as Englishmen, and feeling, we must provide as Englishmen. Your affairs, in spite of us, are made a part of our interest, so far at least as to keep at a distance your panacea, or your plague. If it be a panacea, we do not want it. We know the consequences of unnecessary physic. If it be a plague, it is such a plague that the precautions of the most severe quarantine ought to be established against it.

I hear on all hands that a cabal calling itself philosophic receives the glory of many of the late proceedings, and that their opinions and systems are the true actuating spirit of the whole of them. I have heard of no party in England, literary or political, at any time, known by such a description. It is not with you composed of those men, is it, whom the vulgar in their blunt, homely style commonly call atheists and infidels? If it be, I admit that we, too, have had writers of that description who made some noise in their day. At present they repose in lasting oblivion. Who, born within the last forty years, has read one word of Collins, and Toland, and Tindal, and Chubb, and Morgan, and that whole race who called themselves Freethinkers? Who now reads Bolingbroke? Who ever read him through? Ask the booksellers of London what is become of all these lights of the world. In as few years their few successors will go to the family vault of "all the Capulets." But whatever they were, or are, with us, they were and are wholly unconnected individuals. With us they kept the common nature of their kind and were not gregarious. They never acted in corps or were known as a faction in the state, nor presumed to influence in that name or character, or for the purposes of such a faction, on any of our public concerns. Whether they ought so to exist and so be permitted to act is another question. As such cabals have not existed in England, so neither has the spirit of them had any influence in establishing the original frame of our constitution or in any one of the several reparations and improvements it has undergone. The whole has been done under the auspices, and is confirmed by the sanctions, of religion and piety. The whole has emanated from the simplicity of our national character and from a sort of native plainness and directness of understanding, which for a long time characterized those men who have successively obtained authority amongst us. This disposition still remains, at least in the great body of the people.

XI
BASIS of CIVIL SOCIETY: THE CHURCH

We know, and what is better, we feel inwardly, that religion is the basis of civil society and the source of all good and of all comfort. In England we are so convinced of this, that there is no rust of superstition with which the accumulated absurdity of the human mind might have crusted it over in the course of ages, that ninety-nine in a hundred of the people of England would not prefer to impiety. We shall never be such fools as to call in an enemy to the substance of any system to remove its corruptions, to supply its defects, or to perfect its construction. If our religious tenets should ever want a further elucidation, we shall not call on atheism to explain them. We shall not light up our temple from that unhallowed fire. It will be illuminated with other lights. It will be perfumed with other incense than the infectious stuff which is imported by the smugglers of adulterated metaphysics. If our ecclesiastical establishment should want a revision, it is not avarice or rapacity, public or private, that we shall employ for the audit, or receipt, or application of its consecrated revenue. Violently condemning neither the Greek nor the Armenian, nor, since heats are subsided, the Roman system of religion, we prefer the Protestant, not because we think it has less of the Christian religion in it, but because, in our judgment, it has more. We are Protestants, not from indifference, but from zeal.

We know, and it is our pride to know, that man is by his constitution a religious animal; that atheism is against, not only our reason, but our instincts; and that it cannot prevail long. But if, in the moment of riot and in a drunken delirium from the hot spirit drawn out of the alembic of hell, which in France is now so furiously boiling, we should uncover our nakedness by throwing off that Christian religion which has hitherto been our boast and comfort, and one great source of civilization amongst us and amongst many other nations, we are apprehensive (being well aware that the mind will not endure a void) that some uncouth, pernicious, and degrading superstition might take place of it.

For that reason, before we take from our establishment the natural, human means of estimation and give it up to contempt, as you have done, and in doing it have incurred the penalties you well deserve to suffer, we desire that some other may be presented to us in the place of it. We shall then form our judgment.

On these ideas, instead of quarrelling with establishments, as some do who have made a philosophy and a religion of their hostility to such institutions, we cleave closely to them. We are resolved to keep an established church, an established monarchy, an established aristocracy, and an established democracy, each in the degree it exists, and in no greater. I shall show you presently how much of each of these we possess.

It has been the misfortune (not, as these gentlemen think it, the glory) of this age that everything is to be discussed as if the constitution of our country were to be always a subject rather of altercation than enjoyment. For this reason, as well as for the satisfaction of those among you (if any such you have among you) who may wish to profit of examples, I venture to trouble you with a few thoughts upon each of these establishments. I do not think they were unwise in ancient Rome who, when they wished to remodel their laws, set commissioners to examine the best constituted republics within their reach.

The Church Establishment Consecrates the State

First, I beg leave to speak of our church establishment, which is the first of our prejudices, not a prejudice destitute of reason, but involving in it profound and extensive wisdom. I speak of it first. It is first and last and midst in our minds. For, taking ground on that religious system of which we are now in possession, we continue to act on the early received and uniformly continued sense of mankind. That sense not only, like a wise architect, hath built up the august fabric of states, but, like a provident proprietor, to preserve the structure from profanation and ruin, as a sacred temple purged from all the impurities of fraud and violence and injustice and tyranny, hath solemnly and forever consecrated the commonwealth and all that officiate in it. This consecration is made that all who administer the government of men, in which they stand in the person of God himself, should have high and worthy notions of their function and destination, that their hope should be full of immortality, that they should not look to the paltry pelf of the moment nor to the temporary and transient praise of the vulgar, but to a solid, permanent existence in the permanent part of their nature, and to a permanent fame and glory in the example they leave as a rich inheritance to the world.

Such sublime principles ought to be infused into persons of exalted situations, and religious establishments provided that may continually revive and enforce them. Every sort of moral, every sort of civil, every sort of politic institution, aiding the rational and natural ties that connect the human understanding and affections to the divine, are not more than necessary in order to build up that wonderful structure Man, whose prerogative it is to be in a great degree a creature of his own making, and who, when made as he ought to be made, is destined to hold no trivial place in the creation. But whenever man is put over men, as the better nature ought ever to preside, in that case more particularly, he should as nearly as possible be approximated to his perfection.

The consecration of the state by a state religious establishment is necessary, also, to operate with a wholesome awe upon free citizens, because, in order to secure their freedom, they must enjoy some determinate portion of power. To them, therefore, a religion connected with the state, and with their duty toward it, becomes even more necessary than in such societies where the people, by the terms of their subjection, are confined to private sentiments and the management of their own family concerns. All persons possessing any portion of power ought to be strongly and awfully impressed with an idea that they act in trust, and that they are to account for their conduct in that trust to the one great Master, Author, and Founder of society.

This principle ought even to be more strongly impressed upon the minds of those who compose the collective sovereignty than upon those of single princes. Without instruments, these princes can do nothing. Whoever uses instruments, in finding helps, finds also impediments. Their power is, therefore, by no means complete, nor are they safe in extreme abuse. Such persons, however elevated by flattery, arrogance, and self-opinion, must be sensible that, whether covered or not by positive law, in some way or other they are accountable even here for the abuse of their trust. If they are not cut off by a rebellion of their people, they may be strangled by the very guards kept for their security against all other rebellion. Thus we have seen the king of France sold by his soldiers for an increase of pay. But where popular authority is absolute and unrestrained, the people have an infinitely greater, because a far better founded, confidence in their own power. They are themselves, in a great measure, their own instruments. They are nearer to their objects. Besides, they are less under responsibility to one of the greatest controlling powers on the earth, the sense of fame and estimation. The share of infamy that is likely to fall to the lot of each individual in public acts is small indeed, the operation of opinion being in the inverse ratio to the number of those who abuse power. Their own approbation of their own acts has to them the appearance of a public judgment in their favor. A perfect democracy is, therefore, the most shameless thing in the world. As it is the most shameless, it is also the most fearless. No man apprehends in his person that he can be made subject to punishment. Certainly the people at large never ought, for as all punishments are for example toward the conservation of the people at large, the people at large can never become the subject of punishment by any human hand. It is therefore of infinite importance that they should not be suffered to imagine that their will, any more than that of kings, is the standard of right and wrong. They ought to be persuaded that they are full as little entitled, and far less qualified with safety to themselves, to use any arbitrary power whatsoever; that therefore they are not, under a false show of liberty, but in truth to exercise an unnatural, inverted domination, tyrannically to exact from those who officiate in the state not an entire devotion to their interest, which is their right, but an abject submission to their occasional will, extinguishing thereby in all those who serve them all moral principle, all sense of dignity, all use of judgment, and all consistency of character; whilst by the very same process they give themselves up a proper, a suitable, but a most contemptible prey to the servile ambition of popular sycophants or courtly flatterers.

When the people have emptied themselves of all the lust of selfish will, which without religion it is utterly impossible they ever should, when they are conscious that they exercise, and exercise perhaps in a higher link of the order of delegation, the power, which to be legitimate must be according to that eternal, immutable law in which will and reason are the same, they will be more careful how they place power in base and incapable hands. In their nomination to office, they will not appoint to the exercise of authority as to a pitiful job, but as to a holy function, not according to their sordid, selfish interest, nor to their wanton caprice, nor to their arbitrary will, but they will confer that power (which any man may well tremble to give or to receive) on those only in whom they may discern that predominant proportion of active virtue and wisdom, taken together and fitted to the charge, such as in the great and inevitable mixed mass of human imperfections and infirmities is to be found.

When they are habitually convinced that no evil can be acceptable, either in the act or the permission, to him whose essence is good, they will be better able to extirpate out of the minds of all magistrates, civil, ecclesiastical, or military, anything that bears the least resemblance to a proud and lawless domination.

Provides Stability and Continuity with the Past

But one of the first and most leading principles on which the commonwealth and the laws are consecrated is, lest the temporary possessors and life-renters in it, unmindful of what they have received from their ancestors or of what is due to their posterity, should act as if they were the entire masters, that they should not think it among their rights to cut off the entail or commit waste on the inheritance by destroying at their pleasure the whole original fabric of their society, hazarding to leave to those who come after them a ruin instead of an habitation—and teaching these successors as little to respect their contrivances as they had themselves respected the institutions of their forefathers. By this unprincipled facility of changing the state as often, and as much, and in as many ways as there are floating fancies or fashions, the whole chain and continuity of the commonwealth would be broken. No one generation could link with the other. Men would become little better than the flies of a summer.

And first of all, the science of jurisprudence, the pride of the human intellect, which with all its defects, redundancies, and errors is the collected reason of ages, combining the principles of original justice with the infinite variety of human concerns, as a heap of old exploded errors, would be no longer studied. Personal self-sufficiency and arrogance (the certain attendants upon all those who have never experienced a wisdom greater than their own) would usurp the tribunal. Of course, no certain laws, establishing invariable grounds of hope and fear, would keep the actions of men in a certain course or direct them to a certain end. Nothing stable in the modes of holding property or exercising function could form a solid ground on which any parent could speculate in the education of his offspring or in a choice for their future establishment in the world. No principles would be early worked into the habits. As soon as the most able instructor had completed his laborious course of institution, instead of sending forth his pupil, accomplished in a virtuous discipline, fitted to procure him attention and respect in his place in society, he would find everything altered, and that he had turned out a poor creature to the contempt and derision of the world, ignorant of the true grounds of estimation. Who would insure a tender and delicate sense of honor to beat almost with the first pulses of the heart when no man could know what would be the test of honor in a nation continually varying the standard of its coin? No part of life would retain its acquisitions. Barbarism with regard to science and literature, unskillfulness with regard to arts and manufactures, would infallibly succeed to the want of a steady education and settled principle; and thus the commonwealth itself would, in a few generations, crumble away, be disconnected into the dust and powder of individuality, and at length dispersed to all the winds of heaven.

To avoid, therefore, the evils of inconstancy and versatility, ten thousand times worse than those of obstinacy and the blindest prejudice, we have consecrated the state, that no man should approach to look into its defects or corruptions but with due caution, that he should never dream of beginning its reformation by its subversion, that he should approach to the faults of the state as to the wounds of a father, with pious awe and trembling solicitude. By this wise prejudice we are taught to look with horror on those children of their country who are prompt rashly to hack that aged parent in pieces and put him into the kettle of magicians, in hopes that by their poisonous weeds and wild incantations they may regenerate the paternal constitution and renovate their father's life.

Society is indeed a contract. Subordinate contracts for objects of mere occasional interest may be dissolved at pleasure—but the state ought not to be considered as nothing better than a partnership agreement in a trade of pepper and coffee, calico, or tobacco, or some other such low concern, to be taken up for a little temporary interest, and to be dissolved by the fancy of the parties. It is to be looked on with other reverence, because it is not a partnership in things subservient only to the gross animal existence of a temporary and perishable nature. It is a partnership in all science; a partnership in all art; a partnership in every virtue and in all perfection.

As the ends of such a partnership cannot be obtained in many generations, it becomes a partnership not only between those who are living, but between those who are living, those who are dead, and those who are to be born. Each contract of each particular state is but a clause in the great primeval contract of eternal society, linking the lower with the higher natures, connecting the visible and invisible world, according to a fixed compact sanctioned by the inviolable oath which holds all physical and all moral natures, each in their appointed place. This law is not subject to the will of those who by an obligation above them, and infinitely superior, are bound to submit their will to that law. The municipal corporations of that universal kingdom are not morally at liberty at their pleasure, and on their speculations of a contingent improvement, wholly to separate and tear asunder the bands of their subordinate community and to dissolve it into an unsocial, uncivil, unconnected chaos of elementary principles. It is the first and supreme necessity only, a necessity that is not chosen but chooses, a necessity paramount to deliberation, that admits no discussion and demands no evidence, which alone can justify a resort to anarchy. This necessity is no exception to the rule, because this necessity itself is a part, too, of that moral and physical disposition of things to which man must be obedient by consent or force; but if that which is only submission to necessity should be made the object of choice, the law is broken, nature is disobeyed, and the rebellious are outlawed, cast forth, and exiled from this world of reason, and order, and peace, and virtue, and fruitful penitence, into the antagonist world of madness, discord, vice, confusion, and unavailing sorrow.

Religion Is the Foundation of the English Constitution

These, my dear Sir, are, were, and, I think, long will be the sentiments of not the least learned and reflecting part of this kingdom. They who are included in this description form their opinions on such grounds as such persons ought to form them. The less inquiring receive them from an authority which those whom Providence dooms to live on trust need not be ashamed to rely on. These two sorts of men move in the same direction, though in a different place. They both move with the order of the universe. They all know or feel this great ancient truth: *Quod illi principi et praepotenti Deo qui omnem hunc mundum regit, nihil eorum quae quidem fiant in terris acceptius quam concilia et coetus hominum jure sociati quae civitates appellantur.*[23] They take this tenet of the head and heart, not from the great name which it immediately bears, nor from the greater from whence it is derived, but from that which alone can give true weight and sanction to any learned opinion, the common nature and common relation of men. Persuaded that all things ought to be done with reference, and referring all to the point of reference to which all should be directed, they think themselves bound, not only as individuals in the sanctuary of the heart or as congregated in that personal capacity, to renew the memory of their high origin and cast, but also in their corporate character to perform their national homage to the institutor and author and protector of civil society; without which civil society man could not by any possibility arrive at the perfection of which his nature is capable, nor even make a remote and faint approach to it. They conceive that He who gave our nature to be perfected by our virtue willed also the necessary means of its perfection. He willed therefore the state—He willed its connection with the source and original archetype of all perfection. They who are convinced of this His will, which is the law of laws and the sovereign of sovereigns, cannot think it reprehensible that this our corporate fealty and homage, that this our recognition of a seigniory paramount, I had almost said this oblation of the state itself as a worthy offering on the high altar of universal praise, should be performed as all public, solemn acts are performed, in buildings, in music, in decoration, in speech, in the dignity of persons, according to the customs of mankind taught by their nature; that is, with modest splendor and unassuming state, with mild

---

23 To the great and all-powerful God who rules this whole universe, of the things that take place on earth nothing is more pleasing than the gatherings and societies of men united by law, which are called states.

majesty and sober pomp. For those purposes they think some part of the wealth of the country is as usefully employed as it can be in fomenting the luxury of individuals. It is the public ornament. It is the public consolation. It nourishes the public hope. The poorest man finds his own importance and dignity in it, whilst the wealth and pride of individuals at every moment makes the man of humble rank and fortune sensible of his inferiority and degrades and vilifies his condition. It is for the man in humble life, and to raise his nature and to put him in mind of a state in which the privileges of opulence will cease, when he will be equal by nature, and may be more than equal by virtue, that this portion of the general wealth of his country is employed and sanctified.

I assure you I do not aim at singularity. I give you opinions which have been accepted amongst us, from very early times to this moment, with a continued and general approbation, and which indeed are worked into my mind that I am unable to distinguish what I have learned from others from the results of my own meditation.

It is on some such principles that the majority of the people of England, far from thinking a religious national establishment unlawful, hardly think it lawful to be without one. In France you are wholly mistaken if you do not believe us above all other things attached to it, and beyond all other nations; and when this people has acted unwisely and unjustifiably in its favor (as in some instances they have done most certainly), in their very errors you will at least discover their zeal.

This principle runs through the whole system of their polity. They do not consider their church establishment as convenient, but as essential to their state, not as a thing heterogeneous and separable, something added for accommodation, what they may either keep or lay aside according to their temporary ideas of convenience. They consider it as the foundation of their whole constitution, with which, and with every part of which, it holds an indissoluble union. Church and state are ideas inseparable in their minds, and scarcely is the one ever mentioned without mentioning the other.

Education by the Church Independently Furthers These Principles

Our education is so formed as to confirm and fix this impression. Our education is in a manner wholly in the hands of ecclesiastics, and in all stages from infancy to manhood. Even when our youth, leaving schools and universities, enter that most important period of life which begins to link experience and study together, and when with that view they visit other countries, instead of old domestics whom we have seen as governors to principal men from other parts, three-fourths of those who go abroad with our young nobility and gentlemen are ecclesiastics, not as austere masters, nor as mere followers, but as friends and companions of a graver character, and not seldom persons as well-born as themselves. With them, as relations, they most constantly keep a close connection through life. By this connection we conceive that we attach our gentlemen to the church, and we liberalize the church by an dealings with the leading characters of the country.

So tenacious are we of the old ecclesiastical modes and fashions of institution that very little alteration has been made in them since the fourteenth or fifteenth century; adhering in this particular, as in all things else, to our old settled maxim, never entirely nor at once to depart from antiquity. We found these old institutions, on the whole, favorable to morality and discipline, and we thought they were susceptible of amendment without altering the ground. We thought that they were capable of receiving and meliorating, and above all of preserving, the accessions of science and literature, as the order of Providence should successively produce them. And after all, with this Gothic and monkish education (for such it is in the groundwork) we may put in our claim to as ample and as early a share in all the improvements in science, in arts, and in literature which have illuminated and adorned the modern world, as any other nation in Europe. We think one main cause of this improvement was our not despising the patrimony of knowledge which was left us by our forefathers.

It is from our attachment to a church establishment that the English nation did not think it wise to entrust that great, fundamental interest of the whole to what they trust no part of their civil or military public service, that is, to the unsteady and precarious contribution of individuals. They go further. They certainly never have suffered, and never will suffer, the fixed estate of the church to be converted into a pension, to depend on the treasury and to be delayed, withheld, or perhaps to be extinguished by fiscal difficulties, which difficulties may sometimes be pretended for political purposes, and are in fact often brought on by the extravagance, negligence, and rapacity of politicians. The people of England think that they have constitutional motives, as well as religious, against any project of turning their independent clergy into ecclesiastical pensioners of state. They tremble for their liberty, from the influence of a clergy dependent on the crown; they tremble for the public tranquility from the disorders of a factious clergy, if it were made to depend upon any other than the crown. They therefore made their church, like their king and their nobility, independent.

From the united considerations of religion and constitutional policy, from their opinion of a duty to make sure provision for the consolation of the feeble and the instruction of the ignorant, they have incorporated and identified the estate of the church with the mass of private property, of which the state is not the proprietor, either for use or dominion, but the guardian only and the regulator. They have ordained that the provision of this establishment might be as stable as the earth on which it stands, and should not fluctuate with the Euripus of funds and actions.

Religion for the Humble and Exalted

The men of England, the men, I mean, of light and leading in England, whose wisdom (if they have any) is open and direct, would be ashamed, as of a silly deceitful trick, to profess any religion in name which, by their proceedings, they appear to condemn. If by their conduct (the only language that rarely lies) they seemed to regard the great ruling principle of the moral and the natural world as a mere invention to keep the vulgar in obedience, they apprehend that by such a conduct they would defeat the politic purpose they have in view. They would find it difficult to make others believe in a system to which they manifestly give no credit themselves. The Christian statesmen of this land would indeed first provide for the multitude, because it is the multitude, and is therefore, as such, the first object in the ecclesiastical institution, and in all institutions. They have been taught that the circumstance of the gospel's being preached to the poor was one of the great tests of its true mission. They think, therefore, that those do not believe it who do not take care it should be preached to the poor. But as they know that charity is not confined to any one description, but ought to apply itself to all men who have wants, they are not deprived of a due and anxious sensation of pity to the distresses of the miserable great. They are not repelled through a fastidious delicacy, at the stench of their arrogance and presumption, from a medicinal attention to their mental blotches and running sores. They are sensible that religious instruction is of more consequence to them than to any others—from the greatness of the temptation to which they are exposed; from the important consequences that attend their faults; from the contagion of their ill example; from the necessity of bowing down the stubborn neck of their pride and ambition to the yoke of moderation and virtue; from a consideration of the fat stupidity and gross ignorance concerning what is most important for men to know, which prevails at courts, and at the head of armies, and in senates as much as at the loom and in the field.

The English people are satisfied that to the great the consolations of religion are as necessary as its instructions. They, too, are among the unhappy. They feel personal pain and domestic sorrow. In these they have no privilege, but are subject to pay their full contingent to the contributions levied on mortality. They want this sovereign balm under their gnawing cares and anxieties, which, being less conversant about the limited wants of animal life, range without limit, and are diversified by infinite combinations, in the wild and unbounded regions of imagination. Some charitable dole is wanting to these our often very unhappy brethren to fill the gloomy void that reigns in minds which have nothing on earth to hope or fear; something to relieve in the killing languor and over-labored lassitude of those who have nothing to do; something to excite an appetite to existence in the palled satiety which attends on all pleasures which may be bought where nature is not left to her own process, where even desire is anticipated, and therefore frui-tion defeated by meditated schemes and contrivances of delight; and no interval, no obstacle, is interposed between the wish and the accomplishment.

The people of England know how little influence the teachers of religion are likely to have with the wealthy and powerful of long standing, and how much less with the newly fortunate, if they ap-pear in a manner no way assorted to those with whom they must associate, and over whom they must even exercise, in some cases, something like an authority. What must they think of that body of teachers if they see it in no part above the establishment of their domestic servants? If the poverty were voluntary, there might be some difference. Strong instances of self-denial operate powerfully on our minds, and a man who has no wants has obtained great free-dom and firmness and even dignity. But as the mass of any descrip-tion of men are but men, and their poverty cannot be voluntary, that disrespect which attends upon all lay poverty will not depart from the ecclesiastical. Our provident constitution has therefore taken care that those who are to instruct presumptuous ignorance, those who are to be censors over insolent vice, should neither incur their contempt nor live upon their alms, nor will it tempt the rich to a neglect of the true medicine of their minds. For these reasons, whilst we provide first for the poor, and with a parental solicitude, we have not relegated religion (like something we were ashamed to show) to obscure municipalities or rustic villages. No! We will have her to exalt her mitred front in courts and parliaments. We will have her mixed throughout the whole mass of life and blended with all the classes of society. The people of England will show to the haughty potentates of the world, and to their talking sophisters, that a free, a generous, an informed nation honors the high magistrates of its church; that it will not suffer the insolence of wealth and titles, or any other species of proud pretension, to look down with scorn upon what they looked up to with reverence; nor presume to trample on that acquired personal nobility which they intend always to be, and which often is, the fruit, not the reward (for what can be the reward?) of learning, piety, and virtue. They can see, without pain or grudging, an archbishop precede a duke. They can see a bishop of Durham, or a bishop of Winchester, in possession of ten thousand pounds a year, and cannot conceive why it is in worse hands than estates to the like amount in the hands of this earl or that squire, although it may be true that so many dogs and horses are not kept by the former and fed with the victuals which ought to nourish the children of the people. It is true, the whole church revenue is not always employed, and to every shilling, in charity, nor perhaps ought it, but something is generally employed. It is better to cherish virtue and humanity by leaving much to free will, even with some loss to the object, than to attempt to make men mere machines and instruments of a political benevolence. The world on the whole will gain by a liberty without which virtue cannot exist.

Property of the Church:
Introduction to the Problem of Confiscation

When once the commonwealth has established the estates of the church as property, it can, consistently, hear nothing of the more or the less. "Too much" and "too little" are treason against property. What evil can arise from the quantity in any hand whilst the supreme authority has the full, sovereign superintendence over this, as over all property, to prevent every species of abuse, and, whenever it notably deviates, to give to it a direction agreeable to the purposes of its institution?

In England most of us conceive that it is envy and malignity toward those who are often the beginners of their own fortune, and not a love of the self-denial and mortification of the ancient church, that makes some look askance at the distinctions, and honors, and revenues which, taken from no person, are set apart for virtue. The ears of the people of England are distinguishing. They hear these men speak broad. Their tongue betrays them. Their language is in the patois of fraud, in the cant and gibberish of hypocrisy. The people of England must think so when these praters affect to carry back the clergy to that primitive, evangelic poverty which, in the spirit, ought always to exist in them (and in us, too, however we may like it), but in the thing must be varied when the relation of that body to the state is altered—when manners, when modes of life, when indeed the whole order of human affairs has undergone a total revolution. We shall believe those reformers, then, to be honest enthusiasts, not, as now we think them, cheats and deceivers, when we see them throwing their own goods into common and submitting their own persons to the austere discipline of the early church.

With these ideas rooted in their minds, the commons of Great Britain, in the national emergencies, will never seek their resource from the confiscation of the estates of the church and poor. Sacrilege and proscription are not among the ways and means of our committee of supply. The Jews in Change Alley have not yet dared to hint their hopes of a mortgage on the revenues belonging to the see of Canterbury. I am not afraid that I shall be disavowed when I assure you that there is not one public man in this kingdom whom you would wish to quote, no, not one, of any party or description, who does not reprobate the dishonest, perfidious, and cruel confiscation which the National Assembly has been compelled to make of that property which it was their first duty to protect.

It is with the exultation of a little national pride I tell you that those amongst us who have wished to pledge the societies of Paris in the cup of their abominations have been disappointed. The robbery of your church has proved a security to the possession of ours. It has roused the people. They see with horror and alarm that enormous and shameless act of proscription. It has opened, and will more and more open, their eyes upon the selfish enlargement of mind and the narrow liberality of sentiment of insidious men, which, commencing in close hypocrisy and fraud, have ended in open violence and rapine. At home we behold similar beginnings. We are on our guard against similar conclusions.

XII
CONFISCATION of CHURCH PROPERTY

I hope we shall never be so totally lost to all sense of the duties imposed upon us by the law of social union as, upon any pretext of public service, to confiscate the goods of a single unoffending citizen. Who but a tyrant (a name expressive of everything which can vitiate and degrade human nature) could think of seizing on the property of men unaccused, unheard, untried, by whole descriptions, by hundreds and thousands together? Who that had not lost every trace of humanity could think of casting down men of exalted rank and sacred function, some of them of an age to call at once for reverence and compassion, of casting them down from the highest situation in the commonwealth, wherein they were maintained by their own landed property, to a state of indigence, depression, and contempt?

The confiscators truly have made some allowance to their victims from the scraps and fragments of their own tables from which they have been so harshly driven, and which have been so bountifully spread for a feast to the harpies of usury. But to drive men from independence to live on alms is itself great cruelty. That which might be a tolerable condition to men in one state of life, and not habituated to other things, may, when all these circumstances are altered, be a dreadful revolution, and one to which a virtuous mind would feel pain in condemning any guilt except that which would demand the life of the offender. But to many minds this punishment of degradation and infamy is worse than death. Undoubtedly it is an infinite aggravation of this cruel suffering that the persons who were taught a double prejudice in favor of religion, by education and by the place they held in the administration of its functions, are to receive the remnants of their property as alms from the profane and impious hands of those who had plundered them of all the rest; to receive (if they are at all to receive), not from the charitable contributions of the faithful but from the insolent tenderness of known and avowed atheism, the maintenance of religion measured out to them on the standard of the contempt in which it is held, and for the purpose of rendering those who receive the allowance vile and of no estimation in the eyes of mankind.

But this act of seizure of property, it seems, is a judgment in law, and not a confiscation. They have, it seems, found out in the academies of the Palais Royal and the Jacobins that certain men had no right to the possessions which they held under law, usage, the decisions of courts, and the accumulated prescription of a thousand years. They say that ecclesiastics are fictitious persons, creatures of the state, whom at pleasure they may destroy, and of course limit and modify in every particular; that the goods they possess are not properly theirs but belong to the state which created the fiction; and we are therefore not to trouble ourselves with what they may suffer in their natural feelings and natural persons on account of what is done toward them in this their constructive character. Of what import is it under what names you injure men and deprive them of the just wages of a profession, in which they were not only permitted but encouraged by the state to engage, and upon the supposed certainty of which wages they had formed the plan of their lives, contracted debts, and led multitudes to an entire dependence upon them?

You do not imagine, Sir, that I am going to compliment this miserable distinction of persons with any long discussion. The arguments of tyranny are as contemptible as its force is dreadful. Had not your confiscators, by their early crimes, obtained a power which secures indemnity to all the crimes of which they have since been guilty or that they can commit, it is not the syllogism of the logician, but the lash of the executioner, that would have refuted a sophistry which becomes an accomplice of theft and murder. The sophistic tyrants of Paris are loud in their declamations against the departed regal tyrants, who in former ages have vexed the world. They are thus bold, because they are safe from the dungeons and iron cages of their old masters. Shall we be more tender of the tyrants of our own time, when we see them acting worse tragedies under our eyes? Shall we not use the same liberty that they do, when we can use it with the same safety—when to speak honest truth only requires a contempt of the opinions of those whose actions we abhor?

National Credit of France; Invalid Pretext for Confiscation

This outrage on all the rights of property was at first covered with what, on the system of their conduct, was the most astonishing of all pretexts—a regard to national faith. The enemies to property at first pretended a most tender, delicate, and scrupulous anxiety for keeping the king's engagements with the public creditor. These professors of the rights of men are so busy in teaching others that they have not leisure to learn anything themselves; otherwise they would have known that it is to the property of the citizen, and not to the demands of the creditor of the state, that the first and original faith of civil society is pledged. The claim of the citizen is prior in time, paramount in title, superior in equity. The fortunes of individuals, whether possessed by acquisition or by descent or in virtue of a participation in the goods of some community, were no part of the creditor's security, expressed or implied. They never so much as entered into his head when he made his bargain. He well knew that the public, whether represented by a monarch or by a senate, can pledge nothing but the public estate; and it can have no public estate except in what it derives from a just and proportioned imposition upon the citizens at large. This was engaged, and nothing else could be engaged, to the public creditor. No man can mortgage his injustice as a pawn for his fidelity.

It is impossible to avoid some observation on the contradictions caused by the extreme rigor and the extreme laxity of this new public faith which influenced in this transaction, and which influenced not according to the nature of the obligation, but to the description of the persons to whom it was engaged. No acts of the old government of the kings of France are held valid in the National Assembly except its pecuniary engagements: acts of all others of the most ambiguous legality. The rest of the acts of that royal government are considered in so odious a light that to have a claim under its authority is looked on as a sort of crime. A pension, given as a reward for service to the state, is surely as good a ground of property as any security for money advanced to the state. It is better; for money is paid, and well paid, to obtain that service. We have, however, seen multitudes of people under this description in France who never had been deprived of their allowances by the most arbitrary ministers in the most arbitrary times, by this assembly of the rights of men robbed without mercy. They were told, in answer to their claim to the bread earned with their blood, that their services had not been rendered to the country that now exists.

This laxity of public faith is not confined to those unfortunate persons. The Assembly, with perfect consistency it must be owned, is engaged in a respectable deliberation how far it is bound by the treaties made with other nations under the former government, and their committee is to report which of them they ought to ratify, and which not. By this means they have put the external fidelity of this virgin state on a par with its internal.

It is not easy to conceive upon what rational principle the royal government should not, of the two, rather have possessed the power of rewarding service and making treaties, in virtue of its prerogative, than that of pledging to creditors the revenue of the state, actual and possible. The treasure of the nation, of all things, has been the least allowed to the prerogative of the king of France or to the prerogative of any king in Europe. To mortgage the public revenue implies the sovereign dominion, in the fullest sense, over the public purse. It goes far beyond the trust even of a temporary and occasional taxation. The acts, however, of that dangerous power (the distinctive mark of a boundless despotism) have been alone held sacred. Whence arose this preference given by a democratic assembly to a body of property deriving its title from the most critical and obnoxious of all the exertions of monarchical authority? Reason can furnish nothing to reconcile inconsistency, nor can partial favor be accounted for upon equitable principles. But the contradiction and partiality which admit no justification are not the less without an adequate cause; and that cause I do not think it difficult to discover.

Monied Interests Are against the Church

By the vast debt of France a great monied interest had insensibly grown up, and with it a great power. By the ancient usages which prevailed in that kingdom, the general circulation of property, and in particular the mutual convertibility of land into money, and of money into land, had always been a matter of difficulty. Family settlements, rather more general and more strict than they are in England, the *jus retractus*, the great mass of landed property held by the crown, and, by a maxim of the French law, held unalienably, the vast estates of the ecclesiastical corporations—all these had kept the landed and monied interests more separated in France, less miscible, and the owners of the two distinct species of property not so well disposed to each other as they are in this country.

The monied property was long looked on with rather an evil eye by the people. They saw it connected with their distresses, and aggravating them. It was no less envied by the old landed interests, partly for the same reasons that rendered it obnoxious to the people, but much more so as it eclipsed, by the splendor of an ostentatious luxury, the unendowed pedigrees and naked titles of several among the nobility. Even when the nobility which represented the more permanent landed interest united themselves by marriage (which sometimes was the case) with the other description, the wealth which saved the family from ruin was supposed to contaminate and degrade it. Thus the enmities and heartburnings of these parties were increased even by the usual means by which discord is made to cease and quarrels are turned into friendship. In the meantime, the pride of the wealthy men, not noble or newly noble, increased with its cause. They felt with resentment an inferiority, the grounds of which they did not acknowledge. There was no measure to which they were not willing to lend themselves in order to be revenged of the outrages of this rival pride and to exalt their wealth to what they considered as its natural rank and estimation. They struck at the nobility through the crown and the church. They attacked them particularly on the side on which they thought them the most vulnerable, that is, the possessions of the church, which, through the patronage of the crown, generally devolved upon the nobility. The bishoprics and the great commendatory abbeys were, with few exceptions, held by that order.

In this state of real, though not always perceived, warfare between the noble ancient landed interest and the new monied interest, the greatest, because the most applicable, strength was in the hands of the latter. The monied interest is in its nature more ready for any adventure, and its possessors more disposed to new enterprises of any kind. Being of a recent acquisition, it falls in more naturally with any novelties. It is therefore the kind of wealth which will be resorted to by all who wish for change.

Men of Letters Are against the Church

Along with the monied interest, a new description of men had grown up with whom that interest soon formed a close and marked union—I mean the political men of letters. Men of letters, fond of distinguishing themselves, are rarely averse to innovation. Since the decline of the life and greatness of Louis the Fourteenth, they were not so much cultivated, either by him or by the regent or the successors to the crown, nor were they engaged to the court by favors and emoluments so systematically as during the splendid period of that ostentatious and not impolitic reign. What they lost in the old court protection, they endeavored to make up by joining in a sort of incorporation of their own; to which the two academies of France, and afterwards the vast undertaking of the Encyclopedia, carried on by a society of these gentlemen, did not a little contribute.

The literary cabal had some years ago formed something like a regular plan for the destruction of the Christian religion. This object they pursued with a degree of zeal which hitherto had been discovered only in the propagators of some system of piety. They were possessed with a spirit of proselytism in the most fanatical degree; and from thence, by an easy progress, with the spirit of persecution according to their means. What was not to be done toward their great end by any direct or immediate act might be wrought by a longer process through the medium of opinion. To command that opinion, the first step is to establish a dominion over those who direct it. They contrived to possess themselves, with great method and perseverance, of all the avenues to literary fame. Many of them indeed stood high in the ranks of literature and science. The world had done them justice and in favor of general talents forgave the evil tendency of their peculiar principles. This was true liberality, which they returned by endeavoring to confine the reputation of sense, learning, and taste to themselves or their followers. I will venture to say that this narrow, exclusive spirit has not been less prejudicial to literature and to taste than to morals and true philosophy. These atheistic fathers have a bigotry of their own, and they have learned to talk against monks with the spirit of a monk. But in some things they are men of the world. The resources of intrigue are called in to supply the defects of argument and wit. To this system of literary monopoly was joined an unremitting industry to blacken and discredit in every way, and by every means, all those who did not hold to their faction. To those who have observed the spirit of their conduct it has long been clear that nothing was wanted but the power of carrying the intolerance of the tongue and of the pen into a persecution which would strike at property, liberty, and life.

The desultory and faint persecution carried on against them, more from compliance with form and decency than with serious resentment, neither weakened their strength nor relaxed their efforts. The issue of the whole was that, what with opposition, and what with success, a violent and malignant zeal, of a kind hitherto unknown in the world, had taken an entire possession of their minds and rendered their whole conversation, which otherwise would have been pleasing and instructive, perfectly disgusting. A spirit of cabal, intrigue, and proselytism pervaded all their thoughts, words, and actions. And as controversial zeal soon turns its thoughts on force, they began to insinuate themselves into a correspondence with foreign princes, in hopes through their authority, which at first they flattered, they might bring about the changes they had in view. To them it was indifferent whether these changes were to be accomplished by the thunderbolt of despotism or by the earthquake of popular commotion. The correspondence between this cabal and the late king of Prussia will throw no small light upon the spirit of all their proceedings. For the same purpose for which they intrigued with princes, they cultivated, in a distinguished manner, the monied interest of France; and partly through the means furnished by those whose peculiar offices gave them the most extensive and certain means of communication, they carefully occupied all the avenues to opinion.

Writers, especially when they act in a body and with one direction, have great influence on the public mind; the alliance, therefore, of these writers with the monied interest had no small effect in removing the popular odium and envy which attended that species of wealth. These writers, like the propagators of all novelties, pretended to a great zeal for the poor and the lower orders, whilst in their satires they rendered hateful, by every exaggeration, the faults of courts, of nobility, and of priesthood. They became a sort of demagogues. They served as a link to unite, in favor of one object, obnoxious wealth to restless and desperate poverty.

As these two kinds of men appear principal leaders in all the late transactions, their junction and politics will serve to account, not upon any principles of law or of policy, but as a cause, for the general fury with which all the landed property of ecclesiastical corporations has been attacked; and the great care which, contrary to their pretended principles, has been taken of a monied interest originating from the authority of the crown. All the envy against wealth and power was artificially directed against other descriptions of riches. On what other principle than that which I have stated can we account for an appearance so extraordinary and unnatural as that of the ecclesiastical possessions, which had stood so many successions of ages and shocks of civil violence, and were girded at once by justice and by prejudice, being applied to the payment of debts comparatively recent, invidious, and contracted by a decried and subverted government?

Fraudulence and Madness of the Confiscation

Was the public estate a sufficient stake for the public debts? Assume that it was not, and that a loss must be incurred somewhere. When the only estate lawfully possessed, and which the contracting parties had in contemplation at the time in which their bargain was made, happens to fail, who according to the principles of natural and legal equity ought to be the sufferer? Certainly it ought to be either the party who trusted or the party who persuaded him to trust, or both, and not third parties who had no concern with the transaction. Upon any insolvency they ought to suffer who are weak enough to lend upon bad security, or they who fraudulently held out a security that was not valid. Laws are acquainted with no other rules of decision. But by the new institute of the rights of men, the only persons who in equity ought to suffer are the only persons who are to be saved harmless: those are to answer the debt who neither were lenders nor borrowers, mortgagers nor mortgagees.

What had the clergy to do with these transactions? What had they to do with any public engagement further than the extent of their own debt? To that, to be sure, their estates were bound to the last acre. Nothing can lead more to the true spirit of the Assembly, which sits for public confiscation, with its new equity and its new morality, than an attention to their proceeding with regard to this debt of the clergy. The body of confiscators, true to that monied interest for which they were false to every other, have found the clergy competent to incur a legal debt. Of course, they declared them legally entitled to the property which their power of incurring the debt and mortgaging the estate implied, recognizing the rights of those persecuted citizens in the very act in which they were thus grossly violated.

If, as I said, any persons are to make good deficiencies to the public creditor, besides the public at large, they must be those who managed the agreement. Why, therefore, are not the estates of all the comptrollers-general confiscated? Why not those of the long succession of ministers, financiers, and bankers who have been enriched whilst the nation was impoverished by their dealings and their counsels? Why is not the estate of M. Laborde declared forfeited rather than of the archbishop of Paris, who has had nothing to do in the creation or in the jobbing of the public funds? Or, if you must confiscate old landed estates in favor of the money-jobbers, why is the penalty confined to one description? I do not know whether the expenses of the Duke de Choiseul have left anything of the infinite sums which he had derived from the bounty of his master during the transactions of a reign which contributed largely by every species of prodigality in war and peace to the present debt of France. If any such remains, why is not this confiscated? I remember to have been in Paris during the time of the old government. I was there just after the Duke d'Aiguillon had been snatched (as it was generally thought) from the block by the hand of a protecting despotism. He was a minister and had some concern in the affairs of that prodigal period. Why do I not see his estate delivered up to the municipalities in which it is situated? The noble family of Noailles have long been servants (meritorious servants I admit) to the crown of France, and have had, of course, some share in its bounties. Why do I hear nothing of the application of their estates to the public debt? Why is the estate of the Duke de Rochefoucault more sacred than that of the Cardinal de Rochefoucault? The former is, I doubt not, a worthy person, and (if it were not a sort of profaneness to talk of the use, as affecting the title to the property) he makes a good use of his revenues; but it is no disrespect to him to say, what authentic information well warrants me in saying, that the use made of a property equally valid by his brother, the cardinal archbishop of Rouen, was far more laudable and far more public-spirited. Can one hear of the proscription of such persons and the confiscation of their effects without indignation and horror? He is not a man who does not feel such emotions on such occasions. He does not deserve the name of a freeman who will not express them.

Few barbarous conquerors have ever made so terrible a revolution in property. None of the heads of the Roman factions, when they established *crudelem illam hastam* in all their auctions of rapine,[24] have ever set up to sale the goods of the conquered citizen to such an enormous amount. It must be allowed in favor of those tyrants of antiquity that what was done by them could hardly be said to be done in cold blood. Their passions were inflamed, their tempers soured, their understandings confused with the spirit of revenge, with the innumerable reciprocated and recent inflictions and retaliations of blood and rapine. They were driven beyond all bounds of moderation by the apprehension of the return of power, with the return of property, to the families of those they had injured beyond all hope of forgiveness.

These Roman confiscators, who were yet only in the elements

---

24 That cruel spear.

of tyranny, and were not instructed in the rights of men to exercise all sorts of cruelties on each other without provocation, thought it necessary to spread a sort of color over their injustice. They considered the vanquished party as composed of traitors who had borne arms, or otherwise had acted with hostility, against the commonwealth. They regarded them as persons who had forfeited their property by their crimes. With you, in your improved state of the human mind, there was no such formality. You seized upon five millions sterling of annual rent and turned forty or fifty thousand human creatures out of their houses, because "such was your pleasure." The tyrant Harry the Eighth of England, as he was not better enlightened than the Roman Mariuses and Sullas, and had not studied in your new schools, did not know what an effectual instrument of despotism was to be found in that grand magazine of offensive weapons, the rights of men. When he resolved to rob the abbeys, as the club of the Jacobins have robbed all the ecclesiastics, he began by setting on foot a commission to examine into the crimes and abuses which prevailed in those communities. As it might be expected, his commission reported truths, exaggerations, and falsehoods. But truly or falsely, it reported abuses and offences. However, as abuses might be corrected, as every crime of persons does not infer a forfeiture with regard to communities, and as property, in that dark age, was not discovered to be a creature of prejudice, all those abuses (and there were enough of them) were hardly thought sufficient ground for such a confiscation as it was for his purpose to make. He, therefore, procured the formal surrender of these estates. All these operose proceedings were adopted by one of the most decided tyrants in the rolls of history as necessary preliminaries before he could venture, by bribing the members of his two servile houses with a share of the spoil and holding out to them an eternal immunity from taxation, to demand a confirmation of his iniquitous proceedings by an act of Parliament. Had fate reserved him to our times, four technical terms would have done his business and saved him all this trouble; he needed nothing more than one short form of incantation—"Philosophy, Light, Liberality, the Rights of Men."

I can say nothing in praise of those acts of tyranny which no voice has hitherto ever commended under any of their false colors, yet in these false colors an homage was paid by despotism to justice. The power which was above all fear and all remorse was not set above all shame. Whilst shame keeps its watch, virtue is not wholly extinguished in the heart, nor will moderation be utterly exiled from the minds of tyrants.

I believe every honest man sympathizes in his reflections with our political poet on that occasion, and will pray to avert the omen whenever these acts of rapacious despotism present themselves to his view or his imagination:

> *May no such storm*
> *Fall on our times, where ruin must reform.*
> *Tell me (my Muse) what monstrous dire offence,*
> *What crimes could any Christian king incense*
> *To such a rage? Was't luxury, or lust?*
> *Was he so temperate, so chaste, so just?*
> *Were these their crimes? they were his own much more,*
> *But wealth is crime enough to him that's poor.*

This same wealth, which is at all times treason and *lèze-nation*[25] to indigent and rapacious despotism, under all modes of polity, was your temptation to violate property, law, and religion, united in one object. But was the state of France so wretched and undone that no other recourse but rapine remained to preserve its existence? On this point I wish to receive some information. When the states met, was the condition of the finances of France such that, after economizing on principles of justice and mercy through all departments, no fair repartition of burdens upon all the orders could possibly restore them? If such an equal imposition would have been sufficient, you well know it might easily have been made. M. Necker, in the budget which he laid before the orders assembled at Versailles, made a detailed exposition of the state of the French nation.

---

25 Treason against the nation.

If we give credit to him, it was not necessary to have recourse to any new impositions whatsoever to put the receipts of France on a balance with its expenses. He stated the permanent charges of all descriptions, including the interest of a new loan of four hundred millions, at 531,444,000 livres; the fixed revenue at 475,294,000, making the deficiency 56,150,000, or short of £2,200,000 sterling. But to balance it, he brought forward savings and improvements of revenue (considered as entirely certain) to rather more than the amount of that deficiency; and he concludes with these emphatical words, *"Quel pays, Messieurs, que celui, ou, sans impots et avec de simples objets inappercus, on peut faire disparoitre un deficit qui a fait tant de bruit en Europe."*[26] As to the reimbursement, the sinking of debt, and the other great objects of public credit and political arrangement indicated in Mons. Necker's speech, no doubt could be entertained but that a very moderate and proportioned assessment on the citizens without distinction would have provided for all of them to the fullest extent of their demand.

If this representation of Mons. Necker was false, then the Assembly are in the highest degree culpable for having forced the king to accept as his minister and, since the king's deposition, for having employed as their minister a man who had been capable of abusing so notoriously the confidence of his master and their own, in a matter, too, of the highest moment and directly appertaining to his particular office. But if the representation was exact (as having always, along with you, conceived a high degree of respect for M. Necker, I make no doubt it was), then what can be said in favor of those who, instead of moderate, reasonable, and general contribution, have in cold blood, and impelled by no necessity, had recourse to a partial and cruel confiscation?

Was that contribution refused on a pretext of privilege, either on the part of the clergy or on that of the nobility? No, certainly. As to the clergy, they even ran before the wishes of the third order.

---

26 "What a country, sirs, than one where, without taxes and with only simple unseen schemes, we manage to erase a deficit that has made such noise in all of Europe."

Previous to the meeting of the states, they had in all their instructions expressly directed their deputies to renounce every immunity which put them upon a footing distinct from the condition of their fellow subjects. In this renunciation the clergy were even more explicit than the nobility.

But let us suppose that the deficiency had remained at the fifty-six millions (or £2,200,000 sterling), as at first stated by M. Necker. Let us allow that all the resources he opposed to that deficiency were impudent and groundless fictions, and that the Assembly (or their lords of articles at the Jacobins) were from thence justified in laying the whole burden of that deficiency on the clergy—yet allowing all this, a necessity of £2,200,000 sterling will not support a confiscation to the amount of five millions. The imposition of £2,200,000 on the clergy, as partial, would have been oppressive and unjust, but it would not have been altogether ruinous to those on whom it was imposed, and therefore it would not have answered the real purpose of the managers.

Perhaps persons unacquainted with the state of France, on hearing the clergy and the noblesse were privileged in point of taxation, may be led to imagine that, previous to the Revolution, these bodies had contributed nothing to the state. This is a great mistake. They certainly did not contribute equally with each other, nor either of them equally with the commons. They both, however, contributed largely. Neither nobility nor clergy enjoyed any exemption from the excise on consumable commodities, from duties of custom, or from any of the other numerous indirect impositions, which in France, as well as here, make so very large a proportion of all payments to the public. The noblesse paid the capitation. They paid also a land-tax, called the twentieth penny, to the height sometimes of three, sometimes of four, shillings in the pound—both of them direct impositions of no light nature and no trivial produce. The clergy of the provinces annexed by conquest to France (which in extent make about an eighth part of the whole, but in wealth a much larger proportion) paid likewise to the capitation and the twentieth penny, at the rate paid by the nobility. The clergy in the old provinces did not pay the capitation, but they had redeemed themselves at the expense of about 24 millions, or a little more than a million sterling. They were exempted from the twentieths; but then they made free gifts, they contracted debts for the state, and they were subject to some other charges, the whole computed at about a thirteenth part of their clear income. They ought to have paid annually about forty thousand pounds more to put them on a par with the contribution of the nobility.

When the terrors of this tremendous proscription hung over the clergy, they made an offer of a contribution through the archbishop of Aix, which, for its extravagance, ought not to have been accepted. But it was evidently and obviously more advantageous to the public creditor than anything which could rationally be promised by the confiscation. Why was it not accepted? The reason is plain: there was no desire that the church should be brought to serve the state. The service of the state was made a pretext to destroy the church. In their way to the destruction of the church they would not scruple to destroy their country; and they have destroyed it. One great end in the project would have been defeated if the plan of extortion had been adopted in lieu of the scheme of confiscation. The new landed interest connected with the new republic, and connected with it for its very being, could not have been created. This was among the reasons why that extravagant ransom was not accepted.

The madness of the project of confiscation, on the plan that was first pretended, soon became apparent. To bring this unwieldy mass of landed property, enlarged by the confiscation of all the vast landed domain of the crown, at once into market was obviously to defeat the profits proposed by the confiscation by depreciating the value of those lands and, indeed, of all the landed estates throughout France. Such a sudden diversion of all its circulating money from trade to land must be an additional mischief. What step was taken? Did the Assembly, on becoming sensible of the inevitable ill effects of their projected sale, revert to the offers of the clergy? No distress could oblige them to travel in a course which was disgraced by any appearance of justice. Giving over all hopes from a general immediate sale, another project seems to have succeeded. They proposed to take stock in exchange for the church lands. In that project great difficulties arose in equalizing the objects to be exchanged. Other obstacles also presented themselves, which threw them back again upon some project of sale. The municipalities had taken an alarm. They would not hear of transferring the whole plunder of the kingdom to the stockholders in Paris. Many of those municipalities had been (upon system) reduced to the most deplorable indigence. Money was nowhere to be seen. They were, therefore, led to the point that was so ardently desired. They panted for a currency of any kind which might revive their perishing industry. The municipalities were then to be admitted to a share in the spoil, which evidently rendered the first scheme (if ever it had been seriously entertained) altogether impracticable. Public exigencies pressed upon all sides. The minister of finance reiterated his call for supply with a most urgent, anxious, and boding voice. Thus pressed on all sides, instead of the first plan of converting their bankers into bishops and abbots, instead of paying the old debt, they contracted a new debt at 3 per cent, creating a new paper currency founded on an eventual sale of the church lands. They issued this paper currency to satisfy in the first instance chiefly the demands made upon them by the bank of discount, the great machine, or paper-mill, of their fictitious wealth.

The spoil of the church was now become the only resource of all their operations in finance, the vital principle of all their politics, the sole security for the existence of their power. It was necessary by all, even the most violent means, to put every individual on the same bottom, and to bind the nation in one guilty interest to uphold this act and the authority of those by whom it was done. In order to force the most reluctant into a participation of their pillage, they rendered their paper circulation compulsory in all payments. Those who consider the general tendency of their schemes to this one object as a center, and a center from which afterwards all their measures radiate, will not think that I dwell too long upon this part of the proceedings of the National Assembly.

To cut off all appearance of connection between the crown and public justice, and to bring the whole under implicit obedience to the dictators in Paris, the old independent judicature of the parliaments, with all its merits and all its faults, was wholly abolished. Whilst the parliaments existed, it was evident that the people might some time or other come to resort to them and rally under the standard of their ancient laws. It became, however, a matter of consideration that the magistrates and officers, in the courts now abolished, had purchased their places at a very high rate, for which, as well as for the duty they performed, they received but a very low return of interest. Simple confiscation is a boon only for the clergy; to the lawyers some appearances of equity are to be observed, and they are to receive compensation to an immense amount. Their compensation becomes part of the national debt, for the liquidation of which there is the one exhaustless fund. The lawyers are to obtain their compensation in the new church paper, which is to march with the new principles of judicature and legislature. The dismissed magistrates are to take their share of martyrdom with the ecclesiastics, or to receive their own property from such a fund, and in such a manner, as all those who have been seasoned with the ancient principles of jurisprudence and had been the sworn guardians of property must look upon with horror. Even the clergy are to receive their miserable allowance out of the depreciated paper, which is stamped with the indelible character of sacrilege and with the symbols of their own ruin, or they must starve. So violent an outrage upon credit, property, and liberty as this compulsory paper currency has seldom been exhibited by the alliance of bankruptcy and tyranny, at any time or in any nation.

In the course of all these operations, at length comes out the grand *arcanum*[27]—that in reality, and in a fair sense, the lands of the church (so far as anything certain can be gathered from their proceedings) are not to be sold at all. By the late resolutions of the

---

27 Or mystery.

National Assembly, they are, indeed, to be delivered to the highest bidder. But it is to be observed that a certain portion only of the purchase money is to be laid down. A period of twelve years is to be given for the payment of the rest. The philosophic purchasers are therefore, on payment of a sort of fine, to be put instantly into possession of the estate. It becomes in some respects a sort of gift to them—to be held on the feudal tenure of zeal to the new establishment. This project is evidently to let in a body of purchasers without money. The consequence will be that these purchasers, or rather grantees, will pay, not only from the rents as they accrue, which might as well be received by the state, but from the spoil of the materials of buildings, from waste in woods, and from whatever money, by hands habituated to the griping of usury, they can wring from the miserable peasant. He is to be delivered over to the mercenary and arbitrary discretion of men who will be stimulated to every species of extortion by the growing demands on the growing profits of an estate held under the precarious settlement of a new political system.

When all the frauds, impostures, violence, rapines, burnings, murders, confiscations, compulsory paper currencies, and every description of tyranny and cruelty employed to bring about and to uphold this Revolution have their natural effect, that is, to shock the moral sentiments of all virtuous and sober minds, the abettors of this philosophic system immediately strain their throats in a declamation against the old monarchical government of France. When they have rendered that deposed power sufficiently black, they then proceed in argument as if all those who disapprove of their new abuses must of course be partisans of the old, that those who reprobate their crude and violent schemes of liberty ought to be treated as advocates for servitude. I admit that their necessities do compel them to this base and contemptible fraud. Nothing can reconcile men to their proceedings and projects but the supposition that there is no third option between them and some tyranny as odious as can be furnished by the records of history, or by the invention of poets. This prattling of theirs hardly deserves the name of sophistry. It is nothing but plain impudence. Have these gentlemen never heard, in the whole circle of the worlds of theory and practice, of anything between the despotism of the monarch and the despotism of the multitude? Have they never heard of a monarchy directed by laws, controlled and balanced by the great hereditary wealth and hereditary dignity of a nation, and both again controlled by a judicious check from the reason and feeling of the people at large acting by a suitable and permanent organ? Is it then impossible that a man may be found who, without criminal ill intention or pitiable absurdity, shall prefer such a mixed and tempered government to either of the extremes, and who may repute that nation to be destitute of all wisdom and of all virtue which, having in its choice to obtain such a government with ease, or rather to confirm it when actually possessed, thought proper to commit a thousand crimes and to subject their country to a thousand evils in order to avoid it? Is it then a truth so universally acknowledged that a pure democracy is the only tolerable form into which human society can be thrown, that a man is not permitted to hesitate about its merits without the suspicion of being a friend to tyranny, that is, of being a foe to mankind?

XIII
FRANCE IN LIGHT OF THE REVOLUTION

Government and Abuses

I do not know under what description to class the present ruling authority in France. It affects to be a pure democracy, though I think it in a direct train of becoming shortly a mischievous and ignoble oligarchy. But for the present I admit it to be a contrivance of the nature and effect of what it pretends to. I reprobate no form of government merely upon abstract principles. There may be situations in which the purely democratic form will become necessary. There may be some (very few, and very particularly circumstanced) where it would be clearly desirable. This I do not take to be the case of France or of any other great country. Until now, we have seen no examples of considerable democracies. The ancients were better acquainted with them. Not being wholly unread in the authors who had seen the most of those constitutions, and who best understood them, I cannot help concurring with their opinion that an absolute democracy, no more than absolute monarchy, is to be reckoned among the legitimate forms of government. They think it rather the corruption and degeneracy than the sound constitution of a republic. If I recollect rightly, Aristotle observes that a democracy has many striking points of resemblance with a tyranny. Of this I am certain, that in a democracy the majority of the citizens is capable of exercising the most cruel oppressions upon the minority whenever strong divisions prevail in that kind of polity, as they often must; and that oppression of the minority will extend to far greater numbers and will be carried on with much greater fury than can almost ever be apprehended from the dominion of a single scepter. In such a popular persecution, individual sufferers are in a much more deplorable condition than in any other. Under a cruel prince they have the balmy compassion of mankind to assuage the smart of their wounds; they have the plaudits of the people to animate their generous constancy under their sufferings; but those who are subjected to wrong under multitudes are deprived of all external consolation. They seem deserted by mankind, overpowered by a conspiracy of their whole species.

But admitting democracy not to have that inevitable tendency to party tyranny, which I suppose it to have, and admitting it to possess as much good in it when unmixed as I am sure it possesses when compounded with other forms, does monarchy, on its part, contain nothing at all to recommend it? I do not often quote Bolingbroke, nor have his works in general left any permanent impression on my mind. He is a presumptuous and a superficial writer. But he has one observation which, in my opinion, is not without depth and solidity. He says that he prefers a monarchy to other governments because you can better ingraft any description of republic on a monarchy than anything of monarchy upon the republican forms.

I think him perfectly in the right. The fact is so historically, and it agrees well with the speculation.

I know how easy a topic it is to dwell on the faults of departed greatness. By a revolution in the state, the fawning sycophant of yesterday is converted into the austere critic of the present hour. But steady, independent minds, when they have an object of so serious a concern to mankind as government under their contemplation, will disdain to assume the part of satirists and declaimers. They will judge of human institutions as they do of human characters. They will sort out the good from the evil, which is mixed in mortal institutions, as it is in mortal men.

Your government in France, though usually, and I think justly, reputed the best of the unqualified or ill-qualified monarchies, was still full of abuses. These abuses accumulated in a length of time, as they must accumulate in every monarchy not under the constant inspection of a popular representative. I am no stranger to the faults and defects of the subverted government of France, and I think I am not inclined by nature or policy to make a panegyric upon anything which is a just and natural object of censure. But the question is not now of the vices of that monarchy, but of its existence. Is it, then, true that the French government was such as to be incapable or undeserving of reform, so that it was of absolute necessity that the whole fabric should be at once pulled down and the area cleared for the erection of a theoretic, experimental edifice in its place? All France was of a different opinion in the beginning of the year 1789. The instructions to the representatives to the States-General, from every district in that kingdom, were filled with projects for the reformation of that government without the remotest suggestion of a design to destroy it. Had such a design been even insinuated, I believe there would have been but one voice, and that voice for rejecting it with scorn and horror. Men have been sometimes led by degrees, sometimes hurried, into things of which, if they could have seen the whole together, they never would have permitted the most remote approach. When those instructions were given, there was no question but that abuses existed, and that they demanded a reform; nor is there now. In the interval between the instructions and the revolution things changed their shape; and in consequence of that change, the true question at present is, Whether those who would have reformed or those who have destroyed are in the right?

To hear some men speak of the late monarchy of France, you would imagine that they were talking of Persia bleeding under the ferocious sword of Tahmas Kouli Khan, or at least describing the barbarous anarchic despotism of Turkey, where the finest countries in the most genial climates in the world are wasted by peace more than any countries have been worried by war, where arts are unknown, where manufactures languish, where science is extinguished, where agriculture decays, where the human race itself melts away and perishes under the eye of the observer. Was this the case of France? I have no way of determining the question but by reference to facts. Facts do not support this resemblance. Along with much evil there is some good in monarchy itself, and some corrective to its evil from religion, from laws, from manners, from opinions the French monarchy must have received, which rendered it (though by no means a free, and therefore by no means a good, constitution) a despotism rather in appearance than in reality.

Population

Among the standards upon which the effects of government on any country are to be estimated, I must consider the state of its population as not the least certain. No country in which population flourishes and is in progressive improvement can be under a very mischievous government. About sixty years ago, the Intendants of the generalities of France made, with other matters, a report of the population of their several districts. I have not the books, which are very voluminous, by me, nor do I know where to procure them (I am obliged to speak by memory, and therefore the less positively), but I think the population of France was by them, even at that period, estimated at twenty-two millions of souls. At the end of the last century it had been generally calculated at eighteen. On either of these estimations, France was not ill peopled. M. Necker, who is an authority for his own time, at least equal to the Intendants for theirs, reckons, and upon apparently sure principles, the people of France in the year 1780 at twenty-four millions six hundred and seventy thousand. But was this the probable ultimate term under the old establishment? Dr. Price is of opinion that the growth of population in France was by no means at its acme in that year. I certainly defer to Dr. Price's authority a good deal more in these speculations than I do in his general politics. This gentleman, taking ground on M. Necker's data, is very confident that since the period of that minister's calculation the French population has increased rapidly—so rapidly that in the year 1789 he will not consent to rate the people of that kingdom at a lower number than thirty millions. After abating much (and much I think ought to be abated) from the sanguine calculation of Dr. Price, I have no doubt that the population of France did increase considerably during this later period; but supposing that it increased to nothing more than will be sufficient to complete the twenty-four millions six hundred and seventy thousand to twenty-five millions, still a population of twenty-five millions, and that in an increasing progress, on a space of about twenty-seven thousand square leagues is immense. It is, for instance, a good deal more than the proportionable population of this island, or even than that of England, the best peopled part of the United Kingdom.

It is not universally true that France is a fertile country. Considerable tracts of it are barren and labor under other natural disadvantages. In the portions of that territory where things are more favorable, as far as I am able to discover, the numbers of the people correspond to the indulgence of nature. The Generality of Lisle (this I admit is the strongest example) upon an extent of four hundred and four leagues and a half, about ten years ago, contained seven hundred and thirty-four thousand six hundred souls, which is one thousand seven hundred and seventy-two inhabitants to each square league. The middle term for the rest of France is about nine hundred inhabitants to the same admeasurement.

I do not attribute this population to the deposed government, because I do not like to compliment the contrivances of men with what is due in a great degree to the bounty of Providence. But that decried government could not have obstructed, most probably it favored, the operation of those causes (whatever they were), whether of nature in the soil or habits of industry among the people, which has produced so large a number of the species throughout that whole kingdom and exhibited in some particular places such prodigies of population. I never will suppose that fabric of a state to be the worst of all political institutions which, by experience, is found to contain a principle favorable (however latent it may be) to the increase of mankind.

National Wealth

The wealth of a country is another, and no contemptible, standard by which we may judge whether, on the whole, a government be protecting or destructive. France far exceeds England in the multitude of her people, but I apprehend that her comparative wealth is much inferior to ours, that it is not so equal in the distribution, nor so ready in the circulation. I believe the difference in the form of the two governments to be amongst the causes of this advantage on the side of England. I speak of England, not of the whole British dominions, which, if compared with those of France, will, in some degree, weaken the comparative rate of wealth upon our side. But that wealth, which will not endure a comparison with the riches of England, may constitute a very respectable degree of opulence. M. Necker's book, published in 1785, contains an accurate and interesting collection of facts relative to public economy and to political arithmetic; and his speculations on the subject are in general wise and liberal. In that work he gives an idea of the state of France very remote from the portrait of a country whose government was a perfect grievance, an absolute evil, admitting no cure but through the violent and uncertain remedy of a total revolution. He affirms that from the year 1726 to the year 1784 there was coined at the mint of France, in the species of gold and silver, to the amount of about one hundred millions of pounds sterling.

It is impossible that M. Necker should be mistaken in the amount of the bullion which has been coined in the mint. It is a matter of official record. The reasonings of this able financier, concerning the quantity of gold and silver which remained for circulation, when he wrote in 1785, that is, about four years before the deposition and imprisonment of the French king, are not of equal certainty, but they are laid on grounds so apparently solid that it is not easy to refuse a considerable degree of assent to his calculation. He calculates the *numeraire*, or what we call *specie*, then actually existing in France at about eighty-eight millions of the same English money. A great accumulation of wealth for one country, large as that country is! M. Necker was so far from considering this influx of wealth as likely to cease, when he wrote in 1785, that he presumes upon a future annual increase of two per cent upon the money brought into France during the periods from which he computed.

Some adequate cause must have originally introduced all the money coined at its mint into that kingdom, and some cause as operative must have kept at home, or returned into its bosom, such a vast flood of treasure as M. Necker calculates to remain for domestic circulation. Suppose any reasonable deductions from M. Necker's computation, the remainder must still amount to an immense sum. Causes thus powerful to acquire, and to retain, cannot be found in discouraged industry, insecure property, and a positively destructive government. Indeed, when I consider the face of the kingdom of France, the multitude and opulence of her cities, the useful magnificence of her spacious high roads and bridges, the opportunity of her artificial canals and navigations opening the conveniences of maritime communication through a solid continent of so immense an extent; when I turn my eyes to the stupendous works of her ports and harbors, and to her whole naval apparatus, whether for war or trade; when I bring before my view the number of her fortifications, constructed with so bold and masterly a skill and made and maintained at so prodigious a charge, presenting an armed front and impenetrable barrier to her enemies upon every side; when I recollect how very small a part of that extensive region is without cultivation, and to what complete perfection the culture of many of the best productions of the earth have been brought in France; when I reflect on the excellence of her manufactures and fabrics, second to none but ours, and in some particulars not second; when I contemplate the grand foundations of charity, public and private; when I survey the state of all the arts that beautify and polish life; when I reckon the men she has bred for extending her fame in war, her able statesmen, the multitude of her profound lawyers and theologians, her philosophers, her critics, her historians and antiquaries, her poets and her orators, sacred and profane—I behold in all this something which awes and commands the imagination, which checks the mind on the brink of precipitate and indiscriminate censure, and which demands that we should very seriously examine what and how great are the latent vices that could authorize us at once to level so spacious a fabric with the ground. I do not recognize in this view of things the despotism of Turkey. Nor do I discern the character of a government that has been, on the whole, so oppressive or so corrupt or so negligent as to be utterly unfit for all reformation. I must think such a government well deserved to have its excellence heightened, its faults corrected, and its capacities improved into a British constitution.

Whoever has examined into the proceedings of that deposed government for several years back cannot fail to have observed, amidst the inconstancy and fluctuation natural to courts, an earnest endeavor toward the prosperity and improvement of the country; he must admit that it had long been employed, in some instances wholly to remove, in many considerably to correct, the abusive practices and usages that had prevailed in the state, and that even the unlimited power of the sovereign over the persons of his subjects, inconsistent, as undoubtedly it was, with law and liberty, had yet been every day growing more mitigated in the exercise. So far from refusing itself to reformation, that government was open, with a censurable degree of facility, to all sorts of projects and projectors on the subject. Rather too much countenance was given to the spirit of innovation, which soon was turned against those who fostered it, and ended in their ruin. It is but cold, and no very flattering, justice to that fallen monarchy to say that, for many years, it trespassed more by levity and want of judgment in several of its schemes than from any defect in diligence or in public spirit. To compare the government of France for the last fifteen or sixteen years with wise and well-constituted establishments during that, or during any period, is not to act with fairness. But if in point of prodigality in the expenditure of money, or in point of rigor in the exercise of power, it be compared with any of the former reigns, I believe candid judges will give little credit to the good intentions of those who dwell perpetually on the donations to favorites, or on the expenses of the court, or on the horrors of the Bastille in the reign of Louis the Sixteenth.

New Government's State of Affairs

Whether the system, if it deserves such a name, now built on the ruins of that ancient monarchy will be able to give a better account of the population and wealth of the country which it has taken under its care, is a matter very doubtful. Instead of improving by the change, I apprehend that a long series of years must be told before it can recover in any degree the effects of this philosophic revolution, and before the nation can be replaced on its former footing. If Dr. Price should think fit, a few years hence, to favor us with an estimate of the population of France, he will hardly be able to make up his tale of thirty millions of souls, as computed in 1789, or the Assembly's computation of twenty-six millions of that year, or even M. Necker's twenty-five millions in 1780. I hear that there are considerable emigrations from France, and that many, quitting that voluptuous climate and that seductive Circean liberty, have taken refuge in the frozen regions, and under the British despotism, of Canada.

In the present disappearance of coin, no person could think it the same country in which the present minister of the finances has been able to discover fourscore millions sterling in specie. From its general aspect one would conclude that it had been for some time past under the special direction of the learned academicians of Laputa and Balnibarbi. Already the population of Paris has so declined that M. Necker stated to the National Assembly the provision to be made for its subsistence at a fifth less than what had formerly been found requisite. It is said (and I have never heard it contradicted) that a hundred thousand people are out of employment in that city, though it is become the seat of the imprisoned court and National Assembly. Nothing, I am credibly informed, can exceed the shocking and disgusting spectacle of mendicancy displayed in that capital. Indeed the votes of the National Assembly leave no doubt of the fact. They have lately appointed a standing committee of mendicancy. They are contriving at once a vigorous police on this subject and, for the first time, the imposition of a tax to maintain the poor, for whose present relief great sums appear on the face of the public accounts of the year. In the meantime the leaders of the legislative clubs and coffee-houses are intoxicated with admiration at their own wisdom and ability. They speak with the most sovereign contempt of the rest of the world. They tell the people, to comfort them in the rags with which they have clothed them, that they are a nation of philosophers; and sometimes by all the arts of quackish parade, by show, tumult, and bustle, sometimes by the alarms of plots and invasions, they attempt to drown the cries of indigence and to divert the eyes of the observer from the ruin and wretchedness of the state. A brave people will certainly prefer liberty accompanied with a virtuous poverty to a depraved and wealthy servitude. But before the price of comfort and opulence is paid, one ought to be pretty sure it is real liberty which is purchased, and that she is to be purchased at no other price. I shall always, however, consider that liberty as very equivocal in her appearance which has not wisdom and justice for her companions and does not lead prosperity and plenty in her train.

When I sent this book to the press, I entertained some doubt concerning the nature and extent of the last article in the above accounts, which is only under a general head, without any detail. Since then I have seen M. de Calonne's work. I must think it a great loss to me that I had not that advantage earlier. M. de Calonne thinks this article to be on account of general subsistence; but as he is not able to comprehend how so great a loss as upwards of £1,661,000 sterling could be sustained on the difference between the price and the sale of grain, he seems to attribute this enormous head of charge to secret expenses of the Revolution. I cannot say anything positively on that subject. The reader is capable of judging, by the aggregate of these immense charges, on the state and condition of France; and the system of public economy adopted in that nation. These articles of account produced no inquiry or discussion in the National Assembly.

New Government's View of Previous Governments

The advocates for this Revolution, not satisfied with exaggerating the vices of their ancient government, strike at the fame of their country itself by painting almost all that could have attracted the attention of strangers, I mean their nobility and their clergy, as objects of horror. If this were only a libel, there had not been much in it. But it has practical consequences. Had your nobility and gentry, who formed the great body of your landed men and the whole of your military officers, resembled those of Germany at the period when the Hansetowns were necessitated to confederate against the nobles in defense of their property; had they been like the Orsini and Vitelli in Italy, who used to sally from their fortified dens to rob the trader and traveler; had they been such as the Mamelukes in Egypt or the Nayres on the coast of Malabar, I do admit that too critical an inquiry might not be advisable into the means of freeing the world from such a nuisance. The statues of

Equity and Mercy might be veiled for a moment. The tenderest minds, confounded with the dreadful exigency in which morality submits to the suspension of its own rules in favor of its own principles, might turn aside whilst fraud and violence were accomplishing the destruction of a pretended nobility which disgraced, whilst it persecuted, human nature. The persons most abhorrent from blood, and treason, and arbitrary confiscation might remain silent spectators of this civil war between the vices.

XIV
FRENCH NOBILITY

But did the privileged nobility who met under the king's precept at Versailles, in 1789, or their constituents, deserve to be looked on as the Nayres or Mamelukes of this age, or as the Orsini and Vitelli of ancient times? If I had then asked the question I should have passed for a madman. What have they since done that they were to be driven into exile, that their persons should be hunted about, mangled, and tortured, their families dispersed, their houses laid in ashes, and that their order should be abolished and the memory of it, if possible, extinguished by ordaining them to change the very names by which they were usually known? Read their instructions to their representatives. They breathe the spirit of liberty as warmly and they recommend reformation as strongly as any other order. Their privileges relative to contribution were voluntarily surrendered, as the king, from the beginning, surrendered all pretense to a right of taxation. Upon a free constitution there was but one opinion in France. The absolute monarchy was at an end. It breathed its last, without a groan, without struggle, without convulsion. All the struggle, all the dissension arose afterwards upon the preference of a despotic democracy to a government of reciprocal control. The triumph of the victorious party was over the principles of a British constitution.

I have observed the affectation which for many years past has prevailed in Paris, even to a degree perfectly childish, of idolizing the memory of your Henry the Fourth. If anything could put one out of humor with that ornament to the kingly character, it would be this overdone style of insidious panegyric. The persons who have worked this engine the most busily are those who have ended their panegyrics in dethroning his successor and descendant, a man as good-natured, at the least, as Henry the Fourth, altogether as fond of his people, and who has done infinitely more to correct the ancient vices of the state than that great monarch did, or we are sure he ever meant to do. Well it is for his panegyrists that they have not him to deal with. For Henry of Navarre was a resolute, active, and politic prince. He possessed, indeed, great humanity and mildness, but a humanity and mildness that never stood in the way of his interests. He never sought to be loved without putting himself first in a condition to be feared. He used soft language with determined conduct. He asserted and maintained his authority in the gross, and distributed his acts of concession only in the detail. He spent the income of his prerogative nobly, but he took care not to break in upon the capital, never abandoning for a moment any of the claims which he made under the fundamental laws, nor sparing to shed the blood of those who opposed him, often in the field, sometimes upon the scaffold. Because he knew how to make his virtues respected by the ungrateful, he has merited the praises of those whom, if they had lived in his time, he would have shut up in the Bastille and brought to punishment along with the regicides whom he hanged after he had famished Paris into a surrender.

If these panegyrists are in earnest in their admiration of Henry the Fourth, they must remember that they cannot think more highly of him than he did of the noblesse of France, whose virtue, honor, courage, patriotism, and loyalty were his constant theme.

But the nobility of France are degenerated since the days of Henry the Fourth. This is possible. But it is more than I can believe to be true in any great degree. I do not pretend to know France as correctly as some others, but I have endeavored through my whole life to make myself acquainted with human nature, otherwise

I should be unfit to take even my humble part in the service of mankind. In that study I could not pass by a vast portion of our nature as it appeared modified in a country but twenty-four miles from the shore of this island. On my best observation, compared with my best inquiries, I found your nobility for the greater part composed of men of high spirit and of a delicate sense of honor, both with regard to themselves individually and with regard to their whole corps, over whom they kept, beyond what is common in other countries, a censorial eye. They were tolerably well bred, very officious, humane, and hospitable; in their conversation frank and open; with a good military tone, and reasonably tinctured with literature, particularly of the authors in their own language. Many had pretensions far above this description. I speak of those who were generally met with.

As to their behavior to the inferior classes, they appeared to me to comport themselves toward them with good nature and with something more nearly approaching to familiarity than is generally practiced with us in the relations between the higher and lower ranks of life. To strike any person, even in the most abject condition, was a thing in a manner unknown and would be highly disgraceful. Instances of other ill-treatment of the humble part of the community were rare; and as to attacks made upon the property or the personal liberty of the commons, I never heard of any whatsoever from them; nor, whilst the laws were in vigor under the ancient government, would such tyranny in subjects have been permitted. As men of landed estates, I had no fault to find with their conduct, though much to reprehend and much to wish changed in many of the old tenures. Where the letting of their land was by rent, I could not discover that their agreements with their farmers were oppressive; nor when they were in partnership with the farmer, as often was the case, have I heard that they had taken the lion's share. The proportions seemed not inequitable. There might be exceptions, but certainly they were exceptions only. I have no reason to believe that in these respects the landed noblesse of France were worse than the landed gentry of this country, certainly in no respect more vexatious than the landholders, not noble, of their own nation. In cities the nobility had no manner of power, in the country very little. You know, Sir, that much of the civil government, and the police in the most essential parts, was not in the hands of that nobility which presents itself first to our consideration. The revenue, the system and collection of which were the most grievous parts of the French government, was not administered by the men of the sword, nor were they answerable for the vices of its principle or the vexations, where any such existed, in its management.

Denying, as I am well warranted to do, that the nobility had any considerable share in the oppression of the people in cases in which real oppression existed, I am ready to admit that they were not without considerable faults and errors. A foolish imitation of the worst part of the manners of England, which impaired their natural character without substituting in its place what, perhaps, they meant to copy, has certainly rendered them worse than formerly they were. Habitual dissoluteness of manners, continued beyond the pardonable period of life, was more common amongst them than it is with us; and it reigned with the less hope of remedy, though possibly with something of less mischief by being covered with more exterior decorum. They countenanced too much that licentious philosophy which has helped to bring on their ruin. There was another error amongst them more fatal. Those of the commons who approached to or exceeded many of the nobility in point of wealth were not fully admitted to the rank and estimation which wealth, in reason and good policy, ought to bestow in every country, though I think not equally with that of other nobility. The two kinds of aristocracy were too punctiliously kept asunder, less so, however, than in Germany and some other nations.

This separation, as I have already taken the liberty of suggesting to you, I conceive to be one principal cause of the destruction of the old nobility. The military, particularly, was too exclusively reserved for men of family. But, after all, this was an error of opinion, which a conflicting opinion would have rectified. A permanent assembly in which the commons had their share of power would soon abolish whatever was too invidious and insulting in these distinctions, and even the faults in the morals of the nobility would have been probably corrected by the greater varieties of occupation and pursuit to which a constitution by orders would have given rise.

All this violent cry against the nobility I take to be a mere work of art. To be honored and even privileged by the laws, opinions, and inveterate usages of our country, growing out of the prejudice of ages, has nothing to provoke horror and indignation in any man. Even to be too tenacious of those privileges is not absolutely a crime. The strong struggle in every individual to preserve possession of what he has found to belong to him and to distinguish him is one of the securities against injustice and despotism implanted in our nature. It operates as an instinct to secure property and to preserve communities in a settled state. What is there to shock in this? Nobility is a graceful ornament to the civil order. It is the Corinthian capital of polished society. *Omnes boni nobilitati semper favemus,*[28] was the saying of a wise and good man. It is indeed one sign of a liberal and benevolent mind to incline to it with some sort of partial propensity. He feels no ennobling principle in his own heart who wishes to level all the artificial institutions which have been adopted for giving a body to opinion, and permanence to fugitive esteem. It is a sour, malignant, envious disposition, without taste for the reality or for any image or representation of virtue, that sees with joy the unmerited fall of what had long flourished in splendor and in honor. I do not like to see anything destroyed, any void produced in society, any ruin on the face of the land. It was, therefore, with no disappointment or dissatisfaction that my inquiries and observations did not present to me any incorrigible vices in the noblesse of France, or any abuse which could not be removed by a reform very short of abolition. Your noblesse did not deserve punishment; but to degrade is to punish.

---

28 We all favor good nobility, always.

XV
FRENCH CLERGY

Vices of Present and Past Clergy No Basis for Confiscation

It was with the same satisfaction I found that the result of my inquiry concerning your clergy was not dissimilar. It is no soothing news to my ears that great bodies of men are incurably corrupt. It is not with much credulity I listen to any when they speak evil of those whom they are going to plunder. I rather suspect that vices are feigned or exaggerated when profit is looked for in their punishment. An enemy is a bad witness; a robber is worse. Vices and abuses there were undoubtedly in that order, and must be. It was an old establishment, and not frequently revised. But I saw no crimes in the individuals that merited confiscation of their substance, nor those cruel insults and degradations, and that unnatural persecution which have been substituted in the place of meliorating regulation.

If there had been any just cause for this new religious persecution, the atheistic libelers, who act as trumpeters to animate the populace to plunder, do not love anybody so much as not to dwell with complacency on the vices of the existing clergy. This they have not done. They find themselves obliged to rake into the histories of former ages (which they have ransacked with a malignant and profligate industry) for every instance of oppression and persecution which has been made by that body or in its favor in order to justify, upon very iniquitous, because very illogical, principles of retaliation, their own persecutions and their own cruelties. After destroying all other genealogies and family distinctions, they invent a sort of pedigree of crimes. It is not very just to chastise men for the offences of their natural ancestors, but to take the fiction of ancestry in a corporate succession as a ground for punishing men who have no relation to guilty acts, except in names and general descriptions, is a sort of refinement in injustice belonging to the philosophy of this enlightened age. The Assembly punishes men, many, if not most, of whom abhor the violent conduct of ecclesiastics in former times as much as their present persecutors can do, and who would be as loud and as strong in the expression of that sense, if they were not well aware of the purposes for which all this declamation is employed.

Corporate bodies are immortal for the good of the members, but not for their punishment. Nations themselves are such corporations. As well might we in England think of waging inexpiable war upon all Frenchmen for the evils which they have brought upon us in the several periods of our mutual hostilities. You might, on your part, think yourselves justified in falling upon all Englishmen on account of the unparalleled calamities brought on the people of France by the unjust invasions of our Henries and our Edwards. Indeed, we should be mutually justified in this exterminatory war upon each other, full as much as you are in the unprovoked persecution of your present countrymen, on account of the conduct of men of the same name in other times.

Lessons from History of Clergy

We do not draw the moral lessons we might from history. On the contrary, without care it may be used to vitiate our minds and to destroy our happiness. In history a great volume is unrolled for our instruction, drawing the materials of future wisdom from the past errors and infirmities of mankind. It may, in the perversion, serve for a magazine furnishing offensive and defensive weapons for parties in church and state, and supplying the means of keeping alive or reviving dissensions and animosities, and adding fuel to civil fury. History consists for the greater part of the miseries brought upon the world by pride, ambition, avarice, revenge, lust, sedition, hypocrisy, ungoverned zeal, and all the train of disorderly appetites which shake the public with the same

> *—troublous storms that toss*
> *The private state, and render life unsweet.*

These vices are the causes of those storms. Religion, morals, laws, prerogatives, privileges, liberties, rights of men are the pretexts. The pretexts are always found in some specious appearance of a real good. You would not secure men from tyranny and sedition by rooting out of the mind the principles to which these fraudulent pretexts apply? If you did, you would root out everything that is valuable in the human breast. As these are the pretexts, so the ordinary actors and instruments in great public evils are kings, priests, magistrates, senates, parliaments, national assemblies, judges, and captains. You would not cure the evil by resolving that there should be no more monarchs, nor ministers of state, nor of the gospel; no interpreters of law; no general officers; no public councils. You might change the names. The things in some shape must remain. A certain quantum of power must always exist in the community in some hands and under some appellation. Wise men will apply their remedies to vices, not to names; to the causes of evil which are permanent, not to the occasional organs by which they act, and the transitory modes in which they appear. Otherwise you will be wise historically, a fool in practice. Seldom have two ages the same fashion in their pretexts and the same modes of mischief. Wickedness is a little more inventive. Whilst you are discussing fashion, the fashion is gone by. The very same vice assumes a new body. The spirit transmigrates, and, far from losing its principle of life by the change of its appearance, it is renovated in its new organs with a fresh vigor of a juvenile activity. It walks abroad, it continues its ravages, whilst you are gibbeting the carcass or demolishing the tomb. You are terrifying yourselves with ghosts and apparitions, whilst your house is the haunt of robbers. It is thus with all those who, attending only to the shell and husk of history, think they are waging war with intolerance, pride, and cruelty, whilst, under color of abhorring the ill principles of antiquated parties, they are authorizing and feeding the same odious vices in different factions, and perhaps in worse.

Your citizens of Paris formerly had lent themselves as the ready instruments to slaughter the followers of Calvin, at the infamous massacre of St. Bartholomew. What should we say to those who could think of retaliating on the Parisians of this day the abominations and horrors of that time? They are indeed brought to abhor that massacre. Ferocious as they are, it is not difficult to make them dislike it, because the politicians and fashionable teachers have no interest in giving their passions exactly the same direction. Still, however, they find it their interest to keep the same savage dispositions alive. It was but the other day that they caused this very massacre to be acted on the stage for the diversion of the descendants of those who committed it. In this tragic farce they produced the cardinal of Lorraine in his robes of function, ordering general slaughter. Was this spectacle intended to make the Parisians abhor persecution and loathe the effusion of blood?—No; it was to teach them to persecute their own pastors; it was to excite them, by raising a disgust and horror of their clergy, to an alacrity in hunting down to destruction an order which, if it ought to exist at all, ought to exist not only in safety, but in reverence. It was to stimulate their cannibal appetites (which one would think had been gorged sufficiently) by variety and seasoning; and to quicken them to an alertness in new murders and massacres, if it should suit the purpose of the Guises of the day. An assembly, in which sat a multitude of priests and prelates, was obliged to suffer this indignity at its door. The author was not sent to the galleys, nor the players to the house of correction. Not long after this exhibition, those players came forward to the Assembly to claim the rites of that very religion which they had dared to expose, and to show their prostituted faces in the senate, whilst the archbishop of Paris, whose function was known to his people only by his prayers and benedictions, and his wealth only by his alms, is forced to abandon his house and to fly from his flock (as from ravenous wolves) because, truly, in the sixteenth century, the cardinal of Lorraine was a rebel and a murderer.

Such is the effect of the perversion of history by those who, for the same nefarious purposes, have perverted every other part of learning. But those who will stand upon that elevation of reason which places centuries under our eye and brings things to the true point of comparison, which obscures little names and effaces the colors of little parties, and to which nothing can ascend but the spirit and moral quality of human actions, will say to the teachers of the Palais Royal: The cardinal of Lorraine was the murderer of the sixteenth century, you have the glory of being the murderers in the eighteenth, and this is the only difference between you. But history in the nineteenth century, better understood and better employed, will, I trust, teach a civilized posterity to abhor the misdeeds of both these barbarous ages. It will teach future priests and magistrates not to retaliate upon the speculative and inactive atheists of future times the enormities committed by the present practical zealots and furious fanatics of that wretched error, which, in its quiescent state, is more than punished whenever it is embraced. It will teach posterity not to make war upon either religion or philosophy for the abuse which the hypocrites of both have made of the two most valuable blessings conferred upon us by the bounty of the universal Patron, who in all things eminently favors and protects the race of man.

Clergy Prior to Revolution and the New System

If your clergy, or any clergy, should show themselves vicious beyond the fair bounds allowed to human infirmity, and to those professional faults which can hardly be separated from professional virtues, though their vices never can countenance the exercise of oppression, I do admit that they would naturally have the effect of abating very much of our indignation against the tyrants who exceed measure and justice in their punishment. I can allow in clergymen, through all their divisions, some tenaciousness of their own opinion, some overflowing of zeal for its propagation, some predilection to their own state and office, some attachment to the interests of their own corps, some preference to those who listen with docility to their doctrines, beyond those who scorn and deride them. I allow all this, because I am a man who has to deal with men, and who would not, through a violence of toleration, run into the greatest of all intolerance. I must bear with infirmities until they fester into crimes.

Undoubtedly, the natural progress of the passions, from frailty to vice, ought to be prevented by a watchful eye and a firm hand. But is it true that the body of your clergy had passed those limits of a just allowance? From the general style of your late publications of all sorts one would be led to believe that your clergy in France were a sort of monsters, a horrible composition of superstition, ignorance, sloth, fraud, avarice, and tyranny. But is this true? Is it true that the lapse of time, the cessation of conflicting interests, the woeful experience of the evils resulting from party rage have had no sort of influence gradually to meliorate their minds? Is it true that they were daily renewing invasions on the civil power, troubling the domestic quiet of their country, and rendering the operations of its government feeble and precarious? Is it true that the clergy of our times have pressed down the laity with an iron hand and were in all places lighting up the fires of a savage persecution? Did they by every fraud endeavor to increase their estates? Did they use to exceed the due demands on estates that were their own? Or, rigidly screwing up right into wrong, did they convert a legal claim into a vexatious extortion? When not possessed of power, were they filled with the vices of those who envy it? Were they inflamed with a violent, litigious spirit of controversy? Goaded on with the ambition of intellectual sovereignty, were they ready to fly in the face of all magistracy, to fire churches, to massacre the priests of other descriptions, to pull down altars, and to make their way over the ruins of subverted governments to an empire of doctrine, sometimes flattering, sometimes forcing the consciences of men from the jurisdiction of public institutions into a submission of their personal authority, beginning with a claim of liberty and ending with an abuse of power?

These, or some of these, were the vices objected, and not wholly without foundation, to several of the churchmen of former times who belonged to the two great parties which then divided and distracted Europe.

If there was in France, as in other countries there visibly is, a great abatement rather than any increase of these vices, instead of loading the present clergy with the crimes of other men and the odious character of other times, in common equity they ought to be praised, encouraged, and supported in their departure from a spirit which disgraced their predecessors, and for having assumed a temper of mind and manners more suitable to their sacred function.

When my occasions took me into France, toward the close of the late reign, the clergy, under all their forms, engaged a considerable part of my curiosity. So far from finding (except from one set of men, not then very numerous, though very active) the complaints and discontents against that body, which some publications had given me reason to expect, I perceived little or no public or private uneasiness on their account. On further examination, I found the clergy, in general, persons of moderate minds and decorous manners; I include the seculars and the regulars of both sexes. I had not the good fortune to know a great many of the parochial clergy, but in general I received a perfectly good account of their morals and of their attention to their duties. With some of the higher clergy I had a personal acquaintance, and of the rest in that class a very good means of information. They were, almost all of them, persons of noble birth. They resembled others of their own rank; and where there was any difference, it was in their favor. They were more fully educated than the military noblesse, so as by no means to disgrace their profession by ignorance or by want of fitness for the exercise of their authority. They seemed to me, beyond the clerical character, liberal and open, with the hearts of gentlemen and men of honor, neither insolent nor servile in their manners and conduct. They seemed to me rather a superior class, a set of men amongst whom you would not be surprised to find a Fenelon. I saw among the clergy in Paris (many of the description are not to be met with anywhere) men of great learning and candor; and I had reason to believe that this description was not confined to

Paris. What I found in other places I know was accidental, and therefore to be presumed a fair example. I spent a few days in a provincial town where, in the absence of the bishop, I passed my evenings with three clergymen, his vicars-general, persons who would have done honor to any church. They were all well informed; two of them of deep, general, and extensive erudition, ancient and modern, oriental and western, particularly in their own profession. They had a more extensive knowledge of our English divines than I expected, and they entered into the genius of those writers with a critical accuracy. One of these gentlemen is since dead, the Abbe Morangis. I pay this tribute, without reluctance, to the memory of that noble, reverend, learned, and excellent person; and I should do the same with equal cheerfulness to the merits of the others who, I believe, are still living, if I did not fear to hurt those whom I am unable to serve.

Some of these ecclesiastics of rank are by all titles persons deserving of general respect. They are deserving of gratitude from me and from many English. If this letter should ever come into their hands, I hope they will believe there are those of our nation who feel for their unmerited fall and for the cruel confiscation of their fortunes with no common sensibility. What I say of them is a testimony, as far as one feeble voice can go, which I owe to truth. Whenever the question of this unnatural persecution is concerned, I will pay it. No one shall prevent me from being just and grateful. The time is fitted for the duty, and it is particularly becoming to show our justice and gratitude when those who have deserved well of us and of mankind are laboring under popular obloquy and the persecutions of oppressive power.

You had before your Revolution about a hundred and twenty bishops. A few of them were men of eminent sanctity, and charity without limit. When we talk of the heroic, of course we talk of rare virtue. I believe the instances of eminent depravity may be as rare amongst them as those of transcendent goodness. Examples of avarice and of licentiousness may be picked out, I do not question it, by those who delight in the investigation which leads to such discoveries. A man as old as I am will not be astonished that several, in every description, do not lead that perfect life of self-denial, with regard to wealth or to pleasure, which is wished for by all, by some expected, but by none exacted with more rigor than by those who are the most attentive to their own interests, or the most indulgent to their own passions. When I was in France, I am certain that the number of vicious prelates was not great. Certain individuals among them, not distinguishable for the regularity of their lives, made some amends for their want of the severe virtues in their possession of the liberal, and were endowed with qualities which made them useful in the church and state. I am told that, with few exceptions, Louis the Sixteenth had been more attentive to character, in his promotions to that rank, than his immediate predecessor; and I believe (as some spirit of reform has prevailed through the whole reign) that it may be true. But the present ruling power has shown a disposition only to plunder the church. It has punished all prelates, which is to favor the vicious, at least in point of reputation. It has made a degrading pensionary establishment to which no man of liberal ideas or liberal condition will destine his children. It must settle into the lowest classes of the people. As with you the inferior clergy are not numerous enough for their duties; as these duties are, beyond measure, minute and toilsome; as you have left no middle classes of clergy at their ease, in future nothing of science or erudition can exist in the Gallican church. To complete the project without the least attention to the rights of patrons, the Assembly has provided in future an elective clergy, an arrangement which will drive out of the clerical profession all men of sobriety, all who can pretend to independence in their function or their conduct, and which will throw the whole direction of the public mind into the hands of a set of licentious, bold, crafty, factious, flattering wretches, of such condition and such habits of life as will make their contemptible pensions (in comparison of which the stipend of an exciseman is lucrative and honorable) an object of low and illiberal intrigue. Those officers whom they still call bishops are to be elected to a provision comparatively mean, through the same arts (that is, electioneering arts), by men of all religious tenets that are known or can be invented. The new lawgivers have not ascertained anything whatsoever concerning their qualifications relative either to doctrine or to morals, no more than they have done with regard to the subordinate clergy; nor does it appear but that both the higher and the lower may, at their discretion, practice or preach any mode of religion or irreligion that they please. I do not yet see what the jurisdiction of bishops over their subordinates is to be, or whether they are to have any jurisdiction at all.

In short, Sir, it seems to me that this new ecclesiastical establishment is intended only to be temporary and preparatory to the utter abolition, under any of its forms, of the Christian religion, whenever the minds of men are prepared for this last stroke against it, by the accomplishment of the plan for bringing its ministers into universal contempt. They who will not believe that the philosophical fanatics who guide in these matters have long entertained such a design are utterly ignorant of their character and proceedings. These enthusiasts do not scruple to avow their opinion that a state can subsist without any religion better than with one, and that they are able to supply the place of any good which may be in it by a project of their own—namely, by a sort of education they have imagined, founded in a knowledge of the physical wants of men, progressively carried to an enlightened self-interest which, when well understood, they tell us, will identify with an interest more enlarged and public. The scheme of this education has been long known. Of late they distinguish it (as they have got an entirely new nomenclature of technical terms) by the name of a Civic Education.

I hope their partisans in England (to whom I rather attribute very inconsiderate conduct than the ultimate object in this detestable design) will succeed neither in the pillage of the ecclesiastics, nor in the introduction of a principle of popular election to our bishoprics and parochial cures. This, in the present condition of the world, would be the last corruption of the church, the utter ruin of the clerical character, the most dangerous shock that the state ever received through a misunderstood arrangement of religion. I know well enough that the bishoprics and cures under kingly and seignioral patronage, as now they are in England, and as they have been lately in France, are sometimes acquired by unworthy methods; but the other mode of ecclesiastical canvass subjects them infinitely more surely and more generally to all the evil arts of low ambition, which, operating on and through greater numbers, will produce mischief in proportion.

More on the Confiscation of Church Property

Those of you who have robbed the clergy think that they shall easily reconcile their conduct to all Protestant nations, because the clergy, whom they have thus plundered, degraded, and given over to mockery and scorn, are of the Roman Catholic, that is, of their own pretended persuasion. I have no doubt that some miserable bigots will be found here, as well as elsewhere, who hate sects and parties different from their own more than they love the substance of religion, and who are more angry with those who differ from them in their particular plans and systems than displeased with those who attack the foundation of our common hope. These men will write and speak on the subject in the manner that is to be expected from their temper and character. Burnet says that when he was in France, in the year 1683, "the method which carried over the men of the finest parts to Popery was this—they brought themselves to doubt of the whole Christian religion. When that was once done, it seemed a more indifferent thing of what side or form they continued outwardly." If this was then the ecclesiastical policy of France, it is what they have since but too much reason to repent of. They preferred atheism to a form of religion not agreeable to their ideas. They succeeded in destroying that form; and atheism has succeeded in destroying them. I can readily give credit to Burnet's story, because I have observed too much of a similar spirit (for a little of it is "much too much") amongst ourselves. The humor, however, is not general.

The teachers who reformed our religion in England bore no sort of resemblance to your present reforming doctors in Paris. Perhaps they were (like those whom they opposed) rather more than could be wished under the influence of a party spirit, but they were more sincere believers, men of the most fervent and exalted piety, ready to die (as some of them did die) like true heroes in defense of their particular ideas of Christianity, as they would with equal fortitude, and more cheerfully, for that stock of general truth for the branches of which they contended with their blood. These men would have disavowed with horror those wretches who claimed a fellowship with them upon no other titles than those of their having pillaged the persons with whom they maintained controversies, and their having despised the common religion for the purity of which they exerted themselves with a zeal which unequivocally bespoke their highest reverence for the substance of that system which they wished to reform. Many of their descendants have retained the same zeal, but (as less engaged in conflict) with more moderation. They do not forget that justice and mercy are substantial parts of religion. Impious men do not recommend themselves to their communion by iniquity and cruelty toward any description of their fellow creatures.

We hear these new teachers continually boasting of their spirit of toleration. That those persons should tolerate all opinions, who think none to be of estimation, is a matter of small merit. Equal neglect is not impartial kindness. The species of benevolence which arises from contempt is no true charity. There are in England abundance of men who tolerate in the true spirit of toleration. They think the dogmas of religion, though in different degrees, are all of moment, and that amongst them there is, as amongst all things of value, a just ground of preference. They favor, therefore, and they tolerate. They tolerate, not because they despise opinions, but because they respect justice. They would reverently and affectionately protect all religions because they love and venerate the great principle upon which they all agree, and the great object to which they are all directed. They begin more and more plainly to discern that we have all a common cause, as against a common enemy. They will not be so misled by the spirit of faction as not to distinguish what is done in favor of their subdivision from those acts of hostility which, through some particular description, are aimed at the whole corps, in which they themselves, under another denomination, are included. It is impossible for me to say what may be the character of every description of men amongst us. But I speak for the greater part; and for them, I must tell you that sacrilege is no part of their doctrine of good works; that, so far from calling you into their fellowship on such title, if your professors are admitted to their communion, they must carefully conceal their doctrine of the lawfulness of the prescription of innocent men; and that they must make restitution of all stolen goods whatsoever. Till then they are none of ours.

You may suppose that we do not approve your confiscation of the revenues of bishops, and deans, and chapters, and parochial clergy possessing independent estates arising from land, because we have the same sort of establishment in England. That objection, you will say, cannot hold as to the confiscation of the goods of monks and nuns and the abolition of their order. It is true that this particular part of your general confiscation does not affect England, as a precedent in point; but the reason implies, and it goes a great way. The Long Parliament confiscated the lands of deans and chapters in England on the same ideas upon which your Assembly set to sale the lands of the monastic orders. But it is in the principle of injustice that the danger lies, and not in the description of persons on whom it is first exercised. I see, in a country very near us, a course of policy pursued which sets justice, the common concern of mankind, at defiance. With the National Assembly of France possession is nothing, law and usage are nothing. I see the National Assembly openly reprobate the doctrine of prescription, which one of the greatest of their own lawyers tells us, with great truth, is a part of the law of nature. He tells us that the positive ascertainment of its limits, and its security from invasion, were among the causes for which civil society itself has been instituted. If prescription be once shaken, no species of property is secure when it once becomes an object large enough to tempt the cupidity of indigent power. I see a practice perfectly correspondent to their contempt of this great fundamental part of natural law. I see the confiscators begin with bishops and chapters, and monasteries, but I do not see them end there. I see the princes of the blood, who by the oldest usages of that kingdom held large landed estates, (hardly with the compliment of a debate) deprived of their possessions and, in lieu of their stable, independent property, reduced to the hope of some precarious, charitable pension at the pleasure of an assembly which of course will pay little regard to the rights of pensioners at pleasure when it despises those of legal proprietors. Flushed with the insolence of their first inglorious victories, and pressed by the distresses caused by their lust of unhallowed lucre, disappointed but not discouraged, they have at length ventured completely to subvert all property of all descriptions throughout the extent of a great kingdom. They have compelled all men, in all transactions of commerce, in the disposal of lands, in civil dealing, and through the whole communion of life, to accept as perfect payment and good and lawful tender the symbols of their speculations on a projected sale of their plunder. What vestiges of liberty or property have they left? The tenant right of a cabbage garden, a year's interest in a hovel, the goodwill of an alehouse or a baker's shop, the very shadow of a constructive property, are more ceremoniously treated in our parliament than with you the oldest and most valuable landed possessions, in the hands of the most respectable personages, or than the whole body of the monied and commercial interest of your country. We entertain a high opinion of the legislative authority, but we have never dreamt that parliaments had any right whatever to violate property, to overrule prescription, or to force a currency of their own fiction in the place of that which is real and recognized by the law of nations. But you, who began with refusing to submit to the most moderate restraints, have ended by establishing an unheard-of despotism. I find the ground upon which your confiscators go is this: that, indeed, their proceedings could not be supported in a court of justice, but that the rules of prescription cannot bind a legislative assembly. So that this legislative assembly of a free nation sits, not for the security, but for the destruction, of property, and not of property only, but of every rule and maxim which can give it stability, and of those instruments which can alone give it circulation.

When the Anabaptists of Munster, in the sixteenth century, had filled Germany with confusion by their system of leveling and their wild opinions concerning property, to what country in Europe did not the progress of their fury furnish just cause of alarm? Of all things, wisdom is the most terrified with epidemical fanaticism, because of all enemies it is that against which she is the least able to furnish any kind of resource. We cannot be ignorant of the spirit of atheistical fanaticism that is inspired by a multitude of writings dispersed with incredible assiduity and expense, and by sermons delivered in all the streets and places of public resort in Paris. These writings and sermons have filled the populace with a black and savage atrocity of mind, which supersedes in them the common feelings of nature as well as all sentiments of morality and religion, insomuch that these wretches are induced to bear with a sullen patience the intolerable distresses brought upon them by the violent convulsions and permutations that have been made in property. The spirit of proselytism attends this spirit of fanaticism. They have societies to cabal and correspond at home and abroad for the propagation of their tenets. The republic of Berne, one of the happiest, the most prosperous, and the best governed countries upon earth, is one of the great objects at the destruction of which they aim. I am told they have in some measure succeeded in sowing there the seeds of discontent. They are busy throughout Germany. Spain and Italy have not been untried. England is not left out of the comprehensive scheme of their malignant charity; and in England we find those who stretch out their arms to them, who recommend their example from more than one pulpit, and who choose in more than one periodical meeting publicly to correspond with them, to applaud them, and to hold them up as objects for imitation; who receive from them tokens of confraternity, and standards consecrated amidst their rites and mysteries; who suggest to them leagues of perpetual amity, at the very time when the power to which our constitution has exclusively delegated the federative capacity of this kingdom may find it expedient to make war upon them.

It is not the confiscation of our church property from this example in France that I dread, though I think this would be no trifling evil. The great source of my solicitude is, lest it should ever be considered in England as the policy of a state to seek a resource in confiscations of any kind, or that any one description of citizens should be brought to regard any of the others as their proper prey. Nations are wading deeper and deeper into an ocean of boundless debt. Public debts, which at first were a security to governments by interesting many in the public tranquility, are likely in their excess to become the means of their subversion. If governments provide for these debts by heavy impositions, they perish by becoming odious to the people. If they do not provide for them, they will be undone by the efforts of the most dangerous of all parties—I mean an extensive, discontented monied interest, injured and not destroyed. The men who compose this interest look for their security, in the first instance, to the fidelity of government; in the second, to its power. If they find the old governments effete, worn out, and with their springs relaxed, so as not to be of sufficient vigor for their purposes, they may seek new ones that shall be possessed of more energy; and this energy will be derived, not from an acquisition of resources, but from a contempt of justice. Revolutions are favorable to confiscation; and it is impossible to know under what obnoxious names the next confiscations will be authorized. I am sure that the principles predominant in France extend to very many persons and descriptions of persons, in all countries, who think their innocuous indolence their security. This kind of innocence in proprietors may be argued into inutility; and inutility into an unfitness for their estates. Many parts of Europe are in open disorder. In many others there is a hollow murmuring under ground; a confused movement is felt that threatens a general earthquake in the political world. Already confederacies and correspondences of the most extraordinary nature are forming in several countries. In such a state of things we ought to hold ourselves upon our guard. In all mutations (if mutations must be) the circumstance which will serve most to blunt the edge of their mischief and to promote what good may be in them is that they should find us with our minds tenacious of justice and tender of property.

But it will be argued that this confiscation in France ought not to alarm other nations. They say it is not made from wanton rapacity, that it is a great measure of national policy adopted to remove an extensive, inveterate, superstitious mischief. It is with the greatest difficulty that I am able to separate policy from justice. Justice itself is the great standing policy of civil society, and any eminent departure from it, under any circumstances, lies under the suspicion of being no policy at all.

When men are encouraged to go into a certain mode of life by the existing laws, and protected in that mode as in a lawful occupation; when they have accommodated all their ideas and all their habits to it; when the law had long made their adherence to its rules a ground of reputation, and their departure from them a ground of disgrace and even of penalty—I am sure it is unjust in legislature, by an arbitrary act, to offer a sudden violence to their minds and their feelings, forcibly to degrade them from their state and condition and to stigmatize with shame and infamy that character and those customs which before had been made the measure of their happiness and honor. If to this be added an expulsion from their habitations and a confiscation of all their goods, I am not sagacious enough to discover how this despotic sport, made of the feelings, consciences, prejudices, and properties of men, can be discriminated from the rankest tyranny.

If the injustice of the course pursued in France be clear, the policy of the measure, that is, the public benefit to be expected from it, ought to be at least as evident and at least as important. To a man who acts under the influence of no passion, who has nothing in view in his projects but the public good, a great difference will immediately strike him between what policy would dictate on the original introduction of such institutions and on a question of their total abolition, where they have cast their roots wide and deep, and where, by long habit, things more valuable than themselves are so adapted to them, and in a manner interwoven with them, that the one cannot be destroyed without notably impairing the other. He might be embarrassed if the case were really such as sophisters represent it in their paltry style of debating. But in this, as in most questions of state, there is a middle. There is something else than the mere alternative of absolute destruction or unreformed existence. *Spartam nactus es; hanc exorna.*[29] This is, in my opinion, a rule of profound sense and ought never to depart from the mind of an honest reformer. I cannot conceive how any man can have brought himself to that pitch of presumption to consider his country as nothing but *carte blanche*—upon which he may scribble whatever he pleases. A man full of warm, speculative benevolence may wish his society otherwise constituted than he finds it, but a good patriot and a true politician always considers how he shall make the most of the existing materials of his country. A disposition to preserve and an ability to improve, taken together, would be my standard of a statesman. Everything else is vulgar in the conception, perilous in the execution.

There are moments in the fortune of states when particular men are called to make improvements by great mental exertion. In those moments, even when they seem to enjoy the confidence of their prince and country, and to be invested with full authority, they have not always apt instruments. A politician, to do great things, looks for a power what our workmen call a purchase; and if he finds that power, in politics as in mechanics, he cannot be at a loss to apply it. In the monastic institutions, in my opinion, was found a great power for the mechanism of politic benevolence. There were revenues with a public direction; there were men wholly set apart and dedicated to public purposes, without any other than public ties

---

29 You have obtained Sparta; adorn her.

and public principles; men without the possibility of converting the estate of the community into a private fortune; men denied to self-interests, whose avarice is for some community; men to whom personal poverty is honor, and implicit obedience stands in the place of freedom. In vain shall a man look to the possibility of making such things when he wants them. The winds blow as they list. These institutions are the products of enthusiasm; they are the instruments of wisdom. Wisdom cannot create materials; they are the gifts of nature or of chance; her pride is in the use. The perennial existence of bodies corporate and their fortunes are things particularly suited to a man who has long views; who meditates designs that require time in fashioning, and which propose duration when they are accomplished. He is not deserving to rank high, or even to be mentioned in the order of great statesmen, who, having obtained the command and direction of such a power as existed in the wealth, the discipline, and the habits of such corporations, as those which you have rashly destroyed, cannot find any way of converting it to the great and lasting benefit of his country. On the view of this subject, a thousand uses suggest themselves to a contriving mind. To destroy any power growing wild from the rank productive force of the human mind is almost tantamount, in the moral world, to the destruction of the apparently active properties of bodies in the material. It would be like the attempt to destroy (if it were in our competence to destroy) the expansive force of fixed air in nitre, or the power of steam, or of electricity, or of magnetism. These energies always existed in nature, and they were always discernible. They seemed, some of them unserviceable, some noxious, some no better than a sport to children, until contemplative ability, combining with practical skill, tamed their wild nature, subdued them to use, and rendered them at once the most powerful and the most tractable agents in subservience to the great views and designs of men. Did fifty thousand persons whose mental and whose bodily labor you might direct, and so many hundred thousand a year of a revenue which was neither lazy nor superstitious, appear too big for your abilities to wield? Had you no way of using them but by converting monks into pensioners? Had you no way of turning the revenue to account but through the improvident resource of a spendthrift sale? If you were thus destitute of mental funds, the proceeding is in its natural course. Your politicians do not understand their trade; and therefore they sell their tools.

But the institutions savor of superstition in their very principle, and they nourish it by a permanent and standing influence. This I do not mean to dispute, but this ought not to hinder you from deriving from superstition itself any resources which may thence be furnished for the public advantage. You derive benefits from many dispositions and many passions of the human mind which are of as doubtful a color, in the moral eye, as superstition itself. It was your business to correct and mitigate everything which was noxious in this passion, as in all the passions. But is superstition the greatest of all possible vices? In its possible excess I think it becomes a very great evil. It is, however, a moral subject and, of course, admits of all degrees and all modifications. Superstition is the religion of feeble minds; and they must be tolerated in an intermixture of it, in some trifling or some enthusiastic shape or other, else you will deprive weak minds of a resource found necessary to the strongest. The body of all true religion consists, to be sure, in obedience to the will of the Sovereign of the world, in a confidence in his declarations, and in imitation of his perfections. The rest is our own. It may be prejudicial to the great end; it may be auxiliary. Wise men, who as such are not admirers (not admirers at least of the *Munera Terrae*), are not violently attached to these things, nor do they violently hate them. Wisdom is not the most severe corrector of folly. They are the rival follies which mutually wage so unrelenting a war, and which make so cruel a use of their advantages as they can happen to engage the immoderate vulgar, on the one side or the other, in their quarrels. Prudence would be neuter, but if, in the contention between fond attachment and fierce antipathy concerning things in their nature not made to produce such heats, a prudent man were obliged to make a choice of what errors and excesses of enthusiasm he would condemn or bear, perhaps he would think the superstition which builds to be more tolerable than that which demolishes; that which adorns a country, than that which deforms it; that which endows, than that which plunders; that which disposes to mistaken beneficence, than that which stimulates to real injustice; that which leads a man to refuse to himself lawful pleasures, than that which snatches from others the scanty subsistence of their self-denial. Such, I think, is very nearly the state of the question between the ancient founders of monkish superstition and the superstition of the pretended philosophers of the hour.

Policy of Confiscation vs. Policy of Conservation

For the present I postpone all consideration of the supposed public profit of the sale, which however I conceive to be perfectly delusive. I shall here only consider it as a transfer of property. On the policy of that transfer I shall trouble you with a few thoughts.

In every prosperous community something more is produced than goes to the immediate support of the producer. This surplus forms the income of the landed capitalist. It will be spent by a proprietor who does not labor. But this idleness is itself the spring of labor; this repose the spur to industry. The only concern of the state is that the capital taken in rent from the land should be returned again to the industry from whence it came, and that its expenditure should be with the least possible detriment to the morals of those who expend it, and to those of the people to whom it is returned.

In all the views of receipt, expenditure, and personal employment, a sober legislator would carefully compare the possessor whom he was recommended to expel with the stranger who was proposed to fill his place. Before the inconveniences are incurred which must attend all violent revolutions in property through extensive confiscation, we ought to have some rational assurance that the purchasers of the confiscated property will be in a considerable degree more laborious, more virtuous, more sober, less disposed to extort an unreasonable proportion of the gains of the laborer, or to consume on themselves a larger share than is fit for the measure of an individual; or that they should be qualified to dispense the surplus in a more steady and equal mode, so as to answer the purposes of a politic expenditure, than the old possessors, call those possessors bishops, or canons, or commendatory abbots, or monks, or what you please. The monks are lazy. Be it so. Suppose them no otherwise employed than by singing in the choir. They are as usefully employed as those who neither sing nor say; as usefully even as those who sing upon the stage. They are as usefully employed as if they worked from dawn to dark in the innumerable servile, degrading, unseemly, unmanly, and often most unwholesome and pestiferous occupations to which by the social economy so many wretches are inevitably doomed. If it were not generally pernicious to disturb the natural course of things and to impede in any degree the great wheel of circulation which is turned by the strangely-directed labor of these unhappy people, I should be infinitely more inclined forcibly to rescue them from their miserable industry than violently to disturb the tranquil repose of monastic quietude. Humanity, and perhaps policy, might better justify me in the one than in the other. It is a subject on which I have often reflected, and never reflected without feeling from it. I am sure that no consideration, except the necessity of submitting to the yoke of luxury and the despotism of fancy, who in their own imperious way will distribute the surplus product of the soil, can justify the toleration of such trades and employments in a well-regulated state. But for this purpose of distribution, it seems to me that the idle expenses of monks are quite as well directed as the idle expenses of us lay loiterers.

When the advantages of the possession and of the project are on a par, there is no motive for a change. But in the present case, perhaps, they are not upon a par, and the difference is in favor of the possession. It does not appear to me that the expenses of those whom you are going to expel do in fact take a course so directly and so generally leading to vitiate and degrade and render miserable those through whom they pass as the expenses of those favorites whom you are intruding into their houses. Why should the expenditure of a great landed property, which is a dispersion of the surplus product of the soil, appear intolerable to you or to me when it takes its course through the accumulation of vast libraries, which are the history of the force and weakness of the human mind; through great collections of ancient records, medals, and coins, which attest and explain laws and customs; through paintings and statues that, by imitating nature, seem to extend the limits of creation; through grand monuments of the dead, which continue the regards and connections of life beyond the grave; through collections of the specimens of nature which become a representative assembly of all the classes and families of the world that by disposition facilitate and, by exciting curiosity, open the avenues to science? If by great permanent establishments all these objects of expense are better secured from the inconstant sport of personal caprice and personal extravagance, are they worse than if the same tastes prevailed in scattered individuals? Does not the sweat of the mason and carpenter, who toil in order to partake of the sweat of the peasant, flow as pleasantly and as salubriously in the construction and repair of the majestic edifices of religion as in the painted booths and sordid sties of vice and luxury; as honorably and as profitably in repairing those sacred works which grow hoary with innumerable years as on the momentary receptacles of transient voluptuousness; in opera houses, and brothels, and gaming houses, and clubhouses, and obelisks in the Champ de Mars? Is the surplus product of the olive and the vine worse employed in the frugal sustenance of persons whom the fictions of a pious imagination raise to dignity by construing in the service of God, than in pampering the innumerable multitude of those who are degraded by being made useless domestics, subservient to the pride of man? Are the decorations of temples an expenditure less worthy a wise man than ribbons, and laces, and national cockades, and *petit maisons*, and *petit soupers*[30], and all the innumerable fopperies and follies in which opulence sports away the burden of its superfluity?

---

30 "little houses" and "small dinners."

We tolerate even these, not from love of them, but for fear of worse. We tolerate them because property and liberty, to a degree, require that toleration. But why proscribe the other, and surely, in every point of view, the more laudable, use of estates? Why, through the violation of all property, through an outrage upon every principle of liberty, forcibly carry them from the better to the worse?

This comparison between the new individuals and the old corps is made upon a supposition that no reform could be made in the latter. But in a question of reformation I always consider corporate bodies, whether sole or consisting of many, to be much more susceptible of a public direction by the power of the state, in the use of their property and in the regulation of modes and habits of life in their members, than private citizens ever can be or, perhaps, ought to be; and this seems to me a very material consideration for those who undertake anything which merits the name of a politic enterprise—so far as to the estates of monasteries.

With regard to the estates possessed by bishops and canons and commendatory abbots, I cannot find out for what reason some landed estates may not be held otherwise than by inheritance. Can any philosophic spoiler undertake to demonstrate the positive or the comparative evil of having a certain, and that too a large, portion of landed property passing in succession through persons whose title to it is, always in theory and often in fact, an eminent degree of piety, morals, and learning—a property which, by its destination, in their turn, and on the score of merit, gives to the noblest families renovation and support, to the lowest the means of dignity and elevation; a property the tenure of which is the performance of some duty (whatever value you may choose to set upon that duty), and the character of whose proprietors demands, at least, an exterior decorum and gravity of manners; who are to exercise a generous but temperate hospitality; part of whose income they are to consider as a trust for charity; and who, even when they fail in their trust, when they slide from their character and degenerate into a mere common secular nobleman or gentleman, are in no respect worse than those who may succeed them in their forfeited possessions? Is it better that estates should be held by those who have no duty than by those who have one? By those whose character and destination point to virtues than by those who have no rule and direction in the expenditure of their estates but their own will and appetite? Nor are these estates held together in the character or with the evils supposed inherent in mortmain. They pass from hand to hand with a more rapid circulation than any other. No excess is good; and, therefore, too great a proportion of landed property may be held officially for life; but it does not seem to me of material injury to any commonwealth that there should exist some estates that have a chance of being acquired by other means than the previous acquisition of money.

XVI
CRITIQUE of NATIONAL ASSEMBLY POLICIES

Introduction

This letter has grown to a great length, though it is, indeed, short with regard to the infinite extent of the subject. Various avocations have from time to time called my mind from the subject. I was not sorry to give myself leisure to observe whether, in the proceedings of the National Assembly, I might not find reasons to change or to qualify some of my first sentiments. Everything has confirmed me more strongly in my first opinions. It was my original purpose to take a view of the principles of the National Assembly with regard to the great and fundamental establishments, and to compare the whole of what you have substituted in the place of what you have destroyed with the several members of our British constitution. But this plan is of a greater extent than at first I computed, and I find that you have little desire to take the advantage of any examples. At present I must content myself with some remarks upon your establishments, reserving for another time what I proposed to say concerning the spirit of our British monarchy, aristocracy, and democracy, as practically they exist.

I have taken a view of what has been done by the governing power in France. I have certainly spoken of it with freedom. Those whose principle it is to despise the ancient, permanent sense of mankind and to set up a scheme of society on new principles must naturally expect that such of us who think better of the judgment of the human race than of theirs should consider both them and their devices as men and schemes upon their trial. They must take it for granted that we attend much to their reason, but not at all to their authority. They have not one of the great influencing prejudices of mankind in their favor. They avow their hostility to opinion. Of course, they must expect no support from that influence which, with every other authority, they have deposed from the seat of its jurisdiction.

I can never consider this Assembly as anything else than a voluntary association of men who have availed themselves of circumstances to seize upon the power of the state. They have not the sanction and authority of the character under which they first met. They have assumed another of a very different nature and have completely altered and inverted all the relations in which they originally stood. They do not hold the authority they exercise under any constitutional law of the state. They have departed from the instructions of the people by whom they were sent, which instructions, as the Assembly did not act in virtue of any ancient usage or settled law, were the sole source of their authority. The most considerable of their acts have not been done by great majorities; and in this sort of near divisions, which carry only the constructive authority of the whole, strangers will consider reasons as well as resolutions.

If they had set up this new experimental government as a necessary substitute for an expelled tyranny, mankind would anticipate the time of prescription which, through long usage, mellows into legality governments that were violent in their commencement. All those who have affections which lead them to the conservation of civil order would recognize, even in its cradle, the child as legitimate which has been produced from those principles of cogent expediency to which all just governments owe their birth, and on which they justify their continuance. But they will be late and reluctant in giving any sort of countenance to the operations of a power which has derived its birth from no law and no necessity, but which, on the contrary, has had its origin in those vices and sinister practices by which the social union is often disturbed and sometimes destroyed. This Assembly has hardly a year's prescription. We have their own word for it that they have made a revolution. To make a revolution is a measure which, *prima fronte*, requires an apology. To make a revolution is to subvert the ancient state of our country; and no common reasons are called for to justify so violent a proceeding. The sense of mankind authorizes us to examine into the mode of acquiring new power, and to criticize on the use that is made of it, with less awe and reverence than that which is usually conceded to a settled and recognized authority.

In obtaining and securing their power the Assembly proceeds upon principles the most opposite to those which appear to direct them in the use of it. An observation on this difference will let us into the true spirit of their conduct. Everything which they have done, or continue to do in order to obtain and keep their power is by the most common arts. They proceed exactly as their ancestors of ambition have done before them—trace them through all their artifices, frauds, and violence you can find nothing at all that is new. They follow precedents and examples with the punctilious exactness of a pleader. They never depart an iota from the authentic formulas of tyranny and usurpation. But in all the regulations relative to the public good, the spirit has been the very reverse of this. There they commit the whole to the mercy of untried speculations; they abandon the dearest interests of the public to those loose theories to which none of them would choose to trust the slightest of his private concerns. They make this difference, because in their desire of obtaining and securing power they are thoroughly in earnest; there they travel in the beaten road. The public interests, because about them they have no real solicitude, they abandon wholly to chance; I say to chance, because their schemes have nothing in experience to prove their tendency beneficial.

We must always see with a pity not unmixed with respect the errors of those who are timid and doubtful of themselves with regard to points wherein the happiness of mankind is concerned. But in these gentlemen there is nothing of the tender, parental solicitude which fears to cut up the infant for the sake of an experiment. In the vastness of their promises and the confidence of their predictions, they far outdo all the boasting of empirics. The arrogance of their pretensions in a manner provokes and challenges us to an inquiry into their foundation.

I am convinced that there are men of considerable parts among the popular leaders in the National Assembly. Some of them display eloquence in their speeches and their writings. This cannot be without powerful and cultivated talents. But eloquence may exist without a proportionable degree of wisdom. When I speak of ability, I am obliged to distinguish. What they have done toward the support of their system bespeaks no ordinary men. In the system itself, taken as the scheme of a republic constructed for procuring the prosperity and security of the citizen, and for promoting the strength and grandeur of the state, I confess myself unable to find out anything which displays in a single instance the work of a comprehensive and disposing mind or even the provisions of a vulgar prudence. Their purpose everywhere seems to have been to evade and slip aside from difficulty. This it has been the glory of the great masters in all the arts to confront, and to overcome; and when they had overcome the first difficulty, to turn it into an instrument for new conquests over new difficulties, thus to enable them to extend the empire of their science and even to push forward, beyond the reach of their original thoughts, the landmarks of the human understanding itself. Difficulty is a severe instructor, set over us by the supreme ordinance of a parental Guardian and Legislator, who knows us better than we know ourselves, as he loves us better, too. *Pater ipse colendi haud facilem esse viam voluit.*[31] He that wrestles with us strengthens our nerves and sharpens our skill. Our antagonist

---

31 The father of tilling himself did not wish the way to be easy.

is our helper. This amicable conflict with difficulty obliges us to an intimate acquaintance with our object and compels us to consider it in all its relations. It will not suffer us to be superficial. It is the want of nerves of understanding for such a task, it is the degenerate fondness for tricking shortcuts and little fallacious facilities that has in so many parts of the world created governments with arbitrary powers. They have created the late arbitrary monarchy of France. They have created the arbitrary republic of Paris. With them defects in wisdom are to be supplied by the plenitude of force. They get nothing by it. Commencing their labors on a principle of sloth, they have the common fortune of slothful men. The difficulties, which they rather had eluded than escaped, meet them again in their course; they multiply and thicken on them; they are involved, through a labyrinth of confused detail, in an industry without limit and without direction; and, in conclusion, the whole of their work becomes feeble, vicious, and insecure.

It is this inability to wrestle with difficulty which has obliged the arbitrary Assembly of France to commence their schemes of reform with abolition and total destruction. But is it in destroying and pulling down that skill is displayed? Your mob can do this as well at least as your assemblies. The shallowest understanding, the rudest hand is more than equal to that task. Rage and frenzy will pull down more in half an hour than prudence, deliberation, and foresight can build up in a hundred years. The errors and defects of old establishments are visible and palpable. It calls for little ability to point them out; and where absolute power is given, it requires but a word wholly to abolish the vice and the establishment together. The same lazy but restless disposition which loves sloth and hates quiet directs the politicians when they come to work for supplying the place of what they have destroyed. To make everything the reverse of what they have seen is quite as easy as to destroy. No difficulties occur in what has never been tried. Criticism is almost baffled in discovering the defects of what has not existed; and eager enthusiasm and cheating hope have all the wide field of imagination in which they may expatiate with little or no opposition.

At once to preserve and to reform is quite another thing. When the useful parts of an old establishment are kept, and what is superadded is to be fitted to what is retained, a vigorous mind, steady, persevering attention, various powers of comparison and combination, and the resources of an understanding fruitful in expedients are to be exercised; they are to be exercised in a continued conflict with the combined force of opposite vices, with the obstinacy that rejects all improvement and the levity that is fatigued and disgusted with everything of which it is in possession. But you may object—"A process of this kind is slow. It is not fit for an assembly which glories in performing in a few months the work of ages. Such a mode of reforming, possibly, might take up many years." Without question it might; and it ought. It is one of the excellences of a method in which time is amongst the assistants, that its operation is slow and in some cases almost imperceptible. If circumspection and caution are a part of wisdom when we work only upon inanimate matter, surely they become a part of duty, too, when the subject of our demolition and construction is not brick and timber but sentient beings, by the sudden alteration of whose state, condition, and habits multitudes may be rendered miserable. But it seems as if it were the prevalent opinion in Paris that an unfeeling heart and an undoubting confidence are the sole qualifications for a perfect legislator. Far different are my ideas of that high office. The true lawgiver ought to have a heart full of sensibility. He ought to love and respect his kind, and to fear himself. It may be allowed to his temperament to catch his ultimate object with an intuitive glance, but his movements toward it ought to be deliberate. Political arrangement, as it is a work for social ends, is to be only wrought by social means. There mind must conspire with mind. Time is required to produce that union of minds which alone can produce all the good we aim at. Our patience will achieve more than our force. If I might venture to appeal to what is so much out of fashion in Paris, I mean to experience, I should tell you that in my course I have known and, according to my measure, have co-operated with great men; and I have never yet seen any plan which has not been mended by the observation of those who were much inferior in understanding to the person who took the lead in the business. By a slow but well-sustained progress the effect of each step is watched; the good or ill success of the first gives light to us in the second; and so, from light to light, we are conducted with safety through the whole series. We see that the parts of the system do not clash. The evils latent in the most promising contrivances are provided for as they arise. One advantage is as little as possible sacrificed to another. We compensate, we reconcile, we balance. We are enabled to unite into a consistent whole the various anomalies and contending principles that are found in the minds and affairs of men. From hence arises, not an excellence in simplicity, but one far superior, an excellence in composition. Where the great interests of mankind are concerned through a long succession of generations, that succession ought to be admitted into some share in the councils which are so deeply to affect them. If justice requires this, the work itself requires the aid of more minds than one age can furnish. It is from this view of things that the best legislators have been often satisfied with the establishment of some sure, solid, and ruling principle in government—a power like that which some of the philosophers have called a plastic nature; and having fixed the principle, they have left it afterwards to its own operation.

To proceed in this manner, that is, to proceed with a presiding principle and a prolific energy is with me the criterion of profound wisdom. What your politicians think the marks of a bold, hardy genius are only proofs of a deplorable want of ability. By their violent haste and their defiance of the process of nature, they are delivered over blindly to every projector and adventurer, to every alchemist and empiric. They despair of turning to account anything that is common. Diet is nothing in their system of remedy. The worst of it is that this their despair of curing common distempers by regular methods arises not only from defect of comprehension but, I fear, from some malignity of disposition. Your legislators seem to have taken their opinions of all professions, ranks, and offices from the declamations and buffooneries of satirists; who would themselves be astonished if they were held to the letter of their own descriptions. By listening only to these, your leaders regard all things only on the side of their vices and faults, and view those vices and faults under every color of exaggeration. It is undoubtedly true, though it may seem paradoxical; but in general, those who are habitually employed in finding and displaying faults are unqualified for the work of reformation, because their minds are not only unfurnished with patterns of the fair and good, but by habit they come to take no delight in the contemplation of those things. By hating vices too much, they come to love men too little. It is, therefore, not wonderful that they should be indisposed and unable to serve them. From hence arises the complexional disposition of some of your guides to pull everything in pieces. At this malicious game they display the whole of their quadrimanous activity. As to the rest, the paradoxes of eloquent writers, brought forth purely as a sport of fancy to try their talents, to rouse attention and excite surprise, are taken up by these gentlemen, not in the spirit of the original authors, as means of cultivating their taste and improving their style. These paradoxes become with them serious grounds of action upon which they proceed in regulating the most important concerns of the state. Cicero ludicrously describes Cato as endeavoring to act, in the commonwealth, upon the school paradoxes which exercised the wits of the junior students in the Stoic philosophy. If this was true of Cato, these gentlemen copy after him in the manner of some persons who lived about his time— *pede nudo Catonem*.[32] Mr. Hume told me that he had from Rousseau himself the secret of his principles of composition. That acute though eccentric observer had perceived that to strike and interest the public the marvelous must be produced; that the marvelous of the heathen mythology had long since lost its effect; that the giants, magicians, fairies, and heroes of romance which succeeded had exhausted the portion of credulity which belonged to their age; that now nothing was left to the writer but that species of the marvelous which might still be produced, and with as great an effect as ever, though in another way; that is, the marvelous in life, in

---

32 Reciting Cato barefoot.

manners, in characters, and in extraordinary situations, giving rise to new and unlooked-for strokes in politics and morals. I believe that were Rousseau alive and in one of his lucid intervals, he would be shocked at the practical frenzy of his scholars, who in their paradoxes are servile imitators, and even in their incredulity discover an implicit faith.

Men who undertake considerable things, even in a regular way, ought to give us ground to presume ability. But the physician of the state who, not satisfied with the cure of distempers, undertakes to regenerate constitutions ought to show uncommon powers. Some very unusual appearances of wisdom ought to display themselves on the face of the designs of those who appeal to no practice, and who copy after no model. Has any such been manifested? I shall take a view (it shall for the subject be a very short one) of what the Assembly has done with regard, first, to the constitution of the legislature; in the next place, to that of the executive power; then to that of the judicature; afterwards to the model of the army; and conclude with the system of finance; to see whether we can discover in any part of their schemes the portentous ability which may justify these bold undertakers in the superiority which they assume over mankind.

The Legislature

It is in the model of the sovereign and presiding part of this new republic that we should expect their grand display. Here they were to prove their title to their proud demands. For the plan itself at large, and for the reasons on which it is grounded, I refer to the journals of the Assembly of the 29th of September, 1789, and to the subsequent proceedings which have made any alterations in the plan. So far as in a matter somewhat confused I can see light, the system remains substantially as it has been originally framed. My few remarks will be such as regard its spirit, its tendency, and its fitness for framing a popular commonwealth, which they profess theirs to be, suited to the ends for which any commonwealth, and particularly such a commonwealth, is made. At the same time I mean to consider its consistency with itself and its own principles.

Old establishments are tried by their effects. If the people are happy, united, wealthy, and powerful, we presume the rest. We conclude that to be good from whence good is derived. In old establishments various correctives have been found for their aberrations from theory. Indeed, they are the results of various necessities and expediencies. They are not often constructed after any theory; theories are rather drawn from them. In them we often see the end best obtained where the means seem not perfectly reconcilable to what we may fancy was the original scheme. The means taught by experience may be better suited to political ends than those contrived in the original project. They again react upon the primitive constitution, and sometimes improve the design itself, from which they seem to have departed. I think all this might be curiously exemplified in the British constitution. At worst, the errors and deviations of every kind in reckoning are found and computed, and the ship proceeds in her course. This is the case of old establishments; but in a new and merely theoretic system, it is expected that every contrivance shall appear, on the face of it, to answer its ends, especially where the projectors are no way embarrassed with an endeavor to accommodate the new building to an old one, either in the walls or on the foundations.

The French builders, clearing away as mere rubbish whatever they found and, like their ornamental gardeners, forming everything into an exact level, propose to rest the whole local and general legislature on three bases of three different kinds: one geometrical, one arithmetical, and the third financial; the first of which they call the basis of territory; the second, the basis of population; and the third, the basis of contribution. For the accomplishment of the first of these purposes they divide the area of their country into eighty-three pieces, regularly square, of eighteen leagues by eighteen. These large divisions are called Departments. These they portion, proceeding by square measurement, into seventeen hundred and twenty districts called Communes. These again they subdivide, still proceeding by square measurement, into smaller districts called Cantons, making in all 6400.

At first view this geometrical basis of theirs presents not much to admire or to blame. It calls for no great legislative talents. Nothing more than an accurate land surveyor, with his chain, sight, and theodolite, is requisite for such a plan as this. In the old divisions of the country, various accidents at various times and the ebb and flow of various properties and jurisdictions settled their bounds. These bounds were not made upon any fixed system, undoubtedly. They were subject to some inconveniences, but they were inconveniences for which use had found remedies, and habit had supplied accommodation and patience. In this new pavement of square within square, and this organization and semi-organization, made on the system of Empedocles and Buffon, and not upon any politic principle, it is impossible that innumerable local inconveniences, to which men are not habituated, must not arise. But these I pass over, because it requires an accurate knowledge of the country, which I do not possess, to specify them.

When these state surveyors came to take a view of their work of measurement, they soon found that in politics the most fallacious of all things was geometrical demonstration. They had then recourse to another basis (or rather buttress) to support the building, which tottered on that false foundation. It was evident that the goodness of the soil, the number of the people, their wealth, and the largeness of their contribution made such infinite variations between square and square as to render mensuration a ridiculous standard of power in the commonwealth, and equality in geometry the most unequal of all measures in the distribution of men. However, they could not give it up. But dividing their political and civil representation into three parts, they allotted one of those parts to the square measurement, without a single fact or calculation to ascertain whether this territorial proportion of representation was fairly assigned, and ought upon any principle really to be a third. Having, however, given to geometry this portion (of a third for her dower) out of compliment, I suppose, to that sublime science, they left the other two to be scuffled for between the other parts, population and contribution.

When they came to provide for population, they were not able to proceed quite so smoothly as they had done in the field of their geometry. Here their arithmetic came to bear upon their juridical metaphysics. Had they stuck to their metaphysical principles, the arithmetical process would be simple indeed. Men, with them, are strictly equal and are entitled to equal rights in their own government. Each head, on this system, would have its vote, and every man would vote directly for the person who was to represent him in the legislature. "But soft—by regular degrees, not yet." This metaphysical principle to which law, custom, usage, policy, reason were to yield is to yield itself to their pleasure. There must be many degrees, and some stages, before the representative can come in contact with his constituent. Indeed, as we shall soon see, these two persons are to have no sort of communion with each other. First, the voters in the Canton, who compose what they call "primary assemblies," are to have a qualification. What! A qualification on the indefeasible rights of men? Yes; but it shall be a very small qualification. Our injustice shall be very little oppressive: only the local valuation of three days' labor paid to the public. Why, this is not much, I readily admit, for anything but the utter subversion of your equalizing principle. As a qualification it might as well be let alone, for it answers no one purpose for which qualifications are established; and, on your ideas, it excludes from a vote the man of all others whose natural equality stands the most in need of protection and defense—I mean the man who has nothing else but his natural equality to guard him. You order him to buy the right which you before told him nature had given to him gratuitously at his birth, and of which no authority on earth could lawfully deprive him. With regard to the person who cannot come up to your market, a tyrannous aristocracy, as against him, is established at the very outset by you who pretend to be its sworn foe.

The gradation proceeds. These primary assemblies of the Canton elect deputies to the Commune; one for every two hundred qualified inhabitants. Here is the first medium put between the primary elector and the representative legislator; and here a new turnpike is fixed for taxing the rights of men with a second qualification; for none can be elected into the Commune who does not pay the amount of ten days' labor. Nor have we yet done. There is still to be another gradation. These Communes, chosen by the Canton, choose to the Department; and the deputies of the Department choose their deputies to the National Assembly. Here is a third barrier of a senseless qualification. Every deputy to the National Assembly must pay, in direct contribution, to the value of a mark of silver. Of all these qualifying barriers we must think alike—that they are impotent to secure independence, strong only to destroy the rights of men.

In all this process, which in its fundamental elements affects to consider only population upon a principle of natural right, there is a manifest attention to property, which, however just and reasonable on other schemes, is on theirs perfectly unsupportable.

When they come to their third basis, that of contribution, we find that they have more completely lost sight of their rights of men. This last basis rests entirely on property. A principle totally different from the equality of men, and utterly irreconcilable to it, is thereby admitted; but no sooner is this principle admitted than (as usual) it is subverted; and it is not subverted (as we shall presently see) to approximate the inequality of riches to the level of nature. The additional share in the third portion of representation (a portion reserved exclusively for the higher contribution) is made to regard the district only, and not the individuals in it who pay. It is easy to perceive, by the course of their reasonings, how much they were embarrassed by their contradictory ideas of the rights of men and the privileges of riches. The committee of constitution do as good as admit that they are wholly irreconcilable. "The relation with regard to the contributions is without doubt null (say they) when the question is on the balance of the political rights as between individual and individual, without which personal equality would be destroyed and an aristocracy of the rich would be established. But this inconvenience entirely disappears when the proportional relation of the contribution is only considered in the great masses, and is solely between province and province; it serves in that case only to form a just reciprocal proportion between the cities without affecting the personal rights of the citizens."

Here the principle of contribution, as taken between man and man, is reprobated as null and destructive to equality, and as pernicious, too, because it leads to the establishment of an aristocracy of the rich. However, it must not be abandoned. And the way of getting rid of the difficulty is to establish the inequality as between department and department, leaving all the individuals in each department upon an exact par. Observe that this parity between individuals had been before destroyed when the qualifications within the departments were settled; nor does it seem a matter of great importance whether the equality of men be injured by masses or individually. An individual is not of the same importance in a mass represented by a few as in a mass represented by many. It would be too much to tell a man jealous of his equality that the elector has the same franchise who votes for three members as he who votes for ten.

Now take it in the outer point of view and let us suppose their principle of representation according to contribution, that is, according to riches, to be well imagined and to be a necessary basis for their republic. In this their third basis they assume that riches ought to be respected, and that justice and policy require that they should entitle men, in some mode or other, to a larger share in the administration of public affairs; it is now to be seen how the Assembly provides for the preeminence, or even for the security, of the rich by conferring, in virtue of their opulence, that larger measure of power to their district which is denied to them personally. I readily admit (indeed I should lay it down as a fundamental principle) that in a republican government which has a democratic basis the rich do require an additional security above what is necessary to them in monarchies. They are subject to envy, and through envy to oppression. On the present scheme it is impossible to divine what advantage they derive from the aristocratic preference upon which the unequal representation of the masses is founded. The rich cannot feel it, either as a support to dignity or as security to fortune, for the aristocratic mass is generated from purely democratic principles, and the preference given to it in the general representation has no sort of reference to, or connection with, the persons upon account of whose property this superiority of the mass is established. If the contrivers of this scheme meant any sort of favor to the rich, in consequence of their contribution, they ought to have conferred the privilege either on the individual rich or on some class formed of rich persons (as historians represent Servius Tullius to have done in the early constitution of Rome), because the contest between the rich and the poor is not a struggle between corporation and corporation, but a contest between men and men—a competition not between districts, but between descriptions. It would answer its purpose better if the scheme were inverted: that the vote of the masses were rendered equal, and that the votes within each mass were proportioned to property.

Let us suppose one man in a district (it is an easy supposition) to contribute as much as a hundred of his neighbors. Against these he has but one vote. If there were but one representative for the mass, his poor neighbors would outvote him by a hundred to one for that single representative. Bad enough. But amends are to be made him. How? The district, in virtue of his wealth, is to choose, say, ten members instead of one; that is to say, by paying a very large contribution he has the happiness of being outvoted a hundred to one by the poor for ten representatives, instead of being outvoted exactly in the same proportion for a single member. In truth, instead of benefiting by this superior quantity of representation, the rich man is subjected to an additional hardship. The increase of representation within his province sets up nine persons more, and as many more than nine as there may be democratic candidates, to cabal and intrigue, and to flatter the people at his expense and to his oppression. An interest is by this means held out to multitudes of the inferior sort, in obtaining a salary of eighteen *livres* a day (to them a vast object) besides the pleasure of a residence in Paris and their share in the government of the kingdom. The more the objects of ambition are multiplied and become democratic, just in that proportion the rich are endangered.

Thus it must fare between the poor and the rich in the province deemed aristocratic, which in its internal relation is the very reverse of that character. In its external relation, that is, its relation to the other provinces, I cannot see how the unequal representation which is given to masses on account of wealth becomes the means of preserving the equipoise and the tranquility of the commonwealth. For if it be one of the objects to secure the weak from being crushed by the strong (as in all society undoubtedly it is), how are the smaller and poorer of these masses to be saved from the tyranny of the more wealthy? Is it by adding to the wealthy further and more systematical means of oppressing them? When we come to a balance of representation between corporate bodies, provincial interests, emulations, and jealousies are full as likely to arise among them as among individuals; and their divisions are likely to produce a much hotter spirit of dissension, and something leading much more nearly to a war.

I see that these aristocratic masses are made upon what is called the principle of direct contribution. Nothing can be a more unequal standard than this. The indirect contribution, that which arises from duties on consumption, is in truth a better standard and follows and discovers wealth more naturally than this of direct contribution. It is difficult, indeed, to fix a standard of local preference on account of the one, or of the other, or of both, because some provinces may pay the more of either or of both on account of causes not intrinsic, but originating from those very districts over whom they have obtained a preference in consequence of their ostensible contribution. If the masses were independent, sovereign bodies who were to provide for a federative treasury by distinct contingents, and that the revenue had not (as it has) many impositions running through the whole, which affect men individually, and not corporately, and which, by their nature, confound all territorial limits, something might be said for the basis of contribution as founded on masses. But of all things, this representation, to be measured by contribution, is the most difficult to settle upon principles of equity in a country which considers its districts as members of a whole. For a great city, such as Bordeaux or Paris, appears to pay a vast body of duties, almost out of all assignable proportion to other places, and its mass is considered accordingly. But are these cities the true contributors in that proportion? No. The consumers of the commodities imported into Bordeaux, who are scattered through all France, pay the import duties of Bordeaux. The produce of the vintage in Guienne and Languedoc give to that city the means of its contribution growing out of an export commerce. The landholders who spend their estates in Paris, and are thereby the creators of that city, contribute for Paris from the provinces out of which their revenues arise. Very nearly the same arguments will apply to the representative share given on account of direct contributions, because the direct contribution must be assessed on wealth, real or presumed; and that local wealth will itself arise from causes not local, and which therefore in equity ought not to produce a local preference.

It is very remarkable that in this fundamental regulation which settles the representation of the mass upon the direct contribution, they have not yet settled how that direct contribution shall be laid, and how apportioned. Perhaps there is some latent policy toward the continuance of the present Assembly in this strange procedure. However, until they do this, they can have no certain constitution. It must depend at last upon the system of taxation, and must vary with every variation in that system. As they have contrived matters, their taxation does not so much depend on their constitution as their constitution on their taxation. This must introduce great confusion among the masses, as the variable qualification for votes within the district must, if ever real contested elections take place, cause infinite internal controversies.

To compare together the three bases, not on their political reason, but on the ideas on which the Assembly works, and to try its consistency with itself, we cannot avoid observing that the principle which the committee call the basis of population does not begin to operate from the same point with the two other principles called the bases of territory and of contribution, which are both of an aristocratic nature. The consequence is that, where all three begin to operate together, there is the most absurd inequality produced by the operation of the former on the two latter principles. Every canton contains four square leagues, and is estimated to contain, on the average, 4000 inhabitants or 680 voters in the primary assemblies, which vary in numbers with the population of the canton, and send one deputy to the commune for every 200 voters. Nine cantons make a commune.

Now let us take a canton containing a seaport town of trade, or a great manufacturing town. Let us suppose the population of this canton to be 12,700 inhabitants, or 2193 voters, forming three primary assemblies, and sending ten deputies to the commune.

Oppose to this one canton two others of the remaining eight in the same commune. These we may suppose to have their fair population of 4000 inhabitants and 680 voters each, or 8000 inhabitants and 1360 voters, both together. These will form only two primary assemblies and send only six deputies to the commune.

When the assembly of the commune comes to vote on the basis of territory, which principle is first admitted to operate in that assembly, the single canton which has half the territory of the other two will have ten voices to six in the election of three deputies to the assembly of the department chosen on the express ground of a representation of territory.

This inequality, striking as it is, will be yet highly aggravated if we suppose, as we fairly may, the several other cantons of the commune to fall proportionably short of the average population, as much as the principal canton exceeds it. Now as to the basis of contribution, which also is a principle admitted first to operate in the assembly of the commune. Let us again take one canton, such as is stated above. If the whole of the direct contributions paid by a great trading or manufacturing town be divided equally among the inhabitants, each individual will be found to pay much more than an individual living in the country according to the same average. The whole paid by the inhabitants of the former will be more than the whole paid by the inhabitants of the latter—we may fairly assume one-third more. Then the 12,700 inhabitants, or 2193 voters of the canton, will pay as much as 19,050 inhabitants, or 3289 voters of the other cantons, which are nearly the estimated proportion of inhabitants and voters of five other cantons. Now the 2193 voters will, as I before said, send only ten deputies to the assembly; the 3289 voters will send sixteen. Thus, for an equal share in the contribution of the whole commune, there will be a difference of sixteen voices to ten in voting for deputies to be chosen on the principle of representing the general contribution of the whole commune.

By the same mode of computation we shall find 15,875 inhabitants, or 2741 voters of the other cantons, who pay one-sixth *less* to the contribution of the whole commune, will have three voices *more* than the 12,700 inhabitants, or 2193 voters of the one canton.

Such is the fantastical and unjust inequality between mass and mass in this curious repartition of the rights of representation arising out of territory and contribution. The qualifications which these confer are in truth negative qualifications, that give a right in an inverse proportion to the possession of them.

In this whole contrivance of the three bases, consider it in any light you please, I do not see a variety of objects reconciled in one consistent whole, but several contradictory principles reluctantly and irreconcilably brought and held together by your philosophers, like wild beasts shut up in a cage to claw and bite each other to their mutual destruction.

I am afraid I have gone too far into their way of considering the formation of a constitution. They have much, but bad, metaphysics; much, but bad, geometry; much, but false, proportionate arithmetic; but if it were all as exact as metaphysics, geometry, and arithmetic ought to be, and if their schemes were perfectly consistent in all their parts, it would make only a more fair and sightly vision. It is remarkable that, in a great arrangement of mankind, not one reference whatsoever is to be found to anything moral or anything politic, nothing that relates to the concerns, the actions, the passions, the interests of men. *Hominem non sapiunt.*[33]

You see I only consider this constitution as electoral, and leading by steps to the National Assembly. I do not enter into the internal government of the departments and their genealogy through the communes and cantons. These local governments are, in the original plan, to be as nearly as possible composed in the same manner and on the same principles with the elective assemblies. They are each of them bodies perfectly compact and rounded in themselves.

You cannot but perceive in this scheme that it has a direct and immediate tendency to sever France into a variety of republics, and to render them totally independent of each other without any direct constitutional means of coherence, connection, or subordination, except what may be derived from their acquiescence in the determinations of the general congress of the ambassadors from each independent republic. Such in reality is the National Assembly, and such governments I admit do exist in the world, though in forms infinitely more suitable to the local and habitual circumstances of their people. But such associations, rather than bodies politic, have generally been the effect of necessity, not choice; and I believe the present French power is the very first body of citizens who, having obtained full authority to do with their country what they pleased, have chosen to dissever it in this barbarous manner.

It is impossible not to observe that, in the spirit of this geometrical distribution and arithmetical arrangement, these pretended

---

33 They do not understand man.

citizens treat France exactly like a country of conquest. Acting as conquerors, they have imitated the policy of the harshest of that harsh race. The policy of such barbarous victors, who condemn a subdued people and insult their feelings, has ever been, as much as in them lay, to destroy all vestiges of the ancient country, in religion, in polity, in laws, and in manners; to confound all territorial limits; to produce a general poverty; to put up their properties to auction; to crush their princes, nobles, and pontiffs; to lay low everything which had lifted its head above the level, or which could serve to combine or rally, in their distresses, the disbanded people under the standard of old opinion. They have made France free in the manner in which those sincere friends to the rights of mankind, the Romans, freed Greece, Macedon, and other nations. They destroyed the bonds of their union under color of providing for the independence of each of their cities.

When the members who compose these new bodies of cantons, communes, and departments—arrangements purposely produced through the medium of confusion—begin to act, they will find themselves in a great measure strangers to one another. The electors and elected throughout, especially in the rural cantons, will be frequently without any civil habitudes or connections, or any of that natural discipline which is the soul of a true republic. Magistrates and collectors of revenue are now no longer acquainted with their districts, bishops with their dioceses, or curates with their parishes. These new colonies of the rights of men bear a strong resemblance to that sort of military colonies which Tacitus has observed upon in the declining policy of Rome. In better and wiser days (whatever course they took with foreign nations) they were careful to make the elements of methodical subordination and settlement to be coeval, and even to lay the foundations of civil discipline in the military. But when all the good arts had fallen into ruin, they proceeded, as your Assembly does, upon the equality of men, and with as little judgment and as little care for those things which make a republic tolerable or durable. But in this, as well as almost every instance, your new commonwealth is born and bred and fed in those corruptions which mark degenerated and worn-out republics. Your child comes into the world with the symptoms of death: the *facies Hippocratica* forms the character of its physiognomy, and the prognostic of its fate.[34]

The legislators who framed the ancient republics knew that their business was too arduous to be accomplished with no better apparatus than the metaphysics of an undergraduate, and the mathematics and arithmetic of an exciseman. They had to do with men, and they were obliged to study human nature. They had to do with citizens, and they were obliged to study the effects of those habits which are communicated by the circumstances of civil life. They were sensible that the operation of this second nature on the first produced a new combination; and thence arose many diversities amongst men, according to their birth, their education, their professions, the periods of their lives, their residence in towns or in the country, their several ways of acquiring and of fixing property, and according to the quality of the property itself—all which rendered them as it were so many different species of animals. From hence they thought themselves obliged to dispose their citizens into such classes, and to place them in such situations in the state, as their peculiar habits might qualify them to fill, and to allot to them such appropriated privileges as might secure to them what their specific occasions required, and which might furnish to each description such force as might protect it in the conflict caused by the diversity of interests that must exist and must contend in all complex society; for the legislator would have been ashamed that the coarse husbandman should well know how to assort and to use his sheep, horses, and oxen, and should have enough of common sense not to abstract and equalize them all into animals without providing for each kind an appropriate food, care, and employment, whilst he, the economist, disposer, and shepherd of his own kindred, subliming himself into an airy metaphysician, was resolved to know nothing of his flocks but as men in general. It is for this reason

---

34 The change in the face caused by impending death.

that Montesquieu observed very justly that in their classification of the citizens the great legislators of antiquity made the greatest display of their powers, and even soared above themselves. It is here that your modern legislators have gone deep into the negative series, and sunk even below their own nothing. As the first sort of legislators attended to the different kinds of citizens and combined them into one commonwealth, the others, the metaphysical and alchemistical legislators, have taken the direct contrary course. They have attempted to confound all sorts of citizens, as well as they could, into one homogeneous mass; and then they divided this their amalgam into a number of incoherent republics. They reduce men to loose counters, merely for the sake of simple telling, and not to figures whose power is to arise from their place in the table. The elements of their own metaphysics might have taught them better lessons. The troll of their categorical table might have informed them that there was something else in the intellectual world besides substance and quantity. They might learn from the catechism of metaphysics that there were eight heads more in every complex deliberation which they have never thought of, though these, of all the ten, are the subjects on which the skill of man can operate anything at all.

So far from this able disposition of some of the old republican legislators, which follows with a solicitous accuracy the moral conditions and propensities of men, they have leveled and crushed together all the orders which they found, even under the coarse inartificial arrangement of the monarchy, in which mode of government the classing of the citizens is not of so much importance as in a republic. It is true, however, that every such classification, if properly ordered, is good in all forms of government, and composes a strong barrier against the excesses of despotism, as well as it is the necessary means of giving effect and permanence to a republic. For want of something of this kind, if the present project of a republic should fail, all securities to a moderated freedom fail along with it; all the indirect restraints which mitigate despotism are removed, insomuch that if monarchy should ever again obtain an entire ascendancy in France, under this or under any other dynasty, it will probably be, if not voluntarily tempered at setting out by the wise and virtuous counsels of the prince, the most completely arbitrary power that has ever appeared on earth. This is to play a most desperate game.

The confusion which attends on all such proceedings they even declare to be one of their objects, and they hope to secure their constitution by a terror of a return of those evils which attended their making it. "By this," say they, "its destruction will become difficult to authority, which cannot break it up without the entire disorganization of the whole state." They presume that, if this authority should ever come to the same degree of power that they have acquired, it would make a more moderate and chastised use of it, and would piously tremble entirely to disorganize the state in the savage manner that they have done. They expect, from the virtues of returning despotism, the security which is to be enjoyed by the offspring of their popular vices.

I wish, Sir, that you and my readers would give an attentive perusal to the work of M. de Calonne on this subject. It is, indeed, not only an eloquent, but an able and instructive, performance. I confine myself to what he says relative to the constitution of the new state and to the condition of the revenue. As to the disputes of this minister with his rivals, I do not wish to pronounce upon them. As little do I mean to hazard any opinion concerning his ways and means, financial or political, for taking his country out of its present disgraceful and deplorable situation of servitude, anarchy, bankruptcy, and beggary. I cannot speculate quite so sanguinely as he does; but he is a Frenchman, and has a closer duty relative to those objects, and better means of judging of them, than I can have. I wish that the formal avowal which he refers to, made by one of the principal leaders in the Assembly concerning the tendency of their scheme to bring France not only from a monarchy to a republic, but from a republic to a mere confederacy, may be very particularly attended to. It adds new force to my observations, and indeed M. de Calonne's work supplies my deficiencies by many new and striking arguments on most of the subjects of this letter.

It is this resolution, to break their country into separate republics, which has driven them into the greatest number of their difficulties and contradictions. If it were not for this, all the questions of exact equality and these balances, never to be settled, of individual rights, population, and contribution would be wholly useless. The representation, though derived from parts, would be a duty which equally regarded the whole. Each deputy to the Assembly would be the representative of France, and of all its descriptions, of the many and of the few, of the rich and of the poor, of the great districts and of the small. All these districts would themselves be subordinate to some standing authority, existing independently of them, an authority in which their representation, and everything that belongs to it, originated, and to which it was pointed. This standing, unalterable, fundamental government would make, and it is the only thing which could make, that territory truly and properly a whole. With us, when we elect popular representatives, we send them to a council in which each man individually is a subject and submitted to a government complete in all its ordinary functions. With you the elective Assembly is the sovereign, and the sole sovereign; all the members are therefore integral parts of this sole sovereignty. But with us it is totally different. With us the representative, separated from the other parts, can have no action and no existence. The government is the point of reference of the several members and districts of our representation. This is the center of our unity. This government of reference is a trustee for the whole, and not for the parts. So is the other branch of our public council, I mean the House of Lords. With us the king and the lords are several and joint securities for the equality of each district, each province, each city. When did you hear in Great Britain of any province suffering from the inequality of its representation, what district from having no representation at all? Not only our monarchy and our peerage secure the equality on which our unity depends, but it is the spirit of the House of Commons itself. The very inequality of representation, which is so foolishly complained of, is perhaps the very thing which prevents us from thinking or acting as members for districts. Cornwall elects as many members as all Scotland. But is Cornwall better taken care of than Scotland? Few trouble their heads about any of your bases, out of some giddy clubs. Most of those who wish for any change, upon any plausible grounds, desire it on different ideas.

Your new constitution is the very reverse of ours in its principle; and I am astonished how any persons could dream of holding out anything done in it as an example for Great Britain. With you there is little, or rather no, connection between the last representative and the first constituent. The member who goes to the National Assembly is not chosen by the people, nor accountable to them. There are three elections before he is chosen; two sets of magistracy intervene between him and the primary assembly, so as to render him, as I have said, an ambassador of a state, and not the representative of the people within a state. By this the whole spirit of the election is changed, nor can any corrective which your constitution-mongers have devised render him anything else than what he is. The very attempt to do it would inevitably introduce a confusion, if possible, more horrid than the present. There is no way to make a connection between the original constituent and the representative, but by the circuitous means which may lead the candidate to apply in the first instance to the primary electors, in order that by their authoritative instructions (and something more perhaps) these primary electors may force the two succeeding bodies of electors to make a choice agreeable to their wishes. But this would plainly subvert the whole scheme. It would be to plunge them back into that tumult and confusion of popular election which, by their interposed gradation of elections, they mean to avoid, and at length to risk the whole fortune of the state with those who have the least knowledge of it and the least interest in it. This is a perpetual dilemma into which they are thrown by the vicious, weak, and contradictory principles they have chosen. Unless the people break up and level this gradation, it is plain that they do not at all substantially elect to the Assembly; indeed, they elect as little in appearance as reality.

What is it we all seek for in an election? To answer its real purposes, you must first possess the means of knowing the fitness of your man; and then you must retain some hold upon him by personal obligation or dependence. For what end are these primary electors complimented, or rather mocked, with a choice? They can never know anything of the qualities of him that is to serve them, nor has he any obligation whatsoever to them. Of all the powers unfit to be delegated by those who have any real means of judging, that most peculiarly unfit is what relates to a personal choice. In case of abuse, that body of primary electors never can call the representative to an account for his conduct. He is too far removed from them in the chain of representation. If he acts improperly at the end of his two years' lease, it does not concern him for two years more. By the new French constitution the best and the wisest representatives go equally with the worst into this *Limbus Patrum*.[35] Their bottoms are supposed foul, and they must go into dock to be refitted. Every man who has served in an assembly is ineligible for two years after. Just as these magistrates begin to learn their trade, like chimney sweepers, they are disqualified for exercising it. Superficial, new, petulant acquisition, and interrupted, dronish, broken, ill recollection is to be the destined character of all your future governors. Your constitution has too much of jealousy to have much of sense in it. You consider the breach of trust in the representative so principally that you do not at all regard the question of his fitness to execute it.

This purgatory interval is not unfavorable to a faithless representative, who may be as good a canvasser as he was a bad governor. In this time he may cabal himself into a superiority over the wisest and most virtuous. As in the end all the members of this elective constitution are equally fugitive and exist only for the election, they may be no longer the same persons who had chosen him, to whom he is to be responsible when he solicits for a renewal of his trust. To call all the secondary electors of the Commune to account is ridiculous, impracticable, and unjust; they may themselves have been deceived in their choice, as the third set

---

35 The Father's limbo.

of electors, those of the Department, may be in theirs. In your elections responsibility cannot exist.

Finding no sort of principle of coherence with each other in the nature and constitution of the several new republics of France, I considered what cement the legislators had provided for them from any extraneous materials. Their confederations, their spectacles, their civic feasts, and their enthusiasm I take no notice of; they are nothing but mere tricks; but tracing their policy through their actions, I think I can distinguish the arrangements by which they propose to hold these republics together. The first is the confiscation, with the compulsory paper currency annexed to it; the second is the supreme power of the city of Paris; the third is the general army of the state. Of this last I shall reserve what I have to say until I come to consider the army as a head by itself.

As to the operation of the first (the confiscation and paper currency) merely as a cement, I cannot deny that these, the one depending on the other, may for some time compose some sort of cement if their madness and folly in the management, and in the tempering of the parts together, does not produce a repulsion in the very outset. But allowing to the scheme some coherence and some duration, it appears to me that if, after a while, the confiscation should not be found sufficient to support the paper coinage (as I am morally certain it will not), then, instead of cementing, it will add infinitely to the dissociation, distraction, and confusion of these confederate republics, both with relation to each other and to the several parts within themselves. But if the confiscation should so far succeed as to sink the paper currency, the cement is gone with the circulation. In the meantime its binding force will be very uncertain, and it will straiten or relax with every variation in the credit of the paper.

One thing only is certain in this scheme, which is an effect seemingly collateral, but direct, I have no doubt, in the minds of those who conduct this business, that is, its effect in producing an oligarchy in every one of the republics. A paper circulation, not founded on any real money deposited or engaged for, amounting already to forty-four millions of English money, and this currency by force substituted in the place of the coin of the kingdom, becoming thereby the substance of its revenue as well as the medium of all its commercial and civil intercourse, must put the whole of what power, authority, and influence is left, in any form whatsoever it may assume, into the hands of the managers and conductors of this circulation.

In England, we feel the influence of the Bank, though it is only the center of a voluntary dealing. He knows little indeed of the influence of money upon mankind who does not see the force of the management of a monied concern which is so much more extensive and in its nature so much more depending on the managers than any of ours. But this is not merely a money concern. There is another member in the system inseparably connected with this money management. It consists in the means of drawing out at discretion portions of the confiscated lands for sale, and carrying on a process of continual transmutation of paper into land, and land into paper. When we follow this process in its effects, we may conceive something of the intensity of the force with which this system must operate. By this means the spirit of money-jobbing and speculation goes into the mass of land itself and incorporates with it. By this kind of operation that species of property becomes (as it were) volatilized; it assumes an unnatural and monstrous activity, and thereby throws into the hands of the several managers, principal and subordinate, Parisian and provincial, all the representative of money and perhaps a full tenth part of all the land in France, which has now acquired the worst and most pernicious part of the evil of a paper circulation, the greatest possible uncertainty in its value. They have reversed the Latonian kindness to the landed property of Delos. They have sent theirs to be blown about, like the light fragments of a wreck, *oras et littora circum.*[36]

The new dealers, being all habitually adventurers and without

---

36 [Scattered] around the shores and coasts.

any fixed habits of local predilections, will purchase to job out again, as the market of paper or of money or of land shall present an advantage. For though a holy bishop thinks that agriculture will derive great advantages from the "enlightened" usurers who are to purchase the church confiscations, I, who am not a good but an old farmer, with great humility beg leave to tell his late lordship that usury is not a tutor of agriculture; and if the word "enlightened" be understood according to the new dictionary, as it always is in your new schools, I cannot conceive how a man's not believing in God can teach him to cultivate the earth with the least of any additional skill or encouragement. *"Diis immortalibus sero,"*[37] said an old Roman, when he held one handle of the plough, whilst Death held the other. Though you were to join in the commission all the directors of the two academies to the directors of the Caisse d'Escompte, one old, experienced peasant is worth them all. I have got more information upon a curious and interesting branch of husbandry, in one short conversation with an old Carthusian monk, than I have derived from all the Bank directors that I have ever conversed with. However, there is no cause for apprehension from the meddling of money dealers with rural economy. These gentlemen are too wise in their generation. At first, perhaps, their tender and susceptible imaginations may be captivated with the innocent and unprofitable delights of a pastoral life; but in a little time they will find that agriculture is a trade much more laborious, and much less lucrative, than that which they had left. After making its panegyric, they will turn their backs on it like their great precursor and prototype. They may, like him, begin by singing *"Beatus ille"* but what will be the end?

Haec ubi locutus foenerator Alphius,
Jam jam futurus rusticus
Omnem redegit idibus pecuniam;
Quaerit calendis ponere.[38]

---

37 I sow for the immortal gods.

38 Having said this, Alphius the money-lender, // about to become a farmer // brings back all his money in the ides; // he inquires into investing in the calends.

They will cultivate the Caisse d'Eglise, under the sacred auspices of this prelate, with much more profit than its vineyards and its cornfields. They will employ their talents according to their habits and their interests. They will not follow the plough whilst they can direct treasuries and govern provinces.

Your legislators, in everything new, are the very first who have founded a commonwealth upon gaming, and infused this spirit into it as its vital breath. The great object in these politics is to metamorphose France from a great kingdom into one great play-table; to turn its inhabitants into a nation of gamesters; to make speculation as extensive as life; to mix it with all its concerns and to divert the whole of the hopes and fears of the people from their usual channels into the impulses, passions, and superstitions of those who live on chances. They loudly proclaim their opinion that this their present system of a republic cannot possibly exist without this kind of gaming fund, and that the very thread of its life is spun out of the staple of these speculations. The old gaming in funds was mischievous enough, undoubtedly, but it was so only to individuals. Even when it had its greatest extent, in the Mississippi and South Sea, it affected but few, comparatively; where it extends further, as in lotteries, the spirit has but a single object. But where the law, which in most circumstances forbids, and in none countenances, gaming, is itself debauched so as to reverse its nature and policy and expressly to force the subject to this destructive table by bringing the spirit and symbols of gaming into the minutest matters and engaging everybody in it, and in everything, a more dreadful epidemic distemper of that kind is spread than yet has appeared in the world. With you a man can neither earn nor buy his dinner without a speculation. What he receives in the morning will not have the same value at night. What he is compelled to take as pay for an old debt will not be received as the same when he comes to pay a debt contracted by himself, nor will it be the same when by prompt payment he would avoid contracting any debt at all. Industry must wither away. Economy must be driven from your country. Careful provision will have no existence. Who will labor without knowing the amount of his pay? Who will study to increase what none can estimate? Who will accumulate, when he does not know the value of what he saves? If you abstract it from its uses in gaming, to accumulate your paper wealth would be not the providence of a man, but the distempered instinct of a jackdaw.

The truly melancholy part of the policy of systematically making a nation of gamesters is this, that though all are forced to play, few can understand the game; and fewer still are in a condition to avail themselves of the knowledge. The many must be the dupes of the few who conduct the machine of these speculations. What effect it must have on the country people is visible. The townsman can calculate from day to day, not so the inhabitant of the country. When the peasant first brings his corn to market, the magistrate in the towns obliges him to take the assignat at par; when he goes to the shop with his money, he finds it seven per cent the worse for crossing the way. This market he will not readily resort to again. The townspeople will be inflamed; they will force the country people to bring their corn. Resistance will begin, and the murders of Paris and St. Denis may be renewed through all France.

What signifies the empty compliment paid to the country by giving it, perhaps, more than its share in the theory of your representation? Where have you placed the real power over monied and landed circulation? Where have you placed the means of raising and falling the value of every man's freehold? Those whose operations can take form, or add ten per cent to, the possessions of every man in France must be the masters of every man in France. The whole of the power obtained by this revolution will settle in the towns among the burghers and the monied directors who lead them. The landed gentleman, the yeoman, and the peasant have, none of them, habits or inclinations or experience which can lead them to any share in this the sole source of power and influence now left in France. The very nature of a country life, the very nature of landed property, in all the occupations, and all the pleasures they afford, render combination and arrangement (the sole way of procuring and exerting influence) in a manner impossible amongst country people. Combine them by all the art you can, and all the industry, they are always dissolving into individuality. Anything in the nature of incorporation is almost impracticable amongst them. Hope, fear, alarm, jealousy, the ephemerous tale that does its business and dies in a day—all these things which are the reins and spurs by which leaders check or urge the minds of followers are not easily employed, or hardly at all, amongst scattered people. They assemble, they arm, they act with the utmost difficulty and at the greatest charge. Their efforts, if ever they can be commenced, cannot be sustained. They cannot proceed systematically. If the country gentlemen attempt an influence through the mere income of their property, what is it to that of those who have ten times their income to sell, and who can ruin their property by bringing their plunder to meet it at market? If the landed man wishes to mortgage, he falls the value of his land and raises the value of assignats. He augments the power of his enemy by the very means he must take to contend with him. The country gentleman, therefore, the officer by sea and land, the man of liberal views and habits, attached to no profession, will be as completely excluded from the government of his country as if he were legislatively proscribed. It is obvious that in the towns all things which conspire against the country gentleman combine in favor of the money manager and director. In towns combination is natural. The habits of burghers, their occupations, their diversion, their business, their idleness continually bring them into mutual contact. Their virtues and their vices are sociable; they are always in garrison; and they come embodied and half disciplined into the hands of those who mean to form them for civil or military action.

All these considerations leave no doubt on my mind that, if this monster of a constitution can continue, France will be wholly governed by the agitators in corporations, by societies in the towns formed of directors of assignats, and trustees for the sale of church lands, attorneys, agents, money jobbers, speculators, and adventurers, composing an ignoble oligarchy founded on the destruction of the crown, the church, the nobility, and the people.

Here end all the deceitful dreams and visions of the equality and rights of men. In the Serbonian bog of this base oligarchy they are all absorbed, sunk, and lost forever.

Though human eyes cannot trace them, one would be tempted to think some great offences in France must cry to heaven, which has thought fit to punish it with a subjection to a vile and inglorious domination in which no comfort or compensation is to be found in any, even of those false, splendors which, playing about other tyrannies, prevent mankind from feeling themselves dishonored even whilst they are oppressed. I must confess I am touched with a sorrow, mixed with some indignation, at the conduct of a few men, once of great rank and still of great character, who, deluded with specious names, have engaged in a business too deep for the line of their understanding to fathom; who have lent their fair reputation and the authority of their high-sounding names to the designs of men with whom they could not be acquainted, and have thereby made their very virtues operate to the ruin of their country.

So far as to the first cementing principle.

The second material of cement for their new republic is the superiority of the city of Paris; and this I admit is strongly connected with the other cementing principle of paper circulation and confiscation. It is in this part of the project we must look for the cause of the destruction of all the old bounds of provinces and jurisdictions, ecclesiastical and secular, and the dissolution of all ancient combinations of things, as well as the formation of so many small unconnected republics. The power of the city of Paris is evidently one great spring of all their politics. It is through the power of Paris, now become the center and focus of jobbing, that the leaders of this faction direct, or rather command, the whole legislative and the whole executive government. Everything, therefore, must be done which can confirm the authority of that city over the other republics. Paris is compact; she has an enormous strength, wholly disproportioned to the force of any of the square republics; and this strength is collected and condensed within a narrow compass.

Paris has a natural and easy connection of its parts, which will not be affected by any scheme of a geometrical constitution, nor does it much signify whether its proportion of representation be more or less, since it has the whole draft of fishes in its dragnet. The other divisions of the kingdom, being hackled and torn to pieces, and separated from all their habitual means and even principles of union, cannot, for some time at least, confederate against her. Nothing was to be left in all the subordinate members but weakness, disconnection, and confusion. To confirm this part of the plan, the Assembly has lately come to a resolution that no two of their republics shall have the same commander-in-chief.

To a person who takes a view of the whole, the strength of Paris, thus formed, will appear a system of general weakness. It is boasted that the geometrical policy has been adopted, that all local ideas should be sunk, and that the people should no longer be Gascons, Picards, Bretons, Normans, but Frenchmen, with one country, one heart, and one Assembly. But instead of being all Frenchmen, the greater likelihood is that the inhabitants of that region will shortly have no country. No man ever was attached by a sense of pride, partiality, or real affection to a description of square measurement. He never will glory in belonging to the Chequer No. 71, or to any other badge-ticket. We begin our public affections in our families. No cold relation is a zealous citizen. We pass on to our neighborhoods and our habitual provincial connections. These are inns and resting places. Such divisions of our country as have been formed by habit, and not by a sudden jerk of authority, were so many little images of the great country in which the heart found something which it could fill. The love to the whole is not extinguished by this subordinate partiality. Perhaps it is a sort of elemental training to those higher and more large regards by which alone men come to be affected, as with their own concern, in the prosperity of a kingdom so extensive as that of France. In that general territory itself, as in the old name of provinces, the citizens are interested from old prejudices and unreasoned habits, and not on account of the geometric properties of its figure. The power and preeminence of

Paris does certainly press down and hold these republics together as long as it lasts. But, for the reasons I have already given you, I think it cannot last very long.

Passing from the civil creating and the civil cementing principles of this constitution to the National Assembly, which is to appear and act as sovereign, we see a body in its constitution with every possible power, and no possible external control. We see a body without fundamental laws, without established maxims, without respected rules of proceeding, which nothing can keep firm to any system whatsoever. Their idea of their powers is always taken at the utmost stretch of legislative competence, and their examples for common cases from the exceptions of the most urgent necessity. The future is to be in most respects like the present Assembly; but, by the mode of the new elections and the tendency of the new circulations, it will be purged of the small degree of internal control existing in a minority chosen originally from various interests, and preserving something of their spirit. If possible, the next Assembly must be worse than the present. The present, by destroying and altering everything, will leave to their successors apparently nothing popular to do. They will be roused by emulation and example to enterprises the boldest and the most absurd. To suppose such an Assembly sitting in perfect quietude is ridiculous.

Your all-sufficient legislators, in their hurry to do everything at once, have forgotten one thing that seems essential, and which I believe never has been before, in the theory or the practice, omitted by any projector of a republic. They have forgotten to constitute a senate or something of that nature and character. Never before this time was heard of a body politic composed of one legislative and active assembly, and its executive officers, without such a council, without something to which foreign states might connect themselves; something to which, in the ordinary detail of government, the people could look up; something which might give a bias and steadiness and preserve something like consistency in the proceedings of state. Such a body kings generally have as a council. A monarchy may exist without it, but it seems to be in the very essence of a republican government. It holds a sort of middle place between the supreme power exercised by the people, or immediately delegated from them, and the mere executive. Of this there are no traces in your constitution, and in providing nothing of this kind your Solons and Numas have, as much as in anything else, discovered a sovereign incapacity.

The Executive Power

Let us now turn our eyes to what they have done toward the formation of an executive power. For this they have chosen a degraded king. This their first executive officer is to be a machine without any sort of deliberative discretion in any one act of his function. At best he is but a channel to convey to the National Assembly such matter as it may import that body to know. If he had been made the exclusive channel, the power would not have been without its importance, though infinitely perilous to those who would choose to exercise it. But public intelligence and statement of facts may pass to the Assembly with equal authenticity through any other conveyance. As to the means, therefore, of giving a direction to measures by the statement of an authorized reporter, this office of intelligence is as nothing.

To consider the French scheme of an executive officer, in its two natural divisions of civil and political—in the first, it must be observed that, according to the new constitution, the higher parts of judicature, in either of its lines, are not in the king. The king of France is not the fountain of justice. The judges, neither the original nor the appellate, are of his nomination. He neither proposes the candidates, nor has a negative on the choice. He is not even the public prosecutor. He serves only as a notary to authenticate the choice made of the judges in the several districts. By his officers he is to execute their sentence. When we look into the true nature of his authority, he appears to be nothing more than a chief of bum bailiffs, sergeants at mace, catchpoles, jailers, and hangmen. It is impossible to place anything called royalty in a more degrading point of view. A thousand times better had it been for the dignity of this unhappy prince that he had nothing at all to do with the administration of justice, deprived as he is of all that is venerable and all that is consolatory in that function, without power of originating any process, without a power of suspension, mitigation, or pardon. Everything in justice that is vile and odious is thrown upon him. It was not for nothing that the Assembly has been at such pains to remove the stigma from certain offices when they are resolved to place the person who had lately been their king in a situation but one degree above the executioner, and in an office nearly of the same quality. It is not in nature that, situated as the king of the French now is, he can respect himself or can be respected by others.

View this new executive officer on the side of his political capacity, as he acts under the orders of the National Assembly. To execute laws is a royal office; to execute orders is not to be a king. However, a political executive magistracy, though merely such, is a great trust. It is a trust indeed that has much depending upon its faithful and diligent performance, both in the person presiding in it and in all its subordinates. Means of performing this duty ought to be given by regulation; and dispositions toward it ought to be infused by the circumstances attendant on the trust. It ought to be environed with dignity, authority, and consideration, and it ought to lead to glory. The office of execution is an office of exertion. It is not from impotence we are to expect the tasks of power. What sort of person is a king to command executive service, who has no means whatsoever to reward it? Not in a permanent office; not in a grant of land; no, not in a pension of fifty pounds a year; not in the vainest and most trivial title. In France, the king is no more the fountain of honor than he is the fountain of justice. All rewards, all distinctions are in other hands. Those who serve the king can be actuated by no natural motive but fear—by a fear of everything except their master. His functions of internal coercion are as odious as those which he exercises in the department of justice. If relief is to be given to any municipality, the Assembly gives it. If troops are to be sent to reduce them to obedience to the Assembly, the king is to execute the order; and upon every occasion he is to be spattered over with the blood of his people. He has no negative; yet his name and authority is used to enforce every harsh decree. Nay, he must concur in the butchery of those who shall attempt to free him from his imprisonment or show the slightest attachment to his person or to his ancient authority.

Executive magistracy ought to be constituted in such a manner that those who compose it should be disposed to love and to venerate those whom they are bound to obey. A purposed neglect or, what is worse, a literal but perverse and malignant obedience must be the ruin of the wisest counsels. In vain will the law attempt to anticipate or to follow such studied neglects and fraudulent attentions. To make them act zealously is not in the competence of law. Kings, even such as are truly kings, may and ought to bear the freedom of subjects that are obnoxious to them. They may, too, without derogating from themselves, bear even the authority of such persons if it promotes their service. Louis the Thirteenth mortally hated the Cardinal de Richelieu, but his support of that minister against his rivals was the source of all the glory of his reign and the solid foundation of his throne itself. Louis the Fourteenth, when come to the throne, did not love the Cardinal Mazarin, but for his interests he preserved him in power. When old, he detested Louvois, but for years, whilst he faithfully served his greatness, he endured his person. When George the Second took Mr. Pitt, who certainly was not agreeable to him, into his councils, he did nothing which could humble a wise sovereign. But these ministers, who were chosen by affairs, not by affections, acted in the name of, and in trust for, kings, and not as their avowed, constitutional, and ostensible masters. I think it impossible that any king, when he has recovered his first terrors, can cordially infuse vivacity and vigor into measures which he knows to be dictated by those who, he must be persuaded, are in the highest degree ill affected to his person. Will any ministers who serve such a king (or whatever he may be called) with but a decent appearance of respect cordially obey the orders of those whom but the other day in his name they had committed to the Bastille? Will they obey the orders of those whom, whilst they were exercising despotic justice upon them, they conceived they were treating with lenity, and from whom, in a prison, they thought they had provided an asylum? If you expect such obedience amongst your other innovations and re-generations, you ought to make a revolution in nature and provide a new constitution for the human mind. Otherwise, your supreme government cannot harmonize with its executive system. There are cases in which we cannot take up with names and abstractions. You may call half a dozen leading individuals, whom we have reason to fear and hate, the nation. It makes no other difference than to make us fear and hate them the more. If it had been thought justi-fiable and expedient to make such a revolution by such means, and through such persons, as you have made yours, it would have been more wise to have completed the business of the fifth and sixth of October. The new executive officer would then owe his situation to those who are his creators as well as his masters; and he might be bound in interest, in the society of crime, and (if in crimes there could be virtues) in gratitude to serve those who had promoted him to a place of great lucre and great sensual indulgence, and of something more; for more he must have received from those who certainly would not have limited an aggrandized creature, as they have done a submitting antagonist.

A king circumstanced as the present, if he is totally stupefied by his misfortunes so as to think it not the necessity but the premium and privilege of life to eat and sleep, without any regard to glory, can never be fit for the office. If he feels as men commonly feel, he must be sensible that an office so circumstanced is one in which he can obtain no fame or reputation. He has no generous interest that can excite him to action. At best, his conduct will be passive and defensive. To inferior people such an office might be matter of honor. But to be raised to it, and to descend to it, are different things and suggest different sentiments. Does he really name the ministers? They will have a sympathy with him. Are they forced upon him? The whole business between them and the nominal king will be mutual counteraction. In all other countries, the office of ministers of state is of the highest dignity. In France it is full of peril, and incapable of glory. Rivals, however, they will have in their nothingness, whilst shallow ambition exists in the world, or the desire of a miserable salary is an incentive to short-sighted avarice. Those competitors of the ministers are enabled by your constitution to attack them in their vital parts, whilst they have not the means of repelling their charges in any other than the degrading character of culprits. The ministers of state in France are the only persons in that country who are incapable of a share in the national councils. What ministers! What councils! What a nation! But they are responsible. It is a poor service that is to be had from responsibility. The elevation of mind to be derived from fear will never make a nation glorious. Responsibility prevents crimes. It makes all attempts against the laws dangerous. But for a principle of active and zealous service, none but idiots could think of it. Is the conduct of a war to be trusted to a man who may abhor its principle, who, in every step he may take to render it successful, confirms the power of those by whom he is oppressed? Will foreign states seriously treat with him who has no prerogative of peace or war? No, not so much as in a single vote by himself or his ministers, or by any one whom he can possibly influence. A state of contempt is not a state for a prince; better get rid of him at once.

I know it will be said that these humors in the court and executive government will continue only through this generation, and that the king has been brought to declare the dauphin shall be educated in a conformity to his situation. If he is made to conform to his situation, he will have no education at all. His training must be worse, even, than that of an arbitrary monarch. If he reads—whether he reads or not—some good or evil genius will tell him his ancestors were kings. Thenceforward his object must be to assert himself and to avenge his parents. This you will say is not his duty. That may be; but it is nature; and whilst you pique nature against you, you do unwisely to trust to duty. In this futile scheme of polity, the state nurses in its bosom, for the present, a source of weakness, perplexity, counteraction, inefficiency, and decay; and it prepares the means of its final ruin. In short, I see nothing in the executive force (I cannot call it authority) that has even an appearance of vigor, or that has the smallest degree of just correspondence or symmetry, or amicable relation with the supreme power, either as it now exists or as it is planned for the future government.

You have settled, by an economy as perverted as the policy, two establishments of government—one real, one fictitious. Both maintained at a vast expense, but the fictitious at, I think, the greatest. Such a machine as the latter is not worth the grease of its wheels. The expense is exorbitant, and neither the show nor the use deserve the tenth part of the charge. Oh! but I don't do justice to the talents of the legislators: I don't allow, as I ought to do, for necessity. Their scheme of executive force was not their choice. This pageant must be kept. The people would not consent to part with it. Right; I understand you. You do, in spite of your grand theories, to which you would have heaven and earth to bend—you do know how to conform yourselves to the nature and circumstances of things. But when you were obliged to conform thus far to circumstances, you ought to have carried your submission further, and to have made, what you were obliged to take, a proper instrument, and useful to its end. That was in your power. For instance, among many others, it was in your power to leave to your king the right of peace and war. What! To leave to the executive magistrate the most dangerous of all prerogatives? I know none more dangerous, nor any one more necessary to be so trusted. I do not say that this prerogative ought to be trusted to your king unless he enjoyed other auxiliary trusts along with it, which he does not now hold. But if he did possess them, hazardous as they are undoubtedly, advantages would arise from such a constitution, more than compensating the risk. There is no other way of keeping the several potentates of Europe from intriguing distinctly and personally with the members of your Assembly, from intermeddling in all your concerns, and fomenting, in the heart of your country, the most pernicious of all factions—factions in the interest and under the direction of foreign powers. From that worst of evils, thank God, we are still free. Your skill, if you had any, would be well employed to find out indirect correctives and controls upon this perilous trust. If you did not like those which in England we have chosen, your leaders might have exerted their abilities in contriving better. If it were necessary to exemplify the consequences of such an executive government as yours, in the management of great affairs, I should refer you to the late reports of M. de Montmorin to the National Assembly, and all the other proceedings relative to the differences between Great Britain and Spain. It would be treating your understanding with disrespect to point them out to you.

I hear that the persons who are called ministers have signified an intention of resigning their places. I am rather astonished that they have not resigned long since. For the universe I would not have stood in the situation in which they have been for this last twelvemonth. They wished well, I take it for granted, to the revolution. Let this fact be as it may, they could not, placed as they were upon an eminence, though an eminence of humiliation, but be the first to see collectively, and to feel each in his own department, the evils which have been produced by that revolution. In every step which they took, or forbore to take, they must have felt the degraded situation of their country and their utter incapacity of serving it. They are in a species of subordinate servitude, in which no men before them were ever seen. Without confidence from their sovereign, on whom they were forced, or from the Assembly, who forced them upon him, all the noble functions of their office are executed by committees of the Assembly without any regard whatsoever to their personal or their official authority. They are to execute, without power; they are to be responsible, without discretion; they are to deliberate, without choice. In their puzzled situations, under two sovereigns, over neither of whom they have any influence, they must act in such a manner as (in effect, whatever they may intend) sometimes to betray the one, sometimes the other, and always to betray themselves. Such has been their situation, such must be the situation of those who succeed them. I have much respect and many good wishes for M. Necker. I am obliged to him for attentions. I thought, when his enemies had driven him from Versailles, that his exile was a subject of most serious congratulations—*sed multae urbes et publica vota vicerunt.*[39] He is now sitting on the ruins of the finances and of the monarchy of France.

A great deal more might be observed on the strange constitution of the executive part of the new government, but fatigue must give bounds to the discussion of subjects which in themselves have hardly any limits.

The Judicature

As little genius and talent am I able to perceive in the plan of judicature formed by the National Assembly. According to their invariable course, the framers of your constitution have begun with the utter abolition of the parliaments. These venerable bodies, like the rest of the old government, stood in need of reform, even though there should be no change made in the monarchy. They required several more alterations to adapt them to the system of a free constitution. But they had particulars in their constitution, and those not a few, which deserved approbation from the wise. They possessed one fundamental excellence: they were independent. The most doubtful circumstance attendant on their office, that of its being vendible, contributed however to this independence of character. They held for life. Indeed, they may be said to have held by inheritance. Appointed by the monarch, they were considered as nearly out of his power. The most determined exertions of that authority against them only showed their radical independence. They composed permanent bodies politic, constituted to resist arbitrary innovation; and from that corporate constitution, and from most of their forms, they were well calculated to afford both certainty

---

39   But many cities and public vows conquered them.

and stability to the laws. They had been a safe asylum to secure these laws in all the revolutions of humor and opinion. They had saved that sacred deposit of the country during the reigns of arbitrary princes and the struggles of arbitrary factions. They kept alive the memory and record of the constitution. They were the great security to private property which might be said (when personal liberty had no existence) to be, in fact, as well guarded in France as in any other country. Whatever is supreme in a state ought to have, as much as possible, its judicial authority so constituted as not only not to depend upon it, but in some sort to balance it. It ought to give a security to its justice against its power. It ought to make its judicature, as it were, something exterior to the state.

These parliaments had furnished, not the best certainly, but some considerable corrective to the excesses and vices of the monarchy. Such an independent judicature was ten times more necessary when a democracy became the absolute power of the country. In that constitution, elective temporary, local judges, such as you have contrived, exercising their dependent functions in a narrow society, must be the worst of all tribunals. In them it will be vain to look for any appearance of justice toward strangers, toward the obnoxious rich, toward the minority of routed parties, toward all those who in the election have supported unsuccessful candidates. It will be impossible to keep the new tribunals clear of the worst spirit of faction. All contrivances by ballot we know experimentally to be vain and childish to prevent a discovery of inclinations. Where they may the best answer the purposes of concealment, they answer to produce suspicion, and this is a still more mischievous cause of partiality.

If the parliaments had been preserved, instead of being dissolved at so ruinous a charge to the nation, they might have served in this new commonwealth, perhaps not precisely the same (I do not mean an exact parallel), but nearly the same, purposes as the court and senate of Areopagus did in Athens; that is, as one of the balances and correctives to the evils of a light and unjust democracy. Everyone knows that this tribunal was the great stay of that state; everyone knows with what care it was upheld, and with what a religious awe it was consecrated. The parliaments were not wholly free from faction, I admit; but this evil was exterior and accidental, and not so much the vice of their constitution itself, as it must be in your new contrivance of sexennial elective judicatories. Several English commend the abolition of the old tribunals, as supposing that they determined everything by bribery and corruption. But they have stood the test of monarchic and republican scrutiny. The court was well disposed to prove corruption on those bodies when they were dissolved in 1771. Those who have again dissolved them would have done the same if they could, but both inquisitions having failed, I conclude that gross pecuniary corruption must have been rather rare amongst them.

It would have been prudent, along with the parliaments, to preserve their ancient power of registering, and of remonstrating at least, upon all the decrees of the National Assembly, as they did upon those which passed in the time of the monarchy. It would be a means of squaring the occasional decrees of a democracy to some principles of general jurisprudence. The vice of the ancient democracies, and one cause of their ruin, was that they ruled, as you do, by occasional decrees, psephismata. This practice soon broke in upon the tenor and consistency of the laws; it abated the respect of the people toward them, and totally destroyed them in the end.

Your vesting the power of remonstrance, which, in the time of the monarchy, existed in the parliament of Paris, in your principal executive officer, whom, in spite of common sense, you persevere in calling king, is the height of absurdity. You ought never to suffer remonstrance from him who is to execute. This is to understand neither council nor execution, neither authority nor obedience. The person whom you call king ought not to have this power, or he ought to have more.

Your present arrangement is strictly judicial. Instead of imitating your monarchy and seating your judges on a bench of independence, your object is to reduce them to the most blind obedience.

As you have changed all things, you have invented new principles of order. You first appoint judges, who, I suppose, are to determine according to law, and then you let them know that, at some time or other, you intend to give them some law by which they are to determine. Any studies which they have made (if any they have made) are to be useless to them. But to supply these studies, they are to be sworn to obey all the rules, orders, and instructions which from time to time they are to receive from the National Assembly. These if they submit to, they leave no ground of law to the subject. They become complete and most dangerous instruments in the hands of the governing power which, in the midst of a cause or on the prospect of it, may wholly change the rule of decision. If these orders of the National Assembly come to be contrary to the will of the people, who locally choose judges, such confusion must happen as is terrible to think of. For the judges owe their places to the local authority, and the commands they are sworn to obey come from those who have no share in their appointment. In the meantime they have the example of the court of Chatelet to encourage and guide them in the exercise of their functions. That court is to try criminals sent to it by the National Assembly, or brought before it by other courses of delation. They sit under a guard to save their own lives. They know not by what law they judge, nor under what authority they act, nor by what tenure they hold. It is thought that they are sometimes obliged to condemn at peril of their lives. This is not perhaps certain, nor can it be ascertained; but when they acquit, we know they have seen the persons whom they discharge, with perfect impunity to the actors, hanged at the door of their court.

The Assembly indeed promises that they will form a body of law, which shall be short, simple, clear, and so forth. That is, by their short laws they will leave much to the discretion of the judge, whilst they have exploded the authority of all the learning which could make judicial discretion (a thing perilous at best) deserving the appellation of a sound discretion.

It is curious to observe that the administrative bodies are

carefully exempted from the jurisdiction of these new tribunals. That is, those persons are exempted from the power of the laws who ought to be the most entirely submitted to them. Those who execute public pecuniary trusts ought of all men to be the most strictly held to their duty. One would have thought that it must have been among your earliest cares, if you did not mean that those administrative bodies should be real, sovereign, independent states, to form an awful tribunal, like your late parliaments, or like our king's bench, where all corporate officers might obtain protection in the legal exercise of their functions, and would find coercion if they trespassed against their legal duty. But the cause of the exemption is plain. These administrative bodies are the great instruments of the present leaders in their progress through democracy to oligarchy. They must, therefore, be put above the law. It will be said that the legal tribunals which you have made are unfit to coerce them. They are, undoubtedly. They are unfit for any rational purpose. It will be said, too, that the administrative bodies will be accountable to the General Assembly. This I fear is talking without much consideration of the nature of that Assembly, or of these corporations. However, to be subject to the pleasure of that Assembly is not to be subject to law either for protection or for constraint.

This establishment of judges as yet wants something to its completion. It is to be crowned by a new tribunal. This is to be a grand state judicature, and it is to judge of crimes committed against the nation, that is, against the power of the Assembly. It seems as if they had something in their view of the nature of the high court of justice erected in England during the time of the great usurpation. As they have not yet finished this part of the scheme, it is impossible to form a right judgment upon it. However, if great care is not taken to form it in a spirit very different from that which has guided them in their proceedings relative to state offences, this tribunal, subservient to their inquisition, the Committee of Research, will extinguish the last sparks of liberty in France and settle the most dreadful and arbitrary tyranny ever known in any nation. If they wish to give to this tribunal any appearance of liberty and justice, they must not evoke from or send to it the causes relative to their own members, at their pleasure. They must also remove the seat of that tribunal out of the republic of Paris.

The Army

Has more wisdom been displayed in the constitution of your army than what is discoverable in your plan of judicature? The able arrangement of this part is the more difficult, and requires the greatest skill and attention, not only as the great concern in itself, but as it is the third cementing principle in the new body of republics which you call the French nation. Truly it is not easy to divine what that army may become at last. You have voted a very large one, and on good appointments, at least fully equal to your apparent means of payment. But what is the principle of its discipline, or whom is it to obey? You have got the wolf by the ears, and I wish you joy of the happy position in which you have chosen to place yourselves, and in which you are well circumstanced for a free deliberation relatively to that army or to anything else.

The minister and secretary of state for the war department is M. de la Tour du Pin. This gentleman, like his colleagues in administration, is a most zealous assertor of the revolution, and a sanguine admirer of the new constitution which originated in that event. His statement of facts, relative to the military of France, is important, not only from his official and personal authority, but because it displays very clearly the actual condition of the army in France, and because it throws light on the principles upon which the Assembly proceeds in the administration of this critical object. It may enable us to form some judgment how far it may be expedient in this country to imitate the martial policy of France.

M. de la Tour du Pin, on the fourth of last June, comes to give an account of the state of his department as it exists under the auspices of the National Assembly. No man knows it so well; no man can express it better. Addressing himself to the National Assembly, he says:

His Majesty has this day sent me to apprise you of the multiplied disorders of which every day he receives the most distressing intelligence. The army (le corps militaire) threatens to fall into the most turbulent anarchy. Entire regiments have dared to violate at once the respect due to the laws, to the king, to the order established by your decrees, and to the oaths which they have taken with the most awful solemnity. Compelled by my duty to give you information of these excesses, my heart bleeds when I consider who they are that have committed them. Those against whom it is not in my power to withhold the most grievous complaints are a part of that very soldiery which to this day have been so full of honor and loyalty, and with whom, for fifty years, I have lived the comrade and the friend.

What incomprehensible spirit of delirium and delusion has all at once led them astray? Whilst you are indefatigable in establishing uniformity in the empire, and molding the whole into one coherent and consistent body; whilst the French are taught by you at once the respect which the laws owe to the rights of man, and that which the citizens owe to the laws, the administration of the army presents nothing but disturbance and confusion. I see in more than one corps the bonds of discipline relaxed or broken; the most unheard-of pretensions avowed directly and without any disguise; the ordinances without force; the chiefs without authority; the military chest and the colors carried off; the authority of the king himself (risum teneatis?)[40] proudly defied; the officers despised, degraded, threatened, driven away, and some of them prisoners in the midst of their corps, dragging on a precarious life in the bosom of disgust and humiliation. To fill up the measure of all these horrors, the commandants of places have had their throats cut, under the eyes and almost in the arms of their own soldiers.

These evils are great; but they are not the worst consequences which may be produced by such military insurrections. Sooner or later they may menace the nation itself. The nature of things requires that the army should never act but as an instrument. The moment that, erecting itself into a deliberative body, it shall act according to its own resolutions, the government, be it what it may, will immediately degenerate into a military democracy—a species of political monster which has always ended by devouring those who have produced it.

---

40 Can you help laughing?

> *After all this, who must not be alarmed at the irregular consultations and turbulent committees formed in some regiments by the common soldiers and non-commissioned officers without the knowledge, or even in contempt of the authority, of their superiors, although the presence and concurrence of those superiors could give no authority to such monstrous democratic assemblies (comices).*

It is not necessary to add much to this finished picture—finished as far as its canvas admits, but, as I apprehend, not taking in the whole of the nature and complexity of the disorders of this military democracy which, the minister at war truly and wisely observes, wherever it exists must be the true constitution of the state, by whatever formal appellation it may pass. For though he informs the Assembly that the more considerable part of the army have not cast off their obedience, but are still attached to their duty, yet those travelers who have seen the corps whose conduct is the best rather observe in them the absence of mutiny than the existence of discipline.

I cannot help pausing here for a moment to reflect upon the expressions of surprise which this minister has let fall, relative to the excesses he relates. To him the departure of the troops from their ancient principles of loyalty and honor seems quite inconceivable. Surely those to whom he addresses himself know the causes of it but too well. They know the doctrines which they have preached, the decrees which they have passed, the practices which they have countenanced. The soldiers remember the 6th of October. They recollect the French guards. They have not forgotten the taking of the king's castles in Paris and Marseilles. That the governors in both places were murdered with impunity is a fact that has not passed out of their minds. They do not abandon the principles laid down so ostentatiously and laboriously of the equality of men. They cannot shut their eyes to the degradation of the whole noblesse of France and the suppression of the very idea of a gentleman. The total abolition of titles and distinctions is not lost upon them. But M. de la Tour du Pin is astonished at their disloyalty, when the doctors of the Assembly have taught them at the same time the respect due to laws. It is easy to judge which of the two sorts of lessons men with arms in their hands are likely to learn. As to the authority of the king, we may collect from the minister himself (if any argument on that head were not quite superfluous) that it is not of more consideration with these troops than it is with everybody else. "The king," says he, "has over and over again repeated his orders to put a stop to these excesses; but in so terrible a crisis your (the Assembly's) concurrence is become indispensably necessary to prevent the evils which menace the state. You unite to the force of the legislative power that of opinion still more important." To be sure the army can have no opinion of the power or authority of the king. Perhaps the soldier has by this time learned that the Assembly itself does not enjoy a much greater degree of liberty than that royal figure.

It is now to be seen what has been proposed in this exigency, one of the greatest that can happen in a state. The minister requests the Assembly to array itself in all its terrors, and to call forth all its majesty. He desires that the grave and severe principles announced by them may give vigor to the king's proclamation. After this we should have looked for courts, civil and martial, breaking of some corps, decimating of others, and all the terrible means which necessity has employed in such cases to arrest the progress of the most terrible of all evils; particularly, one might expect that a serious inquiry would be made into the murder of commandants in the view of their soldiers. Not one word of all this or of anything like it. After they had been told that the soldiery trampled upon the decrees of the Assembly promulgated by the king, the Assembly pass new decrees, and they authorize the king to make new proclamations. After the secretary at war had stated that the regiments had paid no regard to oaths *pretes avec la plus imposante solemnite*,[41] they propose—what? More oaths. They renew decrees and proclamations as they experience their insufficiency, and they multiply oaths in proportion as they weaken in the minds of men, the sanctions of

---

41 "Ready with the utmost solemnity."

religion. I hope that handy abridgments of the excellent sermons of Voltaire, d'Alembert, Diderot, and Helvetius, on the Immortality of the Soul, on a particular superintending Providence, and on a Future State of Rewards and Punishments are sent down to the soldiers along with their civic oaths. Of this I have no doubt; as I understand that a certain description of reading makes no inconsiderable part of their military exercises, and that they are full as well supplied with the ammunition of pamphlets as of cartridges.

To prevent the mischiefs arising from conspiracies, irregular consultations, seditious committees, and monstrous democratic assemblies (*comitia, comices*) of the soldiers, and all the disorders arising from idleness, luxury, dissipation, and insubordination, I believe the most astonishing means have been used that ever occurred to men, even in all the inventions of this prolific age. It is no less than this: the king has promulgated in circular letters to all the regiments his direct authority and encouragement that the several corps should join themselves with the clubs and confederations in the several municipalities, and mix with them in their feasts and civic entertainments! This jolly discipline, it seems, is to soften the ferocity of their minds, to reconcile them to their bottle companions of other descriptions, and to merge particular conspiracies in more general associations. That this remedy would be pleasing to the soldiers, as they are described by M. de la Tour du Pin, I can readily believe; and that, however mutinous otherwise, they will dutifully submit themselves to these royal proclamations. But I should question whether all this civic swearing, clubbing, and feasting would dispose them, more than at present they are disposed, to an obedience to their officers, or teach them better to submit to the austere rules of military discipline. It will make them admirable citizens after the French mode, but not quite so good soldiers after any mode. A doubt might well arise whether the conversations at these good tables would fit them a great deal the better for the character of mere instruments, which this veteran officer and statesman justly observes the nature of things always requires an army to be.

Concerning the likelihood of this improvement in discipline by the free conversation of the soldiers with municipal festive societies, which is thus officially encouraged by royal authority and sanction, we may judge by the state of the municipalities themselves, furnished to us by the war minister in this very speech. He conceives good hopes of the success of his endeavors toward restoring order for the present from the good disposition of certain regiments, but he finds something cloudy with regard to the future. As to preventing the return of confusion, for this the administration (says he) cannot be answerable to you as long as they see the municipalities arrogate to themselves an authority over the troops which your institutions have reserved wholly to the monarch. You have fixed the limits of the military authority and the municipal authority. You have bounded the action which you have permitted to the latter over the former to the right of requisition, but never did the letter or the spirit of your decrees authorize the commons in these municipalities to break the officers, to try them, to give orders to the soldiers, to drive them from the posts committed to their guard, to stop them in their marches ordered by the king, or, in a word, to enslave the troops to the caprice of each of the cities or even market towns through which they are to pass.

Such is the character and disposition of the municipal society which is to reclaim the soldiery, to bring them back to the true principles of military subordination, and to render them machines in the hands of the supreme power of the country! Such are the distempers of the French troops! Such is their cure! As the army is, so is the navy. The municipalities supersede the orders of the Assembly, and the seamen in their turn supersede the orders of the municipalities. From my heart I pity the condition of a respectable servant of the public like this war minister, obliged in his old age to pledge the Assembly in their civic cups, and to enter with a hoary head into all the fantastic vagaries of these juvenile politicians. Such schemes are not like propositions coming from a man of fifty years' wear and tear amongst mankind. They seem rather such as ought to be expected from those grand compounders in politics who shorten the road to their degrees in the state and have a certain inward fanatical assurance and illumination upon all subjects, upon the credit of which one of their doctors has thought fit, with great applause, and greater success, to caution the Assembly not to attend to old men or to any persons who valued themselves upon their experience. I suppose all the ministers of state must qualify and take this test—wholly abjuring the errors and heresies of experience and observation. Every man has his own relish. But I think if I could not attain to the wisdom, I would at least preserve something of the stiff and peremptory dignity of age. These gentlemen deal in regeneration; but at any price I should hardly yield my rigid fibers to be regenerated by them, nor begin, in my grand climacteric, to squall in their new accents or to stammer, in my second cradle, the elemental sounds of their barbarous metaphysics. *Si isti mihi largiantur ut repuerascam, et in eorum cunis vagiam, valde recusem!*[42]

The imbecility of any part of the puerile and pedantic system, which they call a constitution, cannot be laid open without discovering the utter insufficiency and mischief of every other part with which it comes in contact, or that bears any the remotest relation to it. You cannot propose a remedy for the incompetence of the crown without displaying the debility of the Assembly. You cannot deliberate on the confusion of the army of the state without disclosing the worse disorders of the armed municipalities. The military lays open the civil, and the civil betrays the military, anarchy. I wish everybody carefully to peruse the eloquent speech (such it is) of M. de la Tour du Pin. He attributes the salvation of the municipalities to the good behavior of some of the troops. These troops are to preserve the well-disposed part of those municipalities, which is confessed to be the weakest, from the pillage of the worst disposed, which is the strongest. But the municipalities affect a sovereignty and will command those troops which are necessary for their protection. Indeed they must command them or court them. The municipalities, by the necessity of their situation, and

---

42 If this lot offered me to return to childhood, to cry in their cribs, I would absolutely refuse!

by the republican powers they have obtained, must, with relation to the military, be the masters, or the servants, or the confederates, or each successively; or they must make a jumble of all together, according to circumstances. What government is there to coerce the army but the municipality, or the municipality but the army? To preserve concord where authority is extinguished, at the hazard of all consequences, the Assembly attempts to cure the distempers by the distempers themselves; and they hope to preserve themselves from a purely military democracy by giving it a debauched interest in the municipal.

If the soldiers once come to mix for any time in the municipal clubs, cabals, and confederacies, an elective attraction will draw them to the lowest and most desperate part. With them will be their habits, affections, and sympathies. The military conspiracies, which are to be remedied by civic confederacies; the rebellious municipalities, which are to be rendered obedient by furnishing them with the means of seducing the very armies of the state that are to keep them in order; all these chimeras of a monstrous and portentous policy must aggravate the confusion from which they have arisen. There must be blood. The want of common judgment manifested in the construction of all their descriptions of forces and in all their kinds of civil and judicial authorities will make it flow. Disorders may be quieted in one time and in one part. They will break out in others, because the evil is radical and intrinsic. All these schemes of mixing mutinous soldiers with seditious citizens must weaken still more and more the military connection of soldiers with their officers, as well as add military and mutinous audacity to turbulent artificers and peasants. To secure a real army, the officer should be first and last in the eye of the soldier; first and last in his attention, observance, and esteem. Officers it seems there are to be, whose chief qualification must be temper and patience. They are to manage their troops by electioneering arts. They must bear themselves as candidates, not as commanders. But as by such means power may be occasionally in their hands, the authority by which they are to be nominated becomes of high importance.

What you may do finally does not appear, nor is it of much moment whilst the strange and contradictory relation between your army and all the parts of your republic, as well as the puzzled relation of those parts to each other and to the whole, remain as they are. You seem to have given the provisional nomination of the officers in the first instance to the king, with a reserve of approbation by the National Assembly. Men who have an interest to pursue are extremely sagacious in discovering the true seat of power. They must soon perceive that those who can negative indefinitely in reality appoint. The officers must, therefore, look to their intrigues in that Assembly as the sole certain road to promotion. Still, however, by your new constitution they must begin their solicitation at court. This double negotiation for military rank seems to me a contrivance as well adapted, as if it were studied for no other end, to promote faction in the Assembly itself, relative to this vast military patronage, and then to poison the corps of officers with factions of a nature still more dangerous to the safety of government, upon any bottom on which it can be placed, and destructive in the end to the efficiency of the army itself. Those officers who lose the promotions intended for them by the crown must become of a faction opposite to that of the Assembly, which has rejected their claims, and must nourish discontents in the heart of the army against the ruling powers. Those officers, on the other hand, who, by carrying their point through an interest in the Assembly, feel themselves to be at best only second in the good will of the crown, though first in that of the Assembly, must slight an authority which would not advance and could not retard their promotion. If to avoid these evils you will have no other rule for command or promotion than seniority, you will have an army of formality; at the same time it will become more independent and more of a military republic. Not they, but the king is the machine. A king is not to be deposed by halves. If he is not everything in the command of an army, he is nothing. What is the effect of a power placed nominally at the head of the army who to that army is no object of gratitude or of fear? Such a cipher is not fit for the administration of an object, of all things the most delicate, the supreme command of military men. They must be constrained (and their inclinations lead them to what their necessities require) by a real, vigorous, effective, decided, personal authority. The authority of the Assembly itself suffers by passing through such a debilitating channel as they have chosen. The army will not long look to an assembly acting through the organ of false show and palpable imposition. They will not seriously yield obedience to a prisoner. They will either despise a pageant, or they will pity a captive king. This relation of your army to the crown will, if I am not greatly mistaken, become a serious dilemma in your politics.

It is, besides, to be considered whether an assembly like yours, even supposing that it was in possession of another sort of organ through which its orders were to pass, is fit for promoting the obedience and discipline of an army. It is known that armies have hitherto yielded a very precarious and uncertain obedience to any senate or popular authority; and they will least of all yield it to an assembly which is only to have a continuance of two years. The officers must totally lose the characteristic disposition of military men if they see with perfect submission and due admiration the dominion of pleaders; especially when they find that they have a new court to pay to an endless succession of those pleaders, whose military policy, and the genius of whose command (if they should have any), must be as uncertain as their duration is transient. In the weakness of one kind of authority, and in the fluctuation of all, the officers of an army will remain for some time mutinous and full of faction until some popular general, who understands the art of conciliating the soldiery, and who possesses the true spirit of command, shall draw the eyes of all men upon himself. Armies will obey him on his personal account. There is no other way of securing military obedience in this state of things. But the moment in which that event shall happen, the person who really commands the army is your master—the master (that is little) of your king, the master of your Assembly, the master of your whole republic.

How came the Assembly by their present power over the army? Chiefly, to be sure, by debauching the soldiers from their officers.

They have begun by a most terrible operation. They have touched the central point about which the particles that compose armies are at repose. They have destroyed the principle of obedience in the great, essential, critical link between the officer and the soldier, just where the chain of military subordination commences and on which the whole of that system depends. The soldier is told he is a citizen and has the rights of man and citizen. The right of a man, he is told, is to be his own governor and to be ruled only by those to whom he delegates that self-government. It is very natural he should think that he ought most of all to have his choice where he is to yield the greatest degree of obedience. He will therefore, in all probability, systematically do what he does at present occasionally; that is, he will exercise at least a negative in the choice of his officers. At present the officers are known at best to be only permissive, and on their good behavior. In fact, there have been many instances in which they have been cashiered by their corps. Here is a second negative on the choice of the king—a negative as effectual at least as the other of the Assembly. The soldiers know already that it has been a question, not ill received in the National Assembly, whether they ought not to have the direct choice of their officers, or some proportion of them? When such matters are in deliberation it is no extravagant supposition that they will incline to the opinion most favorable to their pretensions. They will not bear to be deemed the army of an imprisoned king whilst another army in the same country, with whom, too, they are to feast and confederate, is to be considered as the free army of a free constitution. They will cast their eyes on the other and more permanent army; I mean the municipal. That corps, they well know, does actually elect its own officers. They may not be able to discern the grounds of distinction on which they are not to elect a Marquis de la Fayette (or what is his new name?) of their own. If this election of a commander-in-chief be a part of the rights of men, why not of theirs? They see elective justices of peace, elective judges, elective curates, elective bishops, elective municipalities, and elective commanders of the Parisian army—why should they alone be excluded? Are the brave troops of France the only men in that nation who are not the fit judges of military merit and of the qualifications necessary for a commander-in-chief? Are they paid by the state and do they, therefore, lose the rights of men? They are a part of that nation themselves and contribute to that pay. And is not the king, is not the National Assembly, and are not all who elect the National Assembly, likewise paid? Instead of seeing all these forfeit their rights by their receiving a salary, they perceive that in all these cases a salary is given for the exercise of those rights. All your resolutions, all your proceedings, all your debates, all the works of your doctors in religion and politics have industriously been put into their hands, and you expect that they will apply to their own case just as much of your doctrines and examples as suits your pleasure.

Everything depends upon the army in such a government as yours, for you have industriously destroyed all the opinions and prejudices and, as far as in you lay, all the instincts which support government. Therefore, the moment any difference arises between your National Assembly and any part of the nation, you must have recourse to force. Nothing else is left to you, or rather you have left nothing else to yourselves. You see, by the report of your war minister, that the distribution of the army is in a great measure made with a view of internal coercion. You must rule by an army; and you have infused into that army by which you rule, as well as into the whole body of the nation, principles which after a time must disable you in the use you resolve to make of it. The king is to call out troops to act against his people, when the world has been told, and the assertion is still ringing in our ears, that troops ought not to fire on citizens. The colonies assert to themselves an independent constitution and a free trade. They must be constrained by troops. In what chapter of your code of the rights of men are they able to read that it is a part of the rights of men to have their commerce monopolized and restrained for the benefit of others? As the colonists rise on you, the Negroes rise on them. Troops again—massacre, torture, hanging! These are your rights of men! These are the fruits of metaphysical declarations wantonly made, and shamefully retracted! It was but the other day that the farmers of land in one of your provinces refused to pay some sort of rents to the lord of the soil. In consequence of this, you decree that the country people shall pay all rents and dues, except those which as grievances you have abolished; and if they refuse, then you order the king to march troops against them. You lay down metaphysical propositions which infer universal consequences, and then you attempt to limit logic by despotism. The leaders of the present system tell them of their rights, as men, to take fortresses, to murder guards, to seize on kings without the least appearance of authority even from the Assembly, whilst, as the sovereign legislative body, that Assembly was sitting in the name of the nation—and yet these leaders presume to order out the troops which have acted in these very disorders, to coerce those who shall judge on the principles, and follow the examples, which have been guaranteed by their own approbation.

The leaders teach the people to abhor and reject all feudality as the barbarism of tyranny, and they tell them afterwards how much of that barbarous tyranny they are to bear with patience. As they are prodigal of light with regard to grievances, so the people find them sparing in the extreme with regard to redress. They know that not only certain quitrents and personal duties, which you have permitted them to redeem (but have furnished no money for the redemption), are as nothing to those burdens for which you have made no provision at all. They know that almost the whole system of landed property in its origin is feudal; that it is the distribution of the possessions of the original proprietors, made by a barbarous conqueror to his barbarous instruments; and that the most grievous effects of the conquest are the land rents of every kind, as without question they are.

The peasants, in all probability, are the descendants of these ancient proprietors, Romans or Gauls. But if they fail, in any degree, in the titles which they make on the principles of antiquaries and lawyers, they retreat into the citadel of the rights of men. There they find that men are equal; and the earth, the kind and equal mother of all, ought not to be monopolized to foster the pride and luxury of any men, who by nature are no better than themselves, and who, if they do not labor for their bread, are worse. They find that by the laws of nature the occupant and subduer of the soil is the true proprietor; that there is no prescription against nature; and that the agreements (where any there are) which have been made with the landlords, during the time of slavery, are only the effect of duress and force; and that when the people reentered into the rights of men, those agreements were made as void as everything else which had been settled under the prevalence of the old feudal and aristocratic tyranny. They will tell you that they see no differ-ence between an idler with a hat and a national cockade and an idler in a cowl or in a rochet. If you ground the title to rents on succession and prescription, they tell you from the speech of M. Camus, published by the National Assembly for their information, that things ill begun cannot avail themselves of prescription; that the title of these lords was vicious in its origin; and that force is at least as bad as fraud. As to the title by succession, they will tell you that the succession of those who have cultivated the soil is the true pedigree of property, and not rotten parchments and silly substi-tutions; that the lords have enjoyed their usurpation too long; and that if they allow to these lay monks any charitable pension, they ought to be thankful to the bounty of the true proprietor, who is so generous toward a false claimant to his goods.

When the peasants give you back that coin of sophistic reason on which you have set your image and superscription, you cry it down as base money and tell them you will pay for the future with French guards, and dragoons, and hussars. You hold up, to chas-tise them, the second-hand authority of a king, who is only the instrument of destroying, without any power of protecting either the people or his own person. Through him it seems you will make yourselves obeyed. They answer: You have taught us that there are no gentlemen, and which of your principles teach us to bow to kings whom we have not elected? We know without your teaching that lands were given for the support of feudal dignities, feudal titles, and feudal offices. When you took down the cause as a grievance, why should the more grievous effect remain? As there are now no hereditary honors, and no distinguished families, why are we taxed to maintain what you tell us ought not to exist? You have sent down our old aristocratic landlords in no other character, and with no other title, but that of exactors under your authority. Have you endeavored to make these your rent-gatherers respectable to us? No. You have sent them to us with their arms reversed, their shields broken, their impresses defaced; and so deplumed, degraded, and metamorphosed, such unfeathered two-legged things, that we no longer know them. They are strangers to us. They do not even go by the names of our ancient lords. Physically they may be the same men, though we are not quite sure of that, on your new philosophic doctrines of personal identity. In all other respects they are totally changed. We do not see why we have not as good a right to refuse them their rents as you have to abrogate all their honors, titles, and distinctions. This we have never commissioned you to do; and it is one instance, among many indeed, of your assumption of undelegated power. We see the burghers of Paris, through their clubs, their mobs, and their national guards, directing you at their pleasure and giving that as law to you which, under your authority, is transmitted as law to us. Through you these burghers dispose of the lives and fortunes of us all. Why should not you attend as much to the desires of the laborious husbandman with regard to our rent, by which we are affected in the most serious manner, as you do to the demands of these insolent burghers, relative to distinctions and titles of honor, by which neither they nor we are affected at all? But we find you pay more regard to their fancies than to our necessities. Is it among the rights of man to pay tribute to his equals? Before this measure of yours, we might have thought we were not perfectly equal. We might have entertained some old, habitual, unmeaning prepossession in favor of those landlords; but we cannot conceive with what other view than that of destroying all respect to them, you could have made the law that degrades them. You have forbidden us to treat them with any of the old formalities of respect, and now you send troops to saber and to bayonet us into a submission to fear and force, which you did not suffer us to yield to the mild authority of opinion.

The ground of some of these arguments is horrid and ridiculous to all rational ears, but to the politicians of metaphysics who have opened schools for sophistry and made establishments for anarchy, it is solid and conclusive. It is obvious that, on a mere consideration of the right, the leaders in the Assembly would not in the least have scrupled to abrogate the rents along with the title and family ensigns. It would be only to follow up the principle of their reasonings and to complete the analogy of their conduct. But they had newly possessed themselves of a great body of landed property by confiscation. They had this commodity at market; and the market would have been wholly destroyed if they were to permit the husbandmen to riot in the speculations with which they so freely intoxicated themselves. The only security which property enjoys in any one of its descriptions is from the interests of their rapacity with regard to some other. They have left nothing but their own arbitrary pleasure to determine what property is to be protected and what subverted.

Neither have they left any principle by which any of their municipalities can be bound to obedience, or even conscientiously obliged not to separate from the whole to become independent, or to connect itself with some other state. The people of Lyons, it seems, have refused lately to pay taxes. Why should they not? What lawful authority is there left to exact them? The king imposed some of them. The old states, methodized by orders, settled the more ancient. They may say to the Assembly: who are you, that are not our kings, nor the states we have elected, nor sit on the principles on which we have elected you? And who are we, that when we see the gabelles, which you have ordered to be paid, wholly shaken off, when we see the act of disobedience afterwards ratified by yourselves—who are we, that we are not to judge what taxes we ought or ought not to pay, and are not to avail ourselves of the same powers, the validity of which you have approved in others? To this the answer is, We will send troops. The last reason of kings is always the first with your Assembly. This military aid may serve for a time, whilst the impression of the increase of pay remains, and the vanity of being umpires in all disputes is flattered. But this weapon will snap short, unfaithful to the hand that employs it. The Assembly keep a school where, systematically, and with unremitting perseverance, they teach principles and form regulations destructive to all spirit of subordination, civil and military—and then they expect that they shall hold in obedience an anarchic people by an anarchic army.

The municipal army which, according to the new policy, is to balance this national army, if considered in itself only, is of a constitution much more simple, and in every respect less exceptionable. It is a mere democratic body, unconnected with the crown or the kingdom, armed and trained and officered at the pleasure of the districts to which the corps severally belong, and the personal service of the individuals who compose, or the fine in lieu of personal service, are directed by the same authority. Nothing is more uniform. If, however, considered in any relation to the crown, to the National Assembly, to the public tribunals, or to the other army, or considered in a view to any coherence or connection between its parts, it seems a monster, and can hardly fail to terminate its perplexed movements in some great national calamity. It is a worse preservative of a general constitution than the *systasis* of Crete, or the confederation of Poland, or any other ill-devised corrective which has yet been imagined in the necessities produced by an ill-constructed system of government.

Having concluded my few remarks on the constitution of the supreme power, the executive, the judicature, the military, and on the reciprocal relation of all these establishments, I shall say something of the ability shown by your legislators with regard to the revenue.

The Financial System

In their proceedings relative to this object, if possible, still fewer traces appear of political judgment or financial resource. When the states met, it seemed to be the great object to improve the system of revenue, to enlarge its collection, to cleanse it of oppression and vexation, and to establish it on the most solid footing. Great were the expectations entertained on that head throughout Europe. It was by this grand arrangement that France was to stand or fall; and this became, in my opinion, very properly the test by which the skill and patriotism of those who ruled in that Assembly would be tried. The revenue of the state is the state. In effect, all depends upon it, whether for support or for reformation. The dignity of every occupation wholly depends upon the quantity and the kind of virtue that may be exerted in it. As all great qualities of the mind which operate in public, and are not merely suffering and passive, require force for their display, I had almost said for their unequivocal existence, the revenue, which is the spring of all power, becomes in its administration the sphere of every active virtue. Public virtue, being of a nature magnificent and splendid, instituted for great things and conversant about great concerns, requires abundant scope and room and cannot spread and grow under confinement and in circumstances straitened, narrow, and sordid. Through the revenue alone the body politic can act in its true genius and character, and, therefore, it will display just as much of its collective virtue, and as much of that virtue which may characterize those who move it and are, as it were, its life and guiding principle, as it is possessed of a just revenue. For from hence not only magnanimity, and liberality, and beneficence, and fortitude, and providence, and the tutelary protection of all good arts derive their food and the growth of their organs; but continence, and self-denial, and labor, and vigilance, and frugality, and whatever else there is in which the mind shows itself above the appetite, are nowhere more in their proper element than in the provision and distribution of the public wealth. It is, therefore, not without reason that the science of speculative and practical finance, which must take to its aid so many auxiliary branches of knowledge, stands high in the estimation not only of the ordinary sort but of the wisest and best men; and as this science has grown with the progress of its object, the prosperity and improvement of nations has generally increased with the increase of their revenues; and they will both continue to grow and flourish as long as the balance between what is left to strengthen the efforts of individuals and what is collected for the common efforts of the state bear to each other a due reciprocal proportion and are kept in a close correspondence and communication. And perhaps it may be owing to the greatness of revenues and to the urgency of state necessities that old abuses in the constitution of finances are discovered and their true nature and rational theory comes to be more perfectly understood: insomuch, that a smaller revenue might have been more distressing in one period than a far greater is found to be in another, the proportionate wealth even remaining the same. In this state of things, the French Assembly found something in their revenues to preserve, to secure, and wisely to administer, as well as to abrogate and alter. Though their proud assumption might justify the severest tests, yet in trying their abilities on their financial proceedings, I would only consider what is the plain obvious duty of a common finance minister, and try them upon that, and not upon models of ideal perfection.

The objects of a financier are, then, to secure an ample revenue, to impose it with judgment and equality, to employ it economically, and when necessity obliges him to make use of credit, to secure its foundations in that instance, and forever, by the clearness and candor of his proceedings, the exactness of his calculations and the solidity of his funds. On these heads we may take a short and distinct view of the merits and abilities of those in the National Assembly who have taken to themselves the management of this arduous concern. Far from any increase of revenue in their hands, I find, by a report of M. Vernier, from the committee of finances, of the second of August last, that the amount of the national revenue, as compared with its produce before the Revolution, was diminished by the sum of two hundred millions, or eight millions sterling of the annual income, considerably more than one-third of the whole.

If this be the result of great ability, never surely was ability displayed in a more distinguished manner or with so powerful an effect. No common folly, no vulgar incapacity, no ordinary official negligence, even no official crime, no corruption, no peculation, hardly any direct hostility which we have seen in the modern world could in so short a time have made so complete an overthrow of the finances and, with them, of the strength of a great kingdom— *Cedo qui vestram rempublicam tantam amisistis tam cito?*[43]

The sophisters and declaimers, as soon as the Assembly met, began with decrying the ancient constitution of the revenue in many of its most essential branches, such as the public monopoly of salt. They charged it, as truly as unwisely, with being ill-contrived, oppressive, and partial. This representation they were not satisfied to make use of in speeches preliminary to some plan of reform; they declared it in a solemn resolution or public sentence, as it were judicially passed upon it; and this they dispersed throughout the nation. At the time they passed the decree, with the same gravity they ordered the same absurd, oppressive, and partial tax to be paid until they could find a revenue to replace it. The consequence was inevitable. The provinces which had been always exempted from this salt monopoly, some of whom were charged with other contributions, perhaps equivalent, were totally disinclined to bear any part of the burden which by an equal distribution was to redeem the others. As to the Assembly, occupied as it was with the declaration and violation of the rights of men, and with their arrangements for general confusion, it had neither leisure nor capacity to contrive, nor authority to enforce, any plan of any kind relative to the replacing the tax or equalizing it, or compensating the provinces, or for conducting their minds to any scheme of accommodation with other districts which were to be relieved.

The people of the salt provinces, impatient under taxes, damned by the authority which had directed their payment, very soon found their patience exhausted. They thought themselves as skillful in demolishing as the Assembly could be. They relieved themselves by throwing off the whole burden. Animated by this example, each

---

43 Tell me, how did you lose your great commonwealth so quickly?

district, or part of a district, judging of its own grievance by its own feeling, and of its remedy by its own opinion, did as it pleased with other taxes.

We are next to see how they have conducted themselves in contriving equal impositions, proportioned to the means of the citizens, and the least likely to lean heavy on the active capital employed in the generation of that private wealth from whence the public fortune must be derived. By suffering the several districts, and several of the individuals in each district, to judge of what part of the old revenue they might withhold, instead of better principles of equality, a new inequality was introduced of the most oppressive kind. Payments were regulated by dispositions. The parts of the kingdom which were the most submissive, the most orderly, or the most affectionate to the commonwealth bore the whole burden of the state. Nothing turns out to be so oppressive and unjust as a feeble government. To fill up all the deficiencies in the old impositions and the new deficiencies of every kind which were to be expected—what remained to a state without authority? The National Assembly called for a voluntary benevolence: for a fourth part of the income of all the citizens, to be estimated on the honor of those who were to pay. They obtained something more than could be rationally calculated, but what was far indeed from answerable to their real necessities, and much less to their fond expectations. Rational people could have hoped for little from this their tax in the disguise of a benevolence—a tax weak, ineffective, and unequal; a tax by which luxury, avarice, and selfishness were screened, and the load thrown upon productive capital, upon integrity, generosity, and public spirit; a tax of regulation upon virtue. At length the mask is thrown off, and they are now trying means (with little success) of exacting their benevolence by force.

This benevolence, the rickety offspring of weakness, was to be supported by another resource, the twin brother of the same prolific imbecility. The patriotic donations were to make good the failure of the patriotic contribution. John Doe was to become security for

Richard Roe. By this scheme they took things of much price from the giver, comparatively of small value to the receiver; they ruined several trades; they pillaged the crown of its ornaments, the churches of their plate, and the people of their personal decorations. The invention of these juvenile pretenders to liberty was in reality nothing more than a servile imitation of one of the poorest resources of doting despotism. They took an old, huge, full-bottomed periwig out of the wardrobe of the antiquated frippery of Louis the Fourteenth to cover the premature baldness of the National Assembly. They produced this old-fashioned formal folly, though it had been so abundantly exposed in the Memoirs of the Duke de St. Simon, if to reasonable men it had wanted any arguments to display its mischief and insufficiency. A device of the same kind was tried, in my memory, by Louis the Fifteenth, but it answered at no time. However, the necessities of ruinous wars were some excuse for desperate projects. The deliberations of calamity are rarely wise. But here was a season for disposition and providence. It was in a time of profound peace, then enjoyed for five years, and promising a much longer continuance, that they had recourse to this desperate trifling. They were sure to lose more reputation by sporting, in their serious situation, with these toys and playthings of finance, which have filled half their journals, than could possibly be compensated by the poor temporary supply which they afforded. It seemed as if those who adopted such projects were wholly ignorant of their circumstances or wholly unequal to their necessities. Whatever virtue may be in these devices, it is obvious that neither the patriotic gifts, nor the patriotic contribution, can ever be resorted to again. The resources of public folly are soon exhausted. The whole, indeed, of their scheme of revenue is to make, by any artifice, an appearance of a full reservoir for the hour, whilst at the same time they cut off the springs and living fountains of perennial supply. The account not long since furnished by M. Necker was meant, without question, to be favorable. He gives a flattering view of the means of getting through the year, but he expresses, as it is natural he should, some apprehension for that which was to succeed. On this last prognostic, instead of entering into the grounds of this apprehension in order, by a proper foresight, to prevent the prognosticated evil, M. Necker receives a sort of friendly reprimand from the president of the Assembly.

As to their other schemes of taxation, it is impossible to say anything of them with certainty, because they have not yet had their operation; but nobody is so sanguine as to imagine they will fill up any perceptible part of the wide gaping breach which their incapacity had made in their revenues. At present the state of their treasury sinks every day more and more in cash, and swells more and more in fictitious representation. When so little within or without is now found but paper, the representative not of opulence but of want, the creature not of credit but of power, they imagine that our flourishing state in England is owing to that bank-paper, and not the bank-paper to the flourishing condition of our commerce, to the solidity of our credit, and to the total exclusion of all idea of power from any part of the transaction. They forget that, in England, not one shilling of paper money of any description is received but of choice; that the whole has had its origin in cash actually deposited; and that it is convertible at pleasure, in an instant and without the smallest loss, into cash again. Our paper is of value in commerce, because in law it is of none. It is powerful on 'Change, because in Westminster Hall it is impotent. In payment of a debt of twenty shillings, a creditor may refuse all the paper of the Bank of England. Nor is there amongst us a single public security, of any quality or nature whatsoever, that is enforced by authority. In fact, it might be easily shown that our paper wealth, instead of lessening the real coin, has a tendency to increase it; instead of being a substitute for money, it only facilitates its entry, its exit, and its circulation; that it is the symbol of prosperity, and not the badge of distress. Never was a scarcity of cash and an exuberance of paper a subject of complaint in this nation.

Well! But a lessening of prodigal expenses, and the economy which has been introduced by the virtuous and sapient Assembly, make amends for the losses sustained in the receipt of revenue. In this at least they have fulfilled the duty of a financier. Have those who say so looked at the expenses of the National Assembly itself, of the municipalities, of the city of Paris, of the increased pay of the two armies, of the new police, of the new judicatures? Have they even carefully compared the present pension list with the former? These politicians have been cruel, not economical. Comparing the expense of the former prodigal government and its relation to the then revenues with the expenses of this new system as opposed to the state of its new treasury, I believe the present will be found beyond all comparison more chargeable.

It remains only to consider the proofs of financial ability furnished by the present French managers when they are to raise supplies on credit. Here I am a little at a stand, for credit, properly speaking, they have none. The credit of the ancient government was not indeed the best, but they could always, on some terms, command money, not only at home, but from most of the countries of Europe where a surplus capital was accumulated; and the credit of that government was improving daily. The establishment of a system of liberty would of course be supposed to give it new strength; and so it would actually have done if a system of liberty had been established. What offers has their government of pretended liberty had from Holland, from Hamburg, from Switzerland, from Genoa, from England for a dealing in their paper? Why should these nations of commerce and economy enter into any pecuniary dealings with a people who attempt to reverse the very nature of things, amongst whom they see the debtor prescribing at the point of the bayonet the medium of his solvency to the creditor, discharging one of his engagements with another, turning his very penury into his resource and paying his interest with his rags?

Their fanatical confidence in the omnipotence of church plunder has induced these philosophers to overlook all care of the public estate, just as the dream of the philosopher's stone induces dupes, under the more plausible delusion of the hermetic art, to neglect all rational means of improving their fortunes. With these philosophic financiers, this universal medicine made of church mummy is to cure all the evils of the state. These gentlemen perhaps do not believe a great deal in the miracles of piety, but it cannot be questioned that they have an undoubting faith in the prodigies of sacrilege. Is there a debt which presses them?—Issue assignats. Are compensations to be made or a maintenance decreed to those whom they have robbed of their freehold in their office, or expelled from their profession?—Assignats. Is a fleet to be fitted out?—Assignats. If sixteen millions sterling of these assignats, forced on the people, leave the wants of the state as urgent as ever—issue, says one, thirty millions sterling of assignats—says another, issue fourscore millions more of assignats. The only difference among their financial factions is on the greater or the lesser quantity of assignats to be imposed on the public sufferance. They are all professors of assignats. Even those whose natural good sense and knowledge of commerce, not obliterated by philosophy, furnish decisive arguments against this delusion conclude their arguments by proposing the emission of assignats. I suppose they must talk of assignats, as no other language would be understood. All experience of their inefficiency does not in the least discourage them. Are the old assignats depreciated at market?—What is the remedy? Issue new assignats—*Mais si maladia, opiniatria, non vult se garire, quid illi facere? assignare—postea assignare; ensuita assignare.*[44] The word is a trifle altered. The Latin of your present doctors may be better than that of your old comedy; their wisdom and the variety of their resources are the same. They have not more notes in their song than the cuckoo, though, far from the softness of that harbinger of summer and plenty, their voice is as harsh and as ominous as that of the raven.

Who but the most desperate adventurers in philosophy and finance could at all have thought of destroying the settled revenue of the state, the sole security for the public credit, in the hope of

---

44 What to do if the malady does not want to be cured? Issue assignats—afterwards issue assignats, then issue assignats.

rebuilding it with the materials of confiscated property? If, however, an excessive zeal for the state should have led a pious and venerable prelate (by anticipation a father of the church) to pillage his own order and, for the good of the church and people, to take upon himself the place of grand financier of confiscation and comptroller-general of sacrilege, he and his coadjutors were in my opinion bound to show by their subsequent conduct that they knew something of the office they assumed. When they had resolved to appropriate to the *Fisc* a certain portion of the landed property of their conquered country, it was their business to render their bank a real fund of credit, as far as such a bank was capable of becoming so.

To establish a current circulating credit upon any Land-bank, under any circumstances whatsoever, has hitherto proved difficult at the very least. The attempt has commonly ended in bankruptcy. But when the Assembly were led, through a contempt of moral, to a defiance of economic principles, it might at least have been expected that nothing would be omitted on their part to lessen this difficulty, to prevent any aggravation of this bankruptcy. It might be expected that to render your land-bank tolerable, every means would be adopted that could display openness and candor in the statement of the security—everything which could aid the recovery of the demand. To take things in their most favorable point of view, your condition was that of a man of a large landed estate which he wished to dispose of for the discharge of a debt and the supply of certain services. Not being able instantly to sell, you wished to mortgage. What would a man of fair intentions and a commonly clear understanding do in such circumstances? Ought he not first to ascertain the gross value of the estate, the charges of its management and disposition, the encumbrances perpetual and temporary of all kinds that affect it, then, striking a net surplus, to calculate the just value of the security? When that surplus (the only security to the creditor) had been clearly ascertained and properly vested in the hands of trustees, then he would indicate the parcels to be sold, and the time and conditions of sale; after this, he would admit the public creditor, if he chose it, to subscribe his stock into this new fund, or he might receive proposals for an assignat from those who would advance money to purchase this species of security.

This would be to proceed like men of business, methodically and rationally, and on the only principles of public and private credit that have an existence. The dealer would then know exactly what he purchased; and the only doubt which could hang upon his mind would be the dread of the resumption of the spoil, which one day might be made (perhaps with an addition of punishment) from the sacrilegious gripe of those execrable wretches who could become purchasers at the auction of their innocent fellow citizens.

An open and exact statement of the clear value of the property and of the time, the circumstances, and the place of sale were all necessary to efface as much as possible the stigma that has hitherto been branded on every kind of land-bank. It became necessary on another principle, that is, on account of a pledge of faith previously given on that subject, that their future fidelity in a slippery concern might be established by their adherence to their first engagement. When they had finally determined on a state resource from church booty, they came, on the 14th of April, 1790, to a solemn resolution on the subject, and pledged themselves to their country, "that in the statement of the public charges for each year, there should be brought to account a sum sufficient for defraying the expenses of the R. C. A. religion, the support of the ministers at the altars, the relief of the poor, the pensions to the ecclesiastics, secular as well as regular, of the one and of the other sex, in order that the estates and goods which are at the disposal of the nation may be disengaged of all charges and employed by the representatives, or the legislative body, to the great and most pressing exigencies of the state." They further engaged, on the same day, that the sum necessary for the year 1791 should be forthwith determined.

In this resolution they admit it their duty to show distinctly the expense of the above objects which, by other resolutions, they had before engaged should be first in the order of provision. They admit that they ought to show the estate clear and disengaged of all charges, and that they should show it immediately. Have they done this immediately, or at any time? Have they ever furnished a rent-roll of the immovable estates, or given in an inventory of the movable effects which they confiscate to their assignats? In what manner they can fulfill their engagements of holding out to public service "an estate disengaged of all charges" without authenticating the value of the estate or the quantum of the charges, I leave it to their English admirers to explain. Instantly upon this assurance, and previously to any one step toward making it good, they issue, on the credit of so handsome a declaration, sixteen millions sterling of their paper. This was manly. Who, after this masterly stroke, can doubt of their abilities in finance? But then, before any other emission of these financial indulgences, they took care at least to make good their original promise! If such estimate either of the value of the estate or the amount of the encumbrances has been made, it has escaped me. I never heard of it.

At length they have spoken out, and they have made a full discovery of their abominable fraud in holding out the church lands as a security for any debts, or any service whatsoever. They rob only to enable them to cheat, but in a very short time they defeat the ends both of the robbery and the fraud by making out accounts for other purposes which blow up their whole apparatus of force and of deception. I am obliged to M. de Calonne for his reference to the document which proves this extraordinary fact; it had by some means escaped me. Indeed it was not necessary to make out my assertion as to the breach of faith on the declaration of the 14th of April, 1790. By a report of their committee it now appears that the charge of keeping up the reduced ecclesiastical establishments and other expenses attendant on religion, and maintaining the religious of both sexes, retained or pensioned, and the other concomitant expenses of the same nature which they have brought upon themselves by this convulsion in property, exceeds the income of the estates acquired by it in the enormous sum of two millions sterling annually, besides a debt of seven millions and upwards. These are the calculating powers of imposture! This is the finance of philosophy! This is the result of all the delusions held out to engage a miserable people in rebellion, murder, and sacrilege, and to make them prompt and zealous instruments in the ruin of their country! Never did a state, in any case, enrich itself by the confiscations of the citizens. This new experiment has succeeded like all the rest. Every honest mind, every true lover of liberty and humanity, must rejoice to find that injustice is not always good policy, nor rapine the high road to riches. I subjoin with pleasure, in a note, the able and spirited observations of M. de Calonne on this subject.

In order to persuade the world of the bottomless resource of ecclesiastical confiscation, the Assembly have proceeded to other confiscations of estates in offices, which could not be done with any common color without being compensated out of this grand confiscation of landed property. They have thrown upon this fund, which was to show a surplus disengaged of all charges, a new charge—namely, the compensation to the whole body of the disbanded judicature, and of all suppressed offices and estates, a charge which I cannot ascertain, but which unquestionably amounts to many French millions. Another of the new charges is an annuity of four hundred and eighty thousand pounds sterling, to be paid (if they choose to keep faith) by daily payments, for the interest of the first assignats. Have they even given themselves the trouble to state fairly the expense of the management of the church lands in the hands of the municipalities to whose care, skill, and diligence, and that of their legion of unknown underagents, they have chosen to commit the charge of the forfeited estates, the consequence of which had been so ably pointed out by the bishop of Nancy?

But it is unnecessary to dwell on these obvious heads of encumbrance. Have they made out any clear state of the grand encumbrance of all, I mean the whole of the general and municipal establishments of all sorts, and compared it with the regular income by revenue? Every deficiency in these becomes a charge on the confiscated estate before the creditor can plant his cabbages on an acre of church property. There is no other prop than this confiscation to keep the whole state from tumbling to the ground. In this situation they have purposely covered all that they ought industriously to have cleared with a thick fog, and then, blindfold themselves, like bulls that shut their eyes when they push, they drive, by the point of the bayonets, their slaves, blindfolded indeed no worse than their lords, to take their fictions for currencies and to swallow down paper pills by thirty-four millions sterling at a dose. Then they proudly lay in their claim to a future credit, on failure of all their past engagements, and at a time when (if in such a matter anything can be clear) it is clear that the surplus estates will never answer even the first of their mortgages, I mean that of the four hundred millions (or sixteen millions sterling) of assignats. In all this procedure I can discern neither the solid sense of plain dealing nor the subtle dexterity of ingenious fraud. The objections within the Assembly to pulling up the floodgates for this inundation of fraud are unanswered, but they are thoroughly refuted by a hundred thousand financiers in the street. These are the numbers by which the metaphysical arithmeticians compute. These are the grand calculations on which a philosophical public credit is founded in France. They cannot raise supplies, but they can raise mobs. Let them rejoice in the applauses of the club at Dundee for their wisdom and patriotism in having thus applied the plunder of the citizens to the service of the state. I hear of no address upon this subject from the directors of the Bank of England, though their approbation would be of a little more weight in the scale of credit than that of the club at Dundee. But, to do justice to the club, I believe the gentlemen who compose it to be wiser than they appear; that they will be less liberal of their money than of their addresses; and that they would not give a dog's ear of their most rumpled and ragged Scotch paper for twenty of your fairest assignats.

Early in this year the Assembly issued paper to the amount of sixteen millions sterling; what must have been the state into which the Assembly has brought your affairs, that the relief afforded by so vast a supply has been hardly perceptible? This paper also felt an almost immediate depreciation of five per cent, which in a little time came to about seven. The effect of these assignats on the receipt of the revenue is remarkable. M. Necker found that the collectors of the revenue who received in coin paid the treasury in assignats. The collectors made seven per cent by thus receiving in money and accounting in depreciated paper. It was not very difficult to foresee that this must be inevitable. It was, however, not the less embarrassing. M. Necker was obliged (I believe, for a considerable part, in the market of London) to buy gold and silver for the mint, which amounted to about twelve thousand pounds above the value of the commodity gained. That minister was of opinion that, whatever their secret nutritive virtue might be, the state could not live upon assignats alone, that some real silver was necessary, particularly for the satisfaction of those who, having iron in their hands, were not likely to distinguish themselves for patience when they should perceive that, whilst an increase of pay was held out to them in real money, it was again to be fraudulently drawn back by depreciated paper. The minister, in this very natural distress, applied to the Assembly that they should order the collectors to pay in specie what in specie they had received. It could not escape him that if the treasury paid three per cent for the use of a currency which should be returned seven per cent worse than the minister issued it, such a dealing could not very greatly tend to enrich the public. The Assembly took no notice of this recommendation. They were in this dilemma: if they continued to receive the assignats, cash must become an alien to their treasury; if the treasury should refuse those paper amulets or should discountenance them in any degree, they must destroy the credit of their sole resource. They seem then to have made their option, and to have given some sort of credit to their paper by taking it themselves; at the same time in their speeches they made a sort of swaggering declaration, something, I rather think, above legislative competence; that is, that there is no difference in value between metallic money and their assignats. This was a good, stout, proof article of faith, pronounced under an anathema by the venerable fathers of this philosophic synod. *Credat* who will—certainly not Judaeus Apella.

A noble indignation rises in the minds of your popular leaders on hearing the magic lantern in their show of finance compared to the fraudulent exhibitions of Mr. Law. They cannot bear to hear the sands of his Mississippi compared with the rock of the church on which they build their system. Pray let them suppress this glorious spirit until they show to the world what piece of solid ground there is for their assignats which they have not preoccupied by other charges. They do injustice to that great mother fraud to compare it with their degenerate imitation. It is not true that Law built solely on a speculation concerning the Mississippi. He added the East India trade; he added the African trade; he added the farms of all the farmed revenue of France. All these together unquestionably could not support the structure which the public enthusiasm, not he, chose to build upon these bases. But these were, however, in comparison generous delusions. They supposed, and they aimed at, an increase of the commerce of France. They opened to it the whole range of the two hemispheres. They did not think of feeding France from its own substance. A grand imagination found in this night of commerce something to captivate. It was wherewithal to dazzle the eye of an eagle. It was not made to entice the smell of a mole nuzzling and burying himself in his mother earth, as yours is. Men were not then quite shrunk from their natural dimensions by a degrading and sordid philosophy, and fitted for low and vulgar deceptions. Above all, remember that in imposing on the imagination the then managers of the system made a compliment to the freedom of men. In their fraud there was no mixture of force. This was reserved to our time, to quench the little glimmerings of reason which might break in upon the solid darkness of this enlightened age.

On recollection, I have said nothing of a scheme of finance which may be urged in favor of the abilities of these gentlemen, and which has been introduced with great pomp, though not yet finally adopted, in the National Assembly. It comes with something solid in aid of the credit of the paper circulation; and much has been said of its utility and its elegance. I mean the project for coining into money the bells of the suppressed churches. This is their alchemy. There are some follies which baffle argument, which go beyond ridicule, and which excite no feeling in us but disgust; and therefore I say no more upon it.

It is as little worth remarking any further upon all their drawing and re-drawing on their circulation for putting off the evil day, on the play between the treasury and the Caisse d'Escompte, and on all these old, exploded contrivances of mercantile fraud now exalted into policy of state. The revenue will not be trifled with. The prattling about the rights of men will not be accepted in payment for a biscuit or a pound of gunpowder. Here then the metaphysicians descend from their airy speculations and faithfully follow examples. What examples? The examples of bankrupts. But defeated, baffled, disgraced, when their breath, their strength, their inventions, their fancies desert them, their confidence still maintains its ground. In the manifest failure of their abilities, they take credit for their benevolence. When the revenue disappears in their hands, they have the presumption, in some of their late proceedings, to value themselves on the relief given to the people. They did not relieve the people. If they entertained such intentions, why did they order the obnoxious taxes to be paid? The people relieved themselves in spite of the Assembly.

But waiving all discussion on the parties who may claim the merit of this fallacious relief, has there been, in effect, any relief to the people in any form? Mr. Bailly, one of the grand agents of paper circulation, lets you into the nature of this relief. His speech to the National Assembly contained a high and labored panegyric on the inhabitants of Paris for the constancy and unbroken resolution with which they have borne their distress and misery. A fine picture of public felicity! What great courage and unconquerable firmness of mind to endure benefits and sustain redress! One would think from the speech of this learned lord mayor that the Parisians, for this twelvemonth past, had been suffering the straits of some dreadful blockade, that Henry the Fourth had been stopping up the avenues to their supply, and Sully thundering with his ordnance at the gates of Paris, when in reality they are besieged by no other enemies than their own madness and folly, their own credulity and perverseness. But Mr. Bailly will sooner thaw the eternal ice of his Atlantic regions than restore the central heat to Paris whilst it remains "smitten with the cold, dry, petrific mace" of a false and unfeeling philosophy. Sometime after this speech, that is, on the thirteenth of last August, the same magistrate, giving an account of his government at the bar of the same Assembly, expresses himself as follows:

> *In the month of July, 1789, (the period of everlasting commemoration) the finances of the city of Paris were yet in good order; the expenditure was counterbalanced by the receipt; and she had at that time a million (forty thousand pounds sterling) in bank.*
>
> *The expenses which she has been constrained to incur, subsequent to the Revolution, amount to 2,500,000 livres. From these expenses, and the great falling off in the product of the free gifts, not only a momentary, but a total, want of money has taken place.*

This is the Paris upon whose nourishment, in the course of the last year, such immense sums, drawn from the vitals of all France, have been expended. As long as Paris stands in the place of ancient Rome, so long she will be maintained by the subject provinces. It is an evil inevitably attendant on the dominion of sovereign democratic republics. As it happened in Rome, it may survive that republican domination which gave rise to it. In that case despotism itself must submit to the vices of popularity. Rome, under her emperors, united the evils of both systems; and this unnatural combination was one great cause of her ruin.

To tell the people that they are relieved by the dilapidation of their public estate is a cruel and insolent imposition. Statesmen, before they valued themselves on the relief given to the people by the destruction of their revenue, ought first to have carefully attended to the solution of this problem—whether it be more advantageous to the people to pay considerably and to gain in proportion, or to gain little or nothing and to be disburdened of all contribution?

My mind is made up to decide in favor of the first proposition. Experience is with me, and, I believe, the best opinions also. To keep a balance between the power of acquisition on the part of the subject and the demands he is to answer on the part of the state is the fundamental part of the skill of a true politician. The means of acquisition are prior in time and in arrangement. Good order is the foundation of all good things. To be enabled to acquire, the people, without being servile, must be tractable and obedient. The magistrate must have his reverence, the laws their authority. The body of the people must not find the principles of natural subordination by art rooted out of their minds. They must respect that property of which they cannot partake. They must labor to obtain what by labor can be obtained; and when they find, as they commonly do, the success disproportioned to the endeavor, they must be taught their consolation in the final proportions of eternal justice. Of this consolation, whoever deprives them deadens their industry and strikes at the root of all acquisition as of all conservation. He that does this is the cruel oppressor, the merciless enemy of the poor and wretched, at the same time that by his wicked speculations he exposes the fruits of successful industry and the accumulations of fortune to the plunder of the negligent, the disappointed, and the unprosperous.

Too many of the financiers by profession are apt to see nothing in revenue but banks, and circulations, and annuities on lives, and tontines, and perpetual rents, and all the small wares of the shop. In a settled order of the state, these things are not to be slighted, nor is the skill in them to be held of trivial estimation. They are good, but then only good when they assume the effects of that settled order and are built upon it. But when men think that these beggarly contrivances may supply a resource for the evils which result from breaking up the foundations of public order, and from causing or suffering the principles of property to be subverted, they will, in the ruin of their country, leave a melancholy and lasting monument of the effect of preposterous politics and presumptuous, short-sighted, narrow-minded wisdom.

XVII
CONCLUSION

The effects of the incapacity shown by the popular leaders in all the great members of the commonwealth are to be covered with the "all-atoning name" of liberty. In some people I see great liberty indeed; in many, if not in the most, an oppressive, degrading servitude. But what is liberty without wisdom and without virtue? It is the greatest of all possible evils; for it is folly, vice, and madness, without instruction or restraint. Those who know what virtuous liberty is cannot bear to see it disgraced by incapable heads on account of their having high-sounding words in their mouths. Grand, swelling sentiments of liberty I am sure I do not despise. They warm the heart; they enlarge and liberalize our minds; they animate our courage in a time of conflict. Old as I am, I read the fine raptures of Lucan and Corneille with pleasure. Neither do I wholly condemn the little arts and devices of popularity. They facilitate the carrying of many points of moment; they keep the people together; they refresh the mind in its exertions; and they diffuse occasional gaiety over the severe brow of moral freedom. Every politician ought to sacrifice to the graces, and to join compliance with reason. But in such an undertaking as that in France, all these subsidiary sentiments and artifices are of little avail. To make a government requires no great prudence. Settle the seat of power, teach obedience, and the work is done. To give freedom is still more easy. It is not necessary to guide; it only requires to let go the rein. But to form a free government, that is, to temper together these opposite elements of liberty and restraint in one consistent work, requires much thought, deep reflection, a sagacious, powerful, and combining mind. This I do not find in those who take the lead in the National Assembly. Perhaps they are not so miserably deficient as they appear. I rather believe it. It would put them below the common level of human understanding. But when the leaders choose to make themselves bidders at an auction of popularity, their talents, in the construction of the state, will be of no service. They will become flatterers instead of legislators, the instruments, not the guides, of the people. If any of them should happen to propose a scheme of liberty, soberly limited and defined with proper qualifications, he will be immediately outbid by his competitors who will produce something more splendidly popular. Suspicions will be raised of his fidelity to his cause. Moderation will be stigmatized as the virtue of cowards, and compromise as the prudence of traitors, until, in hopes of preserving the credit which may enable him to temper and moderate, on some occasions, the popular leader is obliged to become active in propagating doctrines and establishing powers that will afterwards defeat any sober purpose at which he ultimately might have aimed.

But am I so unreasonable as to see nothing at all that deserves commendation in the indefatigable labors of this Assembly? I do not deny that, among an infinite number of acts of violence and folly, some good may have been done. They who destroy everything certainly will remove some grievance. They who make everything new have a chance that they may establish something beneficial. To give them credit for what they have done in virtue of the authority they have usurped, or which can excuse them in the crimes by which that authority has been acquired, it must appear that the same things could not have been accomplished without producing such a revolution. Most assuredly they might, because almost every one of the regulations made by them which is not very equivocal was either in the cession of the king, voluntarily made at the meeting of the states, or in the concurrent instructions to the orders. Some usages have been abolished on just grounds, but they were such that if they had stood as they were to all eternity, they would little detract from the happiness and prosperity of any state. The improvements of the National Assembly are superficial, their errors fundamental.

Whatever they are, I wish my countrymen rather to recommend to our neighbors the example of the British constitution than to take models from them for the improvement of our own. In the former, they have got an invaluable treasure. They are not, I think, without some causes of apprehension and complaint, but these they do not owe to their constitution but to their own conduct. I think our happy situation owing to our constitution, but owing to the whole of it, and not to any part singly, owing in a great measure to what we have left standing in our several reviews and reformations as well as to what we have altered or superadded. Our people will find employment enough for a truly patriotic, free, and independent spirit in guarding what they possess from violation. I would not exclude alteration either, but even when I changed, it should be to preserve. I should be led to my remedy by a great grievance. In what I did, I should follow the example of our ancestors. I would make the reparation as nearly as possible in the style of the building. A politic caution, a guarded circumspection, a moral rather than a complexional timidity were among the ruling principles of our forefathers in their most decided conduct. Not being illuminated with the light of which the gentlemen of France tell us they have got so abundant a share, they acted under a strong impression of the ignorance and fallibility of mankind. He that had made them thus fallible rewarded them for having in their conduct attended to their nature. Let us imitate their caution if we wish to deserve their fortune or to retain their bequests. Let us add, if we please, but let us preserve what they have left; and, standing on the firm ground of the British constitution, let us be satisfied to admire rather than attempt to follow in their desperate flights the aeronauts of France.

I have told you candidly my sentiments. I think they are not likely to alter yours. I do not know that they ought. You are young; you cannot guide but must follow the fortune of your country. But hereafter they may be of some use to you, in some future form which your commonwealth may take. In the present it can hardly remain; but before its final settlement it may be obliged to pass, as one of our poets says, "through great varieties of untried being," and in all its transmigrations to be purified by fire and blood.

I have little to recommend my opinions but long observation and much impartiality. They come from one who has been no tool of power, no flatterer of greatness; and who in his last acts does not wish to belie the tenor of his life. They come from one almost the whole of whose public exertion has been a struggle for the liberty of others; from one in whose breast no anger, durable or vehement, has ever been kindled but by what he considered as tyranny; and who snatches from his share in the endeavors which are used by good men to discredit opulent oppression the hours he has employed on your affairs; and who in so doing persuades himself he has not departed from his usual office; they come from one who desires honors, distinctions, and emoluments but little, and who expects them not at all; who has no contempt for fame, and no fear of obloquy; who shuns contention, though he will hazard an opinion; from one who wishes to preserve consistency, but who would preserve consistency by varying his means to secure the unity of his end, and, when the equipoise of the vessel in which he sails may be endangered by overloading it upon one side, is desirous of carrying the small weight of his reasons to that which may preserve its equipoise.

THE RIME OF THE ANCIENT MARINER

Samuel Taylor Coleridge

ARGUMENT

How a Ship having passed the Line was driven by storms to the cold Country towards the South Pole; and how from thence she made her course to the tropical Latitude of the Great Pacific Ocean; and of the strange things that befell; and in what manner the Ancyent Marinere came back to his own Country.

PART I

It is an ancient Mariner,
And he stoppeth one of three.
'By thy long grey beard and glittering eye,
Now wherefore stopp'st thou me?

The Bridegroom's doors are opened wide,
And I am next of kin;
The guests are met, the feast is set:
May'st hear the merry din.'

He holds him with his skinny hand,
10   'There was a ship,' quoth he.
'Hold off! unhand me, grey-beard loon!'
Eftsoons his hand dropt he.

He holds him with his glittering eye—
The Wedding-Guest stood still,
And listens like a three years' child:
The Mariner hath his will.

The Wedding-Guest sat on a stone:
He cannot choose but hear;
And thus spake on that ancient man,
20   The bright-eyed Mariner.

'The ship was cheered, the harbour cleared,
Merrily did we drop
Below the kirk, below the hill,
Below the lighthouse top.

The Sun came up upon the left,
Out of the sea came he!
And he shone bright, and on the right
Went down into the sea.

Higher and higher every day,
30   Till over the mast at noon—'
The Wedding-Guest here beat his breast,
For he heard the loud bassoon.

The bride hath paced into the hall,
Red as a rose is she;
Nodding their heads before her goes
The merry minstrelsy.

The Wedding-Guest he beat his breast,
Yet he cannot choose but hear;
And thus spake on that ancient man,
40   The bright-eyed Mariner.

'And now the STORM-BLAST came, and he
Was tyrannous and strong:
He struck with his o'ertaking wings,
And chased us south along.

With sloping masts and dipping prow,
As who pursued with yell and blow
Still treads the shadow of his foe,
And forward bends his head,
The ship drove fast, loud roared the blast,
And southward aye we fled.   50

And now there came both mist and snow,
And it grew wondrous cold:
And ice, mast-high, came floating by,
As green as emerald.

And through the drifts the snowy clifts
Did send a dismal sheen:
Nor shapes of men nor beasts we ken—
The ice was all between.

The ice was here, the ice was there,
The ice was all around: 60
It cracked and growled, and roared and howled,
Like noises in a swound!

At length did cross an Albatross,
Thorough the fog it came;
As if it had been a Christian soul,
We hailed it in God's name.

It ate the food it ne'er had eat,
And round and round it flew.
The ice did split with a thunder-fit;
The helmsman steered us through!   70

And a good south wind sprung up behind;
The Albatross did follow,

And every day, for food or play,
Came to the mariner's hollo!

In mist or cloud, on mast or shroud,
It perched for vespers nine;
Whiles all the night, through fog-smoke white,
Glimmered the white Moon-shine.'

'God save thee, ancient Mariner!
80   From the fiends, that plague thee thus!—
Why look'st thou so?'—'With my cross-bow
I shot the ALBATROSS.'

Part II

The Sun now rose upon the right:
Out of the sea came he,
Still hid in mist, and on the left
Went down into the sea.

And the good south wind still blew behind,
But no sweet bird did follow,
Nor any day for food or play
90   Came to the mariner's hollo!

And I had done a hellish thing,
And it would work 'em woe:
For all averred, I had killed the bird
That made the breeze to blow.
Ah wretch! said they, the bird to slay,
That made the breeze to blow!

Nor dim nor red, like God's own head,
The glorious Sun uprist:
Then all averred, I had killed the bird
100   That brought the fog and mist.

'Twas right, said they, such birds to slay,
That bring the fog and mist.

The fair breeze blew, the white foam flew,
The furrow followed free;
We were the first that ever burst
Into that silent sea.

Down dropt the breeze, the sails dropt down,
'Twas sad as sad could be;
And we did speak only to break
The silence of the sea!   110

All in a hot and copper sky,
The bloody Sun, at noon,
Right up above the mast did stand,
No bigger than the Moon.

Day after day, day after day,
We stuck, nor breath nor motion;
As idle as a painted ship
Upon a painted ocean.

Water, water, every where,
And all the boards did shrink;   120
Water, water, every where,
Nor any drop to drink.

The very deep did rot: O Christ!
That ever this should be!
Yea, slimy things did crawl with legs
Upon the slimy sea.

About, about, in reel and rout
The death-fires danced at night;
The water, like a witch's oils,
Burnt green, and blue and white.   130

And some in dreams assurèd were
Of the Spirit that plagued us so;

Nine fathom deep he had followed us
From the land of mist and snow.

And every tongue, through utter drought,
Was withered at the root;
We could not speak, no more than if
We had been choked with soot.

Ah! well a-day! what evil looks
140   Had I from old and young!
Instead of the cross, the Albatross
About my neck was hung.

Part III

There passed a weary time. Each throat
Was parched, and glazed each eye.
A weary time! a weary time!
How glazed each weary eye,
When looking westward, I beheld
A something in the sky.

At first it seemed a little speck,
150   And then it seemed a mist;
It moved and moved, and took at last
A certain shape, I wist.

A speck, a mist, a shape, I wist!
And still it neared and neared:
As if it dodged a water-sprite,
It plunged and tacked and veered.

With throats unslaked, with black lips baked,
We could nor laugh nor wail;
Through utter drought all dumb we stood!
160   I bit my arm, I sucked the blood,

And cried, A sail! a sail!

With throats unslaked, with black lips baked,
Agape they heard me call:
Gramercy! they for joy did grin,
And all at once their breath drew in.
As they were drinking all.

See! see! (I cried) she tacks no more!
Hither to work us weal;
Without a breeze, without a tide,
She steadies with upright keel!   170

The western wave was all a-flame.
The day was well nigh done!
Almost upon the western wave
Rested the broad bright Sun;
When that strange shape drove suddenly
Betwixt us and the Sun.

And straight the Sun was flecked with bars,
(Heaven's Mother send us grace!)
As if through a dungeon-grate he peered
With broad and burning face.   180

Alas! (thought I, and my heart beat loud)
How fast she nears and nears!
Are those her sails that glance in the Sun,
Like restless gossameres?

Are those her ribs through which the Sun
Did peer, as through a grate?
And is that Woman all her crew?
Is that a DEATH? and are there two?
Is DEATH that woman's mate?

Her lips were red, her looks were free,   190
Her locks were yellow as gold:
Her skin was as white as leprosy,

The Night-mare LIFE-IN-DEATH was she,
Who thicks man's blood with cold.

The naked hulk alongside came,
And the twain were casting dice;
'The game is done! I've won! I've won!'
Quoth she, and whistles thrice.

The Sun's rim dips; the stars rush out;
200   At one stride comes the dark;
With far-heard whisper, o'er the sea,
Off shot the spectre-bark.

We listened and looked sideways up!
Fear at my heart, as at a cup,
My life-blood seemed to sip!
The stars were dim, and thick the night,
The steersman's face by his lamp gleamed white;
From the sails the dew did drip—
Till clomb above the eastern bar
210   The hornèd Moon, with one bright star
Within the nether tip.

One after one, by the star-dogged Moon,
Too quick for groan or sigh,
Each turned his face with a ghastly pang,
And cursed me with his eye.

Four times fifty living men,
(And I heard nor sigh nor groan)
With heavy thump, a lifeless lump,
They dropped down one by one.

220   The souls did from their bodies fly,—
They fled to bliss or woe!
And every soul, it passed me by,
Like the whizz of my cross-bow!

PART IV

'I fear thee, ancient Mariner!
I fear thy skinny hand!
And thou art long, and lank, and brown,
As is the ribbed sea-sand.

I fear thee and thy glittering eye,
And thy skinny hand, so brown.'—
'Fear not, fear not, thou Wedding-Guest!   230
This body dropt not down.

Alone, alone, all, all alone,
Alone on a wide wide sea!
And never a saint took pity on
My soul in agony.

The many men, so beautiful!
And they all dead did lie:
And a thousand thousand slimy things
Lived on; and so did I.

I looked upon the rotting sea,   240
And drew my eyes away;
I looked upon the rotting deck,
And there the dead men lay.

I looked to heaven, and tried to pray;
But or ever a prayer had gusht,
A wicked whisper came, and made
My heart as dry as dust.

I closed my lids, and kept them close,
And the balls like pulses beat;
For the sky and the sea, and the sea and the sky   250
Lay dead like a load on my weary eye,
And the dead were at my feet.

The cold sweat melted from their limbs,
Nor rot nor reek did they:
The look with which they looked on me
Had never passed away.

An orphan's curse would drag to hell
A spirit from on high;
But oh! more horrible than that
Is the curse in a dead man's eye!
Seven days, seven nights, I saw that curse,
And yet I could not die.

The moving Moon went up the sky,
And no where did abide:
Softly she was going up,
And a star or two beside—

Her beams bemocked the sultry main,
Like April hoar-frost spread;
But where the ship's huge shadow lay,
The charmèd water burnt alway
A still and awful red.

Beyond the shadow of the ship,
I watched the water-snakes:
They moved in tracks of shining white,
And when they reared, the elfish light
Fell off in hoary flakes.

Within the shadow of the ship
I watched their rich attire:
Blue, glossy green, and velvet black,
They coiled and swam; and every track
Was a flash of golden fire.

O happy living things! no tongue
Their beauty might declare:
A spring of love gushed from my heart,

And I blessed them unaware:
Sure my kind saint took pity on me,
And I blessed them unaware.

The self-same moment I could pray;
And from my neck so free
The Albatross fell off, and sank   290
Like lead into the sea.

PART V

Oh sleep! it is a gentle thing,
Beloved from pole to pole!
To Mary Queen the praise be given!
She sent the gentle sleep from Heaven,
That slid into my soul.

The silly buckets on the deck,
That had so long remained,
I dreamt that they were filled with dew;
And when I awoke, it rained.   300

My lips were wet, my throat was cold,
My garments all were dank;
Sure I had drunken in my dreams,
And still my body drank.

I moved, and could not feel my limbs:
I was so light—almost
I thought that I had died in sleep,
And was a blessed ghost.

And soon I heard a roaring wind:
It did not come anear;   310
But with its sound it shook the sails,
That were so thin and sere.

The upper air burst into life!
And a hundred fire-flags sheen,
To and fro they were hurried about!
And to and fro, and in and out,
The wan stars danced between.

And the coming wind did roar more loud,
And the sails did sigh like sedge,
320   And the rain poured down from one black cloud;
The Moon was at its edge.

The thick black cloud was cleft, and still
The Moon was at its side:
Like waters shot from some high crag,
The lightning fell with never a jag,
A river steep and wide.

The loud wind never reached the ship,
Yet now the ship moved on!
Beneath the lightning and the Moon
330   The dead men gave a groan.

They groaned, they stirred, they all uprose,
Nor spake, nor moved their eyes;
It had been strange, even in a dream,
To have seen those dead men rise.

The helmsman steered, the ship moved on;
Yet never a breeze up-blew;
The mariners all 'gan work the ropes,
Where they were wont to do;
They raised their limbs like lifeless tools—
340   We were a ghastly crew.

The body of my brother's son
Stood by me, knee to knee:
The body and I pulled at one rope,
But he said nought to me.

'I fear thee, ancient Mariner!'
Be calm, thou Wedding-Guest!
'Twas not those souls that fled in pain,
Which to their corpses came again,
But a troop of spirits blest:

For when it dawned—they dropped their arms,   350
And clustered round the mast;
Sweet sounds rose slowly through their mouths,
And from their bodies passed.

Around, around, flew each sweet sound,
Then darted to the Sun;
Slowly the sounds came back again,
Now mixed, now one by one.

Sometimes a-dropping from the sky
I heard the sky-lark sing;
Sometimes all little birds that are,   360
How they seemed to fill the sea and air
With their sweet jargoning!

And now 'twas like all instruments,
Now like a lonely flute;
And now it is an angel's song,
That makes the heavens be mute.

It ceased; yet still the sails made on
A pleasant noise till noon,
A noise like of a hidden brook
In the leafy month of June,   370
That to the sleeping woods all night
Singeth a quiet tune.

Till noon we quietly sailed on,
Yet never a breeze did breathe:
Slowly and smoothly went the ship,
Moved onward from beneath.

Under the keel nine fathom deep,
From the land of mist and snow,
The spirit slid: and it was he
380   That made the ship to go.
The sails at noon left off their tune,
And the ship stood still also.

The Sun, right up above the mast,
Had fixed her to the ocean:
But in a minute she 'gan stir,
With a short uneasy motion—
Backwards and forwards half her length
With a short uneasy motion.

Then like a pawing horse let go,
390   She made a sudden bound:
It flung the blood into my head,
And I fell down in a swound.

How long in that same fit I lay,
I have not to declare;
But ere my living life returned,
I heard and in my soul discerned
Two voices in the air.

'Is it he?' quoth one, 'Is this the man?
By him who died on cross,
400   With his cruel bow he laid full low
The harmless Albatross.

The spirit who bideth by himself
In the land of mist and snow,
He loved the bird that loved the man
Who shot him with his bow.'

The other was a softer voice,
As soft as honey-dew:
Quoth he, 'The man hath penance done,
And penance more will do.'

PART VI

First Voice

'But tell me, tell me! speak again,   410
Thy soft response renewing—
What makes that ship drive on so fast?
What is the ocean doing?'

Second Voice

'Still as a slave before his lord,
The ocean hath no blast;
His great bright eye most silently
Up to the Moon is cast—

If he may know which way to go;
For she guides him smooth or grim.
See, brother, see! how graciously   420
She looketh down on him.'

First Voice

'But why drives on that ship so fast,
Without or wave or wind?'

Second Voice

'The air is cut away before,
And closes from behind.

Fly, brother, fly! more high, more high!
Or we shall be belated:
For slow and slow that ship will go,
When the Mariner's trance is abated.'

I woke, and we were sailing on   430

As in a gentle weather:
'Twas night, calm night, the moon was high;
The dead men stood together.

All stood together on the deck,
For a charnel-dungeon fitter:
All fixed on me their stony eyes,
That in the Moon did glitter.

The pang, the curse, with which they died,
Had never passed away:
440   I could not draw my eyes from theirs,
Nor turn them up to pray.

And now this spell was snapt: once more
I viewed the ocean green,
And looked far forth, yet little saw
Of what had else been seen—

Like one, that on a lonesome road
Doth walk in fear and dread,
And having once turned round walks on,
And turns no more his head;
450   Because he knows, a frightful fiend
Doth close behind him tread.

But soon there breathed a wind on me,
Nor sound nor motion made:
Its path was not upon the sea,
In ripple or in shade.

It raised my hair, it fanned my cheek
Like a meadow-gale of spring—
It mingled strangely with my fears,
Yet it felt like a welcoming.

460   Swiftly, swiftly flew the ship,
Yet she sailed softly too:

Sweetly, sweetly blew the breeze—
On me alone it blew.

Oh! dream of joy! is this indeed
The light-house top I see?
Is this the hill? is this the kirk?
Is this mine own countree?

We drifted o'er the harbour-bar,
And I with sobs did pray—
O let me be awake, my God!   470
Or let me sleep alway.

The harbour-bay was clear as glass,
So smoothly it was strewn!
And on the bay the moonlight lay,
And the shadow of the Moon.

The rock shone bright, the kirk no less,
That stands above the rock:
The moonlight steeped in silentness
The steady weathercock.

And the bay was white with silent light,   480
Till rising from the same,
Full many shapes, that shadows were,
In crimson colours came.

A little distance from the prow
Those crimson shadows were:
I turned my eyes upon the deck—
Oh, Christ! what saw I there!

Each corpse lay flat, lifeless and flat,
And, by the holy rood!
A man all light, a seraph-man,   490
On every corpse there stood.

This seraph-band, each waved his hand:

It was a heavenly sight!
They stood as signals to the land,
Each one a lovely light;

This seraph-band, each waved his hand,
No voice did they impart—
No voice; but oh! the silence sank
Like music on my heart.

500 But soon I heard the dash of oars,
I heard the Pilot's cheer;
My head was turned perforce away
And I saw a boat appear.

The Pilot and the Pilot's boy,
I heard them coming fast:
Dear Lord in Heaven! it was a joy
The dead men could not blast.

I saw a third—I heard his voice:
It is the Hermit good!
510 He singeth loud his godly hymns
That he makes in the wood.
He'll shrieve my soul, he'll wash away
The Albatross's blood.

Part VII

This Hermit good lives in that wood
Which slopes down to the sea.
How loudly his sweet voice he rears!
He loves to talk with marineres
That come from a far countree.

He kneels at morn, and noon, and eve—
520 He hath a cushion plump:

It is the moss that wholly hides
The rotted old oak-stump.

The skiff-boat neared: I heard them talk,
'Why, this is strange, I trow!
Where are those lights so many and fair,
That signal made but now?'

'Strange, by my faith!' the Hermit said—
'And they answered not our cheer!
The planks looked warped! and see those sails,
How thin they are and sere!   530
I never saw aught like to them,
Unless perchance it were

Brown skeletons of leaves that lag
My forest-brook along;
When the ivy-tod is heavy with snow,
And the owlet whoops to the wolf below,
That eats the she-wolf's young.'

'Dear Lord! it hath a fiendish look—
(The Pilot made reply)
I am a-feared'—'Push on, push on!'   540
Said the Hermit cheerily.

The boat came closer to the ship,
But I nor spake nor stirred;
The boat came close beneath the ship,
And straight a sound was heard.

Under the water it rumbled on,
Still louder and more dread:
It reached the ship, it split the bay;
The ship went down like lead.

Stunned by that loud and dreadful sound,   550
Which sky and ocean smote,

Like one that hath been seven days drowned
My body lay afloat;
But swift as dreams, myself I found
Within the Pilot's boat.

Upon the whirl, where sank the ship,
The boat spun round and round;
And all was still, save that the hill
Was telling of the sound.

560   I moved my lips—the Pilot shrieked
And fell down in a fit;
The holy Hermit raised his eyes,
And prayed where he did sit.

I took the oars: the Pilot's boy,
Who now doth crazy go,
Laughed loud and long, and all the while
His eyes went to and fro.
'Ha! ha!' quoth he, 'full plain I see,
The Devil knows how to row.'

570   And now, all in my own countree,
I stood on the firm land!
The Hermit stepped forth from the boat,
And scarcely he could stand.

'O shrieve me, shrieve me, holy man!'
The Hermit crossed his brow.
'Say quick,' quoth he, 'I bid thee say—
What manner of man art thou?'

Forthwith this frame of mine was wrenched
With a woful agony,
580   Which forced me to begin my tale;
And then it left me free.

Since then, at an uncertain hour,

That agony returns:
And till my ghastly tale is told,
This heart within me burns.

I pass, like night, from land to land;
I have strange power of speech;
That moment that his face I see,
I know the man that must hear me:
To him my tale I teach.   590

What loud uproar bursts from that door!
The wedding-guests are there:
But in the garden-bower the bride
And bride-maids singing are:
And hark the little vesper bell,
Which biddeth me to prayer!

O Wedding-Guest! this soul hath been
Alone on a wide wide sea:
So lonely 'twas, that God himself
Scarce seemèd there to be.   600

O sweeter than the marriage-feast,
'Tis sweeter far to me,
To walk together to the kirk
With a goodly company!—

To walk together to the kirk,
And all together pray,
While each to his great Father bends,
Old men, and babes, and loving friends
And youths and maidens gay!

Farewell, farewell! but this I tell   610
To thee, thou Wedding-Guest!
He prayeth well, who loveth well
Both man and bird and beast.

He prayeth best, who loveth best
All things both great and small;
For the dear God who loveth us,
He made and loveth all.

The Mariner, whose eye is bright,
Whose beard with age is hoar,
620   Is gone: and now the Wedding-Guest
Turned from the bridegroom's door.

He went like one that hath been stunned,
And is of sense forlorn:
A sadder and a wiser man,
He rose the morrow morn.

POEMS

William Wordsworth

THE SOLITARY REAPER

Behold her, single in the field,
Yon solitary Highland Lass!
Reaping and singing by herself;
Stop here, or gently pass!
Alone she cuts and binds the grain,
And sings a melancholy strain;
O listen! for the Vale profound
Is overflowing with the sound.

No Nightingale did ever chaunt
More welcome notes to weary bands 10
Of travellers in some shady haunt,
Among Arabian sands:
A voice so thrilling ne'er was heard
In spring-time from the Cuckoo-bird,
Breaking the silence of the seas
Among the farthest Hebrides.

Will no one tell me what she sings?—
Perhaps the plaintive numbers flow

For old, unhappy, far-off things,
20 And battles long ago:
Or is it some more humble lay,
Familiar matter of to-day?
Some natural sorrow, loss, or pain,
That has been, and may be again?

Whate'er the theme, the Maiden sang
As if her song could have no ending;
I saw her singing at her work,
And o'er the sickle bending;—
I listened, motionless and still;
30 And, as I mounted up the hill,
The music in my heart I bore,
Long after it was heard no more.

ODE: INTIMATIONS OF IMMORTALITY FROM RECOLLECTIONS OF EARLY CHILDHOOD

The child is father of the man;
And I could wish my days to be
Bound each to each by natural piety.
(Wordsworth, 'My Heart Leaps Up')

There was a time when meadow, grove, and stream,
The earth, and every common sight,
To me did seem
Apparelled in celestial light,
The glory and the freshness of a dream.
It is not now as it hath been of yore;—
Turn wheresoe'er I may,
By night or day.
The things which I have seen I now can see no more.

10 The Rainbow comes and goes,

And lovely is the Rose,
The Moon doth with delight
Look round her when the heavens are bare,
Waters on a starry night
Are beautiful and fair;
The sunshine is a glorious birth;
But yet I know, where'er I go,
That there hath past away a glory from the earth.

Now, while the birds thus sing a joyous song,
And while the young lambs bound   20
As to the tabor's sound,
To me alone there came a thought of grief:
A timely utterance gave that thought relief,
And I again am strong:
The cataracts blow their trumpets from the steep;
No more shall grief of mine the season wrong;
I hear the Echoes through the mountains throng,
The Winds come to me from the fields of sleep,
And all the earth is gay;
Land and sea   30
Give themselves up to jollity,
And with the heart of May
Doth every Beast keep holiday;—
Thou Child of Joy,
Shout round me, let me hear thy shouts, thou happy Shepherd-boy.

Ye blessèd creatures, I have heard the call
Ye to each other make; I see
The heavens laugh with you in your jubilee;
My heart is at your festival,
My head hath its coronal,   40
The fulness of your bliss, I feel—I feel it all.
Oh evil day! if I were sullen
While Earth herself is adorning,
This sweet May-morning,

And the Children are culling
On every side,
In a thousand valleys far and wide,
Fresh flowers; while the sun shines warm,
And the Babe leaps up on his Mother's arm:—
50   I hear, I hear, with joy I hear!
—But there's a Tree, of many, one,
A single field which I have looked upon,
Both of them speak of something that is gone;
The Pansy at my feet
Doth the same tale repeat:
Whither is fled the visionary gleam?
Where is it now, the glory and the dream?

Our birth is but a sleep and a forgetting:
The Soul that rises with us, our life's Star,
60   Hath had elsewhere its setting,
And cometh from afar:
Not in entire forgetfulness,
And not in utter nakedness,
But trailing clouds of glory do we come
From God, who is our home:
Heaven lies about us in our infancy!
Shades of the prison-house begin to close
Upon the growing Boy,
But he beholds the light, and whence it flows,
70   He sees it in his joy;
The Youth, who daily farther from the east
Must travel, still is Nature's Priest,
And by the vision splendid
Is on his way attended;
At length the Man perceives it die away,
And fade into the light of common day.

Earth fills her lap with pleasures of her own;
Yearnings she hath in her own natural kind,

And, even with something of a Mother's mind,
        And no unworthy aim,   80
The homely Nurse doth all she can
To make her Foster-child, her Inmate Man,
        Forget the glories he hath known,
And that imperial palace whence he came.

Behold the Child among his new-born blisses,
A six years' Darling of a pigmy size!
See, where 'mid work of his own hand he lies,
Fretted by sallies of his mother's kisses,
With light upon him from his father's eyes!
See, at his feet, some little plan or chart,   90
Some fragment from his dream of human life,
Shaped by himself with newly-learn{e}d art
        A wedding or a festival,
        A mourning or a funeral;
            And this hath now his heart,
        And unto this he frames his song:
            Then will he fit his tongue
To dialogues of business, love, or strife;
        But it will not be long
        Ere this be thrown aside,   100
        And with new joy and pride
The little Actor cons another part;
Filling from time to time his 'humorous stage'
With all the Persons, down to palsied Age,
That Life brings with her in her equipage;
        As if his whole vocation
        Were endless imitation.

Thou, whose exterior semblance doth belie
        Thy Soul's immensity;
Thou best Philosopher, who yet dost keep   110
Thy heritage, thou Eye among the blind,
That, deaf and silent, read'st the eternal deep,

Haunted for ever by the eternal mind,—
      Mighty Prophet! Seer blest!
      On whom those truths do rest,
Which we are toiling all our lives to find,
In darkness lost, the darkness of the grave;
Thou, over whom thy Immortality
Broods like the Day, a Master o'er a Slave,
A Presence which is not to be put by;
Thou little Child, yet glorious in the might
Of heaven-born freedom on thy being's height,
Why with such earnest pains dost thou provoke
The years to bring the inevitable yoke,
Thus blindly with thy blessedness at strife?
Full soon thy Soul shall have her earthly freight,
And custom lie upon thee with a weight,
Heavy as frost, and deep almost as life!

      O joy! that in our embers
      Is something that doth live,
      That Nature yet remembers
What was so fugitive!
The thought of our past years in me doth breed
Perpetual benediction: not indeed
For that which is most worthy to be blest;
Delight and liberty, the simple creed
Of Childhood, whether busy or at rest,
With new-fledged hope still fluttering in his breast:—
      Not for these I raise
      The song of thanks and praise
      But for those obstinate questionings
      Of sense and outward things,
      Fallings from us, vanishings;
      Blank misgivings of a Creature
Moving about in worlds not realised,
High instincts before which our mortal Nature
Did tremble like a guilty thing surprised:

But for those first affections,
Those shadowy recollections,
Which, be they what they may 150
Are yet the fountain-light of all our day,
Are yet a master-light of all our seeing;
Uphold us, cherish, and have power to make
Our noisy years seem moments in the being
Of the eternal Silence: truths that wake,
To perish never;
Which neither listlessness, nor mad endeavour,
Nor Man nor Boy,
Nor all that is at enmity with joy,
Can utterly abolish or destroy! 160
Hence in a season of calm weather
Though inland far we be,
Our Souls have sight of that immortal sea
Which brought us hither,
Can in a moment travel thither,
And see the Children sport upon the shore,
And hear the mighty waters rolling evermore.

Then sing, ye Birds, sing, sing a joyous song!
And let the young Lambs bound
As to the tabor's sound! 170
We in thought will join your throng,
Ye that pipe and ye that play,
Ye that through your hearts to-day
Feel the gladness of the May!
What though the radiance which was once so bright
Be now for ever taken from my sight,
Though nothing can bring back the hour
Of splendour in the grass, of glory in the flower;
We will grieve not, rather find
Strength in what remains behind; 180
In the primal sympathy
Which having been must ever be;

In the soothing thoughts that spring
Out of human suffering;
In the faith that looks through death,
In years that bring the philosophic mind.
And O, ye Fountains, Meadows, Hills, and Groves,
Forebode not any severing of our loves!
Yet in my heart of hearts I feel your might;
190   I only have relinquished one delight
To live beneath your more habitual sway.
I love the Brooks which down their channels fret,
Even more than when I tripped lightly as they;
The innocent brightness of a new-born Day
Is lovely yet;
The Clouds that gather round the setting sun
Do take a sober colouring from an eye
That hath kept watch o'er man's mortality;
Another race hath been, and other palms are won.
200   Thanks to the human heart by which we live,
Thanks to its tenderness, its joys, and fears,
To me the meanest flower that blows can give
Thoughts that do often lie too deep for tears.

POEMS

George Gordon, Lord Byron

SHE WALKS IN BEAUTY

She walks in beauty, like the night
Of cloudless climes and starry skies;
And all that's best of dark and bright
Meet in her aspect and her eyes;
Thus mellowed to that tender light
Which heaven to gaudy day denies.

One shade the more, one ray the less,
Had half impaired the nameless grace
Which waves in every raven tress,
Or softly lightens o'er her face;
Where thoughts serenely sweet express,
How pure, how dear their dwelling-place.

And on that cheek, and o'er that brow,
So soft, so calm, yet eloquent,
The smiles that win, the tints that glow,
But tell of days in goodness spent,
A mind at peace with all below,
A heart whose love is innocent!

The Destruction of Sennacherib

The Assyrian came down like the wolf on the fold,
And his cohorts were gleaming in purple and gold;
And the sheen of their spears was like stars on the sea,
When the blue wave rolls nightly on deep Galilee.

Like the leaves of the forest when Summer is green,
That host with their banners at sunset were seen:
Like the leaves of the forest when Autumn hath blown,
That host on the morrow lay withered and strown.

For the Angel of Death spread his wings on the blast,
10   And breathed in the face of the foe as he passed;
And the eyes of the sleepers waxed deadly and chill,
And their hearts but once heaved, and for ever grew still!

And there lay the steed with his nostril all wide,
But through it there rolled not the breath of his pride;
And the foam of his gasping lay white on the turf,
And cold as the spray of the rock-beating surf.

And there lay the rider distorted and pale,
With the dew on his brow, and the rust on his mail:
And the tents were all silent, the banners alone,
20   The lances unlifted, the trumpet unblown.

And the widows of Ashur are loud in their wail,
And the idols are broke in the temple of Baal;
And the might of the Gentile, unsmote by the sword,
Hath melted like snow in the glance of the Lord!

On First Looking into Chapman's Homer

John Keats

Much have I travell'd in the realms of gold,
And many goodly states and kingdoms seen;
Round many western islands have I been
Which bards in fealty to Apollo hold.
Oft of one wide expanse had I been told
That deep-brow'd Homer ruled as his demesne;
Yet did I never breathe its pure serene
Till I heard Chapman speak out loud and bold:
Then felt I like some watcher of the skies
When a new planet swims into his ken;
Or like stout Cortez when with eagle eyes
He star'd at the Pacific—and all his men
Look'd at each other with a wild surmise—
Silent, upon a peak in Darien.

ODE TO THE WEST WIND

Percy Bysshe Shelley

1

O wild West Wind, thou breath of Autumn's being,
Thou, from whose unseen presence the leaves dead
Are driven, like ghosts from an enchanter fleeing,

Yellow, and black, and pale, and hectic red,
Pestilence-stricken multitudes: O thou,
Who chariotest to their dark wintry bed

The winged seeds, where they lie cold and low,
Each like a corpse within its grave, until
Thine azure sister of the Spring shall blow

Her clarion o'er the dreaming earth, and fill   10
(Driving sweet buds like flocks to feed in air)
With living hues and odours plain and hill:

Wild Spirit, which art moving everywhere;
Destroyer and preserver; hear, oh hear!

2

Thou on whose stream, mid the steep sky's commotion,
Loose clouds like earth's decaying leaves are shed,
Shook from the tangled boughs of Heaven and Ocean,

Angels of rain and lightning: there are spread
On the blue surface of thine aëry surge,
Like the bright hair uplifted from the head

Of some fierce Maenad, even from the dim verge
Of the horizon to the zenith's height,
The locks of the approaching storm. Thou dirge

Of the dying year, to which this closing night
Will be the dome of a vast sepulchre,
Vaulted with all thy congregated might

Of vapours, from whose solid atmosphere
Black rain, and fire, and hail will burst: oh hear!

3

Thou who didst waken from his summer dreams
The blue Mediterranean, where he lay,
Lull'd by the coil of his crystalline streams,

Beside a pumice isle in Baiae's bay,
And saw in sleep old palaces and towers
Quivering within the wave's intenser day,

All overgrown with azure moss and flowers
So sweet, the sense faints picturing them! Thou
For whose path the Atlantic's level powers

Cleave themselves into chasms, while far below
The sea-blooms and the oozy woods which wear

The sapless foliage of the ocean, know   40

Thy voice, and suddenly grow gray with fear,
And tremble and despoil themselves: oh hear!

4

If I were a dead leaf thou mightest bear;
If I were a swift cloud to fly with thee;
A wave to pant beneath thy power, and share

The impulse of thy strength, only less free
Than thou, O uncontrollable! If even
I were as in my boyhood, and could be

The comrade of thy wanderings over Heaven,
As then, when to outstrip thy skiey speed   50
Scarce seem'd a vision; I would ne'er have striven

As thus with thee in prayer in my sore need.
Oh, lift me as a wave, a leaf, a cloud!
I fall upon the thorns of life! I bleed!

A heavy weight of hours has chain'd and bow'd
One too like thee: tameless, and swift, and proud.

5

Make me thy lyre, even as the forest is:
What if my leaves are falling like its own!
The tumult of thy mighty harmonies

Will take from both a deep, autumnal tone,   60
Sweet though in sadness. Be thou, Spirit fierce,
My spirit! Be thou me, impetuous one!

Drive my dead thoughts over the universe
Like wither'd leaves to quicken a new birth!
And, by the incantation of this verse,

Scatter, as from an unextinguish'd hearth
Ashes and sparks, my words among mankind!
Be through my lips to unawaken'd earth

The trumpet of a prophecy! O Wind,
70   If Winter comes, can Spring be far behind?

Democracy in America

Alexis De Tocqueville

Translated by Henry Reeve

Introduction

Among the novel objects that attracted my attention during my stay in the United States, nothing struck me more forcibly than the general equality of condition among the people. I readily discovered the prodigious influence that this primary fact exercises on the whole course of society; it gives a peculiar direction to public opinion and a peculiar tenor to the laws; it imparts new maxims to the governing authorities and peculiar habits to the governed.

I soon perceived that the influence of this fact extends far beyond the political character and the laws of the country, and that it has no less effect on civil society than on the government; it creates opinions, gives birth to new sentiments, founds novel customs, and modifies whatever it does not produce. The more I advanced in the study of American society, the more I perceived that this equality of condition is the fundamental fact from which all others seem to be derived and the central point at which all my observations constantly terminated.

I then turned my thoughts to our own hemisphere, and thought that I discerned there something analogous to the spectacle which the New World presented to me. I observed that equality of condition, though it has not there reached the extreme limit which it seems to have attained in the United States, is constantly approaching it; and that the democracy which governs the American communities appears to be rapidly rising into power in Europe.

Hence I conceived the idea of the book that is now before the reader.

It is evident to all alike that a great democratic revolution is going on among us, but all do not look at it in the same light. To some it appears to be novel but accidental, and, as such, they hope it may still be checked; to others it seems irresistible, because it is the most uniform, the most ancient, and the most permanent tendency that is to be found in history.

I look back for a moment on the situation of France seven hundred years ago, when the territory was divided among a small number of families, who were the owners of the soil and the rulers of the inhabitants; the right of governing descended with the family inheritance from generation to generation; force was the only means by which man could act on man; and landed property was the sole source of power.

Soon, however, the political power of the clergy was founded and began to increase: the clergy opened their ranks to all classes, to the poor and the rich, the commoner and the noble; through the church, equality penetrated into the government, and he who as a serf must have vegetated in perpetual bondage took his place as a priest in the midst of nobles, and not infrequently above the heads of kings.

The different relations of men with one another became more complicated and numerous as society gradually became more stable and civilized. Hence the want of civil laws was felt; and the ministers of law soon rose from the obscurity of the tribunals and their dusty chambers to appear at the court of the monarch, by the side of the feudal barons clothed in their ermine and their mail.

While the kings were ruining themselves by their great enterprises, and the nobles exhausting their resources by private wars, the lower orders were enriching themselves by commerce. The influence of money began to be perceptible in state affairs. The transactions of business opened a new road to power, and the financier rose to a station of political influence in which he was at once flattered and despised.

Gradually enlightenment spread, a reawakening of taste for literature and the arts became evident; intellect and will contributed to success; knowledge became an attribute of government, intelligence a social force; the educated man took part in affairs of state.

The value attached to high birth declined just as fast as new avenues to power were discovered. In the eleventh century, nobility was beyond all price; in the thirteenth, it might be purchased. Nobility was first conferred by gift in 1270, and equality was thus introduced into the government by the aristocracy itself.

In the course of these seven hundred years it sometimes happened that the nobles, in order to resist the authority of the crown or to diminish the power of their rivals, granted some political power to the common people. Or, more frequently, the king permitted the lower orders to have a share in the government, with the intention of limiting the power of the aristocracy.

In France the kings have always been the most active and the most constant of levelers. When they were strong and ambitious, they spared no pains to raise the people to the level of the nobles; when they were temperate and feeble, they allowed the people to rise above themselves. Some assisted democracy by their talents, others by their vices. Louis XI and Louis XIV reduced all ranks beneath the throne to the same degree of subjection; and finally Louis XV descended, himself and all his court, into the dust.

As soon as land began to be held on any other than a feudal tenure, and personal property could in its turn confer influence and power, every discovery in the arts, every improvement in commerce of manufactures, created so many new elements of equality among men. Henceforward every new invention, every new want which it occasioned, and every new desire which craved satisfaction were steps towards a general leveling. The taste for luxury, the love of war, the rule of fashion, and the most superficial as well as the deepest passions of the human heart seemed to co-operate to enrich the poor and to impoverish the rich.

From the time when the exercise of the intellect became a source of strength and of wealth, we see that every addition to science, every fresh truth, and every new idea became a germ of power placed within the reach of the people. Poetry, eloquence, and memory, the graces of the mind, the fire of imagination, depth of thought, and all the gifts which Heaven scatters at a venture turned to the advantage of democracy; and even when they were in the possession of its adversaries, they still served its cause by throwing into bold relief the natural greatness of man. Its conquests spread, therefore, with those of civilization and knowledge; and literature became an arsenal open to all, where the poor and the weak daily resorted for arms.

In running over the pages of our history, we shall scarcely find a single great event of the last seven hundred years that has not promoted equality of condition.

The Crusades and the English wars decimated the nobles and divided their possessions: the municipal corporations introduced democratic liberty into the bosom of feudal monarchy; the invention of firearms equalized the vassal and the noble on the field of battle; the art of printing opened the same resources to the minds of all classes; the post brought knowledge alike to the door of the cottage and to the gate of the palace; and Protestantism proclaimed that all men are equally able to find the road to heaven. The discovery of America opened a thousand new paths to fortune and led obscure adventurers to wealth and power.

If, beginning with the eleventh century, we examine what has happened in France from one half-century to another, we shall not fail to perceive that at the end of each of these periods a two- fold revolution has taken place in the state of society. The noble has gone down the social ladder, and the commoner has gone up; the one descends as the other rises. Every half-century brings them nearer to each other, and they will soon meet.

Nor is this peculiar to France. Wherever we look, we perceive the same revolution going on throughout the Christian world.

The various occurrences of national existence have everywhere turned to the advantage of democracy: all men have aided it by their exertions, both those who have intentionally labored in its cause and those who have served it unwittingly; those who have fought for it and even those who have declared themselves its opponents have all been driven along in the same direction, have all labored to one end; some unknowingly and some despite themselves, all have been blind instruments in the hands of God.

The gradual development of the principle of equality is, therefore, a providential fact. It has all the chief characteristics of such a fact: it is universal, it is lasting, it constantly eludes all human interference, and all events as well as all men contribute to its progress.

Would it, then, be wise to imagine that a social movement the causes of which lie so far back can be checked by the efforts of one generation? Can it be believed that the democracy which has overthrown the feudal system and vanquished kings will retreat before tradesmen and capitalists? Will it stop now that it has grown so strong and its adversaries so weak?

Whither, then, are we tending? No one can say, for terms of comparison already fail us. There is greater equality of condition in Christian countries at the present day than there has been at any previous time, in any part of the world, so that the magnitude of what already has been done prevents us from foreseeing what is yet to be accomplished.

The whole book that is here offered to the public has been written under the influence of a kind of religious awe produced in the author's mind by the view of that irresistible revolution which has advanced for centuries in spite of every obstacle and which is still advancing in the midst of the ruins it has caused. It is not necessary that God himself should speak in order that we may discover the unquestionable signs of his will. It is enough to ascertain what is the habitual course of nature and the constant tendency of events. I know, without special revelation, that the planets move in the orbits traced by the Creator's hand.

If the men of our time should be convinced, by attentive observation and sincere reflection, that the gradual and progressive development of social equality is at once the past and the future of their history, this discovery alone would confer upon the change the sacred character of a divine decree. To attempt to check democracy would be in that case to resist the will of God; and the nations would then be constrained to make the best of the social lot awarded to them by Providence.

The Christian nations of our day seem to me to present a most alarming spectacle; the movement which impels them is already so strong that it cannot be stopped, but it is not yet so rapid that it cannot be guided. Their fate is still in their own hands; but very soon they may lose control.

The first of the duties that are at this time imposed upon those who direct our affairs is to educate democracy, to reawaken, if possible, its religious beliefs; to purify its morals; to mold its actions; to substitute a knowledge of statecraft for its inexperience, and an awareness of its true interest for its blind instincts, to adapt its government to time and place, and to modify it according to men and to conditions. A new science of politics is needed for a new world.

This, however, is what we think of least; placed in the middle of a rapid stream, we obstinately fix our eyes on the ruins that may still be descried upon the shore we have left, while the current hurries us away and drags us backward towards the abyss.

In no country in Europe has the great social revolution that I have just described made such rapid progress as in France; but it has always advanced without guidance. The heads of the state have made no preparation for it, and it has advanced without their consent or without their knowledge. The most powerful, the most intelligent, and the most moral classes of the nation have never attempted to control it in order to guide it. Democracy has consequently been abandoned to its wild instincts, and it has grown up like those children who have no parental guidance, who receive their education in the public streets, and who are acquainted only with the vices and wretchedness of society. Its existence was seemingly unknown when suddenly it acquired supreme power. All then servilely submitted to its caprices; it was worshiped as the idol of strength; and when afterwards it was enfeebled by its own excesses, the legislator conceived the rash project of destroying it, instead of instructing it and correcting its vices. No attempt was made to fit it to govern, but all were bent on excluding it from the government.

The result has been that the democratic revolution has taken place in the body of society without that concomitant change in the laws, ideas, customs, and morals which was necessary to render such a revolution beneficial. Thus we have a democracy without anything to lessen its vices and bring out its natural advantages; and although we already perceive the evils it brings, we are ignorant of the benefits it may confer.

While the power of the crown, supported by the aristocracy, peaceably governed the nations of Europe, society, in the midst of its wretchedness, had several sources of happiness which can now scarcely be conceived or appreciated. The power of a few of his subjects was an insurmountable barrier to the tyranny of the prince; and the monarch, who felt the almost divine character which he enjoyed in the eyes of the multitude, derived a motive for the just use of his power from the respect which he inspired. The nobles, placed high as they were above the people, could take that calm and benevolent interest in their fate which the shepherd feels towards his flock; and without acknowledging the poor as their equals, they watched over the destiny of those whose welfare Providence had entrusted to their care. The people, never having conceived the idea of a social condition different from their own, and never expecting to become equal to their leaders, received benefits from them without discussing their rights. They became attached to them when they were clement and just and submitted to their exactions without resistance or servility, as to the inevitable visitations of the Deity. Custom and usage, moreover, had established certain limits to oppression and founded a sort of law in the very midst of violence.

As the noble never suspected that anyone would attempt to deprive him of the privileges which he believed to be legitimate, and as the serf looked upon his own inferiority as a consequence of the immutable order of nature, it is easy to imagine that some mutual exchange of goodwill took place between two classes so differently endowed by fate. Inequality and wretchedness were then to be found in society, but the souls of neither rank of men were degraded.

Men are not corrupted by the exercise of power or debased by the habit of obedience, but by the exercise of a power which they believe to be illegitimate, and by obedience to a rule which they consider to be usurped and oppressive.

On the one side were wealth, strength, and leisure, accompanied by the pursuit of luxury, the refinements of taste, the pleasures of wit, and the cultivation of the arts; on the other were labor, clownishness, and ignorance. But in the midst of this coarse and ignorant multitude it was not uncommon to meet with energetic passions, generous sentiments, profound religious convictions, and wild virtues.

The social state thus organized might boast of its stability, its power, and, above all, its glory.

But the scene is now changed. Gradually the distinctions of rank are done away with; the barriers that once severed mankind are falling; property is divided, power is shared by many, the light of intelligence spreads, and the capacities of all classes tend towards equality. Society becomes democratic, and the empire of democracy is slowly and peaceably introduced into institutions and customs.

I can conceive of a society in which all men would feel an equal love and respect for the laws of which they consider themselves the authors; in which the authority of the government would be respected as necessary, and not divine; and in which the loyalty of the subject to the chief magistrate would not be a passion, but a quiet and rational persuasion. With every individual in the possession of rights which he is sure to retain, a kind of manly confidence and reciprocal courtesy would arise between all classes, removed alike from pride and servility. The people, well acquainted with their own true interests, would understand that, in order to profit from the advantages of the state, it is necessary to satisfy its requirements. The voluntary association of the citizens might then take the place of the individual authority of the nobles, and the community would be protected from tyranny and license.

I admit that, in a democratic state thus constituted, society would not be stationary. But the impulses of the social body might there be regulated and made progressive. If there were less splendor than in an aristocracy, misery would also be less prevalent; the pleasures of enjoyment might be less excessive, but those of comfort would be more general; the sciences might be less perfectly cultivated, but ignorance would be less common; the ardor of the feelings would be constrained, and the habits of the nation softened; there would be more vices and fewer crimes.

In the absence of enthusiasm and ardent faith, great sacrifices may be obtained from the members of a commonwealth by an appeal to their understanding and their experience; each individual will feel the same necessity of union with his fellows to protect his own weakness; and as he knows that he can obtain their help only on condition of helping them, he will readily perceive that his personal interest is identified with the interests of the whole community. The nation, taken as a whole, will be less brilliant, less glorious, and perhaps less strong; but the majority of the citizens will enjoy a greater degree of prosperity, and the people will remain peaceable, not because they despair of a change for the better, but because they are conscious that they are well off already.

If all the consequences of this state of things were not good or useful, society would at least have appropriated all such as were useful and good; and having once and forever renounced the social advantages of aristocracy, mankind would enter into possession of all the benefits that democracy can offer.

But here it may be asked what we have adopted in the place of those institutions, those ideas, and those customs of our forefathers which we have abandoned.

The spell of royalty is broken, but it has not been succeeded by the majesty of the laws. The people have learned to despise all authority, but they still fear it; and fear now extorts more than was formerly paid from reverence and love.

I perceive that we have destroyed those individual powers which were able, single-handed, to cope with tyranny; but it is the government alone that has inherited all the privileges of which families, guilds, and individuals have been deprived; to the power of a small number of persons, which if it was sometimes oppressive was often conservative, has succeeded the weakness of the whole community.

The division of property has lessened the distance which separated the rich from the poor; but it would seem that, the nearer they draw to each other, the greater is their mutual hatred and the more vehement the envy and the dread with which they resist each other's claims to power; the idea of right does not exist for either party, and force affords to both the only argument for the present and the only guarantee for the future.

The poor man retains the prejudices of his forefathers without their faith, and their ignorance without their virtues; he has adopted the doctrine of self-interest as the rule of his actions without understanding the science that puts it to use; and his selfishness is no less blind than was formerly his devotion to others.

If society is tranquil, it is not because it is conscious of its strength and its well-being, but because it fears its weakness and its infirmities; a single effort may cost it its life. Everybody feels the evil, but no one has courage or energy enough to seek the cure. The desires, the repinings, the sorrows, and the joys of the present time lead to nothing visible or permanent, like the passions of old men, which terminate in impotence.

We have, then, abandoned whatever advantages the old state of things afforded, without receiving any compensation from our present condition; we have destroyed an aristocracy, and we seem inclined to survey its ruins with complacency and to accept them.

The phenomena which the intellectual world presents are not less deplorable. The democracy of France, hampered in its course or abandoned to its lawless passions, has overthrown whatever crossed its path and has shaken all that it has not destroyed. Its empire has not been gradually introduced or peaceably established, but it has constantly advanced in the midst of the disorders and the agitations of a conflict. In the heat of the struggle each partisan is hurried beyond the natural limits of his opinions by the doctrines and the excesses of his opponents, until he loses sight of the end of his exertions, and holds forth in a way which does not correspond to his real sentiments or secret instincts. Hence arises the strange confusion that we are compelled to witness.

I can recall nothing in history more worthy of sorrow and pity than the scenes which are passing before our eyes. It is as if the natural bond that unites the opinions of man to his tastes, and his actions to his principles, was now broken; the harmony that has always been observed between the feelings and the ideas of mankind appears to be dissolved and all the laws of moral analogy to be abolished.

Zealous Christians are still found among us, whose minds are nurtured on the thoughts that pertain to a future life, and who readily espouse the cause of human liberty as the source of all moral greatness. Christianity, which has declared that all men are equal in the sight of God, will not refuse to acknowledge that all citizens are equal in the eye of the law. But, by a strange coincidence of events, religion has been for a time entangled with those institutions which democracy destroys; and it is not infrequently brought to reject the equality which it loves, and to curse as a foe that cause of liberty whose efforts it might hallow by its alliance.

By the side of these religious men I discern others whose thoughts are turned to earth rather than to heaven. These are the partisans of liberty, not only as the source of the noblest virtues, but more especially as the root of all solid advantages; and they sincerely desire to secure its authority, and to impart its blessings to mankind. It is natural that they should hasten to invoke the assistance of religion, for they must know that liberty cannot be established without morality, nor morality without faith. But they have seen religion in the ranks of their adversaries, and they inquire no further; some of them attack it openly, and the rest are afraid to defend it.

In former ages slavery was advocated by the venal and slavish-minded, while the independent and the warm-hearted were struggling without hope to save the liberties of mankind. But men of high and generous character are now to be met with, whose opinions are directly at variance with their inclinations, and who praise that servility and meanness which they have themselves never known. Others, on the contrary, speak of liberty as if they were able to feel its sanctity and its majesty, and loudly claim for humanity those rights which they have always refused to acknowledge.

There are virtuous and peaceful individuals whose pure morality, quiet habits, opulence, and talents fit them to be the leaders of their fellow men. Their love of country is sincere, and they are ready to make the greatest sacrifices for its welfare. But civilization often finds them among its opponents; they confound its abuses with its benefits, and the idea of evil is inseparable in their minds from that of novelty. Near these I find others whose object is to materialize mankind, to hit upon what is expedient without heeding what is just, to acquire knowledge without faith, and prosperity apart from virtue; claiming to be the champions of modern civilization, they place themselves arrogantly at its head, usurping a place which is abandoned to them, and of which they are wholly unworthy.

Where are we, then?

The religionists are the enemies of liberty, and the friends of liberty attack religion; the high-minded and the noble advocate bondage, and the meanest and most servile preach independence; honest and enlightened citizens are opposed to all progress, while men without patriotism and without principle put themselves forward as the apostles of civilization and intelligence.

Has such been the fate of the centuries which have preceded our own? and has man always inhabited a world like the present, where all things are not in their proper relationships, where virtue is without genius, and genius without honor; where the love of order is confused with a taste for oppression, and the holy cult of freedom with a contempt of law; where the light thrown by conscience on human actions is dim, and where nothing seems to be any longer forbidden or allowed, honorable or shameful, false or true?

I cannot believe that the Creator made man to leave him in an endless struggle with the intellectual wretchedness that surrounds us. God destines a calmer and a more certain future to the communities of Europe. I am ignorant of his designs, but I shall not cease to believe in them because I cannot fathom them, and I had rather mistrust my own capacity than His justice.

There is one country in the world where the great social revolution that I am speaking of seems to have nearly reached its natural limits. It has been effected with ease and simplicity; say rather that this country is reaping the fruits of the democratic revolution which we are undergoing, without having had the revolution itself.

The emigrants who colonized the shores of America in the beginning of the seventeenth century somehow separated the democratic principle from all the principles that it had to contend with in the old communities of Europe, and transplanted it alone to the

New World. It has there been able to spread in perfect freedom and peaceably to determine the character of the laws by influencing the manners of the country. It appears to me beyond a doubt that, sooner or later, we shall arrive, like the Americans, at an almost complete equality of condition. But I do not conclude from this that we shall ever be necessarily led to draw the same political consequences which the Americans have derived from a similar social organization. I am far from supposing that they have chosen the only form of government which a democracy may adopt; but as the generating cause of laws and manners in the two countries is the same, it is of immense interest for us to know what it has produced in each of them.

It is not, then, merely to satisfy a curiosity, however legitimate, that I have examined America; my wish has been to find there instruction by which we may ourselves profit. Whoever should imagine that I have intended to write a panegyric would be strangely mistaken, and on reading this book he will perceive that such was not my design; nor has it been my object to advocate any form of government in particular, for I am of the opinion that absolute perfection is rarely to be found in any system of laws. I have not even pretended to judge whether the social revolution, which I believe to be irresistible, is advantageous or prejudicial to mankind. I have acknowledged this revolution as a fact already accomplished, or on the eve of its accomplishment; and I have selected the nation, from among those which have undergone it, in which its development has been the most peaceful and the most complete, in order to discern its natural consequences and to find out, if possible, the means of rendering it profitable to mankind. I confess that in America I saw more than America; I sought there the image of democracy itself, with its inclinations, its character, its prejudices, and its passions, in order to learn what we have to fear or to hope from its progress.

In the first part of this work I have attempted to show the distinction that democracy, dedicated to its inclinations and tendencies and abandoned almost without restraint to its instincts, gave to the laws the course it impressed on the government, and in general the control which it exercised over affairs of state. I have sought to discover the evils and the advantages which it brings. I have examined the safeguards used by the Americans to direct it, as well as those that they have not adopted, and I have undertaken to point out the factors which enable it to govern society.

My object was to portray, in a second part, the influence which the equality of conditions and democratic government in America exercised on civil society, on habits, ideas, and customs; but I grew less enthusiastic about carrying out this plan. Before I could have completed the task which I set for myself, my work would have become purposeless. Someone else would before long set forth to the public the principal traits of the American character and, delicately cloaking a serious picture, lend to the truth a charm which I should not have been able to equal.

I do not know whether I have succeeded in making known what I saw in America, but I am certain that such has been my sincere desire, and that I have never, knowingly, molded facts to ideas, instead of ideas to facts.

Whenever a point could be established by the aid of written documents, I have had recourse to the original text, and to the most authentic and reputable works. I have cited my authorities in the notes, and anyone may verify them. Whenever opinions political customs, or remarks on the manners of the country were concerned, I have endeavored to consult the most informed men I met with. If the point in question was important or doubtful, I was not satisfied with one witness, but I formed my opinion on the evidence of several witnesses. Here the reader must necessarily rely upon my word. I could frequently have cited names which either are known to him or deserve to be so in support of my assertions; but I have carefully abstained from this practice. A stranger frequently hears important truths at the fireside.

CHAPTER II

ORIGIN OF THE ANGLO-AMERICANS, AND IMPORTANCE OF THIS ORIGIN IN RELATION TO THEIR FUTURE CONDITION

Utility of knowing the origin of nations, in order to understand their social condition and their laws—America the only country in which the starting-point of a great people has been clearly observable—In what respects all who emigrated to British America were similar—In what they differed—Remark applicable to all the Europeans who established themselves on the shores of the New World—colonization of Virginia—Colonization of New England—Original character of the first inhabitants of New England—Their arrival—Their first laws-Their social contract—Penal code borrowed from the Hebrew—Religious Fervor—Republican spirit—Intimate union of the spirit of religion with the spirit of liberty.

A man has come into the world; his early years are spent without notice in the pleasures and activities of childhood. As he grows up, the world receives him when his manhood begins, and he enters into contact with his fellows. He is then studied for the first time, and it is imagined that the germ of the vices and the virtues of his maturer years is then formed.

This, if I am not mistaken, is a great error. We must begin higher up; we must watch the infant in his mother's arms; we must see the first images which the external world casts upon the dark mirror of his mind, the first occurrences that he witnesses, we must hear the first words which awaken the sleeping powers of thought, and stand by his earliest efforts if we would understand the prejudices, the habits, and the passions which will rule his life. The entire man is, so to speak, to be seen in the cradle of the child.

The growth of nations presents something analogous to this;

they all bear some marks of their origin. The circumstances that accompanied their birth and contributed to their development affected the whole term of their being.

If we were able to go back to the elements of states and to examine the oldest monuments of their history, I doubt not that we should discover in them the primal cause of the prejudices, the habits, the ruling passions, and, in short, all that constitutes what is called the national character. We should there find the explanation of certain customs which now seem at variance with the prevailing manners; of such laws as conflict with established principles; and of such incoherent opinions as are here and there to be met with in society, like those fragments of broken chains which we sometimes see hanging from the vaults of an old edifice, supporting nothing. This might explain the destinies of certain nations which seem borne on by an unknown force to ends of which they themselves are ignorant. But hitherto facts have been lacking for such a study: the spirit of analysis has come upon nations only as they matured; and when they at last conceived of contemplating their origin, time had already obscured it, or ignorance and pride had surrounded it with fables behind which the truth was hidden.

America is the only country in which it has been possible to witness the natural and tranquil growth of society, and where the influence exercised on the future condition of states by their origin is clearly distinguishable.

At the period when the peoples of Europe landed in the New World, their national characteristics were already completely formed; each of them had a physiognomy of its own; and as they had already attained that stage of civilization at which men are led to study themselves, they have transmitted to us a faithful picture of their opinions, their manners, and their laws. The men of the sixteenth century are almost as well known to us as our contemporaries. America, consequently, exhibits in the broad light of day the phenomena which the ignorance or rudeness of earlier ages conceals from our researches. The men of our day seem destined to see further than their predecessors into human events; they are close enough to the founding of the American settlements to know in detail their elements, and far enough away from that time already to be able to judge what these beginnings have produced. Providence has given us a torch which our forefathers did not possess, and has allowed us to discern fundamental causes in the history of the world which the obscurity of the past concealed from them. If we carefully examine the social and political state of America, after having studied its history, we shall remain perfectly convinced that not an opinion, not a custom, not a law, I may even say not an event is upon record which the origin of that people will not explain. The readers of this book will find in the present chapter the germ of all that is to follow and the key to almost the whole work.

The emigrants who came at different periods to occupy the territory now covered by the American Union differed from each other in many respects; their aim was not the same, and they governed themselves on different principles.

These men had, however, certain features in common, and they were all placed in an analogous situation. The tie of language is, perhaps, the strongest and the most durable that can unite mankind. All the emigrants spoke the same language; they were all children of the same people. Born in a country which had been agitated for centuries by the struggles of faction, and in which all parties had been obliged in their turn to place themselves under the protection of the laws, their political education had been perfected in this rude school; and they were more conversant with the notions of right and the principles of true freedom than the greater part of their European contemporaries. At the period of the first emigrations the township system, that fruitful germ of free institutions, was deeply rooted in the habits of the English; and with it the doctrine of the sovereignty of the people had been introduced into the very bosom of the monarchy of the house of Tudor.

The religious quarrels which have agitated the Christian world were then rife. England had plunged into the new order of things with headlong vehemence. The character of its inhabitants, which had always been sedate and reflective, became argumentative and austere. General information had been increased by intellectual contests, and the mind had received in them a deeper cultivation. While religion was the topic of discussion, the morals of the people became more pure. All these national features are more or less discoverable in the physiognomy of those Englishmen who came to seek a new home on the opposite shores of the Atlantic.

Another observation, moreover, to which we shall have occasion to return later, is applicable not only to the English, but to the French, the Spaniards, and all the Europeans who successively established themselves in the New World. All these European colonies contained the elements, if not the development, of a complete democracy. Two causes led to this result. It may be said that on leaving the mother country the emigrants had, in general, no notion of superiority one over another. The happy and the powerful do not go into exile, and there are no surer guarantees of equality among men than poverty and misfortune. It happened, however, on several occasions, that persons of rank were driven to America by political and religious quarrels. Laws were made to establish a gradation of ranks; but it was soon found that the soil of America was opposed to a territorial aristocracy. It was realized that in order to clear this land, nothing less than the constant and self-interested efforts of the owner himself was essential; the ground prepared, it became evident that its produce was not sufficient to enrich at the same time both an owner and a farmer. The land was then naturally broken up into small portions, which the proprietor cultivated for himself. Land is the basis of an aristocracy, which clings to the soil that supports it; for it is not by privileges alone, nor by birth, but by landed property handed down from generation to generation that an aristocracy is constituted. A nation may present immense fortunes and extreme wretchedness; but unless those fortunes are territorial, there is no true aristocracy, but simply the class of the rich and that of the poor.

All the British colonies had striking similarities at the time of their origin. All of them, from their beginning, seemed destined to witness the growth, not of the aristocratic liberty of their mother country, but of that freedom of the middle and lower orders of which the history of the world had as yet furnished no complete example. In this general uniformity, however, several marked divergences could be observed, which it is necessary to point out. Two branches may be distinguished in the great Anglo-American family, which have hitherto grown up without entirely commingling; the one in the South, the other in the North.

Virginia received the first English colony; the immigrants took possession of it in 1607. The idea that mines of gold and silver are the sources of national wealth was at that time singularly prevalent in Europe; a fatal delusion, which has done more to impoverish the European nations who adopted it, and has cost more lives in America, than the united influence of war and bad laws. The men sent to Virginia were seekers of gold, adventurers without resources and without character, whose turbulent and restless spirit endangered the infant colony and rendered its progress uncertain. Artisans and agriculturists arrived afterwards; and, although they were a more moral and orderly race of men, they were hardly in any respect above the level of the inferior classes in England. No lofty views, no spiritual conception, presided over the foundation of these new settlements. The colony was scarcely established when slavery was introduced; this was the capital fact which was to exercise an immense influence on the character, the laws, and the whole future of the South. Slavery, as I shall afterwards show, dishonors labor; it introduces idleness into society, and with idleness, ignorance and pride, luxury and distress. It enervates the powers of the mind and benumbs the activity of man. The influence of slavery, united to the English character, explains the manners and the social condition of the Southern states.

On this same English foundation there developed in the North very different characteristics. Here I may be allowed to enter into some details.

In the English colonies of the North, more generally known as the New England states, the two or three main ideas that now constitute the basis of the social theory of the United States were first combined. The principles of New England spread at first to the neighboring states; they then passed successively to the more distant ones; and at last, if I may so speak, they interpenetrated the whole confederation. They now extend their influence beyond its limits, over the whole American world. The civilization of New England has been like a beacon lit upon a hill, which, after it has diffused its warmth immediately around it, also tinges the distant horizon with its glow.

The foundation of New England was a novel spectacle, and all the circumstances attending it were singular and original. Nearly all colonies have been first inhabited either by men without education and without resources, driven by their poverty and their misconduct from the land which gave them birth, or by speculators and adventurers greedy of gain. Some settlements cannot even boast so honorable an origin; Santo Domingo was founded by buccaneers; and at the present day the criminal courts of England supply the population of Australia.

The settlers who established themselves on the shores of New England all belonged to the more independent classes of their native country. Their union on the soil of America at once presented the singular phenomenon of a society containing neither lords nor common people, and we may almost say neither rich nor poor. These men possessed, in proportion to their number, a greater mass of intelligence than is to be found in any European nation of our own time All, perhaps without a single exception, had received a good education, and many of them were known in Europe for their talents and their acquirements. The other colonies had been founded by adventurers without families; the immigrants of New England brought with them the best elements of order and morality; they landed on the desert coast accompanied by their wives and children. But what especially distinguished them from all others was the aim of their undertaking. They had not been obliged by necessity to leave their country; the social position they abandoned was one to be regretted, and their means of subsistence were certain. Nor did they cross the Atlantic to improve their situation or to increase their wealth; it was a purely intellectual craving that called them from the comforts of their former homes; and in facing the inevitable sufferings of exile their object was the triumph of an idea.

The immigrants, or, as they deservedly styled themselves, the Pilgrims, belonged to that English sect the austerity of whose principles had acquired for them the name of Puritans. Puritanism was not merely a religious doctrine, but corresponded in many points with the most absolute democratic and republican theories. It was this tendency that had aroused its most dangerous adversaries. Persecuted by the government of the mother country, and disgusted by the habits of a society which the rigor of their own principles condemned, the Puritans went forth to seek some rude and unfrequented part of the world where they could live according to their own opinions and worship God in freedom.

A few quotations will throw more light upon the spirit of these pious adventurers than all that we can say of them. Nathaniel Morton, the historian of the first years of the settlement, thus opens his subject:

> *'Gentle Reader, I have for some lengths of time looked upon it as a duty incumbent especially on the immediate successors of those that have had so large experience of those many memorable and signal demonstrations of God's goodness, viz. the first beginners of this Plantation in New England, to commit to writing his gracious dispensations on that behalf; having so many inducements thereunto, not only otherwise, but so plentifully in the Sacred Scriptures: that so, what we have seen, and what our fathers have told us (Psalm lxxviii. 3, 4), we may not hide from our children, showing to the generations to come the praises of the Lord; that especially the seed of Abraham his servant, and the children of Jacob his chosen (Psalm cv. 5, 6), may remember his marvellous works in the beginning and progress of the planting*

of New England, his wonders and the judgments of his mouth; how that God brought a vine into this wilderness; that he cast out the heathen, and planted it; that he made room for it and caused it to take deep root; and it filled the land (Psalm lxxx. 8, 9). And not only so, but also that he hath guided his people by his strength to his holy habitation, and planted them in the mountain of his inheritance in respect of precious Gospel enjoyments: and that as especially God may have the glory of all unto whom it is most due; so also some rays of glory may reach the names of those blessed Saints, that were the main instruments and the beginning of this happy enterprise."

The author continues, and thus describes the departure of the first Pilgrims:

So they left that goodly and pleasant city of Leyden, which had been their resting-place for above eleven years; but they knew that they were pilgrims and strangers here below, and looked not much on these things, but lifted up their eyes to heaven, their dearest country, where God hath prepared for them a city (Heb. xi. 16), and therein quieted their spirits. When they came to Delfs-Haven they found the ship and all things ready; and such of their friends as could not come with them followed after them, and sundry came from Amsterdam to see them shipt, and to take their leaves of them. One night was spent with little sleep with the most, but with friendly entertainment and Christian discourse, and other real expressions of true Christian love. The next day they went on board, and their friends with them, where truly doleful was the sight of that sad and mournful parting, to hear what sighs and sobs and prayers did sound amongst them; what tears did gush from every eye, and pithy speeches pierced each other's heart, that sundry of the Dutch strangers that stood on the Key as spectators could not refrain from tears. But the tide (which stays for no man) calling them away, that were thus loth to depart, their Reverend Pastor, falling down on his knees, and they all with him, with watery cheeks commended them with most fervent prayers unto the Lord and his blessing; and then with mutual embraces and many tears they took their leaves one of another, which proved to be the last leave to many of them.

The emigrants were about 150 in number, including the women and the children. Their object was to plant a colony on the shores of the Hudson; but after having been driven about for some time in the Atlantic Ocean, they were forced to land on the arid coast . of New England, at the spot which is now the town of Plymouth The rock is still shown on which the Pilgrims disembarked.

'But before we pass on,' continues our historian,

let the reader with me make a pause, and seriously consider this poor people's present condition, the more to be raised up to admiration of God's goodness towards them in their preservation: for being now passed the vast ocean, and a sea of troubles before them in expectation, they had now no friends to welcome them, no inns to entertain or refresh them, no houses, or much less towns, to repair unto to seek for succour: and for the season it was winter, and they that know the winters of the country know them to be sharp and violent, subject to cruel and fierce storms, dangerous to travel to known places, much more to search unknown coasts. Besides, what could they see but a hideous and desolate wilderness, full of wilde beasts, and wilde men? and what multitudes of them there were, they then knew not: for which way soever they turned their eyes (save upward to Heaven) they could have but little solace or content in respect of any outward object; for summer being ended, all things stand in appearance with a weather-beaten face, and the whole country, full of woods and thickets, represented a wild and savage hew; if they looked behind them, there was the mighty ocean which they had passed, and was now as a main bar or gulph to separate them from all the civil parts of the world.

It must not be imagined that the piety of the Puritans was merely speculative, or that it took no cognizance of the course of worldly affairs. Puritanism, as I have already remarked, was almost as much a political theory as a religious doctrine. No sooner had the immigrants landed on the barren coast described by Nathaniel Morton than it was their first care to constitute a society, by subscribing the following Act:

IN THE NAME OF GOD AMEN. We, whose names are underwritten, the loyal subjects of our dread Sovereign Lord King James, &c. &c., Having undertaken for the glory of God, and advancement of the Christian Faith, and the honour of our King and country, a voyage to plant the first colony in the northern parts of Virginia; Do by these presents solemnly and mutually, in the presence of God and one another, covenant and combine ourselves together into a civil body politick, for our better ordering and preservation, and furtherance of the ends aforesaid: and by virtue hereof do enact, constitute, and frame such just and equal laws, ordinances, acts, constitutions, and offices, from time to time, as shall be thought most meet and convenient for the general good of the Colony: unto which we promise all due submission and obedience, etc.

This happened in 1620, and from that time forwards the emigration went on. The religious and political passion which ravaged the British Empire during the whole reign of Charles I drove fresh crowds of sectarians every year to the shores of America. In England the stronghold of Puritanism continued to be in the middle classes; and it was from the middle classes that most of the emigrants came. The population of New England increased rapidly; and while the hierarchy of rank despotically classed the inhabitants of the mother country, the colony approximated more and more the novel spectacle of a community homogeneous in all its parts. A democracy more perfect than antiquity had dared to dream of started in full size and panoply from the midst of an ancient feudal society.

The English government was not dissatisfied with a large emigration which removed the elements of fresh discord and further revolutions. On the contrary, it did everything to encourage it and seemed to have no anxiety about the destiny of those who sought a shelter from the rigor of their laws on the soil of America. It appeared as if New England was a region given up to the dreams of fancy and the unrestrained experiments of innovators.

The English colonies (and this is one of the main causes of their prosperity) have always enjoyed more internal freedom and more political independence than the colonies of other nations; and this principle of liberty was nowhere more extensively applied than in the New England states. It was generally allowed at that period that the territories of the New World belonged to that European nation which had been the first to discover them. Nearly the whole coast of North America thus became a British possession towards the end of the sixteenth century. The means used by the English government to people these new domains were of several kinds: the king sometimes appointed a governor of his own choice, who ruled a portion of the New World in the name and under the immediate orders of the crown; this is the colonial system adopted by the other countries of Europe. Sometimes grants of certain tracts were made by the crown to an individual or to a company, in which case all the civil and political power fell into the hands of one or more persons, who, under the inspection and control of the crown, sold the lands and governed the inhabitants. Lastly, a third system consisted in allowing a certain number of emigrants to form themselves into a political society under the protection of the mother country and to govern themselves in whatever was not contrary to her laws. This mode of colonization, so favorable to liberty, was adopted only in New England.

In 1628 a charter of this kind was granted by Charles I to the emigrants who went to form the colony of Massachusetts. But, in general, charters were not given to the colonies of New England till their existence had become an established fact. Plymouth, Providence, New Haven, Connecticut, and Rhode Island were founded without the help and almost without the knowledge of the mother country. The new settlers did not derive their powers from the head of the empire, although they did not deny its supremacy; they constituted themselves into a society, and it was not till thirty or forty years afterwards, under Charles II, that their existence was legally recognized by a royal charter.

This frequently renders it difficult, in studying the earliest historical and legislative records of New England, to detect the link that connected the emigrants with the land of their forefathers. They continually exercised the rights of sovereignty; they named their magistrates, concluded peace or declared war, made police regulations, and enacted laws, as if their allegiance was due only to God. Nothing can be more curious and at the same time more instructive than the legislation of that period; it is there that the solution of the great social problem which the United States now presents to the world is to be found.

Among these documents we shall notice as especially characteristic the code of laws promulgated by the little state of Connecticut in 1650.

The legislators of Connecticut begin with the penal laws, and, strange to say, they borrow their provisions from the text of Holy Writ.

'Whosoever shall worship any other God than the Lord,' says the preamble of the Code, 'shall surely be put to death.' This is followed by ten or twelve enactments of the same kind, copied verbatim from the books of Exodus, Leviticus, and Deuteronomy. Blasphemy, sorcery, adultery, and rape were punished with death; an outrage offered by a son to his parents was to be expiated by the same penalty. The legislation of a rude and half-civilized people was thus applied to an enlightened and moral community. The consequence was, that the punishment of death was never more frequently prescribed by statute, and never more rarely enforced.

The chief care of the legislators in this body of penal laws was the maintenance of orderly conduct and good morals in the community; thus they constantly invaded the domain of conscience, and there was scarcely a sin which was not subject to magisterial censure. The reader is aware of the rigor with which these laws punished rape and adultery; intercourse between unmarried persons was likewise severely repressed. The judge was empowered to inflict either a pecuniary penalty, a whipping, or marriage on the misdemeanants, and if the records of the old courts of New Haven may be believed, prosecutions of this kind were not infrequent. We find a sentence, bearing the date of May 1, 1660, inflicting a fine and reprimand on a young woman who was accused of using improper language and of allowing herself to be kissed. The Code of 1650 abounds in preventive measures. It punishes idleness and drunkenness with severity. Innkeepers were forbidden to furnish more than a certain quantity of liquor to each consumer; and simple lying, whenever it may be injurious, is checked by a fine or a flogging. In other places the legislator, entirely forgetting the great principles of religious toleration that he had himself demanded in Europe, makes attendance on divine service compulsory, and goes so far as to visit with severe punishment, and even with death, Christians who chose to worship God according to a ritual differing from his own. Sometimes, indeed, the zeal for regulation induces him to descend to the most frivolous particulars: thus a law is to be found in the same code which prohibits the use of tobacco. It must not be forgotten that these fantastic and oppressive laws were not imposed by authority, but that they were freely voted by all the persons interested in them, and that the customs of the community were even more austere and puritanical than the laws. In 1649 a solemn association was formed in Boston to check the worldly luxury of long hair.

These errors are no doubt discreditable to human reason; they attest the inferiority of our nature, which is incapable of laying firm hold upon what is true and just and is often reduced to the alternative of two excesses. In strict connection with this penal legislation, which bears such striking marks of a narrow, sectarian spirit and of those religious passions which had been warmed by persecution and were still fermenting among the people, a body of political laws is to be found which, though written two hundred years ago, is still in advance of the liberties of our age.

The general principles which are the groundwork of modern constitutions, principles which, in the seventeenth century, were imperfectly known in Europe, and not completely triumphant even in Great Britain, were all recognized and established by the laws of New England: the intervention of the people in public affairs, the free voting of taxes, the responsibility of the agents of power, personal liberty, and trial by jury were all positively established without discussion.

These fruitful principles were there applied and developed to an extent such as no nation in Europe has yet ventured to attempt.

In Connecticut the electoral body consisted, from its origin, of the whole number of citizens; and this is readily to be understood. In this young community there was an almost perfect equality of fortune, and a still greater uniformity of opinions. In Connecticut at this period all the executive officials were elected, including the governor of the state. The citizens above the age of sixteen were obliged to bear arms; they formed a national militia, which appointed its own officers, and was to hold itself at all times in readiness to march for the defense of the country.

In the laws of Connecticut, as well as in all those of New England, we find the germ and gradual development of that township independence which is the life and mainspring of American liberty at the present day. The political existence of the majority of the nations of Europe commenced in the superior ranks of society and was gradually and imperfectly communicated to the different members of the social body. In America, on the contrary, it may be said that the township was organized before the county, the county before the state, the state before the union.

In New England, townships were completely and definitely constituted as early as 1650. The independence of the township was the nucleus round which the local interests, passions, rights, and duties collected and clung. It gave scope to the activity of a real political life, thoroughly democratic and republican. The colonies still recognized the supremacy of the mother country; monarchy was still the law of the state; but the republic was already established in every township.

The towns named their own magistrates of every kind, assessed themselves, and levied their own taxes. In the New England town the law of representation was not adopted; but the affairs of the community were discussed, as at Athens, in the marketplace, by a general assembly of the citizens.

In studying the laws that were promulgated at this early era of the American republics, it is impossible not to be struck by the legislator's knowledge of government and advanced theories. The ideas there formed of the duties of society towards its members are evidently much loftier and more comprehensive than those of European legislators at that time; obligations were there imposed upon it which it elsewhere slighted. In the states of New England, from the first, the condition of the poor was provided for; strict measures were taken for the maintenance of roads, and surveyors were appointed to attend to them; records were established in every town, in which the results of public deliberations and the births, deaths, and marriages of the citizens were entered; clerks were directed to keep these records; officers were appointed to administer the properties having no claimants, and others to determine the boundaries of inherited lands, and still others whose principal functions were to maintain public order in the community. The law enters into a thousand various details to anticipate and satisfy a crowd of social wants that are even now very inadequately felt in France.

But it is by the mandates relating to public education that the original character of American civilization is at once placed in the clearest light. 'Whereas,' says the law, 'Satan, the enemy of mankind, finds his strongest weapons in the ignorance of men, and whereas it is important that the wisdom of our fathers shall not remain buried in their tombs, and whereas the education of children is one of the prime concerns of the state, with the aid of the Lord....' Here follow clauses establishing schools in every township and obliging the inhabitants, under pain of heavy fines, to support them.

Schools of a superior kind were founded in the same manner in the more populous districts. The municipal authorities were bound to enforce the sending of children to school by their parents; they were empowered to inflict fines upon all who refused compliance; and in cases of continued resistance, society assumed the place of the parent, took possession of the child, and deprived the father of those natural rights which he used to so bad a purpose. The reader will undoubtedly have remarked the preamble of these enactments: in America religion is the road to knowledge, and the observance of the divine laws leads man to civil freedom.

If, after having cast a rapid glance over the state of American society in 1650, we turn to the condition of Europe, and more especially to that of the Continent, at the same period, we cannot fail to be shuck with astonishment. On the continent of Europe at the beginning of the seventeenth century absolute monarchy had everywhere triumphed over the ruins of the oligarchical and feudal liberties of the Middle Ages. Never perhaps were the ideas of right more completely overlooked than in the midst of the splendor and literature of Europe; never was there less political activity among the people; never were the principles of true freedom less widely circulated; and at that very time those principles which were scorned or unknown by the nations of Europe were proclaimed in the deserts of the New World and were accepted as the future creed of a great people. The boldest theories of the human mind were reduced to practice by a community so humble that not a statesman condescended to attend to it; and a system of legislation without a precedent was produced offhand by the natural originality of men's imaginations. In the bosom of this obscure democracy, which had as yet brought forth neither generals nor philosophers nor authors, a man might stand up in the face of a free people, and pronounce with general applause the following fine definition of liberty:

Concerning liberty, I observe a great mistake in the country about that. There is a twofold liberty, natural (I mean as our nature is now corrupt) and civil or federal. The first is common to man with beasts and other creatures. By this, man, as he stands in relation to man simply, hath liberty to do what he lists; it is a liberty to evil as well as to good. This liberty is incompatible and inconsistent with authority, and cannot endure the least restraint of the most just authority. The exercise and maintaining of this liberty makes men grow more evil, and in time to be worse than brute beasts: omnes sumus licentia deteriores. This is that great enemy of truth and peace, that wild beast, which all the ordinances of God are bent against, to restrain and subdue it. The other kind of liberty I call civil or federal; it may also be termed moral, in reference to the covenant between God and man, in the moral law, and the politic covenants and constitutions, among men themselves. This liberty is the proper end and object of authority, and cannot subsist without it; and it is a liberty to that only which is good, just, and honest. This liberty you are to stand for, with the hazard not only of your goods, but of your lives, if need be. Whatsoever crosseth this, is not authority, but a distemper thereof. This liberty is maintained and exercised in a way of subjection to authority; it is of the same kind of liberty wherewith Christ hath made us free.

I have said enough to put the character of Anglo-American civilization in its true light. It is the result (and this should be constantly kept in mind) of two distinct elements, which in other places have been in frequent disagreement, but which the Americans have succeeded in incorporating to some extent one with the other and combining admirably. I allude to the spirit of religion and the spirit of liberty.

The settlers of New England were at the same time ardent sectarians and daring innovators. Narrow as the limits of some of their religious opinions were, they were free from all political prejudices.

Hence arose two tendencies, distinct but not opposite, which are everywhere discernible in the manners as well as the laws of the country.

Men sacrifice for a religious opinion their friends, their family, and their country; one can consider them devoted to the pursuit of intellectual goals which they came to purchase at so high a price. One sees them, however, seeking with almost equal eagerness material wealth and moral satisfaction; heaven in the world beyond, and well-being and liberty in this one.

Under their hand, political principles, laws, and human institutions seem malleable, capable of being shaped and combined at will. As they go forward, the barriers which imprisoned society and behind which they were born are lowered; old opinions, which for centuries had been controlling the world, vanish; a course almost without limits, a field without horizon, is revealed: the human spirit rushes forward and traverses them in every direction. But having reached the limits of the political world, the human spirit stops of itself; in fear it relinquishes the need of exploration; it even abstains from lifting the veil of the sanctuary; it bows with respect before truths which it accepts without discussion.

Thus in the moral world everything is classified, systematized, foreseen, and decided beforehand; in the political world everything is agitated, disputed, and uncertain. In the one is a passive though a voluntary obedience; in the other, an independence scornful of experience, and jealous of all authority. These two tendencies, apparently so discrepant, are far from conflicting; they advance together and support each other.

Religion perceives that civil liberty affords a noble exercise to the faculties of man and that the political world is a field prepared by the Creator for the efforts of mind. Free and powerful in its own sphere, satisfied with the place reserved for it, religion never more surely establishes its empire than when it reigns in the hearts of men unsupported by aught beside its native strength.

Liberty regards religion as its companion in all its battles and its triumphs, as the cradle of its infancy and the divine source of its claims. It considers religion as the safeguard of morality, and morality as the best security of law and the surest pledge of the duration of freedom.

Reasons for Certain Anomalies Which the Laws and Customs of the Anglo-Americans Present

Remains of aristocracy institutions amid the most complete democracy—Why?—Careful distinction to be drawn between what is of Puritanical and what of English origin.

The reader is cautioned not to draw too general or too absolute an inference from what has been said. The social condition, the religion, and the customs of the first immigrants undoubtedly exercised an immense influence on the destiny of their new country. Nevertheless, they could not found a state of things originating solely in themselves: no man can entirely shake off the influence of the past; and the settlers, intentionally or not, mingled habits and notions derived from their education and the traditions of their country with those habits and notions that were exclusively their own. To know and to judge the Anglo-Americans of the present day, it is therefore necessary to distinguish what is of Puritanical and what of English origin.

Laws and customs are frequently to be met with in the United States which contrast strongly with all that surrounds them. These laws seem to be drawn up in a spirit contrary to the prevailing tenor of American legislation; and these customs are no less opposed to the general tone of society. If the English colonies had been founded in an age of darkness, or if their origin was already lost in the lapse of years, the problem would be insoluble.

I shall quote a single example to illustrate my meaning. The civil and criminal procedure of the Americans has only two means of action, committal or bail. The first act of the magistrate is to exact security from the defendant or, in case of refusal, to incarcerate him; the ground of the accusation and the importance of the charges against him are then discussed.

It is evident that such a legislation is hostile to the poor and favorable only to the rich. The poor man has not always security to produce, even in a civil case; and if he is obliged to wait for justice in prison, he is speedily reduced to distress. A wealthy person, on the contrary, always escapes imprisonment in civil cases; nay, more, if he has committed a crime, he may readily elude punishment by breaking his bail. Thus all the penalties of the law are, for him, reduced to fines. Nothing can be more aristocratic than this system of legislation. Yet in America it is the poor who make the law, and they usually reserve the greatest advantages of society to themselves. The explanation of the phenomenon is to be found in England; the laws of which I speak are English, and the Americans have retained them, although repugnant to the general tenor of their legislation and the mass of their ideas.

Next to its habits the thing which a nation is least apt to change is its civil legislation. Civil laws are familiarly known only to lawyers, whose direct interest it is to maintain them as they are, whether good or bad, simply because they themselves are conversant with them. The bulk of the nation is scarcely acquainted with them; it sees their action only in particular cases, can with difficulty detect their tendency, and obeys them without thought.

I have quoted one instance where it would have been easy to adduce many others. The picture of American society has, if I may so speak, a surface covering of democracy, beneath which the old aristocratic colors sometimes peep out.

Chapter III

Social Condition of the Anglo-Americans

Social condition is commonly the result of circumstances, sometimes of laws, oftener still of these two causes united; but when once established, it may justly be considered as itself the source of almost all the laws, the usages, and the ideas which regulate the conduct of nations: whatever it does not produce, it modifies. If we would become acquainted with the legislation and the manners of a nation, therefore, we must begin by the study of its social condition.

THE STRIKING CHARACTERISTIC OF THE SOCIAL CONDITION OF THE ANGLO-AMERICANS IS ITS ESSENTIAL DEMOCRACY.

The first immigrants of New England—Their equality—Aristocratic laws introduced in the South—Period of the Revolution—Change in the laws of inheritance—Effects produced by this change—Democracy carried to its utmost limits in the new states of the West—Equality of mental endowments.

Many important observations suggest themselves upon the social condition of the Anglo-Americans; but there is one that takes precedence of all the rest. The social condition of the Americans is eminently democratic; this was its character at the foundation of the colonies, and it is still more strongly marked at the present day.

I have stated in the preceding chapter that great equality existed among the immigrants who settled on the shores of New England. Even the germs of aristocracy were never planted in that part of the Union. The only influence which obtained there was that of intellect; the people became accustomed to revere certain names as representatives of knowledge and virtue. Some of their fellow citizens acquired a power over the others that might truly have been called aristocratic if it had been capable of transmission from father to son.

This was the state of things to the east of the Hudson: to the southwest of that river, and as far as the Floridas, the case was different. In most of the states situated to the southwest of the Hudson some great English proprietors had settled who had imported with them aristocratic principles and the English law of inheritance. I have explained the reasons why it was impossible ever to establish a powerful aristocracy in America; these reasons existed with less force to the southwest of the Hudson. In the South one man, aided by slaves, could cultivate a great extent of country; it was therefore common to see rich landed proprietors. But their influence was not altogether aristocratic, as that term is understood in Europe, since they possessed no privileges; and the cultivation of their estates being carried on by slaves, they had no tenants depending on them, and consequently no patronage. Still, the great proprietors south of the Hudson constituted a superior class, having ideas and tastes of its own and forming the center of political action. This kind of aristocracy sympathized with the body of the people, whose passions and interests it easily embraced; but it was too weak and too shortlived to excite either love or hatred. This was the class which headed the insurrection in the South and furnished the best leaders of the American Revolution.

At this period society was shaken to its center. The people, in whose name the struggle had taken place, conceived the desire of exercising the authority that it had acquired; its democratic tendencies were awakened; and having thrown off the yoke of the mother country, it aspired to independence of every kind. The influence of individuals gradually ceased to be felt, and custom and law united to produce the same result.

But the law of inheritance was the last step to equality. I am surprised that ancient and modern jurists have not attributed to this law a greater influence on human affairs. It is true that these laws belong to civil affairs; but they ought, nevertheless, to be placed at the head of all political institutions; for they exercise an incredible influence upon the social state of a people, while political laws show only what this state already is. They have, moreover, a sure and uniform manner of operating upon society, affecting, as it were, generations yet unborn. Through their means man acquires a kind of preternatural power over the future lot of his fellow creatures. When the legislator has once regulated the law of inheritance, he may rest from his labor. The machine once put in motion will go on for ages, and advance, as if self-guided, towards a point indicated beforehand. When framed in a particular manner, this law unites, draws together, and vests property and power in a few hands; it causes an aristocracy, so to speak, to spring out of the ground. If formed on opposite principles, its action is still more rapid; it divides, distributes, and disperses both property and power. Alarmed by the rapidity of its progress, those who despair of arresting its motion endeavor at least to obstruct it by difficulties and impediments. They vainly seek to counteract its effect by contrary efforts; but it shatters and reduces to powder every obstacle, until we can no longer see anything but a moving and impalpable cloud of dust, which signals the coming of the Democracy. When the law of inheritance permits, still more when it decrees, the equal division of a father's property among all his children, its effects are of two kinds: it is important to distinguish them from each other, although they tend to the same end.

As a result of the law of inheritance, the death of each owner brings about a revolution in property; not only do his possessions change hands, but their very nature is altered, since they are parceled into shares, which become smaller and smaller at each division. This is the direct and as it were the physical effect of the law. In the countries where legislation establishes the equality of division, property, and particularly landed fortunes, have a permanent tendency to diminish. The effects of such legislation, however, would be perceptible only after a lapse of time if the law were abandoned to its own working; for, supposing the family to consist of only two children (and in a country peopled as France is, the average number is not above three), these children, sharing between them the fortune of both parents, would not be poorer than their father or mother.

But the law of equal division exercises its influence not merely upon the property itself, but it affects the minds of the heirs and brings their passions into play. These indirect consequences tend powerfully to the destruction of large fortunes, and especially of large domains.

Among nations whose law of descent is founded upon the right of primogeniture, landed estates often pass from generation to generation without undergoing division; the consequence of this is that family feeling is to a certain degree incorporated with the estate. The family represents the estate, the estate the family, whose name, together with its origin, its glory, its power, and its virtues, is thus perpetuated in an imperishable memorial of the past and as a sure pledge of the future.

When the equal partition of property is established by law, the intimate connection is destroyed between family feeling and the preservation of the paternal estate; the property ceases to represent the family; for, as it must inevitably be divided after one or two generations, it has evidently a constant tendency to diminish and must in the end be completely dispersed. The sons of the great landed proprietor, if they are few in number, or if fortune befriends them, may indeed entertain the hope of being as wealthy as their father, but not of possessing the same property that he did; their riches must be composed of other elements than his. Now, as soon as you divest the landowner of that interest in the preservation of his estate which he derives from association, from tradition, and from family pride, you may be certain that, sooner or later, he will dispose of it; for there is a strong pecuniary interest in favor of selling, as floating capital produces higher interest than real property and is more readily available to gratify the passions of the moment.

Great landed estates which have once been divided never come together again; for the small proprietor draws from his land a better revenue, in proportion, than the large owner does from his; and of course he sells it at a higher rate. The reasons of economy, therefore, which have led the rich man to sell vast estates will prevent him all the more from buying little ones in order to form a large one.

What is called family pride is often founded upon an illusion of self-love. A man wishes to perpetuate and immortalize himself, as it were, in his great-grandchildren. Where family pride ceases to act, individual selfishness comes into play. When the idea of family becomes vague, indeterminate, and uncertain, a man thinks of his present convenience; he provides for the establishment of his next succeeding generation and no more. Either a man gives up the idea of perpetuating his family, or at any rate he seeks to accomplish it by other means than by a landed estate.

Thus, not only does the law of partible inheritance render it difficult for families to preserve their ancestral domains entire, but it deprives them of the inclination to attempt it and compels them in some measure to co-operate with the law in their own extinction. The law of equal distribution proceeds by two methods: by acting upon things, it acts upon persons; by influencing persons, it affects things. By both these means the law succeeds in striking at the root of landed property, and dispersing rapidly both families and fortunes.

Most certainly it is not for us, Frenchmen of the nineteenth century, who daily witness the political and social changes that the law of partition is bringing to pass, to question its influence. It is perpetually conspicuous in our country, overthrowing the walls of our dwellings, and removing the landmarks of our fields. But although it has produced great effects in France, much still remains for it to do. Our recollections, opinions, and habits present powerful obstacles to its progress.

In the United States it has nearly completed its work of destruction, and there we can best study its results. The English laws concerning the transmission of property were abolished in almost all the states at the time of the Revolution. The law of entail was so modified as not materially to interrupt the free circulation of property. The first generation having passed away, estates began to be parceled out; and the change became more and more rapid with the progress of time. And now, after a lapse of a little more than sixty years, the aspect of society is totally altered; the families of the great landed proprietors are almost all commingled with the general mass. In the state of New York, which formerly contained many of these, there are but two who still keep their heads above the stream; and they must shortly disappear. The sons of these opulent citizens have become merchants, lawyers, or physicians. Most of them have lapsed into obscurity. The last trace of hereditary ranks and distinctions is destroyed; the law of partition has reduced all to one level.

I do not mean that there is any lack of wealthy individuals in the United States; I know of no country, indeed, where the love of money has taken stronger hold on the affections of men and where a profounder contempt is expressed for the theory of the permanent equality of property. But wealth circulates with inconceivable rapidity, and experience shows that it is rare to find two succeeding generations in the full enjoyment of it.

This picture, which may, perhaps, be thought to be overcharged, still gives a very imperfect idea of what is taking place in the new states of the West and Southwest. At the end of the last century a few bold adventurers began to penetrate into the valley of the Mississippi, and the mass of the population very soon began to move in that direction: communities unheard of till then suddenly appeared in the desert. States whose names were not in insistence a few years before, claimed their place in the American Union; and in the Western settlements we may behold democracy arrived at its utmost limits. In these states, founded offhand and as it were by chance, the inhabitants are but of yesterday. Scarcely known to one another, the nearest neighbors are ignorant of each other's history. In this part of the American continent, therefore, the population has escaped the influence not only of great names and great wealth, but even of the natural aristocracy of knowledge and virtue. None is there able to wield that respectable power which men willingly grant to the remembrance of a life spent in doing good before their eyes. The new states of the West are already inhabited, but society has no existence among them.

It is not only the fortunes of men that are equal in America; even their acquirements partake in some degree of the same uniformity. I do not believe that there is a country in the world where, in proportion to the population, there are so few ignorant and at the same time so few learned individuals. Primary instruction is within the reach of everybody; superior instruction is scarcely to be obtained by any. This is not surprising; it is, in fact, the necessary consequence of what I have advanced above. Almost all the Americans are in easy circumstances and can therefore obtain the first elements of human knowledge.

In America there are but few wealthy persons; nearly all Americans have to take a profession. Now, every profession requires an apprenticeship. The Americans can devote to general education only the early years of life. At fifteen they enter upon their calling, and thus their education generally ends at the age when ours begins. If it is continued beyond that point, it aims only towards a particular specialized and profitable purpose; one studies science as one takes up a business; and one takes up only those applications whose immediate practicality is recognized.

In America most of the rich men were formerly poor; most of those who now enjoy leisure were absorbed in business during their youth; the consequence of this is that when they might have had a taste for study, they had no time for it, and when the time is at their disposal, they have no longer the inclination. There is no class, then, in America, in which the taste for intellectual pleasures is transmitted with hereditary fortune and leisure and by which the labors of the intellect are held in honor. Accordingly, there is an equal want of the desire and the power of application to these objects.

A middling standard is fixed in America for human knowledge. All approach as near to it as they can; some as they rise, others as they descend. Of course, a multitude of persons are to be found who entertain the same number of ideas on religion, history, science, political economy, legislation, and government. The gifts of intellect proceed directly from God, and man cannot prevent their unequal distribution. But it is at least a consequence of what I have just said that although the capacities of men are different, as the Creator intended they should be, the means that Americans find for putting them to use are equal.

In America the aristocratic element has always been feeble from its birth; and if at the present day it is not actually destroyed, it is at any rate so completely disabled that we can scarcely assign to it any degree of influence on the course of affairs.

The democratic principle, on the contrary, has gained so much strength by time, by events, and by legislation, as to have become not only predominant, but all-powerful. No family or corporate authority can be perceived; very often one cannot even discover in it any very lasting individual influence.

America, then, exhibits in her social state an extraordinary phenomenon. Men are there seen on a greater equality in point of fortune and intellect, or, in other words, more equal in their strength, than in any other country of the world, or in any age of which history has preserved the remembrance.

POLITICAL CONSEQUENCES OF THE SOCIAL CONDITION OF THE ANGLO AMERICANS

The political consequences of such a social condition as this are easily deducible.

It is impossible to believe that equality will not eventually find its way into the political world, as it does everywhere else. To conceive of men remaining forever unequal upon a single point, yet equal on all others, is impossible; they must come in the end to be equal upon all.

Now, I know of only two methods of establishing equality in the political world; rights must be given to every citizen, or none at all to anyone. For nations which are arrived at the same stage of social existence as the Anglo-Americans, it is, therefore, very difficult to discover a medium between the sovereignty of all and the absolute power of one man: and it would be vain to deny that the social condition which I have been describing is just as liable to one of these consequences as to the other.

There is, in fact, a manly and lawful passion for equality that incites men to wish all to be powerful and honored. This passion tends to elevate the humble to the rank of the great; but there exists also in the human heart a depraved taste for equality, which impels the weak to attempt to lower the powerful to their own level and reduces men to prefer equality in slavery to inequality with freedom. Not that those nations whose social condition is democratic naturally despise liberty; on the contrary, they have an instinctive love of it. But liberty is not the chief and constant object of their desires; equality is their idol: they make rapid and sudden efforts to obtain liberty and, if they miss their aim, resign themselves to their disappointment; but nothing can satisfy them without equality, and they would rather perish than lose it.

On the other hand, in a state where the citizens are all practically equal, it becomes difficult for them to preserve their independence against the aggressions of power. No one among them being strong enough to engage in the struggle alone with advantage, nothing but a general combination can protect their liberty. Now, such a union is not always possible.

From the same social position, then, nations may derive one or the other of two great political results; these results are extremely different from each other, but they both proceed from the same cause.

The Anglo-Americans are the first nation who, having been exposed to this formidable alternative, have been happy enough to escape the dominion of absolute power. They have been allowed by their circumstances, their origin, their intelligence, and especially by their morals to establish and maintain the sovereignty of the people.

The Cask of Amontillado

Edgar Allan Poe

The thousand injuries of Fortunato I had borne as I best could; but when he ventured upon insult, I vowed revenge. You, who so well know the nature of my soul, will not suppose, however, that I gave utterance to a threat. At length I would be avenged; this was a point definitively settled—but the very definitiveness with which it was resolved, precluded the idea of risk. I must not only punish, but punish with impunity. A wrong is unredressed when retribution overtakes its redresser. It is equally unredressed when the avenger fails to make himself felt as such to him who has done the wrong.

It must be understood, that neither by word nor deed had I given Fortunato cause to doubt my good will. I continued, as was my wont, to smile in his face, and he did not perceive that my smile now was at the thought of his immolation.

He had a weak point—this Fortunato—although in other regards he was a man to be respected and even feared. He prided himself on his connoisseurship in wine. Few Italians have the true virtuoso spirit. For the most part their enthusiasm is adopted to suit the time and opportunity—to practise imposture upon the British and Austrian millionaires. In painting and gemmary Fortunato, like his countrymen, was a quack—but in the matter of old wines he was sincere. In this respect I did not differ from him materially: I was skilful in the Italian vintages myself, and bought largely whenever I could.

It was about dusk, one evening during the supreme madness of the carnival season, that I encountered my friend. He accosted me with excessive warmth, for he had been drinking much. The man wore motley. He had on a tight-fitting parti-striped dress, and his head was surmounted by the conical cap and bells. I was so pleased to see him, that I thought I should never have done wringing his hand.

I said to him—"My dear Fortunato, you are luckily met. How remarkably well you are looking to-day! But I have received a pipe of what passes for Amontillado, and I have my doubts."

"How?" said he. "Amontillado? A pipe! Impossible! And in the middle of the carnival!"

"I have my doubts," I replied; "and I was silly enough to pay the full Amontillado price without consulting you in the matter. You were not to be found, and I was fearful of losing a bargain."

"Amontillado!"

"I have my doubts."

"Amontillado!"

"And I must satisfy them."

"Amontillado!"

"As you are engaged, I am on my way to Luchesi. If any one has a critical turn, it is he. He will tell me—"

"Luchesi cannot tell Amontillado from Sherry."

"And yet some fools will have it that his taste is a match for your own."

"Come, let us go."

"Whither?"

"To your vaults."

"My friend, no; I will not impose upon your good nature. I perceive you have an engagement. Luchesi—"

"I have no engagement;—come."

"My friend, no. It is not the engagement, but the severe cold with which I perceive you are afflicted. The vaults are insufferably damp. They are encrusted with nitre."

"Let us go, nevertheless. The cold is merely nothing. Amontillado! You have been imposed upon. And as for Luchesi, he cannot distinguish Sherry from Amontillado."

Thus speaking, Fortunato possessed himself of my arm. Putting on a mask of black silk, and drawing a roquelaire closely about my person, I suffered him to hurry me to my palazzo.

There were no attendants at home; they had absconded to make merry in honor of the time. I had told them that I should not return until the morning, and had given them explicit orders not to stir from the house. These orders were sufficient, I well knew, to insure their immediate disappearance, one and all, as soon as my back was turned.

I took from their sconces two flambeaux, and giving one to Fortunato, bowed him through several suites of rooms to the archway that led into the vaults. I passed down a long and winding staircase, requesting him to be cautious as he followed. We came at length to the foot of the descent, and stood together on the damp ground of the catacombs of the Montresors.

The gait of my friend was unsteady, and the bells upon his cap jingled as he strode.

"The pipe," said he.

"It is farther on," said I; "but observe the white web-work which gleams from these cavern walls."

He turned towards me, and looked into my eyes with two filmy orbs that distilled the rheum of intoxication.

"Nitre?" he asked, at length.

"Nitre," I replied. "How long have you had that cough?"

"Ugh! ugh! ugh!—ugh! ugh! ugh!—ugh! ugh! ugh!—ugh! ugh! ugh!—ugh! ugh! ugh!"

My poor friend found it impossible to reply for many minutes.

"It is nothing," he said, at last.

"Come," I said, with decision, "we will go back; your health is precious. You are rich, respected, admired, beloved; you are happy, as once I was. You are a man to be missed. For me it is no matter. We will go back; you will be ill, and I cannot be responsible. Besides, there is Luchesi—"

"Enough," he said; "the cough is a mere nothing; it will not kill me. I shall not die of a cough."

"True—true," I replied; "and, indeed, I had no intention of alarming you unnecessarily—but you should use all proper caution. A draught of this Medoc will defend us from the damps."

Here I knocked off the neck of a bottle which I drew from a long row of its fellows that lay upon the mould.

"Drink," I said, presenting him the wine.

He raised it to his lips with a leer. He paused and nodded to me familiarly, while his bells jingled.

"I drink," he said, "to the buried that repose around us."

"And I to your long life."

He again took my arm, and we proceeded.

"These vaults," he said, "are extensive."

"The Montresors," I replied, "were a great and numerous family."

"I forget your arms."

"A huge human foot d'or, in a field azure; the foot crushes a serpent rampant whose fangs are imbedded in the heel."

"And the motto?"

"*Nemo me impune lacessit.*"

"Good!" he said.

The wine sparkled in his eyes and the bells jingled. My own fancy grew warm with the Medoc. We had passed through walls of piled bones, with casks and puncheons intermingling, into the inmost recesses of the catacombs. I paused again, and this time I made bold to seize Fortunato by an arm above the elbow.

"The nitre!" I said; "see, it increases. It hangs like moss upon the vaults. We are below the river's bed. The drops of moisture trickle among the bones. Come, we will go back ere it is too late. Your cough—"

"It is nothing," he said; "let us go on. But first, another draught of the Medoc."

I broke and reached him a flaçon of De Grâve. He emptied it at a breath. His eyes flashed with a fierce light. He laughed and threw the bottle upwards with a gesticulation I did not understand.

I looked at him in surprise. He repeated the movement—a grotesque one.

"You do not comprehend?" he said.

"Not I," I replied.

"Then you are not of the brotherhood."

"How?"

"You are not of the masons."

"Yes, yes," I said, "yes, yes."

"You? Impossible! A mason?"

"A mason," I replied.

"A sign," he said.

"It is this," I answered, producing a trowel from beneath the folds of my roquelaire.

"You jest," he exclaimed, recoiling a few paces. "But let us proceed to the Amontillado."

"Be it so," I said, replacing the tool beneath the cloak, and again offering him my arm. He leaned upon it heavily. We continued our route in search of the Amontillado. We passed through a range of low arches, descended, passed on, and descending again, arrived at a deep crypt, in which the foulness of the air caused our flambeaux rather to glow than flame.

At the most remote end of the crypt there appeared another less spacious. Its walls had been lined with human remains, piled to the vault overhead, in the fashion of the great catacombs of Paris. Three sides of this interior crypt were still ornamented in this manner. From the fourth side the bones had been thrown down, and lay promiscuously upon the earth, forming at one point a mound of some size. Within the wall thus exposed by the displacing of the bones, we perceived a still interior recess, in depth about four feet, in width three, in height six or seven. It seemed to have been constructed for no especial use within itself, but formed merely the interval between two of the colossal supports of the roof of the catacombs, and was backed by one of their circumscribing walls of solid granite.

It was in vain that Fortunato, uplifting his dull torch, endeavored to pry into the depth of the recess. Its termination the feeble light did not enable us to see.

"Proceed," I said; "herein is the Amontillado. As for Luchesi—"

"He is an ignoramus," interrupted my friend, as he stepped unsteadily forward, while I followed immediately at his heels. In an instant he had reached the extremity of the niche, and finding his progress arrested by the rock, stood stupidly bewildered. A moment more and I had fettered him to the granite. In its surface were two iron staples, distant from each other about two feet, horizontally. From one of these depended a short chain, from the other a padlock. Throwing the links about his waist, it was but the work of a few seconds to secure it. He was too much astounded to resist. Withdrawing the key I stepped back from the recess.

"Pass your hand," I said, "over the wall; you cannot help feeling the nitre. Indeed it is very damp. Once more let me implore you to return. No? Then I must positively leave you. But I must first render you all the little attentions in my power."

"The Amontillado!" ejaculated my friend, not yet recovered from his astonishment.

"True," I replied; "the Amontillado."

As I said these words I busied myself among the pile of bones of which I have before spoken. Throwing them aside, I soon uncovered a quantity of building stone and mortar. With these materials and with the aid of my trowel, I began vigorously to wall up the entrance of the niche.

I had scarcely laid the first tier of the masonry when I discovered that the intoxication of Fortunato had in a great measure worn off. The earliest indication I had of this was a low moaning cry from the depth of the recess. It was not the cry of a drunken man. There was then a long and obstinate silence. I laid the second tier, and the third, and the fourth; and then I heard the furious vibrations of the chain. The noise lasted for several minutes, during which, that I might hearken to it with the more satisfaction, I ceased my labors and sat down upon the bones. When at last the clanking subsided, I resumed the trowel, and finished without interruption the fifth, the sixth, and the seventh tier. The wall was now nearly upon a level with my breast. I again paused, and holding the flambeaux over the mason-work, threw a few feeble rays upon the figure within.

A succession of loud and shrill screams, bursting suddenly from the throat of the chained form, seemed to thrust me violently back. For a brief moment I hesitated—I trembled. Unsheathing my rapier, I began to grope with it about the recess: but the thought of an instant reassured me. I placed my hand upon the solid fabric of the catacombs, and felt satisfied. I reapproached the wall. I replied to the yells of him who clamored. I re-echoed—I aided—I surpassed them in volume and in strength. I did this, and the clamorer grew still.

It was now midnight, and my task was drawing to a close. I had completed the eighth, the ninth, and the tenth tier. I had finished a portion of the last and the eleventh; there remained but a single stone to be fitted and plastered in. I struggled with its weight; I placed it partially in its destined position. But now there came from out the niche a low laugh that erected the hairs upon my head. It was succeeded by a sad voice, which I had difficulty in recognising as that of the noble Fortunate. The voice said—

"Ha! ha! ha!—he! he!—a very good joke indeed—an excellent jest. We will have many a rich laugh about it at the palazzo—he! he! he!—over our wine—he! he! he!"

"The Amontillado!" I said.

"He! he! he!—he! he! he!—yes, the Amontillado. But is it not getting late? Will not they be awaiting us at the palazzo, the Lady Fortunato and the rest? Let us be gone."

"Yes," I said, "let us be gone."

"For the love of God, Montresor!"

"Yes," I said, "for the love of God!"

But to these words I hearkened in vain for a reply. I grew impatient. I called aloud—

"Fortunato!"

No answer. I called again—

"Fortunato!"

No answer still. I thrust a torch through the remaining aperture and let it fall within. There came forth in return only a jingling of the bells. My heart grew sick—on account of the dampness of the catacombs. I hastened to make an end of my labor. I forced the last stone into its position; I plastered it up. Against the new masonry I re-erected the old rampart of bones. For the half of a century no mortal has disturbed them. In pace requiescat!

POEMS

Edgar Allan Poe

ANNABEL LEE

It was many and many a year ago,
    In a kingdom by the sea,
That a maiden there lived whom you may know
    By the name of Annabel Lee;
And this maiden she lived with no other thought
    Than to love and be loved by me.

I was a child and she was a child,
    In this kingdom by the sea,
But we loved with a love that was more than love—
    I and my Annabel Lee—   10
With a love that the wingèd seraphs of Heaven
    Coveted her and me.

And this was the reason that, long ago,
    In this kingdom by the sea,
A wind blew out of a cloud, chilling
    My beautiful Annabel Lee;
So that her highborn kinsmen came
    And bore her away from me,
To shut her up in a sepulchre
    In this kingdom by the sea.   20

The angels, not half so happy in Heaven,
   Went envying her and me—
    Yes!—that was the reason (as all men know,
   In this kingdom by the sea)
That the wind came out of the cloud by night,
   Chilling and killing my Annabel Lee.

But our love it was stronger by far than the love
   Of those who were older than we—
   Of many far wiser than we—
30   And neither the angels in Heaven above
   Nor the demons down under the sea
Can ever dissever my soul from the soul
   Of the beautiful Annabel Lee;

For the moon never beams, without bringing me dreams
   Of the beautiful Annabel Lee;
And the stars never rise, but I feel the bright eyes
   Of the beautiful Annabel Lee;
And so, all the night-tide, I lie down by the side
   Of my darling—my darling—my life and my bride,
40   In her sepulchre there by the sea—
   In her tomb by the sounding sea.

To Helen

Helen, thy beauty is to me
   Like those Nicéan barks of yore,
That gently, o'er a perfumed sea,
   The weary, way-worn wanderer bore
   To his own native shore.

On desperate seas long wont to roam,
   Thy hyacinth hair, thy classic face,
Thy Naiad airs have brought me home

To the glory that was Greece
And the grandeur that was Rome.

Lo! in yon brilliant window-niche
    How statue-like I see thee stand,
The agate lamp within thy hand!
    Ah, Psyche, from the regions which
    Are Holy-Land!

THE RAVEN

Once upon a midnight dreary, while I pondered, weak and weary,
Over many a quaint and curious volume of forgotten lore—
    While I nodded, nearly napping, suddenly there came a tapping,
    As of some one gently rapping, rapping at my chamber door.
"'Tis some visitor," I muttered, "tapping at my chamber door—
        Only this and nothing more."

Ah, distinctly I remember it was in the bleak December;
And each separate dying ember wrought its ghost upon the floor.
    Eagerly I wished the morrow;—vainly I had sought to borrow
    From my books surcease of sorrow—sorrow for the lost Lenore—   10
For the rare and radiant maiden whom the angels name Lenore—
        Nameless here for evermore.

And the silken, sad, uncertain rustling of each purple curtain
Thrilled me—filled me with fantastic terrors never felt before;
    So that now, to still the beating of my heart, I stood repeating
    "'Tis some visitor entreating entrance at my chamber door—
Some late visitor entreating entrance at my chamber door;—
        This it is and nothing more."

Presently my soul grew stronger; hesitating then no longer,
"Sir," said I, "or Madam, truly your forgiveness I implore;   20
    But the fact is I was napping, and so gently you came rapping,
    And so faintly you came tapping, tapping at my chamber door,

That I scarce was sure I heard you"—here I opened wide the
    door;—
        Darkness there and nothing more.

Deep into that darkness peering, long I stood there wonder-
    ing, fearing,
Doubting, dreaming dreams no mortal ever dared to dream
    before;
    But the silence was unbroken, and the stillness gave no token,
    And the only word there spoken was the whispered word,
        "Lenore?"
This I whispered, and an echo murmured back the word,
    "Lenore!"—
30   Merely this and nothing more.

Back into the chamber turning, all my soul within me burning,
Soon again I heard a tapping somewhat louder than before.
    "Surely," said I, "surely that is something at my window
        lattice;
    Let me see, then, what thereat is, and this mystery explore—
Let my heart be still a moment and this mystery explore;—
        'Tis the wind and nothing more!"

Open here I flung the shutter, when, with many a flirt and
    flutter,
In there stepped a stately Raven of the saintly days of yore;
    Not the least obeisance made he; not a minute stopped or
    stayed he;
40   But, with mien of lord or lady, perched above my chamber
    door—
Perched upon a bust of Pallas just above my chamber door—
    Perched, and sat, and nothing more.

Then this ebony bird beguiling my sad fancy into smiling,
By the grave and stern decorum of the countenance it wore,
    "Though thy crest be shorn and shaven, thou," I said, "art
        sure no craven,
    Ghastly grim and ancient Raven wandering from the Nightly

shore—
Tell me what thy lordly name is on the Night's Plutonian shore!"
    Quoth the Raven "Nevermore."

Much I marvelled this ungainly fowl to hear discourse so plainly,
Though its answer little meaning—little relevancy bore;   50
    For we cannot help agreeing that no living human being
    Ever yet was blessed with seeing bird above his chamber door—
Bird or beast upon the sculptured bust above his chamber door,
    With such name as "Nevermore."

But the Raven, sitting lonely on the placid bust, spoke only
That one word, as if his soul in that one word he did outpour.
    Nothing farther then he uttered—not a feather then he
      fluttered—
    Till I scarcely more than muttered "Other friends have flown
      before—
On the morrow he will leave me, as my Hopes have flown before."
    Then the bird said "Nevermore."   60

Startled at the stillness broken by reply so aptly spoken,
"Doubtless," said I, "what it utters is its only stock and store
    Caught from some unhappy master whom unmerciful Disaster
    Followed fast and followed faster till his songs one burden
      bore—
Till the dirges of his Hope that melancholy burden bore
    Of 'Never—nevermore.'"

But the Raven still beguiling all my fancy into smiling,
Straight I wheeled a cushioned seat in front of bird, and bust and
    door;
    Then, upon the velvet sinking, I betook myself to linking
    Fancy unto fancy, thinking what this ominous bird of yore—   70
What this grim, ungainly, ghastly, gaunt, and ominous bird of yore
    Meant in croaking "Nevermore."

This I sat engaged in guessing, but no syllable expressing
To the fowl whose fiery eyes now burned into my bosom's core;

This and more I sat divining, with my head at ease reclining
On the cushion's velvet lining that the lamp-light gloated
    o'er,
But whose velvet-violet lining with the lamp-light gloating o'er,
    She shall press, ah, nevermore!

Then, methought, the air grew denser, perfumed from an
    unseen censer
80   Swung by Seraphim whose foot-falls tinkled on the tufted floor.
    "Wretch," I cried, "thy God hath lent thee—by these angels
      he hath sent thee
    Respite—respite and nepenthe from thy memories of
      Lenore;
Quaff, oh quaff this kind nepenthe and forget this lost Lenore!"
    Quoth the Raven "Nevermore."

"Prophet!" said I, "thing of evil!—prophet still, if bird or
    devil!—
Whether Tempter sent, or whether tempest tossed thee here ashore,
    Desolate yet all undaunted, on this desert land enchanted—
    On this home by Horror haunted—tell me truly, I implore—
Is there—is there balm in Gilead?—tell me—tell me, I implore!"
90   Quoth the Raven "Nevermore."

"Prophet!" said I, "thing of evil!—prophet still, if bird or
    devil!
By that Heaven that bends above us—by that God we both
    adore—
    Tell this soul with sorrow laden if, within the distant Aidenn,
    It shall clasp a sainted maiden whom the angels name
      Lenore—
Clasp a rare and radiant maiden whom the angels name Lenore."
    Quoth the Raven "Nevermore."

"Be that word our sign of parting, bird or fiend!" I shrieked,
    upstarting—
"Get thee back into the tempest and the Night's Plutonian
    shore!

Leave no black plume as a token of that lie thy soul hath spoken!
Leave my loneliness unbroken!—quit the bust above my door!   100
Take thy beak from out my heart, and take thy form from off my
    door!"
        Quoth the Raven "Nevermore."

And the Raven, never flitting, still is sitting, still is sitting
On the pallid bust of Pallas just above my chamber door;
    And his eyes have all the seeming of a demon's that is dreaming,
    And the lamp-light o'er him streaming throws his shadow on
        the floor;
And my soul from out that shadow that lies floating on the floor
        Shall be lifted—nevermore!

THE BELLS

1

        Hear the sledges with the bells—
            Silver bells!
What a world of merriment their melody foretells!
        How they tinkle, tinkle, tinkle,
            In the icy air of night!
        While the stars that oversprinkle
        All the heavens, seem to twinkle
            With a crystalline delight;
        Keeping time, time, time,
        In a sort of Runic rhyme,   10
To the tintinabulation that so musically wells
        From the bells, bells, bells, bells,
            Bells, bells, bells—
    From the jingling and the tinkling of the bells.

2

Hear the mellow wedding bells
Golden bells!
What a world of happiness their harmony foretells!
Through the balmy air of night
How they ring out their delight!
20   From the molten-golden notes,
And all in tune,
What a liquid ditty floats
To the turtle-dove that listens, while she gloats
On the moon!
Oh, from out the sounding cells,
What a gush of euphony voluminously wells!
How it swells!
How it dwells
On the Future! how it tells
30   Of the rapture that impels
To the swinging and the ringing
Of the bells, bells, bells,
Of the bells, bells, bells, bells,
Bells, bells, bells—
To the rhyming and the chiming of the bells!

3

Hear the loud alarum bells—
Brazen bells!
What tale of terror, now, their turbulency tells!
In the startled ear of night
40   How they scream out their affright!
Too much horrified to speak,
They can only shriek, shriek,
Out of tune,
In a clamorous appealing to the mercy of the fire,
In a mad expostulation with the deaf and frantic fire,
Leaping higher, higher, higher,

With a desperate desire,
And a resolute endeavor
Now—now to sit or never,
By the side of the pale-faced moon.   50
Oh, the bells, bells, bells!
What a tale their terror tells
Of Despair!
How they clang, and clash, and roar!
What a horror they outpour
On the bosom of the palpitating air!
Yet the ear, it fully knows,
By the twanging,
And the clanging,
How the danger ebbs and flows;   60
Yet, the ear distinctly tells,
In the jangling,
And the wrangling,
How the danger sinks and swells,
By the sinking or the swelling in the anger of the bells—
Of the bells—
Of the bells, bells, bells, bells,
Bells, bells, bells—
In the clamour and the clangour of the bells!

4

Hear the tolling of the bells—   70
Iron bells!
What a world of solemn thought their monody compels!
In the silence of the night,
How we shiver with affright
At the melancholy meaning of their tone!
For every sound that floats
From the rust within their throats
Is a groan.
And the people—ah, the people—

80   They that dwell up in the steeple,
           All alone,
        And who, tolling, tolling, tolling,
           In that muffled monotone,
        Feel a glory in so rolling
           On the human heart a stone—
      They are neither man nor woman—
      They are neither brute nor human—
          They are Ghouls:—
      And their king it is who tolls;
90   And he rolls, rolls, rolls, rolls,
           Rolls
          A pæan from the bells!
      And his merry bosom swells
         With the pæan of the bells!
      And he dances, and he yells;
     Keeping time, time, time,
     In a sort of Runic rhyme,
         To the pæan of the bells—
         Of the bells :
100   Keeping time, time, time,
     In a sort of Runic rhyme,
         To the throbbing of the bells—
         Of the bells, bells, bells—
         To the sobbing of the bells;
     Keeping time, time, time,
         As he knells, knells, knells,
     In a happy Runic rhyme,
         To the rolling of the bells—
    Of the bells, bells, bells—
110   To the tolling of the bells,
  Of the bells, bells, bells, bells—
         Bells, bells, bells—
To the moaning and the groaning of the bells.

POEMS

Alfred, Lord Tennyson

THE LADY OF SHALOTT
(1842 version)

PART I

On either side the river lie
Long fields of barley and of rye,
That clothe the wold and meet the sky;
And thro' the field the road runs by
    To many-tower'd Camelot;
And up and down the people go,
Gazing where the lilies blow
Round an island there below,
    The island of Shalott.

Willows whiten, aspens quiver.
Little breezes dusk and shiver
Thro' the wave that runs for ever
By the island in the river
    Flowing down to Camelot.
Four gray walls, and four gray towers
Overlook a space of flowers,

And the silent isle imbowers
   The Lady of Shalott.

By the margin, willow-veil'd
20   Slide the heavy barges trail'd
By slow horses; and unhail'd
The shallop flitteh silken-sail'd
   Skimming down to Camelot.
But who hath seen her wave her hand?
Or at the casement seen her stand?
Or is she known in all the land,
   The Lady of Shalott?

Only reapers, reaping early
In among the bearded barley,
30   Hear a song that echoes cheerly
From the river winding clearly
   Down to tower'd Camelot.
And by the moon the reaper weary,
Piling sheaves in uplands airy,
Listening, whispers ''Tis the fairy
   Lady of Shalott.'

Part II

There she weaves by night and day
A magic web with colours gay.
She has heard a whisper say
40   A curse is on her if she stay
   To look down to Camelot.
She knows not what the curse may be;
And so she weaveth steadily,
And little other care hath she,
   The Lady of Shalott.

And moving thro' a mirror clear
That hangs before her all the year,

Shadows of the world appear
There she sees the highway near
   Winding down to Camelot: 50
There the river eddy whirls,
And there the surly village churls,
And the red cloaks of market girls
   Pass onward from Shalott.

Sometimes a troop of damsels glad,
An abbot on an ambling pad,
Sometimes a curly shepherd lad,
Or long-hair'd page in crimson clad,
   Goes by to tower'd Camelot:
And sometimes thro' the mirror blue   60
The knights come riding two and two:
She hath no loyal knight and true,
   The Lady of Shalott.

But in her web she still delights
To weave the mirror's magic sights,
For often thro' the silent nights
A funeral, with plumes and lights
   And music, went to Camelot:
Or when the moon was overhead
Came two young lovers lately wed;   70
'I am half sick of shadows,' said
   The Lady of Shalott.

Part III

A bow-shot from her bower-eaves,
He rode between the barley-sheaves,
The sun came dazzling thro' the leaves,
And flam'd upon the brazen greaves
   Of bold Sir Lancelot.

A red-cross knight for ever kneel'd
To a lady in his shield,
That sparkled on the yellow field,
    Beside remote Shalott.

The gemmy bridle glitter'd free,
Like to some branch of stars we see
Hung in the golden Galaxy.
The bridle bells rang merrily
    As he rode down to Camelot:
And from his blazon'd baldric slung
A mighty silver bugle hung,
And as he rode his armour rung,
    Beside remote Shalott.

All in the blue unclouded weather
Thick-jewell'd shone the saddle-leather,
The helmet and the helmet-feather
Burn'd like one burning flame together,
    As he rode down to Camelot.
As often thro' the purple night,
Below the starry clusters bright,
Some bearded meteor, trailing light,
    Moves over still Shalott.

His broad clear brow in sunlight glow'd;
On burnish'd hooves his war-horse trode;
From underneath his helmet flow'd
His coal-black curls as on he rode,
    As he rode down to Camelot.
From the bank and from the river
He flash'd into the crystal mirror,
'Tirra lirra,' by the river
    Sang Sir Lancelot.

She left the web, she left the loom
She made three paces thro' the room
She saw the water-lily bloom,

She saw the helmet and the plume:
  She look'd down to Camelot.
Out flew the web and floated wide;
The mirror crack'd from side to side;
'The curse is come upon me,' cried
  The Lady of Shalott.

PART IV

In the stormy east-wind straining,
The pale-yellow woods were waning,
The broad stream in his banks complaining,   120
Heavily the low sky raining
  Over tower'd Camelot;
Down she came and found a boat
Beneath a willow left afloat,
And round about the prow she wrote,
  The Lady of Shalott.

And down the river's dim expanse—
Like some bold seër in a trance,
Seeing all his own mischance—
With a glassy countenance   130
  Did she look to Camelot.
 And at the closing of the day
She loos'd the chain, and down she lay;
The broad stream bore her far away,
  The Lady of Shalott.

Lying, robed in snowy white
That loosely flew to left and right—
The leaves upon her falling light—
Thro' the noises of the night
  She floated down to Camelot: 140
And as the boathead wound along
The willowy hills and fields among,

They heard her singing her last song,
    The Lady of Shalott.

Heard a carol, mournful, holy,
Chanted loudly, chanted lowly,
Till her blood was frozen slowly,
And her eyes were darkened wholly,
    Turn'd to tower'd Camelot;
150 For ere she reach'd upon the tide
The first house by the water-side,
Singing in her song she died,
    The Lady of Shalott.

Under tower and balcony,
By garden wall and gallery,
A gleaming shape she floated by,
A corpse between the houses high,
    Silent into Camelot.
Out upon the wharfs they came,
160 Knight and burgher, lord and dame,
And round the prow they read her name,
    The Lady of Shalott.

Who is this? and what is here?
And in the lighted palace near
Died the sound of royal cheer;
And cross'd themselves for fear,
    All the knights at Camelot:
But Lancelot mused a little space;
He said 'She has a lovely face;
170 God in His mercy lend her grace,
    The Lady of Shalott.'

In Memoriam A.H.H.

Preface

Strong Son of God, immortal Love,
    Whom we, that have not seen thy face,
    By faith, and faith alone, embrace,
Believing where we cannot prove;

Thine are these orbs of light and shade;
    Thou madest Life in man and brute;
    Thou madest Death; and lo, thy foot
Is on the skull which thou hast made.

Thou wilt not leave us in the dust:
    Thou madest man, he knows not why,   10
    He thinks he was not made to die;
And thou hast made him: thou art just.

Thou seemest human and divine,
    The highest, holiest manhood, thou.
    Our wills are ours, we know not how;
Our wills are ours, to make them thine.

Our little systems have their day;
    They have their day and cease to be:
    They are but broken lights of thee,
And thou, O Lord, art more than they.   20

We have but faith: we cannot know;
    For knowledge is of things we see
    And yet we trust it comes from thee,
A beam in darkness: let it grow.

Let knowledge grow from more to more,
    But more of reverence in us dwell;
    That mind and soul, according well,
May make one music as before,

But vaster. We are fools and slight;
30   We mock thee when we do not fear:
    But help thy foolish ones to bear;
Help thy vain worlds to bear thy light.

Forgive what seem'd my sin in me;
    What seem'd my worth since I began;
    For merit lives from man to man,
And not from man, O Lord, to thee.

Forgive my grief for one removed,
    Thy creature, whom I found so fair.
    I trust he lives in thee, and there
40   I find him worthier to be loved.

Forgive these wild and wandering cries,
    Confusions of a wasted youth;
    Forgive them where they fail in truth,
And in thy wisdom make me wise.

1

I held it truth, with him who sings
    To one clear harp in divers tones,
    That men may rise on stepping-stones
Of their dead selves to higher things.

But who shall so forecast the years
50   And find in loss a gain to match?
    Or reach a hand thro' time to catch
The far-off interest of tears?

Let Love clasp Grief lest both be drown'd,
    Let darkness keep her raven gloss:
    Ah, sweeter to be drunk with loss,
To dance with death, to beat the ground,

Than that the victor Hours should scorn
    The long result of love, and boast,

'Behold the man that loved and lost,
But all he was is overworn.'   60

2

Old Yew, which graspest at the stones
    That name the under-lying dead,
    Thy fibres net the dreamless head,
Thy roots are wrapt about the bones.

The seasons bring the flower again,
    And bring the firstling to the flock;
    And in the dusk of thee, the clock
Beats out the little lives of men.

O, not for thee the glow, the bloom,
    Who changest not in any gale,
    Nor branding summer suns avail   70
To touch thy thousand years of gloom:

And gazing on thee, sullen tree,
    Sick for thy stubborn hardihood,
    I seem to fail from out my blood
And grow incorporate into thee.

3

O Sorrow, cruel fellowship,
    O Priestess in the vaults of Death,
    O sweet and bitter in a breath,
What whispers from thy lying lip?   80

'The stars,' she whispers, 'blindly run;
    A web is wov'n across the sky;
    From out waste places comes a cry,
And murmurs from the dying sun:

'And all the phantom, Nature, stands—
    With all the music in her tone,

A hollow echo of my own,—
A hollow form with empty hands.'

And shall I take a thing so blind,
90 Embrace her as my natural good;
  Or crush her, like a vice of blood,
Upon the threshold of the mind?

4

To Sleep I give my powers away;
  My will is bondsman to the dark;
  I sit within a helmless bark,
And with my heart I muse and say:

O heart, how fares it with thee now,
  That thou should'st fail from thy desire,
  Who scarcely darest to inquire,
100 'What is it makes me beat so low?'

Something it is which thou hast lost,
  Some pleasure from thine early years.
  Break, thou deep vase of chilling tears,
That grief hath shaken into frost!

Such clouds of nameless trouble cross
  All night below the darken'd eyes;
  With morning wakes the will, and cries,
'Thou shalt not be the fool of loss.'

5

I sometimes hold it half a sin
110 To put in words the grief I feel;
  For words, like Nature, half reveal
And half conceal the Soul within.

But, for the unquiet heart and brain,
  A use in measured language lies;

The sad mechanic exercise,
Like dull narcotics, numbing pain.

In words, like weeds, I'll wrap me o'er,
    Like coarsest clothes against the cold:
    But that large grief which these enfold
Is given in outline and no more.   120

6

One writes, that 'Other friends remain,'
    That 'Loss is common to the race'—
    And common is the commonplace,
And vacant chaff well meant for grain.

That loss is common would not make
    My own less bitter, rather more:
    Too common! Never morning wore
To evening, but some heart did break.

O father, wheresoe'er thou be,
    Who pledgest now thy gallant son;   130
    A shot, ere half thy draught be done,
Hath still'd the life that beat from thee.

O mother, praying God will save
    Thy sailor,—while thy head is bow'd,
    His heavy-shotted hammock-shroud
Drops in his vast and wandering grave.

Ye know no more than I who wrought
    At that last hour to please him well;
    Who mused on all I had to tell,
And something written, something thought;   140

Expecting still his advent home;
    And ever met him on his way
    With wishes, thinking, 'here to-day,'
Or 'here to-morrow will he come.'

O somewhere, meek, unconscious dove,
   That sittest ranging golden hair;
   And glad to find thyself so fair,
Poor child, that waitest for thy love!

For now her father's chimney glows
150   In expectation of a guest;
   And thinking 'this will please him best,'
She takes a riband or a rose;

For he will see them on to-night;
   And with the thought her colour burns;
   And, having left the glass, she turns
Once more to set a ringlet right;

And, even when she turn'd, the curse
   Had fallen, and her future Lord
   Was drown'd in passing thro' the ford,
160   Or kill'd in falling from his horse.

O what to her shall be the end?
   And what to me remains of good?
   To her, perpetual maidenhood,
And unto me no second friend.

7

Dark house, by which once more I stand
   Here in the long unlovely street,
   Doors, where my heart was used to beat
So quickly, waiting for a hand,

A hand that can be clasp'd no more—
170   Behold me, for I cannot sleep,
   And like a guilty thing I creep
At earliest morning to the door.

He is not here; but far away
   The noise of life begins again,

And ghastly thro' the drizzling rain
On the bald street breaks the blank day.

8

A happy lover who has come
    To look on her that loves him well,
    Who 'lights and rings the gateway bell,
And learns her gone and far from home;   180

He saddens, all the magic light
    Dies off at once from bower and hall,
    And all the place is dark, and all
The chambers emptied of delight:

So find I every pleasant spot
    In which we two were wont to meet,
    The field, the chamber, and the street,
For all is dark where thou art not.

Yet as that other, wandering there
    In those deserted walks, may find   190
    A flower beat with rain and wind,
Which once she foster'd up with care;

So seems it in my deep regret,
    O my forsaken heart, with thee
    And this poor flower of poesy
Which little cared for fades not yet.

But since it pleased a vanish'd eye,
    I go to plant it on his tomb,
    That if it can it there may bloom,
Or, dying, there at least may die.   200

9

Fair ship, that from the Italian shore

Sailest the placid ocean-plains
With my lost Arthur's loved remains,
Spread thy full wings, and waft him o'er.

So draw him home to those that mourn
In vain; a favourable speed
Ruffle thy mirror'd mast, and lead
Thro' prosperous floods his holy urn.

All night no ruder air perplex
210   Thy sliding keel, till Phosphor, bright
As our pure love, thro' early light
Shall glimmer on the dewy decks.

Sphere all your lights around, above;
Sleep, gentle heavens, before the prow;
Sleep, gentle winds, as he sleeps now,
My friend, the brother of my love;

My Arthur, whom I shall not see
Till all my widow'd race be run;
Dear as the mother to the son,
220   More than my brothers are to me.

10

I hear the noise about thy keel;
I hear the bell struck in the night:
I see the cabin-window bright;
I see the sailor at the wheel.

Thou bring'st the sailor to his wife,
And travell'd men from foreign lands;
And letters unto trembling hands;
And, thy dark freight, a vanish'd life.

So bring him; we have idle dreams:
230   This look of quiet flatters thus

Our home-bred fancies. O to us,
The fools of habit, sweeter seems

To rest beneath the clover sod,
    That takes the sunshine and the rains,
    Or where the kneeling hamlet drains
The chalice of the grapes of God;

Than if with thee the roaring wells
    Should gulf him fathom-deep in brine;
    And hands so often clasp'd in mine,
Should toss with tangle and with shells.   240

11

Calm is the morn without a sound,
    Calm as to suit a calmer grief,
    And only thro' the faded leaf
The chestnut pattering to the ground:

Calm and deep peace on this high world,
    And on these dews that drench the furze,
    And all the silvery gossamers
That twinkle into green and gold:

Calm and still light on yon great plain
    That sweeps with all its autumn bowers,   250
    And crowded farms and lessening towers,
To mingle with the bounding main:

Calm and deep peace in this wide air,
    These leaves that redden to the fall;
    And in my heart, if calm at all,
If any calm, a calm despair:

Calm on the seas, and silver sleep,
    And waves that sway themselves in rest,
    And dead calm in that noble breast
Which heaves but with the heaving deep.   260

12

Lo, as a dove when up she springs
  To bear thro' Heaven a tale of woe,
  Some dolorous message knit below
The wild pulsation of her wings;

Like her I go; I cannot stay;
  I leave this mortal ark behind,
  A weight of nerves without a mind,
And leave the cliffs, and haste away

O'er ocean-mirrors rounded large,
270 And reach the glow of southern skies,
  And see the sails at distance rise,
And linger weeping on the marge,

And saying; 'Comes he thus, my friend?
  Is this the end of all my care?'
  And circle moaning in the air:
'Is this the end? Is this the end?'

And forward dart again, and play
  About the prow, and back return
  To where the body sits, and learn
280 That I have been an hour away.

13

Tears of the widower, when he sees
  A late-lost form that sleep reveals,
  And moves his doubtful arms, and feels
Her place is empty, fall like these;

Which weep a loss for ever new,
  A void where heart on heart reposed;
  And, where warm hands have prest and closed,
Silence, till I be silent too.

Which weep the comrade of my choice,
    An awful thought, a life removed,
    The human-hearted man I loved,
A Spirit, not a breathing voice.

Come, Time, and teach me, many years,
    I do not suffer in a dream;
    For now so strange do these things seem,
Mine eyes have leisure for their tears;

My fancies time to rise on wing,
    And glance about the approaching sails,
    As tho' they brought but merchants' bales,
And not the burthen that they bring.

14

If one should bring me this report,
    That thou hadst touch'd the land to-day,
    And I went down unto the quay,
And found thee lying in the port;

And standing, muffled round with woe,
    Should see thy passengers in rank
    Come stepping lightly down the plank,
And beckoning unto those they know;

And if along with these should come
    The man I held as half-divine;
    Should strike a sudden hand in mine,
And ask a thousand things of home;

And I should tell him all my pain,
    And how my life had droop'd of late,
    And he should sorrow o'er my state
And marvel what possess'd my brain;

And I perceived no touch of change,
    No hint of death in all his frame,

But found him all in all the same,
320   I should not feel it to be strange.

15

To-night the winds begin to rise
    And roar from yonder dropping day:
    The last red leaf is whirl'd away,
The rooks are blown about the skies;

The forest crack'd, the waters curl'd,
    The cattle huddled on the lea;
    And wildly dash'd on tower and tree
The sunbeam strikes along the world:

And but for fancies, which aver
330   That all thy motions gently pass
    Athwart a plane of molten glass,
I scarce could brook the strain and stir

That makes the barren branches loud;
    And but for fear it is not so,
    The wild unrest that lives in woe
Would dote and pore on yonder cloud

That rises upward always higher,
    And onward drags a labouring breast,
    And topples round the dreary west,
340   A looming bastion fringed with fire.

16

What words are these have falle'n from me?
    Can calm despair and wild unrest
    Be tenants of a single breast,
Or sorrow such a changeling be?

Or cloth she only seem to take
    The touch of change in calm or storm;

But knows no more of transient form
In her deep self, than some dead lake

That holds the shadow of a lark
   Hung in the shadow of a heaven?   350
   Or has the shock, so harshly given,
Confused me like the unhappy bark

That strikes by night a craggy shelf,
   And staggers blindly ere she sink?
   And stunn'd me from my power to think
And all my knowledge of myself;

And made me that delirious man
   Whose fancy fuses old and new,
   And flashes into false and true,
And mingles all without a plan?   360

17

Thou comest, much wept for: such a breeze
   Compell'd thy canvas, and my prayer
   Was as the whisper of an air
To breathe thee over lonely seas.

For I in spirit saw thee move
   Thro' circles of the bounding sky,
   Week after week: the days go by:
Come quick, thou bringest all I love.

Henceforth, wherever thou may'st roam,
   My blessing, like a line of light,   370
   Is on the waters day and night,
And like a beacon guards thee home.

So may whatever tempest mars
   Mid-ocean, spare thee, sacred bark;
   And balmy drops in summer dark
Slide from the bosom of the stars.

So kind an office hath been done,
    Such precious relics brought by thee;
    The dust of him I shall not see
380   Till all my widow'd race be run.

18

'Tis well; 'tis something; we may stand
    Where he in English earth is laid,
    And from his ashes may be made
The violet of his native land.

'Tis little; but it looks in truth
    As if the quiet bones were blest
    Among familiar names to rest
And in the places of his youth.

Come then, pure hands, and bear the head
390   That sleeps or wears the mask of sleep,
    And come, whatever loves to weep,
And hear the ritual of the dead.

Ah yet, ev'n yet, if this might be,
    I, falling on his faithful heart,
    Would breathing thro' his lips impart
The life that almost dies in me;

That dies not, but endures with pain,
    And slowly forms the firmer mind,
    Treasuring the look it cannot find,
400   The words that are not heard again.

19

The Danube to the Severn gave
    The darken'd heart that beat no more;
    They laid him by the pleasant shore,
And in the hearing of the wave.

There twice a day the Severn fills;
  The salt sea-water passes by,
  And hushes half the babbling Wye,
And makes a silence in the hills.

The Wye is hush'd nor moved along,
  And hush'd my deepest grief of all,   410
  When fill'd with tears that cannot fall,
I brim with sorrow drowning song.

The tide flows down, the wave again
  Is vocal in its wooded walls;
  My deeper anguish also falls,
And I can speak a little then.

20

The lesser griefs that may be said,
  That breathe a thousand tender vows,
  Are but as servants in a house
Where lies the master newly dead;   420

Who speak their feeling as it is,
  And weep the fulness from the mind:
  'It will be hard,' they say, 'to find
Another service such as this.'

My lighter moods are like to these,
  That out of words a comfort win;
  But there are other griefs within,
And tears that at their fountain freeze;

For by the hearth the children sit
  Cold in that atmosphere of Death,   430
  And scarce endure to draw the breath,
Or like to noiseless phantoms flit;

But open converse is there none,
  So much the vital spirits sink

To see the vacant chair, and think,
'How good! how kind! and he is gone.'

21

I sing to him that rests below,
    And, since the grasses round me wave,
    I take the grasses of the grave,
440   And make them pipes whereon to blow.

The traveller hears me now and then,
    And sometimes harshly will he speak:
    'This fellow would make weakness weak,
And melt the waxen hearts of men.'

Another answers, 'Let him be,
    He loves to make parade of pain
    That with his piping he may gain
The praise that comes to constancy.'

A third is wroth: 'Is this an hour
450   For private sorrow's barren song,
    When more and more the people throng
The chairs and thrones of civil power?

'A time to sicken and to swoon,
    When Science reaches forth her arms
    To feel from world to world, and charms
Her secret from the latest moon?'

Behold, ye speak an idle thing:
    Ye never knew the sacred dust:
    I do but sing because I must,
460   And pipe but as the linnets sing:

And one is glad; her note is gay,
    For now her little ones have ranged;
    And one is sad; her note is changed,
Because her brood is stol'n away.

22

The path by which we twain did go,
   Which led by tracts that pleased us well,
   Thro' four sweet years arose and fell,
From flower to flower, from snow to snow:

And we with singing cheer'd the way,
   And, crown'd with all the season lent,   470
   From April on to April went,
And glad at heart from May to May:

But where the path we walk'd began
   To slant the fifth autumnal slope,
   As we descended following Hope,
There sat the Shadow fear'd of man;

Who broke our fair companionship,
   And spread his mantle dark and cold,
   And wrapt thee formless in the fold,
And dull'd the murmur on thy lip,   480

And bore thee where I could not see
   Nor follow, tho' I walk in haste,
   And think, that somewhere in the waste
The Shadow sits and waits for me.

23

Now, sometimes in my sorrow shut,
   Or breaking into song by fits,
   Alone, alone, to where he sits,
The Shadow cloak'd from head to foot,

Who keeps the keys of all the creeds,
   I wander, often falling lame,   490
   And looking back to whence I came,
Or on to where the pathway leads;

And crying, How changed from where it ran
    Thro' lands where not a leaf was dumb;
    But all the lavish hills would hum
The murmur of a happy Pan:

When each by turns was guide to each,
    And Fancy light from Fancy caught,
    And Thought leapt out to wed with Thought
500   Ere Thought could wed itself with Speech;

And all we met was fair and good,
    And all was good that Time could bring,
    And all the secret of the Spring
Moved in the chambers of the blood;

And many an old philosophy
    On Argive heights divinely sang,
    And round us all the thicket rang
To many a flute of Arcady.

24

And was the day of my delight
510   As pure and perfect as I say?
    The very source and fount of Day
Is dash'd with wandering isles of night.

If all was good and fair we met,
    This earth had been the Paradise
    It never look'd to human eyes
Since our first Sun arose and set.

And is it that the haze of grief
    Makes former gladness loom so great?
    The lowness of the present state,
520   That sets the past in this relief?

Or that the past will always win
    A glory from its being far;

And orb into the perfect star
We saw not, when we moved therein?

25

I know that this was Life,—the track
   Whereon with equal feet we fared;
   And then, as now, the day prepared
The daily burden for the back.

But this it was that made me move
   As light as carrier-birds in air;   530
   I loved the weight I had to bear,
Because it needed help of Love:

Nor could I weary, heart or limb,
   When mighty Love would cleave in twain
   The lading of a single pain,
And part it, giving half to him.

26

Still onward winds the dreary way;
   I with it; for I long to prove
   No lapse of moons can canker Love,
Whatever fickle tongues may say.   540

And if that eye which watches guilt
   And goodness, and hath power to see
   Within the green the moulder'd tree,
And towers fall'n as soon as built—

Oh, if indeed that eye foresee
   Or see (in Him is no before)
   In more of life true life no more
And Love the indifference to be,

Then might I find, ere yet the morn
   Breaks hither over Indian seas,   550

That Shadow waiting with the keys,
To shroud me from my proper scorn.

27

I envy not in any moods
    The captive void of noble rage,
    The linnet born within the cage,
That never knew the summer woods:

I envy not the beast that takes
    His license in the field of time,
    Unfetter'd by the sense of crime,
560   To whom a conscience never wakes;

Nor, what may count itself as blest,
    The heart that never plighted troth
    But stagnates in the weeds of sloth;
Nor any want-begotten rest.

I hold it true, whate'er befall;
    I feel it, when I sorrow most;
    'Tis better to have loved and lost
Than never to have loved at all.

28

The time draws near the birth of Christ:
570   The moon is hid; the night is still;
    The Christmas bells from hill to hill
Answer each other in the mist.

Four voices of four hamlets round,
    From far and near, on mead and moor,
    Swell out and fail, as if a door
Were shut between me and the sound:

Each voice four changes on the wind,
    That now dilate, and now decrease,

Peace and goodwill, goodwill and peace,
Peace and goodwill, to all mankind.   580

This year I slept and woke with pain,
 I almost wish'd no more to wake,
 And that my hold on life would break
Before I heard those bells again:

But they my troubled spirit rule,
 For they controll'd me when a boy;
 They bring me sorrow touch'd with joy,
The merry merry bells of Yule.

29

With such compelling cause to grieve
 As daily vexes household peace,   590
 And chains regret to his decease,
How dare we keep our Christmas-eve;

Which brings no more a welcome guest
 To enrich the threshold of the night
 With shower'd largess of delight
In dance and song and game and jest?

Yet go, and while the holly boughs
 Entwine the cold baptismal font,
 Make one wreath more for Use and Wont,
That guard the portals of the house;   600

Old sisters of a day gone by,
 Gray nurses, loving nothing new;
 Why should they miss their yearly due
Before their time? They too will die.

30

With trembling fingers did we weave

The holly round the Chrismas hearth;
   A rainy cloud possess'd the earth,
And sadly fell our Christmas-eve.

At our old pastimes in the hall
610   We gambol'd, making vain pretence
   Of gladness, with an awful sense
Of one mute Shadow watching all.

We paused: the winds were in the beech:
   We heard them sweep the winter land;
   And in a circle hand-in-hand
Sat silent, looking each at each.

Then echo-like our voices rang;
   We sung, tho' every eye was dim,
   A merry song we sang with him
620   Last year: impetuously we sang:

We ceased: a gentler feeling crept
   Upon us: surely rest is meet:
   'They rest,' we said, 'their sleep is sweet,'
And silence follow'd, and we wept.

Our voices took a higher range;
   Once more we sang: 'They do not die
   Nor lose their mortal sympathy,
Nor change to us, although they change;

'Rapt from the fickle and the frail
630   With gather'd power, yet the same,
   Pierces the keen seraphic flame
From orb to orb, from veil to veil.'

Rise, happy morn, rise, holy morn,
   Draw forth the cheerful day from night:
   O Father, touch the east, and light
The light that shone when Hope was born.

31

When Lazarus left his charnel-cave,
    And home to Mary's house return'd,
    Was this demanded—if he yearn'd
To hear her weeping by his grave?   640

'Where wert thou, brother, those four days?'
    There lives no record of reply,
    Which telling what it is to die
Had surely added praise to praise.

From every house the neighbours met,
    The streets were fill'd with joyful sound,
    A solemn gladness even crown'd
The purple brows of Olivet.

Behold a man raised up by Christ!
    The rest remaineth unreveal'd;   650
    He told it not; or something seal'd
The lips of that Evangelist.

32

Her eyes are homes of silent prayer,
    Nor other thought her mind admits
    But, he was dead, and there he sits,
And he that brought him back is there.

Then one deep love doth supersede
    All other, when her ardent gaze
    Roves from the living brother's face,
And rests upon the Life indeed.   660

All subtle thought, all curious fears,
    Borne down by gladness so complete,
    She bows, she bathes the Saviour's feet
With costly spikenard and with tears.

Thrice blest whose lives are faithful prayers,
    Whose loves in higher love endure;
    What souls possess themselves so pure,
Or is there blessedness like theirs?

33

O thou that after toil and storm
    Mayst seem to have reach'd a purer air,
    Whose faith has centre everywhere,
Nor cares to fix itself to form,

Leave thou thy sister when she prays,
    Her early Heaven, her happy views;
    Nor thou with shadow'd hint confuse
A life that leads melodious days.

Her faith thro' form is pure as thine,
    Her hands are quicker unto good:
    Oh, sacred be the flesh and blood
To which she links a truth divine!

See thou, that countest reason ripe
    In holding by the law within,
    Thou fail not in a world of sin,
And ev'n for want of such a type.

34

My own dim life should teach me this,
    That life shall live for evermore,
    Else earth is darkness at the core,
And dust and ashes all that is;

This round of green, this orb of flame,
    Fantastic beauty such as lurks
    In some wild Poet, when he works
Without a conscience or an aim.

What then were God to such as I?
   'Twere hardly worth my while to choose
   Of things all mortal, or to use
A tattle patience ere I die;

'Twere best at once to sink to peace,
   Like birds the charming serpent draws,
   To drop head-foremost in the jaws
Of vacant darkness and to cease.   700

35

Yet if some voice that man could trust
   Should murmur from the narrow house,
   'The cheeks drop in; the body bows;
Man dies: nor is there hope in dust:'

Might I not say? 'Yet even here,
   But for one hour, O Love, I strive
   To keep so sweet a thing alive:'
But I should turn mine ears and hear

The moanings of the homeless sea,
   The sound of streams that swift or slow   710
   Draw down Æonian hills, and sow
The dust of continents to be;

And Love would answer with a sigh,
   'The sound of that forgetful shore
   Will change my sweetness more and more,
Half-dead to know that I shall die.'

O me, what profits it to put
   An idle case? If Death were seen
   At first as Death, Love had not been,
Or been in narrowest working shut,   720

Mere fellowship of sluggish moods,
   Or in his coarsest Satyr-shape

Had bruised the herb and crush'd the grape,
    And bask'd and batten'd in the woods.

36

Tho' truths in manhood darkly join,
    Deep-seated in our mystic frame,
    We yield all blessing to the name
Of Him that made them current coin;

For Wisdom dealt with mortal powers,
730   Where truth in closest words shall fail,
    When truth embodied in a tale
Shall enter in at lowly doors.

And so the Word had breath, and wrought
    With human hands the creed of creeds
    In loveliness of perfect deeds,
More strong than all poetic thought;

Which he may read that binds the sheaf,
    Or builds the house, or digs the grave,
    And those wild eyes that watch the wave
740   In roarings round the coral reef.

37

Urania speaks with darken'd brow:
    'Thou pratest here where thou art least;
    This faith has many a purer priest,
And many an abler voice than thou.

'Go down beside thy native rill,
    On thy Parnassus set thy feet,
    And hear thy laurel whisper sweet
About the ledges of the hill.'

And my Melpomene replies,

A touch of shame upon her cheek:　　　　　　　750
　　'I am not worthy ev'n to speak
　　Of thy prevailing mysteries;

'For I am but an earthly Muse,
　　And owning but a little art
　　To lull with song an aching heart,
And render human love his dues;

'But brooding on the dear one dead,
　　And all he said of things divine,
　　(And dear to me as sacred wine
To dying lips is all he said),　　　　　　　760

'I murmur'd, as I came along,
　　Of comfort clasp'd in truth reveal'd;
　　And loiter'd in the master's field,
And darken'd sanctities with song.'

38

With weary steps I loiter on,
　　Tho' always under alter'd skies
　　The purple from the distance dies,
My prospect and horizon gone.

No joy the blowing season gives,
　　The herald melodies of spring,　　　　　770
　　But in the songs I love to sing
A doubtful gleam of solace lives.

If any care for what is here
　　Survive in spirits render'd free,
　　Then are these songs I sing of thee
Not all ungrateful to thine ear.

39

Old warder of these buried bones,
    And answering now my random stroke
    With fruitful cloud and living smoke,
Dark yew, that graspest at the stones

And dippest toward the dreamless head,
    To thee too comes the golden hour
    When flower is feeling after flower;
But Sorrow—fixt upon the dead,

And darkening the dark graves of men,—
    What whisper'd from her lying lips?
    Thy gloom is kindled at the tips,
And passes into gloom again.

40

Could we forget the widow'd hour
    And look on Spirits breathed away,
    As on a maiden in the day
When first she wears her orange-flower!

When crown'd with blessing she doth rise
    To take her latest leave of home,
    And hopes and light regrets that come
Make April of her tender eyes;

And doubtful joys the father move,
    And tears are on the mother's face,
    As parting with a long embrace
She enters other realms of love;

Her office there to rear, to teach,
    Becoming as is meet and fit
    A link among the days, to knit
The generations each with each;

And, doubtless, unto thee is given
  A life that bears immortal fruit
  In those great offices that suit
The full-grown energies of heaven.

Ay me, the difference I discern!
  How often shall her old fireside   810
  Be cheer'd with tidings of the bride,
How often she herself return,

And tell them all they would have told,
  And bring her babe, and make her boast,
  Till even those that miss'd her most
Shall count new things as dear as old:

But thou and I have shaken hands,
  Till growing winters lay me low;
  My paths are in the fields I know.
And thine in undiscover'd lands.   820

41

Thy spirit ere our fatal loss
  Did ever rise from high to higher;
  As mounts the heavenward altar-fire,
As flies the lighter thro' the gross.

But thou art turn'd to something strange,
  And I have lost the links that bound
  Thy changes; here upon the ground,
No more partaker of thy change.

Deep folly! yet that this could be—
  That I could wing my will with might   830
  To leap the grades of life and light,
And flash at once, my friend, to thee.

For tho' my nature rarely yields
  To that vague fear implied in death;

557

Nor shudders at the gulfs beneath,
The howlings from forgotten fields;

Yet oft when sundown skirts the moor
    An inner trouble I behold,
    A spectral doubt which makes me cold,
840   That I shall be thy mate no more,

Tho' following with an upward mind
    The wonders that have come to thee,
    Thro' all the secular to-be,
But evermore a life behind.

42

I vex my heart with fancies dim:
    He still outstript me in the race;
    It was but unity of place
That made me dream I rank'd with him.

And so may Place retain us still,
850   And he the much-beloved again,
    A lord of large experience, train
To riper growth the mind and will:

And what delights can equal those
    That stir the spirit's inner deeps,
    When one that loves but knows not, reaps
A truth from one that loves and knows?

43

If Sleep and Death be truly one,
    And every spirit's folded bloom
    Thro' all its intervital gloom
860   In some long trance should slumber on;

Unconscious of the sliding hour,
    Bare of the body, might it last,

And silent traces of the past
Be all the colour of the flower:

So then were nothing lost to man;
    So that still garden of the souls
    In many a figured leaf enrolls
The total world since life began;

And love will last as pure and whole
    As when he loved me here in Time,   870
    And at the spiritual prime
Rewaken with the dawning soul.

44

How fares it with the happy dead?
    For here the man is more and more;
    But he forgets the days before
God shut the doorways of his head.

The days have vanish'd, tone and tint,
    And yet perhaps the hoarding sense
    Gives out at times (he knows not whence)
A little flash, a mystic hint;   880

And in the long harmonious years
    (If Death so taste Lethean springs
    May some dim touch of earthly things)
Surprise thee ranging with thy peers.

If such a dreamy touch should fall,
    O, turn thee round, resolve the doubt;
    My guardian angel will speak out
In that high place, and tell thee all.

45

The baby new to earth and sky,
    What time his tender palm is prest   890

559

Against the circle of the breast,
Has never thought that 'this is I:'

But as he grows he gathers much,
    And learns the use of 'I' and 'me,'
    And finds 'I am not what I see,
And other than the things I touch.'

So rounds he to a separate mind
    From whence clear memory may begin,
    As thro' the frame that binds him in
900   His isolation grows defined.

This use may lie in blood and breath,
    Which else were fruitless of their due,
    Had man to learn himself anew
Beyond the second birth of Death.

46

We ranging down this lower track,
    The path we came by, thorn and flower,
    Is shadow'd by the growing hour,
Lest life should fail in looking back.

So be it: there no shade can last
910   In that deep dawn behind the tomb,
    But clear from marge to marge shall bloom
The eternal landscape of the past;

A lifelong tract of time reveal'd;
    The fruitful hours of still increase;
    Days order'd in a wealthy peace,
And those five years its richest field.

O Love, thy province were not large,
    A bounded field, nor stretching far;
    Look also, Love, a brooding star,
920   A rosy warmth from marge to marge.

47

That each, who seems a separate whole,
   Should move his rounds, and fusing all
   The skirts of self again, should fall
Remerging in the general Soul,

Is faith as vague as all unsweet:
   Eternal form shall still divide
   The eternal soul from all beside;
And I shall know him when we meet:

And we shall sit at endless feast,
   Enjoying each the other's good: 930
   What vaster dream can hit the mood
Of Love on earth? He seeks at least

Upon the last and sharpest height,
   Before the spirits fade away,
   Some landing-place, to clasp and say,
'Farewell! We lose ourselves in light.'

48

If these brief lays, of Sorrow born,
   Were taken to be such as closed
   Grave doubts and answers here proposed,
Then these were such as men might scorn: 940

Her care is not to part and prove;
   She takes, when harsher moods remit,
   What slender shade of doubt may flit,
And makes it vassal unto love:

And hence, indeed, she sports with words,
   But better serves a wholesome law,
   And holds it sin and shame to draw
The deepest measure from the chords:

Nor dare she trust a larger lay,
950   But rather loosens from the lip
    Short swallow-flights of song, that dip
Their wings in tears, and skim away.

49

From art, from nature, from the schools,
    Let random influences glance,
    Like light in many a shiver'd lance
That breaks about the dappled pools:

The lightest wave of thought shall lisp,
    The fancy's tenderest eddy wreathe,
    The slightest air of song shall breathe
960   To make the sullen surface crisp.

And look thy look, and go thy way,
    But blame not thou the winds that make
    The seeming-wanton ripple break,
The tender-pencil'd shadow play.

Beneath all fancied hopes and fears
    Ay me, the sorrow deepens down.
    Whose muffled motions blindly drown
The bases of my life in tears.

50

Be near me when my light is low,
970   When the blood creeps, and the nerves prick
    And tingle; and the heart is sick,
And all the wheels of Being slow.

Be near me when the sensuous frame
    Is rack'd with pangs that conquer trust;
    And Time, a maniac scattering dust,
And Life, a Fury slinging flame.

Be near me when my faith is dry,
   And men the flies of latter spring,
   That lay their eggs, and sting and sing
And weave their petty cells and die.   980

Be near me when I fade away,
   To point the term of human strife,
   And on the low dark verge of life
The twilight of eternal day.

51

Do we indeed desire the dead
   Should still be near us at our side?
   Is there no baseness we would hide?
No inner vileness that we dread?

Shall he for whose applause I strove,
   I had such reverence for his blame,
   See with clear eye some hidden shame   990
And I be lessen'd in his love?

I wrong the grave with fears untrue:
   Shall love be blamed for want of faith?
   There must be wisdom with great Death:
The dead shall look me thro' and thro.'

Be near us when we climb or fall:
   Ye watch, like God, the rolling hours
   With larger other eyes than ours,
To make allowance for us all.   1000

52

I cannot love thee as I ought,
   For love reflects the thing beloved;
   My words are only words, and moved
Upon the topmost froth of thought.

'Yet blame not thou thy plaintive song,'
   The Spirit of true love replied;
   'Thou canst not move me from thy side,
Nor human frailty do me wrong.

'What keeps a spirit wholly true
1010   To that ideal which he bears?
   What record? not the sinless years
That breathed beneath the Syrian blue:

'So fret not, like an idle girl,
   That life is dash'd with flecks of sin.
   Abide: thy wealth is gather'd in,
When Time hath sunder'd shell from pearl.'

53

How many a father have I seen,
   A sober man, among his boys,
   Whose youth was full of foolish noise,
1020   Who wears his manhood hale and green:

And dare we to this fancy give,
   That had the wild oat not been sown,
   The soil, left barren, scarce had grown
The grain by which a man may live?

Or, if we held the doctrine sound
   For life outliving heats of youth,
   Yet who would preach it as a truth
To those that eddy round and round?

Hold thou the good: define it well:
1030   For fear divine Philosophy
   Should push beyond her mark, and be
Procuress to the Lords of Hell.

54

Oh yet we trust that somehow good
    Will be the final goal of ill,
    To pangs of nature, sins of will,
Defects of doubt, and taints of blood;

That nothing walks with aimless feet;
    That not one life shall be destroy'd,
    Or cast as rubbish to the void,
When God hath made the pile complete;   1040

That not a worm is cloven in vain;
    That not a moth with vain desire
    Is shrivell'd in a fruitless fire,
Or but subserves another's gain.

Behold, we know not anything;
    I can but trust that good shall fall
    At last—far off—at last, to all,
And every winter change to spring.

So runs my dream: but what am I?
    An infant crying in the night: 1050
    An infant crying for the light:
And with no language but a cry.

55

The wish, that of the living whole
    No life may fail beyond the grave,
    Derives it not from what we have
The likest God within the soul?

Are God and Nature then at strife,
    That Nature lends such evil dreams?
    So careful of the type she seems,
So careless of the single life;   1060

That I, considering everywhere
　　Her secret meaning in her deeds,
　　And finding that of fifty seeds
She often brings but one to bear,

I falter where I firmly trod,
　　And falling with my weight of cares
　　Upon the great world's altar-stairs
That slope thro' darkness up to God,

I stretch lame hands of faith, and grope,
1070　　And gather dust and chaff, and call
　　To what I feel is Lord of all,
And faintly trust the larger hope.

56

'So careful of the type?' but no.
　　From scarped cliff and quarried stone
　　She cries, 'A thousand types are gone:
I care for nothing, all shall go.

'Thou makest thine appeal to me:
　　I bring to life, I bring to death:
　　The spirit does but mean the breath:
1080　　I know no more.' And he, shall he,

Man, her last work, who seem'd so fair,
　　Such splendid purpose in his eyes,
　　Who roll'd the psalm to wintry skies,
Who built him fanes of fruitless prayer,

Who trusted God was love indeed
　　And love Creation's final law—
　　Tho' Nature, red in tooth and claw
With ravine, shriek'd against his creed—

Who loved, who suffer'd countless ills,
1090　　Who battled for the True, the Just,

Be blown about the desert dust,
Or seal'd within the iron hills?

No more? A monster then, a dream,
    A discord. Dragons of the prime,
    That tare each other in their slime,
Were mellow music match'd with him.

O life as futile, then, as frail!
    O for thy voice to soothe and bless!
    What hope of answer, or redress?
Behind the veil, behind the veil.   1100

57

Peace; come away: the song of woe
    Is after all an earthly song:
    Peace; come away: we do him wrong
To sing so wildly: let us go.

Come; let us go: your cheeks are pale;
    But half my life I leave behind:
    Methinks my friend is richly shrined;
But I shall pass; my work will fail.

Yet in these ears, till hearing dies,
    One set slow bell will seem to toll   1110
    The passing of the sweetest soul
That ever look'd with human eyes.

I hear it now, and o'er and o'er,
    Eternal greetings to the dead;
    And 'Ave, Ave, Ave,' said,
'Adieu, adieu,' for evermore.

58

In those sad words I took farewell:
    Like echoes in sepulchral halls,

As drop by drop the water falls
1120   In vaults and catacombs, they fell;

And, falling, idly broke the peace
    Of hearts that beat from day to day,
    Half-conscious of their dying clay,
And those cold crypts where they shall cease.

The high Muse answer'd: 'Wherefore grieve
    Thy brethren with a fruitless tear?
    Abide a little longer here,
And thou shalt take a nobler leave.'

59

O Sorrow, wilt thou live with me
1130   No casual mistress, but a wife,
    My bosom-friend and half of life;
As I confess it needs must be;

O Sorrow, wilt thou rule my blood,
    Be sometimes lovely like a bride,
    And put thy harsher moods aside,
If thou wilt have me wise and good.

My centred passion cannot move,
    Nor will it lessen from to-day;
    But I'll have leave at times to play
1140   As with the creature of my love;

And set thee forth, for thou art mine,
    With so much hope for years to come,
    That, howsoe'er I know thee, some
Could hardly tell what name were thine.

60

He past; a soul of nobler tone:
    My spirit loved and loves him yet,

Like some poor girl whose heart is set
On one whose rank exceeds her own.

He mixing with his proper sphere,
   She finds the baseness of her lot,   1150
   Half jealous of she knows not what,
And envying all that meet him there.

The little village looks forlorn;
   She sighs amid her narrow days,
   Moving about the household ways,
In that dark house where she was born.

The foolish neighbors come and go,
   And tease her till the day draws by:
   At night she weeps, 'How vain am I!'
How should he love a thing so low?'   1160

61

If, in thy second state sublime,
   Thy ransom'd reason change replies
   With all the circle of the wise,
The perfect flower of human time;

And if thou cast thine eyes below,
   How dimly character'd and slight,
   How dwarf'd a growth of cold and night,
How blanch'd with darkness must I grow!

Yet turn thee to the doubtful shore,
   Where thy first form was made a man;   1170
   I loved thee, Spirit, and love, nor can
The soul of Shakspeare love thee more.

62

Tho' if an eye that's downward cast
   Could make thee somewhat blench or fail,

569

Then be my love an idle tale,
And fading legend of the past;

And thou, as one that once declined,
When he was little more than boy,
On some unworthy heart with joy,
1180   But lives to wed an equal mind;

And breathes a novel world, the while
His other passion wholly dies,
Or in the light of deeper eyes
Is matter for a flying smile.

63

Yet pity for a horse o'er-driven,
And love in which my hound has part,
Can hang no weight upon my heart
In its assumptions up to heaven;

And I am so much more than these,
1190   As thou, perchance, art more than I,
And yet I spare them sympathy,
And I would set their pains at ease.

So mayst thou watch me where I weep,
As, unto vaster motions bound,
The circuits of thine orbit round
A higher height, a deeper deep.

64

Dost thou look back on what hath been,
As some divinely gifted man,
Whose life in low estate began
1200   And on a simple village green;

Who breaks his birth's invidious bar,
And grasps the skirts of happy chance,

And breasts the blows of circumstance,
   And grapples with his evil star;

Who makes by force his merit known
   And lives to clutch the golden keys,
   To mould a mighty state's decrees,
And shape the whisper of the throne;

And moving up from high to higher,
   Becomes on Fortune's crowning slope
   The pillar of a people's hope,
The centre of a world's desire;

Yet feels, as in a pensive dream,
   When all his active powers are still,
   A distant dearness in the hill,
A secret sweetness in the stream,

The limit of his narrower fate,
   While yet beside its vocal springs
   He play'd at counsellors and kings,
With one that was his earliest mate;

Who ploughs with pain his native lea
   And reaps the labour of his hands,
   Or in the furrow musing stands;
'Does my old friend remember me?'

65

Sweet soul, do with me as thou wilt;
   I lull a fancy trouble-tost
   With 'Love's too precious to be lost,
A little grain shall not be spilt.'

And in that solace can I sing,
   Till out of painful phases wrought
   There flutters up a happy thought,
Self-balanced on a lightsome wing:

1210

1220

1230

Since we deserved the name of friends,
   And thine effect so lives in me,
   A part of mine may live in thee
And move thee on to noble ends.

66

You thought my heart too far diseased;
   You wonder when my fancies play
   To find me gay among the gay,
1240   Like one with any trifle pleased.

The shade by which my life was crost,
   Which makes a desert in the mind,
   Has made me kindly with my kind,
And like to him whose sight is lost;

Whose feet are guided thro' the land,
   Whose jest among his friends is free,
   Who takes the children on his knee,
And winds their curls about his hand:

He plays with threads, he beats his chair
1250   For pastime, dreaming of the sky;
   His inner day can never die,
His night of loss is always there.

67

When on my bed the moonlight falls,
   I know that in thy place of rest
   By that broad water of the west,
There comes a glory on the walls;

Thy marble bright in dark appears,
   As slowly steals a silver flame
   Along the letters of thy name,
1260   And o'er the number of thy years.

The mystic glory swims away;
   From off my bed the moonlight dies;
   And closing eaves of wearied eyes
I sleep till dusk is dipt in gray;

And then I know the mist is drawn
   A lucid veil from coast to coast,
   And in the dark church like a ghost
Thy tablet glimmers to the dawn.

68

When in the down I sink my head,
   Sleep, Death's twin-brother, times my breath;
   Sleep, Death's twin-brother, knows not Death,
Nor can I dream of thee as dead:

I walk as ere I walk'd forlorn,
   When all our path was fresh with dew,
   And all the bugle breezes blew
Reveillée to the breaking morn.

But what is this? I turn about,
   I find a trouble in thine eye,
   Which makes me sad I know not why,
Nor can my dream resolve the doubt:

But ere the lark hath left the lea
   I wake, and I discern the truth;
   It is the trouble of my youth
That foolish sleep transfers to thee.

69

I dream'd there would be Spring no more,
   That Nature's ancient power was lost:
   The streets were black with smoke and frost,
They chatter'd trifles at the door:

1270

1280

I wander'd from the noisy town,
1290   I found a wood with thorny boughs:
     I took the thorns to bind my brows,
I wore them like a civic crown:

I met with scoffs, I met with scorns
     From youth and babe and hoary hairs:
     They call'd me in the public squares
The fool that wears a crown of thorns:

They call'd me fool, they call'd me child:
     I found an angel of the night;
     The voice was low, the look was bright;
1300   He look'd upon my crown and smiled:

He reach'd the glory of a hand,
     That seem'd to touch it into leaf:
     The voice was not the voice of grief,
The words were hard to understand.

70

I cannot see the features right,
     When on the gloom I strive to paint
     The face I know; the hues are faint
And mix with hollow masks of night;

Cloud-towers by ghostly masons wrought,
1310   A gulf that ever shuts and gapes,
     A hand that points, and palled shapes
In shadowy thoroughfares of thought;

And crowds that stream from yawning doors,
     And shoals of pucker'd faces drive;
     Dark bulks that tumble half alive,
And lazy lengths on boundless shores;

Till all at once beyond the will
     I hear a wizard music roll,

And thro' a lattice on the soul
Looks thy fair face and makes it still.   1320

71

Sleep, kinsman thou to death and trance
    And madness, thou hast forged at last
    A night-long Present of the Past
In which we went thro' summer France.

Hadst thou such credit with the soul?
    Then bring an opiate trebly strong,
    Drug down the blindfold sense of wrong
That so my pleasure may be whole;

While now we talk as once we talk'd
    Of men and minds, the dust of change,   1330
    The days that grow to something strange,
In walking as of old we walk'd

Beside the river's wooded reach,
    The fortress, and the mountain ridge,
    The cataract flashing from the bridge,
The breaker breaking on the beach.

72

Risest thou thus, dim dawn, again,
    And howlest, issuing out of night,
    With blasts that blow the poplar white,
And lash with storm the streaming pane?   1340

Day, when my crown'd estate begun
    To pine in that reverse of doom,
    Which sicken'd every living bloom,
And blurr'd the splendour of the sun;

Who usherest in the dolorous hour
    With thy quick tears that make the rose

Pull sideways, and the daisy close
Her crimson fringes to the shower;

Who might'st have heaved a windless flame
1350   Up the deep East, or, whispering, play'd
A chequer-work of beam and shade
Along the hills, yet look'd the same.

As wan, as chill, as wild as now;
Day, mark'd as with some hideous crime,
When the dark hand struck down thro' time,
And cancell'd nature's best: but thou,

Lift as thou may'st thy burthen'd brows
Thro' clouds that drench the morning star,
And whirl the ungarner'd sheaf afar,
1360   And sow the sky with flying boughs,

And up thy vault with roaring sound
Climb thy thick noon, disastrous day;
Touch thy dull goal of joyless gray,
And hide thy shame beneath the ground.

73

So many worlds, so much to do,
So little done, such things to be,
How know I what had need of thee,
For thou wert strong as thou wert true?

The fame is quench'd that I foresaw,
1370   The head hath miss'd an earthly wreath:
I curse not nature, no, nor death;
For nothing is that errs from law.

We pass; the path that each man trod
Is dim, or will be dim, with weeds:
What fame is left for human deeds
In endless age? It rests with God.

O hollow wraith of dying fame,
   Fade wholly, while the soul exults,
   And self-infolds the large results
Of force that would have forged a name.   1380

74

As sometimes in a dead man's face,
   To those that watch it more and more,
   A likeness, hardly seen before,
Comes out—to some one of his race:

So, dearest, now thy brows are cold,
   I see thee what thou art, and know
   Thy likeness to the wise below,
Thy kindred with the great of old.

But there is more than I can see,
   And what I see I leave unsaid,   1390
   Nor speak it, knowing Death has made
His darkness beautiful with thee.

I leave thy praises unexpress'd
   In verse that brings myself relief,
   And by the measure of my grief
I leave thy greatness to be guess'd;

What practice howsoe'er expert
   In fitting aptest words to things,
   Or voice the richest-toned that sings,
Hath power to give thee as thou wert?   1400

I care not in these fading days
   To raise a cry that lasts not long,
   And round thee with the breeze of song
To stir a little dust of praise.

Thy leaf has perish'd in the green,
   And, while we breathe beneath the sun,

The world which credits what is done
Is cold to all that might have been.

So here shall silence guard thy fame;
1410 But somewhere, out of human view,
  Whate'er thy hands are set to do
Is wrought with tumult of acclaim.

75

I leave thy praises unexpress'd
  In verse that brings myself relief,
  And by the measure of my grief
I leave thy greatness to be guess'd;

What practice howsoe'er expert
  In fitting aptest words to things,
  Or voice the richest-toned that sings,
1420 Hath power to give thee as thou wert?

I care not in these fading days
  To raise a cry that lasts not long,
  And round thee with the breeze of song
To stir a little dust of praise.

Thy leaf has perish'd in the green,
  And, while we breathe beneath the sun,
  The world which credits what is done
Is cold to all that might have been.

So here shall silence guard thy fame;
1430 But somewhere, out of human view,
  Whate'er thy hands are set to do
Is wrought with tumult of acclaim.

76

Take wings of fancy, and ascend,

And in a moment set thy face
　　Where all the starry heavens of space
　　Are sharpen'd to a needle's end;

Take wings of foresight; lighten thro'
　　The secular abyss to come,
　　And lo, thy deepest lays are dumb
Before the mouldering of a yew; 　　　　　　1440

And if the matin songs, that woke
　　The darkness of our planet, last,
　　Thine own shall wither in the vast,
Ere half the lifetime of an oak.

Ere these have clothed their branchy bowers
　　With fifty Mays, thy songs are vain;
　　And what are they when these remain
The ruin'd shells of hollow towers?

77

What hope is here for modern rhyme
　　To him, who turns a musing eye 　　　　1450
　　On songs, and deeds, and lives, that lie
Foreshorten'd in the tract of time?

These mortal lullabies of pain
　　May bind a book, may line a box,
　　May serve to curl a maiden's locks;
Or when a thousand moons shall wane

A man upon a stall may find,
　　And, passing, turn the page that tells
　　A grief, then changed to something else,
Sung by a long-forgotten mind. 　　　　　　1460

But what of that? My darken'd ways
　　Shall ring with music all the same;
　　To breathe my loss is more than fame,

To utter love more sweet than praise.

78

Again at Christmas did we weave
    The holly round the Christmas hearth;
    The silent snow possess'd the earth,
And calmly fell our Christmas-eve:

The yule-clog sparkled keen with frost,
1470   No wing of wind the region swept,
    But over all things brooding slept
The quiet sense of something lost.

As in the winters left behind,
    Again our ancient games had place,
    The mimic picture's breathing grace,
And dance and song and hoodman-blind.

Who show'd a token of distress?
    No single tear, no mark of pain:
    O sorrow, then can sorrow wane?
1480 O grief, can grief be changed to less?

O last regret, regret can die!
    No—mixt with all this mystic frame,
    Her deep relations are the same,
But with long use her tears are dry.

79

'More than my brothers are to me,'—
    Let this not vex thee, noble heart!
    I know thee of what force thou art
To hold the costliest love in fee.

But thou and I are one in kind,
1490   As moulded like in Nature's mint;

And hill and wood and field did print
The same sweet forms in either mind.

For us the same cold streamlet curl'd
    Thro' all his eddying coves, the same
    All winds that roam the twilight came
In whispers of the beauteous world.

At one dear knee we proffer'd vows,
    One lesson from one book we learn'd,
    Ere childhood's flaxen ringlet turn'd
To black and brown on kindred brows. 1500

And so my wealth resembles thine,
    But he was rich where I was poor,
    And he supplied my want the more
As his unlikeness fitted mine.

80

If any vague desire should rise,
    That holy Death ere Arthur died
    Had moved me kindly from his side,
And dropt the dust on tearless eyes;

Then fancy shapes, as fancy can,
    The grief my loss in him had wrought, 1510
    A grief as deep as life or thought,
But stay'd in peace with God and man.

I make a picture in the brain;
    I hear the sentence that he speaks;
    He bears the burthen of the weeks
But turns his burthen into gain.

His credit thus shall set me free;
    And, influence-rich to soothe and save,
    Unused example from the grave
Reach out dead hands to comfort me. 1520

81

Could I have said while he was here,
  'My love shall now no further range;
  There cannot come a mellower change,
For now is love mature in ear'?

Love, then, had hope of richer store:
  What end is here to my complaint?
  This haunting whisper makes me faint,
'More years had made me love thee more.'

But Death returns an answer sweet:
1530   'My sudden frost was sudden gain,
  And gave all ripeness to the grain,
It might have drawn from after-heat.'

82

I wage not any feud with Death
  For changes wrought on form and face;
  No lower life that earth's embrace
May breed with him, can fright my faith.

Eternal process moving on,
  From state to state the spirit walks;
  And these are but the shatter'd stalks,
1540 Or ruin'd chrysalis of one.

Nor blame I Death, because he bare
  The use of virtue out of earth:
  I know transplanted human worth
Will bloom to profit, otherwhere.

For this alone on Death I wreak
  The wrath that garners in my heart;
  He put our lives so far apart
We cannot hear each other speak.

83

Dip down upon the northern shore,
   O sweet new-year delaying long;
   Thou doest expectant nature wrong;
Delaying long, delay no more.

What stays thee from the clouded noons,
   Thy sweetness from its proper place?
   Can trouble live with April days,
Or sadness in the summer moons?

Bring orchis, bring the foxglove spire,
   The little speedwell's darling blue,
   Deep tulips dash'd with fiery dew,
Laburnums, dropping-wells of fire.

O thou, new-year, delaying long,
   Delayest the sorrow in my blood,
   That longs to burst a frozen bud
And flood a fresher throat with song.

84

When I contemplate all alone
   The life that had been thine below,
   And fix my thoughts on all the glow
To which thy crescent would have grown;

I see thee sitting crown'd with good,
   A central warmth diffusing bliss
   In glance and smile, and clasp and kiss,
On all the branches of thy blood;

Thy blood, my friend, and partly mine;
   For now the day was drawing on,
   When thou should'st link thy life with one
Of mine own house, and boys of thine

Had babbled 'Uncle' on my knee;
But that remorseless iron hour
Made cypress of her orange flower,
1580 Despair of Hope, and earth of thee.

I seem to meet their least desire,
To clap their cheeks, to call them mine.
I see their unborn faces shine
Beside the never-lighted fire.

I see myself an honor'd guest,
Thy partner in the flowery walk
Of letters, genial table-talk,
Or deep dispute, and graceful jest;

While now thy prosperous labor fills
1590 The lips of men with honest praise,
And sun by sun the happy days
Descend below the golden hills

With promise of a morn as fair;
And all the train of bounteous hours
Conduct by paths of growing powers,
To reverence and the silver hair;

Till slowly worn her earthly robe,
Her lavish mission richly wrought,
Leaving great legacies of thought,
1600 Thy spirit should fail from off the globe;

What time mine own might also flee,
As link'd with thine in love and fate,
And, hovering o'er the dolorous strait
To the other shore, involved in thee,

Arrive at last the blessed goal,
And He that died in Holy Land
Would reach us out the shining hand,
And take us as a single soul.

What reed was that on which I leant?
  Ah, backward fancy, wherefore wake   1610
  The old bitterness again, and break
The low beginnings of content.

85

This truth came borne with bier and pall,
  I felt it, when I sorrow'd most,
  'Tis better to have loved and lost,
Than never to have loved at all—

O true in word, and tried in deed,
  Demanding, so to bring relief
  To this which is our common grief,
What kind of life is that I lead;   1620

And whether trust in things above
  Be dimm'd of sorrow, or sustain'd;
  And whether love for him have drain'd
My capabilities of love;

Your words have virtue such as draws
  A faithful answer from the breast,
  Thro' light reproaches, half exprest,
And loyal unto kindly laws.

My blood an even tenor kept,
  Till on mine ear this message falls,   1630
  That in Vienna's fatal walls
God's finger touch'd him, and he slept.

The great Intelligences fair
  That range above our mortal state,
  In circle round the blessed gate,
Received and gave him welcome there;

And led him thro' the blissful climes,
  And show'd him in the fountain fresh

All knowledge that the sons of flesh
1640 Shall gather in the cycled times.

But I remain'd, whose hopes were dim,
 Whose life, whose thoughts were little worth,
 To wander on a darken'd earth,
Where all things round me breathed of him.

O friendship, equal-poised control,
 O heart, with kindliest motion warm,
 O sacred essence, other form,
O solemn ghost, O crowned soul!

Yet none could better know than I,
1650 How much of act at human hands
 The sense of human will demands
By which we dare to live or die.

Whatever way my days decline,
 I felt and feel, tho' left alone,
 His being working in mine own,
The footsteps of his life in mine;

A life that all the Muses deck'd
 With gifts of grace, that might express
 All-comprehensive tenderness,
1660 All-subtilising intellect:

And so my passion hath not swerved
 To works of weakness, but I find
 An image comforting the mind,
And in my grief a strength reserved.

Likewise the imaginative woe,
 That loved to handle spiritual strife
 Diffused the shock thro' all my life,
But in the present broke the blow.

My pulses therefore beat again
1670 For other friends that once I met;

Nor can it suit me to forget
The mighty hopes that make us men.

I woo your love: I count it crime
    To mourn for any overmuch;
    I, the divided half of such
A friendship as had master'd Time;

Which masters Time indeed, and is
    Eternal, separate from fears:
    The all-assuming months and years
Can take no part away from this: 1680

But Summer on the steaming floods,
    And Spring that swells the narrow brooks,
    And Autumn, with a noise of rooks,
That gather in the waning woods,

And every pulse of wind and wave
    Recalls, in change of light or gloom,
    My old affection of the tomb,
And my prime passion in the grave:

My old affection of the tomb,
    A part of stillness, yearns to speak: 1690
    'Arise, and get thee forth and seek
A friendship for the years to come.

'I watch thee from the quiet shore;
    Thy spirit up to mine can reach;
    But in dear words of human speech
We two communicate no more.'

And I, 'Can clouds of nature stain
    The starry clearness of the free?
    How is it? Canst thou feel for me
Some painless sympathy with pain?'   1700

And lightly does the whisper fall:
    ''Tis hard for thee to fathom this;

I triumph in conclusive bliss,
And that serene result of all.'

So hold I commerce with the dead;
    Or so methinks the dead would say;
    Or so shall grief with symbols play
And pining life be fancy-fed.

Now looking to some settled end,
1710   That these things pass, and I shall prove
    A meeting somewhere, love with love,
I crave your pardon, O my friend;

If not so fresh, with love as true,
    I, clasping brother-hands, aver
    I could not, if I would, transfer
The whole I felt for him to you.

For which be they that hold apart
    The promise of the golden hours?
    First love, first friendship, equal powers,
1720   That marry with the virgin heart.

Still mine, that cannot but deplore,
    That beats within a lonely place,
    That yet remembers his embrace,
But at his footstep leaps no more,

My heart, tho' widow'd, may not rest
    Quite in the love of what is gone,
    But seeks to beat in time with one
That warms another living breast.

Ah, take the imperfect gift I bring,
1730   Knowing the primrose yet is dear,
    The primrose of the later year,
As not unlike to that of Spring.

86

Sweet after showers, ambrosial air,
   That rollest from the gorgeous gloom
   Of evening over brake and bloom
And meadow, slowly breathing bare

The round of space, and rapt below
   Thro' all the dewy-tassell'd wood,
   And shadowing down the horned flood
In ripples, fan my brows and blow   1740

The fever from my cheek, and sigh
   The full new life that feeds thy breath
   Throughout my frame, till Doubt and Death,
Ill brethren, let the fancy fly

From belt to belt of crimson seas
   On leagues of odour streaming far,
   To where in yonder orient star
A hundred spirits whisper 'Peace.'

87

I past beside the reverend walls
   In which of old I wore the gown;   1750
   I roved at random thro' the town,
And saw the tumult of the halls;

And heard once more in college fanes
   The storm their high-built organs make,
   And thunder-music, rolling, shake
The prophet blazon'd on the panes;

And caught once more the distant shout,
   The measured pulse of racing oars
   Among the willows; paced the shores
And many a bridge, and all about   1760

The same gray flats again, and felt

The same, but not the same; and last
    Up that long walk of limes I past
    To see the rooms in which he dwelt.

Another name was on the door:
    I linger'd; all within was noise
    Of songs, and clapping hands, and boys
That crash'd the glass and beat the floor;

Where once we held debate, a band
1770   Of youthful friends, on mind and art,
    And labour, and the changing mart,
And all the framework of the land;

When one would aim an arrow fair,
    But send it slackly from the string;
    And one would pierce an outer ring,
And one an inner, here and there;

And last the master-bowman, he,
    Would cleave the mark. A willing ear
    We lent him. Who, but hung to hear
1780   The rapt oration flowing free

From point to point, with power and grace
    And music in the bounds of law,
    To those conclusions when we saw
The God within him light his face,

And seem to lift the form, and glow
    In azure orbits heavenly-wise;
    And over those ethereal eyes
The bar of Michael Angelo?

88

Wild bird, whose warble, liquid sweet,
1790   Rings Eden thro' the budded quicks,
    O tell me where the senses mix,

O tell me where the passions meet,

Whence radiate: fierce extremes employ
   Thy spirits in the darkening leaf,
   And in the midmost heart of grief
Thy passion clasps a secret joy:

And I—my harp would prelude woe—
   I cannot all command the strings;
   The glory of the sum of things
Will flash along the chords and go.   1800

89

Witch-elms that counterchange the floor
   Of this flat lawn with dusk and bright;
   And thou, with all thy breadth and height
Of foliage, towering sycamore;

How often, hither wandering down,
   My Arthur found your shadows fair,
   And shook to all the liberal air
The dust and din and steam of town:

He brought an eye for all he saw;
   He mixt in all our simple sports;   1810
   They pleased him, fresh from brawling courts
And dusty purlieus of the law.

O joy to him in this retreat,
   Inmantled in ambrosial dark,
   To drink the cooler air, and mark
The landscape winking thro' the heat:

O sound to rout the brood of cares,
   The sweep of scythe in morning dew,
   The gust that round the garden flew,
And tumbled half the mellowing pears!   1820

O bliss, when all in circle drawn
    About him, heart and ear were fed
    To hear him, as he lay and read
The Tuscan poets on the lawn:

Or in the all-golden afternoon
    A guest, or happy sister, sung,
    Or here she brought the harp and flung
A ballad to the brightening moon:

Nor less it pleased in livelier moods,
1830   Beyond the bounding hill to stray,
    And break the livelong summer day
With banquet in the distant woods;

Whereat we glanced from theme to theme,
    Discuss'd the books to love or hate,
    Or touch'd the changes of the state,
Or threaded some Socratic dream;

But if I praised the busy town,
    He loved to rail against it still,
    For 'ground in yonder social mill
1840   We rub each other's angles down,

'And merge,' he said, 'in form and gloss
    The picturesque of man and man.'
    We talk'd: the stream beneath us ran,
The wine-flask lying couch'd in moss,

Or cool'd within the glooming wave;
    And last, returning from afar,
    Before the crimson-circled star
Had fall'n into her father's grave,

And brushing ankle-deep in flowers,
1850   We heard behind the woodbine veil
    The milk that bubbled in the pail,
And buzzings of the honied hours.

90

He tasted love with half his mind,
   Nor ever drank the inviolate spring
   Where nighest heaven, who first could fling
This bitter seed among mankind;

That could the dead, whose dying eyes
   Were closed with wail, resume their life,
   They would but find in child and wife
An iron welcome when they rise: 1860

'Twas well, indeed, when warm with wine,
   To pledge them with a kindly tear,
   To talk them o'er, to wish them here,
To count their memories half divine;

But if they came who past away,
   Behold their brides in other hands;
   The hard heir strides about their lands,
And will not yield them for a day.

Yea, tho' their sons were none of these,
   Not less the yet-loved sire would make   1870
   Confusion worse than death, and shake
The pillars of domestic peace.

Ah dear, but come thou back to me:
   Whatever change the years have wrought,
   I find not yet one lonely thought
That cries against my wish for thee.

91

When rosy plumelets tuft the larch,
   And rarely pipes the mounted thrush;
   Or underneath the barren bush
Flits by the sea-blue bird of March;   1880

Come, wear the form by which I know
    Thy spirit in time among thy peers;
    The hope of unaccomplish'd years
Be large and lucid round thy brow.

When summer's hourly-mellowing change
    May breathe, with many roses sweet,
    Upon the thousand waves of wheat,
That ripple round the lonely grange;

Come: not in watches of the night,
1890   But where the sunbeam broodeth warm,
    Come, beauteous in thine after form,
And like a finer light in light.

92

If any vision should reveal
    Thy likeness, I might count it vain
    As but the canker of the brain;
Yea, tho' it spake and made appeal

To chances where our lots were cast
    Together in the days behind,
    I might but say, I hear a wind
1900   Of memory murmuring the past.

Yea, tho' it spake and bared to view
    A fact within the coming year;
    And tho' the months, revolving near,
Should prove the phantom-warning true,

They might not seem thy prophecies,
    But spiritual presentiments,
    And such refraction of events
As often rises ere they rise.

93

I shall not see thee. Dare I say
   No spirit ever brake the band
   That stays him from the native land
Where first he walk'd when claspt in clay?

No visual shade of some one lost,
   But he, the Spirit himself, may come
   Where all the nerve of sense is numb;
Spirit to Spirit, Ghost to Ghost.

O, therefore from thy sightless range
   With gods in unconjectured bliss,
   O, from the distance of the abyss
Of tenfold-complicated change,

Descend, and touch, and enter; hear
   The wish too strong for words to name;
   That in this blindness of the frame
My Ghost may feel that thine is near.

94

How pure at heart and sound in head,
   With what divine affections bold
   Should be the man whose thought would hold
An hour's communion with the dead.

In vain shalt thou, or any, call
   The spirits from their golden day,
   Except, like them, thou too canst say,
My spirit is at peace with all.

They haunt the silence of the breast,
   Imaginations calm and fair,
   The memory like a cloudless air,
The conscience as a sea at rest:

But when the heart is full of din,
    And doubt beside the portal waits,
    They can but listen at the gates
1940   And hear the household jar within.

95

By night we linger'd on the lawn,
    For underfoot the herb was dry;
    And genial warmth; and o'er the sky
The silvery haze of summer drawn;

And calm that let the tapers burn
    Unwavering: not a cricket chirr'd:
    The brook alone far-off was heard,
And on the board the fluttering urn:

And bats went round in fragrant skies,
1950   And wheel'd or lit the filmy shapes
    That haunt the dusk, with ermine capes
And woolly breasts and beaded eyes;

While now we sang old songs that peal'd
    From knoll to knoll, where, couch'd at ease,
    The white kine glimmer'd, and the trees
Laid their dark arms about the field.

But when those others, one by one,
    Withdrew themselves from me and night,
    And in the house light after light
1960   Went out, and I was all alone,

A hunger seized my heart; I read
    Of that glad year which once had been,
    In those fall'n leaves which kept their green,
The noble letters of the dead:

And strangely on the silence broke
    The silent-speaking words, and strange

Was love's dumb cry defying change
To test his worth; and strangely spoke

The faith, the vigour, bold to dwell
   On doubts that drive the coward back,
   And keen thro' wordy snares to track
Suggestion to her inmost cell.

So word by word, and line by line,
   The dead man touch'd me from the past,
   And all at once it seem'd at last
The living soul was flash'd on mine,

And mine in his was wound, and whirl'd
   About empyreal heights of thought,
   And came on that which is, and caught
The deep pulsations of the world,

Æonian music measuring out
   The steps of Time—the shocks of Chance—
   The blows of Death. At length my trance
Was cancell'd, stricken thro' with doubt.

Vague words! but ah, how hard to frame
   In matter-moulded forms of speech,
   Or ev'n for intellect to reach
Thro' memory that which I became:

Till now the doubtful dusk reveal'd
   The knolls once more where, couch'd at ease,
   The white kine glimmer'd, and the trees
Laid their dark arms about the field;

And suck'd from out the distant gloom
   A breeze began to tremble o'er
   The large leaves of the sycamore,
And fluctuate all the still perfume,

And gathering freshlier overhead,
   Rock'd the full-foliaged elms, and swung

The heavy-folded rose, and flung
2000 The lilies to and fro, and said,

'The dawn, the dawn,' and died away;
  And East and West, without a breath,
  Mixt their dim lights, like life and death,
To broaden into boundless day.

96

You say, but with no touch of scorn,
  Sweet-hearted, you, whose light-blue eyes
  Are tender over drowning flies,
You tell me, doubt is Devil-born.

I know not: one indeed I knew
2010 In many a subtle question versed,
  Who touch'd a jarring lyre at first,
But ever strove to make it true:

Perplext in faith, but pure in deeds,
  At last he beat his music out.
  There lives more faith in honest doubt,
Believe me, than in half the creeds.

He fought his doubts and gather'd strength,
  He would not make his judgment blind,
  He faced the spectres of the mind
2020 And laid them: thus he came at length

To find a stronger faith his own;
  And Power was with him in the night,
  Which makes the darkness and the light,
And dwells not in the light alone,

But in the darkness and the cloud,
  As over Sinaï's peaks of old,
  While Israel made their gods of gold,
Altho' the trumpet blew so loud.

97

My love has talk'd with rocks and trees;
    He finds on misty mountain-ground   2030
    His own vast shadow glory-crown'd;
He sees himself in all he sees.

Two partners of a married life—
    I look'd on these and thought of thee
    In vastness and in mystery,
And of my spirit as of a wife.

These two—they dwelt with eye on eye,
    Their hearts of old have beat in tune,
    Their meetings made December June
Their every parting was to die.   2040

Their love has never past away;
    The days she never can forget
    Are earnest that he loves her yet,
Whate'er the faithless people say.

Her life is lone, he sits apart,
    He loves her yet, she will not weep,
    Tho' rapt in matters dark and deep
He seems to slight her simple heart.

He thrids the labyrinth of the mind,
    He reads the secret of the star,   2050
    He seems so near and yet so far,
He looks so cold: she thinks him kind.

She keeps the gift of years before
    A wither'd violet is her bliss
    She knows not what his greatness is,
For that, for all, she loves him more.

For him she plays, to him she sings
    Of early faith and plighted vows;

She knows but matters of the house,
2060 And he, he knows a thousand things.

Her faith is fixt and cannot move,
  She darkly feels him great and wise,
  She dwells on him with faithful eyes,
'I cannot understand: I love.'

98

You leave us: you will see the Rhine,
  And those fair hills I sail'd below,
  When I was there with him; and go
By summer belts of wheat and vine

To where he breathed his latest breath,
2070 That City. All her splendour seems
  No livelier than the wisp that gleams
On Lethe in the eyes of Death.

Let her great Danube rolling fair
  Enwind her isles, unmark'd of me:
  I have not seen, I will not see
Vienna; rather dream that there,

A treble darkness, Evil haunts
  The birth, the bridal; friend from friend
  Is oftener parted, fathers bend
2080 Above more graves, a thousand wants

Gnarr at the heels of men, and prey
  By each cold hearth, and sadness flings
  Her shadow on the blaze of kings:
And yet myself have heard him say,

That not in any mother town
  With statelier progress to and fro
  The double tides of chariots flow
By park and suburb under brown

Of lustier leaves; nor more content,
   He told me, lives in any crowd,
   When all is gay with lamps, and loud
With sport and song, in booth and tent,

Imperial halls, or open plain;
   And wheels the circled dance, and breaks
   The rocket molten into flakes
Of crimson or in emerald rain.

99

Risest thou thus, dim dawn, again,
   So loud with voices of the birds,
   So thick with lowings of the herds,
Day, when I lost the flower of men;

Who tremblest thro' thy darkling red
   On yon swoll'n brook that bubbles fast
   By meadows breathing of the past,
And woodlands holy to the dead;

Who murmurest in the foliaged eaves
   A song that slights the coming care,
   And Autumn laying here and there
A fiery finger on the leaves;

Who wakenest with thy balmy breath
   To myriads on the genial earth,
   Memories of bridal, or of birth,
And unto myriads more, of death.

O, wheresoever those may be,
   Betwixt the slumber of the poles,
   To-day they count as kindred souls;
They know me not, but mourn with me.

2090
2100
2110

100

I climb the hill: from end to end
  Of all the landscape underneath,
  I find no place that does not breathe
Some gracious memory of my friend;

No gray old grange, or lonely fold,
  Or low morass and whispering reed,
  Or simple stile from mead to mead,
Or sheepwalk up the windy wold;

Nor hoary knoll of ash and hew
  That hears the latest linnet trill,
  Nor quarry trench'd along the hill
And haunted by the wrangling daw;

Nor runlet tinkling from the rock;
  Nor pastoral rivulet that swerves
  To left and right thro' meadowy curves,
That feed the mothers of the flock;

But each has pleased a kindred eye,
  And each reflects a kindlier day;
  And, leaving these, to pass away,
I think once more he seems to die.

101

Unwatch'd, the garden bough shall sway,
  The tender blossom flutter down,
  Unloved, that beech will gather brown,
This maple burn itself away;

Unloved, the sun-flower, shining fair,
  Ray round with flames her disk of seed,
  And many a rose-carnation feed
With summer spice the humming air;

Unloved, by many a sandy bar,
    The brook shall babble down the plain,
    At noon or when the lesser wain
Is twisting round the polar star;

Uncared for, gird the windy grove,
    And flood the haunts of hern and crake;
    Or into silver arrows break
The sailing moon in creek and cove;

Till from the garden and the wild
    A fresh association blow,
    And year by year the landscape grow
Familiar to the stranger's child;

As year by year the labourer tills
    His wonted glebe, or lops the glades;
    And year by year our memory fades
From all the circle of the hills.

102

We leave the well-beloved place
    Where first we gazed upon the sky;
    The roofs, that heard our earliest cry,
Will shelter one of stranger race.

We go, but ere we go from home,
    As down the garden-walks I move,
    Two spirits of a diverse love
Contend for loving masterdom.

One whispers, 'Here thy boyhood sung
    Long since its matin song, and heard
    The low love-language of the bird
In native hazels tassel-hung.'

The other answers, 'Yea, but here
    Thy feet have stray'd in after hours

With thy lost friend among the bowers,
And this hath made them trebly dear.'

These two have striven half the day,
    And each prefers his separate claim,
    Poor rivals in a losing game,
2180   That will not yield each other way.

I turn to go: my feet are set
    To leave the pleasant fields and farms;
    They mix in one another's arms
To one pure image of regret.

103

On that last night before we went
    From out the doors where I was bred,
    I dream'd a vision of the dead,
Which left my after-morn content.

Methought I dwelt within a hall,
2190   And maidens with me: distant hills
    From hidden summits fed with rills
A river sliding by the wall.

The hall with harp and carol rang.
    They sang of what is wise and good
    And graceful. In the centre stood
A statue veil'd, to which they sang;

And which, tho' veil'd, was known to me,
    The shape of him I loved, and love
    For ever: then flew in a dove
2200   And brought a summons from the sea:

And when they learnt that I must go
    They wept and wail'd, but led the way
    To where a little shallop lay
At anchor in the flood below;

And on by many a level mead,
    And shadowing bluff that made the banks,
    We glided winding under ranks
Of iris, and the golden reed;

And still as vaster grew the shore
    And roll'd the floods in grander space,   2210
    The maidens gather'd strength and grace
And presence, lordlier than before;

And I myself, who sat apart
    And watch'd them, wax'd in every limb;
    I felt the thews of Anakim,
The pulses of a Titan's heart;

As one would sing the death of war,
    And one would chant the history
    Of that great race, which is to be,
And one the shaping of a star;   2220

Until the forward-creeping tides
    Began to foam, and we to draw
    From deep to deep, to where we saw
A great ship lift her shining sides.

The man we loved was there on deck,
    But thrice as large as man he bent
    To greet us. Up the side I went,
And fell in silence on his neck;

Whereat those maidens with one mind
    Bewail'd their lot; I did them wrong: 2230
    'We served thee here,' they said, 'so long,
And wilt thou leave us now behind?'

So rapt I was, they could not win
    An answer from my lips, but he
    Replying, 'Enter likewise ye
And go with us:' they enter'd in.

And while the wind began to sweep
   A music out of sheet and shroud,
   We steer'd her toward a crimson cloud
2240   That landlike slept along the deep.

104

The time draws near the birth of Christ;
   The moon is hid, the night is still;
   A single church below the hill
Is pealing, folded in the mist.

A single peal of bells below,
   That wakens at this hour of rest
   A single murmur in the breast,
That these are not the bells I know.

Like strangers' voices here they sound,
2250   In lands where not a memory strays,
   Nor landmark breathes of other days,
But all is new unhallow'd ground.

105

To-night ungather'd let us leave
   This laurel, let this holly stand:
   We live within the stranger's land,
And strangely falls our Christmas-eve.

Our father's dust is left alone
   And silent under other snows:
   There in due time the woodbine blows,
2260   The violet comes, but we are gone.

No more shall wayward grief abuse
   The genial hour with mask and mime,
   For change of place, like growth of time,
Has broke the bond of dying use.

Let cares that petty shadows cast,
    By which our lives are chiefly proved,
    A little spare the night I loved,
And hold it solemn to the past.

But let no footstep beat the floor,
    Nor bowl of wassail mantle warm;   2270
    For who would keep an ancient form
Thro' which the spirit breathes no more?

Be neither song, nor game, nor feast;
    Nor harp be touch'd, nor flute be blown;
    No dance, no motion, save alone
What lightens in the lucid east

Of rising worlds by yonder wood.
    Long sleeps the summer in the seed;
    Run out your measured arcs, and lead
The closing cycle rich in good.   2280

106

Ring out, wild bells, to the wild sky,
    The flying cloud, the frosty light:
    The year is dying in the night;
Ring out, wild bells, and let him die.

Ring out the old, ring in the new,
    Ring, happy bells, across the snow:
    The year is going, let him go;
Ring out the false, ring in the true.

Ring out the grief that saps the mind,
    For those that here we see no more;   2290
    Ring out the feud of rich and poor,
Ring in redress to all mankind.

Ring out a slowly dying cause,
    And ancient forms of party strife;

Ring in the nobler modes of life,
With sweeter manners, purer laws.

Ring out the want, the care, the sin,
    The faithless coldness of the times;
    Ring out, ring out my mournful rhymes,
2300   But ring the fuller minstrel in.

Ring out false pride in place and blood,
    The civic slander and the spite;
    Ring in the love of truth and right,
Ring in the common love of good.

Ring out old shapes of foul disease;
    Ring out the narrowing lust of gold;
    Ring out the thousand wars of old,
Ring in the thousand years of peace.

Ring in the valiant man and free,
2310   The larger heart, the kindlier hand;
    Ring out the darkness of the land,
Ring in the Christ that is to be.

107

It is the day when he was born,
    A bitter day that early sank
    Behind a purple-frosty bank
Of vapour, leaving night forlorn.

The time admits not flowers or leaves
    To deck the banquet. Fiercely flies
    The blast of North and East, and ice
2320   Makes daggers at the sharpen'd eaves,

And bristles all the brakes and thorns
    To yon hard crescent, as she hangs
    Above the wood which grides and clangs
Its leafless ribs and iron horns

Together, in the drifts that pass
    To darken on the rolling brine
    That breaks the coast. But fetch the wine,
Arrange the board and brim the glass;

Bring in great logs and let them lie,
    To make a solid core of heat;   2330
    Be cheerful-minded, talk and treat
Of all things ev'n as he were by;

We keep the day. With festal cheer,
    With books and music, surely we
    Will drink to him, whate'er he be,
And sing the songs he loved to hear.

108

I will not shut me from my kind,
    And, lest I stiffen into stone,
    I will not eat my heart alone,
Nor feed with sighs a passing wind: 2340

What profit lies in barren faith,
    And vacant yearning, tho' with might
    To scale the heaven's highest height,
Or dive below the wells of Death?

What find I in the highest place,
    But mine own phantom chanting hymns?
    And on the depths of death there swims
The reflex of a human face.

I'll rather take what fruit may be
    Of sorrow under human skies: 2350
    'Tis held that sorrow makes us wise,
Whatever wisdom sleep with thee.

109

Heart-affluence in discursive talk
   From household fountains never dry;
   The critic clearness of an eye,
That saw thro' all the Muses' walk;

Seraphic intellect and force
   To seize and throw the doubts of man;
   Impassion'd logic, which outran
2360   The hearer in its fiery course;

High nature amorous of the good,
   But touch'd with no ascetic gloom;
   And passion pure in snowy bloom
Thro' all the years of April blood;

A love of freedom rarely felt,
   Of freedom in her regal seat
   Of England; not the schoolboy heat,
The blind hysterics of the Celt;

And manhood fused with female grace
2370   In such a sort, the child would twine
   A trustful hand, unask'd, in thine,
And find his comfort in thy face;

All these have been, and thee mine eyes
   Have look'd on: if they look'd in vain,
   My shame is greater who remain,
Nor let thy wisdom make me wise.

110

Thy converse drew us with delight,
   The men of rathe and riper years:
   The feeble soul, a haunt of fears,
2380   Forgot his weakness in thy sight.

On thee the loyal-hearted hung,
    The proud was half disarm'd of pride,
    Nor cared the serpent at thy side
To flicker with his double tongue.

The stern were mild when thou wert by,
    The flippant put himself to school
    And heard thee, and the brazen fool
Was soften'd, and he knew not why;

While I, thy nearest, sat apart,
    And felt thy triumph was as mine;   2390
    And loved them more, that they were thine,
The graceful tact, the Christian art;

Nor mine the sweetness or the skill,
    But mine the love that will not tire,
    And, born of love, the vague desire
That spurs an imitative will.

111

The churl in spirit, up or down
    Along the scale of ranks, thro' all,
    To him who grasps a golden ball,
By blood a king, at heart a clown;   2400

The churl in spirit, howe'er he veil
    His want in forms for fashion's sake,
    Will let his coltish nature break
At seasons thro' the gilded pale:

For who can always act? but he,
    To whom a thousand memories call,
    Not being less but more than all
The gentleness he seem'd to be,

Best seem'd the thing he was, and join'd
    Each office of the social hour   2410

To noble manners, as the flower
And native growth of noble mind;

Nor ever narrowness or spite,
    Or villain fancy fleeting by,
    Drew in the expression of an eye,
Where God and Nature met in light;

And thus he bore without abuse
    The grand old name of gentleman,
    Defamed by every charlatan,
2420   And soil'd with all ignoble use.

112

High wisdom holds my wisdom less,
    That I, who gaze with temperate eyes
    On glorious insufficiencies,
Set light by narrower perfectness.

But thou, that fillest all the room
    Of all my love, art reason why
    I seem to cast a careless eye
On souls, the lesser lords of doom.

For what wert thou? some novel power
2430   Sprang up for ever at a touch,
    And hope could never hope too much,
In watching thee from hour to hour,

Large elements in order brought,
    And tracts of calm from tempest made,
    And world-wide fluctuation sway'd
In vassal tides that follow'd thought.

113

'Tis held that sorrow makes us wise;
    Yet how much wisdom sleeps with thee

Which not alone had guided me,
But served the seasons that may rise;   2440

For can I doubt, who knew thee keen
   In intellect, with force and skill
   To strive, to fashion, to fulfil—
I doubt not what thou wouldst have been:

A life in civic action warm,
   A soul on highest mission sent,
   A potent voice of Parliament,
A pillar steadfast in the storm,

Should licensed boldness gather force,
   Becoming, when the time has birth,   2450
   A lever to uplift the earth
And roll it in another course,

With thousand shocks that come and go,
   With agonies, with energies,
   With overthrowings, and with cries
And undulations to and fro.

114

Who loves not Knowledge? Who shall rail
   Against her beauty? May she mix
   With men and prosper! Who shall fix
Her pillars? Let her work prevail.   2460

But on her forehead sits a fire:
   She sets her forward countenance
   And leaps into the future chance,
Submitting all things to desire.

Half-grown as yet, a child, and vain—
   She cannot fight the fear of death.
   What is she, cut from love and faith,
But some wild Pallas from the brain

Of Demons? fiery-hot to burst
2470   All barriers in her onward race
    For power. Let her know her place;
She is the second, not the first.

A higher hand must make her mild,
    If all be not in vain; and guide
    Her footsteps, moving side by side
With wisdom, like the younger child:

For she is earthly of the mind,
    But Wisdom heavenly of the soul.
    O, friend, who camest to thy goal
2480   So early, leaving me behind,

I would the great world grew like thee,
    Who grewest not alone in power
    And knowledge, but by year and hour
In reverence and in charity.

115

Now fades the last long streak of snow,
    Now burgeons every maze of quick
    About the flowering squares, and thick
By ashen roots the violets blow.

Now rings the woodland loud and long,
2490   The distance takes a lovelier hue,
    And drown'd in yonder living blue
The lark becomes a sightless song.

Now dance the lights on lawn and lea,
    The flocks are whiter down the vale,
    And milkier every milky sail
On winding stream or distant sea;

Where now the seamew pipes, or dives
    In yonder greening gleam, and fly

The happy birds, that change their sky
To build and brood; that live their lives   2500

From land to land; and in my breast
   Spring wakens too; and my regret
   Becomes an April violet,
And buds and blossoms like the rest.

116

Is it, then, regret for buried time
   That keenlier in sweet April wakes,
   And meets the year, and gives and takes
The colours of the crescent prime?

Not all: the songs, the stirring air,
   The life re-orient out of dust   2510
   Cry thro' the sense to hearten trust
In that which made the world so fair.

Not all regret: the face will shine
   Upon me, while I muse alone;
   And that dear voice, I once have known,
Still speak to me of me and mine:

Yet less of sorrow lives in me
   For days of happy commune dead;
   Less yearning for the friendship fled,
Than some strong bond which is to be.   2520

117

O days and hours, your work is this
   To hold me from my proper place,
   A little while from his embrace,
For fuller gain of after bliss:

That out of distance might ensue
   Desire of nearness doubly sweet;

And unto meeting when we meet,
Delight a hundredfold accrue,

For every grain of sand that runs,
2530   And every span of shade that steals,
    And every kiss of toothed wheels,
And all the courses of the suns.

118

Contemplate all this work of Time,
    The giant labouring in his youth;
    Nor dream of human love and truth,
As dying Nature's earth and lime;

But trust that those we call the dead
    Are breathers of an ampler day
    For ever nobler ends. They say,
2540   The solid earth whereon we tread

In tracts of fluent heat began,
    And grew to seeming-random forms,
    The seeming prey of cyclic storms,
Till at the last arose the man;

Who throve and branch'd from clime to clime,
    The herald of a higher race,
    And of himself in higher place,
If so he type this work of time

Within himself, from more to more;
2550   Or, crown'd with attributes of woe
    Like glories, move his course, and show
That life is not as idle ore,

But iron dug from central gloom,
    And heated hot with burning fears,
    And dipt in baths of hissing tears,
And batter'd with the shocks of doom

To shape and use. Arise and fly
  The reeling Faun, the sensual feast;
  Move upward, working out the beast,
And let the ape and tiger die.   2560

119

Doors, where my heart was used to beat
  So quickly, not as one that weeps
  I come once more; the city sleeps;
I smell the meadow in the street;

I hear a chirp of birds; I see
  Betwixt the black fronts long-withdrawn
  A light-blue lane of early dawn,
And think of early days and thee,

And bless thee, for thy lips are bland,
  And bright the friendship of thine eye;   2570
  And in my thoughts with scarce a sigh
I take the pressure of thine hand.

120

I trust I have not wasted breath:
  I think we are not wholly brain,
  Magnetic mockeries; not in vain,
Like Paul with beasts, I fought with Death;

Not only cunning casts in clay:
  Let Science prove we are, and then
  What matters Science unto men,
At least to me? I would not stay.   2580

Let him, the wiser man who springs
  Hereafter, up from childhood shape
  His action like the greater ape,
But I was born to other things.

121

Sad Hesper o'er the buried sun
    And ready, thou, to die with him,
    Thou watchest all things ever dim
And dimmer, and a glory done:

The team is loosen'd from the wain,
    The boat is drawn upon the shore;
    Thou listenest to the closing door,
And life is darken'd in the brain.

Bright Phosphor, fresher for the night,
    By thee the world's great work is heard
    Beginning, and the wakeful bird;
Behind thee comes the greater light:

The market boat is on the stream,
    And voices hail it from the brink;
    Thou hear'st the village hammer clink,
And see'st the moving of the team.

Sweet Hesper-Phosphor, double name
    For what is one, the first, the last,
    Thou, like my present and my past,
Thy place is changed; thou art the same.

122

Oh, wast thou with me, dearest, then,
    While I rose up against my doom,
    And yearn'd to burst the folded gloom,
To bare the eternal Heavens again,

To feel once more, in placid awe,
    The strong imagination roll
    A sphere of stars about my soul,
In all her motion one with law;

If thou wert with me, and the grave
    Divide us not, be with me now,
    And enter in at breast and brow,
Till all my blood, a fuller wave,

Be quicken'd with a livelier breath,
    And like an inconsiderate boy,
    As in the former flash of joy,
I slip the thoughts of life and death;   2620

And all the breeze of Fancy blows,
    And every dew-drop paints a bow,
    The wizard lightnings deeply glow,
And every thought breaks out a rose.

123

There rolls the deep where grew the tree.
    O earth, what changes hast thou seen!
    There where the long street roars, hath been
The stillness of the central sea.

The hills are shadows, and they flow
    From form to form, and nothing stands;   2630
    They melt like mist, the solid lands,
Like clouds they shape themselves and go.

But in my spirit will I dwell,
    And dream my dream, and hold it true;
    For tho' my lips may breathe adieu,
I cannot think the thing farewell.

124

That which we dare invoke to bless;
    Our dearest faith; our ghastliest doubt;
    He, They, One, All; within, without;
The Power in darkness whom we guess;   2640

I found Him not in world or sun,
    Or eagle's wing, or insect's eye;
    Nor thro' the questions men may try,
The petty cobwebs we have spun:

If e'er when faith had fall'n asleep,
    I heard a voice 'believe no more'
    And heard an ever-breaking shore
That tumbled in the Godless deep;

A warmth within the breast would melt
2650   The freezing reason's colder part,
    And like a man in wrath the heart
Stood up and answer'd 'I have felt.'

No, like a child in doubt and fear:
    But that blind clamour made me wise;
    Then was I as a child that cries,
But, crying, knows his father near;

And what I am beheld again
    What is, and no man understands;
    And out of darkness came the hands
2660   That reach thro' nature, moulding men.

125

Whatever I have said or sung,
    Some bitter notes my harp would give,
    Yea, tho' there often seem'd to live
A contradiction on the tongue,

Yet Hope had never lost her youth;
    She did but look through dimmer eyes;
    Or Love but play'd with gracious lies,
Because he felt so fix'd in truth:

And if the song were full of care,
2670   He breathed the spirit of the song;

And if the words were sweet and strong
He set his royal signet there;

Abiding with me till I sail
  To seek thee on the mystic deeps,
  And this electric force, that keeps
A thousand pulses dancing, fail.

126

Love is and was my Lord and King,
  And in his presence I attend
  To hear the tidings of my friend,
Which every hour his couriers bring.

Love is and was my King and Lord,
  And will be, tho' as yet I keep
  Within his court on earth, and sleep
Encompass'd by his faithful guard,

And hear at times a sentinel
  Who moves about from place to place,
  And whispers to the worlds of space,
In the deep night, that all is well.

127

And all is well, tho' faith and form
  Be sunder'd in the night of fear;
  Well roars the storm to those that hear
A deeper voice across the storm,

Proclaiming social truth shall spread,
  And justice, ev'n tho' thrice again
  The red fool-fury of the Seine
Should pile her barricades with dead.

But ill for him that wears a crown,
  And him, the lazar, in his rags:

They tremble, the sustaining crags;
2700   The spires of ice are toppled down,

And molten up, and roar in flood;
   The fortress crashes from on high,
   The brute earth lightens to the sky,
And the great Æon sinks in blood,

And compass'd by the fires of Hell;
   While thou, dear spirit, happy star,
   O'erlook'st the tumult from afar,
And smilest, knowing all is well.

128

The love that rose on stronger wings,
2710   Unpalsied when he met with Death,
   Is comrade of the lesser faith
That sees the course of human things.

No doubt vast eddies in the flood
   Of onward time shall yet be made,
   And throned races may degrade;
Yet, O ye mysteries of good,

Wild Hours that fly with Hope and Fear,
   If all your office had to do
   With old results that look like new;
2720   If this were all your mission here,

To draw, to sheathe a useless sword,
   To fool the crowd with glorious lies,
   To cleave a creed in sects and cries,
To change the bearing of a word,

To shift an arbitrary power,
   To cramp the student at his desk,
   To make old bareness picturesque
And tuft with grass a feudal tower;

Why then my scorn might well descend
    On you and yours. I see in part   2730
    That all, as in some piece of art,
Is toil cöoperant to an end.

129

Dear friend, far off, my lost desire,
    So far, so near in woe and weal;
    O loved the most, when most I feel
There is a lower and a higher;

Known and unknown; human, divine;
    Sweet human hand and lips and eye;
    Dear heavenly friend that canst not die,
Mine, mine, for ever, ever mine;   2740

Strange friend, past, present, and to be;
    Loved deeplier, darklier understood;
    Behold, I dream a dream of good,
And mingle all the world with thee.

130

Thy voice is on the rolling air;
    I hear thee where the waters run;
    Thou standest in the rising sun,
And in the setting thou art fair.

What art thou then? I cannot guess;
    But tho' I seem in star and flower   2750
    To feel thee some diffusive power,
I do not therefore love thee less:

My love involves the love before;
    My love is vaster passion now;
    Tho' mix'd with God and Nature thou,
I seem to love thee more and more.

Far off thou art, but ever nigh;
  I have thee still, and I rejoice;
  I prosper, circled with thy voice;
2760 I shall not lose thee tho' I die.

131

O living will that shalt endure
  When all that seems shall suffer shock,
  Rise in the spiritual rock,
Flow thro' our deeds and make them pure,

That we may lift from out of dust
  A voice as unto him that hears,
  A cry above the conquer'd years
To one that with us works, and trust,

With faith that comes of self-control,
2770 The truths that never can be proved
  Until we close with all we loved,
And all we flow from, soul in soul.

Epilogue

O true and tried, so well and long,
  Demand not thou a marriage lay;
  In that it is thy marriage day
Is music more than any song.

Nor have I felt so much of bliss
  Since first he told me that he loved
  A daughter of our house; nor proved
2780 Since that dark day a day like this;

Tho' I since then have number'd o'er
  Some thrice three years: they went and came,
  Remade the blood and changed the frame,
And yet is love not less, but more;

No longer caring to embalm
    In dying songs a dead regret,
    But like a statue solid-set,
And moulded in colossal calm.

Regret is dead, but love is more
    Than in the summers that are flown,   2790
    For I myself with these have grown
To something greater than before;

Which makes appear the songs I made
    As echoes out of weaker times,
    As half but idle brawling rhymes,
The sport of random sun and shade.

But where is she, the bridal flower,
    That must be made a wife ere noon?
    She enters, glowing like the moon
Of Eden on its bridal bower: 2800

On me she bends her blissful eyes
    And then on thee; they meet thy look
    And brighten like the star that shook
Betwixt the palms of paradise.

O when her life was yet in bud,
    He too foretold the perfect rose.
    For thee she grew, for thee she grows
For ever, and as fair as good.

And thou art worthy; full of power;
    As gentle; liberal-minded, great,   2810
    Consistent; wearing all that weight
Of learning lightly like a flower.

But now set out: the noon is near,
    And I must give away the bride;
    She fears not, or with thee beside
And me behind her, will not fear.

For I that danced her on my knee,
  That watch'd her on her nurse's arm,
  That shielded all her life from harm
2820 At last must part with her to thee;

Now waiting to be made a wife,
  Her feet, my darling, on the dead
  Their pensive tablets round her head,
And the most living words of life

Breathed in her ear. The ring is on,
  The 'wilt thou' answer'd, and again
  The 'wilt thou' ask'd, till out of twain
Her sweet 'I will' has made you one.

Now sign your names, which shall be read,
2830 Mute symbols of a joyful morn,
  By village eyes as yet unborn;
The names are sign'd, and overhead

Begins the clash and clang that tells
  The joy to every wandering breeze;
  The blind wall rocks, and on the trees
The dead leaf trembles to the bells.

O happy hour, and happier hours
  Await them. Many a merry face
  Salutes them—maidens of the place,
2840 That pelt us in the porch with flowers.

O happy hour, behold the bride
  With him to whom her hand I gave.
  They leave the porch, they pass the grave
That has to-day its sunny side.

To-day the grave is bright for me,
  For them the light of life increased,
  Who stay to share the morning feast,
Who rest to-night beside the sea.

Let all my genial spirits advance
    To meet and greet a whiter sun;   2850
    My drooping memory will not shun
The foaming grape of eastern France.

It circles round, and fancy plays,
    And hearts are warm'd and faces bloom,
    As drinking health to bride and groom
We wish them store of happy days.

Nor count me all to blame if I
    Conjecture of a stiller guest,
    Perchance, perchance, among the rest,
And, tho' in silence, wishing joy.   2860

But they must go, the time draws on,
    And those white-favour'd horses wait;
    They rise, but linger; it is late;
Farewell, we kiss, and they are gone.

A shade falls on us like the dark
    From little cloudlets on the grass,
    But sweeps away as out we pass
To range the woods, to roam the park,

Discussing how their courtship grew,
    And talk of others that are wed,   2870
    And how she look'd, and what he said,
And back we come at fall of dew.

Again the feast, the speech, the glee,
    The shade of passing thought, the wealth
    Of words and wit, the double health,
The crowning cup, the three-times-three,

And last the dance;—till I retire:
    Dumb is that tower which spake so loud,
    And high in heaven the streaming cloud,
And on the downs a rising fire: 2880

And rise, O moon, from yonder down,
    Till over down and over dale
    All night the shining vapour sail
And pass the silent-lighted town,

The white-faced halls, the glancing rills,
    And catch at every mountain head,
    And o'er the friths that branch and spread
Their sleeping silver thro' the hills;

And touch with shade the bridal doors,
2890   With tender gloom the roof, the wall;
    And breaking let the splendour fall
To spangle all the happy shores

By which they rest, and ocean sounds,
    And, star and system rolling past,
    A soul shall draw from out the vast
And strike his being into bounds,

And, moved thro' life of lower phase,
    Result in man, be born and think,
    And act and love, a closer link
2900 Betwixt us and the crowning race

Of those that, eye to eye, shall look
    On knowledge, under whose command
    Is Earth and Earth's, and in their hand
Is Nature like an open book;

No longer half-akin to brute,
    For all we thought and loved and did,
    And hoped, and suffer'd, is but seed
Of what in them is flower and fruit;

Whereof the man, that with me trod
2910   This planet, was a noble type
    Appearing ere the times were ripe,
That friend of mine who lives in God,

That God, which ever lives and loves,
    One God, one law, one element,
    And one far-off divine event,
To which the whole creation moves.

THE EAGLE

He clasps the crag with crooked hands;
Close to the sun in lonely lands,
Ring'd with the azure world, he stands.

The wrinkled sea beneath him crawls;
He watches from his mountain walls,
And like a thunderbolt he falls.

CROSSING THE BAR

Sunset and evening star,
    And one clear call for me!
And may there be no moaning of the bar,
    When I put out to sea,

   But such a tide as moving seems asleep,
    Too full for sound and foam,
When that which drew from out the boundless deep
    Turns again home.

   Twilight and evening bell,
    And after that the dark!
And may there be no sadness of farewell,
    When I embark;

   For tho' from out our bourne of Time and Place

The flood may bear me far,
I hope to see my Pilot face to face
When I have crost the bar.

POEMS

Robert Browning

SOLILOQUY OF THE SPANISH CLOISTER

Gr-r-r—there go, my heart's abhorrence!
    Water your damned flower-pots, do!
If hate killed men, Brother Lawrence,
    God's blood, would not mine kill you!
What? your myrtle-bush wants trimming?
    Oh, that rose has prior claims—
Needs its leaden vase filled brimming?
    Hell dry you up with its flames!

At the meal we sit together;
    Salve tibi! I must hear   10
Wise talk of the kind of weather,
    Sort of season, time of year:
Not a plenteous cork crop: scarcely
    Dare we hope oak-galls, I doubt;
What's the Latin name for 'parsley'?
    What's the Greek name for 'swine's snout'?

Whew! We'll have our platter burnished,
    Laid with care on our own shelf!
With a fire-new spoon we're furnished,
    And a goblet for ourself,   20

Rinsed like something sacrificial
   Ere 'tis fit to touch our chaps—
Marked with L. for our initial!
   (He-he! There his lily snaps!)

Saint, forsooth! While Brown Dolores
   Squats outside the Convent bank
With Sanchicha, telling stories,
   Steeping tresses in the tank,
Blue-black, lustrous, thick like horsehairs,
30   —Can't I see his dead eye glow,
Bright as 'twere a Barbary corsair's?
   (That is, if he'd let it show!)

When he finishes refection,
   Knife and fork he never lays
Cross-wise, to my recollection,
   As do I, in Jesu's praise.
I the Trinity illustrate,
   Drinking watered orange pulp—
In three sips the Arian frustrate;
40   While he drains his at one gulp!

Oh, those melons! if he's able
   We're to have a feast; so nice!
One goes to the Abbot's table,
   All of us get each a slice.
How go on your flowers? None double?
   Not one fruit-sort can you spy?
Strange!—And I, too, at such trouble,
   Keep them close-nipped on the sly!

There's a great text in Galatians,
50   Once you trip on it, entails
Twenty-nine district damnations,
   One sure, if another fails;
If I trip him just a-dying,
   Sure of heaven as sure can be,

Spin him round and send him flying
    Off to hell, a Manichee?

Or, my scrofulous French novel
    On grey paper with blunt type!
Simply glance at it, you grovel
    Hand and foot in Belial's gripe;   60
If I double down its pages
    At the woeful sixteenth print,
When he gathers his greengages,
    Ope a sieve and slip it in't?

Or, there's Satan!—one might venture
    Pledge one's soul to him, yet leave
Such a flaw in the indenture
    As he'd miss till, past retrieve,
Blasted lay that rose-acacia
    We're so proud of! Hy, Zy, Hine...   70
'St, there's Vespers! Plena gratia
    Ave, Virgo! Gr-r-r—you swine!

My Last Duchess

FERRARA

That's my last Duchess painted on the wall,
Looking as if she were alive. I call
That piece a wonder, now; Fra Pandolf's hands
Worked busily a day, and there she stands.
Will't please you sit and look at her? I said
'Fra Pandolf' by design, for never read
Strangers like you that pictured countenance,
The depth and passion of its earnest glance,
But to myself they turned (since none puts by
The curtain I have drawn for you, but I)   10

And seemed as they would ask me, if they durst,
How such a glance came there; so, not the first
Are you to turn and ask thus. Sir, 'twas not
Her husband's presence only, called that spot
Of joy into the Duchess' cheek; perhaps
Fra Pandolf chanced to say, 'Her mantle laps
Over my lady's wrist too much,' or 'Paint
Must never hope to reproduce the faint
Half-flush that dies along her throat.' Such stuff
20   Was courtesy, she thought, and cause enough
For calling up that spot of joy. She had
A heart—how shall I say?— too soon made glad,
Too easily impressed; she liked whate'er
She looked on, and her looks went everywhere.
Sir, 'twas all one! My favour at her breast,
The dropping of the daylight in the West,
The bough of cherries some officious fool
Broke in the orchard for her, the white mule
She rode with round the terrace—all and each
30   Would draw from her alike the approving speech,
Or blush, at least. She thanked men—good! but thanked
Somehow—I know not how—as if she ranked
My gift of a nine-hundred-years-old name
With anybody's gift. Who'd stoop to blame
This sort of trifling? Even had you skill
In speech—which I have not—to make your will
Quite clear to such an one, and say, 'Just this
Or that in you disgusts me; here you miss,
Or there exceed the mark'—and if she let
40   Herself be lessoned so, nor plainly set
Her wits to yours, forsooth, and made excuse—
E'en then would be some stooping; and I choose
Never to stoop. Oh, sir, she smiled, no doubt,
Whene'er I passed her; but who passed without
Much the same smile? This grew; I gave commands;
Then all smiles stopped together. There she stands

As if alive. Will't please you rise? We'll meet
The company below, then. I repeat,
The Count your master's known munificence
Is ample warrant that no just pretense   50
Of mine for dowry will be disallowed;
Though his fair daughter's self, as I avowed
At starting, is my object. Nay, we'll go
Together down, sir. Notice Neptune, though,
Taming a sea-horse, thought a rarity,
Which Claus of Innsbruck cast in bronze for me!

FRA LIPPO LIPPI

I am poor brother Lippo, by your leave!
You need not clap your torches to my face.
Zooks, what's to blame? you think you see a monk!
What, 'tis past midnight, and you go the rounds,
And here you catch me at an alley's end
Where sportive ladies leave their doors ajar?
The Carmine's my cloister: hunt it up,
Do,—harry out, if you must show your zeal,
Whatever rat, there, haps on his wrong hole,
And nip each softling of a wee white mouse,   10
Weke, weke, that's crept to keep him company!
Aha, you know your betters! Then, you'll take
Your hand away that's fiddling on my throat,
And please to know me likewise. Who am I?
Why, one, sir, who is lodging with a friend
Three streets off—he's a certain... how d'ye call?
Master—a... Cosimo of the Medici,
I' the house that caps the corner. Boh! you were best!
Remember and tell me, the day you're hanged,
How you affected such a gullet's-gripe!   20
But you, sir, it concerns you that your knaves
Pick up a manner nor discredit you:

Zooks, are we pilchards, that they sweep the streets
And count fair price what comes into their net?
He's Judas to a tittle, that man is!
Just such a face! Why, sir, you make amends.
Lord, I'm not angry! Bid your hang-dogs go
Drink out this quarter-florin to the health
Of the munificent House that harbours me
30 (And many more beside, lads! more beside!)
And all's come square again. I'd like his face—
His, elbowing on his comrade in the door
With the pike and lantern,—for the slave that holds
John Baptist's head a-dangle by the hair
With one hand ('Look you, now,' as who should say)
And his weapon in the other, yet unwiped!
It's not your chance to have a bit of chalk,
A wood-coal or the like? or you should see!
Yes, I'm the painter, since you style me so.
40 What, brother Lippo's doings, up and down,
You know them and they take you? like enough!
I saw the proper twinkle in your eye—
'Tell you, I liked your looks at very first.
Let's sit and set things straight now, hip to haunch.
Here's spring come, and the nights one makes up bands
To roam the town and sing out carnival,
And I've been three weeks shut within my mew,
A-painting for the great man, saints and saints
And saints again. I could not paint all night—
50 Ouf! I leaned out of window for fresh air.
There came a hurry of feet and little feet,
A sweep of lute strings, laughs, and whifts of song,—
Flower o' the broom,
Take away love, and our earth is a tomb!
Flower o' the quince,
I let Lisa go, and what good in life since?
Flower o' the thyme—and so on. Round they went.
Scarce had they turned the corner when a titter

Like the skipping of rabbits by moonlight,—three slim shapes,
And a face that looked up... zooks, sir, flesh and blood,   60
That's all I'm made of! Into shreds it went,
Curtain and counterpane and coverlet,
All the bed-furniture—a dozen knots,
There was a ladder! Down I let myself,
Hands and feet, scrambling somehow, and so dropped,
And after them. I came up with the fun
Hard by Saint Laurence, hail fellow, well met,—
Flower o' the rose,
If I've been merry, what matter who knows?
And so as I was stealing back again   70
To get to bed and have a bit of sleep
Ere I rise up to-morrow and go work
On Jerome knocking at his poor old breast
With his great round stone to subdue the flesh,
You snap me of the sudden. Ah, I see!
Though your eye twinkles still, you shake your head—
Mine's shaved—a monk, you say—the sting's in that!
If Master Cosimo announced himself,
Mum's the word naturally; but a monk!
Come, what am I a beast for? tell us, now!   80
I was a baby when my mother died
And father died and left me in the street.
I starved there, God knows how, a year or two
On fig-skins, melon-parings, rinds and shucks,
Refuse and rubbish. One fine frosty day,
My stomach being empty as your hat,
The wind doubled me up and down I went.
Old Aunt Lapaccia trussed me with one hand,
(Its fellow was a stinger as I knew)
And so along the wall, over the bridge,   90
By the straight cut to the convent. Six words there,
While I stood munching my first bread that month:
'So, boy, you're minded,' quoth the good fat father
Wiping his own mouth, 'twas refection-time,—

'To quit this very miserable world?
Will you renounce'... 'the mouthful of bread?' thought I;
By no means! Brief, they made a monk of me;
I did renounce the world, its pride and greed,
Palace, farm, villa, shop, and banking-house,
100   Trash, such as these poor devils of Medici
Have given their hearts to—all at eight years old.
Well, sir, I found in time, you may be sure,
'Twas not for nothing—the good bellyful,
The warm serge and the rope that goes all round,
And day-long blessed idleness beside!
'Let's see what the urchin's fit for'—that came next.
Not overmuch their way, I must confess.
Such a to-do! They tried me with their books:
Lord, they'd have taught me Latin in pure waste!
110   *Flower o' the clove.*
All the Latin I construe is, 'amo' I love!
But, mind you, when a boy starves in the streets
Eight years together, as my fortune was,
Watching folk's faces to know who will fling
The bit of half-stripped grape-bunch he desires,
And who will curse or kick him for his pains,—
Which gentleman processional and fine,
Holding a candle to the Sacrament,
Will wink and let him lift a plate and catch
120   The droppings of the wax to sell again,
Or holla for the Eight and have him whipped,—
How say I?—nay, which dog bites, which lets drop
His bone from the heap of offal in the street,—
Why, soul and sense of him grow sharp alike,
He learns the look of things, and none the less
For admonition from the hunger-pinch.
I had a store of such remarks, be sure,
Which, after I found leisure, turned to use.
I drew men's faces on my copy-books,
130   Scrawled them within the antiphonary's marge,

Joined legs and arms to the long music-notes,
Found eyes and nose and chin for A's and B's,
And made a string of pictures of the world
Betwixt the ins and outs of verb and noun,
On the wall, the bench, the door. The monks looked black.
'Nay,' quoth the Prior, 'turn him out, d'ye say?
In no wise. Lose a crow and catch a lark.
What if at last we get our man of parts,
We Carmelites, like those Camaldolese
And Preaching Friars, to do our church up fine   140
And put the front on it that ought to be!'
And hereupon he bade me daub away.
Thank you! my head being crammed, the walls a blank,
Never was such prompt disemburdening.
First, every sort of monk, the black and white,
I drew them, fat and lean: then, folk at church,
From good old gossips waiting to confess
Their cribs of barrel-droppings, candle-ends,—
To the breathless fellow at the altar-foot,
Fresh from his murder, safe and sitting there   150
With the little children round him in a row
Of admiration, half for his beard and half
For that white anger of his victim's son
Shaking a fist at him with one fierce arm,
Signing himself with the other because of Christ
(Whose sad face on the cross sees only this
After the passion of a thousand years)
Till some poor girl, her apron o'er her head,
(Which the intense eyes looked through) came at eve
On tiptoe, said a word, dropped in a loaf,   160
Her pair of earrings and a bunch of flowers
(The brute took growling), prayed, and so was gone.
I painted all, then cried ''Tis ask and have;
Choose, for more's ready!'—laid the ladder flat,
And showed my covered bit of cloister-wall.
The monks closed in a circle and praised loud

Till checked, taught what to see and not to see,
Being simple bodies,—'That's the very man!
Look at the boy who stoops to pat the dog!
170　That woman's like the Prior's niece who comes
To care about his asthma: it's the life!"
But there my triumph's straw-fire flared and funked;
Their betters took their turn to see and say:
The Prior and the learned pulled a face
And stopped all that in no time. 'How? what's here?
Quite from the mark of painting, bless us all!
Faces, arms, legs, and bodies like the true
As much as pea and pea! it's devil's-game!
Your business is not to catch men with show,
180　With homage to the perishable clay,
But lift them over it, ignore it all,
Make them forget there's such a thing as flesh.
Your business is to paint the souls of men—
Man's soul, and it's a fire, smoke... no, it's not...
It's vapour done up like a new-born babe—
(In that shape when you die it leaves your mouth)
It's... well, what matters talking, it's the soul!
Give us no more of body than shows soul!
Here's Giotto, with his Saint a-praising God,
190　That sets us praising—why not stop with him?
Why put all thoughts of praise out of our head
With wonder at lines, colours, and what not?
Paint the soul, never mind the legs and arms!
Rub all out, try at it a second time.
Oh, that white smallish female with the breasts,
She's just my niece... Herodias, I would say,—
Who went and danced and got men's heads cut off!
Have it all out!' Now, is this sense, I ask?
A fine way to paint soul, by painting body
200　So ill, the eye can't stop there, must go further
And can't fare worse! Thus, yellow does for white
When what you put for yellow's simply black,

And any sort of meaning looks intense
When all beside itself means and looks nought.
Why can't a painter lift each foot in turn,
Left foot and right foot, go a double step,
Make his flesh liker and his soul more like,
Both in their order? Take the prettiest face,
The Prior's niece... patron-saint—is it so pretty
You can't discover if it means hope, fear,   210
Sorrow or joy? won't beauty go with these?
Suppose I've made her eyes all right and blue,
Can't I take breath and try to add life's flash,
And then add soul and heighten them three-fold?
Or say there's beauty with no soul at all—
(I never saw it—put the case the same—)
If you get simple beauty and nought else,
You get about the best thing God invents:
That's somewhat: and you'll find the soul you have missed,
Within yourself, when you return him thanks.   220
'Rub all out!' Well, well, there's my life, in short,
And so the thing has gone on ever since.
I'm grown a man no doubt, I've broken bounds:
You should not take a fellow eight years old
And make him swear to never kiss the girls.
I'm my own master, paint now as I please—
Having a friend, you see, in the Corner-house!
Lord, it's fast holding by the rings in front—
Those great rings serve more purposes than just
To plant a flag in, or tie up a horse!   230
And yet the old schooling sticks, the old grave eyes
Are peeping o'er my shoulder as I work,
The heads shake still—'It's art's decline, my son!
You're not of the true painters, great and old;
Brother Angelico's the man, you'll find;
Brother Lorenzo stands his single peer:
Fag on at flesh, you'll never make the third!'
Flower o' the pine,

You keep your mistr... manners, and I'll stick to mine!
240 I'm not the third, then: bless us, they must know!
Don't you think they're the likeliest to know,
They with their Latin? So, I swallow my rage,
Clench my teeth, suck my lips in tight, and paint
To please them—sometimes do and sometimes don't;
For, doing most, there's pretty sure to come
A turn, some warm eve finds me at my saints—
A laugh, a cry, the business of the world—
(Flower o' the peach
Death for us all, and his own life for each!)
250 And my whole soul revolves, the cup runs over,
The world and life's too big to pass for a dream,
And I do these wild things in sheer despite,
And play the fooleries you catch me at,
In pure rage! The old mill-horse, out at grass
After hard years, throws up his stiff heels so,
Although the miller does not preach to him
The only good of grass is to make chaff.
What would men have? Do they like grass or no—
May they or mayn't they? all I want's the thing
260 Settled for ever one way. As it is,
You tell too many lies and hurt yourself:
You don't like what you only like too much,
You do like what, if given you at your word,
You find abundantly detestable.
For me, I think I speak as I was taught;
I always see the garden and God there
A-making man's wife: and, my lesson learned,
The value and significance of flesh,
I can't unlearn ten minutes afterwards.

270 You understand me: I'm a beast, I know.
But see, now—why, I see as certainly
As that the morning-star's about to shine,
What will hap some day. We've a youngster here
Comes to our convent, studies what I do,

Slouches and stares and lets no atom drop:
His name is Guidi—he'll not mind the monks—
They call him Hulking Tom, he lets them talk—
He picks my practice up—he'll paint apace.
I hope so—though I never live so long,
I know what's sure to follow. You be judge!   280
You speak no Latin more than I, belike;
However, you're my man, you've seen the world
—The beauty and the wonder and the power,
The shapes of things, their colours, lights and shades,
Changes, surprises,—and God made it all!
—For what? Do you feel thankful, ay or no,
For this fair town's face, yonder river's line,
The mountain round it and the sky above,
Much more the figures of man, woman, child,
These are the frame to? What's it all about?   290
To be passed over, despised? or dwelt upon,
Wondered at? oh, this last of course!—you say.
But why not do as well as say,—paint these
Just as they are, careless what comes of it?
God's works—paint any one, and count it crime
To let a truth slip. Don't object, 'His works
Are here already; nature is complete:
Suppose you reproduce her—(which you can't)
There's no advantage! you must beat her, then.'
For, don't you mark? we're made so that we love   300
First when we see them painted, things we have passed
Perhaps a hundred times nor cared to see;
And so they are better, painted—better to us,
Which is the same thing. Art was given for that;
God uses us to help each other so,
Lending our minds out. Have you noticed, now,
Your cullion's hanging face? A bit of chalk,
And trust me but you should, though! How much more,
If I drew higher things with the same truth!
That were to take the Prior's pulpit-place,   310

Interpret God to all of you! Oh, oh,
It makes me mad to see what men shall do
And we in our graves! This world's no blot for us,
Nor blank; it means intensely, and means good:
To find its meaning is my meat and drink.
'Ay, but you don't so instigate to prayer!'
Strikes in the Prior: 'when your meaning's plain
It does not say to folk—remember matins,
Or, mind you fast next Friday!' Why, for this
320   What need of art at all? A skull and bones,
Two bits of stick nailed crosswise, or, what's best,
A bell to chime the hour with, does as well.
I painted a Saint Laurence six months since
At Prato, splashed the fresco in fine style:
'How looks my painting, now the scaffold's down?'
I ask a brother: 'Hugely,' he returns—
'Already not one phiz of your three slaves
Who turn the Deacon off his toasted side,
But's scratched and prodded to our heart's content,
330   The pious people have so eased their own
With coming to say prayers there in a rage:
We get on fast to see the bricks beneath.
Expect another job this time next year,
For pity and religion grow i' the crowd—
Your painting serves its purpose!' Hang the fools!

—That is—you'll not mistake an idle word
Spoke in a huff by a poor monk, God wot,
Tasting the air this spicy night which turns
The unaccustomed head like Chianti wine!
340   Oh, the church knows! don't misreport me, now!
It's natural a poor monk out of bounds
Should have his apt word to excuse himself:
And hearken how I plot to make amends.
I have bethought me: I shall paint a piece
... There's for you! Give me six months, then go, see
Something in Sant' Ambrogio's! Bless the nuns!

They want a cast o' my office. I shall paint
God in the midst, Madonna and her babe,
Ringed by a bowery, flowery angel-brood,
Lilies and vestments and white faces, sweet 350
As puff on puff of grated orris-root
When ladies crowd to Church at midsummer.
And then i' the front, of course a saint or two—
Saint John' because he saves the Florentines,
Saint Ambrose, who puts down in black and white
The convent's friends and gives them a long day,
And Job, I must have him there past mistake,
The man of Uz (and Us without the z,
Painters who need his patience). Well, all these
Secured at their devotion, up shall come 360
Out of a corner when you least expect,
As one by a dark stair into a great light,
Music and talking, who but Lippo! I!—
Mazed, motionless, and moonstruck—I'm the man!
Back I shrink—what is this I see and hear?
I, caught up with my monk's-things by mistake,
My old serge gown and rope that goes all round,
I, in this presence, this pure company!
Where's a hole, where's a corner for escape?
Then steps a sweet angelic slip of a thing 370
Forward, puts out a soft palm—'Not so fast!'
—Addresses the celestial presence, 'nay—
He made you and devised you, after all,
Though he's none of you! Could Saint John there draw—
His camel-hair make up a painting brush?
We come to brother Lippo for all that,
Iste perfecit opus! So, all smile—
I shuffle sideways with my blushing face
Under the cover of a hundred wings
Thrown like a spread of kirtles when you're gay 380
And play hot cockles, all the doors being shut,
Till, wholly unexpected, in there pops

The hothead husband! Thus I scuttle off
To some safe bench behind, not letting go
The palm of her, the little lily thing
That spoke the good word for me in the nick,
Like the Prior's niece... Saint Lucy, I would say.
And so all's saved for me, and for the church
A pretty picture gained. Go, six months hence!
390   Your hand, sir, and good-bye: no lights, no lights!
The street's hushed, and I know my own way back,
Don't fear me! There's the grey beginning. Zooks!

Dover Beach

Matthew Arnold

The sea is calm tonight.
The tide is full, the moon lies fair
Upon the straits; on the French coast the light
Gleams and is gone; the cliffs of England stand,
Glimmering and vast, out in the tranquil bay.
Come to the window, sweet is the night-air!
Only, from the long line of spray
Where the sea meets the moon-blanched land,
Listen! you hear the grating roar
Of pebbles which the waves draw back, and fling,   10
At their return, up the high strand,
Begin, and cease, and then again begin,
With tremulous cadence slow, and bring
The eternal note of sadness in.

Sophocles long ago
Heard it on the Ægean, and it brought
Into his mind the turbid ebb and flow
Of human misery; we
Find also in the sound a thought,
Hearing it by this distant northern sea.   20

The Sea of Faith
Was once, too, at the full, and round earth's shore

Lay like the folds of a bright girdle furled.
But now I only hear
Its melancholy, long, withdrawing roar,
Retreating, to the breath
Of the night-wind, down the vast edges drear
And naked shingles of the world.

Ah, love, let us be true
30   To one another! for the world, which seems
To lie before us like a land of dreams,
So various, so beautiful, so new,
Hath really neither joy, nor love, nor light,
Nor certitude, nor peace, nor help for pain;
And we are here as on a darkling plain
Swept with confused alarms of struggle and flight,
Where ignorant armies clash by night.

POEMS

Christina Rossetti

SONG

When I am dead, my dearest,
    Sing no sad songs for me;
Plant thou no roses at my head,
    Nor shady cypress tree:
Be the green grass above me
    With showers and dewdrops wet;
And if thou wilt, remember,
    And if thou wilt, forget.

I shall not see the shadows,
    I shall not feel the rain;
I shall not hear the nightingale
    Sing on, as if in pain:
And dreaming through the twilight
    That doth not rise nor set,
Haply I may remember,
    And haply may forget.

A Better Resurrection

I have no wit, no words, no tears;
My heart within me like a stone
Is numb'd too much for hopes or fears;
Look right, look left, I dwell alone;
I lift mine eyes, but dimm'd with grief
No everlasting hills I see;
My life is in the falling leaf:
O Jesus, quicken me.

My life is like a faded leaf,
10   My harvest dwindled to a husk:
Truly my life is void and brief
And tedious in the barren dusk;
My life is like a frozen thing,
No bud nor greenness can I see:
Yet rise it shall—the sap of Spring;
O Jesus, rise in me.

My life is like a broken bowl,
A broken bowl that cannot hold
One drop of water for my soul
20   Or cordial in the searching cold;
Cast in the fire the perish'd thing;
Melt and remould it, till it be
A royal cup for Him, my King:
O Jesus, drink of me.

A Birthday

My heart is like a singing bird
    Whose nest is in a water'd shoot;
My heart is like an apple-tree
    Whose boughs are bent with thickset fruit;
My heart is like a rainbow shell
    That paddles in a halcyon sea;
My heart is gladder than all these
    Because my love is come to me.

Raise me a dais of silk and down;
    Hang it with vair and purple dyes;
Carve it in doves and pomegranates,
    And peacocks with a hundred eyes;
Work it in gold and silver grapes,
    In leaves and silver fleurs-de-lys;
Because the birthday of my life
    Is come, my love is come to me.

POEMS

Gerard Manley Hopkins

THE WINDHOVER

To Christ our Lord

I caught this morning morning's minion, king-
   dom of daylight's dauphin, dapple-dawn-drawn Falcon, in his
     riding
   Of the rolling level underneath him steady air, and striding
High there, how he rung upon the rein of a wimpling wing
In his ecstasy! then off, off forth on swing,
   As a skate's heel sweeps smooth on a bow-bend: the hurl and
     gliding
   Rebuffed the big wind. My heart in hiding
Stirred for a bird,—the achieve of, the mastery of the thing!

Brute beauty and valour and act, oh, air, pride, plume, here
   Buckle! AND the fire that breaks from thee then, a billion
Times told lovelier, more dangerous, O my chevalier!

     No wonder of it: shéer plód makes plough down sillion
Shine, and blue-bleak embers, ah my dear,
   Fall, gall themselves, and gash gold-vermilion.

GOD'S GRANDEUR

The world is charged with the grandeur of God.
   It will flame out, like shining from shook foil;
   It gathers to a greatness, like the ooze of oil
Crushed. Why do men then now not reck his rod?
Generations have trod, have trod, have trod;
   And all is seared with trade; bleared, smeared with toil;
   And wears man's smudge and shares man's smell: the soil
Is bare now, nor can foot feel, being shod.

And for all this, nature is never spent;
   There lives the dearest freshness deep down things;
And though the last lights off the black West went
   Oh, morning, at the brown brink eastward, springs—
Because the Holy Ghost over the bent
   World broods with warm breast and with ah! bright wings.

PIED BEAUTY

Glory be to God for dappled things—
   For skies of couple-colour as a brinded cow;
     For rose-moles all in stipple upon trout that swim;
Fresh-firecoal chestnut-falls; finches' wings;
   Landscape plotted and pieced—fold, fallow, and plough;
     And áll trádes, their gear and tackle and trim.

All things counter, original, spare, strange;
   Whatever is fickle, freckled (who knows how?)
     With swift, slow; sweet, sour; adazzle, dim;
He fathers-forth whose beauty is past change:
        Praise him.

NIGHT HAWK TRILOGY

By

J.E. Taylor

Night Hawk Trilogy© 2024 J.E. Taylor
Includes: Night Hawk, Midnight Vows,
Tigress, Trinity Rising, Lilith

NIGHT HAWK

Sentenced to death at the hands of a demon, Naomi Hawk has a firsthand lesson in betrayal. Now, she thirsts for justice... and revenge.

Selling your soul has never been so charming and Mark throws in a little something to sweeten the pot, his girlfriend Naomi.

Sentenced to death at the hands of a demon, Naomi Hawk has a firsthand lesson in despair and betrayal in Mark's deal for fame with all the trimmings. Deep in the clutches of the underground brotherhood, Naomi's light is coveted for the Master's gain.

When she slips and falls eighty stories from a precarious ledge, Naomi resigns herself to the inevitable impact and death by shattered bones. Before she can escape her demons in eternal slumber, something sinister plucks her from the plummet, stealing her out of the night to sacrifice her forever to the shadows.

Imprisoned in bottomless darkness, Naomi thirsts for justice...and revenge.

Night Hawk
Chapter One
Naomi

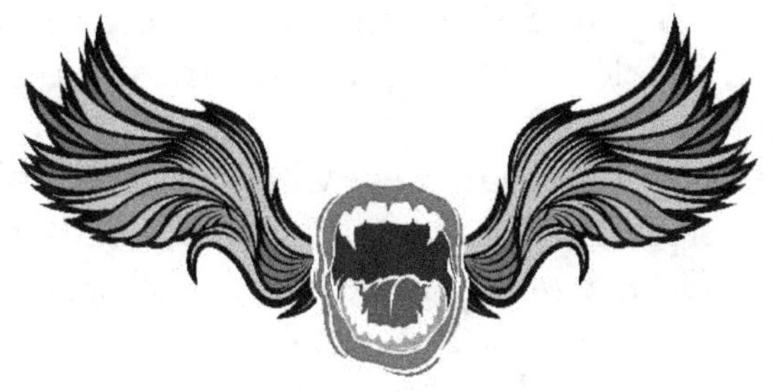

I STILL REMEMBER THE first night.

The full moon illuminated the landscape and I could see for miles from my perch. The eighty-floor drop left me dizzy, and I stepped farther back into the wall. My heart thundered in my chest and the adrenaline warmed my skin against the frigid air.

"There's nowhere for you to go."

His growl yanked my gaze from the busy city street below to his dark and crazed eyes.

My tongue stuck to the roof of my mouth, dry as desert sand, and I shook my head. I didn't want to fall, and I reconsidered my situation. Maybe going inside was a much better alternative, no matter how horrifying death at his hands promised to be. The fear of dying by terminal velocity was even greater, and it cemented my feet to that small ledge.

"I can wait." His evil laugh hung on the air, chilling whatever heat I had left right out of my bones and I clamped my jaw tight against the tears that threatened, leaving my vision warped.

I slid farther away from the open window and the glistening blade in his hand. He ran it slowly along the brick, creating a screaming sound that made my teeth ache.

Either way, I was screwed. A flare of anger shot through the fear, adding to the tremor in my skin. *Damn you, Mark, why did you turn me over to these vultures?*

Demon boy looked up at me and chuckled as if he heard my silent question. His shaded gaze flashed red before it sank back to the sharp blade. "It was the only way my boss would honor his deal," he muttered and glanced back at me. "His soul and your life and your boyfriend will have all the fame and fortune he could ever envision."

"But why me?"

"Your life force is quite a delicacy." The knife scraped against the brick again. "My boss has waited for millenniums to taste the beating heart of a child of the light."

"Fuck you," I said, my voice shook with the flare of anger and I took another step away, however a gale caught me off guard and I teetered on the edge trying to grasp at the brick wall; but my hands were too cold to gain the purchase necessary to catch my balance. All it took was another wind gust, and I slipped, the scream barreling out of my mouth at the sudden weightless freefall.

I had a moment of satisfaction when the demon's expression transitioned into fear-tinted shock at losing what his master coveted.

Gravity pulled, and my hair whipped across my face, blinding me to anything but streaks of light. I thought my heart would catapult out of my chest. It beat so hard, and I drew in a breath, waiting for the impact that would turn out the lights for good.

Pain bit around my waist, and I was yanked from the descent by a powerful grasp. A sharp cry ripped from my throat, and the sound of beating wings filled my world. Before I could focus on what had saved me from certain death, I was tumbling through space again. This time, the hard asphalt of a nearby roof bit into my skin and I rolled away.

When I got my bearings, I brushed the hair from my face in time to see a human form at the edge of the roof. A man in a dark overcoat stepped from the shadows. His intense glare fell on me and he licked his lips, revealing a sharp set of canines.

"Who are you?" I whispered and climbed to my feet. My legs shook under my weight, barely able to hold me up.

He smiled and stepped into the light.

"I've been watching you."

The mere thought of a fiend like him studying me from afar gave me the creeps. The movies always made it quite romantic to be the object of a vampire's affection, but in reality, all they wanted was an entertaining meal.

"Why?" I asked, fumbling for the knife clasped to my belt. When my hand came up empty, he laughed, dangling the weapon from his fingers.

"You really think your little dagger will stop me?" He tossed the knife to the edge of the rooftop and stepped toward me.

Being a demon's meal was bad, but being this bastard's chew toy was worse. I would rather have been splattered on the pavement. I took another shaking step backwards, too aware of my near frozen condition.

"You didn't answer my question," I said, trying to stall him until I could maneuver close enough to dive for my weapon.

He stared me down with hard black eyes. Eyes no more distinct than the shadow he stepped out of.

"Why?" he replied. "Because I swore I'd destroy anything that bastard wants, and you are at the top of that list. I'm sure he's gutting his little lackey right now for not being more subtle. He'll be even more pissed when he finds out I'm the one that stole his dessert."

The bitterness in his voice nearly quelled the fight in me. But when he stepped closer, my survival instinct flared, and I ducked under his reach, swinging my fist, hoping to get a shot in, but my knuckles only grazed his hard cheek.

His vice-like grip clamped on my throat, pulling me close. The burn of his bite seized my muscles, his poison saturating my entire form with exquisite pain. Each beat of my heart hurt, and I screamed. He pulled away from my neck and stared into my eyes.

"My god, you are delicious," he whispered, his voice laced with rough desire and before I could pull another breath in, his teeth ripped at my throat again.

My fading gaze landed on the arch of his neck, and my scream morphed into a growl. I sank my dull human teeth through his skin and was rewarded with a gasp and the gush of black blood filling my mouth. He pressed me closer, still drinking from my throat and pressing my mouth to his neck. I tried to wiggle out of his grasp, but he clamped down hard enough so I had no choice but to ingest his blood.

A wave of dizziness hit and he loosened his grip, stepping away from me. I crumpled to the ground, heaving the blood from my stomach, but I knew it was too late. I had already swallowed too much of the vile poison and no matter how much I threw up, I couldn't stop the infection.

"I bet you never saw that coming," I whispered and sent a glare in his direction.

He no longer held that smug look, instead his handsome face transformed into a mask of horror and his hand clamped his neck, the blood flowing freely over his fingertips.

As the infection spread, it crystallized my cells into a hard shell and transformed my senses into acute hunting weapons. The pain that had gripped me moments ago faded, and I stood with a ravenous need. I ran my tongue over my teeth and winced at the cutting edges that would puncture steel if I so desired.

The human soul inside me cried at the injustice. I should be dead, but instead, I was now one of the undead, all because the bastard before me plucked the demon's meal out of the sky.

I stepped toward him with a growl and his eyes widened, reflecting a blue as crisp as the fall sky, and I stopped.

"You bit me," he whispered, his voice unsteady and shaking.

"Did you think I'd just let you drain me dry without a fight?"

His hand dropped from his throat and he stared at the wet blood covering it before raising his gaze to me. "No one has ever bitten me before," he said.

I crossed my arms and studied him. "Sucks, doesn't it," I said. I couldn't help it. The disbelief on his face made me want to laugh, but I kept a check on my chuckle.

He blinked, and then the smile that spread over his lips sent a shiver through me. Laughter followed, rich and full and as hypnotizing as his smile.

"Yes. It does," he finally said and wiped at his neck again. The flow of blood stopped, and he glanced at me.

"You aren't such a badass after all," I said.

The menacing shadow was gone, replaced by a man barely out of his teens. I studied him, noting the uncomfortable shift along with his worried scan of the surrounding night. It took a minute to understand the hesitation in his gaze.

He glanced back at me, and I knew. This kid was scared shitless, but I wasn't sure if it was me or something else.

"Why do I get the feeling you're in trouble?"

He laughed and caught my gaze, moving faster than I could blink, and I found myself pressed to the wall by his incredibly hard body.

His intense stare left me breathless, but this time, it wasn't food he hungered for, and he leaned in to kiss me.

I swept his feet out from under him and he landed on his back with a thud, surprise plastered across his face.

"Not going to happen." I pointed at him. "You may have turned me into a monster, but that doesn't give you the right to screw me any time you please." I didn't want to rely on any man, never mind a blood-crazed vamp, no matter how good looking he was.

I swallowed, suddenly thirsty, and my gaze dropped to the dried blood on his collar. I knew soon enough the thirst would overwhelm me, but in that moment, I swore I'd never become a shadow dwelling killer.

He climbed to his feet, brushing the roof grit from his jacket. "You're mine now," he said, trying to exude authority.

I laughed and crossed to the knife, picking it up and hesitating. The silver glinted in the moonlight and I sighed, running a fingertip down the length. The metal created a warm glow on my skin unlike anything I had seen before, but it didn't penetrate and draw blood like it should have.

I understood his mocking of my weapons now and glanced over my shoulder at him. "No one owns me." I sheathed the blade and turned toward him, ready for battle.

Night Hawk
Chapter Two
Damian

I STARED AT HER.

Her transformation took seconds, not hours, like mine had. One minute she was human and the next, her beauty transcended anything I'd ever witnessed. I had seen a couple of transformations in the last two millennia, but none of them survived the first pangs of thirst after the sun rose. They burst out of the dark caverns into the burning sun and were reduced to a pile of smoking ash.

I prayed she'd be able to resist, to survive the remainder of the change.

I vaguely recalled that need, but I had been so close to death, I didn't have the strength to pull myself out from under the pile of slaughtered vampires until the next sunset. Lucifer tossed me in that pit, never expecting me to survive, but I fought, just like this vixen before me, sacrificing my soul for vengeance.

I survived the initial bout of thirst by feeding on dead vampires and because of that horrid experience, my taste for humans wasn't as acute as the rest of my shadow kin.

My thirst thrived on the destruction of anything Lucifer coveted.

And Lucifer coveted this beauty.

I stalked her from the shadows, harboring a hatred that clouded my judgment. If I had looked closer, I might have seen the hypnotic power of the life light shining in her heart. That first burst of her blood was sweeter and more soul affirming than any human I had ever tasted, and I lost my focus long enough to let my guard down.

Long enough for her bite to puncture my skin.

I let my gaze travel from her dark locks over her lovely curves all the way to the killer cowboy boots and sighed. Lust was normal for me, but this was beyond lust. I wanted to protect her, to never let her leave my sight.

I was ensnared and there was no escape.

"What's your name?" I asked, hoping to diffuse some of the anger radiating from her.

Her lips thinned and her eyes narrowed. "What?"

I should have expected her hostile response. Hell, when I was in her shoes, I tore the monsters limb from limb, relishing their death, so I don't know why her fury surprised me.

Gulping my unease, I tried again. "I'm Damian," I said and looked at the ground. Unsure if I should offer her my hand or my throat as a peace offering, I shoved my hands into my pockets and did neither.

"So?" Her hands found her hips, and I met her stark glare.

"We need to get out of here," I said, casting a glance at the sky again. Light was just piercing the horizon and the sun would make an appearance within the next hour.

Her gaze followed mine and then snapped back in my direction.

"I refuse to live in the shadows," she snapped.

"And I refuse to let you become a pile of ash," I said and willed myself to morph as I charged toward her. Wrapping my arms around her waist, I jumped from the roof, feeling the change and relishing her gasp as my mighty wings took us higher in the air.

While the subway systems seemed like the most logical place for me to take her, I knew that would be the first place Lucifer would search for us. By now, he knew I screwed up his plans and if he found us during the day, there would be no defense against his strength or fury.

Instead, I turned, heading into the northwest hills of Connecticut, to one of the few places of mine that Lucifer hadn't tracked down. I landed in the backyard just as the sun's rays lit up the horizon. With her in my arms, I swung the door open and rushed her down to the windowless basement, setting her down on the plush couch.

Before I was out of her reach, her palm stung my cheek, sending me back a few steps.

"What makes you think I want to live like this?"

"Maybe you'd like the same shot at vengeance that's kept me alive all these years." I didn't mean for the bitterness to sneak into my tone, but there it was; just as loud as a bullhorn.

My words struck her silent, and she studied me.

Silence descended, and I turned, flipping the switch that filtered the soft glow of fluorescents through the room. I didn't know what else to say, so I took the chair opposite her and fiddled with my hands, folding and unfolding them before shifting in the chair.

"Naomi," her soft voice caught my attention, and I met her gaze.

"My name is Naomi. Naomi Hawk."

My eyebrows rose at the irony.

She allowed a half smile. "I'm hungry," she whispered and her gaze landed on my throat again.

"You can't go out yet," I said, hoping she'd understand. "The sun..." I shrugged and stood. "I'm going to clean up. You're welcome to do the same."

For the first time since I attacked her, she looked down at her blood-soaked shirt. When her gaze lifted, I saw the spark of ravenous hunger.

Night Hawk
Chapter Three
Naomi

BLOOD.
The coppery scent wafted from my shirt and my focus clouded.

Need.

I had never understood what need was until that moment, and my gaze jumped to his. He stepped back, putting distance between us, but it wasn't enough. I could smell the mixture of fear and lust in him, along with the tainted blood that soaked his collar, and I wanted to lick it off his skin.

I blinked at the carnal thoughts flooding my mind and glanced at my surroundings again. I had crossed half the distance between the couch and where he stood without knowledge of moving.

He closed the distance with apprehension and took my hand.

"I think we both need to clean up before you get too far gone."

My gaze dropped to our clasped hand, and I felt the electrical flow it produced through my cells. While I wanted to remain distant and pissed off, this sensation was new and overwhelming. I followed the tight muscles in his arm to his shoulder and stopped at the blackened stain.

Hunger and lust and anger all mixed into a potent concoction, and I snapped my gaze to his.

"You did this to me," I whispered.

He held my gaze and shook his head. "No. I had every intention of killing you."

I yanked my hand from his and stepped back, allowing a fraction of space between us.

"Why didn't you?"

"Because you taste like summer rain," he whispered and reached for me. His fingers fluttered across my cheek and into my hair and before I knew it, his mouth was on mine, his tongue playing with me in a kiss that should have been forbidden.

The burn of it caught me off guard and I pulled away.

"Damn. You still taste like summer rain." His blue eyes flashed, and he stepped closer, crowding me.

I planted my hand on his chest, forgetting about the hunger that throbbed in my teeth. "Maybe we should take a cold shower," I said, trying to diffuse the growing tension between us.

"Together?"

The hope in his eyes made me laugh. "No."

His features fell into a sulk and for a moment, I almost took back my answer, but the stubborn part of me reared up and I stood my ground.

He gave me a nod and turned, leading the way to an enormous bathroom that piqued my interest. Gray marble covered the room from ceiling to floor, and in the corner across from the beautiful walk-in shower was a gas fireplace. The claw-foot tub shined against the gray tiles and a large floor to ceiling mirror was broken with a fine white pedestal sink.

"There are towels and a bathrobe in the linen closet on the other side of the shower that you can use," he said.

I stepped inside and gave him a faint smile before closing the door on his questioning stare. The bank of light switches intrigued me and I played with the dimmers until I had the lighting just the way I liked it, soft shades and, with the flames in the fireplace, it would have been the ultimate romantic setting.

Instead of dwelling on the idea of romance, I stripped the bloody shirt from my back and the rest of the clothing peeled off just as easily. The shower called my attention, and I turned on all the jets as hot as the setting would allow. Steam rose, and I stepped inside, relishing the heat on my cold skin. Pulsing water massaged my muscles, loosening the knots and ridding my skin of any remnants of blood.

I don't know how long I stood soaking in the water, but when I finally opened my eyes, I glanced at the neat little alcove in the shower wall that housed bath wash and shampoo.

Curious, I opened the wash and took a sniff. It reminded me of a bamboo forest and I lathered my body with the luxurious soap.

The shampoo reminded me of cocoa butter and beach lotions. A scent I adored and the reality that I'd never see the sun again hit like the force of a truck. Pain centered in my chest, dropping me to my knees and I buried my face in my hands as the last of my human tears mingled with the hot water.

When the sobs ran dry, I climbed to my feet and turned the water off. A stack of plush towels sat on a small pedestal and I wrapped my drenched hair in one, drying off my body with the other.

A hunger pang hit, almost knocking me to the ground, and I gripped the edge of the sink, clamping my eyes shut and willing the hunger away. I forced myself to breathe in and out until I had some semblance of control, and then I stared at the steam-streaked mirror. Unwrapping the towel from my body, I used it to clear the glass.

My reflection hadn't changed much. I still had curves in the right places and my stomach was as flat as a washboard. I glanced at my new Brazilian wax, wondering if I'd ever have to endure that torture again. If not, that was definitely something positive about being a vampire.

I opened my mouth to inspect my teeth, and a crease appeared between my eyes. They were normal. No sharp canines existed.

"They only go razor at night."

I jumped at his voice and covered my body with the towel, glaring in his direction.

"Get out!"

He grinned and picked up my clothes, leaving without another word.

I hadn't heard him come into the room, and irritation snaked over my skin. *How long had he been there?*

I rummaged through the linen closet, finding a plush bathrobe just like he said and wrapped the cloud-soft fabric around me. I tossed the towels over the side of the tub and hand combed my hair before charging into the living room.

I found him leaning against the bar with his shirt hanging open. The rippled muscles of his stomach glistened in the soft light and I had to tear my eyes away from his god-like form.

"Sorry about that," he said and nodded toward the bathroom, but neither his tone nor his gaze held any regret. He even had the audacity to grin.

"You have no right to spy on me like that," I said, and the words came out in a feral growl.

"I figured you might like clean clothing at some point today."

"But you just walked in without knocking."

He glanced at the floor and nodded. "I guess I'm not used to having houseguests." A bright red hue colored his cheeks and my eyebrow rose.

"You're blushing. I didn't think that was possible."

Damian raised his gaze, meeting mine, and he stood up, crossing to the couch. "I gather you know little about vampires," he said and took a seat.

"I know you like to play with your food," I said with as much snark as possible.

His laugh struck a chord. I crossed my arms and refrained from tapping my foot with impatience at his adolescent behavior.

"How old are you, anyway?" I asked, sending the most derogatory glare I could drum up.

His laughter wound down, but the smile remained.

"Which age? The one I was when I was turned or how many years have I been walking the earth?"

I blinked at his question, debating on which one to ask.

"I was turned when I was twenty-five."

Just a few years older than I am, which explains some of the adolescent behavior, but the wisdom in his eyes told me that his twenty-five was a very long time ago. "How long have you been like this?"

"Longer than you can conceive," he whispered, and any hint of a smile vanished. He turned his head toward the brightly decorated walls. "I've seen the world evolve." When he brought his gaze back to mine, I shivered. In a blink, the shadow hiding his eyes disappeared and the vibrant blue returned.

His evasive answer irritated me, and I tried another tactic. "Where were you born?"

"Greece."

That explained the thick dark hair that I wanted to run my fingers through and even the hint of Mediterranean in his complexion, but I still didn't get a sense of how long he had been like this. I got the impression he didn't really want to discuss the passage of time, and I let it go for now.

Something shifted on the floor above us and my attention snapped to the ceiling, or more specifically, to the heartbeat. I could smell it and the hunger pang hit again.

I didn't realize I had moved until I found myself face down on the stairs with Damian pinning me to the risers.

"No," his whisper hissed in my ear. "They are off limits."

They? I'm surprised his voice cut through the rush of blood I heard pounding in the veins of the humans above. I wanted to drink every drop, to satiate this sudden craving, and I clawed at the stairs, trying to break his grip, my focus on the metal door keeping my meal at bay.

He jammed his wrist in my mouth and at first, I pushed it away, but when he pressed it to my lips a second time, the dull pulse caught my attention. His whisper was lost in the rushing need that gripped my form and I sank my teeth through his flesh, closing my eyes and reveling in the taste of the black blood.

His wince cut through the haze and, with my teeth still embedded in his wrist, I turned, meeting his frantic gaze. My eyes locked with his and the razor incisors in my mouth retracted, but I kept my grip, drinking with greedy slurps.

With each drop came an image, and I saw the world as it was when he was human.

I saw him vibrant and alive and I saw the reasons for the vengeance in his blood.

My betrayal paled compared to his loss.

He watched his lover, Athena, torn to pieces at the hands of a demon, all because she refused to disclose where she hid her daughter.

Damian knew where Zoe hid, but kept silent. He had sworn allegiance to the girl, taking the place of her dead father and loving her like she was his own child. Nothing the demons did would loosen his tongue.

The little girl was an innocent, a child of light descendant, and the demon wanted to feast on her life force even more than he wanted Athena's. It was a coveted delicacy and Damian stood in the demon's path.

When his lover lay in pieces at his feet, her blood smeared across the demon's lips and her heart an empty husk on the ground, Damian swore he would dedicate his life to destroying the demon.

That's when Lucifer threw him into the pit with a hoard of hungry vampires.

He yanked his wrist from me and covered it with his hand, standing and taking an unsteady step backwards. Damian's jumbled thoughts flowed over me like a blanket, suffocating me, and I gasped, my hunger forgotten.

He had walked the earth for over two thousand years, protecting Zoe's bloodline.

Until his fangs sank into *my* neck.

Night Hawk
Chapter Four
Damian

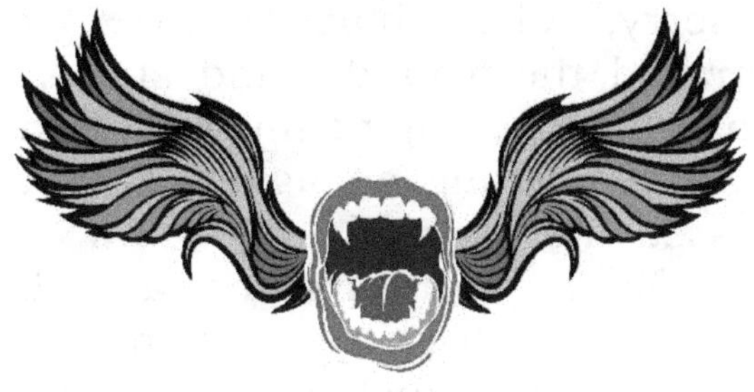

THIS IS WHAT HAPPENS when a light child becomes a shadow.

Her strength outmatched mine, and I had no idea how I subdued her. The moment she sensed human life above, her teeth had flared to sharp weapons of destruction and she had moved like lightning, finding the hidden entrance to the stairwell with ease.

I stared at her, holding my aching wrist and reeling from the mind-union we held as she feasted on my blood. That was an entirely new and unwelcomed experience.

"I, uh, I can't let you go up there," I said, unsure of whether my blood had tempered her thirst. If not, she was screwed. The minute she stepped from our daytime sanctuary, the sunshine would torch her delicate skin, leaving her nothing but a pile of ash.

Naomi wiped her mouth with the back of her hand. Her gaze landed on my wrist and then traveled back to my face. Her eyes carried confusion, and she stepped toward me, pulling my injured wrist toward her.

"I'm sorry," she whispered. Her trembling fingers traced the wounds, and she closed her eyes, inhaling and bringing my wrist to her lips.

Instead of latching on again, as I expected, she pressed her lips to my skin. A warm sensation flooded through me and her eyes opened, her gaze shooting right into my heart. Naomi melted the frost that had built over millenniums and I stifled the urge to take her to my bedroom and do things I hadn't done since the days I spent with Athena.

The light burned in her eyes, too, and she stepped close, crowding me.

"You don't kill humans, do you?" she asked. The lilt in her voice made the phrase more of a statement than a question.

"No. Not usually." I led her out of the stairwell, closing the door and getting my bearings. "I've made exceptions over the years and death is usually warranted, but lately, I've let my hatred get the best of me." I turned back to her. "If I had taken the time to really see you instead of just stalking you for revenge, I would have known why Lucifer wanted you. I would have known you were off limits."

"Off limits?"

"A child of light is off limits," I said and a crinkle of confusion appeared on her forehead. "A child of light is a descendant of the Archangel Michael," I explained. "You're in one of the lines I lost track of." I dropped my gaze to the floor and the heat of my failure filled my cheeks.

"Is that why you looked so scared on the rooftop?"

My gaze snapped to hers and I shrugged.

It was bad enough having Lucifer as an enemy, but pissing off Michael was an automatic death sentence. The righteous were infinitely more brutal than the demons when crossed.

"I'm still here, but that could change at any moment."

Night Hawk
Chapter Five
Naomi

MY LEGS WOBBLED AND he stepped forward, putting his uninjured arm around my waist and led me back to the couch. His touch was gentle, and I wondered just what he would be like in bed.

A different type of hunger accosted me and I pounced, pushing him down on the cushions and his eyes widened, following the line of my neck to the open V of my bathrobe. He blinked and then snapped his gaze from my exposed breasts back to my face. All hesitation in his expression morphed to a desire deeper than mine.

He pulled me to his lips, the first kiss soft as if he was afraid I would run. When his hands threaded into my hair, the kiss became more insistent. His tongue explored my mouth and a low groan escaped him like I was the most precious thing he had ever encountered.

His body responded, and I yanked away at both the jolt of his erection and the shock skittering over my flesh. I blinked down at him and his slow smile made me forget what he was. Nimble fingers unthreaded the tie holding the rest of the bathrobe closed and the coolness of the air slapped me back into control.

Before his shaking hands touched my skin, I hopped off him and pulled the soft material back in place.

"I'm sorry," I said and took a few paces in the opposite direction.

Damian stared at the ceiling with his fists clenched. The muscles in his jaw twitched and I could tell he was grinding his teeth together, fighting for control. When his gaze moved from the ceiling to me, I knew he lost the battle, but I didn't react fast enough.

Within a blink, he had me against the wall. His iron grip held my wrists against the cool fabric covering the concrete beneath. He stared at me, his chest rising and falling with the lust sparkling in his eyes.

"You shouldn't tease me like that."

His voice fanned over me like a delicate shower and instead of struggling, I kept his gaze biting my lip to keep my voice in check. Awareness of how close he was made my heart bang in my chest and the knowledge that it still pumped blood through my body took my attention away from his intense eyes.

"My heart..." I whispered.

His grip loosened, but he didn't let go. "It still beats. So does mine," he said, answering my unasked question.

"I thought..."

He laughed and dropped my hands, taking a step back. "You thought vampires were dead and cold and soulless?"

I raised a shoulder in response.

"We're ageless whether or not we feed on humans and we are alive. I'll admit the degree of alive varies, but we are alive and not the walking dead you're imagining."

"Un-dead," I said.

He smiled and shrugged. "Until your luck runs out, then you're just as dead as the next cadaver."

"Why?"

"The virus crystallizes our cells, freezing them in time, but they still require oxygen, so we breathe. Blood moves the oxygen through the body, so our hearts continue to beat. There hasn't been an ounce of decomposition in my system since I turned. The ability to heal is accelerated as well and I haven't quite figured out why."

His explanation intrigued me. "If that's the case, why can't vampires go out in the sun?"

"The crystallization reacts badly with ultraviolet rays," he said, understating the dangers.

I skirted around him and wandered through the room, digesting his words and examining my surroundings. The tapestries hanging over the concrete provided a lively and warm feel to the space and I reached out, running my fingers over the silky, vibrant fabric. His gaze followed me, heating a spot on my back, and I flexed my shoulders, trying to dislodge the burn.

"I've never known vampires to shape shift," I finally said, stopping in front of a mural of a castle with a pair of hawks flying overhead.

His huff took my attention away from the wall and I turned, meeting his gaze.

"What, exactly, do you know about vampires?"

"You have super human speed and strength, you heal like that," I snapped my fingers. "And you survive by drinking blood. The perfect monster." Sarcasm wrapped its hands around each of my words, and he rolled his eyes.

He crossed his arms and waited for me to continue.

"I used to think a silver blade to the heart would kill them."

His smile surfaced. "Silver will leave a nasty welt, but it's not strong enough to pierce through our skin. However, any blade made from a derivative of platinum, especially when thrust through the heart, kills."

"Why platinum?"

"There's something about the purity of the metal that allows it to pierce our skin, but the blade doesn't have to be forged from pure platinum. It can be forged of steel and dipped in platinum."

"You never answered my question about shape shifting."

He sighed and his gaze lifted to the tapestry. "I didn't think it was a question."

"Well, is that normal?"

He shook his head and his less than cursory glance in my direction made my skin flush.

"So, what? You're special?"

His chuckle caught me off guard, and he shrugged. "I never thought of it that way."

Night Hawk
Chapter Six
Damian

*C*URSED IS MORE LIKE *it,* I thought and met her stare. I could tell she had a boatload of questions pinging around behind those beautiful eyes, but I wasn't in the mood for speculating about why I could morph into a mammoth, predatory bird at will. Whether it was a divine gift or a demonic curse, I wasn't sure, but that unique gift saved my ass a time or two.

"Well?" Her hands found their way to her waist and her head cocked to the side.

Her stance allowed the V in the bathrobe to widen, giving me just enough of a glimpse of her breasts to jump-start my overactive libido. I forced my gaze back to her face and shoved my hands into my back pockets. Even though it had been centuries since I had a houseguest, I hadn't totally lost sight of my manners.

"I'm sorry, Naomi, but I don't have an answer for you."

Her perfect pout surfaced, and I turned, stalking out of the room before I acted on the overwhelming urges wracking my form. Instead, I busied myself with the laundry, pulling the soaking garments from the spiffy new front-loader I had purchased recently, and throwing them into the dryer.

I'd have to take her shopping tonight because there was no way I could resist another day of her lounging in that bathrobe.

I turned away from the machine and stopped. Naomi stood in the doorway, her hands gripping the frame, all her earlier curiosity gone. Her face transformed into a mask of lust-filled hunger.

"I should get you something to drink," I whispered, reacting to her proximity and the knowledge that she could drain me dry if she wanted to.

She didn't budge, and I stepped back in the small space, my back finding another concrete wall.

"I'm hungry," she said in a feral growl that revealed her sharp fangs. Her hands dropped to her sides, and she stepped into the room, blocking my exit.

Memory of how sweet her blood had been bubbled my thirst to the surface, and I licked my lips, my gaze falling to the slow pulse visible in her neck. God, I wanted to drink from her again, but I knew how wrong it would be.

"Naomi," I started, keeping my voice reasonable. "You don't want to do what you're thinking."

Her laugh filled the small space, and she lunged, pinning me to the wall. I tilted my chin to my chest, so she didn't have a clear bite, and stared at her.

"Killing me won't change you back," I whispered.

She snapped her teeth together in a growl, and then her crazed grin faltered. She blinked, and her sharp incisors retracted. "Who says I want to kill you?" she asked, her voice barely a whisper.

I raised a questioning eyebrow.

She let go and stepped back. "I don't know what came over me..."

"You're a newborn. It happens," I said, dismissing the danger and stepping around her. "Your clothes will be dry in a little while, then you can get out of that bathrobe." I started walking away.

The ruffle of fabric made me turn, and she stood in the entryway again, but this time it wasn't bloodlust in her gaze. The bathrobe lay crumpled around her feet and I stumbled, almost falling on my ass at the shock.

She was divine, and I followed her curves before returning my gaze to hers.

"What are you doing?" It took everything in my power not to move to her, to take her in my arms. This need singeing my blood was foreign and unwelcomed. It was far greater than any need the blood-hunt created, and I didn't understand why.

I stepped backwards, putting more distance between me and this goddess.

She spread her arms out. "You don't want me?"

The hysterical laughter that spouted from my mouth was so out of character, and it offended Naomi, setting her into action. She snatched the bathrobe from the ground, wrapping it around her before she stormed off.

I didn't follow until a door slammed and momentary panic filled my bones. I bolted to the stairwell and yanked the door open. The stairs were empty and the upper door still latched from the inside. Relief swept through me and I closed the access door, leaning against it with my eyes closed.

I focused, training my ear to locate her heartbeat, and followed the sound to my bedroom. Tentatively, I turned the knob and opened the door.

Naomi lay face down on the king size bed, her face buried in my pillows and the distinct shake in her shoulders told me she was crying.

What the hell is the etiquette for this? I cleared my throat.

"Go away," she said, her voice muffled by the pillow.

"Um...this is my bedroom."

The glare she leveled at me made me second-guess the living arrangements.

"How long till sunset?"

I waved toward the clock. "It's not even noon yet."

She turned away, and I hung my head, debating on whether I should leave her alone. History and my instincts told me not to leave her unattended, but I didn't want to set her off. Dealing with a newborn was as volatile as dealing with a bomb. One wrong move and you'll find yourself in pieces.

I looked up, meeting her stark stare.

"What?"

I bit the snide comment that surfaced at her snotty tone, opting to stare her down instead.

"Are you just going to stand there?"

"Maybe," I offered with a snideness of my own.

"I don't need a babysitter."

"I beg to differ."

"Screw you," she snarled and turned away again.

The venom in her voice set me into action and I moved across the room, flipping her over on the bed, and slammed her wrists over her head before I could blink. I straddled her, staring down into her wide, dark eyes.

"You have no idea how *much* I want you, so cut the crap."

She struggled, and I squeezed my thighs into her hips, keeping her still beneath me. Naomi twisted her wrists, trying to break my hold, and I clamped harder.

"Why?" she screamed in my face. The fury was back, and I could deal with this much better than the hungry seductress.

"Why what?" I snarled down at her.

"Why don't you just kill me?" she roared, her struggles continued, and she screamed a long, lonely wail before she lay still, her chest rising and falling rapidly.

"Killing you is the last thing on my mind," I whispered, and her exhausted gaze flicked to mine.

A sheen of tears covered her eyes, and I sighed, letting go of her wrists. I sat back on my heels, running my fingers into my hair, holding the back of my head to get control of the torrent flooding my senses.

"But you laughed," she whispered.

I met her gaze, dropping my hands to my thighs. "I laughed because your question was ludicrous." Hurt flashed in her eyes. "Stop doing that."

"Doing what?"

"Assuming the worst."

Her lips pressed together, and she blinked away the sheen.

"You're not running on all cylinders right now," I said. "You haven't finished the transition and while you're in this state..." I trailed off, not knowing how to tell her she might feel differently once everything clicks into place. Instead, I climbed off her and stretched out next to her on the bed, staring at the ceiling.

"So, you're trying *not* to take advantage of me?" she asked, and I smiled, nodding without looking her way.

"Well, doesn't that just beat all?" Naomi sat up. "A chivalrous blood sucker."

"Would you prefer I just fuck you?" I asked, sending a glare in her direction, although just saying it sent tendrils of heated anticipation through my body.

I guess the question turned her on as well because she met my gaze and offered a come-hither smile. She shifted, swinging her thigh over me and straddled my lap like I had done to her moments ago. A wicked gleam filled her eyes, and she took my hands, placing them on her bare thighs.

"I'd like that very much," she purred and circled her hips on my groin.

The feel of her silky skin under my fingertips just about did me in.

"Naomi," I whispered, my voice raspy with want.

"Damian," she whispered back, and leaned forward. Her lips breezed over mine and trailed down my jaw to my neck.

A trail of butterfly kisses lined my throat, and a low grumble started in my chest until the sharp stab of her incisors pierced my skin. Her bite burned and, without thinking, I sank my fangs into her exposed throat. Her blood still tasted like summer rain and I groaned under the pulse of it.

She whimpered against my throat, and I couldn't help myself. My hand found her delicate folds and my fingers circled, playing with her and turning her whimper into a lust filled moan.

"Damian," she whispered, and I realized she wasn't biting anymore. I relinquished my hold on her, the release flooding me with disappointment until our eyes met. My gaze dropped to the thin line of blood trailing down her throat, sliding between her breasts, and I lost control.

I flipped her under me, pushing the bathrobe open and licked the trail away until her skin was pristine again. Her body responded to my touch and the heat between us increased, turning my heart into a frantic drum in my chest.

She fumbled with my belt, and I stopped my exploration, raising my gaze to hers.

"You realize, hawks mate for life," I said.

Her hands paused, and it took her a few seconds to digest my words. Her eyes narrowed.

"You mean to tell me you haven't fucked anyone for over two thousand years?"

I laughed and raised an eyebrow. "I've fucked thousands of women, but none of them were vampires." I chuckled at her wide-eyed reaction, enjoying her shock, and then my laughter faded. "None of them were my own kind." When my gaze locked with hers, I saw the hesitation, and it was enough to dampen my lust.

Night Hawk
Chapter Seven
Naomi

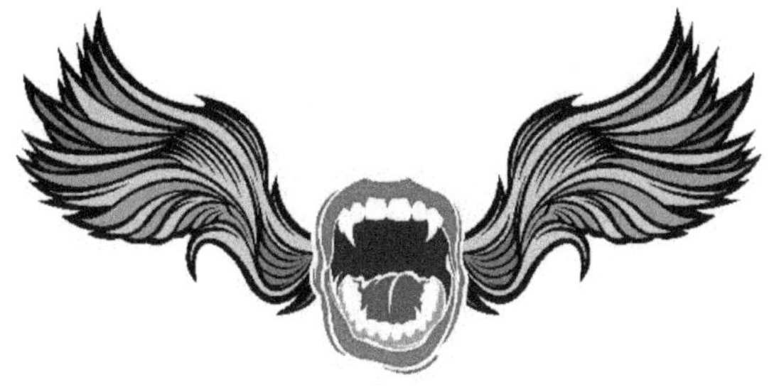

HE PULLED AWAY, GENTLY setting my bathrobe back in place, and the disappointment overwhelmed me. I covered my face and rolled away from him, the volatility in my range of emotions grating on my nerves. On some level, I knew this was a normal part of the transition between being mortal and turning into an immortal monster.

"You don't have to be a monster," he said with his back to me. "It's a choice."

I didn't see how, not with the waves of hunger that kept knocking me senseless. Without elaborating, he got up and left me alone in the bedroom. I reached up and pulled the pillow from under the covers, hugging it. Burning tears choked my throat, and I nuzzled into the soft down with the sweet taste of his blood still in my mouth.

Exhaustion settled in, and I closed my eyes.

Night Hawk
Chapter Eight
Damian

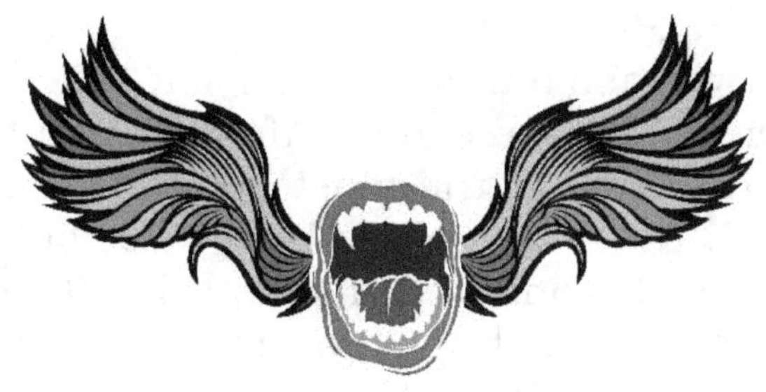

I CROSSED TO THE bar in the corner of the living room and pulled the stopper out of the flask, holding an aged brandy. I poured myself a drink, swirling the amber liquid in the glass, watching as it coated the crystal before retreating in a sensuous liquid dance. I sighed and closed my eyes, downing the alcohol, feeling the heat spread through my system like a wildfire spreading through the dry California timber.

I slammed the glass on the counter and gripped the edge of the bar, feeling the burn now. I clenched my jaw against the sudden pain in my abdomen, knowing it would abate but relishing the momentary punishment. It took a few minutes before the burning agony subsided and I stumbled to the easy chair, dropping into it with relief.

Alcohol always made me feel more human than demon and I sighed, rubbing my face and looking toward the bedroom. Just the thought of her almost brought me to my feet, but I resisted. Instead, I analyzed what made her so damn hypnotizing.

Beauty wasn't the reason I felt like a horny teenager in her presence. After all, I had held court with some of the most beautiful women in the world. No, it was something more subtle and elusive and I wondered if it was her blood that connected me to her, that made me want to protect her, even from herself...even at my peril.

Guilt bit at the lining of my stomach and I shifted in the chair, keeping my eye on the hall in case the hunger overwhelmed her again. She had exercised a great deal of restraint already, showing coherent thought as opposed to ravenous rants.

I glanced at the clock and raised an eyebrow. Naomi had made it far longer than any of my other doomed bids for partnership.

Of course, none of them drank my blood beyond that first minor infusion.

My eyes widened, and I snapped the chair closed.

None of them had wanted my blood the way Naomi did.

Was it just newborn syndrome, or did she crave me as much as I craved her?

I stood and crossed the distance, pushing the bedroom door open. A slight rise and fall in her chest, the rhythm of sleep, greeted me and I sighed, leaning on the threshold and just watched her. My gaze traveled to the ceiling, and

I wondered if Michael would smite me the moment I stepped out of this hideaway.

If I were in his shoes, I would.

The shuffle of fabric caught my attention, and I dropped my gaze. Naomi rolled toward the door, tucking her hands neatly under her cheek in an angelic pose that slammed the point home.

I turned away, heading to gather her clothing before she woke. When I returned to the room, her breathing transitioned into a light snore that shattered the angelic vision and I smiled. I placed the pile at the foot of the bed and started out of the room.

"Don't go," her soft voice stopped me in my tracks.

"I can't stay," I said without turning.

"Why not?" she asked, the lilt in her voice that of curiosity as opposed to either hunger or lust, and I tensed, glancing back at her.

"Because."

It wasn't the answer she was looking for, but instead of the open hostility that would have brought to the surface a few hours ago, a vulnerable disappointment shifted through her features.

"Damian?" she said as I started out of the room again.

This time I turned. She sat with the covers pulled over her chest, her shoulders bare and the bathrobe hanging half in and half out of bed. Her disheveled hair and breathy pout set my heart on fire.

"What?" I tried to keep my voice from shaking, to keep the fear that now pounded in my veins away. The speed of her transition was not possible, there wasn't an ounce of bloodlust left in her gaze, what was there now was a curiosity that leaped from the depths of her mind like a beacon.

She looked around the room and back at me.

"This isn't a dream, is it?"

The sincerity and sweetness in her voice caught me off guard, and a lump formed in my throat. I shook my head slowly, and the guilt came crashing down, mowing me over like a rogue bulldozer. Overwhelming sadness hit and I stumbled from the room, falling to my knees in the hallway from the power of it.

The wrongness of it all tossed me into a dark pit of despair and I covered my face, horrified at what I had done.

When her hand slid onto my shoulder, I couldn't meet her gaze.

"I'm sorry," I whispered.

She didn't speak. She didn't tell me it was okay. Instead, she kneeled beside me and wrapped her arms around my shoulders and leaned her head against mine.

I turned, meeting her gaze, and she offered a conciliatory smile.

Jesus, how I wanted her, and I couldn't help myself this time. This time when I kissed her, it was met with surrender and I soared with the gentleness of it. This creature was so different in demeanor than the woman I turned. I wondered if it was indeed a dream.

"It's not," she whispered against my lips.

"Not what?" I pulled away, meeting her gaze.

"Not a dream," she answered, sending chills through my frame and before I could react, she pulled me into another kiss.

Night Hawk
Chapter Nine
Naomi

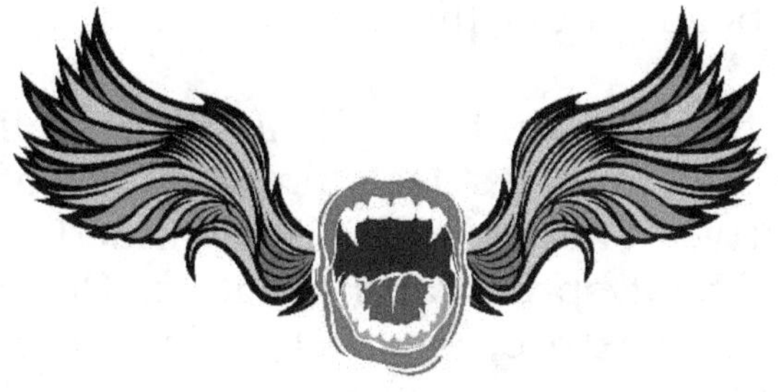

HE PICKED ME UP in his muscular arms and carried me to the bed. This time I was lucid and in control of all my faculties as opposed to the volatile she-devil that took over the moment his blood slammed down my throat. His touch ignited my skin, and his blue eyes sparkled with mischief and lust.

He stripped the bathrobe before he laid me on the satin sheets. He paused, taking a moment to scan me from head to toe, and the rapture in his expression left me breathless. No man had ever looked at me the way he was and when his gaze locked with mine, I couldn't help the thrill that blanketed me.

He stripped his shirt and my gaze traveled over his chiseled torso. The view was magnificent, and he crawled on the bed, straddling me and planting one of those kisses that should be illegal. My entire body melted into him.

When his lips left mine and trailed down the line of my neck, I tensed and he moved to my ear, taking my lobe in his mouth, sucking gently, before he whispered, "I'm not going to bite you."

The hushed timber of his voice lulled me, making my muscles feel like a mass of warm, silly putty. Wherever his lips landed, a small bloom of heat spread and I sighed. Damian was a volatile mixture, but at this moment, he displayed gentleness and tenderness I didn't think capable of a vampire. The way he teased with his hands and mouth drove me farther into the land of pleasure than I had experienced in my human life.

He took his sweet time with me; his slow progression south only heightened my anticipation. I couldn't help my comparison of him to my ex and I think I even chuckled, because Damian paused, meeting my gaze and offering a slow smile that promised so much more.

There was no comparison. Perhaps it was Damian's two thousand years' worth of experience versus the self-centered bastard who sold me out. This was miles away from the "if you won't fuck me, you better damn well suck me" attitude Mark had.

I could get used to this pampering.

Damian stopped at my belly button and tilted his head, sending a questioning stare in my direction, pulling my attention back to him.

"He really treated you like that?"

I blinked and raised an eyebrow. The idea that Damian heard my thoughts sent another wave of chills over me, hardening my nipples further. I didn't speak, but I nodded, confirming his question.

Damian's eyes flashed with a brutal anger and he took a deep breath, closing his eyes a moment before he leveled his gaze at me. "Let me show you how a goddess should be treated," he said and continued his slow progression.

Did he just call me a goddess?

The sideways glance and sudden appearance of dimples confirmed he could read my mind just as easily as if I had spoken aloud. When his mouth dropped between my legs, all thought ceased and only the tendrils of erotic pleasure remained. Slow circles of his tongue caressed my clit, and I voiced the thrill with a wordless purr.

He toyed with me, licking, stroking until I couldn't catch my breath and a hot wave started in my toes, traveling with lightning speed.

"Oh...my...god!" I gasped as aftershocks wracked my form.

He slid his finger inside me and stopped. His eyebrows arched and his mouth dropped open just before his gaze shot to mine. "You're a virgin?" his breathless question caught me off guard and I met his shocked stare.

Consuming heat still filled my form, and I nodded, not understanding the shadow that passed over his face. He slowly pulled away from me; the absence of him cooling my fiery skin and slamming a layer of disappointment over my already raw nerves.

"Is..." I started and swallowed the question back. Mark hated that I was a virgin, and he tried to undo that at every opportunity. I wondered if it would be the same with Damian. "Is that a bad thing?"

Damian laughed, settling over me, his jeans still on, but I could feel the hard outline of him against my crotch and, for a second, I wanted to throw my virginity to the wind and give Damian exactly what Mark coveted.

Damian caught me with another kiss, tender and soft. When he pulled away, he studied my face, tracing his fingers over the skin, and a set of small chills traversed my spine.

"No, it isn't a bad thing. Besides, I wouldn't dream of forcing you into anything you're not ready for," he said.

Blue eyes that held the secrets to this dark world stared at me. His heart pounded against mine and the feel of him on top of me was more natural than anything I imagined. He was right, there was so much I didn't know about vampires and this was one facet I never believed existed.

Night Hawk
Chapter Ten
Damian

HER LIPS WERE SOFT under my fingertips, and I sighed, looking back into her dark eyes. She wasn't ready for this and the thought of the mind games that bastard played on her turned my lust into a simmering anger that I couldn't wait to unleash. If I ever ran into him on the street, I'd make him suffer before I killed him.

A slow, evil smile surfaced. Instead of waiting for a chance, maybe I'd seek him out.

"What are you thinking?" she asked.

"You don't want to know." I glanced at the clock and then back at her. "Congratulations, you've made it longer than any other human I've had the misfortune of turning."

She ran her palm over my cheek. "You know, I'm usually not this easy." Her gaze flicked between us and back to mine. "And I'm surprised you didn't take advantage of the situation earlier when I was in she-devil mode."

"I'm not a shallow bastard like your ex," I said, and her eyes flashed. Her body stiffened under me and I tilted my head, studying her emotional state, wondering if I had pushed the button that would bring the crazy fiend back.

"I'm not sure what I'm going to do about him," Naomi said, her teeth raked her lower lip as she contemplated different forms of revenge.

Every single thought that rang through her mind brought a smile to my lips. She certainly knew how to deliver justice, and when her gaze cleared and she met mine, her cheeks flushed with embarrassment.

"Your ideas on vengeance are quite unique," I said and rolled off her. "Remind me never to piss you off."

Her laugh filled the room, and she sat up, reaching for her clothing. Much to my disappointment, she covered her delectable form. Naomi turned and leveled a glare in my direction.

"It's too late for that. I am already pissed at you because I'll never feel the warmth of the sun on my face ever again."

My smile faded, and I shrugged. "But you will own the night."

Night Hawk
Chapter Eleven
Naomi

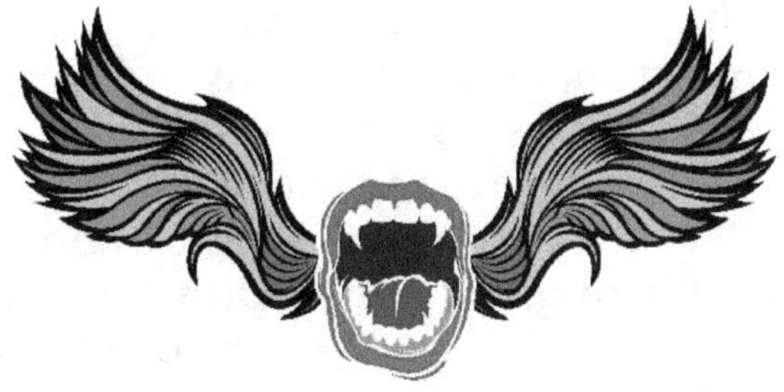

DAMIAN PROPPED HIMSELF ON his elbow, offering another smile. "You will," he added when I just stared at him.

The clock display flipped to five o'clock. I couldn't remember if it was dark at five at this time of year and I wanted to get out of this cave. Tendrils of claustrophobia tickled my psyche, and I shifted.

"How long?" I nodded toward the clock.

"Just a few more minutes. I want to make sure there is no more light in the sky." He rolled off the bed, grabbing the crumpled shirt off the ground and slipped it on. "We need to get you some clothes tonight."

"You trust me around people?" I asked, thinking about the uncontrollable rush I had earlier when I realized humans were just a floor away. I could only imagine the damage I could do in a crowded store.

"I think you'll be okay," he said, but the crease between his eyes said otherwise.

"Really." I crossed my arms and raised an eyebrow.

He smiled and focused on buttoning his shirt, and then he crossed to me. "We'll find out."

Discomfort made me shift my stance. "I don't relish the idea of losing control."

"The constant driving need for blood is a fallacy. The only time a vampire has insane cravings is during the day. That's why there are so few of us still alive. Most give in and go in search of food and once they step into the sun, bam, they're dead. I've learned that feeding at least once at night makes the daylight hours more bearable," he said. "Also, a shot of whiskey helps temper the urge."

I stared at him, his words sinking in, and I narrowed my gaze. "You said the teeth only go sharp at night, but earlier when I attacked you, mine came out."

He grinned and shrugged. "Under normal circumstances, they only come out at night. Last night wasn't normal." He reached over and wiped a stray hair out of my face. "We're vulnerable during the day. Not just from sunlight, but from our enemies. That's why I brought you here. This is one of the few places Lucifer doesn't know I have."

That name sent a flush of fury through me and my jaw tensed. "He is on the top of my hit list."

Damian laughed at me and leaned really close. "Get in line."

The menace in his voice made me recoil, and I stepped away from him.

"Let's go get you a new wardrobe," he said and took my hand, leading me out of the bunker and into a beautiful two-story atrium enclosed in glass.

Views of a full moon met us and I sighed, looking around toward the door to our daytime sanctuary. My gaze traveled over an ornately painted wall, and I turned my attention back to Damian. "Where's the door?"

He smiled. "It's a secret." With that, he led me outside and pulled a set of keys from his pocket, opening a door to another extensive building. Even in the darkened enclosure, I could see just as clearly as if it was daytime, and I gasped at the site before me.

Damian settled on a specific key and led me to an Aston Martin, opening the door for me. I scanned the rest of the cars and met his gaze.

"I collect cars." He gave me a half-shouldered shrug and waved me into the Aston.

"But these are rare," I said, finally finding my voice. He even had a mint condition Benz Motorwagon and a Ford Model T.

"Sweetheart, I was here even before chariots were the bomb." He pointed to an ornate chariot in the far corner and returned his amused gaze to mine.

He closed the passenger door and trotted around to the driver's side, settling in and pushing a button on a remote attached to the visor. The doors slid open, and he pulled out into the night, waiting for the doors to close again before speeding off.

When he pulled into the garage at the Stamford Town Center, I raised an eyebrow.

"It isn't Fifth Avenue, but it's close and you have your choice of designer shops."

"I can't afford this," I said, waving my hand at the fancy shops. I was lucky to afford Wal-Mart.

"I can. Besides, I can't have you walking around all day in a bathrobe."

"I never asked you to do this," I snapped. His audacity unnerved me.

He smiled. "I know you didn't."

"Why don't you just take me to my apartment and I'll pack up my stuff."

His smile vanished. "Because the demons will wait for you there and until you learn the ropes, I'm not letting you anywhere near those sadistic bastards."

"I can take care of myself." I saw the flash of aggravation in his eyes and the muscle in his jaw jumped. "You're not my keeper," I added, pushing his buttons.

He stopped and leveled a glare at me, pulling me close to him. "I am your keeper. I became your keeper when you sank your teeth into my throat last night. You became my responsibility instead of my victim." He let go of my wrist and stepped away, putting a little distance between us and diffusing the building tension.

I kept my instinctual response to myself, waiting for him to calm down. Instead, I studied him under the bright interior lights. His wavy black hair fell in haphazard swirls, framing a face that should have been accompanied by angel wings. Muscles rippled under his shirt as he fought the growing frustration. He obviously wasn't used to a self-sufficient woman.

He rolled his eyes at me.

"Are you in my head again?"

Damian's cheeks bloomed red, and his gaze snapped away from mine. "Just pick out a couple of outfits, so we can get out of here," he said.

I considered telling him to go to hell, but then I thought of another day hanging in his sanctuary with only a bathrobe and his hungry gaze. That clinched it and I turned, stomping into the upscale mall and scanning the store names, unsure of where I should go.

He decided for me, steering me into Saks Fifth Avenue.

I approached a rack of blouses and glanced at one of the price tags. My jaw dropped. Over two hundred dollars for just a simple blouse, and my gaze shot to Damian's.

"Damian, I'm sorry, but I can't let you spend this kind of money on me. All I need is a comfortable pair of yoga pants and a few t-shirts." I bit my lip. "And maybe a quick stop at Victoria's Secret so I can get some underwear."

He scoffed at me. "Money isn't an issue. Besides, I'd like you to have the opportunity to wear something dressier than yoga pants when we go out. So, if you won't choose a few outfits, I'll choose for you." He strolled through the store, casually inspecting the clothing displays. When he stopped at a rack with a beautiful blue cocktail dress, one that I secretly envied, he glanced at me, his eyes sizing me up before he pulled one from the group.

"I think that's your size," he said, and I glanced at the label, nodding. The man had impeccable taste in clothing and when my arms were full, he sent me to the dressing room, taking a seat outside the entrance, waiting for me to model his choices.

I slid the blue dress on and after maneuvering the zipper up my back; I turned and looked in the mirror. While the dress was stunning, it didn't quite go with my cowboy boots. I smiled at the mismatched combination and strode out to where he sat.

Night Hawk
Chapter Twelve
Damian

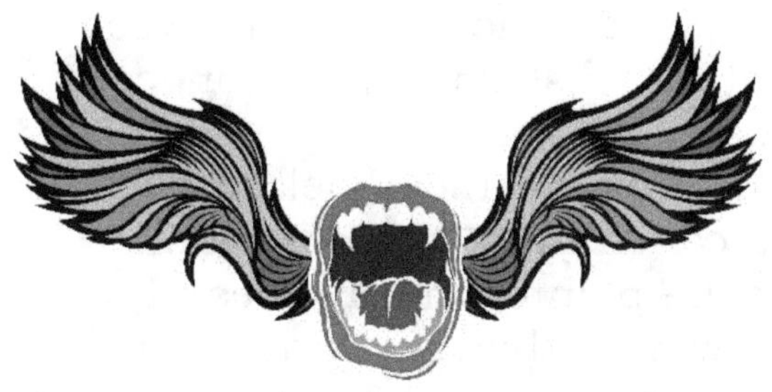

WHEN NAOMI STEPPED INTO the doorway wearing the blue designer dress I picked out for her, my breath locked in my throat. Stunning was an understatement and I'm sure my face reflected the shock because she grinned and twirled, her eyes sparkling with humor.

"You like?" she asked.

I did my best to pull myself together, but my voice still cracked when I said, "Yes."

With each mini-catwalk display of hers, I got hornier and hornier and I could tell by the way she flipped her hair and flaunted her body in the form fitting clothing that she knew the effect she was having on me.

I glanced around and made sure none of the salespeople were within range and slipped into the dressing room. When the dressing room door swung opened, I pushed her back inside, latching the door and planting a hungry kiss. My hands traveled over the silky fabric of the tank top and yoga pants she had donned.

"You are the hottest thing this side of Eden," I whispered when she pushed me away.

"Damian, this is the women's dressing room," she whispered, the crease between her eyes along with the stern expression conveying her disdain.

"I don't care. You look delectable." I licked my lips and leaned in to kiss her again.

Her palm planted on my chest, holding me far enough away to thwart my attempt. "Buying me shit doesn't give you the right to do anything you please," she said.

The admonishment hit home, and I stepped back, my libido in check and aggravation replacing the heat burning inside me. Putting my palms up, I took another step. "Sorry, you just...I just..." Frustration at not being able to articulate swelled. "Shit, Naomi, do you have any idea just how fucking hot you are?"

"So you think I'm hot, big deal? Mark thought I was hot, too. Look where that got me," she snapped, her voice turning feral. "And it doesn't give you the right to come in here and pin me to the wall. That may have been fine and dandy when you were human, but it doesn't work that way these days. You do not own me."

I stared at her and a new thought formed, one I hadn't considered. Maybe she didn't feel the same electricity I did.

"So...you're not feeling the same connection. I get it," I said and reached for the door.

"Damian?" Her exasperated voice stopped me.

"What?"

"It has only been one day..." she whispered. "Give it a rest."

The desperation in her eyes clinched it and I nodded, sneaking out of the dressing room and running smack into a salesclerk at the entrance.

"Excuse me, sir, but you can't be in here," the platinum blonde said, her hands on her hips and her lips pursed in reprimand.

"I'm sorry, but my friend needed a hand with her zipper," I said, just as Naomi stepped from the dressing room with her arms full of clothing. "We'll take everything she has," I added, nodding in Naomi's direction.

Naomi traded an awkward smile with me and handed over the pile to the beaming salesclerk.

I slipped my wallet from the inside of my coat and handed the clerk a credit card. Naomi snickered and turned away, but I caught the dimples before her hair covered her smirk. I shrugged at the saleswoman and offered my best smile, the one I reserved for charming the pants off unsuspecting women, and it worked wonders. She immediately focused just on me, almost salivating, as she rang up the purchase.

Once the transaction was completed, the slip signed and the card back in my wallet, I gave her a nod and took the bags, leading Naomi out of the store with a sideways glance.

"What's your problem?" I asked.

"A vamp with a credit card. It just struck me as funny."

"I'm not a thief." My voice carried a measure of defensiveness and I snapped my mouth closed and tossed the bags into the trunk, slamming it shut.

"Lighten up, dude," she said when I got into the driver's seat and I turned on her.

"Part of surviving is blending in."

"Oh yeah, turning into a giant hawk certainly constitutes blending in." She rolled her eyes.

"Keep pushing and I'll bend you right over my knee."

She burst out laughing. "I'd like to see you try," she said and crossed her arms.

I didn't take kindly to anyone laughing at me and put the car in gear, tearing out of the garage in frustration. I couldn't recall a woman ever getting under my skin the way Naomi did, and I slid my glance in her direction. The chemistry between us was certainly volatile, and I didn't know whether it would ignite or explode.

"Aren't you supposed to be teaching me how to survive?" she asked after a few minutes of strained silence.

I refocused on the road ahead of me and sighed. "Yes. I need to teach you to hunt, otherwise tomorrow will be more of a challenge than today was and I'm not sure I can function after another night of offering myself up as an alternative whenever you get hungry." I met her gaze. "Unless your intention *is* to kill me."

Night Hawk
Chapter Thirteen
Naomi

MY EYES WIDENED AND the anger flared at his thinly veiled accusation, my skin heating with a burning sensation. "If I wanted you dead, you would be," I snapped and looked out at the passing scenery.

He laughed and sent a raised eyebrow in my direction. I could almost hear the response, but he never voiced the words. The look was enough.

"I know how to hunt," I mumbled under my breath, thinking how nice it would be to have my twelve-gauge right about now. I'd pump a round into his pompous ass.

When he pulled into the garage, he turned to me.

"Wait here," he said and grabbed the clothing from the trunk, disappearing with the pile and coming back a few minutes later with the leather jacket I wore last night along with his black trench coat. He tossed the leather jacket to me and waited while I slipped it over my shoulders.

"It's time to learn to be a shadow," he said in a low growl, stepping from the dark corner and flashing a mouthful of sharp fangs. And his bright blue eyes were shrouded in blackness.

I took a step back, and before I realized it, my skin had broken out in a full rash of gooseflesh. The persona he wore scared me as much as it had last night, and I had to remind myself he couldn't hurt me. Not now that I was just like him, but it still didn't alleviate most of the unease racking my bones.

He took a predatory step toward me and tilted his head. "You should be nervous," he snarled.

His voice promised pain, and I took another step back, swallowing the lump of fear blocking my throat. "Cut it out, Damian." I tried to keep my voice steady, but I failed, and the shakes came through loud enough for him to chuckle.

Even his chuckle resounded with pure evil. I turned and ran.

He stalked me through the maze of cars, catching me as I made a run for the door. Instead of tearing my throat open with his teeth, he stopped when the sharp points grazed my skin. With his hand still holding a fistful of my hair, he pulled away, meeting my frightened gaze with a quizzical one of his own.

"Naomi," he started and sniffed me, "I suggest you start defending yourself, otherwise I am going to drain every drop of your sweet blood." He clacked his teeth together and let out a vicious purr.

This was the fiend that attacked me last night. Not the sweet and sexy man I spent the day with and a fury I couldn't control welled up. With a growl, I shoved him away from me and shock gripped me as he flew across the garage, into the cement column between two of the doors.

He was slow to get up, and the persona fell back to Damian, the man instead of the shadow monster. He ran his hand over the back of his head and brought the blood-covered appendage into view before his eyes rolled back in his head and he dropped.

I caught him before he hit the ground. My heart pounded in my chest and my mouth ran dry. A different type of fear took hold, and I laid his injured head on my lap, tapping his cheeks and whispering his name. He didn't respond and I could feel the rising panic.

"Please wake up, Damian," I said. "Please, please wake up!" I glanced toward the ceiling, praying silently for him to wake, for him not to die and leave me here without a clue of how to get into his sanctuary and away from the imminent sunrise.

Without thinking, I ripped my wrist open, placing the flowing wound over his mouth. At first, nothing happened, and a sob escaped my chest. Finally, his throat constricted, swallowing, and his hand grabbed the outside of my wrist, clamping it to his mouth, sucking the blood in one hard pull that burned through my veins.

I tried to break his grasp, but he was just too strong and my sob turned to a frightened gasp.

His eyelids fluttered open and his gaze met mine before widening. He let go of my wrist, licking his lips and blinking in confusion as I covered the wound with my hand.

"I didn't know what else to do," I whispered.

Damian slowly sat up and leaned against the wall, staring at me.

"I could have killed you, Naomi," he said, his voice raspy and unsteady.

I narrowed my eyes and hopped to my feet, unsure of where my fury was coming from. "Wasn't that your intent with this little game?" I waved at the interior of the garage.

"No," he said and felt the back of his head again.

His tone diffused me completely and when his gaze returned to mine, I couldn't help taking a step toward him.

"You never offer your open wrist to a wounded vampire." He pushed himself to his feet and took an unsteady step toward the door.

"Why not?"

"Because when we're wounded, we rarely have the sense to stop."

"But you..." I started, thinking about how he offered himself up to me more than once last night.

"Yes, and you could have killed me, but you seem to have a powerful sense of self-discipline," he stumbled out into the night.

I followed, letting his words sink in as well as all the ramifications of what he had done since he sank his fangs into my skin struck me silent.

"I need to eat," he whispered and headed toward the wood line.

"Is that what I'll turn into?" I asked, pointing back toward the garage as I caught up with him.

He offered a tired smile. "Honestly, I have no idea what you'll turn into. The fangs are supposed to come out as a defense mechanism, but yours didn't."

"They came out on the roof last night and I think they made an appearance during the day, didn't they?" I asked.

"Yeah, I guess," he said and stopped as we stepped into the forest.

"So…"

"Shush." He closed his eyes and sniffed the air. A slow smile spread across his lips. "I'll be right back," he said and sprinted. Within three paces, magnificent wings pounded the air, and he soared into the treetops, leaving me alone and acutely aware of the silence surrounding me.

Night Hawk
Chapter Fourteen
Damian

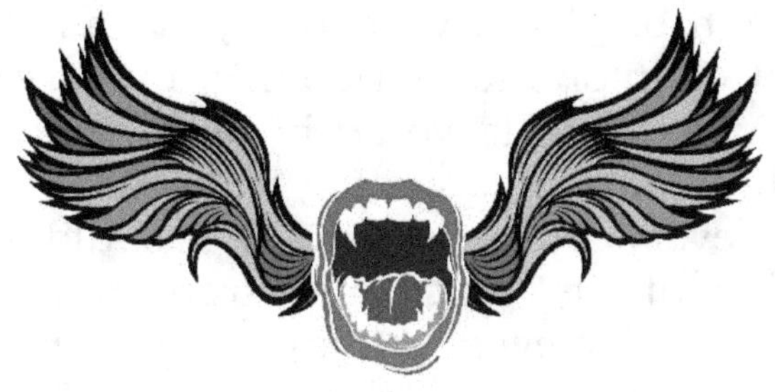

THE COOL NIGHT AIR shuffled through my feathers and I glanced down at her as I pounded the wings, taking me higher over the forest top, heading toward dinner. The forest opened to a small glen filled with deer and I swooped down from the heavens and snatched the largest doe in my talons before any of them understood the danger.

The flight back was harder considering my already exhausted state of mind and when I landed, pinning the deer beneath my talon, I turned my hawk gaze to Naomi.

She stared at the deer and then brought her shocked gaze to mine.

It was clear she didn't understand, and I willed myself back into human form. Without the strength of my talon holding her to the ground, the doe struggled to her feet.

"Food," I said to Naomi and again I got the dumb stare. "If you won't take her down, I will," I snarled and caught the deer before she was able to find her footing, my teeth buried in the soft flesh of her throat, and I was rewarded with the warm rush of blood. Of course, it wasn't nearly as sweet or hypnotic as Naomi's, but it was food none-the-less and it would bring me back to full strength, which I desperately needed.

With every ounce I drank, I could feel the expansion of my cells, the strength returning, and I closed my eyes, pulling every ounce of the hundred ounces out of the carcass. When there was no more, I dropped the dead husk on the ground and wiped my mouth with my shirtsleeve, willing my teeth to retract.

Naomi still stared, and I approached her, exhilarated by the blood. Her gaze pulled from the dead deer to me, and I had to remind myself she was new at this, but the horror reflected in her eyes caught me off guard.

"It's more palatable than tearing a human's throat and draining them," I said. "Besides, this will give the people living in the house a couple week's worth of venison, so it's a bonus."

Her eyebrows rose and her glance jumped from mine to the deer.

"I thought you said you had been hunting before."

She nodded and licked her lips, still unable to speak.

"Naomi, you have to eat tonight."

"Why?" she asked with a whisper of a voice.

"Because come daylight, your training begins and you will need all the strength you can get," I said and pulled her into my arms and planted a kiss, exploring her mouth with my tongue, letting her taste the remnants of blood. I prayed that would set her appetite on fire and I smiled at the shift. Her fangs finally made an appearance.

When I pulled away, the feral hunger in her eyes sent a warning siren through me and I pointed toward the glen. Her gaze landed on my throat and I stepped back, turning and taking flight, drawing her toward the herd.

She sounded like a hungry pride of cats running through the woods and I knew with that approach, she would find herself standing in the field alone. I swooped behind her, wrapping my talon around her waist, and started toward the treetops. When we cleared the brush, I soared, hearing her gasp at the dizzying height.

She held onto my talons like a frightened child and I wanted to tell her she was safe, but a hawk can't speak, at least not in the way human ears would understand. I made a lazy pass over the glen, making sure the herd was still there and Naomi panted in my grasp, her eyes locked on our prey. Her hunger and impatience overwhelmed me and I dove toward the meadow, dropping her right on the back of a large buck.

I swooped, landing on a thick branch at the edge of the woods, turning in time to see the remainder of the herd galloping into the forest underneath my perch. Naomi had her hand wrapped around one antler and her face nuzzled into the deer's throat despite the animal's struggles. She wrestled it to the ground, still drinking as the beast huffed and tried to shake her off.

The death throes of the buck slowed, and then stopped altogether, but Naomi kept her grip, tilting the massive head to get better access until she finally released, and slowly stood.

I transitioned and jumped off the branch, landing on the soft grass in a crouch, my gaze locked on her in case she was still overwhelmed by the shadow thirst. Her chest rose and fell, signs that the blood was working her muscles and when her dark gaze shifted to mine, her lips stretched into a feral smile, revealing the razor-sharp teeth we were known for.

She moved faster than I did, and the hard ground met my back with the force of her tackle. I stared up into her wild eyes and grabbed a fistful of her hair, keeping her teeth away from my throat with brute strength. They snapped together in a click, followed by a growl so fierce it struck fear in me.

"Naomi!" I yelled and rolled, pinning her below me.

She struggled, snarling like a wildcat caught in a snare and I held fast, knowing the effects would wear off in a matter of minutes, but I was exposed, with my hands wrapped around her wrists and my knees squeezing her hips.

She lunged, her teeth scratching my arm, and I shifted, widening her span.

"Naomi." This time I whispered, soft and seductive, hoping my charm would calm her.

Her eyes locked with mine, and her struggling ceased. The fangs retracted, and she blinked up at me before her gaze turned to the meadow surrounding us in confusion.

I released her wrists and sat back on my heels, mopping my face with my palm.

"What happened?"

Chuckling, I swung to the side and took a seat on the grass next to her, pointing at the massive antlers peeking out of the long grass.

She sat up and stared, her eyebrows arching before her head swung in my direction.

"I did that?" she asked, her graceful finger pointed toward the dead buck.

"Yes."

Silence settled.

"I remember nothing beyond you kissing me," she whispered.

I stretched out on the grass and stared up at the stars, trying to remember those first days and nights, and I came up blank as well. In two thousand years, I never got through more than a couple days with a fledgling before disaster struck in some form, so I never had a chance to really talk to those I cursed with this existence.

"I don't remember much about those first few days either," I said, and she turned her beautiful brown eyes in my direction. When she stretched out next to me, I continued, "Of course I was locked in a pit and when I came to my senses, every vampire was in pieces."

She reached over and pulled my hand off my chest, lacing her fingers through mine. The gesture silenced me and I stared at her. I realized in that moment that I really wanted nothing bad to happen to this girl, and I swallowed the lump in my throat. Being associated with me seemed to be bad luck and I pulled my hand out of her grasp, getting to my feet without meeting her gaze.

I crossed to the buck and stared at the carcass.

"Do you want the head mounted?" I asked when she joined me and she flinched. "You don't want a trophy of your first kill?"

"God, no," she gasped and disappointment flushed my skin. "My father asked me the same thing when I shot my first deer a few years ago. I said no to him, too." She met my gaze.

It was nice to know it wasn't just this situation, and I nodded. I glanced around the meadow and sighed. "I'm not going to be able to bring you and the buck back in one trip."

Her eyebrows rose.

"Deerskin and venison," I said and glanced at the buck. "Although I think it'll take me the rest of the night to skin these and pack the freezer."

"Damian?"

I turned to her. "Hmm?"

"When arc we going after Luc..."

I clamped my hand over her mouth and shook my head. "Not here," I whispered, and her eyebrows creased. "When I think you're ready," I answered and waved her back, "Until then," I closed my eyes and the transformation took hold.

Night Hawk
Chapter Fifteen
Naomi

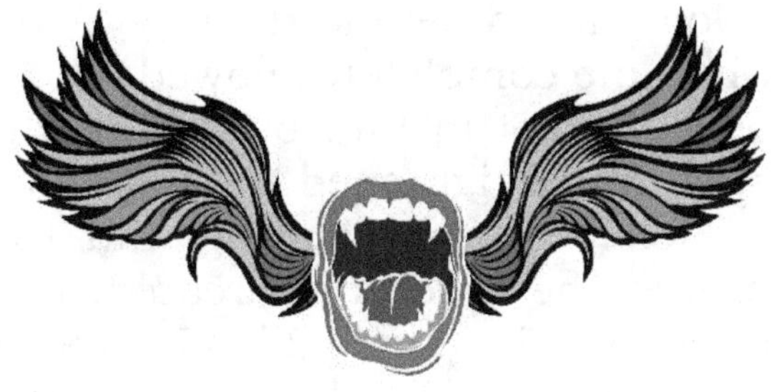

ONE MOMENT HE WAS in human form and the next, the giant hawk spread his wings and, with the buck in his claw, he took off, leaving me alone in the quiet meadow. I glanced up at the unobstructed view of the stars and sighed. I had never seen them so clear and crisp and I stretched on the grass, waiting for him to return.

My thoughts wandered back to the prior evening. The last thing I remembered was sitting at dinner with Mark and sipping the wine he ordered. A black rage gripped me and I sat up, my fists clenching and my skin tingling with the power of the vengeance filling my soul.

The bastard drugged me and the walk from the restaurant to the apartment building across the street was a haze. I don't remember the elevator ride or much of the conversation Mark had, but I remember his unfeeling gaze when he handed me over to that crazy demon.

His words pulled a growl from my throat.

"I don't know why you want her. She's nothing but a tease anyway," he had said and then the door closed behind them.

Mark had me completely snowed.

My foolish belief in him burned in the pit of my stomach and I tightened my jaw. The flap of his wings fell over the clearing and the grass swayed under the breeze he created. Instead of gripping me in his talons like I expected, his hand landed on my shoulder and he took a seat next to me.

He didn't speak. Instead, his hands fidgeted until he finally sighed. "Your ex is a supreme asshole."

I burst out laughing, giving Damian a sideways glance. "Right now, I think all men are assholes." The fallen expression and quiet "oh" amused me and he looked away. I studied him without the flush of hunger roiling in my blood. He had a handsome profile and when his lips formed a smirk, I knew he was hearing my thoughts, but this time I continued staring, trying to figure this creature out.

"Have you been alone all this time?"

He twitched and picked a blade of grass, twirling it around his finger slowly, not answering right away. "Yes and no," he said and stood. "Come on." He reached a hand out to me and I took it, surprised when he led me into the thick woods by foot.

"You must have been very lonely," I said as the forest swallowed us.

His light laugh filled the air. "You have no idea."

"So, no vamp mistresses in all this time?" I teased.

He sent a silent grin in my direction, but as we walked, his smile faded, and his expression turned contemplative. "No," he said and ran a hand through the loose waves of his thick hair. "I've destroyed every vampire that has crossed my path and anyone I turned only lasted a couple of days before something bad happened."

The admission stunned me. "Have you ever been in love?"

His gait slowed, and he turned toward me. "Once, when I was human," he said and shrugged. "I vaguely remember the feeling, but the crushing devastation of losing her can still drop me to my knees if I let it."

Truth rang in his words and the emptiness in the center of my body grew along with a profound sadness. I crossed the distance and wrapped my arms around him. Damian stiffened under the warm hug.

"I'm so sorry," I whispered in his ear and his arms encircled me, holding me tight.

"I haven't felt any deep emotion except rage since she died," he whispered with a trembling voice, and his hands dropped to my waist, pushing me away. "Until you bit me." He offered a crooked smile. "And since then, I've pretty much been scared senseless."

"You afraid of dying?"

He laughed and his shoulders relaxed. "No. I'm not afraid to die."

I believed him. "Then why are you scared?"

His smile slowly faded, and he took a deep breath. "Because you are someone I don't want to lose."

My mouth popped open, and I stared into the bright blue of his irises. Something deep within me stirred, and I reached up, running my hand over his smooth cheek. His eyes closed, and he leaned his forehead against mine.

"Well, well, well," a voice boomed, and Damian reacted, spinning around to face the owner of the voice.

I stood on my tiptoes to get a glimpse over Damian's shoulder, and he blocked part of my view, but what I saw chilled me to the core. Pristine white wings fluttered, and I had a good idea about who interrupted the tender moment.

The sudden shift in Damian's stance, along with the tightening of the muscles in his back, conveyed the growing tension.

"What in the name of heaven do you think you're doing?" the angel growled, his voice rippling through the trees like a hurricane gale.

"Michael, I, uh," Damian stuttered but stood his ground.

He trembled under my hand and I moved to his side, jutting my chin out in defiance at the angry angel.

The angel was as glorious as Damian was, and his dark eyes snapped to mine. For a moment, the angry features softened, but then the hardness returned and he glared at Damian.

"I should have ground you to dust years ago," he growled.

The sudden wave of heat hit and I stepped in front of Damian, blocking whatever punishment this angel was hell bent on delivering. "Don't!"

Michael blinked, and his hands dropped to his side. Chilly air settled between the three of us.

"Why not?"

"Because he didn't intend to turn me."

"I know. He intended to kill you," the angel said. "And that goes against every rule I set down when I pulled him out of that dark pit."

"No matter what his original intent was, he saved me from Lucifer," I said. "If he hadn't been blinded by his hatred, he wouldn't have been there to pluck me out of the sky." I could tell my argument was softening the mighty archangel. "I am still alive." I spread my arms.

"You are a shadow," he spit.

"Damian says I still contain the light."

Michael studied me, his eyes narrowing. "He would have been there to save you if he hadn't lost sight of my bloodline."

I couldn't find a sound argument for that except that Damian couldn't be everywhere at once, and I wondered how many distant relatives I had. "How can you expect one man to be everywhere, overseeing all of us at once?" I asked, voicing the thought as it popped into my head.

"I gave him wings to oversee my lineage."

That's why he can shapeshift into a hawk. I glanced over my shoulder at Damian. His gaze was glued to the forest floor at his feet, and shame heated his cheeks. I turned back toward Michael.

"Why aren't *you* protecting your lineage?"

Anger transitioned back into his features. "Watch your tone, child."

"Naomi, don't," Damian whispered, and his hand settled on my shoulder at the same time Michael spoke. I shook it off, sending a glare at him before turning back to my distant kin.

"Damian may be immortal in some respects, but you can't expect him to be everywhere like you can be. After all, he still is human." A raw anger bubbled up inside me at the audacity of this being.

"I am not God. I can't be everywhere, either," Michael growled.

"Why weren't you there to protect me?"

His jaw tightened, and he leveled his intimidating stare at me. "I think it's time to send you back to hell." His gaze transitioned to Damian.

I reacted before either of them could. When my fangs sank into Michael's throat, both Damian and the angel gasped. Knowledge flowed with the archangel's blood, overwhelming me. Snapshots of information danced on my eyelids.

The promise of heaven.

Michael's love for humankind.

His hatred for Lucifer and every nocturnal creature the demon created.

His joy and love for Athena's mother.

The creation of my bloodline.

His devastation at his daughter's death.

His fury when he pulled Damian from the pit of slaughtered vampires.

The covenant Damian made to protect Zoe and the bloodline.

Pure light fused with my shadow cells, and I moaned. Arms grasped me around the waist, yanking me away. Stunned, I stared at Michael, while Damian whispered softly in my ear, begging for me to stop before Michael lost his temper and reduced me to ashes.

"You were Athena's father?" I asked when I found my voice. I realized how stupid that question was, considering the amount of information his blood infused in me.

Michael stared, just as dumfounded as Damian was when I bit him that first time. He blinked, swiping the remnants of blood still speckling his neck. Michael stared at his hand, and then his gaze snapped to mine.

Damian still held me in his grasp, and the tremors of fear flowing through him were palpable in the air. I wrapped my arms over his to calm him while keeping Michael's gaze.

"Damian has done your bidding for over two thousand years," I said. "What makes you think he won't continue for another two thousand years?"

"He made a fatal mistake," Michael said.

"Yes. He made a mistake, but I wouldn't categorize it as fatal. If you decide to destroy him, you'll have to go through me." I took a breath, wondering whether that would put a stay of execution in play or not. I shifted my weight, waiting for Michael's judgment.

Night Hawk
Chapter Sixteen
Damian

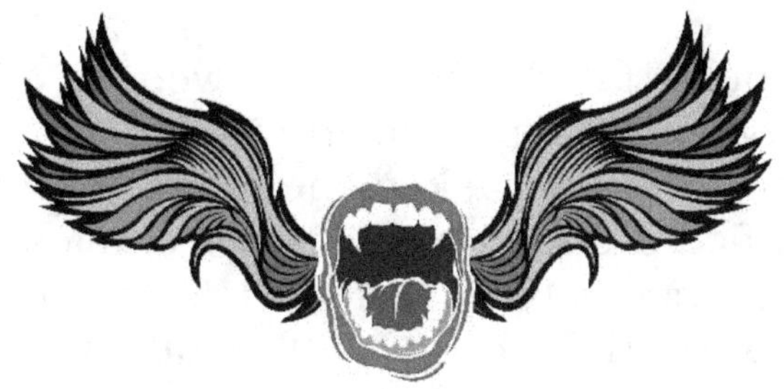

HER BLATANT DISREGARD FOR how dangerous an archangel was astounded me, and her ultimatum left every muscle in my body trembling, expecting the flash and then the nothingness of death that followed.

I unwrapped my arms from around her and pushed her to the side. "I can't let you do that," I said, despite the scream of every cell in my body fighting for self-preservation. If I had to sacrifice for her, I would.

I met Michael's glare, straightening my posture against the urge to cower. My heartbeat thundered in my ears, the pace much higher than its normal dormant beat, announcing my unease like a tribal drum.

"I need him," Naomi shouted as Michael's gaze narrowed.

Her declaration snapped my head in her direction and I arched my eyebrows. *She needs me?*

"Why?" Michael asked.

"Because he is going to help me take down Lucifer."

Michael's laugh filled the woods. "Darling, child. *You* cannot take down Lucifer."

"Why not?" she asked, her tone incredulous, and I stifled a smile at the sweet cluelessness of her innocence. My gaze found Michael's, and I offered a partial shrug at the question in his eyes.

"Do you not know who Lucifer is?" he asked and his arms fell to his sides, his posture relaxing and more quizzical than the deadly coil it was a moment ago.

"He's the king of hell. A fallen angel and all that hoopla," she said, waving her hand like it was just a trifle myth. "Can he not be destroyed, just like the rest of us?"

"Only I can destroy Lucifer," he started, and Naomi interrupted him.

"What about a descendent that has your blood pumping through her?"

She tilted her head, and I couldn't help the chill that layered over me, turning my skin into a relief map of gooseflesh.

Was that your real purpose in biting him?

She glanced in my direction and then back at Michael. "I'm not talking by birthright either," she added softly and licked her lips before flashing that heart-stopping smile.

Maybe she wasn't so innocent after all.

Michael crossed his arms, studying her. The seeds of possibility bloomed in his eyes and, for the first time since I spotted his angry glare, hope found its way into my heart.

Maybe we would make it through the night after all.

"What makes you so sure you can kill Lucifer?" he asked, his voice filled with a level of sarcasm I have never heard from him, and the hope I embraced moments ago evaporated.

She stepped closer to him, positioning herself between us. "I got to you, didn't I?" When she stepped into a familiar ready pose, I nearly laughed aloud.

Was she really challenging the archangel Michael to a fight?

Michael's expression mirrored mine for a fleeting instance, and then it hardened.

"Come on, gramps, let's see what you've got," she said, waving him in with her fingers.

Before her words sank in, Michael was in motion, his fists meant to inflict a lesson on this smart-ass child, but she parried, blocking his swings with a grace and speed that left me breathless. Instead of retreating, she stepped close, using the natural flow of her body and a sweep of her foot to knock Michael's feet out from under him. The angel fell to the ground with a thud that sent a tremor through the earth.

Naomi stood over him with a smug smile on her lips.

A moment later, she was on her back, the smile wiped from her lips, replaced by a shocked 'o', and Michael stood over her with a stern finger pointed in her direction. His lips pressed together, and he waved the finger at her before he stepped back, his face a mask of fury and frustration. But even he couldn't deny the talent she just displayed.

In two thousand years, I hadn't seen anyone, angel, demon, or human, take Michael down.

Silence blanketed the woods and then he turned on me with that fierce glare. "Make sure she goes for the kill when she does that, otherwise Lucifer will have her heart in his hand and that will be the end."

With that, he disappeared.

I stared at the spot he had occupied and swallowed, turning my gaze to her and reaching my hand out in silence. She stared at me for a moment and then accepted my hand, letting me help her to her feet.

"Gramps?" I asked after she brushed herself clean.

She chuckled and shrugged. "It was the first thing that came to mind," she admitted.

"You are insane," I said and joined her with a nervous chuckle.

I took her hand and resumed our journey back to the house. The walk would take us another hour and I considered flying, but I needed the quiet to digest what had just happened.

"Why did you try to protect me?" I asked after we covered half the distance.

She didn't answer right away.

"I don't know," she said, just when I thought she would not give me an answer.

I stopped and swung her to face me. "How do you not know your place in the universe?" I asked, the simmering anger surfacing. "He could have killed you like that." I snapped my fingers, voicing the fear that had shaken the very foundations of my soul.

"I'm part of his bloodline," she answered.

"Naomi, he has stamped out members of his bloodline before. Anyone who crosses the line and embraces evil is destroyed just on principle alone," I said, and she paled. "Thinking you're immune to his wrath is foolish."

I couldn't help the laugh that surfaced. "God, Naomi, that was one of the stupidest things I have ever seen!" I ran my hand through my hair and let her hand go, taking a seat on a nearby stump before my legs gave out from the sudden absence of stress. The complete relief of living through one of Michael's ultimatums took control of my form, sending tremors all the way to my bones.

Night Hawk
Chapter Seventeen
Naomi

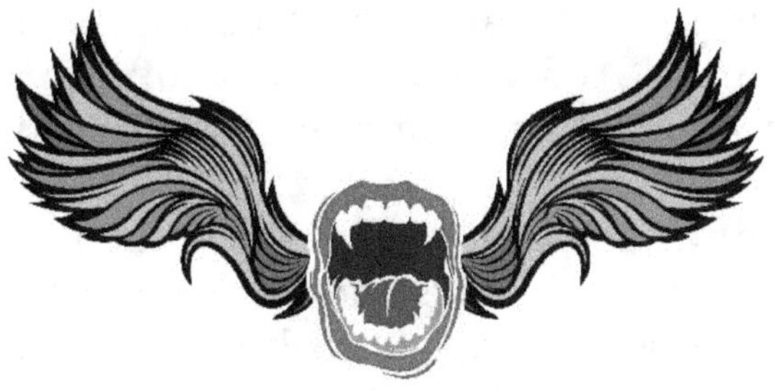

HIS TEETH CHATTERED AS IF it was below freezing, but the cold didn't penetrate our crystallized skin. I crossed and put my hand on his shoulder; the shakes gripping his muscles sending waves up my arms and when he glanced up at me; I saw the depth of his relief under the annoyed glare.

"I didn't know," I said, trying to diffuse him.

He took a breath that expanded his chest and he stood, towering over me. "Well, now you do," he said and stormed away.

I trotted after him, catching up and matching his stride.

"So, what next?"

"I have two deer to clean," he said.

"That's not..."

He interrupted me, swinging into my path. "I know that's not what you were asking and just as soon as I'm done, we can talk about what's next, but for now, I'm going to do something normal and mundane before I step back into the save-the-world mode."

He got right in my face, the biting anger sparked in his eyes and my hands clenched. I wanted to hit him, and I wanted to kiss him. The juxtaposition of opposite emotions rippled through me and I reached out, pulling him to my lips.

My hand laced into his thick hair, forcing him to stay in place, to kiss me back even though he tried to break my grip. It took a few seconds and then I found myself wedged against a tree, his kiss hot and deep and his hands already yanking my shirt out of my pants.

He broke the kiss and glared at me, his hands freezing before they found my skin. "You are infuriating," he whispered and stepped away.

His brash attitude sparked the frustration in me as well, and I stomped past him in the direction we were heading without another word. The truth of the matter was, at that moment, if we had dropped to the forest floor, I would have let him take me.

I guess living through an encounter with an archangel made me just a wee bit reckless. I should be glad Damian stopped, but it just fanned the flame in the middle of my body, tightening my muscles. His silent denial burned my skin as I imagined the sun would.

The flap of wings filled my ears, and I didn't turn completely before the talons grabbed my waist, lifting me off the ground and speeding me to the entry of the garage where the two gutted deer carcasses lay. He dropped me and I landed in a crouch, looking up at the graceful curve he made in the sky above. He didn't stay and transform like I expected, instead; he let out a loud and intimidating screech before swooping up and diving into the woods like a bullet.

I stared at where he disappeared, my heart leaping into my throat as his warning call penetrated my mind. I took an indecisive step toward the woods and stopped to listen, closing my eyes in concentration. Battle sounds reached my ears and my gaze snapped open. I reacted, letting my savage heart take control.

The sight of a demon wielding a knife in Damian's direction ripped a snarl from my throat and I lunged through the air, my teeth tearing right through the bone, severing the arm holding the knife. I slid to a stop on four large white claw-clad paws and turned, aware that I was no longer in human form, and the fear I saw in Damian's expression matched that of the demon. I snarled and attacked, ripping the demon's head from his body in one snap of my jaws. It rolled away, and I sank my teeth into the decapitated body, shaking it back and forth. My battle cry bounced off the trees and I tossed the body away, turning my gaze to Damian.

He stood frozen to the spot, and I approached, adopting a more casual gait. He stared at me and I rubbed against him, bringing my gaze to his. His fear transitioned, and he dropped to a squat, taking my head in his hands.

"Naomi?" he whispered, and I chuffed back, leaning into the fingers that scratched gently behind my ear.

The scent of his blood filled my senses and my gaze dropped to the slash in his shirt, the blood-soaked edges of the fabric bringing another panic attack. This time when I reached for him, it was my beautifully manicured hand that touched him. He still held my head between his palms, and he tilted my chin up.

"I'll be fine," he said and glanced toward the demon before bringing his gaze back to mine. "We need to go before more of them come."

I nodded, and we both stood, sprinting toward the house. Damian hung the deer up in the large walk-in refrigerator at the back of the garage and locked the door before leading me inside.

The atrium was dark, and he crossed, placing his hand on a spot on the wall behind a large plant. A light filled the room, scanning his palm, and I cocked my head in his direction.

"I'm the only one that can get in right now," he said to my quizzical gaze.

The mural slid on hydraulics, revealing a metal door. Damian swung it open and gestured for me to head down the stairs. I didn't hesitate and at the landing below, I glanced up in time to see him punch a combination. The whir of the hydraulics sounded until the scenery above locked back in place.

Damian unbuttoned his shirt as he descended, wincing as he pulled the fabric away from the skin. When he reached me, he peeled the shirt off his shoulders and stared down at the nasty welt traversing his chest. He sighed and met my gaze, his mouth working, but no words came out.

"What was I?"

He laughed. "A massive Siberian tiger," he said and led me into the living room. "And you scared the shit out of me."

"But my paws were white."

"Yes, a White Siberian," he said and sat on the couch. "It is by far the biggest and rarest of all the wild cats, and you dispatched that demon like he was nothing more than a giant stuffed animal." He met my gaze. "Maybe you should be the one teaching me things instead of the other way around."

I smiled at the awe in his eyes. "Do you need me to get anything for that?" I pointed at his chest and he looked at the seeping scar.

"I guess I should get cleaned up," he said and stood, heading out of the room without further comment.

The shower went on and I looked around the room. Last night's escapades down here were a blur, and I wondered if it would be like that every day. I remembered the carnal electricity between the two of us and my gaze traveled over the murals, landing on one that made my heart stop.

It was a winter scene with a white Siberian tiger crossing a meadow and a hawk soaring in the sky.

I turned, crossing the expanse and stepped into the bathroom. "You painted those murals?"

He turned his head toward me, looking over his shoulder and away from the pulsing spray of the shower, and his eyebrows rose. "What?"

I crossed, opening the glass door. "The murals?" I asked, and my gaze couldn't help but wander down to his hard, smooth ass. I felt the smile and blinked, looking back into his eyes.

"What about them?"

"You painted them, right?"

He nodded.

"You painted us," I whispered, and his gaze traveled toward the door. The crease between his eyes deepened and then it smoothed and his eyes widened, returning to mine.

"The tiger," he said.

"And the hawk."

Night Hawk
Chapter Eighteen
Damian

DAMN. I PAINTED THAT mural close to a thousand years ago. My skin broke out in gooseflesh, despite the exquisitely hot water pounding on me and filling the room with steam.

Her gaze wandered down my back and over my ass before bouncing back to my face again. This time her inspection was a little less subtle than the first time and I considered turning and giving her the full frontal view, but I decided against it.

"You're more than welcome to join me," I said when she showed no signs of moving.

Her mouth opened, and she glanced back toward the living room. "When?"

"Right now," I said, knowing she wasn't referring to my offer.

She rolled her eyes. "When did you paint that mural?"

"A long time ago," I said. "Now, are you going to join me or not?" This time I turned toward her, giving her the full view and I smiled at the way her gaze bounced, her eyes widening a fraction before inching their way back up my chest to my face. Her cheeks bloomed, and I cocked an eyebrow at her.

She pressed her lips together and slammed the door, marching out of the room in a huff.

I chuckled and ran the soap over my chest, running my fingers over what was left of the welt on my skin. The vampiric healing powers still amazed me enough that I missed the shift in the air around me.

Nails scraped my back, and I jumped, swinging my head toward the disturbance. Her wide eyes met mine, and I turned, drinking her in from head to toe. Exquisite was the only word that popped into mind and when her fingers touched my chest, I reached, covering her hand and holding it against my skin.

"What are you doing?" I whispered, because having her undressed, and this close, put me at a major disadvantage.

"I'm saying thank you," she said, and her hands moved lower.

Catching her wrists, I warned, "Naomi, don't start something you can't finish." My body responded anyway, and she closed the distance. Her lips grazed my chest, and I closed my eyes, releasing her and surrendering to her exploration.

When her tongue trailed lower, I recalled the memories of her ex and my eyes snapped open. As much as the thought of her taking me in her mouth thrilled me, I didn't want to be *that* memory and I grabbed her by the shoulders, pulling her up to face me. She wasn't one of the common harlots from my past that I let drop to their knees before me.

No, Naomi was different, and I wanted more.

"You do not have to do this just because you aren't ready for anything else."

Her dark eyes met mine, and I traced the frame of her face with my fingertips, studying every curve. Leaning down, I took her lower lip in my mouth, sucking gently before shifting and delivering a kiss that started as tender and rich as her blood, but soon escalated into an all-consuming heat and I could envision living in this bliss for the rest of eternity.

I had lied to her today.

Fear wasn't the only deep emotion I had encountered since I plucked her out of the sky. This need to connect, to love again, overwhelmed me. The irony of her name and the form she turned into added to the feel that fate had prepared this feast just for me.

I reveled in the feel of her, the taste of her, and the sound of her. Each stroke of her hand, each swipe of her tongue, gave me new life.

The shower transitioned to the bedroom and when she whispered, "I'm not doing this because I have to." I nearly lost my mind. Her mouth was the closest I'll ever get to heaven. I couldn't recall ever feeling this out of control with a woman, this lost in the sensation, this deep even with the taste of blood passing over my palette.

"Good lord, girl," I whispered when she crawled next to me and curled up in the crook of my shoulder. Shudders still shot through my form in aftershocks of pleasure, and I met her gaze, hungry for more. I pushed her onto her back and stretched on top of her, clasping her hands in mine and raising them above her head while I explored the recesses of her mouth, our tongues playfully dancing with the rhythm of my heart.

When the kiss broke, I stared down at her with a grin.

"You know, hawks mate for life," she said, her tone laced with amusement.

"You know, I think I heard that somewhere," I answered. Her laugh filled the room, and I turned serious before we did something she didn't fully comprehend. "Are you really ready for this, Naomi?"

Her smile faded. "You drew a mural of us. It's almost like..." she trailed off.

When her eyes closed and that crease formed between them, the heat building inside me doused to a low simmer and I shifted, pulling her back into the crook of my arm as I rolled to my back. She sighed and ran her fingers over my chest.

"Are you angry?" she asked after a few moments.

"No."

"Disappointed?" She raised her head and met my gaze.

I gave her the warmest smile I could muster. "No," I said, even though my soul ached for her. "When you're ready, we'll cross that bridge." I glanced at the clock and peeled her from me, sitting up and taking a deep breath.

"I need to do a quick scout of the area before sunrise."

Her expression became guarded, and she folded her arms over her chest, like I was pulling away on purpose. A flash of a thought brought my attention to her.

"I'm not running out on you, Naomi. I have to make sure the family above is safe. Demons can't get in the house, neither can angels. I saw to that, but my safeguards don't apply to the yard and if demons are hanging around, that could put these people in danger. I can't let that happen."

Naomi unfolded and rolled off the bed, reaching for one of the shopping bags.

"What are you doing?" I asked as she pulled on a pair of jeans from the bunch.

"I'm getting dressed so I can help."

Her offer amused me and I laughed. "You are staying put."

She spun, sending a glare in my direction.

"Lucifer knows I took you, but I'm not sure he knows you're alive, and I'd rather not divulge that fact just yet."

"What if there are more demons out there?" She yanked on the new hiking boots we bought and stood.

"Baby, I could have handled that demon."

It was her turn to laugh. "You weren't handling him when I got there."

"I'm serious, Naomi. I'd rather not have to worry about protecting you if I run across another demon. Please, just stay put."

"What if something happens to you? How would I get out of here and, more importantly, back inside if you don't come back?"

I crossed and grabbed her by the arm, bringing her to my computer. With a few quick keystrokes, the scanner beeped, and I put her right hand on the surface. The machine catalogued her handprint into the security system. "There, you can get in whenever you need to," I said. "As far as the keypad, the number is seven, one, nine, two. Can you remember that?"

She started laughing. "You're kidding, right?"

"What's so funny?" I asked and glanced at the clock. I had a little over three hours before the sun broke the horizon and I wanted to cover a large circumference before I got back.

"That's the day I was born."

My gaze snapped from the clock to her face as another coincidence raked a chill across my skin. "What?"

"Seven, one, ninety-two," she said. "How long have you had that security code?"

"Forever," I said. Anytime I needed a pass code, that was my default.

"Any significance?" she asked and pulled on her coat.

"It's a combination of my birthday and the day Athena died."

Night Hawk
Chapter Nineteen
Naomi

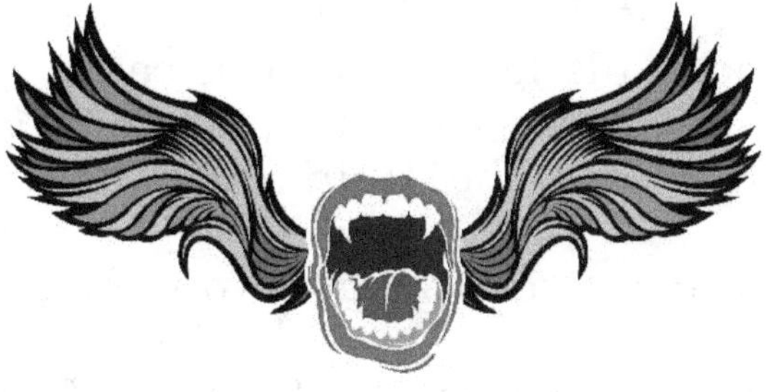

A SHIVER STARTED AT the base of my neck and I resisted the urge to rub the chill from my arms. If I didn't know better, I would think all of this was etched on some ancient tablet somewhere. The intersection of Damian and me was written in the folds of fate.

"You were born on July first?" I asked, and he nodded, his wide blue eyes never leaving mine. Certainty swept through my blood and I took a step back. I needed to sit down, and I turned, crossing to the couch and slumping in the soft cushion.

"Holy shit," I whispered and my gaze found the mural. The thing that triggered the intense sexual romp in the bedroom, and I wondered if I should have said yes, if I should have sealed our fates beyond the blood bond.

He stepped out of the office, running his hand through his thick hair, his face a shade paler than a moment ago.

"I need to do my sweep of the area," he said. "If I'm not back in an hour..." he trailed off.

"I'll come looking for you."

He shook his head. "No. You can't. If you go running out looking for me and don't get back here in time for the sunrise, I'd never forgive myself."

"What about you? What if you don't get back in time?"

He sent a smile in my direction. One meant for the addlebrained, and I tightened my jaw at the flush of anger that seeded in my chest.

"Just stay put," he said and turned to go.

Irritation racked my bones, and I almost followed him, but the warning glare he shot over his shoulder before he disappeared up the stairs stopped me. When the rattle of the door settled, I turned and stared at the clock. If he wasn't back by four, I'd go looking for him regardless of whether he wanted me to or not.

I wandered back into the office and slid into the chair behind the computer monitor, pulling the keyboard out. The minute I moved the mouse, the monitor came to life and a password prompt came up. My fingers paused, and I looked toward the stairwell before I typed the four digits he told me operated on the keypad upstairs.

My hands closed into fists as I waited, and the little hourglass flipped on the screen. After a few tilts of the timer, the familiar windows screen appeared. I huffed at the non-personalized screen and opened up the browser. I logged into my email account and stared at the latest message.

It was from Mark and I hesitated, knowing that the moment I opened it, he would know I wasn't dead and if he knew, Lucifer would know as well. I moved the mouse over the entry, waiting for the preview to show me the first line, but no preview was available.

"Damn it," I whispered to the empty room. "What the hell could he possibly have to say to me, anyway?" Pushing away from the desk, I crossed my arms and stared at the screen. After the internal debate of whether to open the stinking email, I reached for the mouse, moving it to the top corner and closed the browser.

The last thing I wanted to do was lead Lucifer to this house, and I knew enough about computers and email accounts to know that would be exactly what I was doing if I gave in and opened his email.

Thoughts of what I'd do to Mark when I got hold of him accosted my brain and made me smile. I caught my reflection in the monitor and my heart jumped. The visions of tearing Mark to pieces brought forth a set of razor-sharp teeth and I laughed at the image, knowing he'd shit his pants if I showed up at his door like this.

I opened the browser again and brought up the news just to see what was going on in the world. The political climate disgusted me, so I switched from CNN and FOX over to the entertainment news. My fingers itched to jump back into my email or log onto my facebook page, but again, that was dangerous and I wanted to talk with Damian before I endangered all of us by doing something stupid.

My gaze dropped to the clock at the thought of Damian, and my eyes widened. The hour had already passed, and he wasn't back.

I shut down the computer and tore up the stairs, impatiently waiting for the door to unlatch. Once the click signaled, I shot out the door and put my hand on the scanner hidden behind the shrubbery, engaging the mechanics to make the doorway disappear.

I stepped out into the cool morning and scanned the sky. The absence of a hawk in any direction clenched my heart. Losing him now would be devastating, and I almost laughed at the lurch in my stomach, especially since I had only known him for a full day. This kind of attachment usually takes a lifetime.

I closed my eyes and lifted my nose in the air, letting the wind bring all sorts of scents into my consciousness. I stepped into the middle of the large yard, repeating the process, scanning the air over the forest and then inhaling the scents hanging on the air. Neither brought me answers.

I turned in the direction where the demon attacked and a twinge in my spine told me it was the right direction to look. Willing the change, I bounded in the same direction I had earlier, crashing through the forest and sending the wildlife in all directions. I slowed and lifted my snout, testing the air again.

This time, my tiger senses overflowed with information. Damian was in the woods and he wasn't alone.

The knowledge almost sent me into a full charge, but there was more than one demon here and I needed to be stealthy in order to intercept. My heart knocked in my chest and I slunk toward the meadow, leaving a wide berth around the area where I thought they were.

Snow dropped from the sky, helping me blend into the dark forest and when I reached the meadow, I turned my attention to the opening closest to the house. What I saw sent a visceral fury through my frame, and I snarled.

Damian kneeled between two trees, his arms stretched wide and his wrists bound in glinting chains that wrapped around the tree trunks. A demon was pacing in front of him, glancing between the field and Damian as he paced.

A flicker lit the night behind Damian and he winced, his back arching and a pain-filled growl peeled from his throat. Why didn't he just transition and fly away?

My gaze dropped to the chains, and then the demon behind him gleefully cracked the whip against his skin again. It was the same bastard that taunted me from the window last night.

This time, when the whip bit into his back, Damian didn't react. His head lolled on his shoulders.

I took a moment to test the air again. The scent of Damian's blood drifted on the wind, along with the stench of demons. I only saw two, but there were more in the area. One guarded the perimeter of the glen and I slunk farther away from Damian, toward the offensive beast.

The kill was quick and silent. One snap of my jaws severed his head, the taste of the blood reminiscent of fire and brimstone and I didn't linger. I dragged the body into the underbrush and stalked closer.

My senses overloaded with Damian's blood and the continued crack of the whip, and my rage built. I flexed my paws and a line of razor-sharp claws appeared, itching to slice through the bastards.

"Wake him," the order captured my attention, and I lowered close to the ground, still maneuvering closer, using the woods and the shadows to my advantage. Whatever they waved under his face made his head snap back in disgust.

The bastard took a handful of his hair and leaned close. "I want you alive when the sun bakes you to dust," he growled. "You shouldn't have intervened yesterday."

"Fuck you," Damian whispered, but his voice shook with the pain that filled his senses.

I angled myself in the outcrop of trees directly across from him and every muscle in my body tightened. My gaze traveled between the closest demon and the one delivering pain in the form of a whip.

The next snap of the lash acted like the gunshot at the start of a race and I shot out of my crouch, pushing the envelope of speed, and Damian's eyes widened at my approach. The demon in front of him turned just in time for my claws to shred his throat and I coiled, launching myself in the air.

The demon holding the whip didn't even have time to reach back with the weapon before I was on him. His screams were like a twisted elixir and I relished each one until he was in pieces all around me.

"Naomi," his voice cut through my carnage and I spun, licking the blood from my chops. My gaze landed on his shredded back and two conflicting emotions took hold of my form: hunger and horror.

Damian turned his head to the east, and I followed his gaze. The color painting the sky gave my heart a shot of adrenaline and my gaze snapped to the chains holding him in place. I launched at the one on his right, clamping my powerful jaws on the material, even as Damian yelled, "No!"

The metal snapped under the vicious clench of my teeth, and the motion silenced Damian. I repeated with the other chain and then stepped next to him, nudging him. He was in no condition to walk back, never mind run, and I didn't think he could transition with the strips of platinum still wrapped around his wrists. It took him a moment and a second nudge to understand my intention.

He draped his leg over my back and wrapped his arms around my neck. "Go," he whispered in my ear and I took off like a shot, flying over the thin layer of snow with the speed of a cheetah. I slid to a stop just shy of the back door and put my paw on his arms, feeling the transition.

Damian was dead weight on my back, and I stumbled into the atrium with his feet dragging behind me. It was a struggle to cross, but I made it to the keypad, slamming my hand on it and praying it would be fast enough. A quick glance over my shoulder at the morning sky sent a skeptical rush through my veins, and I dragged Damian to the door, impatiently tapping my foot as the mural moved at a snail's pace.

As soon as it stopped, I pushed the door open, nearly falling down the stairs with the weight of him. I caught the railing and closed the door, punching the code before I worked my way downstairs. I didn't stop until I collapsed under his weight on the bathroom floor.

I crawled from underneath him and my hands shook as I unraveled the chains, flinging them across the room in disgust. Damian didn't flinch, or groan, or utter any signs of being alive, and the panic attack started gripping every one of my muscles and twisting.

"Damian, wake up!" My voice shook with an edge of the panic fluttering in my stomach. I glanced at the floor under him. The puddle of blood expanded, and I rolled him over, studying his injuries. The damage was catastrophic, and I found my feet, pulling a towel off the rack and soaking it in cold water before laying the wet fabric across his shredded back.

I rolled him onto his back, with the towel soaking up his blood, and laid his head in my lap. His beautiful face was pale and slack, almost peaceful, and my heart cried out for him. Without more than a fleeting thought, I ripped my wrist open and put it to his mouth, stroking his cheek with my free hand and whispering a prayer.

When he latched on, I gasped at the pain. He pulled the blood from me with a vengeance that made me swoon. I tried to pull away, but he held my wrist in place, sucking around a low growl that started in the center of his chest.

"Damian," I yelled, struggling to pull away.

His eyes flew open, and they were dark shadows of the demon that attacked me on the rooftop until they focused in my direction. The snarl in his throat quieted, and he blinked. The rush of blood slowed, and he looked around the room, his gaze landing back on me before his teeth retracted from my skin. His lips remained in place, but he stopped sucking. Instead, I felt the soft swipe of his tongue. His eyes closed again, and he pulled my wrist away from his mouth.

"I told you never to feed an injured vampire," he whispered and tilted his head back so he could see my face.

I shrugged at him, shaking off the waves of dizziness and offering a smile. "I couldn't let you die."

"Baby, you're lucky I care about you so much," he whispered. "Otherwise, I would have drained every last drop of your blood."

His admission stunned me, and my eyebrows rose. He shifted, lifting his head to sit up, but the strength of my blood hadn't taken hold of him yet and he dropped back in my lap.

"You didn't listen to me, either," his raspy voice cut through my shock.

"If I hadn't come, you would be a pile of dust on the forest floor right now."

He let out a shaky laugh and nodded, easing himself into a sitting position next to me. "I'm not used to having to be saved." He glanced at me. "And you're a hot mess," he grinned and glanced at the blood-soaked towel on the floor. His smile faded, and a sigh replaced it.

I climbed to my feet and glanced in the mirror. My eyes widened in the reflection. Hot mess was an understatement. I looked like a blood-soaked ghost. He straightened next to me in the image, looking every bit as horrid as I did.

"Quite the pair," he said, and I turned a skeptical eye in his direction. He went to strip the shredded shirt and winced. "This is going to take a little longer than the duration of a shower to heal."

I didn't speak, but I reached out and helped him strip the fabric off.

Still clad in his blood-drenched jeans, he maneuvered us into the stall and turned on the shower. His jaw clenched against the whimper of pain when the spray doused his back and he pulled me into his arms, nuzzling his head in the crook of my neck. I wrapped my arms around his waist, careful not to disturb the cuts on his back.

Streaks of red flowed off both of us and I closed my eyes, just holding on and letting the hot water wash away the blood. A twinge of hunger struck at the sweet smell filling the shower stall and I pressed my eyes tight, turning my head away from Damian and willing the thirst away.

"I don't understand how you could snap the chains in half," he whispered and pulled away, meeting my gaze.

"Yeah, well, I still don't understand a whole hell of a lot either," I said. His blue-eyed gaze pulled me in and I sighed and stretched up on my tiptoes, pressing a gentle kiss on his lips.

"Thank you," he said when I dropped to my heels. His gaze traveled over my shoulder at the mess on the bathroom floor. "I made a hell of a mess."

Chuckling, I followed his gaze. "Yes, and I'm not sure I can help you clean it without losing control."

"I've got some emergency reserves that'll help both of us get some strength back."

My gaze snapped to him as the statement sank in. He met my gaze with a shrug. "I've had a run in or two before," he said.

"Like that?" I swung my thumb over my shoulder.

"No, not like that. I've been lucky enough to stay out of range of Lucifer's henchmen." His fingers traced my lips. "Until tonight. I walked right into their ambush like a rookie. I should have known there would be more than one." He pulled away from me and reached for the knob, turning the water off. His hands dropped to his belt, and he unbuckled, peeling his soaking jeans from his skin and dropping them in the corner. Closing his eyes, he leaned his hand on the wall to steady himself.

"You should leave your clothes in here, too," he whispered with his eyes still closed. His chin dipped to his chest, and he drew in a deep breath.

I watched as he gathered himself to take another step. I followed his advice and dropped my clothing on the pile, leaving only my bra and underwear in place. I stepped to his side and took hold of his arm.

He glanced at me. The question in his expression made me smile.

"You look like you need a hand," I said.

We stepped out of the shower, careful to avoid the tacky blood on the floor, and I led him to the bedroom. When he turned to his dresser, I bit back the gasp. His back was still traversed with oozing wounds.

"Do you have any bandages?" I asked with my gaze locked on the thin trails of blood running down to the waistband of his underwear, where it soaked into the fabric, creating a pattern I couldn't tear my eyes from.

He paused with a t-shirt in his hand and cocked his head, like he was thinking through the catalog of items he had in this daytime sanctuary. Finally, he shook his head. "I don't even think I have Band-Aids," he said, glancing over his shoulder at me. "Why? Is it still that bad?"

I laughed, yanked from my thirsty stare by his question. "Whatever you put on, you'll ruin."

"Shit," he said and dropped the shirt back in the drawer. He peeled off the wet underwear and switched it for a dry pair. Rummaging around the drawer, he finally found an old pair of cut off sweats, pulling them on before he turned toward me.

"Are you just going to stand and stare, or are you going to get dressed?"

His curt attitude slapped me into action and I changed into one of the more comfortable lounging accessories I bought and turned.

Damian stood with his hand gripping the top of the chair next to the dresser like it was the only thing holding him upright.

"Do you need my help?" I asked, crossing to him, and he sent a weak smile in my direction. I took that as a yes and wrapped my arm around him and he steered us toward the small kitchenette that I didn't know existed.

"You haven't seen the entire place yet," he said and hobbled to the refrigerator. When he opened the door, I gasped at the content.

"What'd you do, raid a blood bank?"

He shrugged and took out two bags of O positive from the stash. "I only took the most common blood type, and it's just for emergencies." He met my gaze and hobbled to the counter across the small expanse. He reached into the cabinet and pulled out two large goblets that looked like they came from ancient times.

The moment he ripped open the bag, the sweet scent settled in my head and my thirst went from a whisper to a scream. I was at his side, reaching before he was done pouring. He intercepted my wrist long enough to squeeze out the last drop and then he handed the cup to me. I didn't wait for him; I drank in greedy gulps; the liquid fueling a new energy in my tired cells.

"Kind of like crack, isn't it?" he asked, licking his lips. I saw the same renewed energy in his eyes that ran amok in my body. He dropped the empty packages in the garbage under the sink and took the glass from my hands, cleaning both of them and putting them in the drain before turning back to me.

My gaze traveled back to the refrigerator. I wanted more, but he took a grip on my upper arm, pulling me away from the source of my craving. I let him, knowing he was right, but the base animal at my core let out a growling groan and he stopped.

"That's all we need to recharge," he said, and I found his hard gaze. "Any more and you won't be able to resist attacking a human."

His words pierced through the hunger, dissolving it into a twitching itch at the base of my spine, and I nodded, understanding his warning. I didn't want to kill the innocent, and he gave me a nod.

"Neither do I," he whispered.

He was in my head again, and I pulled out of his grip.

"I can't help it, Naomi, and I don't know how to shut it off." He offered a shrug. "This is as new to me as being a vampire is to you."

"You've never read other's minds?"

Damian shook his head. "No. That's been another unique development, and it's only you I can read."

I thought about the flood of information I received when he offered his blood to me yesterday, and I nodded. I had experienced nothing like that in my mortal life.

He reached out and took my hand, leading me back to the bedroom.

"What are you? A sex addict?" I said.

"No, I need some sleep," he said. "And I don't want you to get into trouble." I didn't resist when he pulled me close, his form wrapped around me, fitting around me in the perfect spoon, like we had done this a thousand times before. The natural ease of it sparked in my soul, and I sighed. His lips trailed down my neck and over the back of my shoulder. "Thank you for saving my life," he whispered.

I let the silence settle until his soft snores caressed my neck, tickling, and I smiled, closing my eyes and letting sleep take over.

Night Hawk
Chapter Twenty
Damian

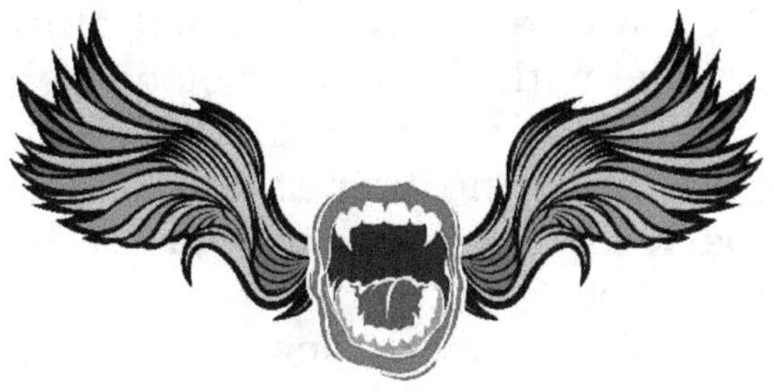

*F*IRE RIPPED THROUGH MY *back again and my heart leaped into my throat at the sight of the white tiger launching over my head.*

I sat up in the bed, my eyes adjusting to the darkness before my gaze landed on her warm form stretched out beside me. The soft rhythm of her breath told me she was still in the grips of slumber and I rubbed my face. She had saved my life today and I couldn't comprehend what would have happened if they had caught her.

The thought produced a shudder, and I stood, collecting our dirty garments and heading to the bathroom to clean up the mess.

I stood in the doorway staring at the blood-soaked towel on the floor, and my heart ached. I could have killed her today and I have no idea what stopped me. All I remember is the visceral craving for more, and then the soft whisper of her voice triggered strength at the core of my soul, commanding me to stop pulling the blood from her veins.

I turned away from the blood-soaked floor and headed into the kitchen, pulling the garbage can from under the sink and the mop from the closet. The towel and my shredded shirt landed in the garbage with the empty blood containers. I tossed the clothing from the shower into the washing machine and turned the load on before I went back to mop up the tacky layer still covering the floor.

Naomi walked in with her nose wrinkled just as I started my third pass with the mop.

"Smells like bleach."

"Yep," I said, more convinced now that I should have died on the floor than when I started cleaning. The fact I was still alive and had enough strength to do this raked over my skin as brutally as that demon's whip.

The shift in her mood hung on the air. "What the hell is your problem?"

I dropped the mop and crossed the room, taking her by the upper arms and slammed her into the wall. "I could have killed you," I snapped, the emotions swarming through me surfaced like a tornado flattening a Midwestern town.

"But you didn't," she answered in a small voice that paled behind her wide eyes.

I leaned in close, snarling; the storm taking hold and turning me into a thoughtless bastard intent on making her regret her decision to sacrifice herself for me. "You don't understand how fucking dangerous that was!" I pointed to the sparkling floor that no longer held the evidence of my near demise.

Her eyes darted from mine to the spot and back.

"And what if they had gotten hold of you out there?" I pointed toward the ceiling. "I would have had to watch you die," I said, and my voice cracked. For the first time in at least a thousand years, my eyes misted, and I let go, turning my back on her. "They would have made me watch you die," I repeated and walked away from her, trying to figure out why that thought nearly brought me to my knees.

She came to me, stepping into my line of sight and raising my chin until I met her gaze.

"I will not apologize for saving you," she said, and the warmth in her eyes made my jaw clench and my eyes blink against the wavering view.

I reached up and took her face in my hands, the warm skin stirring the need deep in me, and I kissed her. "Why did God deliver an angel to me?" I asked when I pulled away.

She laughed, and it brought a smile to my lips.

"I'm no angel," she said. "I want vengeance just as much as you do." She pulled out of my grip and turned me, so my back faced her. The trail of her fingers down my skin sent a spark to a region lower than my beltline. "Your back healed up nicely while we slept."

"Changing the subject?" I turned back to her and her cheeks flushed.

"Kind of," she said and spun, heading into the living room. She slumped on the couch and I glanced at the mop and bucket in the bathroom, deciding it could wait. When I took the seat across from her, she picked at the cuticle on her thumb.

"The demon whipping you was the same one from the other night," she said.

"I gathered from your reaction."

She looked up at me.

"I hope I'm never on the receiving end of your wrath."

She cracked a small smile. "Just don't cross me."

I couldn't fathom crossing her. Quite the opposite. I'd gladly lay down my life for her and that certainty wasn't driven by responsibility or Michael's ultimatum. It was driven by something much deeper. I was just beginning to realize how much her strength and beauty reminded me of her distant grandmother.

"You remind me of Athena," I blurted and then pressed my lips together, looking away from the surprised gaze she had leveled at me.

"Mark sent me an email."

That got my attention, and I nearly gave myself whiplash, turning my head back in her direction. Every level of emotion inside my core turned the black shade of anger. There was a man I'd willingly tear limb from limb just for fun, and the closer I got to Naomi, the bigger that fury grew.

"What did he say?" I asked.

"I didn't open it yet. I don't want him to know I'm alive." She shifted on the couch. "And I wasn't sure if I opened the email, if it would lead them to us."

I sent a smile her way. "I've already thought of that. I've got so many ghost URLs that they'd never find the source. They're more likely to attack my Paris home than anything in the states."

"You understand technology?"

I laughed. "What else is there to do during the day?"

"So, what, you take online classes?"

"Yes. It keeps my mind sharp, and I have to admit the computer revolution has been a blessing. Getting educated prior to online courses was a pain in the ass." I stood and reached out. "Come on; let's see what he has to say."

She stood, allowing me to take her hand and lead her to the office, where she took the seat and I stood behind her, leaning on the back of the black leather seat while she logged into her account.

"Should I open it?" She glanced up at me.

"Hang on." I waved her from the seat and pulled up the virus program I wrote, scanning her email account for hidden code, deleting any Trojan horse I found. I typed a few more commands blocking any return receipts notifying the sender that she opened the email and then gave her the seat. "No one will know you opened any of the messages now."

Naomi moved the mouse over the message and hesitated, her hand pulling away from the controls like the message was going to deliver her news that she couldn't stomach. She took a deep breath and I could feel her nervous energy.

"It will be okay," I said, and she gave me a glare.

"In what world is what he did, okay?" she asked, and I put my hands on her shoulders.

"He can't hurt you anymore," I said, but the doubt in her gaze left me cold.

The click of the mouse pulled my attention to the screen, and we both stared at the message. It was an apology of sorts. One meant to cover his ass if her body was ever found and my fists clenched.

"He called my grandfather?" she whispered in the seat. "That bastard."

My intuition prickled. "Is he..."

"No, he's a tribal elder of the Mohegan Indian tribe." She glanced at me. "That's where my last name originates."

I stared at the screen. "You think he's sending you some sort of warning?"

Naomi shook her head. "No. He's expecting that if I'm alive, I'll run to my grandfather to make sure he's okay. It's a trap."

Another email popped into her box and she opened it.

Mark's words leaped off the screen, producing a growl in my throat.

"Now he's just fishing," Naomi whispered and leaned back in the chair with her arms crossed. The glare she sent at the screen matched mine.

"He called you a slut," I said.

She glanced up at me. "He's doing it to get a response."

"I'll give him a fucking response." The back of the chair creaked under my crushing grip. My gaze moved from the screen to her. A smile played on her lips as her gaze met mine. "What are you smiling at?"

"You getting all protective of my honor," she teased.

I relaxed my grip on the chair and chuckled.

"So when are we going after the dickwad?"

My smile faded. "We have to give it a few weeks." Disappointment transformed her lovely features. "We have to wait until he stops sending you emails. That'll mean he believes you're dead and his guard will drop. Besides, I'd be willing to bet Lucifer has one of his more diligent details tagging along with your boyfriend there, and if we strike while they're around, today will seem like a walk in the park in comparison." I let that settle between us.

Her gaze held mine, and she nodded, glancing back at the screen. "The demons today..."

"I told the truth," I said, answering her before she finished the question and her head snapped around. "I said you were delicious." I couldn't help the grin that surfaced.

"So they thought I was dead?"

"Yes, they made that assumption," I said, offering her a shrug. "Otherwise, they would have used me as bait to flush you out."

The way her eyes widened made me want to kiss her fears away, and I leaned down, planting a peck on her forehead.

"What if Lucifer finds out I'm alive?"

I stood and walked out of the office. The question brought forth a wealth of images, none of which I wanted to discuss with her. She followed and grabbed my shoulder, turning me toward her.

"What will he do?"

I laughed and looked at the ceiling. "Before he cut your heart out, he'd shatter what's left of your innocence just to spite me."

"Why?"

"Because he'd assume the only reason you were alive was because I fell in love with you."

Night Hawk
Chapter Twenty-one
Naomi

HIS WORDS CREATED A warm ripple through my form. "Are you?"

"Am I what?" he asked, but the softness in the question told me much more than I anticipated.

I put my hands on my hip, cocking my head and raising an eyebrow.

He laughed, turning away.

"Damian?"

His shoulders tightened, and he glanced to the side, not quite meeting my inquisitive stare.

"Talk to me."

"I have to finish cleaning the bathroom," he said and sauntered away.

My gaze landed on the mural, and I crossed, studying the intricate detail. The familiarity of the setting chilled me and set me on fire at the same time. It was the snow-covered glen I circled around to save his life, however; the snow was much deeper than the dusting today and my posture in the picture was relaxed, almost playful, while I tracked the hawk in the sky above.

I turned at the rustle behind me. Damian carried the empty bucket and mop toward the laundry area.

"You might want to check the stairway, too," I said.

He stopped and scanned the dark tiles that led from the entry to the bathroom and swung the mop from its resting place on his shoulder. Watching him clean created a peculiar heat in me and he sent a sideways glance in my direction, accompanied by a knowing smirk.

"This turns you on?" he asked without diverting his attention from his task.

"A little," I answered. I hadn't seen Mark lift a finger to clean anything up in all the years we were together, and the sight of a man cleaning just warmed my soul. My eyes traveled over his form, sparking a carnal hunger, and I licked my lips.

Damian stopped and crossed his arms, leaning them on the mop, sending a grin my way. "Will you please get your mind out of the gutter so I can finish this?"

It was my turn to grin.

"Ah, fuck it," he said, letting the mop drop to the floor and crossing the room in a flash, tackling me onto the couch.

I giggled as he settled over me and grinned, looking exactly like a normal impulsive twenty-five-year-old, and for a moment, I lost the ability to breathe. His eyes sparkled with a light humor that I hadn't seen from a man since high school.

"You are insatiable," he said.

I let out a breathy laugh, my gaze locked with his. "What would happen if I let you shatter my innocence?" I asked with a coy teasing tone.

His reaction wasn't what I expected.

Damian's smile faded, and the sparkle in his eyes turned into a burning flame. He pressed his lips to mine for the briefest instant and then pulled away.

"If you were to allow me the honor, any man, mortal or otherwise, who dared to lay a finger on you from that point forward, would be signing his own death warrant."

"Oh, really?" I toyed with him. "And what about all those women who throw themselves at your feet?"

He laughed, and chills traversed my skin.

"Baby, they don't matter," he said and leaned in to kiss me again.

I put my hand between his lips and mine, narrowing my eyes. "Does that mean you can play the field, but I have to be all saintly?"

His eyebrows arched in surprise. "No, that means it would only be you. You'd be my playing field." He let the silence fill the space and then added, "The only field I'd ever play on." And with that, he grinned. "Does this mean you're considering it?"

His grin was infectious and I couldn't help the curve of mine, but I offered a shrug in answer because I couldn't say yes to him. I wasn't in love with him. Sure, I depended on him, but I had to be in love before I made that kind of commitment.

Forever was a long time, especially since we were both immortal.

Night Hawk
Chapter Twenty-two
Damian

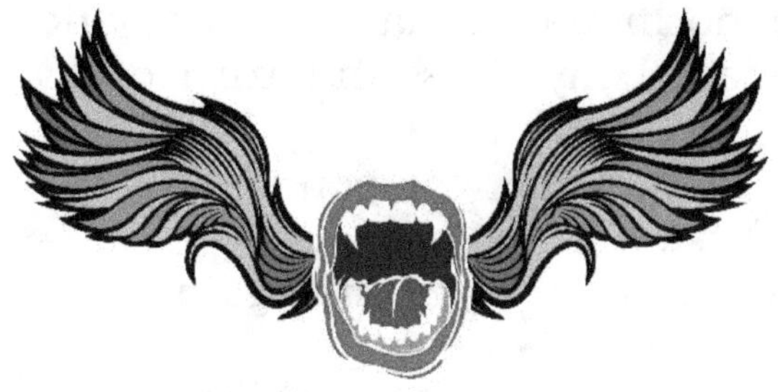

A BLAST OF ARCTIC air couldn't have doused the heat any faster, and I pulled away, giving her a nod and some space. I realized this was going to be a very complicated relationship, one that was going to test my patience.

"What happens if I never get to that point?"

The dread in her voice smoothed the aggravation, and I sighed, meeting her gaze. What happens, indeed? I didn't have an answer, so I went back to cleaning the last of my blood from the slate.

"Damian?"

"I don't know," I answered, watching the slow swipes of the mop on the floor. I didn't turn at the shift in the air around me, nor did I when her fingers ran down my bare back. I just kept up the slow movement across the floor, cleaning all traces of my close call from view.

"Are you angry?"

The mop stopped, and I closed my eyes, giving a shake of my head as an answer. My heart ached, and I sighed, analyzing the emotions sweeping through me. The pendulum swung from one extreme to another, almost as if I was a hormonal teenager again, and it irked me. I opened my eyes and turned my gaze to her.

"I am sorry," she whispered.

"Don't be."

Her eyes drifted over me again and I saw the spark light up in her eyes.

"Maybe I should get dressed," I said, her hungry gaze tempting fate, and I had to distance myself a little from this crazy brew in my blood.

"Maybe you shouldn't," she said and crossed her arms, cocking her head, her teasing tone getting under my skin.

"You better decide, girl, because this hot and cold shit is going to drive me up the fucking wall." I turned and grabbed the bucket, heading into the laundry room and stashing the cleaning equipment. I leaned against the wall with my back to the door, regretting the harshness in my tone. But she didn't comprehend the pending storm.

"Damian?" her soft voice implored.

I turned, leveling my best stay away glare, and she took a step back. The fear that flashed in her tight features diffused the ticking bomb inside me. When she turned and ran toward the bedroom, I didn't follow.

Instead, I went back into my office and slumped at the computer, pulling up my latest online class. I hadn't checked the lesson plans in over a week, and the number of lessons stacked up yanked a groan from my throat. The last thing I wanted to do right now was homework, not with Naomi sulking in the bedroom.

"Damn it," I cursed and pushed the chair back, storming across the expanse and pushing the door open.

She lay stomach down on the bed with her face buried in her crossed arms. "Look," I started, and her glare shut me up.

"Maybe I should find another place to stay," she said and rolled to her side. Her tear-stained face tugged at my nerves just as much as her statement.

I glanced at the ceiling, trying to find the right words, before I brought my gaze back to hers. "You don't need to do that. I can find somewhere else to go if that makes you more comfortable."

She tensed and under the aggravation, I saw a flare of pain.

"It's not that I don't want to be here with you," I started back-tracking and stopped, blinking away the need to babble until that hurt look evaporated from her eyes. *Jesus, what the hell is wrong with me?*

Her lips pressed together, and I sighed.

"Naomi, this whole thing is new for me and I'm not entirely sure what to do with you," I said, laying it out for her with no excuses.

Her face relaxed, and she sat up, crossing her legs Indian style. "You're overwhelming to me, too," she said.

I laughed and crossed the floor, taking a seat on the bed facing her. "Well, I guess it's good that's mutual."

She smiled and studied me for a moment. "Are you in love with me?"

Her question took me by surprise, so did the silent plea in her eyes, and I shrugged. "I don't know. Logically, it's way too soon." I dropped my gaze, not adding that I would be if I could figure out how to break down the last of the crumbling brick around my heart. Instead, I asked, "Are you?"

"I'm at the same place you are," she said, and I glanced into her eyes, seeing the conflict. "Being with you feels right. Natural. Like it was meant to be, but I can't fathom that." She glanced around the room. "I can't fathom any of this."

I nodded, dropping my gaze. "It's funny how things turn out."

"I can't reconcile my feelings right now, Damian," Naomi whispered, and I met her stare. "On one hand, I am still very pissed off that you did this to me and on the other..." She trailed off and her gazed drifted over my still bare chest. She inhaled and continued, "And on the other, you create such a heat in my soul that I can't ignore it, but I'm not sure if it's going to ignite or explode."

The smirk came naturally, and she swatted my arm.

"I'm serious."

"I know. It's just your description is dead on and you're not telling me anything that hasn't crossed my mind."

Dimples appeared in her cheeks and she fought the smile, but lost and I shifted, crawling over to her with a predatory hunger, and she giggled.

"Heat, huh?" I said and pushed her back, nuzzling my face into her neck. "I can show you a heat that's out of this world."

Her laughter filled the room, and I joined her, tickling her sides with my fingers and nipping at her neck, and she squirmed under me. Naomi's hands found my only ticklish spot, an obscure spot on my natural waist, and I jerked away, my laughter turning to a squeak of surprise. The mischief in her eyes bloomed, and she went on the offensive, tickling relentlessly, until I caught her wrists and stretched them over her head.

Both of us continued to shake with laughter and I moved to nip her neck again. She pulled her shoulder up, blocking access. I tried the other side, and she blocked me again, the game repeating through a half dozen times before I let go of her wrists and settled over her, propping myself up on my elbows.

The laughter wound down, and she reached out, sliding her palm over my cheek.

"Thank you."

"For?"

"For making me laugh," she said.

I turned my lips to her hand, placing a kiss at the heart of her palm. "I can't remember the last time I laughed like that," I said and sighed.

Her smile faded, and she stared at me with those beautiful chocolate eyes.

"What's wrong?"

"Nothing," she said and offered a ghost of a smile.

I inhaled her sweet scent and then pulled away. "I'm way behind in my studies," I said and rolled off her and glanced at the clock. "And I only have a few more hours before nightfall, so..."

"So, you're bailing on me?"

"Yes. If you want something to read, I can show you to my library."

Her eyebrows rose.

"Either that or you could go exploring. There are quite a few sections of this place you haven't seen."

"Really?" she asked and smirked. "And here I thought you were shallow and just had places to screw around."

I couldn't help but grin. "I'm sure you'll find more than enough intriguing places for us to screw around, if that's what you desire." With that, I slipped off the bed and headed out of the room.

Night Hawk
Chapter Twenty-three
Naomi

THE VIEW OF HIS back was mighty fine, and when he shot that twinkling smile back at me before disappearing around the corner, I thought my skin would catch fire. I dropped onto my back and stared at the ceiling.

He was smashing almost every notion I had about vampires, although I wondered if it was just his innate ability to charm that had me smitten. And I had to admit, I was smitten, maybe more than smitten now, that he'd let his guard down and laughed with me.

Rough housing impressed his sense of humor, and that was a rarity in the vampire realm. From what I had heard, vampires were cold, with no depth of personality; all they wanted was blood, and that trumped being civil. The disease burned out any hint of fun.

Damian was different. He was as full of life as a twenty-five-year-old should be, like turning the sands of time stopped not only his body, but his mind from aging. He was a strange contradiction. His normal persona was so charismatic and bright, but his shadow form, well, frankly, that terrified me.

I wondered if being an Archangel's lackey had some influence on his demeanor.

Damian stepped back in the doorway.

"I'm not his lackey," he said, the aggravation making his features hard.

"That's what you got from my silent ramblings?"

His cheeks transitioned to embarrassed red, and his gaze dropped to the floor. When his mouth opened and closed a couple times, trying to form a rebuttal, I stifled a chuckle. However, in the end, he just offered me a shy smile.

"Your notion of what a normal vampire is like isn't that far off. They crave blood more than you and I do, and it turns them into uncontrollable monsters."

"Why are we different?"

Damian bit his lip and met my gaze with a shrug. "Probably because you and I survived on vampire blood that first day, and we've both been infused with angel blood."

My eyes widened. "You bit Michael, too?"

The bitter smile surfaced, and he nodded. "He nearly took my head off."

I thought about how pissed he was when I bit him, and I'm part of his bloodline. "Why didn't he kill you?"

"He got a mental viewing of what happened to his daughter and knew how hell bent I was on revenge." Damian leaned on the doorjamb and crossed his arms. "I also think the fact I didn't divulge where Zoe was held some weight."

"So it wasn't just a pity thing," I said and grinned.

His eyes narrowed, and he leveled a glare in my direction before disappearing down the hall. This time, I scrambled after him, catching him halfway across the living room.

"I didn't mean to offend you," I said.

He looked up at the ceiling before bringing his gaze to me. "You didn't offend me. It's just still a sensitive subject," he said.

"Even after all these years?"

His lips pressed together, and he nodded. For a brief instant, I saw the underlying pain flogging his soul, and I reached out, cupping his cheek with my palm. I wanted to erase every drop of strife in him and the soft smile that appeared tugged at my heartstrings.

I moved closer and allowed my hand to drop to his chest. His heartbeat tapped a soft rhythm at my proximity.

"Do you know why the connection between us is so…" I trailed off, unsure of the proper way to describe it. Strong wasn't the right word, but it was the only one I could come up with, and the thought prompted his smile to gain traction.

"Electric?" he asked, his voice lilting in a pleasant question.

My face heated, and I nodded.

"I don't know," he said. "But when you get this close, I can't think straight."

His admission made me smile. I liked the fact that I pushed him to the edge of control, because he certainly had that effect on me.

"Is this a supernatural side effect to being a vampire?"

He laughed. "No," he said when the laughter wound down. "You were out with people last night. Did you feel this connection with anyone else?"

I thought about the stroll through the mall and the number of people surrounding us. Not one of them captured my attention, and I shook my head.

"I really have studying to do," he said, but instead of moving away, he wrapped his arms around my waist, pulling me close. When his lips touched mine, I swear a bolt of lightning pierced through my soul, searing me to him for all eternity.

Night Hawk
Chapter Twenty-four
Damian

THE TASTE OF A summer rainstorm washed over me, and I couldn't help myself. The kiss transitioned into the flash over zone and before I knew it; I had her pressed against the wall. My hormones went into overdrive and all I wanted was to hear her cry my name with her throaty, sex-laden voice.

The reality of our connection sucked the air from my lungs and I pulled away, meeting her gaze.

"I really have to study," I mumbled, trying to convince myself more than her.

She giggled, and the sound made my muscles tingle.

"You've said that three times already," Naomi whispered and licked her lips. That simple act may have been done in innocence, but it erased all thought from my brain, reducing me to the base animalistic tendencies so pronounced in my blood.

I think I growled, but I can't be sure. All I knew is the night was coming and I could feel the pulse of it in my mouth and my cock, both begging for satiation. Cloth tore, and I blinked, staring down at her wide eyes, my body poised over her now naked form laid out on the hard floor, ready to take her without consideration.

My muscles tensed, and I exhaled. "I'm sorry," I whispered and went to pull away.

Naomi grabbed a handful of my hair and yanked my head back. When her teeth closed on my throat I moaned her name, but she didn't break the skin, instead her tongue danced over my carotid, the flutter as pronounced as my pulse. It took every ounce of self-restraint not to bury myself inside her.

For every swipe of her tongue, a little piece of my control chipped away and the burning need to have her stripped my skin of hesitation.

"Ah, fuck, Naomi, you have got to stop that," I said.

"Why?" she asked against my neck just before her teeth punctured my skin.

Her gentle sucking crashed through me and I dipped my mouth to the line of her throat, piercing her skin at the same moment I thrust my hips. Her sharp gasp slapped my mind back in place and my teeth retracted, breaking contact with her skin. The feel of her tight around my throbbing member nearly sent me over the edge and I closed my eyes, relishing the all-consuming heat.

"Damian," her voice cut through my stupor, the moment bringing with it a sharp clarity at what I had done.

I raised my head, meeting her gaze, and then looked down at our coupled bodies. I'm sure my eyes were just as wide as hers, but I made no move to pull out. Instead, I circled my hips slowly and my eyes rolled at the sheer bliss. I leaned down and licked the blood from her neck before bringing my lips to hers.

"I'm sorry, baby," I whispered and punctuated it with another swirl of my hips, bringing a gasp from her, but this time there was an underlying hint of pleasure and her body responded, moving with me.

Her fingers dug into the back of my head, pressing my mouth to hers, our tongues mingling, drenching my senses with blood and summer mist, our bodies sinuous and languid in our rhythm. Not one encounter in my entire existence prepared me for this moment. Even the memories of my time with Athena paled compared to this exquisite creature.

We rolled, and I let her take over the pace, whispering her name accented with my ancient Greek, forming long-forgotten words of affection. Her features transitioned, saturating with ecstasy, and her throaty breath with my name on it led me right into oblivion.

I opened my eyes to the ceiling, blinking before lowering my gaze to her body draped over me. Her knees still tightly hugged my sides, and both her arms curled around my shoulders. Her chest heaved with exertion and her dark hair tickled my neck.

My first coherent thought sent a shock wave spinning through my body. *What the fuck have I done?*

I licked my lips, afraid to speak. I knew I'd have to eventually, so I bit the bullet. "Naomi?"

She lifted her head a fraction, but didn't look at me. Instead, she used her luxurious mane to hide her features and when I went to move her hair from her face; she stopped me with one word.

"Don't."

"I..." I started, but she whipped her hair away from her face and the glare that pierced me shut off any further attempt at an apology.

She lay her head back down on my chest and fear channeled into my cells. My fingers found her hair, and I combed them slowly through her locks. My mind shifted to the feel of the silky strands and the warmth of her stretched out on me. I wasn't sure I'd ever get the chance to feel her this way again, so I took the time to burn it to memory.

When she finally lifted her head and propped her chin on her fist, I met her gaze.

"This doesn't mean you own me," she said, her voice still carrying a hint of anger.

"I know. It means *you* own me." I traced her lips and met her gaze.

Naomi's features softened, and she sighed, allowing a small smile to form. "I guess Lucifer can't shatter my innocence anymore," she said and offered an eye roll.

I smiled, unwilling to speak, unwilling to tell her that Lucifer could now shatter my world. And if he ever got his hands on her, that's exactly what would happen. Making love to Naomi had sealed my fate. My life was now devoted to keeping her safe. Michael would have to enlist someone else to keep tabs on the rest of his bloodline, because this beauty in my arms was my future.

"I could stay like this forever," I whispered.

Night Hawk
Chapter Twenty-five
Naomi

A STORM OF EMOTIONS swept through me and my gaze remained locked on his bright blue eyes. I grinned at the irony. It took two days with a vampire for me to open my legs and welcome him inside me, an action that Mark had been unable to get me to do in over two years.

I had heard horror stories of the first time from my girlfriends, and now I wondered if it was just an elaborate lie. One that I bought into enough to cling to my virginity into my twenties and, I'm sure it probably saved me the same un-enchanted fate as my friends.

While I had felt that initial stab of pain everyone described, Damian had bitten me at the same time, consuming all other sensations. The shock of it was as overwhelming as the flow of his blood had been, and every movement after had been sweet bliss.

My god, it was amazing. He was amazing.

I dropped my head back to his chest, listening to the dull drum of his heart. Resting on his chest felt natural, like we were an extension of each other. His arms wrapped around me and his lips pressed to the top of my head.

"I still have to study," he whispered.

Lifting my head, I stared at him, dumbfounded. "Really?"

He grinned. "Yeah," he said and pushed my hair away from my face. He planted a kiss and sat up, keeping his arms wrapped around me. "If I don't, I won't have time for anything else tomorrow, and I think my boss will go ballistic if I don't check in."

"Your boss?" The notion of Damian holding down a job made me laugh.

"Yes. I freelance. Computer programming, website design, stuff like that."

The more I found out about this man, the more I was intrigued.

"How do you think I maintain my properties?" he asked and pulled me off his lap. The sudden disengagement of our bodies made me whine, and I saw the same wince from him. Our detachment left me empty in more than one respect.

Damian stood, helping me to my feet while he surveyed the clothing carnage scattered across the room. He gestured toward my shredded bra. "It looks like we'll have to make another trip to Victoria's Secret tonight."

My mind was still stuck on the fact he had a job, and I stared at him for a moment before glancing around the room. "Looks that way," I muttered and began picking up my clothing, assessing the damage. Nothing was salvageable, and I turned toward him, holding the pile out to him. "You destroyed everything."

He shrugged, pulling his shorts on, and leveled a shy smile in my direction. "Sorry," he said, and he smirked, turning and disappearing into the office.

I turned and headed back to the bedroom, dropping the ripped clothing in the chair by the door before getting dressed. A quick glance at the clock told me we didn't have much longer cooped up in this underground establishment, and instead of donning jeans and a t-shirt, I opted for a sexier look.

When I walked into the office, Damian's quick glance froze, and his eyes widened in appreciation. I saw the spark ignite, and he leaned back in the chair as I crossed and took the seat on the opposite side of the desk.

"You really know how to distract a man." His appraisal of me continued, and I shifted under his blatant study.

"I want to see if Mark sent another email," I said, changing the subject.

He nodded, and I stood, walking around to his side of the desk. Instead of relinquishing the chair to me, Damian pulled me onto his lap and then closed the course menu he had up, leaving the browser open for me.

He pushed my hair to the side and ran his tongue from my exposed shoulder to the curve of my neck. I tried to shrug him off, but I couldn't ignore the heat. My fingers slipped on the keyboard, and it took me three tries to type in the correct URL and he chuckled in my ear.

"It looks like my homework will have to wait," he whispered.

I stared at the latest note from Mark, my blood running cold despite Damian's attempts at seduction. His hands stopped on my waist and the low growl that formed in his throat told me he was reading the same thing I was.

The words sank in and I tried to stand, but Damian clamped down on my waist.

"It's a bluff," he growled at the screen.

My heart had already started that panicked pulse and my mouth ran dry. "He's got my grandfather, Damian." I turned, meeting his gaze.

Damian's jaw tightened and his glance flicked back to the screen. "What's your grandfather's name and phone number?" he asked, reaching for the phone.

"Nathan Hawk," I said and rattled off the number.

He pressed a few numbers and then dialed my grandfather's line and put his finger on my lip, his eyes carrying the warning to be quiet.

"Hello, is Nathan Hawk available?" he asked. "Oh, okay, can you tell me when he will be home?" He paused and listened. "This is Connecticut Light and Power calling regarding his electric bill." Another pause. "I'll try back then, thank you." He disconnected the call and put the phone on the desk before meeting my gaze.

"My grandfather lives alone," I said and my skin flushed against the chill settling into my bones.

"It's an ambush, Naomi. A set up to draw you out."

"I can't let them torture my grandfather." I pointed at the screen and the promise of the things that would happen to my grandfather if I ignored the email.

"Would your grandfather want you to sacrifice yourself for him?"

The sharp tone in Damian's question along with his stern piercing stare clamped my lips closed. I glanced at the screen and shook my head, although it didn't settle well in my stomach. "I can't let him die in my place," I finally said.

He shook his head. "I'm not letting you go there."

"You don't have a say," I snapped.

"The hell I don't," he growled, his grip on me tightened. "It is a setup."

"I'm well aware it's a setup, but I can't let him take the fall." I struggled out of his grip and spun toward him. "I told you; you don't own me."

He shot to his feet, his eyes blazing, and his fists clenched. The muscles in his arms twitched, and he just glared at me. His chest rose and fell with aggravation. "If I have to lock you up for the next two weeks, I will."

"Bullshit!" I stepped toe-to-toe with him, my fists clenching hard enough for my nails to dig into my palms.

He closed his eyes and hung his head. "I can't." His hands unclenched and he stepped around me, heading out of the office, leaving me with my building fury.

"What do you mean you can't?" I stormed after him.

"I can't walk you into an ambush," he spun and glared at me. "Not in this lifetime."

I raised my eyebrows. "It isn't your choice."

"God damn it, Naomi, I've dealt with these assholes before. You haven't."

"Can you guarantee they won't hurt my grandfather?"

Damian clenched his teeth, his gaze dropping to the floor. "He's already dead," he said, his voice barely a whisper, and when his glance met mine, I saw the truth in his eyes.

I stumbled back, my legs losing all control to hold me upright, and Damian reached out, grasping me around the waist. The shock of his words bled through the numbness and pain hit like a razor to my skin. I shook my head to wipe away the black rim, closing down my vision and met his gaze.

"How do you know?" I asked.

"Because they were there," he said.

Rage burned from the base of my spine to the nape of my neck and a growl formed in my throat. It started low and Damian pulled me close, trying to hold me together, but it was too big, too dark and I wanted blood. I spun, flipping him over my hip and onto the floor, and I shot to the door, my focus only on tearing Lucifer's throat out with my bare hands.

Damian caught me on the stairs, tackling me to the risers.

"No," he growled in my ear, in the voice of his shadow form. "You are not ready to go charging after Lucifer yet."

"Damian, let me go," I screamed and a crash in the house above froze us both in place.

I turned my head, and his shadow glare met mine, sending a shiver up my spine.

"What..."

"Shut up," he muttered and his hand slid over my mouth, his gaze transitioning to the door and the sounds of shuffling above.

"Open it!" a male voice snarled, and Damian picked me up, carrying me back into the house. He closed the door at the bottom of the stairs and set me down. Taking my hand, he stalked through the office to a panel on the wall, punching in the familiar numbers. A door popped open. He led me down another set of concrete stairs into an underground maze.

I lost track of how many turns he took and the complete blackness surrounding us didn't give me any hint of what direction we were going. All I knew was he was practically dragging me. When he stopped, he turned toward me, slamming me against the wall.

Without warning, his body pressed against mine, and he kissed me.

I pushed him away. "What the fuck, Damian,"

His husky laugh filled the dark. "Before we go barreling out of here, I need you to know..."

"Don't give me this sentimental bullshit. Just tell me what you need me to do," I snapped, cutting him off and blinking at his dark shape.

"I need you to run," he whispered.

"Right," I said with all the sarcasm I could muster. "You said the house is demon and angel proof, so that means those are human thugs."

Silence met my comment.

"Who do they have up there?"

"The family's daughter," he whispered.

"How old is she?"

"I think she's eighteen," he said.

"What's her name?"

"Valerie, why?"

"Because I have an idea and I'm dressed for it. Can you get me to the front door?"

His hesitation annoyed me.

"Damian, you know damn well I can hold my own, and even if the idiots upstairs are working for Lucifer, I'll make sure they send back a hell of a message."

"You can't let Lucifer know you're alive."

"Isn't it a little late for that?"

"No. He doesn't know you are alive."

Damian shifted and reached beyond me, pushing a stone. The back wall slid, revealing another stairwell. He took the lead and when we reached the top; he pushed up on the floor. Ambient light filtered in and he scanned the length of the opening before lifting the floorboard up enough for me to slip through.

I slid out of the cavern, crawling under the chassis of a truck. Damian caught my foot before I rolled out into the open garage. I glanced back, and he shook his head, putting a finger to his lips and crawled next to me, closing the hatchway with his foot.

The gentle click echoed, and we both stiffened.

When no one came running, he shimmied out from under the truck and offered his hand. I hesitated and took it. Damian helped me to my feet and wiped the dust off the front of the dress. "They don't know what we are," he whispered.

"Don't worry, I will not go all fangs and rip their throats out in front of Valerie." I glanced around the garage and my gaze landed on a small motorcycle. "Can you get that down the road for me without clueing them in?"

Damian raised an eyebrow.

"Trust me," I whispered and gave him a peck on the lips.

"Okay," he said, but I could tell there wasn't a comfortable bone in his body. We rolled the motorcycle out the side door at the farthest point from the house and with a quick glance; he transitioned and wrapped one talon around the bike and the other around my waist. I argued, but he lifted off, flying low enough to keep the garage as a buffer to the view. When we reached the woods, he set me on the ground and snapped back into human form.

"I don't know what the hell you're up to..."

"Damian, I'll get Valerie out of danger without her knowing what we are, I promise. Okay," I said and his jaw tightened. "I need you to cool your jets."

His lips pressed together.

"Give me ten minutes, that's all I'm asking for, okay?"

He sighed and nodded.

"Where's the road?"

"A few yards that way." He pointed over my shoulder and I pushed the bike onto the tar, straddling it and kicking the starter on.

The engine purred beneath my legs, and I sent a smile in his direction. As soon as I was within distance of the driveway, I whooped and hollered, pulling right up the walkway to the front door, and turned the beast of a motorcycle off.

I vaulted up the stairs and pounded on the door. "Val?" I yelled, continuing to pound on the door. "Val, it's freezing. Let me in!" I pressed the doorbell, shifting my weight and rubbing my arms.

When the girl opened the door with wide, scared eyes, I winked at her.

"Hey Val, I know I said I was grounded, but Jake's party sounds way too good to pass up," I said and stepped into the entry. "I hope like hell we can use your car, because it's way too cold to ride my brother's motorcycle."

I closed the door and glanced at her. "You're not wearing that to the party, are you?" I met her shocked gaze and shivered, still running my hands over my arms as if I was cold.

She blinked and shook her head. "Um, I didn't think you were going to make it so..." she trailed off, picking up on my little sham. Her eyes darted toward the back hallway, the one that led to the atrium and Damian's hideaway below.

"Well, go change," I pointed upstairs, and she nodded, taking a step toward the stairs.

"And who do we have here?" a deep voice said from where her eyes had darted.

Valerie's entire form stiffened, and she reached for the banister.

"I'm Anna. Who the hell are you?" I asked, bringing my hands to my hips as the stranger stepped into the hallway. When he pulled the gun out from behind him, my eyes widened and my hands dropped to my sides. "Whoa, I don't want any trouble," I said, putting my hands up in front of me and stepping back against the door.

"It's a little too late for that," he smiled and waved the gun, motioning me toward Valerie.

My gaze jumped to Valerie. "Did he..." I let the question trail off and added just the right tremor into my voice to carry across to the man with the gun.

Valerie shook her head, and I moved toward her on what appeared to be shaky legs. When I got to her, I threw my arms around her with a dramatic, "Oh god."

The man chuckled.

"When I say run, you run and hide, understand?" I whispered in Valerie's ear. She met my gaze and offered the slightest of nods. I pulled away, putting my hands on her cheeks. "He didn't hurt you?"

Shifting, I put myself between her and the thug.

"No, neither of them hurt me," she said, and I got the message. "They want me to open my father's safe and I don't have the combination."

I turned toward the approaching man with the gun. "You're a fucking thief?"

He laughed and waved for us to step into full view.

I glanced at Valerie. "It's time to run, Val," I said and directed her upstairs with my eyes before turning back to the man. Valerie's footfalls echoed as she scrambled upstairs.

"You bitch," the man snarled and pointed the barrel at me.

The report of the gun filled the space, and I spun. The heat from the bullet grazed my shoulder and before he could get off another shot, I had his wrist in my grip.

Raw power surged in my veins, and I twisted, nearly tearing his wrist off. The gun fell from his hand and I snatched it from the air before it hit the ground. I didn't hesitate. When his accomplice appeared in the doorway, I pulled the trigger.

The bullet hit him between the eyes and he was dead on the ground before I turned the gun on the thug, trying to crawl away. I crossed to him, slamming my stiletto into the small of his back. He cried out.

The hinges on the front door broke and Damian stumbled into the foyer, his eyes crazed and darting around the brightly lit hall until they landed on me. He skidded to a stop and the complete surprise in his features made me burst out laughing.

"I told you I could hold my own."

The click behind me sent a skitter of shock through me and I aimed the gun at the man below my heel before sending a glance over my shoulder. "I'll kill him," I said, meeting the hard gaze of the third culprit and pressed my heel harder into the man's back.

Another anguished cry filled the room.

He stepped into my field of view, and my gaze landed on the gun. It wasn't pointed at me; instead, it was aimed toward the doorway. Toward Damian.

"A platinum bullet will kill him," he said.

I pulled the trigger, killing the man underneath me and spinning so my gun was now aimed at the bastard threatening Damian. No one moved. The shock on his face was complete, like he never expected me to call his bluff and before he could recover, I squeezed the trigger again.

His shot went wild, but mine was true and he landed on his back, his dead surprised gaze locked on the ceiling. A harsh gasp caught my attention, and I turned toward the door.

Damian clutched his shoulder and blood ran over his hand. I stepped toward him.

"Make sure there aren't anymore," he said, and I nodded, spinning and moving like a professional from room to room. The house was empty, and I came back to the foyer, picking up the guns as I went.

Damian was still conscious when I approached, but his complexion was ashen.

"What's wrong?"

"The bullet is still in there," he whispered, meeting my gaze.

I set the guns down and squatted next to him, ripping open the shirt and inspecting the wound. The smell of his blood sent a wave of hunger through me and I clamped my mouth closed, taking a deep breath.

"This is going to hurt," I said, and before he could react, I sank my teeth into his shoulder, tearing at the wound. I leaned back and reached into the gash, extracting the platinum-plated bullet.

He stared at me, his breath ragged as he glanced down at the bullet in my hand.

"You shouldn't even be able to touch platinum," he whispered and then his eyes rolled up into his head and he slumped. I ripped a strip of his shirt and wrapped his shoulder before I wiped my face.

Her eyes burned into my back and I pivoted, glancing at the top of the staircase at Valerie. Now that I wasn't trying to save her life, I took a moment to study her and the light shining from her was almost blinding. I now understood why Damian protected this girl.

She was a child of light like I had been.

"It's okay now."

Valerie's eyes jumped from the dead man by the stairwell to Damian, and her eyes narrowed. "Are you here to hurt my family?"

I stood and stepped to the stairs, meeting her gaze. "No. I'm here to protect you."

"Are you a cop?"

I sighed and glanced at Damon's unconscious form, wondering if I should lie, but I opted not to. "No, I'm not a cop." I met her gaze.

"You sure shoot like one."

I smiled. "My father was a cop and taught me how to shoot," I said, and my smile faded. "He's dead now," I added and dropped my gaze. The smell of fresh blood was overwhelming, and I wanted a drink. "Why don't you go upstairs and wait while I clean up this mess?" I waved to the dead men.

Her glance fell on Damian. "Will he be okay?"

The concern in her voice hit a chord, and I nodded. "I'll see that he is, now go. I'll let you know when it's clear."

Valerie nodded, and I waited until a door latched upstairs before my gaze landed on the expanding pools of blood. I had to get these men out of here, and Damian was in no shape to help. I left him there and jumped into action, using my speed to carry the relatively weightless bodies into the woods. When I stepped back in the house, the bloodlust took control and I closed my eyes, transitioning.

Padding up to the first puddle, I licked it clean, even though the taste disgusted me. It wasn't like the blood bags Damian had and I wondered if the fiends had been human or if they were vampires like we were, or something all together different. I cleaned the first two puddles and stepped to the third, the one closest to Damian. A gasp caught my attention, and I raised my head, my gaze falling on Valerie. She smelled delicious, and I closed my eyes, dipping my head to the puddle of tacky blood before I did something Damian would hate me for.

"Naomi," his voice cut through my concentration and I lifted my head. Damian had gotten to his feet, his hand still clamped on his shoulder, and he stepped to the edge of the stairwell, blocking the path to Valerie. I glanced in her direction before returning my attention to the puddle, swathing up the blood with my tongue.

"Is that yours?" Valerie whispered.

"Yes. Where'd the girl go?" he asked.

"She said she was going to clean up the mess and when I came down, the dead men were gone and that tiger was cleaning the floors."

"She must have let my cat out when she took the bodies out," he said. "Naomi won't hurt you," he added, and I caught the glare he sent my way.

With the last of the intruder's blood mopped up, I padded over to the puddle Damian left. His blood was richer and more full-bodied than the others were, but it still had that tainted quality that screamed vampire. Had these things arrived after sundown? I needed to know and once I finished licking the floor clean; I turned and bolted out of the room.

In the atrium, I transitioned back and whistled.

"There you are," I called out and shut a door.

I walked back into the foyer and glanced at Damian. "Your tiger got loose," I said, hooking my thumb over my shoulder.

"I saw."

Valcrie stepped into view. "Where did you go?"

"I moved the bodies outside, and I didn't realize I let the cat loose," I said, and Valerie put her hands on her hips.

"I'm not stupid, you know," she said and glanced between Damian and me.

"Valerie," Damian began, and she turned on him.

"I know damn well what you are, Damian. I've always known," she said. "And they confirmed it." Her gaze transitioned to me. "I just don't know what the hell you are."

I traded a glance with Damian, his features hard and unreadable as he took a step back.

"You knew?"

"Dude, you haven't aged a day since I was born, and my father believes you've been here since before he was born. We know you're not human, either that or you have one hell of a plastic surgeon." She crossed her arms, and I stifled a smirk. "The blood trail you left this morning freaked us all out and now my parents are out looking for another place to stay."

Damian hung his head and took a deep breath. "Have you talked to them recently?"

"No, why?" her clipped voice answered.

"You don't think?" I interrupted, and Damian's pained gaze met mine.

"Call them," he said and pointed to the living room where the phone sat.

Valerie's features transitioned from annoyed to wide-eyed fear and she bolted down the steps, her dark hair streaming behind her as she tore past me and slid to a stop by the phone. Ripping it from the cradle, she dialed and waited. After half a dozen rings, she said, "Dad?"

Valerie pulled the phone away and stared at it, before spinning and handing it to Damian. "They want to talk to you," she said and her voice shook.

Night Hawk
Chapter Twenty-six
Damian

I STARED AT THE phone and then met her dark and frightened gaze. Naomi shifted behind me and I stepped forward, taking the handset from Valerie. I tried to swallow, but my mouth was devoid of saliva and my shoulder still throbbed where the bullet shattered the bone.

"Hello," I managed, and the chuckle on the other end of the line bit under my skin. I snapped my gaze to Naomi.

"You took something that belonged to me," Lucifer said, his voice holding a measure of anger along with a mocking joy. "I want the girl in exchange," he said.

"Not on your life," I growled.

"What about her parents' lives?"

"That's a joke, right?" I said, and he chuckled, making sucking sounds that disgusted me with their familiarity. I could see the still beating heart he clutched and the monument of my failure hit. "You're a bastard, you know that?" I whispered and met Naomi's gaze.

"Is my original meal still alive?"

"She tasted better than anything on this earth," I said, speaking the truth and knowing Lucifer would take that as a no.

He laughed. "So you're not only running from me, you've got Michael on your ass, too?"

I remained quiet.

"And now, with another of his descendants dead, I'm sure he's going to step up his game."

"Probably," I conceded. There was no reason to lie. Michael was going to be fired up, even with Valerie still breathing.

"I've got a bounty out for your head," he snickered, and I looked at the floor, taking a deep breath. "You won't get out of that house alive and I'll have my pure virgin heart that I've waited so long to taste."

"Fuck you," I whispered and disconnected the call. I put the phone down, trying to frame a way to tell this sweet girl her parents were dead, and it was my oversight that caused it. I should have never had them so close, but I figured I could keep them safe in this remote setting.

What a fucking joke.

"Damian?" Naomi asked.

I sat on the couch and ran my hands through my hair, resting my elbows on my knees while I grappled for words. When I came up empty, I just shook my head without bringing my gaze to either of them.

"What's he saying?" Valerie asked, and I kept my gaze locked on the floor.

"He's saying they're dead," Naomi answered, and I nodded.

"What do you mean, they're dead?" The hysterics in her tone brought my gaze to hers. Naomi had moved to her side and wrapped her arm around the girl.

"Just like my grandfather," she said, meeting my gaze.

I nodded. "And Lucifer has issued a bounty for my head."

"Lucifer?" Valerie's voice rose. "As in the devil?"

"Yes," I said, straightening my back. "You're a delicacy to him."

"Why?" she asked in a voice filled with pain and sorrow.

"Because of your lineage," Naomi said, taking over the conversation. "But neither Damian nor I will let anything happen to you." She led Valerie to the overstuffed chair. "I know this all sounds crazy and unreal, but we won't let your parent's sacrifice be in vain."

I laughed and stood, turning my back on their surprised gaze, surveying the landscape. The buildings were protected from angels and demons, but that's not what he was sending to collect. He was sending his hybrid monsters to bring back his bounty.

Her hand on my arm pulled my attention away from the darkness.

"What is it?"

"He knows where we are," I said. "And he knows how to kill me."

Night Hawk
Chapter Twenty-seven
Naomi

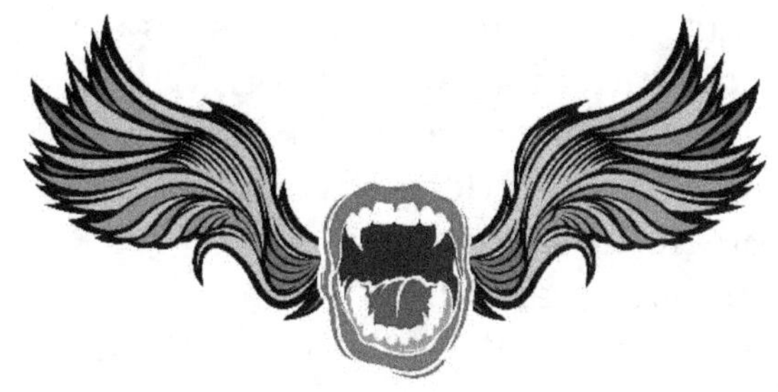

"YOU CAN TAKE HER away from here," I said, ignoring the devastating twinge his words carried.

"I wouldn't get a hundred yards," he said and wiped his face. "I'm surprised we got the motorcycle out and back without being shot."

My gaze landed on the glass he stood in front of and I turned, sweeping his feet out from under him a moment before the window disintegrated in a hailstorm of bullets. Valerie dove to the ground, shrieking, with her arms over her head.

"We have to get her downstairs," I said to Damian, and he nodded.

We crawled to her, each taking an arm, and we got to our feet, running toward the back of the house, keeping low so the bullets passed over our heads. The atrium was off an enclosed mudroom, but the distance between the doorway and the security panel seemed like an impossible feat. The front of the atrium had a line of plants that would help shelter us, but the back wall that gave a clear view all the way to the wood line.

"Damian, you have to do this as a shadow," I whispered, and his gaze fell on Valerie. "It's the only way you'll get across the distance. I can get Valerie through the door if you can get it open," I said when he hesitated.

"Naomi," he started.

"We will all die if you don't," I said, my gaze planted on a line of advancing shadows.

"I don't want to die," Valerie said, pulling his gaze from mine.

One minute Damian was the blue-eyed man that held my heart, and the next, he was the fiend that almost killed me, and Valerie gasped. He shot out into the opening and I wrapped my arms around Valerie and whispered, "He won't hurt you, neither will I, but those things closing in on the house will. When he hits that panel, climb on my back and hold on, understand?" I met her frantic gaze.

"What?"

I wrapped her arms around my neck. "Hold on!" I yelled as the bullets rained on the glass. The door slid far enough, and I saw Damian slip inside and I closed my eyes. Valerie's arms tightened around my neck and I waited a moment before darting out, my paws hitting the tile with intent, and when I slid through the opening, I didn't stop until I stood on the landing with Valerie sobbing into my fur.

I glanced up in time to see the wall close, and Damian shut the door. He stumbled down the steps and closed the door, leaning on it with his breath wheezing. I padded into the room and stopped, putting my paw on the arms grasping me, like I had done with Damian the other night.

Valerie cried into my fur, and I traded a glance with Damian.

"We have to get out of here," he said and stumbled, falling to his hands and knees. I shook Valerie off and sniffed her to make sure there were no bullet holes in her, and then I licked her cheek in a gesture that stopped her tears.

I left her huddled and shaking and turned to Damian. It took me two strides to be back in my human form and I crouched next to him.

"Baby, where are you hit?"

He glanced up at me with a cocked eyebrow. "Baby?" he asked, his breath wheezed again.

I offered him a soft smile. "Where?" I asked again, not acknowledging his questioning gaze. Instead, I pushed him into a sitting position and peeled off his shirt. "Fuck," I whispered. "Is the bullet still inside you?"

He shrugged. "You have to get her out of here," he repeated.

I leaned him forward and didn't find an exit wound on his back. Closing my eyes, I sighed. His shoulder was one thing, but his chest was another. I couldn't just tear that open with my teeth and reach in and grab the bullet poisoning him. "I'll get you both out of here as soon as I get that bullet out," I said. "Do you have a knife in the kitchen?"

He nodded.

"How long before they get through that wall upstairs?"

"I don't know. The outer shell is made of platinum."

"In that case, I'll assume I have the time to fix you up." I hopped to my feet and glanced at Valerie. "Think you've got your shit together enough to help me?"

"Naomi," Damian whispered.

"What?"

"Just leave me," he said, his blue eyes pleading.

I hunched down and ran my palm over his cheek. "Not on your life." My heart thundered at the request, fear biting me from the inside out. I wasn't willing to lose him, to lose either of them; and the longer I chatted with him, the more likely that bullet would make it impossible for me to bring him back.

"Come on," I ordered Valerie and, to her credit, she stood and followed me. Her eyes were still wide amidst the pallor of her face.

"What are you?" she whispered as I rummaged through the drawers until I found a couple specially made steak knives that reminded me of scalpels. I grabbed one and handed it to Valerie. "Hold this a minute," I said and opened the refrigerator.

It took all my willpower not to dig into the bags sitting on the shelf; instead, I grabbed three of them and turned toward her wide eyes.

"He's going to need blood when I'm done," I explained.

"What are you going to do?"

"I have to get that bullet out before it kills him," I said and plucked the knife from her hand, trading the blood for the blade, and made my way back to Damian.

He tried to shake his head, to deter me, to get me to leave, but I met his panicked stare. "I can't just leave you like this," I whispered and laid him down. "I think the bullet is in your lung. Just don't move, okay?" I bit my lip and placed the blade on his skin at the point of entry. "I'm sorry, baby." I met his gaze and pressed, slicing a slit an inch long from the base of the entry wound.

Damian screamed, but didn't move. The second cut was just as painful for both of us, and I heard the slump on the floor behind me, assuming Valerie had passed out. My heart slammed against my chest and I prayed I would be able to get the bullet out. I dropped the knife on the floor and slid my fingers into the cut. The bullet was there, wedged between two of his ribs, spreading toxic poison through his abdomen.

"I'm so sorry," I whispered again and pushed down on the rib. He cried out again, but this time it was weaker and the snap of the bone released the bullet. I yanked it out and tossed it across the room, like it was kryptonite and distance would help Damian.

He panted, blinking, and I could tell he was barely hanging on. I turned and reached for the blood, ripping one end open with my teeth and pouring the bag into his mouth. Damian choked and coughed, and then his reflex took hold and he gulped, hanging onto my hand in a death grip until the bag was empty. I did the same with a second one and the haze over his eyes sharpened, his breath coming in a more natural, un-wheezing rhythm.

When I reached for the third bag, he grabbed my arm. "No," he whispered.

"You need it," I said, and his gaze traveled beyond me. I glanced over my shoulder at Valerie, still laying unconscious on the floor, and turned back to Damian. "You won't hurt her," I said, unsure if it was true or not. All I knew is he needed blood, now, in order to have the strength to run.

"Naomi," he started, and I ripped the bag open, bringing it to his lips. He didn't hesitate and when the bag was empty, I dropped it with the other two. The adrenaline that had propelled me drained, leaving me shaking.

"I need to check on her," I said, and he nodded, leaning his head back against the floor. The wound on his chest was already patching itself up, and I crawled to Valerie, turning her over. I tapped her cheeks lightly with the cleaner of my two hands. "Valerie?"

Her eyes blinked open and when they landed on me, her face scrunched.

"It wasn't a dream?" she asked, the tears springing forth from her eyes.

"No sweetie, it isn't," I said and climbed to my feet. It was my turn to wince, and I glanced at my thigh. Blood streaked my right leg, and I took another step before the room spun into blackness.

Night Hawk
Chapter Twenty-eight
Damian

NAOMI FALTERED AND I was up and moving, catching her before she hit the tile. I traded a glance with Valerie and then focused on Naomi. She had saved my life twice tonight, and I marveled at her speed and cunning, but now she lay bleeding and unconscious and my heart thundered as loud as hers had when she was trying to get the bullet out of my chest.

"Valerie, I need you to get me a couple pints of blood, okay?" I asked, meeting her wide stare.

She nodded without speaking and crossed to the kitchen, coming back with two more bags from the refrigerator. I poked a hole in the bottom of one bag and slipped it between Naomi's slack lips. It only took a few drops before her eyes snapped open and she drank in greedy pulls. When she only sucked air, she let out a growl, and I pointed to the hallway.

"Go to the bedroom down that hall and close the door."

Valerie didn't move.

"Go!" I yelled before Naomi lost all control. Valerie listened this time, and I slid the second bag between Naomi's lips. By the time she finished the second bag, the hole in her leg had closed and I picked her up, bringing her into the shower, and blasting the water while I peeled off her clothes and mine as well.

"What are you doing?" she asked and glanced around.

"I'm getting the blood off both of us before we get dressed and get the hell out of here."

She glanced at my chest, tracing the angry scar with her fingers. "I'm sorry I had to hurt you," she said, and when she raised her gaze to mine, her eyes were filled with tears.

I pressed my lips to her forehead and switched the water off. Sweet moments could wait until after we got through the night. I tossed her a towel and grabbed one of my own, leading her to the bedroom and stepping inside to Valerie's wide gaze.

"The bullet hole..." she trailed off, pointing at my chest.

I nodded in her direction and opened the closet, tossing Naomi a duffel bag. "Pack up your stuff."

I slipped on underwear and jeans under the towel before letting it drop and slamming a handful of outfits into a second duffel bag.

"What about me?" Valerie asked, and I turned.

"I'll buy you new clothing when we find a safe place to hole up."

I stalked out of the room, leaving the women alone. In the office, I slid into the controls and flipped open my laptop, connecting the two with a cord. After a few keystrokes, the hard drive started the transfer. I had five minutes before I could do the self-destruct sequence. I dropped my duffel bag on the floor and headed to the kitchen, grabbing the cooler under the sink and sweeping the contents of the refrigerator into it. I had a feeling we might need some backup.

Anger burned in my veins, and I stormed across the room. Catching sight of Naomi and Valerie stopped in the hallway.

"What?" I snarled, and Valerie shrunk into Naomi.

Naomi cocked an eyebrow.

"I'm pissed, and I'm trying to get my shit together so we can get moving."

"I get it, but you don't have to snarl like a rabid dog," she said, and I stopped moving.

I hadn't realized I was snarling.

She smirked. "Between the snarling and swearing, I could have sworn we were at an illegal dog fight."

"Oh, fuck you, Naomi," I said and stormed back into the office to hear her laughter.

"Are you two related?" Valerie asked, just before I stepped into the office.

"No, we're not," Naomi answered.

"How long have you been together?"

I stopped and turned, meeting Naomi's gaze. "Not long enough," I said, dispelling the questions before I slipped into my chair. I had a minute left, and I dropped the cooler by the door, pointing in that direction.

"What's burning?" Valerie asked.

"The house," I answered and sighed, glancing at Valerie before moving my gaze to Naomi. "Go get some blankets for her. It's going to be cold where we're heading." I received a nod and then she disappeared, coming back a few minutes later with the chenille blanket at the same time the download finished. I stood and pushed the commands and the door opened.

"Take her down, I'll be there in a second," I said and disconnected the laptop, slipping it into my backpack along with the cords I would need. Once I had that zipped, I pressed the destruction commands and took a deep breath, slinging the backpack and duffel bag over my shoulder. I hit enter and grabbed the cooler. I stopped long enough to close and latch the door before jumping down the stairs.

At the bottom, I didn't wait; I grabbed Valerie around the waist, whispering, "Hang on tight," and then bolted. Naomi kept up, running alongside me and I grabbed her when I took the sharp turn away from the property and stopped, my hand running across the wall before I found the release. The squeak of metal met us and I pushed Naomi through, dropping Valerie in her arms before I forced the door back in place.

"Run," I said. The timer in my head ticked off the seconds as we bolted. The fact that neither one questioned my command gave me more speed, and I traded Valerie for the cooler when Naomi started trailing behind. We had to make the outer door before the charges blew, otherwise we'd be buried alive.

I heard the first explosion and turned on the speed. "Hustle!" I yelled, and Naomi grunted. I could see the end of the tunnel now that my eyes had become accustomed to the blackness and put on the brakes, skidding to a halt and reaching for the latch. I swung the door in and stepped aside, letting Naomi skid to a stop beyond me, and I slammed the door before setting Valerie down and leaning my back against the metal.

The ground rocked underneath us and I kept my back to the door. My gaze locked with Naomi's as she held Valerie against her. I closed my eyes, gritting my teeth together. The thought of the murals burning hit harder than I expected, especially the one of Naomi and I crossing a snow-covered glen. The rest were ancient and reminded me of my youth, but that one, that was special and outshone everything. Even my auto collection, which I had taken great pains to buy, came a close second to that painted mural. But I had made allowances for the cars. The security sequence lowered iron plates lined with platinum across all the doorways and windows, securing the building from the pending blast.

"Damian," Naomi said, and I opened my eyes. She unfolded the blanket and held it up. Tucked inside was the mural, and I bit my lip against the gratitude that swept through me, lifting my eyes to the ceiling in a silent prayer of thanks.

"We need to keep going," I said once we caught our breath.

"How long is this tunnel?" Naomi asked.

"A couple miles," I answered. What I didn't tell her was I had no idea what we would do when we came to the end.

"I don't like the dark," Valerie whined.

I dug my cell out of my pocket and took her hand, placing the phone in her palm and curling her fingers around it. "It's not much," I said and took the lead, walking at a slower pace so Valerie could keep up.

Naomi followed behind Valerie, and I could tell by her silence that her brain was trying to wrap around the events of the last few days. The number of lives that had been destroyed since I plucked her from the sky was unprecedented and I sighed, glancing over my shoulder at her.

The cell light kept going on and off, casting an eerie glow through the metal encased tunnel.

"How many do you think the explosion took out?" Valerie asked.

"I don't know."

"I hope it took them all," she said, the darkness in her tone echoing my sentiments.

"I hope so, too," I replied, even though I highly doubted it.

"But you don't think it did," Naomi said, and I stopped, turning toward them.

"No, I don't. I'm not sure if we're walking into an ambush or not, either. And while you and I have something to keep us alive," I started, holding up the cooler. "We have nothing here for Valerie, so we can't just hole up here until this blows over."

Naomi's mouth dropped open and her eyes softened. "And daylight isn't that far off," she said.

"Yep." I nodded, and she closed her eyes.

"So, where does this dump us off?" Naomi asked when she got her composure back.

"A hunting cabin on the edge of the state forest."

"Uncle Nick's cabin?" Valerie asked, her eyebrows arching.

"No, sweetheart, the opposite direction of your uncle's place. I didn't want an escape route they would track down."

Her eyes widened. "Are you telling me…"

I inhaled and shrugged. "I don't know."

"Well, what the fuck do you know?" Valerie snarled at her first display of anger.

"Not a whole hell of a lot at the moment," I answered, knowing it wasn't the least bit reassuring, but I needed them to know the score. To understand that we were alone in this and nobody any of us knew was safe. It was a morbid fact that I could see settling in her eyes. "We are all we have at this moment," I said, pointing between the three of us. "And that could change the instant we step out of this cavern."

Night Hawk
Chapter Twenty-nine
Naomi

DAMIAN'S HAUNTING GAZE SENT a chill up my spine and I could see it had the same reaction in Valerie. Her laugh hit a nerve. It was the high-pitched laugh of someone on the edge and I reached out to touch her arm, but she withdrew.

"What are we going to do?" I asked. This was no life for a teenage girl and we both knew it, but we couldn't just cut her loose in the woods. Not with all the monsters looking for her.

Damian met my gaze. "I'm hoping Michael can help us."

"Jesus, Damian, that isn't an alternative. He'll turn you into dust," I said, and Damian's nonchalant shrug sparked a rage inside me.

"Who's Michael?"

I pressed my lips together and met her gaze. "The Archangel Michael," I said. "He is your ancestor."

Valerie's eyes widened.

"That's why Lucifer considers us such a delicacy." Bitterness laced my voice, and when I glanced at Damian, he lowered his gaze.

"Us?" she asked.

"You and I. We are both descendents of Michael's."

Valerie blinked a few times and turned toward Damian. "Where do you fit into all this?" She crossed her arms, and I pressed my lips together at the smile that threatened. This girl was a pistol and one that had the rare quality of being able to reason during a shit storm.

"I'm supposed to protect the bloodline," he answered. "Keywords are supposed to. That doesn't always go as planned." Damian turned and resumed his gait into the dark tunnel.

Valerie watched him go and then turned in my direction. "So, we're related?"

"In some distant way, yes," I said and took her arm, following Damian's shadow.

"So how long have you been..." she started and paused, glancing at me. "I don't even know what you are," she added.

"I'm a vampire, like Damian." The admission caused Damian to pause and glance back in my direction. His gaze told me I wasn't like him at all, but he kept his mouth shut and turned away before Valerie caught the look in his eyes.

"Oh," Valerie whispered and continued walking; the silence broken only by our shuffling footsteps. "How long have you been like this?"

"Two days," I answered, and she stopped. "Well, almost three at this point." I sent a smile in her direction. "If I smelled anywhere near as sweet as you do, I have no idea how Damian missed it."

"You were nearly frozen to death," he mumbled and his head dipped lower in the posture I was understanding was his "beating himself up" stance.

"You mean to tell me you're new at this?"

I couldn't help the laugh that rang out. "Yes, I'm brand spanking new at this."

"Am I in danger?"

Her voice held a tremor, and I glanced at Damian before looking her way. "I don't think so, but just to put your mind at ease, Damian will protect you from me if it comes to that."

He scoffed and kept moving. His derisiveness irked me and I traded a glance with Valerie.

"He will or I'll kick his ass."

That brought forth a ghost of a laugh, and he glanced over his shoulder. "I'd like to see you try, and I'm talking you, not the tiger."

"When all this is settled, I'll take you on," I shot back.

The grin he sent over his shoulder sent a shiver of anticipation down my spine.

He slowed and stopped, putting the cooler and computer bag down at his feet. Apprehension replaced the grin, and he looked at the ceiling for a moment before facing us.

"I don't think anyone is up there," he whispered.

"Then why are you whispering?"

Valerie looked down to hide the smirk. I wasn't so kind and Damian sent a glare in my direction, his displeasure in my mocking as pronounced as the silence above.

"This isn't a joke," he said, pointing his finger in my face. "You're going to stay put while I check things out.

"Like hell I am," I shot back, dropping everything in my grasp. The sound of my duffel bag hitting the dirt echoed in the small space.

"I don't want to be down here alone," Valerie said, her voice quiet and timid amidst our posturing.

Both our gazes snapped to hers and I could feel Damian's discord. He was not happy with the situation at all.

"We all go together," I said, and Damian opened his mouth to argue. "Or we don't go at all," I added.

Damian put his hands on his waist and stared at the ground, his jaw tight with frustration. When his gaze returned to mine, he nodded. He didn't need to tell me just how dangerous it was to bring Valerie out of here. Any vampire within a hundred yards would pick up her scent. But I also didn't want to be stuck down here if something happened to him.

"If you insist on coming up with me, I want the tiger," he said, leveling a glare.

I narrowed my eyes. "Why?"

"Because if anything *is* out there and gets away, Lucifer won't know it's you."

"Why the hell does that matter now?"

He leaned in close. "Because no matter what happens to me, I'd like to have some sliver of hope that you're going to survive. If Lucifer knows you're alive, all bets are off."

I inhaled at his intensity. But it wasn't the intensity that made me comply. It was the underlying plea in his gaze. Within a blink, I was fur and fury in the small alcove. Valerie took a step back, giving me some space. I chuffed and rubbed against her to ease the fear radiating from her.

Valerie hesitated and then ran her hand over my massive head, finding the spot behind the ear that seemed to make everything all right. She even let out a small laugh when I nuzzled into her further. I wanted her to know I was there to protect her and when she leaned down, wrapping her arms around my neck, I knew I had conveyed the message.

Damian took a deep breath and unlatched the door. The creak of the hinges made me cringe and a low growl came from deep in my throat at the disruption announcing our presence. Another stairway greeted us, and Damian led the way.

He paused at the top door and sent a glance back at us. I saw him clearly and dread filled his features for a moment before he closed his eyes and pushed the door open. Darkness greeted us, along with a draft of frigid air.

I padded ahead with Valerie's hand on my back. Her scent drifted on the air, thick enough that I couldn't get a clear bead on even Damian. Her teeth started chattering, and I glanced around the dark interior of the cabin. Damian crossed the small space, slipping into a side room before returning, his tension melting, and he offered a nod.

"I'll go grab our stuff," he whispered and disappeared. I padded through the rooms of the cottage, sniffing every corner out before feeling secure enough to transition back to human form. The windows in the bedroom were covered with plywood, and no natural light penetrated this room. I wondered if the door was as secure as the windows. In the living space, the windows were covered with only wood-slatted blinds. I crossed and opened the one on the door, scanning the dense forest surrounding the cabin. Nothing stirred, and I closed the slats.

The kitchen offered very few amenities. The stove was one of those mini-two burner blind stoves that really shouldn't be used indoors, but it was my only option for heating something up for Valerie. The cabinets carried a few canned goods and some half-empty water bottles that were frozen solid. A mismatched pair of dishes sat opposite the canned goods and I reached for one of the dust-covered cans.

"It looks like Damian has a few cans of chicken noodle soup," I said, turning toward her. "And we've got some bottled water, too."

Damian dumped the stuff on the floor and wrapped the blanket around Valerie, trading a glance with me. She still had the phone as her night light and he reached over her shoulder, plucking it out of her hand.

"We don't want the battery to die," he said and pocketed the phone, ignoring her gasp at the sudden darkness. "Before we attempt to get that stove going, let me see if I can get you some help."

Nerves punched my lungs, and I intercepted him before he reached the door.

"Damian," I whispered.

"I have to," he said, meeting my gaze. "She'll freeze to death if I don't get her out of here."

"What about starting a fire?"

He pressed his lips together and shook his head. "Not with the demon's henchmen, only a few miles away."

"Don't I have a say?" Valerie asked through her chattering teeth, blindly crossing the room until her hands landed on Damian.

"Val," Damian started.

"Come on, those bastards killed my parents. I want them dead!"

"I promise, they'll pay, but I need to make sure you are somewhere safe that they can't get to you and the only person I know that can make that happen is Michael."

"You're not going out there alone," I said.

"Baby," he sighed.

"Don't baby me, Damian. If Michael has another shit fit..." I stopped and glanced at Valerie, offering a smile. "Michael is a bit of a jerk," I explained and turned back to Damian. "You aren't going alone."

"At least let me do a quick scan of the area," he said, holding his hand up to any argument I might start. "Please."

I gave a nod and put my arm around Valerie's shoulders, not just to settle her nerves. "Two minutes," I said as he opened the door.

He gave a nod, and the door closed behind him.

Night Hawk
Chapter Thirty
Damian

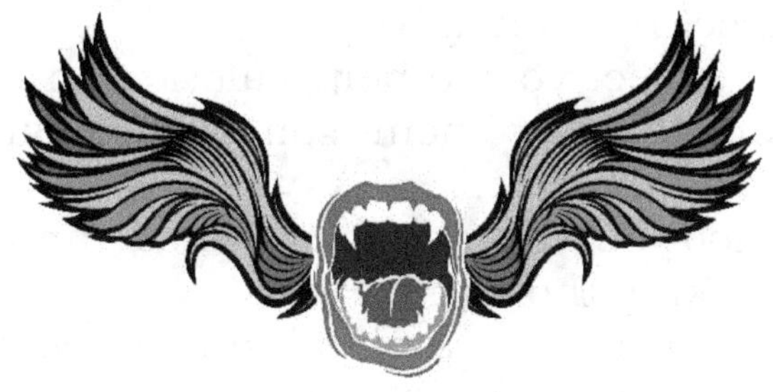

THE QUIET FOREST MET my glance, and I lifted my head, inhaling. Nothing alarming hung on the air, but I didn't trust that. I hadn't smelled the danger closing in on us at the house either, and I wondered if I should take a quick fly-over.

I stepped toward the woods, and the rustle of wings behind me froze me in my tracks. My heart thundered in my chest and I prayed the lesser of two evils stood behind me and not Lucifer.

"You fucked up, again," his voice growled and relief spread over me. I turned toward Michael.

"Yes." I didn't see any reason to talk my way out of it, especially since I had underestimated Lucifer. I should have gotten everyone out after the whipping in the woods. Three demons in such close proximity to the house should have set off my internal alarms, but I was too busy trying to survive the beating. I led them straight to the house.

"I need your help," I said before he could say anything more.

His jaw tightened and his gaze narrowed. "You expect me to help you?"

"No, I expect you to help Valerie and Naomi. I need you to take them somewhere far away, where they'll be safe."

The door to the cottage opened, and Naomi stood blocking the entry.

"I'm not leaving, Damian," she snapped, and I sent a glare in her direction. I wasn't getting out of here in one piece and there was no way in hell I was taking her down with me.

Instead of acknowledging her disagreement, I met Michael's glare. "Will you take them?" I asked, desperation filling my voice because now that he had shown up, the demon hoard would soon follow.

Michael's hand shot out and his fingers wrapped around my neck. Before I could react, a white blur tackled him and I blinked, staring at the white tiger growling in Michael's face.

"Naomi," I started, and Michael's gaze flicked from the teeth inches away from his neck to mine, widening a fraction, and I wasn't sure if his shock would bode well for either of us. I cleared my throat and continued, "Baby, he's the only one that can get Valerie to safety."

The snarl in her throat faded, and she licked her chops, stepping off Michael's chest and positioning herself between Michael and me. I almost rolled my eyes, but the anger settling on

Michael's features gave me pause and I kneeled, pulling Naomi into my grasp.

Michael climbed to his feet, glaring down at the two of us. I flinched at the clench in his jaw and another snarl built in Naomi's throat.

"Please," the soft voice in the doorway caught all our attention. "Please don't hurt them," she said, and Michael glared at her.

"Why not?"

"Because they saved my life," she said.

"That's his job," Michael said, waving in my direction. "And he failed to save your mother."

Valerie inhaled and closed her eyes. "I know."

"So why should I let him live?"

Valerie's eyes opened. "Because he's all the family I have left."

"He isn't family," Michael said, spitting the words out like a bitter pill.

"There's more to family than just blood," Valerie argued and took another step. "At least *he's* been there," she added, with a hint of an attitude that took Michael's full attention. Valerie had the audacity to cross her arms, and I suddenly felt the need to intervene before Michael annihilated all of us.

"Mind your tone," he said.

The teenage attitude came out in full force and I scrambled to my feet just as she spouted out a curse that made Michael's face turn bright red.

"Valerie."

She turned and stared me down with the same glare Naomi had given me that first night. The same glare present in her ancient grandfather's features.

"Shut up, Damian. My family is dead, and this asshole has the fucking nerve to threaten you?"

I put up my hands to settle her down, and the shift in the air caught my eye. Naomi stood next to me, back in human form, and her hand settled on my arm.

"She's grieving," Naomi whispered soft enough to catch my ear, and I saw the subtle change in Michael as he glanced her way before returning his attention to Valerie.

"Valerie, Michael is here to protect you," I said, trying to diffuse the situation.

"Yeah, right," she said, and the first sign of tears surfaced. The glaze in her eyes overflowed, streaking down her cheeks in a silent flood and for the first time in my lifetime, I saw the fire sputter in Michael.

He crossed and wrapped his arms around her. "You'll never be alone," he whispered and glanced at Naomi before his gaze moved to me and hardened.

Before I could tell him to wait, he disappeared, taking Valerie with him. I turned on Naomi and a sudden wave of fear shut down my ability to speak. My gaze traveled over her shoulder to the woods and back to her. They were coming and I could feel it.

"We have to go," I said and spun toward the cottage. She followed me inside and closed the door. I grabbed my backpack and slipped it over her arms, meeting her gaze. "Grab the cooler and then I need to fly you out of here."

"Why?"

"Michael leaves a distinct signature, and this place isn't protected like the house was."

She shoved the blanket and mural into her duffel bag and slung the strap over her head. "What about your clothes?" Naomi asked as I pulled her out of the house.

"I'll be fine," I said and forced the transition, grabbing her around the waist in my talon. I took to the air heading northwest; away from the hungry pack closing in on the cottage from the south. The risk of being shot out of the sky crossed my mind and I ascended higher into the thickening clouds and out of range of rifle fire.

I wasn't sure just how much time we had and my choices of where to go were limited. If I made a mistake, we'd be dead by sunrise. And if I didn't find shelter before then, we'd be just as screwed.

Night Hawk
Chapter Thirty-one
Naomi

FLYING IN THE CLOUDS held a dream-like quality that drenched my senses as much as the condensation soaking my clothing. I clung to the cooler handle, wondering how long I could hold it in the high winds produced by his massive wingspan.

Instead of worrying, I closed my eyes and chose to enjoy the ride. The wind whipped my hair in wet strands and the cold penetrated deeper than it normally would. I found myself shivering and Damian slowed, dipping down into the open air. Lights speckled the landscape and in the distance, I could see a brighter glow.

Damian descended to just above the treetops, scanning the landscape as the glow increased to a cityscape. When he passed a low group of buildings, he dove, landing us in the middle of a deserted lot. The sign announced a self-storage facility, and I glanced at Damian as he walked through the yard, looking both ways at the windowless buildings. He stopped in front of one of the units toward the back of the lot and studied the padlock. Before I could ask what he was doing, he reached into his pocket, pulling a pocketknife from his jeans and kneeled with the lock in his hand.

I took a minute to scan the area as he picked the lock, wondering what the hell we were doing here. A hundred questions flitted through my mind and my arm ached from the weight of the cooler. The click of the lock caught my attention, and I looked back in time to see Damian sliding it out of the clasp.

When he lifted the gate, waving me inside the dark container, I slipped past him with a questioning stare. His lock-picking skills certainly clashed with his statement of not being a thief, and he shrugged, keeping silent as he scanned the grounds and followed me inside.

Once the door closed behind us, he slid the lock through the track, preventing the possibility of thc door being lifted during the day. I dropped the bags on the floor and took a seat on the cooler, unsure of what to do. The water dripped from my body and I wrapped my arms around my chest, trying to find some heat, but there wasn't any left and my teeth started chattering.

The darkness enveloped us and when he opened his phone to scan the interior; I squinted and looked around at the haphazardly packed belongings. Furniture and boxes graced the space, and he moved to the center, pushing boxes to the side and creating a little alcove for the two of us. With another quick scan, his gaze landed on a mattress set leaning in the far corner and he sent a raised eyebrow in my direction.

"It might be more comfortable than the floor," I whispered through my chattering teeth.

He shuffled some more things around and then cut through the path he made to where I sat.

"You need to get out of those wet clothes," he said.

The deep timber of his voice filled the small space and created another chill down my spine. He helped me to my feet and then grabbed the cooler along with the computer bag and my duffel bag, disappearing through the maze again. I had barely started unzipping the fleece jacket when he was at my side, helping me peel the soaking fabric from my chilled skin. Each garment found a resting place on the edges of the boxes lining each side of the container, far enough away from the door for the puddles not to leak outside and trigger the storage unit owner's curiosity.

"Your clothes are that way," he said, pointing through the maze as he stripped his coat and hung it up to dry with the rest of the clothing.

I didn't wait for him. I shuffled down the path, finding the opening he created. A few chairs lined the alcove and a bare mattress lay on the ground with the chenille blanket laid out on it. The thought of being wrapped in the soft fabric overwhelmed me and I nearly dove onto the waiting refuge. It was every bit as heavenly as I thought it would be, and I wrapped the blanket around myself in a tight cocoon. When

Damian rounded the corner in only his underwear, he stopped.

"Are you going to share?" he asked, standing over me.

My teeth chattered in answer and he took a seat next to me, drawing me onto his lap. His powerful arms wrapped around me, while his breath tickled my shoulder, but it still didn't warm my core.

"I am so cold," I said.

"I know. So am I."

The admission caught me off guard and I turned, meeting his shivering stare. Instead of elaborating, he reached over and popped the cooler open, pulling out one of the bags of blood. He sank his teeth into the bag, tearing a hole in the top before tipping it to my lips.

"This will help," he said, and the cold blood flowed into my mouth.

I drank until there wasn't anything left and he dropped the empty into the cooler, taking one out for himself. He drank as quickly as I had and discarded his empty into the box before closing it.

It took a little while for the blood to settle into my system, warming the chill as much as Damian's slow caress of my arms and his lips finding the arch of my neck. I shifted, unwrapping myself from the blanket and letting him take the fabric. He draped it over his shoulders, enclosing both of us in chenille.

"Thank you," he whispered in my ear and just by his tone, I knew it was for more than sharing the blanket and I turned my head, meeting his gaze.

A hunger blazed in his eyes and he offered the slightest of smiles before crushing my lips under his.

Damian's kiss stopped time and made the storage unit disappear.

When his mouth left mine, he was stretched out over me, our bodies melded together on the soft mattress. I don't even remember shifting from his lap or removing my bra and underwear, for that matter. Dimples appeared in his cheeks and he dipped his head, finding my neck. The raw power of him knocked me senseless, and his touch ignited my skin, bringing with it a fever of pleasure.

His slow sensual descent from my throat to my breasts left me dizzy and when his lips trailed even lower, I purred my approval. His mouth and tongue created magic on my skin. Each swipe, each trailing caress, sent tendrils of heat between my legs. When he pushed my thighs wide and buried his mouth between my legs, I moaned.

"Shush," he whispered, his gaze shooting to mine.

I shoved the back of my wrist to my lips, cutting off the moan and he chuckled, resuming his blissful seduction. He took his time, loving me like I had never experienced, until every nerve ending begged for him. When he shifted, crawling back up my body, anticipation quickened my breath and he grinned down at me. The thrust of his hips and sudden fullness of him pulled a gasp from my chest.

"Baby, being inside you is better than heaven," he whispered and crushed my lips under his.

Heaven wasn't in the same league as this. This transcended and thrilled at the same time. The way Damian made love to me today was beyond comprehension, making yesterday's frantic bid feel like an awkward mess. He took his time, his slow grind sending my eyes rolling back into my head and pulling soft pants from my throat.

I opened my eyes and met his bright-blue gaze, his eyes almost glowing in the darkness and his teeth shining in a grin that accompanied a rush of wetness between my thighs. I arched into him, unable to stop the moan this time.

"Oh, god, Damian!" I cried, my voice husky from the orgasm gripping my body. I trembled under him and he picked up the pace, his smile fading into the serious gaze that pierced my soul.

He pressed his lips together against his own groan of gratification just before his eyes clamped closed and every single one of his muscles tightened. He collapsed onto me, his breath as ragged as mine.

I held him tight against me, my fingers lazily tracing his back, content to just be in his arms. Finally, he propped himself up on his elbows and met my gaze, and a warmth I couldn't put words to encompassed me.

"I have waited my entire life for you," he said, and the tear that slipped from the corner of his eye cut me deeper than I could imagine. He tried to smile, but it didn't quite form and he dropped his head to my shoulder, cursing under his breath at the emotional display.

His reaction brought a smile to my face, and I wondered why I wasn't a mess like he was. Maybe two thousand years alone had prompted this. I planted a kiss on his temple and he squeezed me closer in response.

Damian's body relaxed, melting into me, and his breath slowed into that soft rhythm of sleep. His weight became heavy and suffocating, and I squeaked out his name.

"Damian?"

He jerked, his head rose, and he blinked his eyes. Instead of moving off me, he rolled, wrapping us in the blanket before giving me a sleepy smile. His eyes drifted closed, sleep tugging him under.

I studied the lines of his face, the contours of his cheekbones and the strong curve of his chin. The man was beautiful, like an exquisite work of art, and I wondered if I would live up to his expectations.

His brow crunched, and he opened his eyes, meeting my gaze.

"Baby, you surpass all of my expectations."

I stiffened and pressed my lips together. "Stop listening to my thoughts." I rolled off him and out of the warmth of the blanket, annoyed that he could still set my temper on edge.

Crawling to my bag, I rifled through it until I found some underwear and an oversized t-shirt, dressing. I glanced toward the door and froze. Light bled through the perimeter, penetrating the darkness like a halo.

"How much light can hurt us?"

Damian got to his feet with the blanket wrapped around his waist. "That isn't enough," he said and slid on his underwear, taking a seat again. This time, he pulled out his computer and booted it up.

"What are you doing?" I folded up next to him, glancing at the screen.

"I'm praying I can tap into a wireless connection because I need to check the news and our email accounts in case our friends are phishing." He glanced at me. "And I need to find another place for us to go. This isn't safe."

"You said you had other places," I started and before I finished, he was shaking his head.

"I can't risk it." He bit his lip at the wireless accounts that appeared within range and glanced at me. "They're all secure," he said and sighed. He took a moment to rub his face and crack his knuckles, and then his fingers flew over the keyboard. A half hour later, he had hacked into the strongest signal and pulled up a local Connecticut news station.

We scanned the article, our gazes zeroing in on the names of the deceased, and Damian smiled. A name I didn't recognize, along with the three family members, were listed as found dead in the rubble.

"Why are you smiling?"

"Because that's one of my aliases, which means the information was fed to the press by one of our friends."

"You mean Lu..."

He slapped his hand over my mouth. "No, don't. Saying their names is a death sentence."

My eyes widened, and I gulped. "Then why were we able to talk in your place before?"

"I had it angel and demon proofed, remember?"

I nodded.

"This place isn't. Saying the names aloud gives away your location."

He went back to reading the story online while I tried to get a grip on my racing heart.

"It means he's looking for us, whether it was the beast or his brother who leaked the information. He's still looking, but maybe not as diligently." His nimble fingers played on the keys again. "Just need to check one more thing."

When he brought up his email account, he paused, and I swallowed the fear building in my throat. We traded a glance, and he closed his eyes, clenching his fists before opening the email.

"Fuck," Damian whispered and tossed the computer onto the edge of the mattress before throwing himself on his back.

I stared at the words, the threat, the knowledge that I didn't die, and I slid my gaze to Damian's.

Someone witnessed our escape.

Night Hawk
Chapter Thirty-two
Damian

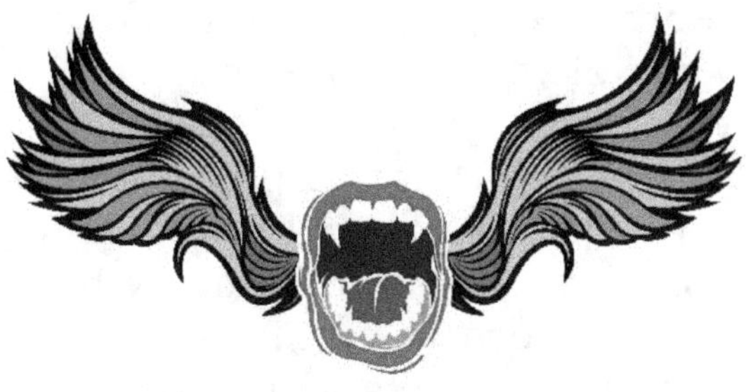

I CAN'T WATCH HER die. That isn't even an option, and the grisly details of what Lucifer would do when he found us were spelled out in black and white on my screen. Each word pummeled my heart and if he ever got hold of us, I would wish for death long before it came. The crush of his promise made my skin burn with fear.

"He doesn't know you turned me," Naomi said, scrolling down the page.

"What difference does that make?"

"To him, I'm just a weak human." She waved at the screen. "I say we go after him instead of waiting for the ball to drop."

Laughter shot from my chest. She was out of her fucking mind and all I could do was shake my head. My laughter choked when she climbed on top of me, straddling my lap, her eyes filled with that wicked twinkle.

My hands landed on her waist and my laughter wound down. "I can't."

"What do you mean, you can't?"

"I've already witnessed the death of someone I loved. I'm not doing it again."

Her eyebrows rose and her mouth dropped open.

Irritation raked over my skin. She still didn't get the depth of our connection, of what all this meant to me, of what she meant to me.

"Did you just..."

"Shut up," I growled and pressed my palms to my eyes. I didn't want to be forced to say the words, not right now when everything in our future was so precarious. The reality of happily ever after was a farce, and the passage of each second brought us closer to the end.

She shifted off me and without removing my hands from over my eyes, I could still picture her with her knees to her chest and her arms wrapped around her legs, wearing that pouting expression that made me want to put my fist through a wall.

With Naomi, it was fire and ice, and I couldn't seem to regulate the emotional impact she had on me. I sighed, pulling my palms away from my face and sure enough, she sat with her arms around her legs and her chin resting on her knee like the sweet child she was at heart, but instead of a pout, she just studied me with interest.

"What?" I asked.

"Sometimes you can be just as juvenile as a teenager."

"Oh, and you can't be?" My comeback brought forth a sour expression, and she dropped her hands, reaching for the computer. I didn't stop her and as she scrolled down the message, taking in everything that I had scanned, her face paled and her gaze rose from the screen.

"He's a real prick, isn't he?"

"Yes." No argument from me there.

When her gaze dropped back to the screen and her fingers started plucking on the keyboard, I sat up.

"What are you doing?"

"Responding in kind," she said and offered me a sly smile. "Since he knows I'm alive, I have a few choice words for him."

"Don't," I snapped, grabbing for the computer and she pulled it away from me. Messing with Lucifer wasn't a prudent thing to do.

"Why the hell not?" she asked.

Her glare said it all, and I rolled my eyes, snatching the laptop from her before she had the chance to hit send. I went to close the browser and paused, raising an eyebrow at the equally disturbing descriptions she typed. I moved my gaze from the screen to her and pressed my lips together, shutting off the smirk.

The temptation to send her scathing prose was just too much, and I hovered the mouse over the command, at the last second I move away from the button and closed the window, opting for at least one more night of safety before sending Lucifer on an all out manhunt. I shut down the computer and dropped it back in my bag.

"What are we going to do for the rest of the day?" she asked, glancing around at the small space.

I sensed her unease, her inability to sit still, and smiled. There were a thousand and one things I could think of to pass the time, none of which included a stitch of clothing.

Her eyes narrowed. "Get your mind out of the gutter."

I raised my hands in the air and laughed. "You're the one who asked the stupid question."

"When the sun sets, I want to go after Mark," she said, and all humor in me evaporated.

"That's not a good idea," I said.

"They won't expect it and I'll be able to dole out a bit of revenge." She sent that sexy smile that sent my blood into overdrive, but underneath there was a deadly streak. "Besides, he's the only human I want to drain dry. He sold me out thinking he'd find fame. Well, I'll give him the headlines he's searching for. He just won't be alive to see it."

"You are a very evil little girl," I purred and got to my hands and knees, crossing the distance between us.

"Not," she said with a laugh and shuffled away, hopping to her feet and retreating far enough to avoid my reach.

Catching her scent, I moved, slamming her into the nearest wall, pinning her to the flimsy metal. "You like to play games, don't you," I whispered and met her gaze.

She sent a shrug my way, and I raised her arms over her head, enjoying the feel of her against my chest, even with the t-shirt.

"Are you always this way?"

"What way?"

"As horny as a tomcat with a room full of females in heat."

I chuckled, not because of the analogy, but because it had been my MO for as long as I could remember. And even though the situation with her was worlds away from the whores I bedded, the basic fact that sex and revenge ruled my world wasn't a mystery.

"Yes," I admitted. "Although you have ignited an entirely new desire."

"And what might that be?" she teased, trying to weasel out of my grip.

"The will to live," I whispered and crushed her lips under mine.

Night Hawk
Chapter Thirty-three
Naomi

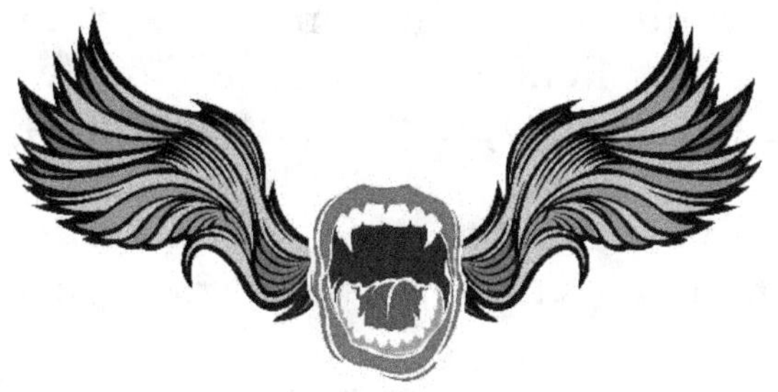

BREATH STEALING HAD BECOME the norm with his kisses, but this time, it was the words uttered before his mouth found mine. When he pulled away, I met his gaze. All teasing and fun slipped away.

"What do you mean?" I searched his smoldering features.

Damian paused, running his hands down my arms before pulling me into a tight grasp, all of which clouded my focus and doubled my heart rate, but I needed to know. When he leaned in to kiss me again, I moved back.

"Well?" I asked.

"I didn't care whether I lived or died until I sank my teeth into your throat."

He kept my gaze, striking me speechless.

"You changed that," he added, shifting under my silent stare.

"Why?"

All I got in answer was a shrug and my eyebrows rose. His gaze dropped and for a moment, I saw underneath his façade, into the pain in his soul.

"What is it?"

"I'm wondering if at some level I knew you were one of Michael's bloodline," he whispered and shifted again, pulling away. "Like I knew it was a suicide mission." His hands dropped, and he went to turn away.

"Damian," I said, and he turned, meeting my gaze.

"I never bet on you biting me," he whispered. "And I sure as shit never thought I'd fall in love with you." He reached out and ran the back of his knuckles over my cheek. "And now that I have, I don't want this to end."

"Who says it has to?"

His gaze softened, and he tilted his head, looking at me as if I was a four-year-old child that had just asked for the impossible. "We both know how this ends," he said.

The hell I did, and I sent him a silent challenge that made him chuckle.

"God, you're so fucking naïve," he whispered.

"Don't be so condescending," I snapped, my mood souring at his tone.

"I'm not trying to be," he said and pulled me back to the mattress, waving for me to take a seat before he continued. "Before all this, I was an annoyance to..." He pointed at his computer. "But I've now upgraded to a bona fide member of his hit list. No one survives that, even with Michael on their side, and I don't even have him in my court now." Damian rubbed his face and sat down next to me. "Honestly, if he catches up to us...I wouldn't want to survive after the things he'll make me witness."

He took my hand and brought it to his lips.

"So, right now, I'm unwilling to walking into a position where he could trap us."

"Look, I am a big girl, and I know how dangerous it is out there, but Luc..." I clamped my mouth closed on the name and started again. "But he knows you wouldn't walk me into that situation. That's why we should strike tonight. Because it will not be expected."

I could see my logic chipping away at his reluctance, and he sighed. When he met my gaze, I knew I had won my argument, and I tried not to gloat.

"Hell hath no fury?" he said, and dimples made a brief appearance.

I pushed him and he smiled, yanking me to him as he stretched out on the mattress.

"If I'm walking you into the lion's den tonight, I better take advantage of every second I have with you today."

"Oh, really?"

He didn't answer with words, instead; he grinned and pulled me to his lips.

Night Hawk
Chapter Thirty-four
Damian

HOURS LATER, I LAY with her sprawled across my chest, her light snores bringing a smile to my lips, but it was fleeting as I let my mind drift to the approaching sunset. My gaze drifted to the fading light leaking through the doors, painting shadows on the ceiling, and I wondered what the sun would feel like.

If Lucifer found us, that's exactly what the morning would bring and I had seen enough vampires reduced to dust to know it wasn't a pleasant end.

Her head rose, and she met my gaze.

"Stop worrying," she whispered and stretched.

"Easy for you to say. You've never seen Lucifer in action," I said, and she stiffened, her eyes widening. It took me a moment to understand her reaction and then what I had said slapped into my brain.

"Oh, fuck," I muttered and slid her off me. "Get dressed," I ordered and crossed to the front of the container, grabbing my damp clothing and sliding them on. A glance at my watch told me we didn't have much time before sunset, but it was enough to trap us in this metal tomb.

I heard the click of a gun and turned toward Naomi as she came around the boxes with her jeans, weapons belt and the skintight black camisole that made me want to forget about the coming danger. When she tossed me the gun in her hand, I stared at it and snapped my gaze back to her.

"You know how to shoot a gun, right?"

"Where did you get these?"

"From those assholes that broke into Valerie's house," she said, flipping the safety on her gun and slipping it into her waistband. "You know how to shoot, right?"

I nodded. It was one of the things I had learned over the years, but from her display at the house, I was sorely lacking in skill in comparison. I made sure the safety was on and slid the gun into my coat pocket before dragging her back through the maze. She kept glancing at her watch and the door while I packed up my computer, zipping the backpack before cracking open the cooler. A half dozen blood bags sat in the bottom and I pulled three out, tossing them to Naomi.

"Power up," I said and did the same.

Naomi handed me her empties and slid on the black bomber jacket she had shoved in the duffel bag and stood looking every bit as formidable as she had that first night. She folded the mural and handed it to me.

"Do you have room for this?"

It fit neatly on top of the computer and I zipped the bag closed. My heart clanged in my chest with each passing minute and I stepped toward her, sliding my backpack over her arms and clipping it across her stomach before giving her a kiss.

I handed her the gun. "You'll have to do the shooting. I'll do the flying." With a big inhale, I glanced at the watch again. "I'm not sure if we should open the door or barrel through it."

"Will going through the door hurt?"

"No, but it will leave no doubt about where we had been."

She pulled the clip out of the gun and stared at the neatly lined bullets before snapping it back in. "If you fly farther north, will you be able to loop around to the city without being seen?"

"We'll find out."

"How accurate is his intuition on where we are?"

I shrugged and took a deep breath, attempting to settle the nerves skittering over my skin like a hoard of spiders. "I don't know."

"Then let's chance going out the door. That way, if no one is there, we can at least lock the place up," she said.

I debated, weighing our chances. Another glance at my watch told me I only had seconds to decide before the sun dipped below the horizon. "Okay," I whispered, and she offered me a smile of support. "I won't be able to fly far, not at twilight, but I think I can get us to a shopping center and then we'll have to procure a car."

"Procure?"

"It sounds nicer than steal," I said, and her dimples appeared.

"I thought you weren't a thief?"

"This isn't the time to razz me, love." I turned and plucked the lock out of the track. "You ready for this?" I asked, and she stepped close, flipping the safety off and positioning herself in a ready stance, with the gun aimed toward the door.

"Go," she said.

I leaned down and gripped the door, sending one more glance in her direction before I pulled it up and slid outside with her leading the way. It took me a second to flip the lock, and I didn't wait for her to give the all clear. Instead, I wrapped my arms around her and launched us over the building into the woods to the north.

No bullets flew in our direction and I landed at the edge of the woods near a strip mall. My heart still clanged in my chest, but the overwhelming fear abated a fraction. It had been years since I hot-wired a car and I scanned the slim pickings and then glanced back at Naomi.

"None of these will work," she muttered.

"Why not?"

"These shoppers aren't planning on being here for a long time. We need more than fifteen minutes to get out of town," she said, and my curiosity bloomed.

"When we get out of here, you'll have to fill me in on how you know that," I said and unclipped the backpack, slipping it off her back and slinging it over my shoulder before taking her hand. "If not here, then where?"

"A mall garage would be best, but it doesn't look like that'll be easy to find here, so let's look for something covered in frost or with a thin layer of snow. That's a vehicle that hasn't been used and the likelihood of it being reported right away is lower."

"Okay," I said, and let her lead the way. She handed me the gun, and I stashed it in the backpack before we stepped out from the woods. We crossed through the parking area and circled behind the building. A car with a frost-bloom pattern on the windshield sat behind the building. "Like that?"

"No."

"Why not?" I asked, trying to squelch the budding irritation.

"Because I'm willing to bet the owner works here and is just about ready to leave."

As if on cue, the door on the back of the store swung open and a man with gray-speckled hair and a weathered face stepped into the alleyway, taking a moment to light a cigarette. With it hanging from his lips, he pointed his remote at the car and it beeped.

We were in the shadows, less than ten paces away, and I traded a glance with Naomi, seeing the spark in her eyes. Perhaps our luck had changed and when the car door opened, I nodded my head in his direction. Naomi understood, and she stepped out of the shadows, clearing her throat.

The man spun, and his eyes widened, but the cigarette didn't move from his lips. When his gaze focused on her, it softened.

"What's a sweet thing like you doing hanging out here?" he asked.

Naomi shrugged. "I think I'm lost," she whispered, and the confused pout she wore even suckered me in. When she slowly stepped toward the man, I almost laughed at his incredulous expression. "The last thing I remember was taking a drink at a party and then I woke up in a deserted car. I don't have any idea where I am. Can you help me?" She stopped a few feet from him.

"Are you hurt?" he asked and concern laced his voice.

Naomi shook her head. "I don't think so. Can you tell me where I am?"

"You're in Albany, darling."

Naomi let out a sharp laugh and looked around, raking her fingers through her hair. "Oh my god," she whispered. "I'm from Pittsburgh."

Her ad-lib was priceless, and I covered the grin.

"How in god's name am I going to get home?" she said, her voice rising with panic.

"I can take you to the bus stop if you'd like," he offered and pulled the cigarette from his lips.

Naomi blinked at him and then rummaged through her pockets. I swore her chin quivered. "I don't have, I don't have any money," she whispered, her voice lilting the way a girl about to cry does. She crossed her arms and shivered.

"Look, let me get you out of the cold and if you'd like, you can use my cell phone to call someone." He waved to the car, and she hesitated before offering a nod and rounding to the passenger side. When she closed the passenger door and took the cell phone from his hand, I moved, opening the back door and sliding in before either of them could react.

Her eyes widened when I placed the barrel of the gun to the back of his head.

"Drive," I snarled and had to hand it to the old man. He kept his cool and slid the keys into the ignition.

Naomi clung to the phone and moved herself against the passenger door, her expression one of absolute fright, and I nearly lost the glare in my expression.

"Is he with you?" the man snarled at Naomi, and her gaze moved from the gun to his face.

She shook her head and whispered, "No."

Even I believed the lie.

He stared at her a moment and then met my gaze in the rearview mirror. "Son, I suggest you put that gun away before someone gets hurt."

"I suggest you drive before someone gets hurt," I snapped back.

His lips thinned, and he put the car in gear, pulling out on the road.

"Where exactly am I driving?"

"South, towards New York City," I said and glanced at Naomi. "What are you looking at?"

Her gaze dropped to the phone in her hand and she turned toward the windshield.

"You don't have to be rude," she muttered, and I almost burst out laughing.

"Why don't you show me what you have in your hands before I blow your friend's brains through the windshield?"

Naomi stiffened in the seat and she slowly raised the phone. I reached forward and plucked it out of her grip. She gave the driver another one of those forlorn looks.

"What's your name?" I asked, and she glanced at me.

"Anna," she whispered, using the same name she had with Valerie.

"Well, Anna, stow the attitude, otherwise this is going to be a very long three-hour ride."

"What are you going to do with us once we get there?" the man asked as he pulled onto the freeway.

"Nothing. You're just on a six-hour joy ride as long as you both cooperate."

"Bullshit," he muttered and glared at me.

"What are you doing with such a hot thing, anyway?" I narrowed my eyes at him.

"I was taking her to the police station," he said, sending me a challenging stare.

"I thought..." she began and stopped. Instead of continuing, she crossed her arms and slumped in the seat. "New York City, Albany, it doesn't matter," she muttered. "It's still a long ass way from home."

"What's your name?" I asked and tapped his head with the barrel.

"None of your fucking business," he snapped, and I smiled in response.

"Okay, in that case, I'll just call you Lebaron, after your shitty car."

THE REST OF THE ride was quiet and despite Lebaron's less than subtle attempts at flagging for help, Naomi remained subdued in the front seat. Staying in character despite the silence.

The wall of stopped cars ahead made me pause, even though we were approaching the George Washington Bridge. Traffic here wasn't uncommon, but my internal alarms started tripping and my gaze shot beyond the traffic to the red and blue flashing lights beyond.

I swiveled my gaze to the man. "Pull over."

He saw the red and blues too, and his hands tightened on the wheel.

"Pull over or she dies," I said, moving the barrel in Naomi's direction. I played the bluff, and it worked. Muttering under his breath, Lebaron pulled to the side of the road. "Now please step out of the car." I kept my gaze on Naomi. "I'm talking to you, not him," I clarified.

Her jaw dropped. "But," she started.

"Get out," I growled, and she blinked before sliding out of the car. She shut the door, and I swung the barrel against Lebaron's head. "Step on the gas."

Lebaron hesitated, and when Naomi reached for the door handle, he peeled away from her. I got a quick glimpse at her aggravated features before I focused on the man in the front seat.

"You're going to drive right by that barricade unless they wave you over to the side of the road. If they do, then I'll keep them busy and you just drive away. Understand?" I asked, and he looked at me like I had sprouted another head. "I was desperate, okay? I needed to get to the city as fast as humanly possible, and I really need to get through that barricade."

"What about the girl?" Lebaron asked, and I inhaled, looking out the window at the approaching checkpoint.

"I didn't want her caught in the middle if this gets nasty."

He leveled another glare in the rearview mirror and gave a curt nod.

"I'm gonna fade into the shadows back here, but I still have the barrel of the gun aimed at your back, so please don't make this any uglier than it already is." I leaned back in the seat, using the shadows to my advantage. Lebaron glanced back at me and his eyebrows creased. "Drive," I said, and he snapped his gaze back at the road.

The closer we got to the checkpoint, the more the supernatural chill bit at my bones. The bastard was here and when the state trooper turned his flashlight on our vehicle; I clenched my teeth.

Lucifer stared right at me before moving his gaze to Lebaron.

"Sir, please pull to the side of the road and put your hands on the wheel where I can see them."

As Lebaron pulled to the side, I dropped the gun on the seat next to him and whispered, "As soon as you hear the door, hit the gas." I met his gaze. "I'm serious. If you don't, you'll die tonight."

When Lucifer had crossed half the distance, I opened the back door and rolled onto the pavement, landing in a crouch, facing the devil himself. I rose to my feet, irritated that the car still idled behind me.

"Where is she?" Lucifer asked and unclasped his gun.

"Gone," I answered and my heart slammed in my chest as I looked around at the number of demons converging on the scene, every one of them wearing the skin of a cop.

"Hands on the wheel!" a voice growled behind me and I closed my eyes.

"I held a gun to his head and made him drive me down here," I said.

"Why would you do that?"

"Because I want to skin the bastard who sold her out."

"Get on your knees and put your hands on your head," Lucifer growled.

The click of a hammer made my teeth clench, and I dropped to my knees on the cold pavement, putting my hands on my head. The burn of platinum bit my skin and I winced as one of the officers secured my wrists in specially designed handcuffs.

Lebaron started arguing with one of the demon officers, and I heard the click of another pair of handcuffs.

Lucifer yanked me to my feet and surveyed the onlookers. He shoved me in the back of the squad car and leaned in. "You're going to wish I had shot you before this night is over."

The door slammed, and I leaned back, closing my eyes. All manners of torture danced over my eyelids and I ground my teeth together to keep them from chattering. When the door on the opposite side of the cruiser opened and Lebaron was shoved into the cage next to me, I met his gaze.

"You should have listened," I said, and he just glared at me. The poor soul thought we were going to the nearest precinct. I knew better and when the car pulled into an abandoned warehouse, I let out a breath of air at the chains glinting in the center of the building.

My gaze rose to the upper level, specifically to the upper wall of windows on the east side of the building.

"What time is it?" I whispered to no one in particular.

Lucifer pulled the keys out of the ignition and turned. "You have a little over eight hours before sunrise."

"This isn't the police station," Lebaron snapped, interrupting Lucifer's concentration. "And why is my car here?"

I looked at Lebaron. "Because they don't leave loose ends."

Lucifer stepped out of the car and opened the back. He reached in and grabbed a handful of my hair, dragging me from the car before tossing me toward the waiting chains. Platinum utensils glowed on the table and I swallowed the fear constricting my throat.

Two demons stepped out of the shadows, yanking me to where the chains lay. I struggled, and when they unclasped the handcuffs, I twisted out of their grasp. My right fist landed in the middle of one of the demon's faces and I had a moment of satisfaction at the feel of bones crunching under my knuckles.

All those years of different martial arts disciplines kicked in and I used the momentum of the second demon and spun him, tossing him into the first asshole. More demons came out of the woodwork and I have no idea how many I took down before the click of a hammer caught my attention. I turned toward the noise.

Lucifer held the barrel of the gun against Lebaron's temple.

"I think that's enough, don't you?" he asked.

"Fuck you," I snarled.

"Let me put it a different way. If you don't cut the shit, I'll blow his brains out."

My fists clenched as tight as my jaw and I sent a glare, but when the remaining demons grabbed me, I didn't struggle. Instead, I let them pull me into the center of the warehouse, over the dead bodies of over a dozen demons to where the chains awaited.

My chest rose and fell with the fury filling my cells, making the fear seeded in my stomach abate. Fabric ripped, and I jerked my shoulder away, reviving a fraction of my fight as they stripped the shirt off my back.

A growl formed in my chest until Lucifer clucked his warning, tapping the gun on Lebaron's temple as a reminder. When the first stab ripped through my left shoulder, a protest of pain peeled from my throat.

The burn of the platinum hook locked my ability to reason and when they pierced my right shoulder, I started spouting curse after curse, alternating between my native Greek and English. Each wrap of the chain around my arms burned, and the fuckers had the audacity to laugh. There wasn't a goddamn thing I could do now, and I struggled to remain standing under the crippling pain.

Lucifer gave a nod and one of his henchmen turned a crank, tightening the chains until my arms stretched to the sides.

Lebaron just stared at the spectacle, his eyes blinking rapidly and his mouth hanging open in shock. I could tell he didn't have a clue what was coming.

"You've made your point. Let him go," I said, mustering up enough anger to send a glare at Lucifer.

The report of the gun silenced Lebaron for eternity and I bit down on the flash of envy that gripped me at his quick death. What I had coming was worlds away from quick and I ground my teeth together, grasping at the fleeting fury, trying to hold on to some semblance of sanity.

Lucifer glanced into the darkness to my right and I followed his gaze. A man stepped out of the shadows. A human, and the anger came back full force, enough so I lunged against the chains, the motion creating a ripping agony in my shoulders and I thundered my discontent.

I knew exactly who this fucker was, and he waltzed up in front of me, his smug expression just as infuriating as the memories of how he treated Naomi.

"You're the asshole who sold her out," I said, my voice raw from pain.

"Yes, and you made the mistake of intervening."

I allowed a smile to form. "The mistake was yours." I straightened, standing tall. I narrowed my eyes, inspecting him in a way that made him shift uncomfortably, his eyes bouncing from my face to the barbed hooks piercing my skin.

"What kind of loser sells out his girlfriend because he can't get into her pants?"

"Shut up," he snapped.

"And while we're talking about that, why was it you couldn't get her to do the deed? Oh yeah, it must be because you're a world class dick," I taunted, pushing his buttons and watching his aggravation grow.

"Like she would ever sleep with a vampire," he laughed.

I raised an eyebrow and produced a knowing smile, letting my mind flow over every nuance of her. The memory gave me strength, and I inhaled.

"Mhm, and she was so fucking good."

I let the words hang on the air, enjoying the effect they had on her ex. His face turned a shade of red that I wasn't readily familiar with, one usually reserved for heart attack victims.

"Worth dying for?" Lucifer asked.

"Yes."

Both Lucifer and Mark blinked, not expecting my immediate answer or the smile that accompanied the single syllable.

It took a second, and Mark's face scrunched into a mask of anger. His brass-knuckle-clad fist slammed into my cheek hard enough for me to stumble back a step, but the chains kept me in place. He didn't stop with just one swing either, and the brass knuckles he wore were platinum-plated for maximum damage.

I blinked away the gray spots in front of my vision in time to see Mark pick up a whip from the table. He had worked himself into a frenzy while Lucifer leaned against the car, watching the beating with amusement. The rest of the demon horde had spread out around the perimeter to watch the show.

The first snap of the whip sliced a trail through my back, dropping me to my knees and forcing a bellow of anguish from me. A pain-filled haze gripped me, tearing at every cell, and my gaze rose to the windows.

"Michael, keep her safe," I whispered at the night sky and another crack of the whip followed.

The sunrise couldn't come fast enough.

Night Hawk
Chapter Thirty-five
Naomi

Pissed didn't describe the fury cramping my muscles as I stomped down the breakdown lane toward the distant police strobes. The frigid winter wind tossed my hair behind me, but I hardly felt the bite of it. It wasn't until I got closer to the checkpoint that I noticed the effect of the chill and my gaze shot to the barricade, now within sight.

I slowed, listening to my internal alarms instead of barreling through like a crazy banshee. When the procession of cop cars rolled away from the scene, I glimpsed the Lebaron and I almost sprinted, until I saw the driver's profile.

A chill settled over me and I could feel the growl form in my throat.

Mark was driving the car, which meant only one thing.

They had Damian.

I took a step toward the cars and stopped, unsure of what to do next. All of my instincts told me to turn and run in the opposite direction, and I knew that's exactly what Damian wanted. He wanted to die knowing I was safe, and I bit down at the flare of anger.

That's why he ditched me.

And I was damned if I'd let him die at the hands of Lucifer.

By the time I got to where the police barricade had been, all traces of the demons and Damian were gone, and the flow of traffic had picked up again. I stomped my foot on the pavement and cursed under my breath. There was only one person who I could think of that could help, and I turned, crossing into the small outcrop of woods lining the road.

"Michael?" I asked, hoping I had the ability to call my long-lost relative.

The wind shifted around me and I turned, meeting the angel's questioning gaze.

"They have Damian."

"I know," he said, crossing his arms.

My mouth dropped open. "So, what are you going to do about it?"

His gaze narrowed. "Watch your tone with me."

I stepped closer, leveling a glare. "You can't let him die."

He closed the distance, towering over me. "I can't intervene," he said through clenched teeth, and I caught the measure of frustration in his tone.

"Why the fuck not?" I shot back, challenging him.

"Because they have the facility marked. I can't get in, and Lucifer can't get out."

His answer wasn't what I expected, and I saw the anguish in Michael's gaze instead of the anger he displayed earlier in Damian's presence. It was almost akin to a father's grief, and I raised my eyebrows, unable to voice the questions that flooded into my head.

"He was supposed to be my son-in-law," Michael said to my questioning stare.

"So, you care about what happens to him?"

Michael nodded.

I looked down at the ground for a minute, digesting the conversation, and then my gaze snapped back to his. "You know where they took him." It wasn't a question and when he looked away, he confirmed it.

"Take me there," I said, and Michael laughed. "I'm serious. I can get him out."

"Damian was right about you being naïve," he said.

"I have to try," I whispered, my lilt on the cusp of begging. "Please."

His lips pressed together, and he shook his head. "I can't protect you and neither can he."

"Did it ever occur to you I can hold my own? After all, I've been able to get the drop on you several times."

Wings fluttered, and he sighed. "If I agree to this, the first thing you have to do is find the mark that looks like this." Michael turned and drew a symbol on the tree that looked like a complex and detailed Chinese symbol. "And destroy it."

"How?"

"If it's on the glass, break the glass. If it is on the wall, scratch it so you put a break in the pattern. That will allow me to get inside."

I looked at the symbol. "And it will allow Lucifer to get out."

He nodded, and I shook my head. "I want to tear his head off myself."

"Damian expects me to protect you," he started, and I opened my mouth to argue, but he put his hand up, stopping me. "He expects me to protect you and considering how much he has done for me over the years, I need to honor that."

"I cannot let him die," I said. The thought of losing him made my heart hurt, like a bullet tore through my chest, producing an overwhelming panic. "I love him."

Michael's eyes closed and his chin dropped to his chest. "Naomi," he started.

"I will not let him die," I said. The force of my words brought his gaze back to mine. "Whether or not you help me, I'll find them and I'll stop them." I turned to leave, and his hand clamped down on my arm.

The transition of time and space warped my brain, and when I blinked, we stood at the edge of a deserted parking lot. At the far end stood a large building made of brick and glass and steel. The second-floor windows caught my attention, and I turned, meeting Michael's gaze.

"They're going to let him burn, aren't they?"

Michael inhaled. "Yes, that's if he doesn't bleed to death first."

I took a step toward the building, unaware that Michael still held my arm. I looked at the grip that stopped me and then up into his eyes. "Let go," I whispered.

"You're not going to wipe out that symbol, are you?"

I debated on giving him a line of crap but somehow I knew he'd see through me, so I shook my head. "If I can't save him, my choice is to die with him."

Michael's eyes misted over, and he looked at the building before returning his gaze to me. "If you get out of there alive, I expect you to keep this information to yourself. Anger works with us and has for millenniums. If he knew I loved him like a son, he might not stay on the righteous path he's on."

"So all your threats?"

"Were serious. If he steps over the line again, I will destroy him whether I want to or not. I made an exception with you, but I won't in the future. He cannot spill innocent human blood." Michael raised his eyebrows. "Neither can you."

"I have no intention of doing that."

He smiled and, with a nod, he held out his arm, exposing his wrist to me. "If you're damn sure you aren't going to destroy that mark, you will need some extra magic to have a prayer of pulling this off. But understand, if you drain me, I won't have the strength to intervene," he clarified when I took his hand.

"You won't die?"

Michael shook his head. "No, I'll just be out of commission for a few days. Take what you need, child."

I hesitated and then brought the soft flesh to my lips. His sweet scent brought forth my fangs, and I bit, closing my eyes and drinking his pure blood, feeling it fuse into my muscles like an armor plate. Revelation after revelation fed into my consciousness, things he had blocked the last time I bit him, and I sighed at the depth of the angel's mercy.

Damian's pain-filled voice echoed in Michael's head. "Michael, keep her safe."

I stiffened and my eyelids flew open, meeting Michael's gaze before my teeth retracted and my head swiveled toward the warehouse. I dropped his hand and bolted toward the building. Within two paces, I transitioned, and my fury and panic melded into the perfect cocktail, giving me the speed and focus I needed.

Scanning the front of the building, I honed in on a lower level window next to the left corner and headed straight for it. The glass disintegrated the moment I launched and, when I landed inside the small room, I rolled, coming to a standing position in my human form. I glanced over my shoulder and gave a nod of thanks to Michael. He returned it with a look that begged for me to be careful, and then he was gone.

I stood in the dark room, letting my eyes adjust and mapping out my strategy, debating on what to enter the belly of the warehouse as. I knew my tiger form was a force to be reckoned with, but not knowing how many demons were on the other side of the office door left me at a disadvantage. I needed to get close to where they held Damian, and that clinched my decision.

If they thought I was human, I'd have a better chance of getting to him.

I reached behind me, digging the gun out of my waistband, and checked the clip. I had four bullets left, and I inhaled, steadying myself for what would come after they ran out. I closed my eyes and flipped off the safety before stepping to the door.

A short hallway greeted me, and the creak of the hinges was masked by another sharp cry. I bit down on my lip, forcing myself to move slowly instead of listening to the building panic inside my muscles, willing me to rush.

I knew once the first bullet flew, my element of surprise would shatter. I stepped into the shadows and got my first look at the setup, focusing on the exterior walls instead of the spectacle in the center.

I counted a half dozen within range and steeled myself for action. Lining up the closest demon's head in the gunsight, I exhaled and pulled the trigger. My shot was true, and he went down. The burn of glares hit me and I ignored it, turning and taking out the second demon before he could step in my direction. They moved fast, and I got the last two shots off before my gun clicked empty.

Tossing the useless shell away, I yanked both knives from my belt, wielding them as the demon hoard approached. My mind raced, and I had to keep the strength pounding my muscles in check. Everything I did had to scream human, otherwise my chances of getting to the center of the floor where Damian was would be killed just as efficiently as I had killed the first demon.

I slashed out, giving the impression of desperation until I was overwhelmed and disarmed. They dragged me, kicking and cursing, all the way to where a police car sat and a darker version of Michael stood with arms crossed and lips pressed together in an amused smirk.

I landed at his feet and glared up at him from my hands and knees.

He looked to his right and an eyebrow rose. I followed his gaze and gasped. Damian was in worse shape than he had been in the woods. The sharp hooks piercing his shoulders sent a wave of nauseous fury through me and I kept it in check, storing it away for when I made my move. When his gaze met mine, I saw defeat and sorrow that stripped my soul down to my base instincts.

"You bastard," I snarled and scrambled to my feet, glaring at Lucifer.

Lucifer's hand reached out and grabbed a handful of my hair, pulling me close and inhaling through his nose. "My god, she smells heavenly," he said, glancing at Damian. "How did you not feast on this girl?"

Damian's gaze shifted to me and he forced himself to his feet, his features morphing into a grimace, and I silently swore they all would pay dearly for torturing him. I glanced at the demons surrounding us, counting a meager five left to defend the building, and they were close by, watching my struggle with interest.

"She's Michael's bloodline," he whispered as if it was a reason, but I could see the confusion in his expression, confusion that Lucifer mistook as pain.

"You fucked this monster?" The question shot from the dark behind Damian, and I tensed, letting my mouth drop open with just the right amount of shock. Mark stepped from the shadows, a bloodied whip in his hand, and I almost changed, just for the sheer joy of ripping him to pieces.

The hand gripping my hair stopped me from doing anything rash just yet, but I had to give a show, so I lunged toward him, yanked back by the hair, allowing a stream of unladylike curses fall from my lips.

Mark threw the whip on the table and approached me, his features contorted in rage. Lucifer pushed me toward him and I stumbled, catching myself to stand tall and defiant.

"You fucked him?" he repeated, pointing at Damian.

I shrugged. "What do you care? You sold me out," I snapped and shifted, putting enough distance between Lucifer and me so I was now out of his reach.

Mark scanned me and then gazed at Lucifer. "I want to fuck her before you kill her," he said, just like I thought he would. The prick was so predictable.

Lucifer gave a go-ahead wave and Damian growled a warning, but I focused on Mark.

"I'd like to see you try," I said, daring him to step within range. I closed my mouth, ignoring the pulse in my teeth and the desire to tear into this bastard. No one in the room besides Damian knew what I was, and when Mark stepped forward, I nearly smiled at his stupidity.

Instead, I shifted my weight, taking a ready stance.

"You think your little self-defense classes are going to save you?" he said, laughing.

"Maybe, maybe not, but I'll at least get a couple shots in, maybe even ruin that pretty face of yours," I said, and the vain asshole paused, nodding to the beasts surrounding us.

"You fucking coward!" I yelled when arms gripped me, holding me in place as he approached.

He stepped close, his hands grabbing my coat and pushing it over my shoulders. The grip on my arms loosened as the demons stripped the garment. I jerked away from Mark's touch, but the demons held me in place. He squeezed one of my breasts through the camisole and grinned.

"I've been waiting years for this," he whispered, and his fingers trailed to my belt.

I brought my knee up, but he expected it, grabbing a hold of my knee, his eyes narrowed in a way that chilled me. The thought that I once thought I loved this asshat made me want to puke.

"So predictable," he said and stepped close, holding my thigh to his hip, and his free hand gripped my ass. He smiled and pressed his crotch to mine, his hard shaft suggesting exactly what he had in store. "And so fucking hot," he whispered.

I tried to wriggle free, giving the impression that the grip on my arms was as good as iron shackles. He laughed and leaned forward, kissing my bare shoulder. His lips followed the line of my neck to my ear, and I glanced at

Damian before my gaze landed on Mark's exposed neck.

It was time, and I sank my teeth into the flesh bared before me, relishing the hot stream that filled my mouth as much as Mark's scream. At the same time I bit, I yanked both demons, knocking their skulls together in a teeth-shattering thud. I spun Mark, throwing him against the stunned demons.

I didn't hesitate; I lunged and when I landed on the trio, claws ripped flesh and screams filled the room. I focused on the demons, leaving Mark for later. I wanted him to live with a few minutes of terror before I tore his head off. I wanted him to feel death's breath, to know how fucking terrifying it was to know he was only a few moments away from dying.

The rest of the hoard charged, and I leaped from the dead bodies, focusing on the chains holding Damian before dispatching the rest of the beasts. The metal holding his right arm snapped in my jaws and before I could reach the second chain, the remaining demons surrounded me.

Lucifer bellowed commands. They were not about to kill me. That I was his, but I didn't wait for them to ensnare me at his orders. I went on the offensive, tearing them apart before turning to Lucifer and Mark. I launched toward them, snapping the second chain in half on my way past Damian.

Lucifer stepped to my right, and I snarled, undecided who to go attack. The scent of Mark's blood drew my attention, and I focused on him. Fury filled every cell and my haunches tightened, springing me onto him. His dying screams of terror fueled my anger, heightening my need to kill, and I clawed and bit, relishing the taste of fear in his blood until all that was left echoing in the warehouse was my snarl and the ripping of flesh.

"Naomi," his voice cut through the rage and I turned.

Lucifer held a handful of Damian's hair and the barrel of a gun rested on his temple. My heart stopped, and the breath locked in my lungs. When I took a step toward them, Lucifer cocked the hammer back. I hesitated, letting the transition take hold.

"Please, don't," I whispered, lifting my gaze from Damian's, meeting Lucifer's furious eyes.

Lucifer smiled and pulled the trigger. The snap of an empty clip filled the room and his smile faded.

I launched from my spot before Lucifer could recover from the shock of his failure, hitting him full in the chest and knocking him away from Damian. I dug in with both claws and teeth, delivering what should have been mortal wounds.

Unfortunately, Lucifer was neither mortal nor demon, and he found the strength to throw me aside. I scrambled, putting myself between the king of hell and my suffering vampire.

"Naomi," Damian's voice attempted to pull my attention, and I ignored him, keeping my eyes on Lucifer circling the perimeter, limping, and leaving a significant trail of blood.

Damian's grip on my fur finally pulled my attention away, and I turned my head.

"Sun," his gaze rose, and I followed it to the growing light in the window.

Lucifer's laughter rang out, and I snarled, crouching so Damian could climb on my back. He seemed to understand and the moment he had a grip; I took off toward the back of the warehouse, away from the sunrise. The only thing between us and the dark water of the Hudson River was glass, and I didn't hesitate. I leaped, smashing the window and tumbling through the air with Damian still holding tight.

White light filled my senses, and then darkness descended.

Night Hawk
Chapter Thirty-six
Damian

PAIN SCRAPED EVERY CELL of my body and my eyes blinked open to black so thick I couldn't see anything. Our tumble into oblivion still sharp in my mind. I tried to sit up, but hands pushed me back.

"Don't move," Naomi said, her voice drowning all my other senses, layering a blanket of relief over me. Tears burned my throat and traced hot paths down my face, blurring the darkness and dulling the agony.

Wire snapped, and I groaned at the fire burning my shoulder, choking me. I clamped my eyes closed, pressing my teeth together while she pulled the metal shard from my shoulder, unwrapping my arm before placing it on my stomach over my other freed appendage.

"Where are we?" I asked once the ability to articulate returned.

"I don't know," she answered and something delectable pressed against my lips.

The minute my teeth pierced her skin, power flowed into me and I had to temper the burn, the need to suck every last drop from her. The knowledge that she'd let me, if it meant my survival, brought a fresh wave of tears to my eyes and after a few draws on the angel infused blood, I released her wrist, opting to pull her against me in the darkness instead of feasting on her blood.

Crying was not normal for me. It was something that I hadn't done since I was a little boy and the strange outpouring gripped me, flooding my ears with hot liquid. My arms tightened around Naomi, my form shaking to the core with silent sobs. I buried my face in her shoulder and her tender lips found my ear.

"I love you," she whispered, and I squeezed tighter.

Light filled the space, and I opened my eyes, staring up into Michael's magnificent form. His melancholy expression blurred, and I blinked the sheen of tears from my eyes, meeting his hard gaze. I scrunched my eyebrows together, wondering if I had seen the warm expression or if it was just the tears that distorted his features.

Naomi pulled out of my arms and stood, crossing to the angel and giving him a hug.

"Thank you," she said and placed a kiss on his cheek. Michael closed his eyes and gave her a quick squeeze before meeting my gaze.

"How's Valerie?" I asked.

"She's with her uncle in a safe place," Michael answered, and then looked at Naomi. "Lucifer is still alive."

Naomi nodded and looked at the floor.

"My sources tell me he's in bad shape," he said and slid his gaze to me. "So it looks like you've got a reprieve while he heals."

Confusion clouded my already emotionally charged brain, and I attempted to sit up again, succeeding, despite the protest of every muscle. I glanced around at the familiar surroundings of the cottage bedroom and the bags on the floor, including my computer bag, before my gaze snapped back to Michael.

"How?" I asked and pointed to the luggage, but really what I wanted to know was why he saved me. I just didn't know how to ask without setting him off.

Michael's eyebrow rose in that arrogant gesture that always infuriated me.

I bit down on a derogatory remark and traded a glance with Naomi. "Okay, then why?" I asked, finding the curiosity too overwhelming not to ask.

"Because she asked for my help," he said, but I saw something underneath the sternness that told me there was more to it than that. He sent a warning glare in Naomi's direction and added, "The bloodline still needs protection." Which sounded logical considering, but it didn't explain the underlying fatherly vibe I was getting.

"You sure it isn't because you care?" I asked, offering a smirk as compensation for the dig.

Michael's laughter filled the room and then he was gone, leaving Naomi and me alone in the dark.

I stood on shaking legs and crossed to where she stood, wrapping my arms around her. "What you did was stupid and foolish," I whispered, and she stiffened in my arms. "And insanely brave," I added and before she could voice any argument, I crushed her lips under mine, kissing her with every ounce of love and passion filling my soul.

Night Hawk
Epilogue
Naomi

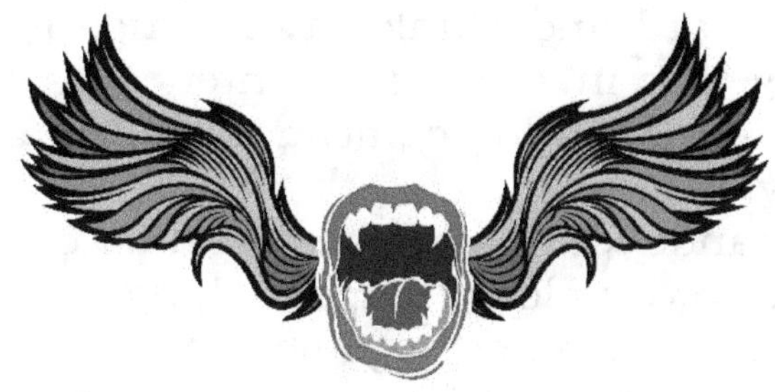

DAMIAN AND I FLED from the east coast as soon as he was healthy enough to move. We found solace in one of his hunting cabins in the Colorado Rockies and carved ourselves a proper living space in the mountain behind the cabin.

It wasn't long after our home was completed that Damian took me out to one of our favorite spots. He made me sit on one of the downed trees while he paced in front of me under the full moon. His constant nibbling on his bottom lip had me concerned.

"Is everything okay?"

He stopped pacing and offered me a soft smile. "Yes, everything is fine," he said, but the nervous expression belied his calm words.

"Are you sure? Because everything about you right now screams nerves."

"Yes. Everything is okay. Just be quiet for a minute. I have something I need to say," he said, exasperated, and then began that incessant gnawing on his lip.

He moved in front of me and I couldn't tell if he tripped or was trying to decide whether to stand or drop to his knees. The entire approach was awkward and clunky, two things I thought I'd never put in the same sentence as Damian Andreas. His entire demeanor pulled a laugh from my lips.

His hands found his waist, and he cocked his head. "Can you please stop laughing?"

I pressed my lips together, but all that did was produce a snort from my nose, which didn't help matters in the least. My incessant giggles turned into a full-bodied laugh.

He stared at me as if I had lost my mind, and then turned, muttering under his breath as he started back towards our cottage.

"Damian, wait," I said, out of breath from laughter. He stopped and the deep breath he took lifted his shoulders before he turned back to me.

"I have a question for you, and I will not ask you if you insist on laughing at me."

The seriousness in his expression squashed my giggles. "I'm sorry. It's just I have never seen you this fidgety. What's bothering you?"

This time when he approached, any sign of nerves had vanished and he stopped right in front of me, staring down at me with such intensity that it was my turn to fidget.

"I know we have only known each other a short time, but I can say with certainty that I love you with all my soul."

He dropped to one knee in front of me, and my heart thumped in my chest.

"I never thought I'd find this kind of passion, this kind of love, again."

His hand slipped under mine, and he brought it to his lips. Just his touch turned my insides to a hot mess, but when he produced a velvet box in his right hand, my breath locked in my chest.

"I want to see every moonrise and moonset with you. I want to dance with you and make love to you under the starlit sky. I want a partner that is my equal on every level." He flipped the box open, and I stared down at the stunning diamond ring. "I honestly don't know why the gods sent you my way, but I cannot imagine a forever without you by my side. So, Naomi Hawk, will you do me the honor of becoming my wife?"

Tears blurred my vision, and my hand moved to cover my mouth. The perfection in his proposal, along with the adoration in his eyes, sealed my answer. He stayed on his knee, but his sincere gaze clouded with worry when a few beats of silence passed. I dropped my hand and nodded, forcing my voice to squeak from my tight chest.

"Yes. Yes, Damian, I will marry you!"

His face transformed into the brightest smile I have ever seen adorned on his lips and he slid the ring on my finger. Damian leaned in and placed a soft kiss on my lips. He pulled away far enough to meet my gaze, and the fire in his irises blazed with the same tornado of need burning through my bloodstream. He swept me off my perch and into his powerful arms, planting a searing kiss that melded our souls into one. With me nestled against his chest, he headed towards the cottage, pledging a forever filled with passion and promise.

THE END

Continue Damian and Naomi's story with MIDNIGHT VOWS.

MIDNIGHT VOWS

Welcome to the wedding of the millennium.

Before she met Damian Andreas, Naomi Hawk always envisioned her wedding on a beach at sunset.

She never thought she'd get married in the mountains under a canopy of stars, but being a vampire bride makes logistics, such as dress shopping and finding a location willing to book a midnight ceremony, difficult to navigate.

Is her wedding going to be everything she dreamed, or a disaster of epic proportions?

Midnight Vows
Chapter 1

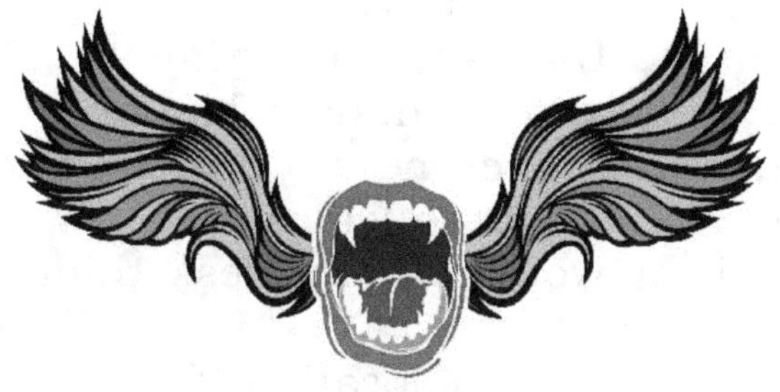

I SLAMMED THE PHONE down, letting out a yell of frustration. Damian came sliding into the room, his eyes all frantic like perhaps Lucifer had shown up instead of me going all banshee because I couldn't find a place that would book a midnight wedding.

"What's wrong?"

"These stupid people don't want to stay later than eleven at night and keep suggesting an earlier wedding. At this point, I'd settle for city hall, which, of course, closes at five," I snapped and waved my hand around like a damn princess.

It was as close to a true hissy fit as Damian had ever seen from me, and his lips twitched. The man was trying his damnedest not to laugh, but he was obviously losing the battle. Which aggravated me even more.

I went to lick my lips before I admonished him, but my tongue ran across my sharp incisors. Crap, my crazy was showing. I had transitioned into a shadow form from all the burning irritation cascading through my blood.

He burst out laughing.

"Damn it, Damian, I'm trying to plan our wedding, and all you can do is laugh?"

"Would you like me to find a place?" he asked, curtailing his chuckles.

"Yes. That would be one less thing to deal with."

"Any preferences of locations?"

"Outdoors. Preferably in some garden setting with a view. And we don't need a reception, just a bottle of champagne for after the ceremony."

He gave me a nod and turned to leave.

"And if the place has a photographer, that would be a bonus. We also need a minister and a couple of folks willing to act as witnesses."

He paused at the door. "Are you sure you don't want to run down to Las Vegas?"

"Yes. I don't want to have a drive-through wedding," I snapped. I didn't. I wanted something worthy of forever, and Las Vegas was just not it. Besides, a Las Vegas wedding seemed cheap and tawdry, and more like something thrown together at the last minute. I wanted something more meaningful. Something put together with care.

Except I was failing miserably at this.

"Honey, the place doesn't matter. The fact we say I do does."

Men had no fricken' clue. I glared at him.

He hurried out of the room to escape my wrath.

The wedding I had dreamed of as a kid involved a beach just as the sun kissed the horizon. That wasn't happening. Not with the shadow virus running amok in my system. Sunshine would turn us both into a pile of ashes, and I was sure Damian would be none too pleased by that, not after waiting twenty-five hundred years for me to come along and steal his heart.

I sighed and opened anther web browser. After searching Denver bridal salons, only two offered hours past 6pm, and I snagged a 7:30 appointment at Emma and Grace Bridal Studio for the following Monday. Thankfully, it was early enough in March to allow us to get to Denver in time for the appointment. Any later in the year and I'd be screwed.

I prayed I'd be able to find a dress that didn't need alterations, because I was sure the in-house seamstress probably worked bankers' hours. Instead of harping on that possibility, I perused their dress offerings, trying to settle my frazzled nerves. There were quite a few that interested me, and I jotted them down on paper and just prayed they would have them onsite for me to try on. I wanted a dress that clearly stated I was the bride, and not one that could be confused with an evening gown. I also wanted a gown that would make Damian's heart stop the minute I stepped within his line of sight.

Damian walked into the room and dropped a piece of paper on the desk. "We are booked at the Secret Garden on Saturday, May 5th, for a midnight ceremony under the full moon. You have the bridal suite starting at 10 p.m. I figured two hours ought to be enough for hair and makeup, right?"

I nodded, dumbfounded.

"I also booked a photographer and a justice of the peace to perform the ceremony. Do you need me to do anything else?"

I stared at him, and then my gaze dropped to the paper before bouncing back to him. "How in the world did you get all that so quickly?"

He grinned. "Money talks," he said and gave me a wink.

My brain ran down all the options for the ceremony. "Does the place have any music for me to walk down the aisle to?"

"I can ask when the curator sends the contract. He also said we could take a look at the venue any evening this week if we'd like. There are a couple of spots we can choose to hold the ceremony onsite. I told him it would have to be after 8 p.m., and he said that was fine as long as we give him a day's notice."

"Maybe we can go on Monday after my dress appointment? It might be later than eight, though."

"Why don't we go on a different night so you're not rushed?"

That was why I loved the man. I smiled, thinking of how rushed I'd already be if the store wanted me out by eight. I just hoped they would let me stay later so I can try on the dresses I had jotted down.

"Tuesday?" I asked, and he gave me the thumbs up before he left the room.

I leaned back in the chair, staring after him. He just pulled off what I hadn't been able to after hours of begging and pleading. I glanced at the paper and stared at the venue name. Secret Garden. That was one I just bypassed because I thought the website was cheesy and not well done.

I hoped it offered what I was looking for. I sighed, glancing at the dress list. I had a dozen dresses listed and I would have to narrow that down based on what I saw in the mirror. If they ran true, I might actually wear it off the rack.

Midnight Vows
Chapter 2

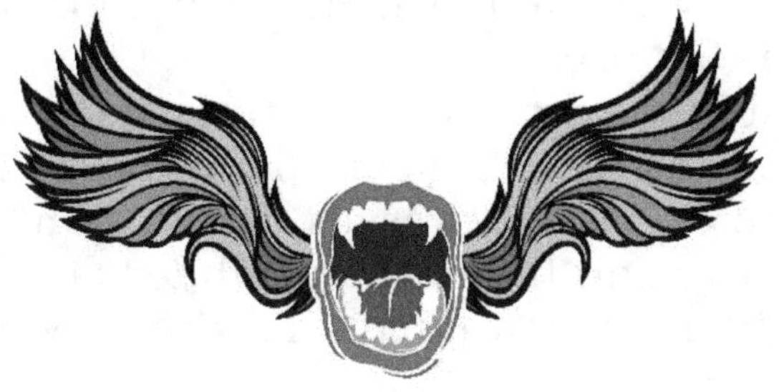

"THIS IS THE DRESS," I said as I stared in the mirror. It was the last dress on my list, and I had one other hanging on the maybe bar. It struck me as funny that the first dress I tried on and the last dress were the two that tickled my fancy.

I twirled in the dress, letting it settle around me before I turned to the saleswomen surrounding me.

"This is the one!" I repeated. It fit snug and was exquisite. I could actually wear the sample dress out of the shop with zero alterations, and the shoes that I had been trying the dress on with fit beautifully.

Annabel, my salesgirl, clapped with a broad smile. "Let me get you a veil that will match that dress perfectly," she said and disappeared.

I turned to the other saleswoman. "This looks better than the other one, right?" I asked, worried that I might have made a mistake between the two. My gaze jumped to the dress hanging against the wall.

"You look lovely in all the dresses, but Angeline looks like it was made just for you. You shine in that dress."

I'm sure the price may be the reason she said that, because the Angeline by *WToo* was one of the more expensive dresses. But I didn't have a budget. Damian had said get whatever I wanted, and right now, I wanted this dress with these shoes.

Annabel came back with the veil and slipped it into my hair. She was right—the details in the veil made it a perfect choice and the half length was perfect.

"I'll take it all. Dress, shoes, veil and corset," I said, turning and smiling at the two women before returning my gaze to the mirror. "My wedding is on May 5th. Can you get this in that fast?" I asked while I was still studying my profile. While I was paler than I used to be, my Native American heritage made my skin look more natural than I imagined most suffering with the shadow virus dealt with. In other words, I didn't look like a pasty white vampire.

"Let me check," Annabel said, and both she and the other saleswoman stepped away, leaving me to change into my street clothes. I glanced at the clock and winced. It was a little after nine, and guilt flooded my bones. These two women had stayed much later than they had to in order to help me.

By the time they came back, I was pulling on my cowboy boots.

"Unfortunately, that dress can't be here in less than twelve weeks," Annabel said. Her cheeks bloomed red.

"However, you could buy the sample," the woman next to Annabel said. "It just came in last week, and you are only the second bride to try it on. I'd be willing to part with it along with the accessories so you can have the dress you were meant to have. I can always order another one for our stock, but even that won't make it here on time for your wedding day."

I stood and walked over to the sample, holding the hem to make sure there wasn't any dirt or snags in the fabric. I wanted this dress. "I'll take it. Can you store it here until the wedding, or do I need to take it today?"

"We would prefer that you take it, and then the week of the wedding bring it back to be pressed. You have a choice of picking it up on either Friday or the day of the wedding. We close at five both days."

I bit my lip and sighed. "I can drop it off the Monday before the wedding, but it will be very close to closing time. I rarely get out of work until after eight at night, so..." I gave her a shrug.

"If you call that day, I'll stay an extra fifteen minutes if that helps," the woman said. "I own the shop, so I don't mind."

I smiled. "Are you Emma or Grace?"

"Emma," she said and took the dress and the veil, shoes, and corset to the counter to bag them up.

The dress was tucked into a large garment bag I hoped would fare well on the flight home.

"Can I have another one of those big shopping bags to fold the garment bag into?" I asked. "I'm meeting my fiancé for dinner and I don't want him to see the dress."

Emma packed the garment bag into one of their large shopping bags. "Just make sure to hang it up once you get home, okay?"

"Absolutely. As far as picking up the pressed dress, I'll probably have a courier pick it up for me. What will they need to pick up the dress?" I asked, wondering about the logistics again. However, if Damian could book a venue and all those other things in less than an hour, I should be able to hire a reliable courier to deliver my dress to the Secret Garden.

"As long as the courier shows us a copy of your dress press receipt and a note allowing us to release the dress to them, we can let them take it."

That worked for me. I left the shop with two large bags and a grin, and crossed to the sports bar across the street where Damian had parked his fine ass for the duration of my shopping.

"Hey, sweetheart," I whispered from behind him.

He glanced over his shoulder and then turned to see the bags.

"Success?"

"Oh, yes. That was the perfect dress shop," I said and caught a kiss. "I was thinking it might be nice to stay at a hotel here in town for the night before the wedding. I'll need to hire a courier to pick up my dress and if I'm at a hotel, at least I can have it dropped off in the room instead of having it delivered to the venue."

He bit his lip. "That might not be such a bad idea, but..."

I knew what was coming next, and I sighed.

"Our friends might get wind of our whereabouts if we do that," he said.

He had a point, but as much as I wanted to avoid detection by Lucifer and his henchmen, I wanted our wedding to be special and as normal as I could make it.

"Do you really think two nights will be an issue?"

He shrugged and palmed my cheek. "It could be."

"I doubt they would put two and two together if we got separate rooms for both nights."

His hand dropped, and a crease appeared between his eyes, signaling his familiar look of confusion.

"You aren't seeing me on our wedding day," I said, and he huffed a laugh. "I'm serious. I'm doing this right, so either we get separate hotel rooms or you stay at the cabin."

He balked. "I'm not staying that far away from you."

"Fine, then it's settled. We'll stay in a hotel."

He chewed his lip, visibly annoyed with my backing him into a corner.

"You can get a town car to take me to the venue, and one to take us back to the hotel, too," I added with a grin.

His dimples appeared. "You're really going to town with this wedding, aren't you?"

"It's the only one I'll ever have, so you bet your ass."

He grinned at me and the spark in his eyes meant one of two things—either he was hungry for food, or he was hungry for me. He threw cash on the bar for the whiskey he nursed while I was trying on dresses and took my hand, leading me outside.

HE DROPPED ME OFF at the cabin with my bags in tow, and I stepped inside to hang up my dress and other items. He didn't follow me in, so that spark was more about sustenance than sex.

I stepped outside a moment later, and he glanced at me before he closed his eyes and sniffed the air. I did the same. This winter had provided slim pickings for us, and I was glad for the early break in temperature because the wildlife had started to move around again, giving us more palatable options for food sources.

"Moose," he said with a grin, and pointed to the east.

A moose had more than enough blood to fill us both up. I grinned as well. We broke out in a run and I closed my eyes, willing my transition. When my eyes opened again, I felt the snow under my huge white paws. Damian's wings beat above me and his shadow moved faster in flight than I did, bounding through the snow.

I was the huntress of the two of us. Damian wouldn't take down a moose because neither hawk nor man wanted to tango with a thirteen-hundred-pound menace. But my alter ego was a seven-hundred-pound white Siberian tiger. At a full sprint, I could hit fifty miles per hour easily, and the force at which I could hit a moose of average size could knock it over. I just have to watch out for the antlers.

Damian loved to watch me go in for the kill. He said I was a force beyond imagination. To him, it was like an exquisite dance, one he never wanted to be a participant of. After all, I almost took down Lucifer, but the sunrise saved his ass.

I caught the moose off guard, hitting him square in the shoulder with a force of nearly two tons. He teetered and fell to the ground, creating a snow puff, but before he could regain his senses, my teeth sank in, severing his jugular. My reward was a fountain of lifeblood.

The hot liquid poured into my mouth, but instead of lapping it, I let it fill my mouth and swallowed. I could feel the strength building in my bones, replenishing my cells and giving me that heady high.

Damian landed next to me and grabbed the antlers, pulling the head farther to the side so he could get a drink of warm blood. I growled at him without removing my teeth. When I was in my primal form, I didn't like sharing.

"Deal with it," he said and leaned in next to me, biting into the fading fountain of life.

When the carcass was drained, I yanked my teeth from the fur and licked my chops. Damian retreated as well, taking the spot next to me, and his hand landed on my head, caressing me behind the ear. My wild cat loved it when he scratched behind my ears, and I leaned into him, almost knocking him on his ass.

"I think it's time we go satisfy our other appetite," he said.

I licked the last of the blood from my paws before glancing up at him. Right now, my inner cat had other ideas. I just wanted to run and play in the snow for a little while. When I was in this form, the feline urges took over, and I wasn't in a position to contradict them. I bounded into the snow before turning and swaying my tail.

He rolled his eyes and then darted straight at me, tackling me into a roll in the snow. This time, he ended up underneath me, and I mopped his face with my tongue until he was laughing and pushing my snout away.

"Enough! If you want to get kinky and lick me all over, let's go home and you can have at it, but only as my fiancé, not a tiger, okay?"

I chuffed at him and stepped off, letting him get to his feet and pat the snow from his clothing.

"Are you ready to go back now?"

I shook the snow from my fur and gave him a nod.

He took a couple of running steps towards our cabin, and then the hawk came out. I ran in the same direction, feeling freer than I had ever felt in my life. While the shadow virus had its drawbacks, it also had its benefits, like being able to run at high speeds through Colorado's frozen mountain terrain.

HE BEAT ME TO the cabin and stood in the doorway as I skidded to a halt. The transition back to human took hold, and after a moment, I stretched upright. I was sure the grin on my face echoed his.

"So, are you going to lick me all over?"

The playful lilt in his voice pulled heat into my cool cheeks, and I stepped inside. "I was thinking we should wait until our wedding night," I said, and braced for his reaction.

He stopped short and stared at me, calculating the days until we said I do in his head. The disappointment showed in every one of his muscles as they slackened in disbelief.

"You honestly want me to keep my sex drive in check for two months?"

"It's a little under two months," I said, trying to soften the blow.

"Can we start tomorrow?" he asked, stepping closer.

"That kind of defeats the purpose of let's wait," I said, planting my palm on his chest. Not that I didn't want to rip his clothes off and take him on the floor right then and there; I just thought the agony of waiting that both of us would deal with would make us almost feral on our wedding night.

He let out a half laugh. "Are you joking right now, or are you serious?"

"I'm serious."

"Oh," he muttered, and his hands found solace in his pockets. He looked like a little kid who dropped his ice cream cone on the street. Dejected. Almost destroyed.

"Damian," I started, and he met my gaze. "I love you and would like nothing more than making love to you right now, but I want our wedding night to be special."

"Every time I make love to you, it's special," he said, his blue eyes pleading.

I almost caved. "That's sweet, but I want the buildup, the anticipation. I want to be half out of my mind for you."

"And you're not like that now?"

I could tell my explanation wasn't coming out the right way, and he was getting defensive. "I am. God knows I am, but I want to wait because I want that night to be memorable, and not like every other night we've ever shared." I held my hand up when his jaw tensed. "I am not saying every night has been less than memorable. I'm saying I want our wedding night to impact both of us in ways that a normal night doesn't. Make sense?"

He blinked and sucked in his bottom lip, chewing on it while he mulled my words over. Instead of standing in the outer cabin, he retreated into the belly of the mountain, where our luxury escape stood beneath the bedrock and away from the sunshine.

I followed him in, hanging up my coat and ditching my boots.

He sat on the couch staring at the blank television screen before he finally turned to me.

"I get what you're saying," he said.

I took the spot next to him. He was usually the soft and sappy one of the two of us, but even though I could be bad-ass, I was a girl. And I wanted to come as close to my wedding dream as I could. That included abstinence before the wedding.

"Have I been moving too fast?" he asked, and worry lines painted his forehead.

"Neither of us has ever moved slow. But with this, I need to do it right. I need our wedding to be as perfect as your proposal."

The slow smile that produced his deep dimples appeared, and he leaned in, planting the softest kiss on my forehead.

"It will be," he whispered and gave my hand a squeeze. "And if I have to keep my desire under wraps until after we wed, then so be it," he added with a grimace meant to be a grin.

"Thank you," I said and pecked his cheek.

"Just don't be surprised if I tear through your dress on our wedding night."

"Buy the tuxedo, because that may end up in shreds, too," I said and retreated into the bedroom to keep my own desires in check. I wanted to lick every inch of him and wasn't sure I would be able to abide by my own rules.

Midnight Vows
Chapter 3

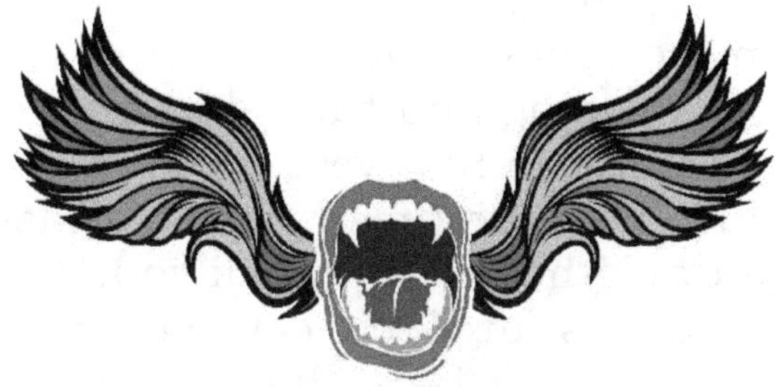

EIGHT WEEKS CRAWLED BY and we both kept our word, but I was as horny as a she-devil in heat. The fantasies of what I wanted to do to Damian when we got back to the cabin had gone into the triple X realm. I could not wait for tomorrow night to come, and just the thought of making love to him made me wet.

I had dropped my dress off on Monday and had a courier scheduled to pick it up today and drop it off at the Crawford Hotel. Damian had booked two rooms for both tonight and tomorrow night, so neither one of us would have to leave before the sun went down.

I paced across the cabin floor, impatiently waiting for sunset. I needed to get away from Damian, from this want scratching under my skin.

"Are you okay?" he asked from his perch on the couch.

"I will be," I said under my breath.

Just under thirty hours before I could ravage him. I had resorted to being snippy to deal with the lack of activity, and it amused the hell out of him. Here I thought he would be the one to have a difficult time with abstinence, but I failed to remember he had gone decades without sex, so my meager eight-week challenge was a no brainer for the man.

"Having second thoughts?"

I stopped pacing and turned to him, catching the glint of worry in his eyes.

"No, just wishing time would go faster so I can rip your clothes off and fuck you."

His eyebrows arched. I rarely resorted to crude language, but I also hadn't gone this long with no real physical contact since we met. It was difficult and frustrating and had me on edge.

He stood and crossed to where I stood. He flashed me his bemused smile, and I wanted to wipe it off his lips.

"You want to know what I am going to do tomorrow night?" he purred, staring at me with such intensity, I dared not ask. He stepped closer, crowding me. "I'm going to make you come so hard you can't breathe. I'm going to take my time with you until you are out of your mind and begging me to fuck you." He grinned and caressed my cheek. "And then I'll make you come again before I give you what you crave. You know why?"

I shook my head, barely able to draw a breath at the sweet thoughts he just planted in my brain.

"Because you made me wait this long."

He gave my cheek a soft pat and walked away, leaving me in the living room. My breath drew ragged in my chest, and my nipples hardened with each of his insinuations. My panties became uncomfortably wet with the vision of his tongue teasing me into oblivion.

I realized I wasn't the only one on edge and I smiled. One more day. All we had to do was endure one more day, and then he better make good on his promises.

He came out from the bedroom with the bag I had packed earlier and a light carryon bag, which I assumed had his stuff packed.

"My tuxedo is being delivered to the hotel," he said when I met his gaze. "You sure you have everything you need?"

I went through my list. I had a handkerchief of Damian's that was from the early 1700s, so old was covered. My garter was blue. My dress was new. The only thing I didn't have was borrowed, and I bit my lip.

"Do you think the handkerchief makes up something borrowed?"

His lips toyed with a smile. "It is mine, so you could say you were borrowing it."

"Then yes. I have everything. Do you have the rings?"

"Of course." He glanced at his watch. "Are you ready to head into Denver?"

I glanced over my shoulder at the clock. It wasn't quite eight yet, so the sky would still have the streaks of color and be light enough for someone to see a giant hawk carrying a woman along with luggage.

"Is it going to be dark enough?"

"I got us a snowmobile last night," he said and grinned. "So all I have to do is get us a few miles from town, and then we've got ourselves a ride."

"Did you steal it?" I asked in a hushed whisper.

"No. I bought it and have it stowed in the woods on the other side of the mountain." He produced a key from his pocket. "It's got a small wrack for luggage, too."

It seemed like a decent idea and one that wouldn't put us in a position to be seen flying. I just had no idea how long it would take to get to town on a snowmobile.

"We should get to the hotel by ten at the latest," he said, reading my thoughts correctly.

I swear he actually heard what I was thinking, but our ability to read each other's minds had faded since the abstinence started, and I couldn't wait for this to be over. I couldn't wait to be his wife.

"Tomorrow night," he whispered as he passed me, heading for the door.

THE HOTEL WAS AS grand as he promised. The shades were thick and so were the curtains, so theoretically, the sun wouldn't breach the room, but I was still nervous. My dress hung on a special dress hanger they brought in, and I stared at it from my perch on the bed.

Hunger wrestled in my stomach, and I glanced at the clock, wondering if I could catch a quick meal before sunup. A knock came on the adjoining door, making me jump. Damian knew how adamant I was at him not seeing me on our wedding day, so his knock surprised me. Still, I crossed and cracked the door, keeping my body hidden from view.

"I thought you might need this." Damian's whisper came through the crack, and then his hand appeared with a bag of blood.

I could have kissed him and I snatched the package from his hand, and my incisors instinctively bared. I pierced the plastic and sucked the bag dry. The fiery burn of human blood blazed through my system. I closed my eyes, leaning against the wall in rapture.

"Thank you," I whispered when my hunger abated.

"Pass back the empty. I've got a little cooler I can put it in."

I handed it back, and his hand disappeared.

"One more thing," he said.

"What's that?" I replied with my eyes closed.

"Make sure you bring all your stuff to the venue because we aren't coming back here after the wedding."

I smile. "The walls are too thin for you?"

He laughed just before the door closed and the locks engaged. It was the kind of laugh that fueled my imagination.

I closed my door and licked my lips, hoping for any remnants, but I had drained the bag clean. Not a drop had been spared, and I felt more alive and energetic than I had in a while.

I picked up my phone and sent a simple text. 'I love you!'

'I know,' came back a moment later, followed by, 'I love you, too.'

WAITING WAS THE WORST. We both had the Do Not Disturb signs hung on the door, but the inability to sleep sucked. At least if I could take a nap, time would pass much quicker than it did when you wanted it to. I had to refrain from opening the curtains to see if it was still daytime. The room clock showed the same time as my phone, but I thought it should be much later than three in the afternoon.

I was sure I wore a path in the carpet and had to keep my fingers away from my mouth. Gnawing on them would ruin the manicure I had last night before we settled in our rooms.

My phone buzzed.

'Relax.'

I picked it up and dialed his number because I had no patience for texting right now. "Who says I'm not relaxed?"

"I can hear you shuffling back and forth," he said, and even he sounded edgy.

"Having doubts?" I asked, stopping my incessant pacing.

"No. I just don't like being in hotels where I might not be able to control the situation. Besides, I have to be careful of where I step in here. My curtains don't close all the way, and I have to keep avoiding the sliver of light traveling across the room."

"Oh, babe," I said, glancing at mine securely closed and letting zero light through. "Did you pull the shade down last night?"

He huffed. "No. I should have, but I was staring out the window wondering what you were doing most of the night, and then I opened my computer and dove into work. Before I knew it, my hand was scorched by the rising sun." He paused and let out a breath. "I was able to get the curtain closed, so at least my exposure is minimized. But damn, I forgot just how painful the sun actually is.”

My mind filled with all the possible what ifs and I shivered, stepping closer to the adjoining door. “I’m glad it wasn’t worse,” I said, wondering what his hand looked like.

“I’m fine. It just looks like a sunburn now, and by tonight, it should be completely gone. The blood from last night helped. If I had been lying on the bed, it would have been much worse.”

I thanked the stars above for our uncanny healing ability. I could just imagine the initial burn. I shivered and pulled my hand to my chest like I shared his pain. “I wish I was there with you,” I whispered.

“We only have a few more hours, hon,” he said. “I’ve got the car scheduled to pick you up at a little after nine. I’m planning on being there at eleven. We don’t have to wait until midnight. Whenever you’re ready, we can start.”

“What about the justice of the peace?”

“I asked him to arrive at eleven, same with the photographer. I like the idea of a May 5th wedding instead of May 6th, so...”

“Wishful thinking,” I laughed. “But I think they’ll be able to do my hair within an hour.” I had picked a Greek goddess hairdo that was fairly complex with part up-do and part cascading curls, so I certainly hoped they would finish in an hour, but I was skeptical, especially with makeup following the hair. Eleven thirty was probably a more accurate time. “But if you want to wait in the garden gazebo for me, I think I will be ready by eleven thirty at the latest.”

"I can't wait," he whispered and disconnected the call.

"Neither can I," I said and glanced at the gorgeous dress, imagining his reaction to seeing me all decked out.

The closest I'd come to looking stunning was trying on the cocktail dresses at the mall right after Damian turned me. His expression then was hotter than a four-alarm fire, and I couldn't wait to see him tomorrow night. If I could, I would have willed time to fly by.

THE PHONE BUZZED AT a little after nine, telling me my car was here to pick me up. I grabbed my small suitcase with my wedding garments, making sure everything was inside, from the shoes to the handkerchief, along with all my toiletries from the hotel, before I zipped it up. I slid the dress back into the garment bag and hauled it over my shoulder.

The town car was big enough to hang my dress on one side while I sat on the other with my bag on the seat next to me. I fidgeted. Both my nerves and the scent of the driver had me on edge. Perhaps it hadn't been the best thing for Damian to feed me human blood last night. I closed my eyes and took a deep breath, pushing the hunger down into the depths, ignoring the pulse of a hot meal in the body in the front seat.

I arrived at the Secret Garden and was whisked into what the owner referred to as the bridal suite. It was a small room with a bathroom off to the side. A far cry from a suite, but it would do. My hairdresser, Jamie, was already set up and waiting with a table full of hairpins and curling irons.

"It's just you?" she asked as the door closed behind me.

"Yes. Why?" I thought I made it clear when we spoke it was just me and no one else. But maybe she misunderstood.

"I thought you might have an attendant or two with you even though they weren't having their hair done," she said.

"Damian and I wanted a small private ceremony," I said, feeling awkward. "Unfortunately, our family lives out east, and they couldn't make the trip." I slid into the chair. "Do you think you'll be able to do what we discussed in an hour?"

Jamie looked at the photo I pulled out and then took a strand of my hair between her fingers. "I think we can do that," she said and started the transformation from everyday hair to wedding hair.

As she dabbed gloss on my lips for the final touches of makeup, my gaze dropped to her throat. I couldn't lick my lips, but I also knew what the shadow virus did to people. That was the only reason I didn't bite her right there. A vampire bite is a death sentence to humans, and I was not a murderer.

I took a deep breath and closed my eyes.

"There," she said as she scrutinized her work. When she was satisfied, she swung me around so I could see her masterpiece.

The woman in the mirror was stunning, with her dark hair piled on her head and ribbon curls falling gracefully from the bun. I blinked at my reflection, and even the makeup was perfection. Understated and soft to match the hair.

"Holy cow," I said and grinned. "This is fantastic!"

"Do you have anyone to help with your dress?" she asked, and I shook my head. "I can stay and help if you'd like."

She had done my hair a few times since we moved here, and she had always been chatty and sincere. I could use a hand and since she offered, I felt compelled to say yes.

"I'd like that, and if you'd like to stay and watch the ceremony, you are welcome to."

She actually beamed and stood, rushing to get the dress. I slipped into the corset bra and my heels while she got the dress ready for me to step into. I slid on the garter, then stepped into the beautiful *WToo* gown. She zipped me up and stepped in front of me.

"You are absolutely beautiful," she said and smiled.

I leaned over and pulled the veil from the bag, smoothing it out.

"May I?" she asked with reverence.

I handed it to her, and she put it on for me and then pulled me to stand in front of the mirror. I hardly recognized the stunning bride in the mirror, and I hoped I had the same effect on Damian as I seemed to have on Jamie.

"Can you tell them I'm ready?"

She nodded and hurried out. I grabbed the handkerchief and waited at the door for Jamie to return.

Jamie came in holding a small bouquet of roses. "Your husband-to-be said you might need these."

I grinned. Flowers. I had completely forgotten flowers, but he seemed to have it covered.

The music started. I detected violins. More than one, and they played Canon in D, one of my favorites. My eyes welled up. I blinked the mist away and stepped out of the little bridal suite.

Jamie fixed my train, and I began walking towards the small glen on the other side of the stream where a gazebo stood, surrounded by wildflowers. My heart thrummed in my chest, and I had to keep my steps in time with the music, slowing my pace regardless of my feet wanting to rush. I turned the corner, centering myself on the path leading directly to the gazebo, and looked up. The view of him in a finely tailored tuxedo stalled my brain and my footing.

Even from this distance, I saw the sparkle in his eyes as he slowly scanned me from head to toe and back. He smiled and turned to face me, his arms falling by his sides in disbelief. He was as enthralled with me as I was with him.

"Beautiful," he whispered, and his voice found my ears even with the music playing.

Jamie fixed my train, reminding me I should cross the distance, and I resumed walking towards my future. Towards everything dear to me. All our planning ended in this sweet perfection. When he stepped forward, taking my hands in his with a satisfied sigh, I smiled with the joy penetrating my entire form.

"In all the centuries I've passed through, I have never seen a more beautiful bride," he whispered. He planted a kiss on my cheek and led me under the canopy of lights to the gazebo.

Jamie stood to the side, and on the other side stood the venue curator, acting as our witnesses. I sighed, wishing it was Valerie and Michael instead. I handed Jamie my bouquet and focused on Damian, forgetting everything else with one glance at him.

The justice of the peace cleared his throat. "A wedding is such a wonderful occasion filled with hopes, dreams, and excitement. We are here today to celebrate the love that Damian and Naomi have for each other, and to recognize and witness their decision to journey forward in their lives as husband and wife." He smiled and flipped the page in the book he was reciting from.

"May your love create a haven for you both on the journey that lies ahead. Lead with your hearts and take the time to do the simple things that will nurture your love. Deeply listen to each other. To your dreams, and to your frustrations. Be playful in finding new ways to give your love anew to each other every day. It is your love that has brought you together. May it grow deeper and sweeter with each passing year."

He turned to Damian.

"Do you, Damian, take Naomi to be your wife? Do you promise to walk by her side forever, and to love, help, and encourage her in all she does? Do you promise to take time to talk with her, to listen to her, and to care for her? Will you share her laughter, and her tears, as her husband, lover, and best friend? Do you take her as your lawfully wedded wife for now and forevermore?"

Damian grinned and looked straight into my eyes. "I do."

The justice turned to me.

"Do you, Naomi, take Damian to be your husband? Do you promise to walk by his side forever, and to love, help, and encourage him in all he does? Do you promise to take time to talk with him, to listen to him, and to care for him? Will you share his laughter, and his tears, as his wife, lover, and best friend? Do you take him as your lawfully wedded husband for now and forevermore?"

"I do," I replied and squeezed Damian's hands.

"Do you have the rings?" The justice asked Damian.

Damian reached into his pocket, pulled out two wedding bands, and placed them in the justice's palm.

"And now, seal your promises with these rings, the symbol of your life shared together," he started and turned to Damian. "Repeat after me: Naomi, this ring I give as a token and pledge, as a sign of my love and devotion. With this ring, I thee wed."

Damian took the ring from his palm and slid it on my left ring finger as he repeated the words, his voice steady and strong, and as gentle as the grip he had on my hand.

The justice looked at me, instructing me to repeat the same words.

I took the ring from his palm and slid it on Damian's left hand ring finger. "Damian, this ring I give as a token and pledge, as a sign of my love and devotion. With this ring, I thee wed."

"Damian and Naomi, by the power invested in me by the great state of Colorado, I now pronounce you husband and wife," the justice announced and smiled. "You may kiss your bride," he added.

Damian pulled me into his arms and delivered a searing kiss that jolted me into a heat-filled mass. It wasn't the tender altar kiss you see at most weddings. It was one that claimed me at the cellular level. I wasn't aware of the clapping from either Jamie or the curator at first, but as soon as it registered, Damian pulled away from my lips.

The smile that donned his face promised me all sorts of trouble, and I couldn't wait to step out of this dress and into his arms.

The End

Continue Damian and Naomi's story with
TIGRESS.

TIGRESS

The antidote to the shadow virus turns Naomi's blood into a lethal elixir, making her toxic to all vampires, including Damian.

Naomi's immortality is nullified, making her vulnerable to the ones who consider her their conquest. If she wasn't already walking over the hot coals of misfortune, she would be obsessed with the next ambush.

The shadow vaccine is hell in a syringe, the antidote turning Naomi's blood into a lethal elixir, rendering her toxic to all vampires, including Damian.

Archangel Michael reveals a long-buried secret of her heritage and cautions Naomi against triggering the apocalypse. If Lucifer discovers just how unique she is, death at his hands will become her most appealing escape.

Tigress
Chapter One
Naomi

HE STOOD ON THE snow-covered peak, his dark hair flowing in the breeze with his face tilted toward the moon. Damian Andreas was one fine-looking man, and I sighed at his eternal beauty. His posture stiffened and his eyes snapped open, scanning the landscape until they landed on me. The slow smile that spread over his lips sent a shiver up my spine, ending with a rush of heat that warmed me to my very soul.

We'd played in the mountains of Colorado for the last five years without the threat of retribution, but both of us knew the hourglass was running out of sand. Our cabin near the south shore of Rainbow Lake made for the perfect hiding spot, blending into the woods and surrounding mountain side. From the outside, it looked like a simple hunting cabin built into the mountainside, but it was far more than just a three-sided hut. Using the natural slope of the mountain, he'd carved us a comfortable sanctuary with all the modern conveniences. Water piped in from the lake, heat and electricity courtesy of solar and geothermal heating and even cell signals strong enough to connect to the internet. It wasn't the haven we left, but it was enough to make a life together.

Damian dropped from the ledge, morphing into the form of a giant hawk; his wingspan blocked the moon as he circled, descending in a graceful arc until he was within a few feet of the ground. He dropped the last few inches in his human form, his intense gaze locked on mine.

"I thought you were reading," he said when his hiking boots touched the snow.

"I was, but I thought the fresh air would do me some good."

He pulled me into his arms and his cool lips brushed mine. His kisses still stunned me as much as they did when we first met. My bones turned to soft clay, melting into him, into his kiss.

The moment our lips separated, the playfulness in his eyes faded and his gaze rose from mine to the trees behind me. His features tensed and he straightened, his eyes narrowing into a glare that bit at my nerves.

"What are you doing here?" he asked in a voice I hardly recognized and I turned, taking in the feral blonde standing at the edge of the woods.

She approached and my pulse jumped at her red eyes and the set of razor teeth gleaming in the moonlight.

"I know your hiding places, Damian," she said in a sensual purr that hung on the night air. "And so does *he*."

Damian's grasp tightened, and he did a quick scan of the area before bringing his gaze back to the woman.

"Don't worry your pretty little head over it, honey. I took care of his hunters a few days ago." Her eyes dropped to mine, and she licked her lips. "She smells wonderful."

"The way my wife smells is of no interest to you," he said, releasing his hold around my waist, taking my hand and stepping in front of me in a protective stance.

"Wife. Wow." Her perfect brow arched as she renewed her study of me. "And you're not going to introduce me?"

"Naomi, this is Lilith," he said, with a voice clipped with an underlying warning.

The name Lilith brought forth a wealth of religious information, but this couldn't possibly be the same as the reference in the old testament. The first woman. The first demon.

I stared at her and she cocked her head, her lips spreading in a sly smile that chilled.

"The story is so much more sordid than those old monks scribed," she said, flipping her hair over her shoulder and igniting my curiosity. "Isn't that right, Damian?"

Damian squeezed my hand and sent a glance in my direction before sliding it back to Lilith. "What are you doing here?" he asked again, this time measuring each word, conveying his distaste.

"Lucy is back on the prowl, and he is in one of the foulest moods this universe has ever seen."

"What does that mean?" I asked.

"It means he's hunting and hellbent on finding the two of you."

"Let him come. This time I won't stop until he's dead," I said and her sharp gaze met mine.

"Sweetheart, if Lucy finds you, you won't have the strength to fight him."

"Why the hell not?" I asked and tried to step to Damian's side, but he shot me a glare that froze my feet in place.

"Because he has the last dose of antidote." Her gaze snapped from mine to Damian's. "If he uses it on you, you'll die like that," she said and snapped her fingers. "But that's not his intent. He plans on stealing her immortality, and her death will be slow and painful."

Damian took a step backwards, forcing me to move. "You found a cure?"

"It took me a while, considering I created the damn virus, but I finally found the right mix. Unfortunately, for those of us who have lived longer than the normal human lifespan, the instantaneous aging process means death." Lilith let out a laugh filled with sarcasm and bitterness, and her gaze landed on me. "But for you, my dear, it will strip you of your strength and make you immune to the virus for the rest of your mortal life."

Damian didn't respond, but his eyes narrowed and his grip on my hand tightened.

The information took a moment to sink in and I blinked at the sudden flurry of questions flooding my mind. "What do you mean by immune?" I asked, a little surprised at the question that actually popped out of my mouth.

"It means no superior strength or speed and your ability to heal would revert to the normal human timeframes." Her gaze flipped back to Damian's. "And it means she's toxic to any vampire." A slow, sadistic smile crossed her lips.

The gaze Damian sent my way reflected a level of trepidation I hadn't seen in years.

Lilith's laugh pulled my attention back to her.

"Baby, no one dances with the devil and lives to tell about it," she said and slid her gaze to Damian's. "Isn't that right, Damian?"

His jaw clenched, and his grip on my hand turned to nearly bone crushing. "You mean no human lives through his wrath," he said.

Lilith's teeth flashed for a moment and I swore I saw a hint of sorrow pass over her features before they hardened.

Damian's head cocked to the side and then he scanned the landscape again. "Where's Eve?"

Lilith's face pinched together, and she turned her gaze away. But I caught the glossy shine of tears in the moonlight.

Damian caught it as well, and his hard posture softened. He released my hand, stepping toward the ancient vampire. "Lilith, what happened?" he asked, touching her shoulder.

Her head snapped in his direction and she glanced at his hand before she spoke. "I had two doses of the antidote," she said in a voice no louder than a whisper.

When he pulled her into a hug, she stiffened and before either of us could react, Lilith pulled a gun from behind her and shot. A burning pain filled my abdomen, and I looked down at the tranquilizer dart sticking from my stomach.

"What the hell have you done?" Damian growled and the grin Lilith shot his way sent a shock wave through my already pain-ridden form. Fury filled his features and before she could answer him, his fist smashed into her face.

"You were always so fucking gullible," she whispered from where she fell.

My knees buckled under the agony filling every cell in my body. This was far worse than the pain of Damian's initial bite. My lungs seized, and I fell forward with Lilith's crazy cackling following me into oblivion.

Tigress
Chapter Two
Naomi

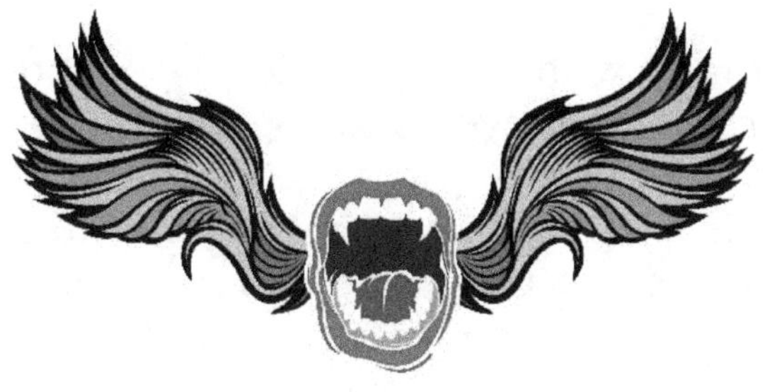

A CRAMP PULLED ME from the dark and I curled my knees to my chest, moaning my discontent. Coolness wiped across my forehead and I opened my eyes. Damian's gaze met mine, and he offered me a grimace that was meant as a smile.

"Am I dying?" I whispered.

The slow shake of his head, along with the sadness in his eyes, brought me further awake, and I glanced at the familiar surroundings of our mountain home.

"What happened?"

He continued to stroke my forehead with a damp cloth, but he wouldn't meet my gaze.

Before I could press further, heat burned through my skin and I screamed, tightening into a compact ball. Drawing a breath seemed like an impossible feat, and I clamped my eyes shut, turning my face into the pillow and away from Damian's pained gaze.

Finally, my chest eased, and I drew in a breath, and then another, concentrating on this one thing and tuning out the agony wrestling my muscles.

"Damian, what happened?" I turned, taking in his bright blue eyes once again.

"Lilith shot you with the antidote," he said and picked up a cup from the nightstand. He lifted my head, tilting the glass to my lips.

Cold water flowed over my tongue, quenching the dryness I hadn't noticed until then. I grabbed his wrist and drank, trying to tip the cup further, but he stopped me.

"You need to go easy," he said, pulling the glass away and putting it on the table.

I stared at him, at the conflict in his features, and when he popped a thermometer in my mouth, my eyebrows rose.

"You've been running a fever," he said, and the thermometer beeped. He pulled it out and checked the reading. The subtle close of his eyes and sigh that escaped gave me an indication of relief, and when he brought his gaze back to mine, I knew. Damian's relief washed over me like soft, subtle waves.

"How long have I been like this?"

"A week."

His answer gave me a start, and I attempted to sit up, but he pushed me back onto the bed.

"You're still sick," he said, showing me the readout.

"It's only a hundred and one," I said and shifted, stretching out of the ball I'd remained curled in. The pressure in my lower abdomen surprised me. "Besides, I think I have to go to the bathroom," I said and did my best to sit up.

The room spun, and he threw the covers back, reaching to pick me up.

"I can do this on my own," I said, knocking his hands away.

Damian stood and waved toward the bathroom. Irritation transforming the worry into a hard stare.

I stumbled into the bathroom on wobbly legs and took a seat on the commode. The unfamiliar burn of urine passed, and I closed my eyes. This was one of the human elements that I had not missed, and I had laughed at Damian for putting a toilet in when neither of us needed one. Now, I was glad to have the convenience. I finished and slowly got to my feet, shuffling to the mirror.

The reflection showed a sickly pale face with dark circles encasing my deep brown eyes. My hair lay in a stringy, matted mess that made me cringe. A shower, that's what I needed, and I turned, twisting the nozzles until steam filled the small space. With a great deal of effort, I stripped the stained and soiled night-shirt off and stepped under the stream of water.

I exhaled and closed my eyes, letting the water cascade down my skin. The effort of just standing there sucked whatever energy I had right from my bones and I reached for the wall. His soft hand took mine instead. I opened my eyes and stared at his fully dressed and soaking form. A chill blanketed me and I cocked my head, too tired to articulate.

Instead of explaining why he was standing in the shower fully dressed, he reached for the shampoo and poured some in his hand. The silence unnerved me just as much as the torture in his gaze. He lathered up my hair, running his fingers through my locks in slow patterns, and I succumbed to his pampering, letting him clean me from head to toe without the usual sexual foreplay.

When I was squeaky clean, he pulled me into his arms and just held me, pressing his lips to the top of my head. It was only after dozing off in his arms did his tremors break through my hazy brain. I pushed away and looked into his eyes.

Tears slowly traced down his cheeks.

His tears sent my heart into overdrive and vaporized the fog surrounding me.

"What is it?"

His hand came to rest on my cheek and the depth of his agony ripped at my soul, leaving it in tatters.

"I gave Lilith the chance to explain what she meant by toxic before I ripped her to pieces." He reached and turned off the water.

I wasn't sure I had the strength for an explanation, but after he tucked me in a towel and sat me down on the toilet lid with no further words, I cleared my throat. Damian turned toward me, his fingers nimbly unbuttoning his shirt, and he shrugged.

"Bullshit," I whispered with the first bite of anger. He was completely avoiding the subject. "Tell me what it means," I said, my voice sounding much stronger.

"You know what toxic means," he said, nearly ripping the dripping shirt off his well-defined chest. His pants came next, and he hung them over the side of the shower before reaching for a towel and meeting my gaze.

"My blood is poison to you."

He let out that sarcastic laugh that set my nerves on edge. "God, if only it was that simple." A sheen of tears covered his blue eyes, and he inhaled. "It isn't just your blood that could kill me," he whispered and stepped closer, stopping in the middle of the floor.

A low growl came from my stomach, settling over the silence of the room.

"I stocked the kitchen," he said in response, but I was still staring at him, trying to figure out the meaning of his words.

I blinked a couple of times and studied the distance between us, the dripping clothing over the shower, and then my gaze shot to his. Understanding crushed my heart to bits. "You mean...I'm your kryptonite?" The words rushed out in a gasp.

His chin dropped to his chest, and he turned, walking out of the bathroom with his shoulders sagging.

"Damian," I whispered, and he stopped in the doorway without turning.

"I need to make you something to eat," he said.

"Look at me."

He spun, gripping the doorway with both hands, and his gaze locked with mine.

"Is being near me..." My throat tightened, cutting off my voice, and I pressed my lips together. He held my gaze and kept silent. I swallowed and pushed the word out. "Painful?"

He shook his head. "No, baby, being near you isn't."

"But?"

"But touching you burns like you're made of platinum," he said and walked away.

I glanced at the dripping clothing and they blurred through my fresh tears.

Tigress
Chapter Three
Naomi

ONCE I FOUND THE strength to pull clean clothing on, I stumbled to the kitchen and found Damian standing over the stove, reading the label on a can of chicken noodle soup.

"You just add a can of water to the soup and heat it up," I said and collapsed into the chair.

"Thanks, captain obvious," he said and shot a glance in my direction.

I was too tired for a verbal spar with him. What I really wanted was to cuddle in his arms and I bit my lip, blinking away the sudden sheen blurring my vision. "What time is it?"

"It's almost ten in the morning."

Morning. I turned toward the door and then back to him, suddenly full of energy. "Can I go outside?"

The way his eyebrows arched when he turned toward me made my excitement fizzle.

"Not until your fever is gone, and then we'll have to head somewhere warmer."

"But I can go out in the sun?" I asked, feeling like I was a child again, asking my father to go out and play.

His huff and nod told me enough. "Yes, you're no longer in danger of turning into a smoking pile of cinder." He stirred the soup in the pot. "Come nightfall, I'll have to go out for a few," he said.

My stomach clenched, and it wasn't because I was hungry. "Why?"

He glanced back at me. "I need to eat and I need to get you something warm enough to fly you out of here, otherwise you'll freeze to death before I can get you to civilization."

"What if he's out there?" I couldn't help asking.

Damian turned off the small burner and sighed, pouring the soup into a bowl and bringing it to me with a spoon. "There isn't a goddamn thing I'll be able to do if he's waiting for me," he said and sat down across from me. "But with the mess I made out there, I'm sure he'll figure we moved on."

"Mess?"

He met my gaze. "I was more destructive than you in tigress mode," he said. "When I was done, there were pieces of her scattered over a hundred-yard radius." His laugh filled the small space. "Lilith actually thought I'd let her walk away after what she did."

His eyes flashed with anger so deep I wanted to shrink into the chair.

"Stupid bitch thought I'd drop to my knees and just give up." He let out a harsh laugh, meeting my gaze. "She thought she'd be able to hand us over to that bastard and win his favor." His head swayed from side to side. "She grossly miscalculated my strength and fury."

I reached out and ran my finger over the back of his hand and he winced, jerking away from my touch. A red welt appeared where my finger traced and I stared as it faded away. When I lifted my gaze to his, the anger was gone, replaced by melancholy.

"But the shower?" I whispered, and he turned his palms toward me.

His palms were red and raw, like he'd held them over the open flame, and my hand shot over my mouth to cover my gasp.

"Oh, my god, Damian," I whispered from behind my hand.

"I'll live," he said.

The reality of our situation fully sank in and pain deep in my core laced outwards, encompassing every fiber. I dropped the spoon into the bowl and pushed it away, crossed my arms on the table and buried my face in the crook of my arm. At first, only silent tears came, but then the sobs started, coming from the well of my soul. Long burning sobs that shook the foundation of my existence.

My husband, my soul mate, could never hold me in his arms again.

Tigress
Chapter Four
Damian

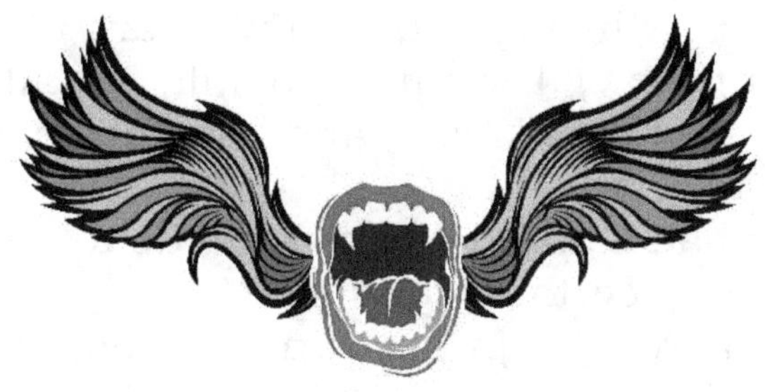

I STEPPED OUT INTO the cool night, inhaling the fresh mountain air and scanning the horizon. My heart hammered with each step away from the cabin, and my gaze bounced, expecting Lucifer's thugs to jump out at any moment. Fresh snow covered the carnage from a week ago, but I could still smell Lilith's blood hanging on the air.

Despair attempted to creep in again, and I shook my head, pushing it away. There would be time to wallow in it later, but for now, I still needed to get her to safety, otherwise she would die in this harsh wilderness and that's the last thing I wanted.

The constellations speckled the dark sky, and I started toward the woods, snow crunching with each step. The farther I got from the cabin, the more my anger blasted to the surface. My hands curled into fists and my jaw ached from my tightly clenched teeth. The injustice burned.

My nerves were raw from Naomi's grief and the fact I couldn't just hold her and comfort her, kiss her or make love to her shattered my sanity. With every wincing touch, my heart blackened and right now, I wanted to kill, to allow the shadow to take over and destroy whatever crossed my path.

Lilith had said Lucifer wanted us to suffer.

Well, this certainly qualified.

With a roar, I picked up the pace, running and jumping and letting the transition take hold. Wings unfurled, taking me higher into the darkness. I banked southeast, toward Denver, hoping to find a less than innocent soul, because right now, wildlife would not satisfy my pummeling hunger.

I landed on the dark soccer field of the East High School and turned north toward the park and the dark windy paths within; praying trouble would find me. The snowy pathways wcre as welcoming as Lucifer's den and with each step, my mood worsened. The absence of criminals pissed me off. This differed from Central Park, where thugs prowled after dark.

A shuffle behind me caught my attention, and I stopped.

"Are you lost or just stupid?"

I turned slowly, facing my attacker, and my gaze dropped to the blade in his hand and back to the hooded figure standing in the path behind me like he was invincible. Steel glinted in the dark, and I raised my palms toward him, playing the game.

"I thought I'd take a shortcut," I whispered. My mouth salivated at the scent of human flesh and the thrill of turning the tables on this asshole.

"Just give me your money and you won't get hurt."

I couldn't help it. I laughed, and he lunged, the knife coming close enough to tear fabric and then he pulled away.

"I'm serious. If you don't give me your wallet, I'll gut you like a fish." His black eyes peered out from under the hood.

"I'd like to see you try," I said and my hands dropped to my sides, waiting for the next lunge. The man snarled and attacked. I turned, letting the knife sail by me, and I grabbed his wrist, yanking him closer. Before he could recover, my teeth sank into his throat.

The sudden rush of fresh blood filled my mouth, and I sucked, swallowing his life in pulses timed with his frantic heartbeat. He didn't have the chance to scream. Instead, he just moaned as death claimed him. When I had drained every drop from his thieving heart, I dropped him to the ground and wiped my mouth, relishing the warm renewal of strength filtering into my muscles.

It had been years since I hunted humans, and now I remembered why. One was never enough. I turned away from the stiff corpse and continued north, my gait strong and my focus on one thing.

Blood.

It wasn't until I walked past the local strip club that someone in the alley hissed for my attention. I stopped and turned, taking in a well-insulated man whose eyes kept darting around.

"You looking for a good time tonight?" he asked in a hushed whisper and nodded toward the van parked farther down the alley.

I glanced at the van and the word "Ménage-mobile" stenciled on the doors. My gaze traveled back to his jumpy eyes. The idea of a van full of whores set my appetite on fire and I licked my lips. "How many are we talking about?"

"I have three girls ready to take care of your every need," he grinned, flashing a mouthful of crooked teeth.

Somehow I doubted that, but I stepped into the alley with him and he waved me forward. When we got alongside the van, he turned and slid the door open. He did indeed have three girls, bound and gagged and spread out for any twisted mind. Their frightened gazes told me more than I wanted and I turned toward the lech in the alley.

"Today is not your lucky day," I said and closed the door on the girls. Before he could draw the gun in his waistband, I snapped his neck and drained him of blood. When there was nothing left to drink, I rummaged through his pockets and found the car keys.

Their frightened gazes met mine when I stepped into the van and closed the door. As much as I wanted to drain them of precious blood, I couldn't. They were what Michael deemed innocents and as I unbound each girl, they crumpled on the floor of the van in tears.

"Are you hurt?" I asked after I untied the last girl.

Their aimless gazes met mine, and I sighed, slipping into the front seat and starting the vehicle. I drove to the emergency room parking lot of St. Luke's Hospital and parked the van.

"You're in the St. Luke's parking lot," I said and opened the driver's side door.

"Wait, Mister," one girl said.

I turned, meeting her teary green gaze.

"Thank you."

I offered a nod and closed the door, walking away and into the shadows. All the anger and homicidal recklessness that ran rampant before burned off on the drive and now all I wanted was to find a decent snow suit for Naomi and get back.

Nothing was open at this time of night, which meant I'd have to break into the Sports Authority and steal what she needed. I took to the sky, landing on the dark roof a few minutes later. A white layer of rooftop snow met my scan, and I sighed, putting my hands on my hips while the aggravation mounted. I walked the grid, looking for the entry, and finally found the edging of the mechanical shaft. I had to dig to uncover the entry and with one yank, I nearly pulled it off its hinges. I dropped from the rafters to the top floor, glancing around in the darkness, blinking until my eyes adjusted.

My first procurement was a heavy-duty duffel bag that I was sure would survive the bitter wind of flight and I tore the tab off, unzipping it and emptying the paper stuffing onto the floor. Another scan of the store and I honed in on the women's section. Within minutes, I had a pair of long underwear and a ski outfit that guaranteed against frostbite shoved into the duffel bag. I found gloves and boots that had a similar frost bite rating and those disappeared into the bag. The only thing left unprotected was her face. I found a sleek full-coverage helmet with goggles included, and between that and a ski mask, I thought that would be enough to protect her. As I passed the rack of boot warmers, I stopped, grabbing a handful and shoving them into the bag along with a thick pair of wool socks.

I crossed to the cash register and piled the tags from each item, pulling out enough cash to cover the bill and then some, and slipped it into an envelope I found under the counter. Before sliding it into the cash register slot, I carefully scrawled, Thank You on the envelope and then slipped it into the slot.

With the roof door secured, I grasped the duffel bag and transformed, taking off to the north once again. The duffel bag made it without fraying in the wind, and I dropped it at the doorway before escaping to my favorite peak.

I knew I shouldn't leave Naomi alone for much longer, but I needed the peace of the night before I dealt with the crushing blow of not being able to touch her.

Tigress
Chapter Five
Damian

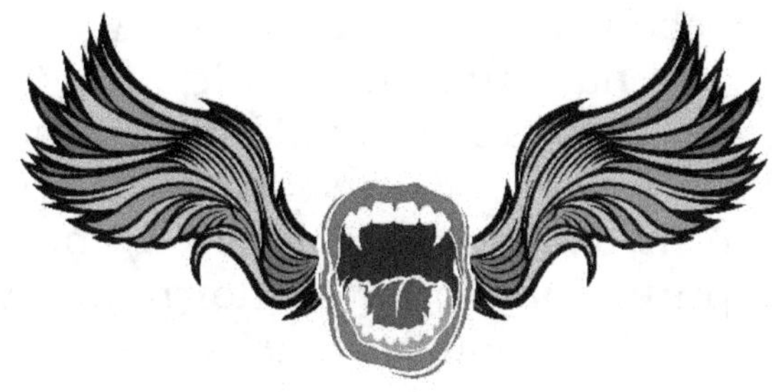

THE LIGHTENING SKY WAS my cue, and I dropped to the cabin, picked up the bag and headed inside. I locked the door behind me and tossed the bag into what Naomi called the mud room before heading to the bedroom.

She slept, and I put my palm close to her forehead, trying to determine if the fever still gripped her. No heat radiated from her and I wondered if it finally broke or if I was just cold enough to not feel it. With a sigh, I crouched next to the bed and crossed my arms on the edge, just watching her sleep.

Naomi was as beautiful now as she had been when I first laid eyes on her. An ache began in my chest and I dropped to my knees, resting my chin on my arms. Her analogy to kryptonite was very appropriate and the anger at the situation bloomed, turning the ache in my chest to a burning pit.

Her eyes blinked open and landed on mine. A small welcoming smile formed, followed by the bite of her lower lip.

"Hi," she whispered.

"Hi." I couldn't tear my gaze away and we stared at each other for a while. My thoughts drifted to the last time we made love. The heat and passion this woman could create in me was more than I ever believed I was capable of. Nothing in my existence matched it and I closed my eyes, putting my forehead down on my arms.

"I'm sorry I was such a mess yesterday," she whispered, and her fingertips ran through my hair, singeing my scalp before she pulled away.

I clenched my teeth and forced control over the emotional storm raging in my heart.

She shifted, and I looked up at her, studying her rosy complexion for a moment.

"You look much better," I said.

"I think the fever broke some time during the night." She sat up and crossed her legs under the covers, patting the bed.

I climbed onto the mattress and took a seat, leaning my back against the post at the end of the bed. "I've got a snow suit and stuff for you in the mudroom. We can head out tonight."

"Where?"

"Anywhere you want to go."

She smiled and glanced around the room, her internal conflict of leaving this place etched into the tight lines at the corners of her mouth. "What about New York?"

Somehow, I knew she was going to say that and I crossed my arms. It was too close to Lucifer's home base. He liked the city. It provided him with a wealth of derelicts to pull into his demonic fold. But it also provided the invisibility of sheer numbers, the ability to hide in plain sight.

I tossed around the idea, and finally, the proximity to Lucifer clinched it. I couldn't take that chance, especially since she was now at a disadvantage.

"I don't know about that, honey," I finally said after weighing the dangers. "We could look for something on the ocean, down south, if you'd like?" I shrugged. "Or we could go southwest into Arizona or southern California."

She crossed her arms. "Just because I'm no longer a vampire doesn't mean I can't hold my own. I want to go home, Damian. I want to go back to the city. It will be the last place he looks."

I laughed at her logic and she swung her legs out from under the covers. For the last five years, we talked about where we wanted to go after Colorado and we could never agree then, so I don't know why I thought now would be any different.

She stood and stretched; the shirt lifting high enough for me to see her cute round butt cheeks and I closed my eyes, turning my head away and getting the sudden swell of lust under wraps.

"New York is not an option. Pick somewhere else," I said, swinging my gaze back to hers. "And remember, wherever we go, if the trip is longer than twelve hours, the ride is going to be interesting."

Her brow creased in that cute questioning way that got my blood going, and I smiled.

"We have to find a vehicle that has somewhere for me to go during the day if you want to keep driving. Or hotels that offer blackout shades."

Dimples appeared. "You mean I get to lock you in the trunk?"

The playful cock of her brow brought forth the first genuine smile I've displayed in the last seven days and I chuckled.

"If that's what you want to do..." I stood, crossing the distance and towering over her.

Her smile faded. "I can't do what I want anymore," she whispered, and her hand moved to my chest. The fabric buffered my skin from the sting of her flesh and I stared down into her brown eyes, debating on just how painful a kiss would be.

"So, what did you eat last night?" she asked, stepping away and putting a damper on my desire.

My gaze dropped to the floor before returning to hers. I knew she wouldn't approve of my meal choice and instead of answering; I turned away, crossing out of the room. "I'm not sure what you want for breakfast..."

"Damian?"

I glanced back at her, leveling my best *leave-it-alone* stare.

Her features transitioned into disappointment and my fists clenched against the denial poised on my lips. I turned away before the lie slipped between us.

"You didn't," she said, and the muscles in my back stiffened. She knew me as well as anyone, and my reaction was a dead giveaway.

"Yes, I did," I said, my voice lowering into that feral quality that always scared her.

"Jesus, Damian."

I turned, letting the frustration boil over. The anger loomed over the room and I crossed, grabbing her arms and pushing her against the wall, ignoring the scream of pain jolting up my arms from where my palms pressed against her skin.

"I needed to kill something, Naomi," I said through my clenched teeth. "Because if I didn't find an outlet, I would have walked out into the daylight and let the sun reduce me to ash."

Her eyes widened.

I pulled my hands away, trying to hide the wince, but blisters on my palms flared an angry red. "This," I held them up for her to see, "this is going to drive me insane." I stepped back, my chest moving up and down with each frustrated inhale and exhale.

The woman had no idea what being near her without the ability to touch her was doing to me, and it had only been a week. I can only imagine the basket case I'm heading for after a month of this or what part of my sanity will be left after a year. Nothing in my twenty-five hundred years compared to this rawness scraping my nerves.

"Lucifer knew damn well what he was doing when he sent Lilith on this mission. He knew this would drive me over the edge." I took another step back, distancing myself.

Her lips thinned and her eyes narrowed.

"And you don't think this whole situation doesn't piss me off too?" Her hands flew to her waist, and she glared at me. "I want to skin that bastard alive," she snarled, her growl very similar to that of the feral tiger form she used to transform into. "We are going to New York," she added, and this time, there was no negotiation in her glare.

Tigress
Chapter Six
Damian

I STOOD IN THE shadows, at least a foot away from the edge of the sun streak on the floor. Naomi stood in the doorway with her face tilted into the sun and a blanket wrapped around her to ward off the frigid wind. My gaze kept scanning what I could of the opening for any sign of danger; although I had no idea what I would do if a demon showed up and grabbed her off the threshold.

"Naomi?"

She turned and smiled. The sheer joy in her expression dug into my stomach like a bullet.

This was the closest to daylight I had been in years. Sure, I had seen the beginning of a sunrise before it hit the horizon, but that light was wrapped in a rainbow of colors. This whiteness beyond Naomi's form actually stung my eyes, and I squinted into it.

My heart throbbed in my throat every second the door was open with Naomi in the full view of the brutal mountainside. She finally shivered and stepped inside, closed the door and engaged the locks. Naomi nearly skipped across the distance and stopped in front of me with that sparkle in her eyes that she used to get whenever I walked into a room.

"As soon as the sun sets, we'll head east." I turned, escaping back to the depths of the cave I built. I sank onto the couch and leaned my head back on the headrest, running my hands through my hair.

Naomi took a seat next to me and put her hand on my thigh. The heat of it filtered through my jeans and she looked at me. "Damian, we'll figure this out."

I met her gaze. "How?"

She shrugged. "We'll find a way."

"Baby, what if there isn't?" I had to know what was on her mind, even though deep down, I knew she would be my undoing.

Her hand withdrew, and she sighed, glancing around the room and then back at me. "I married you for better or worse. Till death do us part, remember?"

I rolled my eyes and stood, crossing the room to the mural. I stared at the likeness of us on canvas, the painting that I created around the time Christ was born.

"You'd stay married to a man who can't be with you in the sun and kills for sport when the sun sets?" I said, skirting the actual issue that was digging a hole in my stomach.

"You do not kill for sport."

I raised an eyebrow in her direction.

"You don't, so don't try to convince me otherwise." Her no-bullshit tone made me smile. "So what exactly are you worried about?" she asked.

I studied the patterns in the silk and then focused on the tiger in the snow, almost laughing at the hawk. Both animals carried the same amusement in their features, the same happiness—everything struck at once. We would never be those carefree creatures I painted.

Ever.

"Damian?"

"I'm worried I'm going to lose you." There, I said it out loud, and it hung over the room like a dark cloud.

Her silence just layered on the unease and when I turned to gauge her reaction, she was standing next to me, studying me just as acutely as I had been studying the portrait.

"Why?" she asked. It held no forcefulness, yet the strength of her soft inquisition made it impossible not to answer.

I laughed. "Because you're as passionate as I am and without that piece of the puzzle, you may come to realize I'm not what you want."

"Granted, our physical relationship has been as intense as everything else between us, but it isn't the only reason I want to be with you. Besides, we can get creative and make that work. It might mean latex and clothing, but it isn't the end of the world."

"So if we never kissed again..."

She pressed her lips together in a thin line of contemplation. "I'd be heartbroken, but it's because of what that does to me. What you do to me on every level. I'd find another way for you to create that same weak-kneed response."

"And if you can't, that's when you'll start looking elsewhere," I replied.

"No," she said.

I wasn't convinced. I knew I'd never touch another soul, but she was human and not bound to me the way I was to her. The heat between us wasn't something either of us could deny and, god help me, it might be just be the thing that finally kills me. The insanity of it all burned and I turned away from her, letting the bite of anger come back full force.

"This time, I'm taking Lucifer down," I said and retreated to my computer, checking my various email accounts. I pulled up my oldest one and froze, staring at the most recent subject line.

Oh, how the mighty have fallen...

But it wasn't the subject that turned my blood into liquid fury. It was the sender. Lucifer had the gall to bait me. My hands curled, my nails slicing through the flesh of my palm at the obvious mock.

"Mother fucker," I whispered and kept my hands clenched so the flurry of responses couldn't find their way onto the screen. I flexed and squeezed in slow increments until the insane urge to answer him with an equally infuriated response died.

When I was sure I wouldn't do anything stupid, I opened the email and pushed the chair back, just in case my hands acted of their own accord.

I gather from the mess you made, Lilith hit her mark. I'm looking forward to chatting with the two of you again. I have a feeling next time will have quite a different...and more satisfying outcome.

Until we meet again.

Lucifer

I shut the computer down and pressed my palms to my eyes. The urge to smash everything within reach settled in my skin and I let out a roar, planting my feet on the floor so I didn't kick the table clear across the space.

When I pulled my hands away, Naomi stood waiting for an explanation.

I slammed my fist down onto the desk. The crack of wood splintered the stale air, and I snarled, "Lucifer just fucked with the wrong person!"

Tigress
Chapter Seven
Naomi

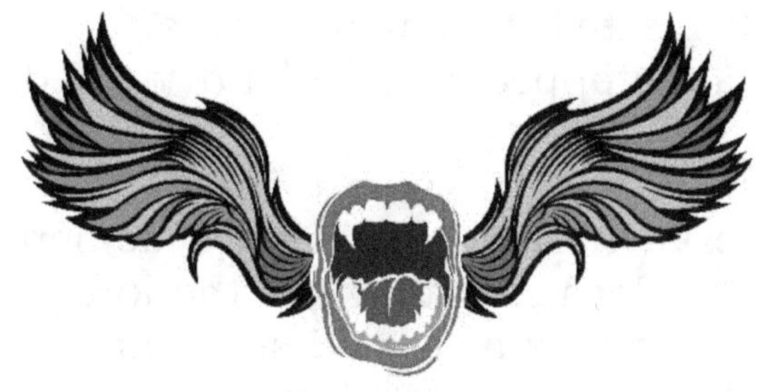

DAMIAN GROWLED AND PACED. Curses in both English and Greek spilled from his lips, crowding the already charged air. If Lucifer showed up at our door at this moment, he wouldn't make it two paces before Damian tore into him.

"Do you think Michael can help?"

Damian's gaze stopped on mine. "With what?"

"Do you think he can make it so you're not allergic to me?"

His bitter laugh filled the room. "I already tried that avenue. Michael can't help."

"You called Michael?"

"I thought you were dying, so yes, I called Michael."

I bit my lip and nodded, understanding how frightened he had to be to call on Michael. He still believed the archangel tolerated him because he was the protector of the bloodline.

He had no clue what Michael really thought of him, and I sighed, setting that secret aside. Instead, I occupied his mind with conversation so he wouldn't go into another tirade and destroy the place.

"Lilith created the shadow virus?"

Damian stopped pacing and turned to me, nodding.

"How?"

"Bacteria, herbs, blood and a demon curse," he said. "At least, that's what the lore says. She practiced the dark arts, and she was in search of immortality." He shrugged and crossed his arms before sliding onto the couch. "She certainly found the right cocktail, but it was her relentless pursuit that got Lucifer kicked out of heaven. For years, she tested her concoctions on unsuspecting victims and I guess the heavenly host got pissed."

"Lilith and Lucifer?" I asked, my mind still locked on that tidbit.

"Yep. And she's the reason Lucifer and Michael hate each other."

He had my curiosity on hyper-drive, and I slid into the chair across from him. "Love triangle?" I asked.

"No. More like a case of jealousy. Lucifer had taken an interest in Lilith around the same time Michael started courting Athena's mother." He shifted, stretching his legs out on the couch, and leaned back with his head on the armrest. "Lucifer never fully understood why he got hurled from heaven and Michael didn't. What started as bitterness turned into all out hatred. Lilith was obsessed with finding immortality, and his brother was busy popping out kids with a mere mortal. Lilith and Lucifer had a sort of falling out around the time Athena was born, so not only was he locked out of heaven, the woman for whom he had been exiled decided she didn't want to be subservient to the likes of Lucifer." He glanced over at me and sent a twist of a smile. "Michael had everything, and Lucifer had nothing but a pit full of blood thirsty fiends from all of Lilith's experiments."

He stopped talking, staring at the ceiling with a faraway expression and what he said next sent a chill all the way to my bones. "Eve was Athena's mother."

Silence settled over the room, and I waited with my heart in my throat.

"Lilith had just created a new batch of elixir when Lucifer decided he had had enough. By this time, he was bitter and alone and the jealousy of his brother and of Lilith carving a life for herself just exploded. In his rage, he grabbed both Eve and Lilith and forced them to be the guinea pigs. This batch had a little extra something." Damian's chuckle made the temperature in the room plunge, and I shivered. "Not only did it contain Lilith's brew, it also had a dose of demon blood and a curse straight from Lucifer's lips." He glanced my way. "But that wasn't the end of his tirade. He wasn't done doling out justice, and what he did next broke whatever alliance he had with Lilith, turning her into a bitter adversary."

His gaze moved back to the ceiling and his jaw tightened at his thoughts and instead of prying, I waited, knowing he would eventually spill the information. Finally, when I couldn't stand it anymore, I asked, "What did he do?"

"Lucifer took Michael's firstborn. Watching him devour that little boy drove Lilith right into Eve's arms."

I was not prepared for the answer, and my arms broke out in a hot rash of gooseflesh. I swallowed the disgust blooming in my stomach along with the endless questions, but the fundamental question that swirled came blurting out, anyway. "Lucifer killed his nephew?"

Damian sent a nod in my direction. "Sick bastard," he muttered and shifted. "Anyway, Michael fled with Athena bringing her to Greece, to my neck of the woods. He found an honorable family to watch over her, and you know the rest."

"How did you meet her?"

Damian sighed. "Her husband was my best friend until he was killed in battle with Carthage." He met my gaze. "Before he took his last breath, I promised him I'd look after Athena and Zoe. It didn't hurt that I was smitten with her already and had been since we met, but Icarus laid claim to her first." He shrugged.

"So, when did you meet Michael?"

"When I got back from the war. And let me tell you, that was an interesting meeting," he started and shifted on the couch, rolling so he faced me.

"I'll bet."

"I nearly shit my pants," he admitted, his cheeks turning the rose color of embarrassment.

I grinned, imagining his reaction. "Did you cower?" I prodded, my tone teasing enough to draw a smile.

"No. I didn't." The spark of humor glinted in his eyes. "I held my ground and promised to watch after his daughter and granddaughter. I didn't realize what I was promising, or the consequences of failure, but I was sincere. I would have gladly laid down my life to protect them if it came to that and he knew it, so I received his blessing." He shrugged his shoulder and rolled on his back again. "A lot of good that did." His expression transitioned from those fond memories to the dark day, Lucifer tore Athena to bits.

"You protected his granddaughter," I said. "Besides, you can't blame yourself for her death."

He turned toward me. "I couldn't stop it, therefore I failed."

It was a simple statement that had ruled his life for centuries, and while I wanted to argue with him, I let it go. I stood and crossed the distance, dropping to my knees by the side of the couch. His haunted gaze tore at my heart, and all I wanted to do was wrap my arms around him and erase all that pain.

He reached for me, his hand halting just before he touched my cheek. His fingers slowly curled into a fist and he let his arm drop across his chest. Breaking my gaze, he turned his frustrated stare to the ceiling and his features hardened.

I dropped my forehead into the curve of his elbow, resting it on the soft fabric of the chambray work shirt he wore. The muscles in his arm flexed and the unmistakable sound of teeth grinding filled the room just before his fingers laced into my hair. The tender stroke of his thumb caught me off guard and I yanked away, knowing his fingers would bear blisters.

I stared into the depths of his blue eyes, wondering why the hell he would put himself through that kind of pain just to comfort me. He reached for me again and I grabbed his arm through the shirt, stopping him with a shake of the head.

"Don't," I whispered. "Intentionally hurting yourself doesn't help."

His inhale filled the space between us and an instant later, he stood on the other side of the room, his movement complete within a blink.

"Then I need space," he said, his voice choked in his throat and I kept his gaze offering a nod. I understood, because being near him was like a time bomb. The closer we were, the less likely we could resist the building tension between us, and I didn't know what kissing him would do. If my skin produced blisters, what in god's name would my saliva do?

Instead of going to him, I slipped back into the chair, my mind going over everything he just told me. I turned my gaze to him, thinking about Lilith and the vampires we ran into at Valerie's house five years before. They looked very different from Damian, especially Lilith. They were essentially around the same age, give or take a few decades, but she was pale as the snow, beautiful, but still pale. Damian, on the other hand, hadn't lost the natural skin tones. It was almost as if...

My eyes widened.

"You're not from the same batch as Lilith, are you?"

His head shook slowly. "I'm a result of the multitude of her failed experiments, and I'm not sure why I survived without becoming a mindless killing machine, like those poor bastards in the pit."

"Are you the only one that ever survived?"

He nodded. "I don't think any of the others thought to bite back. I'm just amazed they didn't destroy themselves long before I was thrown in, but maybe Lucifer kept them fed, so they didn't turn on one another."

"What about Lilith and Eve? Weren't they just as menacing to society?"

"No. They seemed to have some level of control, sort of like I did once Michael freed me. But they were cunning and sly and always together. I scared the shit out of them at first," he said and shot me a grin that faded after a moment. "We crossed paths a couple of times and all three of us had the same goal to destroy Lucifer. Lilith was curious as to how I survived and wanted to run some experiments, but I wasn't about to let her cage me so she could figure out what made me tick. And neither was Eve when she found out I was the protector of her bloodline." He stopped speaking, chewing on his lower lip in contemplation, and then his head turned toward the doorway.

"Eve isn't dead," he said, swinging his gaze in my direction.

"Why do you say that?"

"Because Lilith would have torn into Lucifer and never done his bidding without something on the line, and the only thing she cares about is Eve." He collapsed onto the cushions of the couch, running both his hands into his hair. "Which means I'll be on Eve's hit list regardless of my role as protector of her bloodline."

"So, Lucifer still has another dose of the cure?"

He shrugged. "I have no idea."

Something about the story didn't settle right with me and then the disconnect shot into my mind and out of my mouth. "What about Michael and Eve?"

Silence fell between us, and Damian kept my gaze. "Michael found Eve and Lilith drinking what remained of his son's blood."

Just the thought gave me a start, and I could see the disgust written in the tight lines around Damian's clamped lips.

"That was the end of it. He never forgave her, but he couldn't bring himself to kill her either."

"I'd have to side with Michael on this one," I said, my stomach rolling at the thought of draining the blood from my lifeless child. "But I wouldn't have been so kind. She'd be just as dead as her child."

Damian kept my stare. "Think of it this way. If you found me in that situation, devastated from watching Lucifer kill our child and starving enough to succumb to the scent of blood filling the room, would you kill me?"

"Yes," I said with no hesitation, and his eyebrows rose.

"I'm not sure I'd be able to if the tables were turned," he said.

Irritation snaked over my skin and he caught it easily enough.

He put his hand out, stopping my ramp up to a rant. "Don't get me wrong, I'd be livid, but I just don't have it in me to kill you. There's nothing that would make me want to kill you."

Struck by the sincerity in his eyes, the bite of aggravation nipping at my skin softened. "That's very sweet, but at one time, that wasn't the case."

A combination of irritation and guilt flashed in his eyes, and he turned away. "I wasn't in my right mind," he muttered and stalked out of the room.

Watching his backside as he headed toward the bedroom wiped the smile off my face. He has such a fine ass and my hands clenched in response to the pain that accompanied the thought of never touching him again.

A quick glance at the clock told me we had just a couple of hours left, and I followed him into the bedroom. He shoved clothing into a duffle bag like the garments had offended him in some manner.

"Are you trying to murder your clothes?"

He looked up at me and there was a clear warning in his gaze before he continued packing.

I couldn't help the smirk that captured my lips and his muttering growl told me he saw it, too. "Come on, where's your sense of humor?" I opened one of my bureau drawers.

"I don't want to go to New York," he said.

I paused with a shirt half folded in my hands and met his gaze. "You don't have an option."

His bitter laughter rang out, and he zipped his bag. "I'm the only one with options at the moment."

My hands clenched the shirt, and I slammed it into the open bag with the same ferocity he had because he was right. Even wrapped up in the get up he brought in last night wasn't enough for me to get to civilization on my own. He was the only one who could get me out of here.

"Now look who's murdering their clothing."

I met his gaze and bit back the expletive that broadcast in my mind. Instead of dwelling on my anger, I sighed. "What about your place in Litchfield?"

A spark lit up his eyes and a dimple appeared. "I think the only thing standing was the garage."

"And your cars," I added.

He sat on the side of the bed with his back to me. I finished packing up the clothing that I wanted and waited while he tossed around the idea. I knew it would appeal to him and I also knew he'd weigh the options over and over in his mind. The zip of my bag caught his attention, and he glanced over his shoulder.

"Okay."

I gave him a nod of satisfaction and glanced at the clock. We still had a good hour before the sun set and his silence gave me time to mull over all he said.

"So we differ from the rest of the species?" I asked and his eyebrow cocked along with his head.

"Vampire, humans, whatever?"

"I guess so."

"Is that why my transition was so quick?"

Damian reached over, grabbed my bag, and hauled it off the bed along with his. "I don't know. I made a couple of attempts at companions over the years, and none of them changed like you did. They all ended up like those beasts in the pit. Mindless and driven for blood, and I had no choice but to let them into the daylight. The only explanation I have is it probably had to do with Michael's bloodline, but that's just an educated guess."

"The other vampires you ran into. Did they look like Lilith did?"

Damian's brow knit into confusion.

"You still look human unless you're in your shadow form. Lilith looked like a porcelain doll."

Damian blinked several times and shifted, hiking the bags up on his shoulders. "I guess. They were all products of Lilith and Eve." He crossed to the doorway.

"But shape shifting is unique only to you and I."

He stopped and turned back to me. "What are you getting at?"

"Maybe my blood won't kill you."

"Naomi..." he started, but his gaze dropped to my throat and then bounced back to my eyes. "Even if it doesn't, you don't have the ability to heal and last time I checked, a severed carotid is fatal."

"Who says it has to be my throat?" I said and turned my wrist in his direction.

He took a step forward; the hunger flaring in his features. "What if you're wrong?" he asked and stopped.

"Then we die here," I said with a shrug.

The hardness that captured his features made me step backwards. "I will not sentence you to death."

Damian stormed out of the room and I sank onto the bed and my heart followed, sinking into the depths of my belly. I wasn't trying to doom us to annihilation; I just wanted to figure out a way for both of us to survive.

Together.

Tigress
Chapter Eight
Naomi

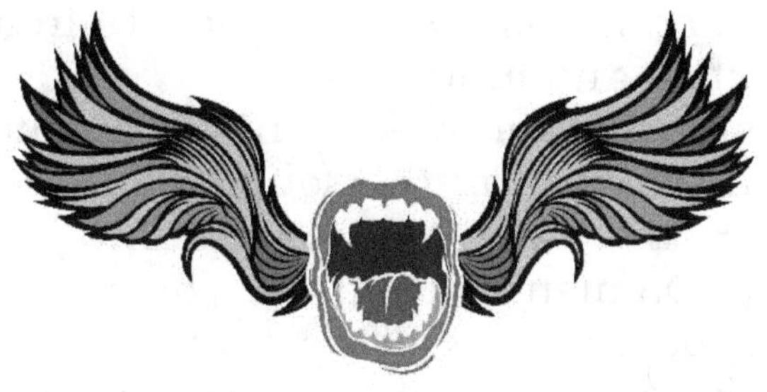

DAMIAN STOOD IN THE doorway with his back to me, scanning the landscape. "I'll be back in a little while," he said.

"Where are you going?" I asked, pulling the snow pants over my jeans and long underwear.

He glanced back at me. "I need to rent a car," he said and smiled back at me. "Any preferences?"

"Something fast with a big trunk."

Dimples appeared and he turned, taking a few steps onto the snow, and then he morphed into that beautiful hawk, cutting through the sky carrying the duffel bags with our clothing. All that was left behind was me and the computer backpack. I sighed and closed the door, deciding to do one last walk through of our home. I wandered around the cavern and stopped in front of the mural, shaking my head at my idiocy. There was no way I was leaving this behind, and I slid it off the hooks. After neatly folding it, I slid it into the bag with Damian's computer equipment. There wasn't much left, and I opened and closed drawers, wandered into the kitchen and opened the cabinet, finding only soup, which I already had for breakfast and lunch.

My stomach growled, and I debated, but closed the cabinet on the soup when I heard the shuffle in the cabin. I stepped into the living room as Damian opened the door. Flakes of snow peppered his dark hair and the bloom on his cheeks told me it was colder than usual. He smiled and dangled a key attached to a U-Haul key ring.

"It isn't fast, and it isn't a luxury sports car, but it will provide a dark space where I can hang during the day."

I rolled my eyes. "You've got to be kidding me?"

"Nope, and we'll need to drop it off in New Haven when we get there. Of course, we'll have to wait until just after sunset."

"But a U-Haul?"

Now he was laughing at me. "Yes, baby, a U-Haul."

I sighed and nodded. "I packed the mural."

"I knew I was missing something. I'm going to do one more walk through while you finish getting dressed," he said.

I let him do his last search of our home without me looking over his shoulder. Instead, I stepped into the cabin where a gas lamp sat on the rustic table. The soft glow filled the room, and I slid into the warm coat and slipped the helmet over my head, tightening all the components until I had a snug fit. The gloves actually snapped onto the parka, creating a buffer between me and the frigid air outside, and I got one on and had to wait for Damian to help me snap the other one in place.

He stepped out with the backpack in his hand and gave me a quick scan before his lips twisted into a smile.

"I guess that is a look," he mumbled and slid the backpack over my arms and secured it around my waist before he snapped the gloved hand I raised to him. Damian crouched down and snapped the pants to my boots as well before standing and staring at me through the dark helmet glass.

"Are you ready?"

Ready. The question gave me pause, and I glanced around at the barren cabin before giving him a nod. The knot in my stomach twisted the moment he reached for the doorknob, and I almost stopped him. Instead, I closed my eyes and took a deep breath. My exhale steamed up the visor, and I stepped out into the night behind him.

Before the fog cleared, the firm grasp of his talon wrapped around me, and I was flying. With each beat of his mighty wings, we rose higher into the sky and I forgot about my pang of sadness in leaving our home behind. I forgot just about everything except for the exquisite rush filling my blood and the panoramic view of the mountains below. I had never experienced flying with Damian from human eyes, and it was even more exhilarating than I recalled, especially with little more than a chill penetrating the cocoon of fabric wrapped around me.

Damian seemed to understand my joy, and he swooped like a rollercoaster. His cry sounded much more like a laugh than the scream of a hawk. When he went into a roll, my scream bounced around the interior of my helmet, nearly drowning out his cry. If I was prone to a weak stomach, this flight would have been my undoing, but the moment we landed, I flipped my visor back and spun to face his bemused expression.

"Can we do that again?"

His laugh filled the dark alley and the beep of a security system answered my question.

"Maybe, when we get settled, wherever we end up," he said and opened the passenger door for me, helping me strip off the backpack before I climbed into the cab.

He slid into the driver's seat and grinned at me. "I keep forgetting just how much you like to fly," he said and started the engine.

"I hate airplanes," I mumbled and pulled the helmet off, putting it behind the seat in the small storage space. I shook my head, freeing the curls from the make-shift bun and running my fingers through my hair before I glanced in his direction.

"What?" I asked at his intense stare.

"Nothing," he said and put the vehicle in gear, navigating the side streets until he pulled onto Interstate 76, heading east.

I peeled off the snow pants and tucked them behind the seat, shifting the jeans to make the remaining layers of clothing fall into a more comfortable position. The radio was useless and after fifteen minutes of fiddling with it, I gave up and turned the static off. Damian glanced at me and then back at the road, that amused expression still formed on his handsome face.

"You don't need to stay up with me if you don't want to," he said and pat his thigh. "And if you need a pillow, you can use my leg."

"Why are you being so accommodating all of a sudden?"

He exhaled and glanced at me. "I'm not. I'm just thinking you'd like to get some rest if you were planning on driving all day."

It made sense, but I wasn't the least bit tired. "It's way too early for me to go to sleep," I said. "Besides, I'm getting hungry, so you'll have to stop at the next rest area."

I caught the dimple in his cheek and the slight shake of his head like he forgot I was human and needed food. He nodded, meeting my gaze for an instant before focusing back on the road.

"I'll stay in the car while you grab something."

"You don't want to come in with me?"

His eyebrows rose. "No," he said and kept his gaze on the road.

I wish I could still get a glimpse of what was on his mind because, outside of the silent challenge in his raised eyebrow, I couldn't read him. It frustrated the hell out of me and I just wanted to know what was going on behind that stormy expression.

His gaze slid to mine. "I'm hungry too," he said.

"Ah. And you don't trust yourself around that many people?"

"I do, but I would rather not tempt fate."

"Did you pack the blood?"

He shook his head. "It would have frozen in the back of the truck."

"Are you going to be okay back there?" I hadn't considered the temperature. With all our romps in the woods in Colorado, I never thought about what ten hours in the back of a van would do to Damian.

"We'll find out," he mumbled.

"We can find a hotel, instead, if you'd prefer."

"I'll be fine. Besides, once we get there, I'll have a ton of things to do, like building a house and finding somewhere for you to stay while I'm doing that."

"I can stay in the garage with you."

"Not until I make the property demon and angel-proof again," he said.

"Can you make it vamp-proof while you're at it?" I asked and got a dimpled grin in return.

"Did you want me exiled from the property?"

I exhaled and rolled my eyes. "I guess not," I said and pointed toward the sign for the rest area. "How exactly does one demon-proof a property?" I asked. I knew about the order of ancient symbols needed to angel-proof a property, but we never demon-proofed the camp in Colorado.

"I need enough rock salt to surround the property."

I envisioned a circle of salt lining the property and laughed. "But won't it wash away?"

He must have gotten some of my thoughts because he chuckled. "It won't for quite a few years, especially when it's sealed and buried in a ditch surrounding the property," he said. "Unfortunately, I had waited too long to refresh the original defenses last time and once the circle is broken, it becomes useless."

The van pulled to a stop in front of a gas pump, and Damian shut it down. "I'll park over there after I fill up," he said and pointed toward the parking spaces in front of the building before peeling a twenty from his wallet. "Will this be enough?"

"Yes, thanks," I replied and took the cash, stuffing it into my pocket and jumped out of the cab. I glanced at him over my shoulder and he had already gotten out of the cab and started pumping gas. The moment I walked in the building, the scent of burgers and fries assaulted my senses and my stomach growled; pushing me toward the McDonald's counter. It had been five years since I ate anything other than blood and broth and I was ravenous.

But I also had to take care of business, so I diverted into the bathroom first. As I washed my hands, I studied my reflection. I couldn't detect any change from before Lilith shot me with the antidote and I wondered if I did age five years or not.

My stomach growled again, and I grabbed a paper towel, wiped my hands and headed to the McDonald's counter to satisfy the food cravings that took control. My hunger pangs were nowhere near as painful as the blood pangs of a vampire; however, they were just as compelling.

I ended up with two Big Macs, large fries, and a large chocolate milkshake. The minute I sat down in the cab, I dug in. Fast food never tasted so delicious, and I didn't look up at Damian until I finished both burgers. He sat with one hand on the steering wheel and the other on the stick shift, just staring at me.

"What?" I asked with a mouthful of French fries.

"I've seen wild dogs eat with more manners," he said.

"Fuck you." I wiped my mouth with a napkin. "I haven't eaten in five years. What'd you expect?"

He started laughing and put the vehicle in gear, pulling back on the road before addressing me again.

"I have no idea what I expected, but that certainly wasn't it."

"Normally I have manners," I said and licked my lips. "It's just this was delicious."

"I guess so." He licked his lips and inhaled. "I'm going to have to eat something before sunrise."

The way he gazed at me set my body on fire and I had to look out the window. While he was talking about hunting, my mind went to the last time he made love to me with his mouth, to the heat he created that went to a cellular level and I sighed, taking a sip of the chocolate shake like it could quell the fire he set with his innocent statement.

Silence filled the cab and after I finished my meal, I tucked the garbage into the bag and took Damian up on his offer to use his leg as a pillow.

"Sing something for me," I said and our eyes met for a moment and he offered a slight nod before looking back at the road. He pressed his lips together in contemplation and then took a breath and his incredible voice filled the cab. I swear his voice would put the heavenly host to shame. He could easily walk into a recording studio and put out a number one album and the women would swoon, just like I always do. He crooned through a collection of my favorite songs, lulling me to sleep.

Tigress
Chapter Nine
Naomi

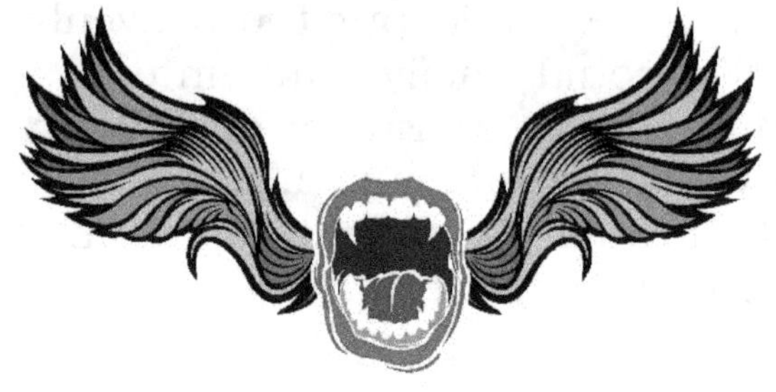

A CHILL TICKLED THE back of my neck and I burrowed further into my coat and shifted, opening my eyes to the empty cab and the night beyond. I sat up, rubbing the sleep from my eyes, and stared at the almost deserted rest stop. The lights were on in the restrooms and I bit my lip, looking at the key ring hanging from the ignition. It held half the keys that it had earlier and I knew Damian was hunting.

I stretched and pulled the remaining keys from the ignition, pocketing them and sliding out of the cab. I made sure I had the right one to unlock the truck before I locked it and headed inside to pee and rinse my mouth out.

When I stepped out of the stall, movement caught my attention and my head snapped toward the door. I stepped back at the hovering shadow. Sharp teeth gleamed, and the form stepped toward me. It wasn't Damian, and my heart thundered in my chest, announcing my fear to this fiend.

Instead of retreating into the stall and limiting my options, I stepped into the center of the space, facing the vampire. She chuckled when I took a defensive posture, tucking my chin to my chest, and Michael's name popped into my head.

"Michael," I whispered, calling on my ancient grandfather, who could toast her on sight.

The air shifted as the vampire attacked, but the moment her fangs dug into my arm, her feral growl turned into a scream of agony. She pulled away, her hands clawing at her throat as my blood spread like poison through her.

Michael's hand descended on my shoulder and he stood watching exactly what my cured blood did to descendants of Lilith and Eve. The angry blisters on Damian's skin were nothing compared to the complete breakdown of this vampire's cells. It was as if she swallowed a gallon of battery acid. A bloody froth bubbled from her mouth and her skin looked as if it were boiling. Her dying screams echoed off the tiled walls. The entire ordeal horrified me, and I turned my face into Michael's chest.

All I could think of was, what if I had let Damian drink my blood?

The screams subsided, but the stench of death hung on the air like a thick bank of fog. When the door banged open, I turned my head, meeting Damian's frantic gaze. A drop of fresh blood still graced his lips and when he glanced at the pile of bloody froth on the floor and back to Michael and me, his brow scrunched in confusion.

"She bit Naomi," Michael said.

"So you did that to her?" his breathless question settled over the room.

"No, my blood did that," I said and wiped the wetness from my cheeks. I hadn't realized I was crying, but the shake in my voice confirmed it, along with the traces of tears on my fingers.

His gaze dropped to the floor, and he closed his mouth, pressing his lips together before his eyes rose to mine. They moved past me to Michael.

"And you just let her suffer?"

"I was curious," Michael said, and I pushed away from him. "And I wanted her to know what would happen if you ever bit her," he added and met my gaze.

I shivered at the thought, but there was something underneath Michael's gaze, something akin to a plea for me not to allow Damian to self-destruct. I sent a reassuring smile his way before turning back to Damian.

"Where are you going?" Michael directed toward Damian.

"Home," Damian said, squaring his shoulders and putting on that rebellious expression that I associate with Michael's presence.

"Home, as in Greece?" Michael asked, his hands finding his hips, and a warning flared in his eyes.

"No, home as in Connecticut."

"You would be better suited to go to Greece."

"She wants to go to New York," Damian said, focusing Michael's displeasure in my direction instead of his.

"No."

"That's what I said." Damian sent a smug smile in my direction and then glanced back at Michael. "Although right now I'd like to tear your brother to pieces for what he's done to us."

Now that the adrenaline had died, the stench of death made me gag and I shuffled around the steaming puddle and out into the frosty night. Damian and Michael followed and for the first time, I noted Michael was wearing regular clothing instead of bare-chested with his majestic wings and I sent him a sideways look.

"I'm tagging along for the ride," he said, and both Damian and I stopped in our tracks. "Someone needs to keep her safe during the day now that my brother is back in action," he added to Damian.

"But won't you give us away?" Damian asked, narrowing his eyes.

"No, not while I take a completely human form." He spread his arms out to prove his point. "No wings, no angelic powers, no beacon, but I still can kick ass."

Damian circled him and the spark in his eyes made me want to warn Michael, but I kept my mouth shut, watching the dynamics. I was sure there was more at play here than just my safety, and as soon as Damian was tucked safely away in the truck, I'd get to the bottom of Michael's intentions.

The hellacious grin that spread on Damian's lips, just before his shadow form morphed, was enough to make me step between the two supernatural beings.

"No," I said, pointing at Damian, knowing his first instinct was to break free of Michael's bond. His mad gaze landed on me and he smiled with a mouthful of razor-sharp teeth.

"Move, baby," he said, but the feral growl that accompanied it made me stand my ground. I knew more about Michael than he did.

Michael put his hand on my shoulder to clear the path, but I shook it off, meeting Damian's glare.

"He cares a great deal about you, you stupid moron," I growled back at Damian. "So I'm sure part of it is keeping you safe, too."

The transition out of shadow form happened in a blink, and the confusion clouding Damian's face made me smile, even with Michael's less than silent curses behind me. I glanced back at him. "Don't you think it's time he knows what he means to you? I know you said this angry shit between you two worked, but it doesn't work for me."

Michael's arms crossed, and he glared at me before he moved his gaze to Damian's.

"What exactly does she know that I don't?" Damian asked.

Michael threw a curveball that neither Damian nor I saw coming.

"That I've been watching over you for a very long time," he said, and his gaze bounced from Damian's to mine and back.

"I failed to save your daughter. Why the hell would you watch over me?"

"Because you are Gabriel's son."

Damian shrugged. "What does my father have to do with this?"

I stared at Michael and my mother's catholic upbringing brought forth the names of the archangels. Understanding sank in and I gasped. "You mean to tell me Damian is your nephew?"

Silence descended between the three of us and when Michael nodded, I stepped back, digesting the implications. Angel blood bound us, and that was the principal difference between Damian and the rest of the vampires.

"But...my parents died when I was a child," Damian whispered.

"Yes, unfortunately, they did. My bringing Athena to Greece wasn't a coincidence. Our brother didn't know about you because he had been exiled from heaven before you were born and Gabriel had seen what kind of destruction he was capable of. If our brother knew about you, I think you would have had the same fate as my son."

"Athena was my...cousin?"

"Yes," Michael said.

Damian shivered and turned away, stalking toward the van without another word.

"You let him screw around with his cousin?"

"Times were different back then, and I knew he had a strong need to protect her," Michael said. "I knew he'd die for her and that's the best a father could hope for, especially with my brother on the warpath."

I paused with my hand on the door handle. "So while you're in human form, you can die like Gabriel?"

A bitter smile surfaced. "Yes."

"And if your other brother was to find you in this form?"

"I would be just as screwed as the two of you." He reached past me and opened the door, holding it so I could climb into the cab.

Damian glared beyond me at the being who had kept him in the dark for millenniums. The hostility in the cab was enough to make me take a deep, settling breath. Anger traced its way through the muscles in his face and the tightness of his jaw. His lips presented a thin white line and the only thing holding more resentment was his challenging blue eyes.

"Fucking angels," he muttered and pulled out of the parking lot like a bat out of hell.

I still had a wealth of questions pinging through my brain, and when Damian lowered his hand to my knee and gave it a squeeze, I glanced at him. The sheen covering his eyes told me more than any words could have, and I went to cover his hand and stopped myself just before our skin touched.

Gritting my teeth, I pulled my hand away, opting to squeeze his arm through the fabric instead, and found my vision distorted by my own tears. I didn't give a damn if he was an angel or a vampire or some weird half-breed like me. I just wanted to hold him and love him again.

Tigress
Chapter Ten
Damian

I GLANCED AT THE clock on the dashboard and her hand on the crook of my arm before refocusing on the road ahead of me. My mind still reeled from Michael's revelation and I couldn't bring myself to look at him, never mind speak. For thousands of years, he played me for a fool and I wondered if this was just another part of his twisted game.

The steering wheel creaked, and I dropped my gaze to my hands. My knuckles were white from squeezing the metal and I inhaled, forcing my muscles to relax and the grip on the wheel to loosen. I chanced a glance at Naomi and the tear slowly tracking down her cheek shot straight to my heart.

I sent a glare at Michael and focused back on the road.

"Why now?" I asked once I was sure I could speak without lashing out.

Michael didn't answer and when I glanced in his direction, he was busy studying the landscape.

"Well?"

When his gaze slid to mine, I clenched my teeth, expecting another ultimatum, but his sigh and the shift of his gaze told me all I needed.

"So, if Naomi hadn't played the 'he cares about you' card, I would still be left in the dark?"

"Pretty much."

"What kind of family were we born into?" I muttered and glanced at Naomi.

"A colossally dysfunctional one," she answered. "At least mine is buffered by umpteen generations. You're the only firstborn angel offspring, so you are totally fucked."

Her answer was just as unexpected as Michael's, and I started laughing. Leave it to my lovely wife to say it like it is. I bumped her with my shoulder and she bumped me back.

The humor faded as I turned over the facts and I pulled off the highway onto a deserted country road, putting the car in park.

"So, the only reason I survived that pit is because I'm half angel?" I slid my gaze from out the windshield to Michael. He didn't acknowledge the question. "And Naomi didn't freak the fuck out like some of my earlier disasters for the same reason?"

Michael leveled a glare in my direction. One meant to silence my oncoming tirade, but I was already too far gone into the land of fury to let it go. I wanted a piece of this asshole and there wasn't anything on this earth that could stop me. Not even Naomi.

"Get out," I snarled and received identical dropped jaws from both Naomi and Michael.

"Damian," she started, and I dropped my glare to her.

"Don't give me that Damian crap. It's high time I kick my uncle's ass."

Michael's face morphed into a mask of anger, and his door opened. I don't think his feet even touched the ground before I was on the other side of the cab. Naomi started to speak, and I slammed the passenger door on her, shutting off her ability to divert my attention.

Michael backed onto the field, his features hard and unreadable, his hands clenched in tight fists by his sides. I considered shifting into shadow form, but I really wanted to see just how good a fighter he was without his angelic powers. I had the advantage in speed and strength, even without my shadow form, and we circled like a couple of prizefighters.

With each step, a low growl emitted from my chest, matching the roaring fury filling my muscles. There were just too many events where I nearly shit my pants in his presence, thinking I was walking a thin line between life and death any time he showed up. I didn't give a damn about respecting my elders at this moment. All I wanted was a few solid hits and, from his expression, he wanted the same.

We both stepped in, but Michael sidestepped, using my inertia to his advantage, and delivered a fist to my ribs as I passed. It wasn't like a normal human swat; this was full of the same power living in my veins. I stumbled and caught myself, turning back in his direction, and this time, I was more cautious with my approach.

My ribs throbbed where his punch landed, and I silently cursed my sloppy attack. I'm sure if any of the multitude of sensei I've had over the years saw my last attempt, I'd be doing a thousand push-ups while being lectured on the virtue of patience. This time, I took a deep breath and concentrated, focusing on Michael's movement and when an opportunity presented itself, I stepped in, throwing my right fist from my waist instead of the wild swing I tried to deliver the first time.

He parried, but his block wasn't fast enough to deflect the blow aimed at his chest. Instead, it knocked my aim to the right, connecting with his shoulder. He spun from the power of it. Unfortunately, he used the natural flow to his advantage, circling around and swinging a shot to my ribs. I think he actually lifted me off the ground with it and the breath shot from my lungs in a groan.

Naomi's yell for us to stop broke through and I sent a glare her way. I should have known better. When I turned back toward Michael, his fist slammed into my cheek. The shock of it sent me flailing backwards, and I fell on my ass. Before the pain flared, I was up and charging. This time, I hit him like a linebacker, driving him to the earth.

Somehow, I ended face down in the dirt with his knee pressing into my lower back and my arm twisted painfully behind me.

"Gabriel never knew how to fight either," Michael mumbled under his breath, but I caught it. "Are you done with your little temper tantrum?" Michael asked.

Just his tone bit my nerves and I bellowed, bucking and rolling, but not before the sickening crack filled the air and pain spread like wildfire from my wrist to my shoulder. I cried out as I rolled onto my broken arm, but that didn't stop me from slamming my good elbow into his chest and sending him onto his ass.

"You broke my fucking arm," I snapped as I got to my feet, cradling the throbbing appendage to my chest.

"You'll heal by nightfall," Michael shot back at me. He dusted himself off and stood, waiting for me to make another move.

I thought twice about taking another swing, especially with the throb in my arm. I didn't dare look at what the actual condition was right now, not with the anger still so embedded in my flesh.

Instead, I turned and headed back toward the truck, passing Naomi only a few paces away with her hand over her mouth and her eyes wide with concern.

"I'll be fine," I said and passed by her, leaving them both in the field while I worked my way back to the van. I leaned against the side and waited for them to follow, the anger still present, but now only at a dull throb that matched the flare in my cheek and ribs.

I took time to assess my arm and attempted to set it myself. My teeth clamped together with the pain and before I could get it right, Michael stepped in and took my arm in his hands, twisting it back into the right alignment before gently setting it against my chest.

I closed my eyes at the wave of dizziness that accompanied the pain and took a few deep breaths to get my bearings. When I opened my eyes, I glanced at the sky before bringing my gaze to his.

"Why did you lie to me?"

"Watch your tone," Michael warned.

"Just answer the fucking question!" I slammed my teeth together, resisting the urge to go into shadow form and tear into him, but as I learned, he was better at predicting my moves than I was and I'd probably end up with another broken bone if I went on the attack.

"I was protecting you," he said, his voice soft and calm, telling me the fight in him had already burned out.

"From what?"

Michael raised his eyebrows. "Lu..." He stopped himself and pressed his lips together in the all too familiar way I've seen in the mirror a thousand times. It was the same expression I got when I catch myself from screwing up.

"Lilith, Eve, my brother, all of hell's demons, you name it," he said.

I lost some of the fire as I digested his answer and I stared at him before glancing up at the sky again, gauging the time I had before the sun hit the horizon. The stars weren't as bright, and I dropped my gaze back to Michael's. "If you were trying to keep me out of the line of fire, why in god's name did you put me in charge of your bloodline?"

He smiled. "That's the safest place for you. Considering the sheer number of descendants and the fact that my brother has only found a handful of them in over two thousand years, I'd say that was a good call." He glanced at Naomi. "Until you crossed paths with her."

I glanced at her and pain flared in her eyes before she dropped her gaze.

"Baby, don't blame yourself," I said and reached my good hand to her. I traced her cheek with my fingertips, and my skin burned with pain, but I didn't pull away until I tilted her chin to look at me. I curled my blistered fingers away from her. "I'd be dead by now if it wasn't for you," I added.

"You would never have been in danger if it wasn't for me," she said and glanced at the sky, just as aware of the time as I was. "You need to get in back." Then her gaze slid from me to Michael. "I suggest you join him. I'm not in the mood for company right now, especially since you decided that breaking his arm was a lesson in humility."

The underlying hostility was clear, and I sighed, not sure how Michael was going to react. He sent a barely suppressed smirk my way and headed toward the back of the van without an argument.

"It might be better if Michael is in the cab with you," I said.

"You want me to break your other arm?" she asked with a flare of venom in her voice that made me shake my head. "Good," she added and crossed to the back of the truck, undoing the latch and sliding the door open to the six-foot container.

I followed and hopped into the barren space filled with only our duffel bags and a queen mattress that spanned most of the space. She raised an eyebrow.

"I figured I'd at least have something soft to land on while you throw me all over the back with your erratic driving."

Michael snorted a small laugh and hopped up into the truck. And she sent a clear warning at us. The one I knew meant to behave. I nodded, and the door slid down. The only sound above the idling engine was the sound of the lock clicking into place.

Tigress
Chapter Eleven
Damian

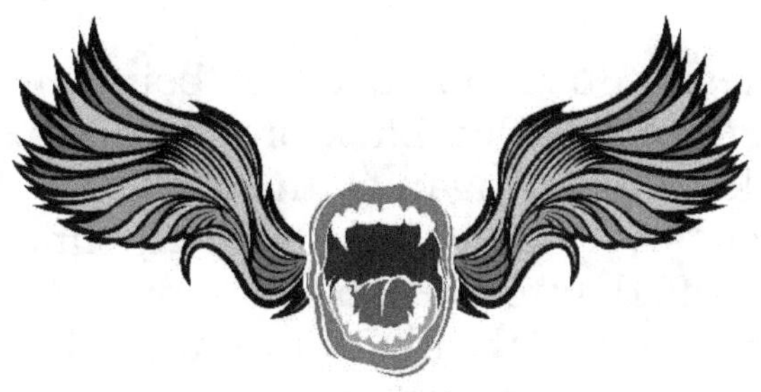

"IT'S COLD IN HERE," Michael said from the other side of the mattress. He had folded his knees in and crossed his arms to find some body heat in the frigid space.

I checked the time on my phone and glanced at him in the dim light. We had only been in the truck for a couple of hours, and while I was just as chilled as he was, I wasn't about to admit it. Instead, I climbed to my feet and crossed to the duffel bags.

The light was dim but enough for me to make out the meager pickings, and I wondered why I hadn't had the forethought to grab a few sweatshirts while I was at it. I found a couple of thick work shirts that would help us deal for the next few hours. Stripping my coat, I slipped one on before tossing the other one to Michael. I slid my coat on just as my phone dropped into sleep mode.

My eyes took a few minutes to adjust to the dark while I repacked the bag and then I grabbed the phone and pressed the button to brighten the space. Michael had followed my lead and zipped up his down vest over the layers.

"I guess you're not used to being human," I mumbled and settled back on the mattress with my back propped against the wall. I pulled the backpack over and unzipped it, finding the mural stuffed into the space. I pulled it out of the bag along with my computer. "This might help as well," I said and tossed the fabric to him.

His expression bordered on grateful, and I rubbed my face before opening my laptop. The light illuminated the space, and I plugged my phone in and started the web browser. Typing commands, I pulled up the same email address that Lucifer sent the note to yesterday and gritted my teeth. Another unopened email sat in my inbox and I put the laptop aside, ignoring it for the time being.

"Come lunchtime, I'm sure Naomi will let you out," I said, and Michael met my gaze.

"It's been a very long time since I took human form," he said. "I forget how fragile the human body is, along with all the other needs that go along with it."

"I'm sure," I said and sent a text to Naomi so she wouldn't forget that Michael needed to eat and use the facilities just like she did, so she would be wise to remember that at the next rest area. I didn't want to deal with a mess back here if I could help it. I raised my gaze and studied him.

He had the same physique as I did, along with the dark curls that matched mine, and my limited recollection of my father carried the same qualities.

"I gather you and Gabriel looked a lot alike," I said, and he nodded. "So, what happened to your other brother?" Lucifer was the polar opposite, with the more traditional Viking complexion as opposed to the decidedly Greek aura of Michael.

"God only knows," he sighed. "He's always been different, rebelling in heaven long before he was cast out." He shivered and brought the mural together around his shoulders. "Gabriel was the musician and much more sensitive than either of us were. He used to disappear for months on end, and finally, when he had decided to be with your mother, he came back to share the news. As I said before, by that time, our brother was no longer welcome in heaven and had already turned bitter, so I suggested Gabriel keep his decision to himself for now and I wouldn't say anything either."

"You mean keep me a secret?"

Michael nodded. "I didn't know just how important that decision was until after my brother killed my son." He paused and blew on his hands to warm them. "I should have known Greece wasn't far enough away from his wrath, but I knew you were there and because of the family bond, you would be compelled to protect Athena."

"I still can't get past the fact that she was my cousin, and you never said a word. You just gave us your blessing and let us live as man and wife," I said, finally voicing my disdain.

"Things were very different back then and yes, I allowed it because it was my best option of protecting my daughter."

"But I failed," I said, and he met my gaze with a shake of his head.

"No, you didn't. I was the one who failed both of you. I didn't make it back in time to stop my brother from slaughtering Athena, but I got there in time to pull you from that pit before you were too far gone to survive. I let you drink from my veins and the double infusion of angel blood made you into what you are instead of a raving, mad killing machine."

I stared at him for a long time before my gaze dropped to the computer.

"Is that why Naomi turned out the way she did?"

"I don't know. She's so far removed from Zoe that I can't be sure. It could be a combination of my bloodline along with her Indian heritage, which has its own unique qualities that are just as rich as my bloodline. Or it could be a wild fluke, but she's just as unique as you are." He offered a shrug. "It could also be because she bit me as well."

"You know, she was stronger than I've ever been," I said.

Michael smiled at me. "She's a descendant of multiple warrior bloodlines. You, on the other hand, are a musician's son."

"Fuck you," I said at the condescending tone in his voice.

"Considering your bloodline, you aren't as lame at fighting as I expected," he said and rubbed his shoulder, offering a grin.

"I'm a mixed breed. What'd you expect?" I sent back, opting for humor instead of letting the aggravation eat away at me. Besides, my head was throbbing and my arm was itching up a storm. I shifted and forced myself not to scratch my mending arm. I knew from experience, once I started, I'd only succeed in the tearing welts on my skin. "So do I call you Uncle Mike?" I asked and sent a tired grin in his direction.

He just laughed and wrapped the mural tighter around his shoulders. "This truce doesn't mean you have free rein to kill innocents, though."

The beginnings of good humor vanished, and I sent a glare in his direction. "I know."

With the irritation already forming over me, I reached for the computer and opened the email, sucking wind through my teeth at the words spilling over the page. Lucifer's plans were far worse than I ever imagined and I turned the computer toward Michael, sliding it along the mattress until he took it from me.

Michael's expression morphed into guarded fury, and he glanced up at me.

"This cannot happen," he said and slid the computer back to me. There was no leeway in his statement and absolutely no argument from me.

Tigress
Chapter Twelve
Damian

THE DECELERATION OF THE van, along with the sharp turn, gave me a clue that Naomi was pulling off the highway. A few minutes later, the cut of the engine confirmed it and I closed my laptop and got to my feet, stretching to get the kinks out of my muscles. The swelling in my arm had gone down, and I could move it without sharp pain. There was still some discomfort, but Michael was right. By the time the sun set tonight, it would be fine.

The lock on the back was unclasped and, as the door rose, I backed up until there was nowhere else to go. The bright sunlight colored half the floor, and I exhaled when the upward progression of the door stopped halfway. Naomi peered inside.

"I figured if I was hungry, you'd have to be, too," she said to Michael and her gaze shifted to me while Michael stood and handed me the mural. He gave me a nod, and I returned it before glancing back at Naomi.

"You doing okay?" she asked as Michael climbed out of the vehicle.

"Yeah," I said. There was no reason to tell her how fucking cold it was in here, because there was nothing she could do right now to warm me up. She gave a nod and closed the door. The lock clicked into place, leaving me drenched in darkness.

No more than ten minutes went by and the lock unlatched again and the tail lifted part way. She stood with an armful of blankets, sliding them inside with a smile.

"I thought these might help."

If I could have kissed her at that moment, I would chance the blisters, but both she and the blankets sat in the direct sun.

"Thank you, babe," I said, and the door dropped again. The moment the lock engaged, I scrambled to the pile. She bought six heavy blankets with different Indiana sports teams on them. I didn't even look at the logos. Instead, I stretched out on the mattress, wrapping myself in the warm fleece, thankful she had given it some thought.

Soon after, both doors to the cab slammed shut, and I sighed, curling tighter into a ball to keep warm and dragged the laptop closer to me. I stared at the email, reading Lucifer's ultimate threat again. Each word shot pain through my entire form and I closed the cover, rolling onto my back and staring into the dark.

I had to make damn sure he never got a hold of her, otherwise I'd relish facing the sun.

My arm ached, and I held it to my chest, letting myself drift off. Sleep seemed to be the secret to the ultra-healing and, with the lull of the engine, I drifted off into a plague of nightmares.

Each one was in excruciating detail of every deviant act Lucifer promised. It was far more vivid than any other nightmare I could remember and I woke in a cold sweat, with my chest constricted to where drawing a breath was nearly impossible.

The hum of the engine brought me around and my lungs opened. I sucked in a mouthful of cold air, thankful for the burn, and I closed my eyes, pressing my palms to them until the images from my nightmares surfaced.

My phone buzzed, and I pulled it from my pocket and glanced at the text.

"You okay back there?"

Naomi's question took me by surprise.

"Yes, why?" I sent back.

"I could have sworn I heard you yell."

"Sorry. Nightmare." I texted back and glanced at the time. I still had a few more hours before I could be set free from this tin can.

"How are things going up there?" I added.

"Good. Michael's driving and I got a nap in. He said you two had a nice talk."

I burst out laughing. I learned a great deal, but I'm not sure I would categorize it as nice. That simmering anger was still present, and I wondered if it would ever go away. I dropped back on the mattress and inspected my motivations.

Tigress
Chapter Thirteen
Naomi

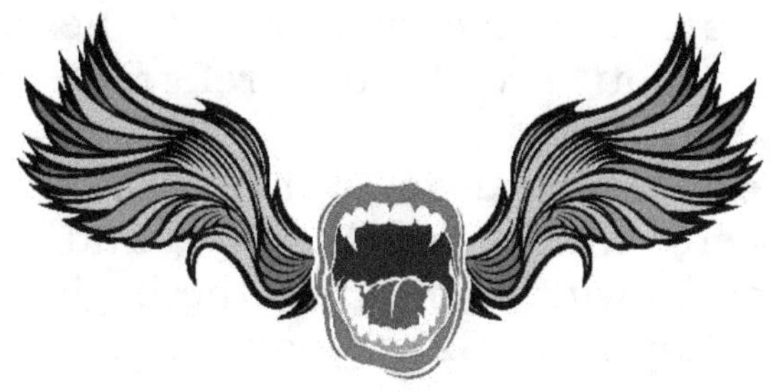

"HE JUST HAD A nightmare," I said, trading a glance with Michael. "You know, I can take over driving if you'd like."

"I'm fine," Michael said with his gaze locked on the road, but ever since I fished him out of the back, conversation had been scarce.

"So, what did you and Damian talk about all morning?"

He slid his gaze to me and then back to the road. "You."

I glanced out the passenger window with a head full of questions and bit my lip. "What about me?" I finally asked when he didn't continue.

"He asked why you were different," Michael said, pulling my attention to him. "Why you were stronger your first day as a vampire than he was after over two thousand years?"

"And you said?" I wanted to hear the explanation because it was something that intrigued me as well.

"Because he's the offspring of a musician and you, you're the offspring of warrior bloodlines."

I glanced out the window at the crowded highway. "You aren't just referring to your bloodline, are you?"

He sent his hard gaze in my direction. "No. There were many angels who had intimate relationships with humans in the beginning," he started. "Raphael, Gabriel and I are the only ones who were blessed with offspring." He paused, slowing down for traffic. "Damian is Gabriel's only child, so his bloodline ended when my brother threw him into that pit. But both Raphael and I have quite vast bloodlines, and until you were conceived, they never intersected," he said and glanced at me, offering a smile that cascaded a wave of chills down my back. I hugged myself to ward off the tremor. "You're Indian heritage is much richer than you thought."

Silence filled the cab as I gawked at him.

"And the moment you bit Damian, Gabriel's blood was introduced into the equation."

"How does that make me stronger than he is?"

"You are a trinity, not a pure trinity, but close enough. You are a mixture of three angelic bloodlines and that is why you are different." He let that settle as he navigated the afternoon traffic. "Imagine if it was possible for you and Damian to have a child?"

The statement stunned me, and my jaw dropped.

"This world has not encountered a pure trinity in over two thousand years," he said with a sigh and focused back on the road.

"I thought you said that this was the first time the bloodlines converged."

He nodded. "I did, and it is. But the only pure trinity born to a human was not created from angel blood," he said.

My brain tried to wrap around what he was saying, but I kept drawing a conclusion that was insane. "Are you referring to the holy trinity?" I asked, voicing the unlikely conclusion.

He nodded, and my pulse quickened. The idea that I could produce the second coming was as farfetched as this conversation, and I let out a frantic laugh. "You mean I could..." I trailed off, unable to voice the mad idea, but the look Michael sent me confirmed my thoughts.

"Either that or the other side of the equation." His gaze bore into me and I shivered.

His assumption irritated the hell out of me. "Damian's not evil," I snapped.

"No, but my brother is. If he ever got it in his head to use you as a fertility experiment, what kind of monster do you think that would create?"

My eyes widened, and a wave of nausea flowed through my form. Just the thought of being Lucifer's baby-maker made me want to vomit. "Does he know about our heritage?"

Michael exhaled. "He does not know about Damian's."

"What about mine?" I asked, and a shadow passed over Michael's face.

"I don't know, but you can damn well bet that if he does, your death would no longer be his highest priority."

I stared at him, turning as cold as the frigid winter air. "You didn't tell Damian this, did you?"

Michael pressed his lips together and offered a sideways glare before concentrating on driving again. "No."

"Why not?"

"Because he's still overwhelmed with this morning's revelation," he said. "And I shouldn't have told you, but you need to know in the event Luc..." he stopped talking, his features morphing into that same expression Damian gets when he almost screwed up.

When he regained composure, he continued, "In the event my brother gets a hold of you, there is really only one option for you if you can't escape."

"I have to kill him?" I said, hoping that was what he was driving at.

When his gaze slid in my direction, my heart lurched into my throat and I bit my lip to keep it from quivering.

"You have to die."

Tigress
Chapter Fourteen
Naomi

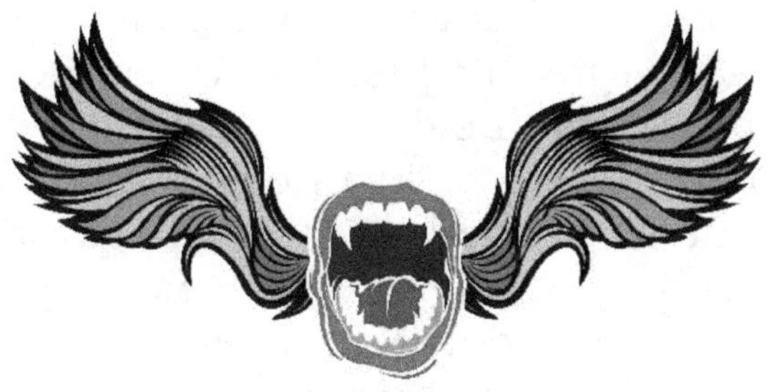

SHOCK STILL FILTERED THROUGH my form at Michael's words and the sun couldn't set fast enough. I glanced at the magnificent colors painting the sky and couldn't find the calmness they should have instilled in me. Instead, death loomed, casting its dark hand over the earth.

The Welcome to Ohio sign loomed less than a tenth of a mile away and I shifted in the seat, trying to find a comfortable position.

When we passed the sign for the upcoming rest area, I said, "I need to hit the next rest area," with a voice that sounded foreign and strained.

He didn't acknowledge that I had spoken, but he took the gently curved exit into the rest area.

"We're going to need gas too," I said when he pulled into a parking space.

"You can get that after we do our business and grab a bite to eat." He waved toward the building and I sighed, giving him a nod of ascent.

He pulled the keys out of the ignition and handed them to me before exiting the cab, leaving me to lock up as he hightailed it toward the restrooms. I thought about seeing if Damian was okay, but my bladder had other ideas and I made a mad dash inside.

By the time we had finished our business and bought our food, the sun had dipped below the horizon and I found my pace picking up as I headed toward the truck. Even though I was only awake for a few hours with Michael in the cab, the relief of having Damian back in the front with us drove my feet forward.

I threw the latch and pushed the gate up. Damian was already on his feet, pacing in the small space between the door and the mattress, and the moment the door cleared his head, he jumped down on the pavement and looked at the bag in my hand before meeting my gaze.

"I'm ravenous," he said. His voice soft and raspy and every bit as sexy as ever.

"Get in the cab," Michael said as he walked past us. There was no leeway in his command, and Damian and I exchanged a look.

Instead of issuing a smart comeback, Damian reached up and slammed the door down, locking it before escorting me to the truck. He opened the door and let me slide into the middle of the bench seat before he slid next to me. The first thing he did after Michael turned the engine over was to crank the heat.

"We still need gas," I said and pointed to the low fuel light.

"Damn machines," Michael muttered and pulled into one of the gas lines. He drummed his fingers impatiently on the steering wheel and I traded a glance with Damian and he rolled his eyes at me.

A strained silence filled the cab and when we pulled up to the pump, Damian slid out and took care of gassing up the truck and then knocked on the driver's side window.

"I can drive," he said when Michael rolled the window down.

Michael kept his gaze for a minute and then nodded, relinquishing the driver's seat to Damian and crossing around to the passenger side. No one spoke as we pulled out onto the highway.

The hum of the truck lulled me into a sleepy trance and my eyelids kept drifting closed.

"You're welcome to use my thigh as a pillow," Damian said, cutting into the thick silence.

"I'm fine," I said and yawned.

A dimple appeared in his cheek and he sent a sideways glance that all but said 'yeah, right". I shook my head and rubbed my face to get the cobwebs out of my brain.

"I'm sorry I was such a prick earlier," he said, looking over my head at Michael.

Michael met his gaze and nodded, accepting the apology in silence, and then he yawned and settled into the corner of the cab with his head against the headrest.

"I'm sorry I broke your arm," he said and closed his eyes.

Both Damian and I exchanged a glance. Getting an apology from Michael was more progress than either of us had hoped for, and it eased some of my angst relating to our last conversation.

I wondered how Damian would take the news when we told him about my being a trinity.

"How long until we reach Connecticut?" I asked.

Damian glanced at the road signs and his lips moved as he silently calculated the distance. "We should get home before the sun rises," he said. "Even with a hunting break." He licked his lips. "I won't make it through the day without blood."

Michael's arm shot across the space. "We don't have time to stop."

Damian glanced at the offering and then back at the road.

"As much as I'd like to tear into you, Uncle Mike, I can't. You are in human form, remember?" He didn't even look our way.

Michael pulled his exposed wrist back and crossed his arms. "Then you'll have to catch up to us," hc said.

Damian cocked his head, considering this before he sighed. "Okay, but you need to stay on this route and if you pull off for any reason, you'll call and leave a message?"

"That's reasonable," Michael agreed. "But I think I need some rest before I take over driving again."

"I can drive," I said, and stretched, reminding both men that I was still in the car.

"You're sure?"

"Yes, I had enough sleep to be okay for a little while," I said, glancing at the sparsely populated highway. "And I'd like to drive, anyway. I hate being a passenger unless I have a book or something, otherwise I just drift off."

"Okay, I'll get off at the next rest area," Damian said.

It turned out to be another hour and a half before the next highway rest area, and I was ready for a bathroom break from dinner. Michael snored against the door, and I took the keys from Damian and headed inside. When I returned, Damian stood by the driver's side and gave me a small smile, nodding toward the cab and a still sleeping Michael.

"You might have to stop somewhere along the way for him. If you do, just text the mile marker and I'll meet up with you. I'll try to get ahead of you once I'm done hunting and I'll text you what exit I'm at. Okay?"

"Are you okay?" I asked before he stepped away. We hadn't had a moment since Michael joined us and his gaze flickered to the interior of the truck and back.

"I had some time to think today and, while I'm still angry about the bullshit games he played, I think I can understand it. Especially when I step back and think of what I would have done in his shoes." He shifted and reached for me, stopping just short of contact before lowering his hand. Frustration filled his features, and he closed his eyes. "So yes, I'm okay. Are you?"

He opened his eyes and met my gaze.

"I'm fine," I said and gave him a reassuring smile. I wasn't about to tell him about the trinity or Michael's ultimatum. Not until we were settled in the safety of a new home away from Michael and all the complications that came with dragging around an archangel in human form.

He pulled the door open for me and shut it as I settled into the seat. Before I turned back to the window, the shuffle of feathers crossed over the windshield and he was gone, disappearing into the night.

Michael stirred, shifted, and after a few minutes, the snoring began again. With no radio to drown out the offensive noise, my nerves jumped on edge and my jaw tightened against the rising bitch factor.

Tigress
Chapter Fifteen
Naomi

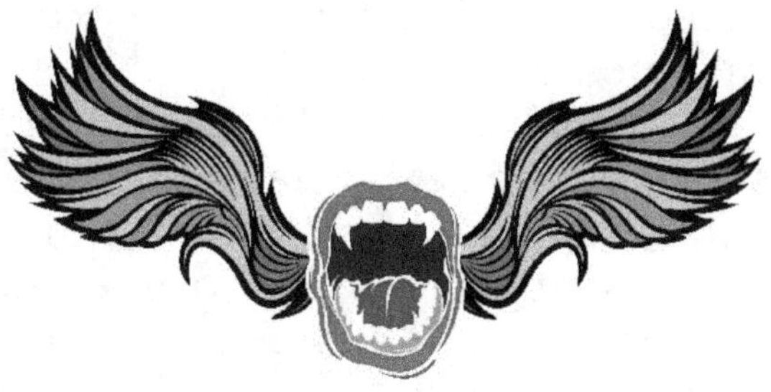

I FLEXED MY HANDS and gripped the steering wheel, grateful for the silence now that Michael's snoring had ceased. He's lucky I didn't smack him at the height of my irritation, but he had been up since the middle of the prior night, so I gave him a break.

A quick glance at the clock told me Damian had been at it for longer than normal. It had been over an hour since he flew off and I picked up my cell, pressing the button to see if he left a message, but my inbox was empty.

"Shit," I muttered and Michael grunted.

"What are you cursing about?" he asked, his voice scratchy with sleep and grumpiness.

"Damian hasn't checked in."

Michael wiped his face and sat up, blinking the sleep from his eyes. "How long has he been gone?"

"A little over an hour."

Michael shifted in the seat, stretching his muscles before he glanced out at the night. "I wouldn't worry."

I handed him the phone. "Text him and see if he's okay."

He stared at my iPhone and then at me like he had no clue how to text.

"Oh, for the love of God," I said and pulled over into the breakdown lane. I grabbed the device out of his hand and showed him how it operated. I sent the text during the basic instruction and Michael offered me a half-assed smile of apology when I handed it to him and pulled back on the road.

"It will buzz when he replies, so you just need to touch the screen and you'll see it," I said and while he nodded, I kept looking over every few seconds. The burning in my stomach increased with each minute that passed and my foot got heavier on the gas, increasing my speed well beyond the speed limit.

Red and blue lights flared in the side mirror.

"Crap," I muttered and sent a sideways grimace in Michael's direction.

His expression morphed into a grin and he glanced away.

The gravel bit underneath the tires, and I slowed to a stop on the shoulder. I leaned over and opened the glove compartment, pulling out the rental forms before I rummaged in my small pocketbook for my license. A knock on the window pulled my attention away, and I rolled down the glass, giving the officer an embarrassed smile as I handed over the documents.

"Do you know how fast you were going?"

"No, I'm sorry officer, I'm supposed to meet a friend at one of these exits and I haven't heard from him. I guess I got a little...anxious."

The officer nodded and sent a cursory glance at Michael before bringing his gaze to the paperwork. He turned and trotted back to his cruiser and I sighed, trading a glance with Michael.

"You were going fast," he said and held up the phone. "And Damian is amused."

My lips tightened at my response to Damian's text.

I leave you alone for five minutes...

I grabbed the cell from Michael and texted, "Where are you?"

The passenger door opened, and he tilted a brow at me, before making Michael slide to the middle. The door closed almost soundlessly under the slam of the police car behind us.

"Ma'am, there seems to be a problem with your license," he started, and his brow scrunched when he glanced in the cab. His gaze landed squarely on Damian before jumping back to me.

"What's the matter?"

He flicked the license on his fingernails and then held the plastic between his index and middle finger. "Well, for a dead girl, you look pretty damn spry."

My face drained of all heat and I met his gaze, covering my mouth and trying desperately to think of something to say that would erase the trouble that was brewing. A nervous energy started in my toes and affected my eyelids, making them flutter with the stress.

"Oh," I whispered from under my hand and I dropped it to my lap. "I must have given you my sister's ID." I added and pressed my lips together, reaching for the license. "I keep it with me..." My voice trailed off in what I hoped was a sad note.

His expression softened from the hard, stern gaze, and he handed me the license. I gave him a ghost of a smile and reached for my pocketbook, wondering just what in the hell I would give the officer in exchange. I didn't have another driver's license, and I rummaged around the depths of my pocketbook and flipped through my wallet twice before I turned my panicked glare toward Damian.

He obviously was enjoying this, and I squinted an evil eye in his direction. "Please tell me you packed my other purse," I said, letting the stress bleed through in my voice. I widened my eyes in a silent plea for help and then glanced back to the officer.

"I packed everything," he said and shifted, pulling his wallet from his pocket and slipping me his license instead. "Officer, it seems my wife's license is packed in the back. You should be able to look her up by our address and last name. Her name is Anna. Anna Andreas," he said, using the alias we agreed upon when we got married. He sent a disarming smile toward the officer.

"She can't continue driving this vehicle," the officer said and snapped Damian's license from my hand before disappearing to the squad car.

Damian got out of the vehicle and crossed around the front to the driver's side, and I slid over, letting him take the helm again. A simmering anger built, aimed at Damian and his piss poor timing. If he had sent a text earlier, we wouldn't be in this predicament.

He glanced at me, sensing my irritation, before swinging his gaze back to the open window. The officer returned a moment later, handing both the license and paperwork to Damian. "Because this rental agreement checks out with your license, I'll give you a break this time around. But you shouldn't let speed demon, there, drive this rig."

He pointed at me, and heat filled my cheeks. I dropped my gaze to the floor and then slid it to Michael, who had kept unusually quiet this entire time.

"Thank you, sir," Damian said and took the paperwork, handing it to me without a glance. As soon as we were underway and the police car sped into the distance, I smacked Damian's arm.

"You scared the shit out of me."

"You need to be more patient," he snapped back. "And not drive like you're in the Indy 500."

"Fuck you."

Damian grinned like Michael wasn't even in the vehicle. Michael cleared his throat, and Damian's smile faded.

"How much longer will we be cooped up in this vehicle?"

We both turned to Michael and his impatient tone, like he was a child asking, *Are we there yet?* He just raised an eyebrow, waiting for one of us to answer.

"We'll get there before sunrise," Damian answered and focused on the road heading toward the unknown.

Tigress
Chapter Sixteen
Damian

THE CONCERT OF SNORES filling the cab made me smile. Naomi's was sporadic, but Michael's was that steady bass that nearly shook the quiet cab. I had tried to sing for a while just to drown them out, but that was futile and they both needed rest.

I wasn't sure what we'd find in Litchfield and as we got closer to New York; I started second guessing this trip.

Naomi stirred in the seat next to me, her sleepy eyes opening to the dark road ahead. When her gaze landed on me, she bit her lip, studying my expression, trying to read my mind like she used to, but now that she was cured, that psychic connection seemed to be disconnected.

"What's wrong?" she asked, and I glanced at her before nodding toward the approaching signs, specifically the one for the George Washington Bridge.

The last time we were there, I almost bit the dust and to this day, I still have nightmares.

She didn't speak, but her hand found my thigh and squeezed. For her, that day was an exercise in revenge, but for me, it was a reminder that Lucifer almost won. The proximity to his home base just reinforced the danger.

The next time we faced him, I wouldn't make it out alive and Naomi's future was even bleaker, but I wasn't about to voice Lucifer's threats. I didn't want to entertain the thoughts at all because, if it came right down to it, I would tear her throat out before I would allow her to become his indentured slave.

"I don't know what we'll find when we get home. I imagine the explosion left one hell of a crater."

Michael's snore ceased, and he shifted. "It did," he said before the rumbling sound of sleep kicked back in.

I traded a glance with Naomi, raising my eyebrow. She shrugged, and I decided to see what kind of information I could draw out of Michael in his sleep state.

"Has it been cleaned up?" I asked, knowing the property reverted to Damian Andreas, the only surviving member of the owner's family. I had claimed the property via email contact and did all the transfer of ownership through a lawyer in Denver, but I hadn't thought to rebuild.

"Yes." Came his answer between the baritone snores.

"Are you asleep?"

Michael's eyes opened, and he sent a glare my way. "Not with you asking questions every five seconds."

"Well, you both slept most of the night and let me tell you, you both snore loudly enough to wake the dead." I glanced at them. "You're lucky I didn't wake you sooner."

"How much longer?" Michael asked.

"We're only a couple of hours away," I answered and glanced at the clock. "There's a rest area up ahead. Do you want me to stop?"

"Please," Naomi said and shifted in the seat a few times. I sent a smirk in her direction. The benefit of this virus meant that the body's elimination cycle was eons slower than normal. I think mine is now in the years range, not days or hours like the unaffected body, and I always forget that necessity until it comes along like a speeding freight train.

The moment they disappeared into the building, I hopped out of the cab and went around to the back of the truck. I slid the top open and grabbed my computer. Sitting on the edge of the truck bed, I logged into my email account. My teeth clenched in a growl at Lucifer's latest taunt. This one burning me enough to head in any other direction than east.

When I looked up, Michael stood a few feet away with his arms crossed.

"He caught the police scan of Naomi's license," I said, feeling the need to explain myself.

Michael just raised a challenging brow.

"What the hell am I supposed to do?" I said, slamming the computer and shoving it into the backpack and disappearing into the darkness to set it down on the other side of the mattress.

"Perhaps we should head somewhere else," Michael's voice drifted on the darkness and I glanced over my shoulder at him.

"Even if I turned us in a different direction, you know damn well I don't have enough time. The minute the sun rose and I'm back here, she'll just turn back in the direction we're headed." I stalked across to the door and hopped down on the pavement, pausing long enough to see her open-mouthed response. "Yeah, I'm talking about you," I said, unable to hide the irritation. If I could have carried her a half a world away, I would have.

"What about me?" she asked, her voice lined with a combination of hesitation and aggravation.

"If I had my way, I'd haul your ass to Australia." I couldn't help it. Lucifer knew how to push my buttons.

The way she dropped her hands to her hips and jutted her chin out was like pouring gas on a bonfire. The effect was explosive, and I slammed the back, locking it before I ran my mouth off. I had a habit of screwing up when I was this angry and it was more prudent to remain silent, but that didn't mean I couldn't make as much noise as I could without destroying the truck.

Doors lent a certain satisfaction when slammed and I nearly inverted the driver's door with the force. Naomi stood at the opening to the passenger door, her expression guarded.

"Damian, I'm not running away," she said in that quiet tone that left no leeway for negotiation, and I looked from her to Michael.

"You talk some sense into her."

He just laughed at me. I think he may know more about her than I gave him credit for, but that was no help to me right now.

"What got your panties in a bunch?" Naomi asked as she climbed into the cab and settled next to me.

"That little expedition with the cop clued him in. When they ran your license through the system, he got the notice, so he knows we're heading east." I glared at her.

She had the audacity to snap at me. "The east coast is a pretty large ground to cover."

As soon as Michael shut the door, I threw the truck in gear and drove to the pumps. The small distance didn't satisfy the budding anger and fear thrumming through my veins. Neither did the time to fill up the truck. Lucifer was hell bent on taking everything from me, including my sanity, and as the figures increased on the gas pump, I started dissecting motives. By the time I got into the cab, my fury had softened, replaced by questions, and I sent a sideways glare at Michael.

"Why exactly does he insist on driving me crazy?" I asked before I put the car in gear. "I mean, he's notorious for hunting down his enemies, but this is beyond that. This is more than personal, and I just don't understand."

When Naomi and Michael exchanged a glance, my jaw tightened in anger.

"What are you hiding from me?"

"Now that Naomi has been infused with your blood, she's a trinity. Not a true one, but close enough. The details he put in that email lead me to believe he knows about Naomi's background and if he catches her, he will produce an army of monsters."

"What the fuck is a trinity?"

"I mentioned her Indian background, but I wasn't specific. Naomi is not only a descendant of mine, but she also is a descendant of Raphael."

Shock skittered over my skin like someone just crossed over my grave. "Two archangels?"

"And with your blood, three." Michael said. "If you two could produce offspring, you would create the first pure trinity." Michael stared at me. "That would be akin to the second coming of Christ."

I had to pull the truck onto the shoulder and put it in park because my brain just couldn't wrap around what he was telling me.

"So this is why she was stronger than I was," I muttered, still trying to put the pieces together.

"Gabriel's son," Michael whispered. "Raphael and my daughter. Three angel bloodlines combined."

The statement sent a shiver up my spine, and I snapped my head in his direction. The full meaning of what would happen if Lucifer got a hold of her settled in my skin and I shivered.

"If he gets a hold of her, we are talking an army of..." I couldn't express the thought out loud. It was inconceivable. If the bible carried any truth to it, offspring created from that union would mean the end of the world, and not just my world.

Silence filled the cab, and I pulled back on the road, unable to entertain even the slightest possibility.

"Revelations," Michael whispered.

"Yup," was all I could muster. "And I'm standing in his way." I let that settle. "I'm no longer sure Connecticut is the right place for us to go. It's way too close."

"I told you, I'm not running away," Naomi said and crossed her arms.

Her sulk was enough to bring forth my shadow self, and I snarled at her. Michael pulled her protectively to his side, only adding to my fury.

"Is there anything else you're keeping from me, Uncle Mike?" I asked with as much contempt in my tone as I could muster, and Naomi's features transitioned to fear. "Or should I just drain you dry in order to capture all your secrets?"

"If you want to tango, son, I'd be more than willing to kick your ass again," Michael said, his eyes narrowing into that silent dare that nearly tore my hands from the steering wheel.

"Ah, but you didn't battle my shadow form." I pulled the truck to the shoulder when Naomi grabbed my wrist.

"No," she commanded, and between the burn of her touch and the tone of her voice, my shadow form melted away. I winced, pulling my blistered wrist from her grip.

"Damn it, Naomi," I cursed, but stayed on the course we were heading. She could be the most infuriating woman on earth.

"Valerie and her uncle live on the property," Michael said after we crossed over the Tappan Zee Bridge.

The declaration made me swerve and shoot him my open-mouthed gape.

"You let Valerie move back there?" Naomi asked, stealing the words I was about to pose.

"Yes," Michael answered. "I took precautions."

"But still..."

"She wanted to go back, and I was skeptical, but I let her uncle rebuild under the condition that he played by my rules. As far as any of the building crew knew, he was alone, and this was family property that was handed down to him after his brother died. The garage was to be left alone and while on the property footprint, it was not to be included in the new building."

"The house is set farther back toward the wood line, and while there is an underground basement, there are no escape tunnels." He sent a smile at the two of us. "It wasn't until I was sure that my brother's snitches had reported back that there was nothing of interest on the property that I allowed her to move in. And once she moved in, I went to work."

"The property is now surrounded by a fence secured by hollow concrete blocks filled with salt. There is a complete unbroken line keeping the house safe, but it does not extend around the garage."

"So, you faked him out," I said and received a curt nod in response. "And the garage?"

"The garage is still intact, but no one has got through the building's defenses," he said and offered a shrug. "And the grounds are...unkept," he added.

"Damn it," I muttered, still focused on the fact that Valerie was where we were headed and with us there, that meant we were putting her in danger.

Tigress
Chapter Seventeen
Damian

WE TURNED THE BEND in the road, and I saw my old property for the first time since the night I blew it to bits. When Michael said the area around the garage was un-kept, he wasn't kidding. Grass that hadn't been mowed in what looked like five years stretched halfway up the sides of the building and the well-manicured driveway I remembered now looked like a forgotten mine field with tufts of grass sprouting from the crumbling pavement.

The chain-link fence separating the garage property from the rest reached almost ten feet high and disappeared into the woods. And appeared a few acres beyond the house, looping around to the edge of the property lining the sidewalk. It even crossed the driveway. I turned my gaze to Michael.

"Remote entry," he said and pulled a small keychain from his pocket, holding it up.

"Platinum?"

Michael grinned. "As far as I know, you're the only vampire that can fly over that fence."

"Yeah, but I've seen a few jump that high," I said, and his smile faded. "Still, it's an impressive setup," I added. I didn't tell him it was better than what I had in place, but then again, I had been here for years and I couldn't very well put up a fence made of platinum like he did. "Angel-proof?" I asked and got a nod in response.

"When the gate opens, it breaks the seal," he said, jingling the keys again.

I glanced up at the brightening sky and opted to pull the truck up onto the crumbling pavement to the side of the garage under the dilapidated awning.

"I'll move this stuff into the garage and then I'll let you return the truck." I said and hopped out of the cab before they could argue.

"You can't stay in the garage," Michael said as I peeled away a sheet of overgrown vines.

"Why not?"

"Because, if they decide to do a drive by, they are expecting the garage to be in this condition."

Shit, he was right. "So, where do you suggest I go?"

"We can move the stuff into their basement for now. I made a small area for you in the event you ever came back."

I looked at the house and back at Michael. It would take a few minutes to empty the contents of the van and get it out of there, but if they were curious enough to do a drive by, they might be out here right now. I couldn't let him take the van inside the fence.

"I may have to stay in the truck one more day," I said and met Michael's stare before transitioning to Naomi. "We'll return the van to either upstate New York, Vermont, or New Hampshire." I glanced at Michael. "They don't happen to have a pickup truck?"

Michael paused, playing with the keys in his hands until he held a single key. "How'd you know?"

"Does it still have a utility locker in back?" The thought of being stuck in that for twelve hours wasn't at the top of my list, but sometimes you have to suck it up.

"Yes."

"Get it and we'll meet you at Valerie's uncle's cabin down the road."

Michael took a deep breath and nodded, turning away from the two of us.

I backed the van up and drove away from the house. I didn't wait for Michael to get through the gate; I just wanted to put as much distance between us and this house as possible before sunrise.

Tigress
Chapter Eighteen
Damian

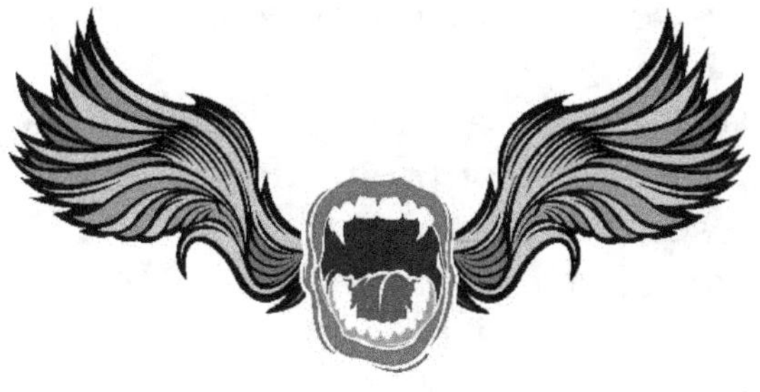

THE HUNTING CABIN HAD one road in and I paced next to the back of the van. The mattress leaned against the side of the opening and our three duffel bags were lined up neatly waiting for the truck bed. I gnawed on my thumbnail as we waited, my gaze jumping from the driveway to the pending sunrise and back.

When the truck rounded the corner, I stopped dead, staring at the three occupants. Valerie was out of the cab even before her uncle could set the brake. I opened my arms on instinct and braced myself for impact. Even with the forethought, the slam of her body against mine nearly knocked all the wind from my lungs.

Her joy at seeing us tempered the panic throbbing in my temple and I offered her a smile and a peck on the cheek before I got down to business.

"I don't have much time," I said and peeled her off me. She immediately turned and flung herself into Naomi's arms with just as much zest as she had with me. Instead of relishing the moment, I hauled the mattress over to the truck bed and tossed it in, offering her uncle a slight nod.

"Hi, Ted," I said as he approached the back of the truck with one of the duffel bags.

He tossed the bag into the back and stared at me before offering his hand. "Thank you for saving Valerie's life," he said.

Michael hauled the last two bags over the side and handed me my computer bag.

"What's the plan?" he asked.

I dug the keys out of my pocket and handed them to him. "I need you to return the van to somewhere in Buffalo."

"Buffalo, New York?" both Ted and Michael said in unison.

"Yes, this way your brother will think we skipped into Canada," I answered and I saw Michael's expression smooth out. "I'm not sure how you'll get back though," I added and glanced at the sky.

"Let me worry about that. Now go get in that oversized toolbox."

I smiled and tossed him the keys. "Naomi, give him your phone so we can keep in touch."

Naomi handed Michael her phone and showed him how to access my phone number, and then she gave me a nod. I turned away from the mini-reunion and hopped into the truck bed, opening the tool chest. They had lined the container with a soft down blanket and I closed my eyes at the thoughtfulness before slipping inside.

My first reaction as the cover dropped was immediate panic. This was worse than a coffin and I had to squeeze my eyes shut and concentrate on slowing my breathing to normal. The sounds of chains clipping closed increased my unease until the pat on the metal came along with her voice.

"We're just securing everything in place," Naomi said, and I knocked back, letting her know I was okay.

I closed my eyes when the hum of the engine resumed. I didn't hear the truck come to life either, so I'm sure Michael was waiting for us to get a reasonable distance. I sighed, feeling some of the stress melt from my muscles. My phone buzzed, and I glanced at the unknown number on the screen, debating on whether or not to answer. I highlighted the number and exhaled, praying it was Naomi and not Lucifer. I accepted the call.

"You okay back there?" Her voice filled the line, and I chuckled.

"Yeah, just didn't realize how claustrophobic I've become," I said.

"Well, we will be back at the house in a few minutes. Valerie tells me the garage doesn't have any windows. Only the back door has a six panel window that faces the east, and the light only covers half of the garage footprint."

"That's good to know." Relief flooded through me.

"Val said the truck is always parked on the dark side of the garage too, so getting out shouldn't be an issue. So I'll see you in the garage."

"Thanks, babe," I said and ended the call.

Tigress
Chapter Nineteen
Naomi

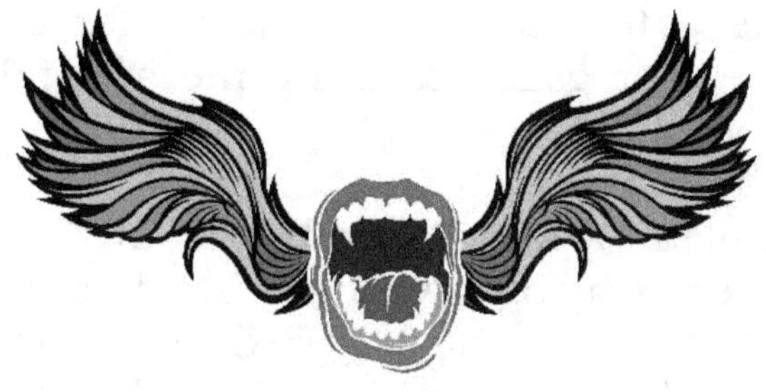

I COULD FEEL VALERIE'S stare as I ended the call.

"Why aren't you back there with him?" she asked when I handed her the phone.

"I'm no longer a vampire," I said, and the truck swerved slightly before Valerie got her shock under control.

"Is that why you went away?"

I met her gaze and shook my head. "No, we were on the run and still are."

"From..." Valerie started and closed her mouth. Michael must have schooled her in the fact that saying an archangel's name can bring them to you. Especially a fallen archangel.

I met her gaze, and she inhaled.

"He did this to me," I said with enough venom in my voice for her to know exactly who I was referring to. "And it comes with a hell of a price."

Valerie slowed as she pulled up to the gate and pressed the button on the remote attached to her visor. The gate slowly opened, and she rolled the truck through, engaging the remote again once we cleared the space. She waited until the gate latched and studied me for the first time, her gaze scanning me and falling on my left hand.

"You're married?"

I smiled and glanced at the elaborate engagement ring and wedding band adorning my finger. "Yes. We got married as soon as he recovered..." I whispered. My mind drifted back to his fumbling proposal in the thicket near where we built our mountainside cottage. He wasn't sure whether to get down on one knee, and his fidgety posturing had me laughing so hard that he almost didn't continue.

I can still hear his exasperation when he told me to please stop. He had something important to say and he couldn't while I was laughing at him. When I wound down, he dropped to his knee and took a deep breath before uttering the most perfect proposal, sending packing the last piece of my heart that still had doubts. I couldn't help but love him even more, and the certainty that we were meant to be together brought forth the only logical answer. Yes.

His expression morphed from the unsure and sincerely timid one he delivered when he asked me to marry him to the brightest, most dazzling smile I had ever seen. The fond memories of his proposal and the wild lovemaking that followed brought forth a wave of fresh tears that I blinked away.

I already missed that all-consuming passion.

"Were you cured then?" she asked.

I shook my head. "I've only been cured for a week," I said. God, it's only been a week? Seven days since we last made love, since we last touched without him wincing. How am I going to survive without his touch for the rest of my life? The thought gripped me as the garage doors opened and we drove into the darkness.

"You know, we could prop the mattress against the back door," Valerie said, and I glanced at the doorway and the ambient light filtering through the windowpanes, glad for something else to focus on.

"That would work," I said, and we got out of the cab, crossing to the tailgate. After Valerie lowered the gate, we pulled the mattress out and maneuvered it between the truck and her little fusion, leaning it on the wall so that it covered the entire back doorway and part of the back wall.

I returned to the truck and unhooked the utility straps around the tool chest. Within seconds of release, the top popped open and Damian sat up, blowing air out of his lungs like he was attempting to control an all out anxiety attack.

"So, I hear you got married," Valerie said, as she leaned on the edge of the tailgate.

Damian sent a smile her way and then met my gaze. "Yes, I did."

"So, what's going to happen now that she's back to normal?"

His gaze never left mine. "Honestly, I don't know," he said in all sincerity and my throat constricted, the lump getting bigger by the second.

Silence filled the space and Damian broke eye contact, glancing around the garage.

"Where's your Uncle Ted?"

"He went with Michael," I said, and Damian pressed his lips together before he climbed out of the box. That was a look I was accustomed to receiving, and I gave him my signature eyebrow raise in response.

"He shouldn't have gone with Michael; that was a big risk."

"Showing up here was a gigantic risk," I countered. "If I had known Valerie was living here, I never would have suggested we come home."

"Hey," Valerie interrupted, and we both turned our gaze toward her.

"No offense, it's just wherever we go, trouble seems to follow," Damian said, diffusing the flash of irritation in our host's face.

"Well, I am offended. I've missed your company. Uncle Ted means well, but he's never played a game of chess in his life and he certainly isn't as well read as you are." Valerie's glanced moved from Damian to me. "And I can take care of myself," she added, bringing her gaze back to Damian.

He stared at Valerie and then turned toward me. "I have never met two more stubborn and pigheaded women as the two of you."

"Well, I've never met anyone so moody who didn't have PMS," I said and sent him a saccharine smile before hopping down to the ground next to Valerie. "Maybe we should leave him alone for a bit," I said and glanced over my shoulder, meeting his exasperated gaze.

"Naomi, you know the dangers, but she doesn't fully understand."

Valerie turned on him. "I took quite a few advanced courses in theology for my undergrad degree, Damian, and I've had endless conversations with Michael about vampires and angels, so I know much more than you give me credit for. I know where you came from," she said. "I know what kills vampires and demons. I know incantations to bring Michael here if we ever need him and I'm far enough along in my medical degree to understand genetics too, so don't treat me like a child."

All I could think was, Damian just got served, and I had to hide the smile that surfaced. Once I was sure I could keep my face neutral, I chanced a glance in Damian's direction. He had taken a seat on the tool chest and ran a hand through his hair. I could tell he was measuring his response because his gaze was locked on the truck bed and not Valerie.

"I'm sorry," he finally said and met her glare. "You've accomplished a lot in five years."

Valerie softened. "I had to grow up real fast," she said, reminding both of us of the hardship she had survived.

"I know," he whispered, his gaze dropping and that all too familiar expression of blame crossing his handsome features.

"It wasn't your fault," both Valerie and I said in unison, and we traded a glance. I guess she knew his expressions as well as I did. After all, she had known him all her life until I entered the equation.

He allowed a brief twist of a smile and he sighed. "Wireless?" he asked, pulling the computer out of the backpack.

"Yes. The pass phrase is Angels with a capital A," Valerie answered.

"Thanks. Why don't you two go visit," he said and tossed me my duffel bag. "I've got some work to do."

I nodded and hauled the bag over my shoulder. "I'll check on you in a little while," I said.

He rolled his eyes and settled down on the truck bed, flipping the laptop open, and started hammering on the keys.

Valerie gave us a strange look and then headed into the house, holding the door and waving me inside. She gave me a tour of the house, which was larger than the front indicated. The ranch sprawled out in a horseshoe, with the living area covering most of the side where the garage attached and the sleeping quarters covered the opposite side. The family room opened to a u-shaped courtyard with a beautiful patio which surrounded a covered in-ground pool.

She led me to the guest suite, and I sighed at the more than modest accommodations.

"This is the guest room and I don't think Michael will mind letting you have it now that you're back to being human," she said and waved at the king size bed decorated with soft blues. "The bathroom reminds me of Damian's in the old house." Valerie swung the bathroom door open, showcasing a marble bathroom that could have been a replica of the one we used to have.

"Oh, Valerie, this is beautiful," I whispered, and the tears sprouted again, but this time I wasn't able to stop them with a flurry of blinks. I dropped the bag on the floor and covered my face.

Her warm arms wrapped around me and I melted into her, letting myself succumb to the soul-strangling sobs.

Tigress
Chapter Twenty
Naomi

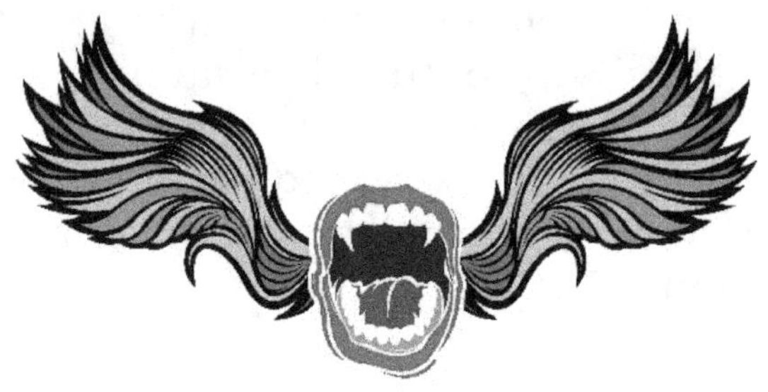

I DON'T KNOW HOW long I cried, but when my tears dried up, I hardly had the strength to stand. Valerie led me to the bed and sat me down before disappearing into the bathroom. She came back with a damp washcloth and handed it to me before taking the spot next to me.

"What happened to you two?"

I wiped my face and balled up the cloth, tossing it into an empty laundry basket that sat by the bureau. "The cure. Damian's allergic to me now." I detested the whiny quality of my nasally voice and sniffled, meeting Valerie's gaze. "And if he ever bites me, it will kill him."

"Jesus," she said. "How did you ever drive together in the truck?"

"It's not like hay-fever." I gave her a smile. "Being around me isn't the problem. We just can't touch; otherwise, he breaks out in blisters wherever our skin comes into contact. It has to hurt like hell, but it does nothing to me," I said, and the tears threatened again.

"Oh, Naomi," Valerie said and took my hands.

"We had five extremely passionate and affectionate years and now..." I clenched my jaw as the anger flare. "Now I want to hurt that bastard as much as he's hurt us," I said and met Valerie's gaze.

"I heard you hurt him pretty bad," she said.

"Unfortunately, I didn't succeed in killing him," I countered. If I had killed Lucifer, we would still be playing in the snow in Denver or wherever our hearts led us, but now we were forever separated by sun and blisters.

"Michael said you saved Damian."

"Yeah. Damian tried to ditch me to keep me safe. He fully expected to die for me."

"I think he would have," she said, and I cocked my head. "I could see how deeply he loved you just by the way he looked at you. That's why it surprised the hell out of me that you had only known each other for a couple of days. The way he looked at you was the way my father always looked at my mother."

"And now?"

Valerie stared at me and sighed. "It's still there, under a layer of soul-wrenching pain."

Soul-wrenching pain. How damned accurate, and it made me crack a smile.

"It's the same way you look at him."

My chin quivered, and I nodded. "I can't go for the rest of my life without touching him, Valerie. What the hell am I going to do?"

"Can he turn you again?"

I shook my head. "I'm immune to the virus and I've seen what happens when a vampire bites me. It's a horrific death..." I closed my eyes and hung my head, unable to relay the details despite Valerie's questioning stare.

She took my hand and squeezed. "Somehow, I'm sure it will all work out in the end."

I met her gaze, but kept my mouth shut. There was no fairytale ending to our story, and I didn't want to burst Valerie's bubble, so I just offered a smile and a nod.

"I think I'll take a shower, if you don't mind. I'm sure I'm a bit ripe after being in a truck for a little over thirty hours."

Valerie grinned. "I'm in med-school, so I've smelled worse."

"I'm sure," I said and took my leave, scooping up my duffel bag on the way.

The heat of the shower lulled me into an exhausted trance, so much so that the ritual of showering went by without my knowledge and when I looked down at my hands, the shrivel lines of being in water too long creased my fingertips. I turned the water off and wrapped myself in an oversized towel.

Valerie had left the bedroom, and I was grateful. I needed sleep. The down comforter and fluffy pillows were more than inviting. I crawled under the warm blankets and was out before my head hit the soft cotton.

Tigress
Chapter Twenty-One
Damian

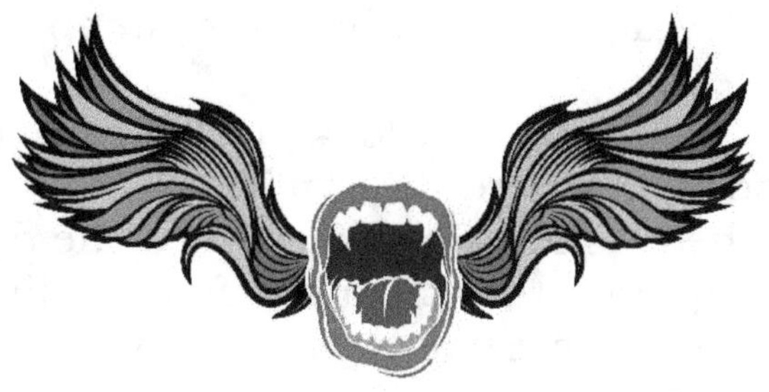

THE GARAGE WASN'T EXACTLY warm, but it was miles beyond the frigid slap the box of the moving van contained.

I pulled the blanket tighter around my shoulders before resuming the web design I was already late delivering. My client wasn't happy with the delay, but when I explained we'd moved across country and had run into complications that I hadn't foreseen, they graciously gave me a couple of days more.

My fingers flew over the keyboard and I concentrated on the code string I was creating instead of the flurry of information I had gotten over the last two days. It was easier to drown in work instead of dwelling on scenarios for the future. All of them bleak and lonely.

My hands curled into fists and I closed my eyes, taking a deep breath and shifting my weight, forcing the thought brigade back.

"If you want this thing done by sunset," I muttered, reminding myself again of the self-imposed deadline I set.

I opened my eyes and the creak of a door caught my attention.

"Hey," Valerie said when she stepped out of the house.

"Hey," I replied and looked behind her at the empty space. "Where's Naomi?"

"Crashed," she said and crossed the distance, hopping up onto the tailgate before settling down on the end of the truck bed. "Are you okay?"

This conversation was going to take longer than normal and I sighed, glancing down at my screen. I saved my work and put the computer aside, still trying to figure out what to say to Valerie's question.

"Not entirely," I said, opting not to bullshit her. She always could read through it anyway, and I could see from the pity written in her expression that Naomi must have done some talking before sleep tackled her.

She just stared at me, waiting for me to continue.

"What do you want me to say?" I asked after a few minutes of silence.

"I don't know." She shifted so her back was against the tire-well. "Maybe you should start at the beginning?"

I narrowed my eyes and bit the inside of my lip against a snide remark. Valerie wasn't the enemy, and I couldn't aim my anger in her direction. "What exactly do you know about me?"

Her smile accompanied a challenge in her eyes. "Everything." She crossed her arms to punctuate her meaning.

"Bullshit," I called her bluff. It had been ages since I'd had a mental spar with Valerie, and I believe the last time she had just turned sixteen and we had a debate about cars. And the girl won.

"Son of Gabriel. Protector to my bloodline. The only vampire who can shape shift and the only one who looks like a normal human, even though you're older than dirt."

I felt the snort of laughter burn my nose. "Sweetie, knowing my history and knowing me are worlds apart," I returned. "And dirt was around before I was born."

All humor faded from her features. "I know you love Naomi and not being able to touch her is slowly killing you."

I spoke and paused, closing my mouth because she was right.

"I've seen this recklessness in you before," she said, and I cocked my head. Before I could ask, she continued, "A couple of nights before all hell broke loose here. I saw you stalk out of the house and your expression is the same one you have now."

"Excuse me?"

"You have the expression of someone who has nothing to live for." She put her hand up to stop my argument. "There's anger, just like you had back then, but underneath it, you've already given up."

I pressed my lips together and stared at my feet stretched out in front of me.

"What the fuck is that all about?"

My gaze snapped to hers and whatever sympathy she displayed earlier was replaced with a harsh anger.

"I..."

"Don't give me a fucking excuse. If you really love her, you'll make this work."

"I love her," I snapped, my defenses going into overdrive. "I love her so much it feels like a blade's been shoved in my chest every time I go to reach for her. And it's only been a fucking week. What kind of basket case am I going to be after a year? Besides, how fair is this to her?" I pointed at the door, my voice rising with the fury filling me.

"And you don't think it's driving her just as crazy as it is you?"

"She'd be happier without me," I growled.

"Oh, that's bullshit, and you know it. True love is much more than a good fuck," she said, shocking the hell out of me. The Valerie I left didn't talk so bluntly or crudely.

"I know that," I muttered. "But I can't even hold her hand."

"It's winter. Wear driving gloves and hold her hand. Jesus, Damian, it's like you were born yesterday. You've got a creative mind. Why the hell aren't you using it?"

"Because I'm angry right now. At every fucking little thing. It took twenty-five hundred years to find my soul mate, and that bastard has succeeded in tearing us apart."

"You need a good swift kick in the ass," she glared at me.

"Why?"

"Because he isn't the one tearing you two apart. You are," she said and stood, hopping off the tailgate. "For such a smart man, you can be a fucking dumbass," she added when her shoes slapped the garage floor.

"What the hell do you mean by that?"

She stopped halfway to the door and turned, taking a deep breath. "Look at it as a challenge for you to overcome instead of a loss. It's up to you to decide whether you will overcome it or not. If you don't, Lucifer wins."

My eyes widened at the drop of his name.

"Chill, the place is angel-proof, remember," Valerie said before she turned, leaving me alone with the hum of my computer.

Valerie was always smarter than a human had a right to be and as soon as the shock wore off, her words bit at my nerves because she was absolutely right. It wasn't what was thrown at us that mattered; it was how we chose to handle it.

Naomi had rolled with it, even in Denver. Even with the building frustration of not being able to touch, she handled it better than I did.

I, on the other hand, resorted to the equivalent of a two-year-old's belligerent rant.

"What the hell is wrong with me?" I muttered and pulled the computer back onto my lap, putting the answer to my question aside and focusing back on the web design.

Tigress
Chapter Twenty-Two
Damian

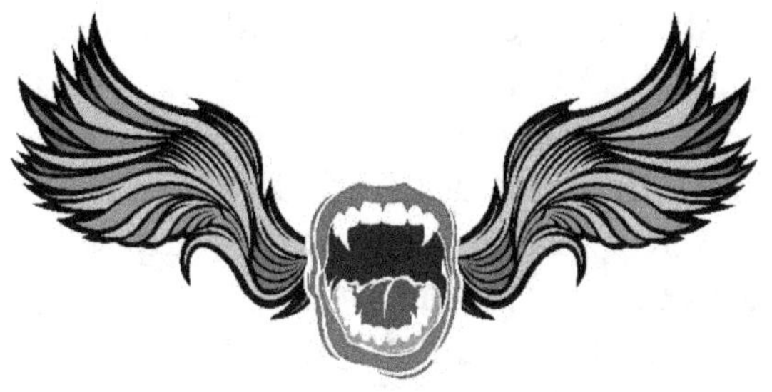

THE RESULTS OF THE day's programming pleased me and I stretched, cracking my knuckles and shaking the cold ache out of my fingers. After I saved the program, I glanced at the clock on the toolbar. It was almost five, and I glanced at the dark phone next to me.

Michael hadn't checked in and I punched in my passcode, sending off a quick text to see if he was okay. Now that the sun had set, I packed up the computer and grabbed my duffel bag, hauling it over my shoulder.

Before I reached the door, my phone buzzed. I glanced at the text and exhaled. The relief swept through my tight muscles like an infusion of blood. They had just boarded a bus headed for Hartford and someone would need to pick them up around two in the morning.

I shot off a text saying that I'd pick them up at the bus station and pocketed my phone.

When I stepped into the house, I glanced at the L-shaped open concept kitchen and family room. Valerie sat on the couch with an array of books open; she didn't look up from scribbling on her notepad until I crossed the room.

When she raised her gaze, she nodded toward the hallway.

"She is still asleep."

I bit my lip and looked at the hallway for a second. "Your uncle wouldn't happen to have driving gloves, would he?"

Dimples appeared on her cheeks. "I have no idea, but I'm glad you're thinking outside the box." Valerie leaned over and rummaged in the bag at her feet. She sat up with a package of micro-thin latex surgical gloves and handed them to me. "I can get more at the hospital tomorrow, so...enjoy," she said and grinned.

I rolled my eyes, but I would not pass up an opportunity to get creative, and I took the box. Heading down the hallway she nodded toward.

"The last bedroom on the left," she called as I rounded the corner.

I didn't need to be told where Naomi was in the house. I could smell her sweet scent the minute I opened the garage door. Quietly, I entered the room and set my bags down, closing the door behind me. Naomi didn't stir, and I stared at her curled up on her side with her hand under her cheek, looking more like a child than the sexy woman I married.

The scratch of the gloves against the cardboard sounded like sandpaper against wood and I winced, praying she wouldn't wake. I wanted to surprise her, wake her with something pleasurable for a change. Just the thought of it made my heart rate rise along with something much lower. A wicked grin formed on my lips and I slunk across the room, slipping one glove on and then the next, trying to not snap the latex.

The minute I lifted the covers, she rolled on her back, muttering in her sleep, but I caught my name on her exhale and I wanted to kiss her sweet lips, but I refrained, settling for running my gloved finger over them instead. Initially, she let out a soft purr, but then her eyes flew open, darting around the room until they landed on me.

I lifted my hand into her field of vision. "Medical gloves."

She stared at the latex for a moment and then at me; the smile gaining traction as she pulled my fingers back to her lips. She sucked on my index finger in a way that made me long for her mouth and I almost said to hell with it all, but I stayed put, relishing the tightness of my jeans at this moment.

I ran my fingers down her neck, stopping over the strong pulse, intrigued at just how much I could feel with the gloves on and for the first time since she collapsed in the snow, I understood what she had said about creativity. While this wasn't quite the same level as skin on skin, it was close, and I knew I had the talent to make her wetter than the ocean.

As my hand trailed lower, stopping to explore each ample breast, her grin widened.

"You have a pair of those gloves for me?" she whispered.

I shook my head. "Tonight it's just about you," I answered and I stopped just short of her clit, teasing her in a way that was just as powerful as my mouth used to be. The roll of her eyes and the quickening of her breath guided me and I slid my gloved fingers over her clit, back and forth, like playing a complex sting of chords, and she replied with a musical moan that thrilled every nerve in my body.

Flush filled her cheeks, deepening to blooming roses the closer she got to orgasm. Music filled the house, and I chuckled.

"I guess you were being a little too loud," I whispered with a chuckle.

She just grinned and her eyes rolled back in her head. Her back arched and her hand grabbed the sheet, balling it in her fist. Now, I had seen her cum before, but this time, her entire body trembled with the strength of it, reminding me of that first night when she had nearly drenched the bed she was so wet.

And her moan, god her moan, almost sent me over the edge, but the lack of sensation when I slid my fingers into her slick canal tempered it. If I continued, I just might throw caution to the wind, so I backed off when her body relaxed and her pants softened. I pulled away, despite her whine of protest, and rolled onto my back, staring at the ceiling, trying to gain control.

Before I could even catch my breath, Naomi swung her leg over me and smiled as she settled right on top of my throbbing cock. The jeans provided a layer of protection between us, and when she circled her hips, I closed my eyes.

"God, Naomi," I whispered. My gloved hands grabbed her waist, guiding her motion, and the friction it created started the spark in my soul, turning it into a burning need. The way she moved, grinding into me in that slow circular flow drove me over the edge.

As soon as my muscles relaxed, I opened my eyes, meeting her gaze.

"I love you," I whispered and pulled my hands away from her.

She smiled and climbed off me, curling up on the bed until her stomach growled. "I guess I should get up and eat something," she said, stretching like a cat.

"I should too, but I need a shower before I go hunting."

"That's probably a good idea." She patted my shirt-clad chest and rolled out of bed. I watched her dress before I got up and headed for the shower.

For the first time since Lilith's visit, I actually felt like myself and I smiled under the warm spray. Naomi had been right. There were ways to get creative and still feed the fire of our passion.

It still wasn't as satisfying as making love to my wife, but it was enough. For now.

When I walked out into the living room, dressed in my jeans and Naomi's favorite bomber jacket, both she and Valerie gave me a cursory glance before going back to flipping pages in a book in the kitchen.

"What are you two doing?" I asked.

"Trying to figure out what we want to make for dinner," Valerie said and glanced at me.

"Sometimes cooking can be fun, but most of the time it's just a pain in the ass."

"You want some fresh venison?"

Valerie bit her lip, and Naomi's eyebrows rose in contemplation.

"You really shouldn't go out just yet," Valerie said.

"I have to eat," I replied, stressing the point. She may have had Michael as a mentor over the last five years, but he didn't understand the cravings that came with the virus. If I didn't eat tonight, I wasn't sure I could go a full day in the basement without stressing.

"Why don't you look at the room downstairs? If you want to trade up the mattress, feel free, but I'm not sure you're going to want to."

"I'll do that later," I said and started toward the door.

"Michael said not to let you go out until he got back," Valerie challenged.

"I'm picking him up at the train station in Hartford at two."

"No. I'll pick them up," Valerie said.

Irritation snaked over my skin and I glared at her. "Am I a prisoner here?"

Valerie laughed. "If that's the way you want to look at it..."

I crossed my arms and met Naomi's amused gaze.

"What?"

"I'm sorry, but your expression is priceless."

"If I don't eat..."

"Just go check out downstairs," Valerie said, her voice filled with the same level of exasperation as her face.

I don't know what made me hesitate, but Naomi pointed toward the door just to the right of the hallway leading to our bedroom. I rolled my eyes and stalked toward the door, nearly ripping it off the hinges in my aggravation. The stairway leading down looked like every other old New England basement, with barren wooden stairs leading into a dark and gray concrete cellar. I glanced over my shoulder and Naomi nodded for me to continue.

Skeptical, I climbed down the surprisingly solid staircase. Lights turned on and I glanced over my shoulder. Valerie and Naomi crowded in the doorway, gauging my reaction. I stepped to the cold floor and glanced at the small space. The furnace sat on the far wall below a small window that I guessed faced the south. When I stepped closer, I squinted, almost laughing out loud. The window, while probably working, was painted with a deep blue, so no sun would penetrate it, but I'm sure when light hit it during the day, it probably emitted a pleasant blue across the room. A massive electrical panel sat on the wall below the staircase and I followed the pipes from the furnace and the wires from the panel along the ceiling, where they disappeared into the wall almost three feet from the end of the stairs.

The cellar I stood in covered a ten foot by ten-foot square, which was a fraction of the blueprint of the house, and I glanced up the stairs at Valerie.

"Where's the rest?" I waved at the small space.

They traded a grin and pointed to the generator panel next to the staircase.

I flipped open the panel and along with the generator switches was a separate keypad. I bit my lip and looked up the stairwell again. The nod I got from Naomi confirmed the passcode and I punched in my favorite four-digit code.

The slow creak of the wall caught my attention and the concrete at the base of the stairs slid inward. I hadn't even seen the break in the concrete and I studied the construction, smiling at the ingenuity. The concrete seams bubbled inward, hiding the cut block. Several seams covered the walls at the same four-foot intervals, so this setup wasn't immediately identifiable. I stepped into the catacomb of rooms they built and let out a whistle.

Michael had said it was small.

His sense of space is truly fucked up, because just this single room was monstrous and I couldn't imagine what lay beyond.

I scanned the room in awe, ignoring the shuffle behind me. The opening dropped me into a massive great room I guessed was roughly three-thousand square feet. The section to my left was an open concept office, with a great mahogany desk and all the modern gadgets laid out across the immaculate desk blotter, including a slick laptop that probably cost three times the one in my bag upstairs. Across from the office space was a large screen television with a plush, leather multi-section couch facing it.

But my gaze was drawn to the wall beyond the office. A full mural of an ocean-side beach. I crossed to it and ran my fingers along the peaks of the breaking waves and scanned the scene all the way to the ceiling. I turned, glancing at the entire expanse of the room, and my eyebrows rose. The vibrant blue of an afternoon sky, broken by fluffy clouds, covered the ceiling, highlighted by randomly placed recessed lights. I dropped my gaze to Valerie and pointed to the fake sky.

"My idea," she said with a wide grin.

My gaze dropped to the kitchenette on the opposite side of the room. But the little tiled alcove wasn't what caught my attention and got my saliva glands running over. The clear glass refrigerator revealed a half dozen blood bags and before I was aware, my feet started moving across the plush sand-toned carpet.

As I passed Valerie and Naomi, I met Valerie's gaze and nodded toward the refrigerator.

"Michael," Valerie said, as if that explained it.

"Really?" I didn't wait for her to answer. Instead, I stopped in front of the display and opened the door, pulling out a bag before the hunger overwhelmed me. Once I drained every drop of blood from the bag, I opened the cabinet under the sink and smiled. A lined garbage can sat exactly where I would have put it and I tossed the empty in the trash.

I closed my eyes and let the blood run through my system. I shivered as it cooled me from my core out. That was one drawback of bagged blood. While it rejuvenated me, it left a distinct chill that would take hours to shake.

I turned back to the spacious room, and I took everything in, stopping my inspection of the living space at the ornately crafted pool table with felt the color of the ceiling. I picked up one of the balls, studying the unique details before rolling it toward the corner pocket. It rolled true and before it plunked into the pocket; I turned back to the two of them gawking at me from the doorway.

"So do you like it?" Valerie asked.

I chuckled and ran my gaze from one side of the room to the other and back to her. "What's not to like?" I said and spread my arms out. "It's amazing."

"We haven't seen everything," Naomi said and pointed toward the hallway.

"By all means." I waved her forward, and she didn't hesitate, but Valerie hung back.

"Aren't you going to give us the grand tour?"

"No. I think you two should explore. Besides, I've got to cook something for dinner, so..." She looked at her watch. "If you could bring her back to reality in a half hour, I should have our dinner all set."

"Will do," I said, and Valerie disappeared back up the stairs.

I followed the curve of the hall and found two closed doors facing each other. I had no idea if Naomi slipped into one or the other or if she continued down the short hallway that dipped down a staircase. I sniffed the air and caught her scent, continuing down the hall instead of exploring either room.

The staircase descended to a small platform and another keypad. The door was still open, so I imagined Naomi had ventured into the darkness beyond. I blinked, letting my eyes adjust, and took a step.

"Boo!"

The sudden volume in the small space gave me a start, and I spun, the growl already purring in the back of my throat until her laughter followed.

"Jesus, Naomi," I whispered and stepped back, gaining control over the sudden shadow mentality that almost took over.

"Sorry, sweetheart, but I couldn't help it."

"I would think by now you'd know not to jump out of dark corners at me," I said, trying to sound stern, but the fact that she actually got my heart pumping pulled a smile to the corners of my lips.

The light from her cell illuminated her grin, and then she nodded toward the opening of the rough-round tunnel. "What do you suppose is down that way?"

I rubbed my chin, contemplating the direction, and then shook my head.

"Michael said there weren't any underground tunnels."

"He also said the place down here was small," she said, and I actually laughed.

"You think?" I stopped and looked into the blackness.

"Only one way to find out," she said and started into the darkness with only the light from her cell as the guide.

Tigress
Chapter Twenty-Three
Damian

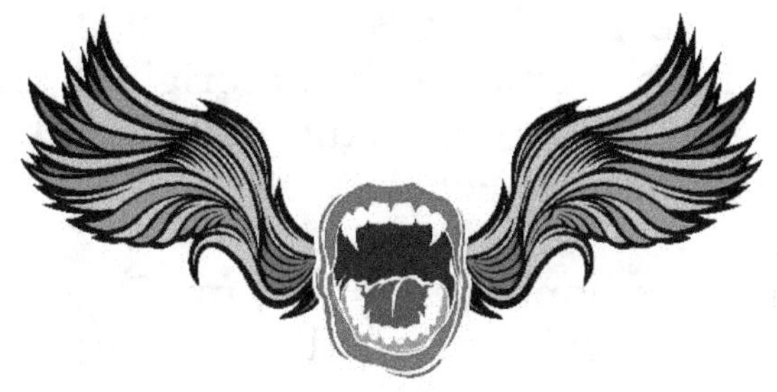

WE STOOD STARING AT the wall of dirt blocking the end of the last pipe. Naomi's phone winked out and a moment later, the light returned.

"I guess Michael was serious when he said they didn't do the underground tunnels," Naomi said.

I bit my lip, contemplating, mentally calculating the distance. If memory served me correctly, we were very close to where my original tunnel system dropped us under the garage. I turned and looked into the darkness behind me, rubbing my forehead where I had clocked a jut in the ceiling. Naomi had found that hysterical, her lovely five-foot-five form just waltzed right under the outcrop without touching the ceiling, the seven-inch difference in height benefitting her for a change.

My guess was that the outcrop was the foundation for the fence. If so, this was where my original doorway was that led to the inside of the garage. I spun back toward the dirt and started digging with my hands.

"What are you doing?"

"This is the remains of the original tunnel to the garage. I'm betting he didn't know what to do when he hit the steel door. Especially with the angel hex."

After three handfuls of dirt, my fingers hit the solid barrier, and I grinned. "I'm surprised this door didn't blow inward from the blast," I mumbled as I uncovered more of the solid steel. The top half of the door was intact, but as I made my way lower, the metal became more deformed, like a boulder hit the center and bent it inward.

It took close to a half hour to uncover the doorway, and I stepped back, aiming Naomi's phone at the door. The outer edges seemed to be fine, but the center was bent inward and I exchanged a glance with Naomi before I stepped forward and felt along the edges.

The latch was stuck, and I sighed. I'd need a wheelbarrow to clean up the mess, and I'd need a crowbar to pry open the door. I had time. Naomi's stomach rumbled in the dark and I chuckled. I had forgotten Valerie's instructions.

"I'll get the rest of this later. We need to get you back so you can eat," I said, wiping my dirty hands on my thighs.

"Are you sure?"

"Yeah, I'll have the rest of the night and all day tomorrow to clean this up and get this section reinforced before I open that door."

"Reinforced?"

I met her gaze. "This could collapse and I'd venture to guess we're at least eight feet below the grass. That's a lot of dirt and we don't want that falling on our heads."

I pressed my lips together to stop the smile that wanted to form at Naomi's worried glance and her hasty retreat. I followed, trying to study the construction of the tunnel, but the lack of light made any close inspection impossible. I'd have to bring a more illuminating light down when I returned. I knew the concrete cylinders were normally used for water channels and these looked dry enough, so it was obvious nothing was getting through the seams. I just wanted to make sure if I opened the steel door, it wouldn't do anything to disrupt the landscaping.

We stepped into the kitchen a few minutes later, and Valerie's eyes narrowed in my direction.

"What in god's name happened to you?"

"We went exploring," Naomi said and glanced at me. "And he decided to dig at the end of the tunnel."

"I see." A dimple appeared in her cheek as she slowly appraised me. "He's something all dirty like that," she said in a tone I never heard from her before.

One that left me speechless, and I traded a glance with Naomi. Hunger reflected in her eyes and I had to blink because Naomi's expression mirrored Valerie's and just the thought of Valerie finding me hot gave me an awful chill. It was as bad as having my child wanting to bed me, and I shifted my stance, meeting Naomi's gaze.

"Does it make you uncomfortable that I notice you?" Valerie said and put two plates piled with pasta on the table.

Naomi answered for me. "I'm pretty sure it does," she said and slid into the seat next to Valerie. "You know that I'll kick your ass if you ever make a move, though," she added with a smile, and picked up her fork.

Valerie grinned. "I assumed, but it's still fun to make him all uncomfortable like that."

She pointed at me and both women nodded, grins playing on each of their lips.

"What did I ever do to you?" I muttered and headed to the garage without waiting for an answer. The wheelbarrow and a shovel sat in the corner and I picked up both, hauling them through the living area without a word, but both their gazes burned into my back. After depositing them at the entry of the tunnel, I climbed back to the kitchen and took a seat across from Valerie, and waited for a break in the conversation.

"So you lived in the mountains for the last five years?" Valerie directed the question at me instead of Naomi.

"Yes," I answered. "Do you have some flashlights?"

"Michael put some down in the walk-in storage area across from the bedroom downstairs. He said most everything you'd ever need is in there."

"I haven't finished looking around down there." I shrugged and went to stand.

"Stay and visit," Naomi said, and it was presented in such a way that I couldn't refuse without offending them.

"What? So the two of you can gang up on me?" I allowed a smile to form despite the discomfort grating on my nerves. I didn't want to think of Valerie as anything but a little girl, and her less than subtle stare was driving me nuts.

"No, so we can talk and be good guests before Valerie has to run out and pick up Michael and her Uncle Ted."

"When we finish dinner, maybe we can play a game of chess before I have to leave," Valerie said. "It will give me a break from studying."

"What specialty are you studying?" Naomi asked and finished the last bite of spaghetti.

"Pediatrics. I love kids," Valerie said as she stood to take Naomi's plate, but I stopped both of them.

"Let me get the dishes, while you two talk," I said and reached across the table, pulling the plates from Valerie.

"Is he for real?" Valerie asked, while I went into the kitchen.

"Yes," Naomi said and I could tell she wore that proud possessive grin without even turning. "He doesn't mind cleaning up. Which is all the better for me because I hate to clean."

I snorted a laugh from the sink. That was an understatement. Naomi would rather do anything else, and had resorted to some really creative bribes to get out of cleaning. Not that I minded at all, especially since her bribes were usually worth every ounce of sweat I shed.

"Are you laughing at me?" she called, and I sent a grin her way before focusing on cleaning up the pots and pans in the sink.

Silence filtered over the room and I shifted, looking out the window in front of me at the woods and then at the reflection in the windowpane.

"Oh, for Christ's sake, stop looking at me like that," I said to the reflections of both Naomi and Valerie staring at me. At my ass in particular.

"You sure you're not willing to share?" Valerie posed the question to Naomi, and I almost dropped the plate in my hands.

Naomi's head tilted as she studied me and the breathless sigh that came sent a heated tingle through me. "Yes. I'm quite territorial. Besides, hawks mate for life. Isn't that right, sweetheart?"

I met her gaze in the reflection and offered a single nod. Even if she had been willing to share, I couldn't conceive of it.

Tigress
Chapter Twenty-Four
Naomi

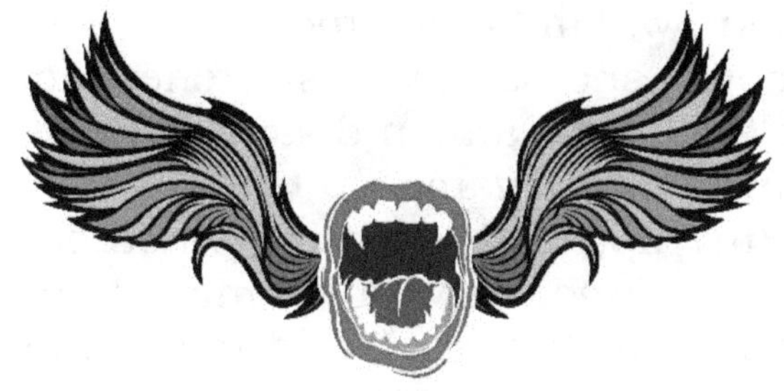

DAMIAN DISAPPEARED AFTER HE finished the dishes. Valerie chuckled at his obvious discomfort and as soon as I thought he was out of range, I stared her down.

"I hope like hell you're just having fun at his expense."

Her jaw dropped, and I leaned back, crossing my arms. She had no clue how territorial I was where he was concerned. Hell, I pretty much had him all to myself for the last five years, so the idea of sharing him in any way irritated me.

Her mouth popped closed as she dropped her gaze. "Naomi, I wouldn't dream of sleeping with him." When she met my glare, I softened at the sincerity in her eyes. "Besides my uncle, Damian's the only family I have."

"So you're yanking his chain for the pure joy of seeing him squirm?"

The slow smile that spread across her lips, along with the glint of humor in her eyes, made me laugh. Valerie had a way of disarming me that no one else had, and I could tell in time we would be the best of friends.

"You know, I'm family, too."

"I know," she said and stretched, looking at the clock. "Since Damian disappeared on us, did you want to play a game?"

I bit my lip, contemplating whether to hang with Valerie or go see what Damian was up to. A quick glance at the clock told me she had some time to kill before she headed out to pick up Michael and Uncle Ted. "I'm not a big chess player. Damian tried to teach me and I just don't have the patience for it. I play cards though, so if you're up for a game of rummy or canasta, I'm game."

"I'm up for a game of Rummy-five hundred," she said and stood, retreating to the living room and coming back a minute later with a deck of cards.

We played Rummy until a little after eleven. I beat her two out of three games and the last one was a draw because she had to get ready to go pick up Michael and her uncle.

"Did you want me to come?"

Valerie shook her head. "Michael was very clear. He didn't want either of you leaving the house for a few days or until he could deem the place safe."

"Oh, so I'm just as much of a prisoner as Damian?" I asked. I didn't like the thought of being sequestered inside, especially during the day, now that I had that kind of freedom.

"You're not prisoners," she sighed. "He just wants to make sure it's safe for all of us."

The reality that we were putting Valerie in as much danger as us settled and I nodded. She was as much a child of the light as I was, and I didn't want Lucifer to target her. If one of his minions reported we were back here, then both Valerie and her uncle would be in danger.

I gave her a small hug. "Be safe," I said, and she smiled, heading out the door and once the garage closed and the headlights faded down the road, I turned, heading down into the basement to see what Damian was up to.

The bulkhead to the basement was open, and I shivered in the cold draft before heading into the living space. Halfway down the dark hallway, a form appeared in the dark. I waited with the light of my cell as company until he stood in front of me.

"This is the last of the dirt," he said and poked his chin toward the mound on the wheelbarrow.

"Ah," I answered and started following him back toward the apartment.

"What have you two been doing?"

"We played some cards before she headed out. I offered to go with her, but apparently, Michael has us on lockdown."

"I understand his discomfort," Damian said and trudged across the living area and out into the basement. For a moment, I wondered how he'd get the heaping wheelbarrow up the stairs, but then he bent down and slid his hand under the bed, lifting it without so much as a strain in any of his muscles. I sighed. It had only been a week, but I missed that raw strength.

He disappeared into the night and, a few minutes later, came back with the empty wheelbarrow, closing the bulkhead doors and latching them before he came back in the basement and closed the door, engaging those locks as well. He wiped his cheek, leaving a streak of dirt, and I smiled. His rugged good looks wore dirt well.

"What?"

"You look sexy when you're all grubby," I said and received a flash of white teeth and a chuckle before he skirted by me.

"The gloves are upstairs in the bedroom," he said. "Feel free to grab them and when I'm done getting the tunnel supports in place, you can do some exploring of your own."

He winked at me and I considered high tailing it upstairs. Instead, I followed him into the dark tunnel.

"Michael did an exceptional job putting this together," he said as we walked toward the glow at the end of the tunnel. "He sealed the concrete connectors almost like a welder connects pieces of steel. I don't have a clue what he used, but the likelihood of water getting in is slim and I think the base is set up like a curtain drain anyway, so water will flow away from the pipes."

He rattled on about the construction and when we approached the end of the tunnel, the pile of dirt had been replaced by a stack of thick wood planks and a crowbar. Damian glanced over his shoulder at me.

"Do me a favor and just stay in the pipe until I can get the door open, okay?"

I glanced at the dirt ceiling and the bent door before I stepped back into the security of the concrete pipe. Damian picked up the crowbar, and I took another step back when he carved the hook into the crease of the door.

The only time I ever saw his muscles strain was when he was chained in the warehouse but the moment he leaned on the bar, the fabric of the shirt pulled taut across his shoulders and the ripple of muscle across his back and arms left me hotter than hell.

His gaze turned away from the door and a crease appeared between his eyes.

"Really?"

"What?" I shrugged.

"The strangest things turn you on," he answered and focused on the crowbar, putting his back into it. The tearing of fabric masked the creak of the door and I was so focused on the frayed seam encasing his shoulder that I didn't see the fruits of his labor until the metal swung open and smashed into the dirt wall, creating a plume of dust.

When the air cleared, Damian stood in the opening, his gaze locked on the top of the stairwell and his chest rising and falling in the pattern of excitement. He glanced at me and smiled, both his teeth and his eyes shining amidst the grime.

He looked like a little boy who rolled in dirt, and I couldn't help but grin back.

The moment he turned back, he vaulted up the steps two at a time and I scrambled after him, catching up to him just as he pushed the hatchway open. It banged into the undercarriage of the truck and his smile faded.

"Flat tires," he said and held the hatch so I could crawl through.

Once I rolled out of the way, he crawled out from under the truck and stood, scanning the garage from floor to ceiling, sighing at the tall platinum covered plates blocking all entry and exits. He opened the driver's door of the truck and put the vehicle in neutral, rolling it away from the opening before resetting the brake and then looked at his undisturbed stock.

I shivered in the cold room, drawing his attention.

"You're more than welcome to go wait in the house where it's warm," he said and glanced at the dark room. "This is going to take me the rest of the night."

"Can I help?" I asked and rubbed my hands together, blowing on my fingers to warm them.

I could see the slight rise of his eyebrow as he met my gaze. He glanced around again and then shook his head. "Not tonight. I have to figure out what I need before I can enlist your help. I'm sure all the cars will need oil changes, batteries and new tires, but I won't know what else until I clean the place up and tinker under the hoods." He glanced up at what was visible of the windows. "And I don't have unlimited time."

I glanced around at the shadows of the cars before turning and climbing back down the stairs into the well-lit alcove. When I passed under the jog in the tunnel ceiling, I had to use my phone for lighting. The warmth of the apartment penetrated the dark and by the time I got back upstairs into the heart of the house, the chill biting my skin in the garage had all but vanished.

Tigress
Chapter Twenty-Five
Naomi

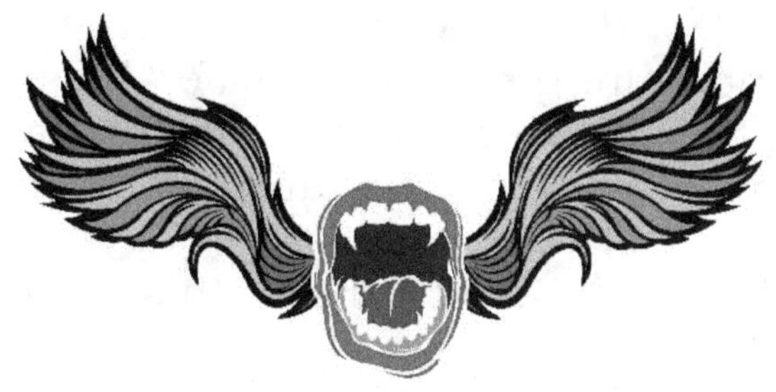

T HE BANG OF THE garage door brought me out of my sleepy stupor. I shifted to a sitting position on the couch and rubbed my eyes before turning my attention to the homeowners.

"I'm heading to bed," Valerie said and disappeared down the hall without so much as a glance at the noise emanating from the television. I reached for the remote and turned the tuner off, silencing the idiotic monologue of late night tv.

Ted just gave me a tired nod and headed the same direction Valerie went.

Michael took a seat on the couch next to me and yawned.

"Where's Damian?" he asked once his yawn and stretch ceased.

"He opened the tunnel to the garage."

His eyes popped open, and he sat stalk straight, turning his irritated gaze in my direction.

"I think he's taking stock of what he'll need to fix up the cars," I added. When Michael's glare continued, I added, "What?"

"I'm not sure the garage is safe," he said.

"Oh, bullshit." I stood and started toward the basement door. "It's probably safer than this place."

"Nothing is safer than this place," he snapped.

"Damian's fine."

"When was the last time you checked on him?"

Michael's condescending tone was irritating me, and I glanced at the clock. "I've only been up here for an hour and a half."

Michael shot to his feet and stalked off toward the basement.

Anger burned through my reason, and I stormed after him. "We aren't children, you know," I said when I caught up to him.

"You most certainly are."

I should have expected his response. Even so, it had the same effect as pouring gasoline on a fire. I huffed and stomped forward in the dark, muttering under my breath until his hand clasped my upper arm and stopped me.

"What?" I snapped, and he covered my mouth.

"Shush," he whispered, and I stopped my struggles and listened.

The sound of rattling chains set my heart into hyper-drive and my body followed. I yanked out of Michael's grasp and bolted into the dark. The scene in the warehouse five years before kept flashing in front of my eyes, propelling me forward faster than I thought possible.

Michael's footfalls echoed behind me, but I didn't stop. Instead, I barreled up the stairs and skidded to a stop in the middle of the floor. It took a second for my mind to catch up, and when it did, I pressed my lips together.

Damian glanced around the body of the car; the crease between his eyes conveyed his confusion.

"Are you okay?" he asked as he wiped his hands on a cloth.

Michael stepped beside me, scanning the array of vehicles in the dimly lit garage. Each one elevated on jacks or hanging from chains. Not one of the bunch had tires, and a line of batteries lay flush against the wall. The room stunk like oil and grease, and Damian's jeans sported oil splatter.

"You did all this in an hour and a half?" I waved my hand around the room.

Damian gave me a shrug. "It's not like I did a tune up on each. I just stripped tires, batteries and drained the oil."

"Yeah, but you've got, like, a dozen cars here."

A smirk appeared on his lips and he glanced at his watch.

"Do you think having any light in here is wise?" Michael asked.

Damian looked at the tall windows almost covered with platinum-steel plates, and then back down at us. "I wouldn't worry too much. No one can get in."

"But they will notice the light. This place has been dark for ages and this gives an indication of activity. That's going to spark some interest from a host of beings."

Damian reached over and flipped the flashlight balanced on the hood off. "Better?" he asked, but did nothing to disguise the snark in his voice as we were drenched in darkness.

Michael huffed and headed toward the stairs, where a fan of light bled from the tunnel, creating long shadows on the steel. "You need to tread lightly for a while, boy," he said. He climbed down the stairs and a moment later, the pure black of a moonless night encompassed the garage.

"He is such a dick," Damian muttered.

I stood still, blinking and trying to get my bearings. I didn't know how many paces away from the hole I was and I couldn't make out a thing. Normally, I would give Damian grief for his slight, but the total absence of light left me blind and uneasy.

The distinct tick of a ratchet wrench filled the thick air.

"Um, Damian, you think you can give me a hand so I don't fall down the stairs and break my neck?"

"Oh, sorry." The clink of metal on metal informed me he put down the wrench. He was almost soundless as he approached, and I jumped when his hand clasped around my upper arm.

"I keep forgetting you don't have the benefit of vampire vision anymore." He led me down the stairs and through the dirt entry to the concrete pipes. "Do you have your phone with you?"

"Yes," I said, and his hand released my arm. I dug in my pocket and pulled the phone out, engaging it and illuminating the small space. "Thank you," I added and stood on my tiptoes to give him a peck on his cheek.

He stepped back in a flinch before my lips even touched his flesh and his eyes flashed in a wince. I lowered my heels, stunned at both his conditioned response and the pain that flared in my chest. The reality of our situation hit home yet again, leaving me hollow.

Tigress
Chapter Twenty-Six
Naomi

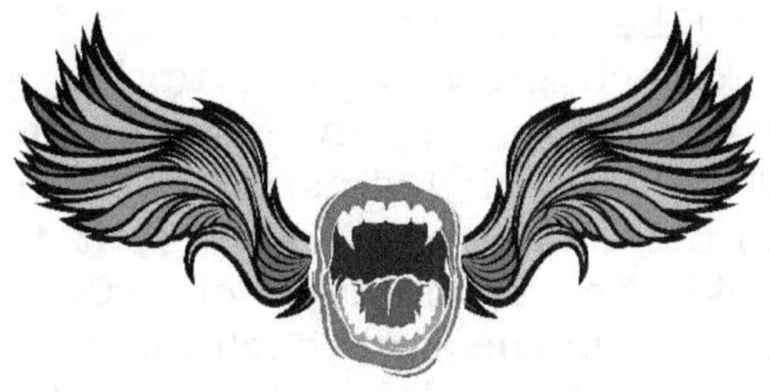

EXHAUSTION TOOK CONTROL OF my muscles, and I made it to the bedroom upstairs, stripping down to my underwear before climbing into bed. It was already half-past three and my eyelids wouldn't stay open. For the first time since we met, we didn't spend the night together.

Brightness and warmth woke me from a sound sleep and I gasped, my heart thundering in my chest as I pressed my back against the headboard. Sunshine painted the end of the bed and it took me a few breaths to remember the sun wouldn't turn me to dust.

When that realization settled into my skin and my heartbeat returned to normal, I actually chuckled. I don't remember dreaming, but the covers were crumpled and twisted like I had been fighting with the fabric.

I glanced at the clock, and my eyebrows rose. It was a little after one in the afternoon and the house was silent. A bout of melancholy hit and I ran my fingers over the pillow next to me. The one that Damian should have occupied if it weren't for the damn sun.

My stomach growled, interrupting my little pity party, and I swung my feet over the side of the bed. Instead of addressing my stomach, I cleaned up first. The prior evening left me feeling like my skin had a hefty layer of dirt and sweat. The hot water in the shower felt like heaven and I scrubbed my body clean and donned a pair of sweats and a torn t-shirt that Damian was partial to, and headed to the kitchen to find something to quell the stomach pangs.

Once my appetite was satiated, I headed down to Damian's lair, finding it dark and empty, and a moment of icy panic bit at my skin before I took a deep breath, calming my nerves. I headed down the tunnel and the sounds of hammering calmed any remnants of worry.

Light filtered from where he was working, making the need for the cell phone light obsolete, and I followed the path easily. I stopped and leaned against the concrete and watched the sweat trickle down Damian's back as he hammered nails into a fancy trellis designed to keep the pathway from collapsing. The muscles in his back rippled, and I smiled.

The hammer stopped halfway from hitting the nail, and Damian shot a glance back at me. Dimples lining his cheek gave away his lighthearted mood and I'm sure my carnal thoughts fueled his playful grin.

"It's about time you got your lazy ass out of bed."

"Give me a break. I'm just getting used to being human again."

"Well, if being human means sleeping for days at a time, then I'll pass," he mumbled and returned to the task he started. As soon as he set the nail, he stepped back next to me and scanned his work. With a satisfied nod, he said, "That ought to do it."

He gathered up the scraps on the floor and dumped them into a wheelbarrow. The hammer, nails, and spotlights followed. With a light leading the way, he strolled toward the underground apartment.

"How far did you get with the cars?"

Without missing a step, he reached into his back pocket and handed me a folded piece of paper. "I need a couple of batteries before I can do any further assessment of the cars. They'll all need one eventually, along with tires, but if you could have someone pick up the things on the list for starters, I should have at least a couple of vehicles working by the end of the night."

"Really?"

"I put the batteries in the basement so you could trade them up for new ones. If you go to Napa, they'll give you a credit on the new purchase for these."

The fact that Damian even thought about discounts made me want to laugh, especially with his accumulation of wealth. His job provided what he called petty cash, but most people would consider his six-figure income a damn good living.

"What?" he asked as I mulled over this contradiction.

"Nothing. I'll give Ted the list once he gets home. I think he's at work."

"I need a shower," Damian said as we rolled the barrow through the living area. He parked it at the entrance and glanced at me. "Do you mind parking this by the hatch and I'll get it up to the garage after sunset?"

"Sure," I said and started out the door.

"Can you grab my bag too?" he called as he headed back toward the hallway.

"Sure," I called and deposited the wheelbarrow where he asked before heading upstairs to retrieve his duffel bag. I left the list on the kitchen table before trotting back downstairs.

When I stepped into the bedroom downstairs, I wondered why they bothered building the bedroom upstairs. The only distinction between the two rooms was the room upstairs actually had windows that allowed the sun to light the room. Down here, the decor was similar to upstairs, but the mural on the back wall was as breathtaking as the beach scene in the living room. Here it showcased a large picture window that looked out over a spring meadow with the bright sunshine painting the array of colorful wildflowers. The rest of the walls were a mix of white and brown and black with green speckled in and, after a couple of blinks, I realized it was a forest of birch trees. The ceiling was a canopy of leaves with a bright blue sky filtering through.

Valerie and Michael had amazing painting skills. I dropped Damian's duffel bag on the small ottoman and headed toward the bathroom, curious about what type of decor that held. A tropical underwater world met me when I pushed open the door and my gaze landed on Damian, wrapping a towel around his waist. His gaze scanned the walls and landed on me.

"Amazing, isn't it?" he asked and ran his hand through his wet hair, hand combing it into less of a disheveled mess.

"Yes." I know he meant the artwork, but his sculpted form always left me speechless.

"The walls," he answered my less than subtle inspection.

"I know what you were referring to. This should be in highlighted in Architectural Digest."

"Have you looked at the details? This must have taken years to do." He ran his fingers over the school of rainbow fish, and their scales shimmered against the trail of light.

"The bedroom is just as incredible."

"If I had taken the time to look at this last night, I never would have made it to the garage," he said and passed by me.

I took a few minutes to inspect the artwork and I couldn't find a flaw in anything, from the coral reef to the seahorses to the array of fish. Even the sinks and shower were in the aquamarine motifs. Valerie must have missed her calling. Interior design came naturally to her based on the designs throughout the house.

"Valerie has quite a bit of talent," I said when I stepped into the bedroom.

Damian laughed. "Valerie didn't do this." He waved at the room. "It might have been her idea, but her talent ends with drawing stick figures."

"Then her uncle?"

His eyebrows rose, and he shook his head.

"No way," I whispered and scanned the art. "I just assumed..."

"I know. It may have been her idea, but Michael painted these scenes just for us." Damian's smile faded and he sighed. "As amazing as it is, it just makes me miss the sunshine even more." He finished buttoning his shirt and walked to the light switches near the door. "Want to see something cool?"

I nodded.

He flipped the master switch off, dropping the room into darkness. Little by little my eyes adjusted and then I realized light was filtering in the window like it would right after sunrise. It brightened to that of mid-day and then faded like a sunset and I turned to him. The longing in his face forced a lump into my throat.

When his gaze dropped from the window just before the last of the light faded, I saw the mist of unshed tears shimmering over his bright blue eyes. I never knew just how much he ached for the sun and my feet shuffled across the floor, finding the fabric of his shirt after a few paces. I wrapped my arms around his waist and tucked my head against the breast of his shirt, careful to not to connect with his skin.

His arms wrapped around me, and we stood still, embracing in the dark.

Tigress
Chapter Twenty-Seven
Damian

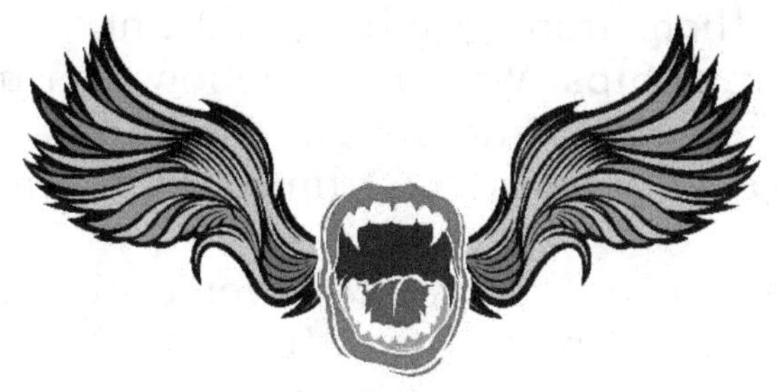

I SQUEEZED HER TIGHTER, blinking the god damn tears from my eyes. When I flipped the lights off earlier and the wall did its passing daylight trick, a rock formed in my throat that the shower did little to erase. It's not like I haven't seen some beautiful scenes on the web, but having the light surrounding me like the living room and the bedroom left me wanting the sunshine as much as I wanted Naomi.

I pushed her away and flipped the overhead lights on. Her dark gaze met mine, and I tried on a smile to appease the worry lines creasing her forehead. They smoothed, and she sent a smile back.

"So, the crew is out?"

"It appears that way. I wish I could just go out. Michael asked me to chill for a while too, just to make sure Lucifer's henchmen weren't in the vicinity."

"As annoying as it is, he's right." I couldn't see any way around it. If we suddenly appeared here, and Lucifer got wind of it, he'd send his entire army to gather us. And even though the property was monster-proofed, that wouldn't prevent them from grabbing Ted and Valerie as bargaining chips. We had to lie low and until we were sure Lucifer had bought the bait.

"Have you heard anything from him?" she asked.

I shook my head. "I haven't checked my emails today. I have a few things to do for work, but I figured none of it was critical yet. So I fixed up the tunnel." I headed into the living room and crossed to the desk, flipping open the new computer to see what it offered. My backpack sat to the side of the desk, just in case this one didn't have everything I needed.

The internet connection was already set up, so I ventured into my email, pushing the sense of dread away as the screen loaded. My jaw clenched at the sight of another email from the same source, and I raised my gaze to Naomi.

"You know he's going to kill me if he gets a hold of us," I said. "But I'm going to make damn sure I get a few licks in before he does."

Her face paled, and her lips pressed together in the telltale sign of apprehension. I know she hated when I talked like this, but she had to know. His tracking us down was inevitable. It might take years, but the time would come when we'd both have to face the music.

"You can't think like that, Damian," she said, and I laughed.

"He's on the hunt, baby. And Lilith was right. When you choose to dance with the devil, the song eventually ends."

She rolled her eyes at my analogy. "We can beat him."

I loved her with my entire being, but even after everything we've encountered, her naivety still amused me.

"The tiger could beat him, but that's lost to us now." I said, finally admitting something I've kept inside for five years. If we had another five or ten minutes in that warehouse before the sun rose, she would have ripped him to shreds.

"You can beat him," she said with all the confidence I lacked.

"No, I can't. I couldn't even take down Michael."

"You weren't in shadow form," she countered, and her hands found her waist. I hated her argumentative stance. It completely undermined my train of thought because when she stood like that, her perky breasts strained against the fabric of her shirt and the dare in her eyes always fanned a heat deep inside me.

It was completely unfair how this woman could derail me. From the moment we met, she could melt and infuriate me at the same time. I was sure if I had a thousand years with her, it would be the same. Naomi made me feel alive and significant. Not just some beast trained to be a watchdog.

Before I opened the email or said anything derogatory to Naomi, I decided to staunch my hunger. I stalked across the room and opened the refrigerator, taking the blood bag. Instead of opening the top and pouring it into a glass, I opted to tear the corner with my teeth and gulp it down like it was a severed arterial spray instead of a civilized drink.

The need to hunt ate at my bones and I closed my eyes, letting the cold human blood quench my nerves and cool the burning pit in my stomach. When the bag was empty, I tucked it into the garbage under the sink and turned back to Naomi and the computer beyond her.

With the blood spreading a warm chill through my body, I crossed to the computer and opened the email. My legs turned to jelly, and I sat down in the chair.

"What's wrong?"

I guess my face registered the shock at Lucifer's words and I could almost hear him chuckling. "He didn't buy my attempt to snow him," I said. "Someone saw the lights in the garage last night. The good news is he hasn't connected us to the house yet. He thinks we're in the garage and he knows I'll eventually have to come out." I chuckled at the last question, raising my gaze to hers. "He'd like to know how I got in."

I pulled out my computer because I knew it had mechanisms that rendered it untraceable and opened the email. I pressed the reply button and typed, *'Isn't it amazing what fingerprints can do?'* and sent the email. I smiled at my wit, wondering if my question would stump him or not.

"Did you just confirm where we are?"

I met her gaze. "I confirmed where he thinks we are."

"Do you have a fucking death wish?" Naomi snapped and stomped out of the room. I tried to catch up to her, but she was up the stairs and into the belly of the house before I could stop her. I found myself halfway up the basement stairs before my internal alarms sounded.

"That's not fair!" I yelled at the cracked door and made my way back to the underground sanctuary. She didn't understand how long this game with Lucifer had been going on or how tired I was of always being at the shit end of the stick.

I sat down behind my computer and brought up the reply prompt again and typed another message. *You know where I am, but are you so sure that drop off in Buffalo didn't contain a very special package of mine? Did you check all the northbound traffic?*

I sat back and smiled. Punching the send button gave me a moment of pure satisfaction. Lucifer would spend the next several days hunting down all the rental agencies and ticket counters in Buffalo, looking for Naomi. When he finally came to the realization I led him on a wild goose chase, I had better buckle down for a long quiet stay underground.

Tigress
Chapter Twenty-Eight
Damian

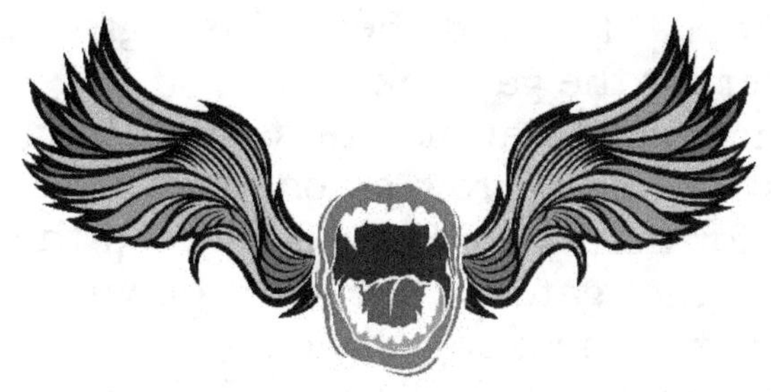

THE SUN SET WHILE I tinkered with the new computer, building it out with everything I needed for both the day job and the URL bounce I built for the laptop we've had for years. A yawn caught me off guard and I stretched, arching my back in the chair to get the stiffness out of the muscles. A glance at my watch told me it was safe to proceed upstairs and find Naomi.

I stepped into the family room, finding Michael and Valerie engaged in a game of chess and Ted in the kitchen whipping up food.

"Where's Naomi?"

All three of them looked at me like I should know and my skin flushed hot. I turned toward the bedrooms and skidded into the empty room. The bathroom was empty, too.

"God damn it," I muttered and inspected her clothing. Her jogging shoes, along with the parka

I bought her, were gone, and I spun around, stalking to the living room.

"She went out jogging," I said, and the shocked silence filled the room. Then everyone scrambled at once and I put out my hands to stop them. "I'll find her. Just give me the controller for the gate, okay?"

Michael glared at me but said nothing.

"Just let me borrow a coat and a hat and I'll go look for her," I said. "And I'll need the remote to open the gate." I headed downstairs and grabbed my sneakers, slipping them on before returning to the living room. Ted handed me a coat and a hat and then he offered another item that made my eyebrows rise. A nine-millimeter.

I met his gaze.

"Platinum rounds just in case," he said.

"If a vampire bites her, they're doomed." Both Valerie and Ted registered slack jaws. "I'm not the only one that's allergic to her." I offered a smile, but I took the gun, anyway. A bullet would do just as much damage to a demon, regardless of the metal components.

I made sure the safety was on and slid it into the inside pocket of Ted's jacket. He handed me a Red Sox cap, and I tucked my black curls under the hat before looking at the group. "A remote?" I asked and put my hand out.

Valerie crossed to the kitchen and pulled a small key ring from the pegs, tossing it to me. I slid it into my pocket and headed out the front door. Walking down the driveway with my attention focused on the asphalt, I sniffed the air, letting my sense of smell dictate the direction Naomi had headed.

DAMIAN

I stepped through the open gate and pressed the remote, securing the property behind me. Turning left, toward the path that headed into the woods, I adopted the slow gait of a jogger warming up. The urge to take flight and soar over the area took hold, and I squashed it. That would give away our tie to the house. Instead, I forced myself to maintain the slow, casual pace.

My heart thundered with each step and after I had traveled a little over a mile, the scent on the air thickened, mixing her natural musk with an undertone of fear. It drove my feet faster and when I turned the blind bend in the road; I saw her. She stood between two men, her hands clenched in fists and her stance defensive.

I stopped and inhaled, assessing her attackers. They were more than mere mortals, and anger bloomed under my skin. Demons toyed with her, circling and laughing at the weak human girl. I caught a hint of wariness in their stance, like she had already delivered a couple of blows, and they treated her with caution.

All upper level brain functions ceased and the animal in my heart took over. I growled as I darted toward the closest demon, but he turned, prepared, like this had been a setup all along. I dodged the glinting blade, ignoring Naomi's cry of caution.

I should have listened to what she said because pain bloomed in my temple. The bastard had a knife in one hand and a hammer in the other. I stumbled from the blow, but was able to react quickly enough to deflect the knife from my chest. It cut through the layers of the coat and seared my arm.

A chain wrapped around my neck, burning my skin as the second demon pulled me against his chest, holding me in place as the one I attacked stepped closer. My gaze flicked from the knife to Naomi and both fear and wild fury filled her features.

She launched at the demon, screaming like a banshee, but something happened halfway through the leap. The demon was so intent on running me through with the knife that he ignored Naomi's war cry. When the white tiger hit him, it knocked him on his side and the hammer shot from his hand, but he still had the knife.

A shot of adrenaline ran through me and I yanked the chain forward, bringing the demon's hand into view. With no hesitation, I sank my fangs into the meat of his thumb and he yelped, dropping the chain, and I used the surprise to flip him over my head and onto the ground with my teeth still embedded in his hand. As much as I hated demon blood, I still drew a mouthful in and swallowed before I released. Instead of going in for a more lethal bite, I drew the gun and flipped off the safety, planting a bullet into the bastard's brain.

The shot stunned both Naomi and the second demon enough so I had a second to train the gun on the demon, but he rolled away, putting Naomi in the way. His attempt to swipe the knife across her abdomen missed doing the damage he'd hoped, but it broke through the skin under her fur and the smell of her sweet blood filled the air. She didn't yelp, instead; she roared and her teeth caught his wrist, snapping it. The knife tumbled away, and he punched Naomi with his free hand. She snarled and yanked at the wrist her teeth were embedded in.

I still didn't have a clear shot and the demon's punches were connecting with her torso hard enough for me to hear the bone on bone connections.

"Naomi, off!" I yelled, praying she would listen and for once, my prayers were answered. She moved to the right, and the demon lunged to the left, reaching for the knife. He never made it. The bullet shattered the back of his skull, exploding out the front of his face, leaving him unrecognizable.

I flipped the safety on the gun and turned toward Naomi. She lay on her back in human form with her hands clutching her stomach. A trickle of blood flowed through her fingers, igniting my hunger and the fear in my soul. I tucked the gun inside the pocket and ran toward her, transitioning and wrapping my talons around her. I took flight, ignoring the burn of her blood against my talons.

As the crow flies, I had less than a mile back to the house and I made it to the backyard within minutes, setting her down on the frozen ground before transitioning back into human form. I scooped her up, carrying her to the door, kicking it and waiting for someone to open it up.

Valerie opened the door, shuffling us both inside. I placed Naomi on the couch and stepped back, letting Valerie take over, inspecting her wounds.

"What happened?" Michael asked as he took the space next to me.

I looked down at my blistered hands before returning my gaze to Naomi. "She was attacked by a couple of demons," I said, and shifted. "I got there just in time."

"If you hadn't..." she started and winced as Valerie swabbed the cut on her abdomen.

"Well, if you hadn't been dumb enough to go jogging alone, they wouldn't have known you were here," I snapped before she could continue. "The only thing I confirmed was that I was in the garage. Not you. Do you really think I'm that much of an idiot?

Her lips pursed, and my fists clenched in response, despite the pain.

"Val, are you going to be able to get any more blood this week?" I asked.

She shook her head without looking my way, and I inhaled. I'd have to hunt to heal my wounds, and I turned away from them. I stripped the coat and the hat, tossing it on a kitchen chair before heading toward the back door.

"Where do you think you're going?"

"Hunting. I'm ravenous."

Tigress
Chapter Twenty-Nine
Damian

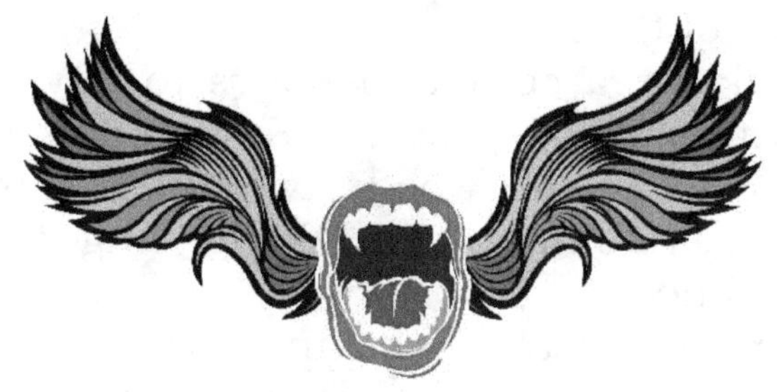

THE DOOR SLAMMED AND I took flight before anyone could stop me. I wanted to hunt for human blood, but I knew better. Right now, I needed to lie low and even taking flight was risky, but the distance to the meadow was far enough to drive me to the air.

I was rewarded with a herd of deer, and I didn't hesitate. Swooping down, I plucked one from the midst before the others knew what happened and turned back into the woods. I landed far enough away not to spook the herd, and before the animal got its bearings, I sank my teeth into his throat, relishing the hot pulse of blood.

Hunger still sang in my veins and I took flight, repeating the ritual until I had half a dozen carcasses at my feet and the blisters on my hands were healed. I wiped my face and turned back toward the house, opting to walk instead of fly. I needed the time to plot out our next move and as much as I didn't want to leave, that was probably the best for all of us.

Lucifer would assume Naomi went where I did, and I could draw his attention away from the three of them.

It took me a couple of hours to navigate the thick winter woods, even without snow cover. I stepped out of the woods twenty feet from the fence line. Naomi stood with her fingers looped into the fence.

"We need to leave," she announced.

"I need to leave," I corrected after I covered half the distance.

Her face transitioned to that hard stubborn stare I knew too well, and I knew if I went inside the fence to our underground escape, I wouldn't get out of there without her. Movement behind her caught my attention, and I met Michael's worried gaze.

I offered him a half-hearted shrug and took a step backwards.

"This is the way it has to be," I whispered. "My presence is lethal. I can't bring that down on everyone." Another step back and the panic formed in her eyes. She had no idea how much strength it took not to give in to her. An invisible hand reached into my chest and squeezed my heart to the point tears sprung from my eyes.

"Don't you dare leave me," she begged, but my mind was made up the moment I rounded the corner and saw the demons playing with her like they were poking sticks at a caged animal.

I took another few paces backwards, sensing the edge of the woods within a couple of feet now. "I have to."

"Bull shit!" she screamed.

"I love you, baby," I said and went to turn. A sharp pain shot through my leg and I stumbled, not understanding what had just happened. My gaze snapped to my thigh. To the blade sticking out of my flesh. Hands grabbed me, but I fought. Unfortunately, I wasn't hungry enough to override the platinum and change into my shadow form, but I was able to slip from their grasp and I bolted toward the fence.

I had no idea what the plan was as I limped forward. Scaling the fence wouldn't work, but I might be able to jump it if I got enough speed. Naomi was going bat-shit on the other side of the platinum barrier, but Michael held onto her, keeping her from climbing out.

I only got a few steps before a crack filled my head and then nothing.

Tigress
Chapter Thirty
Naomi

"DAMIAN!" I SCREAMED AND laced my fingers into the fence. I could scale this in a matter of seconds and I got my foothold when Michael's arms grabbed me around the waist.

"You can't help him right now," he said, but I struggled.

I refused to let him pull me away, to stop me from trying to save my husband; but it was futile. Michael's grip was as strong as iron, and the clan that blindsided Damian dragged him into the woods and out of my line of sight.

I let out a wail of distress that sounded more like the cry of a child than a grown woman and released the fence, collapsing in Michael's grip. Numbness settled over me, right down to the core. Damian was now in Lucifer's hands, and there wasn't a thing I could do to save him this time.

Michael carried me back to the house, but I didn't care. The man I loved was as good as dead. Despair crept in over the numbness, cramping my muscles and forcing sobs from my throat. Nothing on earth could take this pain away.

"Naomi," Valerie whispered, and I turned my face into my hands, unwilling to acknowledge anyone. I just wanted Damian back. As hard as the last few days of not touching were on us, we were still together. I understood how crippling it was to lose your soul mate.

Was this what Damian endured when Athena was slain in front of him?

God, how did he survive all those years with this emptiness as big as a fathomless gorge?

The questions circled through my brain, drowning out the people in the room and I curled tighter in a ball, trying to escape from this pain.

Damian's stupid email today probably set the vultures in motion.

I sat up like I had suddenly been reanimated and before anyone could ask what was going on in my head; I bolted downstairs. They followed, like a posse of body guards protecting me from falling to a million pieces.

"What are you doing?" Michael asked when I propped open Damian's laptop.

"Nothing. I'll be up in a few minutes." I didn't want Michael to know what I was doing. I didn't want to argue or explain myself. I just wanted to find out what Damian said to Lucifer.

When no one moved, I looked up. "I will not do anything stupid. I just want to find out where Lucifer's emails came from."

They still didn't move.

"I promise I will not engage him or do anything foolish." I focused on Ted. "Whatever you're cooking smells wonderful. I'd love to have some when I'm through here," I added for good measure. Valerie and Ted nodded and traded a glance before heading upstairs.

Michael's lips pressed together and his gaze bounced between the computer and me like there was something on the computer I shouldn't see. He crossed his arms and waited.

"I promise I'll be fine," I said, and he met my gaze. "All I'm going to do is open the last email and run a trace."

Whether or not he realized it, relief softened his features. "Fine, but if you're not back upstairs in five minutes, I'm coming to get you."

I rolled my eyes. "Tracers take a little longer than five minutes." Besides, five minutes wasn't enough time for me to look through the other emails from the same address. Michael sparked my interest, whether he wanted to or not.

"Ten minutes," he said and pointed at me.

"Fifteen would probably be better," I said, and he crossed his arms again. "I have to analyze the ping," I added, even though I had no clue how someone traced email. Michael didn't know that, and he nodded.

"I'll check in fifteen," he agreed and headed upstairs, leaving me with a bogus task.

I opened up Damian's email account and stared at the latest message. It was unopened and the subject line sent ice through my blood.

"If you want to see him alive…"

Instead of opening the email, I sorted on the sender and filtered through the messages to the one that set Damian off in the cave. Each message was short and chilling, but one outlined Lucifer's twisted plans for me, including a demon fuck-fest, just for Damian's benefit. The nauseatingly detailed scenario ended with Lucifer ripping my heart from my chest and draining it at sunrise. Long enough for Damian to feel the loss just before the sun cooked him into oblivion.

I closed my eyes and took a deep breath. The outlined scenario gave me a glimmer of hope. Lucifer didn't know that I could produce a trinity, and it also didn't indicate that he knew what Damian was, either. I could work with that.

I glanced at my watch and exhaled. I had five more minutes, and I opened the latest email.

The directive along with the address set me in motion. I snapped the laptop closed and bolted down the hall toward the garage. It was time to plan a full out rescue mission, starting with a hijacking.

Tigress
Chapter Thirty-One
Naomi

I RUMMAGED AROUND IN the dark of the garage, looking for the fucking control panel and getting more frustrated by the minute. Lucifer gave me twenty-four hours to make a decision. If I didn't show up at the address, he specified within twenty-four hours, Damian would suffer a great deal before the following sunrise, and Lucifer would send me Damian's ashes.

And then he'd come after me and everyone living in the house. He knew it was vampire-proof and angel-proof and suspected it was probably demon-proof, but he promised we didn't account for the things he'd send and there was no known defense against them.

I shivered at the thought of what type of a mutant monster that would be.

Shuffling behind me caught my attention, and I stiffened.

"Where the hell do you think you're going?" Michael's voice penetrated the darkness.

"I'm going after him," I said, just as my fingertips found the box I was looking for. I turned on my phone and punched in the familiar numbers. When the hand pad lit up, I put my palm to the glass and held my breath.

I'd never felt as alive as I did the moment the scanner finished and the lights flooded the garage. Platinum plates shifted, disappeared into the flooring with one exception. A panel as wide as the underground tunnel slid to the ceiling and clasped into place.

I turned and scanned the vehicles. Not one was in working condition and my heart sank. Michael hadn't said a word, but his scan of the collection revealed an appreciation in his eyes and he sighed when he brought his gaze back to me.

"I need help to get one of these vehicles back in shape. Did Ted pick up what Damian asked?" I shot the question at Michael and I received a blank stare.

"Damian's list that was on the table." Even I could hear the near hysterical note in my voice.

When he didn't answer, I huffed and climbed back down the stairs. Nothing was going to stop me from getting to Damian. Not now that I had a location and if I couldn't get us free, at least we'd die together, but I'd make sure it was on our terms and not what Lucifer's sick fantasy dictated.

As I navigated the dark tunnels, I couldn't help but shrink away from imagined creatures in every shadow. The itchy, uncomfortable sensation of spiders crawling on my skin overcame me and I shuddered, picking up the pace. When I stepped into the brightly lit hallway, I sighed with relief, rubbing my arms and then the back of my neck.

I glanced over my shoulder and met Michael's gaze.

"You have no idea how much the paintings down here meant to Damian," I said. "Especially the path of sunshine in the bedroom." I didn't wait for a response, instead I headed right to the kitchen where Ted and Valerie sat eating meatloaf with potatoes and carrots. I glanced at my plate. My stomach growled, and I cursed the needs of my human body.

Instead of following through on my questions, I sat down at the table as a sign of respect. "Thank you," I said.

"You're welcome," Ted said and offered me the bottle of ketchup.

Even with my pulse ticking off the wasted seconds, I ate without much conversation. After taking the last bite, I set my silverware down and wiped my lips.

"Did you pick up the things on the list I left on the table?"

"Not yet, but..." He glanced at his watch. "I might be able to make it to the auto store in Torrington before it closes."

A wave of relief hit.

"I will clean up the kitchen if you pick up what he has listed for the Aston Martin." That was by far the fastest car in the garage, and I know it was one of the top ones on Damian's list. He wiped his hands and pulled out the sheet, scanning the list before he nodded.

"Is it safe out there?" Ted asked, but he looked beyond me to Michael.

"Yes," I said, not knowing if Lucifer was bluffing or not, but he was explicit with his directions and while he promised Damian would suffer, he also promised that he would leave the occupants of the adjoining property alone for the duration of the twenty-four hours.

I didn't want to take either of their vehicles. It was bad enough they were targets, but Lucifer didn't know Valerie lived here. He knew about Uncle Ted and the inheritance of the land from Valerie's deceased family. He assumed he was alone and if I showed up with one of their cars, their identity could be compromised.

"You're going after Damian?" Valerie asked after her uncle left.

"Yeah, assuming I can get the car started."

"I could understand why you would do that before, especially with the tiger thing, but now you're just human. You're no match for demons."

I leveled a sarcastic smile in her direction, remembering some conversations I had with my grandfather over the years. All his warnings about the darkness in the world, stories about demons and bloodsuckers and the pending war. And most of all, his description of the savior, the one who makes the darkness flee.

A tiger born of pure blood.

A trinity.

I had no idea those stories were reality until Mark sold me to Lucifer. All my assumptions about vampires were based on those stories, and Damian certainly hadn't fit any of the cold-dead-blood-thirsty fiends my grandfather described, but then again, he was born of a pure bloodline too.

"I seem to still turn into the tiger," I said, and both Valerie and Michael froze in place, staring at me like I sprouted another head.

"What?" their voices rang in unison.

"When they were attacking Damian," I started and ran my hand over my stomach. The skin was still sensitive where the knife had torn flesh. "I guess I got angry and attacked, and my fur protected me from the knife." I offered a shrug and collected the dinner plates, heading into the kitchen to let them digest both their food and that little nugget of information.

IT TOOK THE FOUR of us the better part of the night to get the Aston Martin to turn over and even then the engine sounded sluggish and unreliable. I just needed it to last an hour on the road at best. I wasn't going as far as New York this time. I was going south to Candlewood Lake in New Fairfield, and I was going alone.

I leaned my head on the steering wheel and turned the engine off, my eyes closed from the weight of exhaustion wracking my body. I was in no condition for a stand-off.

"Maybe you should get a little sleep before you try to save the world," Valerie said as she leaned on the open window. She looked as tired as I felt and guilt bit at my skin when I glanced up at the light filtering into the windows.

"Do you have to go to school now?"

She glanced at her watch and gave me a pressed-lip smile.

"Jesus, I'm sorry for keeping you up all night," I said and covered her hand with mine.

She sandwiched my hands between hers. "Stay safe, you hear?" Her voice choked on the words that we both knew were a prequel to goodbye.

I climbed out of the car and gave her a warm hug.

"I have to do this," I whispered in her ear, and she squeezed tighter.

"I know," she said and pulled away, wiping her tears away. She gave me a quick smile and made a beeline for the tunnel, leaving me with Michael and Ted.

"Well, I'm going to take a shower and head to work," Ted said, looking every bit as haggard as the rest of us.

"Thank you for your help," I said, feeling small and selfish.

"Just bring Damian back in one piece," he said, like there was no option of failure.

I nodded, and he followed the path Valerie took.

"You need to get some rest before we go after Damian," Michael said.

"Lucifer said I had to come alone," I said, but I let Michael help me from the car and lead me to the bedroom he'd painted for Damian and me. He didn't argue, but I knew he would not let me leave without him. To prove his point, the keys to the car slid into the front pocket of his jeans. He tucked me under the covers and stretched out on the recliner in the corner, crossing his arms.

Michael drifted off before I did and I considered sneaking the keys from his pocket, but before I could muster the energy, my body pulled me into a succession of brutal nightmares.

Tigress
Chapter Thirty-Two
Naomi

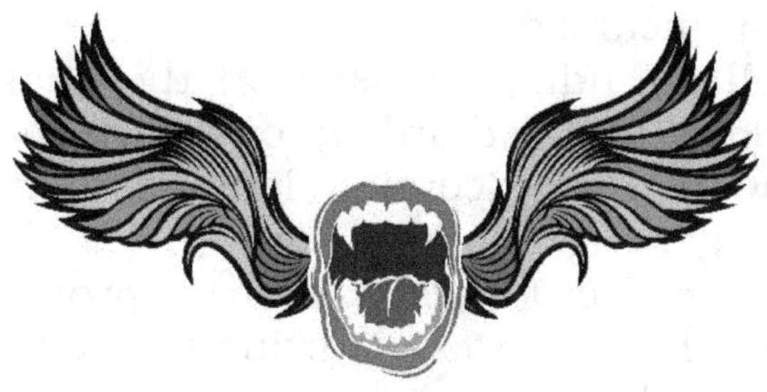

MY SCREAM SHATTERED THE darkness, but they just kept coming and coming, brutally taking me despite my screams while Lucifer laughed and Damian roared. Hands gripped my shoulders, holding me in place, and I broke free from the chains and swung.

"Naomi!" Michael's aggravated voice pierced my dream and my eyes snapped open to the dim light of the bedroom and Michael's firm grip on my wrist.

He stared at me for a moment. "You read the emails," he said when my breathing evened out and my heart beat no longer caused pain.

I dropped my gaze to the covers and then glanced at the clock. It took a moment to register, and then every muscle jumped into action.

"It's after ten at night?" I snarled at Michael, and he nodded.

My body needed relief, and I took two minutes to empty my bladder. I stormed back into the bedroom and pointed at the clock, my nerve endings screaming at me to get moving. "It's been over twenty-four hours. Do you know what that means?"

A dull pounding pressed on the back of my eye sockets and I didn't know if the headache was due to over-sleeping, lack of food or the raging anger wracking my body.

"Damian would want me to protect you," Michael said and stood, putting himself between me and the door.

"Damian will die at sunrise!" I screamed.

Michael's face pinched in pain and he pressed his lips together. His jaw muscles jumped and his eyes sprouted a glaze of tears.

"You don't think I know that?"

"You can save him," I said, grasping at straws. "We can save him, please..." hot tears choked my voice. "There has to be a way," I begged, and a light passed over Michael's irises, but he shook it away.

I wiped the tears from my face and stared him down. "No matter how dangerous or insane, there has to be something we can do," I said, forcing my voice not to shake. "I'd rather make the attempt, even if it means we both die, please."

He slowly shook his head.

Fury blasted through me, and I glared at him. "You can't keep me locked up forever," I growled. "And when I escape this jail, I'm going to let Lucifer do whatever the hell he wants to me. Even if that includes building an army."

The rash remark had the desired effect. Michael's face bloomed red with anger, and his hand shot out. I wasn't sure whether it was in retribution or for comfort, and I didn't wait to find out. I caught his wrist in powerful tiger jaws.

He was stronger than the demon and he tossed me across the room. I twisted and landed on four paws, my teeth bared in derision.

"Don't you ever threaten me with that," he snarled, pointing a shaking finger in my direction. "I don't give a damn how angry you are with me, dangling the end of the world as a method of blackmail is wrong."

"Letting Damian die is wrong," I said and stood on my human feet, the transition from fur to human flesh as quick as a blink. It calmed the raging beast in my blood, but I was still hell bent on saving Damian. "I know you knew how to save him. I saw it in your eyes, so give up the ghost."

He laughed and his hands found his hips as he studied me. When his laughter wound down, he inhaled and blew out a stream of air. Michael closed his eyes and recited an ancient verse. Light filled the room and wings fluttered as he transformed into his true celestial form.

I took an involuntary step backwards, and he cocked his head, silently questioning my actions.

"I'm not going to smite you." His sigh rustled the fabric covering the bed, and I wondered if Lucifer was as intimidating in angel form.

Michael's lips twitched into a smile. "I'm a pussycat compared to my brother."

"Well, that just makes me feel so much better." I couldn't stop the sarcasm. After all, it was my default defense mechanism and right now I had no idea whether Michael took the form to help me or to stop me.

"Sit," he ordered and pointed at the side of the bed.

My feet obeyed, and I crossed, taking a seat facing him.

"What came to mind is highly unorthodox and extremely dangerous," he started and crossed the room, taking my hands in his. "If we fail, the worst case is both Damian and I die and you fulfill the dark prophecy."

I shivered with revulsion and the flash of nightmares I had was nothing compared to the stark fear that drained the blood from my face.

"Another more likely scenario is we all die." He paused, keeping eye contact. "But if this works, there is a slim chance of saving Damian."

"What about you?"

His exhale told me more than I wanted to know.

"It's been a very long time since Lucifer and I stood face to face. It's apt to get very bloody for both of us. He was a formidable sparring partner before he was cast out of heaven and with so many years of resentment built up in him, I'm not sure I'll be in a condition to last for long, but I will do damage. Perhaps as much as you did." He smiled and placed his finger under my chin.

"What do you need me to do?" I asked and bit my lower lip, quelling the dread building in my stomach and tightening the muscles in my throat and chest.

"Get me into the house."

"What if I can't find the markings?"

His sad smile made me recoil. "That's not what I'm suggesting."

"Then how?" my mouth asked while my brain screamed to run, to shut up, to let all this go because whatever it was promised pain and anguish for all of us.

"Do you remember what I said to transform?"

I shook my head. "It sounded like Latin."

"Meque his exsolvite humanae gloriae caelestis exercitus ad vincula," he whispered and placed his hands on my head. The words echoed through my brain, forming a Braille pattern on my tongue as I spoke them over and over with him.

My cranium hurt when he released his hands, and he tilted my chin so our eyes met.

"I need to ride you into that house."

A vision of the tiger with Michael clinging to my back flashed before my eyes and Michael chuckled.

"No, I need to ride in your bloodstream."

"What?"

"And you can't transition to the tiger because you can't recite the incantation to bring my form into that room with you."

I stared at him, blinking and still not understanding how that was possible.

"You can't call me until the moment the sun hits the horizon."

Shock filtered through me like a jolt of electricity. "But if I wait until sunrise, how will that help, Damian?"

"He has to bite you and drink your blood before the sun rises."

"But that will kill him," I gasped and recoiled.

"This is where we have to have some blind faith. Yes, it could kill him like it did that vampire who attacked you at the rest station, but he's got angel blood in him, trinity blood at that because of your infusions into him, so I think there's a slight chance you could be his cure."

"If I'm not the cure, he will suffer and if I am the cure, he'll die of old age."

"If you aren't the cure, the sun will turn him to dust," Michael said. "It's a gamble, Naomi, but either way, his death will be on your terms, not Lucifer's. If by some miracle he doesn't die, you need to get him out of there. You'll have to release me first, otherwise this will be in vain."

I nodded slowly. A slim chance was still a chance, and I had to take it.

He drew in a deep breath. "One more thing. If my human form is rendered useless, all bets are off."

"What do you mean by useless?"

"If my human heart no longer beats, then I can't regain my celestial form. When you release me, I'll ascend into heaven."

"You mean you'll die?"

"Yes. If that happens and you can't escape, you know what you have to do."

I remembered the conversation in the car and nodded. "I have to die," I whispered.

When Michael nodded, I hung my head, preparing myself for battle.

I PULLED THE CAR over a half mile away from the end of Misty Brook Lane in New Fairfield and glanced at Michael before killing the engine.

"Now what?" I asked as we stepped out of the car.

"We need to find a place where you can hide me. I don't physically have to be in the house when you recite the incantation," he said, and I glanced at my watch and then the plumes of air escaping from my mouth and nodded, praying an unconscious human body wouldn't freeze over the course of an hour.

"I won't freeze. Just cover me with leaves and pine limbs and then head to the house," he said to my thought process.

We tromped through the woods toward the house and when we'd covered half the distance; he stopped in the center of a small thicket.

"This will do," he said and pulled a knife from his pocket along with two oversized Band-Aids. He handed the bandages to me and said, "Your left arm." I held it to him and he pushed the jacket up, revealing the soft flesh of my wrist. "This will not be pleasant for either of us. Just try not to make a sound."

I nodded and clenched both my teeth and lips together, bracing myself for the pain. He sliced my wrist and then his in quick succession. The pain was bearable. After all, I had had worse in my lifetime, but when he pressed his open wrist to mine, my breath sucked in and out of my lungs with the burn. It was more debilitating than the agony of the vampire virus. The air shimmered and then his wings disappeared and his eyes rolled up into his head. I caught his slack body at the same time his power merged with my cells, making me dizzy and nauseous.

I quickly put a bandage over his wrist and then mine. The flow of blood already slowed, as he had told me, the itch of healing taking hold. Before I covered him, I leaned my ear against his chest just to make sure. The steady thrum of his heart calmed my vertigo, and I took a deep breath, praying that this would work, otherwise it was the end of my world.

Tigress Chapter Thirty-Three Damian

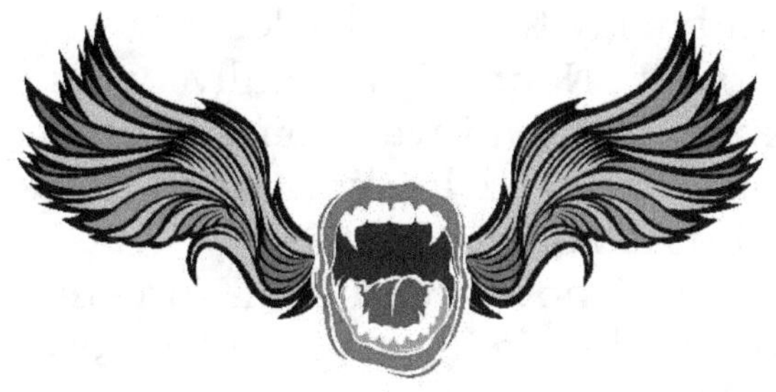

MY EYES BLINKED OPEN, and I glanced around at the darkness surrounding me. My shoulders ached. Hell, my entire body ached, and I shifted, rattling the chains holding me in place. The last thing I remember was running toward the house, praying I'd be able to hurdle over the fence, but with the platinum blade still embedded in my thigh, I highly doubted it. The moment I broke from their grip, something clocked me in the head and everything went black.

"You're awake," a husky female voice penetrated the dark, and it took me a minute to identify the voice.

"Eve?"

The light laugh confirmed it.

"Lucifer said you were the one who killed my Lilith," she said, and the feral snarl in her voice made me want to shrink into the wall, especially with the bonds that held me in place. I was helpless, and I wondered exactly how she would kill me.

I didn't answer right away and just let the silence settle over the room while I formed words that would delay the inevitable.

"She shot Naomi," I finally whispered. "I didn't know if Naomi was going to survive and I went a little nuts." I knew it wasn't much of an answer, but it was the truth.

When her hot breath fell on my face, I swallowed and looked into the black eyes I could just about make out. "So when I tear Naomi apart, we will be even," she said and grinned, revealing her jagged teeth.

I stared at the eyes an inch from my own. "You'd kill your own kin?" I said, playing the only card I had left and betting on the recoil.

The crazed smile faded, but she stayed close, her eyes narrowing to slits that mingled with the blackness.

"What do you mean?"

"Naomi is one of Zoe's bloodline," I said and her eyes widened before she moved back into the darkness. "I guess Lucifer left that little detail out, didn't he?"

No movement filled the space and then a wind drummed up and Eve slammed me against the wall, her hand squeezing my throat and only a feral snarl bled into the darkness.

"Did he forget to mention that she's not only a descendent of yours and Michael's, but she's also a descendent of Raphael's? She's capable of producing a trinity," I said and her hand squeezed tighter, her teeth moved closer to my throat.

"Don't lie to me," she growled.

"I'm not." I shook my head, trying not to let her see the sudden well of fear in my soul. If I died now, there was no hope for Naomi or this world. I wanted to live long enough to explain, but with the crazed madness in her eyes, I knew it was a slim chance.

"You turned her," she said, and I nodded under the suffocating grip.

"I didn't know. I didn't know my blood would turn her into a trinity," I croaked, and the grip on my throat lessened.

Confusion clouded her eyes and the grip on my throat stayed in place, but not restricting like before.

"I'm Gabriel's son," I whispered as softly as I could.

She dropped her grip and stepped back into the shadows. Feet shuffled back and forth in the dark, and then she stepped close again. A crease carved the skin between her eyes.

"I love Naomi, but I'm willing to make whatever sacrifice is necessary if it means Lucifer doesn't get a hold of her. If he does, he'll use her to build an army of his evil spawn," I said and gritted my teeth. "It will mean the end of times," I added, to bring my point home.

Her hand palmed my cheek, and she stared into my eyes.

"Did you hear what I said?" I asked.

"Gabriel?" she asked, and I rolled my eyes.

"Eve, focus," I said, and the inquisitive expression altered to annoyance.

"You're my…" she started and pressed her lips together.

"I'm Michael's nephew," I finished the sentence for her. "And the keeper of Zoe's bloodline," I added for good measure. "And until I met Naomi, I had done a pretty damn good job of it, but since then, things have gone to hell in a handbasket."

"You're lying," she said, but there was no conviction in her words.

I did something that took both of us by surprise. I turned my head, raising my chin so she had access to tear my throat to pieces. "Go ahead. I'm sure you'll know the instant you taste my blood."

Instead of biting my throat, she used her sharp nail to cut a slit in my chest and she leaned forward, sniffing first before she licked the slow flow of blood off my skin. She closed her eyes and groaned.

"You are delectable," she purred and her seductive tone gave me the chills. That tone was filled with raw hunger and I knew I should be scared, but I stood still and said a silent prayer. A foul-smelling cloth covered my mouth and nose and she leaned her head against the crook of my neck. "You taste like my son did," she said in a hushed whisper before the fumes rendered me unconscious.

Tigress
Chapter Thirty-Four
Damian

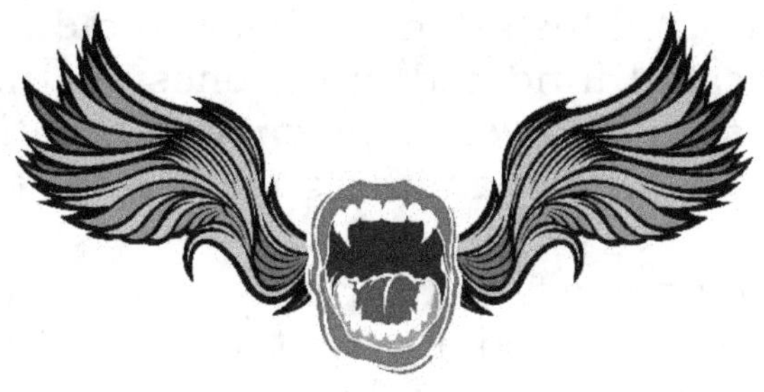

LIGHTS BLINDED ME AND I clamped my eyes closed against the bright fluorescents. An ominous chuckle filled the room, and I shivered despite the hot rush of fear in my blood. I squinted and a formidable shadow was cast across the spotlight and all I could muster was an, "Aw, fuck."

Lucifer.

Lucifer in angel form, not human form.

I was beyond fucked and my body quaked against my will, rattling the chains holding me in place. My gaze moved from him to Eve standing by his side, her arms crossed and a bitter smile filling her features.

"You fucking bitch," I growled.

"Did you know Damian is Gabriel's son?" Eve asked, and Lucifer's head snapped in her direction before focusing back on me.

"Gabriel's son," his voice rumbled through the room and he swatted Eve, sending her catapulting through the room. The crunch of bone filled the air as she smashed into the wall and crumpled, unconscious, to the ground. Lucifer turned his attention back to me.

My heart thundered in my chest at the spark of interest in his eyes as he crossed the distance. I clenched my jaw; anything I said now would be futile.

"Funny, your father never mentioned you," he said as he towered in front of me. "But then again, he was too busy begging for his wife and unborn child."

I blinked and actually took a step back, his words slapping me harder than a physical blow. "My...my parents died because of a...a volcano," I stuttered, hating that I stumbled over the words. My brain couldn't wrap around this new fact.

"Your father died in the blast, but your mother's death triggered the eruption. He was actually trying to kill me, but without his angel form, he was at a distinct disadvantage. He burned in the explosion that was intended to take me out." Lucifer had the audacity to chuckle.

I clamped my jaw against the curses posed on my tongue and mustered up a glare instead.

"I never thought to look for another child," he added just before his fist shot out, connecting with my cheek and sending me back against the restraints.

The dig of platinum tore at my shoulders, pulling an unwanted grunt from my chest. In angel form, Lucifer could deliver the kind of damage I couldn't walk away from, and the grinding throb of the smashed bone in my cheek was just the beginning. The burn of anger rushed through me, tempering the pain.

"You sadistic bastard," I whispered. "Why don't you let me out of these chains and we can see just how well you'd stand in a fair fight?"

He raised his eyebrow and snapped his fingers. The sudden release of burning tension made me stumble, but I caught myself. Lucifer stepped back and waved me in. My gaze jumped to the glint of on his fingers and shock snaked over my skin. His nails were as sharp as Naomis when she donned her tiger form, but it was the platinum sheen that made my throat constrict. I shifted and refocused, standing in ready form, swallowing the bloom of fear.

As we circled, I got a better look at my surroundings. This wasn't the dark dungeon I last awoke in. This was a living space with dark curtains blocking the outside world. The spotlight used to disorient me sat in a round alcove and to my right stood a bright entry way. My gaze lingered on that doorway and Lucifer's clucking pulled my attention back to him.

"Tsk, tsk," he said. "Before you make a run for it, I suggest you take a good look at that escape route."

I glanced back at the entry and what he was saying sank in.

Daylight.

My gaze snapped back to him and then the curtains beyond.

"Why the fuck are you toying with me?" I asked, my thoughts registering out loud in the barren room.

"You are my bait," he answered. "And now that I know who your father was, I understand my brother's need to protect you. As long as you're alive, he'll move heaven and earth to save your ass. I'm betting he'd even send that little minx into the lion's den because he thinks his secret is safe. He has no idea that I'm aware of her lineage. That she has the bloodline of not just one, but two angels." He grinned and continued circling, toying with both his words and his footwork. "I can't think of anything more delightful than building an army of dark trinities, can you?"

The mocking tilt of his eyebrow set a rash of rage through my bloodstream. His dirty insinuations were clear in the knowing smile passing over his lips.

"I hear she's a tigress in bed," he taunted.

A couple of weeks of not being able to touch my wife without blisters because of this lunatic sent me over the edge. Fury filled every fiber, and I launched at him, letting the anger drive me forward. But it wasn't enough to get the jump on Lucifer. He easily blocked my swing and delivered a bone-crunching punch to my ribs. My feet left the ground with the power of it and I landed on my knees, coughing up blood between the painful draws of breath.

I forced myself to my feet, still trying to pull in oxygen through sporadic wheezes. "You will not get the chance," I managed to say, but speaking took more effort than I realized and when he swung at me, my delayed reaction cost me a cracked eye-socket.

Pain flared in the left side of my face despite the rage wracking my form. I growled from my position on the floor and I stood, retreating into shadow form. This time my fist connected, and I was greeted with the sickening crack of bone. It took a moment to realize it was my hand and not his chest that broke.

The power of his next punch connected with my nose, sending me onto my back. I wasn't sure if my eyes were open or not, but the star pattern blinking on the black canvas gave me a hint of my current state. The last sensation that registered in my brain was pure agony.

Tigress
Chapter Thirty-Five
Damian

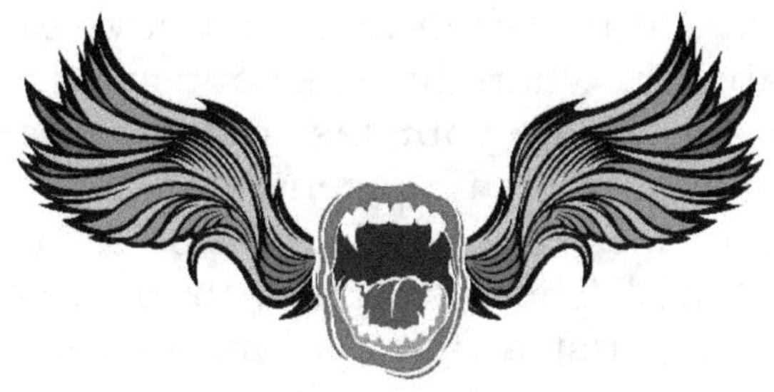

IGHTS DANCED ON WATER, and I pulled myself to my feet, shaking the cobwebs from my head. My face felt like I had put it through a meat grinder and I closed my eyes for a moment, assessing the rest of the damage. The platinum chains were back, but I couldn't feel the burn of it anymore, just the restraint.

My eyelids fluttered open, and I scanned the magnificent view. If I hadn't been on the edge of catatonic, I might have been able to appreciate the scenery. I scanned the night image and then the room.

Eve still lay crumpled where she had landed, and I suspected she might actually be dead.

A burning sensation crossed my chest, and I clamped my teeth together against the bellow of pain. Warm liquid scaled down my stomach, and I glanced down at the cuts across my chest before raising my gaze.

"Tic-tac-toe?" I rasped.

Lucifer stood with his back to me. His wings fluttered as he glanced over his shoulder. "I had to keep myself entertained," he smiled.

"Sadistic bastard," I whispered under my breath, and it occurred to me I'd have to expand my vocabulary where he was concerned.

"Tonight will be your last night on earth," he said, refocusing on the scenery in front of him. "The sunrise over Candlewood Lake is breathtaking." There was no humor or mocking in his voice, just a quiet calmness that left my skin numb and meant only one thing.

"Naomi," I whispered. The ache in my soul grew, and I slumped in the chains.

"She and my brother are planning a half-assed rescue mission," Lucifer said and swiped his finger across the space again.

The immediate burn made me gag, and I hitched my breath in. More warm liquid slid down to the edge of my jeans. This time it continued down, tickling through the fine hairs on my legs.

"If she doesn't get here soon, you may end up bleeding out before sunrise." This time he turned and stared me down, crossing the distance. "You may even miss the opportunity to witness our union."

This was the one weapon he had to crush me and he knew it. I was beyond physical pain, but the mental anguish of his intent grew through me as fast as the bloodstains on my jeans. I snarled and lunged, but the chains kept me in place. My teeth made a brief appearance, driven by both hunger and fury, but exhaustion won out and I slumped against the chains again. I didn't know when the last time I ate was and the smell of my blood made my mouth water.

"How long has it been since you've been able to taste her," he said, tapping his finger on his lips. "A couple of weeks? It is really too bad you couldn't suffer longer."

I pressed my lips together, refusing to play his game. If I had a chance, I'd rip her throat out so she wouldn't have to succumb to his diabolical plan.

He leaned closer. "I'm not talking about her blood, either," he said, and winked.

The moan on the floor pulled both our attention away. Distaste carved into his features and he brought his gaze back to me.

"I have no idea what my brother saw in her," he said, waving toward the semi-conscious vampire. "And I don't understand why Lilith chose her over me, either."

I snorted and glanced away. I could think of a million and one reasons, and one of them slipped from my lips before I could catch it. "Perhaps it's because you were a royal bastard even back then."

The stab in my side drew a wince, and I looked down. Four fingernails were embedded between the bones of my ribcage. He tilted his head and smiled as he yanked them from my flesh. Lucifer stared at the blood streaking his nails and slipped them one by one in his mouth, tasting and raising an eyebrow.

"She was right. You taste a little like her son."

I could see the wheels turning in his head and his gaze dropped to my chest. The image of him drinking blood from Athena's beating heart flashed in my memory just before his eyes flicked back to mine.

"You're lucky," he said and stepped back.

"Why am I lucky?"

He smiled, crossing to the spot in front of the window with his back to me.

My gaze scanned the sky, and I sighed at the ambient light signaling the imminent sunrise. The report of a gun snapped my head toward the entryway. Naomi's voice rang through the ruckus, spouting the foulest curses, and my heart shriveled.

Tigress
Chapter Thirty-Six
Naomi

I STOOD WITH MY back to the wall, forcing my breathing back to normal. The sprint across the open front yard left me exposed, but there was no sign that anyone saw me approach. Perhaps they believed a mere human no longer provided a threat to them or their diabolical plans. I smiled at the thought and glanced toward the woods, wondering if Michael's body would stay hidden until I could release him. I did my best to hide the body in the dense foliage surrounding the pristine house. Twenty-five acres of forest swallowed the white waterfront monstrosity, enough to provide the right amount of solitude needed for torturing Damian until the sun rose.

The angelic power pressed against my skin, and I closed my eyes, reining it in. I still had to be careful. If Lucifer got a whiff of what I had done, he would never let me near Damian, and all three of us would be as good as dead.

I checked the guns on my belt, making sure the safety was set on each pistol before I slid through the open window. I had a moment of déjà vu. My mind reeling back to the warehouse five years ago and I squatted, closing my eyes and getting my bearings. I wasn't sure where I was in relation to where Lucifer had Damian, but I'd bet my life that he was on the far side of the house. The back faced due east with a magnificent view of Candlewood Lake's western shoreline and the full force of the sunrise.

I slid the safety off each gun and scanned the small room. Another office, and I inhaled, blinking my eyes against the change in lighting. Shadows startled me and I had to keep a check on my reflexes. If I let a round go before I had the demons in sight, I'd be overwhelmed, and that would be the end of my little rebellion. God, how I wished for the clarity of my vampire eyes right now, and I bit back on the uncertainty flooding through my veins. I had Michael with me, along with all the knowledge of shooting that my father armed me with, never mind the silent stalk of the Mohegan tribe in my feet. My heritage was built for this, and I clung to that thought as I made my way through the open space of the office. The door wasn't closed, but cracked just enough for the sounds of torture to reach my ears.

I considered trying to transition, but I wasn't sure if I would be able to. I still don't know what triggered it, whether it was seeing Damian get blindsided by the second demon or if it was my overwhelming fury. Even in tiger form, I had a bear of a time with those lowly demons without the vampire strength, and Damian had been beyond frantic when he finally got a clean shot.

Michael said if I transitioned into the tiger and Lucifer got the upper hand, this rescue mission would fail. I needed my human cunning more than sharp claws, and the thirty-two bullets I had would eviscerate at least thirty-two demons. I just hoped like hell there weren't more than that; otherwise, this rescue mission would indeed be an epic failure.

The moment I slid into the hall, I knew something wasn't right. No demons were within sight, but the icy chill in the air told me they couldn't be far. I closed my eyes and tried to tap into my tiger psyche, to sense where the bastards were, but a frigid hand clamped down on my wrist before I had the chance and I knew I was just as doomed as Damian, even with Michael riding my bloodstream.

I got off three shots before my guns were stripped from my hands and none of the self defense moves Damian taught me over the last five years worked against the superhuman strength of the dozen demons now surrounding me.

Still, I fought, scratching and thrashing in their grasp until I was thrown to the floor in the middle of a semi-circular row of windows. I didn't dare move, or take my gaze off the formidable man standing with his back to me. Lucifer looked so much more deadly than he had before and when he sent a raised eyebrow over his shoulder at me, fear struck my breath in place.

He flicked his index finger to the side, and it took a moment for me to understand the sharp instrument fitted over his finger tip. A platinum blade formed a single deadly claw and when he flicked it to the side again, Damian's curses filled the room.

Five years had made Lucifer a much deadlier foe. Instead of relying on the personal touch or a loaded gun, or even his demon horde, he was using every ounce of his power to inflict pain without touching Damian, and his glare promised I was next.

Even Damian's pained cry didn't unlock my muscles. It wasn't until Lucifer fully turned that I found the strength to stand and adopt a glare, forcing my quaking muscles to still. No matter what happened, I couldn't act until the sun hit the horizon and even then, Michael wasn't sure it would be enough to save Damian.

Lucifer's features filled with fury and he swatted his hand to the side like he was flicking an annoying fly out of his way.

An invisible hand hit my cheek, rocking my head to the side and spinning me with the force of a power punch. In the time I took to sprawl on my hands and knees, the pain flared, locking the air in my lungs. I felt like a hot iron branded my cheek and when the burn abated; I raised my hand to the spot, wincing at my touch. When my vision cleared, I blinked at the image of Damian's bare feet.

My heart jumped into my throat at the odd streaks of color running down his jeans and the pool of deep crimson liquid at his feet. I forced my gaze up and a pain deeper than that branding my cheek shot through me at the full view of my broken husband. Deep, angry welts covered his torso and arms in patterns that set my blood boiling. The bastard played with him, carving crude tic-tac-toe games across his torso, drenching him in blood. The waistband of his jeans soaked the trails, turning the blue into a saturated purple that matched the patterns on his face where he had been beaten. Only his bright-blue eyes and the dark curls of his hair told me it was Damian suffering before me.

A wordless scream of fury erupted, and I stood, spinning in Lucifer's direction. The scream cut off along with the flow of air and my glare dropped from the sadistic smile on his face to his hand, curling like the invisible fingers crushing my windpipe. The tear of fabric accompanied the slow and deliberate progress of his clawed finger through the air.

Dark spots flared in front of my eyes, and I blinked at the sound of Damian's growling roar. The grip on my throat ceased, and I crumpled to the floor, wondering how the hell I was going to beat this asshat.

I looked down and understood Damian's growl. My clothing was now hanging by shreds, exposing my flesh to the roomful of demons and Lucifer alike. I glanced at Damian and if pain racked his beaten form, I couldn't tell. He was straining against the platinum chains, his face a mask of fury that went beyond anything I had ever seen, and I understood what Lucifer had in mind, or at least I thought I did, until he spoke.

"I am not going to kill you," Lucifer said and curled his finger, willing me to crawl to him. I tried to resist the hands dragging me forward, but it was as futile as wishing the sunrise away.

"Instead, you will be my slave. My concubine." He sent a wicked grin as I kneeled at his feet, my gaze locked on the crotch of his pants and the bulge that appeared like a poisonous snake curled and ready to strike. "My whore."

I shivered as his fingers touched my face and tilted it so I looked up at him. "Until you've delivered an army of children and your womb can no longer conceive." He glanced up at Damian. "Then I'll let all the demons in hell have a turn at her."

"You fucker," Damian whispered.

"Once they've used her to within a breath of death, that's when I'll tear out her heart and drink the last drops of her precious trinity blood."

"Fuck you," I growled, but his laugh sent me into a fit of shivers.

Lucifer's hand clamped under my chin, his clawed finger piercing my cheek as he squeezed and pulled me to my feet. "If you insist," he said and slammed me against the wall, his body pressing against me in an all too suggestive manner.

"But, before I take what is rightfully mine, I want you to indulge me and give your husband a blow job before the sun cooks him alive." The smile that accompanied the request sent terror through me.

"I can't," I whispered.

"Oh, come now. Mark told me you had a mouth that won't quit. I'd like to see you in action," he sneered and glanced at Damian. "I'll give you a dying wish. Would you like a blow job...or would you prefer to watch?"

Damian blinked at the question, and I had a moment of clarity when his eyes met mine. He pressed his lips together, and they quivered, and then his eyes met Lucifer's gaze.

"I think I'll watch," he whispered, and a tear slid out of the corner of his eye.

Lucifer's eyebrow rose, and he threw me toward Damian. I landed on my hands and knees at his feet and a quick glance over my shoulder into Lucifer's malignant glare told me I didn't have enough stall left. It was now or never, and there was no way I would be reduced to Lucifer's whore for the foreseeable future.

Before the command left Lucifer's lips, I shot to my feet, throwing myself toward Damian. I had a second where Damian's gaze met mine, and I knew he would do anything to avoid Lucifer's plans, even if it screwed both of us. The minute my skin came in contact with his, I heard his sharp inhale and I flipped my hair out of the way, giving him full access to my throat.

"Bite me," I whispered, and I saw the brief passage of lust overcome the pain just before he sank his teeth into my throat. Raw agony flared, and I tightened my grip on him, knowing each pull of blood brought us closer to death.

Death on our terms. Not Lucifer's.

With a yank, I found myself on the floor, dizzy and disoriented, and Damian stood, defiant despite his blistered skin and the raw guttural groan of pain coming from his chest. His knees gave out, and he collapsed, trying to draw his arms in as his body spasmed, his groan turning to a scream as my blood ate him from the inside out.

I blinked at the ray of light filtering in the window, illuminating the wall behind Damian.

"Please Michael," I whispered, too softly for anyone to hear, but Lucifer turned toward me anyway and the glare in his gaze froze my blood in place. I pushed with my legs, putting more distance between us, and prayed that I could set Michael free before Lucifer reached me.

Something to my right caught my attention, and I nearly gasped when a demon tossed Michael's unconscious body onto the floor. His face was the pale pallor of death and his chest lay still. I couldn't even detect a pulse in his neck and despair wrapped around my heart.

"You really think he can help you now?" Lucifer asked with a grin as wicked as my husband's dying screams.

My gaze darted from Michael's prone body to Lucifer. Movement in the corner pulled my attention and Eve's wide eyes met mine before falling on Michael. A wealth of emotion crossed her pale features and when her gaze transitions from me to Lucifer, her face scrunched into a feral snarl, making my focus snap in the same direction.

Lucifer stood over Michael with a dagger clasped in his hands. He raised it over his head and closed his eyes, reciting an ancient alchemy.

The stench of burning flesh filled the room, and my gaze landed on Damian. Rays of sunshine encompassed his black curls, but he wasn't burning.

It was Eve, and I swore my heart stopped. Her dark eyes held knowledge and love when they passed over me and the moment they took in Lucifer, her gaze altered, becoming silent and fierce. She streaked across the room with deadly intent written across her fiery features.

Lucifer didn't have a chance to react before Eve hit him full force, knocking him through the plate-glass window, but not before she ripped a mighty gash in his throat.

I didn't wait for him to return or for the shell-shocked demons to react. I crawled to Michael's body and grasped his head in my hands, praying his heart still carried a beat. The incantation tumbled from my lips and the flow of power drained from me. Within a blink, Michael was on his feet in full angel form, and every demon in the room fell under the heavenly burst of white light.

The last thing that registered in my shell-shocked brain was Damian framed in sunshine, but before I could move, my vision flashed white and then faded.

Tigress
Chapter Thirty-Seven
Naomi

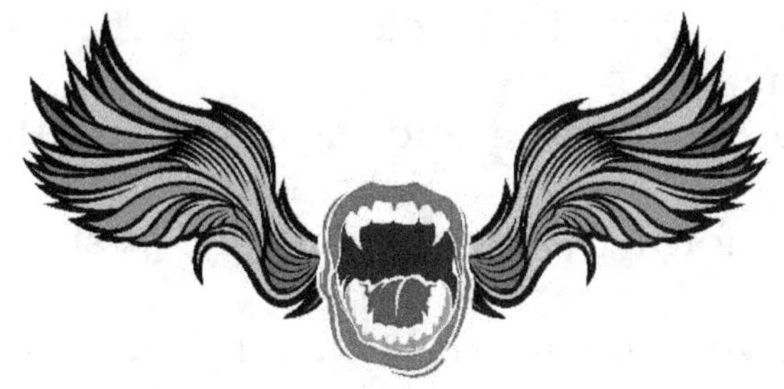

MY EYES OPENED TO a cloth wiping my forehead, and I focused on the owner of the hand. Valerie smiled down at me.

"Michael wasn't able to heal you completely. He stopped the bleeding, but you're going to have a scar."

"Damian?" I asked, pushing the cloth away. Sitting up wasn't as easy as I assumed, and when the dizziness gripped me, Valerie offered a hand to steady me.

"He's in your bedroom," she whispered.

"Where is Michael?"

Valerie bit her lip and shrugged. "He said he needed to recharge and left me to watch over both of you."

I could tell from her tone, she wasn't thrilled with our winged grandfather. I could only guess where an archangel went to recharge, and I looked up at the ceiling. Michael must have gone back home to heaven, and I sighed.

"Did he say anything about Lucifer?"

Valerie sent a rueful smile in my direction. "He said to tell you that Eve did as much damage as you had before she died, so you've got some time."

I closed my eyes and let out a breath before meeting her gaze. "How long have we…" I couldn't form the words and she just offered a smile.

"You've been in and out for a few days, but this is the first time you've been lucid." Valerie picked up the cup from the coffee table and offered it to me. I took it and was rewarded with the cool tartness of an orange-pineapple blend.

After a few sips, I handed it back to her.

"Can you take me to see him?"

Valerie hesitated and met my gaze. "He doesn't look that great," she said.

After what I witnessed at the house, I'd say he probably looked about as appealing as one of the victims of a nuclear holocaust, but I needed to see him, to touch him, to make sure he still drew a breath. I gave a curt nod and pushed to my feet.

Valerie took hold of my elbow and steadied me as she led me to my bedroom. The images playing in my head of what might be beyond the door made my feet as heavy as brick slabs and I forced myself forward. Valerie pushed the door open and stayed in the entry. I met her gaze, then took a deep breath and stepped into the room.

I wasn't prepared for the sight in front of me. My gaze landed on Damian painted in sunlight; his torso was visible and devoid of any evidence of Lucifer's torture. Scar-free and beautiful under a thick sheen of sweat and my hand drew over my mouth, covering the gasp of surprise.

Bags of ice rested along his body and an IV drip hung from a metal rod next to the bed. I followed the line of clear liquid and my gaze landed on his wrist.

His bound wrist. Both arms were bound in soft restraints that reminded me of those in a mental institution, and I glanced over my shoulder at Valerie, cocking an eyebrow in a silent question.

"We strapped him down so he wouldn't hurt himself," she said, answering my question before I could voice it.

"Oh," I whispered and shuffled across the floor with the last of my energy. The exertion took what little strength I had, sapping it from my bones, and I collapsed in the soft cushioned chair next to the bed.

I have no idea how long I stared at his perfect form, still trying to piece together all that had happened since Lilith shot me with the antidote. Slowly, I reached for his hand, but the heat radiating from him sent my blood racing. My heart tripped in my chest and fear dried my mouth. No human could radiate that much heat, and I shot my gaze to Valerie.

"Fever?" I asked, knowing it was an asinine question, but looking for confirmation anyway.

Valerie just nodded.

"How high?"

"Last I checked, he was at one hundred and five, which is much better than when Michael first brought him in." She stepped into the room. "I've got enough intravenous drips to last a month and if he hasn't woken by then, I'll have to figure out how to get more."

I dropped my gaze to my fingertips for a moment, wondering if my touch would spawn angry blisters like before. Dread encompassed me and I reached for his hand again, hesitating before I touched his hot skin. Holding my breath, I dropped my hand on top of his and glanced at his slack face for a reaction, any reaction, and received nothing.

When I pulled my hand away, my gaze locked at his unblemished skin and my heart started a drumbeat in my chest that I felt through my entire form. He wasn't allergic to my touch anymore. I'm not sure if it was the sob that broke from my chest or the look on my face that set Valerie in motion, but I launched myself on top of Damian, planting kisses from his forehead all the way down his face, leaving a trail of tears along my frantic path.

"Naomi, he's burning up and your body heat will not help," Valerie whispered after a few minutes of my emotional display.

I turned toward her. Of all the people in the world, she had to understand what the ability to touch him without harm meant to me. She had to understand my need to be near him right now, but all I saw was her soft concern, along with the underlying warning.

"I'll make you a deal. If he starts the chills again, you can warm him, okay?"

Begrudgingly, I pulled myself off his prone form and slid back into the chair. Valerie picked up his wrist and checked his pulse. "This isn't covered in medical school," she said with a hint of a smile, and met my gaze. "I'm not sure what to do with him beyond keeping him hydrated and keeping his fever in check."

I sighed. "How much school have you missed?"

"I'm on break until Monday, so your timing worked out. Once you get your bearings, I'll need to go over what you need to do when I go back to class."

"Did Michael say when he should wake up?"

Valerie met my gaze, but she didn't speak. Not at first, and then she sighed.

"Michael didn't know if he'd ever wake up."

Tigress
Chapter Thirty-Eight
Damian

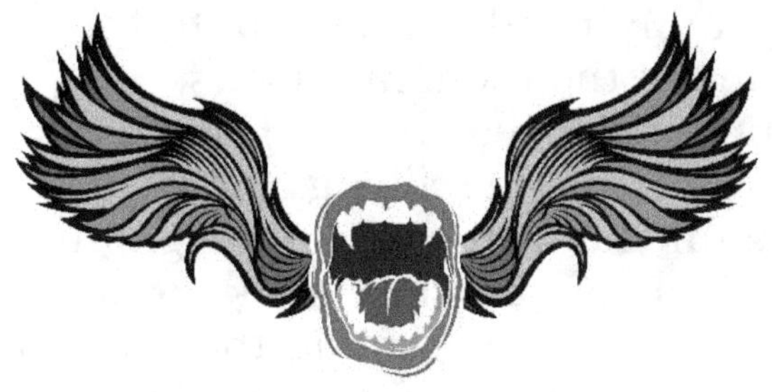

I OPENED MY EYES and squinted, disoriented. Moving my head brought a fresh wave of pain and I closed my eyes against the brightness. A cool breeze swept over my skin and I curled tighter into a ball, my stomach clenched, and I ground my teeth against the groan that formed in my throat.

I must be in hell, I thought, but the soft stroke of fingers that ran across my forehead and into my hair, dulling the throbbing pain in my temple, told me otherwise and I chanced opening one eye.

Naomi smiled down at me in a brightly lit room.

"Hey, babe," she whispered, and my gaze dropped to the bandage on her throat and then back to her dark and concerned eyes.

I tried to move, but my muscles protested, screaming in a new agony.

Her hand came to rest on my chest, and I found the strength to lift my head for a moment and stare at the contact. Her hand on my skin and my gaze snapped back to hers, but not before the fact my chest was clear of all scars registered. My head fell back onto the soft down and I blinked the room into focus.

My breath locked in my throat at the yellow streaks of sunshine filling the room, creating patterns on the wall and creeping onto the bed. Millenniums of instinct took over and fear gripped my muscles, forcing them into action. I pushed myself into a sitting position, right into the shard of light, and I tensed, waiting for the pain.

Expectations of burning flashed over my skin, creating a wetness that I didn't comprehend, but no fire, no stench of burning flesh, and then I realized Naomi was speaking, and her hands were on my shoulders, pushing me back into the bed.

Neither the sun nor her touch burned, and my jaw dropped with surprise. It had been over two thousand years since the sun hit my face and the only logical explanation popped out as a question.

"Is this heaven?"

Her chuckle and the sparkle in her eyes gave me pause, and then she shook her head. "No, sweetheart, this isn't heaven, and the last few weeks have been a nightmare. I thought I lost you at least a dozen times." Her eyes filled with tears and she pulled me into a fierce hug that made me wince.

"What the hell happened?" I asked when she broke free.

"Do you remember biting me?"

I shivered and nodded. I had intended to drain the life from her so Lucifer wouldn't get the chance to defile her, but he caught onto that and yanked her from my lips. I barely hung on because, while her blood was as sweet as I remembered, it roasted my insides more than a straight fifth of Jack Daniels.

"I remember," I said and reached up, running my fingers over the bandage. It was her turn to wince, and I pulled my hand away. "But that still doesn't explain this?" I moved my fingers into the sunlight.

"I guess my blood delivered the cure without killing you."

The cure?

My hands flew to my face, expecting a wrinkled mass of skin, but all I felt was the scratch of wiry hair. I sent a question in her direction.

"Three weeks in a coma," she whispered and ran her hand down my cheek. "You've got a pretty thick layer of stubble."

All I could think about was Lilith's warning that the cure ages vampires, and I swallowed the growing sphere of dread.

"How old..." I couldn't finish and my gaze dropped to my hands. They didn't seem to have aged, but the way my body felt, who the hell knew?

"You haven't aged a day. You're still twenty-five."

The shock hit harder than I could handle, and I forced my legs over the side of the bed. I needed to see, and she seemed to understand. Coming to my side and wrapping her arm around my waist, she helped me to my feet. Every muscle ached, and I nearly collapsed when I tried to take that first step, but she held on.

When she crossed over the threshold of the bathroom and positioned me in front of the mirror, I stared at the disheveled image. The scraggly beard, the matted and greasy hair, the sweat stained shorts and the perfect, unmarked chest.

My gaze traveled over my human image and landed on sharp blue eyes. The eyes that have gazed back at me from mirrors for the last two and a half millennia. I glanced at her reflection, and her beauty hadn't diminished. In fact, it had increased tenfold.

"You could use a shower," she said and glanced up at me.

It had been close to five weeks since I held my wife in my arms and the fact she had her arm slung around me without burning pain accompanying it gave me enough strength to smile down at her.

"I'm not sure I have enough energy to take a shower alone," I said and my voice sounded strange, thick and scratchy, but she just grinned and led me into our shower.

I wondered if I could still shift into the hawk the way she could still transform into a tiger and was about to ask, but she turned on the water and all other thought left me. I stood under that warm spray, my eyes closed and my hands limp at my side while she washed me with a loufah filled with my favorite musk body wash.

She even washed my hair and steadied me when the world spun. She made me sit on the stone bench while she carefully shaved the stubble from my cheeks and when her hands left me; I blinked my eyes open.

She ran a cloth over my cheeks and I pulled her into my arms, resting my head against her chest and listened to the steady beat of her heart. A surge of emotions filtered through me, rendering me speechless and immobile with her in my grasp. Gratitude and fear kept me silent and holding my breath, sure if I let go and opened my eyes, I'd witness Lucifer doing unspeakable things to her.

That was the only thought that made sense. I lost it in the final seconds of life and instead of seeing the horror in front of me; I cooked up this fantasy to go into death with.

Her fingers caressed my scalp in slow soft circles and only the sound of running water accompanied us, not the horrific screams I imagined behind my tightly shut eyes.

"Damian," she whispered.

I finally forced my eyes open and looked up into her dark gaze.

"We are alive," she said and tilted my chin up. When her lips pressed gently to mine, I understood, and the kiss went from the innocent peck it was meant to be into the all-encompassing heated kiss of passion. Fueled by desire, I stood and pushed her against the back wall, my hands finding the places on her body that I longed to touch. Soon my mouth followed and her seductive purr filled the bathroom.

The End

Continue Damian and Naomi's story with Trinity Rising.

TRINITY RISING

Plans for a bright future disintegrate when Lucifer comes to claim Damian and Naomi's trinity child.

Mornings are a challenge, with Damian being mortal. He instinctively dives for the floor when dawn's light illuminates the bed. The scald of whiskey, and the way Naomi feels, are the only constants which haven't changed. However, his mortal world shines when fatherhood hits his horizon.

Plans for a bright future disintegrate when Lucifer comes to claim their Trinity child, playing dirty by framing Damian for murder. Now, Damian and Naomi are on the run from both Lucifer and the law. They find an ally in a most unlikely source, ex-FBI agent Steve Williams and his family; a family with enough psychic energy to wage a war and realign the universe.

With their new friends as part of the dynamic, Damian and Naomi are desperate for victory against the devil. One wrong step and they could trigger Armageddon, or worse, the hope for our future could fall into Lucifer's greedy grip.

Trinity Rising
Chapter One
Damian

SUNSHINE.

I rolled onto the floor with my heart in my throat and panic gripping my muscles. It wasn't until I was on my hands and knees that I realized I had done it again. Naomi's chuckle from the bed immediately set the irritation switch in my head, and I glared over the edge of the mattress at her amused smile.

"That's never going to get old," she said and rolled on her side, propping her cheek in her palm.

I could have said something crude, but the humor in her eyes soothed the nasty comments right out of my vocabulary. Being human sucked much more than I remembered. The only thing that remained the same was the burn of a shot of whiskey and the way Naomi felt when we made love.

Everything else was a constant challenge, including taming my conditioned response to sunlight. You'd think after a little over a month, I wouldn't be throwing myself for cover when the sun hit the bed, but apparently, twenty-five-hundred years of fearing the fiery orb really did a job on my head.

"I'm glad I could amuse you," I said, opting to slip under the covers again for just a little longer before I had to crack open my computer to work on a few coding jobs thrown my way. Now that I was mortal, I didn't need to save like I had in the past. Because of my frugal nature, I had amassed more money than we could ever hope to spend in one lifetime, but even with the ridiculous sum in my bank account, I couldn't just sit on my ass doing nothing.

Naomi started writing. I think it's a form of therapy for her, especially considering the hell she's been through since she met me. Her purging of dark things onto the pages of a book seemed to quiet the nightmares.

I reached for her, pushing a strand of her dark hair behind her ear before giving her a quick morning kiss. When I pulled away, the soft smile on her lips morphed into a grimace and her hand shot over her mouth. Before I knew what was happening, she was out of the bed and running for the bathroom.

Retching sounds came from the half-closed door and I slid out of bed, crossing the distance.

"Sick?" I asked, even though the answer was obvious.

She nodded, wiping her mouth with a tissue before flushing the bile away. I crossed and put my wrist to her forehead. Cool skin met mine.

"You don't feel like you've got a fever."

She climbed to her feet and stepped to the sink, brushing her teeth and spitting before she dignified my comment with an answer.

"My stomach has been queasy for a couple of days."

"Maybe Val can look at you," I offered and grabbed my toothbrush, washing my morning breath away.

"I'm feeling better now; maybe it was just something I ate."

I turned toward her, raising a brow. "Are you complaining about my cooking already?"

"No." Her light laugh filled the bathroom.

The music of her laugh set me in motion and I caught her by the waist, pulling her close.

"You don't want to catch this," she said, arching away from me.

"I don't really care." I kept my grip on her waist, holding her against me and letting my hands wander to the edge of the baby-doll nightgown. She wiggled in my grasp and all I could do was smile at the color filling her cheeks.

"Come on," she whispered, but this time she was less resistant and trying to suppress a smile.

I dipped my mouth to the side of her neck, nibbling my way from her ear to her shoulder. "Are you sure I can't interest you in a nice, long, hot shower?" I asked and worked my way back up the same line to her earlobe. She didn't object, and her sigh of concurrence brought a grin to my lips. I knew I probably should let her go back to bed and rest, but my appetite for her had grown since my transition from immortal to human and I couldn't seem to get enough.

What little clothing we had fell onto the floor and I navigated her into the shower. The water seemed to rejuvenate Naomi, and she was the one to push me against the wall, covering my mouth with the kind of kiss that made me want to sink to my knees in worship.

She knew how to make me forget everything with a touch—forgetting millennia and all that came before her. She erased it all and I could only fathom the moment. Making love to her was a slice of heaven, a dance of rhythms and movement in such unity that I swear this is what fate had planned for me all along.

Music blasted in the living room, and I chuckled against Naomi's neck.

"I think we disrupted Valerie's studies again," I whispered and kissed her exposed throat.

Naomi purred in that erotic way that made my skin tingle and I pulled away, studying her flushed features and the dripping mane of hair, running my hands through the silky strands before covering her mouth in an all-consuming kiss.

Trinity Rising
Chapter Two
Damian

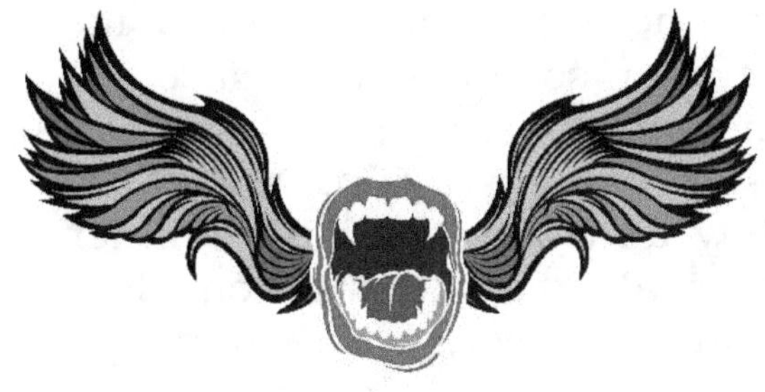

NAOMI STEPPED INTO MY office holding something plastic in her hand. The way she bit her lip as she stared at the thing pulled my full attention. I hated that worried look; it plagued my mind and brought up unpleasant memories of life on the run.

"What?"

She turned the front of what she held towards me and I stared at the little plus in the middle of the plastic before bringing my gaze to hers. I had seen enough commercials over the years to have an idea of what I was looking at, but I wasn't prepared for the onslaught of emotion that little plus sign sent parading through my bloodstream.

"Is that what I think it is?"

She nodded, and joy burst from the center of my being. I had no memory of crossing the distance, but when I came back to reality, I had her in my arms, twirling in a circle, and my smile actually made my cheeks ache.

"Are you sure?" I asked, setting her down.

"Yes. Valerie made me do the test twice."

Naomi was more subdued than I would have expected and I put my enthusiasm in check, lifting her chin so she met my gaze.

"Aren't you excited?"

She bit her lip again, and I dialed it in completely as a new worry bit under my skin. We'd never talked about children. Ever.

Even after we were both cured of the shadow virus, so maybe my assumptions that she wanted the same thing I did was flawed.

"Did you... want children?" I asked. I tried to keep the strained hesitation out of my voice, but I didn't do a very good job.

The tension in her body loosened. "Yes, I want to have children with you, it's just..." she trailed off, and the conflict danced over her features, twitching her eyelids as she tried to articulate all that was going on under the surface.

"You're afraid," I finished, understanding her fears. Hell, I had them too, but mine were more about what sort of child we would produce as opposed to what Lucifer would do when he found out.

Her nod confirmed my statement. "If he ever got his hands on my child..." Naomi couldn't finish, and she pulled me into a fierce hug. "I don't know what I'd do."

I wrapped my arms around her and kissed her temple. "I have a feeling that'll be the least of our worries."

She glanced up. The seriousness in her steady gaze told me she didn't quite understand my point.

"I'm not sure what's involved in raising a trinity," I said. "Especially if our child has some of the same... gifts that you have." For a moment, I envisioned being cornered by an angry tiger cub and couldn't help grinning.

"What's with that look?"

"What if the baby can change forms at will?" I opted to ask the question as opposed to sharing my little imagery.

Naomi sighed. "What if she can't?"

"She?"

Her lips pressed together, and I refocused on what she asked.

"Well, then *she* would be normal."

Her eyes rolled, and she laughed for the first time since she gave me the news. "You really think we're capable of having a normal child?"

I answered with an almost imperceptible lift of my shoulders, along with a grin. "As long as the child is healthy, who the hell cares if she's normal or not?"

Her cheeks dimpled and laugh lines appeared at the corner of her eyes. Any worry that had been there a few minutes ago seemed to evaporate in her budding glow.

"Have I told you I loved you lately?"

She beamed and nodded, pulling me into another hug. "I love you, too," she said and unwrapped her arms. Naomi literally bounced out of the room and I imagined she continued that flighty step all the way to the family room upstairs.

I stared after her, and my smile slowly faded. She had every right to be afraid and so did I. If Lucifer got wind of this, regardless of whatever condition he was in, he'd crawl out of hell to stop it. God only knows what would happen then.

I closed my eyes, and my chin dropped to my chest. I've never been a praying man, but right now, we needed all the protection the angels in heaven could provide.

"Michael, she's pregnant," I whispered, knowing damn well he couldn't hear me from within our sanctuary. Just saying it aloud sent a jolt of excitement along with a profound stab of fear through my body, tingling through my cells and producing a rash of gooseflesh.

I shivered and saved my work, shutting down my computer before putting on an appropriate smile and heading upstairs into the loud music and laughter.

AFTER DINNER, NAOMI BEGGED off early, looking every bit as tired as she said she was. I gave her a goodnight peck and settled into the couch with the remote. I must have clicked through the channels twice before Valerie cleared her throat. I glanced in her direction.

"Feel like a game of chess?" Valerie asked, closing her medical books.

"Sure." I hadn't played a game with her since we came back from Colorado and now that both Naomi and I were back in what Valerie dubbed healthy-land, I figured I could go without a night of aimless television and I turned it off.

She retrieved the beautifully carved chess set I had given her for her birthday and sat down on the couch next to me. I took the black marble pieces and set them up opposite her light set. I caught her glancing toward the hallway and cocked my head, sending her a silent question. She shook her head and tapped her watch.

"What's up?"

"Not yet," she whispered and picked up the remote for the stereo, turning it on low.

"Okay," I said and nodded toward the board. "It's your move."

She smirked and dropped her gaze to the board. For the first time since we got back, I took a moment to study her. The resemblance to Michael came through in the thick, wavy hair and the perfectly proportioned facial features, both qualities that also resonated in my wife, but unlike Naomi, Valerie didn't have a hint of Native American in her complexion or raven-black hair.

She made her first move and leaned back into the cushions, meeting my gaze.

"Are you checking me out?"

I chuckled and glanced at the chessboard. "I never noticed just how much you look like Naomi," I said and countered her move without much thought.

A dimple appeared in her cheek and she pressed her lips into a tight smile.

I crossed my arms and leaned back, challenging her to say what was behind that look. When she said nothing, I smiled. "Wasn't it a couple of months ago that you were checking me out?"

"So you were checking me out." Her arms tightened across her chest, closing me off with non-verbal cues.

"No, I was studying you a little closer, noticing similarities and differences between you and Naomi. At least I was looking at your face and not your ass." I had to add that last point, especially after her not-so-subtle check of my backside when we first came here.

A rose hue bloomed in each of her cheeks and she looked away. Instead of dignifying me with an answer, she concentrated on the chessboard. After a few moments, a knight moved, and she glanced at me expectantly.

"What did you want to talk to me about?" I said, lowering my voice to barely a whisper before focusing on the game in front of me. I sat staring at the chessboard, contemplating my next move, when Valerie cleared her throat. Reaching out, I moved one of my rooks and then focused back on her.

"I ran a couple of tests," she said, shifting on the seat like she suddenly couldn't find a comfortable position.

"Naomi said you made her do a couple of pregnancy tests."

When she met my gaze and tilted her head in that puppy dog way, it made my blood freeze in my veins. Valerie wasn't talking about the pregnancy tests.

"What?" I hissed.

"Besides coming back as undoubtedly pregnant, the results showed a very high level of glucose."

I shrugged. I had no idea what that meant, but based on the concern written in the crease between her eyes, I knew it couldn't be good.

"I need her to get tested for diabetes."

The answer didn't strike the kinds of alarms it would have if the word had been cancer or something equally as deadly.

"Okay," I said, stretching the word out.

"Damian, diabetes could kill both her and the child if left unchecked."

She now had my full attention, and an icy dread blanketed me. I tried to swallow, but my mouth had gone dry. Instead of speaking, I nodded for her to go on.

"Whether it's gestational diabetes, or regular diabetes, there could be complications with the pregnancy. Serious complications."

I blinked. "You are telling me Naomi could die?"

"Yes, if she has diabetes, there is a much higher chance of... issues."

"Issues?"

"Short term, long term, there's a wide range of problems that can occur for both her and the baby," she said.

The lack of full disclosure grated on my nerves. "Tell me the range," I demanded, leaning my elbows on my knees and just staring at the floor as she went from the least severe consequences of having to watch her diet for the rest of her life, to the most catastrophic, which made my eyelids draw closed and my head dip against the pressure.

I swallowed and tried to ask the question twice before my voice would pass over the sudden block in my throat. "Are you telling me we might have to make a choice between her and the baby?"

She remained quiet, meeting my gaze with neither a nod nor a shake of her head. "I don't know. Let's get her properly tested first before you start turning over the different doomsday scenarios in your head. It could also just be a side effect of her DNA makeup. The ability to still change into a tiger could screw with the tests."

Irritation snaked into my blood and I stood, crossing to the sliders, choosing to stare out at the backyard instead of snapping at Valerie. She was just trying to keep me informed, but I would have much preferred being in the dark on this one.

I knew without a doubt Naomi would choose the baby, and I glanced at the stars spattering the early spring sky, wondering just how many times we could face death before it claimed us.

"It's your turn," Valerie said after a few minutes.

"I know." I didn't return to the game yet, contemplating moves between the chessboard and my life. With a sigh, I walked back and moved my king, giving Valerie a half-hearted shrug before leaving her with my sacrifice.

THE ASTON-MARTIN STILL wasn't running as smoothly as I wanted, especially after the joy ride Naomi took it on when she saved my ass from Lucifer; I always ended up in the garage when something was eating at me. It was better than tossing and turning in bed and disrupting Naomi's sleep.

Valerie didn't bother following me into the basement, and I'm glad. I needed time to figure out exactly what options I had. The more I fiddled under the hood, the more I realized it was as much of a crapshoot as stepping off our property into the unprotected world.

The one thing mortality gave me was perspective.

My time was finite now, and I wanted a long, happy life with Naomi, and a hoard of children. The light flickered above me and I glanced up from the underside of the hood, catching the sway of the single bulb.

I leaned to the side and caught her blank stare.

"What are you doing?" Naomi asked, rubbing her sleepy eyes.

"Tinkering." I grabbed the hand cloth and wiped the grease off my fingers, stepping around the engine into full view.

"Why?"

"Couldn't sleep," I answered and tossed the rag onto the side of the engine block.

Worry bloomed in her eyes and I crossed the distance between us. I stopped and stared down into her upturned face, wondering how in the world I would survive without her. Instead of voicing my concerns, I leaned down, pressing my lips to hers in a soft kiss.

"What are you doing up at this hour?" I asked, changing the subject.

"I had a nightmare." She wrapped her arms around her waist and shivered. "It seemed so real and when I woke up, you weren't there."

I knew what that was like. Our nightmares were a blend of the near-death experiences and Lucifer's promises. She sometimes woke screaming, trying to unwrap from the blanket like they were the beasts assaulting her. Those were the ones that made my blood boil. Even though Lucifer never made good on his promise to make her his whore, it still played havoc with both our minds. The rest of them involved seeing each other die in various excruciating ways. I didn't know which flavor she had tonight, and I really didn't want to know. Not after the real-world news I'd been turning over in my head for the last couple of hours.

"Sorry, babe," I said and lead her back to the stairwell leading to the underground tunnel. I grabbed the flashlight before flipping the switch off on the overhead bulb. Drenched in darkness, I reached for her, finding her hand before flipping the flashlight on.

She didn't speak as I led her back to the bedroom in the main house and I didn't press her for details. We both still had nightmares, and only the word was necessary.

"You died," she said when we reached our room and I closed the door.

Naomi couldn't shake that nightmare. She described it once, saying her blood left me like it had the other vampire and she crumbled, unable to fight Lucifer. It always ended with her scream of terror as he came for her.

I ran my palm over her cheek and pulled her to my chest. My nightmares didn't end with her dying. In mine, I lived long enough for the sun to burn and Lucifer to ravage her before I turned to dust.

"It wasn't the usual."

Her tone surprised me, and I searched the shadows of her gaze, looking for insight, but found none. I lifted my eyebrows, waiting for her to enlighten me.

She shook her head. "Just go clean up and come to bed."

Who was I to argue?

After washing my hands and brushing my teeth, I stripped down to my boxers and climbed into the bed. Her back was to me and I curved around her, pulling her to my chest and planting a kiss on her shoulder.

"Are you all right?" I asked when silence blanketed the room.

I thought she had fallen asleep, but she shifted and sighed.

"I'm not sure."

I waited, knowing if I pushed her, she'd just clam up until she was ready. Finally, when she didn't continue, I propped myself up on my elbow and leaned over her, getting a glimpse of her face in the splintered moonlight. The glistening paths on her cheeks gave me a start.

"Are you crying?"

Naomi met my gaze and the gloss filling her eyes confirmed my question and tugged at my heart.

"Babe, it was only a nightmare."

In a flash, her arms encircled my neck, and she pulled me down into her grasp.

"I lost everything," she whispered.

I held her tight, whispering, "shhh." until the quakes rocking her form settled.

"Naomi," I said when she stopped shaking. She peeled away and stared into my eyes. "I'm not planning on dying for a long time," I added when I had her full attention.

"Sometimes planning and reality don't meet," she said and sniffled.

"Neither one of us is clairvoyant," I pointed out.

She wiped her eyes and nodded. "I know, it's just... it was disturbing."

Her trembling lips propelled me forward, and I covered them with mine, tasting the soft saltiness of tears mingling with her natural sweetness, and I sighed, breaking the kiss. She palmed my cheek and attempted to smile. It didn't work quite as well as she might have thought, but I let it go. I really didn't want to hear about whatever nightmarish horror she could dream up.

Instead, I snuggled down into my pillow, pulled her back into the spoon position, and ran my fingers slowly through her hair. It wasn't long before she dropped into dreamland and her chest started the soft rise and fall of sleep.

Trinity Rising
Chapter Three
Damian

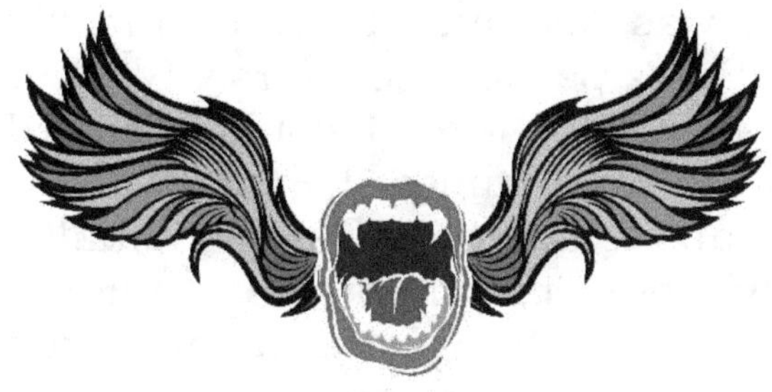

I WOKE FACING AWAY from the window and my gaze landed on the sunlight painting the walls with the outline of the windowpanes standing out like a giant Braille relief map. Instead of the usual freak out, I sighed and studied the patterns that so many take for granted.

The door to the bathroom opened, and I rolled onto my back, looking down beyond the foot of the bed at Naomi. Her hair glistened in the morning sun and the soft smile on her lips created a heat through my entire form. I sat up, returning her smile.

"Valerie is taking me to the doctor. Did you want to come?"

My smile faded. Neither of us had left the safety of the property since the battle with Lucifer and just the thought left me chilled. All the *what-ifs* hit, and I stared at her. Instead of voicing the shit flinging in my head, I gave her a nod and threw the blankets aside. Any hope I had of morning sex went out the window and I headed for the bathroom, catching a quick kiss on my way by.

If she was nervous about leaving, I couldn't tell, but that's par for the course. She could hide her nerves better than I could. Yesterday was one of the first times I had ever seen her hesitant about anything. Naomi usually barrels along without much of a thought to her mortality. It's both refreshing and frustrating, and one of the many reasons I loved her.

The warm water of the shower didn't quell the chill in my bones either, and I wondered if we could get someone to come here instead of venturing out. Sure, I had gone to the garage, but that place was almost as secure as this one. The only saving grace was it was bright and sunny, so the monsters that hunted at night wouldn't be on the prowl.

That left demons.

I hated demons. Those crazy fucks didn't have any sort of moral code. They plundered, tortured, and killed with glee.

By the time I stepped into the living room, I had worked myself up into a foul mood.

"What time is your appointment?" I asked with a clip in my voice that turned both women's heads.

"What crawled up your ass?" Valerie shot back.

I leveled a glare in her direction. "We haven't left the house since..." I stopped, pressing my lips together and shifting my stance. I knew

Valerie's motives were purely to make sure Naomi was okay, but I don't think she considered what could happen on the outside.

"I've been coming to and from without incident."

She had a point. Even with Uncle Ted off on vacation, no one bothered her. I nodded and met Naomi's gaze. "What if demons are watching the place? We have to be prepared for the worst."

That annoyed crease appeared between her eyes and her arms crossed. She didn't need to speak to broadcast her irritation, but underneath the fire burning in her gaze, I saw the first hint of hesitation.

"How does one prepare for a demon attack?" she asked, opting for the snarky sarcasm that always steeled my nerves.

I shrugged. "I used to be able to smell them coming." My hands found their way into my pockets and I dropped my gaze.

"You don't have to come if you don't want to."

My gaze snapped to hers and I bit back my comment. There was no way in hell I was going to let her go without me. I turned to Valerie.

"Do you have your uncle's pistol?"

"You don't have a permit to conceal and carry. Besides, the hospital frowns upon firearms on the premise unless you're a police officer," she said.

I just stared at her because anything that came out of my mouth would have turned into a rant. Instead, I just nodded and clenched my jaw. "Fine," I uttered after her challenging stare down.

Valerie crossed into the kitchen and opened a drawer. It slammed closed, and she stepped back into my line of sight, tossing something in my direction. I caught the small pouch and stared at the pot-pourri wrapped in sheer webbing. "There's already one in her pocketbook. Put it in your coat pocket and whatever badass is in the neighborhood leaves you alone."

"What the hell is this?" I snapped.

"It masks the scent of our bloodline."

"How?" I asked, this time with more patience, bringing the bag up to my nose to take a whiff. I pulled it away fast, but the sickly sweet stench hung on the air, making my eyes water.

"Michael gave them to me."

"He had a way to... hide you from..." I trailed off, looking at the small package again. The scent was repulsive, yet familiar. I blinked, and the origin of that smell slammed into my brain, making my gaze snap back to Valerie. "With demon blood?"

Both Naomi and Valerie blanched at the revelation. Naomi even moved her purse farther away from her body in an unconscious reflex of disgust.

"It works," Valerie said.

I didn't want the thing to touch me and I put it in the side pocket of my jacket, zipping it almost the entire way closed. Wiping my hands on my jeans, I gave a nod. "So, what time is her appointment?" I asked again, but this time without the edge.

VALERIE DROVE WITH NAOMI and me crammed in the small back seat of the truck.

The tiny side windows were tinted, and the back had a stencil of the American Flag blocking the window, so we were virtually invisible to the outside traffic. I still tensed when we got into a more populated area.

The half glances toward the truck had more to do with the rumbling engine than the occupants, and by the time we drove into the medical center in Torrington, I had relaxed enough to let my guard down. The moment the truck shut off, the nerves jumped into action.

Valerie stepped out of the truck and pushed the seat down for us to exit. I got out and my gaze bounced around the quiet parking lot before I turned and helped Naomi out of the cab. I felt like a secret service agent protecting the President in a crowd. My gaze couldn't move fast enough over the blacktop and cars looking for threats. By the time we got to the door, I was wrapped so tight I almost attacked an old woman who pushed open the doors on her way out of the office building.

Valerie and Naomi gave me that shocked expression that I was used to, and I let out a small laugh. I knew my strength and speed were superior to most humans, but if we encountered a demon, I would only be as effective as a fly swatter.

In the waiting room, I sat next to Naomi and my leg bounced in nervous anticipation. My back was safe against a wall, but the office had a half dozen other women in attendance and just the proximity to anything remotely dangerous left me on edge.

Naomi placed her hand on my knee, and I turned, meeting her gaze.

"Everything will be okay," she whispered, pushing down until my leg stopped moving.

I covered her hand with mine and gave it a squeeze, exhaling and offering a tight smile. It was a long half hour wait.

"Anna Andreas?" the nurse asked.

Naomi didn't respond at first, but I gave her hand a squeeze and nodded toward the nurse.

"Oh," she mumbled and collected her purse. She gave Valerie a quick glance and stood. I followed suit, and the nurse gave me that high browed what do you think you're doing glare.

"It's okay if my husband comes in with me, right?" Naomi asked when she caught the nurse's less than subtle glare.

The nurse dropped her gaze to Naomi's, and it softened. She nodded, but when it drifted back in my direction, the hard lines filled in around her mouth. When Naomi disappeared into the bathroom, I started nibbling on my nail, waiting for her to return. The nurse waitcd patiently, but ignored me long enough for my nerve endings to tingle.

"I guess you see a lot of nervous husbands," I finally said to break the ice, but the look she sent my way chilled me further. There would be no ice breaking with this one. I peeled off my coat and hung it on the chair, crossing to the window. I did a quick scan of the asphalt view.

"How old are you anyway?" the nurse asked, and I glanced over my shoulder.

When she asked my age, I caught my smirk in the glass's reflection and wondered how she'd react if I told her my actual age. Instead, I turned, meeting her gaze. "I'm twenty-five."

"Pft. You shouldn't be thinking about a family yet. Get established first," she scoffed at me, but at least the hostility was waning.

I glanced at my coat. Maybe it was the sachet that made her act like the ice princess, and the minute I took my jacket off and put some distance between me and my coat, she thawed. "We're good," I said and crossed my arms, leaning on the windowsill and waiting for Naomi.

"Do you realize just how much raising a child costs?" she chided.

"Yes, ma'am, I'm aware," I said. "I'm also aware of what the projections for college are," I added for good measure, punctuating it with a smile.

Her frown eased, and she gave me a nod just as the door opened and Naomi stepped inside, handing her a cup of urine.

"The doctor will be with you in a moment," the nurse said and stepped out with the offering.

Naomi took a seat, and I stepped to her side, taking her hand in mine.

"I think those things Valerie gave us make normal people hostile," I whispered. "Either that, or the nurse needs lessons in bedside manners."

Naomi giggled and squeezed my hand. "Or she's just reacting to your projected paranoia."

The shock of her words went through me like a sound wave vibrating up my spine and into my teeth. I raised my brow. "It's that obvious?"

"Um...yeah," she answered. Her lips twitched into a smile. "It would be highly amusing if I wasn't just as nervous as you are."

"I think once the baby is born, we should start looking for somewhere else to live," I said.

Her smile faded.

Before she could answer, the door opened and a tall, bespectacled man wearing a white lab coat stepped into the room. He looked from the laptop in his hands to Naomi and me, breaking into a broad grin.

"I guess you two are expecting," he said and placed the computer on the counter before offering Naomi his hand. "I'm Dr. Wolk."

"Na... Anna," Naomi said, catching herself before she revealed her real name. "And this is my husband, Damian."

Dr. Wolk extended his hand to me, and I shook it, meeting his open gaze. His grip was firm, but not overbearing.

"Congratulations," he said and adjusted his glasses before bringing his gaze back to Naomi. "When was your last period?"

Naomi bit her lip and glanced at me. She couldn't very well say five years ago and I'm not sure she had one between being shot with the cure and when I woke from my coma. I just shrugged. She hadn't had one since I came out of it.

"Do you have a calendar?" she asked.

The doctor pointed to the wall behind her.

Naomi hopped off the table and ran her fingers over the dates, silently moving her mouth in thought. She tapped the date that she woke from her delirium in Colorado and ran her finger over the calendar from that point, hesitating over the day we almost died.

A couple of weeks out from that, she tapped the date.

"February third," she said.

I woke up a week later.

"And I'm pretty sure we conceived on the tenth or soon thereafter."

The tenth was that first day in the shower, and the memory stirred my soul. I had mustered up enough energy to make love to her in the shower and then all strength left me. She dried me off and helped me pull on a clean pair of shorts while I sat on the bathroom floor, dizzy and exhausted. Naomi had to enlist Valerie's help to get me back to the bedroom. I remember feeling helpless as they changed the bed, and once I was tucked into the clean sheets, Valerie hooked me back up to the IV. It took me a few days of eating and sleeping to get up the energy to make love to her again, but after those celibate days in the beginning, we haven't missed a daily romp.

She smiled at me and climbed back on the table.

The doctor nodded and typed the information on the computer. "Well, based on that, it looks like you're due around October 20th." He scanned the screen, and a frown formed before he moved his gaze to Naomi.

"I'd like you to have some blood drawn and do a couple of tests before you leave today to make sure we have your glucose levels under control."

"What's wrong with my glucose level?" Naomi asked.

"It's high enough to pass into your urine, which isn't necessarily cause for alarm, but I'd just like to make sure we aren't looking at a potential complication. Did you have anything to eat this morning?"

Naomi shook her head and the flash of concern in Dr. Wolk's eyes before he moved his gaze to the numbers on the screen lit my stomach on fire.

"Is there a history of diabetes in your family?" he asked, scanning the information from the sheet she filled out in the waiting room.

"Not to my knowledge."

She reached out and took my hand in a grip that I had encountered before. The one that announced her nerves jumping into overtime.

The doctor glanced up at her and offered a smile. "I'll send Leticia back in to take some blood," he said and stood. "It will take a few minutes to run the tests and then I'll be back in and see if we can detect a heartbeat, okay?"

We both nodded and the moment the door closed, she turned her dark gaze in my direction. The worry there made me swallow and try on a smile.

"Everything will be just fine," I said, and the conviction in my voice surprised me. Based on the conversation with Valerie, I had my doubts, but it was something under our control and it was my turn to be strong.

I leaned forward and planted a kiss on her forehead, smoothing her hair back with my free hand. She closed her eyes and leaned her cheek on my palm in that endearing way that squeezed my heart.

The door opened, and a different nurse stepped inside. The way she glanced into the hallway and shut the door prickled my nerves. When she turned full toward us, I knew we were in trouble.

"Where's the other nurse?" Naomi asked, her eyes dropping to the tray the nurse set on the counter. The needle and glass vials were expected, but the glistening scalpel was not.

Her red-eyed glare snapped to both of us and she reached for the knife, but I was faster. I slapped my hand down on the corner of the tray, sending everything across the room with a loud clatter. The only thing between this demon and Naomi was me. And she stepped forward, her face transforming into an angry growl.

"What do you think you're doing?" she snarled.

A sound behind her drew her attention and her expression transitioned to embarrassment for the benefit of the head nurse now standing in the open door.

"I was just about to ask you the same question." The head nurse glanced beyond her subordinate without any of the attitude she had given me earlier. Instead, her underling looked down at the mess on the floor and back in her direction.

"Isn't this the room for the D-and-C?"

"We don't have a D-and-C patient today, Clara," the nurse said. There was a clear warning in her tone and her icy glare landed on the younger nurse. "This isn't the first time you've made that mistake." She crossed her arms.

Clara sent visual daggers in my direction before glancing back at her superior.

"Please leave," the head nurse said in a tone that left no negotiation.

"But, Leticia," Clara started, but Nurse Leticia pointed toward the exit.

"Now."

I stepped closer to Naomi, still buffering her from the inept demon and, for a moment, I thought the bitch was going to lash out at Leticia. Her fists clenched, and she shot a glare in my direction before stomping out of the office.

Leticia sighed and stepped inside. "I'm sorry about that. Clara is new, and she's been a disaster since she started." She squatted to pick up the syringe and the vials and hesitated when her gaze fell on the scalpel. A dark shadow crossed her features, and she shook her head, picking up the instrument with her thumb and forefinger, like it carried a nasty disease.

She sat back on her haunches, and the crease between her eyes grew. She glanced up at me before standing. I still blocked Naomi, but when the offending knife and needle dropped into the sharps container, I stepped aside.

"I'll need to get a clean syringe and vials," she said and slipped out of the room, leaving the door open.

I glanced at Naomi.

"What the hell was that?" she whispered.

"A demon," I answered, and the remaining splotches of color in her cheeks faded.

Naomi's hand slid over her abdomen in a protective gesture and I stepped closer, reaching for her hand.

"How'd you know?"

I smiled and glanced over my shoulder at the door before answering. "I've been around a lot longer than you, hun."

She nodded, and her gaze moved behind me.

"Okay, let's see if I can get some blood for those tests the doctor ordered," Leticia said, and I yielded, letting her approach Naomi. She gave me a nod of approval and I locked my gaze with my wife's.

"Are you okay?" I asked. She still hadn't regained any color, and when she shrugged, I followed her gaze to the needle. Reaching out, I turned her chin toward me so she didn't have to watch the drawing of blood. It didn't bother me in the slightest, hell it actually made my stomach growl. I offered her a smirk when she tilted her head in a silent question.

The nurse finished and left the room.

"Are you serious?"

I laughed and gave her a shrug of my own. "What'd you expect?" I asked. "I'm still freaked by sunshine, so it's not odd that the sight of blood still makes me hungry. Twenty-five-hundred years of conditioning."

"You are too funny sometimes," she whispered and pulled me to her lips.

I didn't want to dampen her light mood with what I expected waited for us outside, but I also didn't want Valerie to be hit in the crossfire. After Naomi pulled away, I crossed to my coat and dug my phone out of the inside pocket. I typed a quick text that I was sure would draw a tremor of fear through Valerie, but she had the sachet on her, so the demons might not take notice of her.

"Valerie?" Naomi asked when I turned and dropped the phone in my shirt pocket.

"Yes. I told her to meet us out back. We aren't going in the way we came."

The door opened, interrupting our conversation, and I turned to see Dr. Wolk stepping into the room with what looked like a small stereo speaker. "The initial blood tests don't look as bad as I anticipated; however, we are sending a couple of the vials out for more tests just to make sure you are not at risk. I will want you to do the glucose screening at 24 weeks, but in the meantime, I'd like to take a listen." He slid into the chair next to the bed and lowered the back before pulling up Naomi's shirt to reveal her abdomen. He tucked a sheet in her pants, tugging them down so her entire belly showed.

I stared at her and for the first time; I saw the slight change in her stomach. It was no longer the flat washboard I was used to, and I wondered how I could have missed the nuance of change in her. Of course, I had been dealing with the strangeness of being human again after so long, but that still didn't excuse my lack of noticing the changes in her body.

The doctor ran a thin line of clear gel on Naomi's belly and pulled a thick wand from the side of the speaker. "I'm just warning you, it's extremely rare to hear the heartbeat at this early stage, so if we can't find it, I don't want you to worry."

"Okay," Naomi said.

I squeezed her hand as she tucked the pillow under her head and stared at the ceiling. A smile formed, and I glanced up. Taped above the table was one of those posters of Anne Geddes baby gardens.

Dr. Wolk glanced up and echoed both our smiles. "I try to give my patient's something unique. There's a different picture in each room," he said and the wand touched Naomi, running slowly across the path of gel.

The volume was turned to high and the noises echoing from the speaker sounded like an underwater wonderland. A slight fluttering sound came and went, and the doctor retraced his path, finding the flutter again. He looked up at Naomi with a grin.

"You are one lucky girl. Six weeks is usually early for a heartbeat, but there it is," he said and pulled the wand away from her belly, wiping the gel with a cloth and pulling her shirt down once she was clean. "I'll want to see you next week so we can go over the test results. You can set up your next appointment at the front desk before you leave." Dr. Wolk stood and gave a nod as he exited the room.

The reality that the woman I loved was carrying my child hit, and I bit down on my lip to push the swirl of emotions away. I smiled at her and brought her hand to my lips. Her eyes sparkled with unshed tears and she wrapped her arms around me, using my height to get to her feet.

"We're having a baby," she said and her voice cracked. She buried her face in my chest and the first wave of tears struck.

I blinked my eyes clear and kissed the top of her head. "I love you," I said when I was sure I had a handle on my voice. Since I met her, she was the more emotionally stable of the two of us. Now it was my turn to be strong.

After scheduling Naomi's next appointment, I checked my phone; there was nothing from Valerie, so I stuck my head into the waiting room. Her seat was empty and my gaze shot to the parking lot. The truck still sat where we parked it and icy dread filled my veins.

Instead of heading out of the office area, I turned toward the desk.

"We have a bit of a drive. Is there a restroom my wife could use before we get on the road?"

Naomi's lips pressed into an embarrassed smile. The girl pointed toward the way we had come.

"Down the hall and around the corner on your right."

I took Naomi's hand and led her farther into the office, looking for one specific thing; when we turned the corner, my nerves relaxed a fraction. Before we could be intercepted, I pulled her through the exit, into a small stairwell and put my hand over her mouth, shaking my head before closing the door as quietly as I could.

I glanced between her and the stairs leading down to a lower entrance before maneuvering her into the darkest corner. I pulled my phone out without speaking and typed a text to Valerie, telling her they were running another test, so we would be another fifteen minutes.

I put my finger on my lips and showed Naomi the text before making sure my phone was on silent. She didn't understand until I hit send and Valerie's ringtone echoed through the stairwell.

"Fuck," an unfamiliar voice muttered from below, and Naomi's eyes widened.

I glanced at the stairs leading up and pulled her with me, silently climbing to the next floor. The door didn't have a handle, so we continued to the third floor.

This one had a knob, and I closed my eyes, saying a small prayer, and turned. It gave, and I opened it to another hall, moving Naomi into the carpeted stretch before shutting the door.

"What is going on?"

"Demons have Valerie," I whispered and continued down toward the other end of the hall. I wanted Naomi out of the building before they figured out our game, but I had no idea how I was going to get Valerie away from the bastards. I stopped at the next exit and leaned against the door, running my hand down my face before meeting Naomi's gaze.

"I wish she had let me take the gun," I said, pushing the fear down into my already knotted stomach.

"What are we going to do?" she asked and her hand went into that protective reflex, covering her abdomen without knowledge of the move.

"We aren't going to do anything. You are going to stay here and I'm going to take care of those bastards." I recognized the shadow that traveled over her features before they hardened into that stubborn aggravation I was used to. I shook my head before she opened her mouth to argue. "No. You're carrying my child. You aren't going out there until I know it is safe."

Naomi's lips thinned and she turned her back on me, crossing her arms and surveying the hall. She glanced over her shoulder, sending a glare at me before she marched away. Halfway down the hall sat a fire alarm box and when she reached for it, I almost laughed. Leave it to my wife to find a valid way out that wouldn't leave us alone in the parking lot with the enemy.

She pulled down and as the alarms broke out, wailing throughout the building, she passed in front of me and pushed open the door leading to a set of stairs on the opposite side of the floor. We joined a group of people clearing the building in an orderly fashion.

We exited at the far side of the parking lot, and I didn't want to leave Naomi alone in the crowd. At least one demon knew what she looked like and if I left her alone, I'm sure that's when all hell would break loose.

"Follow me," I whispered and navigated the parking lot, which was easier than I thought, especially with all eyes on the building, including the demon bitch that sat in the passenger seat.

Valerie sat still, her gaze locked in front of her, unfocused, even as we passed her line of sight. Her waxy skin glistened with sweat and I wondered what the hell held her in place. When we were a car away, I pulled Naomi lower.

"Stay here."

She glanced at the truck and then back to me, her eyes pleading in that way that made me hesitate, but I put my hand up and turned, focusing on the truck. From our vantage point, we couldn't see the building, and I didn't know who else was working with the demon bitch of a nurse holding Valerie hostage.

I did a quick scan and then stepped to the side of the truck, yanking the passenger door open. The bitch's head snapped in my direction, but I reacted faster than she did. My fist connected, breaking her nose before she removed the knife buried in Valerie's side.

The anger that flared pulled a growl from my lips and I yanked the psycho nurse from the car, twisting her neck as I turned. The sickening crunch of bone bounced off the car and I dropped the limp body, turning toward Naomi.

"Hurry," I said and as soon as she was in the car, I closed the door and ran to the driver's side. Without thinking, I slid Valerie to the middle of the bench seat and turned the key hanging from the ignition.

The truck revved to life and I hit the gas, tearing through the parking lot as fast as I dared. The hospital emergency room wasn't far, and I chanced a glance at Valerie. The girl still stared out the window, almost like she was already...

I shook the thought out of my head. "Check her pulse," I ordered.

Naomi's shaking fingers reached into my peripheral vision, landing on Valerie's throat as I took the turn into the emergency room entrance.

"Does she have a pulse?" I barked and glanced around Valerie, meeting Naomi's frightened stare.

"I, I don't know," she said. I slammed the brakes, stopping the vehicle within a hair of the ambulance sitting in front of me, and jumped out.

"You can't park here," a heavy-set officer said as he stepped out of the sliding doors.

"My friend was stabbed," was all I said, yanking the passenger door open. Naomi hopped out and moved aside, so I could reach in for Valerie. I didn't hesitate; I scooped her up so the hilt of the blade faced the hospital. My heart dropped when she didn't react with even a grunt from the change in position. I marched past the cop without another look. Each step brought back a random memory of Valerie. Years of memories, of watching her grow, flooded my senses and I carried her right past the desk and into one of the exam rooms. I didn't have to speak. The blade and blood dripping a path from the car was all the hospital needed.

The emergency room staff descended like a pack of wild eagles, pushing us aside while they assessed the damage. Naomi pulled me back against the wall as they barked commands that didn't register. The sound of a heartbeat pulled me out of my stress-filled trance, yanking a breath of relief from my chest. The nursing staff herded us from the room, despite my protests.

"They are bringing her to surgery," someone said, and I glanced down at the owner of the voice. A petite nurse stood with her hand on my chest. The name tattooed on her shirt read Sara H - RN.

"Is she going to make it?" I asked, my voice unsteady. I cleared my throat, glancing at

Naomi, who stood next to me with the same shell-shocked stare I imagined I wore.

"Are you family?"

"She's my cousin," Naomi said, gaining the nurse's attention. "Is she going to be okay?"

"We have the best doctors working on her right now," she answered.

I closed my eyes, finding the wall with my hand.

"The waiting room is that way. I will come find you when I get word as to her condition. Okay?"

I nodded and threw my arm around Naomi, turning in the direction the nurse had pointed.

The officer waited by the door, swinging a set of keys from his finger. When I approached, the keys stilled, and he crossed to me.

"What happened, son?" he asked.

"I don't know," I said. "Valerie came into Dr. Wolk's office with us and she was in the waiting room last I knew. The fire alarm was pulled, and we went out to the truck and found her like that." I pointed a shaking finger toward the exam rooms.

"The police are processing your vehicle."

I glanced around him at the cop cars and crime scene tape and nodded. "I hope they find the son of a bitch..." I muttered and glanced back at the cop.

"Did you touch the knife?"

"No. I don't think either of us did." I glanced at Naomi.

"I didn't touch it. The only thing I did was feel for a pulse when you asked me to."

The cop seemed satisfied for the time being and pointed us to the waiting room. Another staff member approached and handed us a clipboard to fill out with Valerie's information. I stared at the blanks and then at Naomi. I had the name, address and date of birth down, but not much else, and I sighed, dropping my head into my hands.

"Michael," I whispered, calling on the power of heaven to perform yet another miracle.

Trinity Rising
Chapter Four
Damian

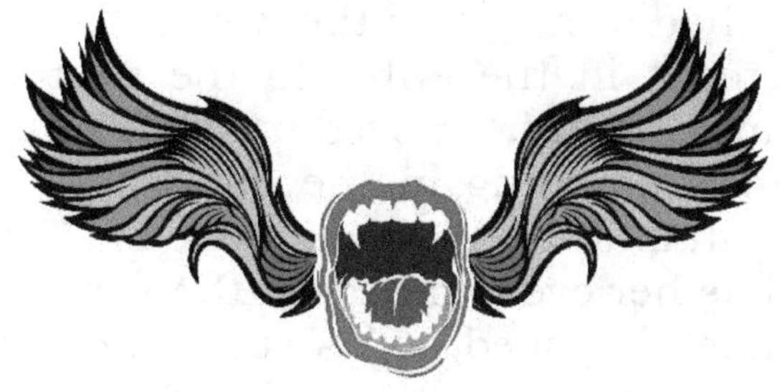

THE ONE GOOD THING about adrenaline is while it's running through your bloodstream; you're pretty much numb to emotions beyond the need to take action. When the battle ends and the adrenaline dries up, the wave crashes, and right now I was drowning in the thought of losing Valerie.

Naomi was doing her best to hold it together, but she barely contained her tears and the lack of response from our angelic relative was biting at my already raw nerves. I reached out, lacing my fingers through Naomi's, gave her my best reassuring smile, and brought the back of her hand to my lips.

Strength in the face of tragedy was not my most reliable trait, but I needed to put on the brave face for her. She sniffled and buried her face in my chest. I wrapped my arm around her and gave a squeeze, knowing damn well it wasn't enough to erase the soul-consuming fear.

I did not know who the other demon was, but I'd bet my fortune that they knew the outcome of Naomi's tests, which meant Lucifer would soon know we had a trinity on the way.

Movement in the entry to the waiting room caught my eye, and I moved my gaze from Naomi to the man standing in the doorway. I lowered Naomi's hand and straightened. Her gasp followed as her eyes landed on the same view.

"Michael?" I asked. I wasn't sure, not with the haggard being leaning on the doorframe. His slight nod kicked me into action and I dropped Naomi's grip, crossing the room and offering him a hand. He glanced at the offer and irritation raked over his face, but he took a hold of my arm and allowed me to lead him to the empty seat next to mine.

The young, vibrant angel I had known for all my days had finally aged... a lot. His once ebony hair was almost pure white and lines carved deep shadows in his face. Even his hands were wrinkled and gnarled. It took me a few minutes to find my voice.

"Can you... help?" I asked.

He gave my leg a pat. "I'm sorry." His chin dropped. "As you can see, I haven't had the chance to rejuvenate yet."

"What happened?" I couldn't help it, even though on some level I already knew.

He turned his gaze to mine. "I spent most of my energy on you, leaving just enough to make sure Naomi didn't bleed out." His gaze moved to Naomi, and he offered the slightest of smiles.

He had performed a miracle. I should have roasted in the sun, or at least dropped dead from the amount of blood loss and crushed bones in my body. But I hadn't because Michael swept in at the last minute and saved both of us. I just didn't realize what it had cost him.

I licked my lips and stared at the tile patterns traversing the floor.

"Will you ever..."

"Recuperate?" Michael finished my sentence and shrugged in a way that left my blood cold. "I honestly don't know."

"Valerie..." I started and fidgeted, picking at the hangnail on my thumb before I cleared my throat. "Valerie was stabbed."

"I know."

"By a demon," I added.

"I gathered it was something along those lines, especially since she asked for your protection," he said. "She wanted to make sure you two survived, even if she didn't."

"She..." Naomi started.

Michael put his hand up, stopping her from asking the question that swarmed my mind as well. "I have no more insight than that."

An angel without insight. Now I've heard it all, but I wasn't in the position to make a snide comment. Instead, I sighed and pinched the bridge of my nose.

Naomi's grip tightened on mine, and I turned. Something outside the window held her gaze. When I followed her gaze to the glass, my already chilled blood froze and my chest constricted like someone tied a complex and tight knot with my lungs.

Outside, the crazy nurse I killed stood next to Valerie's truck, staring at us through the window with a narrowed glare. She cracked her neck and smiled, and then her lips moved, reciting the unmistakable name that would bring the devil to our door.

Lucifer.

The freeze in my blood turned to the burn of adrenaline and I grabbed Michael's arm with my free hand, moving us with a speed I didn't think I still possessed. It wasn't vampire speed, but it was damn fast, especially while dragging an old man and my stunned wife.

I turned toward the belly of the hospital, looking for a way to escape our intertwined fates. My heart hammered in my temple, creating a beat my feet followed. The clap of thunder announced his arrival, but I didn't even chance a look. Instead, I found a staircase leading to the floor below.

It wasn't until I stood in the sparsely populated cafeteria that I stopped. Both Michael and Naomi huffed, their faces as red from exertion as I imagined mine, and I let them rest at the table near the door. Michael collapsed in the chair next to me, and Naomi took the one farthest away from the door.

Her head dropped to the table and the rise and fall of her back was enough for me to grab the nearest garbage can and slide it under her. She spit a couple of times and then nodded, and I moved the can back to the wall by the door. As I approached the table, the air in the cafeteria shifted and I stopped with my gaze locked on Naomi's.

I didn't need to turn to know Lucifer stood behind me, but I wondered if he was in the same condition as his brother. Michael stood and for a brief instance, I saw the fire flare in him, but it flickered and he grabbed the edge of the table to steady his feeble form.

I inhaled, and spun, facing the monster that was hell bent on destroying me. Lucifer stood before me in human form, but unlike Michael, he was still young. A bandage covered his neck and Eve's burning form had left more damage on the right side of the devil's face.

His gaze narrowed as he studied me, and then it transitioned to Michael.

"You fool. You gave him your grace?"

My skin flushed hot with those words. Michael's grace? Holy shit. The old angel stepped to my side, but I couldn't look at him. I was still processing Lucifer's words.

"Now all he needs is yours," Michael snarled, and Lucifer's clawed hand shot out, puncturing Michael's chest.

"He may have your grace, but I am claiming your soul."

Michael somehow produced a smile. "My soul belongs to God," he uttered.

Lucifer yanked, ripping the heart from Michael's body. A scream pierced the room and the shuffle of panicked footsteps filled the cafeteria. Michael collapsed on the floor and Lucifer stared at the heart, mesmerized as the muscle's contractions slowed until it was still.

I stared as well, unable to move, to allow my brain to grasp the death of my uncle or the words he uttered. It wasn't until Lucifer brought the heart to his lips that my paralysis broke and I stepped backwards, running into the table.

The beast ripped the heart in half, his eyes closing as he savored the taste, and I shivered with revulsion. My gaze darted around the now empty room and back to Lucifer. He swallowed the rest of Michael's heart and slowly licked his fingers.

"There's nothing quite like angel blood, even without the grace," he whispered. The burns on his face transformed before my eyes, healing and reforming to what he had been before the flaming vampire attacked him.

With blood dripping from his lips, he turned toward the cafeteria entry, where an officer stood with his gun drawn. The smile that formed set me in motion. Instead of attacking, I turned, grabbed Naomi, and fled.

Naomi tripped on a chair and went down hard on her knees and I stopped to help her up. The boom of a gunshot cut off the crazy cackling laugh behind me. I pulled Naomi off the floor and kept going without looking back.

My throat pounded and burned at the same time and I stopped in the stairwell, leaning over with my hands on my thighs. A high-pitched whine filled my ears, and I grabbed for the iron railing, steadying myself while I caught my breath.

"We have to get out of here," I said, meeting Naomi's gaze. She glanced at the ceiling and then nodded. Valerie crossed my mind too, but we didn't have the luxury of a rescue mission. If we tried, it would put her right in the path of danger.

DAMIAN

Another gunshot rang out, and I caught my breath, blowing out a stream of air before straightening just as a scream pierced the air.

"Time to go, now," I said and took her hand. We vaulted up the stairs and stepped into the back of the emergency room. Into a world of chaos.

We sidestepped out of the way as a group of officers ran by and my gaze landed on the unattended truck. My hand slid into my front pocket and the metal of the spare key ring sent a jolt through my form that moved me forward.

Demon nurse was nowhere to be seen, and I helped Naomi into the front seat and crossed to the driver's side. Ignoring the red stain on the seat and the stench of blood in the small space, I threw the car in gear and peeled out, heading away as fast as possible. I expected to be followed, especially when I was driving like the truck was my Aston Martin and I was on the Audubon.

Naomi gagged, and I glanced at her. "Open the window, it might help," I said and then focused back on the road. I knew the car had markings, so we were untraceable to celestial beings. I wasn't sure about demons or whatever else was out there.

I didn't truly exhale until we were in the dark garage and the door had dropped the last inch and the whine of the motor above shut off. I climbed out of the vehicle and made it to the kitchen sink in time to feel the bile burn the back of my throat. The cold water I splashed on my face didn't stop the onset of the shakes.

For a man who had dealt in death for so many years, this reaction rocked me to the core and I crossed to the table on shaking legs. Naomi was already sitting with her arms crossed on the walnut finish and her face buried in the crook of her elbow. Silent sobs shook her form, and I ran my damp hand over her back, not speaking for fear of splitting into a million pieces.

My phone buzzed, and I pulled it out, staring at the number.

"Fuck," the word spit out, interrupting Naomi's outburst. She stiffened under my hand and lifted her tear-stained face.

I pressed the button and put the phone to my ear.

"I will find you," Lucifer's voice growled on the line.

"I'll be ready when you do." I clicked the off button and put the phone down, shocked at how calm and cold I sounded. My hand continued the slow caress over Naomi's back as I stared out the windows at the beginning signs of spring.

"Who was that?"

I pressed my lips together and flipped the phone over, showing her the display with Valerie's number as the last call received. I couldn't speak yet; I was still dealing with an internal storm that threatened to become a hurricane.

Naomi leaned into me, laying her head on my shoulder. I wrapped my arm around her and set the phone back on the table. Every muscle in my form pounded with the same dull ache that overtook my head. Too much had happened in such a short time and I was still numb.

"I need to call Ted," I said, avoiding most of the swirl inside me. I stood, but Naomi increased her hold on me.

"Don't shut down," she said.

My gaze moved from the backyard to her deep brown eyes.

I couldn't help the laugh that bubbled up, and I peeled her off me, pulling away because with the laughter came a violent anger and I didn't want it aimed at her. The tidal wave swept through me and I clenched my fists, trying to contain the fury and the need to destroy.

Instead of addressing her comment, I stormed away, heading down into the basement. By the time I hit the tunnel, I was in a sprint, trying to run from the emotions wrestling for dominance. The trap door to the garage nearly peeled away from the hinges when I slammed it open and I climbed into the garage, with my chest heaving.

I let out a roar and picked up the closest thing, a socket wrench, and whipped it across the garage. The clang of metal on concrete just fueled my rage. A crow bar was next, but this time I turned, swinging it like I was hitting a grand slam. When the curved edge struck the side of my Ford 150, the satisfying give of metal reverberated up the shaft and into my arms. I didn't stop there. Twenty-five hundred years of fury blew and I beat the truck over and over and over, ignoring the shatter of glass and creak of metal until my arms were too tired to swing anymore.

I stumbled back into the wall, letting the crow bar fall to the floor before I sank to the ground. I folded my arms on my knees and rested my head against them before the sobs overtook me. The rips coming from my chest echoed in the garage, sounding more like an animal than a human.

I don't know how long I sat there sobbing. Time just seemed to fold in on itself and it wasn't until her hand touched the back of my head that I noticed more than just myself. The soft caress of her fingers through my hair silenced me, but they didn't stop the tears and I didn't look up. Shards of glass and metal sprinkled the floor within my vision and I focused on the prisms of light each piece represented through the sheen of my tears.

Her soft coo repeated in time with her fingers and when I raised my head and met her gaze, her bloodshot eyes told me I wasn't the only one experiencing this profound sadness. In silence, I pulled her into my arms and just held her, looking beyond her at the annihilated vehicle.

When I finally let her go, she turned and looked at my destruction.

"At least it wasn't the Aston-Martin," she said.

A smile surfaced. "Luckily, it wasn't the closest vehicle to the opening," I said, my voice raw from my outburst.

"Feel better now?" Naomi asked and wiped my cheeks.

I took a deep breath and exhaled before climbing to my feet and helping her up. I didn't quite know how to answer that question, because, while the fury was gone, a fire still burned in the middle of my chest.

"I'm not going to destroy anything else." I crossed to the closet and pulled out the broom, taking my time cleaning up the mess I made. Naomi took a seat on the stool lining my workbench, and her eyes tracked my movement.

"Imagine if I still had my vampire strength?" I said as I scooped up the first of many debris-filled dustpans and dumped it into the garbage bin.

Her quick laugh echoed, and I met her gaze.

"No, I can't imagine," Naomi said, her eyes still glistening with a sheen of tears. "You ready to talk?"

What was it with women and talking? I stopped mid-sweep and stared at her, weighing my reaction. "There really isn't anything to discuss," I said.

Her eyebrows curved, and her gaze dropped to the remaining pieces of the car. It was her *I-beg-to-differ* look, and I ignored it, returning to my task of cleaning up the mess I created.

She huffed and jumped off the chair, heading for the exit.

"Naomi," I said a little too sharply, and she spun.

"What?"

"I'm trying," I started, and leaned my forehead on the broomstick, pushing the flood waters back down into the well of my soul. "I just need to figure out what the hell is going on inside me before I'll be able to articulate it, okay?"

Her silence brought my gaze from the floor to her face. She gave me a strained smile and nodded before leaving me to finish what I started.

Trinity Rising
Chapter Five
Damian

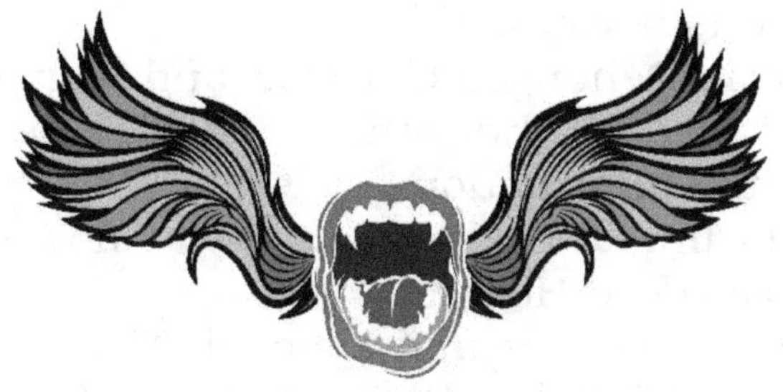

I FOUND NAOMI IN our bedroom, curled up on the bed with a throw blanket covering her. I leaned against the doorjamb, crossing my arms, and contemplated whether or not to interrupt her sleep. Her soft snore permeated through the fringe of the blanket and I sighed, stepping out of the room. She needed rest, and I had a phone call to make.

My stomach growled, and I diverted from the table to the refrigerator, opening it and scanning the contents. Nothing appealed to me and I closed the door, stepping back to the table and my cell phone.

The thought of calling Valerie's uncle left my chest tight, and I opted to call the hospital to find out how she was instead.

"Charlotte Hungerford Hospital. How may I help you?"

"I understand my cousin was brought into the emergency room earlier today," I started. "The last information I was given was that she was in surgery. Can you tell me what her status is now?"

"What is her name?"

"Valerie Denongalis," I said and waited while the person on the other end of the phone entered the information.

"According to the notes, she was flown by Life Star to Hartford Hospital."

I closed my eyes and exhaled. "Thank you." I hung up and did a Google search, finding the number to Hartford Hospital, and repeated the process.

They took down my name and phone number, validating I was on the list of next of kin. Once they were satisfied, they put me on hold. I paced while waiting for a voice, glancing at the clock and calculating the time we first entered the emergency room and now. Seven hours had passed. A hell of a lot more than I thought, and the longer I was on hold, the more unnerved I got.

"Mr. Andreas?" a male voice asked.

"Yes."

"I'm Dr. Browne, the surgeon in charge of your cousin's case," he said and papers shuffled. "She is in the recovery room at the moment, but we will move her to the intensive care within the hour."

"Is she... okay?"

The doctor hesitated. "I'll know more in the morning. I understand her uncle is on the way.

If you have the means to get here..." he drifted off.

"Unfortunately, I'm not in the position to get to Hartford at the moment," I said. "Can you give me some specifics?"

"The knife punctured her right kidney, and we were unable to save it. It also nicked the renal artery, and she lost a great deal of blood."

"She can survive with one kidney, right?"

"Yes, the kidney is the least of her worries," the doctor said. "The blood loss and increased chance of infection are the bigger issues, but now that we've contained the bleeding, she should have a better chance of fighting off whatever bacteria might have been on that knife."

I remained quiet. "Chances of survival?" I asked when he said nothing more.

"If she makes it through the night, I can give you better odds."

"What are her odds of making it through the night?"

"A little better than fifty percent."

"Thank you. I appreciate the information," I said and hung up. My next call was to Ted, and it took a couple of rings before he answered.

"Damian?" he asked after the shuffle sounds stopped.

"Yes, sir."

"I assume you know what happened," he said. A blinker sounded in the background.

"Demons, sir," I said. "They attacked her when we were in Torrington."

"What the hell were you doing in Torrington?"

"Valerie wanted Naomi checked out by a doctor."

"Why?"

"Naomi is pregnant."

Silence. Ted's breathing filled the line and all the prophecies Michael had told came to the forefront of my mind.

"Naomi's due in October and Val was worried that she might be diabetic." I crossed the kitchen and leaned on the window frame, scanning the wood line beyond the fence. "Val took us to the doctor's office."

"Let me guess, the doctor was a demon?"

I blinked at the venom in his question. "No. One of the nurses."

"You think that's a coincidence?"

"I... uh," I stumbled on the words.

"They've been watching the house ever since Michael dropped the two of you on our doorstep, and you can bet they were laying in wait for this day."

The mention of Michael's name tightened my throat. "Michael's dead."

"What?"

"Lucifer showed up at the hospital. So did Michael, and he didn't make it." Just recounting the day sucked the life out of me and I walked to the couch in the living room, dropping into the soft cushions. "I don't know how soon after that they sent Val to Hartford, but I'm glad they did, otherwise Lucifer would have found her and eaten her heart, too."

"How did you get out of there?"

"Cops converged." It was the first time in my life I had been truly happy to see a cop in the vicinity. "And I grabbed Naomi and ran." I paused and licked my lips. "Did you know Michael gave me his grace?"

An exhale filled the line. "No. He didn't mention that, but I knew bringing you back from the dead nearly did him in," Ted said, and the soft purr of the engine cut off. "I'm at the hospital. I'll let you know if her condition changes."

"Thank you."

"And Damian?"

"Yeah?"

"You and Naomi need to look for another place to live."

I huffed a laugh out. "What?"

"I have to keep my niece safe, and I can't with you there."

"Ted..." I trailed off. He was right, and even though the property was mine, it was where Valerie had lived all her life. I couldn't take that away from her, not when association with me had cost her everything else.

"I'm serious. I want the two of you gone before I bring her home from the hospital."

There was no leeway in his statement, and I closed my eyes. "Fine. I'll start looking in the morning."

"I'll let you know if anything changes with Valerie," he said and hung up the phone.

I dropped the phone on the table and rubbed my face. Naomi wasn't going to take this well, and I had no clue how I'd get us out of here without being attacked.

NAOMI STEPPED INTO THE room in the middle of a yawn. I did a quick glance at her and then focused back on my computer without a word. There were so many options on where we could go that I was at an impasse.

"Where do you want to live?" I finally asked, looking up as she took a seat on the couch.

"Here."

"Not an option."

"Damian..."

"Ted wants us gone before he brings Valerie home," I cut her off and glanced back at the computer. "And I have no idea where you want to live." I returned my gaze to her. "New York is not an option," I added before she fell back on her usual location.

"What do you mean, Ted wants us to go?"

I leaned back and kept her stare. I didn't need to speak, either. It was obvious after today. Anyone close to us would always be in danger, and I dropped my gaze to her stomach before looking back at the computer.

My children would always be on the run.

The reality of that statement shot me to my feet, and I crossed, slipping outside onto the patio and into the chill of the falling evening. I longed for the simplicity of life. The cluelessness of not knowing angels or demons or things much darker existed. I wanted a normal life for my children, not this hide to survive bullshit.

I glanced up at the stars and sighed. Maybe it was time to go home.

Naomi stepped next to me, glancing up at the stars in the twilight sky.

"What about Greece?" I said, still scanning the deepening colors of dusk.

The way she sighed pulled my attention to her. She looked between the sky and my face before turning toward me.

"While I'd love to see Greece at some time, this country is my home."

I knew she'd say that and as much as I longed for the white beaches and azure water of my birthplace; I hadn't been back, and I didn't know if it would be the same.

"I can't talk you into some place like Australia or New Zealand?"

She hesitated, studying the colorful sky before she spoke. "Again, those are places I'd like to visit, but I just can't see living there. And before you ask, the same goes for South America and Africa. I love my country. I don't want the devil chasing me out of my home."

"The west coast?"

"California isn't my style either. I enjoy having the seasons."

"Tahoe has seasons," I said, but her head was shaking. "We already did the mountains and while I loved Colorado, I missed home."

"That leaves Alaska or Hawaii," I said, thinking of places as far away from here as possible.

She laughed and met my gaze with a shake of her head.

She wasn't giving me much of the landscape to work with. "Somehow, I can't see you in the south either," I said and gave her a hint of a smile.

Naomi's dimples made an appearance. "You can't see me saying y'all?"

"No, no, I can't," I actually chuckled and pulled her to me. "You definitely are not a mild-mannered southern belle. I can see you as a kick-ass cowgirl, though."

She wrinkled her nose at me and shook her head. "I'm not interested in the wild west."

I tilted my chin toward my chest and raised an eyebrow. "Then where?"

She bit her lip. "Have you ever been to..." She paused and glanced up at the stars. "...Maine?"

I followed her gaze. "It's still too close."

"Have you ever been there?"

I shook my head. That was one state I hadn't been to and the idea of still being in New England didn't sit well with me. Being on this half of the world didn't sit well, but I knew I'd never get Naomi to agree to raise children on a deserted island in the South Pacific.

Hell, Lilith found us in the mountains of Colorado, so really, there wasn't any place safe on Earth and we damn well couldn't populate the moon.

I sighed. "Okay."

"Really?"

I dropped my gaze to hers. "Really. But I have to make it look like we are leaving the country." I planted a kiss on her forehead and led us back inside.

"I'm booking us on as many flights to Greece as I can from airports around here and in Michigan."

"Why Michigan?"

"I own one of the top automobile museums in the country. I'll send most of the car collection to them so they don't rot here."

"I didn't realize you had more than what's in the garage?"

"There are a lot of things you still don't know about me." I sent a grin her way and refocused. "I'm also going to book one flight out of Louisiana."

"Louisiana?"

"It's part of the shell game and he'll assume that's where we settled."

"New Orleans?"

I grinned and nodded.

"Isn't that a bit... cliché?"

"Absolutely, but he won't get it," I said and slid onto the couch. It took me close to an hour to book ten separate flights, ranging from as early as the following week out of Boston to the latest from Louisiana next month. The only flights that didn't have connections in the U.S. originated out of Boston, the rest of the flights had connections in O'Hare, Dulles or Atlanta.

When I finished, I cracked my knuckles and stretched my fingers before switching gears. I sent a note to the museum curator informing him I had a dozen more vehicles coming the following week, including pieces from ancient Greece and Rome. The response came in less than five minutes after I hit send, and I swear the man must have been close to a fucking orgasm with how much he gushed.

I sent a note back saying the vehicles needed some engine work because they had been sitting for most of the last five years, and he assured me they would be attended to when they arrived.

Next, I arranged for transportation of everything except my Aston-Martin; that would go wherever we went. The next couple of days would be busy loading vehicles and when I was done with the arrangements, I turned the computer to Naomi.

"Your turn. You need to look for a place for us to stay," I said and stood up. "I'm going to make sure I have everything I need to finish up the Aston Martin and hide it from view."

"Do I have a budget?" she asked as she pulled the computer onto her lap.

"Find a lease for now."

Disappointment transitioned her mouth into a pouty frown and I turned, leaving her to the task. I found my way through the underground tunnel and stood in the center of the garage, looking at the contents. The dozen vehicles, including the ornate chariots, would be gone by the end of the following day, and the rest of the things needed to be cleared out before we left. The Aston-Martin didn't have a great deal of storage space, so anything I wanted to come with us had to be compact.

I slid into the seat and turned the ignition key. The car jumped to life, purring like she should. All the work I had done over the past month had gotten her into shape and there wasn't anything I could think of that she needed. Even the tires had been replaced. I shut the car off and popped the trunk. I packed a toolbox with the wrench set and all the custom sockets I had for the different engine parts.

When I had everything I needed for future servicing, I closed the lid and placed the toolbox in the trunk, along with the extra oil filters and spark plugs for the car.

I cleared a space in the far right corner and pulled the car as close to the wall as I dared before putting a fitted cover over the vehicle. Then I moved boxes, old tires and two rolling tool chests I had around the car, hiding it from view and giving us the room to maneuver the rest of the vehicles.

I stepped back, scanning the area. It needed more, and I glanced at the ruined truck. Once I found the key, I yanked on the driver's door, but it didn't budge, so I climbed up on the bent foot rail and hauled myself through the empty window.

Despite my skepticism, the truck started, and I moved it, so it blocked the box barricade. I exited the way I entered and walked around to the belly of the garage. The mangled form did a better job of blocking the Aston Martin than the boxes and tool chests. Now it just looked like a normal garage storage space, along with a truck that needed serious bodywork.

Satisfied, I wiped my hands on my jeans and headed back to the house.

"York," Naomi said when I entered the living room.

I raised an eyebrow. "I told you, New York is not an option."

"No, York, Maine. It's a beach community, and I found a couple of rentals that would be perfect and they aren't outrageous."

She spun the computer toward me and I scanned the list of year-round rentals. They weren't bad and a few of the home rentals were downright beautiful. "Where is York?" I asked, hoping she'd say as far north as possible.

"It's like fifteen minutes from Portsmouth, New Hampshire."

I met her gaze and she wet her lips with her tongue and flashed that pleading smile that made it impossible to say no. Fuck it. I tapped the more expensive of the two condo rentals. "See if that's still available."

She picked up the phone, and I crossed into the kitchen to figure out something for dinner. We hadn't eaten much today, and I got that lightheaded feeling that comes with forgetting to eat. Instead of opting for some heavy Greek dish, I went simple and opened a can of tomato soup.

Naomi stepped into the kitchen behind me and wrapped her arms around my waist. Just the feel of her made my heart flutter, despite the day from hell, and I turned my head, catching a quick kiss over my shoulder.

"Do you want grilled cheese with this?"

She glanced at the stove and nodded. "I'll probably only have grilled cheese."

"Keeping it light?"

"Yeah, my stomach is still unsettled and not eating today didn't help."

I just nodded and continued stirring. Now that I wasn't actively doing anything, my mind started wondering about what Michael said today.

"Why did Michael give me his grace?" I asked with my back to Naomi. "And what the hell did he mean by now all I need is Lucifer's?" I didn't expect an answer and when Naomi didn't speak, I took a glance over my shoulder. She stood looking out the back window, her profile carved in thought.

I let it go, focusing back on our dinner. When I set our plates on the table, she turned and sighed, taking the seat opposite me. I brought two bowls and spoons along with the soup pot, just in case she changed her mind.

The minute I set the soup down, she turned ravenous, like she hadn't eaten in years. I had the forethought to make her two sandwiches, and she decided halfway through the first half to add soup to her meal.

"Maybe he's setting you up to be a true trinity." Naomi said around a mouthful of grilled cheese.

"How?"

"Maybe when your father died, you got his grace too."

I burst out laughing. "I still can't get over the fact I was the beneficiary of one angel's grace. I'm certainly not worthy of two."

Naomi's brow knit together and she took another bite of her sandwich. "Why do you do that?" Her eyes flared to match the sharpness in her tone.

"Sweetheart, I killed my fair share of people and some of them did not deserve to die. I'm not worthy of grace."

Her gaze narrowed. "Worthy or not, it sounds like you have it and you need to figure out how to use it."

My hands dropped to the table, and I stared at her. "What do you mean?"

"I might be wrong, but I have a feeling he could have made you better without granting you his grace."

This wasn't an idea I wanted to entertain. I didn't understand why Michael would be so foolish as to put himself in harm's way for me. "So he died for me?" I asked, my voice carrying all the incredulousness that filled my brain.

"Angels don't die, Damian. They just don't get to leave heaven anymore."

"Isn't that the same thing?" I asked her, leaning back in the chair and crossing my arms.

Her gaze turned to a glare. "That isn't the point. There was a reason Michael gave you his grace. We just need to figure it out, and I think his statement may have been the key."

"Look, right now, I want to get us as far from this house as I possibly can. I want you and my child to be safe, and the last thing I want to do is confront Lucifer. You saw just as much as I did. He's almost back to full strength, which means if we cross his path, we have nothing to defend ourselves with."

"There has to be a way to kill that bastard," she said.

"Okay, I'm curious, now that we're human, just how in the hell do you suggest we kill an angel?" I countered, leaning forward on the table because I really had no clue and wanted to hear what she had to say. After all, she had nearly done him in when she was a vampire in tiger form.

"You steal his grace," she said like it was an achievable thing.

I started laughing. "You are out of your fucking mind."

Naomi huffed and pushed her plate in, crossing her arms in that stubborn manner that made me want to take her over my knee. Anger bloomed, and I stood, clearing the table before I said something I'd regret.

"I'm serious."

I spun from the sink. "You had the strength to kill him when you were a vampire; I never had that kind of power."

She stood and cut the distance between us to nothing but a fraction of an inch. "You're the stronger one now."

Her hand landed on my chest, and I stared into her eyes. Into the conviction displayed in her deep chocolate irises and laughed. I looked up at the ceiling, cursing my bloodline as well as hers. I turned away from her, finishing the dishes instead of continuing this insane conversation.

"Have you heard anything more about Valerie?"

I wiped my hands on a dishtowel, realizing that I hadn't told her about the conversation I had with the doctor. "I talked to her doctor before I called Ted. Life Star took Valerie to Hartford Hospital once she stabilized enough to travel. Her doctor said they had to remove her right kidney and they could give us a better idea of her recuperation time in the morning." I left out the fact her odds weren't ideal for making it through the night. Naomi didn't need to know just how close we came to losing her. "And Ted said he'd call me if anything changed."

Naomi just stared at me, her eyelashes batting like she didn't quite understand. "They flew her to Hartford?"

"Yes. She needed a trauma one center, and that's the closest one. If they hadn't, she probably would have died from blood loss." Instead of taking a seat at the table, I left the kitchen and flopped on the couch, turning the laptop towards me. I hadn't logged into the day job at all and when I opened my business email account, I exhaled at the flurry of activity.

The last piece of the shell game needed to be addressed, and I sent a note to my boss, telling him I needed some personal time in order to move. He must have been online because my phone buzzed and I glanced at Naomi.

"What do you mean, you need more time off?" Kevin bellowed in my ear when I answered.

"It's either that or I'll have to give notice," I said and pinched the bridge of my nose to dull the forming headache.

"You're the best damn programmer I have and we need you," he pushed. "The project will not get done in time if you leave."

"Kevin, I'm not in a position to give you a whole hell of a lot of time right now. If you can live with what I can give, when I can give it, then we're good. Otherwise..." I trailed off, trying not to get aggravated with him. I knew I was putting him in a difficult spot, but I just couldn't see a way around it. Juggling everything I had in the air right now needed my concentration, otherwise, I'd screw up.

As trite as it sounded, lives were at stake, and failing was not an option.

A project timeline put in jeopardy just seemed so ridiculously unimportant in comparison, but I didn't want to burn any bridges.

A huff came over the line and I could just imagine him chewing on his lip while overlooking some concrete landscape out the window. He exhaled. "What can you give me?"

I closed my eyes and dropped my chin to my chest. Whatever I promised, I'd have to follow through on, no matter what, and right now that was a nearly impossible commitment. Instead of saying I couldn't give him anything, I said, "I can commit to five hours a week for the next month."

"An hour a day? Are you fucking kidding me?"

"It's what I can commit to. If I find I can give you more, I will."

"Does this have anything to do with the accident?"

My eyes opened, and I met Naomi's gaze. That was the excuse she gave when I was in a coma. A car accident. I wish it had been that instead of Lucifer playing tic-tac-toe on my chest with a razor, or beating me to a pulp with his fist. An accident would have been cleaner and easier to deal with. Instead, I had nightmares every night and now I had to face that bastard again.

"Damian?"

"Yes, there have been some complications that need to be addressed," I answered and just left it at that.

"Are you... okay?" he asked in a voice softened with concern.

"I'm not dying, if that's what you're worried about," I said.

"Oh, okay, that's good," Kevin said, stumbling before he recovered his authoritative boom. "I guess we can work around your schedule," he added.

"Thank you."

"Can you look at the issue the testers found?"

"Yeah, I'll take a look now and shoot over my findings in a few," I said and disconnected the call. "Shit." The last thing I wanted to do was work.

Naomi stretched out on the couch next to me, using my thigh as a pillow. She flipped on the television while I shuffled through the email chain.

After a few minutes, the irony of the situation hit me and I chuckled.

Naomi glanced up at me with her brow scrunched in her what-the-fuck look.

"For someone who's supposed to save the world, being stuck troubleshooting code is completely fucked up."

Dimples appeared even before her giggle and she rolled her eyes, settling back down on my lap to catch the rest of the show.

I had the problem figured out and fixed before the half-hour sitcom ended and sent a note to my boss. I folded the laptop, set it on the table, and stretched.

"Are we all set with that condo?" I asked, and Naomi rolled onto her back, looking straight up at me.

"They weren't there when I called and they haven't called back yet."

"If it doesn't pan out, we can always stay at a hotel until we find something." I cupped her cheek and ran my thumb over her lips, enjoying the silkiness of her skin.

"When are we leaving?"

"Your guess is as good as mine." I shifted and brushed her hair away from her face, tucking the stray hairs behind her ear. "It won't be until after all the cars are on their way to Michigan and we may have to stay downstairs for a few days. Just until I think it's clear to go."

She raised an eyebrow.

"Besides, I have to reprogram the access to the rooms downstairs. I need to make a failsafe that will freeze the lock if someone attempts to override the commands I put in place. I don't want anyone getting in or out of there after we go. I want to make it so they'd have to blast the door off with dynamite to gain access."

"Why?"

"I'm not worried about Ted and Valerie using the place. I'm more concerned with someone finding their way in from the garage." I shrugged, leaving the possibilities open, and she slowly nodded. "Demon's can't get past the entry pipe—but anything else can."

"If you lock it up..." she started, and I raised my eyebrows at her, silently telling her to rethink the statement before she continued. Naomi inhaled and nodded, getting my point.

"I want to leave the garage open. That way, they'll know it's empty and that we've left for good. But before we go, not only do I have to do the reprogramming magic, I also need to solder the door at the bottom of the stairs and do the same to the hatchway so nothing can get through. And, just for good measure, I'll move the truck over the hatch to make it less obvious. Once we're in Maine, I'll make sure the ownership of both the property and the garage is transferred to Valerie and she can do whatever she wants with it."

Leaving unnoticed would not be easy, but if I could pull it off, it would give us time. How much time was the question, and I broke eye contact with Naomi, looking out at the dark settling over the backyard.

If I didn't succeed at this, God only knew what the hell we'd unleash.

Naomi yawned and stretched, pulling my attention away from the outside world, and I smiled down at her. I wish I knew what she was thinking. I missed the mind reading abilities we shared as vampires and I sighed, running my fingertips over her sexy lips.

She grabbed my wrist and pulled my index finger into her mouth. Heat stirred inside me and I closed my eyes for a moment as she slowly released it. When she teased me like this, I could feel the fire between us burn bright. I opened my eyes and allowed the slow grin she adored to form.

It had the desired effect; she propped herself up to meet my hungry lips.

Her mouth tasted like caramel, and she wrapped her arms around my neck, deepening the kiss. Her tongue danced slowly with mine, turning off logical thought. The animal in me reared up, carnal and wanting, and I wrapped my arms around her, pulling her closer.

A distant buzz cut through my lust and I pulled away from her sweet lips, meeting her gaze before transitioning my attention to the phone on the table. It could be Ted and I sighed, pushing her aside and picked up the phone.

Any heat she'd created turned to an icy fury at the caller ID and every muscle tensed into hard knots. I inhaled, closing my eyes before bringing the phone to my ear.

His malignant chuckle drifted over the line.

"What the fuck do you want?" I growled into the phone through clenched teeth. I opened my eyes, meeting Naomi's gaze.

"I want your wife and your unborn child."

"Not on your life."

"My plans have changed a bit since you seemed to have already created the first pure trinity. I'll gladly trade your daughter's soul for your wife's. I can't think of anything more perfect than deflowering a virgin trinity. If you deliver Naomi to me, I'll let you live to watch your daughter grow and become my concubine," he purred, pushing dangerous buttons.

"You must be pretty bad off to think I'd entertain the idea of a negotiation. Why don't we make a deal? You leave us the fuck alone and I won't kill you," I said, and Naomi shivered in my arms. Before he could interject some more horrifying images, I continued, "Did you know when an angel dies, they get locked in heaven? I wonder what happens when the devil dies?"

Naomi's eyes widened, and she shook her head.

In the back of my mind, I wondered why the hell I was poking a sleeping dragon, but for the first time, I seemed in control of the conversation and it gave me the audacity to taunt him.

"I am going to enjoy watching you die," Lucifer growled, pulling a smile from within my anger.

"Yeah, I've heard that before. At least three times, but it doesn't seem to stick, now does it?" I asked and winked at Naomi, enjoying this more than I should.

A roar came over the line. "I'll kill you both, you little shit!"

"You will never get the chance."

"I will hunt you down and rip your heart out," he growled.

"You're such a sadistic bastard, you know that?" I laughed, realizing somewhere along the way the tides had turned in my favor.

"You think you can hide in Greece?" he asked, his voice barely steady.

"It's a big world, my friend, and who knows, maybe I'll organize me a demonic hunting party. I really enjoy killing those bastards and I'm sure eventually the path of dead assholes will lead me to you."

"Damian," Naomi whispered, and I met her panicked gaze. I smiled and palmed her cheek.

"Now, if you don't mind, I'm going to make love to my wife," I said and cut the call, tossing the phone onto the table.

"Are you out of your fucking mind?"

I raised my eyebrow at her outburst. "What?"

"Do you really think pissing off Lucifer is a smart idea?"

"You know what? I've been walking on eggshells for twenty-five hundred years trying not to piss off the legion of angels, and what has it gotten me? I'm done. I'm not taking shit from any of them ever again." I stood, pulling her to her feet and shutting off her argument with my lips.

Fired up was an understatement, and I focused all the built up frustration on her. I swept her up into my arms and turned off the lights, carrying her to our bedroom.

Trinity Rising
Chapter Six
Naomi

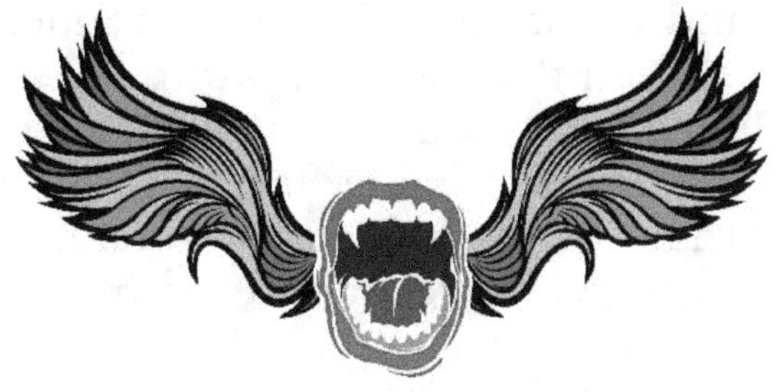

THE ICY FIRE IN his eyes, along with the determined set of his jaw, jumpstarted my heart, spreading a flush over my skin, and I shivered with anticipation. Even with the shitty day we've had and the insane call from Lucifer, one hungry gaze from Damian still sent me into the land of lust.

When he laid me out on the bed, I stared at him, taking in his hard form from head to toe as he stripped. Without clothing, the man screamed perfection, and I caught the twinkle in his eyes as he crawled toward me.

Damian licked his lips and pushed my shirt up, finding my skin with his hot tongue. The magic in his fingertips sent me into orbit and he started unbuttoning my pants and then stripped away every stitch of fabric. A side of him I had never seen came out tonight.

Rough, demanding, in control and hotter than hell.

The things he did to me werc far from the gentle, thoughtful lover I spent the last five years with. I think he even growled at one point, nipping and stroking with such abandon that I got lost between the pleasure and pain.

He claimed my body with a vengeance that left me breathless, filling me with a need so palpable that our room filled with steam.

I don't know how long we went at it, but when it was over, we lay side by side staring at the ceiling, both of us panting for breath. I turned my head and met his satiated gaze. He gave me that one dimple smile that warmed my form and I sent one back, still unable to speak.

My body felt supple and exhausted, exhilarated and thrilled all at the same time. My muscles trembled from exertion and I closed my eyes.

"Damn, boy," I finally said with a breathless sigh.

He chuckled and rolled on his side, pulling me into him.

"I love you, Naomi," he whispered in my ear with a voice as ragged as my own.

"I love you, too," I said and turned so I could accept a kiss. As tired as I was, I couldn't fall asleep, even when his breathing slowed into that soft cadence of sleep.

Being human had changed Damian in more ways than I think he knew. He still had a kind heart, but he now had command over his emotions. They no longer broadcast in his every expression. Most notably, the haunted look that had been in his eyes since I first met him was no longer there.

We've always had an active sex life. Sometimes it got wild, and when we were both vampires, it included sinking our teeth in each other's throat at the moment of orgasm. But even those wild nights paled compared to this.

Not once in our courtship had he ravaged me like he did tonight.

I shifted in his arms and his breathing hitched and then smoothed out. Gently, I moved his hand and rolled out of bed as a different need struck. I made my way into the bathroom, did my business, and stopped at the sink. My hair looked like a bird's nest and I took time to brush it before heading back to bed.

On my way through the bedroom, something in the dark caught my attention, and I crossed to the window, squinting into the darkness. A small spark erupted at the closest point of the fence and I gasped at the face illuminated by a lighter. My arms crossed over my bare breasts and Lucifer took a long drag and blew a stream of smoke into the air, sending the most disturbing smile my way before the flame extinguished, leaving only the glow of the cigarette in the darkness.

I stepped farther into the shadows and swallowed the vile taste of fear.

Damian sat up in bed, staring at me, and our eyes locked. The smile on his face froze my heart in place. It was the same one Lucifer wore just before the lighter went out.

"What's wrong, baby, you don't like dancing with the devil?" he asked in a way that left me frigid. It was Damian's voice, but it was *not* my husband.

A SCREAM PEELED FROM my throat, burning it raw with the force and the nightstand light switched on.

"Naomi?" his hand caressed my arm, and I cranked my head in his direction.

I sat stalk straight in the bed; the covers knotted around me, and his sleepy, worried gaze met mine. It took a full minute to get my breathing under control and I blinked in confusion at the nightmare. The bed trembled with the shakes racking my form, and Damian wrapped his arms around me, kissing my temple.

"Do you want to talk about it?" he asked and I couldn't help the hysterical laugh that came bubbling up.

Complete confusion overwhelmed me and I wondered if I had dreamed the entire night; but the ache in my hips and the pressure in my bladder told me otherwise. Still, I had to ask.

"Was... did..." I couldn't articulate, and I met Damian's gaze. "Did we..."

He grinned, and the blush heightened in his cheeks and then his smile faded, worry replacing it. "You thought that was part of your nightmare?"

My mouth opened to speak and then I closed it, wondering exactly what I was going to say.

"I... I'm sorry," he whispered, coming to the wrong conclusion.

"Don't apologize, you were...beyond fantastic, it's just, you've never been like that before," I started and saw a flare of hurt pass over his face. He shifted the covers and dropped his gaze.

"I dreamed Lucifer had somehow possessed you."

His eyes snapped to mine.

I offered a shrug in my defense. "And you were so... so different than you usually are that I thought—"

"Jesus," he muttered and ran his hands through his hair, the horror of it all reflecting on his face.

"Yeah, it was bizarre." I slipped out of bed, heading for the bathroom to relieve myself. I grabbed a nightgown on my way by the dresser to dilute the discomfort of being exposed. When I came back out, Damian had straightened the covers and sat with his arms crossed and that brooding expression that I immediately recognized.

He was getting more irritated by the second and he met my gaze when I slipped into the bed.

"How can you even think that?" he snapped, taking me by surprised.

"Look, in the dream I saw something out the window that caught my attention. It was Lucifer, and he was outside the fence smoking a cigarette like they do in the old movies, you know, after fucking around. And you, you sat up with that same shit-eating grin and asked me how I liked dancing with the devil."

Damian blinked, and his eyebrows rose.

"Then I woke up screaming."

Damian's gaze moved past me to the window and back, and the tightness in his jaw softened. "I can assure you, that was all me." He blushed.

"But Lucifer was the one who brought out the beast in you," I said.

His gaze dropped to his hands, and he took a deep breath as he analyzed my comment and his head started shaking back and forth. "No. Lucifer had nothing to do with my behavior tonight." He turned his glance toward me. "You had everything to do with it. I'll concede that my anger may have made me a bit more callous than usual, or less inhibited, but you're the one who drives me insane." A dimple appeared. "In the best way possible," he added.

Trinity Rising
Chapter Seven
Naomi

THE MORNING SUN DRENCHED the bedroom, and I blinked, rolling away from the open curtains. Damian's side of the bed was empty, and I pushed myself up into a sitting position. My stomach decided that wasn't the brightest thing to do, and I clamped my hand over my mouth, running to the bathroom as the bile crawled up my throat.

I did not like this side effect of pregnancy. Dealing with an unsettled stomach close to twenty-four hours a day sucked. Exhaustion I could deal with, but this, this was a royal pain. I spit in the toilet and climbed to my feet, flushing before washing the nasty taste from my mouth. I wrapped a warm bathrobe around my body and headed into the living room.

Damian looked up from his position on the couch, his computer propped on his lap and a pencil sticking out of both sides of his mouth.

Papers and a yellow pad lay across the couch and I smiled. He pulled the pencil from between his teeth.

"Hey, how are you feeling?"

"Eh. What are you doing?" I waved toward the mess.

"I figured I'd try to get most of the time I promised to Kevin." He glanced at his watch and stretched.

"How long have you been at it?"

"A little over three hours and I only have another forty-five minutes before the auto-transport company is due to arrive."

I glanced at the clock. "You got up at five?"

"I couldn't get back to sleep," he said, folding the computer and putting it on the table. He arranged the paperwork into a neat pile and then set it on top of his computer before he finally met my stare.

When he didn't offer an explanation, I shrugged and asked, "Why not?"

He stood and retreated to the kitchen, and I followed. After he popped a couple of pieces of bread into the toaster, he turned, leaning on the counter behind him.

"The more I thought about it, the angrier I got," he said.

My mouth went dry, and I wasn't sure I wanted to know, but I asked anyway. "Thought about what?"

"Everything." He didn't continue right away. Instead, he focused on buttering the toast and bringing it to the table, setting it in front of the chair I stood behind. "I'm pissed that we're pawns in their fucking game," he said and sat down.

The toast smelled good, and my mouth watered, so I took a bite. He yawned, covering it with his hand before continuing.

"I've been running for centuries, surviving by hiding away: from the sun, from Lucifer, even from Michael for a time. Every time I thought I found peace, the angels rained down on me, spoiling it in some manner. I will not let that happen this time."

The intensity in his eyes made me swallow hard.

"I'm done being afraid," he added and crossed his arms. "Death is just an end to the running and if I don't stop him this time, my child will never know peace."

An icy fear pierced my heart and spread through my body, almost doubling me over. I dropped the slice I held onto the plate. "I'm not letting you sacrifice yourself for us. I need you just as much as your child does."

He laughed in a way that sparked an irrational irritation.

"I'm not suggesting that I become a martyr, honey. I'm talking about killing him. Ending his reign of terror and walking away from it." He reached over and snatched one slice of toast. "You got me thinking. There has to be a way to kill an angel and with Lucifer, I'm not sure stealing his grace is achievable, but we both know he can be killed. You're the one who's got the closest to that goal, so I just need to figure out how to do it without the tiger."

"I almost beat him because he was in human form."

"We're both painfully aware of the differences between human and angel forms," he said with a sigh. "I think he's stuck in human form until he mends completely. At least that's what I'm hoping."

"He looked pretty whole after eating Michael's heart." My appetite vanished. Damian nodded and he exhaled audibly through his nose.

"I know. I guess I expected Michael to fight back in some way, even in his debilitated state."

"Yeah, I think I expected him to sprout wings and smite that bastard."

Damian let out a small laugh. "I should have taken advantage of the situation and attacked while he was still vulnerable." He met my gaze and shrugged. "I think that's the thing that pisses me off the most. That was probably the best chance I had of beating Lucifer and I ran away like a frightened little girl."

The venom in his voice gave me pause, and I searched his face for a moment. "You were protecting me."

He nodded. "You and the baby."

"And really, what could you have done with the cop there?"

"I could have broken his neck, like I did to that demon," he answered. "It would have at least slowed him down, and maybe he wouldn't have killed that cop."

I jerked with the shock of his statement. "He killed..." I started and trailed off.

"It was on the news this morning, along with my face. Plastered all over the fucking news. I'm apparently a person of interest," he said, using finger quotes around the words person of interest.

I blinked at him, and my eyebrows arched.

"They didn't have a clear picture of you," he said and offered a smile. "But they have one of me, looking shocked as shit."

Muscles I didn't realize I had tensed, relaxed a fraction. I don't look any different from five years ago and I'm sure if this story went national, some of my friends in New York might have been able to provide an identity that would be traced back to a dead girl.

"So, what else did they show?"

"Nothing. No footage of Lucifer, nothing, just my face, which looks like a still from a video feed, and a couple of seconds of us running as the cop yelled freeze."

I couldn't help the laugh that escaped, as if our lives weren't complicated enough. Now we had the police searching for us. My brain caught up, and I gasped, my gaze shooting back to Damian's. "They don't have footage of Lucifer?"

Damian slowly shook his head, and I exhaled, slumping in the chair. We needed a break, but it didn't look like it was coming any time soon.

"The bastard set us up."

I blinked, staring at him. "And he's using the media to find us."

"Bingo. Are you sure you don't want to go to Greece?" he asked, cocking his head. "Because right now, it looks like they're building a case against us."

"With your picture plastered all over the airwaves, there's no way we would get away with leaving the country," I said and he bit his bottom lip with an expression that agreed with my statement.

"The good news is not many people know my face and most of those people know me under an alias. There are only three people who know my name and address, and one is sitting right here."

"And the other two are at Hartford Hospital."

"Yes. I also spoke with Ted this morning. It looks like Valerie is going to be okay. She made it through the night without incident and she even regained consciousness enough to relay her version of the attack."

"Really?"

"Yes. Thankfully, that wasn't picked up by any news stories because Lucifer would put it together and go after her. At this point, he does not know where she went." Damian glanced at his watch and stood. "I have to go meet the auto-transport people." He paused at the doorway to the living room. "Just hang here, okay?"

The worry in his eyes made me nod. I didn't need to help pack the cars, anyway. I had some packing of my own to do. "Be careful," I said.

"I always am."

I huffed, and Damian rolled his eyes.

"I'll try," he added, and disappeared from view.

Trinity Rising
Chapter Eight
Naomi

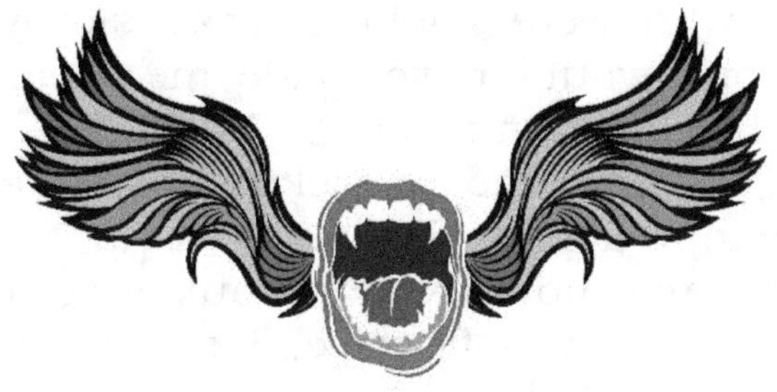

I MADE THE MISTAKE of turning on the television and taking in the news story. The raw anger that bit at me sparked a chuff from my lips and the shock of the feral sound pulled my gaze to the floor, and the white-furred paws.

Shock transitioned through my body and I took another step, still locked in tiger form. I hissed and spat and padded down the stairs. The keypad was difficult to manage with my paw, but I finally had the idea of using one of my razor sharp nails.

The door squeaked open, and I padded my way down the tunnel, turning into a gallop and by the time I reached the stairs, my heart pounded and I was sure Damian was being tortured on the other side of the hatch. I flew up the stairs, using the strength in my massive shoulder to open the hatch. I came to a sliding stop in the middle of the garage, a snarl coming from my mouth.

Damian spun along with one of the work crew. I growled and then chuffed and licked my chops, looking between Damian and the group of workers who were backing away slowly. Their expressions would have made me laugh had I been in human form.

Damian gave me a cocked-head stare and then he approached, slowly.

"Hey, baby, how'd you get out of your cage?" he asked with a soft voice, like one meant to disarm an angry tiger.

"Wo, dude, that's yours?" one of the crew asked.

"Yeah, she's mostly harmless unless you decide to attack me or something," Damian said, coming up to me and running his hand over my head and scratching me behind the ear. I rubbed my head against his leg, knocking him back a step.

"Sit," he said with authority, and I glanced up at him. While I wanted to tell him to fuck off, I obeyed and sat down on my haunches before stretching my paws out.

"That's my girl," he said, and I actually bared my teeth at him for a moment before settling in place.

I wish I could have answered the questions in his eyes, but I didn't quite understand the switch, either. I was angry at the news story, but I had been angry before and never just popped into the tiger like this. It's usually caused by mortal danger, but there was no danger here.

I licked my paws as I watched them load car after car until all the vehicles were loaded. After Damian locked the doors, he turned and stared at me.

"What the fuck?" he asked.

I stood and stretched before crossing to him and rubbing against his leg.

He squatted and held my head between his hands. "Can you change back so we can talk?"

I licked his face, and he sat back on his haunches, concern marking his handsome face. The man smelled wonderful, and I stepped in, nuzzling against him.

"Naomi," he whispered, his voice carrying a warning, and I looked up at his face, but he wasn't looking at me anymore.

I turned my head and followed his gaze to the back door. Paws smashed through the door, breaking the hinges, and the door swung open. The stench of the thing made my nose crinkle. It smelled like a cross between a demon and a wet dog, and it didn't look much better.

The beast filled the exit, and I bared my teeth, positioning myself between this thing and Damian. The sound of metal scraping pulled my attention in Damian's direction and he stepped next to me. The crowbar gripped in his hand.

"What do you want?" Damian asked, like he expected the mutant dog to speak.

"I've been sent to bring your head back to my master," it growled and stepped inside.

The shock of actually hearing a hellhound talk gave me pause, and I measured it up against my formidable size. It wasn't as big as I was, and it certainly didn't have the raw strength I had. It looked more like a mangy mutt than a powerhouse.

It wasn't until the second one stepped in that my confidence wavered. The hatchway to the basement sat open, and I wondered what our chances were of making it to the tunnel opening. Although, I had doubts the salt ring would keep these demon-dogs out. Especially since I thought Damian had reinforced the garage.

The two split up, circling the outside edges, their growls echoing in the empty garage. I flexed my paws, bringing out my deadly claws. That was my advantage against the mangy beasts. They had teeth, but I had both teeth and claws and I tightened my muscles, getting ready to spring.

Damian raised the crowbar like a bat and turned his back toward me, covering me from that side. I focused on the beast closest to me and I didn't think either of them were aware of who I was, so another advantage. They were here to kill Damian, and right now, I stood in their way.

"Let's do this," Damian whispered, and I launched, twisted in the air, and landed on top of the mangy beast. My claws latched onto the dog's torso and I bit down on the back of its neck, hoping for a quick kill. It reared up and his howl of pain filled the garage. I shifted my nails, tearing at the beast's front chest. It tried to turn its head, but my jaws prevented him from reaching me. I ripped until blood started shooting and the thing stumbled to the ground. I shook it with a growl and then released, focusing on the one circling Damian.

The crowbar swung and connected with the beast's shoulder, but it got a piece of Damian's thigh with its teeth. Not enough to latch on, but enough to rip through jeans and flesh, drawing blood. With a roar, I launched. I hit the beast full on, my teeth clamping down on the underside of its throat, ripping through flesh and arteries in one powerful chomp. As we rolled, I raked my claws down its abdomen, tearing strips of flesh out, and then I was on my feet, ready for more. But both hellhounds were down, and Damian stood with the crowbar, waiting for another attack.

It took him a moment, but he looked between the two downed dogs and me.

"Holy shit," he muttered and took a step toward the door.

A flash darted from the door and I moved just as quickly, launching at the same moment the mutt launched at Damian. I caught it in the air and took it the same way I had the other one, quickly, efficiently and bloodily. I didn't let go until the beast's heart stopped and Damian spoke my name.

"Naomi."

I released, turning my attention to him. The taste of demon blood filled my mouth and the smell of death hung on the air.

I glanced toward the door and stepped away from the dead hellhound toward Damian. My paws were soaked red and I'm sure my white coat was sufficiently stained as well. After two paces, my view altered, and I looked down at bloody hands.

"I guess the danger has passed," I said, bringing my gaze back to Damian's wide eyes.

"How'd you know?"

"I didn't. One minute I was watching the news stories and the next I was the tiger. I thought I just changed because I got angry at the thinly veiled accusations on the television. They've even brought in some ex-FBI expert and you'll never guess where the hell he's from." I shifted, trying to make the pants I was wearing more comfortable, but I couldn't. Before Damian could venture a guess, I said, "I need a shower," and headed toward the hatchway.

Damian didn't follow me and I paused halfway down the tunnel, conflicted about going back until he was ready to come with me. The fact I was still human and not a carnivorous tiger clinched the decision. I continued to the downstairs bedroom and stripped when I stepped into the bathroom. The details in the marine mural still captivated me; stepping into the shower was like stepping into an underwater world of vibrant fish and coral reefs.

The water ran red for longer than I expected, even with scrubbing until my skin burned and my hair squeaked when I ran my fingers through it. When the water cleared, I closed my eyes and enjoyed the pummeling heat.

A breeze caressed my skin, creating goose flesh under the hot stream, and I opened my eyes. Damian stood naked in the doorway to the shower stall. His gaze slowly scanned my form, lingering on my breasts before traveling lower. A crease appeared between his eyes and his gaze bounced from my stomach to my face, locking with mine.

The question in his eyes made me drop my gaze to the bump in my belly. I had been so consumed with cleaning off the blood that I hadn't noticed the newly stretched skin. Bump was an understatement. Between the time I pulled on my pants this morning and now, I had popped and my gaze jumped back to his.

"Holy shit," he said and stepped under the spray with me, his hands finding the soft skin stretched over my abdomen. My gaze dropped to the red water running down his thigh and I turned him so I could inspect his wound.

"It's just superficial. Leave it be," he said, studying my belly with the same intensity that I gave the cut on his leg. When he lifted his gaze, there were a hundred unasked questions swirling in his vibrant irises, but I had no answer for him. I looked like someone who was at least six months pregnant and that explained why my pants were so damned uncomfortable when I transitioned back to human form.

"I know how long human incubation is, but how long is a tiger's?" he asked and I stared at him.

"You don't think..." I trailed off and the candor in his expression brought forth an unwelcomed shiver.

"It's not normal to grow this big overnight," he said, running his hands over my stomach. "And you did just change into a tigress." He smiled like he was not at all unsettled by this. "You know, you kicked ass like I've never seen," he added and drew me into a kiss.

I pushed him away, still too preoccupied with the tiger conclusion to get into a romantic tryst with him. "Damian," I said, and his eyes widened into that innocent look, followed by the brief appearance of his dimples.

"What?" He didn't suppress the smirk fast enough.

"This isn't funny," I said. "Do you think I did something bad to our child by changing?"

His smirk faded, and the first shadow passed over his gaze. He looked down at the symmetry under his hands. "No. I don't think you did something bad," he said, meeting my gaze. "We aren't normal, Naomi. To expect a normal pregnancy is asking for a lot, especially since this little bundle is a trinity." He patted my stomach, and I felt more than just a flutter. He pulled his hand away and then placed it back on my belly, awe painted on his features.

"The baby just kicked." He glanced up at me and grinned. "Did you feel it?"

Dumb question. I felt more than just a kick; I felt rotation, as if the child was moving. The sudden appearance of motion meant my child was alive, and I matched Damian's grin, nodding.

The worry was still present, but it dulled compared to the joy I felt. This time, when he pulled me into a kiss, I did not resist.

Trinity Rising
Chapter Nine
Naomi

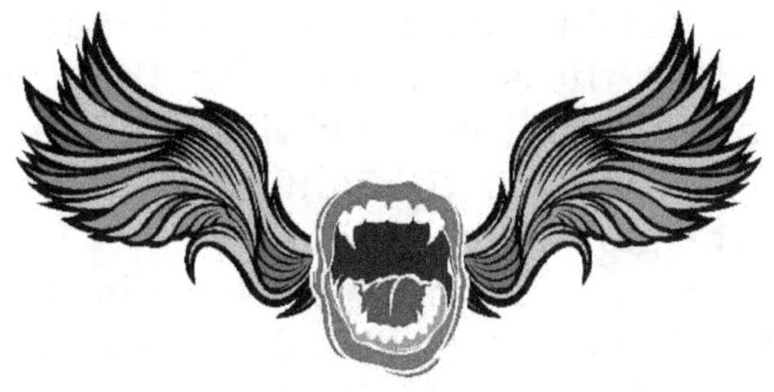

I LAY IN BED, staring at the cloud-covered ceiling as Damian rested his ear on my stomach. He giggled a couple of times as a foot or hand passed over, connecting with his cheek.

"What if I give birth to some sort of hybrid?" I asked, voicing my growing concern.

He propped himself up on his elbow and offered a shrug. "We'll deal with it," he said.

"Aren't you the least bit worried?"

Damian sighed and shook his head. "No. Maybe I should be, but I'm not. It's…" He looked at the ceiling, his eyes moving around the room as he searched for the correct word. "Right," he finally said when his gaze locked on mine. "I know it's strange, but I can feel the rightness of this in my soul. Can't you?"

For the first time since I got the news, a strange calmness settled over me and I nodded. I felt the perfection of this situation just as much as he did. He smiled and studied me for a moment, his features adopting a more serious expression.

"Do you know what prompted you to change today?"

"No, at first I thought it was because I was frustrated by the speculation on the news. But then I couldn't just will myself back into human form. That's when I thought there might be an issue in the garage."

He huffed at me and pressed his lips to my stomach. "You've never had that issue before."

"No, but maybe the hormones are messing me up." That sounded like the most viable theory. It actually made sense, but who knows, it could be some divine intervention for all I knew.

"Do you think the hormones are giving you some level of precognitive ability? Sensing danger and forcing the tiger out?"

I laughed at his flawed logic. "I don't think so," I answered.

His eyebrow rose in a silent challenge.

"Then where the hell was the tiger when we were at the doctor's office, or at the hospital, for that matter?" I asked. While I'd love to believe that, there were just too many holes in the theory. "I think it has to do with getting angry and my not being able to switch back was just a lucky coincidence."

"You only transitioned back when there was no more danger."

"I'm aware of that," I snapped and rolled out of bed. "I need some clothes," I said with my back to him. The bed creaked and a moment later, he wrapped a bathrobe around my shoulders.

"This is all that's down here," he said, crossing into my field of vision and tying the sash to his bathrobe. "Everything else is upstairs and, based on what happened today, I think we should get the hell out of here as soon as possible. I already moved the car. It's in the garage here for now and I didn't lock the workshop, so anyone can get in."

"What about the hatch?"

"The truck is sitting over it and surrounded by boxes. I still need to weld it shut along with the door at the end of the tunnel. But that should take less than an hour. Then we should bolt."

I wasn't ready to leave yet, but we really had no choice, not when Lucifer's hellhounds found us so easily. It stood to reason that he'd soon follow and we didn't want to be anywhere near here when he arrived.

"What about Ted and Valerie?"

"She isn't out of danger and he doesn't have any idea when she'll be ready to be released," Damian said. "And I told Ted to find somewhere else to stay until she was good to come home."

"We might have a problem," I said, shifting and meeting his gaze.

He tensed and crossed his arms. "What?"

"The ex-FBI agent lives in York."

Damian's expression hardened, but before he could balk, I added, "He's the only one on the news who didn't jump to the conclusion that you killed those people. He said he spoke to a witness, a cafeteria worker who saw what happened. He said you weren't responsible for the officer's death, despite the evidence stacked against you. The cops disagree. Considering the surveillance video, they severed the agent's connection to the case. That's when I got pissed. Lucifer is doing a hell of a job setting you up."

"I'm aware of what that bastard is doing, and now we have a garage smeared with blood. I'd bet my left arm there will be a missing person reported and he'll make sure the blood in the garage is matched to the victim."

"But the dogs?"

Damian pointed toward the tunnel. "You missed the coup d'état. The hellhounds disintegrated, so it's just a bloody mess."

"Jesus," I whispered, my mind turning this additional fact over. It was like Lucifer intentionally sent those beasts into the slaughterhouse. "It would have been better if the carcasses were found, even though they would have been a real bizarre find."

Damian sent a sarcastic smile. "That would have made things eons better," he said and ran his hand through his tussled hair. "Should we change our plans and head to Greece?"

I blew a stream of air from my lips, considering his offer, but I knew damn well both cops and Lucifer's henchmen would pack the airports. "No. I think we need to look up that agent. He's the only one who believed you weren't responsible, and both the cops and reporters made him look like a fool."

"He'd hand us over in a heartbeat," Damian said.

"Well, if he tries, I can always turn tiger," I said and forced a smile, but the prospect of hurting a human made me feel sick to my stomach. I swallowed the burn in the back of my throat. "But I don't think he will. Before he got into his car, he said if we wanted someone on our side, to look him up."

Damian rolled his eyes. "It's a bullshit ploy," he said, raising my irritation level.

"I know bullshit when I see it," I said. "This wasn't. Besides, I'd rather take my chances with him than the cops, because you know damn well if we end up in a jail cell, neither one of us will walk out alive." The memory of the roadblock in New York City crossed my mind. The sheer number of police officers Lucifer commanded had chilled my blood, and even the memory made me shiver.

"How do you know this guy isn't in Lucifer's pocket?" Damian asked as if he had got a whiff of my memory.

I focused on him. "I don't."

"Then why the hell do we even chance it?"

We stared at each other, and I sighed. "It's just one of those things, Damian. I trusted him. I don't know how to explain it better than that."

"What's his name?"

"Special Agent Steve Williams."

"As soon as I finish welding the doors, I'll find his address. While I'm doing that, do you mind packing things upstairs?"

I didn't mind, especially with him safeguarding the house from demons and other preternatural creatures. My gaze dropped to his leg. "Do you have any bandages down here?" I pointed to his still oozing wound.

"I don't think so," he said and turned, disappearing into the bathroom. The creak of a door drifted on the quiet, followed by the crinkle of a package being opened. When he stepped out, a six-inch bandage covered the cut. "I guess Michael stocked us up," he added and pressed his lips together.

Damian's hands found his waist, and his head dropped to his chest. It wasn't until I saw the shake of his shoulders that I realized he was crying. I crossed and lifted his chin. His crystal-blue eyes swam with tears and more clear drops traced lines on his face.

"I guess grief hits at the damnedest times," he said and laughed, swiping the tears from his face like they were an unforgiveable offense.

My heart squeezed in my chest and I wrapped my arms around him. He returned the hug for a minute and then planted a kiss on my cheek.

"I don't have time for this right now," he mumbled and stepped away, heading back into the bathroom. This time, when he came out, he wore the clothes he had on when we were attacked and I started to speak, but he held up his hand.

"I'll change after I'm done." He pointed toward the tunnel and then stepped out of the bedroom, leaving me with my own sense of loss.

Trinity Rising
Chapter Ten
Naomi

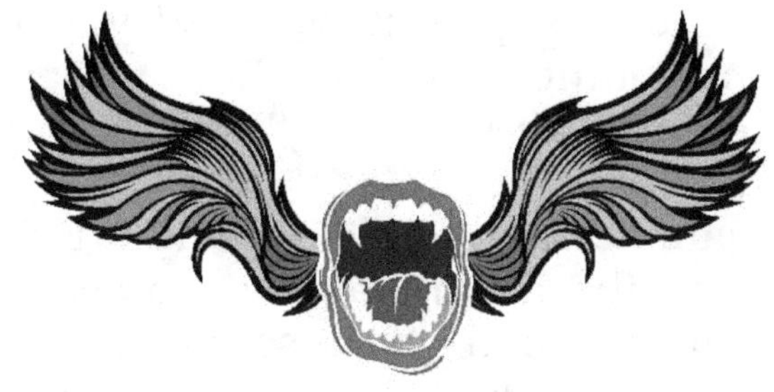

I DROPED THE DUFFEL bags into the trunk of the Aston Martin and retreated to the living room, irritated that the only comfortable thing I found to wear was a pair of Damian's sweat pants. My cell buzzed, and I picked it up from the table, glancing at the caller ID. It wasn't Valerie, so I answered the call.

"Hello?"

"Hello, Mrs. Andreas?"

"Yes," I said, trying to place the vaguely familiar voice.

He cleared his throat. "Mrs. Andreas, this is Dr. Wolk," he said and his tone set off a wealth of alarms through my form, jolting my heart into a pounding rhythm and my grip on my phone tightened.

I swallowed the dry fear from my mouth. "What can I do for you?"

"Well, there seems to be an issue with your blood sample."

"Diabetes?"

"No, at least not in this sample. It looks like someone introduced feline DNA with yours. I'm sorry for the mixup, but we need you to come back in for another blood test."

I stared out the window. "What do you mean feline DNA?"

"The sample had a trace of feline DNA along with yours, like a cat hair was present in the vial, so all we can surmise is that the lab screwed up or the containers were contaminated."

I sat down heavily on the couch. "Um, we're headed out of the country to visit Damian's relatives. Can I follow up with you when we get back?"

There was silence on the line and then a hurried, "That will be fine, thank you for understanding." A dial tone stretched through the line and I disconnected the call.

I was still in shock when Damian stepped into the room with a box in his arms. He put it on the table and met my gaze.

"What's up?"

I stared at the computer and peripherals sticking out of the box and then looked up at him. "I don't have diabetes, but apparently my blood contains traces of feline DNA."

His eyebrows arched and he slid onto the couch.

"They think it's a lab error, or a contaminated vial, but..." I trailed off. I thought the tiger was a left over result of the shadow virus. Damian sat with his mouth open in shock, so he obviously thought the same thing. He blinked and cocked his head.

"Does that mean my blood contains traces of hawk DNA?"

I didn't even want to consider the ramifications of what this meant for the baby in my belly, but one image kept flashing before my eyes. The symbol for my grandfather's specific bloodline: a winged-tiger.

"They wanted me to come down for another blood test, but I told him we were headed out of the country."

"Quick thinking," Damian said and stood, retreating to the bedroom to change. He hadn't said a word about my attire, and I appreciated it. He returned in the clean clothing I had laid out for him and dropped his dirty clothing in the garbage, sealing it and dumping it out in the garage.

"You about ready?" he asked after he finished packing his laptop and note pads that were scattered over the coffee table.

I looked up at him, still in shock from the news. "You did everything, including fixing the keypad?"

He nodded. "It took a little longer than I wanted though," he said and I glanced at the clock.

A little over an hour had passed since I started packing. Of course, it took me forever to find something that fit over my belly. "We might need to go shopping before we find a place to stay," I said and stood, waving toward the sweats. "I had nothing that fit."

He pressed his lips into a tight smile. His attempt at hiding the budding humor lost, and instead of addressing the breach in manners, he picked up the box and disappeared into the garage.

"Did you want to do a quick walk through?" he asked, and I nodded.

"I already packed the mural," I said. That was the one thing that followed us from place to place, and I know it meant a great deal to him. He gave a nod and pulled out his phone. I turned away, heading to the bedroom and scanning the vacant dresser shelves. Opening and closing drawers and dressers before doing the same in the bathroom. On impulse, I grabbed the first aid kit and opened it, dumping the headache remedies, anti-biotic ointment and bandages into the box before clipping it closed.

Damian held my coat open as I stepped into the living room. He had Ted's thick hunting jacket on instead of the sleek leather he usually wore.

"I figured Ted could use something fancier than this. Especially since this one is better for packing," he said. "I also have all the extra ammunition for his nine-millimeter stored in the trunk."

"Does he know?" I said, feeling the first bite of irritation, but it disappeared with a nod from Damian.

"He doesn't know I left him my coat, but I asked if we could take the gun. He has no issue with it and in a few weeks, he'll report it stolen. In the meantime, he'll keep us informed of

Valerie's condition," he said and led me to the car.

"Ready?" he asked once he settled into the driver's seat.

"I'm ready. Are you?" I asked, glancing at his shaking hands.

He followed my gaze and chuckled. "I have to admit, I'm a little nervous. I don't know what's waiting for us out there."

Trinity Rising
Chapter Eleven
Damian

EVERY MUSCLE IN MY body tensed as we pulled out of the garage. I waited until the door had closed before turning the car around in the driveway. I gave Naomi a cursory glance and took a deep breath, pressing the gate controls as I approached.

No one was visible in the vicinity and after pulling through the gate, I pushed the button, waiting until the gate clicked closed, then I gunned it, turning toward the nearest highway route. I kept glancing in my rearview, expecting a tail, but there was nothing on the road behind us, or in front of us, for that matter, and I gave a relieved laugh as the house disappeared from view.

"Knock on wood," I said and gave Naomi's hand a squeeze. She responded with only a strained smile before she continued her darting scan of the landscape.

"I don't think…"

"Shush. Not until we are a safe distance away, okay?"

I nodded consent and focused on the road. The only cars that pulled out behind us turned down different roads and by the time we pulled onto the highway, I relaxed enough to fully exhale.

When we passed the Welcome to Massachusetts sign, I glanced at Naomi again and shrugged. "I guess my checking in for our flight out of Hartford may have given us just enough of a window to get out of there." The muscles in my shoulders relaxed a notch.

"When did you do that?"

"Right before I reprogrammed the basement keypad." I glanced at the clock on the display. "The plane will start boarding in another half hour. Just long enough for us to put a little more distance between us and the airport."

"He's not going to buy that we went to Michigan with the cars?" she asked.

"No, not with us killing his dogs. I have a feeling they were sent on a suicide mission just to prove we were still there." I finally voiced my thoughts and the wound on my leg flared, sending an itch that made my hands grip the wheel tighter.

"I've been meaning to ask. Hellhounds talk?"

Her question made me raise an eyebrow in her direction. "What?"

"When you asked the hellhound what he wanted, he spoke."

I couldn't help the laugh. "No, baby, it just growled up a fucking storm."

She laughed as well, but something about the tone of it pulled my gaze to hers. "Actually, they were sent to bring your head back. At least that's the answer I heard."

The shock of her words left me quiet and I glance at her, wondering just what kind of freak she was. The worry in her eyes calmed me. If she was a freak, it didn't matter. She's the one that saved my sorry ass. Again.

"My head, huh?" I asked, and she nodded. "I can see that," I replied and took her hand, bringing it to my lips. "If you hadn't come, I'd be dog chow by now."

"You were doing a pretty good job with the crowbar."

I chuckled. "If you say so." Whether she admitted it, I knew I wouldn't have survived and the garage floor would have been stained with my flesh and blood. I shivered at the thought.

The traffic was pretty light, and we pulled off the highway exactly three hours later and I pulled into the first gas station off the exit ramp and parked by the pumps. Naomi scuttled out of the car towards the building, walking fast with her thighs together, and I grinned. The car still idled, and I turned the ignition key, shutting off the engine and stretched before I reached down and popped the gas cap. As I pulled my wallet out, I paused, wondering if using a credit card would alert Lucifer to our whereabouts.

"Shit," I mumbled and opted for cash, pulling a twenty out of the billfold and heading inside to pre-pay. While I was inside, I grabbed a couple of bottles of water and stepped to the counter as the bathroom door opened and Naomi came out.

She grabbed a candy bar and some mints and added them to my tab.

I paid just as the door jingled and as I turned; I handed Naomi the bag with the drinks. She took it and looked up at the man in the doorway, freezing on the spot. Her widening eyes made me look closer at the stranger.

The man stared at me, just as wide-eyed as Naomi.

"Oh, hey, Agent Williams, how are you?" the kid behind the counter asked, and the man sent a nod in his direction.

"I'm good, John. Didn't you need to check something in the stockroom?" he said and a cold shiver traversed my spine as the kid nodded and disappeared into the back of the store, leaving the three of us alone.

A base warning in the pit of my stomach said to run, to get away as soon as possible, and my heart clenched in my chest. I reached into my jacket, wrapping my hand around the handle of my revolver, but the flutter of wings caught me off guard and I stepped back, my eyes darting around to find the source.

"Be careful, Steve," the voice whispered, and Naomi stepped back as well, her hand shooting out to grab my elbow.

When my gaze landed on Agent Williams, he was assessing me with narrowed eyes.

"Why don't you give me the gun, son," he said and put out his hand.

I blinked as I pulled the gun out of my pocket, almost as if I had no control, but instead of handing it over, I pointed it at him.

"Damian," Naomi gasped.

"I don't want any trouble," I said, and the agent cocked his head, looking between the gun and me as if perplexed.

"Give me the gun," he said more forcefully, and I felt a tickle in my mind, followed by the instinct to give him our only weapon.

"I don't think so," I said, resisting the urge, and another flutter caught my attention. "Why are you following us?" I asked. That was the only justification I had for him being here at the same time. After all, he was a cop.

He let out a quick laugh. "I wasn't following you. This is completely coincidence and from the look on your faces, you know exactly who I am."

"And you know who I am."

He nodded. "Yes. I suggest you put the gun away before someone else comes in or John figures out he really didn't need anything from the back room." He glanced up at the camera in the corner and then back at me. "If you're not going to give it to me, put the damn thing away."

I laughed. "Why? So you can arrest us?"

The tension in the room mounted and wings fluttered yet again, along with another warning directly to Agent Williams.

"What's with the angel?" Naomi spouted, and both our gazes dropped to hers. She wasn't looking directly at Steve. Instead, her gaze was over his shoulder to the right, as if a ghost I couldn't see stood at his side.

"You can see him?" Steve said, pulling my attention back to him. He looked just as shocked as I felt.

"Sort of, but he doesn't seem to be a dick like Lu..." She stopped and covered her mouth before she conjured the bastard by mistake.

"We have to go," I said and stowed the gun in my pocket. The proximity of any angel to where we were only meant trouble, and I wasn't sticking around to find out whether this man was on our side or not.

"I'm on your side," Agent Williams said and planted his feet, blocking the only exit.

"Bullshit. You're a cop."

"Ex-cop," he said. "And why would being close to an angel be an issue for you?"

A jolt zapped me, creating a prickly tickle all over my skin, and I stared at him. "You... can read minds?"

The cocky smile and nod confirmed it. "I can do a hell of a lot more than that," he said. "Gas up your car and follow me. I need some answers."

I straightened my back. "While that sounds charming, I think I'll pass," I said. "Besides, I don't give a shit what you need. We're out of here." I glanced at Naomi. "This was a bad idea," I said and started for the door. If he didn't get out of my way, I'd run him over and his gaze narrowed, reading my intentions correctly.

"I can be your best friend or your worst fucking nightmare. It's your choice, kid."

I ignored him, but Naomi pulled back on my arm. I peeled her hand off, meeting her frightened gaze. "I'll be fine," I whispered and turned back to Agent Williams.

"I don't think you want to do that," he warned as I approached and I let out a strained laugh as every muscle in my body tightened, ready for battle.

He didn't yield, instead he stood his ground, his hands curling into fists as well and when he shifted into a ready stance, I stopped, recognizing the form.

"Karate?"

He just nodded, and for a brief instant, I thought it might be nice to spar again. I hadn't truly sparred in years.

Agent Williams raised an eyebrow. "Years? What were you, a toddler?"

It was my turn to send a sarcastic smile. "I'm a master in a few different schools," I said, prompting a laugh from him as he sized me up.

"You aren't old enough," he said with authority.

I glanced at Naomi and then back at him. I'm sure my life story would completely blow his mind, but I kept a wrap on my thoughts.

"Please move, Agent Williams," I said. "I need to fill my car."

He shook his head, and I stepped in, throwing the first punch. When his hand closed around my fist, stopping it from connecting, the world swam in front of my eyes and I wasn't the only one who gasped. Like a hyped up download, the man's entire life flashed like a bizarre slide show in my head.

Everything he experienced right up to this moment downloaded into my brain and I inhaled, yanking away as if contact with his skin had produced burning blisters.

His face remained pale and his jaw slack as he stared at me. It took me a moment to understand the transference that occurred.

If I saw his entire life...

"What just happened?" Naomi whispered, and I turned to her.

"Nothing," I said, and we walked past the stunned agent to the car. I helped her into the front seat and pumped the pre-paid amount into my car. I kept glancing at the store, expecting Agent Williams to come out, but he hadn't recovered from the glimpse of my life he received.

Hell, I couldn't blame him. His life was bizarre enough, but the existence of vampires alone must have blown his logical circuitry right out of the water. When I finished, I returned the pump to the holder and closed the gas cap.

Agent Williams still hadn't come out, and I sighed as I slipped into the driver's seat, waiting for him to get his bearings.

"Where are we going?" Naomi asked.

"To his house," I said and nodded toward the store. Agent Williams finally stepped outside, still looking like he had seen a thousand ghosts.

Naomi looked at him and then back at me. "What happened in there?"

I gave her a laugh. "Special Agent Williams isn't normal by any means," I said, and her head snapped to him.

"What is he?"

"Oh, he's human, but he's supercharged." She turned back to me and her brow creased. "Did you ever watch Star Trek?" I asked, and her brow creased even more. "The only description I can think of is he did a Vulcan mind meld on me."

The crease in her brow altered into the incredulous arches. "What?"

"I saw his life and by the look on his face, he saw mine."

Her head snapped in his direction as Agent Williams slipped into his car. His hands visibly shook, and I started laughing, prompting Naomi to bring her gaze back to me.

"What do you mean by supercharged?"

I sighed and started the car, pulling out behind the vintage BMW. "His psychic powers are beyond anything I have ever encountered in a human." I was still digesting all I saw and his life was full of some of the same challenges and devastations as mine. "But you were right. He is on our side." I glanced at her. "And it's a damned good thing."

Trinity Rising
Chapter Twelve
Damian

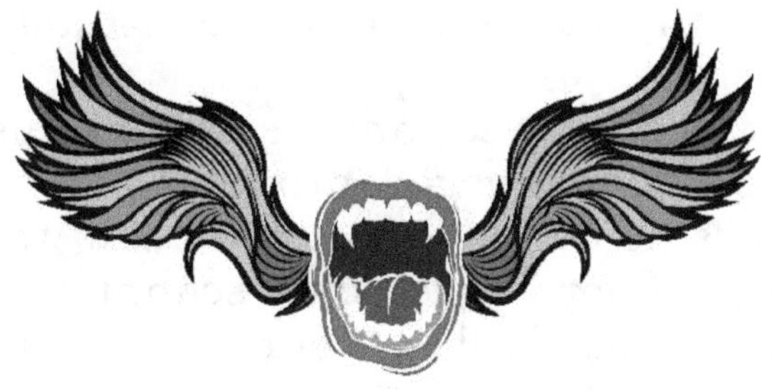

WE DROVE IN SILENCE and by the time we pulled up to the gate surrounding his house, I'd had time to think about our predicament and wondered if this was really a good thing or not. If Lucifer got wind of this man and all his talents, we might end up as a secondary trophy.

I hesitated before following him inside and when I parked in the driveway behind him; I glanced at the gate closing behind us. He got out of his car and just stared at me. After a moment, he shook his head like clearing thoughts and the glare he leveled at me made me second-guess this.

I stepped out of the car and circled around to Naomi, helping her out.

Agent Williams waited in the garage and I approached him.

"What kind of fool do you think I am?" he snarled when I got within the confines of the garage.

"Denial? That's what you're going with?" I huffed. That should have been what I expected based on the man's history, but it still caught me off guard.

His eyes narrowed, and he crossed his arms. The garage door engaged, dropping behind us.

"There's no fucking way what I saw was real."

I thought for a moment, scanning through the contents of his life. "Your life hasn't been a walk in the park, either."

Naomi shifted, and she cleared her throat.

"Can I use your bathroom?" she asked with a small voice that cut through the tension. His gaze dropped to her.

"I'm supposed to believe you..." he waved at her and blinked, his gaze dropping to her belly. He nodded instead and turned, leading us into the family room of his home. "The bathroom is down there." He pointed to a small hallway on the other side of the kitchen.

He waited until she was out of sight and turned to me.

"I'm not sure what to call you, considering," I said. "Special Agent Williams seems a bit formal, don't you think?"

"That shit can't be real," he said and crossed his arms.

"If you don't believe what you saw, have your angel friend ask Michael directly."

Wings fluttered, and the winged man in Agent William's memory appeared for a moment. "I can't. I'm not allowed in heaven. At least, not yet," he said.

I studied him, watching as he faded to nothing, and finally I shook my head, refocusing on Agent Williams. His relationship with his guardian angel was as bizarre as some things in my life and as I focused on those memories, a flood of secondary memories filtered up from a lower level and I raised an eyebrow.

"So you're telling me you're twenty-five hundred years old?"

I nodded, and he sat down on the couch.

"And there are such things as vampires?" he asked, pinching the bridge of his nose.

"Well, there were. I think Eve was the last one."

"And Lu..." he started and pressed his lips closed along with his eyes. "And archangels, fallen or otherwise, exist?"

"Yes."

"And your wife can transform into a white tiger?" He opened his eyes, his voice carrying the incredulous spin of someone whose world was crumbling around them.

I smiled and shrugged. "You forgot demons," I added.

"I already believed in demons." A shadow passed over his face.

The memory filtered up to the forefront of my mind, and I gave him a quick nod. He just stared at me in silent awe that made me uncomfortable. I shifted, unsure of whether I should sit.

"Well, doesn't that just beat all?" He ran both hands through his hair. "So, what I saw in that poor cafeteria worker's mind really happened?"

"Yes. The devil slayed Michael and ate his heart."

Naomi shuffled back into the room with pale cheeks and wet eyelashes. She blinked and gave me that sickly smile. From the looks of it, her morning sickness was acting up again.

"Agent Williams, you wouldn't happen to have any ginger-ale?" I asked.

He stood and crossed to the refrigerator, pulling out a can and handed it to Naomi and then turned back to me. "Call me Steve," he said. "Can I get you a drink?"

I smiled and stuffed my hands into my pocket. "Scotch," I said, knowing that was his drink of choice as well.

He brought two glasses and set them on the coffee table and retrieved a bottle of Glendronach. I nodded my approval, and he poured me a glass.

"It may take me a little while to digest all that I've seen. In the meantime, you might want to do that angel proofing thing." He raised his glass.

"Do you have a bar of soap?"

"I think we have one in the bathroom cabinet." He pointed the same way Naomi came. "Why?"

"I know it works on archangels, but I have no idea if it will trap him here, so I figured you probably don't want the symbols to be permanent."

"I don't know about that," he said and gulped his drink down.

"Fuck you, Williams," the voice spat out, and I couldn't help but smile. His relationship with his guardian angel was one I didn't quite understand, even with the history I received.

"You seem to be a magnet for redeemed killers," I said and received a snort from the air, followed by laughter. Instead of continuing the conversation, I turned in search of soap because, between the three of us, someone was bound to fuck up and say Lucifer's name out loud.

I drew the symbols on all the first-floor windows as low in the corner as possible, trying to make them inconspicuous. I drew it on the front door, garage door and the back sliders as well. Any place that allowed passage between the inside and outside was marked. When I finished, I stepped back into the family room and pointed to the ceiling.

"Yeah, go ahead," Steve nodded and continued his conversation with Naomi.

I took my time; not only drawing the angel hex, but also digesting the memories I had been given. When I completed my rounds, I dropped the soap in the soap dish in the upstairs bathroom, cleaning off my fingertips before returning downstairs.

"When do you think your family will return?" I asked, rounding the last step.

Steve looked at the clock and then at me. "Anytime."

I nodded and slid next to Naomi. "How are you feeling?" I asked and rubbed her belly.

"Okay," she said, and I knew she was lying. Her cheeks were too pale and dark rings appeared under her eyes.

"Did you need to lie down?" Steve asked, and Naomi hesitated.

"We're safe for the moment," I said and moved my gaze to Steve's. "Right?"

He nodded. "We have a couple of guest rooms," he said and stood. "Let me show you where they are. I'm also assuming that you two will be our guests tonight?" he asked, glancing at me.

"Honestly, I hadn't thought that far in advance." I met Naomi's gaze, and she shrugged, leaving the decision to me. She was too tired to function right now and needed sleep. "We'll play it by ear," I replied.

"When my wife was pregnant, she used to shut down all of a sudden, too," I heard Steve say as he escorted her upstairs.

Left to my own devices, I poured another glass of scotch and stepped to the sliding glass doors leading to their backyard. A covered pool took up half of the vast lawn and the ocean view was stellar. I had to give it to Naomi. This place was beautiful. Colder than Greece, but it would do.

The sound of the garage opening pulled my attention to the door we entered and the man who stepped in the house a few minutes later could have passed as my twin. I shuffled through Steve's memories and readily identified him as CJ Ryan.

He blinked and stopped, blocking the doorway as he stared at me with wide eyes.

"Who are you?" he asked and stepped aside, letting the rest of the family into the house.

"Damian Andreas," I said and turned to face them, their names coming just as quickly as their faces appeared. Tom Ryan and his wife Raven followed by Steve's wife, Jennifer.

Raven nearly dropped her bags when her gaze fell on me, and what color had been in her face bled out. The way CJ's gaze shot to her, and then back to me, made me shift. For a moment, I wished for Naomi in tiger form standing next to me. With her formidable force, I'd feel a hell of a lot safer than I did right now.

CJ's eyes narrowed, and he crossed, dumping his bag on the table. I knew enough about him to feel the discomfort prickle through me when he turned a glare in my direction. An unfamiliar tingle encompassed my head, and I realized he was trying to force his way into my mind.

"Your father was nice enough to show my wife to a bedroom upstairs. He should be down in a minute," I said, doing my best to block his probe.

The creak of the stairs pulled my gaze away and Steve appeared.

"I see you've met my family," he said.

"Yes. Is Naomi okay?" I asked and took a sip of the scotch, irritated with the slight shake in my hand that knocked the ice cubes against the glass.

"I think she was out the moment her head hit the pillow. Reminds me of Jen when she was pregnant," Steve said.

He met my gaze, and I swear I saw a flash of sorrow cross his features. After all the years, losing his children still created a visual pain. I doubted my ability to carry on if I lost my children, and they hadn't even been born yet, so the fact that Steve had been able to function at all increased my admiration.

Steve turned to his wife. "They're going to be staying with us for a while," he said.

"Just tonight," I corrected, and an awkward silence filled the room. The rest of Steve's family just stared at me and Raven blanched a little more, shifting, so her husband buffered her from view.

"What is he?" Raven whispered to CJ, thinking she spoke softly enough, but I caught it and glanced at her, trying to stifle a laugh.

"I'm sorry for laughing, Raven, but there really is no straightforward answer to that question." Everyone's eyes widened and their gazes traveled to Steve.

He shrugged. "We had a transfer of sorts," he said.

"Isn't he the one who killed those cops in Connecticut?" CJ asked, pointing in my direction.

"No." Steve stepped into the room and crossed to the table, picking up his glass. "He's being set up."

CJ stared at him, then he wobbled, reaching for the table and sitting in the nearest chair, his eyes widening in shock, and then his gaze traveled to me. "I think maybe you guys should unpack the groceries and go get dinner somewhere."

"Why?" Tom asked, his gaze bouncing between Steve, Raven and CJ before meeting mine, and then they traveled to the fluttering wings next to Steve.

"Steve?" Jennifer asked.

He glanced at me, and I sighed.

"I'm putting you at risk," I said. "They have a right to know what could be coming."

Tom's hands flew in a pattern I didn't recognize, but the question in his gaze was enough.

CJ hadn't stopped staring at me, and even his complexion blanched.

"What might be coming?" Jennifer asked.

"Armageddon," CJ answered, and a silent chill blanketed the room.

Trinity Rising
Chapter Thirteen
Damian

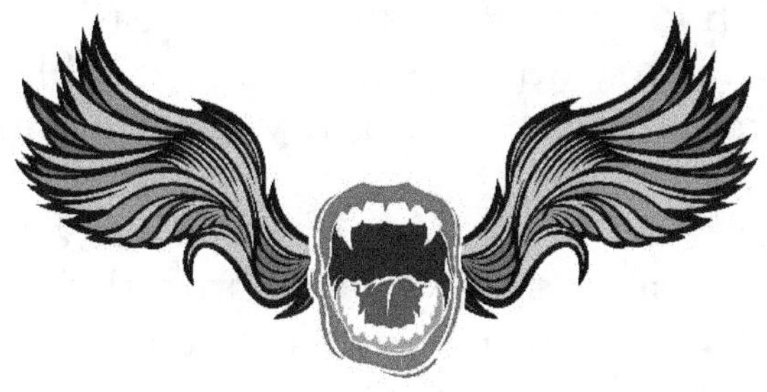

"YOU KNOW I HAVE an open mind, especially with what happened to us in college," Jennifer said as she sat down next to Steve on the couch. "But this. This is way too out there for me to even comprehend."

I had been talking for a couple of hours, trying to recap my life and our plight. The groceries had long been put away, five large pizza boxes sat on the kitchen table picked over, and the remaining half dozen pieces on a plate set aside for Naomi.

Tom and Raven kept their distance, giving me the greatest berth, because even though the others had warmed up to my being in their home, Raven still couldn't look at me and when she did her expression was tense, like I was going to self-destruct at any moment and I focused on her for a minute.

"May I ask you a question?" I asked before her gaze flitted away again.

She pointed at her chest, and I nodded. "I... I guess," she answered.

"What are you seeing that everyone else can't?" I had enough history from Steve to know she saw auras, but she hadn't been able to look at me more than a cursory glance since she came in.

"You're too bright for me to look at for any length of time. It's like looking into the sun," she said. "And if I squint, I can see a shadow of... of wings mingled with it." She squinted and then blinked away. "But it's not like CJ's father's wings, not angel wings."

"When I was a vampire, I could change into a hawk at will," I said, and everyone's gaze jumped back to me. I hadn't included my ability to transition into a wild bird in my conversation, but I had explained the shadow virus and our near demise at Lucifer's hands. They also knew his plans if he ever got a hold of Naomi. "Something about the combination of shadow virus and angel blood."

"I turn into a tiger," Naomi's voice broke everyone's stare, and the relief I had at the sight of her rumpled hair and sleepy eyes was more than in my mind. The knot I developed in the middle of my back loosened and I stood. "Naomi, this is Steve's wife, Jennifer," I started introductions. "And this is Tom and his wife, Raven."

"Nice to meet you," she said and received nods in response. Raven's squint was less pronounced when she viewed Naomi, but it was there.

"She has the same aura?" I asked and Raven glanced in my general direction, but her gaze was averted toward the ground.

"No. It reminds me a little of CJ's aura."

I caught Naomi's gaze. "Michael's grace," we both said at the same time. That was the only logical explanation I could conceive. The grace of an archangel must be glaring.

CJ turned and stood. "I'm CJ," he said, finishing the introductions.

Naomi's eyes widened, flashing between my doppelganger and me. She let out a nervous laugh. "You two could be twins," she said.

A moment passed where their eyes locked, and then he offered her his seat. The blatant interest painted on his face sent a burning irritation through my core, landing in my stomach and churning like a time bomb. He glanced at me and raised an eyebrow and for the first time in over a millennium, I tasted the bitter pill of jealousy.

He returned his gaze to Naomi. "Can I get you some pizza?" he asked and Naomi nodded, still staring at him in a way that burned my insides.

Silence blanketed the room, and Steve's brow creased as he glanced at me. A smirk appeared on his face and he slid his glance to his wife, sharing a silent communication that I was not privy to. By the sudden appearance and suppression of a smile, I guessed he was broadcasting my discomfort with their son's chivalrous behavior.

Naomi's gaze followed him and I set my drink on the table and stood.

"I need some air," I said and turned without explaining. The chill slapped at me as I stepped out of the sliding glass doors into the backyard. The cold Atlantic beckoned in the distance and I crossed the expanse of yard to a quaint rock wall that separated the yard from a fifteen-foot drop into the ocean.

I shoved my hands into my pockets and scanned the vastness before me.

A few minutes passed and despite the frigid breeze, I remained in my spot, trying to isolate why I was suddenly feeling so insecure about Naomi. She was bound to me by marriage and blood, and yet, I was afraid that she'd run to the nearest man with an honest and pure heart.

"You really have nothing to worry about," CJ said, stepping next to me. "Your wife loves you."

I glanced at him and then back at the water. "I know she does, but I've never had any competition before," I admitted, knowing he was privy to my train of thought.

He chuckled in a way that pulled my attention to him.

"I didn't think it was a competition," he said.

"So you're not interested in Naomi," I stated, hoping to put my mind at ease. I glanced back at the sunset painting the clouds, turning everything the purple-pink of twilight.

Silence drifted between us, and I turned toward him, meeting his gaze.

"No comment?" I asked, and he gave me the kind of smile that I always equated with Lucifer; cocky and certain that he held the winning hand. I clenched my teeth, sending a glare at him.

"Look, if this was a competition, you would lose. But it isn't, so just fucking relax, will ya?"

"I wouldn't lose." I crossed my arms and scanned the sea once more before trudging back into the warm house. Naomi looked up from the kitchen table where Jennifer sat with her. She tilted her head, questioning me without words, and I shrugged. She didn't need to know just how unhinged I was right now.

"Where'd everyone go?" I asked, sliding into the seat next to her.

"Steve went to change and Tom and Raven decided to catch a movie in Portsmouth," Jennifer said and we all glanced as CJ stepped inside and took a seat on the couch. "Are you really as old as Steve says?"

"I'm twenty-five," I said. "Of course, I've been twenty-five for over two thousand years, but who's counting?"

She glanced at Naomi for confirmation and got a nod in return. When her gaze landed back on me, she asked, "Did you have a chance to meet Jesus?"

I laughed. "I've met many people, ma'am, and yes; the messiah was one of them."

"What was he like?"

"Interesting. He had a lot of good ideas, and an honest heart. Of course, I had already been introduced to Michael and angel bloodlines, so the idea of God's child wasn't as farfetched as some people thought." I glanced at Naomi. "I can tell you this much though, he has got to be livid that so many acts of violence have been perpetrated in his name. He was a peaceful man, but had no tolerance for those who skewed the word of the Lord for their own gain."

Jennifer looked down at her hands. "And heaven?"

When her gaze returned to mine, I knew where she was going with the questions. Even with the existence of a guardian angel looking over her husband, she still had doubts and worries about where her children's souls were. I sent her a soft smile and a nod. "Yes. There's a heaven," I said, and the relief swept over her face. "And I'm sure your daughters are there."

Jennifer blinked her tears back and gave me a quick nod.

Naomi watched the exchange, her brow furrowing with questions, and I shook my head. She let it go and focused back on the conversation, but I could tell she understood. She blinked, studying the woman at the table with the same admiration as I felt for both Jennifer and Steve.

"What was your favorite era?" Jennifer asked.

My gaze moved to Naomi. "Right now," I said, with no hesitation.

A snort from the couch pulled my attention and CJ sent a glance over his shoulder, his derision snaking over me like a hangman's noose.

I knew it was poor manners, but I shot the question out, anyway. "What the hell is your issue?"

CJ stood, turning toward me. "You. You're my issue," he pointed at me. "They think you're something special, but all I see is someone who killed for sport, like my father did. But in this case, you did it for centuries upon centuries."

"Damian didn't kill for sport," Naomi said before I could form a response.

CJ challenged her with an arch of his eyebrow.

"He's right," I said, pulling her gaze to mine. "I killed with abandon, but I only killed those worthy of death. So, in that way, I differ from your father."

"Who are you to judge?" CJ said.

I stood, crossing the distance, extending my hand.

"Go ahead," I challenged, knowing he had the same power to siphon memories as Steve.

He looked at my hand, and the muscles in his jaw jumped. When his gaze locked on mine, he reached out. The moment our skin contacted, a rush of memories assaulted me. Sound swirled around me and a power I couldn't comprehend gripped every muscle. CJ's memories flooded my mind, just like Steve's had, but there was something else that came with them that hadn't been transferred when Steve did his mind meld.

Just before his grip loosened, I felt the power crawling back into its host and the room came into clear view. In my mind's eye, I reached out, grabbing hold of the last ribbon of magic, feeling a piece tear off and settle inside me.

CJ's gaze hardened, and he yanked his hand from my grip. He stepped back, rubbing his palm, just staring at me. He looked down at his hand and back, like I was still the shadow being, his silence just as unnerving as the flurry of memories.

Whispers, like faint echoes, caressed my ears, but I kept my gaze on CJ, waiting for his judgment. Instead of speaking, he slowly lowered to the couch.

He licked his lips, formulating broken thoughts before speaking.

"You really are an angel's descendent." It wasn't a question, just a statement that I let hang on the air for a full beat.

"Do you think I'd really spend the last few hours bullshitting you?"

"Actually, that's exactly what I thought. I couldn't read much from either of you." He glanced between Naomi and I. "I just thought you were here to pull one over on us and you somehow snowed Uncle Steve. I couldn't figure out what your deal was."

"And now?"

"At least I know you're not a liar," he said.

Trinity Rising
Chapter Fourteen
Damian

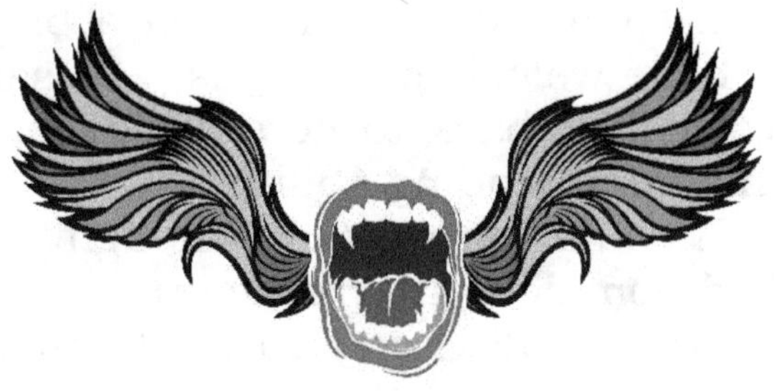

NAOMI OFFERED ME A tired smile as I sat down on the edge of the bed.

"I'm not tired," I said and brushed the hair from her face before planting a soft kiss on her lips. The whispers continued, and I shook my head, wondering just what the hell I was hearing. "Do you hear anything funny?"

She shook her head. "Why?"

"Because I feel like I'm in a theater and everyone is whispering."

Naomi let out a little laugh and I could have sworn she said, *you're so weird sometimes*, but her lips never moved. Still, it was her voice in my head, and I studied her.

"I'm not weird," I said, testing the waters, and her eyes widened.

Holy shit, you can hear me?

I started laughing. It had been a couple of months since I could hear her in my head and I missed being able to read her. On the heels of realizing I could hear her thoughts; I realized the buzz I was hearing were the random thoughts of the others in the household. My smile faded, and I glanced at the door.

"I think I may have transferred a bit of CJ's talent when we shook hands," I said and brought my gaze back to hers. If I'd pulled in a little of his mind reading ability...

Before I could complete the thought, a knock on the bedroom door interrupted us.

"Come in," I called and stood, half-expecting CJ.

When Steve pushed open the door, I met his stare.

"We need to talk," he said.

I nodded and turned to Naomi. "I'll be up in a while," I said and headed out of the room, meeting his gaze as I closed the door.

"CJ thinks you may have gotten some of his shine."

"That's what you're calling it?" I asked, avoiding the question.

"Stop being such a cocky son of a bitch." He turned, expecting me to follow. He stopped at the top of the stairs, and I got a hint of frustration. He wasn't able to read me or command me like a normal human. Transferring memories had been incidental, something he hadn't intended, especially after ordering me to give him my gun, and I didn't comply.

Now he was even more wary of me and instead of pushing his buttons and taking advantage of his hostility, I followed him downstairs, where CJ sat flipping through the television channels.

He tossed the remote onto the table and glared at me.

I didn't give you permission to take any of my juice, he thought, and I shrugged.

"Look, I didn't plan on it either," I said, taking the seat on the opposite couch.

"How did you do that?" Steve asked.

"Honestly, I'm not sure. I felt the infusion of power when we shook hands and when it retreated, I guess I grabbed onto a piece."

They exchanged a glance, and I took a minute to study their histories. Steve had done something similar, but in his case, it was the full absorption of power and it wasn't something he consciously did.

When I refocused on the two of them, I had no more answers than they did.

"Maybe it's the angel's grace. Michael had said I had his and Naomi assumes I also have my father's, so it could be... disrupting the natural order," I said.

CJ burst out laughing. "Disrupting the natural order? Dude, your entire existence disrupts the natural order. We've dealt with a lot in our lifetimes, but the existence of vampires and demons and hellhounds and Lucifer isn't anything we're equipped to deal with."

"CJ," Steve said, his concentration focused on the backyard. "I've had to alter my beliefs more than once during my lifetime. This is just another window that's opened up. A god-awful one, but if we sit in denial and turn our backs on Damian, we're setting up the end of days." He turned from the glass.

CJ sent a glare in his direction.

"We've dealt with angels and ghosts, along with some of the most evil bastards on earth, so what's a few more?"

"All due respect, but after tonight, Naomi and I will find somewhere else to go."

"Why?" Steve asked.

"Look closely at my memories, the ones with Lucifer," I said, moving my gaze between the two of them, waiting as they did as I asked.

CJ blanched a little, but Steve just sighed and refocused on me.

"So?" he said.

"I was no match for him, even in shadow form, so how do you expect to beat him?"

CJ stood and put his hand out, his mind commanding me to fly into the wall. Nothing happened and his face turned red with effort. He dropped his arm to his side, his eyes going wide as he stared at me. *Jesus, you took it all.*

"I didn't. Try moving something else," I said.

He glanced at the coffee table, and it rose off the ground. The relief on his face made me smile. Then he turned his gaze to me.

"Are you consciously trying to stop me?" he asked, trying to dissect why his powers didn't work on me.

"No," I said and thought about it. "I mean, I heard the command and felt what I would categorize as a breeze, but nothing like what you envisioned in your head." I shifted my gaze to Steve. "When you demanded the gun, I felt compelled to give it to you, so that was a conscious choice to ignore your request."

"So you're immune," Steve ventured and traded a glance with CJ.

"If I'm immune, you can bet your ass Lucifer is too."

"I'm not so sure. I've pulled Ty back down to the earth," Steve said, triggering that memory.

"He's not an archangel, is he?"

"No," Ty's voice boomed in the quiet room.

"Then we can't assume your influence or powers or whatever you call it will affect him in any way. I'd rather err on the side of caution and assume that it can't. If I'm wrong, then it will be a pleasant surprise for all of us, but if I'm right, at least we'll be prepared with something else up our sleeves," I said.

"What about trying to trap him?" Steve asked, and even his guardian angel laughed.

"No. I don't want him within a hundred miles of Naomi."

The garage door swung open, and the chill pulled my attention away from the conversation. Tom and Raven stood just beyond the door and they were not alone. The terror in their eyes pulled the air from my lungs; and when two demons stepped through the door holding knives to their throats, the horror of coming here slammed home.

"Put the knife down," all three of us commanded, one voice, three wills, and the knives tumbled from the demon's hands.

The minute the immediate threat neutralized, Tom flipped the bastard holding him and Raven slammed her heel into the demon's foot, but he tightened his grip around her neck.

A white blur shot through the air, hitting the demon holding Raven, peeling him off her and leaving her shaking. Naomi's snarl drowned out the demon's dying screams. Tom grabbed Raven, pulling her to where we stood. I didn't wait for the second demon to react, instead, I tried to do exactly what CJ had willed to happen to me and I blinked in shock as the bastard flew into the wall, cracking the drywall and pulling Naomi's attention away from her dead catch.

"How did you find me?" I asked, and the bastard smiled, his gaze dropping to the cut on my leg. The cut made by a hellhound's teeth.

"You're marked," he said and laughed.

I roared with the anger filling my soul, willing the unthinkable.

Blood mist filled the room, and I blinked, staggering back a step before dropping to the couch. I didn't understand what just happened and Steve waved his hand in front of my gaze, pulling my attention away from the spot the demon had been. My ears buzzed and my gaze dropped to the massive tiger nuzzling my lap. Naomi's tongue ran a warm path across my cheek and she pushed into me again. I scanned her blood-soaked fur and looked up at Steve. He wore the same gory mess that the rest of us did.

"What happened?" I asked, looking from Steve to CJ and then beyond to Tom, holding Raven in his arms. My gaze transitioned from the people to the actual room and my mouth dropped open. Blood even dripped from the ceiling.

"You made him explode."

I turned toward CJ, meeting his horrified gaze, and then I looked beyond him at the pristine angel behind him.

"I did that to someone once," he said, glancing around the room and then back at me. "It's pretty fucking messy."

I let out a bark of a laugh.

"It happens when the juice gets away from you, and I'd say that's exactly what happened here."

Instead of dignifying his comment with an answer, I ran my fingers behind Naomi's ears, glancing up at Tom and Raven. "Where did they ambush you?"

"In the garage, after we got out of the car," Raven said.

"And you didn't warn us?" CJ glared at Tom.

"No time," he signed.

Naomi's ears flattened, and she hissed at the back door.

I turned and stared at the pack of hellhounds keeping watch.

"Fuck," I whispered and chanced a glance in Steve's direction.

He bolted for the training room, his fear hanging on the air and agitating the dogs outdoors. Jennifer argued with him until he pulled her into the family room and then she dropped silent, letting him move her beyond Naomi and me to where the rest of their family stood together.

It wasn't until the air outside shifted and the pack parted I felt the first threads of fear.

"Do you have salt?" I asked. A moment later, a container of Morton's salt appeared. I pulled my gaze away from the man standing amid the hellhounds and looked up at Steve. "Pour a line in front of the doors and on the windowsills. Now."

Steve crossed and laid a patch of salt across the floor in front of the sliders and then the garage door. He disappeared and did the same to the front door and the windowsills, coming back with a near empty container that he set on the counter.

I knew it wouldn't stop Lucifer, but it would stop demons.

The tap on the back window pulled all our gazes, and I stared into Lucifer's angry glare. He scanned the room and his expression turned to disgust, but it wasn't his face that had my attention. It was the wings. Lucifer came calling in his deadliest form.

Wings next to me fluttered into view and Ty Ryan appeared in full glory.

Lucifer bared his teeth at the angel next to me. "Uriel," he growled loud enough to hear through the glass.

Ty laughed, shaking his head. "Try again, asshole," he said.

Lucifer focused on Ty, his gaze narrowing

I met Steve's wide gaze. "Go," I whispered and nodded toward the stairs. "He can't get in and neither can anymore demons."

I wasn't so sure about the hellhounds, but they seemed to be held at bay for the time being. I grabbed the salt and lined the bottom stair, creating a buffer for the rest of the family.

Naomi hissed, pacing in the small space.

Lucifer snapped his fingers, and Ty's smile disappeared. Standing next to the devil was a bloodied and beaten man, his haunted eyes matching that of the angel standing next to me.

"Chris," he whispered, stepping forward.

I reached out and grabbed his arm, my fingers gripping solid flesh and not air like I expected. Ty looked down at my grip and then into my eyes. The window to his soul opened, and I saw even more than what I had gleaned from Steve.

The hellhounds surrounded Chris, toying with him. The first rip of flesh brought forth a soul-crushing scream and Ty struggled against my grip.

"That's my brother," he said.

"He's already dead," I said.

"So am I." He tried to yank from my grip.

"You can't save him." I met his irritated gaze, and I knew where his heart was, but he wasn't thinking straight, not with the brutal spectacle outside the glass. "You cannot open that door."

"I have to try," he said, tears filling his bright blue eyes.

"If he gets into this house, who do you think he'll kill first?"

Ty glared at me. "You."

I shook my head and suddenly the truth hit him and he dropped to his knees, remembering the dark period when he hung between life and death. He glanced up, pain filling his features as the hellhounds tore Chris apart in front of us.

"You can't kill a ghost," I whispered.

"No, but you can torture a soul for eternity," he replied, his voice filled with anguish.

I kept hold of his arm, watching the blood spill, the anger building, agitating Naomi and she charged at the glass, stopping short and putting her claws on the window.

It was a stupid move that exposed her belly, and I saw the hellhound lunge. It hit, cracking the glass into a spider-web fracture. Naomi leaped back, retreating to the spot in front of Ty and me.

"Naomi, go upstairs," I said, and she turned her head, baring her feral teeth. "Go," I whispered and pointed, ignoring her angry stare. I finally dropped my gaze. "I will be fine. I need you to protect our family." I didn't need to expand anymore, and she turned, heading upstairs like I requested.

The second dog hit the glass, sending shards our way. I still had a grip on Ty's arm and we traded a glance. "It's your house," I said, dropping my hand.

He looked around the room and then back at me.

"Vaporize the fuckers," he said, and the power surged in my chest.

His brother's screams bled through the glass and when another dog launched, I let loose.

Lucifer stepped back, shock filling his features and his gaze locked on the spot the hellhound had launched from. All that remained was a back paw; Lucifer was wearing the rest of the creature in a spray of blood and guts.

Lucifer wiped the blood off his face and looked at his hand before leveling a glare at Ty.

He wrongly assumed the angel had killed his hound. Neither of us corrected him, either.

Chris's screams had subsided, but the sound of flesh tearing still permeated the glass. Lucifer pointed to the decimated form. "This is now your brother's fate. He will suffer an eternity of being ripped to shreds by my dogs," he growled, and then his gaze turned to me.

"When I return, there will be nothing you can do to stop me and my army from getting to your precious wife."

In a blink, he was gone, and so were Chris and the dogs.

Ty hung his head. "That should have been me," he whispered.

I stood transfixed, my body trembling. The expenditure of energy didn't diminish the magic flowing in my bloodstream, instead, it magnified.

"Damian?" Naomi's voice cut through the waves of thought, and I glanced at my surroundings until my gaze landed on her at the base of the stairwell.

"He's coming back, and he's bringing... things with him." I didn't know if it would be demon or vampire or something else entirely, but no one in the house was safe. Not even the angel beside me kneeling in defeat.

Trinity Rising
Chapter Fifteen
Damian

"HOW MUCH TIME DO we have?" Steve asked, swiping his clean face with a towel.

"I have no idea, but whatever he's bringing back..." I stopped and closed my eyes for a minute, thinking about some things I knew about Lucifer and the monsters he commanded. "If he brings vampires back, Naomi and I are safe, but you aren't." I met his gaze. "They can get through the symbols and salt and once even one symbol is compromised, Lucifer can get in."

"I thought you said there were no more vampires," he said.

I opened my mouth to speak and then just sighed. "I honestly don't know. I thought Eve was the last, but who the hell knows?"

"He said there were things far worse than vampires," Naomi said, meeting my gaze.

I bit my lip, thinking about what could be worse. "The only thing as deadly as a demon

675

that can break through our defenses is a vampire." I stopped and spun, staring out the window at my car before digging into my pockets. I clasped the key, yanking it out.

"I trust you have a nine-millimeter?" I asked Steve.

His eyebrows arched and he nodded.

"Get the gun out of my jacket," I ordered and headed to the front door.

"Why?"

"Platinum rounds. Heart shot or head shot will kill a vampire."

I grabbed the salt as I passed and poured an arch wide enough for the door to swing open without compromising the integrity of the demon defense.

"What are you doing?" Naomi grabbed my arm as I reached for the door.

"Getting the ammunition from the trunk. Did you want me to grab my bag while I'm out there?" I hadn't brought anything in and we were all in need of changing out of the blood-soaked clothing.

She glanced down at her sodden outfit and nodded. Her stomach had grown enough to stretch the wet fabric. I wondered if my sweats would be enough and then swept the thought aside and swung the door open, stepping out into the quiet night.

I didn't mosey. In fact, I sprinted and popped the trunk when I was still a couple of paces away. Sweeping my hand through handles, I hauled the duffel bags over my shoulder and reached for the boxes of ammunition, sweeping them into one of the smaller environmental-friendly shopping bags. I reached for the top of the trunk and a low growl froze me in place. The feral sound rumbled from behind me and I held my breath, closing the trunk slowly before turning to face whatever was in the driveway.

"Fuck," I whispered as I stared at a beast that looked like a cross between a hellhound and a grizzly. I couldn't back up, so I took a step toward the house. The thing bared its teeth, snarling. A gunshot rang out, and the thing yelped. I didn't wait for it to react; I turned and sprinted toward the open door.

Steve stood on the front step, aiming at the thing behind me. I scanned the front of the house, making sure there wasn't another one of these creatures waiting to pounce. The ground shook, followed by another gunshot. My heart pounded in my chest and I wished for my vampire speed.

Inside. The thought ripped from my mind and Steve took another shot before retreating and holding the door wide. I dove the last few feet, flipping myself into a break-fall, and the door slammed closed before I rolled to my feet. I dropped everything and grabbed the salt as the beast hit the other side of the door. It held, and I drew a shaky line of salt across the entryway and took a step back before the tremors reduced me to a hyperventilating pile on the floor.

"What the hell was that?"

I glanced up at him, trying to catch my breath, and shook my head. Instead of trying to guess, I reached into the bag and tossed him a box of ammunition. "Nice shooting," I breathed.

Naomi stepped into view.

"I guess there are some things that are worse," I said and sat back on my ass, leaning my forearms on my knees, still huffing. I glanced at the gun in Steve's hand and then up at him. "That's not mine." I pointed my chin at the Sig Sauer in his hand.

"Tom has yours."

Steve put his hand out, and I took it, allowing him to help me to my feet. We stepped into the kitchen and I crossed to the refrigerator. I didn't ask like I should have, instead; I opened the door and pulled the first beer within reach. I could have used scotch, but something cold that would stop my hands from shaking without clouding my mind was more appropriate for the situation.

I guzzled half the beer before turning around. A layer of a shock bit at my skin. It looked like Mr. Clean had visited the family room, except for a two-foot diameter of blood on the floor and a few tendrils stretching across the room. CJ's head was bent in concentration as the last of the tendrils pooled together. He exhaled and opened his eyes.

"Now all we need are showers," he said.

I handed Naomi the duffel bags. "Women first," I said and got no argument from anyone. Naomi hesitated, her gaze bouncing between the window behind us and me.

"Go clean up." I didn't leave any leeway in my command and she nodded, following Jennifer and Raven up the stairs.

Tom still held the gun aimed at the sliders, even as I approached.

"Why don't you and CJ go cleanup, as well? I think Steve and I can handle it for a few minutes."

He turned, glancing at me, and then Steve, waiting for the okay. I glanced over my shoulder, but Steve wasn't looking at us. He was busy loading his gun with the new bullets, his gaze jumping from the front entry to the window.

Tom brought his gaze to me. "oo o," he said and his mind echoed the proper enunciation of "You go."

I glanced at CJ, and he gave me a nod. "We've got this."

"I'll only be a few minutes," I said and took the opportunity.

The guest room had a private bathroom, and I stepped into it, peeling off my clothing and dropping them on Naomi's pile. She spun when I opened the door and I paused.

"You got bigger," I said and slipped inside.

I didn't have time to study her swollen belly; instead, I moved her out of the warm spray with a mumbled apology and grabbed the soap, scrubbing as quickly as I could. I didn't even wait until the water ran clear before lathering up my hair and rinsing. She watched from just outside the spray, her arms crossed over her breasts in an effort to keep warm. When my hair squeaked beneath my fingers, I moved her back under the water and captured a kiss.

"Thank you," I whispered and then left her in the warm flow.

I toweled off and stalked into the bedroom, ripping open the darker duffel bag. A hodgepodge of clothing met my search, and I found underwear, an undershirt, and a pair of socks. After I pulled my undergarments on, I found a pair of jeans, sliding them on before grabbing a flannel shirt. I hesitated, glancing between the blood-ridden sneakers by the door and my stocking-clad feet. My work boots were still in the car and there was no way in hell I was going outside again. I jammed my feet into my sneakers and headed out of the bedroom, buttoning my shirt as I descended the stairs. It took me exactly five minutes from the time I entered the bedroom to the time I hit the landing and my heart hadn't stopped slamming the walls of my chest.

"Your turn," I said, hand combing my dripping locks away from my face before putting my hand out for the gun.

Tom nodded and handed over the weapon, slipping upstairs.

"Steve?" CJ asked, putting his hand out for Steve's gun.

"You go," he said.

"There isn't an open bathroom for me," CJ said, and Steve sighed, looking between his adopted son and me. "We can handle five minutes alone," CJ added.

"Fine." He handed over the gun and sprinted the same way I had.

CJ moved toward me, his gun trained on the front of the house, and I stood with mine on the back entry. He stopped at my shoulder and met my gaze. "You need to learn to control it," he said.

I started laughing and looked out at the darkness beyond the glass. The power he had transferred seemed to take on a life of its own inside me, snaking through my cells like a forest fire during a drought. My gaze dropped to my hands holding the gun, specifically the tremor in them. Fear didn't drive the shakes. The tornado inside me was responsible, and I glanced back at CJ.

"How?" I whispered.

He stared at me and then focused on the front again. "How did you control yourself when you were a vampire?"

"I didn't in the beginning," I admitted and shame painted my face with heat. "But I learned to feed when I had to and not just when the need struck. It was a delicate balance. And when they started storing blood, it made things much easier." I glanced at him and shrugged. "Scotch helped, too."

He grinned, his white teeth a stark contrast to the bloody streaks still present on his skin. The water went off overhead and he glanced at me. "Every time you use the destructive ability, it gets stronger and when you lose control, it blooms like a sun flare."

"You've never lost control," I said, thinking about his memories.

CJ shook his head. "No, I haven't. I came close a few times, but I was able to rein it in before I lost it. Let me leave you with something to consider. You took the equivalent of a raindrop compared to the ocean out there, and you're having a rough time controlling that small infusion. Can you imagine the damage that would result if I ever lost control?"

He met my gaze, and I shivered at the possibilities.

Naomi stepped into the room and glanced at the two of us before putting her hand out. "Our bathroom is free," she said and CJ glanced at her hand, raising his eyebrow in question.

"She's a better shot than I am," I said and he glanced at the ceiling, then at me before he relinquished the gun.

Naomi stepped next to me, adopting the same stance CJ had, her focus on the front window as he disappeared up the stairs. When her gaze met mine, she gave me a strained smile. I took the time to glance at her attire, sweats and an oversized t-shirt that stretched over her belly.

"I'm not going to have any clothes left, am I?" I said and refocused on the glass sliders, wondering if we'd get the chance to get maternity clothes. Her belly had grown disproportionately and at this rate, even my oversized bum-around sweats would be too small for her.

"They're the only thing that sort of fits at this point," she said and shifted. "Every time I change into the tiger, it's acting like an accelerant. The good news is I can feel the baby moving. A lot."

I dropped my left hand, placing it on her extended belly and a foot connected, pulling my attention from the glass back to her. The flurries within made me blink and stare at her stomach. I focused and let out a small laugh at the distinct, simplistic thoughts coming from inside.

"They're hungry," I said, raising my gaze to hers.

"They?"

"Yes, you are carrying more than one." I pulled my hand back to steady the gun, my heart feeling both lighter with the new knowledge and fiercer on my intent to defend my family.

"How do you know?" she whispered, her focus on me and not the window in front of her.

"Keep watch," I hissed, and her gaze went back to where it belonged.

"How many do you think?" she asked, even though her mind kept focusing on how I knew.

"Two," I said, analyzing the nuance of thoughts. "Maybe three," I added after a minute. I could identify two distinct voices, but there was an echo on one that made me think it might be three.

"Twins?"

I grinned and nodded. The stairs creaked, pulling my gaze for a moment. Tom and Raven descended into the room with a duffel bag and Naomi relinquished the gun to Tom when he extended his hand. A few minutes later, Steve and Jennifer came down.

"We need to leave," Steve said, and I raised an eyebrow.

"Yes," Jennifer said. "As soon as CJ is done, we need to go."

I nodded. I couldn't blame her. If I were in her shoes, I'd bail as soon as I could, too.

"We're not bailing on you. We're bringing you with us," Steve said, throwing a separate duffel bag on the floor.

"They can track me," I said. "At least that's what the demon said."

"Not where we're going."

The certainty in his voice made me sigh. "You've been wrong before," I pointed out.

"But I've never been wrong," Jennifer said. "Go get your bags. We only have a small window to get out of here."

"There's a demon bear outside. How do you suggest we get past it?" I stood my ground, dropping my gaze to Jennifer's.

She held up a controller. "Bears have sensitive hearing and we have a hell of a house alarm."

Her answer shocked me, and I handed Steve my gun, trotting upstairs and retrieving our bags. CJ met me in the hall with a backpack slung over his shoulder.

"I guess we're going on a road trip," he said.

As we filtered out, I glanced over my shoulder at the angel still standing in the house. With a swipe of my arm, I broke the symbol on the garage door and the angel popped out of sight.

A Tahoe occupied the third garage spot, and I smiled at the large vehicle. We each threw our bags in the back and then piled in. As soon as we had locked and closed all the doors, Jennifer and Steve exchanged a glance. A moment later, the garage door blew to pieces and the house alarm pierced the air.

I don't think I fully appreciated the power of a Chevy engine until this beast roared to life and we hit fifty before the gate blew off the hinges. When Steve's phone rang, he shook his head.

"Don't answer it. Let them send the cops," he said, and I couldn't help but laugh.

"Too bad you cleaned up the family room," I said over my shoulder. Meeting CJ's gaze. He smiled and closed his eyes for a second.

"That should keep the place crawling with people for quite a while."

I thought about my car and the electronics inside and bit my lip. As much as I loved the car, the cops couldn't start digging around in there, and I added to the melee. With controlled focus, I made my car explode, destroying all the electronics along with my prized car. A pang of sorrow hit and I pressed my lips together, watching the plume of smoke retreat into the distance.

"It's just a car," Naomi said, and I nodded, but it still felt like I had taken a gut shot.

"The mural..." I started, and she shook her head.

"I put it in my duffel bag," she whispered and squeezed my hand. "Maybe I'll be able to wear it like a poncho," she added and ran her hand over her stomach.

Jennifer turned in the front seat. "You look much bigger than you did earlier," she said.

Naomi just nodded. Neither of us understood the acceleration and as I gazed at her, I wondered what it was doing to her. I took a moment to study her and then I closed my eyes, listening to the hum of discontent coming from her abdomen. Soon, their demands would bloom into something Naomi would have to answer.

"I may have something you can wear at the cottage," Jennifer said, her gaze dropping to Naomi's belly, and a flash of sadness filled the car. She turned toward the front, staring out the windshield as Steve barreled down the road, his focus on getting us all to what he deemed a place of safety instead of his equally harsh pang of sorrow.

"The cottage?" Naomi asked.

"We own a cottage in New Hampshire. On Paradise Cove," Steve said and glanced in the mirror at me.

The name started a flow of memories. Paradise Cove seemed to be a mystical gateway, one where miracles happened, but I still didn't get why they were leading the devil to such a place. "Why there?"

"Because Paradise Cove will provide us with an army of our own," Jennifer said, turning and meeting my gaze. "An army equipped to bury your nemesis."

Trinity Rising
Chapter Sixteen
Naomi

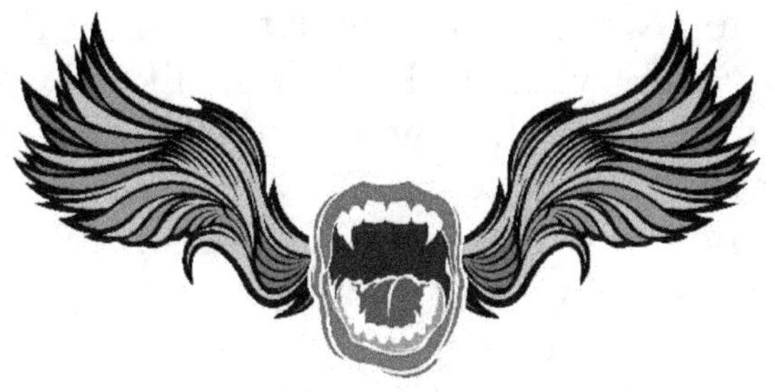

A DEEP CHILL PENETRATED my body, and I shivered, glancing over at Damian. Ever since he shook CJ's hand, something in him had changed. I have no idea what happened with the demon, either. One minute, I was ripping the throat out of one of them and the next; the house was full of red mist. It was as if the bastards were wired with a ton of C-4, but the blast only affected the demons.

Damian leaned over. "I got a little of their magic," he whispered in my ear and kissed my cheek before pulling away.

"What does that mean?" I didn't intend to shout out the question, but he chuckled in response and Steve glanced back at me.

"It means your husband has been touched by more than just angel grace. He's the one who disintegrated those demons, and it was his display of power that made your car blow up like a fireworks disaster," Steve said. "And if I'm not mistaken, he can read your mind."

"But he doesn't have a good handle on controlling it yet," CJ said from the backseat.

I was getting more irritated by the second. It wasn't their words, but their tone, like they were handling me with kid gloves, like I wouldn't understand what they were saying, and I turned, meeting Raven's gaze.

"Do they always talk to women like they're feeble-minded?"

Raven pressed her lips together but didn't hide the snort of laughter. "Aye, especially when they talk about their gifts," she said, her Irish accent coming through with her full-bodied laugh. Tom rolled his eyes and shook his head, but he kept his mouth closed and his hands still. CJ glared at his sister-in-law and then at me.

"We don't think you're feeble-minded," he said. "It's just..."

"Dude, I was a vampire," I said, silencing everyone in the car. "When I get pissed, I turn into a fucking tiger. I've dealt with angels, killed demons and even danced with the fucking devil, so when you toss out lame descriptions for psychic occurrences, I get irritated." I glared at the three in the back and turned to the front, leveling the same disgust in the mirror at Steve. "I am a Mohegan warrior princess, and just because I'm a pregnant, hormonal wreck, doesn't mean you have to treat me like an unstable idiot."

"Mohegan warrior princess?" Damian chuckled, and my glare shot to him. He raised his hands, trying to show he meant no harm, but in his gaze, I saw the years of teasing I'd get for that statement.

I looked out the window, and a smile found my lips. Chuckles erupted from the front passenger seat along with the row behind me.

"My grandfather used to call me his warrior princess," I muttered and slid my gaze to Damian. I couldn't completely suppress my smile. He grinned at me and winked.

"Well, I'm glad you're my warrior princess," he teased in that endearing manner that made me alternate between wanting to slap him and kiss him.

"Damn, she's a pistol," Steve laughed, glancing at Damian.

He grinned and nodded. "Yes, she is," he said, oozing with pride.

Laughter filled the car, and in the midst of it, Steve's phone buzzed again. This time, he didn't ignore the call. He answered, and a panicked voice filled the car.

"Steve?"

"Hi, Sarah," he said and glanced at his wife.

"What the hell?" the woman said, and I smiled, picking up the distinct New York City accent.

"Where are you?" he asked, his laughter now fizzling out, replaced by worry lines.

"I'm on my way to your place. The police said it was a mess."

"Steer clear of there until I call you. It's not safe for anyone we give a damn about."

Silence came over the line and the sound of a car slowing to a stop replaced the hum in the background.

"Did you just admit to giving a shit about me?"

I watched the exchange between Jennifer and Steve before he sighed. There was a history there that piqued my curiosity.

"Yeah. I give a shit," he grumbled.

"Jen?"

"Hi, Sarah," Jennifer said.

"It's that fucking bad?"

Another exchange and then Jennifer glanced back at me as she answered. "Worse than you can imagine, but we're all alive and breathing, so..."

"You know I can't just make excuses and not show up."

"If she has to go, tell her to steer clear of anyone she doesn't know. And don't say anything about talking to us," I said, staring at Jennifer. "Otherwise, you'll never see her again."

"Who the hell is that?" Sarah barked and after that, she said, "Is that the girl from the hospital? Did you find those two psychos?"

"I found them," Steve said, giving me the keep-your-mouth-shut glare. "Trust me on this one," he added.

"And who the hell did they kill? There's blood all over your family room and on the lawn in the backyard, according to the call we got."

"They didn't kill anyone."

I met his gaze in the mirror. He lied better than I expected from a federal agent.

Damian leaned close. "He worked undercover for years," he whispered, his voice tickling my ear. I glanced at him and then my gaze drifted beyond.

Headlights were too close.

"Watch out!" I screamed just as the Ford truck slammed into the side of the Tahoe and we swerved. The back wheel caught dirt and slid, swinging around and then nothing. No sound at all as the vehicle started the beginning of a death roll.

Trinity Rising
Chapter Seventeen
Naomi

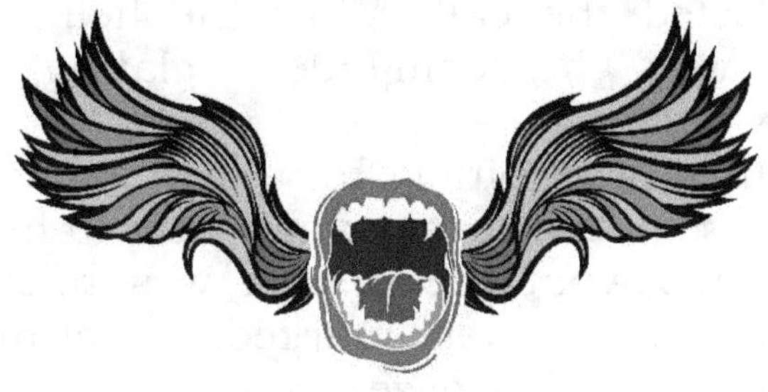

IMAGES REGISTERED BETWEEN BLINKS, and my entire body tensed, waiting for the impact.

The crazed smile of the demon driver who ran us off the road.

The Ford flashing over in a ball of flame and then turning to dust.

Cars swerving to avoid hitting us.

We spun in the air and I could no longer see the traffic behind us. I expected shattered glass and crumpling metal. I expected the jar of the seatbelt and the following whiplash. I didn't expect what happened.

The vehicle completed the revolution, and the tires bounced on the asphalt, finding purchase and propelling us forward.

Cars braking around us were louder than our impact. The only sound was our collective breathing, hard and laborious, like we all had just run the hundred-yard dash.

"What the hell was that?" Sarah roared on the speakerphone.

"I hit a guardrail," Steve answered. "I'm going to have to call you back," he added and disconnected the call. "How the hell are they finding us?" he demanded, glaring in the rearview mirror.

"Damian was bitten by a hellhound earlier today," I said and dropped my gaze to his leg. "I think that's what the demon was referring to when he said you were marked." I met his stark stare and then his gaze dropped to his leg as well. His expression altered, and he closed his eyes.

"Did anyone think to grab the salt?" he asked and silence met his question.

"What were you going to do, pour salt in your cut?"

"Yes. I figure if salt keeps demons out, it might mask my whereabouts."

"Do we need to stop?" Steve askcd.

"There isn't time," Jennifer said.

The bouncing conversation along with the erratic lane changes were making me sick, and I swallowed the acidic taste in my mouth.

"We might need to stop anyway," Damian said and brushed a stray hair behind my ear. "Naomi needs to eat."

"I'll be fine," I muttered, but if I didn't eat soon, I was going to pass out or vomit. The pizza I had before the demons attacked had long been digested and absorbed and the babies were starting to kick.

"You need food," Damian said, and his gaze fell on my stomach. "The dinner you ate wasn't enough to fuel your transformation, never mind the accelerated growth of the babies."

Jennifer glanced over her shoulder. "How far along are you, anyway?"

I laughed and met her gaze. "I'm supposed to be due in October."

Her eyebrows arched and she dropped her gaze to my stomach. Her lips moving silently, forming partial words before she looked back at me. "That means you're a little less than two months?"

I nodded. "I was less than two months before I transformed, but I have no clue how far along I am now. And Damian thinks we're having twins."

"Triplets," CJ and Jennifer said at the same time, and I met her gaze while Damian looked back at CJ.

"How do you know?" I asked Jennifer.

She offered me a strained smile and traded a glance with Steve. "I had a vision."

Even Damian looked surprised with the answer, but he quickly recovered, and his hand found my belly. He caressed my abdomen and smiled. "You need to eat, because they are still hungry."

"I need to get gas anyway," Steve mumbled and veered off toward the next exit. When we stopped, Damian helped me out of the car and I wobbled into the convenience store, heading directly into the bathroom.

"You guys have to calm down. I'm going to get something to eat just as soon as I can," I said, rubbing the swollen skin. Once I had relieved the pressure on my bladder, the babies calmed, almost as if they shared in my relief. I shimmied the sweats back up and stepped to the sink.

My reflection took me by surprise and I stared at my gaunt face and ringed eyes. I hadn't had the time to inspect what I looked like at the house, but I never imagined I looked this bad. No wonder I felt like death.

"Damian?" I said, and the door opened.

"Are you okay?" he asked.

"Look at me." I pointed to the mirror. "I look like a walking skeleton."

He sighed and nodded. "I know. You need to eat."

"No shit," I responded and grabbed a paper towel, wiping my hands before tossing the crumpled paper into the garbage. "No wonder the guy at the counter looked at me like I was a fucking ghost," I muttered and stepped out into the heart of the store.

As I walked by the candy shelf, a hunger pain hit and I doubled over, holding my stomach. My insides felt like a hand was squeezing, trying to make my stomach pop like a balloon, and my knees gave out, hitting the hard floor. I couldn't draw a breath.

I didn't understand what was happening and I couldn't call out.

"Is she okay?" the kid at the counter called.

"She will be," Damian said and swept me up into his arms, carrying me toward the door while I forced small breaths. His gaze bounced, like he was looking for the cause, and then he stopped, pulling me closer. The car wasn't at the pump and the man standing in the darkness beyond the station lights made my stomach clutch tighter.

Lucifer.

Pain seared through me, and I screamed, fighting the darkness threatening to pull me into oblivion.

Trinity Rising
Chapter Eighteen
Naomi

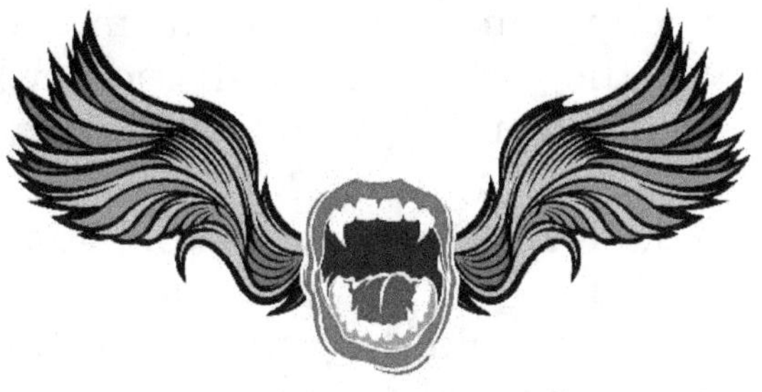

TIRES SQUEALED AND THE Tahoe slammed to a stop in front of us, blocking my view of the bastard pulverizing my insides. The back door swung open and Damian climbed in with me in his arms. Before we even settled in the seat, the door closed, pulled by whatever psychic magic the men in the car possessed. Steve gunned the engine, and I had a moment to capture Lucifer's angry glare as we sped off. The farther away we got, the looser the tightness in my abdomen became.

I hyperventilated, leaning over as far as my oversized stomach would allow, and slowly, my seized lungs released, allowing oxygen to flow until the pain finally abated.

"Why isn't he following?" I asked when I had my voice back.

"I painted the symbols on the ceiling." Steve pointed to the roof of the car and I looked up.

The deep red etched in the gray fabric pulled a gasp from my throat. "Is that blood?"

"Yes," he answered and raised his left hand. I caught the make-shift bandage wrapped around his palm. "It's all we had." He glanced in the mirror, meeting my gaze for a moment. "I'll swing into the drive through somewhere in Brooksfield for you. It won't be much longer. Okay?"

I nodded, despite the incessant rumbling in my stomach.

"Maybe you should drop me off on the side of the highway and take her somewhere safe," Damian said.

I shot an open-mouthed gape in his direction and shook my head. "No! You're not going to be a martyr this time. You've done that too many times before, and every time you decide to make the sacrifice, you come within a hair's breadth of death. It's not happening again."

"But..." he started.

"No," I growled through clenched teeth. The prickling of the transition started, and I pushed it back. I didn't have room to transition in the car and I certainly didn't want to find out how far along I'd be when I snapped back to human form.

"Naomi, it's dangerous for me to be here. I'm the damned magnet that leads them right to us every time."

"You need to be with us, Damian," Steve said. "You're the only one who can stop that maniac."

"CJ could stop him," Damian argued, and I gave him a sideways glance, trying to understand what made CJ Ryan so special, beyond his uncanny similarity to my husband.

"He can't," Ty's detached voice said. "Even on hallowed ground, he's still doesn't have the power to kill the devil."

Fear flashed over Damian's features and he swallowed, dropping his gaze. I didn't have to be a mind reader to know he was replaying every brutal encounter with Lucifer. When he looked out the window, his jaw tightened, followed by his grip on my hand.

The minute his gaze came back to mine, I shivered at the raw fury filling his bright-blue eyes.

Damian's anger filled the car and instead of hitting it head on like I normally would, I curled up on the seat, putting my head in his lap. My stomach had turned to a roiling mess, and I needed a little tender loving care.

He sighed and started slowly hand combing my hair. The triplets had started doing acrobatics in the small space and my back ached from the strain. I just wanted a normal pregnancy and a quiet life raising my children with Damian.

I wanted peace.

My eyelids closed under his continued pampering, and he started singing for my benefit. Soft and sweet, pulling me under the blanket of sleep.

Trinity Rising
Chapter Nineteen
Naomi

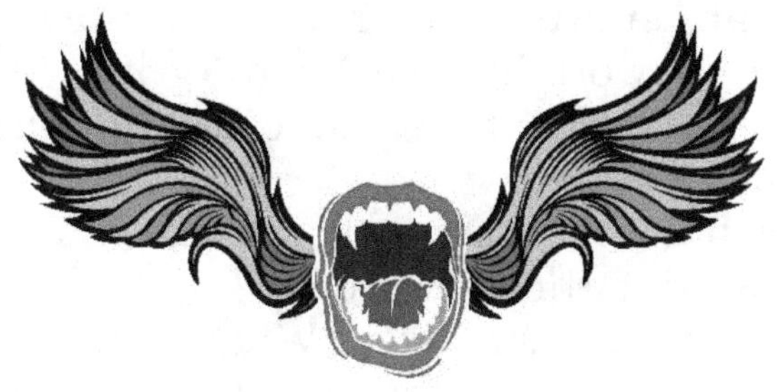

FRENCH FRIES.

The identification of the scent immediately popped me into a sitting position. I have no idea how long I was out, but now I was fully awake and ravenous. A quick glance at my surroundings told me we were in the drive through line of a Wendy's and my mouth salivated.

"What would you like?" Steve asked, meeting my gaze.

"Everything," I said in all seriousness, and he arched a brow. "Fine," I sighed and looked at the approaching board. "Two double bacon cheeseburgers, no, make that three, two large fries, a large chocolate frosty." I scanned the menu. "And maybe spicy chicken sandwich," I added. "Wait, make that three portabella bacon cheeseburgers instead of the double cheeseburgers," I said and smiled. "And a large frosty shake along with the chocolate frosty."

Steve stared at me in the mirror.

"That should do for me," I said and glanced at Damian. "Do you want anything?"

Damian snorted laughter and Steve looked down so I wouldn't see him grin. After the chortle of laughter filled the car, everyone yelled out their orders.

"Just hold on a second," he said as he rolled up to the drive through kiosk.

"Welcome to Wendy's. What can I get you today?" the chipper voice asked.

Steve accurately recounted my order, which impressed the hell out of me, and he continued ticking off what everyone had called out down to the last frosty. It was an impressive list for seven people, but no one had near the volume of food I ordered.

"I got this," Damian said, reaching for his wallet, but his expression fell when his hand came up empty. "Fuck," he muttered, and Steve glanced back at him. "My wallet was in the jeans I had on earlier," he said. "Which are on the floor in the bathroom upstairs."

"That means they're going to assume you had something to do with the disappearance of my family," Steve mumbled, pulling his wallet out and peeling off enough cash to cover the bill at the window.

We didn't linger. The minute the food was in the car and accounted for, Steve pulled out of the parking lot, heading down one of the main thoroughfares right through the middle of a college campus. He pushed the redial button on his phone as soon as he was sure no one was following us.

"Steve?"

"You went to the house, didn't you?" he asked, his voice filled with instant irritation.

"It's my job. There's blood everywhere. What the hell happened?" Sarah snapped back.

"We are all okay."

"You said that earlier. But after seeing this, clearly, someone isn't."

"Something. Not someone."

"What the fuck am I supposed to do with that?"

"Let it go. This is one of those situations where you don't want to know. Just like you don't want to know what the hell happened at the hospital in Torrington. It's way too out there for you to come to terms with."

Silence cascaded on the line.

"More fucked up than your guardian angel?"

"Far more," he said, his voice softening. "It's even more fucked up than what happened at Black Cove."

Jennifer shivered at the mention of Black Cove, encircling herself with her arms as if that could ward off whatever chill accosted her. I traded a glance with Damian and focused on my food, carefully unwrapping the first burger.

"Fine. Can I at least tell Ron that you're okay?"

"Go ahead," Steve answered. "And let him know that video didn't carry the full story. The man in the video was there, but he isn't responsible for those deaths. It's a setup. And I know who is responsible."

"Fine, I'll tell him," Sarah said, and the line went dead.

I tore into my second burger and glanced at Damian. I had a few questions, but my mind focused back on the food and I devoured it with zest, like this was my last meal.

Silence blanketed the car, and I looked up at Damian. His lips pressed together in derision and his gaze jumped between the food in my hands and my face and then he shook his head, taking a spoonful of my chocolate frosty that he held for me.

I glanced in the back and all three of them were staring at me in the same manner as Damian.

"I'm hungry," I said around a mouthful of French fries.

That seemed to break their morbid curiosity, and they all looked down at their own food. I glanced back at Damian. "What?"

"Wild dogs," he whispered and grinned, shaking his head like I was a hopeless case. He handed me my frosty and broke into his meal.

I finished mine before he had the chance to drink half his soda.

We pulled off the main road onto an overgrown dirt path between drifts of snow. I hadn't noticed the shift in the scenery from the snow dusted seacoast to the mountains of New Hampshire until now.

"Where are you taking us?" I asked and covered a burp. The triplets seemed to be falling into the same food coma I was entering, and I yawned.

"Paradise Cove," Steve said just as the woods opened to a clearing with a charming oversized cottage like the ones you'd see the rich and famous slumming in.

The moonlight reflected on the snow and Steve slowed as the garage opened and he pulled inside, throwing the car into park and cutting the engine. He waited until the door closed behind us before he reached up and scratched a line through the symbol, rendering it useless. Steve stepped out of the car and opened the door for me.

"You've got just enough time to hit the bathroom and then we have to move," he said, unlocking the house and waving me inside. The crew unloaded, but no one else came inside with Steve and me.

I did my business and stepped back into the dark room.

"You and Damian will need these," Steve said, handing me a down coat and once I pulled it on, he handed me the one for Damian and I stepped back into the garage.

Damian stepped close, and I offered him the coat. He slipped it on and we waited for Steve. A couple of minutes later, he came out with a metal box along with four coats draped across the top. After handing the coats to Jennifer, Raven, Tom and CJ, Steve set the box down and pulled out his keys.

"Get the ammunition," he said, nodding toward the back of the truck where Damian had stashed the grocery bag of bullets. Damian stepped to the trunk while Steve unlocked the box and handed CJ and Tom two of the revolvers from within the case. When Damian returned, he handed each one of them a box of ammunition.

"Load up, boys," Steve said and took a box himself, making sure his clip was full.

Damian did the same, and I watched each of the platinum bullets fit neatly in the clip and then he pushed it in place, meeting my gaze.

"You ready for this?" he asked me and I nodded, running my hands over my belly.

He offered me a strained smile and leaned down, meeting my lips with his cool ones.

"If something happens to me, make sure they know I loved them as much as their mamma," he whispered and pulled away.

"I hate it when you do that," I snapped. "Nothing's going to happen to you." I straightened, sending a glare in his direction before turning to Steve. "You got another gun?"

"I'm sorry, I don't," Steve answered, showing me the empty case. "Besides, you've got an advantage the rest of us don't."

"The tiger?"

He nodded.

"I'm not so sure that's a good idea," I said, running my hand over my belly.

"It's your best option if the shit hits the fan," he said.

As much as I didn't like that answer, I had to agree. I was a force in tiger form, especially after what I did to the hellhounds in the garage. I gave him a nod and moved next to Damian.

Steve checked the safety on the gun before stepping toward the door. He waited until everyone finished loading their clips, his gaze settling on each one of us as we lined up behind him.

"Game on," Steve said.

All the hairs on the back of my neck stood up. He opened the door, and I clamped my teeth together, steeling myself for battle.

Trinity Rising
Chapter Twenty
Damian

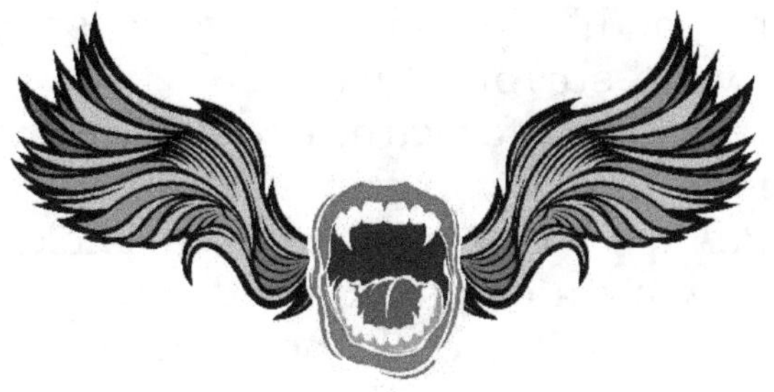

STEVE TOOK THE FRONT with the three women between us and Tom and CJ were at my back. The formation moved as one toward the woods. Each step left a crunching sound as we padded across the snow. Darkness surrounded us, but the moon shone brightly enough to make out shadows on the white landscape. Steve led us quickly onto a narrow path in the woods. The proximity of the trees made my imagination flare. This was the type of pathway I used to like to trap my victims on. With such little room for maneuvering, the victim wouldn't be able to put up much of a fight.

"Give me some credit," Steve said and glanced over his shoulder.

"It's the perfect place for an ambush," I replied, glancing around at the deep wooded boundaries. Muscles in my back tightened in response to the warning bells in my stomach.

Steve picked up the pace, and I glanced behind me, making sure Tom and CJ were still with us.

"We're good," CJ said, his voice soft, falling with the wind surrounding us.

When I turned forward, I could see the woods opening up and my paranoia dropped a notch. We made it to the glen without incident and Steve threw me a canister.

"Make yourself useful," he said.

I raised an eyebrow. "Salt?"

"Yes, make a barrier at the wood line."

"I'm not sure this is going to work," I said, but stepped to the path we just crossed over and poured a thick line across the snow-covered ground, continuing to the frozen water line of the small inlet. I crossed and did the same around the remainder of the perimeter until I shook the last grains of salt out of the container at the opposite shoreline and turned to the group.

"Now what?" I asked.

Steve traded a glance with Jennifer and then started clearing a space with his feet. "Now we make a fire and wait," Steve said. CJ and Tom helped clear the snow off with their feet, revealing a deep green moss that seemed to cover the entire opening.

"You know, for such a brilliant investigator, you can be a complete idiot," I said, and Steve looked up at me. "Step aside." I crossed to a spot just inside the salt line and pushed with my mind, clearing all the snow from the ground and the water, leaving a pile at the far edge of the icy cove.

Steve crossed his arms, glaring at me like I just did a major faux pas.

"What? You've got the power to do this. Why the hell would you do it manually?" I said and moved my gaze to Naomi. Her eyes were wide with awe. I guess she really didn't understand the powers this family harbored. I offered her a smile and a shrug.

"Because it reminds me I'm human, and not some all powerful god," Steve answered, his tone as sharp as his gaze.

I huffed and took a step forward, but something gripped the collar of my jacket, pulling my legs out from under me, and I was yanked backwards into the woods. Naomi's warning followed me into the darkness and I had a moment to flash to a bad horror movie I once saw. It snapped out of my head the moment I hit a tree, knocking the wind out of my chest. Dazed, I stared at a set of fangs dipping toward my neck.

I blocked the bite with my arm, but the beast's teeth sank into my flesh. I roared at the sting, but it was nothing compared to the vampire's scream. I hadn't had the pleasure of seeing what the cure did to a vampire before, like Naomi had, and the frothing blood bubbling from his throat was enough of a view. She hadn't been kidding when she said the cure ate vampires from the inside out. Horrified, I backed away a few steps, then turned and bolted toward the clearing, silently announcing to CJ and Steve that I was okay before breaking through the wood barrier. The burn of the bite faded as my blood flowed, cleaning the puncture wounds, but I was left with a dull throbbing ache.

Naomi stood on all fours, blocking the rest of the group, her growl sending a warning through the woods. I stopped a few steps inside the line and looked down at my arm. Blood dripped from my hand and Naomi's expression changed. Even on a tiger, I saw the concern.

"I'm fine," I said to her, although my heart still hammered from the adrenaline rush that fear afforded me. "I can't say the same for the vampire."

I looked up at the huddled group, Naomi in front and then the three men, guns drawn and pointing in three different directions. Jennifer and Raven stood behind them with the lake at their heels. Even Ty made an appearance, standing in the center of the ice, raining light on the dark alcove.

I crossed to Naomi, and she licked my hand, cleaning off the dark drips before nuzzling her head against my leg.

"It's probably a good idea that you stay in tiger form," I said and crouched down. "I think you can protect yourself better like this." Her tongue swathed my face, and I gave her a hug before pulling back. I stripped the coat and inspected my punctured arm. The bastard's teeth had gone into the meaty flesh of my forearm, but at least he hadn't torn a chunk out.

"Jesus," Steve muttered, and I looked up.

His gaze scanned the woods behind me and I turned, pulling the jacket back on and digging the revolver out of the pocket. At least a dozen vampires stepped into view, brought forward by the smell of my blood. While Naomi and I were immune to the virus, the others weren't, and a bite meant a highly unpleasant death.

They stopped, collectively smiling.

"The great Damian Andreas," one of them growled, and I focused on him. The face looked familiar, like someone I'd met in passing, but it didn't matter when or where. I had to rid the earth of these monsters, otherwise they'd keep multiplying.

"I'll give you to the count of three to leave. Otherwise, you'll be burning in hell before you can blink." I raised the gun, pointing it at a spot on the bastard's forehead. Naomi growled at my side and I heard the click of the safety on all the guns behind me.

Burn them. Torch their asses when I get to three, understand? I sent the thought out to Steve and CJ and got a resounding *Got it* from both of them.

"One," I said and paused when the vampires laughed.

"You're going to shoot us?" the lead asshole said and chuckled. "You should know better."

I smiled, looking over the gun. "Two, and yes, I know better," I said, and his cocky stance waned.

"Platinum?" he gasped and took a step back, fear transitioning his features from shadow back to the pale white of Lilith's brood.

"And we're all expert shots," I said and didn't wait for them to attack or retreat. Instead, I yelled, "Three!"

A wave of heat passed by me, joining with the power that leaped from my core, fanning out to encompass the mass of vampires. The stench of burned flesh filled the air, along with the dust of the decimated vampires.

Trinity Rising
Chapter Twenty-one
Damian

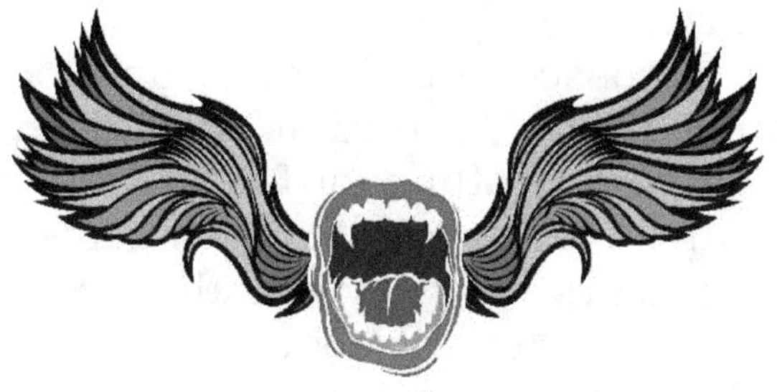

A SHIFT IN THE wind blew the dust into the woods and I turned, my heart lurching at the sight before me. Ty stood on the ice, surrounded by a host of angels. I stared at the assembly and my gaze locked on one pair in particular.

Michael stood revived in his youthful form but without wings. Beside him stood a similar wingless angel with a face I barely remembered, but one that made my arms drop to my side.

"μπαμπάς?" I asked in my native tongue. "Papa, is that really you?" My throat closed around a lump that formed. I hadn't seen my father since I was little and the fact he stood ready to do battle at my side pulled at my heartstrings.

The emotions that flew through my body left me numb. All the wrongs I had done flushed me with shame, and all the heroic actions counteracted, and I dropped my gaze to the ground, not knowing how to react.

"Damian," he whispered, and just his voice triggered fond memories of fishing on the banks of the Mediterranean. "My son," he added, and I met his gaze.

Gabriel crossed the distance and pulled me into a hug. I didn't return it right away, aware that we didn't have time for family reunions, but the warmth of the arms encircling me brought the burn of tears to my eyes and I met Michael's gaze. He gave me a tight nod.

"How?" I asked, scanning the white-winged beings in our midst, two of which were supposed to be trapped behind the gates of heaven.

Two who had sacrificed their grace for me.

Steve cleared his throat, and I pulled away from my father.

"I promised you an army," Steve said and waved his hand at the heavenly host, grinning like he knew a particularly intriguing secret.

Trinity Rising
Chapter Twenty-two
Damian

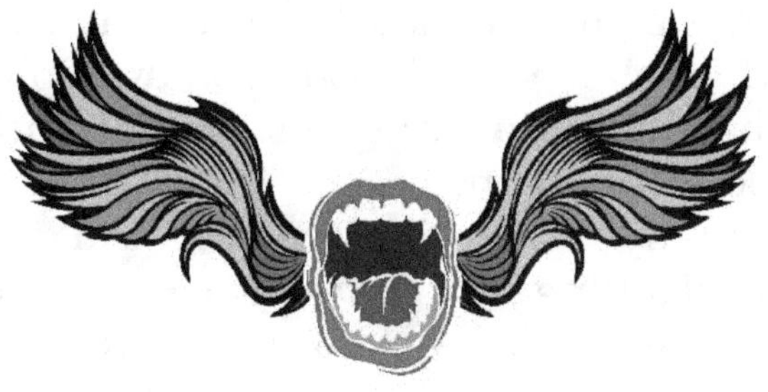

MOVEMENT PULLED MY ATTENTION back to the woods and a chill lit up the area, pressing down on me. I moved away from my father, closer to Naomi. A solid line of demons stepped into view, stopping at the salt line I poured.

The next wave of assailants took up their posts, side by side with a legion of hellhounds. Naomi actually stepped back at the numbers and I felt her fear. It blended with my own and one look at Steve and his family revealed they were in the same place we were.

Terror gripped every one of us and we spread out on the shoreline far enough away from the woods to be safe for the moment. Steve took the left side, and I took the right. CJ stood dead center. Jennifer, Tom and Raven stood a step behind, relying on us to provide a solid wall of defense. I glanced down at Naomi and pointed for her to join them. She hissed at me, but obeyed my silent command to move back.

Angels flanked us, providing a solid line between the innocents behind us and the demon horde. My heart scrambled in my chest, pumping a beat that nearly seized my lungs and I traded a glance with CJ. He swallowed and curled his hands around his revolver, aiming it at the closest demon.

The air sparked with tension and when the demons blocking the path parted; I knew we were in for a nasty battle. Lucifer stepped inside the ring, swiping a clean path through the salt I had laid down, and he wasn't alone.

He dragged a beautiful blonde woman forward, tossing her at his feet in front of him. When she raised her bruised face, Steve cursed under his breath and the gun moved from the line of demons to Lucifer.

Lucifer just grinned at the assembly and his black wings fluttered as he cracked his fingers. His gazed moved over the crowd of angels. "What have we here?" he said, scanning the line until his gaze landed on Gabriel and Michael. He tilted his head in contemplation, and then his gaze moved back to Steve.

"This lovely police officer was particularly useful," he said, meeting Steve's glare and waving his hand in the woman's direction.

Her gaze bounced from the demons surrounding us to the angels in line, landing on the tiger behind me. Then they jumped to Steve.

"What the fuck?" she whispered and Steve offered her a half laugh.

"I told you not to go to the house," he said, and I knew exactly who this was. The abrasive FBI agent Steve had spoken to on the phone. Sarah. Lucifer reached for the woman, grabbing a handful of her hair.

"Let go of me, asshole," Sarah snapped, swatting at his hand. While her voice was defiant and full of moxie, her eyes held a soul-crushing fear that I knew all too well.

He pulled her to her feet, bringing her close to him. Her elbow connected with his stomach, and he chuckled in her ear.

"I like my women feisty," he purred in her ear, keeping his gaze locked on Steve's. This primer was just the beginning of his dance, and I knew the woman was doomed.

We were all doomed.

"I'll tell you what," he said, running a sharp nail lightly down her arm. "I'll let you and your family go, along with this lovely officer, if you leave us to settle our differences," he said, nodding toward Naomi and me, negotiating a deal that would seal me in my grave.

I didn't move, but I made a point of recounting this beast's broken promises. The moment they stepped outside this cove, the hellhounds would tear them to bits.

"That includes leaving the angel and his son," Lucifer clarified, his gaze landing on Ty, narrowing into a hateful expression that I was used to receiving.

Steve's jaw clenched and his gaze dropped to Sarah.

"Do your magic and get me out of this," Sarah said, the panic reaching her voice as Steve's head shook back and forth.

His entire being shook and the frustration and anger pulsing in his veins drifted over me.

"You bastard," I whispered, and Lucifer sent a chilling smile in my direction.

"I can't do that," Steve said, and I glanced at him. Jennifer's hand rested on his shoulder and her forehead rested between his shoulder blades, her form shaking with silent sobs; and pain flashed in my chest.

I should have never let Naomi talk me into coming to Maine. We should have run across the globe, and then these pure souls wouldn't have to sacrifice those they loved for me.

CJ slid a glare in my direction and the mental reprimand resounded in my head like one of those obnoxious air horns. *Stop the fucking pity party.*

I winced at the volume and my gaze dropped to the ground, returning to the woman struggling in Lucifer's grasp.

Lucifer's hand ripped the shirt open, revealing a modest sports bra, and he tilted his head, smiling as his fingernails dimpled the skin over her heart. "Last chance," he said.

"I'm sorry, Sarah," Steve said, his eyes filled with tears and his lips pressed together.

Sarah's scream shattered the night, followed by the report of a gun. Smoke drifted from the end of Steve's revolver and I stared at it before turning toward the deafening silence.

Lucifer's fingers were buried knuckle deep in Sarah's chest, but that's not what silenced her scream. The neat bullet hole between her eyes had sent her to heaven before Lucifer could rip her heart out.

I turned back toward Steve, and his arms lowered. His chin dropped to his chest, and his breath hitched once. With a violent shake of his head, his tear-stained glare landed on Lucifer and the gun rose back in place.

"Get the fuck off my property," he said with a growl.

"As soon as I have my whore," he said.

Steve pulled the trigger again, but this time nothing happened until he moved the aim to the demon closest to Lucifer and then the gun jumped to life, expelling another round. The shot was as true as the one that took Sarah's life, and the first demon fell.

Lucifer yanked his hand from Sarah's flesh and tossed her next to the dead demon. He licked his fingers and scowled, glaring at Steve. The minute he stepped forward, Ty interceded, blocking the devil's path.

That hateful glare reappeared and Lucifer snapped his fingers, Christopher Ryan appeared in the center of the clearing, bleeding and on his knees, his screams filling the silent woods, echoing on the dark lake and the hellhounds tasked with ripping him to shreds continued their attack.

This time, Ty moved; his face filled with a wrath I had only seen once before and my gaze drifted to Michal. CJ took a step toward his father, pulling my attention back to the spectacle before us. Both Steve and I grabbed an arm, keeping him from entering the violent scene in front of us. This was the primer to the war, and I knew it was just an appetizer meant to drive the hounds in line into a frenzy, preparing them for attack.

"You can't stop it," I said when CJ tried to rip out of my grasp.

He turned a pleading gaze in my direction when the first hellhound turned on Ty.

I knew the pain in his gaze. I knew the need to stop the inevitable, and I also knew the futility of any action against what had already been set into motion.

What I didn't expect was for Ty to rip a hellhound in two with his bare hands and from the expression on Lucifer's face, neither did he.

Ty grabbed Chris around the waist and launched toward the heavens, pulling his brother out of range of the hellhounds into the single beacon of light, disappearing from view before Lucifer could yank him back to the earth.

Lucifer's furious gaze dropped from the sky to me, then moved to CJ. His face crinkled and he roared his aggravation, squeezing a fist in front of him, sending out the command to burst the boy's heart. I stepped into the flow of power aimed at Ty's son, deflecting it with a mental wall. Three of the demons next to Lucifer burst, exploding into balls of flame.

The surprise of the back-to-back events stunned everyone, and nothing moved until a streak of lightning flared and Ty landed on one knee in the center of the clearing like Thor arriving for battle. His wings smoldered, sending tendrils of smoke into the air, but when he lifted his head, his fury filled the space and he stood, shifting into a battle stance.

"You've cheated me for the last time," Lucifer growled and pointed at Ty.

"Game on, you bastard," Ty said and leveled the glare I had seen in Steve's mind. The one that dubbed the man as the Angel of Death while he was alive, and it evoked a tremor, a chill that bit at my heels and spread like a four-alarm fire.

Naomi hissed behind me, and the spell that held me in place broke. I remembered the gun in my hand and raised it, aiming at the closest hellhound. I squeezed the trigger and the report of gunfire shattered the stillness, breaking the stalemate between good and evil.

Trinity Rising
Chapter Twenty-three
Damian

THIRTY DEMONS WENT DOWN in the span of the ten seconds it took the four of us to empty our guns and the only one that took the time to re-load was Tom. The angels charged forward meeting the advancing demons in the center, but Steve, CJ and I stayed put, protecting our families behind us.

When Tom stepped between CJ and me, leveling the gun at the melee, I pushed his hand down and shook my head.

"Hold on to those. We might need them," I said, meeting his gaze and pushing him back into the safety of the cocoon we created.

A hellhound launched at us, and I let a targeted power bolt loose. The beast exploded, like the one at the house, and CJ and I traded a glance. I wasn't sure I could target only demons in the battle, but both Steve and CJ nodded.

"We have to try it," Steve said.

"On three," CJ said, and I closed my eyes, concentrating. "One," CJ breathed low over the bellows of fighting angels and demons.

"Two," I said and felt the tight coil in my chest.

"Three!" Steve said.

My eyes snapped open, and the wave rolled across the field, leaving only a bloody mist in its wake, along with four stunned angels.

Ty glanced at the three of us with a maniacal grin.

Lucifer stood at the edge of the field, scanning the gory remains of his army.

Michael and Gabriel stared at the mess with open mouths.

Only the sound of blood rain filled the space and I realize we'd annihilated demons and angels alike. Only archangels remained and my gaze landed on Ty. A shiver caught my soul, turning my blood as cold as the frigid water behind me.

We moved closer to Ty, Michael and Gabriel, squaring up to Lucifer, but he wasn't done with his arsenal of tricks. Naomi howled, and I blinked down at the writhing cat before my gaze jumped to Lucifer.

I charged without thought and got one hit in before his backhand hit me, spinning me onto the ground. The howl turned into an ear-piercing scream, snapping my gaze to my wife. Naomi lay in a ball, in human form, holding her stomach, screaming in pain.

The black power moved from Naomi to CJ, dropping him to his knees as he held his chest. His head dipped and his hands balled into fists.

When he snapped his gaze from the ground back at Lucifer, the devil stumbled back, nearly falling on his ass.

CJ stood, his breath coming in shallow bursts, and I scrambled to my feet, retreating to Naomi and falling on my knees next to her. She turned her head and shock filtered through me at the gaunt face that peered at me. She was too pale, too thin, and my heart pounded in my throat. I put my hand on her swollen belly, praying for signs of life and the moment my hand touched, a foot found it, but with it came the writhing struggle inside the womb. My children were alive, but they were in as much pain as Naomi.

"It hurts," she whispered, and I pushed her hair away from her face, planting a kiss on her cheek.

"It's going to be all right," I said, even though I didn't believe it, not with our dwindling numbers. Michael and Gabriel went on the offensive, launching a fistfight with Lucifer while we tended to Naomi.

"Can you fix her?" I whispered and then sent a glance in Lucifer's direction in time to see Gabriel fall. He went down hard, the side of his face marred by a red welt where Lucifer had connected. He met my gaze for a moment and then returned to the fight.

Steve bent down and delivered a kiss to Naomi's forehead and light danced over her form, rejuvenating her body, filling her hollow cheeks with a healthy glow. She blinked at him and then her eyes rolled back and she went limp.

"What did you do?" I asked, alarmed by her slip into unconsciousness.

"She'll be fine," Raven said, "But we need to get her out of here," she added, watching the movement of the three archangels. "The path isn't blocked anymore," she said, pointing.

I didn't hesitate. I picked Naomi up and headed for the open escape, and the group followed me. I ran as fast as possible with her limp form in my arms, praying I wouldn't slip. When I reached the back door, I used the power growling inside me to open the locks to the house and burst inside, heading toward the nearest soft surface. The couch sat on the sidewall in the family room with a view of the front yard and lake beyond. I laid Naomi on the soft cushions and pushed her hair away from her face.

"Come on, baby," I whispered, pressing my lips to hers. She didn't respond, and I turned, looking at the crowd behind me.

Raven stepped forward, her gaze averted, but she forced eye contact. "She'll be okay; her life force is still strong." She touched my cheek. "Your babies shine just like you."

I dropped my head to my chest, my relief choking me for a moment before I inhaled and stood, shaking off the momentary lapse. The dull ache in my arms reminded me of my human frailty and I scanned the beautiful view, wondering who would win the battle in the blood-filled clearing.

My answer came a few minutes later, when Lucifer stalked onto the property. The severed heads of my father and uncle dangled from each of his hands and he held them up for me to see. His roar of triumph painted my skin with a burn I hadn't felt since I watched Athena die.

I wanted vengeance, and the power inside me screamed for justice.

"Shit," Ty said from behind me and I turned, staring down the only other angel standing.

I pointed to Naomi. "Keep her safe. That's all I ask," I said, moving my gaze across the faces in the room, then I turned and crossed to the door.

"What do you think you're doing?" Steve asked.

I paused with my hand on the doorknob, asking myself the same question. I glanced out the window and then met Steve's stare dead on.

"Ending this," I said and stepped outside, letting the fury of twenty-five hundred years take over.

Trinity Rising
Chapter Twenty-four
Damian

I STALKED TOWARD LUCIFER, getting my mind in fight mode. A shadow moved into step with me and I glanced at my companion.

"I thought I told you to keep Naomi safe."

"CJ and Steve will see to that," Ty said and met my gaze. "They're making the house safe right now," he added, which meant he wouldn't be able to get back in, and neither would Lucifer if he was the last one standing.

I focused on my nemesis, and he dropped the heads on the ground so they faced me. I ground my teeth together at the manner in which he wiped his hands together, like they were nothing more than dirt and grime. He grinned at me, knowing just how angry I was.

"Coming to exact revenge for your family?" he asked, moving his gaze from me to Ty and back. The question was fitting for both of us, and we stopped less than five paces away.

"Vengeance is mine," I whispered, feeling more like a god than a human at the moment. "And you shall behold the full fury of the heavens."

He laughed, leaning back and cackling to the sky. Ty and I traded a glance and then the angel by my side launched his attack, leaving me standing in a place like a shocked little kid. I blinked as Lucifer went flying on his ass. Ty shook his right hand and then curled it up again as Lucifer got to his feet, his smirk long gone and replaced with wariness.

"I've only felt that kind of power from Michael," he said, narrowing his eyes and studying the angelic form of Ty Ryan. "Gabriel wasn't strong enough to wage any sort of decent fight," he added, stepping away from the discarded heads.

Ty grinned. "The world has never seen anything like me," he said, his voice a feral growl that promised all the pain hell could deliver. "And neither has heaven."

Lucifer waved his hand, and I landed on my ass from the invisible sucker punch. The cold snow seeped into my bloodstained jeans and I climbed to my feet, circling away from Lucifer, letting Ty take the lead in this fight, even though he didn't have the same mental power Lucifer had.

Ty's smile faded when he was shoved a step backwards, but he didn't stumble, he only leveled that glare.

"What are you?" Lucifer asked, unnerved by his inability to budge his primary foe.

"I'm your worst fucking nightmare," Ty said, pulling memory after memory of the same line delivered for the past two decades.

The two angels charged, slamming into each other and creating an explosion that knocked me back twenty feet. Dazed, I pushed into a sitting position, shaking the cobwebs from my head and focused on the flurry of snow before me. The only identifier I could see in the blur was black wings. Ty's blended in with the snow tornado they created.

Blows sounded like thunder, shaking the landscape; and I chanced a glance at the picture window behind me. Steve and Tom had a hold on CJ, his mouth crying out, but the glass prevented me from hearing his wail. I turned back in time to witness the fountain of crimson coming from a headless body kneeling on the ground; blood cascaded down, staining the pristine white wings.

A head rolled on the snow, landing at my feet, and I scrambled into a standing position. The sense of loss coming from the house clouded my vision. My heart ached with sorrow, and I raised my gaze.

Lucifer stepped out of the snow cloud, and I reveled in a moment of satisfaction. Ty had done some damage, but none of it was catastrophic. Lucifer limped forward on a bloodied leg. One of his wrists was twisted enough to elicit a wince from me and his right eye was swollen shut. Even with his injuries, he was a dangerous adversary. I exhaled, stepping into a defensive posture. I would not charge into this blinded by fury. That would only result in the same outcome as Ty, and my father, and Michael.

I was rather fond of having my head attached to my body and I had a family inside to defend, so I proceeded with caution, letting the power coil up inside me, looking for the right moment to strike.

I ignored the belligerent curses coming from CJ; the cautions coming from Steve, and the cries of pain coming from Naomi. I ignored everything but the bastard in front of me.

"I got this," I whispered, and the din in my head lowered.

Lucifer raised an eyebrow, waving me in with the fingers on his good hand. I took a tentative step forward with my heart in my throat and the metallic taste of fear lacing my tongue. New cries filled my mind, and I paused, looking at the snow to my side before bringing my gaze back to Lucifer.

"I'm so looking forward to feeding on a trinity heart, no matter how tainted," he said and looked at my chest. "Especially one containing the grace of two angels."

I let a small laugh escape; he didn't know I was now a father. He didn't know just what kind of strength was building in my bones, and I sidestepped, bringing him away from the house. Away from the heads lying in the snow and towards the pretty little gazebo on the edge of the lake.

The full moon sat high overhead, settling a blue hue over the snow covered world. I glimpsed CJ standing in the window, his glare as deadly as the power coiled in my belly. He met my gaze and the order to make the devil pay rocked my form, but CJ didn't have control over me, just like Steve couldn't get me to relinquish the gun, and my gaze dropped to Lucifer.

Despite their lack of control over my actions, I wholeheartedly agreed with CJ's order.

Lucifer would pay, but I needed information. I needed to know how to fulfill the statement Michael made at the hospital. All I needed now was Lucifer's grace.

"Just out of curiosity, what the hell did Michael mean when he said now all I needed was your grace?" I asked as Lucifer advanced.

He smiled, stalking me like a deadly black panther. "You would become a trinity."

"I thought I already was?" I asked, stalling, stepping further from the house.

"By vampire blood, not by angel grace." He took a step in my direction and I countered, backing up into the half wall of the gazebo.

I had run out of space, and Lucifer knew it. He lunged, pinning me against the post with his injured arm. His glare filling me with dread and the ripping pain that gripped my chest pulled a yelp from my lips. I looked down around the arm, pinning me in place at the fingernails piercing my skin.

My jujitsu maneuvers didn't work, it only proved to further increase the penetration. My base instincts took over and I let out a growl, sinking my teeth into his arm. They broke through the flesh and he howled, pulling away from me. I covered my heart with my left hand and shot my right out in the same dagger like formation as his hand had been.

My fingers sank into flesh and I pushed with both my inertia and my mind, crushing the ribs that stood in my way. I met Lucifer's shocked gaze and smiled as my hand wrapped around his heart. His grace.

He stumbled back, and I yanked with everything I had.

Lucifer landed on his ass with a gaping hole in his chest, but he was still lucid. His wide eyes landing on the pulsing muscle in my hand.

Hot blood ran down my wrist and the thing continued to pulse in my grasp. When I looked beyond the still beating heart and met Lucifer's gaze, I knew I only had a minute to react. He was already climbing to his feet, his features transitioning into fury. If I did the wrong thing, I'd be the one lying dead in the snow.

My stomach rolled at the thought of what I had to do, but I inhaled and brought the heart to my lips.

"No!" he yelled and lunged, but I had already sunk my teeth into the slimy muscle.

Trinity Rising
Chapter Twenty-five
Damian

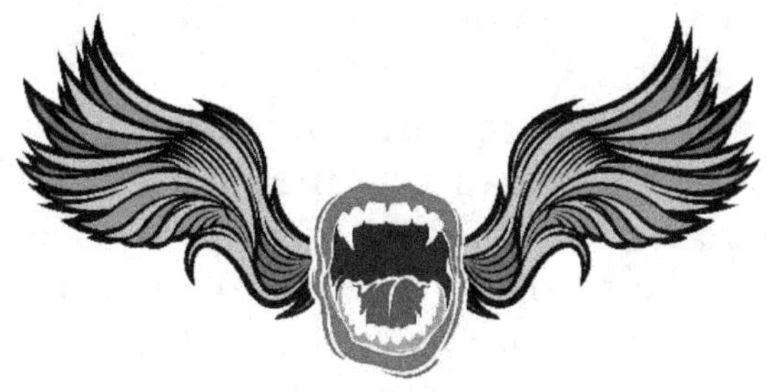

BLOOD BURNED MY TONGUE, sliding down my throat, and I shoved the rest of his heart in my mouth before he could reach me. His face transitioned from fury to shock to pain with each chew. I struggled not to spit it out, knowing I had to eat the whole thing in order to destroy him.

My throat spasmed, and I stepped up onto the gazebo, forcing breaths through my nose as the vile heart broke down between my teeth. Lucifer crawled forward, and I suppressed my gag reflex, swallowing what chunks were left.

My esophagus clenched, and I fell to my knees, folding over at the pain that bloomed in my core. I grabbed a fistful of snow and shoved it in my mouth to calm the burn.

Lucifer grabbed my wrist, and I yanked away from him, falling back onto my butt.

The power encompassed every fiber, and I bellowed, pushing myself to the opposite wall with my feet. The wounds on my chest formed a patchwork-healing pattern and, after a blink, my skin flushed clear. The wounds disappeared and the power inside me flashed beyond comprehension.

Bitter cold sucked into my lungs as I huffed through the pain gripping me. This was far more painful than the shadow virus had been. It felt like two masses of air ramming into each other, creating an internal tornado. White and dark, fighting for dominance as they melded together into one and CJ's power braided through it like a golden lasso, tying it together and bonding it to every cell in my body.

Lucifer chuckled, his gaze still animated and locked on me. I pushed myself into a standing position and he dragged himself up as well.

Another cry filtered through me, and I looked at the window. My second child. The storm settled like rain and I snapped my gaze back to Lucifer and the gaping hole in his chest.

"So that's how you steal grace," I said and stepped forward, slamming my fist into his face. Bones crunched, and this time, I knew they were his. He flew onto his back on the snow and then turned onto his hands and knees, crawling away.

I stared at the withered wings, feeling a level of triumph I had never known. I always assumed I would die at his hands and a just fury wrapped around my heart. I sent the first blast of power at him, crushing him into the ground.

"Go to hell," I whispered, and the power leaped out, striking with the full force of a flamethrower at point-blank range. Nothing was left but a blackened patch and I stared at it.

Freedom.

The word had a new meaning, and I looked up, crossing the bloody snow to the house that held my future.

A future filled with hope.

Trinity Rising
Chapter Twenty-six
Naomi

"WHERE IS HE?" I screamed as another contraction crushed my abdomen.

"He's coming," CJ said, and crossed to the door.

A blinding fear filled me, and I didn't understand why CJ would let Lucifer inside. When Damian stepped in the door with blood dripping from his lips, I gasped and the next contraction gripped my stomach. I cried out, grabbing the sides of the couch as Raven wiped my forehead with a damp cloth.

As quickly as it started, it faded, and I breathed a few deep breaths to prepare for the next one, bringing my gaze back to Damian.

He wiped his sleeve across his face, grimacing at the maroon swath it left on the coat. He peeled the fabric off, dropping it on the floor.

"He won't be bothering any of us, ever again," he said, and I blinked, unable to comprehend his words.

Damian's gaze jumped to Tom, and then the baby wrapped in a towel in his arms. It jumped to Steve and the same type bundle wrapped in his arms. When his gaze returned to me, it was filled with wonder and he moved across the floor, dropping to his knees next to me, and pulled my hand to his chest.

His warm smile settled over me, and the next contraction began in earnest. It was like this child waited until her father was at my side. My face scrunched into a mask of pain and I saw the worry in his eyes.

"It's okay," I squeaked out and relief flooded his features.

"Push," Jennifer said, looking down between my legs with the same excitement she had with the first two boys. Raven helped me curl forward; holding her hands on my shoulder blades like Jennifer told her to do.

Damian starcd at me, awe painting his features.

"Watch for the baby," I said, each word a pant, and he seemed to snap out of his trance, shifting so he could see what was making Jennifer grin like a madwoman.

"Oh my god," Damian said, his face flushing with anticipation. "I can see the baby's head," he added with a smile. "Keep pushing, sweetheart," he added, with a new level of exhilaration sparkling in his eyes.

The pressure gripped me and I pushed with the last ounce of energy I had and suddenly it released. Jennifer wrapped the third child and smiled.

"You have a girl," she said, and my eyes filled with tears as she handed the third bundle to me. I leaned against Raven and showed her the final perfect child. My little angel looked at me and cooed before her eyes roamed to her father.

"Glad you could make it," I said breathlessly, meeting Damian's glossy gaze.

"You've got two boys and a girl," Jennifer said, glancing at Damian as she swiped up the afterbirth. "And you owe me a new couch," she added with a smile.

"Do you have names picked out?" Steve asked as he looked at his watch and scribbled down the time, along with the date on the paper he had recorded the other births on.

I met Damian's gaze and nodded. "You pick," I said, trusting him to pick the perfect names. I was too exhausted to think and in such awe of the miracles bestowed on us.

"Gabriel Alexander for my first-born boy," he said, and I smiled, feeling the lump form at the homage to the two fallen angels. Damian traded a glance with CJ and got a nod in response. Alexander was his father's middle name, and I knew he had caught the significance.

"Michael for the second." I said. I needed to honor the man who saved Damian from death more than once.

"Michael Christopher," Damian replied, completing the homage to those who saved us from Lucifer today, although I could tell CJ wasn't as comfortable with the honor.

"Hey, I wouldn't have been able to do what I did without that little bit of magic I stole from you," Damian smiled and CJ gave a silent nod, looking down at the baby in his arms.

"I guess that's as good a name as any," he sighed.

"What about her?" I asked and pressed my lips to the baby's forehead.

"Grace," he said before I could formulate a name.

I glanced at Damian as Tommy handed Gabriel to him. The way he looked holding my child made me bit my lip, blinking the tears away, and I glanced back at the baby in my arms.

"Grace?" I asked, and the baby cooed. I smiled at her and tried the name once more time. "Hi, sweet baby, Grace."

Trinity Rising
Epilogue
Damian

THE KIDS RAN DOWN the beach. Their little legs pumping and their laughter floating on the breeze. I ran after them, pretending to be a big, bad sand monster, catching each one in my arms and rolling onto my back on the sand. Gracie jumped on my chest and her little fingers found the ticklish spots on my neck as Gabe and Michael yelled for help.

I yielded, letting them go and sitting up. All three children gave me fierce hugs, and I looked beyond my five-year-olds at my wife and friends watching in amusement.

The children ran back to the group, and I sighed, feeling the blessings this life had delivered. I stood, swiping the fine grains of sand from my hands, and crossed the distance, settling into the chair next to Naomi and picking up my beer.

Five years had changed all our lives. I still held the power of the trinity as well as the magic CJ had given me. The months following Lucifer's demise had been tough on all of us. For Naomi and me, it was more trying to juggle three infants and sleepless nights than coming to terms with Michael's death. Even the loss of my father felt surreal, but I suppose that was more easily accepted because he hadn't been in my life for multiple millenniums.

Steve had the toughest time dealing with the guilt of killing Sarah. He still wonders if he did the right thing, even when I tell him it was better than the alternative. When he came back from taking us to the hospital, he said the entire place was clear. No blood, no bodies, nothing except the swath of burned ground where I torched Lucifer. As I understand it, Sarah's disappearance from the house in York is still an open case.

Losing Ty hasn't helped him bounce back either. He took it far worse than either CJ or Tom. Regardless of how much he bitched about being saddled with Ty as his guardian angel, the man had become his confidant and best friend.

CJ and Tom adjusted, but then again, they had other things pulling their attention away from their grief.

I sighed, focusing on my daughter. Grace was special in a way that none of us could pinpoint and my boys were just that; wildly active five-year-old identical twins.

Grace wasn't a third identical twin. She hadn't shared the same sac, only the same womb, and the boys adored her. They were fiercely protective of her, just like the rest of us, and I like to think they know she has an extraordinarily rare gene. I like to think they know she's a trinity.

My gaze landed on the birthmark on her right shoulder blade. Doctors had given us shit for years on that, but it was natural and not a tattoo, as they wrongly assumed. As she got older, the details seemed to get crisper, the coloring bolder. When we had checked in at Brooksfield Hospital after the births, they accused us of drawing on our baby girl. That was the first time we saw the etched details of the white-winged tiger mark.

From that day forward, whenever we have blood work done, they always tell us it's been tainted with feline DNA. I just wonder when that tiger is going to come out. I'm hoping it won't make an appearance, but I know that's just wishful thinking.

I stared at the sun-drenched ocean. The light dancing on the waves captured my attention, and I wondered how I got to this wonderful station in life and why I was so lucky.

Naomi's hand covered mine, and I smiled, moving my attention away from the waves.

Some other things have changed for the better, too, and I glanced at two of my closest friends. One has known me since she was born, and I couldn't have picked a better man for her.

Valerie smiled at me like she knew what I was thinking. She ran her hand down CJ's arm and laced her fingers with his.

He turned toward her, returning her grin before his gaze dropped to her oversized belly.

CJ leaned forward, planting a kiss on the swollen skin under her beach dress.

"How you feeling?" he asked.

"Good, considering I'm overdue," she said. "I swear this boy just doesn't want to come out."

Tom and Raven chuckled, turning toward the squealing laugh of their three-year-old daughter. Hannah approached, her tiny hands grasping one of Steve's and Jennifer's. She planted her feet and then jumped, letting Steve and Jennifer swing her forward. Her giggle tickled all of us and we exchanged glances before returning our gaze to the wild redhead. She broke free and ran to our three kids, sliding to a stop and dropping into the sand next to them.

Steve and Jennifer approached, dropping into the vacant seats nearest the kids.

"She's a handful," Steve smiled.

Tom returned his smile, nodding and signing a simple, "Yes."

"Have you settled on a name yet?" Naomi asked, her eyes locked on our children building a sand castle a few feet away.

"Ty," Valerie said, pulling our gazes to her. "Ty Alexander Ryan."

I smiled, scanning the horizon, wondering if Ty was finally at peace in heaven.

Grace stood and crossed to me, taking my hand and meeting my gaze.

"He is, Daddy," she said, patting my hand, leaving tiny traces of sand with each pat.

A chill drifted over all of us and I traded a glance with CJ. He could read me better than anyone here. And he raised his beer in response. Grace seemed to have a line straight to heaven, one that even a trinity of angelic grace didn't have. I gave her a soft smile, staring into those dazzling big blue eyes, and ran my finger down her nose, tapping the end of it lightly.

"Thank you, Grace," I said and wondered just where her celestial knowledge ended. Her level of comprehension never ceased to amaze me, and her insight was always frighteningly accurate, even at five.

"You're welcome, Daddy." She turned, skipping back to the sandcastle.

I knew someday I'd have to worry about Grace, but today wasn't that day.

The End

Continue with Lilith: A Nighthawk Prequel.

LILITH: A NIGHT HAWK PREQUEL

Obsession puts Lilith within the grasp of immortality, but the price for living forever creates a different, much darker fixation.

Lilith
Chapter One

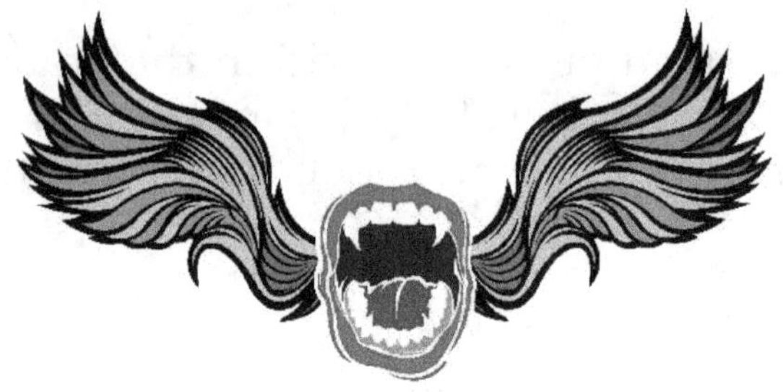

WHO WOULD HAVE THOUGHT my quest for immortality would be the thing that finally killed me?

But I'm not here to talk about my death. I am here to talk about what led me to that dark place where all I craved was life's essence.

It was an age of decadence, when angels mated with humans and God didn't interfere with the unions forged. The hosts of archangels—Michael, Gabriel, Raphael, Uriel, and Lucifer—walked among men, living, instead of locked within the gates of heaven.

Of course, the average human didn't know divinity was in their midst. Even I was clueless for a time.

I remember my first encounter with the light bringer. It was early morning, and the sun had not warmed the day yet. I kneeled by the river with a basket full of soiled clothing sitting nearby. Instead of scrubbing the cloth like I was supposed to be doing, I was studying the plants lining the riverbed. Plucking the ones that interested me.

As I studied the herb in my palm, a throat cleared, making me jump and clasp my hand closed. I was on my feet with my hands behind my back before I realized the man before me wasn't my father. I stared at him. He was perhaps the most beautiful man I had ever laid eyes on. Dark hair, blue eyes, strong jaw, and dimples that only grew deeper with a smile. His teeth were pristine white and his complexion was like fresh cream, and as smooth as silk. His lips were full and inviting. His build was solid but not bulky, and he stood bare-chested with his wrap loosely draped around his hips.

He stepped closer, crowding me as he studied me with as much interest as I was studying him. When he reached out and pulled a handful of my hair towards him, I tried to step away, but instead of a graceful exit, I fell into the river. I gasped as the cold water soaked through my clothing.

His eyebrows arched, and he cocked his head. "Curious little thing," he said and offered me his hand.

His voice warmed my insides. Deep and masculine and as musical as any harp I had ever heard. I reached out, letting him help me out of the water.

He pulled me with such ease that I ended up against his chest. Just touching a man in this manner would have set my father in motion with the whip had he been within eyeshot.

I stared up into the depths of the man's eyes and forgot about any transgression I may have been making against our family. "What's your name?"

"Lucifer. And what do they call you?" he purred and ran the fingers of his free hand through my red hair.

"Lilith," I answered, still captivated by his gaze and the smooth skin under my fingertips.

"Lilith," he repeated softly, as if he were trying it out on his tongue.

The sound of my name on his lips was enough to suddenly make me glad I was dripping frigid water. Without it, I probably would have burst into flame by now. Then he flashed a devastating smile, and the chill was replaced with a stirring heat. My knees wobbled, and his grip around my waist tightened.

My name echoed on the wind, and it took me a second to realize that Lucifer hadn't been the one to call me. With the spell broken, I pushed out of his grip and stepped away, distancing myself. Although every fiber of my form wanted to be back in his arms, I had to heed the warning in the distance. If I didn't, my back would support bloody welts by nightfall.

I turned, squatted next to the basket, and started dipping the soiled clothing into the river, paying Lucifer no mind. His shadow faded away.

"What happened to you?" my father grumbled as he reached my side.

I glanced up at him. "I slipped on the shore and fell in."

"I thought I saw someone with you," he said, glancing around.

I scanned the area and shook my head. "No one is here, Papa," I said and started scrubbing again, wondering where Lucifer had disappeared to.

"Finish your duties here. Once you hang the clothes to dry, your mother needs help in the kitchen."

"Yes, Papa." I hated doing laundry and my father knew it. I would rather help prepare the meals or, better yet, mixing the medicinal herbs for the sick. Curing illness was more satisfying than anything else, and someday I would find a cure for death.

He left me to the unenviable task of scrubbing the dirt out of the clothing in the icy river water. I concentrated on cleaning the clothing until a shadow crossed over my shoulder.

"Tell Mama I am almost done," I said without turning.

"Who is Mama?" he said in that heavenly voice that made me tremble in shock.

I wrung out the last shirt and threw it in the basket before turning towards Lucifer. I scanned the landscape, looking for anywhere he could have disappeared behind, but there was nothing.

"Where have you been hiding?" I asked after my gaze returned to his impossibly handsome face.

He waved his hand nonchalantly and smiled down at me.

I picked up the basket, balancing it on my hip as irritation flushed my skin. His lack of an answer racked my nerves. "I need to go hang these to dry." I hooked my thumb towards where the town proper sat.

He tilted his head and looked from the basket to me. A crease appeared between his intense eyes.

"Chores," I said, and the line deepened as if he had never heard such a word. I turned and headed towards home. When Lucifer fell into step beside me, my heart jumped into my throat. "You cannot follow me home." I gasped, glancing toward the small village. "My father wouldn't approve," I added after a moment.

My father would beat me blind if he saw me walking with a half-naked man, but Lucifer didn't need to know how full of violence my father was. He didn't tolerate my interest in medicinal herbs and potions, and if he had caught me gathering the plants at the river's edge instead of Lucifer, I would have been far worse off than just a fall into the cold water.

Lucifer stopped and reached out, taking my forearm in his warm hand, stopping my progression.

"Your voice shakes," he said. "Do you fear me?"

Astute observation, but it wasn't the man standing next to me who I was afraid of. Although I probably should have been, but I couldn't seem to find reason to tremble at his innocent gaze.

I shook my head. "No. I don't fear you, but I do fear my father."

His lips twitched into a smirk, and he dropped his grip on my arm. "Ah. Fathers." He glanced around and sighed. "Perhaps I will see you again?" he asked when his gaze trained back on me.

My heart picked up at the prospect. "Perhaps." I smiled back at the flash of teeth he gave me and then turned back towards the village. After a few paces, I turned to ask when, but the road and fields beyond me lay empty.

I swallowed the surprise and scanned the area. There was no sign of the strange man. Only stillness, like he had up and disappeared on the breeze.

Lilith
Chapter Two

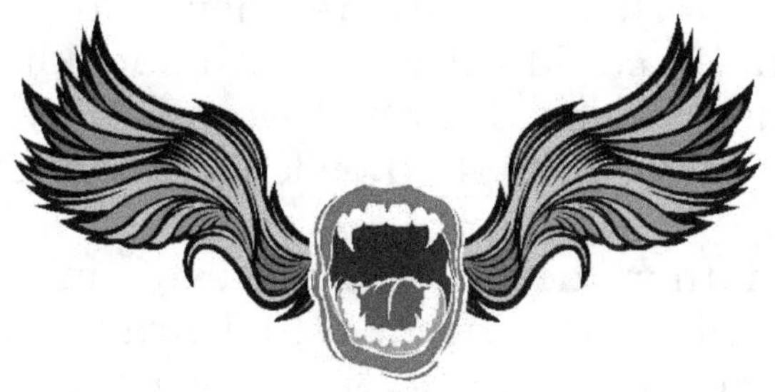

A S SOON AS I pinned the clothing to the lines, I put the basket back in the house. Instead of helping my mother with the meal, I crossed to the shore closest to the town and began foraging different herbs and plants. I knew there had to be a combination that would stave off death, and I was hellbent on finding it.

The ones that I knew were toxic I kept separate from those that were of healing origin. I learned early on the difference between water hemlock and celery. One would kill, and the other added flavor to soups and stews. I could remember my mother berating me after she had seen me cutting up the hemlock for the stew she had on the fire.

She had shaken me and screamed at me, and I swore I didn't put the greens into the pot. I hadn't had a chance. After that day, she made a point of bringing me out to the river's edge and pointing out the different plants. Drilling into me what was safe and what was deadly.

I learned everything about mixing herbs to heal the sick from my mother and the local shaman. If I could get away with sneaking out of the house to visit Josiah, I would. He was even more of a wealth of knowledge than even my mother.

My father never approved of my visiting Josiah. He said I needed to learn trades that were useful to a husband, not wasting my time learning about plants. He didn't appreciate the power found within nature.

With a basket full of both healing and toxic plants, I snuck by our house and slid down the winding path that led to Josiah's cabin. He lived far enough away for the air to still around his little hut. I followed the thin trail of smoke until I rounded a bend in the path. Josiah's home sat amid lush green trees. The ground alternated in circles around his abode. The farthest path was rock, which led to dusty dirt, and then thick moss closest to the cottage.

Josiah sat in the old rocking chair on the porch, whittling a piece of wood. His long white hair stirred in a breeze I hadn't noticed. His gnarled hands seemed much nimbler as he whittled than any other time I had seen him. His dark, wrinkled face was a mask of concentration.

"What did you bring this time?" he asked in a frail, shaky voice, but his concentration never wavered from the wood between his fingers.

"Nightshade, parsnips, and a handful of castor beans."

His fluffy white eyebrow rose. "Quite the deadly combination there, my girl." He stopped whittling and glanced up at me. "Are you still on that silly quest to cure death?"

"It's not a silly quest." I pouted, then made my way across to his porch and put my basket of offerings at his feet.

"It is one thing to ease someone's sufferings with herbs and potions. That is a noble pursuit. But to cheat death... That, my child, cannot be done." His kind gaze met mine. "I will continue to teach you the healing ways if you promise to drop this quest."

My stomach twisted, but I nodded, lowering my gaze to my quarry. I set the basket down in front of him. I wasn't sure I could honor my agreement, though. I still believed there was a way to cure all illnesses. To cure death, as he'd put it.

He raised an eyebrow, as if sensing my lack of commitment.

"Fine." I crossed my arms and leaned against the side of his home.

His eyes narrowed, inspecting me. He seemed to debate. What he saw in my face must have convinced him because he put his whittling knife down and picked up the basket.

"Come," he said and entered his house with my herbs.

When he dumped the basket into the fire in the center of the space, my mouth dropped open. It had taken me a bit of time to find the nightshade, and he burned it to a crisp within seconds. I snapped my mouth closed as he turned in my direction.

"We don't want to grab the wrong herb," he said and flashed a smile.

"What are we mixing today?"

"Honey and ginger." He stepped out the back of the cottage and crossed to the trees where bees swarmed, but that didn't deter him. With slow progression, he reached into the hole in the tree. When his hand came out, he had a small honeycomb between his fingers.

We reentered his house, and he set the honey aside. He started grinding a gingerroot in a bowl.

My mind drifted back to the stranger from the river and I sighed.

"You have not listened since I started breaking this root down," Josiah said.

My gaze snapped from the flames of his fire to him. I raised my eyebrows. I couldn't exactly argue with his assessment because it was correct. I had not been present in the room as he droned on about the process.

"I'm sorry," I said.

"Where is your brain, girl?" he asked, still pummeling the root into a fine powder.

I pressed my lips together and glanced at the door. Trusting Josiah with my aspirations about beating death wasn't as dangerous as trusting him with my secret stranger. He might be inclined to tell my father, and then I would be punished for my transgression.

But Josiah was my only genuine friend.

I sighed. "I met a strange man this morning while I was washing clothes at the river."

His gaze narrowed in the same way I imagined my father's would if he had actually caught me with Lucifer. His root grinding stopped and his inspection of me caused the skin of his face to redden in a way that made my heart pump a frantic beat.

"Did you speak to him?"

I nodded and lowered my gaze. "He surprised me, and I fell in the river."

The arch of Josiah's eyebrow worried me. It planted the seed of doubt that he would indeed keep my secret.

"He helped me out of the water, and then I went back to my chores." I fidgeted under his intense stare.

"Where was he from?" he asked, his voice edged with a bite.

I shrugged.

He pressed his lips together and returned to grinding the ginger into fine powder. When he finished, he picked up his sieve and put the honeycomb into it. He ground that into a sticky mess and set it on top of a deeper bowl. With the honey slowly draining, he turned to me and crossed his arms.

"You expect me to believe you fell into the river because you were washing clothes?"

I pressed my lips against a smirk and glanced towards the fire where my herbs had been reduced to ash. When I slid my gaze back to Josiah, he turned back to the task at hand.

"I did not think so." He looked up from the straining honey with a single raised eyebrow. "Be more careful next time. The river current is strong enough to sweep a girl like you away."

"Like me?"

"You are a wisp of a thing." He waved his hand at me. "And it would be a waste of talent to see you swallowed by the river."

I didn't tell Josiah that I had swum in the river before. That was how I collected some of the more questionable herbs that he had forbidden me to collect.

Lilith
Chapter Three

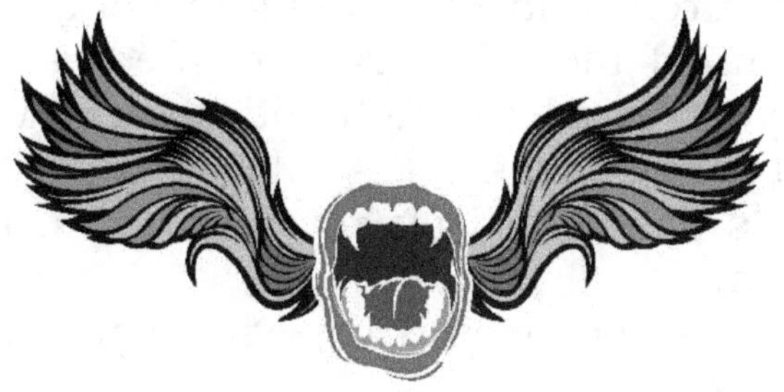

THE NEXT DAY I delivered the ginger honey to one of the village elders. Unice had the whitest hair, and her eyes were nearly opaque with age. She hobbled to the door and snatched the jar from my hand while she covered a phlegmy cough with the other.

Not even a thank you for bringing the medicine to her. She just opened the jar and stuck two fingers inside before she licked them clean. It was one of the vilest actions I had ever seen. I wondered why Josiah would take the time to give this woman relief from whatever ailed her.

"What are you still doing here?" she growled.

I turned and marched away, frustrated with the lack of gratitude. Instead of going back to our hut, I let my mind wander as I walked up the river's edge until the town was just a dot behind me.

Something disturbed the tall grass to my right, and I stopped, scanning the terrain. My skin flushed with fear. I had gone farther than I ever ventured, and the feeling of being watched overwhelmed me. The grass rustled, and green feline eyes stared through the blades. My heart lurched in my chest.

Hands descended on my shoulders. I yelped and spun.

Lucifer stood behind me with a peculiar grin on his face.

I pointed at the crouched jaguar in the grass as panic braised through my body. We needed to run, but I couldn't form the words.

"He won't harm you."

A high-pitched, crazed laugh escaped from my mouth. My laughter died the moment the cat hissed and turned away from us without another glance.

When I'd first looked, it was ready to pounce. Jade eyes zeroed in on me, as if I were a lost gazelle. But after Lucifer put his hands on my shoulders, the jaguar slinked away like a scolded child. It was as if a larger, more dangerous predator had entered its territory.

I glanced up at Lucifer and shivered.

"Where did you come from?" I hadn't heard his approach, but I had heard the rustling of the grass. It made no sense.

"I followed you. Given the dangers lurking, I believe it was the right choice."

I couldn't argue with his logic. I stepped around him, heading back the way I came.

"Do you not collect unique plants?" He waved towards the purple and blue flowers surrounding us.

I scanned the abundant field of wolfsbane and belladonna. My gaze jumped to his in surprise. With the small, empty basket I used to carry Eunice's medicine still perched on the inside of my elbow, I bent, pulled a handful of the deadly plants from the ground, and dropped them into the basket. The belladonna gave way to a small patch of nightshade, and I did the same to it, careful not to disrupt any of the berries from the vines.

I lost track of Lucifer as I headed toward the village. I'd been so focused on the vegetation since he had pointed it out. When the green plants thinned, I found a few castor bean plants, and I added them to my deadly greens.

I rounded a bend, and a small patch of hemlock grew right at the water's edge. I added that to my quarry. This basket wasn't going to Josiah. I needed to store these somewhere safe. I spun on my heels and then bounced off Lucifer's chest.

He grabbed my arms to keep me from falling backwards.

I stared up at his perfect grin. Humor and something else danced in his eyes. His touch stirred a dozen butterflies in my stomach, and I was struck dumb by his intensity.

He cocked his head, studying me before his gaze lowered to the overfilled basket. "What do you plan to do with all that?"

"I want to cheat death," I said. I didn't mean to blurt out my intent.

He laughed. The music of it played over my skin, heating my cheeks and regions south.

"Oh, little thing, there is no cheating death for your kind. When he comes, there is no recourse."

I pulled out of his grip. "I intend to find a way."

I turned and headed back toward the village, still trying to figure out a hiding place for my deadly stash. Josiah would burn it all, and my mother would dump it into the river. If I left it anywhere obvious, the village children would get into it, and I did not want to be responsible for the death of an innocent.

"Silly child," he whispered and fell into step beside me.

"I am not a child." I glared up at him.

He just raised an eyebrow at me.

He kept pace, showing no signs of leaving me to fend for myself. As I drew closer to town, my nerves bundled in my belly. I scanned the road for signs of anyone from my village.

I stopped and faced him. "I cannot be seen with a strange man."

"I am not strange to you." His brow wrinkled in confusion.

"Actually, you are. I shouldn't be talking to you or wandering off alone with you like I have. Even though you somehow saved me from that cat." I nodded in the direction we came from and contemplated my predicament. "I cannot bring you or this basket back home."

"Why not?"

"These are poison, and my mother will get rid of them so no one gets hurt." I lifted the basket.

"But I need to experiment with the herbs. I think there is a way to mix deadly and healthy herbs to create the kind of elixir I am striving for." I glanced at the ground. "But my mother and the local medicine man think I'm just as foolish as you do."

"I can keep them safe for you."

I bit the inside of my lip, considering his offer. "How do I know you will not throw them out?"

"Are they important to you?"

I nodded, and the soft smile that captured his lips nearly sent me to my knees. Something about this man enlisted such trust in me. The only other male figure I had trust in was Josiah. Most of the others were mean and violent, like my father.

"Then I will keep them for you, and all you need to do is to whisper my name and I will bring them to you."

Relief swept through me as I studied his sincere gaze. "Thank you." I handed him the basket and resumed walking.

He continued next to me.

I stopped again. "I still can't be seen with you."

"Do you not like my company?"

I rolled my eyes. Lucifer didn't seem to understand the suspicion of strangers that ran so prevalent in our village. "It has nothing to do with whether I like your company. You are not a part of our community, and they frown upon strangers. Especially strangers who like to keep the company of single women."

He didn't seem to be swayed by my argument.

"My father would have a problem with me talking to you."

Understanding relaxed his features, and he glanced toward the village.

I turned in time to see my father heading in my direction. His face was a mask of anger, even from this distance. My heart jumped into my throat, and I turned to Lucifer. The spot where he had been standing was empty. I glanced around with a start. I circled, scanning the sparse scenery, too preoccupied to notice my father's mad rantings.

Lilith
Chapter Four

I LAY ON MY cot in my room in our hut. Darkness had fallen some time ago, and I was afraid to get up. My cheek still throbbed from my father's fist. If I hadn't been so preoccupied with where Lucifer had disappeared to, I would have recognized an impending beating. But by the time I circled around, my father was within arm's reach. He didn't even ask where I had been. No, the first thing he'd done was beat me, and then he dragged me back to the hut by my hair.

My crime—I had left the house before my morning duties. And Unice was horrible enough to tell him she had seen me wandering off with a strange man and even pointed him in my direction. Her next batch of medicine would have some extra kick in it.

I shook my head and winced. Everything hurt. I knew it would be my luck to find the right ingredients for an immortality elixir, and Unice would be my first test subject. That was not a woman who I would like to have share eternity with me.

I closed my swollen eyes. I needed test subjects, and I knew I would fail many times before I finally found the right mixture. After all, most of the ingredients were toxic to the human species, so my early subjects couldn't be those with a kind disposition.

I sighed and let my mind wander over the combinations.

Peppermint had to be an ingredient. That was an all-encompassing, healing elixir. Dandelions and sunflower tea would need to be incorporated, too. But which deadly herb should be in the mix? Maybe white oleander or water hemlock? I didn't know.

Finally, I rolled onto my side, shifting to find a semi-comfortable position so I could fall asleep. It took a while, but I dozed off, only to be gruffly knocked from my bed just as the sun crested the horizon.

"Get up and go do your chores." My father's harsh voice broke through my stupor.

I climbed to my feet and tried to open my eyes more than just a slit, but I couldn't. I found the laundry basket and stumbled to my normal spot far enough away from the village that I would find peace in the cool morning air.

My side still hurt, and so did my face. I slowly scrubbed the clothes and wrung them out before I dumped them into the basket.

The air behind me shifted, and I looked up through my swollen slits.

"Lilith?"

I turned away, hiding my face from Lucifer, but he crouched down and gripped my shoulders, turning me towards him.

"Child, what happened to you?" he asked as he raised me to my feet. Concern laced his eyes as they inspected my face.

"My father." I looked down at the ground. "I did not do my chores before I went on my foraging expedition, and he punished me."

He hooked his finger under my chin. "Fathers are supposed to be strict, not violent tyrants." He leaned forward and planted the softest kiss on my forehead.

What followed felt like a spring rain shower. It started from the spot Lucifer kissed and cascaded down my body, tingling wherever I was bruised or battered.

He stepped back and scanned my face again. "That's more like it." His gaze went to the basket, and he cocked an eyebrow. "Besides, you should not be doing chores."

I touched my face, and what would have been excruciating a moment ago did not hurt one lick. "What did you just do?"

He pulled me closer, and his fingers traveled over the skin of my cheek, caressing. "I made sure those shameful marks were erased, and I will ensure that this never happens again." His gaze found mine, and there was a fierceness there that overshadowed the moment.

"Thank you, but the way to never allow it to happen again is to let me do my chores." I stepped away and turned to attend to the laundry.

He wrapped his arms wrapped around me and pulled me to his chest. "You should not be doing chores," he said again.

I blinked up into his bright blue eyes, his grip around my waist tight enough for me to lose myself. "And what exactly would you have me doing?"

His grin widened, and he flexed his shoulders. White wings appeared behind him, and his grasp around my midsection tightened in a vise grip. His knees bent, and then he pushed off the ground. We soared into the sky as blue as his irises. I didn't have time to gasp. His lips covered mine in a celestial kiss that would have sent me to the ground had I been standing on dirt.

He landed in a heavily wooded glen. We were surrounded by brush. Soft moss caressed my feet. His lips were still on mine, and his hands threaded into my hair, holding me as his tongue assaulted my mouth in a seductive dance that took my breath from my lungs.

Somehow, I found the strength to push away from him, breaking the kiss. It took me a moment to catch my breath. My chest heaved as if I had run a sprint through town.

Lucifer's eyes danced with mischief. I stared at his folded wings and then met his gaze. My brain wasn't functioning properly at either the flight or the kiss. Both sent my neurons into a tizzy. My hands splayed across his sculpted chest, and his heart beat under my palms, confirming he was flesh and blood, but he was so much more than a man.

"What are you?" I whispered.

"I am the first archangel," he said and dipped his mouth to my neck. "God's chosen to bring the light." His words were muffled against my skin. "But I want to share the light with you."

"You are...divine?" I forced the words out instead of swooning under his kisses. Kisses that lit my skin on fire and weakened my knees.

He pulled away from me and smiled. His grin was as bright as the sun. My knees gave out, but he steadied me. His gaze dropped from my face to the cloth covering my form. Without words, he took the fabric under my chin and ripped until it dropped, leaving me naked in the bright sunlight.

My breath quickened. My father would have me stoned for such a transgression. I crossed my arms over my chest as heat filled my cheeks.

Lucifer stared at my body, taking a step back so he could see all of me. "Perfection," he whispered and met my gaze. His wrap loosened and fell to the ground.

I licked my lips as I took in his angelic form from crown to toe. I could imagine nothing more perfect on earth or in heaven. When he stepped closer, pulling me to him, I allowed him to lower me to the ground and drape himself over me.

My heart clanged in my chest at the intensity of his gaze. His hands caressed my skin, and he gently bit my lower lip before trailing his mouth down my throat to my chest. He kneaded my breasts, pulling a moan from deep within me.

He slid lower, but I was so enthralled with his touch to care. I was being taken by an angel of the Lord, and he knew how to drive me mad. His hands, his mouth, his body—everything he did fueled a fire within me, and by the time he returned to my mouth, I welcomed his hard thrust inside me.

Wonder filled his eyes, and his smile gleamed as his hips circled languidly. I matched his movement, and he groaned, closing his eyes. His expression matched that of anyone who partook in one of my grandmother's treats. The kind of treat that melted in your mouth and left a sweet tingle on your tongue.

Even the sigh that escaped him sounded like he had indulged. When his eyes finally opened, desire brewed in his irises.

"You could convince me to turn my back on heaven," he said, his voice reverent even as his movements increased.

My brain caught up just at the moment, my body clenched with a wave of pleasure.

Lucifer was an angel.

An immortal angel.

I cried out with the force of my release, and white lights blanketed my vision.

His groan followed.

Warmth spread between my legs, and the dots filling my eyes faded. I stared at the sky above us, trying to catch my breath. His wings fluttered, and he propped himself up on his elbows, glancing down at me like a child who had found a most favored toy.

I shivered as the magnitude of my actions slammed into my consciousness. My chest tightened, and my eyes widened. I pushed him off and gathered my clothing in a panicked rush.

I couldn't meet his gaze. Not with his essence dripping down my legs, mingled with the blood of my innocence. Did he not understand what he'd just sentenced me to? Any man who took me as his wife would soon discover I was not pure.

And then I was a dead woman.

I had witnessed the beatings. I had witnessed the group assaults. I had witnessed the stonings. I had witnessed the damages done before death came to take the whores away, and it turned my stomach.

Lucifer grabbed me by the arms, stopping my frantic movement. His eyes were as wide as mine. "Still yourself," he commanded.

I gaped at him. "You have sentenced me to death."

His eyebrows arched, and then he laughed. "Why would you think that?"

"Because I am no longer innocent. Do you know what will happen when I am married off?"

"Married? You would marry another?" His tone turned dark and questioning.

"If my father deems it so, yes. I will have no choice."

He tilted his head back and laughed. "Don't you know God granted you free will?"

"God is not here. He does not have a hand over those who rule the land, and those men say otherwise." I crossed my arms over the ripped fabric of my dress. I had no way to explain my current state, and I did not see a pleasant ending to my day. As a matter of fact, I saw a bloody beating waiting for me, especially with the laundry still sitting on the river's edge and me nowhere to be found.

His laughter wound down and his gaze narrowed. "You will not give yourself to another." His wings fluttered and disappeared, and he stepped close.

I blinked and met his sharp stare. "You may be divine, but you are a stranger here and the village will never understand."

"Then I will raze the village."

I closed my eyes. "No, you cannot destroy my home."

"I will escort you home, and if your father sees fit to punish you, he will meet a very nasty end." He decisively nodded, as if that was the end of the conversation. He put his hands out, his fingers splayed. "Just wait here."

One minute he was before me, and the next, gone. I now understood why I wasn't caught before. I gripped my clothing, trying to figure out how to mend the un-mendable.

He popped back with his wings unfurled. He carried a sheath and kneeled in front of me to secure it to my thigh. "For your protection when I am not with you."

I stared at the ornate blue obsidian handle in the sheath that seemed to refract light even when there wasn't any. When I touched the smooth surface, a thrill ran through me, like a tremor deep in the earth. I pulled the knife out and gasped. The blade curved like a bow, and both sides gleamed sharp. But it wasn't steel. It looked like what I would envision as the ocean. Clear blue crystal, but more deadly than a cobra.

I glanced at Lucifer, raising an eyebrow.

"It is forged from heaven's light. It will obliterate anything you use it on. Including me."

I sheathed the weapon and met his sincere gaze with a nod of thanks, even though I didn't know if I could raise a weapon to my father, despite the beatings.

He leaned down, ripped a strip of fabric from the bottom of my dress, and handed it to me. "Will this help?"

I crisscrossed the torn fabric around me and tied the makeshift sash around my waist. It would have to do until I could retrieve the clothing by the side of the river.

He stepped close and clasped an arm around me. This time when he took flight, my stomach dropped at the height. I clung to him. We landed on the bank of the river. It looked like where I had been this morning, but the clothing basket was no longer there.

A cold certainty bit at my skin, along with a healthy dose of fear.

"Do not worry, child."

I laughed, a high-pitched one, and wrapped the ripped fabric of my dress tighter. I didn't know whether or not to flee.

Lucifer placed his hand on my lower back and pushed me towards the town, stopping my run response dead.

Begrudgingly, I fell into step beside him as he led me down the main street of our town. People stopped to watch us, and their gazes narrowed at my disheveled state. By the time we reached the hut, the rumble of the murmurs behind us had reached a consistent hiss.

The minute we stepped inside, my father turned his glare in my direction. He was up and moving with violent intent, and as he approached with fists already cocked, Lucifer raised his hand. My father stopped mid step.

"Lilith is not to be harmed."

In his frozen form, my father's eyebrows rose, and his face transformed from anger into fury. "Who are you to dictate how I rule my home?"

Lucifer dropped his hand and stepped in front of me. Whatever magic he had exercised dissolved and my father's flying fist resumed until Lucifer caught it in his palm and squeezed.

My father cried out and fell to his knees.

Lucifer leaned down. "I will end you if you harm her again." His tone was feral and harsh.

I shivered, wrapping my hands tighter around my midsection. I hadn't agreed to his claim on me, but I wasn't opposed to it, either, especially if he protected me from my father's wrath.

My father did not assent to Lucifer's will, but he also did not argue with the man standing over him. He sent a glare in my direction, one that promised as soon as this stranger was out of our home, I was going to pay for this humiliation.

"Lucifer," I whispered and put my hand on his shoulder.

He released my father's hand and glanced back at me. "If for some reason this fool thinks it is wise to beat you again, I will revisit every brutality on him threefold." Lucifer sent a look toward my father that should have shriveled the man in his skin, but my father was too preoccupied with his mangled hand to notice. "I will see you tomorrow." He gave me a nod and stepped out of our cottage.

I swallowed the lump of fear that had formed the moment my angel stepped out of the hut. Hatred oozed from my father, blanketing me in discomfort.

His gaze fell to my torn dress and his face turned bright red. "I may not be allowed to touch you, but you have disgraced this family and this community." He climbed to his feet and pointed towards the door. "Whore!" he screamed and tore the shredded material from my shoulders. "Get out of my house!" He pushed me out the door, wearing only the sheath on my thigh.

I stumbled into the dusty street, trying to hide myself from the view of the townspeople, but it was impossible. The single statement of my father created a frenzy out of the quiet town. This was what I had warned Lucifer of.

The first rock hit me on the shoulder blade, ripping a gasp from my chest as the chants of "whore" broke out. More rocks pelted my skin. I covered my face and tried to run, but the crowd pushed me back into the center of the ring of people. A rock hit my temple, and I fell to my knee in a wave of dizziness.

I blinked and reached for the dagger that Lucifer gave me. The sheath was empty, and my chest lurched.

"Looking for this, missy?" One of the older men in the crowd waved it at me.

My vision blurred, and I struggled to rise, but the blow from the rock had left me disoriented. Heat flowed down my face, and I wiped at it. My palm came back into view, covered in blood. If I didn't get up…

The crack of a belt bit into my back and I screamed. It was cut off a second later when the leather wrapped around my throat. Horror washed through me as the younger men stepped forward to do what they were bound to do to the village whores.

"Lucifer," I whispered to the sky with a voice constricted by the tight belt. At this moment, I did not care if the angel leveled the entire village.

A roar rumbled from the blackening sky. The sight of Lucifer descending with wings that spanned the width of the street and lightning rolling off his entire form was enough to make a majority of the crowd back away. All except the stupid one who was focused on violating me. He didn't take any notice until Lucifer landed in front of me.

Lucifer slammed his fist into the ground, and the wave of destruction spiraled out from the spot right under my face. I felt the heat, but it did not hurt. It was like a light from heaven had encompassed me in a safe bubble as Lucifer's wrath burned the rest of the village.

The stench of burned flesh hung on the air, and I flinched when Lucifer reached for me.

He brushed his hand over my cheek and into my hair, studying the cut on my temple. He shook his head and pressed a healing kiss to my forehead.

The sharp pain where every rock had collided with my skin dulled.

"Why did you not use the knife I gave you?" he asked as he jerked my chin up.

"First, the knife can't stop a thrown rock, and second, someone relieved me of it while I was trying to run away." I wiped my face and blinked back the sheen of tears that blurred my vision.

"You lost the knife?" His voice was sharp enough for me to shrink back.

I glanced at the destruction around me and the ash swirling in the breeze. "It's somewhere in the ash, assuming it survived." I waved at the remains of my village. I wasn't even sure which side that scoundrel had ended up on before Lucifer's wrath decimated everything.

He wiped his face and glanced around us. Annoyed creases appeared at the edges of his lips. "Perhaps if you had clothing on, you wouldn't have lost it."

"My father tore the fabric off my back and shoved me out to be dealt with by the village. I told you, you damned me." I crossed my arms over my chest. "I told you I was as good as dead, but you led me back home anyway and now look at my village." Anger seeped into my tone. If I let the rest of the tumult inside reach the surface, I would have fallen to the ground in a puddle of tears.

While I did not mourn my father's death, my mother's was a different story. And there were others in the town who were kind and did not deserve to be smited by an angel of the Lord.

I shook with anguish.

"Why are you lashing out at me?" he asked, clearly perplexed by my actions. "I saved you."

"I have no clothes, no home, and nowhere to go. While I am thankful that I did not die here today, I can't say I won't die tonight from exposure or some wild animals on the prowl." The wind picked up, and I coughed as a swirl of gray dust assaulted us.

I turned away from him and headed towards the river. I needed to feel clean, and then I needed to figure out what the hell I was going to do. Lucifer accompanied me but kept quiet, and when I continued walking into the water, he matched me step for step.

When I dunked under, he did the same. When we both stood, his wings were once again pristine white. They fluttered on his back as he pulled me close while droplets rained down around us.

"You will not be harmed."

I yanked out of his grip. "That is what you promised when you left me at my father's mercy!" I waved towards where our hut used to be. "And how did that turn out?"

Lucifer crossed his arms. "I am sorry I did not intervene sooner. I was in the middle of an argument with *MY* father."

I turned and marched to the shore, wrapping my arms around my naked form, even though there were no eyes for miles. I wanted to be covered, because if Lucifer left me and I crossed by someone who decided they could have me, I was helpless to stop them. At least with clothing, I would be less vulnerable.

I spun back to Lucifer with wicked words on my tongue, and he held out a garment for me. I stared at the red fabric in awe. I had never seen cloth so soft-looking and I reached to touch the dress.

He helped slide it over my head. "Now, that is what a lady should look like."

The soft dress hugged my curves and fell to just below my knees in pleated waves. It was as red as fresh blood and made my exposed shoulders look like cream against the dark, decadent color. I had seen nothing like it, especially something on a woman that revealed so much. Yet it felt so good against my skin, like it was made just for me.

I ran my hands down the front and glanced up at Lucifer. "What is this made of?"

He just smiled and scanned me. Heat radiated from him. Being this close felt like being stranded in the desert on a hot summer's day. Despite my aggravation for him razing my village, I couldn't help but be thankful for his skill to pull things out of nowhere, but there was a nagging deep inside me that told me to run fast and run far.

Too bad I didn't heed that internal alarm.

Lilith
Chapter Five

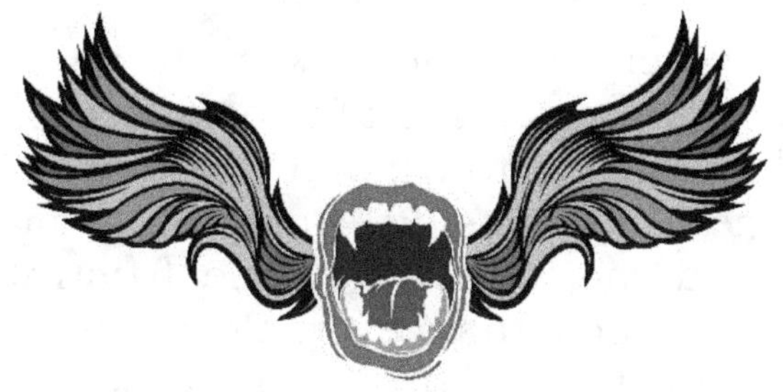

"WHAT DO YOU MEAN I need to stop trying to cheat death?" I slammed my fist on the table in front of me. My various containers laid out on the wood rattled.

He had been asking me to stop for a while now, and it irritated me to no end. I was getting closer to a cure for death, and he was pulling this now?

I spun and glared at Lucifer. "I am almost there!"

Lucifer wiped his hand down his face. "Haven't you failed enough?" he asked softly. "You are turning people into things that cannot be controlled."

"They aren't dying, are they?" I crossed my arms.

"No. But they aren't truly alive anymore. They are monsters that only crave the slaughter."

"You've contained them?" I had asked him to put the subjects somewhere where they couldn't hurt anyone.

"Yes. But it still is not right."

"I am so close!" I didn't want to give this up. Not after so many years of near success. Lucifer had helped me get to where I was now, but there was something missing. Something significant that eluded me, and it left me frustrated and more determined than ever. So much so that I didn't care if Lucifer tired of this mental tug-of-war that we seemed to do daily.

He wanted children, but I would not bring a child into this difficult world. Not when failure meant death. I wanted them to experience everlasting joy without the worry of mortality.

He had set me up in this magnificent hut with an area to practice my herbal concoctions separate from my regular quarters. He provided me with whatever I requested and was good to me in every way, but I was not reliant on him in the same way he seemed to be reliant on me.

Our arguments increased as our lovemaking decreased. I didn't need the physical attention, but I enjoyed it when it occurred. Lucifer was a giving lover, but it was not enough to satiate my need for knowledge.

"You do not realize the ramifications..." His eyes blazed and his face turned red. He turned away from me and ran his hand through his hair.

"Of what, trying to eliminate death? Eliminate disease?" Anger bloomed in my chest in a suffocating heat that must have equaled his frustration.

"You are killing innocents," he yelled and spun back to me. His wings flared on his back, and I stared at the blackened feathers. "I beg of you, please stop. Please let me start a family with you. I want to make love to you night after night and find that bliss we used to have again."

"What happened?" I asked, still focused on his burned wings and not on whatever he was blathering on about.

His lips pressed together, and his glare startled me. "This was my punishment for loving you."

His words burned. "I did not ask you to love me. That was your choice." I crossed my arms and jutted my chin. "You were the one who swooped down and saved me from my life when I didn't need saving. You were the one who put me in danger and then destroyed everything I had ever known."

"I gave up heaven for you!" he yelled.

I blinked at him as frustration boiled in my blood at the unsaid accusations in his tone. "I never asked you to give up heaven. I never asked for anything from you."

He growled and crossed the distance to stand over me. "I gave you everything you ever desired."

I laughed at him. I had traded one overbearing control monger for another. The only difference between Lucifer and my father was that Lucifer never lifted a hand in anger, the way my father so easily had. While he had initially helped me get to this point with my potions, I was feeling very stifled.

"Everything I ever desired?" I stepped back, distancing myself. "You took my virginity and then nearly let me die at the hands of the village."

"Are you ever going to let me live that down?" he growled.

"This was *NOT* my choice. It was yours. I had as much say in this as I had with doing my family's laundry when they were alive."

"I helped you with your strive for immortality," he said, blinking rapidly.

"I would have gotten to this point eventually," I argued, but I knew it would have taken at least twice as long without his help. I was grateful, but that didn't mean the man owned me. "I am not a piece of property to be claimed."

The flash in his eyes frightened me. I tried to take another step away, but he grabbed me by the arms and slammed me into the wall behind me.

"You will stop this!" he bellowed in my face.

Anger boiled to the surface. I would not live the rest of my life in fear of his retribution.

"No," I yelled back. "And you can get out of my hut and never return!"

His eyes widened, and he slowly put me down. "I'm sorry."

"Get out!" I pointed.

"Lilith, please..." he whispered and reached for my face.

I knocked his hand away. "You touched me in anger. Get out!" I was nearly as frenzied as he had been. But I could not go back to the life where beatings were the normal everyday occurrence. I would not live like that ever again.

He dropped to a knee in front of me. "I'm begging you," he said, his voice choked with emotion.

"No. Get out and never return." My voice echoed in the small room, and Lucifer winced.

"Please," he said, climbing to his feet. Tears glazed his eyes.

I shook my head and pointed. "Never again." I said through clenched teeth.

For a moment, I wished I still had that obsidian knife that I'd hunted for repeatedly, but never found, because that would ensure I would never be harmed again.

His lips thinned, and his cheeks turned red, and then he turned and stalked out the door.

Lilith
Chapter Six

IT HAD BEEN A year almost to the day since our falling out. I hadn't seen Lucifer since he walked out my door. Not a peep. Not even a feeling of him watching me. Until this evening, and it was stifling.

I shivered with the sudden certainty he was right there, but the feeling was different, hostile. Like being watched by my father all those years ago. I wrapped my shawl around me tighter and scuttled down the street as I glanced from side to side.

The door to my hut stood ajar. My stomach lurched, and my feet moved faster. I swung the door open and froze. Everything I owned was sprawled out across the place, and every item was smashed or torn or shattered.

My hand flew over my mouth, shutting off my gasp. Before I knew it, I was sprinting across the room, trying to dodge the broken pieces of my life. I slid to a stop at the door of my lab. Nothing remained in one piece.

Cold horror scratched over my skin like a million tiny spiders. My entire collection of herbs and spices, both deadly and beneficial, was smoldering in the center of my lab.

"What have you done?" I cried and ran towards where I'd had my latest batch of magic brewing.

A hand shot out from the darkness and gripped my throat in a vise. He pulled me until my face was near enough for me to feel his hot breath on my skin.

He wore a crazed mask of fury as he growled, "You have been very naughty."

When life with Lucifer had been normal and blessed, those particular words would have started a heat between my legs that would spread through my entire form, but this time, it left me chilled, like I would never be able to warm up again.

I had never seen anyone deranged with anger beyond my father, and seeing it on Lucifer, an angel of the Lord, frightened me to the point my bladder squeezed.

His wings had a layer of soot and grime, and he smelled like hellfire.

I couldn't speak with the grip around my throat. I wasn't sure I would be able to, even if he wasn't choking me. I scratched at his hand as he dragged me towards him. He gripped me tight and bent his knees before launching us through the thatched roof of my hut.

The last thing I saw was the dark entrance of a mountain cave, and then all went dark.

MY EYES OPENED TO a dingy cave with a table strewn with my lab equipment. Lucifer muttered under his breath, and his mangled wings trembled.

"Why?" a woman next to me asked. Her voice sounded as parched as I felt.

Lucifer glared over his shoulder at her and then strode toward me. "Good. You are awake." He grabbed one of two vials, crossed to the woman, grabbed her jaw, and forced her mouth open before dropping the contents in her mouth.

He tossed the empty vial back on the table and took a seat on the stool. He crossed his arms as the woman clawed at her throat. A scream filled the cavern. He smiled like he was enjoying what my potion was doing to the human body.

The woman dropped to her knees and screamed so loud and for so long; I thought her vocal cords would burst. Then the convulsions started, altering the screams into starts and stops as violent as the fits accosting her.

And then she lay silent, her chest hitching breaths in wheezing intervals, rising and falling in a slow cadence.

I had witnessed the same passing of stages time and time again, with one exception. The woman's breath still hissed from her chest. My subjects all stopped breathing before they woke with a mouthful of teeth as sharp as a tiger's.

Lucifer nodded and reached over his shoulder to grab the second vial. He stood and approached me.

"What are you doing?" I asked, my voice carrying the same panic heating every cell in my body. The kind angel whom I had once known was gone, and this crazed being who had bound me to the wall was going to turn me into one of those mindless monsters.

"You wanted immortality?" Lucifer growled and grabbed my jaw, forcing his fingers into my cheek until I had no choice but to open my mouth. He poured the contents of the vial down my throat and held my jaw until I was forced to swallow.

My throat burned like the heart of a fire, and when the liquid hit my stomach, I swore it torched right through my skin. I screamed so loud I thought my neck was going to rupture. Every inch of my form sang with exquisite torture. My hair even felt as if I had been doused in oil and set aflame.

My chest squeezed as if a mighty oak had fallen on top of me, adding to the pain racking every cell. I understood the sheer suffering of the transformations that my subjects had endured.

"There is a steep price for cheating death. I hope you burn with it for eternity," Lucifer whispered in my ear. His voice carried wrath and blackness, and his eyes blazed with hatred.

I couldn't curl up or fall to the floor the way the woman had next to me. She was not bound to the wall the way I was. My body trembled as I tried to pull my arms and legs closer to ease some of this suffering.

"I found your secret ingredient," he added and held up his wrist. A jagged scar traversed his skin. "Blood," he hissed. "Divine blood and a curse that you will suffer as I have. If I'm locked out of heaven, you deserve the same fate. Bound to the darkness, until judgement day. And then you will burn in my hell for the rest of eternity."

My mind wasn't too far gone to comprehend his words, and the sentiment sent a chill of terror through my already taxed form. Every muscle seized, and all I could do was bellow my fear mingled with agony.

I prayed for death. For a release from this horrifying pain. I prayed for unconsciousness or anything that would relieve the burning. I prayed to a god whom I'd angered enough to cast out his son. I knew my prayers fell on deaf ears, but I couldn't stop the begging litany that repeated in my head while I wailed wordlessly.

Somewhere between the pain and fear, hunger bloomed in the mix. I snapped at Lucifer, but he danced out of reach. The copper taste of blood filled my mouth.

The woman next to me looked up with red eyes. Saliva dripped from her mouth. I had seen enough of my failed experiments to know she had gone feral. She was on her feet in a flash, straining against the chains to get to me.

Her screams mingled with mine. The only difference between us was hers were borne of frustration and mine were from the sheer agony of the transformation.

"Cool your jets. I've got something special for you." Lucifer turned and walked out of the room.

To my surprise, the woman calmed, but stared at my chin and licked her lips. My suffering was not lost on her.

"The pain ends," she whispered.

My heart lurched in my chest, adding to my discomfort. I still couldn't utter words, just a long consistent wail, clouding my thoughts and echoing off the rocks surrounding us. My brain processed the fact that she'd spoken coherently. My pain dropped a notch, but the hunger raged. Even the smell of my own bloody lip activated the saliva in my mouth.

Lucifer walked into the room with a young boy. The woman next to me froze in place. Her eyes widened, and saliva dripped from large canine teeth.

"No. Not my baby," she whispered and stepped back against the rocks.

I could smell the child. He smelled like a spring rainstorm, and all I wanted to do was tear open his throat and swallow every drop of that scent. I whimpered.

Lucifer sat the child on his knee a few feet out of reach of the woman. "My brothers and I came down to earth many years ago. And while I was spending time with you, they popped out kids with the women they fell in love with. But I got thrown out of heaven because you wanted to be immortal. Which is forbidden. Only the heavenly host is immortal. Not a creature created by God." He flexed his chest. His burned and molted wings spread over the room. "I was punished for loving you, but my brothers were not. They were allowed to have families." He shook his head in disgust. "They have everything, and I have nothing."

He tore the robe off the child, and without hesitation, his sharp fingernails dug into the child's chest. The boy screamed, but Lucifer just smiled as his fingers buried deeper into the boy's flesh.

"You are hurting him!" the woman next to me screamed. For a moment, her red eyes cooled into a blue inferno of fear and agony.

Lucifer glared at her and punched his hand through, shattering bone. The child's scream cut off, and a moment later, Lucifer held the boy's beating heart in his hand. He licked it, and his wings trembled.

"Angel blood." He shoved that small beating heart into his mouth and closed his eyes as if he were eating a fine meal.

The woman screamed, and time rippled.

When Lucifer stood, he wiped his mouth with his forearm and let the dead boy drop to the floor. "I will destroy every Nephilim."

Lucifer turned. His wings looked better than they had before, but they were as black as the night.

The child's blood flowed into a puddle between the woman and me, and the scent of it cramped my stomach. I wanted that blood. I needed that blood. I thought my soul would burn if I didn't have any of the blood.

From the looks of it, the woman next to me felt the same, although the dead body was her child. The stench of blood mixed in the air, clouded by our moans. I couldn't reach the slowly spreading puddle, but the woman next to me could.

She lapped at the dirt, sobbing as she crawled as far as she could. Her fingertips were just able to glance off his shoulder, but that didn't dissuade her from sucking up the blood pool with greedy slurps.

I trembled in my binds, unable to partake in the feast even though every cell screamed for the blood. Grunts echoed off the walls, and at first, I thought the woman was making the noises. Then a giant slurp carried over the sound, and I realized I was making the animal noises. I closed my mouth and my eyes, tilting my head back to block it all out.

I failed. Every muscle flexed, straining. A snap followed by another, and my eyes went wide. I had broken the binds. The pull of the blood didn't give me any time to digest the kind of strength I had just displayed. I fell to my knees and buried my face into the puddle right next to the child's mother.

Blood flowed over my tongue, cramping my stomach, and I moaned, meeting the woman's pained gaze. Tears cascaded down her bloodstained cheeks.

I swallowed hard. A lump in my throat formed, and my vision blurred. I couldn't stop, and neither could she. I pulled her boy close enough for her to wrap her arms around him, and she buried her face in the hole Lucifer's hand had left.

Sobbing and slurping, she reached out and gripped my hand in a show of solidarity, and I held it while taking my fill from the puddle.

The door slammed open, and we both looked up at the being who had walked in. He looked so very similar to Lucifer. His white wings spread, ruffling as his face turned bright red. His gaze fell on the child and then narrowed on the woman.

I could smell his wrath filling the air, and it reminded me of a forest fire. His hands curled into fists.

"She didn't do this. Lucifer did," I said as he stepped closer.

His gaze moved to me as if he hadn't noticed me before. His gaze landed on the boy again, and he closed his eyes.

"Athena," the woman said.

"Is safe," he said, his voice shaking. "Eve, why are you drinking our child's blood?" he barely choked out.

Eve shook her head. "I cannot help myself." She covered her face.

"Lucifer cursed us with tainted immortality," I whispered and forced myself to ignore the blood puddling between my knees. My hands were covered in it, and I slipped my fingers in my mouth to keep the urge to drink from the ground at bay.

Blood dripped from Eve's chin and he recoiled. Disgust peeled his lips back.

"I should end you," he hissed, but pressed his lips together as tears welled up in his eyes.

"Michael, do it," Eve said softly, her eyes as haunted as I imagined mine were.

A tear spilled down his cheek, and his fists tightened until both hands were blanched as white as his wings.

I thought we were dead. I thought this angel was going to raze the entire kill room. He trembled with barely contained emotions and then turned and left.

I pulled my fingers out of my mouth, catching one on my tooth. It stung like fire, and I gasped, feeling my teeth, especially my incisors. They were long and fanged like Eve's.

I fell back against the wall, exhaling. I wasn't sure if what I felt was relief or not, but at some base level, my survival instinct was stronger than whatever this curse Lucifer passed to us was.

Eve glanced at me. "Why?" She held her bloody hands out for me to see. "Why my son?"

I clenched my teeth. Lucifer and Michael were made from the same cloth. Brothers in heaven, now enemies on earth. I had no idea why he would take his anger out on his brother's child. All I could do was shake my head.

"Why did he do this to us?" she asked and dipped her fingers in the pool of her son's chest.

That was a simpler answer. "I know why he did this to me, but I cannot fathom why he threw you into this."

She licked her fingers and repeated the actions. Dip and then suck. "Why?" she asked after staring at her now clean fingers in abject horror.

"Because my endeavors for finding immortality got him kicked out of heaven, and then when he started showing signs of aggression towards me, I told him to leave."

She closed her eyes and hung her head. A sob ripped from her chest as she stared at her dead son.

"What are we?" she whispered.

"I have no idea. But I think he did it. I think we are immortal." I met her gaze. Horror and excitement ran through me as hot as the cooling blood roiling in my stomach. Possibilities swarmed in my head, but I would never forgive that bastard for killing an innocent child so painfully and callously.

"I need more," she whispered, wiping her fingers around the nearly empty cavern, and a sob broke through her.

I pulled her into my arms, holding her as tight as I could to staunch the shakes that had overtaken her. "I am so sorry," I whispered and smoothed her soiled hair.

Lilith
Chapter Seven

WE FOUND OUT THE hard way that our newly transformed beings were just as volatile in the sunlight as the monsters in Lucifer's pit. Both our arms were scarred from the burns, and it took a long time before I could convince Eve that the moonlight wouldn't harm us. But hunger eventually drove us from our sanctuary.

I stood at the edge of the river with Eve next to me, our hands entwined as the moonlight painted the land. I hadn't been to my village since the day I kicked Lucifer out of our home. But we came back to find the one thing that could destroy Lucifer.

I scanned the newly built village that had replaced the barren charred land we had left. In fact, it looked as though the burning had made the soil rich, bringing with it flowers of all colors and grasses of deep green.

I didn't know where to look, especially with the scent of human blood on the air.

Eve's hand tightened. "I thought you said he destroyed your home."

"He did." I glanced around, trying to staunch the building hunger, but I couldn't. Considering how tight Eve's grip was, she was losing the battle, too. Saliva dripped from my teeth, and I licked my lips.

A group of drunken men weaved through the huts, the beats of their hearts lulling us. We froze in place, and then hunger overtook us.

Death followed, picking up the poor husks we left behind.

The End

If you enjoyed this book, please leave a review!

About J.E. Taylor

J.E. Taylor is a USA Today bestselling author, a publisher, an editor, a manuscript formatter, a mother, a wife, a business analyst, and a Supernatural fangirl. Not necessarily in that order. She first sat down to seriously write in February of 2007 after her daughter asked:

"Mom, if you could do anything, what would you do?"

From that moment on, she hasn't looked back.

Besides being co-owner of Novel Concept Publishing, Ms. Taylor also moonlights as a Senior Editor of Allegory, an online venue for Science Fiction, Fantasy and Horror. J.E. Taylor is also one of the co-hosts of the popular podcast <u>Spilling Ink</u>.

She lives in New Hampshire with her husband and two children and during the summer months enjoys her weekends on the shore in southern Maine.

Visit her at <u>www.jetaylor75.com</u> and sign up for her newsletter for early previews of her upcoming books, release announcements, and special opportunities for free swag!

www.ingramcontent.com/pod-product-compliance
Lightning Source LLC
Chambersburg PA
CBHW060637310726

48982CB00003B/806